IEEE Technology Update Series

Neural Networks Applications

IEEE Technology Update Series

Neural Networks Applications

Dr. Patrick K. Simpson

EDITOR

IEEE Technical Activities Board

A Selected Reprint Volume under the sponsorship of the Products Council of the IEEE Technical Activities Board

The Institute of Electrical and Electronics Engineers, Inc.
New York City, New York

Library of Congress Cataloging-in-Publication Data

Neural networks applications / Patrick K. Simpson, editor.
     p.   cm. — (IEEE technology update series)
     Includes index.
     ISBN 0-7803-2566-4
     1. Neural networks (Computer science)   I. Simpson, Patrick K.
     II. Series.
     QA76.87.N4793   1996
     620 ′ .00285 ′ 63—dc20   96-33928
                                                     CIP

IEEE Technical Activities Board

445 Hoes Lane
Piscataway, New Jersey 08855-1331

Patrick K. Simpson
Editor-in-Chief

Robert T. Wangemann
Executive Editor

Harry Strickholm, Managing Editor
Jayne F. Cerone, Administrative Editor
Lois J. Pannella, Administrative Editor
Eileen M. Reid, Administrative Editor
Patricia Thompson, Administrative Editor
Mark A. Vasquez-Jorge, Administrative Editor
Ann Burgmeyer, Production Editor

FOREWORD

Technological advances and applications in numerous consumer and industrial products have led to rapid growth in the field of neural networks. Neural networks applications can be found in many, if not most, of the fields of electrotechnology. In 1995, fifteen IEEE Societies have shown interest in the field through their participation in the IEEE Neural Networks Council.

For these reasons, neural networks was selected as the topic of this edition of the IEEE Technology Update Series. This Series was developed by the IEEE Technical Activities Board (TAB) and the TAB Book Broker Committee to furnish readers with up-to-date information in specific fields of interest. "Neural Networks: Applications" contains material from IEEE conferences and journals, and targets the use of neural networks in control; power systems; medical systems; information processing; signal processing; manufacturing; production and inspection; and vehicles. A companion volume, "Neural Networks: Theory, Technology and Applications" was published earlier this year.

I would like to thank Patrick K. Simpson for his skilled efforts as Editor-in-Chief of "Neural Networks: Applications." Mr. Simpson served as Chair of the IEEE Neural Networks Council in 1994.

For their guidance and work with the Technology Update Series, I would like to recognize the support of Dr. Bruce Eisenstein, IEEE Vice President - Technical Activities, and Dr. Jan Brown, Chair of the TAB Book Broker Committee.

Finally, I acknowledge the Technical Activities Department staff who gathered the materials for this volume. Thanks to Harry Strickholm, Jayne F. Cerone, Lois J. Pannella, Eileen M. Reid, Patricia Thompson and Mark A. Vasquez-Jorge for their editorial input. I would also like to thank Ann Burgmeyer, Production Editor of the IEEE Publishing Department.

Robert T. Wangemann
Staff Director - Technical Activities

CONTENTS

EDITOR'S INTRODUCTION

In 1987, the IEEE sponsored the First International Conference on Neural Networks (ICNN 87) in San Diego CA. Over 1200 scientists and engineers attended that historic meeting, which included several tutorials, standing room only plenary sessions, and the presentation of over 400 papers. This meeting served as a catalyst for the community. Several government and industry funded efforts emerged as a result of this meeting. In addition, the field began to take shape. Leaders emerged, technical challenges were identified, and literally hundreds of applications were proposed or already being developed.

Since 1987, the IEEE has remained very active in neural networks. There has been at least one ICNN (or IJCNN) each year since. In addition, well over half of the IEEE sponsored meetings held each year includes at least one paper concerned with some aspect of neural networks. Special issues or special sections on neural networks have appeared in sixteen of the 92 archival IEEE publications ranging from Communications to Oceanic Engineering. In 1988, the IEEE formed a Technical Committee that served as the focal group for IEEE neural networks activities. This committee grew and in 1990 became the IEEE Neural Networks Council (NNC). In 1994, the NNC directly involved 15 of the 35 IEEE Societies. The NNC publishes two Transactions (*Transactions on Neural Networks and Transactions on Fuzzy Systems*), has sponsored over a half-dozen books and video tutorials, and honors the best in the field with awards, promotes local activities through regional interest groups and distinguished lecturers, and supports Fellow activities.

A close examination of the neural networks field reveals continued growth. In his September 1993 editorial,[1] Prof. Robert J. Marks II chronicled the growth of neural networks in two areas: archival papers and patents. Using the INSPEC database of archival papers, Marks reported the number of papers published in 1990, 1991, and 1992 was 2720, 4336, and 5574, respectively. Almost half of these INSPEC entries were associated with IEEE activities. In a similar fashion, using the CASSIS database of U.S. Patents, Marks reported 36, 66, and 119 neural network related patents were issued in 1990, 1991, and 1992, respectively.

Clearly, the field of neural networks is expansive and diverse. Each year it becomes more difficult to follow all the advances being made. In recognition of this problem, this book's objective is to provide the practicing engineer with a snapshot of the latest theory, technology, applications, and implementations of neural networks. To achieve this goal, the IEEE Technical Activities Board has collected all of the papers dealing with any aspect of neural networks from any IEEE sponsored or co-sponsored meeting during 1993. Over 1200 papers were published in these IEEE conference records in 1993. This collection included at least one paper in 87 of 137 IEEE sponsored or co-sponsored meetings during the year. Due to the sheer diversity of this field, and the quality of papers presented, it was not possible to reduce 1200 papers to a single volume. As such, a second volume was needed. Two volumes was enough, but just barely.

The paper selection process was done in three steps. First, each of the 1200 papers was reviewed for accuracy, clarity, and completeness. Also, duplicate papers (nearly identical papers presented at two or more different meetings) were eliminated. This process reduced the original 1200 papers to 803 papers. The second pass through the papers was used to create index terms and organize the papers into categories. The results of this second pass included two theory categories, seven technology categories, three implementation categories, and seven application categories. The third and final pass was used to reduce the collection of papers to those found in these first two "Neural Networks Technology and Applications" volumes. The final selection of papers

---

1   Marks, R. (1994). Intelligence: Computational vs. Artificial, *IEEE Trans. on Neural Networks,* Vol. 4, No. 5, pp. 737-739.

emphasized diversity and new results. This volume covers theory, technology, and implementations, and includes 139 conference papers. A second volume is dedicated to applications and includes approximately the same number of papers.

THE STATE OF NEURAL NETWORKS

I have had the privilege of being involved with neural networks since 1986. Over these past nine years, I have witnessed several changes in the field. I have watched the funding for neural network technology dramatically grow. I have seen changes and trends in the technical emphasis of the field. And, I still see many challenges that remain ahead. The following three sections provide my perspectives in each of these areas.

A. Funding

There has been a significant investment in neural network technology since 1987. *Electronic Engineering Times* (March 29, 1993) reported the U.S. Department of Defense has spent $71 M developing neural network technology. Of this $71 M, the Advanced Research Projects Agency has spent $35 M. *Federal Computer Week* (February 15, 1993) reported this number could double by 1996. Neural network programs also exist within the National Science Foundation (basic research), Department of Energy (adaptive control), Department of Transportation (Intelligent Vehicle Highway System), Department of Commerce (process control), Department of Health and Human Services (diagnostic technologies), Federal Bureau of Identification (fingerprint recognition), Internal Revenue System (character recognition), Postal Service (handwriting recognition), and the Environmental Protection Agency (environment monitoring). Neural network programs have also emerged within other countries. The European Community funded a large effort under ESPRIT entitled Pygmalion. In addition, the Japanese have been aggressively funding several efforts in speech processing, control, and character recognition, and Australia has also been very active.

Private industry has also embraced the application of neural networks. When looking at industry's involvement, I am reminded of a comment made by Prof. Robert Hecht-Nielsen during one of his neural network short courses I attended in 1987. When asked to prognosticate and describe where the biggest applications of neural networks would be, Hecht-Nielsen offered a list he felt had good potential, but concluded his answer by stating that the applications with the greatest pay-off may not even be envisioned yet. Hecht-Nielsen proved to be prophetic. Two areas where neural networks are enjoying success are financial forecasting and process control. To my knowledge, neither of these applications were highly touted in 1987, yet both receive strong industrial support today.

B. Trends

There have been many changes over the past eight years. The following list represents some of the trends that I have observed during this period of time. Introductions to the chapters will expand on these items where appropriate.

- **Associative Memory Obsolescence.** Associative memory research has lost its momentum. Although there are still some researchers attempting to shine a spotlight into corners of a well-lit room, this area of research has never met the potential originally projected. Cellular neural networks represent one possible exception to this observation.

- **Optical Implementation Decline**. Optical and Electro-Optical implementations of neural networks have almost disappeared. Only one paper of the 1200 dealt with this area. Through the late 1980s, this was considered to be the implementation of choice. It was felt that light intensity could encode connection weights and dense packaging could be achieved because light nondestructively interferes with itself. Some of this attention deficit can be attributed to the reduction in associative memory interest.

- **MLP Proliferation.** Multi-Layer Perceptrons (MLPs) trained using the backpropagation algorithm encompasses almost half of the 1200 papers reviewed. Many scientists and engineers first exposed to the field are not aware there are other neural network paradigms beyond MLPs trained with backpropagation. Unfortunately, those that have followed such a path and have met limited success might have discarded this approach and retained a poor perspective of neural networks on a whole.

- **Analytical Rigor.** The analytical rigor has steadily improved each year. In particular, this volume will examine sensitivity, fault tolerance, generalization, and approximation in detail.

- **Analog Versus Digital.** The link between digital signal processing (DSP) and neural networks seems to be growing stronger. In particular, DSP chips are used for neural network applications in increasing numbers, resulting in a reduced need for special purpose neural network chips. Neural network integrated circuits have been emphasizing analog operations and the digital operations are being performed by DSP chips.

- **Software Simulations.** There are several excellent neural network simulation packages that are available in the public domain. As a result, companies that provide neural network software are emphasizing full solutions more than a software package.

- **Synergistic Hybrids.** The synergism between neural networks and other technologies is on the rise. Three notable areas include expert systems, fuzzy sets, and evolutionary computation. Expert systems and neural networks are combined to allow *a priori* knowledge to be efficiently and effectively combined with information that is attained through adaptation. Fuzzy sets and neural networks are now regularly combined for pattern recognition and control tasks, and evolutionary computation is often used for network design and training.

C. Challenges

Although the field of neural networks has matured, there are still many challenges that remain. The following list represents some of the most pressing problem areas.

- **Biological Ignorance.** Most of the scientists and engineers in the field of neural networks are biologically ignorant. There is a great body of knowledge in neuroscience that is available that has not been tapped by this community. With a few notable exceptions (such as Terrance Sejnowski, Stephen Grossberg, and Carver Mead), the gap between what is biologically relevant and what is being simulated has not been closed. To achieve truly intelligent machines, there must be more collaboration between engineering and neuroscience.

- **Rapid Learning.** Although there have been notable improvements, neural networks still are not learning fast enough to be of practical use in a great many applications, including adaptive control and communications. The neural networks community is still waiting for an algorithm that trains a three-layer nonlinear neural network as fast as a two-layer linear network.

- **Explanation Facility.** The explanation facilities that are available to neural networks are still primitive. Currently, fuzzy neural networks are closest to achieving this goal. The papers found in Chapter 1: Design give an indication of the progress being made in this area. Until this problem is solved, neural networks will continue to be perceived as an impenetrable black box that provides no hint of how it makes decisions. For many applications, especially in diagnostics, this proves to be a significant barrier.

---

2   Bezdek, J. & Pal, S. Eds., (1992). Fuzzy Models for Pattern Recognition, IEEE Press, Piscataway, NJ.

- **Construction Theorem**. There are several existence theorems that prove some neural networks can approximate a broad class of functions to any desired degree of accuracy.[3] Examples of this work are found in this volume. Knowing that a neural network can approximate a function is an important step, but now a prescription on how to build a network to achieve the mapping is needed. These construction theorems are the next big hurdle for neural networks.

- **Incremental Learning**. With only a few exceptions, if you have new data that you would like to train an existing neural network with, you must add the new data to the old data and completely retrain. This is clearly not how humans learn. New information is added incrementally to the old information immediately. In many neural network applications, incremental learning is an important property. As examples, often an engineer will want to add a new class to an existing neural network classifier, or additional data in a time-series modeling problem will become available and she will want to improve the model with the new data. With the exception of Reduced Coulomb Energy (RCE) networks,[4] Probablistic Neural Networks (PNN),[5] Fuzzy Min-Max (FMM) Neural Networks,[6] and Adaptive Resonance Theory (ART) networks,[7] this property is not widely available. In particular, the most popular neural networks today, the Multi-Layer Perceptron (MLP),[8] the Radial Basis Function (RBF) network,[9] and the Learning Vector Quantization (LVQ) network,[10] are not incremental learning networks.

- **Sparse Data Generalization**. One area of neural network analysis that has made significant progress over the past few years has been the study of generalization.[11] Using the theory of Probably Almost Correct (PAC) learning,[12] bounds on the number of training patterns needed for sufficient generalization have been

---

3   Poggio, T. & Girosi, F. (1990). Networks for approximation and learning, Proceedings of the IEEE, Vol. 78, No. 9., pp. 1481-1497.

4   Reilly, D., Cooper, L., & Elbaum, C. (1982). A neural model for category learning, Biological Cybernetics, Vol. 45, pp. 35-41.

5   Specht, D. (1990). Probablistic neural networks, Neural Networks, Vol. 3, No. 5, pp. 109-118.

6   Simpson, P. (1992). Fuzzy Min-max neural networks - Part 1: Classification, Vol. 3, No. 5, pp. 776-786; Simpson, P. (1993). Fuzzy Min-max neural networks - Part 2: Clustering, Vol. 1, No. 1, pp. 32-45.

7   Carpenter, G. (1989) Neural network models for pattern recognition and associative memory, Neural Networks, Vol. 2, No. 4, pp. 243-258.

8   Haykin, S. (1994). Neural Networks: A Comprehensive Foundation, IEEE Press, Piscataway, NJ.

9   Leonard, J., Kramer, M. & Unger L. (1992). Using radial basis functions to approximate a function and its error bounds, IEEE Trans. on Neural Networks, Vol. 3, No. 4, pp. 624-626.

10   Kohonen, T. (1990). Self-Organization and Associate Memory, Springer-Verlag, Berlin.

11   Hush, D. & Horne, B. (1993). Progress in supervised neural networks, IEEE Signal Processing Magazine, Vol. 10, No. 1, pp. 8-39

12   Vapnik, V. & Chervonenkis, A. (1971). On uniform convergence of relative frequencies of events to their probabilities, Theory of Probability and its Applications, Vol. 16, No. 2, pp. 264-280; Baum, E.

derived. That is the good news. The bad news is that the number of training patterns needed relative to the number of free parameters (neural network weights) grows large very quickly. A new challenge now emerges. Although there are some neural network applications that are abundant with data, there are large number that are not. Training techniques for existing (or new) neural networks need to be devised that will allow good generalization from sparse data sets.

- **Recurrent Network Analysis**. Recurrent neural networks present a whole new class of problems. The foremost problem is learning while remaining stable. When is it best to learn in a recurrent neural network? Once the network has stabilized? While it is stabilizing? What if it is not stable? In addition, learning in recurrent neural networks is slower, sometimes much slower, than learning in purely feedforward systems. How can the learning speed be improved? A special issue of the *IEEE Transactions on Neural Networks*[13] recently addressed many of these issues. Some of the papers found in this volume begin to work on this problem, but a good solution still remains to be found.

& Haussler, D. (1989). What size net gives valid generalization?, Neural Computation, Vol. 1, pp. 151-160.

13   Giles, C., Kuhn, G. & Williams, R. (1994). Guest Editorial: special Issue on Dynamic Recurrent Neural Networks, IEEE Trans. on Neural Networks, Vol. 5, No. 2, pp. 153-156.

IEEE Technology Update Series

Neural Networks Applications

Part I: Control

Control applications represents one of the strongest growth areas of neural networks. As an example of this proliferation, each year since 1988 there has been a special issue on neural networks for control in the prestigious *IEEE Control Systems Magazine*. In addition, the IEEE has published an entire book of edited papers on this subject.

There are four areas where neural networks present an advantage to control applications. Neural networks are model-free function approximators that learn from historical data and can therefore eliminate the dependance on a plant model. They are adaptive, which allows them to modify their behavior in response to changes in the plant. Neural networks are nonlinear, allowing them to perform highly complicated control tasks. And, they can be implemented using high-speed parallel hardware, thus providing real-time operation.

Part I addresses six different control areas. Chapter 1 describes four different neural network applications to electric motor control. Chapter 2 reviews twelve different process control applications from welding and metal cutting to fast food frying. Chapter 3 demonstrates the utility of neural networks to some of the most challenging engineering problems that exist in robotics such as manipulator control and biped locomotion. Chapter 4 offers two applications of neural networks to structure control, one for the stabilization of space platforms and the other for buildings. Chapter 5 illustrates the application of neural networks to various aspects of vehicle control for boats, planes, and automobiles. Chapter 6 illustrates how neural networks can be used to improve power conversion and inversion.

Electric motors are everywhere. They are in our fans, in our heating systems, in our computers, on our boats and in our cars. The future sees this trend continuing. Making the most efficient use of an electric motor is difficult, but the pay-off is tremendous. This chapter includes four different aspects of electric motor control using four different neural network approaches. In **Paper 1.1,** a multilayer perceptron (MLP) is used to learn the inverse plant dynamics of a chopper-fed DC motor. Following some analysis to confirm that this application has promise, a hardware realization of the controller is presented. **Paper 1.2** also utilizes an MLP for plant identification, but the conventional gradient descent training algorithm is replaced with a faster adapting Extended Kalman Filter (EKF) training algorithm. The combination of neural networks and fuzzy systems for electric motor control is found in **Paper 1.3**. In this paper, a robust neuro fuzzy controller is designed, and a Digital Signal Processor (DSP) implementation is described. The final paper in this chapter, **Paper 1.4**, focuses on the adaptive properties of neural networks. In this paper, the CMAC neural network is used to minimize torque ripple in switched reluctance motors.

Chapter 1:   *Electric Motor Control*

Neural Network Control of a Chopper-Fed DC Motor

John Bates   Malik E. Elbuluk   Donald S. Zinger

Department of Electrical Engineering
University of Akron
Akron, Ohio 44325-3904 USA

Abstract -- Neural networks are finding their way into control of power electronics and electric machines. Neural network controllers (NC) possess generalization and learning capabilities that makes them suitable to control of nonlinear, time-variant plants. This paper investigates neural network control of a chopper-fed dc motor. A dynamic NC is used in a direct adaptive control configuration. After proper training, the dynamic NC emulates the inverse plant dynamic mapping. Training requirements of a NC is investigated. Simulation results showing system performance are presented. Hardware implementation of the NC is discussed.

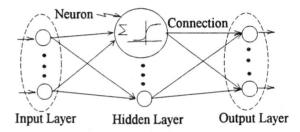

Fig. 1. Feed-forward, multilayered neural network structure showing layers, neurons, and connections.

I. INTRODUCTION

Artificial neural networks (ANN) are described by mathematical models of biological nervous systems. Like these nervous systems, ANNs possess, to some extent, learning and generalization capabilities. Through proper training, ANNs are capable of learning nonlinear mappings between an input space and an output space. By generalization, the trained ANN can map a new input (i.e. an input that was not in the training set) to an output. ANNs, then, are suitable to control applications that require controllers with learning and generalization capabilities. Such applications would include control of nonlinear, time-variant plants and control of plants with uncertainties.

One type of ANN is the multilayered, feed-forward neural network shown in Fig. 1. This type of neural network has a layered structure of neurons. Each neuron contains a summing node and a non-linearity. The neurons of adjacent layers are connected through weighted connections. The connection weights are dynamic through the learning process.

A neurocontroller (NC) is considered to be a nonconventional adaptive controller [1]. The NC is believed to be an improvement over a conventional adaptive controller when dealing with nonlinear systems and systems with uncertainties. For one thing, conventional adaptive control suffers from calculation complication for large numbers of unknown system parameters [2]. If properly trained, a NC is capable of compensating for system uncertainties, such as

parameter drifts, in a relatively short time. In addition, a NC, with a sufficient number of hidden layers and neurons, is fault tolerant. That is, if part of the NC is destroyed then the remaining part can compensate for this and control the system.

One of the main drawbacks of the NC is the large amount of time required to train it. This is due to the slowness (i.e. the slow convergence of the weights) of the training algorithm (e.g. error back-propagation). Attempts are currently being made [1] to improve on-line training algorithms.

The objective of this paper is to contribute to the understanding of neurocontrol of electric motor drives by studying neurocontrol of a chopper-fed dc motor. It is hoped that a sufficient understanding will eventually lead to a determination of the viability of neurocontrol to electric drives. There is little information in the literature addressing this application. References [3] and [4], for example, address specific applications of neurocontrol to inverter drives.

First, the plant (chopper-fed dc motor) is briefly described. A dynamic discrete-time model is presented. Then, the dynamic NC, in the direct adaptive control configuration, is described. NC training requirements are discussed next. Simulations of the system are presented. Included are simulations that show system response during the training process and system response to plant parameter disturbances and NC faults. Finally, hardware implementation of the NC is discussed. Circuit schematics are given for neuron and connection implementation.

9

II. PLANT DESCRIPTION

The plant is a chopper-fed dc motor, shown in Fig. 2. δ is the duty ratio and T is the switching period. The separately excited dc motor is modeled by an armature resistance, R_a, an armature inductance, L_a, and a back emf E as shown. In order to study the plant under load, a dc generator, identical to the dc motor, is used. A resistive load is connected to the dc generator.

The purpose of the controller, in this case, is to control the average speed, $<\omega>$, of the dc motor. Thus an average model of the plant is used, as shown in Fig. 3. The average model is most conveniently described by a sampled-data state space equation where the sampling interval is aligned with the switching period of the chopper. This convenience arises due to the discrete nature of δ. That is, each switching period has one δ associated with it. Thus a state space description in discrete-time is obtained where k, the discrete-time index, is incremented at the end of each switching period.

Using the forward Euler approximation of a continuous-time derivative, an approximate discrete-time model of the plant is obtained:

$$\begin{aligned}
<\omega>(k+1) &= 2.2<\omega>(k) - 1.5<\omega>(k-1) \\
&+ 0.3<\omega>(k-2) + 3.2 \cdot 10^{-3}\delta(k-1) \\
&- 1.1 \cdot 10^{-3}\delta(k-2).
\end{aligned} \quad (1)$$

The following parameter values were used: $R_a = 3\ \Omega$, $L_a = 0.01$ H, $V_{dc} = 24$ V, $R_L = 10\ \Omega$, T = 0.5 msec, J = 0.104 Nms^2, and $k\Phi = 0.54$ Vsec. $k\Phi$ is the motor-flux constant and J is the polar moment of inertia of the motor and generator. Equation (1) specifies that $<\omega>(k+1)$ is a function of $<\omega>(k)$, $<\omega>(k-1)$, $<\omega>(k-2)$, $\delta(k-1)$, and $\delta(k-2)$.

III. INVERSE PLANT DESCRIPTION

Equation (1) can be generalized as

$$\begin{aligned}
<\omega>(k+1) = f(&<\omega>(k), <\omega>(k-1), <\omega>(k-2), \\
&\delta(k-1), \delta(k-2)).
\end{aligned} \quad (2)$$

The function f is the dynamic model of the average plant. f maps $<\omega>(k)$, $<\omega>(k-1)$, $<\omega>(k-2)$, $\delta(k-1)$, and $\delta(k-2)$ to $<\omega>(k+1)$. For the plant under consideration, f is linear.

If f is invertible then $\delta(k)$ can be found as

$$\begin{aligned}
\delta(k) = f^{-1}(&<\omega>(k+2), <\omega>(k+1), <\omega>(k), \\
&<\omega>(k-1), \delta(k-1)).
\end{aligned} \quad (3)$$

f^{-1} maps $<\omega>(k+2)$, $<\omega>(k+1)$, $<\omega>(k)$, $<\omega>(k-1)$, and $\delta(k-1)$ to $\delta(k)$. Equation (3) is an inverse plant dynamic model. Indeed, f as given by (1) is invertible. The inverse function is given by:

$$\begin{aligned}
\delta(k) = 312.5<\omega>(k+2) - &687.5<\omega>(k+1) + 468.75<\omega>(k) \\
&- 93.75<\omega>(k-1) + 0.34\delta(k-1).
\end{aligned} \quad (4)$$

Fig. 4 shows the inverse plant control configuration. At time step k, the input to the plant is $\delta(k)$. The plant output $<\omega>(k)$ and its delayed version $<\omega>(k-1)$ are available for feedback. $<\omega>(k+2)$ and $<\omega>(k+1)$ are not available for feedback at k since they represent measurements that have not been made yet. Thus they are replaced by command values $<\omega>^*(k+2)$ and $<\omega>^*(k+1)$ that are the desired values of $<\omega>$ at (k+2) and (k+1) respectively.

IV. NEUROCONTROLLER DESCRIPTION

The control configuration, shown in Fig. 5, is called direct adaptive control [1]. The inverse plant in Fig. 4 has been replaced by a dynamic NC. The NC is dynamic in the sense that a recurrent feedback loop with time delay operator is used [5]. The input/output functionality of the NC is given by

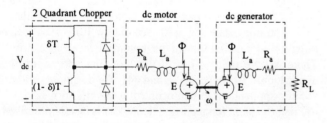

Fig. 2 Plant.

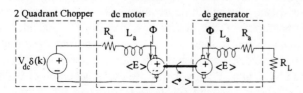

Fig. 3. Average plant model.

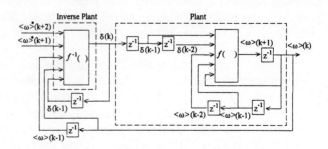

Fig. 4. Inverse plant control configuration.

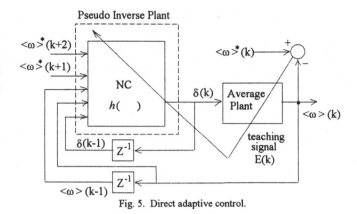

Fig. 5. Direct adaptive control.

$$\delta(k) = h(<\omega>^*(k+2), <\omega>^*(k+1), <\omega>(k),$$
$$<\omega>(k-1), \delta(k-1)). \qquad (5)$$

The objective of training is $h = f^{-1}$. In other words, the NC is taught to mimic the inverse plant.

The NC is trained using error back-propagation. The teaching signal, E(k), is the error in the average speed. That is, E(k) is the difference between the command average speed at k and the actual average speed at k. In direct adaptive control, E(k) is back-propagated directly through the plant and, then, through the NC. The plant is viewed as an additional NC layer [6]. As such, E(k) is back-propagated through the plant using the partial derivative of $<\omega>(k)$ with respect to $\delta(k)$ evaluated at the steady-state operating point.

Prior to training, the NC connection weights can be randomly initialized. Alternatively, off-line training can be used to initialize the connection weights [6]. This usually gives better weight initialization. After weight initialization, the NC is trained on-line. That is, as the NC is learning the inverse plant dynamics, it is controlling the plant.

To train the NC, a training pattern is specified. The training pattern is a specified $<\omega>^*(k)$ that is used to generate E(k), $<\omega>^*(k+2)$, and $<\omega>^*(k+1)$. Possible training patterns are periodic staircase functions and periodic sawtooth functions. The continuous-time versions of these functions are shown in Fig. 6. In this figure, t_n is the beginning of the nth training cycle and T_{tr} is the time duration of each training cycle.

The NC weights are updated using the back-propagation algorithm with frequency f_{ln}. Fig. 7 shows typical relationships between T, T_{tr}, and T_{ln} (i.e. inverse of f_{ln}). T_{tr} usually contains many switching periods. T_{ln} does not have to align with T. It is conceivably possible to update the weights at the end of each switching period or after m switching periods. It is also conceivably possible for the weights to be updated j times per switching period. Results on other

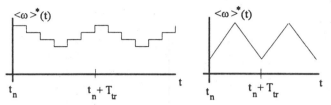

Fig. 6. Periodic training pattern examples.

systems [1] indicate that large f_{ln} is desirable. Practically, f_{ln} will be limited by processing time necessary for one learning iteration.

The training procedure stops once the NC weights have converged. Hopefully, the weights will converge to a global minimum in $E^2(k)$. There is, however, no guarantee that this will be the case [6]. After training, E(k) is used to adapt the NC to system disturbances such as parameter drifts and NC faults. Other results [6] indicate that NCs can compensate for faults after some transition interval.

V. SIMULATION RESULTS

Simulations of the system were done using the NC shown in Fig. 8. The inputs to this NC are $<\omega>^*(k)$, $<\omega>(k-1)$, and $<\omega>(k-2)$. The input/output functionality of this NC is given by:

$$\delta(k) = h(<\omega>^*(k), <\omega>(k-1), <\omega>(k-2)). \qquad (6)$$

This NC gives good results and its training time is significantly less than that for the NC shown in Fig. 5. Hence (6) can be thought of as a reduced order model of (5).

The NC used in the simulations is a multilayered feed-forward neural network [2]. It has one hidden layer with three neurons. The input neurons have a linear signal function. The hidden and output neurons have a signal function that is a piece-wise linear approximation to the sigmoidal function with coefficient equal to 0.9. The learning rate is 0.1. The switching and learning frequencies are both 2 kHz. Thus, the NC weights were updated once at the end of each switching period. The motor and generator parameters are given in section II.

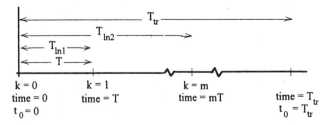

Fig. 7 Typical relationship between training cycle period, switching period, and learning interval.

11

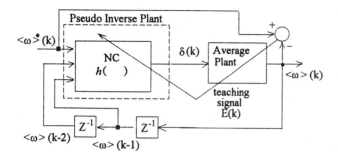

Fig. 8. NC used in the simulations.

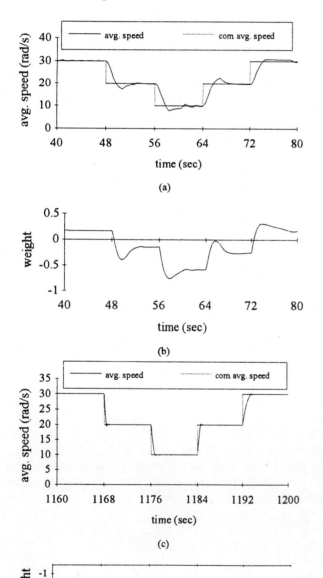

(a)

(b)

(c)

(d)

ı response. (a) Second training cycle. (c) Training cycle #30. NC
'. (b) Second training cycle. (d) Training cycle #30.

The system response during the training process is shown in Fig. 9. The NC weights were randomly initialized. The training pattern (i.e. command average speed) is a periodic staircase function as shown in Figs. 9(a) and (c). Three operating points were chosen: 30 rad/s, 20 rad/s, and 10 rad/s. They form the training set (TS): {30 rad/s, 20 rad/s, 10 rad/s}. Each element of TS appears in the training pattern for 8 seconds at a time. Each training cycle lasts 40 seconds.

Fig. 9(a) shows the average speed, $<\omega>(t)$, during the second training cycle. The NC has not sufficiently learned the inverse plant dynamics at this point and, hence, system response is poor. The NC weight shown in Fig. 9(b) shows no indication that it will converge during the second training cycle.

By the thirtieth training cycle, most of the NC weights have converged. Fig. 9(d) shows one of the twelve weights. Indeed, system response shown in Fig. 9(c) indicates that the NC has learned to mimic the inverse plant. The average speed closely tracks the command average speed.

The trained weights (i.e. the converged weights) can be used to study the system performance, under various scenarios, with a trained NC. Fig. 10(a) shows the system response to command average speeds that are not in TS. This will provide an indication of the NCs generalization capabilities. The response indicates that the trained NC has good generalization capabilities. Close inspection of the NC weight shown in Fig. 10(b) indicates that some learning is taking place as the average speed approaches 5 rad/s. It seems that the NCs ability to generalize to small command

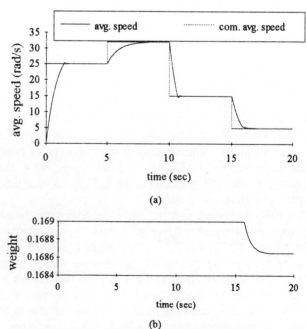

(a)

(b)

Fig. 10. Trained NC. (a) System response to command speeds outside the
training set. (b) NC weight.

average speeds is not sufficient. Thus some additional training is needed. This is, in part, provided by the presence of E(k). The sluggishness of the response to a step in the command average speed from 25 rad/s to 32 rad/s can not be attributed to the NC. 32 rad/s is close to the maximum steady-state operating point attainable under the given conditions. Correspondingly, δ has reached its upper bound of 1.

In a practical application, it might be desirable to command a constant average acceleration. Thus, a ramp average speed, whose slope is the desired acceleration, would be the command average speed. Fig. 11 shows system response to a ramp command average speed. The trained NC performs quite well as indicated by close tracking. In particular, the system has some difficulty at low speeds where some additional fine tuning of the weights is needed. Overall, the accumulated error between command and actual speed is small.

In an actual implementation, the NC will have to utilize its adaptation abilities to compensate for plant parameter changes. For example, it is well known that dc machine armature resistance (R_a) changes with armature current. Fig. 12 shows simulated response, of a pretrained system, to changing R_a. In this case, R_a is a series of 1 Ω steps. The average speed is 0 rad/s at 0 seconds. As R_a steps to 2 Ω at 5 seconds, the response begins to oscillate (indicated by the thicker line) about the command speed. During this time, the NC is learning the new inverse plant dynamics. When R_a steps back to 3 Ω at 10 seconds, the response settles back to the command speed. This would seem to indicate that the NC still remembers the dynamics at 3 Ω. The response dips slightly as R_a steps to 4 Ω. In order to maintain 30 rad/s at this R_a, δ must increase to a value near its upper bound. It takes a short amount of time for the NC to learn this.

One of the advantages of an NC, over conventional controllers, is its tolerance to faults. That is, if part of the NC is destroyed while it is on-line, then it is possible for the remaining part to control the system. Some training, however, might be necessary after the fault occurs. Fig. 13 shows the response, of a pretrained system, to the destruction of one hidden layer neuron at 5 seconds. What remains,

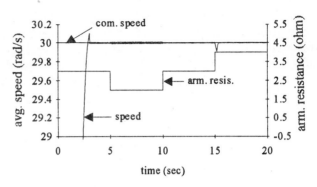

Fig. 12. Pretrained system response to changing armature resistance. Command speed is constant at 30 rad/s.

after the fault, is an NC with one hidden layer having only two neurons. The system response, after the fault, indicates that the inverse plant dynamics are not sufficiently known by the new NC structure. Therefore, some training is required for the NC to relearn the dynamics. The step response shown at 15 seconds is indicative of good control. However, the response at 20 seconds can be improved. Either more training is needed to improve the response or the new NC structure does not contain enough hidden layer neurons to sufficiently learn the inverse plant dynamics.

VI. HARDWARE IMPLEMENTATION

Currently, NC hardware implementation is being pursued, by the authors, to obtain experimental results. One possible implementation, which is being tested, is the hybrid analog/digital implementation [3]. In this type of implementation, the connections between neurons of adjacent layers are implemented by a multiplying DAC. The neurons, on the other hand, are implemented with analog circuitry.

A block diagram of a single neuron and its connections is shown in Fig. 14. Each neuron has its own dedicated microcontroller. Currently, the MC68705P3 is being tested for this application. It coordinates all the activities of its

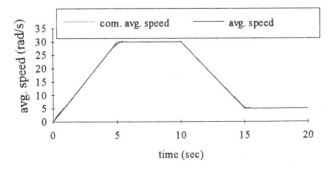

Fig. 11. Pretrained system response to ramp command speed.

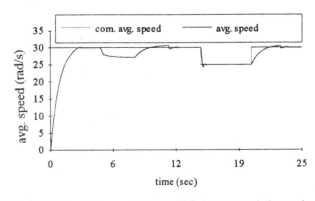

Fig. 13. Pretrained system response to an NC fault. A neuron is destroyed at 5 seconds.

neuron. It also sends and receives information from a personal computer (PC). The PC oversees and coordinates the activities of the entire neural network. It is primarily responsible for implementing the back-propagation algorithm. The connection weights, which are stored in the PC, are downloaded to the corresponding neuron. Each neuron also has its own A/D. The A/D converts the analog neuron activation to a digital representation. This weight is then passed to the PC, through the microcontroller, where it is needed in the back-propagation algorithm. The circuitry implementing the blocks contained within the dashed line can be constructed on one printed circuit board. This allows for modular construction of the neural network.

In order to reduce costs, one DAC is used per neuron as shown in Fig. 15. The connections, to adjacent layer neurons, are multiplexed using an eight channel analog MUX (e.g. 14051). Thus, each neuron has a maximum of eight possible connections. The neuron microcontroller sends a three bit address of one of the input channels. Each channel is connected to the output of a neuron in the left adjacent layer. The channel corresponding to the address is connected to the DAC. At this time, the appropriate connection weight is sent to the DAC from the microcontroller. Now the output of the DAC is the product of the weight and the neuron output. The neuron output is always positive and the weight can be positive or negative. The output of the DAC is a unidirectional current that is converted to a positive voltage via the op-amp with feedback resistor. Circuitry is included to convert this voltage to its negative value if the sign bit of the weight is high. The voltage that represents the weight-neuron output product is sent to the appropriate output channel via an eight channel analog DEMUX. While this voltage is held by a capacitor, the microcontroller sends the address of the next channel to the MUX. The appropriate digital weight is loaded and the product is computed. The voltage, which represents the product, is demultiplexed and held by a capacitor on the appropriate output channel. The microcontroller scans the input channels, in this manner, until all weight-neuron output products have been computed.

There are tradeoffs between this approach (MUX approach) and the approach that employs one DAC for each connection. If full channel capacity (i.e. the neuron is connected to eight neurons of the adjacent layer) is utilized then cost is cut by using the MUX approach. This conclusion is arrived at by considering the cost of eight DACs versus the cost of one DAC, two MUXs, and one microcontroller. On the other hand, the MUX approach is more complicated with respect to programming and interfacing requirements. The "one DAC" approach does not require the degree of neuron coordination that the MUX approach does. Also, NCs implemented with the MUX approach have longer feed-forward processing times than NCs implemented with the "one DAC" approach. The slow processing time, of the MUX approach, is due to eight channels, of each neuron, sharing one DAC. When applied to a chopper switching at 2 kHz, it appears that an NC implemented with the MUX approach is sufficiently fast.

Neuron implementation using analog circuitry is shown in Fig. 16 [3]. A resistor network and one op-amp are used to implement the sum of all input voltages, thus computing the neuron activation. The input channels of the neuron circuitry are the output channels of the connection circuitry as shown in Fig. 14. The neuron non-linearity is implemented using an op-amp with resistive feedback and zener diode clamping circuit. The non-linearity is a piece-wise approximation to the sigmoidal non-linearity. Through proper pot adjustment, a family of non-linearities is attainable. Fig. 17 shows the non-linearity for three wiper settings on pot 1 in Fig. 16: 10 Ω, 5 kΩ, and 10 kΩ. The upper saturation level can be adjusted through pot 2 in Fig. 16. Notice that, unlike the sigmoidal function, the non-linearity shown in Fig. 17 is not symmetrical about a vertical axis through 0 volts.

VII. CONCLUSIONS

Simulations of NC control, in the direct adaptive configuration, of a chopper-fed dc motor indicate good control characteristics. A sufficiently trained NC can achieve small cumulative error between actual and desired speed. Simulations also show that training time of an untrained NC can be long. On the other hand, adaptation time of a trained NC to system disturbances is within the realm of a good controller. This is evident in simulations where motor armature resistance changes. The NC is also seen to be versatile in that it can control the motor to track ramp speeds. Simulations also show that neurocontrol can be tolerant to faults although some additional training might be necessary. Most conventional controllers, on the other hand, are not fault tolerant. Currently, the system is being built in order to experimentally verify the simulation results.

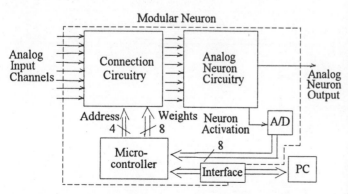

Fig. 14. Block diagram of modular neuron showing interfacing to PC.

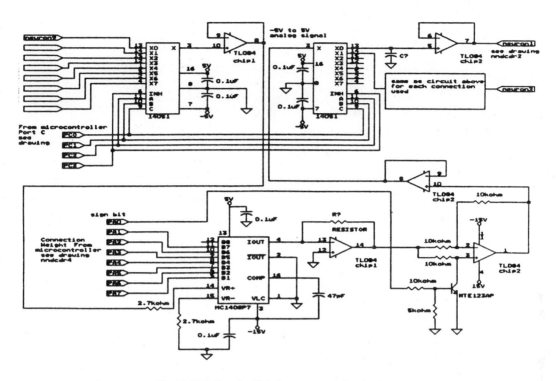

Fig. 15. Hybrid analog/digital neuron connection circuitry.

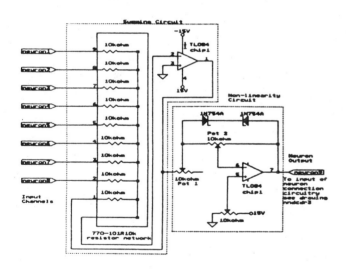

Fig. 16 Analog neuron circuit showing summer and non-linearity implementation.

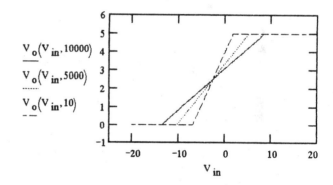

$$\frac{V_o(V_{in}, 10000)}{\overline{V_o(V_{in}, 5000)}}$$

$$V_o(V_{in}, 10)$$

Fig. 17. Family of non-linearities. Slope is adjusted through pot 1 in Fig. 16. Both axis units are volts.

ACKNOWLEDGMENT

The authors would like to acknowledge the participation of Tom Perl, at the University of Akron, in the hardware phase of the project. Discussions with Dr. Bill Timmons were very valuable and highly appreciated.

REFERENCES

[1] J. Tanomaru and S. Omatu, "Process Control by On-Line Trained Neural Controllers," *IEEE Trans. Indust. Elect.,* vol. 39, no. 6, pp. 511-521, Dec. 1992.

[2] T. Fukuda and T. Shibata, "Theory and Applications of Neural Networks for Industrial Control Systems," *IEEE Trans. Indust. Elect.,* vol. 39, no. 6, pp. 472-487, Dec. 1992.

[3] M. Buhl and R. Lorenz, "Design and Implementation of Neural Networks for Digital Current Regulation of Inverter Drives," *Conf. Record of IEEE, IAS Annual Meeting,* 1991, pp. 415 - 421.

[4] Y. Ito, T. Furuhashi, S. Okuma, and Y. Uchikawa, "A Digital Current Controller for a PWM Inverter Using a Neural Network and its Stability," *PESC,* 1990, vol. 1, pp. 219 - 224.

[5] T. Yabuta and T. Yamada, "Neural Network Controller Characteristics with Regard to Adaptive Control," *IEEE Trans. Sys., Man, Cyber.,* vol. 22, no. 1, pp. 170 - 176, Jan/Feb 1992.

[6] P. Raiskila and H. Koivo, "Properties of a Neural Network Controller," *IECON Tutorial Text Book,* 1991, pp. 84 - 88.

Artificial Neural Network Identification of Partially Known Dynamic Nonlinear Systems

Ronald H. Brown, Timothy L. Ruchti, and Xin Feng
(414/288-3501), (414/288-1609), (414/288-3504)

Department of Electrical and Computer Engineering
Marquette University
1515 West Wisconsin Avenue
Milwaukee, WI 53233

Abstract - This paper presents a method for incorporating *a priori* information about an uncertain nonlinear system into the structure of a multilayer feedforward artificial neural network. Known information is incorporated into the activation function of the network output layer. An algorithm is derived for backpropagating the error and updating adjustable parameters within this layer that is consistent with existing supervised learning techniques. The developed technique is applied to the identification of a dynamic system and compared with a conventional feedforward artificial neural network identifier. Results exhibit an improvement in the quality of the identification model and an increase in the rate of convergence. As a practical application, *a prior* information is utilized for identification of switched reluctance motor characteristics on the basis of experimental measurements. The results further demonstrate that artificial neural networks employing *a priori* information converge faster, require fewer adjustable weights, and more accurately predict the system of interest.

1. INTRODUCTION

Although extensive research has been devoted to developing powerful techniques for the identification and control of uncertain dynamic linear systems, analogous methods are yet to be developed for dynamic systems that exhibit significant nonlinearities and uncertainties.

Artificial neural networks (ANNs) are an emerging technology promising to contribute to the solution of the nonlinear system identification and control problems. A principle advantage of ANNs, resulting from their parallel structure and inherent nonlinearity, is the ability to model any piecewise continuous nonlinear mapping to an arbitrary degree of accuracy with properly selected parameters [1,2,3]. Consequently, the suitability of feedforward ANNs for representing mappings in nonlinear identification and control problems has been recognized and recently, several authors have made tremendous contributions to this area by integrating ANNs into identification model and controller structures [4,5,6,7,8,9,10]. In these applications, a feedforward ANN is generally employed as a black box identification model that approximates an unknown nonlinear mapping imbedded in a dynamic plant. Practically, however, a substantial amount of *a priori* information exists and is available regarding the behavior of a particular system that can be exploited to the advantage of the ANN identifier and controller.

The use of *a priori* information has been suggested in the literature [10,11,12,13,14]. Recently, Joerding et. al. [12] established that *a priori* knowledge can be used to constrain the weights of an ANN through modification of the training algorithm. Sartori et. al. [13] suggested that *a priori* knowledge be incorporated in parallel with an ANN identifier. Both Selinsky [14] and Iiguni [11] employed known dynamics about the object of control to train ANNs offline to the advantage of the neurocontrol structure. Pao [15] introduced a technique for enhancing initial representations to an ANN by replacing the linear links with functional links which can be useful for utilizing *a priori* information to the benefit of an ANN based identifier. However, no practical method that integrates such *a priori* knowledge into the structure of an ANN while allowing training of adjacent layers has been reported.

In this paper, a method is extended that allows the incorporation of prior information concerning the nature of an uncertain nonlinear system into the structure of an ANN. Previously [17], weights were constrained in an ANN layer, denoted the gray layer, according to *a priori* information, while the ability to backpropagate error and adaptively modify other parameters was retained. The weights of the gray layer were set to functions of the input that modeled known characteristics of the system being identified. As a result, incorporation of *a priori* information was limited to functions that can be represented by a linear combination of ANN signals. In subsequent sections, this technique is advanced such that the gray layer can include information that is nonlinear in ANN signals. This is achieved by incorporating known plant characteristics into the activation functions of the ANN rather than the weights.

The paper is organized as follows. In Section 2 a brief introduction and review is given on the topic of feedforward ANNs to clarify the notation and serve as a basis for the development of the gray layer. The gray layer technique is proposed in Section 3. The advantage of a gray layer in nonlinear dynamic system identification is demonstrated in Section 4 by integrating it into an identification example outlined in [8] and applied to the identification of the highly nonlinear static torque characteristics of a switched reluctance motor (SRM) as a practical example demonstrating the utility of the new technique in Section 5.

2. FEEDFORWARD ARTIFICIAL NEURAL NETWORKS

The input layer of an ANN will be denoted the *l*st layer and each subsequent layer will be referred to as the $(L+1)$th layer. A given layer, L, consists of a set of weights or synapses { $w_{ij}^L(k)$: i=1 to n^L, j=1 to n^{L-1} } contained in the matrix $W^L(k)$ and n^L neurons or processing elements. Propagation of an observation, $u(k)$, through the

ANN is governed by

$$o_i^L(k) = f\left[\sum_{j=1}^{n^{L-1}} w_{ij}^L(k)\, o_j^{L-1}(k)\right] = f\left[x_i^L(k)\right] \qquad (2.1)$$

where k is the input pattern index, $o_j^{L-1}(k)$ is the output of the jth neuron in the $(L-1)$th layer, and $f(\cdot)$ is the sigmoidal function which maps $[-\infty\ \infty] \rightarrow [-1\ 1]$. Note that $o_j^0(k) \triangleq u_j(k)$, the jth input to the ANN at time k.

Two training algorithms are utilized in this paper including the standard backpropagation algorithm in which the weights are updated according to

$$\Delta W_{ij}^L(k) = \alpha\, \delta_i^L(k)\, o_j^{L-1}(k) \qquad (2.2)$$

where α is the learning rate and δ_i refers to the backpropagated error in the ith layer. In the output layer, the signal error is

$$\delta_i^L(k) = e_i(k)\frac{\partial f_i^L(x_i^L(k))}{\partial x_i^L(k)} = e_i(k)\, f_i^{L'}(k) \qquad (2.3)$$

while for any other layer

$$\delta_i^L(k) = f_i^{L'}(k)\left(W_{col\,i}^{L+1}(k)\right)^T \delta^{L+1}(k) \qquad (2.4)$$

The extended Kalman training algorithm, proposed by [19,20], utilizes an extended Kalman filter by defining weight selection as a nonlinear state estimation problem. Briefly, this involves the consolidation of all adjustable network weights into a state vector, the calculation of the explicit partial derivatives of the output with respect to this vector, and the application of the Kalman filter for each input-output pattern. Although this technique is computationally intensive, the rate of convergence and the ability of the algorithm to locate the global minima is superior to gradient descent techniques.

3. THE GRAY LAYER TECHNIQUE

The availability of *a priori* knowledge is a decided advantage in the identification of uncertain nonlinear systems. The exploitation of such information is usually beneficial, resulting in the selection of more accurate identification models and a faster rate of parameter convergence [21]. While feedforward ANNs have been shown to represent a class of structures suitable for application in a wide range of identification problems, *a priori* information concerning the nature of the uncertain mappings is generally neglected and the system of interest is considered to be a "black box." Although this type of identification scheme has achieved results unattainable by conventional linear approaches, it is shown in subsequent sections that the utilization of all information about a given system will result in superior identification.

In this section a technique is developed for incorporating *a prior* information about an uncertain nonlinear transformation into the structure of an ANN. The strategy employed is to choose the activation functions according to *a priori* knowledge of the plant characteristics. The resulting ANN is then envisioned to model a partially known or "gray" mapping rather than a completely unknown one, hence the layer is designated a "gray layer".

A. Definition

Consider an uncertain nonlinear mapping, $\Gamma:\mathbb{R}^m \rightarrow \mathbb{R}^n$, where $\Gamma(\cdot)$ is known to be roughly approximated by

$$\Gamma(u(k)) \approx \hat{g} = \tilde{\Gamma}\left[u(k),\gamma(u(k))\right] + d(u(k)) \qquad (3.1)$$

where $\tilde{\Gamma}:\mathbb{R}^m \rightarrow \mathbb{R}^n$ is known and well-defined and $\gamma(k)$ is an unknown nonlinear mapping operating on the input vector $u(k)$. The mapping, $\tilde{\Gamma}(\cdot)$, represents an underlying relationship between the input and $\Gamma(\cdot)$

that is known to exist, for example: the periodicity of $\Gamma(\cdot)$ or the variation of $\Gamma(\cdot)$ with respect to the square of $u(k)$. The function $d:\mathbb{R}^m \rightarrow \mathbb{R}^n$ is an unknown nonlinear transformation that accounts for the portion of $\Gamma(\cdot)$ left unmodeled by $\tilde{\Gamma}(\cdot)$. The proposed gray layer technique is a method of estimating $\Gamma(\cdot)$ by incorporating the known function, $\tilde{\Gamma}(\cdot)$, into the activation functions of the ANN output layer and utilizing the prior layers to determine $\gamma(\cdot)$ and $d(\cdot)$. Equation (3.1) is denoted the gray function.

Using the notation of Section 2, the gray layer is defined as the Gth feedforward layer of an ANN consisting of n^G neurons, n^G by n^{G-1} weight matrix $W^G(k)$, and an activation function $\hat{g}(\cdot)$. The product of the weight matrix and the output from the previous layer form

$$x^G(k) = W^G(k)\, o^{G-1}(k) \qquad (3.2)$$

where o^{G-1} is the output of the last layer before the (output) gray layer. The activation function $\hat{g}(\cdot)$, specified by (3.1), performs one or more of the following: a nonlinear mapping, a functional link between the activation levels, and a summation operation. When the output of the nonlinear mapping is a scalar, the first element of x^G is typically assigned to d and the remaining elements to γ. Other mappings of x^G onto d and γ can be devised.

Given an ANN incorporating a gray layer, forward propagation of a pattern though the gray layer occurs by evaluating (3.2), preforming the mapping from x^G to d and γ, and evaluating the gray function, (3.1).

Example 1, part a. A nonlinear mapping is known to be an odd function of $u_i(k) \in u(k)$, with odd half wave symmetry. The gray layer function could be:

$$\begin{aligned} x_1^G &= d \\ x_2^G &= \gamma_1 \\ x_3^G &= \gamma_2 \\ x_4^G &= \gamma_3 \end{aligned} \qquad (3.3)$$

$$\hat{g} = d + \gamma_1 \sin(c u_1(k)) + \gamma_2 \sin(3 c u_1(k)) + \gamma_3 \sin(5 c u_1(k))$$

where c is a constant. An ANN with this gray layer is shown in Figure 1.

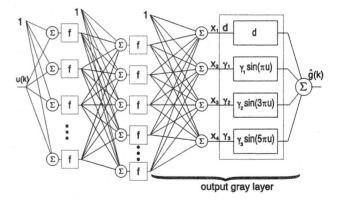

Figure 1. *An ANN with a 4-element gray layer.*

B. Backpropagation Through a Gray Layer

The weights in the gray layer can be updated the same way as any other layer using (2.2) once $\delta^G(k)$ is determined. $\delta^G(k)$ can be determined from (2.3) where

$$\frac{\partial f_i^G(x_i^G(k))}{\partial x_i^G(k)} = \frac{\partial\left[\tilde{\Gamma}(u(k),\gamma(k)) + d(u(k))\right]}{\partial x_i^G(k)} \qquad (3.4)$$

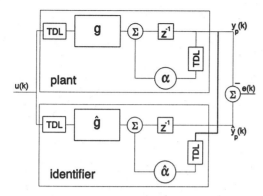

Figure 2. *The unknown system and the series-parallel identifier of Model I.*

Example 1, part b. $\delta^G(k)$ for the gray layer described in Example 1 above is

$$\begin{aligned}
\delta_1^G &= e(k)\cdot 1 \\
\delta_2^G &= e(k)\cdot \sin\big(cu_1(k)\big) \\
\delta_3^G &= e(k)\cdot \sin\big(3cu_1(k)\big) \\
\delta_4^G &= e(k)\cdot \sin\big(5cu_1(k)\big)
\end{aligned} \tag{3.5}$$

C. Discussion

The principle advantage of the gray layer technique is the reduction of the burden placed upon the remaining portion of the ANN through the building of a better identification model. Although feedforward ANNs are structurally capable of modeling any continuous function, the number of basis functions necessary and the burden placed on the estimation technique grows with the complexity of the mapping. Hence, the exploitation of the known characteristics of a system reduces the number of additional identification model components.

4. IDENTIFICATION OF A NONLINEAR DYNAMIC SYSTEM

In this section, results are presented from a nonlinear system identification problem similar to those outlined [8] with the addition of a gray layer. Under consideration is a general class of dynamic systems represented by vector differential or difference equations. For example,

$$\begin{aligned}
x(k+1) &= \Phi\big[x(k), u(k)\big] \\
y(k) &= \Psi\big[x(k)\big]
\end{aligned} \tag{4.1}$$

with $x(k)\in\mathbb{R}^n$, $u(k)\in\mathbb{R}^p$, $y(k)\in\mathbb{R}^m$
and nonlinear mappings $\Phi:\mathbb{R}^n\times\mathbb{R}^p\to\mathbb{R}^n$, $\Psi:\mathbb{R}^n\to\mathbb{R}^m$

According to the convention proposed by [8], when $\Phi(\cdot)$ is separable, i.e., $\Phi(\cdot) = f(\cdot) + g(\cdot)$, and $f(\cdot)$ is linear, the system is a Model I representation and a series-parallel identifier topology can be applied, as illustrated in Figure 2.

It is desired to identify a dynamic plant described of the form given in (4.1) with a known linear element in the feedback path and an unknown nonlinearity in the feedforward path. The plant dynamics are

$$y(k+1) = g\big[u(k)\big] + 0.3y(k) + 0.6y(k-1) \tag{4.2}$$

where the unknown nonlinearity is

$$g\big[u(k)\big] = 1.8\,\frac{10u(k)}{1 + 100u^2(k)} \tag{4.3}$$

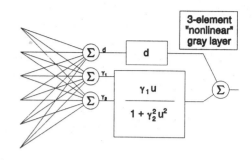

Figure 3. *Depiction of the three-element gray layer (without the prior input and hidden layers).*

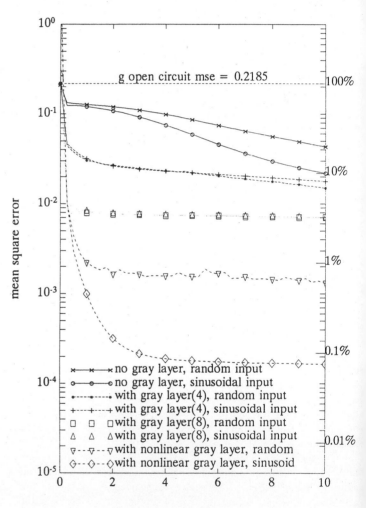

iteration in thousands

Figure 4. *Convergence characteristics for the ANN based identifier without a gray layer, with the 4-element gray layer, with the 8-element gray layer, and with the nonlinear 3-element gray layer.*

The system was simulated with both uniformly distributed random inputs and a sinusoidal input of $u(k)=\sin(2\pi k/10)+\sin(2\pi k/25)$, with a conventional ANN identifier without a gray layer, an ANN with a gray layer consisting of 4-elements as in (3.3) and illustrated in Figure 1, and an ANN with a gray layer containing the 8-elements:

$$\hat{g} = d + \gamma_1 u(k) + \gamma_2 u^3(k) + \gamma_3 \sin(\pi u(k)) + \gamma_4 \sin(2\pi u(k))$$
$$+ \gamma_5 \sin(3\pi u(k)) + \gamma_6 \sin(4\pi u(k)) + \gamma_7 \sin(5\pi u(k))$$

During each simulation, the mean square error (mse) was measured every epoch (250 iterations) for ten different random initializations of the ANN weight matrices. The average convergence characteristics were determined by averaging the mse from the ten simulations. This was performed for each of the six cases (2 inputs, 3 identifiers). The average mse for each case is shown in Figure 4.

The 4-element gray layer is not significant for this problem, and performs only slightly better than the identifier without a gray layer. This shows that if the gray layer is poorly chosen, no significant benefit will result. The more general 8-element gray layer converges to a mse that is an order of magnitude smaller than the identifier without a gray layer in relatively few iterations.

An additional gray layer was simulated in this example. This gray layer, given by

$$\hat{g} = d + a_1\gamma_1 \frac{u(k)}{1 + a_2\gamma_2^2 u^2(k)} \qquad (4.5)$$

is illustrated in Figure 3 and is nonlinear in the neural network output. This gray layer was simulated with random and sinusoidal inputs and the mse versus iteration, also shown in Figure 4, is substantially better than any of the previous simulations.

5. IDENTIFICATION OF SRM STATIC TORQUE CURVES

As a practical example demonstrating the utility of gray layers, consider the identification of the static torque characteristics of a switched reluctance motor (SRM) through the use of a feedforward ANN. SRMs are doubly salient D.C. devices distinguished by their reliability and high torque to inertia ratio. However, widespread use in high performance applications has been hampered because the developed torque is a highly nonlinear function of rotor position and stator current [22]. While the identification of this relationship has proven to be difficult [23], it is a necessary component of recent nonlinear control systems involving the utilization of SRMs for highly dynamic tasks [24].

It is well known that the developed torque of an SRM is periodic and approximately an odd function of rotor position [22] as illustrated by the experimental measurements depicted in Figure 5. This *a priori* information can be exploited to the advantage of an ANN through the addition of a gray output layer consisting of one neuron and weights specified according to:

$$w_1(k) = \beta$$
$$w_{i+1}(k) = \sin(2\pi i\theta(k)) \qquad i = 1, 2, \cdots, p \qquad (5.1)$$

where β is a scaler constant, p specifies the number of harmonic components in the gray layer, and θ specifies the rotor position in electrical radians. The output of the gray layer is then given by

$$y^G(k) = \beta y_1^{G-1}(k) + \sum_{i=1}^{p} y_{i+1}^{G-1}(k)\sin(2\pi i\theta(k)) \qquad (5.2)$$

where $y^{G-1}(k)$ is the output vector of the $(G-1)$th layer.

The ANN identification process which was performed consisted of two steps: the measurement of experimental data, and the supervised training of several feedforward ANNs. Experimental torque versus position measurements for 20 different current levels over a complete rotation of an SRM were taken through an automated data acquisition system. One electrical cycle of the acquired data is shown in Figure 5. Each of the curves contains 270 data points. Five evenly spaced torque curves were selected as a test set to be used exclusively

Table 1 - *Summary of torque characterization results employing training via backpropagation.*

Gray Layer	Network Architecture	Adj. Weights	Its.	$\underline{MSE}^2$
NO	2-30-10-1	370	200k	9.137
YES	2-8-4-(11-1)[1]	92	200k	0.2216

[1] *parentheses denote a gray layer.* [2] *of the 10 seed average.*

Table 2 - *Summary of torque characterization results employing the extended Kalman training algorithm.*

Gray Layer	Network Architecture	Adj. Weights	Its.	MSE^2
NO	2-14-7-1	133	50k	0.1025
YES	2-8-4-(11-1)[1]	92	50k	0.0505

[1] *parentheses denote a gray layer.* [2] *of the 10 seed average.*

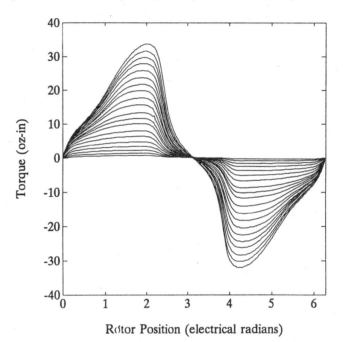

Figure 5. *Measure static torque curves for 20 current levels ranging from 0.25 to 3 amps.*

for the purpose of performance evaluation during and after the ANN training process. The remaining torque data was used to train the identifiers described below.

A total of four separate experiments, summarized in Tables I and II, were performed on ANNs with and without gray layers and utilizing two different learning algorithms. Each experiment was performed for 10 separate random ANN initializations. The tables lists the average 10 seed mean squared error of the test set after training was terminated.

Both conventional and gray layer networks required two inputs because torque is a function of both rotor position and stator current. Even though position is used to set the weights of the gray layer, the gray layer network needed to be presented with current and position input to model error resulting from the truncated Fourier series and to model the Fourier coefficients as functions of position, as evidenced by the nonsymmetric nature of the torque curves in Figure 5.

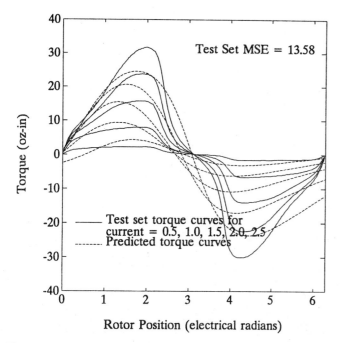

Figure 6. *Actual and predicted test set torque vs. position curves for training via backpropagation and without a gray layer.*

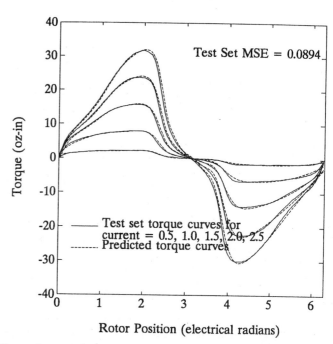

Figure 8. *Actual and predicted test set torque vs. position curves for training via the extended Kalman filter and without a gray layer.*

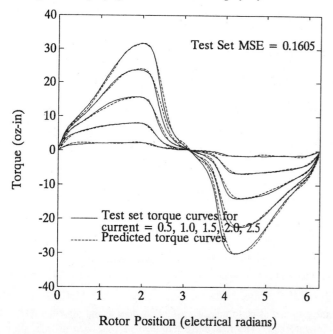

Figure 7. *Actual and predicted test set torque vs. position curves for training via backpropagation and with a gray layer.*

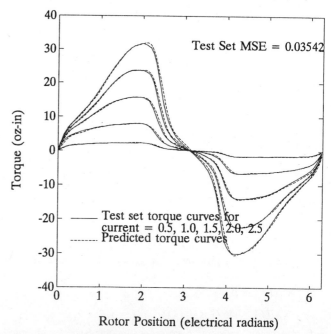

Figure 9. *Actual and predicted test set torque vs. position curves for training via the extended Kalman filter and with a gray layer.*

In the first experiment, training was terminated after 200,000 iterations due to the low rate of convergence even though Figure 6 indicates that the network was not fully trained. Experiment 2 employed an identical learning algorithm (backpropagation), but achieved superior results as shown if Figure 7 with the addition of a gray layer. A comparison of the two experiments reveals that the network with the gray layer required fewer adjustable weights and achieved a much lower error in the same number of iterations.

In experiments 3 and 4 the extended Kalman training algorithm was utilized and achieved improved results in fewer training iterations when compared to the backpropagation networks. The reason for this is that the extended Kalman filter selects its weight adjustment step

size on the basis all observations rather than according to the error of just the present sample. As a result, it approximates a global search technique and is more immune to mechanical and measurement inaccuracies which are part of the training set. A comparison of the two experiments in Table II and Figures 8 and 9 shows that with fewer weights, the network including a gray layer achieved a higher degree of accuracy. In addition, the *training set* mean squared error versus training iteration, depicted in Figure 9, shows that the networks with a gray layer converged faster than the networks without a gray layer.

6. CONCLUSIONS

A new method has been developed for incorporating *a priori*

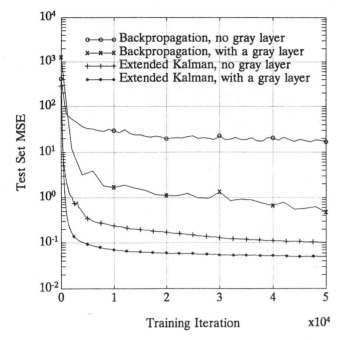

Figure 10 - Training set MSE vs. training iteration of experiments 1-4. Each curve represents the average convergence of 10 different random initializations.

information about an uncertain system into the structure of a feedforward ANN. The technique was applied to the output layer of a feedforward ANN and is transparent to gradient based learning algorithms. The system identification examples illustrated that, in general, ANNs with layers that utilize *a priori* information converged faster and achieved a lower mse than conventional methods as well as other methods of exploiting *a priori* information.

Previous gray layer approaches were extended by integrating a priori information into the activation function of the output layer while retaining the ability to train via backpropagation.

The advantage of this technique over a "black box" modeling approach was further illustrated by examples involving the identification of the static torque characteristics of a switched reluctance motor and of uncertain dynamic nonlinear systems. Feedforward ANNs using the methods proposed in this paper exhibited a faster rate of convergence, were able to more accurately model the systems of interest, and required fewer adjustable weights.

7. REFERENCES

[1] E. K. Blum and L. K. Li, "Approximation Theory and Feedforward Networks," Neural Networks Sci., vol. 4, pp. 511-515, 1991.

[2] R. Hecht-Nielsen, Neurocomputing. Reading, MA: Addison-Wesley, 1990.

[3] K. Hornik, M. Stinchcombe, and H. White, "Multilayer feedforward networks are universal approximators," Neural Networks, vol. 2, pp. 359-366, 1989.

[4] B. Bavarian, "Introduction to Neural Networks for Intelligent Control," IEEE Control Systems Magazine, pp. 3-7, April 1988.

[5] Fu-Chuang Chen and H. K. Khalil, "Adaptive Control of Nonlinear Systems Using Neural Networks," Proceedings: 29th Conference on Decision and Control, Honolulu, Hawaii, pp. 1707-1712, Dec. 1990.

[6] S. R. Chu, R. Shoureshi, and M. Tenorio, "Neural Networks for System Identification," IEEE Control Systems Magazine, pp. 31-35, April 1990.

[7] J. J. Helferty, S. Biswas, and M. Maund, "Experiments in Adaptive Control Using Artificial Neural Networks," Proceedings: IEEE International Conf. on Sys. Eng., Pittsburgh, PA, pp. 339-342, Aug. 1990.

[8] K. S. Narendra and K. Parthasarathy, "Identification and Control of Dynamic Systems Using Neural Networks," IEEE Trans. Neural Networks, vol. 1, no. 1, pp. 4-26, March 1990.

[9] K. S. Narendra and K. Parthasarathy, "Gradient methods for the optimization of dynamical systems containing neural networks," IEEE Trans. Neural Networks, vol. 2, no. 2, pp. 252-262, June 1991.

[10] Neural Networks for Control, W. T. Miller, R. S. Sutton, and P. J. Werbos, Eds. MIT Press, Cambridge, MA, 1990.

[11] Y. Iiguni and H. Sakai, "A Nonlinear regulator design in the presence of system uncertainties using multilayered neural networks," IEEE Trans. Neural Networks, vol. 2, no. 4, pp. 410-417, July 1989.

[12] W. H. Joerding and J. L. Meador, "Encoding *A Priori* Information in Feedforward Networks," Neural Networks, vol. 4, pp. 847-856, 1991.

[13] M. A. Sartori and P. J. Antsaklis, "Implementing Learning Control Systems Using Neural Networks," IEEE Control Systems Magazine, vol. 12, no. 2, pp. 49-57, April 1992.

[14] J. W. Selinsky and A. Guez, "The Role of a priori knowledge of plant dynamics in neurocontroller design," Proceedings: 28th Conference on Decision and Control, Tampa, FL, pp. 1754-1758, Dec. 1989.

[15] R. Yoh-Han Pao, Adaptive Pattern Recognition and Neural Networks, Addison-Wesley, Reading, MA, 1989.

[16] P. J. Werbos, "Neural Networks for Control and System Identification," Proceedings: 28th Conference on Decision and Control, Tampa, FL, pp. 260-265, Dec. 1989.

[17] R. H. Brown and T. L. Ruchti, "Gray Layer Technology: Incorporating *A Priori* Knowledge into Feedforward Artificial Neural Networks," IEEE International Joint Conference on Neural Networks (Baltimore, MD), June 1992, pp. I-806 - I-811.

[18] Rumelhart, D. E., Hinton, G. E., and R. J. Williams, "Learning internal representations by error propagation," Parallel Distributed Processing: Explorations in the Microstructure of Cognition, vol. 1, Cambridge, MA, MIT Press, pp. 318-62, 1986.

[19] S. Chen, C. F. Cowan, S. A. Billings, and P. M. Grant, "Parallel Recursive Prediction Error Algorithm for Training Layered Neural Networks." Int. J. Control, vol. 51, no. 8, pp. 1215-1228, 1990.

[20] S. Singhal and L. Wu, "Training Feed-Forward Networks with the Extended Kalman Algorithm." Proc. ICASSP, pp. 1187-1190, 1989.

[21] L. Lung, System Identification Theory For the User. Englewood Cliffs, New Jersey: Prentice Hall, 1987.

[22] G. Singh and B. C. Kuo, "Modeling and Simulation of Variable-Reluctance Step Motors with Application to a High-Performance Printer System," IEEE Trans. Industry Appl., vol. IA-22, no. 4, pp. 708-715, July/Aug. 1986.

[23] B. K. Bose, T. J. E. Miller, P. M. Szczensy, and W. H. Bicknell, "Microcomputer Control of Switch Reluctance Motor," IEEE Trans. Industry Appl., vol. IA-22, no. 4, pp. 708-715, July/Aug. 1986.

[24] M. Ilic'-Spong, R. Marino, S. M. Peresada, and D. G. Taylor, "Feedback Linearizing Control of Switched Reluctance Motors," IEEE Trans. Automat. Contr., vol. AC-32, no. 5, pp. 371-379, May 1987.

Neuro Fuzzy Robust Controllers
for Drive Systems

Yasuhiko Dote, Miguel Strefezza and Amin Suyitno

Department of Computer Science and Systems Engineering
Muroran Institute of Technology, Mizumoto 27-1,
Muroran 050, Japan. Tel. (0143)-44-4181 ext. 2433
Fax. (0143)-47-3374

ABSTRACT

This paper describes and approximated zeroing with an equivalent disturbance observer and predictive controller for drive systems. Then this linear controller structure is changed by fuzzy logic such that the controller makes the system respond quickly if the error e is large and vice versa in order to obtain a robust controller which is insensitive to both the plant noise and the observation noise. Next, a variable structure PI controller by fuzzy logic for drive systems is introduced. Then, this control scheme is implemented with neural networks. These controllers are realized with digital signal processors. The experimental results are given. Lastly, the applications of neuro fuzzy methods to inverters, converters, motion controls and sensors are explained.

Keywords: Neuro Fuzzy Control, Nonlinear Control, Motion Drive Systems, Inverters Converters and Controls.

1. INTRODUCTION

Neuro fuzzy control is one of the intelligent controls since knowledge engineering is used in the neuro fuzzy control. Neuro fuzzy control is usually utilized for the two purposes [1]. One is for the constructing nonlinear controllers. The other is for adding human intelligence to controllers, such as perception (sensory information process), understanding, recognition, inference, learning, diagnosis and others.

Fuzzy control is like following what a person says by language (fuzzy set). On the other hand neuro control is explained like following what a person does by data. In order to construct nonlinear controllers fuzzy control and neuro control should be combined as shown in Fig.1.

Fuzzy control is useful only if it is simple and low cost and only when human skill is converted into control knowledge by language (fuzzy representation).

This paper concerns with the construction of nonlinear controllers. Linear control design procedure has been almost accomplished. H-infinitive control CAD is now commercially available. Therefore it is high time to consider nonlinear controllers which attack highly nonlinear systems and gives higher control performance than linear controllers.

In this paper neuro fuzzy control is applied to drive systems to obtain robust controllers. Controllers are implemented with digital signal processors [2]. Then the applications of neuro fuzzy approaches to inverters, converters, motion controls and intelligent sensors are surveyed.

2. VARIABLE - STRUCTURED ROBUST CONTROL BY FUZZY LOGIC AND STABILITY ANALYSIS FOR AC DRIVE SYSTEM

2.1 Robust and Fast Speed Controller

Assume that a flux vector control method [3] is applied and the current control loop time constant is small enough to be negligible (1 msec.). Then, the equation (1) describes the machine transient.

$$J\dot{\omega} + B\omega + T_l = k_t i_a \qquad (1)$$

where
J : moment of inertia
B : viscous friction coefficient
K_t: torque constant
T_l: external load torque
ω : motor speed
i_a: motor current

Let $J = \hat{J} + \triangle J$ and $K_t = \hat{K}_t + \triangle K_t$, , where ^ denotes the nominal value and $\triangle$ represents the variation or unknown value. Define the equivalent disturbance $T_e(s)$ as

$$T_e(s) = T_l(s) + B\omega(s) + \triangle Js\omega(s) - \triangle K_t i_a(s) \qquad (2)$$

The first through the fourth term on the right hand side of the equation (2) represent the external load torque, the

22

viscous friction torque, the torque due to the parameter variation and the torque variation due to the flux vector control failure and torque ripples, respectively.

The $T_e(s)$ is obtained in the equation (3) from (1) and (2).

$$T_e(s) = \hat{K}_t i_a(s) - s\hat{J}\omega(s) \qquad (3)$$

The estimate of $T_e(s)$, $\hat{T}_e(s)$ is constructed by using a low pass filter $(1/(T_o s + 1))$. In fact this is an observer. Thus

$$\hat{T}_e(s) = (\hat{K}_t i_a(s) - s\hat{J}\omega(s))/(T_o s + 1) \qquad (4)$$

where T_o is the observer time constant. The signal $\hat{T}_e(s)$ is shown in the Fig.1. $T_e(s)$ is assumed to be slowly time varying.

By some control block simplification, the equivalent block diagram is obtained and shown in Fig.2. It is noted that a PI controller is contained in this controller. The following transfer functions are calculated.

$$\omega(s)/T_e(s) = -(1-1/(T_o s + 1))(1/\hat{J}s + \hat{B}) \qquad (5)$$

Since T_o is very small, $w(s)/T_e(s)$ becomes zero quickly. Therefore this is called "approximate zeroing". The equivalent disturbance has been cancelled. Next,

$$\omega(s)/i_a^*(s) = \hat{K}_t/(\hat{J}s + \hat{B}) \qquad (6)$$

This is shown in Fig.3.

In order to obtain quick command response the following controller is designed. First, put B=0 to make the steady state error zero for step response. Then a proportional gain controller K_p is added. Finally a predict controller $\hat{J}s/\hat{K}_t$ is designed independently of the robust controller [4], since,

$$\omega(s)/\omega^*(s) = 1/(\hat{J}/\hat{K}_t K_p s + 1) \qquad (7)$$

2.2 Variable – Structured Robust Control by Fuzzy Logic

The derived controller is robust to the plant noises (external disturbances and system parameter variations), but sensitive to the observation noises which usually contain high-frequency components. Thus, in this section a variable-structured robust controller whose structure is continuously changed by fuzzy logic such that if the error is large or its rate is large then the controller makes the system respond quickly and vice versa. The design procedure is as follows.

1. Design an approximate fuzzy controller from human being's knowledge (skill).(if the error is large or its rate is large, then the controller makes the system respond quickly and vice versa)

2. Apply Liapunov's method, in order to determine nonlinear controller parameters. Alternatively, implement the

approximate fuzzy controller with neural networks in order to construct a self-tuning controller. A novel real-time learning algorithm is devised.

Fig.4.(b) shows an equivalent control block diagram of Fig.4.(a) except the feed forward controller. The following variable-structure by fuzzy logic is introduced to the controller in order to construct a nonlinear controller which is insensitive to both the plant noise (equivalent disturbance) and the observation noise.

If e is large, then K_p is large
If e is small, then K_p is small
If e is large, then T_o is small
If e is small, then T_o is large

where e is the error, which is defined by $e = \omega^* - \omega$ (see Fig.4.(a)).

By assigning appropriate membership functions to both the situation recognition portion and the action portion, and by inference, nonlinear T_o and K_p with respect to e are obtained as shown in Fig.5.(a) and Fig.5.(b). The membership function for e and K_p is shown in Fig.5.(c), and K_p is inferred by the next equation.

$$K_p = \frac{\omega_1 K_{p1} + \omega_2 K_{p2}}{\omega_1 + \omega_2},$$

T_o and K_c are defined using the same method as K_p.

2.3. Stability Analysis of Overall System and Controller Design Measure

When the command input $\omega^*(s)$ is in the steady state condition and the equivalent block diagram of the closed-loop system is as shown in the Fig.4.(b), the following nonlinear dynamics equation is obtained. Define $e = e_1$; $\dot{e} = e_2$;

$$T_o \hat{J} \dot{e}_2 + (\hat{K}_t K_p T_o + \hat{J}) e_2(s) + \hat{K}_t K_p e_1(s) = 0,$$

or in matrix form can be written as

$$\begin{bmatrix} \overset{o}{e}_1 \\ \overset{o}{e}_2 \end{bmatrix} = \begin{bmatrix} 0 & 1 \\ -\dfrac{K_p \hat{K}_t}{\hat{J} T_o} & -\dfrac{\hat{J} + T_o K_p \hat{K}_t}{\hat{J} T_o} \end{bmatrix} \begin{bmatrix} e_1 \\ e_2 \end{bmatrix} ; \qquad (8)$$

or $\qquad \dot{e} = Ae$; $e = [e_1, e_2]^T$;

where $\qquad K_p = K_p' = k_{p1} - K_{p2} e^{-K_{p3}|e_1|^2}$

$$T_o = T_o' = T_{min} + T_{o1} e^{-T_{o2}|e_1|^2}$$

where K_{p1}, K_{p2}, and K_{p3} are positive constants and T_{min} is the minimum value of T_0. T_o and K_p are monotone decreasing and increasing functions of e_1, respectively.

23

Stability Analysis of Linear System (T_o, K_p are constants)

The eigenvalues λ of A in (8) is obtained as follows.

$$\lambda_1 = -\frac{K_p \hat{K}_t}{\hat{J}} < 0 \quad \text{and} \quad \lambda_2 = -\frac{1}{T_o} < 0 \qquad (9)$$

Therefore, the linear system is stable.

Stability Analysis of Nonlinear System

Liapunov's stability theorem says that if the elements of A(e) are slowly time-varying and all the eigenvalues of A(e) have negative real parts (see the Appendix). Then the nonlinear system $\dot{e} = Ae$ is asymptotically stable.

In this system, if e is slowly time-varying. Consequently the elements of A(e) is slowly time-varying. Therefore from (9), the nonlinear system is asymptotically stable.

Instability of This System

If T_0 exist in the shaded area in Fig.7, instability occurs as shown in Fig.8.(c). This is illustrated in Fig.8 (a) and (b), due to sudden change in T_0. The sudden changes in the parameter violates the Liapunov's stability theory described in this section. Since $\dot{T}_0$ is $(dT_0/de)\dot{e}$, large dT_0/de in Fig. 7 and $\dot{e}$ causes instability.

Control Design Measure

The eigenvalues λ_1, λ_2 in (9) are the function of parameters T_o and K_p which are continuously changed. Thus, the controller design can be performed by examining λ_1 and λ_2 in (9). For stability T_0 versus e curves should exist outside the shaded area in Fig.7.

2.4. Experiment Results

The overall control block diagram is shown in Fig.6 and Fig.9(a) and (b). Guard filters whose time constants are 1.6 msec. for F1 and 12.8 msec. for F2 respectively are utilized. The control object is an induction motor of 7.5Kw, 200V, 600Hz, 4p and 1800rpm. The load is a 11Kw dc machine. The constants are J:0.2 Kgm², K_t:1.0, K_p:10.0, Pulse Generator (PG): 600 pulses per revolution.

All control algorithms and filters are implemented with a digital signal processor, TMS32C14E, including flux vector control. A 8086 is a host computer. A control program is loaded through a 232C interface to the TMS32C14E from the host computer and is executed. The whole sampling time is 100 micro seconds.

Fig.10 and Fig.11 show time responses for the proposed method and for a conventional PI controller respectively. Since the cancellation signals are generated in the proposed controller, it is insensitive to 100 percent load change and 500 percent moment inertia variations. Fig.12 shows that torque ripples are removed for the proposed controller.

3. VARIABLE - STRUCTURED ROBUST PI CONTROLLER BY FUZZY LOGIC FOR SERVOMOTOR

3.1 Control Method

An adaptive (gain scheduling) fuzzy controller is proposed to construct a self-tuning non linear controller. The design procedure is as follows.

1) Design an approximate fuzzy controller from human being's knowledge a proportional (P) controller should dominate a integral (I) controller if the absolute value of the error is large and vice versa or if the time derivative of the error is large then the integrator gains is very large and vice versa to obtain good time response and robustness by assuming a lot of operation data are not enough available.

2) No integrators are used to this variable structured PI controller by fuzzy logic. The integrators used in conventional adaptive mechanisms bring stability problems in the adaptive systems.

3) Apply Popov's stability criterion to the overall system in order to obtain controller parameters.

In order to make the command response quick, the following rules are applied. The overall control block diagram is given in Fig.13, where J: inersia, B: viscous friction coefficient, K: gain, K_p and K_i are changed by fuzzy logic (rules) as follow. Let e be r-y.

If e is small (ISM), then K_i is large (OILG)
If e is large (ILG), then K_i is small (OISM)
If e is small (PSM), then K_p is small (OPSM)
If e is large (PLG), then K_p is large (OPLG)
$$(10)$$

Membership function for e and K_i are shown in Fig.14. K_i is inferred by the following equation.

$$K_i' = \frac{\omega_1 K_{i1}' + \omega_2 K_{i2}'}{\omega_1 + \omega_2} \qquad (11)$$

K_p is also inferred in the same way. Then, K_i and K_p are nonlinear function of $|e|$ as shown in fig 15. Then the following rules are applied to obtain robustness.

If $\dot{e}$ is large for a quite long time, then K_i is very large.
If $\dot{e}$ is small then K_p and K_i are normal. (12)

This rules are induced as follows, consider a high gain controller shows in Fig.16. This was used in the previous section as a robust controller which cancels the external disturbance and the effect of the system parameter variations. The filter time constant, T_0 is 1 msec. This means that high gain integral control must be used to obtain insensitiveness to the equivalent disturbance. Thus, (12) is introduced.

3.2. Stability Analysis and Controller Design

By redefining the nonlinear K_i and K_p as shown in Fig.17 for the nonlinear K_i and K_p in Fig.15, the equivalent of overall control system to the system as shown in Fig.13 is obtain as shown in Fig.18.

By using Popov's absolute stability criterion, the following in equalities must be satisfied for absolute stability.

$$\text{Re } (1+j\omega q)G_1(j\omega) + \frac{1}{K_{pmax}-K_{pmin}} > 0 \quad (13)$$

$$\text{Re } (1+j\omega q)G_2(j\omega) + \frac{1}{K_{imax}-K_{imin}} > 0$$

where

$$G_1(s) = \frac{K\ K_{pmin}}{Js + B + KK_{pmin}} \quad (14)$$

$$G_2(s) = \frac{K\ K_{imin}}{Js^2 + Bs + KK_{imin}}$$

This is shown in Fig.19. The controller parameters K_p, K_i are determined by (13) and (14).

3.3. Experiment Results

The control object is an induction motor of 7.5Kw, 200V, 600Hz, 4p and 1800rpm. The load is a 11Kw dc machine. The constants are J:0.2 Kgm^2, K_t:1.0, K_p:10.0, Pulse Generator (PG): 600 pulses per revolution.

All control algorithms and filters are implemented with a digital signal processor, TMS32C14E, including flux vector control. A 8086 is a host computer. A control program is loaded through a 232C interface to the TMS32C14E from the host computer and is executed. The whole sampling time is 100 micro seconds. This is shown in Fig.9 (a) and (b).

Fig.20 and Fig.21 show time responses for the proposed method and for a conventional PI controller respectively. Since the cancellation signals are generated in the proposed controller, it is insensitive to 100 percent load change and 500 percent moment inertia variations.

4. RADIAL BASIS NEURAL NETWORK ADAPTIVE PID CONTROLLER FOR SERVOMOTOR

4.1 Radial Basis Function Networks

The use of sigmoid function as the transfer function to train a network has been common, now the use of radial basis function is becoming popular [5].

Radial basis function networks were proposed by Moody and Darken . It has three layers: input, hidden and output layer, Fig. 22 shows the basic structure of this network. The input layer is simply directly connected to the hidden layer via unweighted links . Usually the network is fully connected then all outputs from the input layer are connected to all hidden nodes.

The ith radial basis function neuron in the hidden layer of the radial basis network has the following transfer function:

$$h_i = r(\| X - c_i \| / \sigma_i) \quad (15)$$

where h_i is the ith output of the neuron at the hidden layer, $r(.)$ is a radial basis function, X is the input vector ; c_i is the bias vector with the components corresponding to those of X and σ_i is a positive scalar.

Typically Gaussian function units are selected, then

$$h_i = e^{-\| X - c_i \|^2 / \sigma_i^2} \quad (16)$$

where c_i is the center of the ith radial unit in the input space and σ_i the width of the ith radial unit.

Denoting by Y_j the output of the jth neuron in the output layer, is given as:

$$Y_j = \sum_{i=1}^{n} W_{ji}\ h_i \quad (17)$$

where W_{ji} are the weights of the connections between the output layer and the hidden layer, h_i is the output coming from the hidden layer and n is the number of radial basis function neuron.

4.2. Proposed Learning Scheme

The goal of this article is to improve the learning process of an artificial net with an algorithm able to train it in a short period of time and in real time. To prove the proposed learning scheme two cases are presented . First, the basic three layers radial basis function network and second, a two layers radial basis function network.

Three Layers Network

The neural networks used in this

article are trained to control a servomotor, because this the net consists of a single unit in the output layer. Fig. 23 shows the the structure this net.

The output of the hidden layer unit is giving by equation (2). The number of units of the hidden layer as the values of c_i and σ_i are pre-set for the net before the learning process begins. The training process of the net begins with a random initial value of the weights W_{ji}. In this scheme the connection weights are updated by:

$$W_{ji}(t) = W_{ji}(t-1) + \triangle W_{ji} \eta \qquad (18)$$

where $W_{ji}(t)$ is the value of the weight. $W_{ji}(t-1)$ is the value of the weight one iteration before. η is the momentum term which affects the speed convergence and stability of the weights during the learning process. $\triangle W_{ji}$ is a value that determines the change to be made in each weight.

$\triangle W_{ji}$ is updated by using the following expression:

$$\triangle W_{ji}(t) = \sin \beta (t) \qquad (19)$$

$$\beta (t) = h_i \theta(t) / 360 \qquad (20)$$

h_i is the output of each hidden neuron of the net and e(t) is the error between the desired position of the motor and its actual position.

The training of the net continues until the maximum $\triangle W_{ji}$ is acceptably small under the following condition given as:

$$\left| W_{ji}(t) - W_{ji}(t-1) \right| < \tau \qquad (21)$$

τ is the maximum acceptably value for the convergence of the weights. Finally the output of the net is calculated with equation (17).

Two Layers Network

It was explained previously that the basic structure of the radial basis network consists of three layers. Here a two layers radial basis function network is introduced. Equations used before to obtain the output value for the hidden layer and output layer are modified to train the net. The purpose of this is to reduce the learning time of the net. Fig. 24 shows the new structure of the network.

In this structure of the net, the radial basis function is used at the output layer. In this case equations (16) and (17) are modified to train the net. Having only two layers in the net it has to be considered that the weights between them have to produce an influence on the output and also they have to be updated.

The equations used to obtain the output

of the structure are given as:

$$O_n = e^{- \| I - c_i \|^2 / \sigma_i^2} \qquad (22)$$

$$I = \sum_{1}^{n} X_n W_{ji} \qquad (23)$$

O_N is the output of the network, I is the new term introduced in the radial basis function, c_i and σ_i are constants.

The weights are also updated as in the previous case with equations (18),(19),(20) and (21).

4.3 Neuro Controller

In this section is presented the design of the controller by using the proposed training scheme. The block diagram of the controller is shown in Fig. 25. In this type of controller the neural network tunes the parameter of the conventional controller and offers more robustness. The block diagram can be divided into three parts.

Firstly, the neural network controller composed of three nets with the output $Y_1(t)$, $Y_2(t)$ and $Y_3(t)$ respectively. Secondly, the system, a servomotor where the friction is assumed and third a conventional controller, a PID controller. The gains of the PID controller are defined as function of the absolute value of the error ($|e|$) as is shown in Fig. 26. The task of the net is to tune these functions to obtain the input to the system.

Previously two different radial basis networks structures were presented , then two neuro controllers are built with them. Each network consists of four units in the first layer. The teaching signals used to train the nets depend on the error change ,$|\dot{e}|$; the reciprocal of the speed of the motor, $|5/\omega|$; a variable α which is explained later in details and the bias.

The training process of the neural networks start with random initial values of the weights W_{ji}. Then because the nets are untrained, they output an erroneous signal $Y_n(t)$ to control the system.

The weights of the nets are updated with equations (18),(19),(20) and (21).The process continues for T times steps until the weights of the nets converge to the desired values.

In general terms, the equation of a servomotor is:

$$\dot{\theta} = \omega \qquad (24)$$
$$\dot{\omega} = \psi U'/J - \lambda \quad \omega/J - T_L/J$$

where θ is the position of the motor, ω is the speed, λ and ψ are parameters of the motor, U' is the input, T_L is the friction and J is the inertia.

To train the neuro control it is considered unknown the value of λ/J in equation (24) and ψ/J is constant. Then α is

$$\alpha_{(t)} = (\Gamma_{(t)} - \Phi_{(t)})/5 \qquad (25)$$

where $\Gamma_{(t)}$ is given by:

$$\Gamma_{(t)} = \theta_{(t)}/360 - \dot{\theta}_{(t)} - \Gamma_{(t-1)} \qquad (26)$$

e(t) is the error and $\dot{e}$(t) is the error change. The following condition is used to identify λ/J

$$\Phi_{(t)} = \Gamma_{(t)} \qquad (27)$$

this condition is applied until the weights of the nets converge. When the convergence occurs, Φ(t) is obtained and becomes a constant (Φ_c) and must have a value close to the nominal value of λ/J.

After the neuro controller is trained the servomotor is able to reach any desired position between 0 and 360 degrees.

4.4 Simulation Results

In this section simulations results are presented applying the proposed control scheme to control the position of a motor. During the training process of the net is assumed that coulomb friction exists. The initial position of the motor is 0 degree and the final position is 360 degrees during this process.

The first structure of the net has 4 units at the input layer, 3 at the hidden layer and 1 at the output layer. The sampling time is 1msec. η is 0.2, γ is 0.001. The initial values of the weights w_{ji} are set between 0.1 and 0.3.

Supposing in equation (24) λ/J unknown and ψ/J is 135 the controller is trained. The weights of the net converge after 300 cycles approximately .The value of $_c$ after the identification is 29.65, being the nominal value of λ/J 30. Fig. 27 shows the response of the motor during the training process.

After the controller is trained, simulations are done assuming the maximum value of the disturbance in the system. The maximum torque (T_L/J) 50. Fig. 28 shows the response of the motor.

The modified radial basis network structure has 4 units at the input layer and 1 at output layer. η is 0.25. The initial value of the weights are set between 0.05 and 0.09. The rest of the parameters and conditions are not changed.

Simulations with the two layers network are also performed supposing λ/J unknown. The weights of the networks converge after 150 cycles approximately. The value of Φ_c after the weights converge is 29.53 . Coulomb friction is introduced to the system

as before. Figs. 29 - 30 show the response of the motor during the learning process and with the existence of friction.

The results show that with the proposed control scheme the response of the servomotor does not present oscillations. Simulations are also done with linear controllers as PI or PID . The response of the motor is shown in Fig. 31(a) and (b) for each controller respectively when load is applied. The motor shows oscillations before obtaining a stable response signal.

5. NEURO FUZZY APPROACHES APPLIED TO POWER ELECTRONICS SYSTEMS

This section surveys the applications of Neuro-Fuzzy approaches to inverters, converters motion control and sensor based control systems.

5.1 Additions of Intelligence to Controllers and Sensors.

Knowledge Acquisition(Neural Networks)[6]
If a lot of operational data are available fuzzy control knowledge (a set of rules and membership functions) is acquired by using a neural network as is shown in Fig. 32. This neural network is also gives a self tuning controller by its learning capabilities.

Diagnosis (Neural Network)[7]
The bearing and winding damages of an induction motor are detected by using neural network into which motor currents and speeds are fed. This is shown in Fig. 33.

Sensor Fusion (Neural Network)[8]
Controllers and sensors are complementary. Intelligent sensor fusion can be achieved by using neural networks (or fuzzy logic) as shown in Fig.34.

Sensor Failure Detection and Data Recovery (Neural Networks)[9]
By using information at the hidden layer of a neural network, sensor failure detection and data recovery are performed as shown Fig. 35.

5.2 Neuro-Fuzzy Nonlinear Controls Applied to Inverters, Converters and Motion Control.

Inverter Control (Neural Network)[10]
A inverter is usually controlled by using a current-hysteresis controlled PWM method and a subharmonic PWM method as show in Fig. 36. The nonlinear mapping of a neural network is used to control an inverter. This is shown in Fig. 37. It gives less higher harmonics in the output current as shown in Fig. 38 (a) and (b).

Converter Control (Fuzzy Logic)[11]
A nonlinear discontinuous current mode in a converter is linearized by using fuzzy logic.

Induction Motor Flux Observer at Low Speed (Neural Network) [12]

It is very difficult to sense induction motor flux robustly at its low speed. If a lot of operations data are available, it is possible to construct it observer with neural networks for robust induction motor flux vector control as shown in Fig. 39.

Nonlinear Vibration Suppression Control (Neural Network) [13]

Vibration suppression control is always required in any motion control systems. It is performed by using neural networks as shown in Fig. 40.

Elimination of Nonlinearities in Motion Control (Fuzzy Expert System)[14]

Static friction in a motor control system is eliminated by using a fuzzy expert system approach. It is shown in Fig. 41 (a) and (b).

6. CONCLUSION

In this paper firstly, nonlinear neuro-fuzzy motor controls which have been achieved by authors are presented. Next, Neuro-fuzzy approaches applied to power electronics systems are surveyed. More intelligent controls will be applied to power electronics systems in the future in order to obtain higher-performance systems. These will contribute to the construction of high-efficient production lines and the production of high-quality products.

7. REFERENCES

[1]   Y.Dote,"Fuzzy and Neural Network Controllers", Proceedings of the Second Workshop on Neural networks, Academy/ Industrial / Nasa/ Defense Computer Simulation Society, Auburn University, U.S.A., Feb. 1991.

[2]   Y.Dote, Servo Motor and Motion Control Using Digital Signal Processors, Printice-Hall, New Jersey U.S.A., April 1990

[3] I.Takahashi and T.Noguchi, "A New Quick Response and High Efficiently Control Strategy of an Induction Motor", IEEE Trans. on Ind. Appl., Vol. IA-22, 1986.

[4] Amin Suyitno, J.Fujikawa, H.Kobayashi, and Yasuhiko Dote, "Variable-Structured Robust Controller by Fuzzy Logic for Servomotors", IEEE Trans. on Industrial Electronics, Vol.40, No 1, February 1993

[5]   J.Ralpaia and H.N.Koivo, "Self-Generating Radial Base Network in Fault Diagnosis", Proceedings of ICARCV'92, Singapure, Sept. 15-18, 1992.

[6] N. Imazaki, J. Kiji and K. Endo, "Neural Network Structure for Fuzzy Rules" Proceedings of Japanese Fuzzy Society, No. 5, 1992 (in Japanese).

[7]   Chow, Bilbro and Yee, "Using Neural Networks to Detect Incipient Faults in Induction Motors", Journal of Neural Network Computing, Vol. 2, No. 3, 1991.

[8]   F. Harashima and Y. Dote, "Sensor based Robot Systems", Proceedings of the IEEE International Symposium on Industrial Electronics, Xian, China, May 1992.

[9]   C.S. Lin, I.C. Wu and T.H. Guo, "Neural Networks for Sensor Failure Detection and Data Recovery", C.H. Dagli, S.R.T. Kumara and Y.C. Shin Edited: Intelligent Engineering Systems Through Artificial Neural Networks, ASME press, 1991.

[10] B. Linand and R.G. Hoft, "Neural Networks and Fuzzy Logic in Power electronics Systems", Proceedings of the IEEE International Workshop on Neuro Fuzzy Control, Muroran Japan, March 22-23, 1993.

[11] G.C.D. Sousa and B.K. Bose, "A Fuzzy Set Theory Based Control of a Phase-Controlled Converter DC Machine Drive", Proceedings of the IEEE IAS, Dearborn U.S.A., Sept. 28-Oct. 4, 1991.

[12] Theocharis and Petridis, "A Neural Network Adaptive Observer for Field Oriented Control", Proceedings of the IEEE International Symposium on Industry Electronics, Xian, China, May 1992.

[13] D.J. Bozich and H.B. Mackay, "Vibration Cancellation Using Neuro Controllers" from the same book aas [9]

[14] M. Marcos and P.E. Wellstead, "An intelligent Rule-Based Compensator for Control System Input Nonlinearities", Proceedings of the Americal Control Conference, 1991.

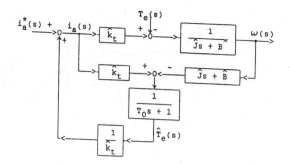

Fig.1, Block diagram of motor and equivalent disturbance
observer.

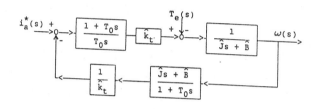

Fig.2, Equivalent block diagram of Fig.1.

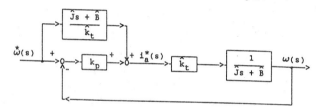

Fig.3, Predictive controller.

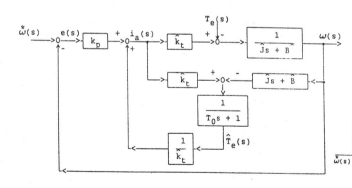

Fig.4.(a), Block diagram of motor and equivalent disturbance
observer with feed-back loop.

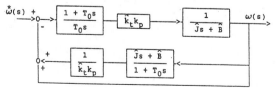

Fig.4.(b), Equivalent block diagrams of Fig.4.(a).

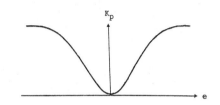

Fig.5.(a), T_o

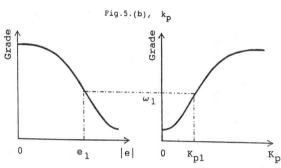

Fig.5.(b), k_p

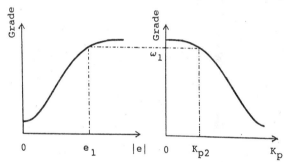

Fig.5.(c), Membership function for $|e|$ and K_p.

Fig.5, Nonlinear k_p and T_o.

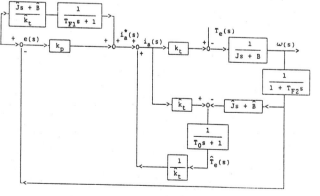

Fig.6, Overall control block diagram.

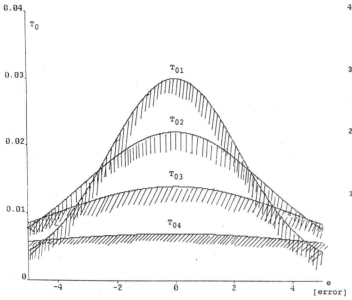

Fig.7, The curve of T_{01}, T_{02}, T_{03} and T_{04}.

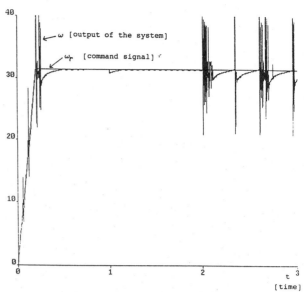

Fig.8.(c), The output of the system in the unstable condition.

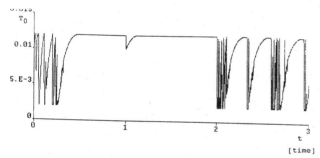

Fig.8.(a), T_0 vs Time in the unstable condition.

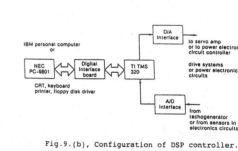

Fig.9.(a), Schematic diagram of overall system.

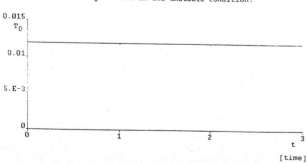

Fig.8.(b), T_0 vs Time in the stable condition.

Fig.8, T_0 vs Time.

Fig.9.(b), Configuration of DSP controller.

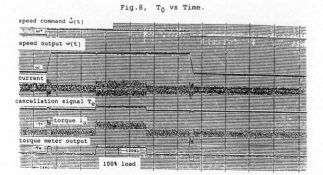

Fig.10.(a), J = 0.2 kg-m².

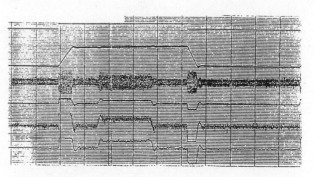

Fig.10.(b), J = 1.0 kg-m².

Fig.10, Time responses for proposed controller.

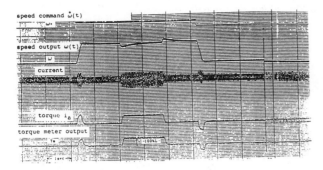

speed command $\overset{*}{\omega}(t)$

ω^*

speed output $\omega(t)$

ω

current

torque i_a

torque meter output

T_m -100%L

Fig.11.(a), J = 0.2 kg-m².

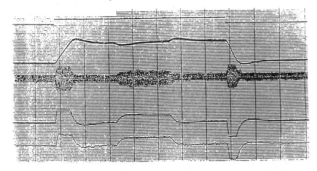

Fig.11.(b), J = 1.0 kg-m².

Fig.11, Time responses for PI controller.

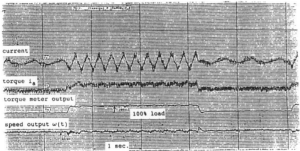

current

torque i_a

torque meter output

T_m 100% load

speed output $\omega(t)$

1 sec.

Fig.12.(a), Proposed controller.

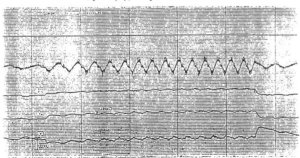

Fig.12.(b), Classical PI controller.

Fig.12, Torque ripple elimination.

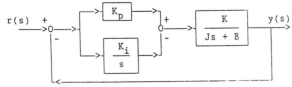

Fig. 13 Overall control block diagram

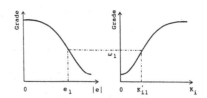

Fig. 14, Membership functions for $|e|$ and K_i.

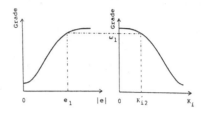

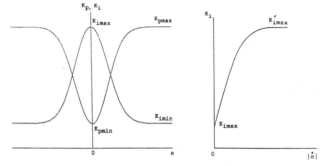

Fig. 15, K_p and K_i versus error.

(a), High gain controller.　　(b), Equivalent controller.

Fig. 16, High gain controller.

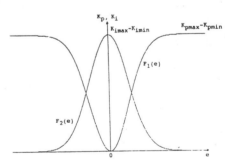

Fig. 17, Nonlinear K_p and K_i.

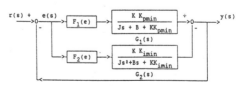

Fig. 18 Equivalent control system to system in Fig.1.

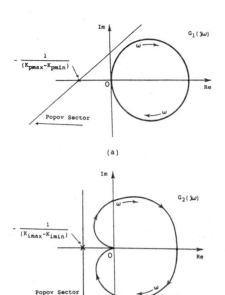

(a)

(b)

Fig. 19 , Popov's absolute stability criteria

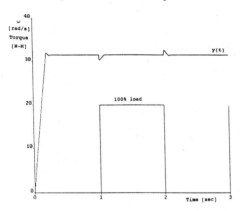

Fig. 20 The result of simulation of the system.

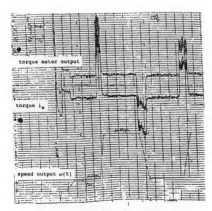

Fig. 21, Command response of the system.

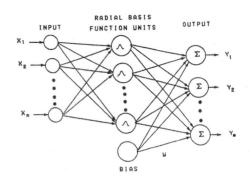

Fig. 22. Basic Structure of a Radial Basis Function Network

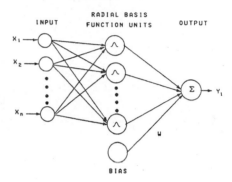

Fig. 23 Structure of three layers Radial Basis Function Network used to build a Neuro Controller.

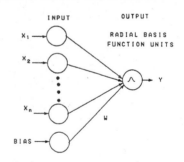

Fig. 24 . Structure of two layers Radial Basis Function Network.

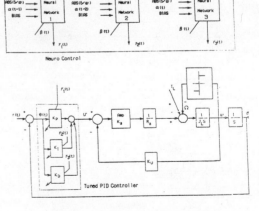

Fig. 25 Block Diagram of the Neuro Controller.

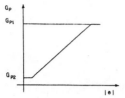

(a) Function for the Proportional Gain

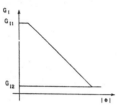

(b) Function for the Integral Gain

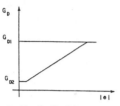

(c) Function for the Differential Gain

Fig. 26   Functions that define the gains of the PID Controller.

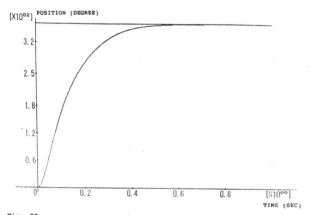

Fig. 27 Response of the motor during the Training process with a three layer Radial Basis Function Network.

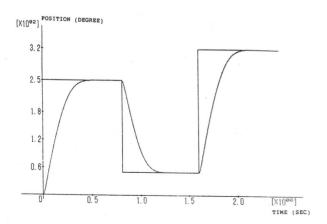

Fig. 28 . Response of the motor when maximum torque is applied.

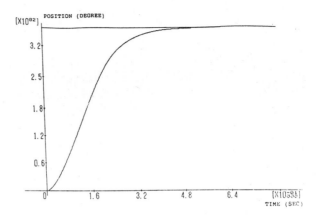

Fig. 29 Response of the motor during the Training process with a two layer Radial Basis Function Network.

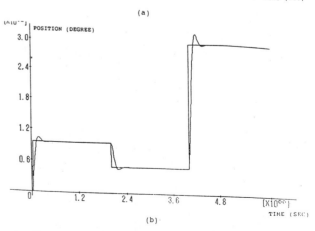

Fig. 30. Response of the motor when maximum torque is applied usin the two layers network.

(a)

(b)

Fig. 31.   Response of the motor when maximum load is applied. (a) PI Controller (b) PID controller.

A) Addition of Intelligence to Controller

1) Knowlege Acquisition (a set of rules and membership functions) and Tuning (Neural Network)

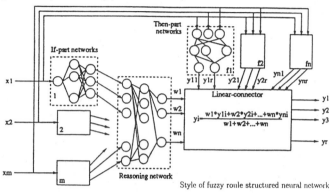

Style of fuzzy roule structured neural network

Fig. 32

2) Diagnosis (Neural Network)
Induction Motor Damage (Winding, Bearing)

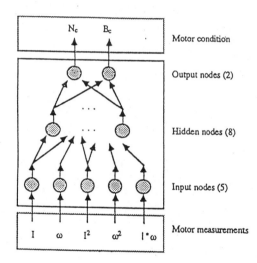

Basic structure of the high-order neural network IFDANN used for incipient fault detection of winding insulation fault and bearing wear in single phase induction motors.

Fig. 33

3) Sensor Fusion (Neural Network)

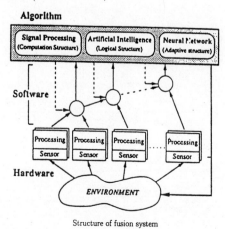

Structure of fusion system

Fig. 34

4) Sensor Failure Detection and Data Recovery (Neural Network)
Use information at the hidden layer

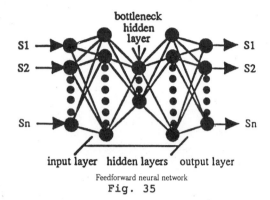

Feedforward neural network

Fig. 35

B) Nonlinear Controls Applied to Power Electronics Systems

1) Inverter Control (Neural Network)

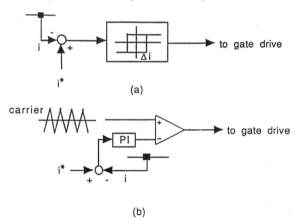

Fig. 36 Conventional current controls
(a) Current hysteresis-controlled PWM
(b) Subharmonic PWM

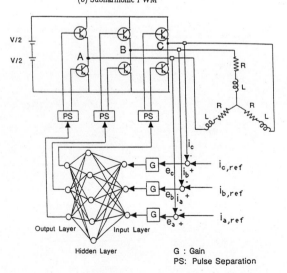

Fig. 37 Neural network control

34

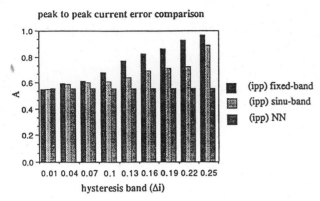

peak to peak current error comparison

Fig. 38(a) Comparisons of the peak to peak current error

- (ipp) fixed-band
- (ipp) sinu-band
- (ipp) NN

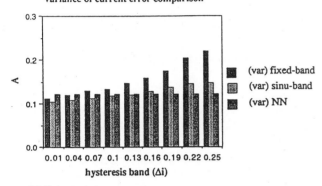

variance of current error comparison

Fig. 38(b) Comparisons of the variance of the current error

- (var) fixed-band
- (var) sinu-band
- (var) NN

4) Induction Motor Flux Observer at low speed (Neural Network)

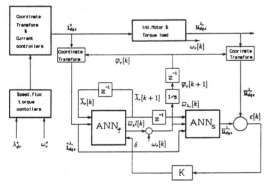

Fig. 39 Neural-net observer

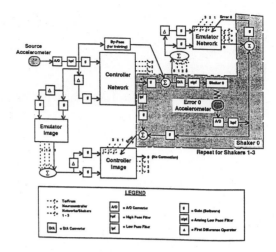

Fig. 40 Multiple network neurocontroller/neuroemulator

6) Elimination of Nonlinearities (Friction) (Fuzzy Expert Approach)

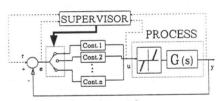

Supervisor Control Structure

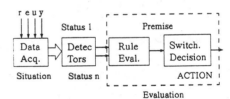

Fig. 41(a) Supervisor Logical Schema

Expert Approach)

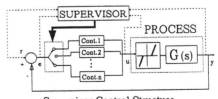

Supervisor Control Structure

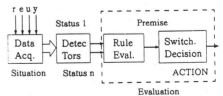

Fig. 41(b) Supervisor Logical Schema

Application of Associative Memory Neural Networks to the Control of a Switched Reluctance Motor

D.S. Reay, T.C. Green and B.W. Williams

Department of Computing and Electrical Engineering,
Heriot-Watt University,
Edinburgh EH14 4AS, UK

Abstract — The application of an associative memory neural network to the problem of torque ripple minimisation in a switched reluctance motor is presented. Conventional techniques for torque linearisation and decoupling are reviewed, after which the application of neural techniques to the problem is described. An instrumented test rig based around a 4 kW IGBT converter and a four phase switched reluctance motor has been constructed. Results obtained experimentally and by simulation demonstrate the effectiveness of the approach. The neural network has been implemented using both digital signal processor and field programmable gate array technologies.

INTRODUCTION

The cost advantages and ruggedness of switched reluctance motor (SRM) drives find favour in many industrial applications. However, the non-linear coupling between the phase current, rotor position and overlap angle as well as the machine design combine to produce high torque ripple. This has limited the use of SRM drives in servo systems. Previously reported methods of torque linearisation and decoupling involve the computation of current profiles *off-line* using either static torque measurements [1] or finite element models of a motor [2]. Problems concerning the choice between possible solutions, cross-saturation effects due to simultaneously conducting phases and the limited bandwidth of current-source power converters remain.

Neural techniques afford the capability to learn the current profiles required to minimise torque ripple and to satisfy other performance criteria *on-line*. In the learning phase, torque measurement is required. The current profiles learned in real-time as a motor rotates in an instrumented test rig could subsequently be stored in either a conventional look up table or a neural network implementation.

A test rig based around a 4 kW IGBT converter and a four phase SRM has been constructed. Results obtained experimentally and by simulation have been successful in verifying the ability of neural networks to learn suitable current profiles. The neural network has been implemented using both digital signal processor (DSP) and field programmable gate array (FPGA) technologies.

SRM DRIVE TORQUE CHARACTERISTICS

The simplest form of commutation, in which constant currents are applied to the different phases in turn leads to an uneven torque-position characteristic. This is due to the non-linear torque production characteristics of each phase, the finite time required for phase currents to switch between their nominal values and zero and saturation effects.

Figure 1 shows an experimentally produced static torque characteristic for a single conducting phase and figure 2 shows a prediction of the torque produced by this motor using a simple commutation scheme. The finite times required for phase currents to commutate and cross-saturation effects are not considered in this model.

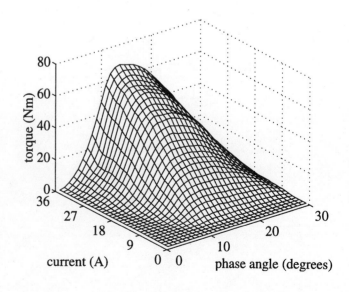

Figure 1. Static torque characteristic for one phase of a switched reluctance motor.

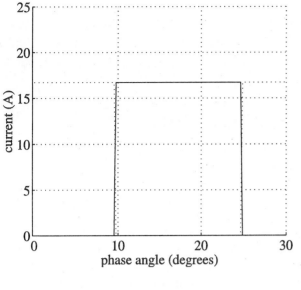

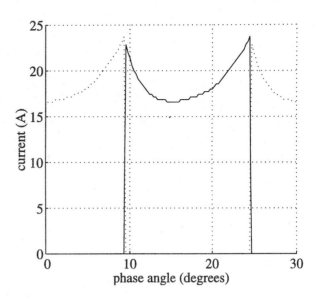

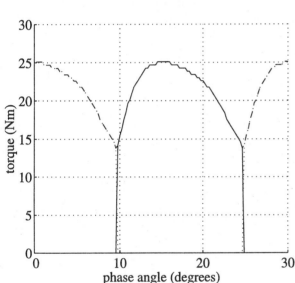

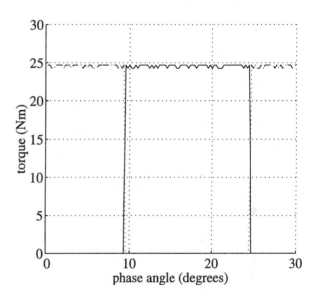

Figure 2. Predicted torque production using a simple method of commutation.

Figure 3. Predicted torque production using current profiles computed off-line.

One approach to the problem of torque ripple minimisation is to replace rectangular current profiles with profiles designed to deliver constant torque over the conduction period of a phase [1]. Such profiles may be derived from the data shown in figure 1.

However, this method has a number of undesirable features. Although addressing the problem of non-linear torque production in each phase, it still attempts to switch torque production from a single conducting phase to another instantaneously. This is not feasible as it implies an infinite rate of change of current in an inductive phase winding. Commutation is at the angles where torque production is least efficient and hence high currents are employed at commutation. Also, for a given torque, the peak current required may be significantly greater than the mean. If the motor is to be used in a position control system, the inverter must be rated for the peak current.

Recently, Schramm et al. [3] have investigated an approach based on constant rate of change of torque during commutation. Here, commutation is designed to take place over a range of phase angles with torque production in one phase decreasing linearly while torque production in the next increases. In other words, torque production by one phase, as a function of phase angle, is specified as a trapezoid rather than as a rectangle. Overall torque, produced by one or two simultaneously conducting phases, is constant.

Having specified a torque profile, the corresponding current profile may be obtained from the data illustrated in figure 1. Torque and current profiles that are optimum in the sense of lowest peak current (or in terms of any other criteria) may be found by computer-aided iteration.

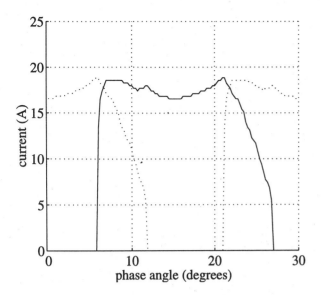

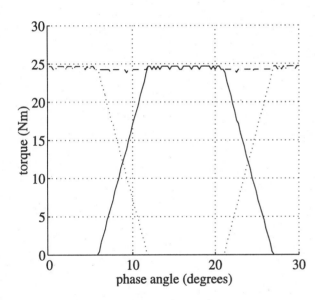

Figure 4. Predicted torque production using the method of constant rate of change of torque.

NEURAL NETWORK BASED APPROACH

An alternative to the technique described above, involves the use of a neural network to learn current profiles that minimise torque ripple. Figure 5 shows the way in which a neural network has been applied to the problem.

Using a neural network to learn current profiles *on-line* it is possible to account for effects ignored by the techniques mentioned previously, e.g. magnetic interaction between simultaneously conducting phases, windage and friction.

The different phases of the motor are assumed to have identical torque production characteristics and therefore the same current profile is used for each one. Commutation logic selects which two of the four phases are active according to the rotor position, θ, i.e. it switches the current demands i_A and i_B to phases k and $(k+1) \bmod 4$ and

provides phase angles θ_A and θ_B to the neural network block. The neural network block comprises a single two-input, one-output network to which the input pairs (Td, θ_A) and (Td, θ_B) are multiplexed in order to obtain outputs i_A and i_B respectively.

Choice of Neural Network Architecture

In this application, a neural network is used to approximate a non-linear function, learning *on-line*. For this task, a network exhibiting local, rather than global generalisation is most suitable. Local generalisation has the advantage that new learning in one region of input space does not affect the function approximation in distant regions of input space where a function may already have been learned satisfactorily (see Tolle et al. [4] for a discussion of the merits of locally generalising networks). Such networks may be viewed as possessing a more sophisticated pattern of connections than those exhibiting global generalisation, e.g. multilayer perceptrons.

Networks, the outputs of which are adjustable linear combinations of fixed non-linear functions of the inputs tend to train faster than those that are non-linear in the parameters adjusted.

Gaussian radial basis function networks have outputs that are adaptable linear combinations of fixed non-linear functions of the inputs and, in so far as the effect of training at one point in input space will have little effect at other distant points, may effectively exhibit local generalisation. However, the network output is the sum of contributions from all basis functions and in general each must be evaluated and its weighting adapted for any input.

The functional link network [5] is linear in the parameters adjusted but does not exhibit local generalisation and requires some prior knowledge of the function to be approximated.

The cerebellar model articulation controller (CMAC) [6] exhibits local generalisation and has the additional property of compact support, which makes it particularly suitable for real-time implementation. A limitation of this network is that its memory requirement increases exponentially with input dimension, rendering individual networks impractical for applications involving many inputs. However, since this application required a network with only two inputs, a CMAC network was considered ideal.

CMAC Network Architecture

The CMAC network architecture may be thought of as comprising two layers of neurons. The receptive fields of the neurons in the first layer span the input space and overlap extensively, such that a fixed number of these neurons will respond to any particular input. Each neuron output is binary, according to whether or not an input falls within its receptive field. The network output, formed by a

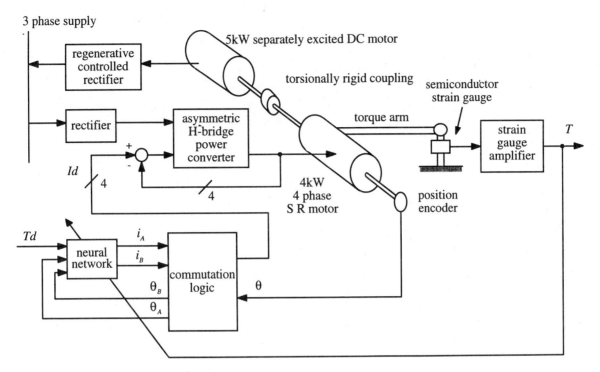

Figure 5. The application of a neural network to the control of a switched reluctance motor

second layer of neurons, is the weighted sum of the outputs of all neurons in the first layer. The output layer is linear and hence the network may be trained using an equivalent of the least mean squares (LMS) rule.

The generalisation characteristics of the network are determined by the shape and arrangement of its overlapping receptive fields. Typically, these are arranged as identical layers of equally sized hypercubes, each layer spanning the input space without overlap. In the work reported here, identical layers of receptive fields were offset relative to one another along a hyperdiagonal in input space although this is not the only pattern of offsets possible [7].

CMAC was developed as a model of neural functions found in the cerebellum. However, to describe CMAC as a neural network is not particularly enlightening. Alternatively, it may be viewed as a non-linear adaptive filter. As such, it is applicable to problems requiring unknown or time-varying functions to be learned, particularly when linear approximations are inadequate. In this application the phase currents required cannot usefully be represented as a linear function of torque demand and phase angle and so a non-linear filter is required.

One method of implementing a non-linear filter is by means of table look up. Another view of CMAC is as a lookup table with generalisation properties. It is a table in which no entry may be altered without affecting a number of other entries. This property is useful in that it allows learning without the need to experience all possible input-output combinations, effectively increasing the learning rate of the filter. It also saves memory over a conventional lookup table.

CMAC is closely related to B-spline networks. The binary receptive field function used in CMAC is effectively a B-spline basis function of order one and hence a CMAC network may be viewed as a set of overlapping first order B-spline networks. Lane et al. [8] have suggested the use of higher order B-spline basis functions for CMAC receptive field functions, resulting in higher order CMAC networks with analytical derivatives.

A charge frequently leveled at neural networks is that they are incapable of giving up the information that they encode. This is not applicable to CMAC. The significance of each weight can be explained and its contribution to the network output as a whole predicted.

Training Method

On-line training of the network was carried out using the techniques described by Albus [9]. The time inversion technique was used for fine training while coarse training was carried out according to the following assumptions.

i) increased current in either of the active phases, at any angle, gives rise to increased torque.
ii) current is applied most profitably at the centre of a phase's conduction period.

Prior to training, the network was loaded with current profiles that embodied these assumptions, i.e. linearly increasing current in the first half of the conduction period, followed by linearly decreasing current in the second half, the peak current being proportional to the demanded torque. These current profiles are shown in figure 6.

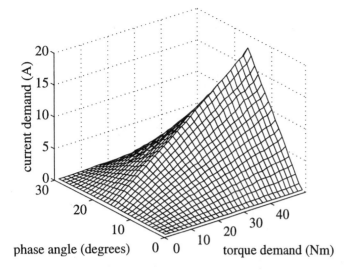

Figure 6. Network output after initialisation with triangular current profiles.

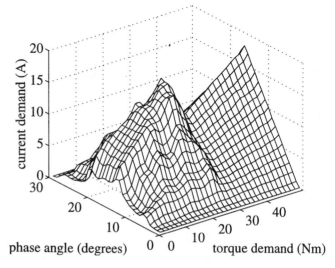

Figure 7. Network output after some training for torque demands in the range 0 to 26 Nm.

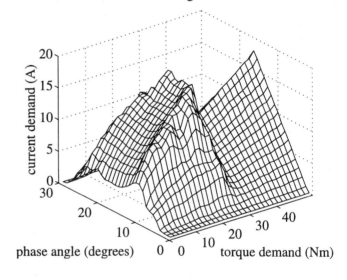

Figure 8. Network output after further training.

Once training began, if the torque, T, produced by the network outputs was so different from that demanded, Td, that training by time inversion at the point (T,θ) had no effect on the network output at (Td,θ) then training was carried out at the latter point according to the following rules. If $T < Td$ then network output was incremented. If $T > Td$ then network output was decremented. The size of the increment or decrement depended on the phase angle. Greater values were used at angles towards the centre of the conduction period.

SIMULATION RESULTS

The system shown in figure 5 was simulated using a two-dimensional lookup table based on experimental static torque measurements to represent the SRM. This is the data shown in figure 1.

Figure 6 shows the initial current profiles embodying the assumptions given in the previous section. It was assumed (and subsequently verified experimentally) that the SRM would rotate under the application of these current profiles and therefore, in the simulation, training proceeded by stepping through all rotor positions sequentially for a range of torque demands.

Figures 7 and 8 show the current profiles learned after different numbers of training cycles with torque demands in the range 0 to 26 Nm. Note that the current profiles outside this range remain as initialised. This illustrates the local generalisation property of the network. The memory requirements of the network used was 2048 words (network weights were stored as 16-bit signed integers).

Figure 9 shows the current profile learned by the neural network for a torque demand of 25.0 Nm. Compared with the profile of figure 4, obtained by the constant rate of change of torque method, the peak current is similar. However, the maximum rate of change of current demanded by the neural network solution is significantly less.

NETWORK IMPLEMENTATION

For experimental purposes, the network has been implemented using a TMS320C25 digital signal processor. The time taken to compute the output of a network and to execute a training cycle depends on the number of weights summed to form an output. In the case of the network, the output of which is illustrated in figures 6 to 8 and which used 8 weights per output, each output computation took 42μs. On the basis of computing an output for every increment of the position encoder, this allows a maximum motor speed of approximately 900 rpm. During training, approximately twice the processing time would be required, i.e. training could take place at motor speeds of up to 450 rpm. The trained networks have been implemented also using a Xilinx FPGA and static RAM. The computation

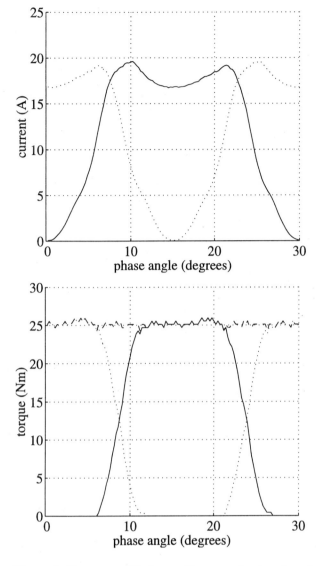

Figure 9. Current profile learned by neural network and predicted torque.

time for a similar network implemented this way is less than 2µs. An accelerator card using this technology is under development.

EXPERIMENTAL RESULTS

At the time of writing, a semiconductor strain gauge based torque sensor is under construction. Experimental results so far are confined to using the neural network to recall current profiles learned off-line using single phase static torque measurement data.

The computer simulation of the SRM drive assumed that a demanded current could be supplied instantaneously. In practice, a converter has a dynamic response. Initial experimental results indicate, however, that the response of the converter used is able to track the current profiles demanded by the neural network at speeds of up to 1200 rpm (figure 10).

DISCUSSION

Figures 4 and 6 illustrate two of the infinite number of different current profiles that would minimise torque ripple. In practice, the suitability of a particular current profile depends on factors such as the rate of change of current with angle, peak and rms values.

The current profiles learned by a neural network are influenced strongly by its initial condition. If pre-loaded with a poor (in terms of rms current and $di / d\theta$ considerations) solution, e.g. a solution found by conventional methods, the network (using a torque-related cost function) would not adapt. Incorporating simple heuristics into both the choice of initial current profiles loaded into the network and the method of coarse training has been successful in generating good solutions. Further

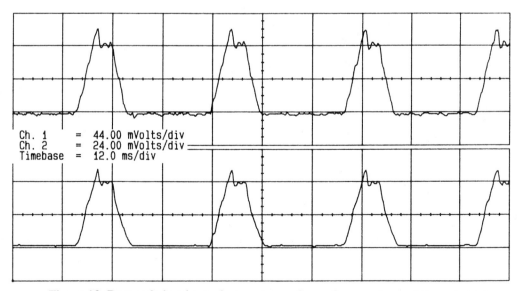

Figure 10. Demanded and actual current waveforms for one phase of the switched reluctance motor, using a DSP implemented neural network. V_{DC} = 150 V.

41

work is necessary on the use of cost functions that include $di/d\theta$ and rms current considerations.

CONCLUSIONS

Simulation, based on experimental torque measurements, has shown neural networks to be capable of learning the current profiles required to minimise torque ripple in SRM drives. A CMAC network has been implemented using both DSP and FPGA technologies and its real-time performance verified as being in excess of that required by the application.

ACKNOWLEDGEMENT

The authors wish to thank Bruno Vilain for his help in commissioning the experimental rig.

REFERENCES

[1] Taylor, G.D., Woolley, M.J., and Ilic, M., Design and Implementation of a Linearizing and Decoupling Feedback Transformation for Switched Reluctance Motors, *Proc. 17th Symposium on Incremental Motion Control Systems and Devices*, Champaign IL, 1988

[2] Wallace, R.S. and Taylor, G.D., Low-Torque-Ripple Switched Reluctance Motors for Direct-Drive Robotics, *Trans. IEEE on Robotics and Automation*, vol. 7, no. 6, 1991

[3] Schramm, D.S., Williams, B.W., and Green, T.C., Torque Ripple Reduction of Switched Reluctance Motors by Phase Current Optimal Profiling, *Proc. ICEM*, Manchester, 1992

[4] Tolle, H., Parks, P.C., Ersu, E., Hormel, M. and Militzer, J., Learning Control with Interpolating Memories - General Ideas, Design Layout, Theoretical Approaches and Practical Applications, *Int. J. Control*, 1992, vol. 56, no. 2, pp 291-317

[5] Pao, Y.H., *Adaptive Pattern Recognition and Neural Networks*, Addison-Wesley, 1989

[6] Albus, J.S, A New Approach to Manipulator Control : The Cerebellar Model Articulation Controller (CMAC), *Trans. ASME, J. DSMC*, 1975, vol. 97, no. 3, pp 312-324

[7] Edgar An, P.C., Miller, W.T., Parks, P.C., Design Improvements in Associative Memories for Cerebellar Model Articulation Controllers (CMAC), *Proc. ICANN*, 1991, pp 1207-1210

[8] Lane, S.H., Handelman, D.A. and Gelfand, J.J., Theory and Development of Higher-Order CMAC Neural Networks, *IEEE Control Systems Magazine*, 1992, vol. 23, no. 2, pp 23-30

[9] Albus, J.S, Data Storage in the Cerebellar Model Articulation Controller (CMAC), *Trans. ASME, J. DSMC*, 1975, vol. 97, no. 3, pp 228-233

Process control is possibly the most ubiquitous type of control utilized today. Every manufacturing and production process must maintain consistency throughout the process. The twelve papers in this chapter attempt to demonstrate the diversity of the process control problems where neural networks have been applied. The first five papers in this chapter utilize various combinations of neural networks and fuzzy systems for processing control, including: tank level control in a dewaxing plant (**Paper 2.1**), thermal control in a heating, ventilation and air conditioning system (**Paper 2.2**), metal-cutting control for industrial machining (**Paper 2.3**), weld pool depth control (**Paper 2.4**), and snack food frying control (**Paper 2.5**). The next five papers describe various applications of the MLP neural network to process control, including: chemical process control of a polymer reactor and a distillation column (**Paper 2.6**), gear backlash hysteresis control in precision position controlled mechanisms (**Paper 2.7**), process planning control and process scheduling control (**Paper 2.8**), plasma gate etch control (**Paper 2.9**), and paper web quality profile analysis (**Paper 2.10**). The last two papers in this chapter demonstrate the utility of variants of the MLP approach to process control. **Paper 2.11** uses a neural network partial least squares algorithm for controlling a municipal waste water process. **Paper 2.12** uses a recurrent neural network for piezo tool positioning.

Chapter 2: *Process Control*

Application of Neuro-Fuzzy Hybrid Control System to Tank Level Control

Tetsuji Tani
Maintenance & System Development Section
Manufacturing Department
Idemitsu Kosan Co., Ltd., Japan

Shunji Murakoshi and Tsutomu Sato
Institute of Information Technology
Information Systems Department
Idemitsu Kosan Co., Ltd., Japan

Motohide Umano
Department of
Precision Engineering
Osaka University, Japan

Kazuo Tanaka
Department of
Mechanical Systems Engineering
Kanazawa University, Japan

Abstract : This paper proposes a practical control method using neural networks and fuzzy control techniques, where neural networks estimate the target of fuzzy control. Neural networks estimate the transient state of the plant which has non-linear process such as refrigerating and filtering. Based on the estimation, the suitable control target pattern for fuzzy control is selected.

This method is applied to the tank level control of the solvent dewaxing plant. And it is shown that this proposed system can control the tank level effectively not only in steady state but also in transient state.

1. Introduction

Since phenomena in the real plant are too complicated to build a theoretical model, it is very difficult to design a control system of such a plant. The operator, however, can control such a plant using his experience. Recently, fuzzy logic, neural network, or both are applied to the real process rather than mathematical models[1, 2, 3]. Fuzzy logic deals with the linguistic and imprecise rules by expert's knowledge. Neural network is also applied to control plants.

This paper deals with a tank level control including non-linear process such as refrigerating and filtering.

A real process often has more than one purpose of control. Our purposes of control are,

(1) to change the flow rate from the tank smoothly,

(2) to keep the tank level stable.

These are contrary to each other.

To overcome these problems, we observe an experienced operator's procedure. He can estimate the suitable target of the tank level and keep the tank level stable. The aim of this paper is to design a neuro-fuzzy hybrid control system which replaces expert's operation. Neural networks estimate the transient state of the plant and based on this estimation the control target pattern of fuzzy control for the smooth change of the flow rate is selected.

This neuro-fuzzy hybrid method is applied to the real tank level control of the solvent dewaxing plant, and good results are obtained not only in steady state but also in transient state.

2. Description of Process

In the process of the vacuum distillation for producing lubricant oil, distillate oil and reduced oil are produced, including wax. Such oils including wax generally have a high

47

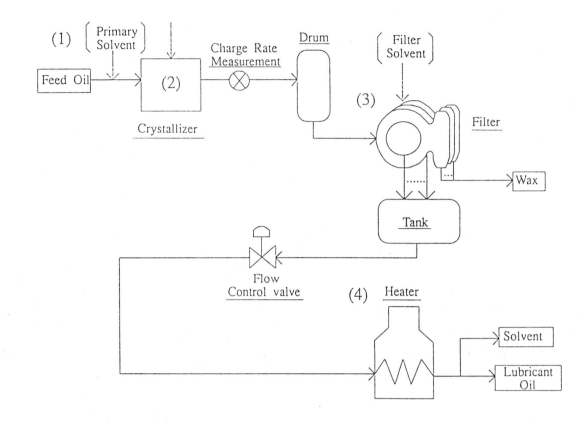

Fig.1. Process flow of the solvent dewaxing plant

solidifying point, so we have to remove the wax not to freeze at low temperature.

The solvent dewaxing plant for removing the wax is outlined in Fig.1. This plant uses solvent to remove the freezed wax easily. We have several steps as follows:

(1) The primary solvent is added to the feed oil.

(2) The feed oil is refrigerated in crystallizer on adding secondary solvent.

(3) The congealed wax is removed by the filter on spraying the filter solvent. The filter is composed of a vacuumed rotating drum which separates the congealed wax from the feed oil. The dewaxing oil, which is a mixture of lubricant oil and solvent, is sent to the tank.

(4) The heater makes solvent evaporate. As a result, low fluid point lubricant oil is produced.

Our control purpose is to keep the tank level constant in all conditions. However, we have the following difficulties for keeping the tank level constant.

(1) The inflow rate to the tank varies with the filter plugging. Since the response of the filter plugging has a long delay time when the feed oil is switched (the delay time also depends on kinds of feed oil), it is difficult to keep the tank level constant using a feed-forward controller.

(2) The heater has a limit in the changing of the flow rate.

(3) We have the feed oil switching frequently (every three or four days).

These factors are combined in a complicated fashion, where an experienced operator used to control the flow rate manually.

3. Operator's Procedure

We have two operation states. One is steady state for everyday operation and the other is transient state of the feed oil switching.

(1) Steady State

Several filters are in operation and one is stopped periodically for washing. The tank level, therefore, goes down and up periodically. An experienced operator,

(a) estimates the flow rate roughly by observing the tank level over several hours,

(b) compensates the flow rate by observing the tank level and the time of filter washing.

(2) Transient State

When the feed oil will be switched, an operator controls the tank level beforehand to make the change of the flow rate more smoothly. For example, if the inflow rate of the tank is expected to be lower after the feed oil switching, the flow rate is beforehand decreased to keep the tank level constant. This prevents the tank from becoming empty and the flow rate from changing rapidly.

We model such experienced operator's procedures to control the tank level as follows:

Step1 : To obtain long-time tendencies of the flow rate, we calculate the average from operation data. This is equivalent to the expert's estimation of rough flow rate.

Step2 : To compensate the flow rate, we use a fuzzy control system based on expert's knowledge. The input variables of this fuzzy control system are the tank level and the time of filter washing.

Step3 : To control the tank level beforehand, we find transient state by using neural networks. This is equivalent to the expert's predictions. The expert predicts the transient state and changes the control target of the tank level.

4. Structure of Neuro-Fuzzy Hybrid Controller

We design neuro-fuzzy hybrid control system which

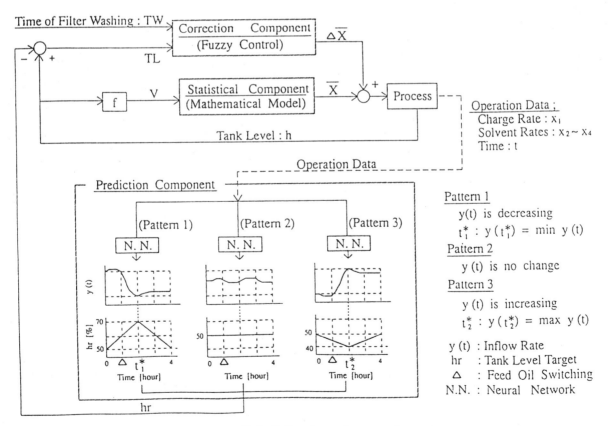

Fig.2. Outline of neuro-fuzzy control system

replaces expert's operation[4, 5, 6]. The controller consists of three components, (1) a statistical component, (2) a correction component (fuzzy controller) and (3) a prediction component (neural networks) in Fig.2.

4.1 Statistical Component

The statistical component is a statistical model for calculating long-time tendencies of the flow rate from operation data. An experienced operator sets the flow rate based on long-time tendencies for the tank level. For example, if the level has a tendency to increase, the flow rate gradually increases.

The difference of the tank amount ΔV is defined as

$$\Delta V(t) = f(h(t)) - f(h(t-1)) \tag{1}$$

where h(t) and h(t-1) are the tank level and f converts its level to the corresponding amount. And the average flow rate $\overline{X}$ is defined as

$$\overline{X}(t) = \overline{X}(t-1) + \alpha \Delta V(t) \tag{2}$$

where α is a real number ($0 < \alpha \leq 1$) and determined by experience. And $\alpha = \alpha_1$ in the steady state and $\alpha = \alpha_2$ is in the transient state, where $\alpha_1 < \alpha_2$.

4.2 Correction Component

The correction component is a fuzzy controller for compensating the flow rate from the statistical component to stabilize the tank level. We use a simplified method of fuzzy reasoning[7].

The control rules of experienced operators to stabilize the tank level are shown in Table 1. These rules mean that,

· when the tank level is near the target, operators focus on the rate of level changing,

· when the tank level is far from the target, operators focus on the time until the next washing.

As a example : If TL is PS and ΔTL is PS then $\Delta\overline{X}$ is PS, where $\Delta\overline{X}$ is compensation of $\overline{X}$.

The tank level target for fuzzy control is 50% of the tank capacity in a steady state. In a transient state, it is set by neural networks which will be described in the next section.

4.3 Prediction Component

When the feed oil will be switched, we have to predict the inflow rate of the tank. But it is too complicated process to build a mathematical model. We use a neural network approach to predict the inflow rate.

The prediction component is neural networks for predicting the inflow rate to estimate the target of fuzzy controller. We use a three layers model whose learning method is back propagation algorithm[8]. Our neural network is shown in Fig.3. The input layer has five units, the hidden layer has ten and output layer has one. We had an interview with experienced operator to decide the input variables. Input are charge rate of

Table 1. Control rule table

		ΔTL					TW		
		PB	PS	ZE	NS	NB	PB	PS	ZE
TL	PB	—	—	—	—	—	PB	PB	PS
	PS	PB	PS	—	ZE	NB	—	—	—
	ZE	ZE	ZE	ZE	ZE	ZE	ZE	ZE	ZE
	NS	PB	ZE	—	NS	NB	—	—	—
	NB	—	—	—	—	—	NS	NB	NB

[Input of fuzzy control]

TL : h - hr , where h is tank level and hr is tank level target
ΔTL : rate of the changing level
TW : time until next filter washing

[Compensation of the average flow rate]

PB : Positive Big
PS : Positive Small
ZE : Zero
NS : Negative Small
NB : Negative Big

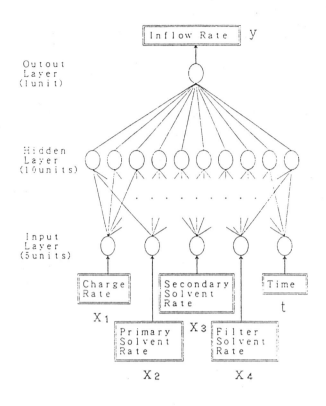

Fig.3. Outline of neural network

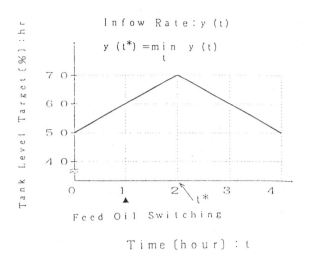

Fig.5. Example of tank level target patten

the feed oil, primary solvent rate, secondary solvent rate, filter solvent rate and time. Output is the inflow rate. We use several neural networks for the different feed oil switching patterns, e.g., oil A to oil B and oil B to oil C.

From the prediction of the inflow rate by the trained neural networks, we can find the followings:

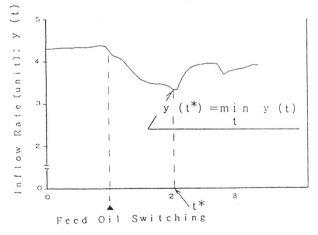

Fig.4. Example of inflow rate pattern

(1) The inflow rate changing pattern after the feed oil switching: increasing, decreasing and no change.

(2) The time of the highest stage or the lowest stage for the inflow rate.

For example, Fig.4 shows a prediction of a inflow rate pattern by using the trained neural network when the oil is switched oil A to oil B. We can find the followings:

(1) The inflow rate of the tank is decreasing.

(2) The inflow rate of the tank becomes the lowest stage about an hour after the feed oil switching.

Fig.5 shows the target pattern when the oil is switched from oil A to oil B. This means that it takes 2 hours that the tank level must be increased for compensation to the lowest stage of the inflow rate, and then it is decreased to 50% of the tank capacity. This is equivalent to the expert's action. He makes the tank level the highest at the lowest stage of the inflow rate.

5. Results

We applied the proposed method to the real plant of the solvent dewaxing plant at Idemitsu Chiba refinery. As results of on-line test, we got the stability for the tank level, and

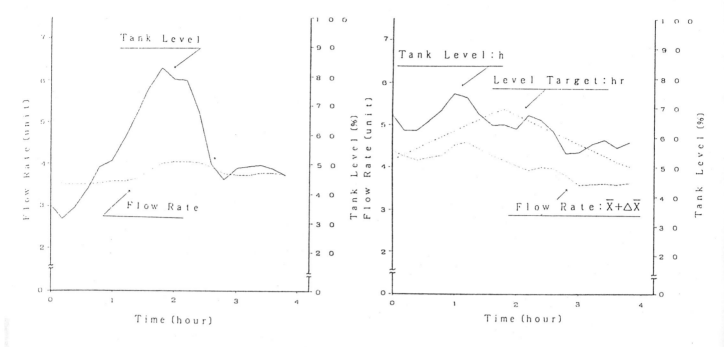

Fig.6. Example of manual operation   Fig.7. Example of neuro-fuzzy control system

smoothness for the flow rate not only in the steady state but also in the transient state.

Fig.6 shows a result of the manual control when oil A is switched to oil B. The experienced operator has raised the tank level before oil switching. On the other hand, Fig.7 shows a result of the proposed method for the same oil switching. The tank level ranges from 35% to 75% by the operation of proposed method, although it raises from 30% to 80% by manual operation. And the flow rate by the proposed method is as smooth as that by the well-experienced operator.

6. Conclusion

A practical control method of neuro-fuzzy hybrid control is proposed. Neural networks are used for estimating the target of fuzzy control.

This method is applied to the tank level control of the real process. The process has two purposes that are contrary each other. The hybrid controller shows its usefulness not only in steady state but also in transient state.

Reference

[1] M. Sugeno, Ed. : Industrial Applications of Fuzzy Control, North-Holland(1985).

[2] A.Guez, J.L.Elibert and M.Kam : Neural Network Architecture for Control, IEEE Control Systems Magazine, Vol.8, No.2, pp.22-25(1988).

[3] K. Suzuki and Y. Nakamori : Model Predictive Based on Fuzzy Dynamic Models, 4th Inter. Conf. on Process Sys. Engg, Vol.II, pp.18.1-18.15(1991).

[4] T. Tani and K. Tanaka : A Design of Fuzzy-PID Combination Control System and Application to Heater Output Temperature Control, Trans.Society of Instrument and Control Engineers, Vol.27,No.11, pp.1274-1280(1991) (in Japanese).

[5] T. Takagi and M. Sugeno : Fuzzy Identification of Systems and Its Application to Modeling and Control, IEEE Trans. on Sys. Man and Cybernetics, Vol.SMC-15, No.1, pp.116-132(1985).

[6] G. T. Kang and M. Sugeno : Fuzzy Modeling and Control of Multilayer Incinerator, Fuzzy Sets and Systems, Vol.18, pp.329-346(1986).

[7] M. Mizumoto : Fuzzy Controls by Product-Sum-Gravity Method, Advancement of Fuzzy Theory and Systems in China and Japan (ed. by X.H.Liu and M.Mizumoto), International Academic Publishers, pp.c1.1-c1.4(1990)

[8] D. E. Rumelhart, G. E. Hinton, and R. J. Williams : Learning internal representations by error propagation, Parallel Distributed Processing, Vol.1, MIT press, Cambridge, pp.318-362(1986)

A Design Methodology for an Intelligent Controller using Fuzzy Logic and Artificial Neural Networks

Alberico Menozzi
Student Member, IEEE
amenozz@eos.ncsu.edu

Mo-yuen Chow
Senior Member, IEEE
chow@eos.ncsu.edu

Dept. of Electrical and Computer Engineering
North Carolina State University
Raleigh, NC 27695
USA

Abstract

The optimal control of nonlinear time-varying systems, particularly when the mathematical model of the system is unavailable or inexact, is an interesting and difficult control problem. This paper outlines a methodology for the design of an intelligent controller to perform optimal control of a nonlinear system adaptively, using emerging technologies of Fuzzy Logic (FL) and Artificial Neural Networks (ANN). FL is utilized to incorporate the available knowledge into the control system, and ANN technology is applied to adaptively provide an optimal control strategy based on some performance criteria. The technique is tested on a system that consists of a DC motor (a linear time-invariant (LTI) system) and a thermal system (a time-varying nonlinear system). Performance criteria such as tracking accuracy, cost, robustness, are considered, and the results are presented in this paper.

I. Introduction

Most *conventional methods*, such as PI control, are based on mathematical and statistical procedures for the modeling of the system and the estimation of the optimal controller parameters. In practice, the plant to be controlled is often highly nonlinear and a mathematical model may be difficult to derive. In such case, conventional techniques may prove to be sub-optimal and may lack robustness in face of modeling error, because they are only as accurate as the model which was used to design them. With the advancement of technology, sophisticated control techniques have been developed to improve the control of systems that cannot be easily handled by conventional control. *Artificial Neural Networks* (ANN) and *Fuzzy Logic* (FL) have been successfully applied to different areas such as fault detection and control [2-4, 8] (giving rise to terminology such as *neural control, fuzzy control*, and *intelligent control*).

Intelligence is an important and delicate word because of its strong association with human behavior, and its introduction in the control systems literature has generated many different reactions. The problem stems from the inability to generally agree on what constitutes intelligence. The approach taken here in the definition of intelligent control comes from trying to understand how human/animal/biological systems achieve certain tasks in order to get ideas about how to solve difficult control problems [1]. An intelligent controller should not be strongly tied to mathematical models. In fact, human beings routinely perform very complicated tasks without the aid of any mathematical representations. A basic knowledge base and the ability to learn by training seem to guide humans through even the most difficult problems. Furthermore, it may be desirable to optimize the performance of the control system with respect to some user-definable criteria. These performance criteria are problem dependent and often consist of a combination of many different factors, each having its degree of importance.

A control system which incorporates human qualities, such as heuristic knowledge and the ability to learn, can be considered to possess a certain degree of intelligence. Such intelligent control system has an advantage over the purely analytical methods because, besides incorporating human knowledge, it is less dependent on the overall mathematical model. For this reason, the methodology described in this paper consists of utilizing FL to incorporate relevant knowledge from human heuristics and from control theory into the control system, and using ANNs to introduce the ability to perfect the control strategy based on some performance criteria. This combination of knowledge, human wisdom, and the ability to learn from experience constitutes an intelligent control system. This paper gives an overview of the proposed methodology and presents the results of applying the intelligent control on a *Heating Ventilation and Air Conditioning* (HVAC) system, which is a highly nonlinear and stochastic system.

II. An Intelligent Control Design Methodology

Figure 1 shows a very general pictorial representation of control engineering that can serve as a guide to understanding the basic reasoning behind the proposed methodology for intelligent controller design. In fact, most problems of interest fall in a category corresponding to the central portion of the problem set in Figure 1. These are the problems that need to be solved by a method which makes use of both the available control theory and the heuristic knowledge/experience of an expert or an operator.

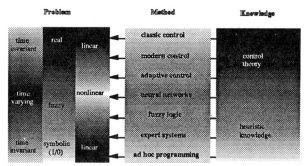

Figure 1. General view of control engineering.

The characteristics of FL [8, 12, 13] make it particularly attractive for control applications because only a linguistic description of the appropriate control strategy is needed in order to obtain the actual numerical control value. Moreover, the description of the control strategy could be derived by examining the behavior of a conventional controller [2, 11]. Thus, FL can be used as a general method to incorporate knowledge, heuristic or theoretical, into a controller. Still, FL by itself lacks the ability to adapt, which is a capability of great interest for adaptive control applications. In fact, current applications of classical control involve tweaking models by hand or periodically tuning controller parameters. This tweaking occurs after the design has been finalized, and represents a great amount of effort in the development of the control system.

Usually, a human operator is responsible for adjusting the controller's parameters in order to approach his/her own idea of good performance. Indirectly, the operator is performing a minimization of a cost function based on his/her knowledge. More generally, when confronted with a problem situation, humans execute a mapping between a set of events and the set of corresponding appropriate actions. The appropriateness of these actions is due to some basic acquired knowledge, or even instinct, which guides the initial stages of the mapping. Then, through experience and a set of implicit guidelines, the human learns to perform a better mapping. This is an on-going process throughout a human being's life. Similarly, an ANN, if given initial guidance, can learn to improve its performance through a set of guidelines, e.g. minimize a cost function. In fact, a properly structured ANN can learn any arbitrarily complicated mapping [5]. The problem becomes that of a) providing initial basic knowledge and b) providing the general guidelines on how to judge the behavior of the control effort, i.e. the cost function to minimize. In the proposed method, the initial basic knowledge is provided by a FL controller, and the cost function is provided by the user and depends on the particular problem to be solved.

Figure 2 is a pictorial representation of the concept of coupling FL and ANNs to implement intelligent control. Because the knowledge from control theory is important, an attempt should

be made to incorporate it into the FL controller along with the heuristic knowledge. Then, the control action performed by this resulting FL controller is used to supply the ANN with a set of training patterns to be used for its initial supervised training. After this supervised training, the ANN will, in effect, have learned the basic control strategy provided by both heuristic knowledge and control theory through the FL controller. Once this basic knowledge has been incorporated, the ANN can undergo on-line unsupervised learning in which the weights are adapted in order to minimize the user-defined cost function. By learning on-line, the ANN controller can adjust to small changes or disturbances in the system.

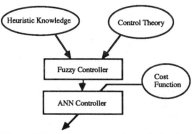

Figure 2. Using a) FL to incorporate knowledge into an ANN (initialize it) and b) a user-defined cost function for on-line learning.

III. HVAC Intelligent Control System Design

The system to be controlled consists of a HVAC system whose main components are a room, a variable speed fan driven by a DC motor, and a heat exchanger (see Figure 3). The conditions within the system are regulated by controlling the heat input in the heat exchanger and the volumetric airflow rate.

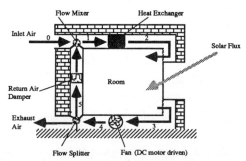

Figure 3. Pictorial representation of the HVAC system.

The system dynamic equations can be derived from conservation of energy principles [6]:

$$\rho c_p V_{he} \frac{dT_2}{dt} = f\rho c_p (T_1 - T_2) + Q_{he}, \tag{1}$$

and

$$\rho c_p V_r \frac{dT_3}{dt} = f\rho c_p (T_2 - T_3) + Q_l \tag{2}$$

where c_p is the constant pressure specific heat of air, f is the volumetric airflow rate, Q_{he} is the heat input in the heat exchanger, Q_l is the thermal load on the room, T_i is the temperature at location i

(see Figure 3), V_{he} is the effective heat exchanger volume, V_r is the effective room volume, ρ is the air density, and t is time. Statements of conservation of mass and energy applied at the flow mixer, with other mild assumptions, yield:

$$T_1 = T_3 + \frac{(T_0 - T_3)}{r} \qquad (3)$$

where

$$r = \frac{f}{f_0} \qquad (4)$$

is the system to outside air volumetric flow rate ratio. For $r = 1$, there is no recirculation and a *once-through* system is considered. By letting $x = [T_2, T_3]^T$, and considering the case in which the outside airflow rate is a constant greater than or equal to 0.0354 m^3/s, the control variables are $u = [Q_{he}, f]^T$, and the state equations of the system are:

$$\dot{x}_1 = \frac{1}{V_{he}} \left[(u_2 - f_0)x_2 - x_1 u_2 + f_0 T_0 + \frac{u_1}{\rho c_p} \right], \qquad (5)$$

$$\dot{x}_2 = \frac{1}{V_r} \left[(x_1 - x_2)u_2 + \frac{Q_l}{\rho c_p} \right], \qquad (6)$$

which describe a nonlinear system. The thermal load into the room is due to the daily solar flux coming through a window, Q_l, which is a time-varying parameter. Another time-varying parameter is the temperature of the outside air, T_0, due to other uncontrollable meteorological factors.

1. DC Motor Control

We first consider the control for the DC motor that drives the fan which can be treated as a nonlinear, time varying and stochastic load. The description of the DC motor system and the procedure for deriving a FL controller from heuristic knowledge and control theory is contained in previous work [2], where a PI controller was designed and used to aid the design of a set of FL control rules and membership functions. The control action from the resulting FL controller was pictorially represented as a control surface. In this paper, using the results from [2], a ANN is pre-trained with the FL control surface through the familiar generalized *delta rule* with *backpropagation* algorithm [10] . After this initial off-line supervised training, the ANN controller executes on-line adaptation and its performance is constantly evaluated via a user pre-defined cost function J. Based on this evaluation, the ANN controller continuously adapts its weights to minimize this cost function.

The specific ANN paradigm used for the DC motor control is a multi-layer feedforward network with two input nodes, fifteen hidden nodes, and one output node, and it is denoted as $\mathfrak{N}_{2,15,1}$. The two input nodes are the tracking error signal and the change in tracking error signal, and the output node provides the signal for the DC motor. During on-line training the generalized delta rule with *dynamic backpropagation* technique [9] is used to adapt the weights

of the network to give optimal performance. Adaptation is achieved by adjusting the ANN's weights in the following manner:

$$\Delta w_{ji}(k+1) = \eta \delta_j o_i + \alpha \Delta w_{ji}(k), \qquad (7)$$

where w_{ji} denotes the weight between node j in a layer and node i in its preceding layer, δ_j is the learning error as seen by node j, o_i is the output of node i, η denotes the learning rate, α is the momentum term, and k indicates the discrete time index. Each weight is updated after every sample instance (*pattern update*). The various values of δ are generated by applying the following equation:

$$\delta_j = -\frac{\partial J}{\partial net_j} = -\frac{\partial J}{\partial o_j} g'(net_j), \qquad (8)$$

where

$$net_j = \sum_i w_{ji} o_i \qquad (9)$$

is the weighted sum of the input signals to node i. In (8) g is a sigmoidal activation function, and J is the cost function which determines performance. The overall effect is that the weights of the ANN are adjusted in the direction of the negative gradient of the cost function in order to converge to a weight configuration which minimizes this cost function.

Of course, if the desired input-output patterns of the controller are available the ANN controller can be trained through supervised training. However, this is not the case for the on-line adaptation process. Nevertheless, the ANN controller can be trained by using the dynamic backpropagation training algorithm based on the chosen cost function. The training then amounts to computing the $\frac{\partial J}{\partial o_j}$ of (8), where j is the outer layer, so that (8) can be rewritten as:

$$\delta_j = -\frac{\partial J}{\partial y} \frac{\partial y}{\partial o_j} g'(net_j), \qquad (10)$$

or

$$\delta_j = -\frac{\partial J}{\partial y} \frac{\partial y}{\partial u} u(1-u), \qquad (11)$$

where y is the output of the DC motor system, and u is the output of the ANN controller. The chosen cost criterion, J, to be minimized is a function of both the error and the change in error, defined as :

$$J(k) = \frac{1}{2} \left[c_1 e^2(k) + c_2(e(k) - e(k-1))^2 \right], \qquad (12)$$

where e is the difference between the desired and the actual output of the DC motor. The relative importance of the terms in the cost function can be adjusted with the factors c_1 and c_2. Given the above cost function, it can be easily shown that

$$\frac{\partial J}{\partial y}(k) = -\left[c_1 e(k) + c_2(e(k) - e(k-1)) \right], \qquad (13)$$

and thus,

$$\delta_j = \left[c_1(E) + c_2(CE) \right] \frac{\partial y}{\partial u} u(1-u), \qquad (14)$$

and the only remaining obstacle is the computation of $\frac{\partial y}{\partial u}$. One approach is to use an approximated mathematical model of the system in question, and compute its derivative. A second strategy involves the use of another ANN to be employed as a system estimator, in which case the derivative is computed by using the familiar backpropagation algorithm on the estimator ANN. In this study, since a differentiable mathematical model is available, the first method is applied. The mathematical model which is used does not need to be exact. In fact, as long as the correct sign of its derivative (i.e. the direction of the gradient) is provided, the ANN controller is able to converge toward the minimum of the cost function. The *learning rate* and the *momentum term* for the ANN training algorithm, as well as the c_1 and c_2 of the cost function J, need to be specified. In this study the values of $c_1 = 0.7275$ and $c_2 = 50$ are used in order to attribute approximately the same importance to both accuracy and smoothness in judging performance. A few trial simulations yielded the acceptable ranges of learning rate and momentum term which allowed satisfactory performance.

2. Room Temperature Controller Design

The room temperature control strategy is also developed by designing a FL controller to initialize an ANN controller. The block diagram of the control system is shown in Figure 4, where e is the temperature tracking error, ce is the change in the temperature tracking error, and d is the time-delay notation. The tracking error and the change in error $\{e, ce\}$ and the volumetric airflow and the heat input in the heat exchanger $\{f, Q_{he}\}$ are used as the two inputs and two outputs of the FL controller, respectively. These quantities are described by fuzzy sets over their universe of discourse.

NB	Negative Big
NM	Negative Medium
Z	Zero
PM	Positive Medium
PB	Positive Big
CC	Very Cold
C	Cold
H	Hot
HH	Very Hot
PS	Positive Small

Table 1. Fuzzy set values and their linguistic meaning.

The membership functions describing the fuzzy sets of all the variables are shown in Figure 5. Table 1 lists the corresponding fuzzy set values and their linguistic meaning for the thermal system. For example, f is a fuzzy *variable* that can take Z, PS, or PB as a fuzzy set *value*.

The heuristic reasoning which dictates the FL control strategy is summarized by two sets of rules: one is directed toward controlling the volumetric airflow rate (f), and the other refers to the control of the heat input in the heat exchanger (Q_{he}). For example, the airflow rate rule set is shown in Table 2.

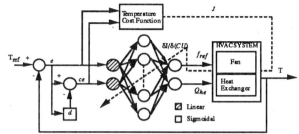

Figure 4. Block diagram of the HVAC control system, d is a delay.

			e		
		NB	NM	Z	PM	PB
	NB	PB	PB	PB	Z	PB
	NM	PB	PB	PS	PS	PB
ce	Z	PB	PB	Z	PB	PB
	PM	PB	PS	PS	PB	PB
	PB	PB	Z	PB	PB	PB

Table 2. Rule set for the airflow f.

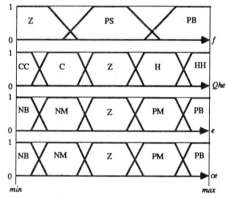

Figure 5. Fuzzy membership functions.

Notice that there is a rule for every possible combination of e and ce that may arise. These rules have the form:

rule i : if $e = A_{e,i}$ and $ce = A_{ce,i}$ then $f = C_{f,i}$ and $Q_{he} = C_{Q_{he},i}$

where $A_{e,i}$ and $A_{ce,i}$ are the fuzzy set values of the antecedent part of rule i for e and ce, respectively. Likewise, $C_{f,i}$ and $C_{Q_{he},i}$ are the fuzzy set values of the consequent part of rule i for f and Q_{he}, respectively. For example:

rule 1: if e = NB and ce = NB then f = PB and Q_{he} = CC

means that "if the error is largely negative (i.e. the temperature is much higher than desired), and it is rapidly getting worse, then the fan should be set at maximum speed and the heat exchanger should be set for maximum cooling".

When actual numerical values for e and ce are obtained, the control values f and Q_{he} are computed, from the set of N rules, as follows:

$$f = \frac{\sum_{i=1}^{N} m_i c_{f,i} I_{f,i}}{\sum_{i=1}^{N} m_i I_{f,i}}, \qquad (15)$$

and

$$Q_{he} = \frac{\sum_{i=1}^{N} m_i c_{Q_{he},i} I_{Q_{he},i}}{\sum_{i=1}^{N} m_i I_{Q_{he},i}}, \qquad (16)$$

where

$$m_i = \min\{\mu_{A_{e,i}}(e), \mu_{A_{ce,i}}(ce)\}, \qquad (17)$$

$$c_{f,i} = centroid(C_{f,i})$$

and

$$\left.\begin{array}{l} I_{f,i} = area(C_{f,i}) \\ c_{Q_{he},i} = centroid(C_{Q_{he},i}) \\ I_{Q_{he},i} = area(C_{Q_{he},i}) \end{array}\right. \qquad (18)$$

In (15) - (18), the subscript i indicates the i-th rule of a set of N rules. In (17), the μs are membership functions, and their subscripts indicate the fuzzy sets that they describe. FL literature refers to the above method as *fuzzy-centroid computation* based on *correlation-product inference* [7, 8]. This technique is not computation-intensive and favors computer implementation.

IV. HVAC Intelligent Control Performance and Discussion

One of the control surfaces, which give a pictorial representation of the overall control strategy, generated by the room temperature FL controller (designed in the previous section) is shown in Figure 6. Without fine tuning the FL controller, these first-try control surfaces will be used to initialize the ANN controller. The ANN configuration used for the room system is $\mathfrak{N}_{2,15,2}$ (see Figure 4). The two input nodes are the tracking error signal (e) and the change in tracking error signal (ce), and the output nodes will provide the signals for the fan (f) and the heat exchanger (Q_{he}). All the nodes used in the ANN have a sigmoidal activation function, with the exception of the two input nodes which have a linear activation function. The learning rate and the momentum term for the ANN training are set to 0.1 and 0.5, respectively.

By training the ANN to reproduce the FL control surfaces, the heuristic knowledge that was used to design the FL controller is transmitted to the ANN. Figures 7a and 7b show the performance of the ANN control system after this supervised training. In this case, the initial weights of the ANN are due only to the FL control surface initialization. The lack of fine tuning of the FL control surface can be noticed as being very influential. In fact, a large overshoot is exhibited in Figure 7b, which is due to the coarseness of the FL controller. In order to improve performance, the ANN was trained on-line in the using the same technique (dynamic backpropagation) that was used for the DC motor sub-system. This

on-line training consisted of presenting 30 random reference temperatures in the range [15°C, 25°C].

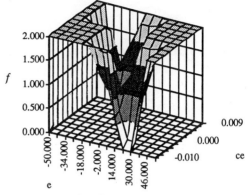

Figure 6. Control surface for the airflow that is generated by the room temperature FL controller.

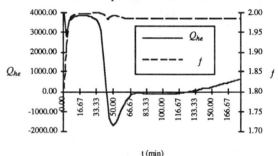

Figure 7a. Fan and heat exchanger action before on-line training.

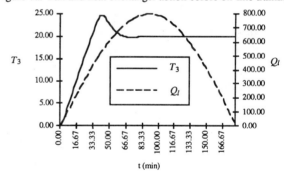

Figure 7b. Temperature and sun flux. The ANN controller has not been trained on-line yet. Its weights are initialized by the FL control surface.

In a similar way, when a human being is confronted with a situation never experienced before, he/she can only rely on some, if any, initial heuristic knowledge about the situation. This knowledge is often too general to be optimal for the specific situation. As time goes on and actual experience is gained, he/she can adjust and perfect the course of actions. Figure 8 shows the ANN fan control surface after the on-line training (compare with Figure 6). Figures 9a and 9b show the performance of the ANN control system after the on-line adaptation for the same operating condition as discussed for the supervised training performance in Figures 7a and 7b. It can be seen that the response has been improved from that of Figures 7a and 7b where the large overshoot has been eliminated. Similar responses were obtained with different reference temperatures.

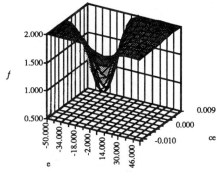

Figure 8. ANN fan control surface after the on-line training.

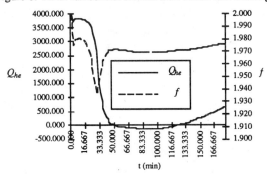

Figure 9a. Fan and heat exchanger action after on-line training.

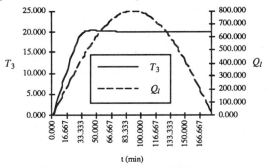

Figure 9b. Temperature and sun flux. ANN controller has been trained on-line.

V. Conclusions

This paper has presented a methodology on designing an intelligent controller using FL and ANN technology which is comparable to installing the human heuristics and other available knowledge about the system into the ANN. The initial knowledge gathered with the help of FL would be of limited usefulness if allowed to remain static. The application of ANN technology to this initially static knowledge introduces the capability to learn from supervised experience. Therefore, the knowledge has become dynamic in nature, and the system, like a human being, can adjust appropriately to situations which were unknown at the beginning. The proposed methodology of control system design has been shown to be virtually free of many conventional mathematical ties

such as system modeling, noise assumptions, and give satisfactory results for the HVAC system control problem that was used as an example.

VI. Acknowledgments

The authors of this paper would like to acknowledge the support of: Electric Power Research Institute - Exploratory and Applied Research Division, for Research Contract RP8004-24.

VII. References

[1] Antsaklis, P. J., K. M. Passino and S. J. Wang, "Towards intelligent autonomous control systems: Architecture and fundamental issues," *J. Intelligent Robotic Syst.*, Vol. 1, pp. 315-342, 1989.

[2] Chow, M. -Y., A. Menozzi and F. Holcomb, "On the Comparison of the Performance of Emerging and Conventional Control Techniques for DC Motor Velocity and Position Control," *Proc. IECON '92*, San Diego, CA, pp. 1008-1013, November 1992.

[3] Chow, M. -Y., R. N. Sharpe and J. C. Hung, "On the Application and Design of Artificial Neural Networks for Motor Fault Detection: Part I & Part II," *IEEE Transactions on Industrial Electronics*, Vol. 40, No. 2, pp. 181-196, April 1993.

[4] Chow, M. -Y. and S. -O. Yee, "An Adaptive Backpropagation Through Time Training Algorithm for a Neural Controller," *Proceedings of the 1991 IEEE International Symposium on Intelligent Control*, Arlington, VA, pp. 170-175, August 13-15, 1991.

[5] Cybenko, G., "Approximations by superpositions of a sigmoidal function," *Mathematics of Control, Signals, and Systems*, Vol. 2, pp. 303-314, 1989.

[6] House, J. M., T. F. Smith and J. S. Arora, "Optimal Control of a Thermal System," *ASHRAE Transactions 1991*, vol. 97, Part 2, pp. 991-1001, 1991.

[7] Kosko, B., *Neural Networks and Fuzzy Systems: A Dynamical Systems Approach to Machine Intelligence*. Englewood Cliffs, NJ: Prentice Hall, 1992.

[8] Lee, C. C., "Fuzzy logic in control systems: Fuzzy logic controller, Part I," *IEEE Transactions on Systems, Man, and Cybernetics*, Vol. 20, No. 2, pp. 404-418, March/April 1990.

[9] Narendra, K. S. and K. Parthasarathy, "Identification and Control of Dynamical Systems using Neural Networks," *IEEE Trans. on Neural Networks*, Vol. 1, No. 1, pp. 4-21, March 1990.

[10] Rumelhart, D. E., G. E. Hinton and R. J. Williams, "Learning internal representations by error propagation," *Parallel Distributed Processing: Explorations in the Microstructure of Cognition. Vol. 1.: Foundations*, D. E. Rumelhart, J. L. McClelland and the PDP research group, Eds., Cambridge, MA: MIT Press, pp. 318-362, 1986.

[11] Tang, K. L., R. J. Mulholland, "Comparing Fuzzy Logic with Classical Controller Designs," *IEEE Trans. on Systems, Man, and Cybernetics*, Vol. 17, No. 6, pp. 1085-1087, Nov/Dec 1987.

[12] Tong, R. M. and P. P. Bonissone, "A linguistic approach to decision making with fuzzy sets," *IEEE Transactions on Systems, Man, and Cybernetics*, vol. SMC-10, pp. 716-723, 1980.

[13] Zadeh, L. A., "The concept of a linguistic variable and its application to approximate reasoning," Parts 1 and 2, *Information Sciences*, Vol. 8, pp. 199-249, 301-357, 1975.

CONTROL OF METAL-CUTTING PROCESS USING NEURAL FUZZY CONTROLLER

M. Balazinski

École Polytechnique de Montréal, Mechanical Engineering,
C.P. 6079, Succ. «A», Montréal (Québec) Canada, H3C 3A7

E. Czogala and T. Sadowski

Institute of Electronics, Technical University of Silesia
Pstrowskiego 16, 44-101 Gliwice, Poland

Abstract—This paper recalls the idea of a neural controller with application to the control of an industrial machining process. Two structures of a neural fuzzy controller, which links the ideas of a fuzzy controller and a neural network, are suggested. Results of simulations comparing performance of such a controller to that of a conventional fuzzy logic controller are shown. The experiment indicates that the performance of the proposed neural fuzzy controller is satisfactory. Hence, using a neural network, it is possible to build a controller that performs equally well as a fuzzy logic controller; moreover, it is more flexible and faster.

Keywords: Neural networks, neural fuzzy controller, fuzzy control, metal cutting.

I. INTRODUCTION

Numerous applications of the fuzzy logic controller to the control of ill-defined complex processes have been reported since Mamdani's first paper [9]. Conventional and modern control theories need a precise knowledge of the model of the process to be controlled and exact measurements of input and output parameters. However, due to the complexity and vagueness of practical processes, the application of these theories is still limited.

In many real processes, control relies heavily upon human experience. Skilled human operators can control such processes quite successfully without any quantitative models in mind. The control strategy of the human operator is mainly based on linguistic qualitative knowledge concerning the behavior of an ill-defined process. Since most machining processes are stochastic, nonlinear and ill-defined, also metal-cutting processes fall into such a category of complex processes which are attractive to be controlled by means of fuzzy logic [10].

Considering the applications of fuzzy logic to control machining processes, the work of Zhu, Shumsheruddin and Bollinger [15] should be mentioned as the first. A simple loop, based on error and change in error was employed to control the surface finish in grinding by changing the feed rate. The knowledge base of the controller consists of thirty one rules based on the operator expertise. Sakai and Ohkusa [12,13] considered the application of the idea of fuzzy logic controller to turning. They obtained a preliminary framework for computing fuzzy control rules. Ralston and Ward have examined fuzzy logic control of turning within the context of computer numerical control and adaptive control [10,11] and, together with Dressman and Karwowski, they have considered a related expert system for machining. In his significant work Dubois [6] introduced fuzzy arithmetics to optimization of cutting conditions. Several knowledge-based systems, including expert systems, have been applied to simulate the fuzzy control of machining as well (cf. [10]).

Some approaches to the concept of a neural-network-based controllers employed to the control of various ill-defined, complex processes have been reported recently [1,2,3,4]. The aim of this paper is to recall this useful concept by pointing out its potential application to the control of machining processes, such as turning, milling, grinding etc.

II. STRUCTURES OF THE NEURAL FUZZY CONTROLLER

A. The idea of a fuzzy logic controller

Fuzzy logic controllers may by considered as a special case of generalized decision tables with finite sets of conditions and actions in the rules [8]. Such controllers can be also viewed as models of a human operator determining the appropriate values of the control signal or its increment based on observation of process variables (e.g. *Error, Change in*

Error, Sum of Errors etc.). The design of a fuzzy logic controller includes, after process recognition, a specification of the collection of control rules consisting of linguistic statements linking the inputs of the controller with the appropriate outputs.

The imprecise knowledge delivered by a human operator is usually expressed by fuzzy rules written in the form:

R_r: If A is $A_i^{(r)}$ and B is $B_j^{(r)}$ and ... and C is $C_p^{(r)}$
then U is $U_k^{(r)}$ and V is $V_l^{(r)}$ and ... and W is $W_q^{(r)}$ $\qquad$ (1)

where $A_i^{(r)}$, $B_j^{(r)}$,..., $C_p^{(r)}$ denote linguistic values of the condition variables defined in universes of discourse: **X**, **Y**, ..., **Z** and $U_k^{(r)}$, $V_l^{(r)}$,..., $W_q^{(r)}$ stand for linguistic values of the conclusion variables defined in universes of discourse **U**, **V**, ..., **W** respectively; finally, r denotes the number of the rule. Such a rule corresponds to a relation which may be represented by a fuzzy implication [8].

Approximate reasoning is performed by means of the compositional rule of inference [14] which may be written in the form:

$$(U',V',...,W') = (A', B',..., C') \circ R \qquad (2)$$

R represents the global relation aggregating all the rules and may be expressed as

$$R = also_r (R_r) \qquad (3)$$

where the sentence-connective "also" may denote any t-, s-norms [8] (e.g. **min**, **max** operators) or average operators. The symbol $\circ$ stands for the compositional rule of inference operation (e.g. **sup-min**, **sup-product** etc.). (A', B',..., C') denote inputs, and (U',V',...,W') stand for outputs.

Taking into account the fact that fuzzy rules are usually formulated for each output separately we may consider the simplified rules (with one conclusion only). In this case the output may be obtained as follows:

$$U' = (A', B',..., C') \circ R \qquad (4)$$

Let us assume that the simplest fuzzy controller contains a knowledge base consisting of a collection of fuzzy control rules which have the form

R_r: $\quad$ **If** Error $= A_i^{(r)}$
$\quad$ **and** Change in Error $= B_j^{(r)}$
$\quad$ **then** Control Action $= U_k^{(r)}$ $\qquad$ (5)

where r stands for the rule index. $A_i^{(r)}$, $B_j^{(r)}$, $U_k^{(r)}$ are linguistic values (fuzzy sets) for the linguistic variables *Error, Change in Error* and *Control Action* defined in universes of discourse

X, Y, U, respectively.

We should mention here the explicit connective 'and' between the variables *Error* and *Change in Error* and the implicit sentence connective 'also' which links all the rules in the knowledge base.

A fuzzy control rule is usually implemented by a fuzzy implication (a fuzzy relation in **X** $\times$ **Y** $\times$ **U**):

$$R_r = (A_i^{(r)} \text{ and } B_j^{(r)}) \to U_k^{(r)} \qquad (6)$$

where $(A_i^{(r)} \text{ and } B_j^{(r)})$ may be interpreted as a fuzzy set $A_i^{(r)} \times B_j^{(r)}$ in **X** $\times$ **Y**.

The input information: A' (error) and B' (change in error) being given, the control action U' can be deduced employing the compositional rule of inference, the definitions of fuzzy implication and connectives 'and' and 'also'. Even if we choose a particular compositional rule of inference, fuzzy implication and both connectives 'and' and 'also', the inference process can still be realized in different ways. Namely, if we consider input information (error and change in error) as vectors, we shall write the compositional rule of inference in the form:

$$U' = B' \circ (A' \circ R) \qquad (7)$$

where R is the global relation obtained by connecting all the rules.

We can also use another notation and apply the following formula:

$$U' = (B' \times A') \circ R \qquad (8)$$

Taking into account, for example, **sup-prod** as composition operator, **prod** for implication, **prod** for 'and' and **sum** for 'also' connectives, we get the same inference result from both formulas (7) and (8) respectively.

Using the membership function representation [8], we can write

$$U'(u) = \qquad (9)$$
$$\sum_r \sup_{x \in X, y \in Y} \left[(B'(y) \cdot A'(x)) \cdot (A_i^{(r)}(x) \cdot B_j^{(r)}(y) \cdot U_k^{(r)}(u)) \right]$$

Taking singletons (Kronecker delta) for A'(x), B'(y), when measurements are available, formula (9) can be simplified:

$$U'(u) = \sum_r \left[A_i^{(r)}(x_0) \cdot B_j^{(r)}(y_0) \cdot U_k^{(r)}(u)) \right] \qquad (10)$$

As a defuzzification method, center of gravity can be used. It should be noted here that a different selection of operators may produce different inference results.

Two possible structures of a neural fuzzy controller will be described below.

B. Discrete (m-h-n) neural controller (neural fuzzy controller)

Taking into account the input information, two versions of the neural fuzzy controller may be considered [2]. The difference between them lies in the shape of the input layer, which can be linear ('vector' version of the controller) or rectangular ('matrix' version).

Let Card(X), Card(Y), ..., Card(Z), Card(U), Card(V), ..., Card(W) denote the respective cardinal numbers of the aforesaid discretized universes of discourse. The number of input neurons for the 'vector' version of a neural network can be determined as [5]

$$m = \text{Card}(X) + \text{Card}(Y) + ... + \text{Card}(Z) \qquad (11)$$

while the number of output neurons

$$n = \text{Card}(U) + \text{Card}(V) + ... + \text{Card}(W) \qquad (12)$$

For the 'matrix' version of a neural network the number of input neurons can be determined as

$$m = \text{Card}(X) * \text{Card}(Y) * ... * \text{Card}(Z) \qquad (13)$$

and the number of output neurons as

$$n = \text{Card}(U) * \text{Card}(V) * ... * \text{Card}(W) \qquad (14)$$

It is easy to show that the approach to the inference process in a fuzzy controller mentioned in the previous subsection leads to the above-described construction of two versions of the neural fuzzy controller which can be trained using the same input information and the control results can be compared.

Considering the discretization of the universes of discourse for error - **X**, change in error - **Y**, and control action - **U**, we can now construct two versions of the neural fuzzy controller. The structure of multilayer perceptron seems to be sufficient for the discussed task [1,5]. The structure of the input layer is considered to be linear for the 'vector' version and rectangular for the 'matrix' version (see Fig. 1)

According to formula (11) and taking into account the discretization of universes of discourse, the vector version will have $m_1 = \text{Card}(X) + \text{Card}(Y)$ input neurons. The number of output neurons is given by $n = \text{Card}(U)$. Denoting the number of units in the hidden layers as h_1, h_2,... , we can annotate the structure of the 'vector' network as $(m_1 - h_1 - h_2 - ... - n)$.

For the 'matrix' version according to formula (13) and

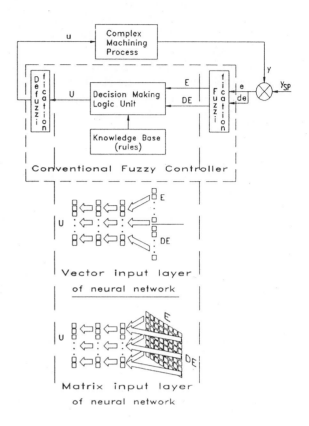

Fig. 1 Control loop employing a fuzzy logic controller and both versions of neural fuzzy controller

using the same discretization as in the vector version, we will have $m_2 = \text{Card}(X) * \text{Card}(Y)$ input neurons. Assuming the same number of output neurons i.e. $n = \text{Card}(U)$ and denoting the number of units in the hidden layers as h_1, h_2, ... , we can also annotate the structure of the network matrix version as $(m_2 - h_1 - h_2 - ... - n)$

For instance, let us consider a 'vector' neural fuzzy controller using 10 input neurons for error and change in error, and 10 output neurons for the control value. Assuming that all the values lie within the intervals (0, 1), for the triple (0.1, 0.4, 0.6) we may write the following input and output vectors:

input: 0100000000 0001000000
output: 0000010000

Note that discretization enforces rounding input and output data to several values, corresponding to input or output neurons. Such a network does not exhibit interpolative properties; however, its advantage is that it may accept 'sampled' fuzzy information, not only crisp (singleton) data.

C. Training and process control

The neural fuzzy controller presented above may be trained

off-line by means of quantitative measurements expressed by triples (*Error, Change in Error, Control Action*) obtained during the observation of the process (sampling its parameters). The structure of the controller forces rescaling and discretization of the input-output data. It should be mentioned here that neural nets may also be initially trained using information obtained from the control rules (qualitative knowledge) [5]. As a learning scheme, the widely used backpropagation algorithm can be applied.

After training, the network can be used to control the process. This is accomplished by feeding process data (error and change in error) to the input layer of the network, which then recalls an appropriate action.

III. NUMERICAL RESULTS

We will present here some numerical results obtained by simulating the control of a machining process.

In order to obtain comparable results we have used a slightly modified knowledge base originating from Zhu et al. [15]. The fuzzy controller used in our experiments employed **sup-prod** for compositional operation, **prod** for the 'and' connective between rule premises, **sum** for the sentence connective 'also'.

As an example let us mention a turning process, in which a constant cutting force (static case) should be assumed to assure the proper wear of the cutting tool. The changeable depth of cutting is compensated by the change of the feed rate. Basing on [7], the relation between the cutting depth, feed rate and the cutting force in the *y*-direction can be approximated by the following formula:

$$F_y = C_y \cdot d^{e_y} \cdot f^{u_y} \qquad (15)$$

where d denotes the cutting depth, f stands for the respective feed rate and C_y, e_y, u_y are constant coefficients.

Under chosen cutting conditions [7], formula (15) takes the form

$$F_y = 876 d^{0.9} f^{0.75} \qquad (16)$$

Assuming a constant force $F_{yo} = 3050.4$ [N], the range of the cutting depth $d \in [3..5]$ [mm] corresponds to the feed rate $f \in [0.75..1.4]$ [mm/s]. In this case the cutting depth was the value controlled, the feed rate being the control value.

In the first stage of our experiment we used a fuzzy controller represented by equations (7) and (10) to simulate a human operator. The set point was preprogrammed to change within the interval [3..5] (see Fig. 2 and 3). The results of control, shown in Fig. 2, were then used to train the neural fuzzy controller. For modeling the controller ('vector' version only) we employed three-layer feedforward

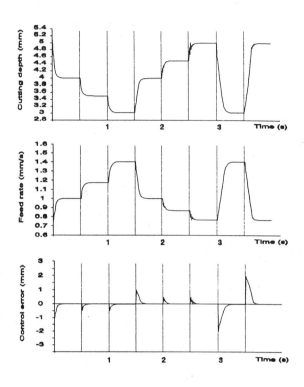

Fig. 2 Results of control using fuzzy logic controller

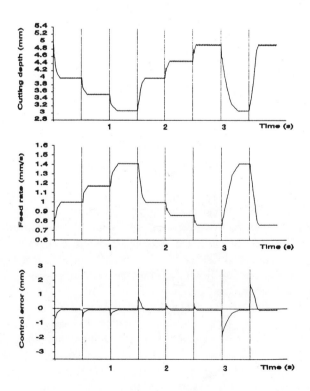

Fig. 3 Results of control using neural fuzzy controller

network with sigmoidal elements arranged in a 20-20-10 structure. A backpropagation algorithm was used for training, with learning rate of 0.6 and momentum factor of 0.3. A random pattern presentation scheme was used for training; 200 training rounds were performed. The connectivity matrices were initially randomized with values from within the interval $[-0.5; 0.5]$. The ranges of error, change in error and drive were rescaled to 'fill' the whole range covered by the input and output neurons; rescaling was performed on the basis of previous observation of the process (i.e. operator's experience). The error and change in error values were clamped to the interval $[-0.5; 0.5]$, while drive values lay within the interval of $[0.75; 1.4]$.

In the second stage the same control program was performed using previously trained neural fuzzy controller. The results are shown in Fig. 3.

For the purpose of comparative study a quality index was defined as below:

$$QI = \sum_{i=0}^{N} \frac{(CD_i - SP_i)^2}{N+1} \qquad (17)$$

where CD_i denotes the controlled value (cutting depth), SP is the set point and N is the total number of observation points.

Comparing both stages we can note that both the fuzzy and the neural fuzzy controller behave similarly. Control performed by the neural fuzzy controller was minimally worse (quality index of 12.546 versus 11.797 of the fuzzy logic controller), and oscillations, resulting from relatively rough discretization, can be observed in steady states. It should be noted that the speed of a neural fuzzy controller is greater than that of a classical fuzzy controller, even though the parallel structure of the neural network is simulated.

IV. CONCLUDING REMARKS

The results of numerical experiments show that the neural controller performs equally well as a conventional fuzzy logic controller. Moreover, it is much more flexible (adaptive) and faster than the latter. The accuracy of control is sufficient, as it results from the performed experiments.

As an objective for future research, the input and output discretization problem should be considered: the larger the number of input (output) neurons, the better the accuracy of the controller; however, the larger the network itself, the longer the training time. Also the number of hidden neurons and learning parameters should be examined deeper.

It should also be noted that the structure of the neural fuzzy controller allows introduction of data expressed as fuzzy sets (which are 'sampled' at its inputs and outputs).

REFERENCES

[1] M. Balazinski, E. Czogala and T. Sadowski, Neural controllers and their application to the control of a machining process, Archives of Theoretical and Applied Computer Science, Polish Academy of Sciences, in press.

[2] U. Brunsmann, E. Czogala, and H. von Koch, On modelling of a fuzzy controller by means of two versions of multilayer feedforward neural networks, BUSEFAL 50, March 1992.

[3] J.J. Buckley and E. Czogala, Fuzzy models, fuzzy controllers, and neural nets, Archives of Theoretical and Applied Computer Science, Polish Academy of Sciences, in press.

[4] J.J. Buckley, Y. Hayashi and E. Czogala, On the equivalence of neural nets and fuzzy expert systems, Fuzzy Sets and Systems, in press.

[5] Czogala E., Sadowski T., A Method of Conversion of Fuzzy Decision Tables into Neural Networks, Biocybernetics and Biomedical Engineering, Inst. of Biocybernetics and Biomedical Engineering, Polish Academy of Sciences, Warsaw, in press.

[6] Dubois D., An Application of Fuzzy Arithmetic to the Optimization of Industrial Machining Processes, Mathematical Modelling, vol. 9, no. 6. 1987, 461-475.

[7] Kaczmarek J., *Principles of Machining by Cutting, Abrasion and Erosion*, Peter Peregrinus Ltd., 1976.

[8] C.C. Lee, Fuzzy logic in control systems: fuzzy logic controller - Part I/Part II, IEEE Trans. on Systems, Man and Cybernetics, vol. 20, No. 2, March/April 1990, 404-435.

[9] E.H. Mamdani, Applications of fuzzy algorithms for simple dynamic plant, Proc. IEE, vol. 121, No. 12, 1974, 1585-1588.

[10] P.A.S. Ralston and T.L. Ward, Fuzzy logic control of machining, Manufacturing Review, vol. 3, No. 3, 1990, 147-154.

[11] P.A.S. Ralston, T.L. Ward, L.M. Lambert, Simulation of Fuzzy Logic Control of a Lathe, Symposium on Advanced Manufacturing, Lexington, Kentucky, September 26-28, 1988, 21-25.

[12] Y. Sakai and K. Ohkusa, A Fuzzy Controller in

Turning Process Automation, Industrial Applications od Fuzzy Control, Elsevier Science Publishers B.V. (North-Holland), 1985, 139-151.

[13] Y. Sakai, K. Ohkusa, On a Control System for Cutting Process, 16th CIRP International Seminar on Manufacturing Systems, Tokyo, 1984, 188-195.

[14] L.A. Zadeh, Outline of a new approach to the analysis of complex systems and decision processes, IEEE Trans. on Systems, Man and Cybernetics, vol. 3, 1973, 28-44.

[15] J.Y. Zhu, A.A. Shumsheruddin, J.G. Bollinger, Control of Machine Tools Using the Fuzzy Control Technique, Annals of CIRP vol. 31, 1982, 347-352.

Neural Network and Fuzzy Control of Weld Pool with Welding Robot

Satoshi Yamane*, Yasuyoshi Kaneko**, Noriyuki Kitahara*,
Kenji Ohshima**,and Mitsuyoshi Yamamoto***

* Maizuru College of Technology, Maizuru, Kyoto 625, Japan
** Saitama University, Urawa, Saitama 338, Japan
*** Takusyoku University, Hachiouji, Tokyo 183, Japan

Abstract - This paper deals with the problem concerning the sensing and the controlling of weld pool. In order to obtain the high quality of the welding result, it is important to control the weld pool depth in the robotic welding. The method of controlling the weld pool depth without mathematical model is discussed.

Since it is difficult to directly measure the depth, the depth can be estimated from the information during the welding. Neural networks are used to estimate the depth : this estimates the depth from the weld pool shape, the groove gap, and the welding current. The output of the neural network, which corresponds to the weld pool depth, is controlled with the fuzzy controller. The validity of the neural network and of the fuzzy controller was verified by the welding experiments.

I. INTRODUCTION

The weld pool depth in the joining part is one of factors to determine the mechanical strength. It is important to keep the weld pool depth constant. In order to directly observe the depth with a TV camera, the sensing of the back side of the base metal needs. In general structures, pipes, steel frame buildings, and so on, it is difficult to prepare the place to set up those in the back side. Moreover, since the welding phenomena are described by partial differential equations[1-3], it is difficult to construct the depth's mathematical model described by state equations. A new method is proposed for measuring the weld pool depth. In the method, the weld pool depth is estimated by using the information obtained from the welding side, i.e. the depth of the weld pool is estimated from the surface shapes of the weld pool, the state of the heat input, which corresponds to the changes of the welding current, and the state of the groove gap.

If the numerical data, which describe the relationship between the input and the output of the unknown plant, are given, the state of the unknown plant can be described by using neural networks trained by back propagation method. The dynamical state of the weld pool depth is described by using the neural network[4,5]. Namely, the depth is obtained without solving the mathematical model described by partial differential equations.

The surface shape of the weld pool and the width of the groove gap can be measured during the welding. The weld pool depth can be also measured after the welding. The training data are constructed from these numerical data.

One of the advantage of the fuzzy controller is easy to describe the expert knowledge[6]. The fuzzy controller is valid for the plant, of which the construction of the mathematical model may be difficult. Therefore, the welding current is controlled with the fuzzy controller so as to keep the output of the neural network constant. The neural network and the fuzzy controller are verified by the welding experiments.

II. SENSING OF WELD POOL

The system to observe the surface shape of the weld pool and the width of the groove gap and to control the weld pool depth is constructed from CCD cameras, the power source, and the computer as shown in Fig.1. The surface shape of the weld pool and the groove gap are taken with the CCD camera 1 and camera 2, respectively. They output the vertical division signal VD after sending the video signal of

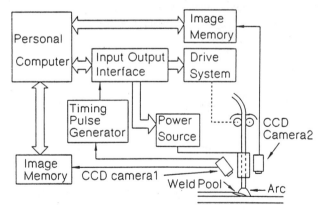

Fig.1 System of observing and controlling the weld pool.

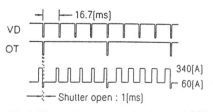

Fig.2 Timing chart to open the shutter of CCD cameras.

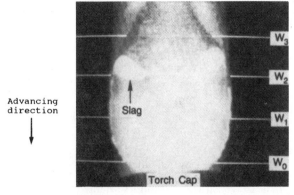

Fig.3 Typical image of the weld pool after processing.

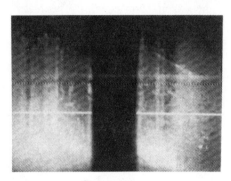

Groove gap
Fig.4 Typical image of the groove gap.

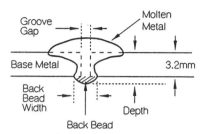

Fig.5 Conception figure of the weld pool depth.

be found from the characteristic of the distribution of the brightness.

III. NEURAL NETWORKS TO DESCRIBE DYNAMICAL SYSTEM OF THE WELD POOL DEPTH

Since it is difficult to directly measure the weld pool depth during the welding, the neural network is used to describe the weld pool depth. That is, the state variables and the output variables which can not be measured directly are found from the state variables and input variable which are easy to measure. The unknown output can be described with the neural network trained by using the relationship between the input and the output. The value of the state variable is found without solving partial differential equations.

The relationship among the molten metal, the groove gap, and the base metal is illustrated in Fig.5. When the base metal melts to the back side, the back bead generates. The width of the back bead becomes wide when the weld pool depth becomes deep.

The dominant factors of the weld pool depth are discussed to find the input of the neural network. The fundamental experiments are performed in the following condition : the thickness of the base metal is the mild steel of the thickness 3.2 mm, the welding speed is 25 cm/min, the range of the current is from 90 to 140 A, the two base metals are jointed without the groove gap. The relationship among the surface shape of the weld pool, the weld pool depth, the welding current is shown in Fig.6. From the result the relationship between the surface shape of the pool and weld pool depth is discussed. The heat input to the base metal becomes big in proportion to the welding current. The surface shape of the weld pool becomes large when the weld pool depth is below about 4.5mm and the heat input increases. When the depth is over 4.5mm and the heat input increase slightly, the much molten metal appears to the back side. Hence the area of the surface shape becomes small.

The fundamental experiments with the groove gap of 1mm is performed in the same conditions as that without the groove gap. The relationship among the surface shape of the weld pool, the weld pool depth, the welding current is shown in Fig.7. The relationship among the surface shape of the weld pool, the width of the groove gap, and the weld pool depth is discussed. The weld pool depth becomes deep as the

the taken image[7]. It takes 1/60s (= 16.7ms) to send the video signal. The personal computer processes the image and calculates the welding current, after the image memory received the video signal. As it takes about 50ms to observe the weld pool and to determine the welding current, the sampling period needs over 50ms. Therefore, the weld pool is taken with the CCD camera and is controlled every 4/60s. The timing signal OT of sensing is generated from VD. The shutter of the CCD camera synchronizes with the signal OT and opens for 1ms as illustrated in Fig.2. Since an arc light is too strong, the welding current is decreased to 20A during opening of the shutter.

The typical image of the weld pool is shown in Fig.3 after processing the image. The pool width, W_0, W_1, W_2, and W_3 at 4 points instead of the surface shape are measured to easily process the image. W_0 corresponds to the pool width just under the electrode. W_1, W_2, and W_3 correspond to the width at 4.17mm, 8.33mm, and 12.5mm behind the electrode against the advancing direction of the welding.

The groove gap is taken with CCD camera 2. The typical image of the groove gap is shown in Fig.4. The surface of the base metal is bright by the arc light of 20A. But, the groove gap is darker than the surface of the base metal, since the reflection of the arc light does not exit in the groove gap. Hence the brightness near the boundary between the base metal and the groove gap changes sharply. The boundary can

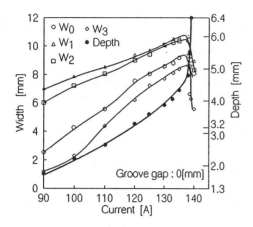

Fig.6   Relationship among the weld pool width, the weld pool depth, and the current in the steady state without the groove gap.

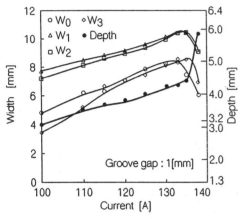

Fig.7   Relationship among the weld pool width, the weld pool depth, and the current in the steady state with the groove gap of 1mm.

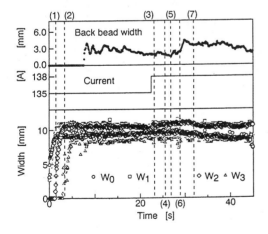

Fig.8 Response of the weld pool width in the transient state.

heat input increases. When the heat input is the same as the case without the groove gap, the weld pool depth of the case with the groove gap of 1 mm is deeper than that without the groove gap, because the molten metals enter into the groove

gap, when the groove gap becomes wide. The weld pool depth becomes deep as the width of the groove gap increases. The fundamental experiment, where the welding current is changed from 135A to 138A like step, is performed to discuss the dynamical response of the weld pool depth. The responses of the surface shape of the weld pool and the width of the back bead is shown in Fig.8. The width of the back bead is easily measured after the experiments were carried out. When the heat input changes, the response of the pool width just under the electrode is the fastest. The response of other width delays. Hence the variation of the welding current, the groove gap, and the variation of the surface shape are used to describe the dynamical system of the weld pool depth. The three layer feedforward neural network is constructed to describe the dynamical system of the weld pool depth as shown in Fig.9.

A. Input layer

The information used to the input layer is illustrated in Fig.10. The width of the groove gap at the position of sensing the pool width can not directly measured, since the molten metal fills the groove gap. The width G_{k+25} of the groove gap at 6.9mm before the electrode, where k is the number of sampling, is measured. As the welding speed is 25 cm/min, the torch moves the distance of 6.9mm in 25 sampling periods. The width G_{k+25} is stored into the memory of the personal computer. The width G_k of the groove gap just under the electrode is obtained by using the stored width of the groove gap. The width of the groove gap at the sensing point W_0, W_1, W_2, and W_3 correspond to G_k G_{k-15}, G_{k-30}, and G_{k-45}, respectively.

The variation of surface shape of the pool is detected by examining the variation of the front part of the surface shape. So that the variation of the width W_0 and W_1 in 1s is adapted as the information of the variation of the surface shape, i.e. the values of the width W_0 and W_1 per 2 sampling periods are given to the neural network : $W_{0,k}$, $W_{0,k-2}$, $W_{0,k-4}$, $W_{0,k-6}$, $W_{0,k-8}$, $W_{0,k-10}$, $W_{0,k-12}$, $W_{0,k-14}$, $W_{1,k}$, $W_{1,k-2}$, $W_{1,k-4}$, $W_{1,k-6}$, $W_{1,k-8}$, $W_{1,k-10}$, $W_{1,k-12}$, and $W_{1,k-14}$, where k is sampling iteration and the sampling period is 4/60s. Similarly, the variation of the welding current, which corresponds to the heat input of the base metal, is represented by using the value per 2 sampling periods : i_k, i_{k-2}, i_{k-4}, i_{k-6}, i_{k-8}, i_{k-10}, i_{k-12}, and i_{k-14}. The input layer is constructed from 30 units.

B. Training of neural network

The neural network is trained by using back propagation method. The performance of the neural network depends on the training data, which is constructed from the relationship between the input and the output. The training data are constructed from the relationship among the surface shape of the weld pool, the welding current, and the weld pool depth in the steady state and the transient state. In general, when the back propagation method is used, the output of the neural network is value from 0 to 1. From the fundamental experiments, the weld pool depth of 6.4mm, which is two times of the base metal's thickness, corresponds to the case in which the base metal is burn through. Therefore, let the output of the neural network be from 0mm to 6.4mm.

First, the training data are constructed from the surface

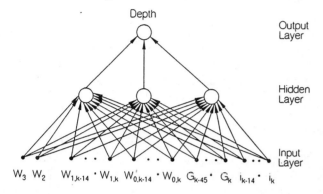

Fig.9 Three layer neural network to describe the weld pool depth.

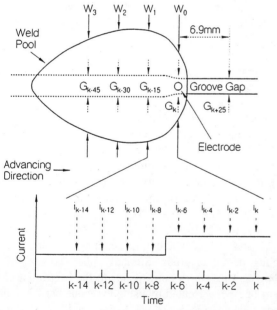

Fig.10 Input variables to the neural network.

shape of the weld pool and the weld pool depth in steady state as shown in Fig.6 and Fig.7. From Fig.6, the surface shape, the width of the groove gap, and the weld pool depth at 90, 100, 110, 120, 125, 130, 133, 135, 138, 139, and 140A are selected as the training data. From Fig.7, the surface shape, the width of the groove gap, and the weld pool depth at 100, 110, 115, 120, 125, 130, 133, 135, and 138A are selected as the training data.

Next, the training data are constructed from the transient response of the weld pool depth for the step change of the welding current in Fig.8, i.e. the response of both the surface shape and the weld pool depth at (1), (2), (3), (4),(5),(6), and (7) in Fig.8 are selected.

The number of units at the hidden layer is decreased while the training error becomes below 3%. The resultant number of the units in the hidden layer is 3.

IV. DESIGN OF FUZZY CONTROLLERS TO CONTROL THE WELD POOL DEPTH

The block diagram of controlling the weld pool depth is shown in Fig.11. Let the desired weld pool depth be D_r. The neural network procedures the weld pool depth D. The deviation e ($= D - D_r$) is calculated from the output of the neural network. The weld pool depth changes by the variation of the width of the groove gap. Since the width before the electrode is taken with the CCD camera 2, the width of the groove gap just under the electrode is already given. In order to control the weld pool depth without the time delay, the feedforward control system is constructed for the variation of the groove gap's width. On the other hand, the feedback control system for the weld pool depth includes the time delay of one sampling period, which needs to process the image and to determine the welding current. The control block diagram is constructed from the feedforward system and feedback system.

First, the design of the fuzzy controller in the feedback part is discussed. It takes one sampling period to process the pool image and to determine the welding current. Namely the time delay T of one sampling period is included to the plant. The plant can be described as first order system with the time delay.

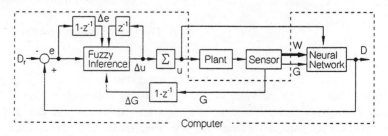

Fig.11 Neural network and fuzzy controller of controlling the weld pool depth.

$$\frac{dx(t)}{dt} = -\lambda x(t) + bu(t-T) \qquad (1)$$

Suppose the coefficient λ to be constant. The fuzzy controller is designed by using the pole assignment method. The desired response of the plant for the step input $r(t) = U_s(t)$ is given by

$$x(t) = U_s(t-T)\{1 - e^{-\alpha(t-T)}\} \qquad (2)$$

where $1/\alpha$ is the time constant.

The characteristic of the controller is

$$\Delta u[n] = a_0 e[n] + a_1 e[n] - b_0 \Delta u[n-1] \qquad (3)$$

The fuzzy controller is designed from the above equation, i.e. the manipulating variable $\Delta u[n]$ is inferred from the deviation $e[n]$, it's variation $\Delta e[n]$, and the prior manipulating variable $\Delta u[n-1]$.

Next, we discuss the fuzzy controller in the feedforward part. When the width of the groove gap becomes wide, the weld pool depth becomes deep. Hence, the heat input must be reduced to keep the weld pool depth constant. On the other hand, when the width of the groove gap becomes narrow, the weld pool depth becomes shallow. The heat input must be increased to keep the weld pool depth constant.

The fuzzy controller is constructed from such knowledge, i.e. the variation $\Delta u[n]$ of the welding current is determined by the variation $\Delta G[n]$ of the groove gap. Let the increasing , the decreasing, and not changing of the welding current be positive, zero, and negative, respectively. The control rules and the fuzzy variables of the fuzzy controller in the feedback part and feedforward part are shown in Table I and Fig.12.

The manipulating variable $\Delta u[n]$ is inferred from the deviation $e[n]$, it's variation $\Delta e[n]$, the prior manipulating variable $\Delta u[n-1]$, and the variation $\Delta G[n]$ of the groove gap.

When the weld pool depth is shallow, the weld pool depth dose not immediately become deep, even if the heat input becomes big. When the weld pool depth is deep, the weld pool depth changes sharply, even if the change of the welding current is small. The gain of the controller must be increased to obtain the quick response. Therefore let the form of the membership function concerning the deviation $e[n]$ be unsymmetry against the origin. When the deviation $e[n]$ is positive, the gain becomes big.

In general, the many control rules are needed, since the manipulating variable is inferred from four kinds of variables. For the simplicity of the calculation, the inference part of the manipulating variable is divided into three parts. $\Delta u_0[n]$ is inferred from the deviation $e[n]$ and its variation $\Delta e[n]$. $\Delta u_1[n]$ is inferred from the variation $\Delta G[n]$ of the groove gap's width just under the electrode. By considering (3), the manipulating

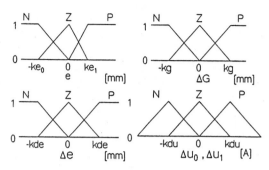

Fig.12 Fuzzy variables.

Table I
CONTROL RULES.

Δe \ e	N	Z	P	
P	Z	N	N	P=Positive
Z	P	Z	N	Z=Zero
N	P	P	Z	N=Negative

	N	Z	P
ΔG	N	Z	P
Δu_1	P	Z	N

$\Delta u[n] = \Delta u_0 + \Delta u_1 - 0.4\Delta u[n-1]$

variable $\Delta u[n]$ is obtained from the following equation.

$$\Delta u[n] = \Delta u_0[n] + \Delta u_1[n] - b_0 \Delta u[n-1] \qquad (4)$$

where let b_0 be 0.4.

V. WELDING EXPERIMENT WITH THE NEURAL NETWORK AND FUZZY CONTROLLER

The welding experiment is performed to verify the performance of the fuzzy controller. The base metal is the same as that used in the fundamental experiments. The welding conditions are as follows:
1) The base metal is the mild steel SS41 of 3.2 mm thickness.
2) The welding speed is 25 cm/min.
3) The shielding gas is the mixing of Ar 98 % and O_2 2%.
4) The reference of the depth is 4.5mm.
5) The width of the groove gap is changed from 0mm to 0.8mm as the disturbance.

First, the welding experiment without the fuzzy controller is performed by using the constant welding current, which is 138A. The variation of the groove gap's width, the response of the surface shape of the weld pool, and the change of the

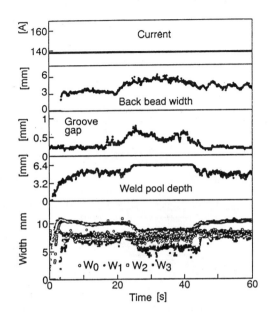

Fig.13 Experimental result with the constant current.

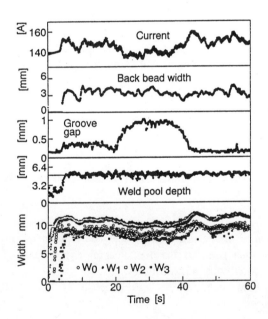

Fig.14 Experimental result with the fuzzy controller.

welding current are shown in Fig.13. When the width of the groove gap is wide, the base metal burn through.

Next, the welding experiment with the fuzzy controller is performed by using the same welding condition as the case of the constant welding current. Let ke_0, ke_1, kde, kdu for Δu_0, kg, and kdu for Δu_1 be 2.5, 1.3, 0.5, 3.0, 1.0, and 20, respectively.

The welding result with the fuzzy controller is shown in Fig.14. The uniform width of the back bead can be obtained. The good performance is obtained, since the weld pool depth measured after the welding is about uniform. Moreover, when the width of the groove gap becomes wide, the welding current is decreasing as shown in Fig.14. On the other hand, when the width of the groove gap becomes narrow, the welding current is increasing.

VI. CONCLUSIONS

The sensing and the controlling of the weld pool depth is discussed. The method to measure the depth is proposed with the neural network, since the depth cannot be directly measured at real time. The weld pool depth is estimated by using the information obtained from the welding side.

The surface shape of the weld pool and the width of the groove gap can be measured during the welding. The weld pool depth can be also measured after the welding. The training data was constructed from these numerical data.

When the width of the groove gap changes, the weld pool depth changes, too. The feedforward control system for the variation of the groove gap's width just under the electrode can be constructed by observing the groove gap's width before the electrode.

The feedback control system was constructed so as to keep the output of the neural network constant. The fuzzy control system was constructed from the feedback control part and the feedforward control part. The validity of neuro-fuzzy controller was verified by doing the welding experiments.

REFERENCES

[1] "Welding Handbook",American Welding Society,vol.1,Miami,Florida 33125(1976).

[2] J.F.Lancaster, "the Physics of Welding", International Institute of Welding", Peramon Press (1984)

[3] H.Maruo, Y.Hirata, "Bead Constitution Phenomenal in Pulsed TIG Welding", Japan Weld.Soc., vol.3, (1985) (in Japanese)

[4] K.Ohshima, Y.Kaneko, Y.Kohashi, T.Kubota, and S.Yamane, "Neuro and Fuzzy Control of Weld Pool in Pulsed MIG welding", 51th National Meeting of Japan Welding Society, Sendai, pp.354-355 (1992) (in Japanese)

[5] K.Ohshima, Y.Kaneko, Y.Kohashi, T.Iizaka, S.Yamane, "Neuro-Fuzzy Control of Weld Pool in Pulsed MIG Welding", 140th Technical Committee of Welding Process of J.W.S.(1992)

[6] Mamdani, E. H., "Application of Fuzzy Logic to Approximate Reasoning Using Linguistic Synthesis", IEEE Transactions on Computers, vol. C-26, no. 12, pp. 1182-1191, (1977)

[7] G.Alzamora, H.Ikeya, Y.Kaneko, K.Ohshima, "Intelligent Welding Robot System", Singapore Int. Conf. on Intelligent Control and Instrumentation, pp.1058-1062 (1992)

Self-Learning Fuzzy Controller with Neural Plant Estimator for Snack Food Frying

Yeong Soo Choi, A. Dale Whittaker, and David C. Bullock
Department of Agricultural Engineering
Texas A&M University, College Station, TX 77843-2117

I. INTRODUCTION

Fuzzy logic-based control has emerged as a promising approach for complex and/or ill-defined process control. However, this approach still has some basic problems of no formal ways to identify the fuzzy inference rules and the lack of adaptability or learning algorithm to tune the membership functions [2]. Also, most of real process control systems are multidimensional and have large time lag. If the fuzzy controller can predict actual plant output by the plant estimator, superior control decision can be obtained because the actual effect of control input changes appear on plant output after time lags.

In this paper, a self-learning fuzzy controller with neural plant estimator is designed for the snack food frying control and the specific objectives are as follows;
1)to find control variables affecting on product quality based on the statistical results of experimental data 2)to employ the neural estimator for the prediction of real plant output related to time lag 3)to construct the adaptive-network-based fuzzy inference system for the fuzzy inference rule extraction and the membepship function tunning 4)to evaluate designed controller performance by simulation

II. DESCRIPTION OF SNACK FOOD FRYING PROCESS

The snack food frying process is composed of dehydration, conveying, and cooling. The product quality is determined in terms of color and moisture content of the final product. Color and moisture content are affected by several factors such as exposure temperature, exposure time, and conditioning time. A main difficulty in designing the this frying process controller is large time lags because the color and moisture content sensors located at the rear of the conveyors are installed far from the control actuators.

III. STRUCTURE OF THE DESIGNED FUZZY CONTROL SYSTEM

The designed fuzzy control system is composed of comparator, fuzzy controller, and neural estimator(Fig. 1).

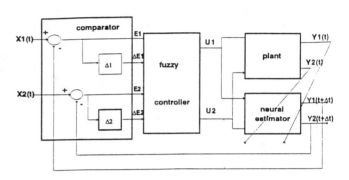

Fig.1. Block diagram of neuro-fuzzy control system

X1 and X2 are desired values of color and moisture content. E1 and E2 are errors between actual and desired color and moisture content. $\Delta E1$ and $\Delta E2$ are error changes of actual color and moisture content. U1 and U2 are exposure temperature and conditioning time. Y1 and Y2 are actual color and moisture content. Δt is the time lag. The neural estimator predicts the actual plant output, $Y(t+\Delta t)$ and the error, $e(t)$ is calculated by the difference between the desired output and neural estimator output which is regarded as actual plant output.

A. Neural Estimator

The neural estimator used in this paper is the time delay multilayer feedforward network with output feedback to process time series data. It is possible to use a static network to represent time series data by simply converting the temporal sequence into a static pattern by unfolding the sequence over time. That is, time is treated as an another dimension in the problem.

$$y(k) = F\left[x(k), x(k-1), \ldots, x(k-n), u(k-1), u(k-2), \ldots, u(k-m)\right] \quad (1)$$

It is essential to construct the effective structure of the neural estimator and to apply on-line learning so that the estimator can produce the minimum error for the real plant predictive output.

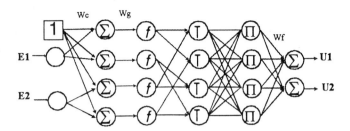

Fig.2. Simplified neuro-fuzzy inference network

B. Adaptive-network-based fuzzy controller

Recently, several approaches of fuzzy inference systems using neural network structure have been proposed for the automatic extraction of fuzzy rules and the tuning of fuzzy membership functions [1],[2]. The basic idea of the composition method of this approach is to realize the process of fuzzy reasoning by the structure of an neural network and to make the parameters of fuzzy reasoning be expressed by the connection weights of an neural network. This methodology can automatically identify the fuzzy rules and tune the membership functions by modifying the connection weights of the networks using Back-Propagation algorithm.

The simplified adaptive-network-based fuzzy controller used in this paper is shown in Fig.2. Main features of the method considered for the snack food frying process control are;

1)Application of the back-propagation gradient descent to find a set of controller weights that minimizes the error function J [4],

$$J = \sum_{k=1}^{n} \|z_d - z_k\|^2 + \lambda \sum_{k=0}^{n-1} \|u_k\|^2 \qquad (2)$$

where, z_d is the desired state in k time steps. z_k is a final state and u_k is controller's output.

2)T-norm operators for generalized AND function.

3)Fuzzy membership functions composed by using sigmoid function with two parameters(w_c, w_g) for each membership function, f in premise part of fuzzy rule. A singular membership function in consequence part[3].

$$f(x_i) = 1/(1 + \exp(-A)), \quad A = w_g(x_i + w_c) \qquad (3)$$

4)Errors and error changes of two plant outputs for controller's inputs.

A technical report[5] is in preparation for IFIS presentation.

IV. REFERENCES

[1] Shin-ichi Horikawa, Takeshi Furuhashi, and Yoshiki Uchikawa. "On Fuzzy Modeling Using Fuzzy Neural Networks with the Back-Propagation Algorithm," *IEEE Transactions on Neural Networks*, vol.3, No.5, pp.801-806, 1992.

[2] Jyh-Shing R. Jang. "Self-Learning Fuzzy Controllers Based on Temporal Back Propagation," *IEEE Transactions on Neural Networks*, Vol.3, No.5, pp.714-723, 1992.

[3] Jyh-Shing R. Jang. "Adaptive-Network-Based Fuzzy Inference System," *IEEE Trans., Man, Cybern*, 1993.

[4] Derrick H. Nguyen and Bernard Widrow. "Neural Networks for Self-Learning Control Systems," *Control Systems Magazine*. pp.18-23, 1990.

[5] Yeong S. Choi, A. Dale Whittaker, and David C. Bullock. "Self-learning Fuzzy Controller with Neural Plant Estimator for Snack Food Frying," *Technical report CFL-93-006*, 1993.

Neural Model Predictive Control of Nonlinear Chemical Processes

Hong-Te Su[†] and Thomas J. McAvoy[‡]

Abstract: Recently, artificial neural networks have attracted much interest as process models for Model Predictive Control (MPC). As pointed out in [12], there are two different neural network dynamic modeling approaches. The paper mainly focuses on the comparison of the two modeling approaches in terms of their MPC performance. Two chemical processes, a polymer reactor and a distillation column, are studied.

1. Introduction

During the past decade, model predictive control (MPC) has been widely accepted by the process industries. Not only have many MPC algorithms using linear or nonlinear models been proposed, but many successful applications have been reported. From the literature, it appears that DMC (Dynamic Matrix Control) [2] forms the basis of many other MPC algorithms, such as QDMC [4]. DMC and QDMC have been applied successfully to industrial processes.

While MPC algorithms using linear models have significant advantages for implementation as well as theoretical analysis, algorithms using nonlinear models are necessary in practice. A number of MPC algorithms using nonlinear models have been proposed, in which a nonlinear model is needed. In stead of developing a nonlinear first principles model, engineers seek to establish a dynamic model directly from the input/output data sampled from the plant. As artificial neural networks have recently become popular in many research areas, control engineers have also started to employ artificial neural networks for modeling nonlinear processes. Among a variety of different neural network architectures, multilayer Perceptron networks are most widely studied. In most of the applications to date, however, Perceptron networks have been adapted as an NARX model, which is essentially a one-step ahead predictive model [1]. The accuracy of a one-step ahead predictive model often deteriorates as the prediction horizon increases [12]. Thus the use of an NARX Perceptron network model with MPC becomes problematic.

This paper thus presents a long-range training approach for a Perceptron network, and the use of the resulting model in Model Predictive Control. The long-range training method is adopted from a training algorithm for recurrent network, known as *backpropagation through time* [13]. The paper treats the Perceptron network as a sub-class of a fully connected recurrent network. Based upon this argu-

ment, the NARX Perceptron network is then modified so that the training can result in a good long-range predictive model. The modified Perceptron network is referred as an *external recurrent network* in the paper. Further investigation of an external recurrent network reveals that the objective of the recurrent training algorithm can become similar to that of the MPC [12].

To demonstrate the advantage of the external recurrent networks, two chemical processes are studied: a ploymerization process and a distillation column. When used with MPC for controlling this nonlinear process, results of the external recurrent network is compared with those of the regular NARX Perceptron network model. The external recurrent neural network leads to significantly better MPC performance than the regular Perceptron network does. Furthermore, the results from a classical decentralized PID is also used for comparison. It is shown the the MPC with an external recurrent network model outperforms the classical PID.

2. Neural Network Dynamic Modeling

A general multilayer Perceptron network can be depicted as in Fig. 1. Such a multilayer Perceptron network can be a universal function approximator [5]. Therefore, many researchers have investigated the use of neural networks for developing a nonlinear dynamic model.

In general, an identification model, regardless of the form of its mathematical representation, can be estimated in two different approaches: a series-parallel and a parallel identification method [8]. Fig. 2 illustrates these two identification approaches. In the case where the switch "sp" is connected, the plant output is fed directly to the model for prediction during the training. This method is referred to as a *series-parallel identification method*. To the contrary, when the switch "p" is connected, the plant output is *not* fed to the model for predicting the plant output. The latter is referred to as a *parallel identification method*. In most of the applications to date, a multilayer feedforward network is employed as an NARX (nonlinear auto-regressive with exogenous input) model, in which the network uses a number of past (delayed) plant inputs and outputs to predict the future system output. For example, Bhat and McAvoy

[†]System & Sensor Development Center, Honeywell Inc., Minneapolis, MN 55418. Email: tedsu@ssdc.honeywell.com
[‡]Institute for Systems Research, and Department of Chemical Engineering, University of Maryland, College Park, MD 20742. Email: mcavoy@eng.umd.edu

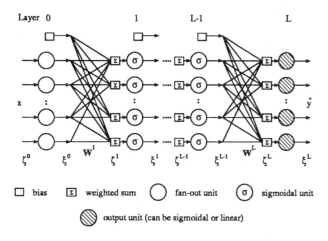

Layer 0   *1*   *L-1*   *L*

☐ bias   Σ weighted sum   ◯ fan-out unit   σ sigmoidal unit

▨ output unit (can be sigmoidal or linear)

Figure 1: *A multilayer Perceptron network.*

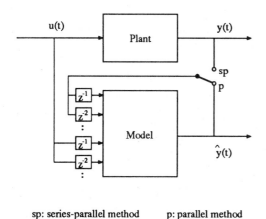

sp: series-parallel method   p: parallel method

Figure 2: *Series-parallel or parallel identification methods.*

[1] have used the series-parallel identification approach for modeling a pH reactor, where the past plant inputs and outputs are fed as the input to the network. As pointed out in [12], the series-parallel identification method leads to a one-step ahead predictive model, which can yield very poor results for long-range prediction. On the other hand, the parallel identification method can lead to a good long-range predictive model.

For the parallel identification method, the input vector to the network contains time-delayed outputs from the network itself. Therefore a perceptron networks in the parallel configuration is referred to as an *external recurrent network* [12]. Hereinafter, a recurrent network refers to an external recurrent network unless otherwise indicated. For convenience, the series-parallel identification method is referred to as FFN modeling approach, and the parallel identification method as RNN modeling approach.

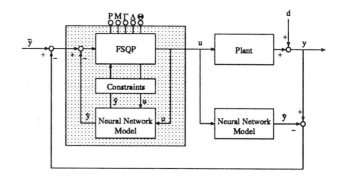

Figure 3: *The architecture of the NNMPC algorithm.*

3. Neural Model Predictive Control

The formulation of a nonlinear model predictive control algorithm is a nonlinear programing problem. The approach presented here is an application of neural networks in the well-established nonlinear model predictive control framework except that the neural network model is used. This approach offers significant computation time savings over other NLMPC methods because integration is not needed.

The MPC problem can be formulated as a standard nonlinear optimization problem

$$\min_{u} \sum ||\theta(y_m - y_{sp})||^2 + ||\lambda\Delta u||^2 \qquad (1)$$

Fig. 3 illustrates a general architecture of the NNMPC. For convenience, the dead time does not appear in the formulation. It is straightforward to account for the process dead time in the formulation.

To solve the NNMPC problem, several NLP techniques can be used [3]. Among others, a modified version of the SQP method proposed in [9, 14], which is referred to as Feasible SQP (FSQP), is used in this study. In FSQP, the feasible solution is assured at each iteration. From a practical point of view, it is more important that the solution be feasible than optimal.

4. Case Study I

In the first study case, a continuous copolymerization process is studied. The process is a 3-input 1-output system. The process contains a PI temperature control loop. The polymer property is the only product quality indicator. The desired polymer property is maintained by manipulating the feed flow rate of the mixture, the ratio of the two monomers in the mixture, and temperature setpoint which is controlled by the PI controller.

In order to develop a neural network dynamic model, each of the three manipulated variables of the simulated plant is perturbed by a sequence of pseudo random signals. A pseudo random multi-state signal (PRMS) is used for data

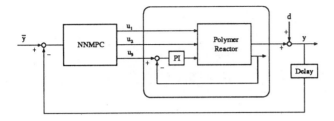

Figure 4: *Block diagram of the polymerization reactor NNMPC control scheme.*

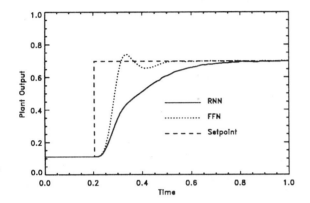

Figure 5: *The FFN model can outperform the RNN model for a short prediction horizon.*

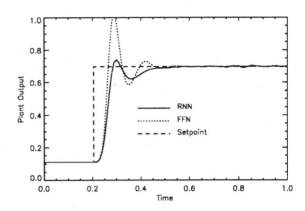

Figure 6: *The FFN model can not always outperform the RNN model for short prediction horizon.*

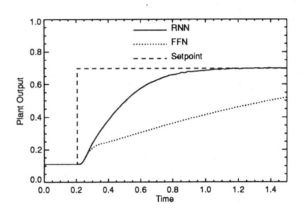

Figure 7: *As the prediction horizon increases, the RNN tends to outperform the FFN model.*

generation [11]. A neural network is then trained on the data using the two modeling approaches (FFN and RNN). During the training phase, the measurement delay is not considered. Since the measurement delay in a real process is not exactly known and can vary over a very wide range, an additional uncertainty of the measurement delay must be accounted for in designing an MPC controller. To account for the actual situations, the measurement delay is assumed to be known within a range. Three cases are studied based upon different assumptions for the measurement delay.

Firstly, the process is assume to have no measurement delay. Thus, the prediction horizon can be as short as one-step. The FFN modeling approach tends to result in a one-step ahead predictive model. It is interesting to see how the FFN model compares to the RNN model. As shown in Fig. 5, the controller using the FFN model *does* yield better results than the one using the RNN model in the case of setpoint tracking. Similarly, the FFN model yields better results than the RNN model for disturbance rejection. Fig. 6 shows the result for different tuning parameters. The FFN model does not necessary yield better result than the RNN model.

In reality, a measurement delay does exist, and its value is not exactly known. To account for the uncertainty of the measurement delay, secondly, a larger prediction horizon is used so as to cover the maximum possible delay. For a large prediction horizon, it has been concluded that the RNN model should outperform the FFN model [12]. Fig. 7 supports this claim. In addition, the performance of the FFN model decreases significantly with increasing prediction horizon. For a large prediction horizon, e.g. $P = 30$ or larger, it is extremely difficult to obtain a set of appropriate tuning parameters for FFN model.

Thirdly, the uncertainty of the measurement delay is studied. In order to account for the uncertainty of the measurement delay, the prediction horizon must be large enough to cover the uncertainty region of the delay. Only the RNN model is studied in this case. The NNMPC controller is first tuned to control a plant where the actual measurement delay is also τ_0. As indicated by the solid line in Fig. 8, the closed-loop performance of the controller is quite aggressive. When the process has a measurement delay $= 3\tau_0$, the closed-loop performance of the system is shown by the dotted line. The controller results in a significant overshoot/undershot and oscillation. Ob-

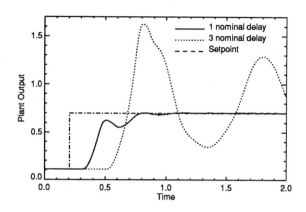

Figure 8: *With the uncertainty of the measurement delay, the performance of the NNMPC deteriorates.*

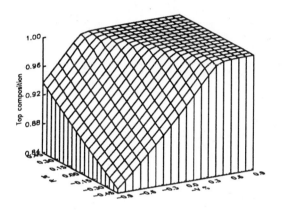

Figure 9: *The high-purity column exhibits extremely high nonlinearity.*

viously, the controller must be de-tuned in order to essure reasonable performance for all possible measurement delays. Although there is currently no general methodology for de-tuning the NLMPC, it is observed that guidelines for tuning the LMPC can be used [7].

5. Example II

The simulation model for the distillation column is taken from [6]. Three binary distillation columns with different product specifications are considered. For illustration purpose, only a high purity (99.5%) column is shown here. It is a benzene/toluene column. From a steady state analysis, the distillation column exhibits significant nonlinearity (see Fig. 9).

Both the top and bottom compositions (x_D and x_B, respectively) are controlled with reflux flow (R) and vapor boilup (V) chosen as two manipulated variables. The feed flow rate and the feed composition are kept constant for

Purity	High	Moderate	Low
Vapor Change	25-100	25-80	20-60
Reflux Change	70-360	90-160	80-150

Table I: *Different settling times under different operating conditions. Unit: min.*

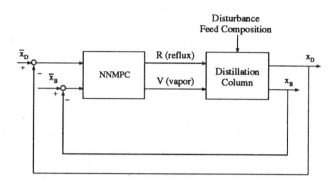

Figure 10: *Control block diagram of the distillation processes.*

generating training data. In order to generate training data, a pseudo random multi-state signal (PRMS) is introduced at each manipulated variable. The data generated consists of successive values of the two manipulated variables and the resulting top and bottom compositions (as the output variables).

The choice of the sampling time is crucial for a sampled-data system. From a good rule of thumb, the optimal sampling time is approximately equal to 1/30 of the open-loop settling time. In this study, it is found that the settling time for the three distillation columns can vary from 25 to 360 minutes depending on the magnitude of input changes and the purity of a column (see Table I). This paper considers a trade-off between the sampling times. For example, one can partially compensate a small sampling time by adding more past values (model order) of that particular input variable to which the system responds slowest. As a result, a sampling time of 6 minutes is used for the high purity column. After the sampling time is chosen, one then determines the number of hidden units by a cross-validation approach [12].

The neural network models resulting from different modeling approaches (RNN and FFN) are used for NNMPC control for the three distillation columns. A control block diagram is shown in Fig. 10. The controlled variables are the top and bottom compositions (x_D and x_B), Reflux flow rate (R) and vapor boilup (V) are the two manipulated variables. In this case, the ability of the NNMPC for disturbance rejection is studied. A 10% drop in the feed composition is considered. The disturbance occurs at time $t = 10$ min.

For the high purity column, the control performance is shown in Fig. 11. As can be seen, the RNN and FFN

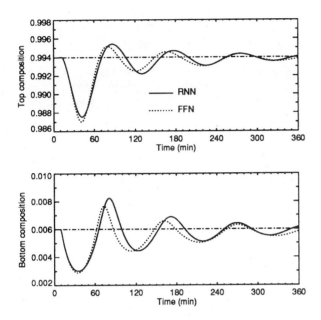

Figure 11: *Comparison of RNN model and FFN model used for short-range prediction in NNMPC.*

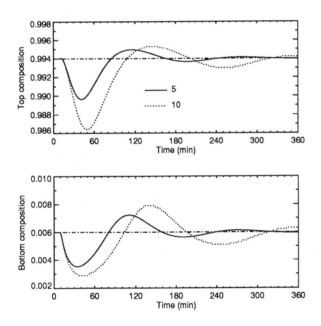

Figure 12: *RNN model used for long-range prediction in NNMPC.*

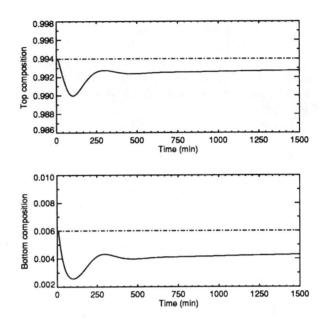

Figure 13: *FFN model can hardly be used for long-range prediction in NNMPC.*

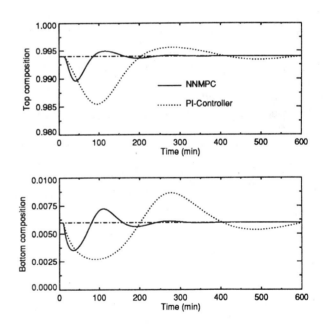

Figure 14: *Comparison with PI Control.*

neural network modeling approaches give similar performance when prediction horizon is small ($P = 1$). Under the specific tuning parameters, the two neural network models give similar performance for controlling the two compositions. For a larger prediction horizon $P = 20$, as shown in Fig. 12, the RNN model becomes less aggressive than it

was for a short prediction horizon. The NNMPC with the FFN model cannot be tuned to give any satisfactory result (e.g. see Fig. 13). In general, the two neural network models give similar control performance for short prediction horizons. The RNN model outperforms the FFN model when the prediction horizon is large. In most cases, when the prediction becomes large, it is very difficult to find a proper set of tuning parameter that can yield satisfactory results for the FFN model.

For comparison, two decentralized PI-controllers are implemented to control the two compositions, where the vapor boilup V controls the bottom composition x_B and the reflux flow rate R controls the top composition x_D. As shown in Fig. 14, the NNMPC significantly out-performs the PI controllers. The PI controllers result in significantly a larger overshoot/undershoot and a longer settling time than the NNMPC (with RNN model). Notice that the parameters of the PI controllers are calculated using Cohen and Coon's method [10] and re-tuned to improve the performance by trial-and-error.

6. Summary

In this paper, the MPC performance of two neural network modeling approaches, a one-step modeling approach and a long-range modeling approach, are compared. The NNMPC control algorithm is used for controlling a polymer reactor and distillation columns. In the first example, uncertainty of measurement delay is considered. It is found that the FFN model is more aggressive than the RNN model when the prediction horizon is one (the shortest prediction horizon) where all other tuning parameters are fixed. To account for the measurement delay, one must increase the prediction horizon. As the prediction horizon increases, however, the RNN model becomes superior to the FFN model in terms of their performance in the NNMPC control scheme and the ease of obtaining an appropriate set of tuning parameters. Similar results are found in the second example, where an FFN model can give a satisfactory result only for a short prediction horizon. The FFN model cannot yield acceptab'e result in most case. Finally, the NNMPC (with RNN model) is shown to outperform the classical PI control strategy in the second example.

References

[1] Bhat, N. & McAvoy, T. J. (1990). "Use of neural nets for dynamic modeling and control of chemical process systems." *Computers & Chemical Engineering*, **14**:(5), 573–583.

[2] Cutler, C. R. & Ramaker, B. L. (1980). "Dynamic matrix control: A computer control algorithm." *Proceedings of American Control Conference*.

[3] Edgar, T. & Himmelblau, D. (1989). *Optimization of Chemical Processes*. Prentice-Hall.

[4] García, C. E. & Morshedi, A. M. (1986). "Quadratic programming solution of Dynamic Matrix Control (QDMC)." *Chemical Engineering Communication*, **46**, 73–87.

[5] Hornik, K., Stinchcombe, M., & White, H. (1989). "Multilayer feedforward networks are universal approximators." *Neural Networks*, **2**:(5), 359–366.

[6] Luyben, W. L. (1973). *Process Simulation, Modeling and Control for Chemical Processes*. McGraw Hill.

[7] Morari, M., García, C. E., & Prett, D. M. (1992). *Model Predictive Control*. in press.

[8] Narendra, K. S. & Parthasarathy, K. (1990). "Identification and control of dynamic system using neural networks." *IEEE Transactions on Neural Networks*, **1**:(1), 4–27.

[9] Panier, E. R. & Tits, A. L. (1993). "On combining feasibility, descent and superlinear convergence in inequality constrained optimization." *Mathematical Programming*, **59**:(2), 261–276.

[10] Stephanopoulos, G. (1984). *Chemical Process Control: An Introduction to Theory and Practice*. Prentice-Hall.

[11] Su, H. T. & McAvoy, T. J. (1993). "Applications of neural network long-range predictive models for non-linear model predictive control." *Journal of Process Control*. To appear.

[12] Su, H. T., McAvoy, T. J., & Werbos, P. J. (1992). "Long-term predictions of chemical processes using recurrent neural networks: A parallel training approach." *Industrial & Engineering Chemistry Research*, **31**, 1338–1352.

[13] Werbos, P. J. (1989). "Maximizing long-term gas industry profits in two minutes in lotus using neural network methods." *IEEE Transactions on Systems, Man, & Cybernetics*, **19**:(2), 315–333.

[14] Zhou, J. L. & Tits, A. L. (1993). "Nonmonotone line search for minmax problems." *Journal of Optimization Theory & Application*, **76**:(3), 455–476.

Neural Network Compensation of Gear Backlash Hysteresis in Position-Controlled Mechanisms

David R. Seidl   Sui-Lun Lam   Jerry A. Putman   Robert D. Lorenz

Department of Electrical & Computer Engineering
University of Wisconsin—Madison
Madison, WI 53706

Abstract – **This paper demonstrates that artificial neural networks can be used to identify and compensate for hysteresis caused by gear backlash in precision position-controlled mechanisms. A major contribution of this research is that physical analysis of the system nonlinearities and optimal control are used to design the neural network structure. Network sizing and initializing problems are thus eliminated. This physically-meaningful, modular approach facilitates the integration of this neural network with existing controllers; thus, initial performance matches that of existing control approaches and then is improved by refining the parameter estimates via further learning. The neural network operates by recognizing backlash and switching to a control which moves smoothly through the backlash when the torque transmitted to the output shaft must be reversed.**

I. INTRODUCTION

The hysteresis caused by gear backlash is a well-understood dynamic nonlinearity. Discussions can be found in several control texts [1-2]. The standard linear feedback (PD or PID) controller ignores the dynamic properties of backlash leading to tracking errors. Specifically,

- the gears must be engaged in the correct direction before transmitting torque,
- the motor acts on only the motor shaft—not the lumped—dynamics when reversing direction, and
- the engaging of the gears is an inelastic collision which, because of its impulsive nature, can excite otherwise benign high frequency resonances if not limited.

Moreover, overshoot caused by improperly referenced, underdamped, or integral error feedback exacerbates these problems, forcing torque reversals. These deficiencies lead to high frequency limit cycles (high controller gains) or poor disturbance rejection (low controller gains).

An adaptive exact inverse backlash model controller was proposed in [3]. The exact inverse requires creating an ideal impulse in the motor shaft velocity to achieve an instantaneous move from one end of the backlash region to the other. This is not realizable since the motor shaft position cannot change instantaneously. The exact inverse does however provide the mathematically ideal control for which we seek the best possible approximation.

The solution examined in this paper uses the desired load shaft trajectory to create corresponding motor shaft and motor torque trajectories. First, the gear torque needed to follow the desired load shaft trajectory is computed; it includes inertia and friction decoupling and position and velocity error feedback. Then a reference trajectory for the motor shaft is created that moves the motor shaft to the correct backlash boundary in a time-optimal fashion (subject to relative acceleration limits) and maintains it there until the desired gear torque is reversed. A torque command for the motor shaft is then created that decouples the motor shaft inertia and friction, provides velocity and position error feedback and, if the gear is engaged, supplies the desired gear torque. Proper feedforward and references are used, and feedback is tuned to avoid overshoot and gear reversals. Avoiding reversals allows the load inertia and friction to hold the shaft against the gear resulting in improved tracking.

This controller's need for fast nonlinear computing and parameter identification suggests the use of a neural network. Neural networks have several useful attributes.
- They can approximate a nonlinear function as accurately as desired if enough neurons are available and the correct weights can be found.
- They can compute quickly (propagation delays in the tens of nanoseconds) when implemented in VLSI due to their structure of simple components in parallel.
- They can be adapted (learn) with gradient-descent, least squared-error algorithms.

However, standard neural network development procedures also have significant drawbacks.
- The number of neurons needed and their proper distribution into layers are unknown requiring experimentation with different configurations until satisfactory results are obtained.
- The gradient-descent weight adaptation algorithms used to iteratively improve the network's approximation of the ideal controller can be slow and stall in poor solutions, particularly when more than one hidden layer is used.
- The adaptation procedure is initialized by random weights which disregards existing system knowledge.
- The resulting network yields no insight into how it

works providing no way to adapt it to related problems.

These problems can be minimized or avoided by directly constructing the neural network to implement a desirable control algorithm. The algorithm is obtained using state space, nonlinear decoupling, and optimal control techniques. The basic operation of the neuron makes it ideal for integrating state error feedback with the switching surfaces produced by time-optimal or sliding mode control algorithms. The neural network backlash controller developed in this paper demonstrates the use of neurons to implement
• linear state error feedback,
• time optimal switching curves, and
• conditional terms to decouple nonlinear friction.

This paper presents the backlash model and derives the control algorithm. Then, neural network basics and construction techniques are discussed and applied to the controller. Finally, experimental results are presented.

II. DETAILS OF THE BACKLASH MODELS

The state equations describing backlash hysteresis are given by (1, ie. 1a-1gvii). The subscripts M and L denote motor and load shaft quantities. The time dependent variables are angular acceleration (α), velocity (ω), position (θ) and torque (τ). The torque terms are the motor air gap torque (τ_M), the friction torques (τ_{FM} and τ_{FL}) and the torque transmitted through the gear to the load shaft (τ_G). The physical constants are the inertias (J_M and J_L), the viscous (B_M and B_L), coulomb (C_M and C_L), and static (S_M and S_L) friction values, the gear ratio (R) and half of the angular deadzone distance between gears on the motor shaft side (σ). The friction torques (1e,f) and gear transmission torque (1g) are functions of the state (ω_M, θ_M, ω_L and θ_L) and the input (τ_M) and receive their time dependence through these variables. The time dependence and state dependence designations are omitted for conciseness except when needed. Time instants just before and after time t are denoted by t^- and t^+.

$$\frac{d\omega_M}{dt} = J_M^{-1} [-\tau_{FM} - R\tau_G + \tau_M] \qquad (1a)$$

$$\frac{d\theta_M}{dt} = \omega_M \qquad (1b)$$

$$\frac{d\omega_L}{dt} = J_L^{-1} [-\tau_{FL} + \tau_G] \qquad (1c)$$

$$\frac{d\theta_L}{dt} = \omega_L. \qquad (1d)$$

where

$$\tau_{FM} = -B_M\omega_M - C_M\text{sgn}(\omega_M)$$
$$- \text{sgn}(\tau_M - R\tau_G)1\{\omega_M=0\}\min(|S_M|,|\tau_M - R\tau_G|) \qquad (1e)$$

$$\tau_{FL} = -B_L\omega_L - C_L\text{sgn}(\omega_L)$$
$$- \text{sgn}(-\tau_G)1\{\omega_L=0\}\min(|S_L|,|-\tau_G|) \qquad (1f)$$

$$\tau_G = 0 \cdot 1\{-\sigma < \theta_M - R^{-1}\theta_L < \sigma\} \qquad (1gi)$$
$$+ \max(0, (J_M + R^2 J_L)^{-1}[RJ_L(\tau_M - \tau_{FM}) + J_M\tau_{FL}])$$
$$\cdot 1\{\theta_M - R^{-1}\theta_L = \sigma \quad \cap \quad \omega_M = R^{-1}\omega_L \neq 0\} \qquad (1gii)$$

$$+ \min(0, (J_M + R^2 J_L)^{-1}[RJ_L(\tau_M - \tau_{FM}) + J_M\tau_{FL}])$$
$$\cdot 1\{\theta_M - R^{-1}\theta_L = -\sigma \quad \cap \quad \omega_M = R^{-1}\omega_L \neq 0\} \qquad (1giii)$$

$$+ \max(0, \tau_M - S_M)$$
$$\cdot 1\{\theta_M - R^{-1}\theta_L = \sigma \quad \cap \quad \omega_M = R^{-1}\omega_L = 0\} \qquad (1giv)$$

$$+ \min(0, \tau_M + S_M)$$
$$\cdot 1\{\theta_M - R^{-1}\theta_L = -\sigma \quad \cap \quad \omega_M = R^{-1}\omega_L = 0\} \qquad (1gv)$$

$$+ J_M J_L (J_M + R^2 J_L)^{-1}(R\omega_M(t^-) - \omega_L(t^-))$$
$$\cdot \delta\{\theta_M - R^{-1}\theta_L = \sigma \quad \cap \quad \omega_M(t) > R^{-1}\omega_L(t)\} \qquad (1gvi)$$

$$+ J_M J_L (J_M + R^2 J_L)^{-1}(R\omega_M(t^-) - \omega_L(t^-))$$
$$\cdot \delta\{\theta_M - R^{-1}\theta_L = -\sigma \quad \cap \quad \omega_M(t) < R^{-1}\omega_L(t)\} \qquad (1gvii)$$

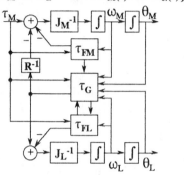

Fig. 1. The Backlash Model

The state equations (1) describe the motor and load shaft velocities and positions and are depicted in block diagram form in Fig. 1. Both shafts include friction torques described in (1e&f). The friction models are comprised of viscous, coulomb and static terms. The gear torque described in (1g) acts on the output shaft and the reflected gear torque reacts on the motor shaft.

The expression for gear torque has several terms. The indicator function used in (1gi-v) equals "1" when the bracketed condition is true and "0" when false. The delta function used in (1gvi-vii) introduces an impulse when the bracketed condition is true causing acceleration impulses and velocity step changes. All achievable state conditions are covered by these mutually exclusive terms.

The first term (1gi) indicates the gear torque is zero when the gear is in the backlash region. The system is fourth order, and the shafts are completely uncoupled.

The second and third terms (1gii-iii) give the transmitted torque when the gears are engaged and moving so that the friction is coulomb and viscous. In this condition, the two shafts act as one lumped shaft with the positions and velocities algebraically fixed reducing the system to second order. The simplified state relations are given by (2), where (2a) comes from using (1giii) or (1giv) to eliminate θ_L and its derivatives from (1c) and using (1c) to eliminate τ_G from (1a).

$$(J_M + R^2 J_L) \frac{d\omega_M}{dt} = - \tau_{FM} - R\tau_{FL} + \tau_M \qquad (2a)$$

$$\frac{d\theta_M}{dt} = \omega_M \qquad (2b)$$

$$\omega_L = R\omega_M \qquad (2c)$$

$$\theta_L = R(\theta_M \pm \sigma) \quad (\text{−=positive, +=negative gear face}) \quad (2d)$$

The reduced system also allows (1a) and (1c) to be solved for τ_G (by eliminating the velocity derivatives) giving the expressions found in the max and min arguments. Taking the max and min with zero indicates that torque can only be transmitted in the direction the gear is engaged. If the τ_G expression derived from (1a) and (1c) reverses sign, τ_G becomes zero and the gears disengage.

The fourth and fifth terms (1giv-v) give the torque transmitted when the gears are engaged but not moving so that the static friction model is used. In this case, the gear reflects to the load shaft that portion of the motor torque—in the direction that the gear is engaged—not canceled by motor shaft static friction.

The sixth and seventh terms (1gvi-vii) introduce torque impulses at the instant when the gears reach the boundaries of the backlash region with sufficient relative velocity to collide. The collisions are inelastic. Thus, the conditions of zero relative velocity after collision (3a) and conservation of angular momentum during the collision (3b) are used to derive the shaft velocities after the collision in terms of the shaft velocities before the collision (3c). Taking the limit of $J\Delta\omega/\Delta t$ as $\Delta t \to 0$ yields the torque impulse in (3d).

$$\omega_L(t^+) = R\omega_M(t^+) \quad (3a)$$

$$(J_M + R^2 J_L)\omega_L(t^+) = J_M R\omega_M(t^-) + R^2 J_L \omega_L(t^-) \quad (3b)$$

$$\omega_L(t^+) = R\omega_M(t^+) = (J_M + R^2 J_L)^{-1}(J_M R\omega_M(t^-) + R^2 J_L \omega_L(t^-)) \quad (3c)$$

$$\tau_G(t) = \lim_{\Delta t \to 0} -R^{-1} J_M \frac{\omega_M(t^+) - \omega_M(t^-)}{\Delta t} = \lim_{\Delta t \to 0} J_L \frac{\omega_L(t^+) - \omega_L(t^-)}{\Delta t}$$

$$= J_M J_L (J_M + R^2 J_L)^{-1} (R\omega_M(t^-) - \omega_L(t^-)) \,\delta(t) \quad (3d)$$

III. The Controller

The nonlinear, state space controller is described by (4) and pictured in Fig. 2. In (4), "*" denotes desired, commanded or reference, "∧" denotes estimated, "~" denotes error (the desired minus the actual value) and "∧" denotes estimation error (the actual minus the estimated).

$$\tau_G^* := (\hat{J}_L \alpha_L^* + \hat{\tau}_{FL}) + B_{AL}(\omega_L^* - \hat{\omega}_L) + K_{AL}(\theta_L^* - \hat{\theta}_L) \quad (4a)$$

$$\tau_M := \hat{J}_M \alpha_M^* + \hat{\tau}_{FM} + B_{AM}(\omega_M^* - \hat{\omega}_M) + K_{AM}(\theta_M^* - \hat{\theta}_M)$$
$$+ R\tau_G^* \cdot 1\{[\theta_R^* = \sigma \cap \tau_G^* > 0] \cup [\theta_R^* = -\sigma \cap \tau_G^* < 0]\} \quad (4b)$$

$$\alpha_M^* := R^{-1}\hat{\alpha}_L + \alpha_R^* \quad (4c)$$

$$\omega_M^* := R^{-1}\hat{\omega}_L + \omega_R^* \quad (4d)$$

$$\theta_M^* := R^{-1}\hat{\theta}_L + \theta_R^* \quad (4e)$$

$$\alpha_R^* := A \cdot [1\{\theta_R^* < SC\} - 1\{\theta_R^* > SC\}] \quad (4f)$$

$$\omega_R^* := \omega_R^*(0) + \int_0^t \alpha_R^*(t)dt \quad (4g)$$

$$\theta_R^* := \theta_R^*(0) + \int_0^t \omega_R^*(t)dt \quad (4h)$$

$$\Theta := \sigma \cdot \mathrm{sgn}(\tau_G^*) \qquad \Omega := 0 \cdot \mathrm{sgn}(\tau_G^*) \quad (4i)$$

$$SC := \Theta + (2A)^{-1}(\Omega^2 - \omega_R^{*2}) \cdot [1\{\omega_R^* \le \Omega\} - 1\{\omega_R^* \ge \Omega\}] \quad (4j)$$

Since relative motion of the shafts facilitates representing backlash, $\theta_R := \theta_M - R^{-1}\theta_L$ is used to simplify the equations. Only state variable estimates are used to avoid specifying a priori which variables are measured and which are estimated using desired or observed values.

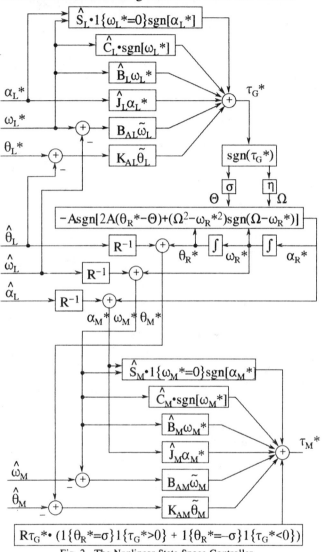

Fig. 2. The Nonlinear State Space Controller

The controller's objective is to make the load shaft follow a desired position trajectory by generating the appropriate motor shaft torque command and reference trajectory. To do this, the gear torque needed to cause the load shaft to follow the desired trajectory is calculated. Then a motor shaft reference trajectory is generated that uses time-optimal control to guide the motor shaft to (and then hold the shaft at) the correct backlash boundary making it possible to apply the desired gear torque. Then the motor torque is computed that decouples the motor shaft dynamics, provides state error feedback and, if the gear is engaged, supplies the desired gear torque.

The desired load shaft trajectory segments should be twice differentiable so that the acceleration is continuous.

This permits the computation of a corresponding continuous desired transmitted gear torque, τ_G^*. This desired torque (4a) provides inertia and friction decoupling and position and velocity error feedback for the load shaft using the model found in [4]. With this definition of τ_G^*, τ_G can be eliminated from the load shaft differential equation (1c) and terms grouped to produce (5), which describes the load shaft dynamics in terms of state and parameter estimate errors. This demonstrates the dynamic correctness of τ_G^* since the state error differential equation is driven only by parameter estimate errors and errors in the production of τ_G^*. When the gears are not engaged, $\tau_G = 0$ and $\tilde{\tau}_G = \tau_G^*$. The gear torque error is then 100%, motivating the use of time-optimal control to minimize the time that this occurs.

$$J_L\alpha_L = -\tau_{FL} + \tau_G \quad \text{and} \quad \tau_G = \tau_G^* - \tilde{\tau}_G \quad \Rightarrow$$

$$0 = \hat{J}_L\tilde{\alpha}_L + B_{AL}\tilde{\omega}_L + K_{AL}\tilde{\theta}_L$$
$$+ \tilde{B}_{AL}\hat{\omega}_L + \tilde{K}_{AL}\hat{\theta}_L - \tilde{J}_L\hat{\alpha}_L - \tilde{\tau}_{FL} - \tilde{\tau}_G \quad (5)$$

The motor torque τ_M in (4b) decouples motor shaft inertia and friction and adds velocity and position error feedback. If the gears are estimated to be engaged in the correct direction, the desired reflected transmitted torque $R\tau_G^*$ is also added. The load shaft decoupling terms are built into $R\tau_G^*$. Solving (1a) and (4b) and combining terms produces (6a) which is the motor shaft analog to (5). The choice of α_M^*, ω_M^* and θ_M^* in (4c-e) causes the state error to be the negative of the estimate of the state error allowing (6a) to be simplified to (6b).

$$0 = \hat{J}_M\tilde{\alpha}_M + B_{AM}\tilde{\omega}_M + K_{AL}\tilde{\theta}_M$$
$$+ \tilde{B}_{AM}\hat{\omega}_M + \tilde{K}_{AM}\hat{\theta}_M - \tilde{J}_M\hat{\alpha}_M - \tilde{\tau}_{FM} - \tilde{\tau}_G \quad (6a)$$
$$= \hat{J}_M\tilde{\alpha}_M - \tilde{J}_M\hat{\alpha}_M - \tilde{\tau}_{FM} - \tilde{\tau}_G \quad (6b)$$

When the gears are not engaged these two equations are independent, but when the gears are engaged the motor shaft states can be expressed algebraically in terms of the load shaft states. Using this and eliminating $\tilde{\tau}_G$ from (5) using (6b) yields the combined shaft error dynamics (7).

$$0 = \hat{J}_L\tilde{\alpha}_L + B_{AL}\tilde{\omega}_L + K_{AL}\tilde{\theta}_L + R^{-2}\hat{J}_M\tilde{\alpha}_L + \tilde{B}_{AL}\hat{\omega}_L + \tilde{K}_{AL}\hat{\theta}_L$$
$$- (\tilde{J}_L + R^{-2}\tilde{J}_M)\hat{\alpha}_L - (\tilde{\tau}_{FL} + R^{-1}\tilde{\tau}_{FL}) \quad (7)$$

The motor shaft reference trajectory is comprised of acceleration (4c), velocity (4d) and position (4e). Each has a first term that matches the trajectory to the reflected load trajectory and a second term that determines the relative trajectory. The relative trajectory is described by (4f-j). The desired relative acceleration α_R^* of (4f) calls for a constant positive acceleration A when θ_R^* is less than SC (the switching condition/curve described below) given in (4j) and a constant negative acceleration $-A$ when θ_R^* is greater than SC. Only on the switching curve is α_R^* zero, and only at the one stable point $(\omega_R^*, \theta_R^*) = (0, \Theta)$ can $\alpha_R^* = 0$ for longer than an instant. The desired

relative velocity ω_R^* of (4g) is the integral of α_R^* and is linear and continuous with respect to time. The slopes of the segments are either A, $-A$ or 0. The desired relative position θ_R^* of (4h) is the integral of ω_R^* and is parabolic and continuous with respect to time with the curvature of the segments being either A, $-A$ or 0.

The switching condition/curve is the solution to minimizing the time required to reach a given $\theta_R^*(t_f) = \Theta$ with $\omega_R^*(t_f) = \Omega = 0$ subject to $\alpha_R^* \in [-A, +A]$. By setting $\theta_R^*(t_f) = \Theta = \sigma \cdot \text{sgn}(\tau_G^*)$ in (4i), the final relative position is the middle of the backlash region if $\tau_G^* = 0$ and the the proper boundary of the backlash region if $\tau_G^* \neq 0$. Thus, the gears are engaged quickly and smoothly with zero relative velocity. Torque can then be transmitted to the load shaft and $R\tau_G^*$ is added to τ_M^*.

In lieu of a formal derivation, a simple argument can be used to justify the result. A calculus of variations proof is found in [5]. Suppose $\theta_R^* < \Theta$. To minimize the time the greatest average velocity must be achieved. Working backward, given ω_R^* there is a minimum distance $\Theta - \theta_R^*$ such that the maximum deceleration $\alpha_R^* = -A$ will cause ω_R^* to just reach zero as θ_R^* reaches Θ. This is the switching condition because prior to this, the maximum acceleration $\alpha_R^* = A$ is used to increase and thus maximize the velocity.

The velocity and position equations for a constant acceleration α are given by (8a) and (9a). The time required to accelerate from $\omega_R^*(t_1)$ to $\omega_R^*(t_2)$ is determined by (8b). Then $t_2 - t_1$ is eliminated from (9a) to give the position trajectory directly in terms of the velocity in (9b). Setting $t_2 = t_f$ (the final or arrival time) and $t_1 = t_s$ (the switching time) in (9b) produces (10a), the switching curve in terms of α. Since $\alpha = -A$ for $\omega_R^*(t_s) \geq \Omega$ and $\alpha = +A$ for $\omega_R^*(t_s) \leq \Omega$, $\alpha = -A \cdot [1\{\omega_R^* \leq \Omega\} - 1\{\omega_R^* \geq \Omega\}]$ giving the final expression for the switching curve in (10b). Although this controller uses $\Omega = 0$, Ω has been retained in the switching curve expression to make it possible to set a small impact velocity to help overcome static friction upon engaging. The most common relative trajectory is to move from one boundary of the backlash region to the other starting and ending with zero relative velocity and without midcourse reversals. The trajectories for $\alpha_R^*(t)$, $\omega_R^*(t)$ and $\theta_R^*(t)$ for the move from the negative to the positive boundary are pictured in Fig. 3.

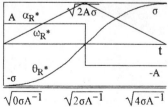

Fig. 3. Acceleration, Velocity, and Position Trajectories in the Backlash Region

$$\omega(t_2) = \omega(t_1) + \alpha(t_2 - t_1) \quad (8a)$$
$$\Rightarrow \quad (t_2 - t_1) = \alpha^{-1}(\omega(t_2) - \omega(t_1)) \quad (8b)$$

$$\theta(t_2) = \theta(t_1) + \omega(t_1)(t_2-t_1) + \alpha(t_2-t_1)^2/2 \qquad (9a)$$

$$\Rightarrow \ \theta(t_2) - \theta(t_1) = (2\alpha)^{-1}(\omega(t_2)^2 - \omega(t_1)^2) \qquad (9b)$$

$$\Rightarrow \ SC: \ \Theta - \theta(t_s) = (2\alpha)^{-1}(\Omega^2 - \omega(t_s)^2) \qquad (10a)$$

$$\Rightarrow \ SC: \ \theta_R^* - \Theta =$$
$$(2A)^{-1}(\Omega^2 - \omega_R^{*2}) \cdot [1\{\omega_R^* \le \Omega\} - 1\{\omega_R^* \ge \Omega\}] \qquad (10b)$$

The relations in (9b) and (10b) provide the basis for a phase plane description shown in Fig. 4.

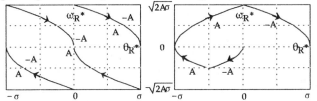

Fig. 4. Phase Plane (a) Switching Curves & (b) Velocity/Position Trajectory

Positive constant acceleration produces a parabolic trajectory symmetric about the zero velocity line with the curvature in the direction of increasing position and with the evolution in the direction of increasing velocity. Negative constant acceleration produces a parabolic trajectory symmetric about the zero velocity line with the curvature in the direction of decreasing position and with the evolution in the direction of decreasing velocity. The switching curves for the backlash boundaries and zero relative velocity are shown in Fig. 4a. To the left of the switching curve $\alpha_R^* = A$, to the right $\alpha_R^* = -A$. Thus, ω_R^* and θ_R^* follow the parabolic trajectory that evolves into the switching curve, then follow this curve to the desired boundary (or middle) of the backlash region. Fig. 4b shows the trajectory for a move from the origin to the negative backlash boundary and then to the positive backlash boundary.

IV. NEURAL NETWORK BACKGROUND

Artificial neural networks are interconnections of artificial neurons. The two basic neuron models discussed in [6] are the Σ, the weighted sum of inputs given by (11a) and the $\Sigma\Pi$, the weighted sum of products of inputs given by (11b), where z is the output (or activation) and $\mathbf{u}$ is the n-component input vector. Both types of neurons are comprised of simple operations that are readily implemented in VLSI with propagation times in the tens of nanoseconds [7].

$$z = \psi(s) \quad s = w_{bias} + \Sigma_{i \in I} \ w_i u_i$$
$$I = \{1,...,n\} \qquad (11a)$$
$$z = \psi(s) \quad s = w_{bias} + \Sigma_{j \in K} \ w_j p_j$$
$$p_j = \Pi_{i \in I} (1 + (u_i - 1) \cdot 1\{\text{ith digit of } j = 1\})$$
$$K \subset 2^n = \{\text{all n-digit binary numbers}\} \qquad (11b)$$

The Σ-neuron forms a biased weighted sum (s) of the input components and then applies a nonlinear "squashing" function ψ. The $\Sigma\Pi$-neuron forms a biased weighted sum of products (p_j) of the input components.

Creating all 2^n products is rarely feasible, so only a subset K (such as all products with two or fewer terms) is considered. The Σ-neuron is a degenerate $\Sigma\Pi$-neuron with only one term products. Product terms with higher powers of a particular u_i are created by supplying u_i on as many input lines as the highest desired power.

The squashing function ψ can be any function that monotonically increases from either -1 (bipolar) or 0 (positive) to 1. Ψ is the "diagonal" operator that takes a vector input and applies ψ to each component. The most common functions are the sigmoid, the linear and the threshhold pictured in Fig. 5. (Subscripts B, P, S, L and T denote bipolar, positive, sigmoid, linear and threshholding.) Bipolar and positive units can be interchanged by applying the appropriate bias and scaling factor to the output. Sigmoidal and linear units function as threshhold units if the input gains are large. The use of different squashing functions is a notational convenience that facilitates interpreting the network. Simple transformations allow implementing the whole network with a single type of linear or sigmoidal unit.

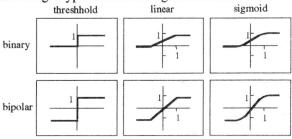

Fig. 5 Possible Neuron Models

Neurons are generally arranged in layers in feedforward networks such as the two hidden layer network of Fig. 7. In this configuration, the inputs to a neuron are the outputs of the neurons in the previous layer. The output of the neuron then feeds forward to the neurons in the next layer. A key neural network property is that any nonlinear function with bounded input and outputs can be approximated arbitrarily well by a network with at least one hidden layer, enough neurons and correct weights [8].

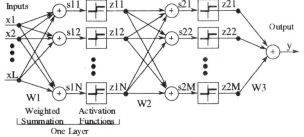

Fig. 7 A Neural Network with 2 Hidden Layers

The usual procedure for finding (training) the weights is an adaptive gradient-descent least squared-error procedure called backpropagation [9]. This process is initialized with random weights which ignores existing knowledge of the system. When the error is linear in the weights, gradient-descent converges quickly and reliably to the best possible solution. However, in the nonlinear case, gradient-descent may converge slowly, not at all or to a poor solution. For neural networks, only the output layer has the linear in error property; thus, output layer adaptation works well, but hidden layer adaptation may be slow or fail. To compound matters, the number of neurons needed is found through trial and error, requiring that the procedure be repeated many times.

V. Neuron Operations - Network Construction

The direct construction of the backlash neural controller is based on a building block approach that dedicates a neuron or neurons to the realization of each individual controller function. This physical model-based approach is similar in concept to the synthesis of analog computers as discussed in [10]. Many desired control functions, including linear feedback, bang-bang and logical AND and OR, have extremely simple neuron realizations. More complicated functions encountered in nonlinear decoupling can be approximated using a piecewise reconstruction procedure.

Affine linear operations (linear operations with a bias) are performed by scaling the sum into the linear region of the squashing function as in (11) where k is the scaling factor. This assumes a linear or sigmoidal bipolar unit.

$$z = \Psi_{(L \text{ or } S)P} \left(k \bullet (w_{bias} + \Sigma_{i \in I} w_i u_i) \right) = k \bullet (w_{bias} + \Sigma_{i \in I} w_i u_i) \quad (11)$$

Therefore, state error feedback and inertia and viscous friction decoupling can be performed by a single neuron.

Symmetric bang-bang control is simply a scaled signum function of an input. This is the definition of the bipolar threshhold neuron as indicated in (12a). The on-off bang-bang control is the scaled threshhold function, which is by definition the positive threshhold neuron in (12b).

$$z = k \bullet \psi_{TB}(u) = k \bullet sgn(u) = k \bullet [1\{u>0\} - 1\{u<0\}] \quad (12a)$$

$$z = k \bullet \psi_{TP}(u) = k \bullet 1\{u>0\} \quad (12b)$$

Technically, the scaling factors k are not on the neuron output but on the input to all the neurons it feeds.

Neurons can perform the logic operations AND and OR. The n-input AND and OR neurons are given by (13a) and (13b).

$$AND(u) = \Psi_{TP}(-n+0.5 + \Sigma_{i=1}^n u_i) \quad (13a)$$

$$OR(u) = \Psi_{TP}(-0.5 + \Sigma_{i=1}^n u_i) \quad (13b)$$

Both neurons start by summing the n binary inputs. Choosing the bias to be −n+0.5 means that all n inputs must be 1 for the sum to be positive and trigger the threshhold producing the AND. Choosing the bias to be −0.5 means that at least one input must be 1 to trigger the threshhold producing the OR.

More complicated functions can be approximated by using a three layer network with positive threshhold neurons in the two hidden layers and bipolar linear neurons in the output layer. Each first layer neuron indicates whether the input is in a particular half space.

Each second layer neuron AND's designated first layer neurons thus indicating whether the input is in the intersection of the designated half spaces. If the input is in the intersection of the designated half spaces, the neuron output is one and the corresponding output weight is added to the linear output; if the input is not in the intersection, the neuron output is zero contributing nothing to the output. Thus, the input space can be carved into convex regions over which the variation of the desired output is sufficiently small. The regions can then be constructed as the intersection of half spaces and the average desired output over the region assigned to the corresponding output weight. If continuous rather than threshholding neurons are used in defining the half planes, this procedure creates fuzzy sets and, hence, a fuzzy set representation of the function.

VI. The Neural Network Controller

The neural network controller is described by (14) and (15). Equation (14) describes the computation of the desired torques from the desired trajectories (τ_G^* from α_L^*, ω_L^* and θ_L^* and τ_M from α_L^*, ω_L^* and θ_L^*). Equation (15) describes the computation of the desired trajectory. As seen by comparing (4a) and (4b) and the controller, Fig. 2, the equations for τ_G^* and τ_M are identical except for the addition of

$$R^{-1}\tau_G^* \bullet 1\{[\theta_R^*=\sigma \cap \tau_G^*>0] \cup [\theta_R^*=-\sigma \cap \tau_G^*<0]\}$$

to the τ_M sum and the use of the appropriate shaft parameters. Therefore, the torque equations are shown only once with a dummy shaft identifier S which equals L for load or M for shaft. An indicator function for S=M adds the gear torque term to τ_M.

$$z1 = \Psi_{TP}(s1) \quad s1 = \begin{pmatrix} 1 & 1 & -1 \\ 0 & -1 & 1 \\ 1 & 1 & 1 \\ 0 & 1 & -1 \\ -1 & -1 & 1 \\ 0 & -1 & -1 \\ -1 & -1 & -1 \\ 0 & 1 & 1 \end{pmatrix} \begin{pmatrix} \alpha_S^*T \\ \omega_S^* \\ \Omega \end{pmatrix} \quad (14a)$$

$$z2 = \Psi_{TP}(s2) \quad s2 = \begin{pmatrix} 1 & 1 & 0 & 0 & 0 & 0 & 0 & 0 & -1 \\ 0 & 0 & 1 & 1 & 0 & 0 & 0 & 0 & -1 \\ 0 & 0 & 0 & 0 & 1 & 1 & 0 & 0 & -1 \\ 0 & 0 & 0 & 0 & 0 & 0 & 1 & 1 & -1 \end{pmatrix} \begin{pmatrix} z1 \\ 1.5 \end{pmatrix} \quad (14b)$$

$$\tau_{FFS} = (\hat{S}_S \quad \hat{C}_S \quad -\hat{C}_S \quad -\hat{S}_S \quad \hat{B}_S \quad \hat{J}_S) \begin{pmatrix} z2 \\ \omega_S^* \\ \alpha_S^* \end{pmatrix} \quad (14c)$$

$$\tau_{FBS} = (B_{AS} \quad -B_{AS} \quad K_{AS} \quad -K_{AS}) \begin{pmatrix} \omega_S^* \\ \omega_S \\ \theta_S^* \\ \theta_S \end{pmatrix} \quad (14d)$$

$$z3 = \Psi_{TP}(s3) \quad s3 = \begin{pmatrix} 1 & 0 & -\sigma \\ 0 & 1 & 0 \\ -1 & 0 & -\sigma \\ 0 & -1 & 0 \end{pmatrix} \begin{pmatrix} \theta_R^* \\ \tau_G^* \\ 1 \end{pmatrix} \quad (14e)$$

$$z4 = \Psi_{TP}(s4) \quad s4 = \begin{pmatrix} 1 & 1 & 0 & 0 & -1.5 \\ 0 & 0 & 1 & 1 & -1.5 \end{pmatrix} z3 \tag{14f}$$

$$z5 = \Psi_{TP}(s5) \quad s5 = (1 \; 1 \; -0.5)\, z4 \tag{14g}$$

$$\tau_G{}^* = \tau_{FFS} + \tau_{FFS} \quad \text{with } s=L \tag{14h}$$

$$\tau_M = \tau_{FFS} + \tau_{FFS} + R\tau_G{}^* {\cdot} z5 \quad \text{with } s=M \tag{14i}$$

$$z6 = \Psi_{TB}(\tau_G{}^*) \tag{15a}$$

$$z7 = \Psi_{LB}(s7) \quad s3 = \begin{pmatrix} 1 & 0 & -\sigma \\ 0 & 1 & \eta \\ 0 & 1 & -\eta \\ 0 & G & -G\eta \end{pmatrix} \begin{pmatrix} \theta_R{}^* \\ \omega_R{}^* \\ z6 \end{pmatrix} \tag{15b}$$

$$z8 = \Psi_{TB}(s8) \quad s8 = \left(1 - \tfrac{1}{2A}\right) p8 \quad p8 = \begin{pmatrix} z7_1 \\ z7_2 {\cdot} z7_3 {\cdot} z7_4 \end{pmatrix} \tag{15c}$$

$$\alpha_M{}^* = R^{-1}\hat{\alpha}_L + \alpha_R{}^* \quad \alpha_R{}^* = -A {\cdot} z8 \tag{15d}$$

$$\omega_M{}^* = R^{-1}\hat{\omega}_L + \omega_R{}^* \quad \omega_R{}^* = \omega_R{}^*(0) + \int_0^t \alpha_R{}^*(t)\,dt \tag{15e}$$

$$\theta_M{}^* = R^{-1}\hat{\theta}_L + \theta_R{}^* \quad \theta_R{}^* = \theta_R{}^*(0) + \int_0^t \omega_R{}^*(t)\,dt \tag{15f}$$

Equations (14a-d) and (14h-i) are essentially the neural network position controller with friction decoupling equations demonstrated in [11]. Two slight changes have been made. To accommodate the continuous time formulation of the controller equations used here $\omega^*(t+1)$ was replaced with $\omega^*(t) + \alpha^*(t)T$. Also, the gear torque term had to be added to the τ_M sum. <u>This illustrates the building block principle by using two single shaft networks from [11] to build a two shaft controller by connecting the networks with the correct torque coupling term.</u>

In (14a), the first and second $z1$ components are the indicators for the two conditions for including positive static friction decoupling. The third and fourth $z1$ components indicate the conditions for including positive coulomb friction decoupling. The fifth and sixth $z1$ components indicate the symmetric conditions for negative coulomb friction decoupling. The seventh and eighth $z1$ components indicate the symmetric conditions for the negative static friction decoupling. In (14b), the four components of $z2$ are the AND's of these pairs of $z1$ components. ANDing set indicators is equivalent to indicating the intersection of the sets as discussed in the piecewise function approximation procedure in the previous section. Thus, the $z2$ components indicate the use of $\hat{S}$, $\hat{C}$, $-\hat{C}$ and $-\hat{S}$, respectively. In (14c), the complete feedforward torque decoupling is computed by appending ω^* and α^* to $z2$ and setting the weights to the corresponding parameter estimates. In (14d), the state error feedback torque is computed.

In (14e), the conditions required to form the $R\tau_G{}^*$ indicator function for the τ_M sum are created. The first $z3$ component indicates the gear is positively engaged, and the second $z3$ component indicates $\tau_G{}^*$ is positive. The third and fourth components indicate the gear is negatively engaged and $\tau_G{}^*$ is negative. In (14f), the first $z4$ component AND's the first two conditions, and the second

$z4$ component AND's the second two conditions. In (16g), $z5$ OR's the two components of $z4$ producing the desired indicator.

In (14h) and (14i), the torque commands are produced by summing the feedforward decoupling and feedback terms. For the motor shaft the gear torque decoupling is also included using $z5$ to switch the term appropriately. This $R\tau_G{}^*$ multiplied by its indicator functioned followed by the summation has the form of $\Sigma\Pi$-neuron.

The relative trajectory and the motor trajectory are formed in (15). In (15a), $z6$ serves as the $\mathrm{sgn}(\tau_G{}^*)$ term used in determining Θ and Ω. In (15b), the first $z7$ component is $\theta_R{}^* - \Theta$. The second and third $z7$ components are $\omega_R{}^* + \Omega$ and $\omega_R{}^* - \Omega$. The fourth $z7$ component is $\mathrm{sgn}(\omega_R{}^* - \Omega)$, where G is assumed to be a large transforming the linear to a threshhold unit. In (15c), the switching condition is formed with a $\Sigma\Pi$-neuron. The first $p8$ product term is $\theta_R{}^* - \Theta$. The second $p8$ product term forms $(\Omega^2 - \omega_R{}^{*2})\mathrm{sgn}(\omega_R{}^* - \Omega)$ as the product of the second, third and fourth components of $z7$. The second product term is scaled by $(2A)^{-1}$ and the scaled products are summed creating the switching condition. The bipolar threshhold activation function performs the switch making $z8$ the indicator for using $+A$ or $-A$ relative acceleration. The relative acceleration is so set in (15d), with (15e) and (15f) giving the corresponding integral relations for the relative velocity and position.

VII. RESULTS

The experiment was performed using a commercial dc motor controlled by a PC-AT with a Burr-Brown data acquisition board operating at a 200 Hz sampling rate. Encoders were mounted on both shafts, but only the motor shaft encoder was used for parameter estimation and control. When the relative trajectory reference indicated the gears were engaged, the algebraic relation between the load and motor shaft was used. When not engaged, the desired load shaft trajectory was used as an estimate. The parameter estimates and gains used are as follows.

$\hat{S}_L = 0.025$	$\hat{S}_M = 0.025$ N·m
$\hat{C}_L = 0.009$	$\hat{C}_M = 0.006$ N·m
$\hat{B}_L = 0.000$	$\hat{B}_M = 0.12 \times 10^{-3}$ N·m/(rad/s)
$\hat{J}_L = 0.10 \times 10^{-5}$	$\hat{J}_M = 0.10 \times 10^{-3}$ N·m/(rad/s²)
$B_{AL} = 6.80 \times 10^{-5}$	$B_{AM} = 6.80 \times 10^{-3}$ N·m/(rad/s)
$K_{AL} = 0.041 \times 10^{-2}$	$K_{AM} = 0.041$ N·m/(rad)
$R=1$ $\quad \sigma = 0.44$ rad	$A = 75$ rad/s²

The estimate $\hat{J}_L$ is not accurate. We only know $\hat{J}_L < 0.02 \hat{J}_M$. Thus, $\hat{J}_L$, B_{AL} and K_{AL} were chosen proportionate to the optimally-tuned corresponding motor parameters.

The results for a 1 Hz parabolic load trajectory are shown in Figs. 8 and 9. Comparisons are made between controllers with feedback only, feedback plus feedforward decoupling using lumped shaft parameter estimates, and

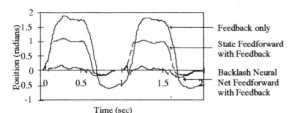

Fig. 8. Error Comparison for 1 Hz Parabolic Trajectory

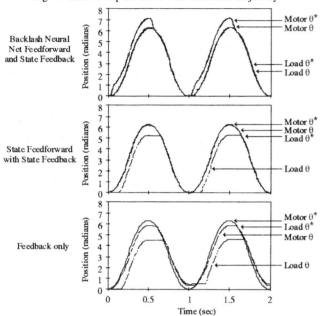

Fig. 9. Motor & Load/Reference & Actual Trajectories

the backlash controller. Note that for convenience the motor shaft was referenced to the negative backlash boundary rather than the center. This creates large error on positive movement and smaller error on negative movement, rather than symmetric error.

The results are consistent for the two cases. With feedback only, the motor shaft lags its desired trajectory in addition to the lag and flat regions caused by failing to alter the motor shaft trajectory. Addition of the feedforward decoupling allowed the motor to track its reference well, but still left the characteristic backlash lag and flat zone. The backlash controller supplied the quickest trajectory correction possible given the current limit of our drive. It left only a short small pulse in the load shaft error while the motor shaft moved to the correct gear face.

In this experiment, the error reductions relative to the feedback only controller are approximately 50% for the addition of feedforward and 80% to 90% for the backlash controller. However, the percent reductions can vary greatly from system to system depending on the relative magnitude of the backlach induced errors to the friction induced errors and how well the parameters can be estimated. Position dependence of the friction and shaft compliance can also be significant factors that have the potential to mask the benefits of this controller.

IX. CONCLUSIONS

A neural network topology that compensates for backlash and friction in precision, position controlled mechanisms has been developed and successfully demonstrated. The control algorithm it implements has several unique features.

- It moves the motor shaft to the proper backlash boundary using a time-optimal control subject to acceleration limits.
- It decouples the inertial, friction (viscous, coulomb and static) and the gear torques.
- It incorporates properly referenced state error feedback.

The method of implementing the neural network embodies several novel features.

- Standard linear control is directly implemented by a neuron operating in its linear region. This allows the corresponding weights to be initialized with the gains of an existing controller.
- The bang-bang control that results from time-optimal control subject to hard constraints can be directly implemented by a threshholding neuron once the switching curve is created.
- State conditions for inclusion of friction decoupling, gear torque decoupling and the optimal relative acceleration were systematically created from Σ-neuron half-spaces and a $\Sigma\Pi$-neuron parabola.
- Logical operations were used to create complicated conditions from more basic, single neuron-generated conditions.

ACKNOWLEDGEMENT

The authors wish to acknowledge the financial support provided by the Rockwell Foundation.

REFERENCES

[1] F.G. Shinskey, Process Control Systems, McGraw-Hill, 1967, pp. 128-130.

[2] J.-J. E. Slotine, W. Li, Applied Nonlinear Control, Prentice Hall, 1991, pp. 171-179.

[3] G. Tao, P.V. Kokotovic, "Adaptive Control of Systems with Backlash," Tech. Report CCEC, UCSB, 1992.

[4] C.T. Johnson, R.D. Lorenz, "Experimental Identification of Friction and Its Compensation in Precise, Position Controlled Mechanisms," In Proc. of IEEE, IAS Annual Meeting, Oct., 1991, pp. 1392-1398.

[5] F.L. Lewis, Optimal Control, John Wiley & Sons, 1986, pp. 252-280.

[6] D.E. Rumelhart, G.E. Hinton, R.J. Williams, "Learning Internal Representations by Error Propagation," Parallel Distributed Processing, MIT Press, 1986, pp.45-76.

[7] C. Narathong, University of Wisconsin-Platteville report, ECE Dept

[8] K. Hornik, M. Stinchcombe, H. White, "Multilayer Feedforward Networks are Universal Approximators," Neural Networks, 2, 1989.

[9] D.E. Rumelhart, G.E. Hinton, J.L. McClelland, "A General Framework for Parallel Distributed Processing," Parallel Distributed Processing, MIT Press, 1986, pp.318-364.

[10] C. L. Johnson, Analog Computer Techniques, McGraw-Hill, 1956.

[11] D.R. Seidl, T.L. Reneking, and R.D. Lorenz, "Use of Neural Networks to Identify and Compensate for Friction in Precision, Position Controlled Mechanisms", In Proc. of IEEE, IAS Annual Meeting, Oct., 1992, pp. 1937-1944.

ANN BASED PROCESS CONTROL IN MANUFACTURING

S.C.Wang   J.X.Dong   G.Shen

Dept. of Manufacturing Engineering
Beijing Univ. of Aero. & Astro.
100083 Beijing P.R.C.

ABSTRACT

Artificial Neural Network (ANN) based expert system in manufacturing control is presented as a new approach used for discrete system. Process planning control and process scheduling control are discussed in detail by multilayer ANN. The weights series of Wij, "i" the layers number , "j" the neurons number , are got initially by learning samples through mapping function and then revised further by competitive learning. The mechanism of competitive learning includes two steps: response and competition, which is only worked among these excited neurons by means of learning rules to revise the weights. The learning rules involve the weights calculation by iterating and the convergence by balance criterion. The expected values in ANN learning system in process planning are obtained by sample learning with mark-giving experiment. But in scheduling control the quantitated items in long term scheduling strategy are used for expected values.

1. INTRODUCTION

Recently, people have been much interested in ANN used in industrial applications, since ANN manifests oneself in three distinguished advantages from traditional AI, that involve knowledge representation by implicit expression, parallel inference by ANN algorithm and self-learning by samples or inputs.

We try to integrate ANN theory with discrete process control in manufacturing to build an advanced production system with higher intelligence in real-time condition. Process planning control and scheduling control play important role in an integrated manufacturing system. If constraints of facilities, production specifications and production processing requirements are given, an arrangement of production processing sequence should be done to make the desired criteria optimal or suboptimal and to provide a real-time supervision to operation for production process. From the system point of view, real-time production scheduling could be regarded as a real-time information based decision-making[1].

It should be mentioned that an ANN based expert systym can be used as an intelligent tool, because there is a strong mechanism in learning samples, which provide the tool for dealing with a certain product-family as well as these samples.

2. PROCESS PLANNING CONTROL IN MANUFACTURING

PROCESS CONTROL IN MACHINING OPERATION

A multilayer ANN model with hierarchical structure is shown in Fig.1(a)(b). The weights series of $[W_{ij}],[W_{jk}],[W_{kl}]$ respectively in Fig.1[a] are initially got by learning samples. The hierarchical ANN shown in Fig.1(b) includes two subsystems: ANN1—sample learning system and ANN2—real application system. The former gives the initial weights by samples, the later gives the real output through mapping function "f".

In discrete events, the neuron nodes are always in independent state, the link between them is in non-linear dynamic mode. The exciting factor is only given by domain engineers according their knowledge. The weights calculation regarding the link between nodes could be operated in accordance with the following rules:

<1> $\sum$ rule: $W = \sum_{i}^{n} W_{i}$.

<2> OR rule: $W = max\{W_{i}\}$,

<3> AND rule: $W = 1 - \prod_{i}^{n}(1 - W_{i})$,

where Wi is the weights of neuron node "i".

Once the neuron nodes are excited in active state, then the competitive mechanism will be worked among these excited nodes by learning rule to revise the weights. The learning rule involves the weights calculation by iterating and the balance criterion by convergence accuaracy.

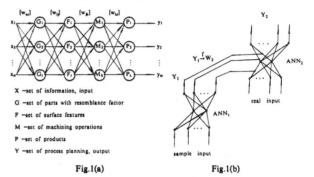

X —set of information, input
G —set of parts with resemblance factor
F —set of surface features
M —set of machining operations
P —set of products
Y —set of process planning, output

Fig.1(a)   Fig.1(b)

PROCESS CONTROL IN MACHINING ROUTING

Process planning control includes machining operation control and machining routing control, of course, routing control should be on the basis of operations. The routing design is related to surface features in a part and locating reference for a workpiece set on machine tool. For example as in Fig. 2(a), the box part should be processed according to the following sequence: machining plane F3 first, machining holes F1 and F2 second, then tapping female screws F4 last, while the locating reference should be considered before.

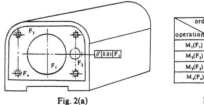

order operation	1	2	3	4
$M_1(F_1)$	0	1	0	0
$M_2(F_2)$	0	0	1	0
$M_3(F_3)$	1	0	0	0
$M_4(F_4)$	0	0	0	1

Fig. 2(a)   Fig. 2(b)

We present an approach using constrained Hopfield network. The approach transforms the reference and feature type constraints into the elements of connection matrix, which specifies the connection strength among neurons in ANN.

The neurons arranged as a matrix with N rows and N columns are coupled together by a set of non-linear differential equations:

$$dU_{ai}/dt = -U_{ai}/\tau - A\sum_{j=1}^{N} V_{aj} - B\sum_{b=1}^{N} V_{bi} - C(\sum_{j=1}^{N}\sum_{a=1}^{N} V_{aj} - N) -$$
$$D\sum_{j=1}^{N}(y_i - y_{i+1})^2(V_{bi+1} + V_{bi-1}) \qquad (1)$$

$$V_{ai} = 1/2(1 + \tanh(U_{ai}/U_0)) \qquad (2)$$

$$P = [V_{ij}] \qquad (3)$$

$$Y^T = PX^T \qquad (4)$$

where V_{ij} are the neural state variables, which may take values from 0 to 1, P denotes permutation matrix, in which the sum is N, X denotes initial array of machining operations. Y is the result output,which means a collated machining routing made by Hopfield neural computation.

In the box part the suitable parameters and initial conditions are given by experience, such as $A = B = D = 600$, $C = 200$, $\tau = 1$, $u_0 = 0.04$ and put them into formula (1),(2),(3), when iteration $n = 200$, the permutation matrix is got as Fig. 2(b), which indicates the machining sequence for the box part: $F_3 \rightarrow F_1 \rightarrow F_2 \rightarrow F_4$.

3. PROCESS SCHEDULING CONTROL IN MANUFACTURING

In job–shop or batch production, there are a great variety of parts which should be scheduled into production line as much as possible. Process scheduling in manufacturing system is always wanted to maintain the production line working smoothly, and be able to handle noice interference in process. The former function is called " scheduling", the later " rescheduling". There are two strategical rules to guide an algorithm in searching the tree .

The first rule is used to find a suitable job to be worked as early as possible for production line. If " $t_{i,1}$ " denotes the time of first–operation for part "i", then $\text{Min}[t_{i,1}| i = 1,2,\cdots,n]$ can be taken as the weights in ANN model shown in Fig.3 .

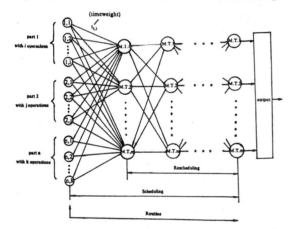

Fig.3

Fig.4

The second rule is used to balance the load of machine tools in production line as smoothly as possible. If " $T_{m,i}^k$ " denotes the remainder machining time, " $T_{w,i}^k$ " denotes the part " i " waiting time for machining (see Fig. 4), where $i = 1,2,\cdots,n$ means job number; $k = 0,1,2,\cdots$, means the sequence of counting cycles .

$$\sum T_{re,i}^k = \sum T_{re,i}^{k-1} - T_{re,i}^k \quad ; \quad (i = 1,2,\cdots,n; k = 0,1,\cdots)$$
$$\sum T_{w,i}^k = \sum T_{w,i}^{k-1} - T_{w,i}^k \quad ; \quad (i = 1,2,\cdots,n; k = 0,1,\cdots)$$
$$\text{and let:} \quad T_i^k = \sum T_{re,i}^k + \sum T_{w,i}^k$$

The search goal is to find the $\text{Max}[T_i^k | i = 1,2,\cdots,n]$, which should be scheduled first with priority. If $t_{idle,i}^j$ denotes the idle time of machine tool j for waiting job i, then $\sum t_{idle,i}^j$ could be accumulated, where $i = 1,2,\cdots,n$, $j = 1,2,\cdots,m$.

Table 1 is an example of three machine tools and five parts with different number of operations . In table 1, m_{ij} indicates the machine number, (i,j) – i part, j opera-

tion, t_{ij} – the machining time of (i,j), $S_{i,j}^k$ – the start machining time of part (i,j) obtained from the calculation of the k times, $E_{i,j}^k$ – the end machining time of part (i,j) obtained from the calculation of the k times. It is clear from table 1 that the total machining time is 26, the idle time of machine 1 is $S_{i,j}^1 - S_{i,j}^0 = 2$, the idle time of machine 2 is $S_{4,4}^6 - E_{3,3}^5 = 1$, the idle time of machine 3 is 0.

Obviously, the time T_i^k is always in progressive decreasement, and in regular dynamic mode. Therefore, any noice or new job inserted can be looked as an interference happened, which only changes T_i^k put in a new rescheduling cycle.

If we set some production norms such as productivity, delivery date and stock as the expected values in long term strategy, all of them should be transformed into function of time as well as the constraint factors in rescheduling cycle.

An iterative algorithm is put forward to find the optimal solution. The procedure of the iterative algorithm is going on ANN model by process of scheduling the part–queue through $t_{i,1}$ and T_i^k, and process of calculating the idle time of machine tools. The procedure of iterating is a procedure of correcting the part–queue by means of the idle time, which , of course, is always expected the less the better. Because of the iterative procedure involved both computing and inferencing, the heuristic information and the search strategy should guarantee the iterative procedure to be convergent.

Table 1

(i,j)	t_{ij}	$S_{i,j}^0$	$E_{i,j}^0$	$S_{i,j}^1$	$E_{i,j}^1$	$S_{i,j}^2$	$E_{i,j}^2$	$S_{i,j}^3$	$E_{i,j}^3$	$S_{i,j}^4$	$E_{i,j}^4$	$S_{i,j}^5$	$E_{i,j}^5$	$S_{i,j}^6$	$E_{i,j}^6$
$m_{ij}=1$															
(1,3)	3									21	24				
(2,2)	5			2	7										
(3,2)	7					7	14								
(4,3)	7							14	21						
$m_{ij}=2$															
(1,1)	3					6	9								
(2,1)	2	0	2												
(2,3)	2									15	17				
(3,3)	3											17	20		
(4,1)	4			2	6										
(4,4)	4													21	25
(5,2)	6					9	15								
$m_{ij}=3$															
(1,2)	6							13	19						
(2,4)	7											19	26		
(3,1)	5			2	7										
(4,2)	6					7	13								
(5,1)	2	0	2												

4. CONCLUSION

ANN based expert system is a higher potential method in manufacturing process to solve the problems in real–time control by means of parallel distributed processing and in knowledge abstraction by means of self–learning. Self–learning and self–organizing functions by ANN could eliminate the difference between expert system and development tool, which provides a more flexible and object–oriented industrial application . In discrete manufacturing system the competitive learning will play an important role in connection weights, by which the domain engineers are able to lead knowledge factors into connection weights. A suitable time–function can give a unified algorithm in static and dynamic scheduling control, then any noice in automatic production can be handled only as an interference inserted in time axis.

REFERENCES

[1] L.W.Bao, Y.Z.Lu, 'Neural Network based time production scheduling for industrial process', Proc. of IFAC second workshop, 1989
[2] J.J.Hopfield, 'Neural Network and Physical Systems with Emergent collective computational Abilities', Proc. Natl. Acad. Sci. USA, Vol.79, 1982
[3] L. C. Jiao, 'The theory of Neural Network systems', The press of Xian Electronics Science & Technology Univ., 1991
[4] Yamamoto, M., 'Scheduling / rescheduling in the manufacturing operating system environment', Int.J. Prod. Res., Vol.23, No.4, 1985

NEURAL NETWORK CONTROL OF A PLASMA GATE ETCH: EARLY STEPS IN WAFER-TO-WAFER PROCESS CONTROL

E. A. Rietman, Bell Labs, Murray Hill, NJ
S. H. Patel, Bell Labs, Orlando, FL
E. R. Lory, Bell Labs, Princeton, NJ

ABSTRACT

We have developed a gate oxide thickness controller for a plasma etch reactor. This controller is for a 0.9 um technology currently being manufactured in our Orlando CMOS fab line. By monitoring certain process signatures aren feeding them forward into a neural network trained by the backpropagation method, it is possible to predict in real time the correct over etch time on a wafer-by-wafer basis. Computer simulations indicate that the neural network is equivalent to humans for this task. The uniqueness of this controllere is compared with a previous controller for a 1.25 um technology gate etch process.

INTRODUCTION

Typical process control, as practiced in integrated circuit manufacturing, consists of open-loop control with statistical analysis to observe changes in some process variable or process signature compared with a mean and variance from a short historical record. This approach to process control does not allow wafer-to-wafer control of the type needed for developing submicron structures, with a good yield at the end of the process. For a high yield some wafer attribute should be correlated to a control variable(s) or an in situ process signature for real time wafer-to-wafer feedback control.

In this paper we describe a controller for the gate etch process, the remaining oxide thickness in the source and drain regions can be controlled by the overetch time. The time computation is based on a neural network mapping of the mean values of the fluctuations about the set points for the control variables and an in situ optical emission monitor. In this paper we describe the controller and its performance. The conclusions of the paper will compare this gate etch controller with previous work (cf. Rietman et al. 1993).

Neural networks are loosely modeled after biological neural networks. They are, in essence, a nonparametric nonlinear learning algorithm. No assumptions are made about the populations of the variables and no assumptions are made about the functional relations of the variables. The only assumption is that there is a cause and effect relation between the inputs and the outputs (cf. Weiss and Kulokowski (1991), Smith (1993)). The training of a neural network consists of adjusting the elements of several matrices in order to minimize the error between the network output and the target response (cf. Rumelhart et al., 1986). Miller et al. (1990) and White and Sofge (1992) have assembled collections of papers on neural networks for control.

THE CONTROLLER

Neural networks have the ability of learn any mapping in which there is a cause and effect relation (cf. Hornik et al. 1990). It is clear that such a relation exists between the remaining oxide thickness in the source and drain regions, and some process signatures. For example, by monitoring one wavelength in the optical emission while the etch is in progress it is possible to collect an emission trace of the process. This emission trace has embedded in it the obvious information about ion concentration in the plasma glow. It also has embedded in it the etch rate, the uniformity of the etch and the pattern density. If an autozero step occurs to correct for fogging of the optical windows, than the emission trace also has embedded in it the history of the cleaning of the reaction chamber or optical emission system drift.

The optical emission trace, from the plasma glow, is an excellent monitor for our controller. Many plasma etch processes use the emission trace to determine the end point. Figure 1 is a plot of a typical emission trace for a polysilicon etch in gate formation. After 21 seconds the intensity drops significantly. At this point an autozero occurs. The intensity then increases until a threshold is reached. The wafer is then process for an overetch time as determined by the control algorithm.

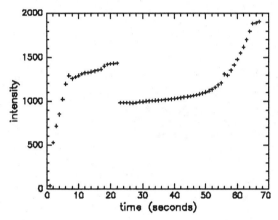

Figure 1: Typical optical emission trace.

We collected vectors of inputs and corresponding outputs (wafer attributes) to develop the neural network mapping. The mapping is basically given by the relation:

$$O = f(\Sigma W1 f(\Sigma W2 * I))$$

Where O is the mapping output, in our case the overetch time to give the desired oxide thickness, I is a vector of inputs and W1 and W2 are two matrices that have been optimized during the learning process. In preforming training (the learning process) we were mapping a vector of inputs (process signatures) to the ideal etch time for a desired oxide thickness. It was therefore necessary to collect real world oxide thickness measurements. The training is done with the process signatures as the network input (see Figure 2) and the ideal etch time as the target. The ideal etch time is computed from a simple linear corrector by the equation

$$t_{ideal} = t_{obs} + \frac{T_{obs} - T_{des}}{E_R}$$

Where t_{ideal} and t_{obs} are the ideal and observed etch times, T_{obs} and T_{des} are the observed and desired thicknesses, and E_R is the etch rate. The neural network was a backpropagation network (cf. Rumelhart et al. 1986) with 36 inputs, 5 nodes in one hidden layer and 1 output node. The input and hidden layer each had one constant bias node for self adjustment of the network.

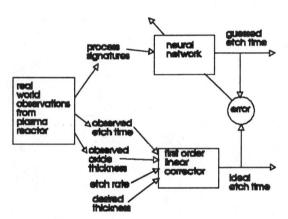

Figure 2: Training method.

In order for this linear correction to work it should be kept in mind that the observed over etch time is close to the ideal and the first order corrections are small. This linear correction is valid only near the end of the etch process. The earlier steps in the etch sequence, which encounter different layers and transient effects at turn-on time, are highly nonlinear andless well-behaved.

After the network is trained no linear corrections need to be computed. The network will see several process signatures in real time and compute the ideal over-etch time.

In a previous publication we described a controller for a 1.25 micron, TaSi-Poly gate etch (cf. Rietman et al. 1993). That controller used as its input a portion of the emission trace.

For the present controller, a 0.9 micron poly gate etch process, it was necessary to include the mean values of the fluctuations about the set points of the control variables for the second step in a three step process. The neural network computes the ideal overetch time for the third etch step. In the first etch step the wafer is quickly etched during a timed etch. The second step is called by the emission trace endpoint algorithm and generates the emission trace shown in Figure 1. It is from the process signatures generated in this second etch step that the over-etch time is computed for the third etch step.

In order to get the network to converge during the learning phase it was necessary to include, in addition to the emission trace, the mean values of the fluctuations about the set points for: the applied rf power, reflected rf power, dc bias, flow rate of four gases, reactor pressure, and the total time for completion of step two. In addition to these live process signatures the network uses information from an on-line and in real-time interrogation of a database to retrieve the mean values of the following: the observed oxide thickness, the observed over-etch time, the applied rf power (step 2) and dc bias (step 2), from the previous lot etched on this machine. From the mean value of the observed oxide thickness and the over-etch time of the previous lot the ideal over-etch time can be computed and used as another input. All these inputs are listed in Table 1.

PERFORMANCE OF THE CONTROLLER

In developing the controller and studying its performance we collected 1660 input/output tuples. This dataset was randomized and partitioned into subsets for training and testing. The training consisted of repeated random selection of examples from the training set and back-propagating the resulting errors to update the connection matrices. After the error converged the training was stopped and the network was evaluated with the data set aside for testing. The performance vs. the size of the training set is shown in Figure 3.

Table 1: Inputs to neural network controller

1. dc bias (mean from last lot).
2. thickness (mean form last lot).
3. applied rf (mean from last lot).
4. ideal over-etch time (mean from last lot).
5. total time for step two (current wafer).
6. gas 1 flow rate (current wafer).
7. gas 2 flow rate (current wafer).
8. gas 3 flow rate (current wafer).
9. gas 4 flow rate (current wafer).
10. reactor pressure (current wafer).
11. applied rf (current wafer).
12. reflected rf (current wafer).
13. dc bias (current wafer).
14-34. the last 21 data points from the emission trace for the current wafer.

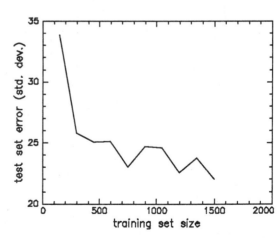

Figure 3: Network performance vs. size of training set.
This plot shows that as the training set size increases, the standard deviation of the network error decreases. The human equivalent for this task results in a standard deviation of 23 Angstroms. From this

figure it is clear that the neural network has achieved human equivalent.

CONCLUSIONS

Although it wasn't discussed to any length in this paper the previous gate etch controller (Rietman et al. 1993) was for a 1.25 micron two step gate etch in which the first step was for removing TaSi and the second step was the removal of polysilicon. Of interest to note is the initial gate oxide for that technology was 208 A and the post etch oxide thickness between the source and drain was 153 A with a standard deviation of 15 A. The current controller is for a 0.9 micron polysilicon gate etch with the initial gate oxide thickness about 150 A and the post etch thickness 83 A with a standard deviation of 23 A. If these trends continue down to 0.15 micron technology with an initial gate oxide thickness of 40-50 A, further improvements in process control will be required.

Proud et al. (1991), Barna and Tovell (1992) and Elta (1993) have all argued for wafer-to-wafer control of the processing steps. In this paper we have described an approach to achieving this result for the gate etch.

ACKNOWLEDGMENTS

We thank R. C. Frye, R. A. Gottscho, Y. Le Cunn, S. Neston and J. S. Denker for many stimulating conversations. We further thank T. R. Harry for graphics and database support, G. J. Vorhis for SECS interfacing studies, M. Beachy for database support and, J. Sniegowski, and J. L. Keen for enthusiastic support.

REFERENCES

Barna, G. and Tovell, N. "Wafer-to-Wafer Process Control", TI Tech. J., 76-86, Sept-Oct (1992)

Elta, M. "Developing 'Smart' Controllers for Semiconductor Processes", R&D Magazine, 69-72, Feb., (1993)

Hornik, K., Stinchcombe, M. and White, H. "Universal Approximation of an Unknown Mapping and its Derivatives Using Multilayer Feedforward Networks", Neural Networks, 3, 551-560, (1990)

Miller, W. T., III, Sutton, R. S., and Werbos, P. J., NEURAL NETWORKS FOR CONTROL, MIT Press, Cambridge, MA, (1990)

Proud, J., Gottscho, R. A., Bondur, J., Garscadden, A., Heberlein, J. V., Herb, G. K., Kushner, M. J., Lawler, J. E., Lieberman, M. A., Mayer, T. M., Phelps, A. V., Roman, W., Sawin, H., and Winters, H. F., PLASMA PROCESSING OF MATERIALS: SCIENTIFIC OPPORTUNITIES AND TECHNOLOGICAL CHALLANGES, National Research Council, National Academy Press, Washington, D.C. (1991)

Smith, M., NEURAL NETWORKS FOR STATISTICAL MODELING, Van Nostrand Reinhold Publishers, New York, (1993)

Rietman, E. A., Frye, R. C., Lory, E. R. and Harry, T. R., "Active Neural Network Control of Wafer Attributes in a Plasma Etch Process", J. Vac. Sci. and Tech. part B, in press (1993)

Rumelhart, D. E., McClelland, J. L. and the PDP Research Group, PARALLEL DISTRIBUTED PROCESSING: EXPLORATIONS IN THE MICROSTRUCTURE OF COGNITION, Vol. I: Foundations, MIT Press, Cambridge, MA, (1986)

Weiss, S. M. and Kulikowski, C. A., COMPUTER SYSTEMS THAT LEARN, Morgan Kaufmann Pub., San Mateo, CA, (1991)

White, D. A. and Sofge, D. A., HANDBOOK OF INTELLIGENT CONTROL: NEURAL, FUZZY AND ADAPTIVE APPROACHES, Van Nostrand Reinhold Publishers, New York, (1992)

Paper Web Quality Profile Analysis Tool Based on Artificial Neural Networks

Jukka Vanhala[1], Pekka Pakarinen[2], and Kimmo Kaski[1]

[1]Tampere University of Technology,
Microelectronics Laboratory,
P.O.Box 692, 33101 Tampere, Finland

jv@ee.tut.fi

[2]Technical Research Centre of Finland,
Combustion and Thermal Engineering Laboratory,
P.O.Box 221, 40101 Jyväskylä, Finland

PEKKA.PAKARINEN@vtt.fi

Abstract

In order to guarantee the uniform quality of paper across the whole cross direction of the paper machine, on-line measurements and control equipment related to different paper quality profiles are necessary. In modern paper machines only the basis weight, the moisture and the caliber profiles are controlled by an on-line control system. However, there are several important profiles that can not be easily measured or controlled directly. As an example, the fiber-orientation profile is difficult to measure on-line and in addition to this the control mechanism is not clear. This is mainly due to the insufficient knowledge about the complex relationship between the orientation profile and the other profiles. Artificial Neural Networks can be used to model such difficult complex systems where only input-output data is available. In this case study the artificial neural network methods are applied to the fiber-orientation profile analysis and its control. The same method can be used to control other profiles as well.

1. Introduction to the problem area

The schematic structure of the paper machine *wet end* is shown in Fig. 1. The *header* is for even cross-machine introduction of stock into the *headbox*. The header tapers to provide uniform pressure gradient across the whole width of the headbox. *Inlet tubes* are designed to give high velocity even rectangular flow of stock into the *attenuation chamber*. Also the turbulence will break flocks and provides complete blending of the suspension. The role of the attenuation chamber is to dampen the temporal variations of the flow velocity and pressure. Pressure drop and high velocities in small diameter tubes, the *turbulence generator*, provide final, controlled flow rate of the stock into the *converging channel*. Tube inlet and outlet configuration and tube discharge velocity absorption generate the final homogenizing micro-turbulence. The velocity of the stock is increased substantially in the converging channel and the *slice opening*. The slice opening is provided with a precise control over the whole width of the headbox, Fig 2. The stock ejects onto the *wire* where the paper *web* is formed. This is the main control mechanism for the various quality profiles. The wire is made of yarn and it has small holes through which the water can filtrate. Most of the fibers are retained on top of the wire. The basis-weight profile and the fiber-orientation profile will be fixed after the free water has been removed from the suspension on the wire. After that the fibers do not move or turn markedly. The drying process only removes the excess moisture from the paper.

The quality properties of the paper are described with several variables that are dependent on the cross-machine position. These kind of profiles are *e.g.* basis-weight profile, fiber-orientation profile, moisture profile, and caliber profile. Of course these profiles depend on each other but the relation may be very complex and it is understood only at a qualitative level. Some of the profiles are controlled on-line, the most important being the basis-weight profile. The requirement for on-line control is that the profile can be measured in real time. The time constants in the paper quality parameter control are of the order of 1 to 10 minutes. Some of the profiles are easy to measure on-line and some impossible. The basis-weight profile is an example of the former and the output velocity profile of the turbulence generator is an example of the latter [1, 2].

Cross-machine flow causes changes in the fibre orientation. Cross-machine flow can be due to *e.g.* adjustments to the slice opening or irregular flow from the turbulence generator, see Fig 3. Where the slice opening is wider a larger amount of stock runs onto the wire because the wider slice opening causes a smaller pressure behind the slice bar which gives rise to cross flow inside the converging channel and on the wire [3]. The fiber-orientation profile can be adjusted to a near optimal shape but only on the cost of the basis weight and formation profiles. Since the latter are normally more important factors and also easier to control, the fiber orientation is not optimized [4]. When the paper machine is run on the drag side, *i.e.* the velocity of the wire

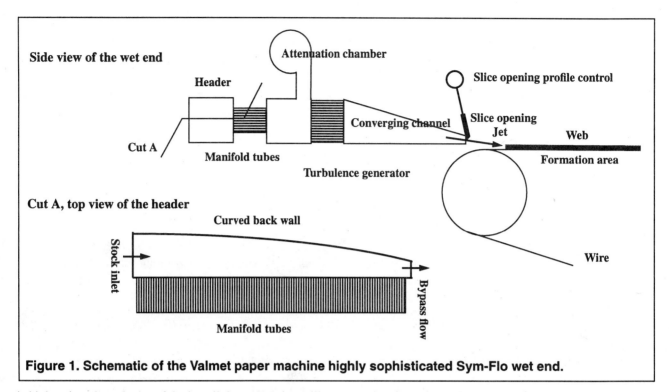

Figure 1. Schematic of the Valmet paper machine highly sophisticated Sym-Flo wet end.

is higher than the velocity of the jet, all the suspension will filtrate in a same manner and the cross-machine component of the flow will show up in the fiber-orientation profile. If the profile is adjusted in this situation the paper machine may be run also on rush side *i.e.* with lower wire velocities without generating cross-machine flow.

2. Wetsim, the paper machine wet end profile simulator

In the first step the training data for the Quanet profile analyzer is provided by a simulator. The paper machine wet end simulator, Wetsim, simulates the flow of the sus-

pension from the outlet of the turbulence generator trough the slice area and up to the formation area of the wire. The simulator is based on the physical model of the wet end modelled with Newtonian, Navier Stokes and continuity equations. Wetsim provides among other quality profiles also the basis-weight profile and the fiber-orientation profile. To collect enough information of the whole dynamic range of the paper machine the simulator is run with widely modified run parameters. The resulting profiles are collected into a database which is used to train the neural network.

Wetsim runs on a Unix workstation and has a graphical user interface. Several parameters can be tuned. The physi-

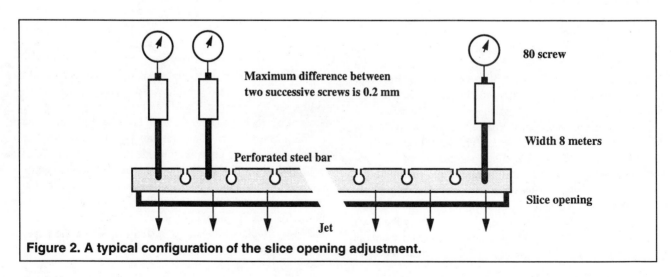

Figure 2. A typical configuration of the slice opening adjustment.

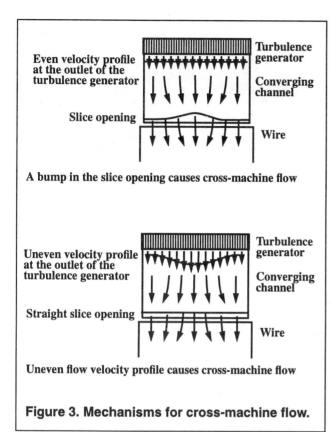

Even velocity profile at the outlet of the turbulence generator

Turbulence generator

Converging channel

Slice opening

Wire

A bump in the slice opening causes cross-machine flow

Uneven velocity profile at the outlet of the turbulence generator

Turbulence generator

Converging channel

Straight slice opening

Wire

Uneven flow velocity profile causes cross-machine flow

Figure 3. Mechanisms for cross-machine flow.

cal structure of the wet end must be given describing *e.g.* the geometry of the slice and the retention and friction of the wire. Also the simulator needs the parameters for running the paper machine such as the speed of the wire and the characteristics of the stock. Finally the normal control parameters including the screw positions are also given.

There are two advantages in using a simulator instead of real measured data. First the measurements needed to collect the required database are very tedious and expensive to make. A whole paper machine should be dedicated for several days to serve only the measurements. Also it is not straightforward to run a paper machine with parameters which differ largely from the optimal state for the machine. The data obtained are not clean, they are plagued with periodic and unperiodic noise which arise both from the paper machine itself and from the limited accuracy of the measurements. Of course, when simulated training data are used the results must be checked against the real world situation; the system must eventually be taken into a paper mill for evaluation in the field.

3. Quanet, the neural network based quality profile analyzer

Quanet is intended to be used for various paper machine quality profile analysis and control tasks. Typically there is

a large database containing measured profile data from the paper machine or generated data from the Wetsim simulator. Since all this data are collected from the same physical system there is some, probably unknown, mapping between the profiles. Quanet is used for extracting this mapping from the measurements and for predicting new output profiles from previously unseen input profiles.

Quanet runs on Unix-workstations and on PC-hardware under DOS operating system. The workstation environment is used mainly for system development and for teaching the system which requires large computational resources. PC-class machines are used mainly for product runs. Quanet is intended to be used in the control room of a paper mill either as a stand-alone version running on dedicated hardware or as an embedded application integrated into the control system of the paper machine.

We have used a back-propagation type network with two hidden layers for profile data analysis [5]. The training algorithm employs both adaptive learning rate and momentum terms. The case is a typical mapping task where the input and output are large vectors. We have used from 30 to 100 cross-machine points on both input and output. The number of units in the hidden layers vary from test to test from ten to one hundred. The training set was generated using the Wetsim paper machine wet end simulator. The profiles are not given to the network as such but instead we calculate differences between successive profile pairs for both input and output. This way the absolute value of the profiles is hidden and the system processes only changes in the profiles.

4. The Test Case

As a test case we have created a system which is intended to help the paper machine operator to control the fiber-orientation profile. The fiber-orientation profile is measured in the laboratory using the standard methods of ultra-sound velocity measurements. Using this profile the neural network system will give the required change to the basis-weight profile which will correct the fiber-orientation profile. The operator checks that the change to the basis-weight profile is acceptable and feeds the change into the control system of the paper machine.

Quanet is able to learn the training set and also to make accurate generalizations when given an input profile that has not been included in the training set, Figs 4 and 5. In Fig 4 the basis-weight output profile is accurate over the whole width of the web. In Fig 5 the output is only qualitatively correct but can still be used to make the fiber-orientation profile better. Both cases shown use data from the simulator.

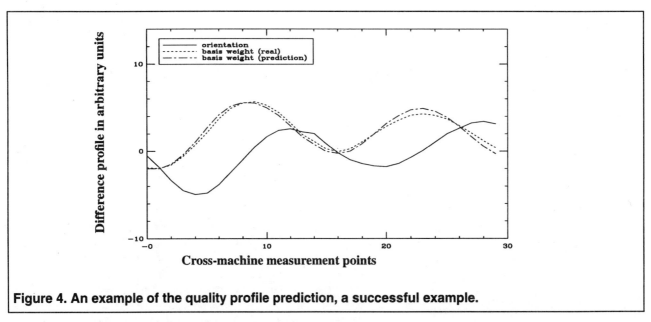

Figure 4. An example of the quality profile prediction, a successful example.

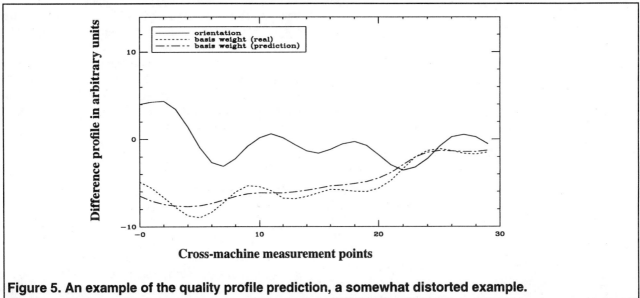

Figure 5. An example of the quality profile prediction, a somewhat distorted example.

5. Conclusions

The neural network approach seems promising in paper profile data analysis. The approach is by no means limited to the case presented here (the mapping between the fiber-orientation profile and the basis-weight profile). There are several other important profile quality measures that can be analyzed with neural networks. Here we have demonstrated the success of one example. Other applications could include the fault diagnosis of the wet end of a paper machine, and the drying mechanisms. The results obtained seem to be encouraging enough to continue the work in this field.

References

[1] Smith, K.E., "Cross-direction control is still top process automation trend," Pulp and Paper, February 1985.
[2] Brewster D.B and Robinson W.I., "How computers are controlling functions on the paper machine," Pulp and Paper, November 1973.
[3] Turunen R. "Experiences of Sym-Flo headbox and automatic profile control," Papermakers conference, 1986.
[4] Brewster D.B., "Interactions in CD control," Symposium on Systems in the pulp and paper industry, May 1986.
[5] Rumelhart, D.E., Hinton, G.E., and Williams, R.J. (1986). "Learning internal representations by error propagation," in D.E. Rumelhart and J.L. McClelland (Eds.), Parallel Distributed Processing: Explorations in the Microstructure of Cognition, Volume 1: Foundations, MIT Press, Cambridge, MA, pp. 318-362.

Neural Net Modeling and Control of a Municipal Waste Water Process

Peter A. Minderman, Jr, and Thomas J. McAvoy*
Dept. of Chemical Engineering and Institute for Systems Research
University of Maryland
College Park, MD 20742-2111

Abstract

One municipal facility is beginning to consider the benefits of using model predictive control as a means of improving product quality and reducing energy costs. To date, the initial steps of this project have been completed. The first step was to upgrade the basic control and data acquisition systems. The second step was to collect experimental data in order to build a process model. The third step was to build this model; a dynamic nonlinear finite impulse response model was constructed using the neural network partial least squares algorithm. This model has been used to analyze the steady state behavior of the plant, and this analysis has helped identify an improved control strategy which lowers annual operating costs. The implementation of these ideas awaits the completion of a process retrofit. After this expansion, the modified process will be remodeled, and the suggested control strategy will be experimentally verified.

Introduction

Waste water reclamation facilities (WRFs) are under pressure to maintain a high quality effluent while minimizing energy costs. Strategies for improving the process control of such facilities are constantly being considered. One approach for developing an improved control system is to model the process, and then one can design and optimize the control system based on this plant model.

Mechanistic models, e.g. [1], of the activated sludge process have been developed. However their complex structure and high number of unmeasured variables make it difficult to use such models in control systems. Input-output models are more amenable for these applications, but the challenge is to develop a model that fits a wide range of process conditions. Because of their ability to represent any nonlinear relationship, neural networks are promising general purpose modeling tools for such applications.

Earlier modeling results [2] have shown that a recurrent neural network model can adequately predict the effluent compositions of nitrite/nitrate, phosphate, and ammonium ions in a heavily instrumented pilot plant at the Technical University of Denmark. An alternative neural network modeling scheme [3] is analogous to the linear models used in traditional DMC implementations, but the model is nonlinear. This approach (NNPLS-NFIR) builds nonlinear finite impulse response models using the neural network partial least squares algorithm [4]. The resultant model lends itself well to steady state analysis and to on-line control applications.

Plant Description

The plant under investigation is the Patuxent Water Reclamation Facility in Crofton, Maryland. This facility uses activated sludge technology in an unconventional flow scheme. The municipal raw wastewater enters the plant through a pumping station and is passed through a screening step and through a grit-removal step. At this point, caustic soda can be added to ensure proper alkalinity before the nitrification/denitrification process. The water then flows to one of two Innovated barrier oxidation ditches. These ditches are the focus of this project, and one is illustrated in Figure 1. In an oxidation ditch, the pretreated wastewater mixes with a large internal recycle stream, and the mixed liquor is forced down a draft tube into which air is sparged. The effluent overflows to the clarifiers, where the activated sludge is separated and returned to the oxidizers.

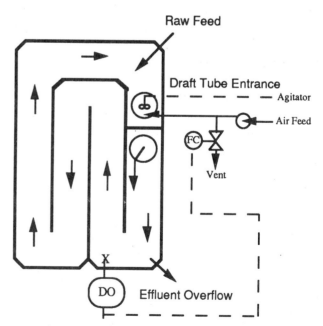

Figure 1: Oxidizer Process Flow Diagram

The nominal hold-up time of the oxidation ditch is 16-24 hours. The system is under a repeatable daily, weekly, and seasonal feed flow cycle. A sample daily flow variation is illustrated in Figure 2.

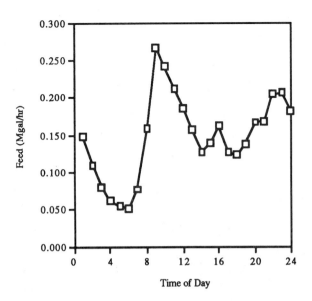

Figure 2: Typical Daily Influent Flow Variation

The plant is well instrumented, and it uses PLCs for the low-level control and has a distributed control system for higher levels of control. As illustrated in Figure 1, the air vent is manipulated by a simple controller to achieve a desired downstream dissolved oxygen (DO) set point. DO set point trajectories have been determined by plant experience, and changes are made to these trajectories as lab quality measurements dictate. A sample DO set point trajectory is listed in Table 1. The agitator speed is set to 100%, and it is not manipulated.

Table 1: Sample DO Set Point Trajectories		
Time Window		DO Set Point
Weekday	00:00–09:00	1.2
	09:00–11:00	1.4
	11:00–20:00	1.3
	20:00–24:00	1.4
Weekend	00:00–10:00	1.2
	10:00–22:00	1.4
	22:00–24:00	1.2

Modeling Technology

Dynamic system identification has been extensively studied in the past two decades [5]. Most methodologies assume a linear or linear-in-parameter structure, noise distributions, and an ideal experimental input signal. However biological systems are known to be highly nonlinear and multivariable, and the process noise and measurement noise typically are poorly known and do not follow a presumed probabilistic distribution. Also the process data tend to be highly correlated, and this may lead to ill-conditioning and parameter estimates with large variance.

In this work, nonlinear finite impulse response dynamic models are constructed using the Neural Network Partial Least Squares algorithm [3, 4]. This technique can rep-

resent nonlinear data mappings directly, and our laboratory has observed several cases in which the model estimates from this direct method are more accurate than classical methods in which the nonlinear transformation and the parameter identification steps are sequential.

This algorithm also handles the problems of over-parameterization and ill-conditioning. The NNPLS method projects the input space onto a number of one-dimensional latent structures. These structures can also be used to visualize the goodness-of-fit and to determine outliers.

The algorithm has a well defined implementation procedure, i.e. the model identification step determines all of the parameter values. Traditional neural network models have several design variables such as the number of input nodes and hidden nodes. The NNPLS algorithm explicitly determines these variables. The resultant NNPLS-NFIR model does not have any "tuning" parameters.

Open Loop Model Development

After some preliminary process improvements were completed, a controlled open-loop experiment was conducted on September 17, 1992 in a single ditch under an artificially high feed flow condition. Two manipulated variables, agitator speed (S) and air feed rate (F_A), were forced as shown in Figure 3. The wastewater feed flow variations represent normal process variations. The DO response is shown as the top curve in Figure 3.

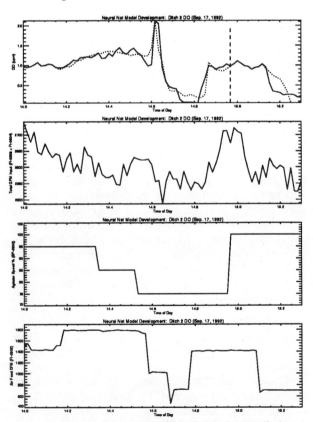

Figure 3: Comparison: Plant Data & Model Predictions
Top Curve is Output DO Data and Prediction
Bottom Three Curves are Input Variables (F_W, S, F_A)

These data were used to develop an open-loop process model. In this particular case, the desired outcome was a model of the effects of the agitator speed on the dissolved oxygen. As illustrated in Figure 4, all three input variables contribute to the DO variance. Qin [6] discussed the relative sensitivity ratio.

The outcome of the model identification is a structure of the form:

$$DO_k = NN(F_{W,k-1}, F_{W,k-2}, ... F_{W,k-10}, \qquad (1)$$
$$S_{k-1}, S_{k-2}, ..., S_{k-10},$$
$$F_{A,k-1}, F_{A,k-2}, ..., F_{A,k-10})$$

where

DO_k is the dissolved O_2 (ppm) at time t_k
NN is the neural network mapping
$F_{W,k}$ is the influent flow rate (gpm) at t_k
S_k is the agitator speed drive (%) at t_k
$F_{A,k}$ is the air flow rate (cfm) at t_k
t_k is the time (minutes)

The model predictions of the DO are compared with data in Figure 3. One can see that the model predictions are reasonable.

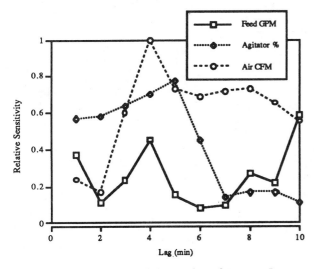

Figure 4: Relative Sensitivity Ratios of Process Inputs

Steady State Model Analysis

One can perform steady state model analysis of the nonlinear finite impulse response model quite easily. In this section, the model is used in its steady state form, i.e. all the dynamic input variables have constant values. The goal of this analysis is to optimize the steady state operating cost.

Figure 5 illustrates the model prediction of the steady state dissolved oxygen by varying the air flow and the agitator speed. These steady state predictions qualitatively agree with plant experience.

An operating cost model can be developed from plant characteristics. This model is based on the following data and assumptions.

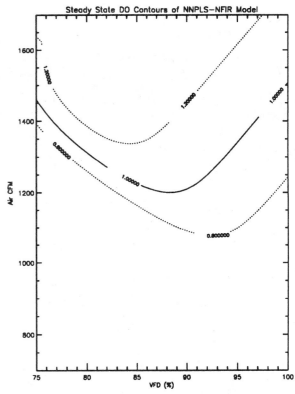

Figure 5: Steady State DO Contours

The agitator motor is 250 hp, and the speed is linearly related to the motor's electrical consumption.

There are two 60 hp air blowers. The second blower turns on when the air flow reaches 1400 cfm.

The electricity cost is $0.07 / kW-hr.

The cost model is expressed in [$/yr] as follows:

$$C = 457.26 \left(250\,S + 60 \left\{ \begin{array}{l} 1 \text{ if } F_A < 1400. \\ 2 \text{ otherwise} \end{array} \right\} \right) \qquad (2)$$

Figure 6 illustrates the operating costs in variables by which the process is manipulated, i.e. dissolved oxygen set point and agitator speed. In this case, the air feed rate is manipulated to achieve the desired dissolved oxygen set point.

This analysis suggests that there are significant cost savings which may be realized. For example, Figure 6 illustrates the savings which may be achieved by reducing the agitator speed from 100% to 80% for a dissolved oxygen set point of 1.2 ppm. Over an annual period, this represents a $ 50,000 (per ditch) savings.

The model is also useful in quantifying the benefits of additional capital improvements to the plant. For example, plant personnel have considered the idea of replacing the air blowers' constant speed drives with variable speed drives. In Figure 7, the operating costs of this upgrade are compared with the costs identified in the previous optimization. One can see that the cost savings of this upgrade are significant when compared to the current process, but the savings are a small improvement

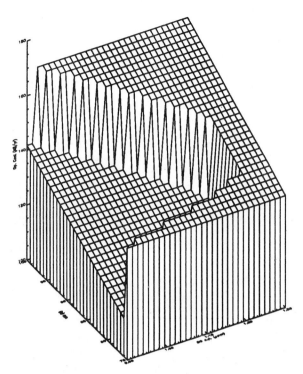

Figure 6: Steady State Operating Cost vs.
DO Set Points and Agitator Speed

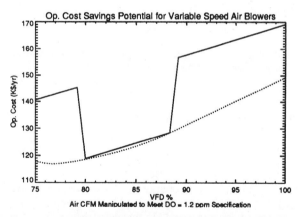

Figure 7: Operating Cost Savings Potential for Variable
Speed Air Blowers Upgrade

over the proposed new operation as discussed above.
The upgrade would save only an additional $2000/year.

Discussion

This modeling and analysis effort has convinced plant
personnel of the benefits of process modeling. More
work now remains in order to validate and implement
the proposed control strategy. During the first quarter of
1993, the Crofton plant is undergoing a major retrofit to
the oxidizer air distribution system; these changes should
significantly increase the plant's oxygen delivery capacity. When the capital expansion has been completed,
this model development and analysis effort will be repeated with new experimental data. A larger training
database will be collected, thus one should be able to develop a process model which spans a wider range of process conditions. With this process model and the operating cost objective function (Eq. 2), one could then implement an on-line steady state optimization to manipulate the agitator speed subject to the current dissolved
oxygen set point.

Future Work

Process experience suggests that this process is not difficult to control under normal operations, i.e. the manipulation of the air vent rapidly brings the dissolved oxygen
back to set point. Thus there is probably very little incentive for a traditional application of model predictive
control, i.e. a procedure in which the disturbances in the
prediction horizon are set to the present value. Possibly
there might be benefits from predictive control if the disturbance (raw wastewater feed) is described by a stocas-
tically-known trajectory. Then one could implement an
optimal feedforward control strategy based on "known"
future disturbances. This possibility is being investigated.

The area in which an optimal control approach may have
the greatest payback is the higher-level optimization, i.e.
the determination of the dissolved oxygen set point.
Currently the operating cost is not being optimized at
this level; i.e. the dissolved oxygen set points are set by
plant experience with daily feedback from lab quality
assays. With a mechanistic process model, one could
pose the constrained optimization problem of minimizing the operating cost via manipulation of the air vent
and agitator speed subject to the known product quality
specifications. One can envision scenarios in which it
may be cost effective to "store" dissolved oxygen, e.g.
during the summer, it may make sense to build up dissolved oxygen at night, when electricity is more available, for use in the high BOD morning surge.

Conclusions

General purpose nonlinear modeling tools have been
used to develop a reasonable nonlinear finite impulse
response model of an activated sludge oxidizer ditch.
This model has been used to suggest a new steady state
process control strategy for reducing operating costs.
This project awaits the completion of a plant retrofit to
validate and implement the proposed strategy.

While the results discussed above are specific to one
particular wastewater reclamation facility, the approach
is general. The modeling techniques used in this work
can be easily applied to other activated sludge processes.

Acknowlegements

The authors gratefully acknowlege the support of the
Crofton WRF personnel, Mr. Daniel R. Rumke and Mr.
Chip Yanaga; and finacial support from the Maryland
Sea Grant College grant R/P-77-PD under the NOAA/
Maryland Sea Grant omnibus grant, NA90AA-D-SG063.

Nomenclature

C — annual operating cost ($/yr)

DO_k — dissolved O_2 (ppm) at time t_k

$F_{A,k}$ — air flow rate (cfm) at t_k

$F_{W,k}$ — influent flow rate (gpm) at t_k

S_k — agitator speed drive (%) at t_k

t_k — time (min)

References

[1] Henze, M., C.P.L. Grady, Jr., W. Gujer, G. v. R. Marais, and T. Matsuo, "Activated Sludge Model No. 1," International Association on Water Pollution Research and Control, (1986).

[2] Su, H.T., T. J. McAvoy, and P. Werbos. "Long-Term Predictions of Chemical Processes Using Recurrent Neural Networks: A Parallel Training Approach," *I&EC Res.*, **31**, 1338-1352, (1992).

[3] Qin, S. Z. and T. J. McAvoy. "Building Nonlinear FIR Models Via a Neural Net PLS Approach for Long Term Prediction," AIChE 1992 Annual Meeting, Miami, FL, (1992).

[4] Qin, S. Z. and T. J. McAvoy. "Nonlinear PLS Modeling Using Neural Networks," *Comp. & Chem. Eng.*, **16** (4), 379-391, (1992).

[5] Box, G.E.P. and G. M. Jenkins. Time Series Analysis–Forecasting and Control. San Francisco: Holden Day, (1976).

[6] Qin, S. Z. "Integration and Comparison of Neural Networks and Conventional Modeling Techniques," Ph.D. Dissertation, University of Maryland, (1992).

Neural Network Control of a Piezo Tool Positioner

J.-H. Xu

Systems Research Laboratories
2800 Indian Ripple Road
Dayton, OHIO 45440

Abstract   The major technical challenge to the application of piezo crystal as an actuator is concerned with its hysteresis behavior. This would result in a nonlinear and multi-valued mapping between the actuator input and output and hence influence the desired control precision. This problem was solved by using closed-loop robust neural network control technology.

1. Introduction

For the design of an accurate cutting tool positioning system we need a stiff and precise actuator to orient the cutting tool in response to the profile measurement of a partially completed work piece. Various applications suggest that a piezo-electric crystal could be used as such an actuator, because of its stiffness and high resolution.

The major technical challenge to the application of piezo crystal as an actuator is concerned with its hysteresis behavior. This would result in a nonlinear and multi-valued mapping between the actuator input and output and hence influence the desired control precision. This problem was solved by using neural network technology.

Our approach was to globally linearize the piezo behavior by training a recurrent neural network to model the inverse of the piezo crystal and then connecting this trained network in series with the piezo. Due to the inevitable modelling error of the neural network [1], this might result in a quasi-linear system (a system with small nonlinearity) after neural network compensation instead of a linear one as we expected. For dealing with this problem, a robust regulator was designed for the compensated system which can guarantee both the feedback system stability and the desired precision in spite of certain small system nonlinearity.

For demonstrating our control strategy via computer simulation, we used a recurrent neural network trained using operation data to model the piezo actuator as a dynamic system. This aimed to get rid of the multi-valued mapping between the piezo input and output. The robust neural control strategy described above was realized with C source code on an IBM PC utilizing an ANZA board containing a neuro-coprocessor for speeding the calculation. The control concept was studied via a simulation designed to illustrate the performance of the tool position control system. With a positioning error 0.00082 degree, our tool position control system has satisfied the 5 arc minute (0.08333 degree) accuracy requirement.

2. Modelling of Piezo Translator Using Neural Network

Piezo translators are electrically activated units, which, without rotating parts, change their dimensions by utilizing only the piezoelectric effect. Depending on the external applied voltage, a piezo translator can change its length from a fraction of micron up to the millimeter range. The maximum expansion, the stiffness, as well as the force a piezo translator is capable of exerting, depends on the construction of the element. They can be optimized for almost every application. The resolution of a piezo element is theoretically unlimited, and depends merely upon the stability of the applied voltage. However, its practical application has been greatly constrained by its hysteresis behavior.

As with magnetic materials, hysteresis also occurs between the applied voltage and expansion of piezo translator. A plot of the input and output data we collected from a tool-actuator assembly model built using a piezo translator is shown in Figure 2.1. Here we can see that the piezo expansion (converted to tool angle by the tool assembly) vs. applied voltage is not a straight line, but a slightly bent curve which implies the nonlinearity. Another point we can see is that the map between the piezo expansion and applied voltage is a multi-valued function, because the same operating voltage can result in different expansions depending on what kind of voltage was applied previously. The size of the hysteresis depends on the amplitude of the voltage change. Obviously, the hysteresis behavior will reduce the positioning precision of the piezo actuator.

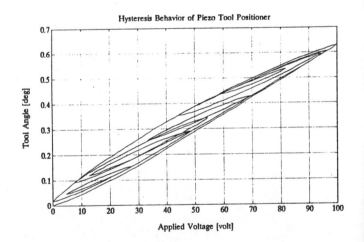

Figure 2.1 Hysteresis Characteristics of Piezo

Since our objective for this approach was to verify the neural network positioning idea via a simulation, it was necessary to develop a mathematical model of the piezo element, i.e. we were to find out the mathematical relation between the piezo expansion and the applied voltage.

With the multi-valued mapping behavior, it has been impossible to obtain the required control precision with a piezo actuator, so the technique was rendered impractical. Fortunately, a solution comes from the observation which shows that the next tool angular position (piezo expansion) $A(k+1)$ depends only on the present angular position $A(k)$, present applied voltage $u(k)$ and the next applied voltage $u(k+1)$. Therefore we can form a single-valued mapping between measurements [u(k), A(k), u(k+1)] and A(k+1) as a function of the internal model of the piezo translator (Figure 2.2, where Z^{-1} denotes a delay operator). Note that the number of the internal model inputs is three.

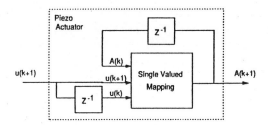

Figure 2.2 Single-Valued Internal Model of Piezo

It has been shown by Hecht-Nielsen [1] that any nonlinear map can be approximated with a neural network to any predefined degree. This result can be utilized to model the piezo translator which is now a single-valued process but still nonlinear. Using the input and output data collected from a tool-actuator assembly model built using a piezo translator, we successfully trained a neural network model using NeuralWorks Professional II Plus software package. This neural network model has 3 inputs, 1 output and 2 hidden layers with 10 neurons on the first hidden layer and 5 on the second. The RMS modelling error is less than 0.003. This neural model is in C source code and will be used to represent the real piezo actuator in the following study and simulation. A comparison of the behavior of the neural network model and the real piezo translator is shown in Figure 2.3.

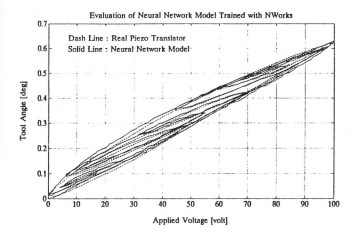

Figure 2.3 Comparison of Neural Model and Piezo Translator

Note that the accuracy of a neural network model depends strongly on the network structure (e.g., number of hidden layers, number of neurons, connection between neurons), sort of neuron transfer functions (e.g., sigmoid, tanh, sin), algorithms for training, initial values of weights, and so on. We experimented with many different combinations of parameters until we found this model.

3. Neural Control of Tool Positioning Actuator

3.1   Open-Loop Neural Inverse Control

Conventional control of a physical system typically takes advantage of a priori information about the system, for example, the

system transfer function. The goal of the control problem is to determine an input which when applied will elicit the desired output. In the open-loop control case the known (or assumed) transfer function is simply inverted and used to preprocess the desired output to produce a set of inputs to the system to make it behave in a manner desired. This inverted transfer function is the controller.

As mentioned before, a neural network can be used to model any nonlinear transfer function, therefore, it can be used as well to model the inverse of the system transfer function and hence to serve as an open-loop controller. The application of this idea to our tool positioning problem leads to the following block diagrams for a neural network inverse controller (Figure 3.1) and for an open-loop neural network inverse control system (Figure 3.2).

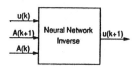

Figure 3.1 Neural Network Inverse Controller

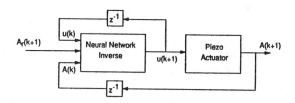

Figure 3.2 Open-Loop Neural Network Inverse Control

In this case and also in the following study and simulation, the neural network controller was initially trained on an IBM PC with the help of ANZA, a general purpose neuro-coprocessor made by HNC Inc., and was realized in C source code. The ANZA board can operate in parallel with the host computer and acts to accelerate the execution of neural networks, hence it should be a good tool for real time neural control. The modeling accuracy of the neural network inverse controller is shown in Figure 3.3, and the simulation of neural inverse control is shown in Figure 3.4.

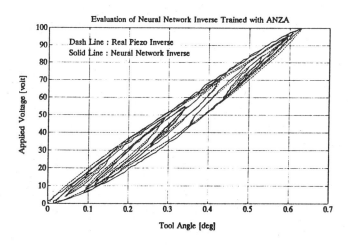

Figure 3.3 Modeling of Neural Network Inverse Controller

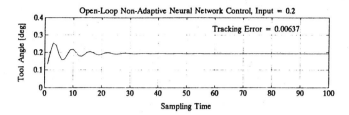

Figure 3.4 Simulation of Neural Inverse Control

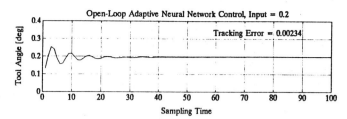

Figure 3.6 Simulation of Adaptive Neural Inverse Control

3.2 *Open-Loop Adaptive Neural Control*

Of course the trouble with the open-loop neural inverse control becomes evident when the system transfer function is either uncertain or time-variant, or a precise inverse of the transfer function cannot be found because of computation difficulties. All these problems may happen in our neural network tool position control, and hence an alternative is required which should be able to adapt to these cases. To solve the problem we used Adaptive Neural Inverse Control strategy (see Figure 3.5) to continually monitor the piezo actuator and use the measurements collected on-line from the piezo actuator to update the inverse transfer function (re-train) so that the real angular position A(k) can follow the desired angular position $A_r(k)$.

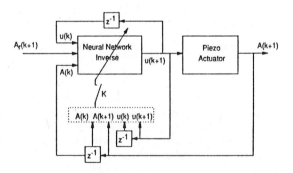

Figure 3.5 Open-Loop Adaptive Neural Inverse Controller

The desired tool position is given by the operator. The current tool position and applied voltage can be measured by the capacitance probe and voltage sensor, respectively. The desired angle A_r drives the initially trained neural inverse controller, and the output of the neural controller activates the piezo actuator. Both the control signal u(k) and the corresponding response A(k) of the piezo actuator are collected and used as input-output pairs to re-train the neural network for improving the precision of the inverse of piezo actuator. These input-output pairs allow modification to be made to the neural network controller which in turn will provide better inputs to the piezo actuator even if its behavior may change. In practice this training is done continuously as the system is running so that the neural network can always represent the current inverse transfer function of the piezo actuator. The adaptation frequency can be controlled by a switch K in Figure 3.4. The simulation result for adaptive neural inverse control is shown in Figure 3.6.

It can be seen in Figure 3.4 and Figure 3.6 that both control strategies worked well. However, the adaptive control strategy obtained better accuracy than the non-adaptive neural control with a positioning error of 0.00234 degree as opposed to 0.00637 degree. We believe that the observed effect was due to the fact that the adaptive neural controller was adjusted automatically using the on-line information [2] while the non-adaptive one was not. This means that in the non-adaptive case, the modelling error of the neural network resulting from the initial training stage never changed whereas the adaptive network continued to improve its performance with experience. Nevertheless, both control strategies were much better than the 5 arc minute (0.08333 degree) accuracy requirement.

Note that in the simulation above we only showed the positive adjustment of the cutting tool angle (0.0 - 0.6 degree). Both the positive and negative adjustment can be obtained if we set A_r = 0.3 degree for the normal operation. The neural control system might dynamically respond differently when initialized with a different applied voltage, because the system is nonlinear.

3.3 *Closed-Loop Neural Control*

As discussed in Section 3.1 and Section 3.2, the problem with open-loop neural control, no matter adaptive or non-adaptive, is that an exact inverse of the transfer function can never be found because of the modelling error of neural network. This will in general degrade any tracking control system (the system output is required to follow the system input) by the amount of modelling error that remains.

Actually, using the open-loop neural inverse control scheme as shown in Figure 3.2, we do not get a completely linear output from the inverse controller because of residual modelling error, but we get a neural network compensated quasi-linear system with its input-output behavior shown in Figure 3.7. Mathematically this small nonlinearity may be expressed as $A = (1 + \delta) \times A_r$, where δ is unknown, but $(1 + \delta) \times A_r$ is bounded inside the sector with angle α. It is obvious from Figure 3.7 that only with certain amplitude of A_r can we have A equal to A_r (where $\delta = 0$). This is not desired if we would like the tool angle be continuously adjustable.

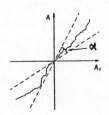

Figure 3.7 Input-Output Behavior of Neural Inverse Control

To improve the open-loop neural inverse control, we introduce here the concept of closed-loop robust neural control (see Figure 3.8). The basic idea is to compare the desired Angle A$_r$ and the real measured angle A and then use the error signal to activate a robust regulator which in turn generates a control signal u for the compensated quasi-linear system to get rid of the tracking error [3]. Note that the real controller consists of the neural network inverse and the robust regulator. The function of a regulator is to make the system output follow the given system input. A controller is robust if it can, without changing itself during the control procedure, maintain certain system performances in spite of some uncertainties. Using the robust regulator, we expected to guarantee bounded performance of the system without the necessity of re-training the neural network inverse controller. Here the uncertainty considered is the unknown nonlinearity δ, the small nonlinearity remaining after the action of the neural network inverse compensator.

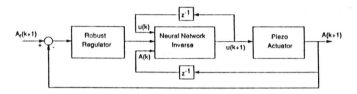

Figure 3.8 Closed-Loop Robust Neural Control

Theoretically, it is still unknown how to design such a robust regulator for handling nonlinear uncertainty. However, using the servo-control idea and through trial and error, we designed a PI controller

$$G_c(s) = 0.03 + 0.6 \times \frac{1}{s}$$

to serve as the desired regulator. Here the integral part is to guarantee the regulation (tracking error tends toward zero as time increases) and the proportional part is to increase the stability of the closed-loop system. The simulation of the closed-loop robust neural control system is shown in Figure 3.9.

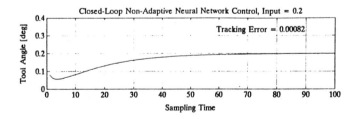

Figure 3.9 Simulation of Closed-Loop Robust Neural Control

It can be seen in Figure 3.9 that the closed-loop robust neural control resulted in a positioning error 0.00082 degree. This control precision is already far beyond the 5 arc minute (0.08333 degree) accuracy requirement.

As in the open-loop case, we can also have a closed-loop adaptive neural control system if the neural network inverse is re-trained during the control procedure.

4. Conclusion

The major technical challenge to the application of piezo crystal as an actuator is concerned with its hysteresis behavior. This would result in a nonlinear and multi-valued mapping between the actuator input and output and hence influence the desired control precision. This problem was solved by using closed-loop robust neural network control technology.

Our approach was to globally linearize the piezo behavior by training a recurrent neural network to model the inverse of the piezo crystal and then connecting this trained network in series with the piezo. Due to the inevitable modelling error of the neural network [1], this might result in a quasi-linear system (a system with small nonlinearity) after neural network compensation instead of a linear one as we expected. For dealing with this problem, a robust regulator was designed for the compensated system which can guarantee both the feedback system stability and the desired precision in spite of certain small system nonlinearity.

For demonstrating our control strategy via computer simulation, we used a recurrent neural network trained using operation data to model the piezo actuator as a dynamic system. This aimed to get rid of the multi-valued mapping between the piezo input and output. The robust neural control strategy described above was realized with C source code on an IBM PC utilizing an ANZA board containing a neuro-coprocessor for speeding the calculation. The control concept was studied via a simulation designed to illustrate the performance of the tool position control system. With a positioning error 0.00082 degree, our tool position control system has satisfied the 5 arc minute (0.08333 degree) accuracy requirement.

Acknowledgement

The author would like to thank Dr. Don Birx at Systems Research Laboratories, Mr. James Johnson at Netrologic Inc. and Dennis Locke at Mechanical Technology Inc. for their support and help with this work. Of course, the generous support of US National Science Foundation is greatly appreciated.

References

[1] R. Hecht-Nielsen, "Neurocomputing", Addison-Wesley Publishing Company, 1991.

[2] K.S. Narendra and A.M. Annaswamy, "Stable Adaptive Systems", Englewood Cliffs, NJ: Prentice-Hall, 1989.

[3] J.-H. Xu, "Synthesis of H∞-Optimal Robust Regulator for Linear Systems", Ph.D. Dissertation at Swiss Federal Institute of Technology (ETH), Zurich, 1989.

Chapter 3
Robotic Control

The promise of robots able to replace menial, tedious, or dangerous human tasks has motivated many engineers. Neural networks are being applied to some of the difficult aspects of robotics, and the result has led to an advancement in the field on several fronts. This chapter includes eight papers that address different aspects of robotic control. In **Paper 3.1**, the combination (or fusion) of multiple data sources to create an internal representation is achieved using the multilayer perceptron (MLP) neural network. The control of a deburring robot using an MLP neural network is described in **Paper 3.2**. The next two papers apply neural networks to quadraped and biped robot locomotion. **Paper 3.3** uses a combination of reinforcement learning, adaptive resonance theory, and temporal difference learning to create a distributed adaptive control system for quadraped robots. **Paper 3.4** uses a neuro oscillator to generate trajectories for a biped robot. The last four papers in this chapter focus on the development of neural network-based controllers for robotic arms and robotic hands. **Paper 3.5** describes the structure and stability of radial basis function and MLP neural networks for a general serial-link robot arm. **Paper 3.6** explores the application of neural networks to position and differential kinematic control of robot manipulators. **Paper 3.7** applies recurrent neural networks to a flexible space manipulator. **Paper 3.8** applies the combination of fuzzy sets and neural networks to robotic hand control.

Chapter 3: *Robotic Control*

A Sensory Information Processing System
Using Neural Networks *
—Three-Dimensional Object Recognition with Sensorimotor Fusion—

D. Masumoto, T. Kimoto, and S. Nagata

Open Systems Division, Fujitsu Limited,

1015 Kamikodanaka Nakahara-ku, Kawasaki 211, Japan

Abstract— In order to carry out actions particular to the goals, a robot processes sensory information, that is, it transforms sensed data to internal representation. In some cases, however, the robot's internal representation cannot be determined uniquely from the sensed data. We propose an architecture for sensory information processing system that overcomes this ill-posed problem. The system uses an artificial neural network which was trained to transform internal representation to sensory data. Applying an iterative scheme to the network, the unique internal representation can be determined. The scheme is comparing the network's output (sensory data) with the sensed data and by backpropagating the difference through the layers, updating an input (internal representation) which could have created the applied output (sensed data) based on gradient descent method. Besides, by predicting the resulting state based on the intention of the system's own movement, accuracy and speed of sensory information processing can be improved. We also show simulation results for three-dimensional object recognition.

I. Introduction

In order to carry out actions particular to the goals, a robot processes sensory information, that is, it transforms sensed data to an internal representation. Environmental information obtained by a sensor is limited and the robot may lack the information required for uniquely transforming the sensed data [1]. In addition, sensed data often contain deviations, distortion, or some noise.

When the robot lacks the required information and the sensed data is not accurate, one unavoidable consequence of sensory information processing is that the robot's internal representation cannot be determined uniquely from the sensed data. In other words, the robot's internal representation confounds external world states. If we used a multilayered neural network to process sensory information directly, the network would learn different outputs for identical input and would not converge.

On the other hand, the inverse transformation, that is, the transformation from internal representation to sensory data, can be uniquely done. The inverse transformation can thus be captured by a multilayered neural network with error backpropagation learning [2].

Applying an iterative scheme to the network, the proposed sensory information processing system uniquely transforms sensed data to internal representation.

II. Sensory Information Processing System

A. Architecture

The system has a top-down model and a prediction model (Figure 1).

The top-down model is a multilayered neural network which was trained to transform internal representation to sensory data. When an initial value of internal representation is given in some way, the network transforms the value to sensory data. It then calculates the difference between the sensory data and the actually sensed data. By repeating backpropagation of the difference and update of the internal representation, we can search for an internal representation that is more consistent with actual observation.

When the initial value is in the basin of attraction for the solution, the value converges to the solution. Otherwise the value may converge into a local minimum or diverge or oscillate. To overcome this problem, the system refers to the motor command for predicting its own movement and can use it for sensory information processing.

*This study was performed partially through Special Coordination Funds of the Science and Technology Agency of the Japanese Government.

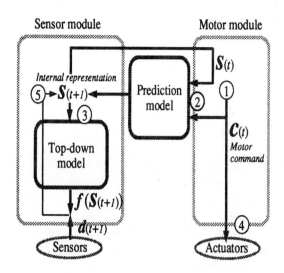

Figure 1: System diagram

When the actuator executes a motor command, the prediction model, can be a multilayered neural network, predicts the resulting state based on the current internal representation and the motor command. The top-down model uses the prediction as an initial value to improve accuracy and speed. This procedure is an instance of sensorimotor fusion [3].

The illustration in Figure 1 explains the actions of the system.

1. The motor module orders a motor command $c(t)$ based on the intended motion.

2. Enter the internal representation $s(t)$ and a copy of the motor command $c(t)$ into the prediction model.

3. Enter the predicted internal representation $s(t + 1)$ to be output from the prediction model as an initial value into the top-down model.

4. The motor module executes the motor command $c(t)$ and activates the actuator.

5. Calculate the difference between the sensory data $f(s(t + 1))$ output from the top-down model and the actually sensed data $d(t + 1)$. Update the internal representation to minimize the difference with an iterative scheme.

Repeating this procedure, the system processes sensory

information while moving.

B. Iterative Scheme

The illustration in Figure 2 explains the iterative scheme adopted by the model.

1. Assume an initial value of internal representation s is given in some way and enter the value into the network.

2. Calculate the sum of squared errors between $f(s)$ output from the network and the presented data d.

$$U(s, d) = \sum_j \{f_j(s) - d_j\}^2 \qquad (1)$$

3. If $U(s, d)$ is greater than a constant ϵ, update the internal representation s to minimize $U(s, d)$ (gradient descent method).

$$s_i(t + \triangle t) = s_i(t) - K \frac{\partial U(s, d)}{\partial s_i} \qquad (2)$$

where K is a constant.
Considering the second term on the right,

$$\frac{\partial U(s, d)}{\partial s_i} = 2 \sum_j \{f_j(s) - d_j\} \frac{\partial f_j(s)}{\partial s_i} . \qquad (3)$$

The partial derivative on the right indicates how the data $f_j(s)$ changes as a s_i varies. That is, it represents the degree to which a change in the value of one input layer unit(i) influences the change in the output value of output layer unit(j). This influence can be calculated as follows.

This yields

$$
\begin{aligned}
\frac{\partial f_j(s)}{\partial s_i} &= \frac{df_j}{dF_j} \frac{\partial F_j}{\partial s_i} \\
&= \sigma'(F_j) \sum_k v_{jk} \frac{\partial h_k}{\partial s_i} \\
&= \sigma'(F_j) \sum_k v_{jk} \sigma'(H_k) \frac{\partial H_k}{\partial s_i} \\
&= \sigma'(F_j) \sum_k v_{jk} \sigma'(H_k) w_{ki} \qquad (4)
\end{aligned}
$$

$$\frac{\partial U(s, d)}{\partial s_i} = 2 \sum_j \{f_j - d_j\} \sigma'(F_j) \sum_k v_{jk} \sigma'(H_k) w_{ki} .$$

$$(5)$$

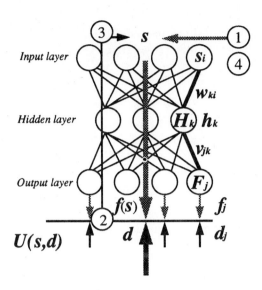

Figure 2: The iterative scheme

s_i: Input layer unit i's value,

w_{ki}: Connection weight between input layer unit i and hidden layer unit k,

$H_k = \sum_i w_{ki}s_i$: Hidden layer unit k's value,
$h_k = \sigma(H_k)$: Output value from hidden layer unit k, (σ is an I/O function of unit),

v_{jk}: Connection weight between hidden layer unit k and output layer unit j,

$F_j = \sum_k v_{jk}h_k$: Output layer unit j's value,
$f_j = \sigma(F_j)$: Output value from output unit j.

4. Enter the updated value s into the top-down model and go back to step 2.

Repeating this process, we can search for an input which could have created the presented data.

III. Experiments and Results

To verify the system, we experimented with three-dimensional object recognition on the basis of their shape [4].

The object is projected on a camera as a series of feature points. The coordinates (x_i, y_i) on the projection image are regarded as sensed data and the object attitude (θ_s, ϕ_s) with respect to the camera is regarded as internal representation.

The recognition problem is to decide whether the shape of the object is the same as that of the known one and, if so, to identify the object attitude with respect to the camera.

The majority of approaches to this problem employ 3-D models of objects, but the learning of 3-D models requires a separate process to recover the 3-D structure of objects [5] [6].

Abu-Mostafa and Pslatis [7] used 2-D viewer-centered representations for the recognition problem. They developed a neural network that stores a large number of observed views of objects. The network was used as associative memories. Given a new view, it retrieves the stored representation which most colsely resembles it. The system is limited in its ability by the notion of similarity used in associative momories.

We suggest a different kind of representations to model the objects. An object is modeled by a set of its perspective views.

Such a representation was used by Poggio and Edelman [8] to develop a network that recognizes objets using radial basis functions (RBFs) and was used by Ullman and Basri [9] to build a linear operator that can distinguish views of a specific object from views of other objects.

A. Setup

As shown in Figure 3, the end of a shaft is fixed at the origin of the world coordinate system. A camera is mounted at the top of the shaft. The shaft attitude can be identified by $\theta_a (0 \le \theta_a < 360 \deg)$ and $\phi_a (0 \le \phi_a < 180 \deg)$. The command to change the $\triangle\theta_a$, $\triangle\phi_a$ angles is given as a motor command.

A.1. Top-down model

Creating a training set

1. Define the position of the object within the range of the camera. Assume the four points can be viewed from any viewpoint and that the object is defined by the four points $p_0 = (1, -1, 2), p_1 = (2, -1, -1), p_2 = (-1, -1, -2), p_3 = (1, 2, 1)$.

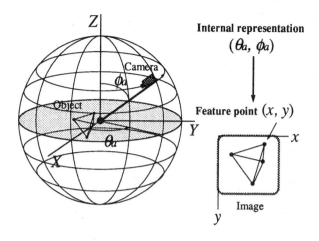

Figure 3: The setup of the experimental system

2. Divide the sphere into meshes for every 30 degrees of θ_a and ϕ_a. Place viewpoints at the intersection points ($12 \times 6 = 72$). In this setup, we can define the object attitude with respect to the camera as the corresponding shaft attitude. That is, $\theta_s = \theta_a$, $\phi_s = \phi_a$.

3. From each viewpoint, measure the coordinates of the four feature points to be projected onto the image. A training set is composed of the attitude and the coordinates pairs.

Network architecture We use a three-layered neural network for the top-down model.

The input layer has four units corresponding to $cos\theta_s$, $sin\theta_s$, $cos\phi_s$ and $sin\phi_s$ which represent the object attitude. The hidden layer has fifteen units. The output layer has eight units corresponding to the image coordinates $(x_0, y_0), (x_1, y_1), (x_2, y_2), (x_3, y_3)$.

Training We train the network until the maximum error in the training sets is less than 3%.

A.2. Prediction model

In this setup, we can assume $\theta_s(t+1) = \theta_s(t) + \triangle\theta_a$ and $\phi_s(t+1) = \phi_s(t) + \triangle\phi_a$. In this experiment, we use these formulas as the prediction model.

B. Recognition

The recognition experiment procedure is indicated below.

1. Enter $cos\theta_s, sin\theta_s, cos\phi_s$ and $sin\phi_s = 0$ as input unit initial values into the trained top-down model ($t = 0$).

2. Assign the coordinates of the feature points to the output of the trained top-down model.

3. Using the above mentioned iterative scheme($K = 0.8$), we update these input values until the maximum output error among the proposed sets is less the 1% or until they have been updated one thousand times.

4. The motor control module orders the motor command $\triangle\theta_a = 30(deg), \triangle\phi_a = 0(deg)$ and activates the actuator. That is, $\theta_a(t+1) = \theta_a(t) + 30(deg)$ and $\phi_a(t+1) = \phi_a(t)$.

5. The prediction model predicts the next $\theta_s(t+1), \phi_s(t+1)$. Enter the value as an initial value into the top-down model.

6. Go back to step 2 and add 1 to t.

B.1. Data Sets

We prepared four data sets for the evaluation.

- Training set: divide the sphere into meshes for every 30 degrees of θ_a and ϕ_a. Viewpoints are placed at the intersection points($12 \times 6 = 72$).

- Test set: meshes set at every 7.5 degrees. Viewpoints ($48 \times 24 = 1152$).

- Hidden point set: We hide a point by not backpropagating from the output unit corresponding to the point $(1, -1, 2)$. Meshes set at every 7.5 degrees. Viewpoints ($48 \times 24 = 1152$).

- Unknown object set: the feature point $p_4 = (1, 2, 1)$ of the known object is exchanged with $(-1, 2, -1)$. Meshes are set at every 7.5degrees. Viewpoints ($48 \times 24 = 1152$).

B.2. Generalization

We evaluate generalization performance by the following criteria.

1) How accurately did the system identify the object attitude which is not in the training set?

2) How accurately did the system identify the object attitude that has a hidden feature point?

Figure 4 shows the percentage of the set in which an accuracy of 3.75 degrees or less was achieved (attitude identification rate).

As is suggested from the results of this experiment, almost the same attitude identification rate can be achieved

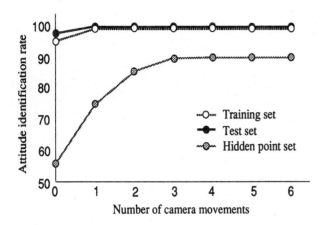

Figure 4: Attitude identification rate

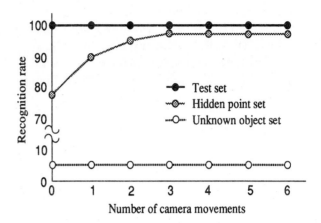

Figure 6: Recognition rate

shows the percentage of the set in which the sum of the squared errors is smaller than 0.01 after iterations. We assume that this percentage indicates the recognition rate.

The results of this experiment suggests that the system can reject unknown object.

IV. CONCLUSION

We have proposed a sensory information processing system that can solve the ill-posed problem of sensory information processing.

The estimated generalization performance indicates that we can improve accuracy and speed of the sensory information processing with sensorimotor fusion. The estimated discrimination performance indicates that the system can identify unknown objects by observation from multiple viewpoints.

We will experiment with the system for adaptation to more realistic environments.

Acknowledgment.

Thanks are due to Prof. Masatoshi Ishikawa (Univ. of Tokyo) for his insightful discussions.

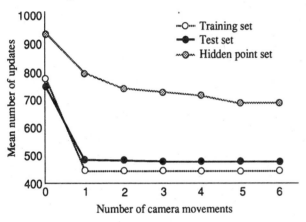

Figure 5: Mean number of updates

for the test set as for the training set. While moving, we can improve accuracy of the sensory information processing. This advantage is common to each of the sets. It is especially effective for the set in which the object has a hidden feature point.

B.3. Speed

We evaluate recognition speed by the mean number of update with the iterative scheme. Simulation results are presented in Figure 5.

While moving, we can improve speed of the sensory information processing.

B.4. Discrimination

We evaluate discrimination performance based on how accurately the system can decide whether the shape of the object is the same as that of the known one. Figure 6

REFERENCES

[1] J. J. Clark and A. L. Yuille, "Data Fusion for Sensory Information Processing Systems," Kluwer Academic Publishers (1991).

[2] D. E. Rumelhart, G. E. Hinton, and R. J. Williams, "Learning Internal Representations by Error Propagation," eds. D. E. Rumelhart and J. L. McClelland, Parallel distributed processing: Explorations in the microstructure of cognition, 1, chap. 8, MIT Press (1986).

[3] D. Masumoto, T. Kimoto, and S. Nagata, "A neural network approach to sensorimotor fusion - Intentional sensing for recognizing three-dimensional objects," In Proceedings of the IMACS/SICE International Symposium on Robotics, Mechatronics and Manufacturing Systems '92 Kobe, 1105-1110 (1992).

[4] S. Ullman, "Aligning pictorial descriptions: An approach to object recognition," *Cognition*, 32 193-254 (1989).

[5] T. J. Fan, G. Medioni, and R. Nevatia, "Recognizing 3-D objects using Surface Descriptions," In *Proceedings of IEEE 2nd International Conference on Computer Vision*, 474-481 (1988).

[6] W. E. L. Grimson and T. Lozano-Pérez, "Localizing Overlapping Parts by Searching the Interpretation Tree," *IEEE Transactions on Pattern Analysis and Machine Intelligence*, Vol. 9, No. 4, 469-482 (1987).

[7] Y. S. Abu-Mostafa and D. Pslatis, "Optical neural computing," *Scientific American*, 256, 66-73 (1987).

[8] T. Poggio and S. Edelman, "A network that learns to recognize three-dimensional objects," *Nature*, 343 263-266 (1990).

[9] S. Ullman and R. Basri, "Recognition by Linear Combinations of Models," *IEEE Transactions on Pattern Analysis and Machine Intelligence*, Vol. 13, No. 10, 992-1006 (1991).

Teaching and Learning of Deburring Robots Using Neural Networks

Sheng Liu   Haruhiko Asada

Center for Information-Driven Mechanical Systems
Department of Mechanical Engineering
Massachusetts Institute of Technology

Abstract

This paper describes a method for applying an advanced robot adaptive control to manufacturing processes. The method does not require complex programming, but the robot control system is easily constructed with human teaching data, and is refined automatically through a learning process using neural networks. The techniques are developed for deburring robots, but they can be extended to other manufacturing tasks.

First, the teaching method for constructing a sensor-based, task-level adaptive control system is briefly described. Based on demonstration data acquired from a human, adaptive control laws that elucidate human motions are identified and stored in a multi-layer neural network. At the same time, the resultant task performance is evaluated, and the relationship between the human actions and the performance index is stored in the second neural network. Based on the initial teaching data, the robot begins to perform a task. While performing a task repeatedly, the robot acquires additional data and improves its performance. Errors with respect to the performance index are propagated through the second network to modify the adaptive control law represented by the first network. This allows the robot further improve its performance and excel the human operator who has provided the initial teaching data. A proof-of-concept demonstration and simulation are presented at the end.

1   Introduction

Robotics has not been exploited successfully in manufacturing, despite tremendous research efforts and potential needs in industries. It is said that today's robots are still limited in performance. They need costly peripheral devices such as jigs, fixtures, positioners, and part feeders even for performing simple tasks. Advanced robot systems with visions and force sensors have been used in some industries, but have not been deployed in a large scale. A great amount of investment capital is required not merely for the equipment itself but for engineering, maintenance, and job training associated with the deployment. In most cases, it is not justifiable to use complex robot systems due to the limited utility. To overcome this difficulty, we need to be concerned with how robots are used in industries and what are stumbling blocks in the deployment of the technology.

In this paper, we will develop techniques to alleviate difficulties in using robots and deploying advanced technologies in the real manufacturing environment. Specifically, we will address: (1) an effective teaching method for communicating human intentions, strategies and skills to robots, and (2) a learning method for tuning and refining control strategies without human assistance. We will develop an integrated teaching and learning method and apply the method to sensor-based deburring robots. Our goal is to develop an effective tool and aids that will allow factory floor personnel to easily comprehend and effectively use sophisticated robots.

For successful deployment of robotics, active participation and cooperation by factory floor personnel are indispensable. They are the individuals who know the manufacturing process and are the archives of useful knowledge. If the robots can acquire their expertise and skills, the utility and performance of the robots will increase significantly. In this paper we will develop a new type of teaching-by-showing method using a neural network. Neural networks allow us to code human expertise and skills through data acquired from human teaching operations. This method does not require explicit, formal programming, nevertheless, necessary information about human intentions and skills can be transferred effectively from the human to a robot. This teaching method makes it much easier for humans to communicate with the robots.

Another critical aspect in improving the utility of manufacturing robots is to reduce time and effort required for debugging, tuning and maintenance, all the jobs other than the initial programming. In particular, fine tuning and adjustment at start-ups and changeovers are time consuming and labor intensive tasks.

117

Effective methods are necessary for eliminating this problem. In this paper, we will also explore a learning method in order to reduce the fine tuning and adjustment operations. Learning allows a robot to improve its performance based on past experience and supplement incomplete *a priori* knowledge. Although a robot starts up a given task with limited knowledge provided by a human, it will be able to perform the task satisfactorily, if the robot can correct and amend the original program. As tasks become complicated, it is difficult to generate complete control programs in the off-line teaching and programming stage. It requires substantial modifications, corrections and fine tuning after the initial programming is completed. The elimination or reduction of these labor intensive tasks leads to a significant improvement in productivity and reliability.

In this paper we will develop an effective method for integrating teaching and learning by using neural networks. The method will be developed for deburring robots as a case study. The basic concept, however, can be applied to other types of tasks without difficulty.

2 Off-Line Teaching of Human Skills to Deburring Robots

Teaching is to communicate human intentions and task strategies to robots. For simple tasks, teaching is simply to provide a series of reference inputs, mostly positional trajectories, for the robot to follow. As for more complex tasks such as assembly and grinding, reference trajectories alone are not sufficient. Task goals and control strategies for achieving the goal must be taught. It is, however, difficult for factory workers and technicians to formulate control strategies and code them to robot command lines. It is necessary to assist them in expressing their expertise and skills and translating them into control strategies that are readily executable for robots.

To communicate with robots in a natural manner, the technique broadly termed "teaching by showing" is an effective method that fits the manufacturing environment. For force-controlled robots, several groups have developed techniques for teaching force and motion trajectories to robots, e.g. [Asada and Hanafusa, 1979], [Aramaki, 1983], [Hirzinger and Heindl, 1983], and [Deschutter and Leysen, 1987]. In these works, the force and motion trajectories are known prior to the teaching, and modification of these trajectories during playback is not needed. [Liu and Asada, 1992] developed a high level control strategy which includes on-line modification of force/motion trajectories by translating human skills to robots through the observation of human demonstrations. The demonstration data is analyzed to extract useful control strategies and build

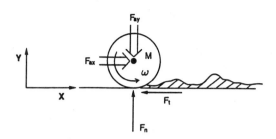

Figure 1: Schematic diagram of a deburring process

a task-level adaptive control system based on the extracted strategies. It is a direct method to communicate with robots, and does not need detail, formal coding of task strategies. In this paper, we will extend this method to the integration of teaching/learning by incorporating off-line teaching into on-line learning. The method will be developed for a deburring task again. Before we address the learning method, the deburring task and the basic teaching method are first described below.

Figure 1 shows a schematic diagram of a deburring process on a two dimensional plane, where the x-axis is aligned with the workpiece surface. In the present work, we study deburring on a workpiece with a straight line contour, while burr size and hardness may change along the contour. The task goal of a deburring system is to remove excess material from a workpiece and to generate a smooth surface. For removing burrs we need to take into account the wear of tools and thermal effects. We need a strategy to achieve the goal in an appropriate way. To describe the strategy, the two essential control parameters that affect the overall performance are the tool feedrate in the tangential direction and the tool stiffness in the normal direction, that is, the equivalent stiffness in the normal direction with which the tool is held. The tool feedrate relates directly to the material removal rate, while the tool stiffness in the normal direction maintains a desirable depth of cut and avoids chattering. A human expert in deburring can effectively combine an appropriate tool feedrate with a tool holding stiffness to remove all excess material and generate a fine surface finish without damaging the tool and the workpiece. Let V_o denote a tool feedrate selected by a human for some burr characteristics. The corresponding tool holding stiffness can be expressed as

$$k_y y + F_o = F_n \qquad (1)$$

where k_y is the stiffness coefficient, y is the tool displacement in the normal direction, F_o is a reference normal force, and F_n is the reaction force in the normal direction, as shown in the figure.

For regulating the tool feedrate and tool stiffness,

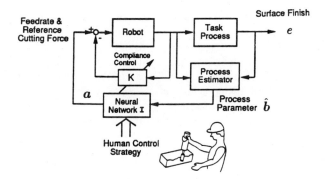

Figure 2: Teaching human skills to robot. The adaptive compliance-feedrate controller is constructed based on human teaching data.

the following control laws are considered:

$$
\begin{aligned}
F_{ax} &= b_x(V_o - \dot{x}) &\qquad(2)\\
F_{ay} &= b_y\dot{y} + k_y y + F_o &\qquad(3)
\end{aligned}
$$

where F_{ax} and F_{ay} are actuator forces, and b_x and b_y are constant velocity gains. For this control system, the vector of control parameters can be defined as $a^T = [V_o\ k_y\ F_o]$, whose components are to be adjusted dynamically in response to variations in burr characteristics.

For the purpose of parameterizing burr characteristics, the following model based on a metal cutting theory is introduced [King and Hahn, 1986].

$$
F_t\omega = b_1\dot{x} + b_2\dot{y} + b_3 \qquad(4)
$$

For this process model, the vector of process parameters can be written as $b^T = [b_1\ b_2\ b_3]$.

The beauty of human expertise and skills is to adaptively modify control actions by monitoring changes in the task process. In [Liu and Asada, 1992], such skills are described as an adaptive control law that varies the vector of control actions, a, in relation to the process parameters, b, which are estimated in the process. As shown in Figure 2, an indirect adaptive control system is then constructed, where the functional relationship between a and b is represented by unsing a neural network associative mapping.

To identify the associative mapping, a set of teaching data pairs are obtained as $T = \{(a, b)_p \mid p = 1, ..., N\}$ from a series of human demonstrations. When all data pairs have been tested and satisfy Lipschitz's condition, it can be confirmed that equation (4) is an effective model for characterizing human perception of process conditions [Liu and Asada, 1992]. Based on the training set T, a mapping can be recovered as in the following function form for each compo-

nent of vector $a^T = [V_o\ k_y\ F_o]$.

$$
\begin{aligned}
V_o &= V_o(b) &\qquad(5)\\
k_y &= k_y(b) &\qquad(6)\\
F_o &= F_o(b) &\qquad(7)
\end{aligned}
$$

where $b \in B$, and B is the space of all possible values that b may take in deburring.

As discussed in [Liu and Asada, 1992], a three-layered neural network can approximate the above mapping to a desired accuracy. Figure 2 shows a block diagram of a control system using the trained neural network to operate the computation of control parameters, V_o, k_y, and F_o.

3 On-Line Learning for Improving Task Performance

Through the off-line teaching described above, an indirect adaptive control system is obtained from human demonstration data. Human expertise and skills are imbedded in this control system, which are useful and effective for performing complex tasks such as deburring. However, to meet rigorous performance specifications such as accuracy, human skills alone may not be enough to guarantee the performance. In precision deburring, for example, the surface smoothness and final workpiece dimensions are specified rigorously. To eliminate manual tuning, which is ineffective and time consuming, we consider a learning method for fine tuning the controller. In the off-line teaching phase, the indirect adaptive controller has been constructed, which includes a multilayer neural network. Learning can be performed simply by retraining this neural network controller using on-line data. Also important to note is that the off-line demonstration data provide useful information for constructing the learning controller. We will utilize those data for expediting the learning process.

The mapping represented by the neural network used in the indirect adaptive controller can be written as follows.

$$
a = C[\hat{b}; W] \qquad(8)
$$

where a represents the vector of reference inputs and the feedback gain, $\hat{b}$, is the vector of process parameter estimates, and W represents the matrix whose elements are all the weights involved in network C. As discussed before, matrix W is obtained by using human demonstration data as teaching data. It is desired to improve the surface finish performance of the deburring system by modifying the mapping relationship between vectors a and $\hat{b}$. In other words, it is intended to adjust weight matrix W in network C so that the mapping between a and $\hat{b}$ can be more effective for obtaining a smooth, accurate surface.

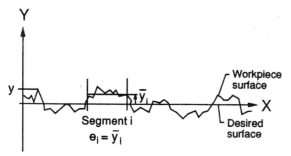

Figure 3: Definition of the surface finish measure e

During the off-line teaching phase, weight matrix W in controller network C can be identified based on a set of input-output training pairs obtained from human demonstrations. Now for on-line learning, there is no sample training pair readily available for further fine adjustment of weight matrix W, since for every burr characteristics, $\hat{b}$, it is unclear what should be the target output a for the controller network so that the surface finish criterion can be optimized. Obviously, what is lacking here is the knowledge of the relationship between the surface finish criterion and control vector a.

In a deburring process, the workpiece surface finish depends on burr characteristics as well as how the deburring tool is manipulated. As discussed before, the tool manipulation strategy in a deburring task can be completely characterized by a vector of control parameters a. Under a certain burr condition, parameterized by vector b, the deburring tool that operates with a strategy a will produce a result of the workpiece surface finish with a measure denoted e, and $e \in \mathcal{R}$. As shown in Figure 3, surface finish can be measured as the deviation, denoted y, of the final workpiece surface from the desired contour line. Obviously if at every point along the workpiece contour the deviation is minimized, then the workpiece surface will be accurate and smooth. For the present study, we are concerned with the surface finish only on an average scale. That is, we don't try to minimize deviation y at every point along the workpiece contour, although that is the ultimate goal. Instead, along the x axis in Figure 3, we divide the workpiece into several small segments and take the *average* value of y within each segment as the value of e, as shown in Figure 3. With this simplification, the objective is to minimize the *average* deviation, e. Therefore, we consider only the quasi-static phenomena in a deburring process and model the relationship between e and a as well as b by a static map:

$$e = f(a, b) \qquad (9)$$

Function f is presumably nonlinear, and it is difficult to identify in a constructive manner using principal laws of physics. Since sample data pairs are available from a deburring process, function f can be approximated based on a set of training data. For the pos-

sible nonlinear nature of function f, a neural network is employed to learn and approximate this mapping.

Using a neural network to represent the plant model has been widely used in the field of connectionist (neural network) learning for control, e.g. [Widrow, *et al.*, 1978], [Kuperstein, 1987], and [Werbos, 1988]. In the case of using a neural network to describe forward plant dynamics, it is often call "forward model", since it forwards control commands into a simulated plant dynamics and predicts plant output [Jordan and Rumelhart, 1991]. In the present case, the forward model describes a function of control command a as well as the characteristics of the plant itself, b, which varies with time. Let us rewrite equation (9) with a neural network notation:

$$e = F[a, \hat{b}; V] \qquad (10)$$

where $\hat{b}$ is used to replace b in equation (9), since b can only be estimated from measured signals, and V is the weight matrix. The same set of human teaching data used to acquire initial value of W can also be used to identified weight matrix V. After V is identified, it's value will remain fixed throughout the on-line learning process. Substituting equation (1) into equation (10), we have

$$e = F[C[\hat{b}; W], \hat{b}; V] \qquad (11)$$

For a certain selection of W, e is a function of $\hat{b}$ only. For simplicity, we discretize the burr characteristics space, B, and assume that the total number of pattern of burr characteristics is finite. Define a performance index function as:

$$E = \sum_p E_p = \sum_p e_p^2 \qquad (12)$$

where p is an index for the pattern of burr characteristics, and $e_p = F[C[\hat{b}_p; W], \hat{b}_p; V]$. To optimize E with respect to W, the gradient descent method can be applied for adjusting W:

$$\triangle w_{ij} = -\eta \frac{\partial E}{\partial w_{ij}} = -\eta \sum_p \frac{\partial E_p}{\partial w_{ij}} \qquad (13)$$

where η is the learning rate. When the learning rate is set very small, each element w_{ij} in the weight matrix W can be adjusted based on each performance measurement E_p, and the result is a close approximation to the gradient descent in E. Therefore, consider the learning rule:

$$\triangle_p w_{ij} = -\eta \frac{\partial E_p}{\partial w_{ij}} = -2\eta e_p \frac{\partial e_p}{\partial w_{ij}} \qquad (14)$$

Equation (11) shows that e_p is an implicit function of w_{ij}. Therefore, the chain rule is applied in order to

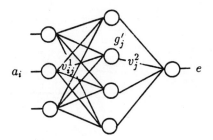

Figure 4: Neural Network structure for the forward model

compute $\frac{\partial e_p}{\partial w_{ij}}$.

$$\frac{\partial e_p}{\partial w_{ij}} = \frac{\partial e_p}{\partial \mathbf{a}} \frac{\partial \mathbf{a}}{\partial w_{ij}} \qquad (15)$$

The term $\frac{\partial e_p}{\partial \mathbf{a}}$ can be readily computed as follows. Suppose that the forward model F is represented by a three layer network with one hidden layer, as depicted in Figure 4. In each hidden unit, the sigmoid function, denoted g, is used as the activation function. The output of the network is simply a linear combination of the outputs from all hidden units. The computation of partial derivative of e_p with respect to each component of $\mathbf{a}$ can be expressed as:

$$\frac{\partial e_p}{\partial a_i} = \sum_{j=1}^{n} v_{ij}^1 g_j' v_j^2 \qquad (16)$$

where n is the total number of hidden units, v_{ij}^1 is the weight for the connection between the ith input unit and the jth hidden unit, g_j' is the derivative of the sigmoid function with respect to its argument at the jth hidden unit, and v_j^2 is the weight for the connection between the jth hidden unit and the output unit. The term $\frac{\partial \mathbf{a}}{\partial w_{ij}}$ in equation (15) can be computed by using the controller network (equation (8)). The overall learning process that backpropagates performance error e for refining the controller network is depicted in Figure 5.

4   Implementation Results

As shown in Figure 1, the tool displacement in the direction normal to the workpiece surface is closely related to the surface finish. Namely, if the tool fluctuates very much in the normal direction, it is expected that the workpiece surface after cutting by the tool will be rough. Therefore, the tool displacement y can be used as an approximate measure of the surface smoothness.

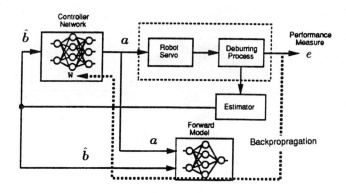

Figure 5: Backpropagation of performance error e for refining the controller network

Figure 6 is an example plot of tool displacement y measured from an actual robot deburring motion. In this operation, the associative mapping, as shown in equation (8), was used in the adaptation loop to compute control vector $\mathbf{a}$. In Figure 6, $y = 0$ corresponds to a reference or the desired contour of the workpiece surface after deburring. High frequency fluctuation can be clearly seen in the tool displacement, and this can be attributed to spindle motor vibration, tool flexibility as well as measurement noise. Beside the high frequency oscillation, the average trace of tool displacement deviates from the reference contour line from time to time. It can be found that the deviation takes place at times when the tool encountered large size burrs on the original workpiece. This observation implies that the neural network controller shown in equation (8) needs to be fine tuned in order to generate control vector $\mathbf{a}$ that always well matches the time-varying burr characteristics. The main objective for the present study is to decrease the deviations of the mean trace of the tool when cutting a large burr. The deviation takes place on a much slower time scale than that of the high frequency fluctuation; therefore, it is considered as a quasi-static tool behavior which is directly affected by burr characteristics and control commands.

As mentioned before, the same set of human teaching data, $T = \{(\mathbf{a}, \mathbf{b})_p \mid p = 1, ..., N\}$, used to acquire the initial value of $\mathbf{W}$ can also be used to identify the forward model. For each process characteristics pattern $\hat{\mathbf{b}}_p$, we calculate e_p by taking the time average of tool displacement y within a period of time during which burr characteristics remain the same pattern $\hat{\mathbf{b}}_p$. A set of 50 training pairs $\{(\mathbf{a}, \hat{\mathbf{b}})_p, e_p\}$ was used to train a three-layer neural network with 20 units in the hidden layer. After the training had converged, the weight matrix $\mathbf{V}$, defined in equation (10), is fixed, and will be used to compute $\frac{\partial e_p}{\partial \mathbf{a}}$ in the learning process.

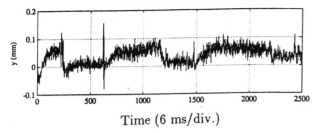

Figure 6: Tool displacement in a robotic deburring process

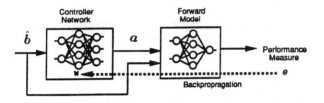

Figure 7: Simulation of the learning process

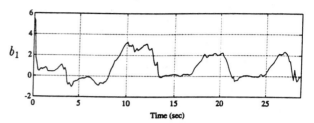

Figure 8: Process parameter estimate $\hat{b}_1(t)$ obtained from an actual deburring process

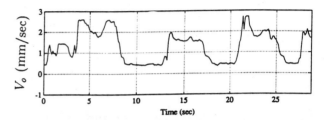

Figure 9: Reference feedrate V_o corresponding to the process parameter shown in Figure 8

Using the identified forward model to back propagate performance error, the learning process proposed in Section 3 is simulated as the following. Figure 7 depicts this simulation process. A time series of process parameter estimate $\hat{b}(t)$, obtained from an actual deburring motion, was used in the simulation as if it were obtained from a real time operation. The neural network that describes the associative mapping, equation (8), was used to compute control command $a(t)$. As discussed before, the forward model describes only the quasi-static phenomena in a deburring process. Therefore, we take time average of $a(t)$ and $\hat{b}(t)$ over every period in which $\hat{b}(t)$ remains relatively unchanged. The pth averaged control vector a_p and the corresponding $\hat{b}_p$ were then fed to the forward model to compute performance error e_p. For each performance error e_p, the value of $\frac{\partial e_p}{\partial a}$ is computed, which was then back propagated through the network C to modify the weight matrix W based on equations (14) and (15). One learning cycle was completed by back propagating all patterns of e_p. The refined weight matrix W was then used to begin another cycle of simulating control vector $a(t)$ as well as performance error e_p.

Figure 8 is a sample plot of component $\hat{b}_1(t)$ of process parameter estimate $\hat{b}(t)$ obtained from an actual deburring motion by a robot. The on-line estimation scheme used to produce $\hat{b}(t)$ is the recursive least square algorithm incorporated with the Bayesian approach for tracking [Ljung and Söderström, 1983]. Figure 9 shows the first component of control vector $a(t)$, i.e. $V_o(t)$, calculated by using $\hat{b}(t)$ and equation

(15). The $\hat{b}(t)$ plot in Figure 8 was divided into 16 segments in a manner that in each segment $\hat{b}(t)$ is very much constant. Therefore, each segment corresponds to one pattern of burr characteristics $\hat{b}$. Taking time average of $\hat{b}(t)$ and $a(t)$ over each segment, we have 16 pairs of $\{a, \hat{b}\}_p$.

Figure 10 shows the result of the simulated learning process based on the same series of process parameter estimate, $\hat{b}(t)$, as shown in Figure 8. The abscissa in Figure 10 is the segment index. The performance of the controller is indeed improved after every learning iteration with respect to the same burr characteristics. This result confirms that the controller can be gradually refined after the control system practices a number of operations over the same workpiece. In an actual deburring task, two workpieces can never be found having exactly the same burr characteristics. Therefore, this learning process is useful only when the controller can learn and improve its performance at every iteration even when a new workpiece with different burr characteristics is used in each iteration. Figure 11 is the simulated result of a learning process in which a new series of burr parameter estimate $\hat{b}(t)$ is used for each iteration. The ordinate is the performance measure E computed using equation (12), and the abscissa is the iteration number. It is clear that after the first and second iterations, the controller performance is improved. However, at the third iteration, the performance error becomes higher than the second one. In each iteration, a new series of burr parameter estimate is used for simulation. If the forward

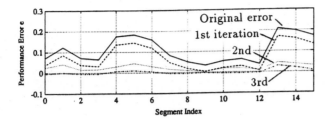

Figure 10: Result of learning when the same series of process parameters estimate

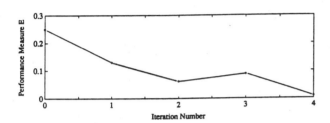

Figure 11: Result of learning when a different series of process parameters estimate is used in each iteration

model (equation (10)) through which the performance error is back propagated does not properly approximate the actual mapping shown in equation (9) for all burr characteristics, then the controller may not learn properly from the performance error under the burr conditions unknown to the forward model. The simulation result shown in Figure 11 suggests that the learning algorithm proposed in this paper relies heavily on the validity of the forward model to approximate the functional relationship between performance error e and control vector a as well as burr characteristics $\hat{b}$.

5 Conclusions

This paper presents an experimental approach to teaching and learning of adaptive control of deburring robots. The method of teaching adaptive control to deburring robots based on human demonstration data has been well documented in [Liu and Asada, 1992]. When high accuracy is required as the performance objective, human skills alone may not suffice to be the basis for constructing an effective robot controller. To improve system performance for higher accuracy, learning is introduced to fine tune controller parameters. Using a forward model for back propagating task-level performance error is found to be effective. However, a crucial condition for the learning algorithm to be effective is that the forward model must be a valid representation of the mapping between the performance error and the control vector as well

as burr characteristics. For further study on this indirect learning technique applied on robotic deburring, the critical issues are:
(1) the validity of the forward model,
(2) the conditions under which the learning will converge, and
(3) a more efficient learning algorithm that involves a time-varying learning rate.

References

[Aramaki, 1983] S. Aramaki, "Flexible Playback Control of an Artificial Hand", *Trans. Society of Instrument and Control Engineer*, Vol. 19-6, 1983.

[Asada and Hanafusa, 1979] H. Asada and H. Hanafusa, "Playback Control of Force Teachable Robots", *Trans. Society of Instrument and Control Engineer*, Vol. 15-3, 1979.

[DeSchutter and Leysen, 1987] J. DeSchutter and J. Leysen, "Tracking in Compliant Robot Motion: Automatic Generation of the Task Frame Trajectory Based on Observation of Natural Constraints", *Proc. 4th Int. Symp. of Robotics Research*, pp. 215-223, 1987.

[Hirzinger and Heindl, 1983] G. Hirzinger and J. Heindl, "Sensor Programming - A New Way for Teaching Robot Parts and Forces/Torques Simultaneously", *Proc. 3rd Int. Conf. on Robot Vision and Sensory Controls*, pp. 549-558, 1983.

[Jordan and Rumelhart, 1991] M. I. Jordan and D. E. Rumelhart, "Internal World Models and Supervised Learning", *Machine Learning: Proc. of the 8th International Workshop*, edited by L. Birnhaum and G. Collins, 1991.

[King and Hahn, 1986] R. King and R. Hahn, *Handbook of Modern Grinding Technology*, pp. 34-38.

[Kuperstein, 1987] M. Kuperstein, "Adaptive Visual-Motor Coordination in Multi-joint Robots Using Parallel Architecture", *Proc. of 1987 IEEE Int. Conf. on Robotics and Automation*, pp. 1595-1602, 1987.

[Liu and Asada, 1992] S. Liu and H. Asada, "Transferring Manipulative Skills to Robots: Representation and Acquisition of Tool Manipulative Skills Using a Process Dynamics Model", *ASME Journal of Dynamic System, Measurement and Control*, Vol. 114, No. 2, pp. 220-228, June 1992

[Ljung and Söderström, 1983] L. Ljung and T. Söderström, *Theory and Practice of Recursive Identification*, MIT Press, 1983.

[Werbos, 1988] P. J. Werbos, "Generalization of Bach Propagation with Applications to Recurrent Gas Market Model", *Neural Networks*, Vol. 1, pp. 339-356, 1988.

[Widrow, et al., 1978] B. Widrow, J. McCool, and B. Medoff, "Adaptive Control by Inverse Modeling", *Twelfth Asilomar Conference on Circuits, Systems, and Computers*, 1978.

A Distributed Adaptive Control System for a Quadruped Mobile Robot

Bruce L. Digney and M. M. Gupta
Intelligent Systems Research Laboratory, College of Engineering
University of Saskatchewan, Saskatoon, Sask. CANADA S7N 0W0
E_mail: digney@dvinci.usask.ca

Abstract— In this research, a method by which reinforcement learning can be combined into a behavior based control system is presented. Behaviors which are impossible or impractical to embed as predetermined responses are learned through self-exploration and self-organization using a temporal difference reinforcement learning technique. This results in what is referred to as a distributed adaptive control system (DACS); in effect the robot's artificial nervous system. A DACS is developed for a simulated quadruped mobile robot and the locomotion behavior level is isolated and evaluated. At the locomotion level the proper actuator sequences were learned for all possible gaits and eventually graceful gait transitions were also learned. When confronted with an actuator malfunction, all gaits and transitions were adapted resulting in new *limping* gaits for the quadruped.

I. INTRODUCTION

Although conventional control and artificial intelligence researchers have made many advances, neither ideology seems capable of realizing autonomous operation. That is, neither can produce machines which can interact with the world with an ease comparable to humans or at least higher animals. In responding to such limitations, many researchers have looked to biological/physiological based systems as the motivation to design artificial systems. As an example are the behavior based systems of Brooks [1] and Beer [2]. Behavior based control systems consist of a hierarchical structure of simple behavior modules. Each module is responsible for the sensory motor responses of a particular level of behavior. The overall effect is that higher level behaviors are recursively built upon lower ones and the resulting system operates in a self-organizing manner. Both Brooks and Beer's systems were loosely based upon the nervous systems of insects. These artificial insects operated in a hardwired manner and exhibited an interesting repertoire of simple behaviors. By *hardwired* it is meant that each behavior module had its responses predetermined and was simply programmed externally. Although this approach is successful with simple behaviors, it is obvious that many situations exist where predetermined solutions are impossible or impractical to obtain. It is subsequently proposed that by incorporating learning into the behavior based control system, these difficult behaviors could be acquired through self-exploration and self-learning.

Complex behaviors are usually characterized by a sequence of actions with success or failure only known at the end of that sequence. Also, the critical error signal is only an indication of the success or failure of the system and no information regarding error gradients can be determined, as in the case of continuous valued error feedback. Thus the required learning mechanism must be capable of both reinforcement learning as well as temporal credit assignment. Incremental dynamic programming techniques such as Barto's [3] temporal difference (TD) appear to be well suited to such tasks. Based upon Barto's previous adaptive heuristic critic [4], TD employs adaptive state and action evaluation functions to incrementally improve its action policy until successful operation is attained. The incorporation of TD learning into behavior based control results in a framework of adaptive (ABMs) and non-adaptive behavior modules which is referred to here as a distributed adaptive control system (DACS). The remainder of this report will be concerned with a brief description of the DACS and ABMs, and implementing of the locomotion level ABM within the DACS of a simulated quadruped mobile robot. This level is considered appropriate because the actuator sequences for quadruped locomotion are not intuitively obvious and difficult to determine. Other levels such as global navigation, task planning and task coordination are implemented and discussed by Digney [5].

II. DISTRIBUTED ADAPTIVE CONTROL SYSTEMS

The DACS shown in Figure 1 is comprised of various adaptive and non-adaptive behavior modules. Non-adaptive modules are present as inherent knowledge and are used where adaptive solutions are not required. All modules receive sensory inputs and respond with actions in an attempt to perform a command specified by a higher level. The performance of commands in most cases will require a sequence of actions by the lower level system and possibly the cooperation of many lower level systems. The coupling between ABMs is shown in Figure 2. In this configuration, the action from level $l+1$ becomes the command for level l. Level $l+1$ also supplies goal based reinforcement, r_g, to drive level l towards successful completion of that command. Level l in turn issues actions to level $l-1$ and receives environmental based reinforcement, r_e, from level $l-1$. This environment based reinforcement is representative of the difficulty or cost incurred while performing the requested actions and is included to drive level l to a cost effective solution. While operating, level l may enter a state which is in some way damaging or dangerous. To drive the system away from such a state, sensor based reinforcement, r_s, is used. Sensor based reinforcement is supplied from sensors at level l. It is analogous to *pain or fear* and will ensure that level l operates in a safe manner. These three reinforcements are combined into a total reinforcement signal, r_t, according to Equation 1.

$$r_t = \alpha_e \cdot r_e + \alpha_g \cdot r_g + \alpha_s \cdot r_s \qquad (1)$$

where: α_e, α_g and α_s are the relative importance of the reinforcements.

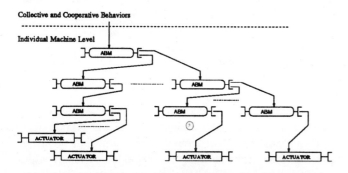

Figure 1: Schematic of DACS

It can be seen from Figure 2 that the flow of environmental and sensor based reinforcement is in the upward direction. This will result in lower level skills and behaviors being learned first, then other higher level behaviors, converging in a recursive manner toward the highest level. Figure 1 shows this highest level as existing within a single physical machine. However, in the case of multiple machines operating in a collective, higher abstract behavior levels are possible. Within the context of this paper, only behaviors relevant to individual machines will be discussed. In the absence of higher collective behaviors con-

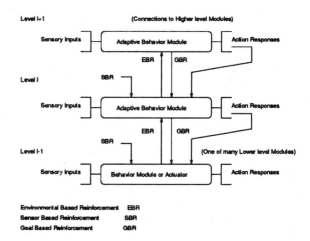

Figure 2: Hierarchy of Three ABMs

trolling individual machines, the purpose or task of the machine is embedded within the DACS as an *instinct or drive*. This instinct is the high level action which results in a feeling of accomplishment or positive reinforcement within the DACS. It is then the responsibility of the adaptive behavior modules within the DACS to learn the skills and behaviors necessary to fulfill this drive. This concept as well as the self-organizing characteristics that result from such interactions are further discussed by Digney [5].

The ABM is the primary adaptive building block for the DACS. Within it exist computational mechanisms for state classification, learning and the combination of reinforcement signals. Figure 3 shows a schematic of an ABM complete with incoming command, sensory and reinforcement signals. For clarity the outgoing reinforcement signals have been removed. For any particular level, say l, the ABM observes the relevant system states through appropriate sensors. For a perception system consisting of N sensors, the state S_l, is defined as

$$S_l = \begin{bmatrix} s_0 & \cdots & s_n & \cdots & s_N \end{bmatrix}^T \qquad (2)$$

where: s_n is the individual sensor reading, $0 < n < N$

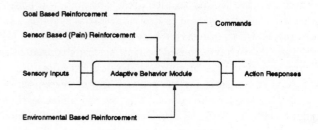

Figure 3: Single ABM

State transitions are detected and the resulting states are classified using an idealized neural classification scheme. This classification embodies the macroscopic operating principles of unsupervised neural networks such as ART2-A [6] and will be assumed adequate in the context of these simulations. The Temporal Difference (TD) algorithm as developed by Barton [7] learns by adjusting state and action evaluation functions then uses these evaluations to choose an optimum action policy. It can be shown that these two evaluation functions can be combined into a single action dependent evaluation function, say $Q_{s,u}$, similar to that described by Barto [7]. Given the system at state s, the action taken, u^*, is the action which satisfies

$$\max_u \{Q_{s,u} + \zeta\} \Rightarrow u^* \tag{3}$$

where: ζ is a random valued function.

In Equation 3, $Q_{s,u}$ and ζ can be thought of as the goal driven and exploration driven components of the action policy respectively. Taking the action u^* results in the transition from state s to state v and the incurring of a total reinforcement signal r_t. The action dependent evaluation function error is obtained by modifying the TD error equation and is

$$e = \gamma \cdot Q_{virtual} - Q_{s,u^*} + r_t. \tag{4}$$

where: $Q_{virtual}$ is the virtual state evaluation value of the next state v and γ is the temporal discount factor.

If action, u^*, does not achieve the desired goal, the virtual state evaluation is,

$$Q_{virtual} = \max_u \{Q_{v,u}\}. \tag{5}$$

It is easily seen that $Q_{virtual}$ becomes the minimum action dependent evaluation function of the new state, v, (remember the evaluation functions are negative in sign) and in effect corresponds to the action most likely to be taken when the system leaves state v.

If the action, u^*, achieves the desired goal, the virtual state evaluation is,

$$Q_{virtual} = 0. \tag{6}$$

This provides relative state evaluations and allows for openended or cyclic goal states. This is illustrated by considering that for cyclic goals it is the dynamic transitions between states that constitutes a goal state and not simply the arrival at a static system state(s).

This error is used to adapt the evaluation functions according to LMS rules as follows

$$Q_{s,u=u^*}(k+1) = Q_{s,u=u^*}(k) + \eta \cdot e \tag{7}$$

$$Q_{s,u \neq u^*}(k+1) = Q_{s,u \neq u^*}(k) \tag{8}$$

where: η is the rate of adaption and k is the index of adaption.

As the evaluation function converges, the goal driven component begins to dominate over the exploration driven component. The resulting action policy will perform the command in a successful and efficient manner. Generally, an ABM will be capable of performing more than a single command. For an ABM capable of c_{max} commands, the vector of the evaluation functions is defined as:

$$Eval_l = \begin{bmatrix} Q_{s,u,0}, & \cdots & Q_{s,u,c}, & \cdots, & Q_{s,u,c_{max}} \end{bmatrix}^T \tag{9}$$

where: $Q_{s,u}$ is the evaluation function and c the particular command $0 < c < c_{max}$.

III. DACS FOR A QUADRUPED MOBLE ROBOT

To evaluate the DACS, the simulated quadruped shown in Figure 4 was used. This mobile robot was placed inside a simulated three dimensional landscape where it is left to develop skills and behaviors as it interacts with its environment. This world is made up of ramps, plateaus, cliffs and walls, as well as various substances of interest. In the absence of any predetermined knowledge it is the responsibility of the DACS and in particular the ABMs to acquire the skills and behaviors for successful operation.

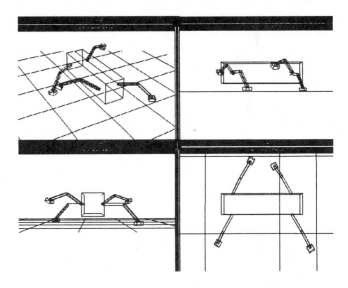

Figure 4: Simulated Quadruped

Although not the most efficient method of locomotion, the learning of quadruped walking provides interesting and challenging problems. Involved is the learning of complex actuator sequences in the midst of numerous false goal states and modes of failure. Figure 5 shows the locomotion ABM with the appropriate sensory, reinforcement and motor action connections.

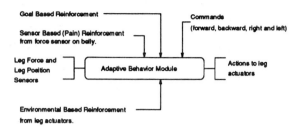

Figure 5: Locomotion ABM

The commands, $c_{locomotion}$, are issued from the ABM above and are dependent upon the possible sensory states of that module. In this case these sensors are capable of detecting all realizable modes of body motion. The commands for the locomotion level are defined in Equation 10.

$$c_{locomotion} = \begin{cases} 0 & \text{forward} \\ 1 & \text{left turn} \\ \vdots & \vdots \\ c_{max} & \text{all possible modes} \end{cases} \quad (10)$$

For any specific command the locomotion ABM will issue action responses, $u_{locomotion}$, to the actuators driving the legs in the horizontal, h, and vertical, v, directions. Within this action vector are the individual actuator commands to extend, ex, or retract, rt, as shown in Equation 11 and 12.

$$u_{locomotion} = \begin{bmatrix} c_{leg_0}, & c_{leg_1}, & c_{leg_2}, & c_{leg_3} \end{bmatrix}^T \quad (11)$$

where

$$c_{leg} = \begin{cases} h & \text{hold} \\ v_{ex} & \text{extend vertical} \\ v_{rt} & \text{retract vertical} \\ h_{ex} & \text{extend horizontal} \\ h_{rt} & \text{retract horizontal} \end{cases} \quad (12)$$

Each leg is equipped with sensors for measuring the forces on each foot and the positions of each leg. The forces on the foot are are biased such that $-f_{max} < f_{leg} < f_{max}$, where f_{max} is the highest force magnitude expected. Similarly the position sensors are biased such that $-l_{max} < l_{leg} < l_{max}$, where l_{max} is half the stroke of the linear actuator. For an arbitrary leg, leg_n, and direction, d, the force and position descriptions of state are

$$s_{force,d,leg_n} = \begin{cases} -1 & \text{if } f_{leg_n,d} < 0 \\ 0 & \text{if } f_{leg_n,d} = 0 \\ +1 & \text{if } f_{leg_n,d} > 0 \end{cases} \quad (13)$$

$$s_{pos,d,leg_n} = \begin{cases} -1 & \text{if } l_{leg_n,d} < 0 \\ +1 & \text{if } l_{leg_n,d} > 0 \end{cases} \quad (14)$$

The reinforcement signals are defined as

$$r_g = \begin{cases} 0 & \text{if } c_{locomotion} \text{ is performed,} \\ -R_g & \text{otherwise} \end{cases} \quad (15)$$

$$r_e = \begin{cases} -R_{low} & \text{easy operation} \\ -R_{high} & \text{difficult operation} \end{cases} \quad (16)$$

$$r_s = \begin{cases} -R_s & \text{if } f_{belly} > 0, \\ 0 & \text{otherwise} \end{cases} \quad (17)$$

where: f_{belly} is a force sensor on the bottom of the robot and R_* are appropriate positive values.

The net effect of these reinforcements is to drive the locomotion system to learn efficient actuator sequences that will perform the specified gaits while maintaining the quadruped's balance. At this level of abstraction the quadruped is said to lose balance when the line drawn between any two legs in contact with the ground does not pass through the quadruped's center of gravity.

Equations 13 and 14, when combined into Equation 18, define the complete state of the locomotion system. For the transition between any pair of past and present states, the total reinforcement can be determined by combining Equations 15, 16 and 17 into Equation 1. The total reinforcement is then used to adapt the command specific evaluation functions of Equation 19 according to Equations 4, 7 and 8. As these evaluation functions converge, all realizable gaits should be achieved.

$$S_{locomotion} = \begin{bmatrix} s_{force,d,leg_0} \\ \vdots \\ s_{pos,d,leg_0} \end{bmatrix} \quad (18)$$

$$Eval_{locomotion} = \begin{bmatrix} Q_{s,u,forward} \\ Q_{s,u,backward} \\ Q_{s,u,rightturn} \\ Q_{s,u,leftturn} \end{bmatrix} \quad (19)$$

IV. SIMULATION AND RESULTS

Using the reinforcement scheme described above, the locomotion ABM was simulated and its abilities to learn in an initially unknown environment and adapt to changes and malfunctions were evaluated. In the following section results from the locomotion tests are presented. Note that the temporal discount factor and the adaption rate chosen for these tests was 0.9 and 0.5 respectively. The reinforcements R_g, R_{low}, R_{high} and R_s were set to 1.0, 1.0, 2.0 and 4.0 respectively.

All possible gaits, including forward, backward, right turn and left turn were discovered and eventually mastered. Figure 6 shows the quadruped's performance while learning the four gaits. Shown on the vertical axis is the cumulative negative reinforcement per step, which can be thought of as the difficulty encountered while performing a single step. The number of steps taken is shown on the horizontal axis. Improvement is obvious as the quadruped initially functions poorly, then eventually learns the optimum actions necessary to perform and maintain a particular gait. In the simulation, the quadruped alternates between all possible gaits, making it possible to evaluate the quadruped's ability to learn graceful transitions between the gaits. In the performance graph of Figure 6, a zone of slow improvement is evident. It is here where the graceful gait transitions are being learned. A mechanical malfunction was simulated by deactivating the horizontal actuator on a single leg. This effectively made the leg able to support only a vertical load and unable to apply any horizontal force to the body of the quadruped. Figure 7 shows the performance of the quadruped under both intact and crippled conditions. Initially, the intact quadruped learns the four standard gaits. Once crippling occurs, a recovery period is required as the quadruped relearns all gaits, this time with a limp. As before, graceful transitions are eventually learned for the new limping gaits. For an intact quadruped Figures 8 and 9 show the individual leg movements that comprise forward and right turning gaits respectively. The corresponding leg commands and reinforcement signals are shown in Tables 1 and 2 for these forward and right turning gaits respectively. In these simulations the end of the quadruped closest to the reader is the front and leg_0, leg_1, leg_2, and leg_3 are considered the front right, front left, rear left and rear right legs respectively. Also, the actuator extensions v_{ex} and h_{ex} cause the leg to move downward and towards the front. The actuator retractions v_{rt} and h_{rt} cause the leg to move upward and towards the rear.

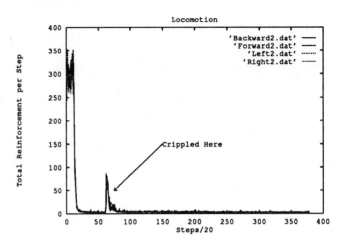

Figure 7: Performance of Crippled Quadruped

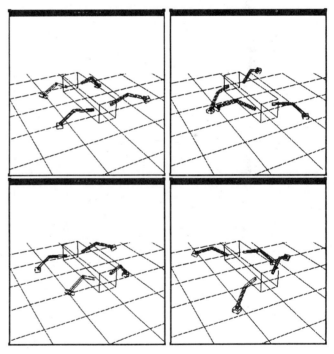

Figure 8: Forward gait(motion towards the reader). Note frame sequence: top left (frame 1) → top right (frame 2) → bottom left (frame 3) → bottom right (frame 4) → top left (frame 1).

Table 1: Command Sequence: Forward Gait

Frame	Commands				Reinforcements		
k	leg_0	leg_1	leg_2	leg_3	r_e	r_g	r_s
$1 \rightarrow 2$	v_{rt}	v_{ex}	v_{rt}	v_{ex}	R_{low}	R_g	0
$2 \rightarrow 3$	h_{ex}	h_{rt}	h_{ex}	h_{rt}	R_{low}	0	0
$3 \rightarrow 4$	v_{ex}	v_{rt}	v_{ex}	v_{rt}	R_{low}	R_g	0
$4 \rightarrow 1$	h_{rt}	h_{ex}	h_{rt}	h_{ex}	R_{low}	0	0

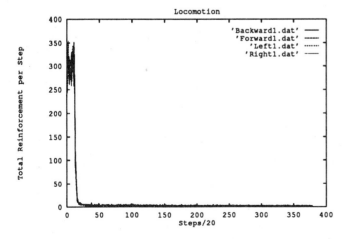

Figure 6: Performance of Intact Quadruped

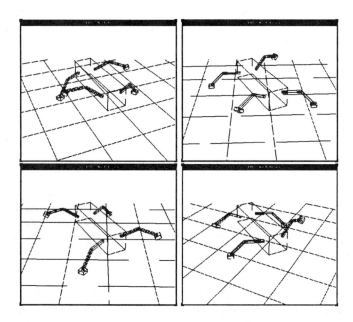

Figure 9: Right Turn Gait(rotation is clockwise as viewed from top) Note frame sequence: top left (frame 1) → top right (frame 2) → bottom left (frame 3) → bottom right (frame 4) → top left (frame 1).

Table 2: Command Sequence: Right Turn Gait

Frame	Commands				Reinforcements		
k	leg_0	leg_1	leg_2	leg_3	r_e	r_g	r_s
$1 \to 2$	h_{ex}	h_{ex}	h_{rt}	h_{rt}	R_{low}	0	0
$2 \to 3$	v_{ex}	v_{rt}	v_{ex}	v_{rt}	R_{low}	R_g	0
$3 \to 4$	h_{rt}	h_{rt}	h_{ex}	h_{ex}	R_{low}	0	0
$4 \to 1$	v_{ex}	v_{ex}	v_{rt}	v_{ex}	R_{low}	R_g	0

V. DISCUSSION

The results achieved in the locomotion tests showed initial poor performance followed by rapid improvement and eventual convergence to an optimum solution. It is during the initial poor performance that the ABM explores the state space, discovering all the obtainable states of the system. For the locomotion ABM, these states are the leg positions and the force on each foot. During this exploration, the learning system refined the initially random action policy to a policy that achieves the specified command. These commands themselves are not supplied to the system as predetermined knowledge but are discovered as realizable commands by the system above. If the quadruped had been placed in water, then it would learn to swim or had the physical configuration allowed it to perform other gaits then these gaits would be learned also.

In response to actuator malfunctions the ABM, after a period of recovery, adapted to the changes and converged to another optimum action policy, in this case a limping leg sequences. This malfunction is labeled as *non-severe* because the adaption required for the DACS to recover is confined to a single ABM. If the malfunction was such that some gaits became impossible to perform, then adaption of higher ABMs would be required for recovery, and what is called a *severe* malfunction would have occurred.

VI. CONCLUSIONS

The ABM for locomotion successfully learned the complex action sequences for all realizable gaits. The locomotion ABM was able to successfully recover from a non-severe malfunction. The success of a single ABM can not be extrapolated to imply the success of the entire DACS. Work is currently being performed in the simulation of other behaviors such as body coordination, local navigation, global navigation, task planning, and task coordination. Once these other levels can be incorporated into the DACS, the concepts of self-organization and self-configuration can be explored.

REFERENCES

[1] Brooks, R (1991) Intelligence Without Reason, *AI Memo No. 1293*, MIT Artificial Intelligence Lab.

[2] Beer, R.D., Chiel, H.J., and Sterling, L.S. (1990) A biological perspective on autonomous agent design, *Robotics and Autonomous Systems 6*, pp 169-186.

[3] Barto, A.G., R.S. Sutton and C.H. Watkins (1989) Learning and Sequential Decision Making, *COINS Technical Report*

[4] Barto, A.G., Sutton, R.S., and Anderson, C.W. (1983) Neuronlike adaptive elements that can solve difficult learning control problems, *IEEE Transactions on Systems, Man, and Cybernetics SMC-13*, pp 834-846.

[5] Digney, B.L. (1992) Emergent Intelligence in a Distributed Adaptive Control System, *Ph.D. Thesis* circulated in draft, University of Saskatchewan, Saskatoon, Saskatchewan.

[6] Carpenter, G.A., S. Grossberg, and D., Rosen, (1990) ART2-A: An adaptive resonance Algorithm for rapid category learning and recognition, *IJCNN 1991 Seattle Washington*, Vol II pp 151-156.

[7] Barto, A.G., S.J. Bradtke and S.P. Singh (1991) Real-time Learning and Control Using Asynchronous Dynamic Programming *University of Amherst Technical Report 91 - 57*

Autonomous Trajectory Generation of a Biped Locomotive Robot Using Neuro Oscillator

Yasuo Kurematsu, Takuji Maeda and Shinzo Kitamura
Department of Computer and Systems Engineering, Faculty of Engineering, Kobe University

Abstract— The trajectory of a biped locomotive robot is generated using a neuro oscillator. This oscillator consists of four neuron cells which are mutually coupled with inhibitory connections. This model shows a stationary periodic oscillation for an appropriate set of parameters. Stability analysis of the neuro oscillator can be done by the linearization method. A stationary periodic oscillation appears in the unstable region for equilibrium states and this periodic oscillation generates a trajectory for stationary walking by assigning the state variables of neuron cells to joint angles of robot. The simulation studies assured the relevancy of the proposed method.

I. Introduction

Robots in future will be expected to work in the extreme environment, for example on the sea bottom or on the rough terrain, where a human cannot work. Biped locomotive robots will provide an efficient moving mechanism in such conditions. But there are difficulties in this mechanism, and many reserchers have attempted to develop prototypes of walking mechanism.[1, 2, 3, 4] Also the research on autonomous trajectory generation are important in order to develop intelligent and human-like robots, because a simple procedure cannot cope with the change of gait modes or with the disturbances caused by floor conditions. Some attempts in this direction have already been discussed.[5]

From a physiological viewpoint, some studies simulating the motion of animals by a neuron model have been reported.[6, 7]; further, dynamic biped locomotion by utilizing a stable limit cycle[8], the modeling of a neural pattern generator with coupled nonlinear oscillators [9], a biped locomotive motion using van der Pol oscillators[10], and the stable and flexible locomotion by global entrainment between the rhythmic activities of neural oscilltors and the rhythmic movements of a musculo-skeletal system.[11]

Under the background mentioned above, we have studied a neuro oscillator model consisting of four neuron cells, which generates the trajectory of a biped locomotive robot. Stability of the neuro oscillator was analyzed by the linearization around the equilibria. The walking modes were also examined in relation to the parameters in the model.

II. Model of neuro oscillator

A neuro oscillator consists of inhibitory connected neuron cells as in Figure 1 is considered. The ith neuron cell satisfies the following equations, which have been discussed in detail by Matsuoka.[12]

$$T_r \frac{dx_i}{dt} + x_i = -\sum_{j=0}^{n-1} a_{ij} y_j + s_i - b f_i$$

$$y_i = m_i x_i$$

$$m_i = \begin{cases} 1 & x_i \geq 0 \\ 0 & x_i < 0 \end{cases}$$

$$T_a \frac{df_i}{dt} + f_i = y_i$$

$$i = 0, 1, 2, \cdots, n-1 \tag{1}$$

where

x_i	: internal state variable of the ith neuron
y_i	: output variable of the ith neuron
f_i	: variable that represents the degree of fatigue of the ith neuron
b	: coefficient of the degree of fatigue
s_i	: constant input to the ith neuron cell
a_{ij}	: a weight of inhibitory synaptic connection from jth neuron to ith neuron
T_r, T_a	: time constant
n	: the number of neurons

When an appropriate set of parameters b, T_r, T_a, and a_{ij} is given to eqs.(1), they yield a periodic solution. The stability of this neuro oscillator is discussed in the section 5.

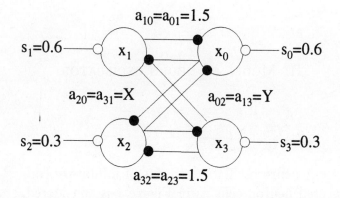

Figure 1: Structure of four neuron cells model

III. APPLICATION TO THE TRAJECTORY GENERATION OF A BIPED LOCOMOTIVE ROBOT

The trajectory generation system is shown in Figure 2.

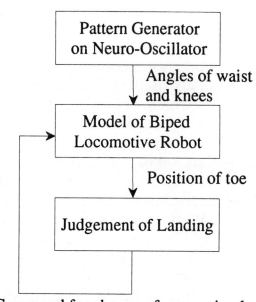

Figure 2: Trajectory generation system

The state variables of the neuro oscillator correspond to the absolute angles of robot's joints as in Figure 3. In this study, only the single leg supporting phase is assumed. Therefore, a supporting leg should be switched, when it lands at the floor, by another swinging leg. The stationary walking here was defined by the conditions;

- A knee does not bend reversely.

- The robot moves forward.

IV. SIMULATION RESULTS

A stick diagram of stationary walking yielded by the neuro oscillator with the parameters in Table 1 is shown in Figure 4. Lower four charts in Figure 4 are the waveforms corresponding to the time courses of the variables x_0 to x_3. Such

sign of joint angles

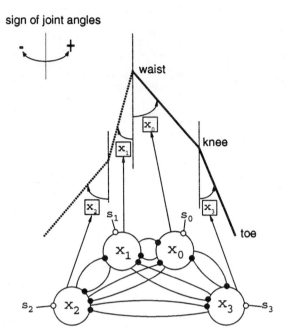

Figure 3: Correspondence between the neuro oscillator and the link model of a biped locomotive robot

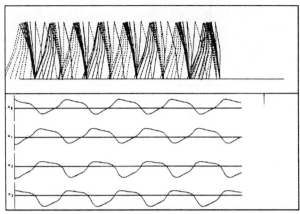

Figure 4: Simulation result for stationary walking

trajectories are robust in the sense that the generated limit-cycle in the phase-plane is asymptotically stable. An example is shown in Figure 5 where an impulsive disturbance was added to the waist joint angle at the point *, and the recovery process to the stationary walking can be observed there.

As for the parameter b in eqs.(1), the period of the solution becomes shorter, as a result, the step width becomes larger for tuning b to be small, and vice versa. However, it happened that the normal walking pattern could not be obtained, even if the eqs.(1) yield a periodic solution. For example, a strange walking patterns is shown in Figure 6 , for which $(X, Y) = (2.0, 1.3)$ is assigned in the unstable zone which will be discussed in the next section.

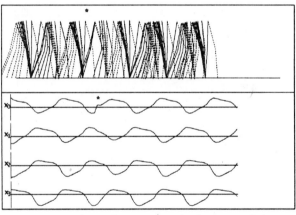

Figure 5: Simulation result for impulsive disturbance

Table 1: Parameters in the simulation studies

i	s_i	a_{0i}	a_{1i}	a_{2i}	a_{3i}	T_r	T_a	b
0	0.6	0.0	1.5	1.0	0.0			
1	0.6	1.5	0.0	0.0	1.0			
2	0.3	0.2	0.0	0.0	1.5	1.0	12.0	2.5
3	0.3	0.0	0.2	1.5	0.0			

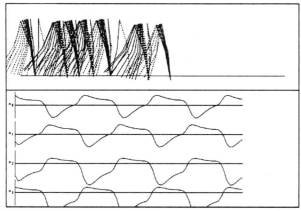

Figure 6: Simulation result for strange walking patterns

$$\mathbf{A_{21}} = \begin{pmatrix} m_0 & 0 & 0 & 0 \\ 0 & m_1 & 0 & 0 \\ 0 & 0 & m_2 & 0 \\ 0 & 0 & 0 & m_3 \end{pmatrix}$$

$$\boldsymbol{B} = \begin{pmatrix} \frac{1}{T_r} & 0 & 0 & 0 \\ 0 & \frac{1}{T_r} & 0 & 0 \\ 0 & 0 & \frac{1}{T_r} & 0 \\ 0 & 0 & 0 & \frac{1}{T_r} \\ 0 & 0 & 0 & 0 \\ 0 & 0 & 0 & 0 \\ 0 & 0 & 0 & 0 \\ 0 & 0 & 0 & 0 \end{pmatrix} \qquad (6)$$

V. STABILITY ANALYSIS

The neuro oscillator in the section 1 could generate the trajectories for the walking robot as shown in the previous section. However, the selection of parameters in eqs.(1) by simulation studies has been ineffective. Since the boundedness of the solution of eqs.(1) was already proved by Matsuoka [13], the analysis of the existence of equilibrium states and their stability is important in this study. Let

$$\boldsymbol{u} \equiv \begin{pmatrix} x_0 & x_1 & x_2 & x_3 & f_0 & f_1 & f_2 & f_3 \end{pmatrix}^t \quad (2)$$

$$\boldsymbol{s} \equiv \begin{pmatrix} s_0 & s_1 & s_2 & s_3 \end{pmatrix}^t \qquad (3)$$

then we obtain a representation as

$$\dot{\boldsymbol{u}} = \boldsymbol{A}\boldsymbol{u} + \boldsymbol{B}\boldsymbol{s} \qquad (4)$$

where $\boldsymbol{A}$ is an 8×8 matrix and $\boldsymbol{B}$ is an 8×4 matrix in the following.

$$\mathbf{A} = \begin{pmatrix} -\frac{1}{T_r}\mathbf{A_{11}} & -\frac{b}{T_r}\mathbf{I_4} \\ \frac{1}{T_a}\mathbf{A_{21}} & -\frac{1}{T_a}\mathbf{I_4} \end{pmatrix} \qquad (5)$$

$$\mathbf{A_{11}} = \begin{pmatrix} 1 & a_{01}m_1 & a_{02}m_2 & a_{03}m_3 \\ a_{10}m_0 & 1 & a_{12}m_2 & \dot{a}_{13}m_3 \\ a_{20}m_0 & a_{21}m_1 & 1 & a_{23}m_3 \\ a_{30}m_0 & a_{31}m_1 & a_{32}m_2 & 1 \end{pmatrix}$$

The equilibrium states of eq.(4) are obtained by the condition $\dot{\boldsymbol{u}} \equiv 0$. Then, the linearized equations can be obtained around an equilibrium and their stability can be examined by the *Hurwitz* criterion. In the following, we take two parameters $a_{20} \equiv a_{31} \equiv X$ and $a_{02} \equiv a_{13} \equiv Y$ (other parameters are shown in Figure 1 and Table 1).

Under the given conditions, it could be clarified that three equilibria exist in the quadrants of $(m_0, m_1, m_2, m_3) = (1,1,1,1), (1,1,0,0)$ and $(1,1,0,1)$. The stability chart is shown in Figure 7. In the unstable zone, oscillations appear. However, note that, as stated previously, all the oscillations in this zone cannot accommodate to the stationary walking patterns for the biped locomotive robot. Also, note that chaotic oscillations may appear. This situation is difficult for theoretical analysis, and we used simulation studies. As a result, a zone corresponding to the mode of stationary walking is depicted by two black circles in Figure 7.

VI. CONCLUSION

A trajectory for the biped locomotive robot has been generated using a mutually coupled neuro oscillator with four cells. Its relevancy was studied by stability analysis and simulation. The existence of equilibria and their stability were found by theoretical analysis, while the stationary walking zone in the parameter plane could be obtained by the computer simulation. With the parameters in this walking zone, the neuro oscillator can generate various modes for the biped locomotion.

Achnowledgement

The research was financially supported by the grant-in-aid for scientific research on priority areas, "Autonomous Distributed Systems (Nos.03234109 and 04218109)", by the Ministry of Education, Science and Culture of Japan.

REFERENCES

[1] H.Miura(*ed.*): Status of the Research on the Mechanism and Control of Biped Locomotive Robots; Report for the Grant-in-Aids for the Scientific Research by the Ministry of Education, Science and Culture of Japan. (1987) (in Japanese)

[2] Y.Kurematsu, S.Kitamura and Y.Kondo: Trajectory Planning and Control of a Biped Locomotive Robot-Simulation and Experiment-; Robotics and Manufacturing, Recent Trends in Research, Education, and Applications, M.Jamshidi (*ed.*), pp.65-72, ASME Press. (1988)

[3] A.Takanishi, M.Ishida, Y.Yamazaki and I.Kato: The Realization of Dynamic Walking by the Biped Walking Robot WL-10RD, Journal of the Robotics Society of Japan, Vol.2, No.4, pp.67-78 (1985) (in Japanese)

[4] E.Igarashi and T.Nogai: Study on the Lower Level Adaptive Walking in Sagittal Plane by a Biped Locomotion Robot, Journal of the Robotics Society of Japan, Vol.7, No.6, pp.12-22, (1989) (in Japanese)

[5] S.Kitamura, Y.Kurematsu and M.Iwata: Motion Generation of a Biped Locomotive Robot Using an Inverted Pendulum Model and Neural Networks, Proc. 29th IEEE Conference on Decision and Control, pp.3308-3313 (1990)

[6] H.Yuasa, Y.Ito and M.Ito: Autonomous Distributed Systems which Generate Various Patterns Using Bifurcation, Trans.

Region for existence of an equilibrium state in the quadrant of (1111), (1101) and (1100).

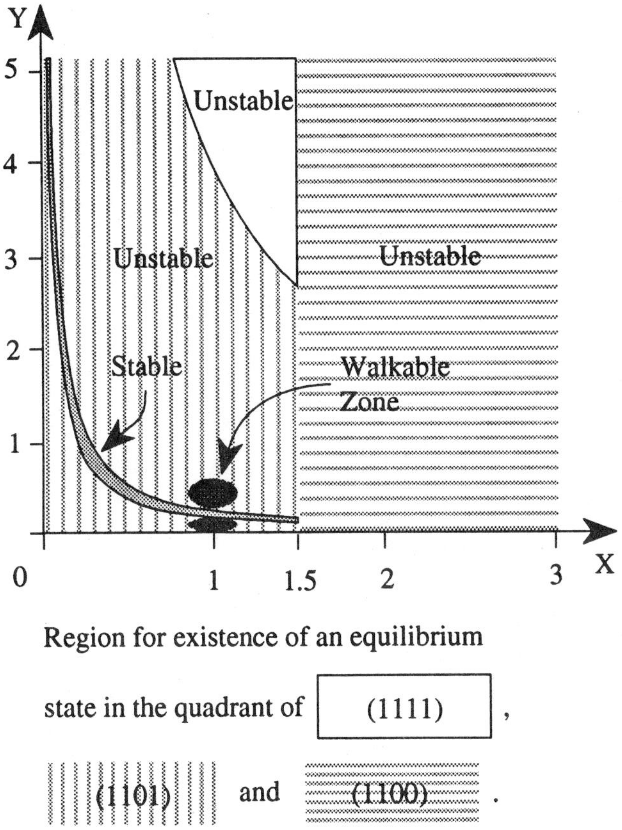

Figure 7: Stability chart for equilibria of eqs.(1) and the walking zone in the region $[0, 3] \times [0, 5]$

of the SICE, Vol.27, No.11, pp.1307-1314
(1991) (in Japanese)

[7] S.Kumagai et al: Coupling Between Respiratory and Stepping Ryhthms during Controlled Locomotion in Decerebrate Cats, MBE88-165, Institute of Electronics, Information and Communication Engineers, pp.57-62 (1988) (in Japanese)

[8] R.Katoh and M.Mori: Control Method of Biped Locomotion Giving Asymptotic Stability of Trajectory, Automatica., Vol.20, No.4, pp.405-414 (1984)

[9] J.S.Bay and H.Hemami: Modeling of a Neural Pattern Generator with Coupled Nonlinear Oscillators, IEEE Transactions on Biomedical Engineering, Vol. BME-34, No.4 pp.297-306 (1987)

[10] M.Frik: A nonlinear pattern generator for legged locomotion systems, The 4th Japanese-German Seminar on Nonlinear Problems in Dynamical System - Theory and Applications -, K.Hirai and E.Shimemura(*eds.*) ,pp.12-20 (1989)

[11] G.Taga, Y.Yamaguchi and H.Shimizu: Self-organized control of bipedal locomotion by neural oscillators in unpredictable environment, Biol. Cybern. 65, pp.147-159 (1991)

[12] K.Matsuoka: Mechanisms of Frequency and Pattern Control in the Neural Rhythm Generators, Biol. Cybern. 56, pp.345-353 (1987)

[13] K.Matsuoka: The Dynamic Model of Binocular Rivalry, Biol. Cybern. 49, pp.201-208 (1984)

NEURAL NET ROBOT CONTROLLER: STRUCTURE AND STABILITY PROOFS

F. L. Lewis, A. Yesildirek, and K. Liu
Automation and Robotics Research Institute
The University of Texas at Arlington
7300 Jack Newell Blvd. S
Ft. Worth, Texas 76118

Research supported by NSF Grants MSS-9114009, IRI-9216545

ABSTRACT

A multilayer neural net (NN) controller for a general serial-link robot arm is developed. The structure of the NN controller is derived using a filtered error/passivity approach. No learning phase is needed. It is argued that standard backpropagation tuning, when used for real-time closed-loop control, can yield unbounded NN weights if: (1) the net cannot exactly reconstruct a certain required nonlinear control function, (2) there are bounded unknown disturbances in the robot dynamics, or (3) the robot arm has more than one link (i.e. nonlinear case). Novel on-line weight tuning algorithms given here include correction terms to backpropagation, plus an added robustifying signal, and guarantee tracking as well as bounded weights. Notions of NN passivity are given.

1. INTRODUCTION

Much has been written about NN for system identification (e.g. [8]) or identification-based ('indirect') control, little about the use of NN in direct closed-loop controllers that yield guaranteed performance. Some results showing the relations between NN and direct adaptive control, as well as some notions on NN for robot control, are given in [3,6,9,11,13,14,17]. See also [5].

Persistent problems that remain to be adequately addressed include ad hoc controller structures and the inability to guarantee satisfactory performance of the system. Uncertainty on how to initialize the NN weights leads to the necessity for 'preliminary off-line tuning'. Some of these problems have been addressed for the 2-layer NN, where linearity in the parameters holds [11,13,14].

In this paper we confront these deficiencies for the full nonlinear 3-layer NN. Some notions in robot control [4] are tied to some notions in NN theory. The NN weights are tuned on-line, with <u>no 'learning phase' needed</u>. Fast convergence of the tracking error is comparable to that of adaptive controllers. The controller structure ensures good performance during the initial period if the NN weights are initialized at zero. Tracking performance is guaranteed using a Lyapunov approach even though there do not exist 'ideal' weights such that the NN perfectly reconstructs a required nonlinear function.

It is shown here that the <u>backpropagation tuning technique generally yields unbounded NN weights</u> if the net cannot exactly reconstruct a certain nonlinear robot function, or if there are bounded unmodelled disturbances in the robot dynamics, or if the robot function is not linear (which it never is for arms with more than one link). Modified weight tuning rules introduced here guarantee tracking and bounded weights for the general case. The modifications consist of: (1) the e-modification in [7], and (2) a term corresponding to a second-order <u>forward propagating wave</u> in the backprop tuning network [8]. Also required is a robustifying extra control signal.

2. BACKGROUND

Let R denote the real numbers, R^n denote the real n-vectors, R^{mxn} the real m x n matrices. Let S be a compact simply connected set of R^n. With map f: $S \to R^m$, define $C^m(S)$ as the space such that f is continuous. We denote by $\|.\|$ any suitable vector norm. When it is required to be specific we denote the p-norm by $\|.\|_p$. Given A= $[a_{ij}]$, B $\in R^{mxn}$ the <u>Frobenius norm</u> is defined by

$$\|A\|_F^2 = tr(A^TA) = \sum_{i,j} a^2_{ij} ,$$

with tr() the trace. The associated inner product is $<A,B>_F= tr(A^TB)$. The Frobenius norm cannot be defined as the induced matrix norm for any vector norm, but is <u>compatible</u> with the 2-norm so that $\|Ax\|_2 \le \|A\|_F \|x\|_2$, with $A \in R^{mxn}$ and $x \in R^n$.

2.1 Neural Networks

Given $x_k \in R$, a three-layer neural net (NN) (Fig. 2.1) has a net output given by

$$y_i= \sum_{j=1}^{N_2} \left[w_{ij} \; \sigma[\sum_{k=1}^{N_1} v_{jk}x_k + \theta_{vj}] + \theta_{wi} \right]; \; i= 1,..,N_3 \quad (2.1)$$

with $\sigma(.)$ the activation functions, v_{jk} the first-to-second layer interconnection weights, and w_{ij} the second-to-third layer interconnection weights. The θ_{vl}, θ_{wl}, $l= 1,2,...,$ are threshold offsets and the number of neurons in layer l is N_l, with N_2 the number of hidden-layer neurons.

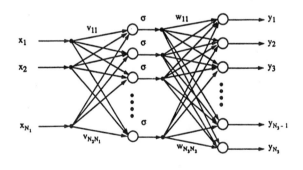

Figure 2.1 Three Layer Neural Network

The NN equation may be conveniently expressed in matrix format by defining x= $[x_0 \; x_1 \; x_2 \; ... \; x_{N1}]^T$, y= $[y_1 \; y_2 \; ... \; y_{N3}]^T$, and weight matrices $W^T= [w_{ij}]$, $V^T= [v_{jk}]$. Including $x_0= 1$ in x allows one to include the thresholds θ_{vj} as the first column of V^T, so that V^T contains both the weights and thresholds of the first-to-second layer connections. Then,

$$y= W^T \sigma(V^Tx) \quad (2.2)$$

with the vector of activation functions defined by $\sigma(z)= [\sigma(z_1)...\sigma(z_n)]^T$ for a vector $z \in R^n$ with components z_i (c.f. [13]). Including 1 as the first element of $\sigma(z)$ (i.e. above $\sigma(z_1)$) allows one to incorporate the thresholds θ_{wi} as the first column of W^T. Any tuning of W and V then includes tuning of the thresholds as well. Although, vectors x and $\sigma()$ may be thus augmented, we loosely say that $x \in R^{N1}$ and $\sigma: R^{N2} \to R^{N2}$.

A general function $f(x) \in C^m(S)$ can be written as

$$f(x) = W^T \sigma(V^T x) + \varepsilon(x), \qquad (2.3)$$

with $N_1 = n$, $N_3 = m$, and $\varepsilon(x)$ a <u>NN functional reconstruction error</u> vector. If there exist N_2 and constant 'ideal' weights W and V so that $\varepsilon = 0$ for all $x \in S$, we say $f(x)$ is <u>in the functional range of the NN</u>. In general, given a constant real number $\varepsilon_N > 0$, we say $f(x)$ is <u>within ε_N of the NN range</u> if there exist N_2 and constant weights so that for all $x \in R^n$, (2.3) holds with $\|\varepsilon\| < \varepsilon_N$.

Various well-known results for various activation functions $\sigma()$, based, e.g. on the Stone-Weierstrass theorem, say that any sufficiently smooth function can be approximated by a suitably large net [10,14]. In fact, the functional range of NN (2.2) can be shown to be dense in $C^m(S)$.

Typical selections for $\sigma()$ include the sigmoid, hyperbolic tangent, radial basis functions, etc. The issues of selecting σ, and of choosing N_2 for a specified $S \subset R^n$ and ε_N are current topics of research (see e.g. [10]).

2.2 Stability and Passive Systems

Consider the nonlinear system

$$\dot{x} = f(x,u,t) \ , \ y = h(x,t).$$

We say the solution is <u>globally uniformly ultimately bounded (GUUB)</u> if for all $x(t_0) = x_0$ there exists an $\varepsilon > 0$ and a number $T(\varepsilon, x_0)$ such that $\|x(t)\| < \varepsilon$ for all $t \geq t_0 + T$.

A system with input $u(t)$ and output $y(t)$ is said to be <u>passive</u> [4,16] if it verifies an equality of the so-called 'power form'

$$\dot{L}(t) = y^T u - g(t) \qquad (2.4)$$

with $L(t)$ lower bounded and $g(t) \geq 0$. That is,

$$\int_0^T y^T(\tau) u(\tau) \, d\tau \geq \int_0^T g(\tau) \, d\tau \ - \ \gamma^2 \qquad (2.5)$$

for all $T \geq 0$ and some $\gamma \geq 0$.

We say the system is <u>dissipative</u> if it is passive and in addition

$$\int_0^\infty y^T(\tau) u(\tau) \, d\tau \neq 0 \ \text{implies} \ \int_0^\infty g(\tau) \, d\tau > 0. \qquad (2.6)$$

A special sort of dissipativity occurs if $g(t)$ is a monic quadratic function of $\|x\|$ with bounded coefficients, where $x(t)$ is the internal state of the system. We call this <u>state strict passivity</u>, and are not aware of its use previously in the literature. Then the L_2 norm of the state is overbounded in terms of the L_2 inner product of output and input (i.e. the power delivered to the system). This we use to conclude some internal boundedness properties of the system without the usual assumption of persistence of excitation.

2.3 Robot Arm Dynamics

The dynamics of an n-link robot manipulator may be expressed in the Lagrange form [4]

$$M(q) \ddot{q} + V_m(q,\dot{q}) \dot{q} + G(q) + F(\dot{q}) + \tau_d = \tau \qquad (2.7)$$

with $q(t) \in R^n$ the joint variable vector, $M(q)$ the inertia matrix, $V_m(q,\dot{q})$ the coriolis/centripetal matrix, $G(q)$ the gravity vector, and $F(\dot{q})$ the friction. Bounded unknown disturbances (including e.g. unstructured unmodelled dynamics) are denoted by τ_d, and the control input torque is $\tau(t)$.

Given a desired arm trajectory $q_d(t) \in R^n$ the <u>tracking error</u> is

$$e(t) = q_d(t) - q(t) \qquad (2.8)$$

and the <u>filtered tracking error</u> is

$$r = \dot{e} + \Lambda e \qquad (2.9)$$

where $\Lambda = \Lambda^T > 0$ is a design parameter matrix, usually selected diagonal. Differentiating $r(t)$ and using (2.7), the arm dynamics may be written in terms of the filtered tracking error as

$$M\dot{r} = -V_m r - \tau + f + \tau_d \qquad (2.10)$$

where the <u>nonlinear robot function</u> is

$$f(x) = M(q)(\ddot{q}_d + \Lambda \dot{e}) + V_m(q,\dot{q})(\dot{q}_d + \Lambda e) + G(q) + F(\dot{q}) \qquad (2.11)$$

and, for instance,

$$x = [e^T \ \dot{e}^T \ q_d^T \ \dot{q}_d^T \ \ddot{q}_d^T]^T. \qquad (2.12)$$

Define now a control input torque as

$$\tau_0 = \hat{f} + K_v r \qquad (2.13)$$

with $\hat{f}(x)$ an estimate of $f(x)$ and a gain matrix $K_v = K_v^T > 0$. Note that τ_0 incorporates a PD term $K_v r = K_v(\dot{e} + \Lambda e)$. The closed-loop system becomes

$$M\dot{r} = -(K_v + V_m)r + \tilde{f} + \tau_d = -(K_v + V_m)r + \zeta_0 \qquad (2.14)$$

where the functional estimation error is given by

$$\tilde{f} = f - \hat{f} \qquad (2.15)$$

This is an error system wherein the filtered tracking error is driven by the functional estimation error.

In the remainder of the paper we shall use (2.14) to focus on selecting NN tuning algorithms that guarantee the stability of the filtered tracking error $r(t)$. Then, standard techniques [16] guarantee that $e(t)$ exhibits stable behavior.

The following properties of the robot dynamics are required [4].

<u>Property 1</u>: $M(q)$ is a positive definite symmetric matrix bounded by $m_1 I \leq M(q) \leq m_2 I$, with m_1, m_2 known positive constants.

<u>Property 2</u>: $V_m(q,\dot{q})$ is bounded by $v_b(q)\|\dot{q}\|$, with $v_b(q) \in C^1(S)$.

<u>Property 3</u>: The matrix $\dot{M} - 2V_m$ is skew-symmetric.

<u>Property 4</u>: The unknown disturbance satisfies $\|\tau_d\| < b_d$, with b_d a known positive constant.

<u>Property 5</u>: The dynamics (2.14) from $\zeta_0(t)$ to $r(t)$ are a state strict passive system.

<u>Proof of Property 5</u>: Take the nonnegative function

$$L = \tfrac{1}{2} r^T M r$$

so that, using (2.14)

$$\dot{L} = r^T M \dot{r} + \tfrac{1}{2} r^T \dot{M} r = -r^T K_v r + \tfrac{1}{2} r^T (\dot{M} - 2V_m)r + r^T \zeta_0$$

whence skew-symmetry yields the power form

$$\dot{L} = r^T \zeta_0 - r^T K_v r. \qquad \blacksquare$$

3. NN CONTROLLER

In this section we derive a NN controller for the robot dynamics in Section 2. We propose various weight tuning algorithms that guarantee tracking, including standard backpropagation. It is shown that with backpropagation tuning the NN can only be guaranteed to perform suitably in closed-loop under ideal conditions (which require e.g. $f(x)$ linear). A modified tuning algorithm is then proposed so that the NN controller performs under realistic conditions.

Thus, assume that the nonlinear robot function (2.11) is given by a neural net as in (2.3) for some constant 'ideal' NN weights W and V, where the net reconstruction error $\varepsilon(x)$ is bounded by a known constant ε_N. <u>We only need to know that such ideal weights exist; their actual values are not required.</u> For notational convenience define the matrix of all the weights as

$$Z = \begin{bmatrix} W \\ V \end{bmatrix}, \qquad (3.1)$$

with padding by zeros for dimensional consistency.

3.1 Some Bounding Assumptions and Facts

Some <u>bounding assumptions/facts</u> are now stated.

<u>**Assumption 1**</u>

The ideal weights are bounded by known positive values so that $\|V\|_F \le V_M$, $\|W\|_F \le W_M$, or

$$\|Z\|_F \le Z_M \qquad (3.2)$$

with Z_M known.

<u>**Assumption 2**</u>

The desired trajectory is bounded in the sense, for instance, that for some known constant $Q_d \in R$,

$$\begin{Vmatrix} q_d \\ \dot{q}_d \\ \ddot{q}_d \end{Vmatrix} \le Q_d. \qquad (3.3)$$

∎

<u>**Fact 3**</u>

For each time t, $x(t)$ in (2.12) is bounded by

$$\|x\| \le c_1 Q_d + c_2 \|r\| \qquad (3.4)$$

for computable positive constants c_i (c_2 decreases as Λ increases.)

∎

The next discussion is of major importance in this paper (c.f. [12]). With V, W some estimates of the ideal weight values, define the weight deviations or <u>weight estimation errors</u> as

$$\tilde{V} = V - \hat{V}, \quad \tilde{W} = W - \hat{W}, \quad \tilde{Z} = Z - \hat{Z} \qquad (3.5)$$

and the <u>hidden layer output error</u> for a given x as

$$\tilde{\sigma} = \sigma - \hat{\sigma} = \sigma(V^T x) - \sigma(\hat{V}^T x). \qquad (3.6)$$

The Taylor series expansion for a given x is

$$\sigma(V^T x) = \sigma(\hat{V}^T x) + \sigma'(\hat{V}^T x)\, \tilde{V}^T x + O(\tilde{V}^T x)^2 \qquad (3.7)$$

with $\sigma'(\hat{z}) = d\sigma(z)/dz |_{z = \hat{z}}$, and $O(z)^2$ denoting terms of order two. Denoting $\hat{\sigma}' = \sigma'(\hat{V}^T x)$, we have

$$\tilde{\sigma} = \sigma'(\hat{V}^T x)\tilde{V}^T x + O(\tilde{V}^T x)^2 = \hat{\sigma}'\tilde{V}^T x + O(\tilde{V}^T x)^2. \qquad (3.8)$$

Different bounds may be put on the Taylor series higher-order terms depending on the choice for $\sigma(\cdot)$. Noting that

$$O(\tilde{V}^T x)^2 = [\sigma(V^T x) - \sigma(\hat{V}^T x)] - \sigma'(\hat{V}^T x)\,\tilde{V}^T x \qquad (3.9)$$

we take the following.

<u>**Fact 4**</u>

For sigmoid, RBF, and tanh activation functions, the higher-order terms in the Taylor series are bounded by

$$\|O(\tilde{V}^T x)^2\| \le c_3 + c_4 Q_d \|\tilde{V}\|_F + c_5 \|\tilde{V}\|_F \|r\|$$

where c_i are computable positive constants. ∎

Fact 4 is direct to show using (3.4), some standard norm inequalities, and the fact that $\sigma(\cdot)$ and its derivative are bounded by constants for RBF, sigmoid, and tanh.

3.2 Controller Structure and Error System Dynamics

Define the <u>NN functional estimate</u> of (2.11) by

$$\hat{f}(x) = \hat{W}^T \sigma(\hat{V}^T x), \qquad (3.10)$$

with $\hat{V}$, $\hat{W}$ the current (estimated) values of the ideal NN weights V, W. With τ_0 defined in (2.13), select the control input

$$\tau = \tau_0 - v = \hat{W}^T \sigma(\hat{V}^T x) + K_v r - v, \qquad (3.11)$$

with $v(t)$ a function to be detailed subsequently that provides robustness in the face of higher-order terms in the Taylor series. The proposed NN control structure is shown in Fig. 3.1, where $\underline{q} = [q^T \quad \dot{q}^T]^T$, $\underline{e} = [e^T \quad \dot{e}^T]^T$.

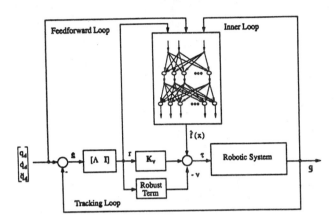

Figure 3.1 Neural Net Control Structure

Using this controller, the closed-loop filtered error dynamics become

$$M\dot{r} = -(K_v + V_m)r + W^T \sigma(V^T x) - \hat{W}^T \sigma(\hat{V}^T x) + (\varepsilon + \tau_d) + v.$$

Adding and subtracting $W^T \hat{\sigma}$ yields

$$M\dot{r} = -(K_v + V_m)r + \tilde{W}^T \hat{\sigma} + W^T \tilde{\sigma} + (\varepsilon + \tau_d) + v.$$

with $\hat{\sigma}$ and $\tilde{\sigma}$ defined in (3.6). Adding and subtracting now $\hat{W}^T \tilde{\sigma}$ yields

$$M\dot{r} = -(K_v + V_m)r + \tilde{W}^T \hat{\sigma} + \hat{W}^T \tilde{\sigma} + \tilde{W}^T \tilde{\sigma} + (\varepsilon + \tau_d) + v. \qquad (3.12)$$

The key step is the use now of the Taylor series approximation (3.8) for $\tilde{\sigma}$, according to which the closed-loop error system is

$$M\dot{r} = -(K_v + V_m)r + \tilde{W}^T \hat{\sigma} + \hat{W}^T \hat{\sigma}' \tilde{V}^T x + w_1 + v \qquad (3.13)$$

where the disturbance terms are

$$w_1(t) = \tilde{W}^T \hat{\sigma}' \tilde{V}^T x + W^T O(\tilde{V}^T x)^2 + (\varepsilon + \tau_d). \qquad (3.14)$$

Unfortunately, using this error system does not yield a compact set outside which a certain Lyapunov function derivative is negative. Therefore, write finally the error system

$$M\dot{r} = -(K_v + V_m)r + \tilde{W}^T (\hat{\sigma} - \hat{\sigma}'\hat{V}^T x) + \hat{W}^T \hat{\sigma}' \tilde{V}^T x + w + v$$

$$= -(K_v + V_m)r + \zeta_1. \qquad (3.15)$$

where the disturbance terms are

$$w(t) = \tilde{W}^T \hat{\sigma}' V^T x + W^T O(\tilde{V}^T x)^2 + (\varepsilon + \tau_d). \qquad (3.16)$$

The next key bound is required. Its importance is in allowing one to overbound $w(t)$ at each time by a <u>known computable function</u>; it follows from Fact 4 and some standard norm inequalities.

<u>**Fact 5**</u>

The disturbance term (3.16) is bounded according to

$$\|w(t)\| \le (\varepsilon_N + b_d + c_3 Z_M) + c_6 Z_M \|\tilde{Z}\|_F + c_7 Z_M \|\tilde{Z}\|_F \|r\|$$

or

$$\|w(t)\| \le C_0 + C_1 \|\tilde{Z}\|_F + C_2 \|\tilde{Z}\|_F \|r\| \qquad (3.17)$$

with C_i known positive constants. ∎

3.3 Weight Updates for Guaranteed Tracking Performance

We give here some NN weight tuning algorithms that

guarantee the tracking stability of the closed-loop system under various assumptions. It is required to demonstrate that the tracking error r(t) is suitably small and that the NN weights V, W remain bounded, for then the control $\tau(t)$ is bounded.

Note that the problem of <u>net weight initialization</u> occurring in other approaches in the literature does not arise, since if W(0), V(0) are taken as zero the PD term $K_v r$ in (3.11) stabilizes the plant on an interim basis. A formal proof reveals that K_v should be large enough and the initial filtered error r(0) small enough.

Ideal Case- Backpropagation Tuning of Weights

The next result details the closed-loop behavior in a certain idealized case that demands: (1) no net functional reconstruction error, (2) no unmodelled disturbances in the robot arm dynamics, and (3) no higher-order Taylor series terms. The last amounts to the assumption that f(x) in (2.10) is <u>linear</u>. In this case the tuning rules are straightforward and familiar.

Theorem 3.1

Let the desired trajectory be bounded and suppose the disturbance term $w_1(t)$ in (3.13) is equal to zero. Let the control input for (2.7) be given by (3.11) with v(t)= 0 and weight tuning provided by

$$\dot{\hat{W}} = F\hat{\sigma}r^T \tag{3.18}$$

$$\dot{\hat{V}} = Gx(\hat{\sigma}'^T\hat{W}r)^T \tag{3.19}$$

and any constant positive definite (design) matrices F, G. Then the tracking error r(t) goes to zero with t and the weight estimates V, W are bounded.

Proof:

Define the Lyapunov function candidate

$$L= \tfrac{1}{2}r^T Mr + \tfrac{1}{2}\, tr(\tilde{W}^T F^{-1}\tilde{W}) + \tfrac{1}{2}tr(\tilde{V}^T G^{-1}\tilde{V}) \tag{3.20}$$

Differentiating yields

$$\dot{L}= r^T M\dot{r} + \tfrac{1}{2}r^T\dot{M}r + tr(\tilde{W}^T F^{-1}\dot{\tilde{W}}) + tr(\tilde{V}^T G^{-1}\dot{\tilde{V}}),$$

whence substitution from (3.13) (with w_1= 0, v= 0) yields

$$\dot{L}= -r^T K_v r + \tfrac{1}{2}r^T(\dot{M}-2V_m)r + tr\,\tilde{W}^T(F^{-1}\dot{\tilde{W}} + \hat{\sigma}r^T)$$
$$+ tr\,\tilde{V}^T(G^{-1}\dot{\tilde{V}} + xr^T\hat{W}^T\hat{\sigma}')$$

The skew symmetry property makes the second term zero, and since $\tilde{W}= W-\hat{W}$ with W constant, so that $d\tilde{W}/dt= -d\hat{W}/dt$ (and similarly for V), the tuning rules yield

$$\dot{L}= -r^T K_v r.$$

Since L> 0 and $\dot{L}\leq 0$ this shows stability in the sense of Lyapunov so that r, $\tilde{V}$, and $\tilde{W}$ (and hence V, W) are bounded. Moreover,

$$\int_0^\infty -\dot{L}\, dt < \infty . \tag{3.21}$$

Boundedness of r guarantees the boundedness of e and $\dot{e}$, whence boundedness of the desired trajectory shows q, $\dot{q}$, x are bounded. Property 2 then shows boundedness of $V_m(q,\dot{q})$. Now, $\ddot{L}= -2r^T K_v \dot{r}$, and the boundedness of $M^{-1}(q)$ and of all signals on the right-hand side of (3.13) verify the boundedness of $\dot{r}$, and hence the uniform continuity of $\dot{L}$. This allows one to invoke Barbalat's Lemma [4,16] in connection with (3.21) to conclude that $\dot{L}$ goes to zero with t, and hence that r(t) vanishes. ∎

Note that (3.18), (3.19) is nothing but the continuous version of the <u>backpropagation algorithm</u>. In the scalar sigmoid case, for instance,

$$\sigma'(z)= \sigma(z)(1-\sigma(z)), \qquad \hat{\sigma}'^T\hat{W}r = \sigma(\hat{V}^T x)[1 - \sigma(\hat{V}^T x)]\,\hat{W}r,$$

which is the filtered error weighted by the current estimate $\hat{W}$ and multiplied by the usual product involving the hidden layer outputs.

Theorem 3.1 reveals the failure of standard backpropagation in the general case. In fact, in the 2-layer NN case V= I (i.e. linear in the parameters), it is easy to show that, using update rule (3.18), the weights W are not generally bounded unless the hidden layer output $\sigma(x)$ obeys a stringent <u>persistency of excitation (PE)</u> condition. In the 3-layer (nonlinear) case, PE conditions are not easy to derive or guarantee as one is faced with the observability properties of a certain bilinear system. Thus, <u>backpropagation used in a net that cannot exactly reconstruct f(x), or on a robot arm with bounded unmodelled disturbances, or when f(x) is nonlinear, cannot be guaranteed to yield bounded weights in the closed-loop system</u>.

General Case

To attack the stability and tracking performance of a NN robot arm controller in the thorny general case we require the modification of the weight tuning rules as well as the addition of a robustifying term v(t).

Theorem 3.2

Let the desired trajectory be bounded by (3.3). Take the control input for (2.7) as (3.11) with

$$v(t)= -K_z(\|\hat{Z}\|_F + Z_M)\, r \tag{3.22}$$

and gain

$$K_z> C_2 \tag{3.23}$$

with C_2 the known constant in (3.17). Let weight tuning be provided by

$$\dot{\hat{W}}= F\hat{\sigma}r^T - F\hat{\sigma}'\hat{V}^T xr^T - \kappa F\|r\|\hat{W} \tag{3.24}$$

$$\dot{\hat{V}}= Gx(\hat{\sigma}'^T\hat{W}r)^T - \kappa G\|r\|\hat{V} \tag{3.25}$$

with any constant matrices F= F^T> 0, G= G^T> 0, and scalar design parameter κ>0. Then the filtered tracking error r(t) and NN weight estimates V, W are GUUB.

Proof:

Selecting the Lyapunov function (3.20), differentiating, and substituting now from the error system (3.15) yields

$$\dot{L}= -r^T K_v r + \tfrac{1}{2}r^T(\dot{M}-2V_m)r + tr\,\tilde{W}^T(F^{-1}\dot{\tilde{W}} + \hat{\sigma}r^T - \hat{\sigma}'\hat{V}^T xr^T)$$
$$+ tr\,\tilde{V}^T(G^{-1}\dot{\tilde{V}} + xr^T\hat{W}^T\hat{\sigma}') + r^T(w+v).$$

The tuning rules give

$$\dot{L}= -r^T K_v r + \kappa\|r\|\, tr\,\tilde{W}^T(W-\tilde{W}) + \kappa\|r\|\, tr\,\tilde{V}^T(V-\tilde{V}) + r^T(w+v)$$
$$= -r^T K_v r + \kappa\|r\|\, tr\,\tilde{Z}^T(Z-\tilde{Z}) + r^T(w+v).$$

Since $tr\,\tilde{Z}^T(Z-\tilde{Z}) = \langle\tilde{Z}, Z\rangle_F - \|\tilde{Z}\|_F^2 \leq \|\tilde{Z}\|_F \|Z\|_F - \|\tilde{Z}\|_F^2$, there results

$$\dot{L}\leq - K_{vmin}\|r\|^2 + \kappa\|r\|\,\|\tilde{Z}\|_F (Z_M - \|\tilde{Z}\|_F) - K_z(\|\hat{Z}\|_F+Z_M)\|r\|^2$$
$$+ \|r\|\,\|w\|$$

$$\leq - K_{vmin}\|r\|^2 + \kappa\|r\|\,\|\tilde{Z}\|_F (Z_M - \|\tilde{Z}\|_F) - K_z(\|\hat{Z}\|_F+Z_M)\|r\|^2$$
$$+ \|r\|\,[C_0 + C_1\|\tilde{Z}\|_F + C_2\|\tilde{Z}\|_F\|r\|]$$

$$\leq -\|r\|\,[K_{vmin}\|r\| + \kappa\|\tilde{Z}\|_F (\|\tilde{Z}\|_F-Z_M) - C_0 - C_1\|\tilde{Z}\|_F],$$

where K_{vmin} is the minimum singular value of K_v and the last inequality holds due to (3.23). Thus, $\dot{L}$ is negative as long as the term in braces is positive.

Defining $C_3= Z_M+C_1/\kappa$ and completing the square yields

$$K_{vmin}\|r\| + \kappa\|\tilde{Z}\|_F (\|\tilde{Z}\|_F-C_3) - C_0$$
$$= \kappa(\|\tilde{Z}\|_F - C_3/2)^2 - \kappa C_3^2/4 + K_{vmin}\|r\| - C_0,$$

which is guaranteed positive as long as either

140

$$\|r\| > \frac{\kappa C_2^2/4 + C_0}{K_{vmin}} \qquad (3.26)$$

or

$$\|\tilde{Z}\|_F > C_3/2 + \sqrt{C_3^2/4 + C_0/\kappa} \quad . \qquad (3.27)$$

This demonstrates the GUUB of both $\|r\|$ and $\|\tilde{Z}\|_F$. ∎

The first terms of (3.24), (3.25) are nothing but the standard backpropagation algorithm. The last terms correspond to the e-modification [7] in standard use in adaptive control to guarantee bounded parameter estimates. The second term in (3.24) is very interesting and bears discussion. The standard backprop terms can be thought of as backward propagating signals in a nonlinear 'backprop' network [8] that contains multipliers. The second term in (3.24) corresponds to a <u>forward travelling wave in the backprop net</u> that provides a second-order correction to the weight tuning for W.

Note from (3.26), that <u>arbitrarily small tracking error bounds may be achieved</u> by selecting large control gains K_v. On the other hand, (3.27) reveals that <u>the NN weight errors are fundamentally bounded</u> by Z_M (through C_3). The parameter κ offers a design tradeoff between the relative eventual magnitudes of $\|r\|$ and $\|\tilde{Z}\|_F$.

Note that there is <u>design freedom in the degree of complexity (e.g. size) of the NN</u>. For a more complex NN (e.g. more hidden units), the bounding constants will decrease, resulting in smaller tracking errors. On the other hand, a simplified NN with fewer hidden units will result in larger error bounds; this degradation can be compensated for, as long as bound ε_N is known, by selecting a larger value for K_z in the robustifying signal $v(t)$, or for Λ in (2.9).

4. PASSIVITY PROPERTIES OF THE NN

The <u>closed-loop error system</u> appears in Fig. 4.1, with the signal ζ_2 defined as

$$\zeta_2(t) = -\tilde{W}^T\hat{\sigma} \qquad \text{, for error system (3.13)}$$
$$\zeta_2(t) = -\tilde{W}^T(\hat{\sigma} - \hat{\sigma}'\hat{V}^Tx), \text{ for error system (3.15).} \qquad (4.1)$$

(In the former case, signal $w(t)$ should be replaced by $w_1(t)$.) The NN appears here in standard feedback configuration.

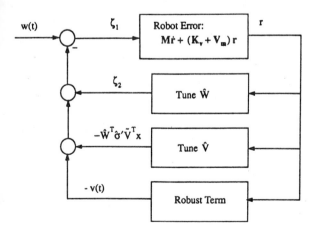

Figure 4.1 Neural Net Closed-loop Error System

Passivity is important in a closed-loop system as it guarantees the boundedness of signals, and hence suitable performance, even in the presence of <u>additional unforseen disturbances</u> as long as they are bounded. In general a NN cannot be guaranteed to be passive. The next results show, however, that the weight tuning algorithms given here do in fact guarantee desirable passivity properties

of the NN, and hence of the closed-loop system.

The first result is with regard to error system (3.13).

<u>Theorem 4.1</u>

The backprop weight tuning algorithms (3.18), (3.19) make the map from $r(t)$ to $-\tilde{W}^T\sigma$, and the map from $r(t)$ to $-\hat{W}^T\hat{\sigma}'\tilde{V}^Tx$, both passive maps.

<u>Proof</u>:
The dynamics with respect to $\tilde{W}$, $\tilde{V}$ are

$$\dot{\tilde{W}} = -F\hat{\sigma}r^T \qquad (4.2)$$

$$\dot{\tilde{V}} = -Gx(\hat{\sigma}'^T\hat{W}r)^T \qquad (4.3)$$

1. Selecting the nonnegative function

$$L = \frac{1}{2} \, tr \; \tilde{W}^TF^{-1}\tilde{W}$$

and evaluating $\dot{L}$ along the trajectories of (4.2) yields

$$\dot{L} = tr \; \tilde{W}^TF^{-1}\dot{\tilde{W}} = -tr \; \tilde{W}^T\hat{\sigma}r^T = r^T(-\tilde{W}^T\hat{\sigma}),$$

which is in power form (2.4).

2. Selecting the nonnegative function

$$L = \frac{1}{2} \, tr \; \tilde{V}^TF^{-1}\tilde{V}$$

and evaluating $\dot{L}$ along the trajectories of (4.3) yields

$$\dot{L} = tr \; \tilde{V}^TF^{-1}\dot{\tilde{V}} = -tr \; \tilde{V}^Tx(\hat{\sigma}'^T\hat{W}r)^T = r^T(-\hat{W}^T\hat{\sigma}'\tilde{V}^Tx).$$

which is in power form. ∎

Thus, the robot error system in Fig. 4.1 is state strict passive (SSP) and the weight error blocks are passive; this guarantees the dissipativity of the closed-loop system [16]. Using the passivity theorem one may now conclude that the input/output signals of each block are bounded as long as the external inputs are bounded.

Unfortunately, though dissipative, the closed-loop system is <u>not</u> SSP so, when disturbance $w_1(t)$ is nonzero, this does not yield boundedness of the internal states of the weight blocks (i.e. $\tilde{W}$, $\tilde{V}$) unless those blocks are observable, that is <u>persistently exciting (PE)</u>. PE is very difficult to check or guarantee for a NN.

The next result shows why a PE condition is not needed with the modified weight update algorithm of Theorem 3.2; it is in the context of error system (3.15).

<u>Theorem 4.2</u>

The modified weight tuning algorithms (3.24), (3.25) make the map from $r(t)$ to $-\tilde{W}^T(\sigma - \sigma'\hat{V}^Tx)$, and the map from $r(t)$ to $-\hat{W}^T\hat{\sigma}'\tilde{V}^Tx$, both state strict passive (SSP) maps.

<u>Proof</u>:
The revised dynamics relative to $\tilde{W}$, $\tilde{V}$ are given by

$$\dot{\tilde{W}} = -F\hat{\sigma}r^T + F\hat{\sigma}'\hat{V}^Txr^T + \kappa F \|r\| \hat{W} \qquad (4.4)$$

$$\dot{\tilde{V}} = -Gx(\hat{\sigma}'^T\hat{W}r)^T + \kappa G \|r\| \hat{V}. \qquad (4.5)$$

1. Selecting the nonnegative function

$$L = \frac{1}{2} \, tr \; \tilde{W}^TF^{-1}\tilde{W}$$

and evaluating $\dot{L}$ yields

$$\dot{L} = tr \; \tilde{W}^TF^{-1}\dot{\tilde{W}} = r^T[-\tilde{W}^T(\hat{\sigma} - \hat{\sigma}'\hat{V}^Tx)] - \kappa\|r\| \, (\|\tilde{W}\|_F^2 - <\tilde{W},W>_F)$$

$$\leq r^T[-\tilde{W}^T(\hat{\sigma} - \hat{\sigma}'\hat{V}^Tx)] - \kappa\|r\| \, (\|\tilde{W}\|_F^2 - W_M\|\tilde{W}\|_F)$$

which is in power form with the last function quadratic in $\|\tilde{W}\|_F$.

2. Selecting the nonnegative function

$$L = \frac{1}{2} \, tr \; \tilde{V}^TF^{-1}\tilde{V}$$

and evaluating $\dot{L}$ yields

$$\dot{L} = \text{tr } \tilde{V}^T F^{-1} \dot{\tilde{V}} = r^T(-\hat{W}^T\hat{\sigma}'\tilde{V}^Tx) - \kappa\|r\| \, (\|\tilde{V}\|_F^2 - <\tilde{V},V>_F)$$

$$\leq r^T(-\hat{W}^T\hat{\sigma}'\tilde{V}^Tx) - \kappa\|r\| \, (\|\tilde{V}\|_F^2 - V_M\|\tilde{V}\|_F)$$

which is in power form with the last function quadratic in $\|\tilde{V}\|_F$. ∎

It should be noted that SSP of both the robot dynamics and the weight tuning blocks <u>does guarantee SSP of the closed-loop system</u>, so that the norms of the <u>internal states</u> are bounded in terms of the power delivered to each block. Then, boundedness of input/output signals assures state boundedness without any sort of observability requirement.

We define a NN as <u>passive</u> if, in the error formulation, it guarantees the passivity of the weight tuning subsystems. Then, an extra PE condition is needed to guarantee boundedness of the weights [?]. We define a NN as <u>robust</u> if, in the error formulation, it guarantees the SSP of the weight tuning subsystem. Then, no extra PE condition is needed for boundedness of the weights. Note that (1) SSP of the open-loop plant error system is needed in addition for tracking stability, and (2) the NN passivity properties are dependent on the weight tuning algorithm used.

5. ILLUSTRATIVE DESIGN AND SIMULATION

A planar 2-link arm used extensively in the literature for illustration purposes appears in Fig. 6.1. The dynamics are given, for instance in [4]; no friction term was used. The joint variable is $q = [q_1 \quad q_2]^T$. We should like to illustrate the NN control scheme derived herein, which will require no knowledge of the dynamics, not even their structure which is needed for adaptive control.

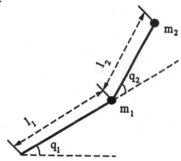

Fig 6.1 2-Link Planar Elbow Arm

<u>Adaptive Controller: Baseline Design</u>

For comparison, a standard adaptive controller is given by [15]

$$\tau = Y\hat{\psi} + K_v r \tag{5.1}$$

$$\dot{\hat{\psi}} = FY^T r \tag{5.2}$$

with $F = F^T > 0$ a design parameter matrix, $Y(e, \dot{e}, q_d, \dot{q}_d, \ddot{q}_d)$ a fairly complicated matrix of robot functions <u>that must be explicitly derived from the dynamics for each arm</u>, and ψ the vector of unknown parameters, in this case simply the link masses m_1, m_2.

We took the arm parameters as $\ell_1 = \ell_2 = 1$ m, $m_1 = 0.8$ kg, $m_2 = 2.3$ kg, and selected $q_{1d}(t) = \sin t$, $q_{2d}(t) = \cos t$, $K_v = \text{diag}\{20,20\}$, $F = \text{diag}\{10,10\}$, $\Lambda = \text{diag}\{5,5\}$. The response with this controller when $q(0) = 0$, $\dot{q}(0) = 0$, $\hat{m}_1(0) = 0$, $\hat{m}_2(0) = 0$ is shown in Fig. 6.2.

The (1,1) entry of the robot function matrix Y is $\ell_1^2(\ddot{q}_{d1} + \lambda_1 e_1) + \ell_1 g \cos q_1$ (with $\Lambda = \text{diag}\{\lambda_1, \lambda_2\}$). To demonstrate the deleterious effects of unmodeled dynamics in adaptive control, the term $\ell_1 g \cos q_1$ was now dropped in the controller. The result appears in Fig. 6.3 and is

very bad. It is emphasized that in the NN controller <u>all the dynamics are unmodeled.</u>

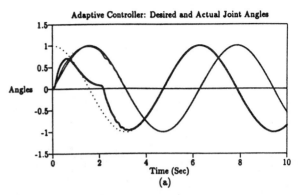

(a)

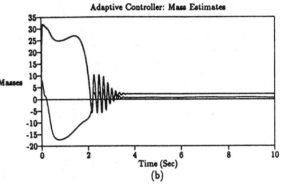

(b)

Figure 6.2 Response of Adaptive Controller. (a) Actual and Desired Joint Angles. (b) Parameter Estimates.

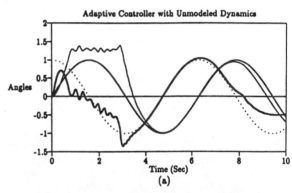

(a)

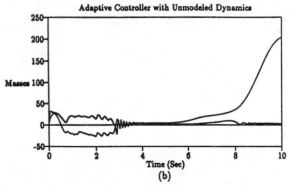

(b)

Figure 6.3 Response of Adaptive Controller with Unmodeled Dynamics. (a) Actual and Desired Joint Angles. (b) Parameter Estimates.

NN Controller With Backprop Weight Tuning

The NN controller appears in Fig. 3.1, with the NN input x(t) given by (2.12) and $\zeta_1 = \dot{q}_d + \Lambda e$, $\zeta_2 = \ddot{q}_d + \Lambda \dot{e}$. We selected 10 hidden-layer neurons. The sigmoid activation functions were used.

The response of the controller (3.11) (with $v(t) = 0$) with backprop weight tuning (e.g. Theorem 3.2) appears in Fig. 6.4. In this case the NN weights appear to remain bounded, though this cannot in general be guaranteed.

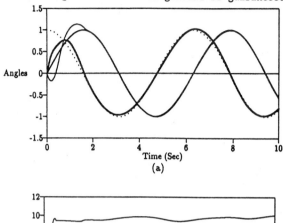

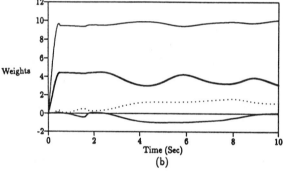

Figure 6.4 Response of NN Controller with BP Weight Tuning. (a) Actual and Desired Joint Angles. (b) Representative Weight Estimates.

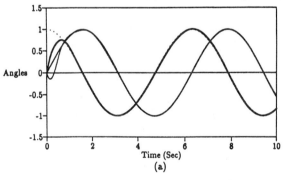

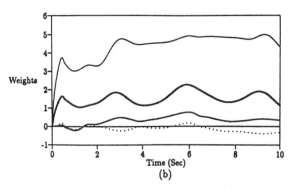

Figure 6.5 Response of Improved NN Controller. (a) Actual and Desired Joint Angles. (b) Representative Weight Estimates.

NN Controller With Improved Weight Tuning

The response of the controller (3.11) with the improved weight tuning in Theorem 3.2 appears in Fig. 6.5, where we took $\kappa = 0.1$. The tracking response is better than that using straight backprop, and the weights are guaranteed to remain bounded even though PE may not hold. The comparison with the performance of the standard adaptive controller in Fig. 6.2 is impressive, even though the dynamics of the arm were not required to implement the NN controller.

No initial NN training or learning phase was needed. The NN weights were simply initialized at zero in this figure.

REFERENCES

[1] R.G. Bartle, _The Elements of Real Analysis_, New York: Wiley, 1964.
[2] J.J. Craig, _Adaptive Control of Robot Manipulators_, Reading, VA: Addison-Wesley, 1988.
[3] Y. Iiguni, H. Sakai, and H. Tokumaru, "A nonlinear regulator design in the presence of system uncertaities using multilayer neural networks," _IEEE Trans. Neural Networks_, vol. 2, no. 4, pp. 410-417, July 1991.
[4] F.L. Lewis, C.T. Abdallah, and D.M. Dawson, _Control of Robot Manipulators_, New York: Macmillan, 1993.
[5] W.T. Miller, R.S. Sutton, P.J. Werbos, ed., _Neural Networks for Control_, Cambridge: MIT Press, 1991.
[6] K.S. Narendra, "Adaptive Control Using Neural Networks," _Neural Networks for Control_, pp 115-142. ed. W.T. Miller, R.S. Sutton, P.J. Werbos, Cambridge: MIT Press, 1991.
[7] K.S. Narendra and A.M. Annaswamy, "A new adaptive law for robust adaptation without persistent adaptation," _IEEE Trans. Automat. Control_, vol. AC-32, no. 2, pp. 134-145, Feb. 1987.
[8] K.S. Narendra and K. Parthasarathy, "Identification and control of dynamical systems using neural networks," _IEEE Trans. Neural Networks_, vol. 1, pp. 4-27, Mar. 1990.
[9] T. Ozaki, T. Suzuki, T. Furuhashi, S. Okuma, and Y. Uchikawa, "Trajectory control of robotic manipulators," _IEEE Trans. Ind. Elec._, vol. 38, pp. 195-202, June 1991.
[10] J. Park and I.W. Sandberg, "Universal approximation using radial-basis-function networks," _Neural Comp._, vol. 3, pp. 246-257, 1991.
[11] M.M. Polycarpou and P.A. Ioannu, "Identification and control using neural network models: design and stability analysis," Tech. Report 91-09-01, Dept. Elect. Eng. Sys., Univ. S. Cal., Sept. 1991.
[12] M.M. Polycarpou and P.A. Ioannu, "Neural networks as on-line approximators of nonlinear systems," _Proc. IEEE Conf. Decision and Control_, pp. 7-12, Tucson, Dec. 1992.
[13] N. Sadegh, "Nonlinear identification and control via neural networks," _Control Systems with Inexact Dynamics Models_, DSC-vol. 33, ASME Winter Annual Meeting, 1991.
[14] R.M. Sanner and J.-J.E. Slotine, "Stable adaptive control and recursive identification using radial gaussian networks," _Proc. IEEE Conf. Decision and Control_, Brighton, 1991.
[15] J.-J.E. Slotine and W. Li, "Adaptive manipulator control: a case study," _IEEE Trans. Automat. Control_, vol. 33, no. 11, pp. 995-1003, Nov. 1988.
[16] J.-J.E. Slotine and W. Li, _Applied Nonlinear Control_, New Jersey: Prentice-Hall, 1991.
[17] T. Yabuta and T. Yamada, "Neural network controller characteristics with regard to adaptive control," _IEEE Trans. Syst., Man, Cybern._, vol. 22, no. 1, pp. 170-176, Jan. 1992.

Position and Differential Kinematic Neural Control of Robot Manipulators: A Comparison Between Two Schemes

J. M. Ibarra Zannatha[1], D. F. Bassi[2], R. A. García[1]

[1]Cinvestav; A.P. 14-740; 07000 México, D.F., MEXICO. jibarra@cinvesmx.bitnet
[2]Universidad de Chile; República 701, Casilla 2777; Santiago, CHILE. dbassi@dcc.uchile.cl

Abstract. **In this paper two schemes for kinematics robot control based on neural networks are presented and compared. The first scheme is straightforward, it tries to find directly the inverse coordinate vector given a desired cartesian position. The second scheme is a differential approach. It tries to find the inverse Jacobian using a context network and a cartesian feedback. This scheme takes advantage of the function decomposition of the differential kinematics, since we are using information about the structure of the kinematic equations. The neural networks used are three layer feedforward networks trained with a modified backpropagation error algorithm, whose hidden layer is non linear (based on sigmoid or gaussian neurons), and its output layer is linear. We simulate both schemes and compare their results, concluding that the first scheme provides a good approximation for the kinematic problem without cartesian position feedback; while the differential scheme combined with a good cartesian coordinates measurements, gives a high precision robot motion.**

I. INTRODUCTION

In the specialized literature we find mainly two classes of robot control algorithms: dynamic- and kinematic-based algorithms. To cope with the nonlinear behaviour of robotic manipulators working at high velocity, the dynamic-based algorithms are used, normally designed on a exact cancellation of the nonlinear dynamic model. Nevertheless, the kinematic-based control laws offer good performances in fine motion when it is performed at a low speeds. Moreover, the inverse-kinematic problem solution has application in control schemes with cartesian path input, where trajectory generation is needed. In these schemes both kinematic models are used: Trajectory conversion based on geometric model and differential displacements (velocity) conversion or force-torque conversion based on Jacobian [1].

In the other hand, the recent resurgence of research and application of artificial neural networks (NN) to a diverse range of disciplines includes robotics. Solutions have been presented for the kinematics, dynamics, trajectory planning, sensing, control and visual-motor integration. In robot control applications mainly two classes of neural networks are used: recurrent networks and multilayer neural networks. From a systems theoretic point of view, recurrent networks are represented by nonlinear dynamic feedback systems, while multilayer networks represent static nonlinear maps [2]. Multilayer neural networks have proved extremely successful solving pattern recognition problems and recently, their learning capability of non linear functions is also used to design connectionist controllers [3]. Then, for solving the inverse kinematic problem, multilayer networks are very usefull [4].

The bases to implement a neural mapping that approximates the inverse kinematic of a robot, may be finded in several works: in [5], the relation between learning process in NN and classical approximation theory is showed; in [6], is reported that any continuous mapping may be approximated with a three layer NN with any continuous sigmoidal activation function in the hidden layer; while in [2] is presented an unified approach to use NN in design of identification and controller structures for control of unknown nonlinear dynamical systems.

In this paper we propose the use of the multilayered neural networks to approximate the inverse geometric model and the contextual neural networks to aproximate the inverse Jacobian, in a kinematic neural control scheme of robot manipulators. We propose the use of this kind of approximators to take advantage of one of the main properties of the multilayered feedforward neural networks: their capabilities to approximate a wide range of complex (including nonlinear) functions [7].

The paper is organized as follows: Section II deals with basic robot kinematic concepts showing the associated problems. In Section III, neural networks, backpropagation method for adjustement of their synaptic weights and their function approximation capabilities are presented. Section IV is devoted to presentation of the position and differential kinematic neural schemes for robot control proposed in this paper. Finally, in Section V, the simulation results are presented and commented.

The work of R.A. García corresponds to his Master Thesis at Cinvestav-IPN and it is supported by CONACyT (Mexican Council of Science and Technology). The autors would like to acknowledge the CYTED-D support to their SiProFlex project.

II. ROBOT KINEMATICS

A robotic manipulator is a kinematic chain formed by a combination of rigid links and revolute or prismatic joints, where one end is fixed while the other end is free. In order to move the end-effector along a desired path, the joints, generally six, are to be moved to track this path. To do that, it is necessary to know the displacements of the joints at each instant of time with respect to a fixed reference frame (base frame), corresponding to the end-effector's path described in the base frame. A kinematic model defines the position and velocity of each link and the end-effector without the consideration of mass or forces. The direct kinematics problem deals with finding the cartesian position of the end-effector defined in base frame, given the joint displacements and the link parameters. Thus for a given joint coordinate vector $\mathbf{q}$ and the cartesian position vector $\mathbf{x}$ of the end-effector, we are to solve:

$$\mathbf{x} = f(\mathbf{q}) \tag{1}$$

where f is a nonlinear, continuous and differentiable function. Equation (1) has a unique solution. In the inverse kinematic problem, given position and orientation of the end-effector expressed in cartesian coordinates, the correspondent joint displacements must be finded solving:

$$\mathbf{q} = f^{-1}(\mathbf{x}) \tag{2}$$

The solution of (2) is in general not unique. The robot motion control problem consists in bringing the end-effector from the actual to the desired position and orientation in cartesian coordinates, along a prescribed trajectory. Since the desired position and trajectory are usually specified in cartesian coordinates, whereas the joint actuators are to be controled with desired joint positions, the inverse kinematic model must be solved.

A. Homogeneous Transform.

Let be a robot with n joints or dof (degrees of freedom), and $A_i \in \Re^{4x4}$ the Denavit-Hartenberg's homogeneous transform matrix that describes the position and orientation of the ith joint frame with respect to the $(i-1)$th one. Then, the displacement and rotation between the base frame and the n-th frame is given by the matrix ${}^0T_n$ which is the product of an $A_1, A_2,..., A_n$ matrices:

$$\prod_{i=1}^{n} A_i(q_i) = {}^0T_n(\mathbf{q}) \tag{3.a}$$

$$
{}^0T_n(\mathbf{q}) = \begin{bmatrix} n_x & o_x & a_x & p_x \\ n_y & o_y & a_y & p_y \\ n_z & o_z & a_z & p_z \\ 0 & 0 & 0 & 1 \end{bmatrix} \tag{3.b}
$$

where the vector $\mathbf{p}^T = (p_x, p_y, p_z)$ is the end-effector cartesian position and the three vectors $\mathbf{n}$, $\mathbf{o}$ and $\mathbf{a}$ represents its orientation with respect to base frame. Each A_i matrix is a function only of a single joint variable q_i, but the twelve significative composants of the entire transformation ${}^0T_n$ are function of the n joint coordinates. Then, given desired values for cartesian position and orientation (3.b), the inverse kinematic problem means to find the corresponding values of n joint coordinates, solving this set of twelve equations (3.a).

Usually more than one solution is obtained for some of of the joint variables. A selection of one of the multiple solutions obtained requires certains criteria and constrains robot dependant, such as range of joint displacements, manipulability, robot attitudes, obstacle avoidance, etc. [8]. Due to this customization, a new algorithm has to be found and reprogramed every time a new manipulator is to be controlled. The complexity of the problem is increased not only with dof number of manipulator, but with the number of iterations needed to solve the problem when a closed form solution does no exist [8]. Even for the non-redundant arms, use of iterative methods, very time consuming, are the only way to solve the inverse kinematic problem.

B. Jacobian

The Jacobian is a multidimensional form of the derivative. Suppose, for instance, that we have six functions, each of which is a function of six independent joint variables, like in (1). If we wish to calculate the differentials of x_i as a function of differentials of q_j, we simple use the chain rule to calculate, and we get:

$$\delta \mathbf{x} = \frac{\partial f}{\partial \mathbf{q}} \delta \mathbf{q} = J(\mathbf{q}) \delta \mathbf{q} \tag{4}$$

The matrix, $J(\mathbf{q}) \in \Re^{6x6}$, of partial derivatives in (4) is what we call the Jacobian, whose components are function of q_j, because the functions f_i are nonlinear. The Jacobian is a time varying linear transformation, used, in robotics, to mapping joint to cartesian velocities

$$\dot{\mathbf{x}} = J(\mathbf{q})\dot{\mathbf{q}} \tag{5}$$

or joint torques τ to cartesian forces F:

$$\tau = J^T(\mathbf{q})F \tag{6}$$

If we wish to move end-effector with a given velocity vector in cartesian space, we can calculate the joint rates at each instant along the path, using the inverse relationship of (5):

$$\dot{\mathbf{q}} = J^{-1}(\mathbf{q})\dot{\mathbf{x}} \tag{7}$$

But, often the manipulators have values of $\mathbf{q}$ where the Jacobian becomes singular and it is no possible to find joint velocities. These singularities occur at the workspace boundary or when two or more axes are lining up.

III. NEURAL NETWORKS.

Neural Networks (NN) are massive parallel networks of simple neuron-like computing units. Each unit outputs a response which is a function, so-called *transfer function* or *activation function*, of the weighted sum of its inputs plus a bias. The inputs correspond either to external imposed values or the outputs of the other units. The output of each unit is given by:

$$y_j = \phi_j \left(\sum_i w_{ji} y_i + bj \right) \tag{8}$$

where y_j is the response of *j*th unit, ϕ_j is the activation function, w_{ji} is the weight of the conection from *i*th unit to *j*th unit and b_j is the bias. This *synaptic weight* represents the strength of the connection between two units and, if it is positive, it is known as *excitatory*, while a negative one is known as *inhibitory*. A zero weight means that the corresponding units are not connected. The transfer function is commonly a simple nondecreasing function like threshold, identity or sigmoid; however other more complex functions are also considered, like gaussian. In general, a NN is given by the following vectorial equation:

$$\mathbf{y} = \phi(\mathbf{W} \cdot \mathbf{y} + \mathbf{V} \cdot \mathbf{u} + \mathbf{b}) \tag{9}$$

where $\mathbf{y}$ is the output vector, $\mathbf{u}$ the input vector (external signals), $\mathbf{W}$ is the matrix of internal connection weights, $\mathbf{V}$ is the matrix of external input weights, $\mathbf{b}$ is the vector of bias and $\phi = [\phi_i]$ is the vectorial transfer function.

According with its architecture (neurons interconnection), there are recurrent networks with *feedback* and *feedforward* networks. In the last one, the output depends only on the inputs. We are interesed in a particular feedforward NN, so-called multilayer, in such away that only interconnections between subsequent layers of neurons are allowed. For each layer an activation vector is defined. The input layer is the first and the output is the last one, while the layers non connected to the output nor the input are the *hidden layers*. The following recursive equations define a *k+1* layer NN:

$$\mathbf{y}_0 \equiv \mathbf{u} \tag{10}$$

$$\mathbf{y}_l = \phi_l(\mathbf{W}_l \cdot \bar{\mathbf{y}}_{l-1}), \, l = 1, 2, \cdots k \tag{11}$$

where $\mathbf{y}_{l-1}$ is the activation vector of *l*th layer ($\mathbf{y}_k = \mathbf{y}$ being the output of a *k+1* layer NN), $\mathbf{u}$ is the input, ϕ_l is the activation function of the lth layer, $\mathbf{W}_l$ is the weight matrix between layers *l-1* and *l*, and $\bar{\mathbf{y}}_j = [\mathbf{y}_j, 1]^T$ is the associated homogeneous vector of $\mathbf{y}_j$. In (11) the bias vector was included in the weight matrix.

A. Supervised Learning: Back-propagation Rule.

With a continuous activation function, the feedforward multilayer NN can be conveniently used as a parallel computational model of a continuous mapping. The desired mapping is usually obtained by doing adecuate incremental adjustments of the weight matrix, process known as *learning*. The main learning paradigms used in NN are *reinforcement learning, unsupervised learning,* and *supervised learning*. In this paper we use the last one; that paradigm consist of the acquisition of a mapping by presentation of an input/output pair: For each input value, called *pattern,* the NN evaluates an output wich is compared with the target output, whereupon an adjustment on the NN weights is attempted in order to reduce some network error. The most widely used supervised learning scheme for multilayer feedforward NN is the *back-propagation* algorithm (BP). The goal of the BP procedure is to minimize the average sum-squared errors measured between the target value $\hat{\mathbf{y}}^p$ and the network output $\mathbf{y}^p$ for a given pattern set (the *p* superscript refers to the *p*th input pattern), over the all training patterns:

$$\mathbf{E} = \sum_{p \in P} \mathbf{E}^p = \frac{1}{2} \sum_{p \in P} \left| \hat{\mathbf{y}}^p - \mathbf{y}_k^p \right|^2 = \frac{1}{2} \sum_{p \in P} \sum_{i=1}^{M} \left| \hat{y}_i^p - y_{ki}^p \right|^2 \tag{12}$$

based on gradient of this error measured with respect to the weights. Thus it requieres a differentiable activation function. This description begins after the pth input pattern has been propagated through the network from inputs to outputs. We are now ready to begin the backpropagation of the error to update the weights on both output and hidden layers. Their adjustement is proportional to the error gradient:

$$\Delta w_{lij} = -\eta \frac{\partial \mathbf{E}}{\partial w_{lij}} = \eta \sum_{p \in P} \delta_{li}^{p} \, \overline{y}_{l-1j}^{p} \qquad (13)$$

$$\Delta w(t+1) = w(t+1) - w(t)$$

$$\delta_{ki}^{p} = \left(\hat{y}_{i}^{p} - y_{ki}^{p} \right) \phi'_{ki} \left(x_{ki}^{p} \right), \text{ for output layer} \qquad (14)$$

$$\delta_{li}^{p} = \sum_{r=1}^{M} \delta_{l+1r}^{p} \, w_{l+1ri} \, \phi'_{li} \left(x_{li}^{p} \right), \; l = 1, 2, \cdots k-1 \qquad (15)$$

$$x_{ki}^{p} = \sum_{r=1}^{M} w_{kir} \, \overline{y}_{k-1r}^{p} \qquad (16)$$

where w_{kij} are the weight wich connects jth unit in layer k-1 with ith unit in (output) layer k; the subscripts ki means ith unit in layer k; and $\eta > 0$ is the learning rate, which allows an increased learning speed. These equations allows for a recursive computation of the gradient, starting in the output layer and going inwards, i.e. the errors (δ's) are propageted back through the network from the output. A modification of the BP algorithm introduces a *momentum* term:

$$\Delta w(t+1) = -\eta \frac{\partial \mathbf{E}}{\partial w} + \alpha \, \Delta w(t) \qquad (17)$$

where $1 > \alpha > 0$, the *momentum factor*, helps to avoid local minima.

B. *Aproximation of Continuous Functions.*

In recent years, several researchers have published results proving the general representation capabilities of NN, drawing an important conclusion upon the usefulness of this networks as general function approximators. In [3] we can find a résumé of results of the main works in this area. All these results may be synthetized in one approximation theorem, wich is given herein without proof:

Theorem. *For any continuous function f defined in a compact set, where $f: A \subset \Re^{n} \to \Re$, for any $\varepsilon > 0$, and $\Re \to \Re$, discriminatory, there exists N, $\{a_i \in \Re\}_{i=1}^{N}$, $\{\mathbf{w}_i \in \Re^{n}\}_{i=1}^{N}$ and $\{b_i \in \Re\}_{i=1}^{N}$ such that $\forall \mathbf{x} \in A \subset \Re^{n}$:*

$$\left| f(\mathbf{x}) - \sum_{i=1}^{N} a_i \, \phi(\mathbf{w}_i \cdot \mathbf{x} + b_i) \right| < \varepsilon \qquad (18)$$

The discriminatory function in this theorem may be any of the activation function commonly used in NN models: sigmoidal or probabilistic functions (like gaussian).

The available results give an existance proof of the approximation theorem. However the feasibility of such approximation is not yet answered: How many terms are necessary to achieve a given approximation quality? How do the choice of the activation function and the properties of the approximated function affect the approximation? For traditional approximation theory some of those answers are known. For example, using Fourier Analisys, the approximation error for a truncated series may be related to the bandwidth of the approximated function. For power series (Taylor's), the knowledge of a high order derivative allows finding a bound in the approximation error. In [5], the relation between the learning process in NN and classical approximation theory is shown. In particular, a three-layered NN with gaussian hidden units is an implementation of a technique called regularization, well known in approximation theory, equivalent to generalizad splines, and closely related to classical radial basis function used for interpolation tasks. Regularization means that the approximation is a smoother version of the original function. These relations point towards a unified theory, where well known results of classical approximation theory could be applied to more complex neural approximations.

C. *Context Neural Networks.*

If we want to use a NN to approximate the function in (7) we require the actual position q and desired cartesian velocity $\dot{x}$ as inputs to calculate the joint velocity $\dot{q}$. This mapping is highly nonlinear, since the transformation depends on the location of the end-effector in generalized frame. It is well known that learning in highly nonlinear mappings is very time-consuming [9]. As shown in [10], the set of input variables can be partitioned into two groups: one set is used in a NN wich approximates the basic transformation being represented (the function network), while the second set determines the context within wich the function is calculated. In our differential inverse kinematic problem, the function network transforms the desired cartesian velocity to joint velocity, and the context is the spacial location of the end-effector expressed in internal coordinates.

The context-sensitive NN are composed of two multilayered feedforward networks: The **context network**, using nonlinear units and a BP learning process, whose outputs are used to set up the weights of the **function network**, generally with linear units. The first one has a many outputs as there are weights in the function network. Since this number may be very large, the function network should be as simple as possible [9].

IV. KINEMATIC NEURAL CONTROL OF ROBOTS

In Section II of this paper several inverse kinematic problems was pointed out, they consist basicaly in to find one solution (and only one) for (3.b) and [7] in spite of singularities and lack of closed form solutions or their complexity. To tackle these problems we propose the use of well known approximation capabilities of NN [6] and other NN features like: A NN can de trained by being shown examples (programming may then be eliminated); With a NN completly trained, the time required to obtain a solution to a problem is independent of the number of dof; The ability of the NN to generalize from a scarce set of data points and giving good results at a new data points; Self organizing gives the ability to adapt to changes occurring within the system; Fault tolerance [4].

In the first problem we must get generalized joint coordinates given the cartesian end-effector coordinates. Although this problem can be analitically solved, it is complicated because it needs a lot of computations and very precise geometric parameters [8], [10]. From earliest works in neural control schemes applied to robotics in 1975 [11], in latest 80's several researches developped kinematic controllers based on NN, demonstrated on robots with either 2 or 3 dof [3], [5], [8] and [10].

V. SIMULATION RESULTS

In order to show the feasibility and performances of the proposed kinematic neural control schemes, a simulation study was carried out with a simplified model of a two dof planar manipulator with 1 m. links articulated by revoluted joints. First, a three layered NN was designed

and trained to control the end-effector with a position kinematic neural controller. Second, for the differential kinematic controller based on a NN, a contextual network was designed and trained to realize this controller. Finally, simulation results for both schemes are presented and commented.

A. NN for the position kinematic control scheme.

This scheme is straighforward, it tries to find directly the inverse coordinate vector given a desired cartesian position. We are using a three layer feedforward network with three linear units (x, y and bias) in the input layer, eight nonlinear units in hidden layer and two linear units (q_1 and q_2) in the output layer. The nonlinear activation function used in hidden layer are either sigmoid or gaussian. The NN is trained with a modified BP error algorithm, where the learning rate η is variated in function of the errors changes. The proposed modification consist in to reduce the learning rate to a half of its actual value if the errors do not decrease enough in a horizon of n steps. In our case, the initial value of learning coefficient is $\eta= 0.02$ and the horizon is $n=5$ steps. In learning process, this NN is trained with a little number (sixteen) of samples obtained by choosing four random values for each joint in a reduced workspace, defined by:

$$q_1 \in \left[0.5\pi - 0.1\pi, 0.5\pi - 0.1\pi\right]$$

$$q_2 \in \left[-0.5\pi - 0.1\pi, -0.5\pi + 0.1\pi\right]$$

in wich the input is the cartesian position (x,y) of the robot end-effector plus a unit bias, and the output is the corresponding joint values.

We found differences between learning speed of the two NN (with sigmoidal and gaussian units). In a 1000 epochs learning process the use of gaussian activation functions increases the convergence speed (Fig. 1), in relation with that obtained with sigmoidal transfer functions (Fig. 2) and we obtain a littlest error. Moreover, the use of nu-modification accelerates the learning speed without divergence risk, and produces a smoother behaviour of error. Fig. 3 shows the error evolution with a

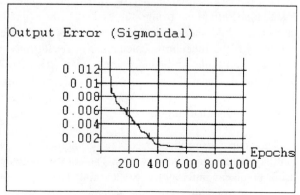

Fig. 1. Learning error of NN with sigmoidal units.

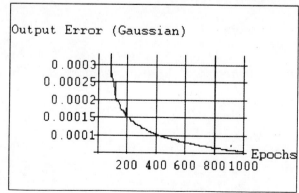

Fig. 2. Learning error of NN with gaussian units.

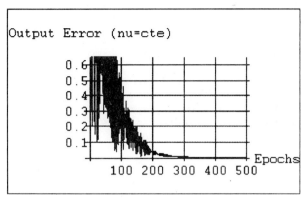

Fig. 3. Learning error with a constant learning rate

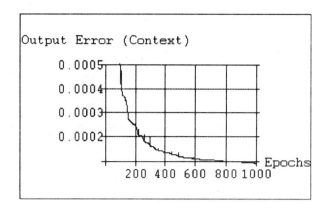

Fig. 4. Learning error in a Context Sensitive NN.

constant learning rate. Using gaussian units with a more localized response, the NN is able to minimize the interaction among its neurons and can deal efficiently with the high non linearity of problem, thereby allowing a speed up of the learning process.

B. NN for the differential neural control scheme.

The second kinematic neural control scheme used is a differential approach. It tries to find the inverse Jacobian in (7) using a context-sensitive network with a cartesian feedback. This scheme takes advantage of the function decomposition of the differential kinematic, i.e. we are using information about the structure of the kinematic equation given by (7). In this scheme the fuctional part of the context network realize the product between the desired cartesian velocity vector (or differential displacements) and the inverse Jacobian. The last one is approximated by the context part of the network, whose input is just the joint angles vector. The context network is a three layer feedforward NN trained with a η-modified BP error algorithm, whose hidden layer is nonlinear (based on gaussian units), while output layer has 24+16 linear units to adjust the corresponding weights in the functional network. This is a three layer NN with eigth linear units in his hidden layer and two linear units in his output layer. The results obtained in learning process are showed in Fig. 4.

C. Conclusions.

Comparing both schems, we can conclude that the differential scheme combined with a good cartesian coordinates measurements, gives a high precision robot motion. Moreover, this results can be enhanced by using smaller increments, proportional to the displacement magnitud. In the other hand, the first scheme provides a good approximation for the kinematic problem without cartesian position feedback. This case correspond to the *ballistic motion* with no external sensorial feedback.

REFERENCES

[1]   J. J. Craig, *Introduction to Robotics: Mechanics and Control.*. 2nd edition, Addison-Wesley Publishing Co. 1989.

[2]   K. S. Narendra, K. Parthasarathy, "Identification and Control of Dynamical Systems using Neural Networks." *IEEE Trans. on Neural Networks,* Vol. 1 N° 1, pp. 4-27, 1990.

[3]   D. F. Bassi, "Connectionist Dynamic Control of Robotic Manipulators." Ph. D. Thesis, U. of Southern California, 1990.

[4]   A. Guez, Z. Ahmad, "Solution to the Inverse Kinematic Problem in Robotics by Neural Networks," *Proc. of 2nd IEEE Int. Conf. on Neural Networks,* Vol. 2, pp. 617-624. San Diego, CA, USA, 1988.

[5]   T. Poggio, F Girosi, "Regularization Algorithms for Learning that are Equivalent to Multilayer Networks." *Science, N° 247, pp. 978-982, feb. 1990.*

[6]   G. Cybenko, "Approximation by Superposition of a Sigmoidal Function." *Mathematics of Control, Signals and Systems,* Vol. 2, N° 2, pp. 303-315. 1989.

[7]   K. Hornik, "Multilayer Feedforward Networks are Universal Aproximators," *Neural Networks.* Vol. 2, pp. 359-366, 1989.

[8]   R. P. Paul, H. Zhang, "Computationally Efficient Kinematics for Manipulators with Spherical Wrist, Based on the Homogeneous Transformation Representation," *The Int. J. of Robotics Research,* Vol. 5, N° 2, Summer 1986.

[9]   B. Kosko, Ed. *"Neural Networks for Signal Processing"* Prentice Hall, Englewood Cliffs, NJ, EUA. 1992.

[10]   D. Yeung, G. A. Bekey, "Using a Context-Sensitive Learning Network for Robot Arm Control." *Proc. of 1989 IEEE Int. Conf. on Robotics and Automation,* Vol. III, pp. 1441-1447, may 1989.

[11]   D. Psaltis, A. Sideris and A. Yamamura, "Neural Controllers." *Proc. of IEEE Int. Conf. on Neural Networks,* pp. 551-558, 1987.

Real-time Implementation of Neural Network Learning Control of a Flexible Space Manipulator

R. Todd Newton and Yangsheng Xu

Abstract: This paper presents a neural network approach to on-line learning control and real-time implementation for a flexible space robot manipulator. An overview discusses the motivation and system development of the Self-Mobile Space Manipulator (SM^2). The neural network learns control by updating feedforward dynamics based on feedback control input. Implementation issues associated with on-line training strategies are addressed and a simple stochastic training scheme is presented. A new recurrent neural network architecture with improved performance is proposed. By using the proposed learning scheme, the manipulator tracking error is reduced by 85% compared to conventional PID control. The approach possesses a high degree of generality and adaptability in various applications and will be a valuable method in learning control for robots working in unconstructed environments.

Introduction[1]

Robotic technology is useful in space exploration, both for eliminating the need of astronauts working in inhospitable environments, and for promoting the productivity that astronauts might achieve. In designing a space manipulator, energy efficiency and micro-gravity effects must be considered. For this reason, the robot manipulator is normally designed as a light-weight structure which presents a significant flexibility between links and results in a challenge in control. The flexibility of a multi-degrees of freedom manipulator providing three dimensional motion is difficult to model, and thus most model-based control schemes are unfeasible. On the other hand, because of the light-weight structure and micro-gravity condition, the joint torque is relatively much lower than in industrial manipulators; thus joint friction is relatively much higher. For the space robot manipulator developed in our laboratory, the torque for friction compensation is more than 30% of the total torque applied, compared to about 3% for normal industrial manipulators.

The structural flexibility and joint frictions cause extreme difficulty in modeling the manipulator dynamics and providing a stable, efficient motion. To eliminate the high order vibrations of the structure, we apply a low-pass filter to the measured joint values. The system bandwidth, however, is decreased by the low-pass filters, and hence the speed of the manipulator motion is greatly limited. At the same time, relatively low feedback gains must be selected for each joint to prevent low-mode vibration and maintain stable manipulation. Although the effects of friction are decreased by the use of a moving-sum integral error feedback term, the gains associated with these terms are limited to low values to avoid creating instabilities resulting from underdamped control. Working within these limitations, control of the

1. The authors are with the Robotics Institute, Carnegie Mellon University, Pittsburgh, PA 15213. This work is supported by the Space Projects Office, Shimizu Corporation, Japan. We would like to thank the following colleagues for their technical contributions and support: Ben Brown, Mark Friedman, Randy Casciola, Greg White, David Stewart, Jie Yang, Shigeru Aoki, and Takeo Kanade.

self-mobile space manipulator (SM^2) without an accurate dynamic model yields large tracking errors.

We have been working on several adaptive control schemes, but the result depends on the structure of the model and computation is expensive. The approach of neural networks to dynamic modeling is not restricted by a model and is computationally efficient. This paper focuses on a neural network approach to real-time learning control and implementation for a flexible space manipulator. First, we overview the Self-Mobile Space Manipulator (SM^2) project testbed. We then introduce the concept of feedback-error-learning as a method of training a neural network. Details associated with the implementation and training are discussed. By using the proposed neural network scheme, the manipulator trajectory error is reduced by 85%.

Self-Mobile Space Manipulator Testbed

Basic Concept

In the Robotics Institute at Carnegie Mellon, we have developed a light-weight and low-cost robot [1,2] that provides independent mobility on the Space Station exterior and at the same time is capable of accomplishing manipulation tasks. We call this robot the Self-Mobile Space Manipulator, or SM^2. This robot would primarily be used for visual inspection, material transport, and light assembly. To achieve the mobility of the robot on the Space Station trusswork, the robot walker is of minimum size and complexity. As shown in Figure 1, SM^2 is a symmetric robot having nine joints, two slender links, two feet and two grippers at both ends. The foot (node gripper) is used to attach to trusswork providing mobility, and the gripper serves as a general purpose part gripper during manipulation tasks. Walking is accomplished by alternate attaching and releasing at the trusswork attachment locations, and swinging of the feet from one truss attachment location to the next. Using such steps with alternate feet, SM^2 can move across the exterior of the trusswork. At any given time one foot is attached to a truss beam, fixing the two degrees of freedom associated with the gripper on the same end. This provides a seven degree-of-freedom (7-DOF) serial configuration for manipulation. Thus, the gripper defines the tip of the robot, while the foot at the other end acts as the robot's base.

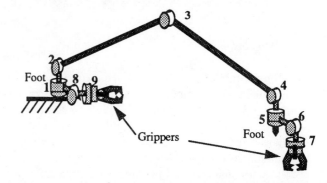

Figure 1: Concept picture of the self-mobile space manipulator (SM^2). While one end is attached to the trusswork fixing joints 8 and 9, the remaining joints 1-7 provide a seven-degree-of-freedom (7-DOF) manipulator configuration.

Design and Hardware

In order to perform realistic experiments in the laboratory, we designed and built a 1/3-size laboratory robot based on a hypothetical, full-size, self-contained robot to be used on the Space Station (see Figure 2). We used scaling rules to keep the dynamics parameters (masses, stiffness, natural frequencies, linear speeds) of the scaled-down robot similar to those of the hypothetical one. Overall dimensions of the truss and robot were reduced to 1/3, while local dimensions (joints and grippers) were kept equal. This allows the testbed to be used in an average size laboratory, yet mechanisms are not unworkably small. Each joint contains a rare-earth-magnet DC motor; a harmonic-drive speed reducer (60:1 or 100:1 ratio); and an optical encoder on the motor shaft to measure a joint angle. The motors and the drive components were selected and arranged to give maximum power and torque in a small, light-weight package. Presently, the robot is tethered to the computer hardware. The software has been developed on the Chimera III experimental real-time system. We also have installed a BIT3 bus adapter which controls communication on the VME bus between the real-time processors (2 Ironics CPUs) and the host Sun computer.

Gravity Compensation System

The absence of gravitational forces in orbit has a dramatic effect on the design and operation of robots. To permit realistic testing on Earth we have developed two gravity compensation systems (GCI and GCII) that balance the significant gravitational effects on the robot. Each system includes a vertical counterweight system and an actively controlled horizontal system. The vertical system comprises a counterweight mechanism, and a series of pulleys and cables that provide a constant upward force to balance the robot while increasing the inertia of the system by only 10%. Horizontal motions are servocontrolled to keep the support point above the robot. An optical sensor mounted on the carriage of the GC measures the deviation from the vertical of the support cable connecting the carriage to the robot. A servocontroller tries to null this deviation by driving motors causing the above gantry to move. The first system (GCI), having a Cartesian XY based axis gantry, is used for mobility experiments. The second system (GCII) shown in Figure 2, which operates in cylindrical coordinates, has a boom pivoted above the fixed end of the robot, and a carriage that moves along the boom to match the radial movements of the robot. Although the GCII system does not permit mobility, it is more suited for delicate manipulation experiments since the gantry axis coincides with the principle axis of movement of the robot in the horizontal plane. All experiments in this paper are conducted using the GCII system.

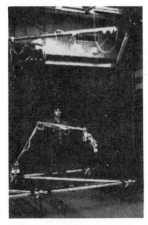

Figure 2: Photograph of SM² supported by gravity compensation system GCII. The axis of rotation of the GCII is aligned with the fixed end of the robot.

Learning Control with Neural Networks

Feedback-Learning Concept

To learn the dynamic model of SM² we employed the method of neural network feedback-error-learning [3]. Inspired by the proficiency of learned control demonstrated in biological systems, the neural network develops an inverse dynamics model through experience. In fact there is a separate neural network responsible for modelling each joint, and the inputs of each network are, of course, also dependent on the other joints. Although mutual information could be utilized by modelling all of the joints in a single larger network, the use of an individual network for each joint allows a better framework for experimentation and simplifies analysis of the internal network representations. Throughout this paper the reader should note that each joint has its own neural network. More specifically, this neural network scheme uses the error obtained from the linear controller (i.e., PID or PD) to adapt the weights of the neural network (Figure 3). Using the common feedforward neural network architecture trained using backpropagation [4] (we assume the reader has a basic understanding of this algorithm), the network learns to become what is commonly referred to as the feedforward term of the system. The uniqueness of learning through feedback lies in the ability to learn mappings where the target values are not known, and only a signal estimating the error in the present output is available. Therefore, the network learns by continually estimating the target from the feedback error signal received from the controller. Equation (1) shows the target estimation, $\hat{\tau}^t_{target}$, as a function of u and τ^t_{net} representing the feedback error and the actual output of the network at time t.

$$\hat{\tau}^t_{target} = \tau^t_{net} + u^t \qquad (1)$$

The process of modeling the manipulator dynamics is accomplished on-line during system execution. After each system cycle the weights of the network are updated to minimize the error feedback. During actual real-time trajectory execution the weights of the network are updated via backpropagation at approximately 30% the control loop operating frequency. Thus learning is actually taking place on-line, as the robot moves around. In time the neural network learns the correct network output to produce the desired/reference output of the plant, and in turn the feedback signal decreases. Teaching neural networks by error feedback has been shown to yield improved performance by several simulation studies [3,5,6]. However, there has been little work regarding the real-time implementation, and the advantages of the approach as well as various implementation issues cannot be revealed from simulation. Presented in this paper, the approach of neural networks trained by feedback-error-learning is implemented in a flexible space robot and shown to greatly reduce both tracking errors and steady state errors.

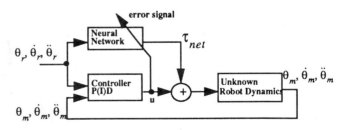

Figure 3: Block diagram of the general concept of learning control through error feedback learning. The angles θ_r and θ_m describe the reference output of the plant and the measured output of the plant, respectively. τ_{net} and u describe the output signal of the neural network and the feedback signal of the controller, respectively. Note that the feedback from the controller is used to teach the neural network.

151

Neural Network Control Architecture

The first three joints from the base of the SM^2 position the end-effector and payload in gross motion. Thus, these joints are the most difficult to control because they are restricted to low controller gains to maintain stability, avoiding excitation of structural vibrations. For this reason, our experiments will be restricted to learning control of these first three joints from the base, and therefore we will have three neural networks employed, one for each joint. Since the configuration of the remaining dorsal joints remains constant throughout the experiments, none of the networks are given inputs dependent on the dorsal joints. As a result, the networks are forced to view the dorsal joint system as a lumped mass. Each network has as inputs the particular reference velocity and reference acceleration associated with that joint and several additional terms which are dependent on the other two remaining joints. All inputs are normalized such that each maximum input value is less than one. The scaling constants are determined by the robot before learning starts. By normalizing all inputs, we provide each input with an equal chance to be utilized while discouraging potential saturation problems of neurons in the proceeding layers. Each network has one output representing the feedforward torque term. Internally each network has two hidden layers of 13 and 20 neurons. The neurons of the hidden layers possess sigmoid transfer functions with activation range [-1,1] while the output neuron has a linear transfer function. As is usually the case, the sigmoid transfer function was selected to aid in modeling the nonlinearities of the system. On the other hand, since it is unclear what the desired range of the output activations should be, the output neurons are given a linear transfer function resulting in an unbound activation range. The torque applied to each joint is the sum of the network activation torque and the controller feedback torque. A diagram of the system as applied to SM^2 is shown in Figure 4.

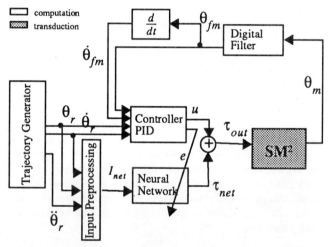

Figure 4: Block diagram of control flow for SM^2 using a neural network. The variables θ_m, θ_{fm}, and θ_r represent the measured joint angle position, the filtered measured joint angle position, and the reference joint angle position respectively. u and e represent the PID feedback signal used for motor control and the PD feedback signal used to correct the network. τ_{net} and τ_{out} represent the output torque value of the network and the composite torque to be sent to the joint. I_{net} represents the input vector to the neural network produced by the preprocessing step (i.e. normalizing and subcomponent composition).

Since the dynamics of each joint are dependent on more than simply the reference velocity and reference acceleration of that joint, we provide each network with several additional input terms that describe some of the stronger dependencies on the other joints. The terms chosen are subcomponents of the dynamics equations for the first three

joints when using a lumped-mass, rigid-body model. We could use a model for the flexible manipulator, but this would be much more complex and also this may not yield an ideal result since any model is an approximation. The preprocessed input terms provide dependencies between joints. They also allow the network to implicitly assume some known nonlinear relations among joints. As a result, the speed and accuracy at which the network may learn the correct dynamics increases. Table 1 shows the inputs for each of the three joints. Each term represents a subcomponent used in the derivation of the inertial, centripetal, Coriolis, or frictional components of the joints, and was used in an earlier study [3].

Trajectory Training Scheme

A common problem found in training neural networks is ensuring that the training patterns are evenly distributed across the problem domain. In the case of training three joints of a manipulator the domain is trajectories. There are several challenges that are specific to training neural networks on-line. One problem is that repeatedly training over a fixed sequence of distributed trajectories is overlearning the sequence which has been shown to lead to poor generalization [7]. Another problem is that the method of teaching a task by presenting local portions of the task one at a time is not suitable for on-line training of neural networks [7]. The lack of diversity for a sustained period of time results in the degeneration of information previously encoded within the network. In essence, the network "forgets". Both of these factors discourage the use of deterministic schemes.

Training through on-line feedback also places challenges on how the networks should update their weights. Most off-line training in large, complex domains is done by updating the network using the accumulated gradient across a set of training patterns. This method enhances learning by increasing the network's ability to reach the global solution. Unfortunately, for on-line training of manipulator dynamics, this is difficult since defining what patterns should be in a training set is not straightforward. Furthermore, since the networks are training on error signals and not known targets, the actual error signal is itself only an estimation. The estimations of the target values change over time; therefore, reexperiencing old patterns used in a training set to gain new estimations is essential for convergence. If learning over a training set is applied here, difficulties arise in determining how to sequence the execution of the trajectories to include the input patterns of the training set and how to determine what members of the set should be replaced or reexperienced.

Considering these issues, the option of training by a simple scheme of stochastically-generated trajectories appears to avoid many of the potential problems pointed out earlier. At the same time, the stochastic approach described below ensures a more continuously distributed sequence of training trajectories. For this reason training over a trajectory set, or epoch, is less essential. Instead, updating the network continuously based on only the previous error gradient is sufficient.

The most obvious approach to a pseudo-random trajectory generating scheme is to repeatedly produce a random point in the 3 degrees-of-freedom workspace and execute the trajectory from the present configuration to the produced endpoint configuration. The workspace of the manipulator is defined not by physical joint limitations but by polar coordinates. Because there are stability limitations due to the degree of extension of the manipulator tip, and physical limitations due to the placement of the trusswork, specifying trajectory endpoints in polar coordinates as shown in Figure 5 is the easiest way to define the legal workspace for training. The polar endpoint is then transformed into joint space for trajectory calculations. There is still a problem with training using sequences of trajectories defined by connecting random points in the workspace. Although the configuration

Joint 1	Joint 2	Joint 3
$\sin(\theta_{J1} + \theta_{J2})(\dot{\theta}_{J1} + \dot{\theta}_{J2})^2$	$\sin(\theta_{J1} + \theta_{J2})\cos(\theta_{J1})\dot{\theta}_{J0}^2$	$\sin\theta_{J1}\cos(\theta_{J1} + \theta_{J2})\dot{\theta}_{J0}^2$
$(\sin\theta_{J1})^2\dot{\theta}_{J0}$	$\sin\theta_{J2}\dot{\theta}_{J2}^2$	$\cos\theta_{J2}\dot{\theta}_{J1}$
$sgn(\dot{\theta}_{J0})$	$sgn(\dot{\theta}_{J1})$	$sgn(\dot{\theta}_{J2})$
$\dot{\theta}_{J0}$	$\dot{\theta}_{J1}$	$\dot{\theta}_{J2}$
$\ddot{\theta}_{J0}$	$\ddot{\theta}_{J1}$	$\ddot{\theta}_{J2}$

Table 1: Inputs to the three neural networks for joints 1, 2, and 3, respectively.

endpoints are evenly distributed, the actual trajectory defined by the difference between the two bounded random endpoints is not evenly distributed (when integrated over all endpoint possibilities). The probability distribution of the differences is biased toward smaller values.This is illustrated by a one dimensional example in Figure 6. As a partial solution to this problem, a critical difference value (in radians) has been defined for each joint. In order for a random endpoint to be valid, at least one joint must have a movement greater than the critical value for that joint. The test is repeated until a valid new endpoint is found. In short, this solution does not give an even distribution, but it does provide a simple solution which does not bias toward smaller trajectories.

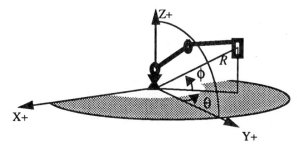

Figure 5: The representation of polar coordinates defined by θ, ϕ, and R. Each parameter has a selected minimum and maximum. For SM^2, the workspace defined by the limits forms a quartersphere with a hollow center.

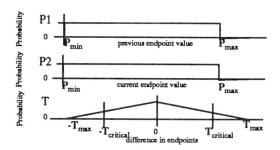

Figure 6: Example of the relative probability distribution of two discrete parameter endpoints (P1 and P2) and the probability distribution of the difference of the two endpoints (T).

The trajectory is interpolated in joint space using the trigonometric functions (2-4) for each joint.

$$p = nt - \sin(2\pi * nt) * (1/2\pi) \quad (2)$$

where nt is normalized time between [0,1] during trajectory execution. Note all joints use the same nt. The current value of nt is defined as

$$nt = i/(\omega\alpha) \quad (3)$$

where ω is the sampling frequency, α is the specified period of the trajectory, and i is the index counter which is incremented after each iteration of execution.The trajectory is then defined

$$\theta = \theta_0 + \Delta\theta * p \quad (4)$$

where θ is the present reference position, θ_0 is the initial position, and $\Delta\theta$ represents the difference between the initial and end positions.

An upperbound velocity magnitude is selected for each joint. The period of the actual trajectory is defined by the period of whichever joint is found to take the most time at the upperbound velocity. In this way, each trajectory will contain at least one joint which is executing at maximum velocity. Although we have limited the variety of trajectories by selecting a specific trajectory scheme of interpolations and period selection, the portion of the trajectory domain has been selected to most closely match the required types of trajectories used by most applications of the manipulator. Below is an outline of the trajectory generation process:

Algorithm

1. Select a random point in polar coordinates and transform the point into joint space coordinates.

2. Check to see if the magnitude of the difference between the present position and candidate endpoint is greater than the critical amount for each of the joints. If no difference is above the threshold, repeat Step 1, else proceed to Step 3.

3. Select the time period of the trajectory by using the maximum of the periods computed from each individual joint executing the joint trajectory at maximum velocity.

4. Generate actual trajectory and execute.

5. Return to Step 1.

Initial Issues

Before discussing particular experiments, several of the initial issues encountered regarding learning convergence are discussed. One of the first problems experienced during learning was the saturation of neurons in the hidden layers. This resulted from backpropagating from the linear neuron with an unbounded error signal to the hidden layer neurons possessing bounded activation levels and expecting bounded error signals. To avoid saturations, we have lowered the learning rate for all the connections other than the output neuron connections. This allows the output connections to establish the large weight values needed to generate the desired range of output activations before the hidden layer connections saturate in an attempt to create activations which are out of their range.

Since we are training on-line, the initial state of the network must maintain the manipulator's stability. Therefore, it is difficult to initialize the network with random weights having large ranges (i.e. |x| > 1) since this results in random outputs of larger magnitudes creating instabilities in control. On the other hand, initializing the network with random weights having a small range (i.e. |x| < 0.05) slows learning since the weight changes are proportional to the weight value. To overcome the delay in learning associated with the use of small initial weight values, the network's learning rate is amplified by a factor of five for the first 20 seconds. This brief "shock" period allows the weights to more quickly overcome the period where little learning is accomplished due to the small magnitude of the connection weights, and to establish a coarse but stable model. Note that if a "shock" is applied for too long then this also results in saturation of the hidden units.

In preliminary experiments, using the error signal generated by the PID controller was found to cause large trajectory endpoint overshooting during learning. Since the integral term of the controller causes large increases in error feedback for near-static errors, the network was led to believe that more torque should be applied during the final portion of the trajectories. Over the learning phase, the network slowly converges to the correct action by alternating between undershooting and overshooting the target over the training trajectories. In view of these observations, manipulators with low bandwidth operation and high frictional effects should use PD feedback signals, not PID feedback signals, as the network teaching signal. For our experiments we use a PID signal to control the manipulator and a PD signal to teach the network.

Implementation

For each of the following experiments, the manipulator is autonomously trained in the manner previously described. The learning period is selected as the minimal learning time required until observed improvement in performance ceases (observed from the mean square error (MSE)). This time interval was found to be 600 seconds. After the learning phase the network adaptation is turned off, and a test trajectory sequence of 60 seconds is executed. The results of the test sequence are shown for each experiment. The control frequency of the manipulator is 40 Hz. Because of computational limitations, the neural networks are limited to a feedforward frequency of 25 Hz and a backpropagation frequency of 12.5 Hz. Controller gains were empirically determined to provide the best conventional performance possible without creating instabilities.

Experiment I

The first experiment uses the standard network architecture shown in Figure 7 for each of the three joints. As learning commences the mean controller feedback signal decreases as the neural network plays an increasing feedforward role. By the end of the training phase, the mean feedback signal for each joint has typically decreased by 65%.

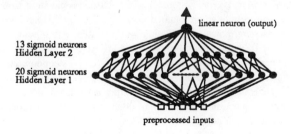

Figure 7: The neural network architecture used for each of the three joints in Experiment I. Each layer is fully connected.

There is an obvious improvement in tracking using the neural networks, but there is a problem in the latter portions of several trajectory segments in the test sequence of joint 1. The errors are due to over-deacceleration outputted by the network, causing a reverse in motion

and resulting in static errors. Because the ratio of inertial mass to friction is large for joint1 relative to the other joints, joint 1 relies more on applying reverse torques to deaccelerate, while joints 2 and 3 rely more on frictions to deaccelerate. As would be expected from this observation, the other two joints do not exhibit this problem. Rather, both tracking error and steady-state error decrease for joints 2 and 3. To overcome some of the limitations of this network's architecture, the next experiment focuses on providing a network architecture with temporal context to improve the modeling capacity.

Experiment II

The major limitation of the network used in Experiment I was that its output torque was dependent only on the inputs applied at that instant. In other words, the network did not possess the ability to evaluate the new inputs using any context obtained from previous inputs. Investigations into recurrent networks have proven successful in providing context which improves the network's capacity to learn [4,5]. Some of the more popular approaches feed back activation levels of output neurons or hidden neurons as input for the next feedforward cycle. For our network application, recurrence of the hidden layer activation vector is investigated since it has more information capacity in comparison to the output scalar. Network instability problems associated with directly feeding back the previous hidden layer 1 state as inputs were avoided by feeding them instead into hidden layer 2 as shown in Figure 8. The hidden layer 1 consists of two sets of neurons. The activations of the neurons constituting the first set are determined by the inputs as usual, but the second set is determined by applying a transfer function to the activations of each neuron in the first set to determine the activation of the corresponding neuron in the second set. In this way, the second set allows the network architecture to take advantage of temporal context in the "feature space" expressed by the first set of hidden layer 1. Hidden layer 2 provides a second level of processing which extracts a representation which is dependent on both the present input and the present inputs and the temporal context of those inputs.This network architecture was applied to SM^2 using the standard transfer function z^{-1} (1 iteration delay). Unfortunately, the network had the same performance as that of Experiment I. The input values between the previous and present iterations differ so little that the feature roles between the corresponding neurons of two halves were identical.

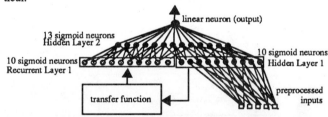

Figure 8: The new neural network architecture used for each of the three joints in Experiment II. Note that the first hidden layer is composed of two halves. The activations of the right half (black neurons) are determined as before, but the activations of the left half (gray neurons) are determined by individually applying a transfer function to neurons of the right half. Note that each level is fully connected.

Two modifications are made to aid the network in utilizing temporal knowledge. First, use the recurrent vector to present the difference between the current and previous states of hidden layer 1. Second, increase the temporal interval being applied. Combining these modifications amounts to taking the difference of the moving average of the activations over a fixed time period. In summarizing the modification, we use the same architecture as in Figure 8, but the transfer function has been modified to that shown in Equation (5).

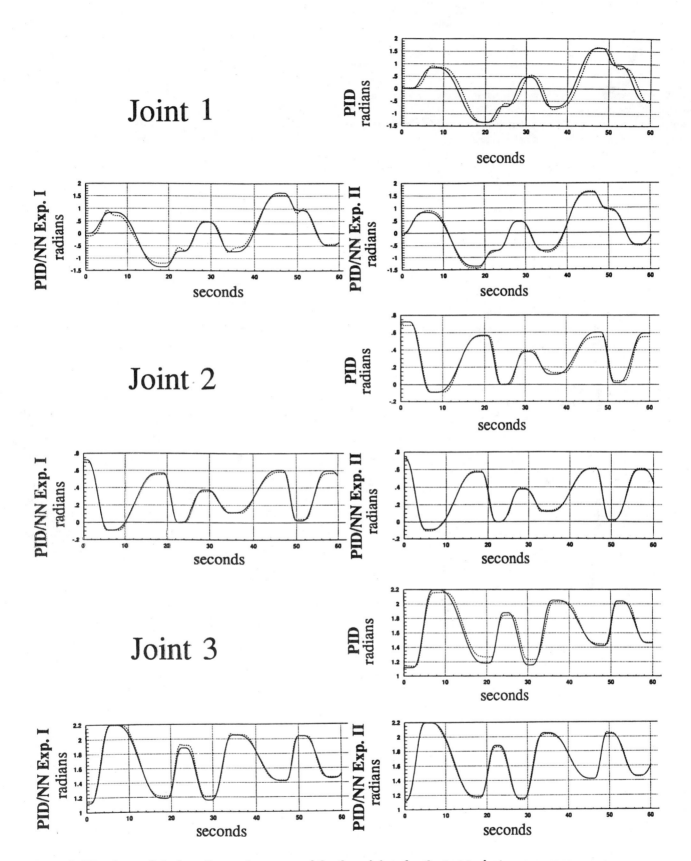

Figure 9: The above plots show the performance of the three joints for the test trajectory sequence over various control architectures. Reference trajectories are shown in solid and measured are in dashed.

$$\frac{1 - z^{-b}}{b} \qquad (5)$$

Note b represents the interval size in iterations of the window used in computing the moving average. At second glance, this transfer function is just a two-point differentiation where b adjusts the time interval between the two points used to compute the difference. If the value of b is too large, making the interval too large, then the differential approximations become erroneous, particularly for high-frequency components of trajectories. Since our robot is limited to low feedback gains, responses to rapid changes in reference position are invariably delayed. Considering this delay in response, the interval used in calculating the differential approximation must be large enough to sustain the differential signals long enough for the physical robot system to be able to utilize them. As would be expected from these comments, no improvement in performance was observed when applying extremely large (> 2.0 seconds) or extremely small (< 0.05 seconds) intervals. The optimal moving average interval was found to be 0.5 seconds, or 12 iterations at 25 Hz. After applying this architecture, the performance improved over that of Experiment I by 50%. A comparison can be made between Experiment I and Experiment II using Figure 9. Most notably, the problems observed in joint 1 have been overcome. At the same time several noticeable static errors existed in joint 2 and Joint 3 using the architecture of Experiment I, but are now overcome using the recurrent architecture of Experiment II.

Experimental Results

Because the training involves no fixed set of trajectories and the types of errors reflected by the mean square error (MSE) are ambiguous, one can draw little from plotting the joints' MSE over time during the learning stage. For this reason, results are more easily explained by observing plots of reference and measured joint positions across a standard test trajectory sequence taken after the learning period. Shown in Table 2 is a comparison of the mean square error over the entire test trajectory sequence using various control architectures. Learning was turned off for the test trajectory sequence execution. One notices that the addition of integral control decreased the controller error by typically 74%. Even so, errors are still visible from the trajectory plots using PID. The introduction of neural networks into the control scheme was found to reduce the MSE by typically 85% in comparison to PID, and 96% in comparison to PD.

Although the MSE is an effective method of measuring performance, there is ambiguity in what types of errors the MSE value is reflecting because the MSE is a mixture of both steady state errors (errors still present when the reference is constant) and tracking errors. When observing the joint trajectory plots for PID in Figure 9, we see the primary problem with joint 1 is tracking error, and in joints 2 and 3 the problems are more results of steady state error. The error plot of joint 2 is similar to joint 3 and is not shown in Figure 9 for simplicity. The network architecture of Experiment I decreased the MSE by primarily improving the tracking errors, but steady state errors still remained noticeable.

Control Type	Joint 1	Joint 2	Joint 3
PD	0.1342	0.0064	0.0089
PID	0.0350	0.0012	0.0030
PID/NN Exp I	0.0101	0.0004	0.0010
PID/NN Exp II	0.0046	0.0001	0.0005

Table 2: Comparison of the mean square error (radians).

The modeling required to overcome the remaining errors was first hypothesized to be the most context dependent. This hypothesis was verified by using a recurrent network to provide context information to successfully overcome the (near-)steady state errors. Looking at the plots from Experiment II (Figure 9), we see that the differential moving-average recurrent network architecture was able to improve the control such that both types of errors decreased substantially.

Conclusions

We have presented a real-time learning control scheme using neural networks and have successfully implemented the scheme for a light-weight space manipulator. The approach significantly improves the motion precision of the manipulator by learning the flexible robot dynamics on-line. The trajectory error is reduced by 85% compared to the results obtained from conventional linear control. The approach may be applied to different manipulators or even to different domains. The neural networks approach also provides rapid adaptability implicitly. This is particularly crucial where changes in payloads or in actual manipulator configuration may cause substantial dynamics model updating. Particular to a light-weight space robot, the approach overcomes the difficulty in real-time dynamics modeling in a micro-gravity environment.

We have discussed issues associated with on-line training strategies and presented a simple stochastic training scheme. We have presented a novel recurrent neural network architecture which improves performance in comparison to the standard neural network. The proposed moving-average differential recurrent network succeeds in utilizing context to improve performance over the original network architecture by 50% where commonly used recurrent network approaches fails. Our future research will involve a more formal and thorough investigation of the effects of varying the window of the moving average.

References

[1] Y. Xu, B. Brown, S. Aoki, and T. Kanade, Mobility and Manipulation of a Light-Weight Space Robot, *IEEE International Conference on Intelligent Robots and Systems*, 1992.

[2] H. Ueno, Y. Xu, B. Brown, M. Ueno, T. Kanade, On Control and Planning of a Flexible Space Manipulator, *IEEE International Conference on System Engineering*, 1990.

[3] H. Miyamoto, M. Kawato, T. Setoyama, and R. Suzuki, Feedback-Error-Learning Neural Network for Trajectory Control of a Robotic Manipulator, *Neural Networks*, Vol.11, pp. 251-265, 1988.

[4] J. McClelland, D. Rumelhart, and PDP research Group, *Parallel Distributed Processing*, Volume 1, Cambridge, MA: MIT Press, ISBN 0-262-18120-7, 1986.

[5] K. Wilhelmsen and N. Cotter, Neural Network Based Controllers for a Single-Degree-of-Freedom Robotic Arm, *International Joint Conference on Neural Networks*, 1990.

[6] K. S. Narendra and K. Parthasarathy, Identification and Control of Dynamical Systems Using Neural Networks, *IEEE Transactions On Neural Networks*, Vol 1 No. 1, 1992.

[7] D. Pomerleau, *Neural Network Perception for Mobile Robot Guidance*, PhD thesis, Carnegie Mellon University, 1992.

INTELLIGENT CONTROL OF A ROBOTIC HAND
WITH NEURAL NETS AND FUZZY SETS

A. Tascillo[1], V. Skormin[1], J. Crisman[2], and N. Bourbakis[1]
[1] Department of Electrical Engineering
T.J. Watson School of Engineering and Applied Science
Binghamton University
Binghamton, NY 13902

[2] Department of Electrical Engineering
Dana Research Center
Northeastern University
Boston, MA 02115

ABSTRACT

In this paper, an efficient first grasp for a wheelchair robotic hand with pressure sensing is determined and learned by combining the advantages of neural networks and fuzzy logic into a hybrid control algorithm. Modifications to standard approaches are outlined, and basic approaches are demonstrated in preparation for future physical implementation.

KEYWORDS: Robotic Hand Control, Neural Networks, Fuzzy Logic, Genetic Algorithms, and Robotic Hand Grasp Planning

1.0 INTRODUCTION

In many situations, classical and modern control theory is inadequate to control complex systems. The system to be controlled may be partially or totally unknown, parameters within the plant may drift, and highly nonlinear behavior within the system may drive an algorithm based upon linearization unstable. A primary example of such a complex system is a robotic hand. Not only are robotic hands redundant joints which complicate classical six axis kinematic and dynamic control schemes, but the motions required must be intricately dexterous and adaptive to loads of variable weight, center of mass, orientation, friction, stiffness, and grasp stability.

If an adaptive robotic control system is to be trusted for implementation, it must reliably outperform humans. Like a human, it must be able to follow fast, low precision movements with slow, high precision movements, and be able to estimate when first faced with a task, and then learn from that experience for recall at a later time. Applying this to a robotic hand entails the coordination of several dedicated algorithms, each controlling with a simplified yet flexible and adaptive algorithm.

1.1 BACKGROUND

Before any grasping is to be attempted by a robotic hand, it is advisable to use a "rougher" algorithm to approach an object from a distance away, allowing the desired task to be optimized for more intricate motions. Hu, et. al. [1] conclude that local reference frames aid in the navigation of an autonomous robot via a Kalman filter approach. Once in the proximity of the object, however, two challenges arise, "How should the object be approached?", and once grasped, "How can stable and reliable control be maintained?".

An initial grasp can be estimated simply as a direct computation based upon sensory feedback, or it can draw from past experience based upon object features. One example of the first case can be found in [2], which employs a frictionless point contact model (best applicable to objects large compared to the fingers) of an object to evaluate quality as a function of the disturbance to the object caused by the fingers. The algorithm assumes small grasp adjustments and is most accurate for objects approaching the size of the hand itself. Prior to this approach one could apply that of [3], who define a grasp as a combination of possible subconfigurations and use a knowledge base to search for an optimal grasp from the initial approximation. If the experience gained from the first approach can be used to add data to the knowledge base, the controller could continue grasp learning unsupervised.

One way to accumulate knowledge could be by matching object features in the database, and adding the experience gained. One example is [4], where object profiles, based upon polygonal approximations of two dimensional visual data, are compared with object polygons in a database via a Hopfield network. Classification is successful with objects which are rotated and whose estimated polygon vertices outnumber those of the object in the database. Physical contact could be utilized in a similar way. If the data is hard to match from the sensory data available, [5] offer an enhancement. Because a neural feature extraction network often has problems identifying highly noisy detailed patterns, a pattern is sectioned up into blocks, sub-blocks of which are clustered by dissimilarity and then entered into the neural network. The final layer of the network consists of noise filtering fuzzy membership functions, which compare their results to patterns in a database.

Once the object has been grasped in a perceived optimal manner, it must be lifted successfully, and factors such as tip and slip must be compensated for. Adaptive control is necessary both for grasp stability and for negotiating through cluttered environments. Classical control techniques may not be adequate to compensate for extremely nonlinear behavior. One example of classical feedback control, [6], employs finger tip pressure and position feedback control to move a peg from one hole to another. The peg must be dragged along the worksurface between the holes to obtain necessary feedback information. Neural networks and fuzzy logic show promise in tandem with or when compared to classical approaches. In [7], an adaptive fuzzy robotic trajectory tracker compares favorably to continuous and quantized input PID controllers. In [8], a neural network design with nonlinear feedback decoupling is used to control a biped robot that is robust to disturbances. Sub-functions in the walking task are controlled with small dedicated networks.

Demonstrations of what is possible with fuzzy logic are many. The classic inverted pendulum has been a favorite, where as many as three pendula have been balanced in series [9]. As another control problem [10], a monorail cart is commanded to balance an inverted pendulum while the cart follows a desired trajectory. Due to the integral inference block that has been added, a step disturbance exists in the angle attained for the pendulum. Soon balancing will lose center stage to walking demonstrations. In [11], with no inverse kinematics model, overlapping gaussian fuzzy membership functions approximate the nonlinear functions of a biped walking step with continuous derivatives. Adaptive fuzzy systems are already challenging older neural network designs. In [12], an adaptive fuzzy logic tractor trailer backer upper controller outperforms a one hidden layer neural network.

Fuzzy sets, although very fast to implement, depend upon the designer's prior knowledge for performance (at least initially, if they are adaptive). Although neural networks can learn an unknown functional relationship, choice of and design of an appropriate adaptive control scheme can be difficult. For instance, networks can be designed to operate with binary or continuous inputs, and can vary widely in their structure and training. In [13], a competitive adaptive resonance theory (ART) network is used to quickly control prey avoidance along a one dimensional path (various degrees to the left or right) in a simulated rabbit. Due to the binary nature of the outputs, each response requires a dedicated node. For systems with complex output possibilities, this approach may prove ungainly. For a backpropagation training scheme and architecture in [14], a force control servomechanism is used to demonstrate that stability of the one hidden layer network depends upon a trial-and-error choice of learning rate and connection weight values.

Researchers have attempted to overcome some of the training difficulties inherent in neural networks, especially the much feared local minima. In [15], the dynamics of a manipulator are approximated with small neural networks joined by a final layer trained with a least squares method. The same researchers in [16] employ a steepest descent autotuning method to vary the shape of the sigmoidal activation function. And in [17], a genetic algorithm is used to swap weight values within a neural network controller which has been held initially stable by a fixed feedback controller.

1.2 THE ROBOTIC HAND

Fuzzy logic and neural networks are employed to control a robotic hand with two three-jointed fingers and a two-jointed thumb. The hand algorithm is expected to estimate a grasp for an unknown object, adjust its grasp until one that is most stable is found, and then lift the object, adjusting for tip and slip.

Additionally, vision cannot be depended upon in a cluttered environment (i.e. a refrigerator), so the algorithms must be able to operate with little or no support from camera data. Instead, pressure and force feedback are used. This paper is organized into six sections, three of which concentrate on a specific task within the hand grasp algorithm. Section 2 introduces the hand problem and outlines the approach. Section 3 discusses a stability hierarchy for choice of a best tentative grasp. In Section 4 the tip and slip algorithms are overviewed, and a simplified tipping controller is demonstrated. Section 5 introduces a custom neural network algorithm for the class of problems with constraints similar to a neural initial grasp estimator. Finally, Section 6 concludes with future directions.

2.0 PROBLEM APPROACH

The required grasp orientation and pressure are determined by repeating a procedure where, after the hand makes three tentative test grasps, a look-up table stability hierarchy is referenced to determine whether a lift should be attempted with one of these grasps for a given tip or pad contact scenario (Figures 1 and 2), or another three should be tried. Once a grasp is attempted, fuzzy logic tip and slip routines correct for the errors in desired orientation for the object (usually defined as the orientation it was found in). When no tip or slip registers, a true lift will be attempted and independent trajectory following routines can be initiated. After several such lifting attempts, a neural network learns a best approach angle and hand orientation for a category of objects it has defined from experience. If a set of three test grasps triggers recognition from the neural network, this approach angle and orientation will be implemented and the control algorithm will resume as before with the fuzzy tip and slip algorithms.

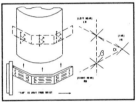

Figure 1: Pad Contact Scenario.

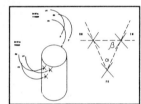

Figure 2: Tip contact scenario.

In order to overcome the constraints of time and complexity, simplifications are made to the approach which will not, for the time being, compromise the effectiveness of the control, and may in fact improve it. The first step toward simplification is to minimize the number of sensors and actuators, and then secondly, to break the control sequence into smaller manageable routines. Thirdly, an approach or combination of approaches must be chosen which can best handle each task.

Each joint on the finger is assumed to have two parallel pressure sensors (assumed here to be strain gauges), a number adequate to sense a change in orientation perpendicular to the joint grasping surface, as well as to register an absolute value to compare to an acceptable threshold. For the preliminary calculations, placement is first calculated for the first finger and thumb only, leaving the second finger free for balancing of the object.

When one of the two digits contacts the object, the second closes in to make contact. Pressure readings are taken, and if a grasp is to be attempted, the third finger contacts the surface. Tentative grasps can be helpful not only in learning the smallest practical diameter of the object (usually most stable), but also help avoid locations with sudden changes in diameter, such as a handle on a mug or a pocket clip on a pen.

3.0 THE GRASP STABILITY HIERARCHY

Some grasps are intuitively more stable than others, and should be given a higher priority when several trial grasp options are available. Assuming no open vessels of liquid, a scheme was devised that agrees with one's intuitive perception of which grasps are most stable. The method is demonstrated with an example of four trial grasps shown in Figure 3 (note that the second finger is neglected at first, to be used for extra stability). Figure 4 outlines the membership values assigned to grasps A through D for each criterion. The second joint of grasp B does not touch the object; instead it reaches behind it as if it were a mug handle, for instance.

A grasp hierarchy can be determined once applicable assumptions are made and applied. There are many ways that a grasp can be perceived more stable. The first to be considered is the number of pressure contacts made per finger or thumb. It was also assumed that joints farther away from the wrist can

take advantage of supporting objects against the "palm," and are therefore more stable that those objects held by more proximal joints. The two hierarchies in Figures 5 and 6 resulted, and membership function values were assigned, ranging from 1 for the first ranked, and zero for the last, where the finger or thumb makes no contact. The order for the finger ran {1,.9,.8,.7,.3,.2,.1,0}, and the thumb ran {1,.7,.3,0}.

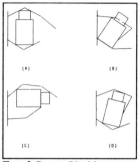

Figure 3: Four possible trial grasps.

GRASP	F HIER	T HIER	TH4	TH1 F	TH1 T	TOTAL
A	.7	1	.7	.4	.6	3.4
B	.9	.3	.5	.8	.2	2.7
C	.9	1	.3	.2	.8	3.2
D	.8	1	.9	.6	.4	3.7

Figure 4: Grasp membership values and total ranks.

Other criteria also contribute to a more stable grasp. Assuming that the largest positive theta 1 (base grasp) angle corresponds to a clenched fist, and that this would imply a tighter grasp, all candidate grasps were ranked, highest theta one as .8, lowest as .2, and all others equally spaced between. This was done separately for both finger and thumb. Based on the premise that if an object is grasped at two points 180 degrees apart it is most stable, the highest rank of .9 was assigned to finger and thumb combinations that most closely satisfied the equation:

$$(\theta_4)_{finger} = -(\theta_4)_{thumb} \qquad (1)$$

and the lowest rank was assigned .3. All others were spaced equally as before. A tie breaking criterion was used only if two of the sums from the above criteria were equal. The grasp that allowed more room for the second balancing finger was chosen as the final grasp to move onto the fuzzy tip and slip controller. Grasp D of Figure 5 wins handily with a total of 3.7 and does not require the tie breaking criterion. The addition of the fuzzy membership values from each individual criterion resulted in ranking the four grasps the same way a human volunteer did, implying that the human added up the contributions of various factors in coming to a perceived stability ranking.

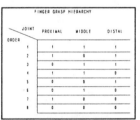

Figure 5: Finger Grasp Hierarchy.

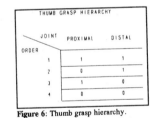

Figure 6: Thumb grasp hierarchy.

4.0 FUZZY LOGIC FOR TIP AND SLIP CONTROL

While neural networks can adaptively estimate a function, fuzzy logic excels at quick, rough human approximation when a fast and adequate control action is required [18]. For the simplest fuzzy controller, common sense is used to build rules that, given normal "crisp" sensory values (i.e., position, velocity, torque, or pressure), percentage memberships in various categories are determined. A logical process (often max-min decomposition) is used to choose the dominant category, and a resulting control effort is determined through defuzzification to a crisp value. Because fuzzy logic obtains its commands from additions and multiplies of non-zero set membership values, classical control mathematics violations are avoided, and time is optimized.

In order to adjust the grasp for object tip and slip employing fuzzy set theory, a three step algorithm is followed. First, it is assumed that excessive pressure on one member of a pair of pressure sensors for a finger in Figure 7 signals a possible tipping of the object. The bottom member of each pair is subtracted from the top, and the values are entered along the horizontal axis of the membership function in Figure 8. A membership value is found on the vertical axis for every category that is nonzero at that horizontal value. Category values are found for each sensor pair that exceeds a minimum tolerance, ϵ. This tolerance ignores pairs that do not register a significant pressure as well as pairs that are practically identical and do not need adjustment.

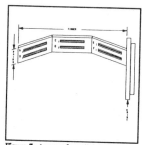

Figure 7: Array of parallel strain gauges on one of the fingers.

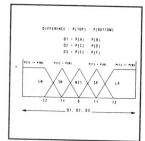

Figure 8: Tip membership function.

Sensor input categories must now be defined, and possible controller responses determined. The minimum membership values for each category, large negative (LN), small negative (SN), near zero (NZ1), small positive (SP), and large positive (LP) are found, and the category that possesses the maximum of these surviving minimums is the category chosen for control. In the cases of LN, LP, and NZ1, the PUMA arm that supports the hand will be given the command to move the finger up or down the object (assuming a loosing and subsequent tightening of the finger some small amount). If the winning category is SN or LP, the fingers themselves can adjust their yaw angles to compensate. The actual adjustment command is found by entering the associated membership into the vertical axis of a function such as Figure 9, retrieving the desired command value at the horizontal. Humans do not react symmetrically in each direction, so in order to avoid a limit cycle, avoid symmetry in the fuzzy controller command function.

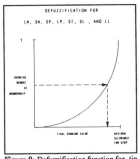

Figure 9: Defuzzification function for tip and slip.

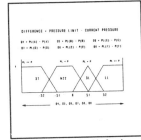

Figure 10: Slip membership function.

The second major focus in the algorithm, the slip problem, is very similar to that for tip, but the incoming pressure information must be interpreted differently. Each pressure sensor is compared to a suggested pressure limit, and these limits may vary due to individual sensor characteristics or to expected pressures for a perceived familiar shape. It is assumed that a little too tight of a grasp is better than a little too loose, so no adjustment is made for anywhere from just right to a little too tight. Much too tight, however, could damage the finger or grasped object, so the finger is carefully loosened. Loose grasps are tightened to approach the desired limit. In a manner similar to that for tip, each individual pressure is subtracted from its limit and the values are entered onto the horizontal axis of Figure 10.

For slip, the choice of control signal must be considered carefully in case the shape of the grasped object produces confusing inputs. This time, instead of employing a maximum of the minimums to decide on a prevailing control effort, a priority hierarchy is followed. If any membership value for small tight (ST) is equal to 1, all other values are overruled and the grasp is loosened. Otherwise, if the minimum for ST is greater than .1, that value is entered into a function similar to Figure 9, and that command is used for adjustment. Otherwise, the .1 criterion is applied to near zero (NZ2) if true, or small loose (SL) if false. Finally, if no previous category has a minimum greater than .1, the appropriate adjustment is found by inserting the minimum for large loose (LL).

An example of a confusing slip situation is illustrated in Figure 11. Here the middle finger pair has exceeded the suggested pressure limit, ostensibly crushing the object, while a small offshoot of the object barely makes contact with one of the two sensors proximal to the wrist. In this case the two middle sensors would probably have overruled the proximal sensor nonetheless, but an object with many projections could draw attention away from a critical stress situation.

If an adjustment for tip or slip is not necessary, the third phase, lifting of the object, may be attempted. First, the algorithm checks to see if the winning categories for the two prior steps were NZ1 and NZ2. If so, an attempt is made to lift or continue lifting the object before repeating steps 1 and 2. If large negative (LN) or large positive (LP) are resulting commands for tip after the object has been lifted, an attempt should be made to set the object down before readjusting, and the estimated neural grasp should be recalculated before lifting the object again.

4.1 FUZZY LOGIC TIPPING CONTROLLER

A simplified tipping case was demonstrated by a simulation written in C, which will be extended to three dimensions. Some assumptions have been made to approximate reality. First, the motion of the soda can is modelled as an inverted pendulum with a stable equilibrium state at topmost vertical (within ± 1.7 degrees). Friction at the soda can's bottom pivot is assumed strong enough to ignore slipping on the supporting surface.

Tipping is confined to movement into or out of the screen, and only one finger is being used to counter the tipping. The thumb is fixed in the location estimated by the neural net, which is a useful assumption if the thumb is within a mug handle, for instance. The finger adjusts with a vertical up or down movement, pushing the can backward by a number of degrees in proportion to its vertical movement. The finger adjustments are slow to avoid drastic overshoot and to allow an overworked controller to catch up. The can is allowed to continue in its motion before the next adjustment.

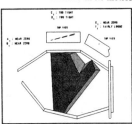

Figure 11: A challenging slip problem.

Figure 12: Initial angle of 45 degrees chosen.

Results of the simulation program for this control is demonstrated in Figures 12 through 16. First, the user is asked for an initial tipping angle theta, positive or negative any amount. Of course, anything beyond about 45 degrees is not realistic for a can of soda on a counter top, but the controller demonstrates that it is capable of following its rules for multiple revolutions of 360 degrees, suggesting that it could accomplish complex movements such as tying shoelaces, possibly with neural tuning of the fuzzy membership functions.

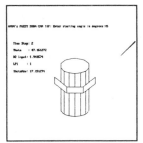

Figure 13: First fuzzy correction at time step 2.

Figure 14: Can continues under its own momentum.

Next, the soda can, the adjusting finger, and a side view of the inverted pendulum modelling the can are displayed. The program lets the soda can continue to tip from its initial or adjusted position before applying a control effort. If the can lingers within 1.7 degrees either side of vertical, the control is considered a success and the program stops. Otherwise, the pressure difference between upper and lower joint sensors of the middle joint (D2 = PC - PD) is entered into a membership function and its associated degree of membership (between 0 and 1) is displayed. A vertical adjustment along the edge of the can is obtained by entering the above results into a nonsymmetrical output function, and the final angle is the difference between a virtual adjustment angle and the movement the can would have made without adjustment. Motion is again monitored for convergence before another control effort is applied.

5.0 THE NEURAL NETWORK ALGORITHM

Neural networks excel at learning relationships based upon little available information, and due their parallel nature and adaptability, make them well suited to approximating relationships that may not be obvious to a human.

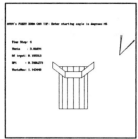

Figure 15: Second and final fuzzy correction.

Figure 16: Algorithm stops at time step 4, as angle was within the wobble tolerance of 1.7 degrees.

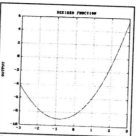

Figure 17: Desired Function.

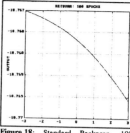

Figure 18: Standard Backprop, 100 Iterations (Epochs) through the training set.

An attempt is made here to determine an optimal approach angle and hand orientation for a range of similar objects, with little regard for features that humans might insist on considering. For the hand an architecture and algorithm based upon backpropagation was chosen, for its relative stability and ability to provide continuous output values.

Backpropagation utilizes a weight update method that is based upon the gradient descent error minimization technique. Because this relies upon the rate of change of the error, it is performs best for functions of second order and lower. Higher order functions possess many nonoptimal local minima potentially trapping backpropagation, despite enhancements such as adaptive learning rate and momentum. The popular method of minimizing the sum of the individual squared errors for each training set example can result in a network that minimizes an overall error, leading to a solution which is less than optimal over the region of interest within the target function.

Currently neural network researchers will repeatedly reintroduce a training set of input examples to the network for weight update. Unfortunately, a network started down an inopportune path is not likely to be corrected after tens of thousands of cycles, or epochs, of additional training. Due to the unpredictable nature of the error surface, progress is inconsistent from one set of random initial conditions to the next, impairing the effective implementation of neural networks for the demanding and stability sensitive control of dynamically changing nonlinear systems. A method is necessary which guarantees a fast, reasonably accurate estimate of an unknown functional relationship, independent of its degree of nonlinearity or the number of linearly dependent inputs.

After considering the above mentioned factors, the architecture that resulted was partially derived from Scott Fahlman's cascade correlation [19]. Fahlman's approach of incrementally adding one hidden unit at a time during training may be slower at first, but will result in an efficient function representation with is not under constrained with too few weights (leading to a flattening or simplifying of the true function), or over constrained with too many weights (resulting in an erroneous representation that serendipitously minimizes the error criterion). Unfortunately, one hidden unit is forced to minimize the error for all outputs, even if they vary widely in magnitude. The hand algorithm devotes a minimum number of hidden units in two hidden layers to each output. This arrangement blended efficiency and accuracy.

5.1 A GENETIC APPROACH

In order to overcome backpropagation's difficulty in avoiding local minima, the modified algorithm preconditioned the trainable weights and biases by arranging them in a vector, varying and evaluating them via a quality measure. The winning vector was then introduced or returned to the network for further optimization. This method, based upon the genetic algorithm concept, excels when desirable performance criterion values are surrounded by undesirable values, a trap for a gradient-based algorithm. The organized randomness of the genetic algorithm jumps over this "moat" by utilizing the concepts of mutation and crossover [20]. Such discontinuous moves are possible by choosing offspring based on diversity as well as optimality.

In a commonly implemented genetic algorithm, all variables are arranged into a vector called a chromosome. Individual entries, or genes, in the vector are mutated by varying one increment up or down to create offspring chromosomes. At a randomly chosen breakpoint, a chromosome trades a section of itself with a sibling, approximating the crossover that occurs as a result of mating. All candidate offspring are then evaluated by a performance measure, (i.e., an absolute distance from a target), and are ranked. The best ranked offspring is then compared to every other offspring to yield diversity values, and another ranking is performed. Performance rank and diversity rank are then combined in a user-defined fashion to yield a final rank to which probability values are assigned. Offspring passing on to the next step are chosen

with a higher probability from the higher ranks, and a lower probability from the lower ranks. Normally half of the offspring are chosen to continue, maintaining a constant population. Repeat mutation, crossover, and ranking continues until either performance stops improving or an error tolerance is reached.

Although related to the standard, the modified implementation of the genetic algorithm varies in several respects. In the modified hand algorithm, all neural net variable weights are arranged into a vector. One weight is randomly varied, creating an offspring of the original vector to approximate mutation. Variation of one weight is continued across the length of the vector until there are as many offspring as weights, plus the original parent. A few more offspring are then created by randomly varying all weights to approximate diversity. Output values are obtained for distance from the target, rate of change of that distance ("velocity"), and curvature of that distance ("acceleration"). The resulting values (or normalized versions) are added together and the offspring with the lowest overall score is chosen to continue for optimization by the neural network. If the original parent is chosen, a flag can be set to stop or modify the genetic portion for later. Otherwise, when progress in error reduction of the backpropagation has slowed, the weights will return to the genetic portion.

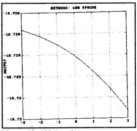

Figure 19: 600 Iterations.

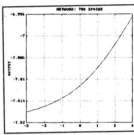

Figure 20: 700 Iterations.

When backpropagation was alternated with periodic genetic rearrangement of the weights, significant progress was made in learning. The original backpropagation, with adaptive learning rate, momentum, adjustable bias, and variable hidden layer architecture, would stop learning around 800 iterations (Figures 17 through 21). No significant progress occurred as far as 9900 iterations (Figure 22).

First, a genetic algorithm that compared distance away from the target was employed. The curve was better approximated for the positive x axis, but remained flat for the negative x axis (Figure 23). With a rate of change ("velocity") factor added into the performance measure, the negative side lifted up (Figure 24), and with acceleration added, the curve was even better approximated (Figure 25). The genetic algorithm is surely worth investigating for practical applications such as the hand. Because the estimation strays at the edges, training beyond the expected operation range is recommended to get the closest fit where crucial.

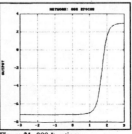

Figure 21: 800 Iterations.

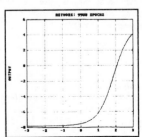

Figure 22: 9900 Iterations.

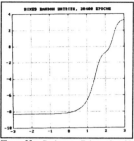
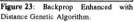

Figure 23: Backprop Enhanced with Distance Genetic Algorithm.

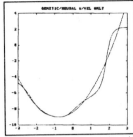

Figure 24: Distance and Velocity, with desired function superimposed.

As of this writing an enhancement has been added to the genetic algorithm to consistently ensure a desired set of weights that can be refined with the backpropagation algorithm, regardless of linearly dependent inputs. With this preconditioning, significant progress toward the function shape occurs as soon as 500 backprop iterations, and after 2000 iterations the estimation is closer to the target than in Figure 25.

5.2 OBJECT CATEGORY NETWORK

In order to avoid an extensive search for an optimal grasp each time an object is lifted, a learning mechanism is triggered. As the robotic hand, through trial and error, determines the quality of a trial grasp as a function of the number of tip and slip corrections as well as a hierarchy emphasizing more stable configurations, a history is accumulated for a given object category. A neural network for that object, or class of objects, is trained under the supervision of a fuzzy grasp quality classifier, which will assign a crisp value between -1 and 1 as the target value for the set of trial grasp input conditions. These nine inputs are components of the hand approach vector as well as the pitch and yaw base angle positions of the two fingers and thumb. Repeated exposure to training examples can begin as soon as the first set of three trial grasps is performed.

After a suitable training period has passed, the neural knowledge base, consisting of several object grasp quality rankers, will receive a new set of trial grasps one at a time, assigning a grasp quality value for each possible object. The object network with the highest quality is chosen for each grasp, and the results are compared by a fuzzy classifer. If all three grasps are classified as the same object, the grasp with the highest rank is chosen. If the value of that quality is high, the hand will attempt a lift, triggering the tip and slip controller algorithms. If the quality of the winner is not satisfactory, another set of trial grasps is performed, and the process is repeated. If a set of trial inputs does not correlate well with the types of inputs seen by existing categories, the fuzzy classifier will assume ignorance, create a new category network, and immediately trigger a lift attempt. The final number of categories is determined by how strict the correlation criterion is set.

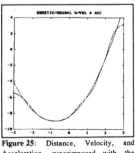

Figure 25: Distance, Velocity, and Acceleration, superimposed with the desired function.

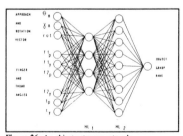

Figure 26: An object category network.

When the physical hand and arm system has been constructed, details of the control algorithm will be customized for the real world physical parameters. To this point, simulation has been instrumental in demonstrating optimal algorithms. Neural network training, for example, has shown that a neural network with two hidden layers populated with fewer hidden units is a faster and more accurate estimator of higher order nonlinear functions than a one layer network with many units. Also, three test grasps is an efficient compromise as an three dimensional approximation of an object surface in a particular region. It is hoped that the implemented control algorithms will prove to be adaptive to time dependent concerns such as wear and fluctuating loads.

For any given problem, the best neural network and fuzzy logic controllers can compete head-to-head, implying, that at present, neither is superior and both should be given equal consideration. Capable of "winging it,"

fuzzy logic control can react reliably and quickly, given a minimum of often unreliable and noisy information. Because of its fast implementation realization, many feel that neural networks are too complex for fast and accurate reaction. Fast fuzzy implementation assumes, however, that a human expert is ready and available to give complete and accurate rules for the fuzzy logic controller to follow, and that these rules still apply to a system with drifting parameters.

For the highly nonlinear control of a robotic hand, however, neural networks are indispensable in learning the relationship of a system where the parameters may not be available or accessible. The parallel aspects of neural networks, especially once implemented in custom hardware, should be able to equal or exceed the performance of fuzzy logic, despite the longer initial neural training. The modified training algorithms presented here show promise in attaining this goal. By employing a combination of advanced adaptive control concepts to deal with all anticipated situations in the limited case of object grasping, these techniques could be extended to a full range of tasks.

REFERENCES

[1] Hu, Huosheng, Michael Brady, and Penelope Probert, "Navigation and Control of a Mobile Robot Among Moving Obstacles," Proceedings of the 30th Conference on Decision and Control, Brighton, England, December 1991.

[2] Gongliang Guo, William A. Gruver, and Qixian Zhang, "Optimal Grasps for planar Multifingered Robotic Hands," IEEE Transactions on Systems, Man, and Cybernetics, Vol. 22, No. 1, January/February 1992.

[3] Nguyen, Thang N., and Harry E. Stephanou, "A Continuous Model of Robot Hand Preshaping," IEEE International Conference on Systems, Man, and Cybernetics, New York: Institute of Electrical and Electronic Engineers, Inc., pp. 798-803, 1989.

[4] Nasrabadi, Nasser M., and Wei Li, "Object Recognition by a Hopfield Neural Network," IEEE Transactions on Systems , Man and Cybernetics, Vol. 21, No. 6, November/December 1991.

[5] Takagi, Toshiyuki, and Shohachiro Nakanishi, "Pattern Recognition Based on the Extraction of Features by Neural Networks and Fuzzy Set Theory," Part VI, Fuzzy and Neuro, Fuzzy Engineering toward Human Friendly Systems, IFES 1991.

[6] Eng, Victor J., "Modal Segments for a Peg Insertion Task," IEEE Robotics: Challenges in Motion Control, Planning, and Vision, The 29th Videoconference Seminars via Satellite, Thursday, April 6, 1989.

[7] Scharf, E.M., and N.J. Mandic, "The Application of a Fuzzy Controller to the Control of a Multi-Degree-of-Freedom Robot Arm," Industrial Applications of Fuzzy Control, M. Sugeno, editor, North-Holland: Elsevier Science Publishers B.V., 1985.

[8] Wang, H., T.T. Lee, and W.A. Gruver, "A Neuromorphic Controller for a Three-Link Biped Robot," IEEE Transactions on Systems, Man, and Cybernetics, Vol. 22, No. 1, January/February 1992.

[9] Schwartz, Daniel G., and George J. Klir, "Fuzzy Logic Flowers in Japan," IEEE Spectrum, July 1992.

[10] Kawaji, Shigeyasu, and Teruyuki Maeda, "Fuzzy Servo Control System for an Inverted Pendulum," Fuzzy Engineering toward Human Friendly Systems, Part VII, Fuzzy Logic Control, IFES 1991.

[11] Ashida, Hitoshi, and Hidetomo Ichihashi, "Fuzzy Learning Control of a Biped Locomotive Robot," Fuzzy Engineering toward Human Friendly Systems, Part VIII, Application, IFES 1991.

[12] Kong, Seong-Gon and Bart Kosko, "Comparison of Fuzzy and Neural Truck Backer-Upper Control Systems," Neural Networks and Fuzzy Systems: A Dynamical Systems Approach to Machine Intelligence, Englewood Cliffs, NJ: Prentice Hall 1992.

[13] Winter, C.L., "Bugs: An Adaptive Critter," Journal of Neural Network Computing, Summer 1989.

[14] Yamada, Takayuki, and Tetsuro Yabuta, "Neural Network Controller Characteristics with Regard to Adaptive Control," IEEE Transactions on Systems, Man, and Cybernetics, Vol. 22, No. 1, January/February 1992.

[15] Guez, A., Z. Ahmad, and J. Selinsky, "The Application of Neural Networks to Robotics," Neural Networks: Current Applications, edited by P.G.J. Lisboa, New York: Chapman & Hall, 1992.

[16] Yamada, Takayuki, and Tetsuro Yabuta, "Neural Network Controller Using Autotuning Method for Nonlinear Functions," IEEE Transactions on Neural Networks, Vol. 3, No. 4, July 1992.

[17] Ichikawa, Yoshiaki and Toshiyuki Sawa, "Neural Network Application for Direct Feedback Controllers," IEEE Transactions on Neural Networks, Vol. 3, No. 2, March 1992.

[18] Zadeh, L.A., "Fuzzy Sets," Information and Control, No. 8, 1965, pp. 338-353.

[19] Fahlman, S.E., and C. Lebiere, "The Cascade-Correlation Learning Architecture," School of Computer Science, Carnegie Mellon University, Pittsburgh, Pennsylvania, February 14, 1990.

[20] Winston, Patrick Henry, Artificial Intelligence. New York: Addison-Wesley, 1992.

Chapter 4
Structure Control

The application of neural networks to control large structures such as buildings and space structures has not been as popular as the preceding three applications areas, but its application here could be quite pervasive if shown to be successful. This chapter includes two structure control applications. **Paper 4.1** uses a multilayer perceptron (MLP) neural network for parameter identification in a five story building. Once these parameters can be identified, the damping of building motion is possible. **Paper 4.2** uses recurrent neural networks to control flexible space structures. The stabilization of space structures is considered a critical technology for the successful development of space.

Chapter 4:   *Structure Control*

Neural networks for the Identification of Linear Dynamical Model of a Five Story Building

M. Elkordy,   R. Ghanem,   G.C. Lee

Department of Civil Engineering
State University of New York at Buffalo
Buffalo, NY 14260.

Abstract

In this paper, neural networks are used for parameter identification of multistory buildings. The networks are trained and tested using experimental data measured on building models. The measurements consist of acceleration time histories taken at the base of the buildings and at the various floor levels. It is demonstrated that once the initial learning phase is completed, the network can provide instantaneous identification of system parameters when presented with different acceleration record.

1 Introduction

Associated with any system identification process, two major issues can be identified whose adequate treatment is crucial for the results to be of practical value. The first of these consists of identifying a mathematical model which is completely determined by a finite set of parameters. This model should be able to anticipate the behavior of the system within an acceptable tolerance. The second issue is to identify these parameters based on the observed behavior of the system. The identification of nonlinear relationships between the measured input and output of a given system is still in its infancy, particularly as related to structural engineering systems. This is in sharp contrast with the expected nonlinear behavior of structural systems, particularly those subjected to extreme loading conditions forcing them to sustain a certain amount of damage. Due to this differential in the state-of-the-art between identification and analysis, system identification has traditionally focused on estimating a linearized model of the structural system, which is equivalent, in some sense, to the original nonlinear system. Once a linear model for the system has been decided upon, any of a number of algorithms can be used to identify the parameters which will completely determine this model. Each of these algorithms is the computational incarnation of a theoretical effort which minimizes a certain norm of a certain error. The specific error and the associated norm are, obviously, dependent on the particular algorithm. In general, these algorithms fall into two categories, depending on whether they operate on the data in the time domain, or on the Fourier transform of the data,

in the frequency, or more generally, the wave number domain. Frequency domain algorithms have been the most popular, mainly due to their simplicity, and also for historical reasons. These algorithms, however, involve averaging temporal information, thus discarding any of the details thereof. For structural systems, whose parameters are expected to degrade with time, this tradeoff of temporal information for frequency information is not always justifiable. Other, time domain algorithms, also aim at identifying linear models with time invariant parameters. These have the same shortcoming as the frequency domain approach mentioned above, albeit they make use of the details of the temporal variation in the measured data. Given the restriction of identifying a linear model of a given structure, it is apparent that the model which is capable of extracting the most information out of the available data, is one that identifies a linear model which is evolving in time. Such a model would be linear in its parameters which are themselves, time varying, and therefore have to be repeatedly updated through an identification process. Recent research efforts in structural system identification have aimed at further developing and validating the structural engineering applications of recursive and other time domain algorithms capable of tracking the variation in time of the parameters of a given system [11][10].

An experiment was performed using a scaleed model of a steel building. The data sets from the experiment consisted of acceleration records measured at various floor levels. Each of these records was analyzed using a number of different system identification techniques.

The system identification technique which used in this study consisted of a variant of the recursive least squares variable methods. This methods was recommended in the literature by various investigators. It provides for an exponential phasing out of old data. A detailed analysis of the system identification aspects of this problem are provided elsewhere [4] [5] [10].

This paper presents the results of utilizing neural networks to provide an efficient computational model for a dynamical system. The neural networks are trained with acceleration records measured at the various floors in the five story building. Each training session is performed by adjusting the internal connections of the network until it is capable of mapping a certain acceleration records to the corresponding set of coefficients. These coefficients can then be utilized for the expeditious prediction of the motion of the structure when subjected to various loading conditions.

2 Models of the Dynamical Systems

The class of structures that fall within the scope of the present investigation can be adequately modeled by the following N-dimensional system of equations which describes the motion of the structure,

$$\mathbf{M\ddot{u}} + \mathbf{C\dot{u}} + \mathbf{Ku} + \mathbf{g}[\mathbf{u}, \dot{\mathbf{u}}] = \mathbf{f}(t) + \boldsymbol{\omega}(t) . \quad (1)$$

Here, $\mathbf{M}$ denotes the inertia matrix associated with the structure, $\mathbf{C}$ denotes the corresponding viscous damping matrix and $\mathbf{K}$ the stiffness matrix. Furthermore, the vector $\mathbf{f}(t)$ denotes the externally applied forces, and $\mathbf{g}[\mathbf{u}, \dot{\mathbf{u}}]$ is a vector whose components are nonlinear functions of the structural displacement $\mathbf{u}$ and its first derivative $\dot{\mathbf{u}}$. In the above equation, the term $\boldsymbol{\omega}(t)$ represents errors due to modeling approximations. Obviously, it can also be used to model an additive noise to the excitation process $\mathbf{f}(t)$ in which case, the noise may be attributed to unmeasured environmental factors. The most useful form for this noise process has proven to be a zero-mean stationary Gaussian white noise.

For the purpose of structural identification, measurement devices are placed at certain locations throughout the structure. Their number is usually less than the number of degrees of freedom of the structure. This is due to both the expense associated with additional measurements, as well as to the fact that theoretically, each measured record contains enough information to permit the identification of all the unknown parameters. Furthermore, measurement noise is usually associated with the measurement process, leading to the following observation equation which relates the observation vector at the ith observation time interval to the response vector at that instant,

$$\mathbf{y}_i = \mathbf{H\ddot{u}}_i + \mathbf{e}_i . \quad (2)$$

In the above equation, $\mathbf{H}$ is a matrix which reflects the location of the measurement devices in relation to the structural nodes, and the associated amplification or attenuation factors, and $\mathbf{e}_i$ is a vector denoting the measurement noise and is usually assumed to be a zero-mean Gaussian white noise.

Alternatively, the identification problem can be cast completely in terms of the observed input and output, without any reference to the underlying mechanics or the associated differential equation. This approach provides an algorithm which permits forecasts of the response of the structure that are compatible, in some sense, with measured past input and output data. A general class of models referred to as the prediction error models is obtained using the following equation [6]

$$\mathbf{y}_i = \mathcal{Y}_i(\mathbf{y}_{i-1}, \ldots, \mathbf{y}_{i-k}, \mathbf{f}_i, \ldots, \mathbf{f}_{i-l}) + \mathbf{e}_i . \quad (3)$$

Obviously, the more complicated the form of the functional $\mathcal{Y}_i$, the more sophisticated the model is, but also the more specialized and less robust it is. In the important case of a linear functional relationship, equation (3) can be conveniently rewritten as

$$\mathbf{y}_i = \boldsymbol{\theta}_i^T \mathbf{x}_i + \mathbf{e}_i \quad (4)$$

where $\boldsymbol{\theta}_i$ is a matrix of the coefficients in the linear expansion, and

$$\mathbf{x}_i = [\mathbf{y}_{i-1}, \ldots, \mathbf{y}_{i-k}, \mathbf{f}_i, \ldots, \mathbf{f}_{i-l}] . \quad (5)$$

Since equations (1) and (3) are mathematical expressions of the same physical problem, an equivalence, in some sense, should be anticipated between them. Depending on the dimension of the observation space, this equivalence can take one of many forms. Also, the extent of the desired equivalence is problem dependent and is usually limited to the equivalence of the predicted output of a linearized version of these equations. Such equivalence can be achieved by matching the spectral density of the response of a linearized version of equation (1), with that of an appropriate linear difference equation model. Thus the difference equation associated with a scalar observable can be written as

$$\sum_{k=0}^{2N} a_k y_{i-k} + \sum_{k=0}^{2N} b_k f_{i-k} = 0 . \quad (6)$$

Equating the transfer function associated with equations (6) and (1) after its linearization, results in the following expressions for the physical parameters in terms of the regression coefficients,

$$\omega_j = \frac{\sqrt{\lambda_j^2 + \delta_j^2}}{\Delta t} , \quad \xi_j = \frac{\delta}{\sqrt{\lambda_j^2 + \delta_j^2}} \quad (7)$$

where Δt denotes the sampling rate, and

$$\lambda_j = \text{Arg}[z_j] , \delta_j = -\frac{1}{2}\ln|z_j|^2 . \quad (8)$$

In the above equation, ω_j and ξ_j denote the modal frequency and damping ratio of the jth mode, respectively. Also, z_j denotes the jth pole, in the upper half of the complex plane, of the transfer function of the model in equation (6). The equivalence given by the above equations is based on the assumption that modal superposition applies to the dynamical system under consideration. This assumption may lead to spurious results when trying to recover the physical parameters from the regression coefficients. In particular, it is noted that for z_j real, a value of 100% is obtained for the corresponding critical damping ratio ξ_j.

3 Recursive Least Squares

The recursive least squares method consists of updating a least squares fit to the available data, as more data is made available. It can be shown that the estimates obtained using a least squares algorithm tend to be biased unless the prediction errors are uncorrelated, which is seldom the case. The bias is generally associated with the propagation of the initial error in the estimates. The effect of this error can be substantially reduced by implementing a process whereby less weight is given to older data. An exponential weighting function has been successfully implemented to this end in a number of investigations. This technique is mathematically based on minimizing the following loss function [?],

$$S_k(\theta_k) = \alpha S_{k-1}(\theta_k) + \left(y_k - \mathbf{x}_k^T \theta_k\right)^2 , \quad (9)$$

where the second term represents the error associated with the current observation, and $0 < \alpha < 1$. It can be shown that the cost function given by the above equation is equivalent to the cost function given by the equation

$$S_k(\theta) = \sum_{i=1}^{k} \left(y_i - \mathbf{x}_i^T \theta\right) \alpha^{k-i} n \quad (10)$$

which better explains the role of the parameter α as a decay factor for older observations. The prediction equation and the gain matrix $\mathbf{K}$ are given by

$$\hat{\theta}_{k+1} = \hat{\theta}_k + \mathbf{K}_{k+1} \left[y_{k+1} - \mathbf{x}_{k+1}^T \hat{\theta}_k \right] , \quad (11)$$

and

$$\mathbf{K}_{k+1} = \frac{\mathbf{P}_k \mathbf{x}_{k+1}}{\alpha + \mathbf{x}_{k+1}^T \mathbf{P}_k \mathbf{x}_{k+1}} , \quad (12)$$

respectively. Furthermore, the recursion for matrix $\mathbf{P}$ appearing in the above equation is given by

$$\mathbf{P}_{k+1} = \frac{1}{\alpha} \left[\mathbf{I} - \mathbf{P}_k \frac{\mathbf{x}_{k+1} \mathbf{x}_{k+1}^T}{\alpha + \mathbf{x}_{k+1}^T \mathbf{P}_k \mathbf{x}_{k+1}} \right] \mathbf{P}_k . \quad (13)$$

In the implementation of this algorithm, a zero initial guess for the regression coefficients, and a diagonal matrix with large elements (1000) for the matrix $\mathbf{P}$ were used. In the course of the present research, values of α ranging from 0.7 to 0.99 were tested. A value of 0.99 was found to be most suitable for this application, agreeing with the published literature. Table (1) shows the estimated auto-regressive coefficients of an order 10 predictive model as given by equation (6). Figure (1) shows graphically depicts these coefficients. It should be noted at this point that these values of the coefficients correspond to the values estimated at the end of the observation time interval. Thus these numbers do not reflect the time variation of the coefficients.

4   Back Propagation Neural Networks

Inspired by the neuronal architecture of the brain, an artificial neural network is a computational model that is composed of simple processors, called neurons

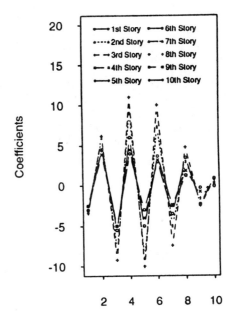

Figure 1: Coefficients of the Prediction Model as Estimated Using Recursive Least Squares; Data Collected at Five Different Stories in Building.

or nodes, that are inter-connected with each others. These connections have weights, consisting of numerical values, associated with them. Each neuron has an activation value that is a function of the weighted sum of inputs received from other neurons through the various connections. Neural networks are capable of self organization and learning. This usually involves modifying connection weights via a learning rule. Many types of neural networks have been proposed by changing the network topology, node characteristics, and the learning procedures. Examples of those are the Hopfield network [7], the Kohonen network [8], and the back propagation network [9]. In civil engineering, back propagation networks have been used by researchers to solve different types of problems. For example, Ghaboussi et al. [3], used back propagation networks for modeling material behavior. Another example is the work done by Chen and Shah [1], in which they used back propagation neural networks in dynamic analysis of bridges. Garrett [2] provides an overview of possible neural networks applications in civil engineering. A back propagation network consists of an input layer, hidden layers, an output layer and adaptive connections between successive layers. Back propagation networks can learn when presented with input-target output pairs. Learning or training involves modifying the connection weights until the network is capable of reproducing the target output, within a specified error margin, for the respective input patterns. Training takes place in an iterative fashion. Each iteration cycle involves a forward propagation step followed by backward propagation of the error to update the connection weights. The forward propagation step starts when the input nodes receive their activation levels in the form of an input pattern. Then, forward propagation proceeds through the hidden layers up to the output layer by computing the activation levels of the nodes in those layers. Activation levels are computed as follows:

- Each node receives its input from other nodes impinging on it and computes the net input N_j from the equation

$$N_j = \sum_{i=0}^{n} a_i W_{ji} \, , \qquad (14)$$

where a_i is the output of the nodes impinging on node j, and W_{ji} is the weight of the connection between nodes i and j.

- The activation level of each node is computed from the relation,

$$a_j = F(N_j) \, , \qquad (15)$$

where F is the sigmoid function defined by the equation,

$$F(x) = \frac{1}{1 + e^{-x}} \, . \qquad (16)$$

In the network used in this study, the output value of the node is the same as its activation value. The outputs of the network are the activation values of the output nodes. For all the nodes in the output layer during training, an error value δ_j is computed from the equation [?]

$$\delta_j = (t_j - a_j) F'(N_j) \, , \qquad (17)$$

where t_j is the target output of node j, a_j is the network output of node j, After those values are computed, the error back propagation step starts. The purpose of the back propagation step is to modify the connection weights such that the difference between the output of the network, computed from the forward propagation step, and the target output, is reduced. Connection weights are updated through the generalized delta rule [9],

$$\Delta W_{ji} = \eta \delta_j a_i \, , \qquad (18)$$

where η a constant referred to as the *learning rate*, and the value of δ_j associated with the nodes in the hidden layers is estimated from the equation,

$$\delta_j = F'(N_j) \sum_i \delta_i W_{ji} \, . \qquad (19)$$

[9], provide a detailed description of the back propagation networks.

5 Design, Training and Testing of the Proposed Networks

A total of 10 neural networks were used, each associated with a coefficient in the linear predictive model. The ith network was trained to predict the value of a_i. The time history of the response after the initial 13.5 seconds was used to train each network. That was done to allow for the response to be free of the initial noise. The time history between 13.5 seconds and 21 seconds was divided in 23 time segments of 0.5 seconds each. Each segment contained 50 observations. An overlap of 0.2 seconds was used between each two consecutive time segments. All ten networks were designed as back propagation networks with 50 input nodes (one node for each observation), 40 hidden nodes and one output node representing the respective a_i value. The networks were trained with the time histories and the a_i values for the 1st, 2nd, 3rd, and 5th floors. During training, the network adjusts its connection weights until it is able to reproduce the target a_i value for the training samples within an error margin. If the training set contained all the information relevant to making accurate predictions of the a_i value, the trained network would be capable of not only reproducing the a_i values for the time histories used in training, but also giving highly accurate estimates of a_i values for time histories different than those used in training. Upon completing the training, each network was tested using the time history of the response recorded at the fourth floor which was not used in training the network. Upon presenting the ith network with the observations obtained from the fourth floor, it produced a prediction of a_i. The prediction obtained from the neural networks are sketched in Fig. (2) and (3), and their values are shown in Table (2). A comparison between the output from the networks and the values of coefficients calculated through the system identification technique is presented in Table (3)

6 Summary and Conclusions

In this paper, a neural network was utilized for the development of a computational representation of a five story building model. The neural network was trained using data collected from the building, at four different floor levels, during an experiment. Using data from the fifth floor (which was not used in training the networks), the trained networks were subsequently able to identify the coefficients of a dynamical model of the structure with reasonable accuracy. A knowledge of these coefficients permits the prediction of the motion of the structure for control purposes, as well as allowing for the detection of damage during the vibration of the structure under extreme loading conditions. The advantage of using neural networks instead of traditional system identification methods is that once the network is trained, it requires virtually no computation time to estimate the coefficients of the dynamical model. This is a crucial advantage of the approach, specially for on-line control problems.

	a(1)	a(2)	a(3)	a(4)	a(5)	a(6)	a(7)	a(8)	a(9)	a(10)
1st Floor	-2.5	4.5	-5.5	6	-5	3.7	-2.5	1.25	-0.3	-0.1
2nd Floor	-3.1	˙6	-8	9	-9	7.3	-5	3	-1.6	0.52
3rd Floor	-3.4	6.2	-9.2	11	-10	10	-7.4	4.8	-2.5	0.7
4th Floor	-2.5	3.9	-5	4.5	-4	3.2	-2.4	1.8	-0.8	0.2
5th Floor	-3	4.5	7 -5	4	-3	3	-3.5	3.5	-2.3	0.9

Table 1: Coefficients Measured Using Recursive Least Squares with Exponential Decay

a1	a2	a3	a4	a5	a6	a7	a8	a9	a10
-2.87	4.23	-4.93	4.47	-4.07	3.31	-3.10	2.28	-1.73	0.90
-2.86	4.22	-4.92	4.41	-4.12	3.35	-3.11	2.28	-1.65	0.90
-2.86	4.21	-4.91	4.22	-4.10	3.30	-3.06	2.28	-1.61	0.90
-2.88	4.18	-4.88	4.36	-4.01	3.32	-3.11	2.28	-1.63	0.90
-2.87	4.19	-4.89	4.21	-4.02	3.36	-3.15	2.28	-1.51	0.90
-2.84	4.13	-4.86	4.30	-3.97	3.27	-2.97	2.28	-1.47	0.70
-2.87	4.12	-4.86	4.39	-4.05	3.35	-2.97	2.28	-1.49	0.62
-2.82	4.09	-4.85	4.25	-3.97	3.37	-2.97	2.28	-1.41	0.60
-2.82	4.10	-4.87	4.41	-4.02	3.35	-2.81	2.27	-1.39	0.47
-2.80	4.06	-4.84	4.40	-3.90	3.34	-2.76	2.26	-1.43	0.38
-2.77	4.07	-4.85	4.51	-4.08	3.45	-2.72	2.25	-1.38	0.41
-2.77	4.06	-4.84	4.50	-3.87	3.31	-2.65	2.22	-1.40	0.26
-2.75	4.06	-4.85	4.64	-4.00	3.42	-2.59	2.20	-1.41	0.28
-2.75	4.07	-4.85	4.59	-3.94	3.40	-2.64	2.23	-1.42	0.31
-2.75	4.07	-4.84	4.58	-3.86	3.38	-2.64	2.22	-1.45	0.30
-2.75	4.08	-4.85	4.57	-3.93	3.41	-2.70	2.25	-1.48	0.39
-2.76	4.13	-4.86	4.57	-3.93	3.38	-2.72	2.26	-1.49	0.44
-2.79	4.12	-4.87	4.59	-3.96	3.37	-2.77	2.27	-1.54	0.49
-2.80	4.14	-4.88	4.51	-3.99	3.39	-2.85	2.27	-1.53	0.59
-2.81	4.16	-4.89	4.48	-3.98	3.35	-2.89	2.28	-1.53	0.63
-2.83	4.17	-4.89	4.49	-4.02	3.35	-2.91	2.28	-1.54	0.66
-2.84	4.18	-4.90	4.44	-4.05	3.37	-2.94	2.28	-1.51	0.69
-2.84	4.10	-4.87	4.53	-4.00	3.37	-2.70	2.25	-1.40	0.39

Table 2: Coefficients as Calculated from the Neural Network; Data from 4th Story

Neural Networks	Rec. Least Squares
-2.81	-2.5
4.13	3.9
-4.87	-5
4.45	4.5
-3.99	-4
3.36	3.2
-2.86	-2.4
2.26	1.8
-1.50	-0.8
0.57	0.2

Table 3: Comparison Between a_i Produced by the Neural Network and Recursive Least Squares

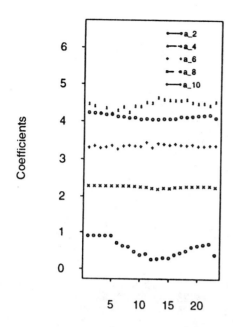

Figure 2: Coefficients of the Dynamical Model as Predicted by the Data from the Fourth Floor; Odd Coefficients.

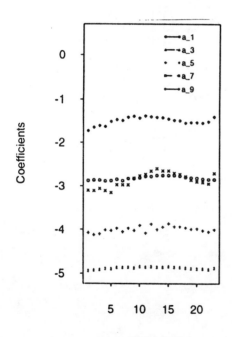

Figure 3: Coefficients of the Dynamical Model as Predicted by the Data from the Fourth Floor; Even Coefficients.

Acknowledgements

Part of this research was supported by the National Center for Earthquake Engineering Research through project number 92-5001F and National Science Foundation grant number BCS-9222710.

Bibliography

[1] Chen, Stuart, and Shah, Ketan, (1992) "Neural Networks in Dynamic Analysis of Bridges," *Proceedings of the Eighth Annual Conference of Computing in Civil Engineering, ASCE*, June, 1992

[2] Garrett, James H. JR., (1992) "Neural Networks and their Applicability within Civil Engineering," *Proceedings of the Eighth Annual Conference of Computing in Civil Engineering, ASCE*, June, 1992

[3] Ghaboussi, J., Garrett, J. H. Jr., and X. Wu., (1991) "Knowledge-Based Modeling of Material Behavior with Neural Networks," *Journal of Engineering Mechanics*, Vol 117, No. 1, January 1991. 132-153.

[4] Ghanem, R., Gavin, H., and Shinozuka, M., *Experimental Verification of a Number of Structural System Identification Algorithms*, NCEER Report, 1991.

[5] Ghanem, R., and Shinozuka, M., "A Comparative Analysis of System Identification Techniques for Earthquake Engineering Applications," *International Conference on Structural Safety and Reliability*, Innsbruck, August 1993.

[6] Goodwin, G.C. and Payne, R.L., *Dynamic System Identification: Experiment Design and Data Analysis*, Academic Press, New York, San Francisco, London, 1977.

[7] Hopfield, J. J., (1982), "Neural Networks and Physical Systems with Emergent Collective Computational Abilities," *Proceedings of the National Academy of Science*, 79, pp. 2554-2558, 1982.

[8] Kohonen, T. (1988) "Self-Organization and Associative memory, Springer-Verlag," Berlin, 1988

[9] Rumelhart, D. E. Hinton, G. E. and Williams, R. J. (1986), "Learning Internal Representation by Error propagation," in *Parallel Distributed Processing, Vol. 1: Foundations*, D. E. Rumelhart and J. L. McClelland, eds., The MIT Press, Cambridge, Mass.

[10] Shinozuka, M., Ghanem, R., and Gavin, H., "Recursive system Identification in earthquake engineering," pp. 2737-2742, *Proceedings of the Tenth World Conference on Earthquake Engineering*, 19-24 July 1992, Madrid, Spain.

[11] Young, P., *Recursive Estimation and Time-Series Analysis: An Introduction*, Springer-Verlag, Berlin, Heidelberg, New York, Tokyo, 1984.

MODELING AND CONTROL OF FLEXIBLE SPACE STRUCTURES USING NEURAL NETWORKS

Liang Jin, Madan M. Gupta, Peter N. Nikiforuk
Intelligent Systems Research Labroatory,
College of Engineering, University of Saskatchewan,
Saskatoon, Saskatchewan, Canada S7N 0W0.

ABSTRACT

Intelligent control of flexible space structures using neural network approaches is an exciting and innovative field of research with potantial applications in space systems such as large modern satellites, space station, and space robotic and maniputators. This paper intends to present some primaary studies in the field of modeling and control for flexible space structures using neural networks. The discussions include the state-of-the art in three areas: (i) on-orbit learning modeling of flexible dynamics using neural networks, (ii) neural learning and control scheme of flexible space structures, and (iii) setting of an experiment for the purposes of implementing the neural learning modeling and control for flexible structures on-ground.

1. INTRODUCTION

Future utilization of space is expected to require large space structures in low-earth as well as geosynchronous orbits. Examples of such future missions include: electronic mail systems, earth observation systems, mobile satellite communication systems, solar power satellites, large optical reflectors, and space stations. Such missions typically require large antennas, platforms and solar arrays. These missions would be feasible because of the launching capability of the Space Shuttle, which can be expanded by augmentation with Orbit Transfer Vehicles (OTV) for placement in the geosynchronous orbit.

The dimensions of such structures would typically range from 450 meters (m) to possibly several kilometers (km). For example, one mobile personal communcation system concept, for the entire continental United States, would require a space antenna with a diameter of 122 m. To establish such structures in space at minimum cost would require that their weight be minimized. It will also be necessary to compactly package them in sub-assemblies, each of which is deployable and can fit in the shuttle cargo bay. Some of the structures (e.g., space station) will require on-orbit assembly using components such as deployable beams.

Because of their light weight and expansive sizes, these structures will tend to have extremely low-frequency, lightly damped structural (elastic) modes. Natural frequencies of the elastic modes would be generally closely spaced, and some natural frequencies may be lower than the controller bandwidth. In addition, the elastic mode parameters (natural frequencies, mode shapes and damping ratios) would not be known accurately. For these reasons, control systems design for large flexible space structures (LFSS) is a difficult and challenging problem [1-3].

Advances in the area of artificial neural networks have provided the potential for developing new approaches to the control of complex and unknown nonlinear dynamic systems through learning processes. An artifical neural network as shown in Figs.1 and 2 consists of many interconnected identical simple processing units called neurons or nodes. An individual neuron sums its weighted inputs and yields an output through a nonlinear activation function with a threshold .

The main potentials of the neural network approaches for control applications can be summarized as follows:

(i) they can be used to approximate any continuous mapping to any desired degree of accuracy;

(ii) they perform this approximation through learning;

(iii) parallel processing and fault tolerance are easily accomplished.

The objective in the field of neural networks based adaptive control systems for complex flexible space structures is to develop adaptive control systems using neural networks that are used to approximate the dynamic input-output systems through a on-line learning process. To avoid modeling difficulties for flexible space structures, the neural learning and control approach provides a natural framework for the design of on-orbit intelligent control systems for flexible space systems. A number of neural networks based adaptive learning control systems have been recently proposed by the researchers at the Intelligent Systems Research Laboratory [12-17]. These studies promise to make theoretical contributions as well as practical applcations to complex space robotic systems whose dynamics are changing continuously or discontinuously, and sometimes drastically, making the system inherently unstable.

The main purpose of this paper is to present some primary studies in the field of on-orbit modeling and intelligent control techniques for flexible space structures using neural network approach. The discussions in this paper include the state-of-the art in three areas:

(i) on-orbit learning modeling of flexible dynamics using neural networks;

(ii) neural learning and control scheme of flexible space structures;

(iii) setting an experiment for the purposes of implementing the neural learning modeling and control for flexible structures on-ground.

2. BASIC STRUCTURES OF COMPUTATIONAL NEURAL NETWORKS

2.1 Multilayered Feedforward Neural Networks (MFNNs)

As a computational architecture, the multilayered feedforward neural structure which is one of the main classes of artificial neural networks plays an important role in system identification, control, equalization, and pattern recognition. The backpropagation (BP) algorithm is based on the gradient descent algorithm an d has been used widely to train multilayered neural networks for performing desired tasks since BP learning algorithm, including several extensions was developed. The advantages of BP algorithm include the parallel structure of computation, its ability to store many more patterns than the number of network inputs, and its ability to acquire arbitrarily complex nonlinear mappings.

In a multilayered feedforward network the neurons are organized into layers with no feedback or lateral connections. A basic structure of multilayered neural networks (MNNs) with feedforward connections is shown in Figs. 3 and 4. Let M be total number of layers of the MNN including the input and output layers, the $i-th$ neuron in the $s-th$ layer be denoted by $neuron(s,i)$, n_s be total number of neurons in the $s-th$ layer, x_i be the input of the $neuron(1,i)$, x_i^s be the output of the $neuron(s,i)$, $w_{i,k}^s$ be the linkweight coefficient from the $neuron(s,k)$ to the $neuron(s+1,i)$, and $\hat{w}_i^s$ be the threshold of the $neuron(s,i)$. Mathematically, the operation of the $neuron(s,i)$ is defined as

$$z_i^s = \begin{cases} x_i, & if \quad s = 1 \\ \sum_{k=1}^{n_{s-1}+1} w_{i,k}^{s-1} x_k^{s-1}, & if \quad 2 \leq s \leq M \end{cases} \quad (1)$$

and

$$x_i^s = \begin{cases} z_i^s, & if \quad s = 1 \ or \ M \\ h(z_i^s), & if \quad 2 \leq s \leq M-1 \end{cases} \quad (2)$$

where $x_{n_{s-1}+1}^{s-1} = 1, 2 \leq s \leq M$, and

$$w_{i,n_{s-1}+1}^{s-1} = \begin{cases} \hat{w}_i^s, & if \quad 2 \leq s \leq M-1 \\ 0, & if \quad s = M \end{cases} \quad (3)$$

It is convenient to lump all of the weights of the network into a vector that is denoted by w. The output equation of the MNN at time k may then be represented by the input x and the weight vector w as follows

$$y(k) = f(w, x(k)) + v(k) \quad (4)$$

where $y(k)$ is a $n_M \times 1$ vector of the output of the network at time k, $x(k)$ is a $n_1 \times 1$ vector of the input of the network at time k, $f(.)$ is a $n_M \times 1$ smooth vector function, $v(k)$ is assumed to be a white noise vector with the covariance matrix $R(k)$ due to the modelling error, and the diagonal components of $R(k)$ are equal to or slightly less than 1.

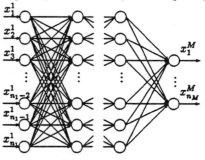

Figure 1. The multilayered neural networks

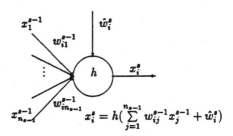

Figure 2. The i-th neuron of the s-th layer

The neural activation function $\sigma(.)$ may be chosen as the continuous and differentiable nonlinear sigmoidal function satifying the following conditions:

(i) $\sigma(x) \longrightarrow \pm 1$ as $x \longrightarrow \pm\infty$;

(ii) $\sigma(x)$ is bounded with the upper bound 1 and the lower bound -1;

(iii) $\sigma(x) = 0$ at a unique point $x = 0$;

(iv) $\sigma'(x) > 0$ and $\sigma'(x) \longrightarrow 0$ as $x \longrightarrow \pm\infty$;

(v) $\sigma'(x)$ has a global maximal value $c \leq 1$.

Typical examples of such a function $\sigma(.)$ are

$$\sigma(x) = \frac{e^x - e^{-x}}{e^x + e^{-x}} = tanh(x)$$

$$\sigma(x) = \frac{1 - e^{-x}}{1 + e^{-x}}$$

$$\sigma(x) = \frac{2}{\pi} tan^{-1}(\frac{\pi}{2}x)$$

$$\sigma(x) = \frac{x^2}{1+x^2} sign(x)$$

where $sign(.)$ is a sign function, and all the above nonlinear activation functions are bounded, monotonic, non-decreasing functions as shown in Figure 3.

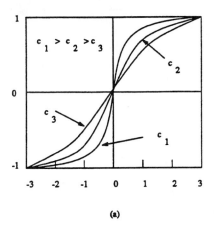

(a)

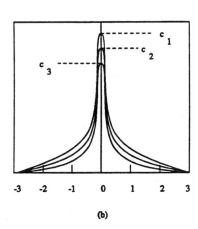

(b)

Figure 3. Sigmoid function $\sigma(cx)$ and its derivative $\sigma'(cx)$: (a) $\sigma(c_1x)$, $\sigma(c_2x)$ and $\sigma(c_3x)$, where $c_1 > c_2 > c_3$; (b) $\sigma'(c_1x)$, $\sigma'(c_2x)$ and $\sigma'(c_3x)$.

Some structures of the *time delay neural networks* (TDNNs) are shown in Figure 4, the input-output equations of the TDNNs given in Figure 4 can be summarized as

$$y(k+1) = f(w, y(k), ..., y(k-n), u(k)) \quad (5)$$

$$y(k+1) = f(w, y(k), ..., y(k-n), u(k), ..., u(k-m)) \quad (6)$$

$$y(k+1) = f_1(w, y(k), ..., y(k-n), u(k-1), ..., u(k-m)) \quad (7)$$
$$+ f_2(w, y(k), ..., y(k-n), u(k-1), ..., u(k-m))u(k)$$

These neural network structures have a good ability to represent a class of nonlinear input-output mappings of unknown nonlinear systems, and have been successfully applied to design adaptive control systems [4].

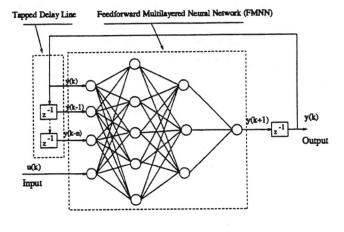

(4a)

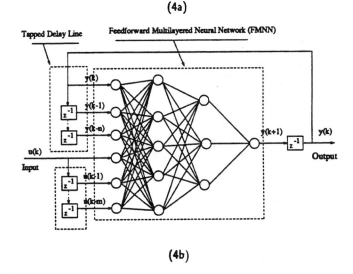

(4b)

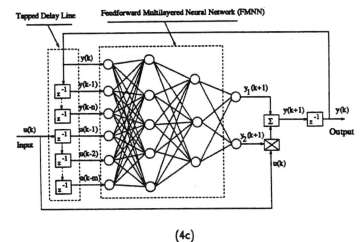

(4c)

Figure 4. Time delay neural networks (TDNNs).

2.2 Multilayered Recurrent Neural Networks (MRNNs)

An artifical neural network consists of many interconnected identical simple processing units called neurons or nodes. An individual neuron sums its weighted inputs and yields an output through a nonlinear activation function with a threshold. A novel multilayered recurrent neural network (MRNN) architecture is proposed in this section. The MRNN is a hybrid feedforward and feedback neural network, with the feedback represented by the recurrent connections and cross-talk, appropriate for approximating a nonlinear dynamic system. The MRNN is composed of an input layer, a series of hidden layers, and an output layer. It allows for feedforward and feedback among the neurons of neighboring layers, and cross-talk and recurrency in the hidden layers.

A basic structure of the multilayered recurrent neural networks (MRNNs) with feedforward and feedback connections is shown in Figure 5. Let M be total number of hidden layers of the MRNN, the $i-th$ neuron in the $s-th$ hidden layer be denoted by $neuron(s,i)$, N_s be total number of neurons in the $s-th$ hidden layer, u_i be the $i-th$ input of the MRNN, $x_{s,i}(k)$ be the state of the $neuron(s,i)$, y_i be the $i-th$ output of the MRNN, $w_{s,j}^{s,i}$ be the intra-layer linkweight coefficient from the $neuron(s,j)$ to the $neuron(s,i)$, $w_{s-1,j}^{s,i}$ be the feedforward linkweight coefficient from the $neuron(s-1,j)$ to the $neuron(s,i)$, $w_{s+1,j}^{s,i}$ be the feedback linkweight coefficient from the $neuron(s+1,j)$ to the $neuron(s,i)$, and $w_T^{s,i}$ be the threshold of the $neuron(s,i)$. Mathematically, the operation of the $neuron(s,i)$ is defined by following dynamic equations

For the first hidden layer:

$$
\begin{aligned}
x_{1,i}(k+1) =& \ \sigma[\sum_{j=1}^{N_2} w_{2,j}^{1,i} x_{2,j}(k) \\
&+ \sum_{j=1}^{N_1} w_{1,j}^{1,i} x_{1,j}(k) + \sum_{j=1}^{l} w_{0,j}^{1,i} u_j(k) + w_T^{1,i}] \quad (8)
\end{aligned}
$$

$$
i = 1, 2, ..., N_1
$$

For the s-th hidden layer:

$$
\begin{aligned}
x_{s,i}(k+1) =& \ \sigma[\sum_{j=1}^{N_{s+1}} w_{s+1,j}^{s,i} x_{s+1,j}(k) \\
&+ \sum_{j=1}^{N_s} w_{s,j}^{s,i} x_{s,j}(k) + \sum_{j=1}^{N_{s-1}} w_{s-1,j}^{s,i} x_{s-1,j}(k) + w_T^{s,i}] \\
=& \ \sigma[\sum_{h=-1}^{1} \sum_{j=1}^{N_{s+h}} w_{s+h,j}^{s,i} x_{s+h,j}(k) + w_T^{s,i}] \quad (9)
\end{aligned}
$$

$$
s = 2, 3, ..., M; \quad i = 1, 2, ..., N_s
$$

Note that there are no feedback actions from the output layer in the $M-th$ hidden layer; that is, $w_{M+1,j}^{M,i} \equiv 0$. If the activation function $\sigma(.)$ is a *symmetric ramp function*, the MRNN is then a special type of the brain-state-in-a-box (BSB) model with a nonsymmetric weight matrix. The terms on the right side of above equation represent respectively the feedback from the upper hidden layer, the intra-layer connections, and the feedforward from the lower layer. Indeed, the output equations of the MRNN are derived as

$$
y_i(k) = \sum_{j=1}^{N_M} w_{M,j}^{M+1,i} x_{M,j}(k), \quad i = 1, 2, ..., m \quad (10)
$$

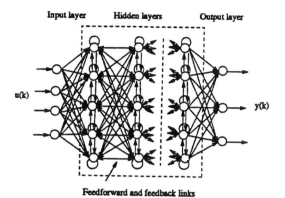

(5a) The network structure.

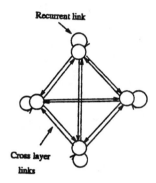

(5b) The intra-layer connections.

Figure 5. The multilayered recurrent neural network (MRNN).

Since the function $-1 \le \sigma(.) \le 1$, the state vector $x(k)$ of the system (8)-(10) exists in the "box" $H^n = [-1,1]^n$, which is a closed n-dimensional hypercube, and the output $y(k)$ is uniformly bounded for the bounded input $u(k)$. For the adaptive learning control purposes, the number of input u_i of MRNN is assumed to have the same number as the output y_i. Furthermore, in order to obtain the I/O relationship of the MRNN shown in Figure 5, let $x_i = [x_{i,1}, x_{i,2}, ..., x_{i,N_i}]^T$ be the state of the neurons in the $i-th$ hidden layer of the MRNN. The dynamic neural system (8-10) can then be represented in the vector difference equations

$$
\left\{
\begin{aligned}
x_1(k+1) =& \ \sigma[W_1^1 x_1(k) + W_2^1 x_2(k) + W_0^1 u(k) + w_T^1] \\
\equiv& \ \sigma_1[x_1(k), x_2(k), u(k)] \\
x_i(k+1) =& \ \sigma[W_{i-1}^i x_{i-1}(k) + W_i^i x_i(k) + W_{i+1}^i x_{i+1}(k) + w_T^i] \\
\equiv& \ \sigma_i[x_{i-1}(k), x_i(k), x_{i+1}(k)], \quad i = 1, 2, ..., M-1 \\
x_M(k+1) =& \ \sigma[W_{M-1}^M x_{M-1}(k) + W_M^M x_M(k) + w_T^M] \\
\equiv& \ \sigma_M[x_{M-1}(k), x_M(k)] \\
y(k) =& \ W_{M+1}^{M+1} x_M(k)
\end{aligned}
\right.
$$

The block diagram of the MRNN is given in Figure 6. Moreover, the relationship between the state $x(k)$, input $u(k)$ and the output $y(k)$ may be derived as follows

$$\begin{cases} y(k+1) &= W_M^{M+1}\sigma_M[x_{M-1}(k), x_M(k)] \\ &\equiv T^1[x_{M-1}(k), x_M(k)] \\ y(k+2) &= T^1[x_{M-1}(k+1), x_M(k+1)] \\ &\equiv T^2[x_{M-2}(k), x_{M-1}(k), x_M(k)] \\ &\vdots \\ y(k+M) &= T^{M-1}[x_1(k+1), ..., x_M(k+1)] \\ &\equiv T^M[x_1(k), ..., x_M(k), u(k)] \end{cases} \qquad (11)$$

Therefore, for the MRNN with m-inputs and m-outputs, and M-hidden layers, the relative degree of the dynamic system (8)-(10) at some point (x^0, u^0) is then $r_j = M$, $j = 1, 2, ..., m$.

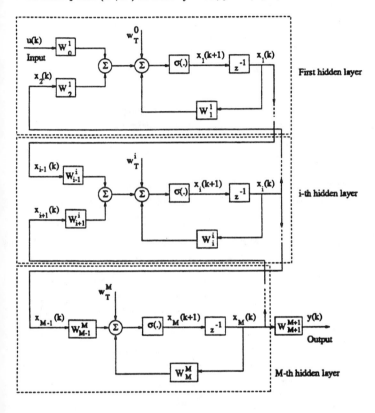

Figure 6. The block diagram of multilayered recurrent neural network (MRNN).

2.3 General Dynamic Neural Networks

Consider a general form of a dynamic recurrent neural network described by a discrete-time nonlinear system of the form

$$\begin{cases} x(k+1) &= f(x(k), W, \theta) \\ y(k) &= h(x(k)) \end{cases} \qquad (12)$$

where $x = [x_1, ..., x_n] \in R^n$ is the state vector of the dynamic neural network, x_i represents the internal state of the $i - th$ neuron, $W = [w_{i,j}]_{n \times n}$ is the real-valued matrix of the synaptic connection weights, θ is a threshold vector or a so-called somatic vector, $y = [y_1, ..., y_m]^T$ is an observation vector or output vector, $f: R^n \times R^{n \times n} \times R^n \longrightarrow R^n$ is a continuous and differentiable vector valued function, $f_i(.)$ and $\partial f_i / \partial x$ are respectively bounded and uniformly bounded, and $h(x): R^n \longrightarrow R^m$ is a known continuous and differentiable vector valued function.

The recurrent neural network consists of both feedforward and feedback connections between the layers and neurons forming complicated dynamics. In fact, the weight $w_{i,j}$ represents a synaptic connection parameter between the $i - th$ neuron and the $j - th$ neuron, and θ_i is a threshold at the $i - th$ neuron. Hence, the nonlinear vector valued function on the right side of system (12) may be represented as

$$\begin{cases} x_i(k+1) &= f_i(x(k), w_i, \theta_i) \\ y(k) &= h(x(k)) \end{cases} \qquad (13)$$

where

$$W = \begin{bmatrix} w_{1,1}, & ..., & w_{1,n} \\ \vdots & \vdots & \vdots \\ w_{n,1}, & ..., & w_{n,n} \end{bmatrix} = \begin{bmatrix} w_1^T \\ \vdots \\ w_n^T \end{bmatrix} \qquad (14)$$

and

$$w_i = \begin{bmatrix} w_{i,1} \\ \vdots \\ w_{i,n} \end{bmatrix}, \qquad i = 1, ..., n \qquad (15)$$

Equation (13) indicates that the dynamics of the $i - th$ neuron in the network are associated with all the states of the network, the synaptic weights $w_{i,1}, ..., w_{i,n}$ and the somatic threshold parameter θ_i.

The four main types of discrete-time dynamic neural models are given in Table 1. These neural models describe the different dynamic perporties due to the different neural state equations. Models I and II consist of complete nonlinear difference equations. Models III and IV are, howeven, the se mi-nonlinear equations which contain the linear terms on the right of the models . In these neural models, $W = [w_{i,j}]_{n \times n}$ is the synaptic connection weight matrix, β_i is the neural gain of the $i - th$ neuron, $0 < \alpha_i < 1$ is the time-constant or linear feedback gain of the $i - th$ neuron, and θ_i is a threshold at the $i - th$ neuron.

3. NEURAL MODELING OF FLEXIBLE DYNAMICS

A class of flexible structures can be generically described by a system of partial differential equations (PDEs) such as

$$m(s)\frac{\partial^2}{\partial t^2}u(s, t) + D\frac{\partial}{\partial t}u(s, t) + Au(s, t) = F(s, t) \qquad (16)$$

where $u(s, t)$ is a displacement (translational or rotational) of the structure from its equilibrium position, as a function of space variable s and t. $m(s)$ is the mass density, A is a time-invariant differential operator, whose domain consists of all smooth functions satisfying (1) with appropriate boundary conditions, and is thus dense in the infinite dimensional Hilbert space $L_2(\Omega)$, where Ω denotes the structure. The operator A is generally self-adjoint and non-negative. $F(s, t)$ is the distribution of the applied generaalized force (i.e., forces and moments). D represents the inherent damping operator, which is a property of the structure (materials, joint design, etc).

Table 1. Four Discrete-Time Dynamic Neural Models

No	Dynamic Neural Models	
	State Equations	Region of Equilibrium Points
I	$x_i(k+1) = \beta_i \sigma_i(\sum\limits_{j=1}^{n} w_{i,j} x_j + \theta_i)$	$[-|\beta_i|, |\beta_i|]^n$
II	$x_i(k+1) = \sigma_i(\sum\limits_{j=1}^{n} w_{i,j} x_j) + \theta_i$	$[|\theta_i| - 1, |\theta_i| + 1]^n$
III	$x_i(k+1) = \alpha_i x_i(k) + (1-\alpha_i)\sigma_i(\sum\limits_{j=1}^{n} w_{i,j} x_j + \theta_i)$ $0 < \alpha_i < 1$	$[-1, 1]^n$
IV	$x_i(k+1) = \alpha_i x_i(k) + \beta_i \sigma_i(\sum\limits_{j=1}^{n} w_{i,j} x_j + \theta_i)$ $0 < \alpha_i < 1$	$[-\beta_i/(1-\alpha_i)|, |\beta_i/(1-\alpha_i)|]^n$

Using the finite element method (FEM), a mode coordinate form of equation (1) is expressed as

$$\ddot{q}(t) + D\dot{q}(t) + \Lambda q(t) = \Gamma^T f(t) \qquad (17)$$

where $D = 2diag[\rho_1 \sigma_1, ..., \rho_n \sigma_n]$ and $\Lambda = diag[\sigma_n^2, ..., \sigma_n^2]$, and ρ_i and σ_i denote the inherent damping ratio and the natural frequency of the $i - th$ elastic mode. For large space structures, ρ_i is typically on the order of 0.001-0.01.

An appropriaate mathematical model for studying control problem of flexible spacecraft can be obtained using the hybrid coordinate approach as follows

$$J\dot{\omega}(t) + \delta^T \ddot{q}(t) + \omega(t) \times H_m(t) + g_1(\omega, \dot{q}, q)$$
$$= u_t(t) + B_1 f(t) \qquad (18)$$
$$\ddot{q}(t) + D\dot{q}(t) + \Lambda q(t) + \delta\dot{w} + g_1(\omega, \dot{q}, q) = \Gamma^T f(t) \quad (19)$$

where ω is a vector of attitude angular velocity, J is a inertia matrix of the total spacecraft in undeformed state, δ is a coupling matrix, H_m is a vector of total angular momentum of the flexible spacecraft, u_t is a control torque acting on the rigid main body, and $g_1(.)$ and $g_2(.)$ are the nonlinear terms in the dynamic equations.

Conventional control system synthesis techniques for flexible space structures require a reasonably good knowledge of the design model, usually a finite element model of flexible structures, as well as the uncontrollable modes. Determination of the parameters, (e.g., using finite element methods) generally does not give sufficiently accurate parameter estimates. This is particularly true for damping ratios, because finite element methods have no means of computing inherent damping ratios. The inherent damping ratios play a vital role in the control system design process.

Ground testing for parameter estimation is almost impossible for two reasons: a) many of the flexible space structures will be assembled in space, and b) deployable structures, 100 m or larger in size, would be too large to test on ground. They are not designed to withstand stresses of the 1-g environment (i.e., gravity). In addition to these, physical constraints, because of the sheer size, it would be impractical to construct the necessary test facilities such as vaccum chambers. Thus it is important to have an effective technique for on-orbit learning and control, and this is the main purpose of this proposed studies.

In this project, an on-orbit learning modeling technique for flexible space structures is proposed for the purpose of designing as intelligent control system using the dynamic neural networks with parallel structures. Both the parallel and series-parallel learning schemes for modeling unknown flexible dynamics are shown in Figure 7. Also, the fast learning algorithms based on decoupled recursive estimaton is studied; such an approach brings major reductions in the computational and storage requirements of the on-orbit modeling process. Furthermore, the software implementation as well as the hardware experimental studies of the neural modeling process for flexible space structures will be conducted extensively.

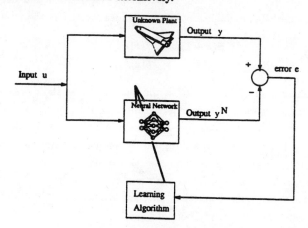

(7a). Parallel modeling process

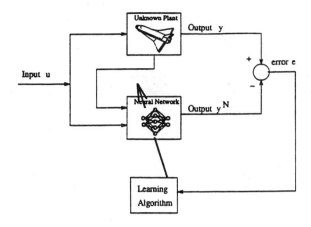

(7b). Series-parallel modeling process

Figure 7. On-Orbit modeling process for flexible space structures using neural networks

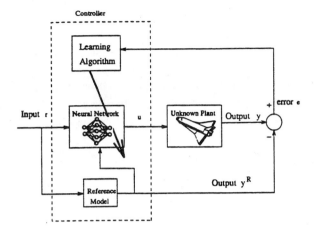

(8a). Direct adaptive control

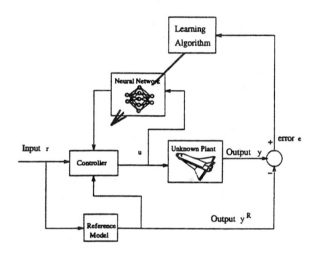

(8b). Indirect adaptive control

Figure 8. Adaptive control of flexible space structures using neural networks.

4. NEURAL CONTROL SCHEMES OF FLEXIBLE SPACE STRUCTURES

Two of the most important control problems for flexible space structures are:

i) Fine-pointing of flexible space structures in space with the required precison in attitude (that is, the three pointing angles) and shape,

ii) Large angle maneuvering ("slewing") the flexible structures to orient to a different target [13].

The later is a typical nonlinear system control problem. The performance requirements for both of these problems are usually very high. In order to achieve the required performance, it is of utmost importance to be able to control such structures in a highly uncertain space environment with high precision in attitude and shape. Intelligent control of such structures is a challenging problem because of their special dynamics characteristics, which result from their large size and light weight.

The proposed research on neuro-control for both of the linear and nonlinear flexible dynamics is an important theoretical problem, as well as it has many applied implications. This work involves the contributions to neural learning and intelligent control using fuzzy logic and neural networks. The dynamic neural network schemes studied in this project provide the potential for the learning and control of general unknown plants such as flexible space structures. The ability of neural networks to model arbitrary dynamic nonlinear systems is incorporated to approximate the unknown flexible dynamics using on-orbit learning process. The model based neural control systems are developed with simultaneous on-line identification and control for flexible space structures as shown in Figure 8.

5. DEVELOPMENT OF A GROUND-BASED EXPERIMENTAL TEST FACILITY

As the second stage studies, a ground-based experimental test facility as given in Figure 9 will be established to study the dynamics and control of flexible space structures. The objective of such a facility is to examine the effectiveness of the neural modeling and control for flexible space structures using the real-time computer control technique as well as to investigate sensor and actuator placement problem.

This goal required the design of a suitable test structure that could, in an earth gravity environment, physically mimic the characteristic dynamic behavior of a flexible structure. The experimental flexible structure will be designed to include a number of attributes associated with large flexible space structures. These include lightly damped, closed spaced modes, colocated and non-colocated sensors and actuators, and numerous modes in the controller cossover region.

In addition to the physical specification of the experiment facility, there are requirements for the control elements. The sensors must offer sufficient resolution to provide desired pointing accuracy, whereas the actuators must have sufficient power output and bandwidth to implement effective control. The computer and data acquisition system must be powerful enough to maintain a consistently high controller update rate necessary for the implementation of real-time learning control.

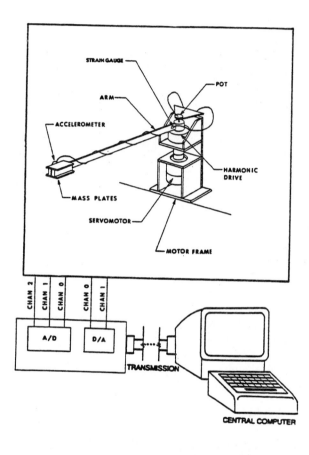

Figure 9. An example of experimental schemes for flexible structure control

References

[1] C. Hsieh, J.H. Kim, K. Liu, G. Zhu, and R. Skelton, " Control of Large Flexible Structures-An Experiment on the NASA Mini-Mast Facility", *IEEE* Control Systems Magazine, Vol. 11, No. 10, pp. 13-21, 1991.

[2] G. Crocker, P. Hughes, T. Hong, " Real-time Computer Control of a Flexible Spacecraft Emulator", *IEEE* Control Systems Magazine, Vol. 10, No. 1, pp. 3-8, 1990.

[3] K.R. Lorell, J.N. Aubrun, D.F. Zacharie, and E. Perez, " Control Technology Test Bed for Large Segmented Reflectors", *IEEE* Control Systems Magazine, Vol. 9, No. 6, pp. 13-20, 1989.

[4] K.S. Narendra and K.Parthasarathy, "Identification and Control of Dynamical Systems using Neural Networks," *IEEE* Trans. Neural Networks, Vol. NN-1, No. 1, pp. 4-27, March, 1990.

[5] D.E. Rumelhart and J.L. McCelland, " Learning Internal Representations by Error Propagation ", Parallel Distributed Processing : Explorations in the Micr ostructure of Cognition, Vol. 1: Foundations, MIT Press, 1986.

[6] R. Hecht-Nielsen, "Theory of the Back-propagation Neural Network' ", Proc. Int'l. Joint Conf. on Neural Networks, pp. I-593-605, June 1989.

[7] P.K. Simpson, Artifical Neural Systems, Pergamon Press, 1990.

[8] K. Hornik, M. Stinchcombe and H. White, " Multilayer Feedforward Networks are Universal Approximators", Neural Networks, Vol. 2, pp. 359-366, 1 98 9.

[9] B.Widrow and M.A.Lehr, "30 Years of Adaptive Neural Networks: Perceptron, Madaline, and Backpropagation", Proc. *IEEE*, Vol. 78, No. 9, pp. 141 5-1441, 1990.

[10] R. Williams and D. Zipser, "A Learning Algorithm for Continually Running Fully Recurrent Neural Networks", *Neural Computation*, 1, 270-280, 1989.

[11] R.M. Sanner and J.J.E.Slotine, "Gaussian Networks for Direct Adaptive Control," *IEEE* Trans. Neural Networks, Vol. 3, No. 6, pp. 837-863, 1992.

[12] L. Jin, " Robust Attitude Control of a Large communication Satell ite with Flexible Solar Arrays", Presented at the 35th International Astronauti cal Federation (IAF) Congress, IAF-84-340, Lausanne, Switzerland, Oct., 7-13, 19 84.

[13] L. Jin, "Nonlinear Control Strategies of Flexible Multibody Spa cecraft Slewing Maneuvers", Presented at the 41st International Astronautical F ederation (IAF) Congress, IAF-90-332, Deesden, Germany, Oct., 6-12, 1990.

[14] L. Jin, P.N.Nikiforuk and M.M. Gupta, "Adaptive Tracking of SISO Nonlinear Systems Using Multilayered Neural Networks", Proc. of the 1992 American Control Conference, pp. 56-60, Chicago, June 24-26, 1992.

[15] L. Jin, P.N. Nikiforuk and M.M. Gupta, "Direct Adaptive Output Tracking Control Using Multilayered Neural Networks", *IEE* Proc.-D, 1993 [In Press].

[16] L. Jin, P.N. Nikiforuk and M.M. Gupta, "Adaptive Control of Nonlinear Systems Using Multilayered Recurrent Neural Networks", *IEE* Proc.-D, 1993 [to appear].

[17] L. Jin, P.N. Nikiforuk and M.M. Gupta, "Multilayered Recurrent Neural Networks for Learning and Control of Unknown Nonlinear Systems", J. Dynamics, Measurements and Control [to appear].

Controlling a moving vehicle is one of the most obvious application areas for control to the layman. Making our cars more efficient at high speeds and yet still able to stop on a dime, or making the cross country flight smoother are instantly understood as control application areas. In this chapter, the application of neural network control to three different vehicles is presented. In **Paper 5.1**, a neural network-based controller design that integrates airframe and engine is described for a fighter aircraft. **Paper 5.2** combines neural networks and expert systems to produce an optimal cruise control for an automobile. **Paper 5.3** introduces the use of recurrent neural networks for heave compensation on marine exploration platforms that require stability for accurate bottom mapping.

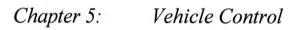

Chapter 5:   *Vehicle Control*

INTEGRATED FLIGHT/PROPULSION CONTROL SYSTEM DESIGN VIA NEURAL NETWORK

C. M. Ha
Department of Mechanical Engineering
The University of Texas at Arlington
P.O. Box 19023
Arlington, Texas 76019-0023

ABSTRACT

Neural network design methodology is utilized to design an integrated airframe/engine control system for a modern, statically unstable, fighter aircraft in landing. The resulting neural controller structure consists of a feedback compensator and a feedforward filter formulated in the form of a 3-layer feedforward network whose parameters are trained by a static back-propagation method. The number of parameters are chosen by an ad hoc procedure. The feedback compensator satisfies closed-loop stability while the feedforward filter provides command shaping. Once training has been completed, and the parameters are fixed, overall system performance evaluation results are then presented.

I. INTRODUCTION

Numerous classical and modern, standard as well as non-standard control law design methodologies have been proposed for designing continuous-time or discrete-time longitudinal and lateral-directional control laws for aircraft (Ref. 1-2). These time- and frequency-domain design techniques usually apply to linear, time-invariant state-space dynamic models of the aircraft from either single-input-single-output (SISO) or multi-input-multi-output (MIMO) point of view. However, the aircraft's equations of motion are highly nonlinear in six-degree-of-freedom (6-DOF) throughout its operating envelope. Thus, those who design flight control laws for aircraft face formidable challenges because of the inadequacies of these design techniques to address atmospheric turbulence, sensor noise, time delay, time-varying parameters (structured uncertainty), and poorly-modeled high-frequency dynamics (unstructured uncertainty).

The traditional corrective procedure for nonlinearity has been "gain scheduling." In this approach, the resulting nonlinear control law is realized by interpolating between various linear controllers as a function of speed, altitude, and wing loading. However, in normal operation, the resulting nonlinear control law may not be adequate due to expected changes in loading or unexpected surface damage/actuator and sensor failures which are only addressed through the robustness designed into the linear controller. These problems have motivated the search for a type of flight control system that is capable of learning from flight experience, i.e., the more it is flown, the better it becomes.

In recent years, increased interest in neural network has developed in aerospace applications (Ref. 3-6) as the aircraft flight control design community became aware of the feasibility of rapid and inexpensive implementation through very large scale integrated technology. Ref. 3 shows how a 3-layer neural network can be used as a real-time gain adjuster in a longitudinal stability augmentation system. A multi-layer neural network for the preliminary development of an autopilot model to precisely control a high performance aircraft during its flight maneuvers was conceptually demonstrated in Ref. 5-6. A gradient descent algorithm was utilized to train the neural controller to learn to function as a closed-loop flight control system and to force the dynamics of the aircraft to match that of a specified reference model. If the aircraft's dynamics are time-varying, then the training would require the learning algorithm to adjust the neural controller accordingly.

Maneuvering envelopes of future fighter aircraft are expanding into low speed, high angle-of-attack regime over which conventional aerodynamic surfaces lose their effectiveness. The use of forces and moments produced by the aircraft's propulsion system is needed to augment the flight control function in order to maintain maneuvering capabilities in this low dynamic pressure flight region. An integrated flight/propulsion control (IFPC) system is, therefore, required in order to achieve an effective augmentation system so as to reduce pilot workload. Two approaches to integrated flight/propulsion control design have appeared recently (Ref. 7-8). They are the Linear Quadratic Gaussian/Loop Transfer Recovery (LQG/LTR) and the H_∞ control synthesis techniques. Both of these two control law design procedures were utilized to design a compensator for the full integrated airframe and engine system to meet some high level performance criteria, then the high-order compensator was partitioned into lower-order controllers that can be implemented separately on the airframe and the engine without any significant loss of overall system performance and robustness characteristics.

In this paper, the application of neural network design methodology to integrated flight/propulsion control system design for a fighter aircraft is investigated. The objective is to gain an insight into the integrated control design approach of neural network. The paper is organized as follows. A background on neural network is first described. The linear model of a fighter aircraft in landing to be used for integrated neural network flight/propulsion control system design and evaluation is then presented along with some description of the structure of the neural controller. Detailed closed-loop evaluation results of the neural controller are given. They demonstrate the applicability of the neural network design methodology to the centralized feedback controller design.

II. 3-LAYER FEEDFORWARD NETWORK

In this study, a 3-layer feedforward neural network with an input layer, a hidden layer, and an output layer is considered. This neural network structure can approximately realize any nonlinear continuous mapping to a degree of accuracy over some compact domain (Ref. 9). However, this is only an existence proof because it does not show how to find the correct interconnection weights, nor does it indicate how many neurons should be in each layer. Also, Ref. 9 mentioned that using more than one hidden layer may have the advantage of significantly reducing the number of hidden neurons needed for the same task.

2.1 3-Layer Neural Network Equations
a. Output layer:
$$y_k = f(y_k), \quad k = 1,2,...,ny \tag{2.1}$$
$$y_k = \sum_{i=1}^{n2} \gamma_{ki} v_i$$
b. Hidden layer:
$$v_i = f(v_i) \tag{2.2}$$
$$v_i = \sum_{j=1}^{n1} \alpha_{ij} z_j$$
c. Input layer:
$$z_j = f(z_j) \tag{2.3}$$
$$z_j = \sum_{l=1}^{nu} \beta_{jl} u_l$$
ny: number of outputs
nu: number of inputs
n_1: number of neurons in input layer
n_2: number of neurons in hidden layer
γ_{ki}, α_{ij}, and β_{jl} are interconnection weights
f is the sigmoid function defined by $f(x) = (2/\mu)\{(1 - e^{-\mu x})/(1 + e^{-\mu x})\}$ with x is the input and μ is the parameter determining the shape of f(x) (Ref. 10-11)

2.2 Neural Network Training
Here, the interconnection weights γ_{ki}, α_{ij}, and β_{jl} are adjusted by some learning algorithm to optimize an appropriate performance function. Let's suppose the outputs $y_k(t)$ of the network are desired to be $yd_k(t)$ where t runs from 1 to L. The performance function to be optimized is the following mean square error

$$J = 0.5 \sum_{t=1}^{L} \sum_{k=1}^{ny} (y_k(t) - yd_k(t))^2 \tag{2.4}$$

The interconnection weights γ_{ki}, α_{ij}, and β_{jl} are then updated when training according to a quasi-Newton procedure:

$$\theta_{i+1} = \theta_i - \eta_i H_i \nabla_\theta J_i \tag{2.5}$$

$\theta_i = [\gamma_{ki} \ \alpha_{ij} \ \beta_{jl}]$ at iteration i
η_i: step size that leads to a minimum of J along the search direction given by $H_i \nabla_\theta J_i$
H_i: an estimate of the inverse Hessian matrix for θ_i
$\nabla_\theta J_i = [\partial J/\partial \gamma_{ki} \ \partial J/\partial \alpha_{ij} \ \partial J/\partial \beta_{jl}]$ is the gradient of J with respect to θ's at iteration i

A numerical approximation of H_i can be obtained from the values of $\nabla_\theta J_i$ evaluated with two sets of parameters at successive iterations. If p_i and q_i are defined as

$$p_i = \theta_{i+1} - \theta_i \tag{2.6a}$$
$$q_i = \nabla_\theta J_{i+1} - \nabla_\theta J_i \tag{2.6b}$$

where $\nabla_\theta J_{i+1}$ is the gradient of J for the new values of θ_{i+1}. The estimate H_i of the inverse Hessian matrix is then updated as

$$H_{i+1} = H_i + (1 + q_i^T H_i q_i / p_i^T q_i)(p_i p_i^T / p_i^T q_i)$$
$$- (1/p_i^T q_i)(p_i q_i^T H_i + H_i q_i p_i^T) \tag{2.7}$$

The initial value of the Hessian matrix H_0 can be chosen as any symmetric positive definite matrix. The identity matrix is commonly used, causing the first parameter update to be in the steepest descent direction. Equation (2.5) can be expressed as follows.

$$\gamma_{ki(new)} = \gamma_{ki(old)} - \eta_\gamma [H_i]_{ki} \partial J/\partial \gamma_{ki} \tag{2.8a}$$
$$\alpha_{ij(new)} = \alpha_{ij(old)} - \eta_\alpha [H_i]_{ij} \partial J/\partial \alpha_{ij} \tag{2.8b}$$
$$\beta_{jl(new)} = \beta_{jl(old)} - \eta_\beta [H_i]_{jl} \partial J/\partial \beta_{jl} \tag{2.8c}$$

where η_γ, η_α, and η_β are step size gains taking values in the range (0,1); and H_i is an estimate of the inverse Hessian matrix

$$\partial J/\partial \gamma_{ki} = (\partial J/\partial y_k)(\partial y_k/\partial \gamma_{ki}) \tag{2.9a}$$
$$\partial J/\partial \alpha_{ij} = (\partial J/\partial y_k)(\partial y_k/\partial \alpha_{ij}) \tag{2.9b}$$

$\partial J/\partial\beta_{jl} = (\partial J/\partial y_k)(\partial y_k/\partial\beta_{jl})$ (2.9c)

and

$\partial J/\partial y_k = \sum_{t=1}^{L}(y_k(t) - yd_k(t))$ (2.10)

with

$\partial y_k/\partial\gamma_{ki} = [f'(y_k)]\partial[\sum\gamma_{ki}v_i]/\partial\gamma_{ki}$

$\partial y_k/\partial\gamma_{ki} = [f'(y_k)]\partial[\sum\gamma_{ki}v_i]/\partial\gamma_{ki}$ (2.11a)

$\partial y_k/\partial\gamma_{ki} = [f'(y_k)]v_i$ (2.11b)

$\partial y_k/\partial\alpha_{ij} = (\partial y_k/\partial v_i)(\partial v_i/\partial\alpha_{ij})$ (2.12a)

$\partial y_k/\partial v_i = [f'(y_k)]\gamma_{ki}$ (2.12b)

$\partial v_i/\partial\alpha_{ij} = [f'(v_i)]\partial[\sum\alpha_{ij}z_j]/\partial\alpha_{ij}$

$\partial v_i/\partial\alpha_{ij} = [f'(v_i)]\partial[\sum\alpha_{ij}z_j]/\partial\alpha_{ij}$ (2.12c)

$\partial v_i/\partial\alpha_{ij} = [f'(v_i)]z_j$ (2.12d)

$\partial y_k/\partial\alpha_{ij} = \{[f'(y_k)]\gamma_{ki}\}.\{[f'(v_i)]z_j\}$ (2.12e)

$\partial y_k/\partial\beta_{jl} = (\partial y_k/\partial v_i)(\partial v_i/\partial z_j)(\partial z_j/\partial\beta_{jl})$ (2.13a)

$\partial v_i/\partial z_j = [f'(v_i)]\alpha_{ij}$ (2.13b)

$\partial z_j/\partial\beta_{jl} = [f'(z_j)]\partial[\sum\beta_{jl}u_l]/\partial\beta_{jl}$

$\partial z_j/\partial\beta_{jl} = [f'(z_j)]\partial[\sum\beta_{jl}u_l]/\partial\beta_{jl}$ (2.13c)

$\partial z_j/\partial\beta_{jl} = [f'(z_j)]u_l$ (2.13d)

$\partial y_k/\partial\beta_{jl} = \{[f'(y_k)]\gamma_{ki}\}.\{[f'(v_i)]\alpha_{ij}\}.$
$\{[f'(z_j)]u_l\}$ (2.13e)

Combining Equations (2.10) with Equations (2.11b), (2.12e), and (2.13e), Equations (2.9a-2.9c) become

$\partial J/\partial\gamma_{ki}=\{\sum(y_k(t)-yd_k(t))\}.\{f'(y_k).v_i\}$ (2.14a)

$\partial J/\partial\alpha_{ij}=\{\sum(y_k(t)-yd_k(t))\}.\{f'(y_k).\gamma_{ki}\}.\{f'(v_i).z_j\}$ (2.14b)

$\partial J/\partial\beta_{jl}=\{\sum(y_k(t)-yd_k(t))\}.\{f'(y_k).\gamma_{ki}\}.\{f'(v_i).\alpha_{ij}\}.$
$\{f'(z_j).u_l\}$ (2.14c)

Equations (2.8a-2.8c) can then be expressed as follows.

$\gamma_{ki(new)}=\gamma_{ki(old)}-\eta_{\gamma}[H_i]_{ki}\{\sum(y_k(t)-yd_k(t))\}.\{f'(y_k).v_i\}$ (2.15a)

$\alpha_{ij(new)}=\alpha_{ij(old)}-\eta_{\alpha}[H_i]_{ij}\{\sum(y_k(t)-yd_k(t))\}.\{f'(y_k).\gamma_{ki}\}.$
$\{f'(v_i).z_j\}$ (2.15b)

$\beta_{jl(new)}=\beta_{jl(old)}-\eta_{\beta}[H_i]_{jl}\{\sum(y_k(t)-yd_k(t))\}.\{f'(y_k).\gamma_{ki}\}.$
$\{f'(v_i).\alpha_{ij}\}.\{f'(z_j).u_l\}$ (2.15c)

As can be seen in Equations (2.15a-2.15c), the interconnection weights γ_{ki}, α_{ij}, and β_{jl} are updated in the direction of decreasing J by the steepest descent algorithm. Also, it is seen that all signals used to compute the partial derivatives $\partial J/\partial\gamma_{ki}$, $\partial J/\partial\alpha_{ij}$, and $\partial J/\partial\beta_{jl}$ of Equations (2.14a-14c) seem to be identical to those in the network except flowing in the opposite direction, justifying the use of the term "back-propagation." In all the simulations carried out in this study, the initial weights $\gamma_{ki(old)}$, $\alpha_{ij(old)}$, and $\beta_{jl(old)}$ are selected randomly between +0.5 and -0.5. If $\gamma_{ki(old)}$, $\alpha_{ij(old)}$, and $\beta_{jl(old)}$ are initially set to 0.0, then the network will never learn. This is because the steepest descent algorithm is propagated

back through the neurons in proportion to $\gamma_{ki(old)}$, $\alpha_{ij(old)}$, and $\beta_{jl(old)}$ (Equations 2.11b, 2.12e, and 2.13e). Thus, the network starts out at a local minimum and will remain there. It should be noted that the steepest descent gradient search technique is known to have problems with local minima and saddle points, and to have a slow rate of convergence.

III. APPLICATION

Application of the neural network design methodology to designing an integrated flight/propulsion control law for a modern high-performance fighter aircraft powered by a two-spool turbofan engine and equipped with a 2-D thrust vectoring and reversing nozzle is now discussed. The integrated neural network control law capabilities are demonstrated using a linear simulation of the aircraft longitudinal equations of motion in landing. Numerical results are then presented after linear dynamic models of longitudinal are described.

3.1 Linearized Aircraft Equations of Motion

From linearization of the full nonlinear rigid aircraft equations of motion about a trim flight condition (flight path angle=-3 degrees and airspeed= 120 kts), the rigid, linear equations for longitudinal motion consist of an integrated airframe and propulsion system state-space mathematical model

$\dot{x} = Ax + Bu$, $x(0)$ given (3.1)
$y = Cx + Du$

The preceding equations represent a continuous-time process model. The use of this model in a digital integrated neural network flight/propulsion control system requires a discrete-time model representation. Here a sampling time of $\Delta t=1/32$ second is selected, and Equation (3.1) is transformed into the following equivalent discrete form

$x(t+1) = Fx(t) + Gu(t)$, $x(0)$ given (3.2)
$y(t) = Hx(t) + Ju(t)$

A, B, C, and D are listed in Ref. 7 whereas $F = e^{A\Delta t}$, $G = \int e^{A\Delta\tau}Bd\tau$, $H = C$, and $J = D$

$x = [u$, aircraft body axis forward velocity, ft/sec$]$
$[w$, aircraft body axis vertical velocity, ft/sec $]$
$[q$, aircraft pitch rate, rad/sec $]$
$[\theta$, pitch angle, rad $]$
$[h$, altitude, ft $]$
$[N2$, engine fan speed, rpm $]$
$[N25$, core compressor speed, rpm $]$
$[P6$, engine mixing plane pressure, psia $]$
$[T41B$, engine high-pressure turbine blade temperature, °R $]$

$u = [\delta_{FL}$, leading-edge flap deflection angle, deg$]$
$[\delta_{FT}$, trailing-edge flap deflection angle, deg $]$
$[WF$, engine main burner fuel flow rate, lb/h $]$
$[A78$, thrust reverser port area, in.^{2} $]$

[A8, main nozzle throat area, in.^{2}]
[δ_{TV}, nozzle thrust vectoring angle, deg   ]

y = [V, aircraft airspeed, ft/sec   ]
[q_v, pitch variable = q + 0.1θ, deg/sec   ]
[N2P, engine fan speed (% of maximum allowable rpm at operating condition)   ]
[EPR, engine pressure ratio   ]

The choice of q_v reflects the desire to track pitch rate q commands at high frequencies and pitch attitude θ commands at low frequencies (Ref. 7-8). The primary goal of the integrated neural network flight/propulsion control system design is to provide the aircraft with a maneuvering capability that exhibits a level I short period characteristics (well-damped, minimal overshoot, and rapid settling time). In transfer function form, the desired response from pilot's pitch stick command, $\delta_{pitch\ stick}$, to pitch rate, $q_{desired}$, should be approximately second order (Ref. 7), i.e.,

$$q_{desired}/\delta_{pitch\ stick} = \frac{35.12(s+0.5)}{(s^2+2*0.89*2.24s+2.24^2)} \qquad (3.3a)$$

$$q_{desired}/\delta_{pitch\ stick} = \frac{(1.0393z-1.0231)}{(z^2-1.8782z+0.8828)} \qquad (3.3b)$$

for a sampling time $\Delta t=1/32$ second

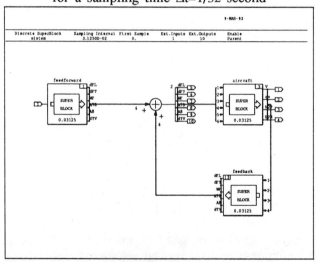

Figure 3-1: Closed-Loop System

In an effort to achieve this goal, a neural network flight/propulsion control configuration shown in Fig. 3-1 is proposed. The configuration consists of a feedback compensator and a feedforward filter. The compensator ensures a stable closed-loop response and good feedback properties such as settling time and damping. Then, freedom to specify the response to pilot's pitch stick command, $\delta_{pitch\ stick}$, such as zero steady-state tracking error is provided through the feedforward filter.

3.2 3-layer neural network equations for feedback compensator:
a. Output layer:
$$y_k = f(\sum_{i=1}^{n2} \gamma c_{ki}\ v_i),\ k=1,2,...,ny \qquad (3.4)$$
b. Hidden layer:
$$v_i = f(v_i) \qquad (3.5)$$
$$v_i = \sum_{j=1}^{n1} \alpha c_{ij}\ z_j$$
c. Input layer:
$$z_j = f(z_j) \qquad (3.6)$$
$$z_j = \sum_{l=1}^{nu} \beta c_{jl}\ u_l$$
ny = 6, nu = 4, n_1 = 8, n_2 = 8
total number of interconnection weights γc_{ki}, αc_{ij}, and βc_{jl} = (6+8+4)*8 = 144
[$y_1\ y_2\ y_3\ y_4\ y_5\ y_6$] = [$\delta_{FL}(t)\ \delta_{FT}(t)$ WF(t) A78(t) A8(t) $\delta_{TV}(t)$]
[$u_1\ u_2\ u_3\ u_4$] = [V(t) $q_v(t)$ N2P(t) EPR(t)]
with $q_v(t) = q(t) + 0.1\theta(t)$

3.3 3-layer neural network equations for feedforward filter:
a. Output layer:
$$y_k = f(\sum_{i=1}^{n2} \gamma f_{ki}\ v_i),\ k=1,2,...,ny \qquad (3.7)$$
b. Hidden layer:
$$v_i = f(v_i) \qquad (3.8)$$
$$v_i = \sum_{j=1}^{n1} \alpha f_{ij}\ z_j$$
c. Input layer:
$$z_j = f(z_j) \qquad (3.9)$$
$$z_j = \sum_{l=1}^{nu} \beta f_{jl}\ u_l$$
ny = 6, nu = 1, n_1 = 8, and n_2 = 8
total number of interconnection weights γf_{ki}, αf_{ij}, and βf_{jl} = (1+8+6)*8 = 120
[$y_1\ y_2\ y_3\ y_4\ y_5\ y_6$] = [$\delta_{FL}(t)\ \delta_{FT}(t)$ WF(t) A78(t) A8(t) $\delta_{TV}(t)$]
$u_1 = \delta_{pitch\ stick}(t)$

The number of neurons in each layer was chosen by trial and error. In this study, 8 neurons were found to be satisfactory.

3.4 Neural Network Training
Our objective is to train (144+120+1=265) interconnection weights γc_{ki}, αc_{ij}, βc_{jl}, γf_{ki}, αf_{ij}, βf_{jl}, and μ so that the integrated neural network flight/propulsion control system responds properly to pilot's pitch stick command, $\delta_{pitch\ stick}$. Here, the following mean square error is minimized

$$J = 0.5 \sum_{t=1}^{L} \{(q_v(t)-q_{desired}(t))^2\} \qquad (3.10)$$

with $q_v(t) = q(t) + 0.1\theta(t)$ and

$$q_{desired}/\delta_{pitch\ stick} = \frac{(1.0393z-1.0231)}{(z^2-1.8782z+0.8828)} \qquad (3.3b)$$

where a typical step response of $q_{desired}(t)$ is shown as dotted lines in Fig. 3-2. For the pitch stick command, Fig. 3-2 shows that the back-propagation technique produces J≈0.009 in 100 iterations, as evidenced in Fig. 3-3 where the integrated neural network flight/propulsion control system provides a good tracking of pitch rate command. On the other hand, the propulsion system actuation requirements

WF, A8, and δ_{TV}, shown in Fig. 3-4, are quite reasonable.

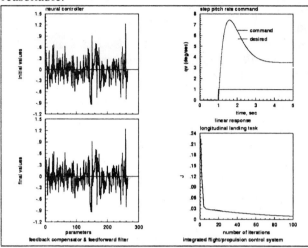

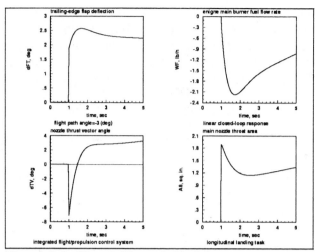

Figure 3-4: Neural Network Training
Closed-Loop Response - δ_{FT}, WF, A8, and δ_{TV}

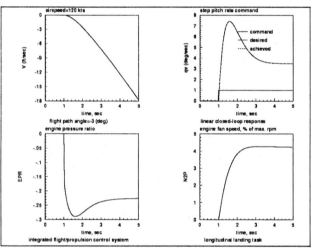

Figure 3-2: Neural Network Training

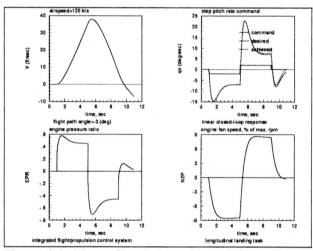

Figure 4-1: Linear Simulation - V, q_v, N2P, and EPR

Figure 3-3: Neural Network Training
Closed-Loop Response - V, q_v, N2P, and EPR

IV. RESULTS

Once training has been completed (Fig. 3-2), and the interconnection weights γc_{ki}, αc_{ij}, βc_{jl}, γf_{ki}, αf_{ij}, βf_{jl}, and μ are fixed (tabulated in the Appendix), stability and performance of the integrated neural network flight/propulsion control system is evaluated in a linear time-domain simulation for the following maneuver: starting from a trim condition, a ± 2 (deg/sec) step pitch rate with a 4-second duration is commanded. The desired $q_{desired}$ and achieved pitch rate q_v to a step pilot stick command, $q_{pitch\ stick}$, are compared in Fig. 4-1. A good agreement is observed between the desired response and that achieved using neural network. The propulsion system control activities WF, A8, and δ_{TV} are shown in Fig. 4-2. Although deflection and rate limits were

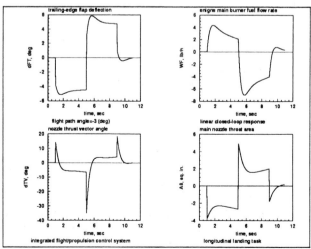

Figure 4-2: Linear Simulation - δ_{FT}, WF, A8, and δ_{TV}

not incorporated in the linear simulation, the results are quite encouraging in that they demonstrate that neural network has the promise to meet the requirements of an integrated flight/propulsion control design.

V. CONCLUSIONS

An example application of the neural network-based design methodology to integrated flight/propulsion control system design for a modern, statically unstable fighter aircraft in landing has been presented in this paper. The integrated neural network controller which is of low-order provides good tracking of pitch rate command without integral control action and input/output scaling. Since the integrated neural network flight/propulsion control system is nonlinear, its robustness against nonlinearities, parameter variations, unmodeled actuator and sensor dynamics requires a nonlinear simulation evaluation over the design portion of the flight envelope.

APPENDIX

$[\beta c]_{8 \times 4} =$

-0.0208	0.2237	0.4363	0.0613
0.1041	-0.1017	-0.5031	0.2559
-0.0649	-0.1117	-0.0006	0.4864
-0.3251	-0.2554	-0.4483	0.0756
-0.1547	-0.2569	0.0104	0.1066
-0.1315	-0.3596	0.5951	-0.1731
-0.0645	0.2507	0.6503	-0.1549
-0.0456	0.0993	-0.1201	-0.3082

$[\alpha c]_{8 \times 8} =$

-0.3655	0.0257	-0.2042	0.1772	-0.0152	0.4940	-0.1256	-0.1127
0.1434	-0.4228	0.2252	-0.0853	0.1286	0.1528	0.3007	-0.2686
-0.0669	0.2564	-0.1286	-0.0748	-0.0573	-0.1666	0.2716	0.3825
-0.0818	-0.2844	-0.0726	-0.4099	-0.0043	0.2673	0.6300	0.1236
-0.1232	-0.0939	-0.0443	0.2878	-0.2094	-0.2752	-0.3671	0.1443
-0.3151	0.1822	-0.0441	0.1033	0.2280	0.0372	-0.0493	0.2027
0.0711	0.0625	-0.2125	-0.4118	0.0522	0.3589	0.1805	0.0332
-0.4603	0.4071	0.0095	0.1568	0.1046	-0.4392	-0.5734	-0.3275

$[\gamma c]_{6 \times 8} =$

-0.0587	-0.0118	-0.2514	-0.1397	-0.2205	0.0557	0.3294	-0.4004
-0.3368	-0.0260	-0.2827	-0.0462	-0.0601	-0.1178	-0.1163	-0.0500
0.2300	0.0618	-0.1893	-0.2364	-0.0095	-0.0127	-0.0711	0.0309
-0.3724	0.1159	0.2603	0.4305	-0.2570	-0.3705	0.0974	-0.2220
0.1811	0.1958	0.3836	0.0486	0.2772	-0.0904	-0.2156	0.0878
0.0638	0.4969	-0.1898	0.5381	-0.2640	-0.1328	0.4242	-0.7039

$[\beta f]_{8 \times 1} =$
$[-0.7707 \ -0.8167 \ -0.9335 \ -0.5140 \ -0.0747 \ -0.9410 \ 0.9219 \ -0.0529]^T$

$[\alpha f]_{8 \times 8} =$

-0.2545	0.2783	-0.1508	0.0664	0.1558	0.1045	0.1560	0.2460
0.5521	0.4264	0.7085	0.0885	-0.0500	0.6924	-0.7540	-0.0446
0.4922	0.4311	0.2576	0.1123	0.1620	0.5905	-0.5025	0.1110
-0.3808	-0.5965	-0.5082	-0.4232	0.1167	-0.3119	0.2300	-0.1632
0.1433	-0.0931	-0.2049	-0.4674	0.1364	-0.4426	-0.2754	-0.1145
-0.1340	-0.3410	-0.2597	-0.2570	-0.0306	0.0055	0.1144	0.2696
0.1000	-0.0200	-0.0576	0.0775	-0.1118	-0.4570	0.0301	0.1025
-0.1333	-0.2398	-0.2524	-0.4151	-0.2174	-0.2665	0.2018	0.1829

$[\gamma f]_{6 \times 8} =$

-0.0566	0.1355	0.3022	-0.2399	0.2674	0.0947	-0.0127	0.2146
0.0794	-0.0863	-0.4428	0.2854	0.1485	0.2720	-0.0174	-0.1124
-0.2576	0.1466	-0.0372	0.3085	0.0029	-0.2747	-0.0239	-0.2979
-0.0896	-0.4596	-0.7403	0.2787	0.2913	0.3343	0.2778	0.6140
-0.2401	-0.4955	-0.0028	0.1100	0.4151	0.0673	-0.1477	0.0597
-0.2145	1.2435	0.6344	-0.8053	-0.0641	-0.2673	-0.0521	-0.3324

$\mu = 5.0000D-04$

REFERENCES

[1] McRuer, D. and Graham, D., "Eighty Years of Flight Control: Triumphs and Pitfalls of the Systems Approach," *AIAA Journal of Guidance, Control, and Dynamics*, Vol. 4, No. 4, July-August 1981, pp. 353-362.

[2] Bryson, A. E., Jr., "New Concepts in Control Theory, 1959-1984," *AIAA Journal of Guidance, Control, and Dynamics*, Vol. 8, No. 4, July-August 1985, pp. 417-425.

[3] Josin, G. M., "Preliminary Development of A Neural Network Autopilot Model For A High Performance Aircraft," Neural Systems, Inc., 2827 West 43rd Avenue, Vancouver, B.C., V6N 3H9, CANADA, June 12, 1989.

[4] Caglayan, A. K. and Allen, S. M., "A Neural Net Approach To Space Vehicle Guidance," *Proceedings of the 1990 American Control Conference*, San Diego, California, May 1990, pp. 1839-1842.

[5] Burgin, G. H. and Schnetzler, S. S., "Artificial Neural Networks In Flight Control And Flight Management Systems," *Proceedings of the 1990 NAECON*, Dayton, Ohio, May 1990, pp. 567-573.

[6] Ha, C. M., "Neural Networks Approach To AIAA Aircraft Control Design Challenge," AIAA Guidance, Navigation and Control Conference, AIAA-91-2672, August 12-14, 1991, New Orleans, Louisiana.

[7] Garg, S., Mattern, D. L., and Bullard, R. E., "Integrated Flight/Propulsion Control System Design Based on a Centralized Approach," *AIAA Journal of Guidance, Control, and Dynamics*, Vol. 14, No. 1, January-February 1991, pp. 107-116.

[8] Garg, S., "Robust Integrated Flight/Propulsion Control Design for a STOVL Aircraft Using H_∞ Control Design Techniques," *Automatica*, Vol. 29, No. 1, pp. 129-145, January 1993.

[9] Chen, F. C., "Back-Propagation Neural Networks for Nonlinear Self-Tuning Adaptive Control," *IEEE Control Systems Magazine*, pp. 44-48, April 1990.

[10] Yamada, T. and Yabuta, T., "Neural Network Controller Using Autotuning Method for Nonlinear Functions," *IEEE Transactions on Neural Networks*, Vol. 3, No. 4, July 1992, pp. 595-601.

[11] Napolitano, M. R. and Chen, C. I., "Failure Detection and Identification Via Neural Networks and Analysis of Cross-Correlation Function," submitted for publication in the *AIAA Journal of Guidance, Control, and Dynamics*.

Neuro Fuzzy Optimal TransmissionControl for Automobile with Variable Loads

K.Hayashi,Y.shimizu,S.nakamura,Y.dote,A.Takayama* and A.Hirako*

Department of Computer Science and Systems Engineering Muroran
Institute of Technology, Mizumoto 27-1,Muroran 050, Japan.
Tel. (0143)-44-4181 ext. 2433, Fax. (0143)-47-3374
E-mail: dote@jumit.crd.muroran-it.ac.jp

*Isuzu Advanced Engineering Center LTD.
8 Tsuchidana, Fujisawa-shi, Kanagawa-ken 252, Japan

ABSTRACT

An optimal transmission controller for an automobile with variable loads is designed and tested by using a transmission system (Isuzu NAVi-5) which consists of actuators and sensors beside gears, a throttle and a clutch. This system engages and disengages the clutch and gears up and down automatically. In other words a manual gear shift system is automated.

As neuro and fuzzy approaches are promising methods to interface between a vehicle operator and an automobile, they are used to design an optimal transmission controller.

The automobile loads are estimated from the signals of the status sensors by fuzzy logic. The vehicle operator's intention is inferred by fuzzy logic using the information from the automobile status sensors on which the operator's intention is reflected. Then,these are fed into a neural network. An experienced driver(a lot of data) teacher the neural network an optimal gear shift scheduling such that a vehicle operator feels comfortable even when the automobile loads change (for example when an automobile is traveling up and down hill).

1.INTRODUCTION

Neuro fuzzy control has one of the intelligent controls since knowledge engineering is used in the neuro fuzzy control. Neuro fuzzy control is usually utilized for the two purposes[1][2]. One is for the constructing nonlinear controllers. The other is for adding human intelligence to controllers, such as perception (sensory information process), understanding, recognition, inference, learning, diagnosis and others.

Fuzzy control is like following what a person says by language (fuzzy set). On the other hand neuro control is explained like following what a person does by data. In order to construct nonlinear and intelligent controllers fuzzy

control and neuro control should be combined as shown in Fig.1.

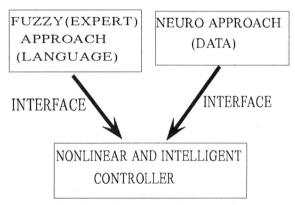

Fig.1 Neuro Fuzzy approches to construct nonlinear and intelligent controllors.

Fuzzy control is useful only if it is simple and low cost and only when human skill is converted into control knowledge by language (fuzzy representation).

Neuro control is useful if a lot of operational data are available. Then by using its nonlinear mapping a skillful operator's control action can be realized. Thus both neuro and fuzzy approaches are promising interface methods between human and automobiles.

In this paper, neuro fuzzy approaches are used to design an optimal gear shift controller. The automobile loads are estimated from the signals of the automobile status sensors by fuzzy logic. The vehicle operators intention is also inferred by fuzzy logic using the information indirectly, from the vehicle status sensors on which the vehicle operator's intention is reflected. Then these are fed into a neural network. An experienced driver(a lot of data) teaches the neural network an optimal gear shift scheduling such that a vehicle operator feels comfortable even when the automobile loads change during urban street test or during uphill driving and downhill driving. This control scheme saves gas consumption and reduces harmful exhaust gas and gives smooth driving since "shift-busy" is a voided.

2.SYSTEM DESCRIPTION [3]

An automated gear shift system is illustrated in Fig.2. This system is operated by twenty vehicle state sensor signals and vehicle operator's accelerator pedal command or gear shift command Throttle control, clutch control and gear shift control are achieved. The control objective is to determine the most appropriate gear position. A microprocessor MC68HC11, with a 16 Kbyte EPROM is used as digital controller. The necessary interface circuits are shown in Fig.3.

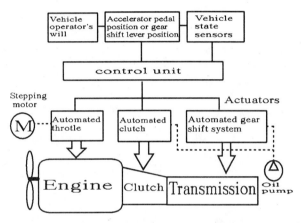

Fig.2 Automated gear shift control system.

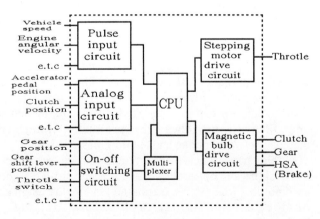

Fig3. interface circuits.

3.FUNDAMENTAL CONTROL [3]

Firstly, fundamental gear shift maps which describe gear positions according to accelerator pedal displacement versus vehicle speed are constructed as shown in Fig.4. They are stored in the memories.Fig.4.c) shows how to be geared up. Suppose that the accelerator pedal position is now a, then according to the

vehicle speeds V1, V2, V3, and V4, the gear position is shifted to 2, 3, 4 and 5 respectively. In addition to this map, the accelerator pedal position displacement rate is introdused as shown in Fig.5. This is stored in the memory. The control due to this variable is added to the fundamental control.

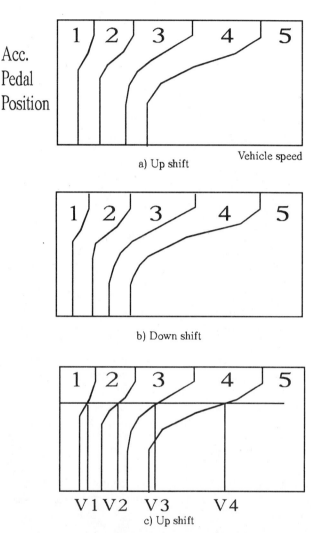

a) Up shift

b) Down shift

c) Up shift

Fig.4 Fundamentals gear shift maps.

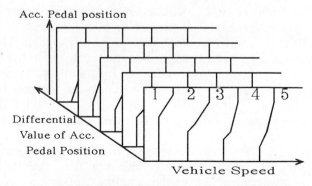

Fig.5 Gear shift map with additional variable.

4. NEURO FUZZY OPTIMAL GEAR-SHIFT CONTROL

4.1. Control Objectives
"Shift-busy" occurs when there is interactions between speed decrease due to applied loads and vehicle operator's accelerator operations. The control objective is to avoid this "shift-busy" by using neuro-fuzzy control.

4.2. Automobile Load Estimation
Automobile loads are estimated by fuzzy logic from the input shaft speed and accelerator position displacement as shown in Fig.6. f1 and f2 are functions to adjust the signal levels. The rules used here are as follows.

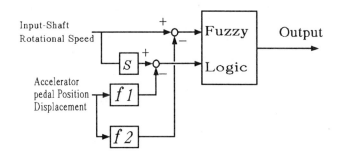

Fig.5 Vehicle loads estimation.

IF IS = NB and △IS = NB THEN OUT = PB
IF IS = NB and △IS = NM THEN OUT = PM
IF IS = NB and △IS = ZO THEN OUT = ZO
IF IS = NB and △IS = P   THEN OUT = N
IF IS = NM and △IS = NB THEN OUT = PB
IF IS = NM and △IS = NM THEN OUT = PM
IF IS = NM and △IS = ZO THEN OUT = ZO
IF IS = NM and △IS = P   THEN OUT = N
IF IS = ZO and △IS = NB THEN OUT = ZO
IF IS = ZO and △IS = NM THEN OUT = ZO
IF IS = ZO and △IS = ZO THEN OUT = N
IF IS = ZO and △IS = P   THEN OUT = N
IF IS = P and △IS = NB THEN OUT = N
IF IS = P and △IS = NM THEN OUT = N
IF IS = P and △IS = ZO THEN OUT = N

where,
NB : negative big	P : positive
PB : positive big	N : negative
PM : positive medium	IS : speed
NM : negative medium	△IS : acceleration
ZO : zero	OUT : estimated load

Fig.7 shows membership functions for these rules.

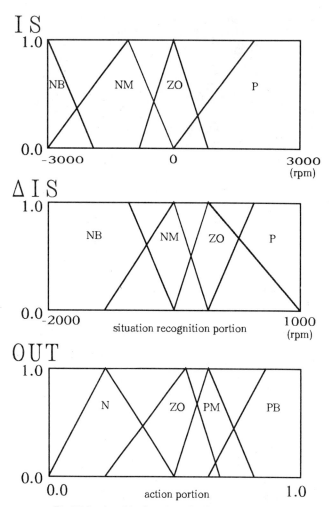

Fig.7 Membership functions for load estimation.

4.3. Operator's Intention Inference
Driver's intention is inferred by fuzzy logic from the accelerator position displacement and its rate as shown in Fig.8. f3 is a function to adjust the signal levels.

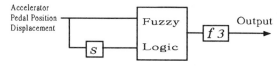

Fig.8 Driver's intention estimation.

The rules used here are as follows.
IF AC = ZO and △AC = NB THEN OUT = ZO
IF AC = ZO and △AC = NM THEN OUT = ZO
IF AC = ZO and △AC = ZO THEN OUT = ZO
IF AC = ZO and △AC = PM THEN OUT = PM
IF AC = ZO and △AC = PB THEN OUT = PB
IF AC = PM and △AC = NB THEN OUT = N
IF AC = ZO and △AC = NM THEN OUT = ZO
IF AC = PM and △AC = ZO THEN OUT = ZO
IF AC = PM and △AC = PM THEN OUT = PM
IF AC = PM and △AC = PB THEN OUT = PB
IF AC = PB and △AC = NB THEN OUT = N
IF AC = PB and △AC = NM THEN OUT = N

IF AC = PB and △AC = ZO THEN OUT = ZO
IF AC = PB and △AC = PM THEN OUT = PM
IF AC = PB and △AC = PB THEN OUT = PM

where
AC : accelerator position displacement
AC : AC rate.
Fig.9 shows **membership functions for driver's intention inference.**

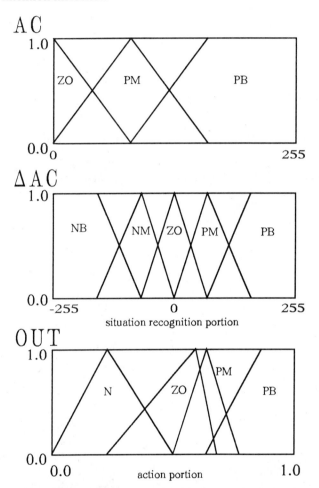

Fig.9 Membership functions for driver's intention estimation

4.4. Optimate Gear Shift Position Determination

Optimal gear shift position are determinate by using a neural network from the estimated load, the inferred driver's intention, the car speed and the accelerator pedal position displacement as shown in Fig.10. f4 is a function to adjust the original levels. The neural network used here is a 3-layers back propagation type network. It has four neurons for the input layer, nine neurons in the hidden layer and five neurons for the output layer as shown in Fig.11. A standard gear shift scheduling map, date in uphill driving and experienced operator's knowledge are used to train this neural network with "off-line".

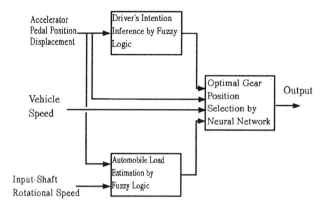

Fig.10 Optimal gear shift position selection.

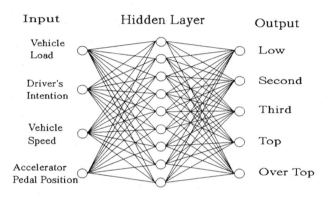

Fig.11 Neural Network for gear shift positions determinations

4.5. Experimental Results

The proposed neuro fuzzy control is implemented with a personal computer PC-9801. Actual uphill driving tests are performed on the slop shown in Fig.12. Fig.13 shows the test results for conventional method. Fig.14 shows the test results for this neuro-fuzzy control. The proposed method gives more smoothing driving, less fuel consumption and less harmful exhaust gas.

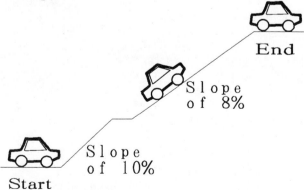

Fig.12 Experiment course conditions

194

5. CONCLUSION

Neuro-fuzzy control is a promising approach to interface between a vehicle operator and an automobile. Uphill driving tests are achieved by this neuro-fuzzy optimal gear-shift control. The test result show that this approach give consumption and less harmful exhaust gas than conventional approaches. This is also applicable to downhill driving and driving with variable loads on the plain road.

6. REFERENCES

[1] P.J.Werbos, "Neuro Control and Fuzzy Logic: Connections and Design", International Journal of Approximate Reasoning, May 1991.
[2] Y.Dote, "Fuzzy and Neuro Controllers", Proceeding of the WANN'91, Auburn University, U.S.A., February 1991.
[3] Y.Dote, K.Hayashi, J.Nasu, M.Strefezza, A.Takayama and A.Hirako, "Neural Fuzzy Transmission Control for Automobile", Proceedings of the IEEE Round Table Discussion on Neural Network, Fuzzy, and Vehicle Applications, Inst. on Industrial Science, Univ. of Tokyo, 1991.

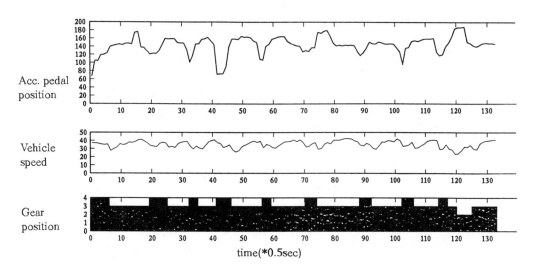

Fig.13 Driving test results for conventional control.

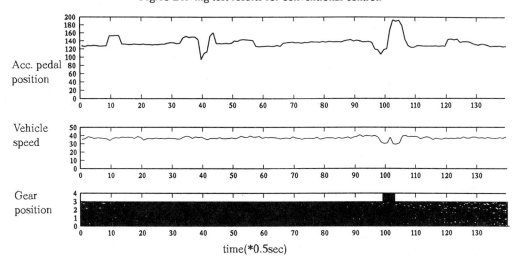

Fig.14 Driving test results for neuro-fuzzy control.

ADAPTIVE HEAVE COMPENSATION VIA DYNAMIC NEURAL NETWORKS

D.G. Lainiotis, K.N. Plataniotis, Dinesh Menon, C.J. Charalampous

Florida Institute of Technology

MELBOURNE, FLORIDA

ABSTRACT

This paper discusses the problem of Adaptive heave compensation. A new estimator based on dynamic recurrent neural networks is applied to this problem. It is shown that the new algorithm is well suited for on-line implementation and has excellent performance. Computational results via extensive simulations are provided to illustrate the effectiveness of the algorithm. A comparative evaluation with conventional methods is also provided.

I. INTRODUCTION

Dynamic heave compensation arises in many sea-related problems such as seismic experiments for oil exploration [1], control of autonomous underwater vehicles [2], underwater target tracking, and float wave data analysis [3]. The physical models of the heave process can be found in [4]. Frequency methods have been used in the past to identify models of source heave. The model is based on the frequency content of the heave record and it is used as the basis to formulate the heave extraction problem as one of optimal linear estimation.

A lot of studies have been reported for the solution to this problem, most of them utilizing Kalman Filter based approach. The state-space formulation of heave dynamics make the Kalman Filter an obvious first choice. The design of the Kalman estimator is based on the assumption of the complete structural knowledge of the model which describes the heave dynamics. Its recursive form is based on the gaussian assumption of the state space noise statistics. It is well known that there is a degradation of the estimate quality, when a mismatch between the structure and noise statistics used to design the Kalman Filter, and the actual model exists [5]. In order to overcome such drawbacks, another approach was followed in [5]. Based on the Lainiotis

Multimodel Partitioning Approach [6], [7], the highly parallel, Adaptive Lainiotis Filter was used to provide adaptability in a changing environment and reduced processing time.

It is obvious, an estimator that can handle more realistic assumptions about the dynamic model, can provide more meaningful estimates of the desired states in real time situations. On the other hand, the emphasis on parallel processing capabilities in the new estimator designs, and the availability of powerful parallel computers, indicates the importance of a parallel, decoupled structure, like that of the ALF [8]. Taking all these into consideration, a neural estimator is proposed, that can also take advantage of the new hardware capabilities.

Specifically this paper is organized as follows: In Section II the structure of the proposed neural estimator, the details of the construction of the network, the training method used, and a comparison with conventional techniques via extensive simulations are given. Finally Section III summarizes the conclusions.

II. NEURAL NETWORKS FOR HEAVE COMPENSATION

Recently, neural networks have been used to estimate states of dynamic systems [9], [10], [13]. Recurrent neural networks seem to be an answer to these estimation problems, where the applicability of other statistical estimators, like the Kalman filter, are limited. The neural estimators provide improved performance, especially when the system model violates the assumptions about the structure and the statistics, upon which the Kalman filter is based.

In this work, a recurrent multilayer network trained via the back-propagation method [12], has been used as neural estimator. The neural estimator is an input recurrent dynamic network that allows information to flow from the output nodes to the input nodes [9], [11], [14].

Neural and conventional estimators have been used here in order to estimate the states of the heave compensation state space model. The heave compensation model had been obtained from field data records off the coast of Newfoundland and discussed in [4]. The heave compensation process involves two steps. In the first a mathematical model is obtained from the available heave data, and then a filtering method is applied to estimate the heave state.

A second order transfer function model which had been obtained in [4] is used here

$$T(s) = \frac{12566.375}{s^2 + 12566.375 \cdot s + 6.316547 \times 10^8}$$

(1)

The model is based on an oscillatory system with center frequency, F_q=4 KHz and Q_o=2. A time scaling is used in order to avoid aliasing in the Fourier Transform operation. The overall dynamics is converted from the s-domain transfer function to a stable z-domain transfer function using a zero-order hold device and a sampling period [4].

The equivalent time domain representation [6], in a state space observable canonical form is:

$$x(k+1) = \begin{bmatrix} 1.559 & 1 \\ -0.777 & 0 \end{bmatrix} \cdot x(k) + \begin{bmatrix} 0.213 \\ -0.213 \end{bmatrix} \cdot w(k)$$

(2)

$$z(k) = \begin{bmatrix} 1 & 0 \end{bmatrix} \cdot x(k) + v(k)$$

(3)

where,
w(k) is assumed to be zero-mean gaussian noise with covariance Q=10.0
v(k) is assumed to be zero-mean gaussian observation noise with covariance 10.0
The initial state vector, x(0) is assumed to be a gaussian vector with known mean, x(0/0), and error covariance matrix, P(0/0). The initial state is also assumed independent of the noise.

Statistical or neural estimators can be used to generate estimates of the heave record from data observed through the above model. In most of the cases, the filter estimates are based on data records gathered together from different sensors, or the same sensors recording at different time intervals. These measurements are obtained using mechanical or electronic instruments. It is well known that the environment around the measurement sensors might introduce unknown bias terms in the measurement sequence. Moreover failures in instrumentation may randomly occur. Therefore the assumption that the filter designer has a complete knowledge of the measurement equation dynamics and statistics is not always true in real situations. The above measurement biases can be modeled either as unknown constant parameters, or as additive measurement noise with unknown characteristics.

In an ideal situation where the above model is completely known, the Kalman filter is the optimal estimator in the mean square sense. However when the dynamics of the measurement equation or the statistics of the measurement noise are not available the Kalman filter fails to provide accurate estimates. More powerful statistical estimators like ALF [6], [7] that can handle model uncertainties must be used.

In this paper a similar situation is introduced. The state equation that describes the heave phenomenon is known. However unknown measurement bias exists. The objective of the different estimators is to estimate the system state with partial knowledge of the measurement equation. The above two statistical estimators are compared in terms of performance, with a neural estimator which is derived without any specific assumption about the statistics and the dynamics of the measurement model. The experimental set -up is given below:

● System model:

The structural model that describes the heave phenomenon is linear and time-invariant, but the measurement dynamics, and the statistics of the measurement noise are not completely known. In this experiment the following model is assumed:

$$x(k+1) = \begin{bmatrix} 1.559 & 1 \\ -0.777 & 0 \end{bmatrix} \cdot x(k) + \begin{bmatrix} 0.213 \\ -0.213 \end{bmatrix} \cdot w(k)$$

(4)

$$z(k) = \begin{bmatrix} 1 & 0 \end{bmatrix} \cdot x(k) + b(k) + v(k)$$

(5)

where, b(k) is unknown measurement bias, uniformly distributed over the interval [-2.5, 2.5]. The statistics of the bias term is unknown to the filters designer. In order to overcome the uncertainty, the designer has assumed that different models represent the physical phenomenon. Since the unknown parameter is the bias term the following assumptions are made about its statistics.

- Model I

The bias term is white gaussian noise with $R_b = 2.083$

- Model II

The bias term is white gaussian noise with $R_b = 3.12$

- Model III

The bias term is white gaussian noise with $R_b = 4.51$

In the experiment it is assumed that the real data are generated using the Eqs. (4),(5). The Kalman filter, the Adaptive Lainiotis filter, and a dynamic recurrent neural network are used to estimate the states of the above state space model. More specific the different filter configurations are summarized below:

—Statistical estimator: Kalman Filter (KF)

In this simulation two Kalman filters are used. The first one is matched to the Model I. In other words it is a Kalman filter that knows the exact dynamics of the model and assumes that the bias term is gaussian with variance the actual variance of the uniform noise. The second Kalman filter does not know the statistics of the bias term. It assumes that the bias is gaussian with mean the actual sample mean, and covariance the actual sample covariance. Both the recursive algorithm start with initial state estimate, $\hat{x}(0/0)=0$ and initial covariance, $P(0/0)=100$.

—Statistical Estimator: Adaptive Lainiotis filter (ALF)

The Adaptive Lainiotis Filter (ALF) [6], [7], is used to provide state estimates. The ALF filter employs two different Kalman filters. The first one is matched to Model II, and the other uses the assumptions of Model III. In this way each of the filters in the ALF's bank is an optimal estimator. The nonlinear filter combines their estimates in an adaptive sense, providing the overall estimates [7]. The same initial conditions as above have been used to initialize the filter.

—Neural Estimators: Input recurrent neural networks

The dynamic recurrent neural estimator has the following structure.
- Network topology:
  - 2 input nodes: the current and the previous

measurements are used as input signals.
- 3 hidden layers with 4-4-2 nodes respectively.
- 2 output linear nodes: the number of output nodes depends on the dimensionality of the state vector. The output nodes provide the desired estimates of the system's states.

—learning parameters:
- learning rate: 0.05, momentum term: 0.2

—Training method:
- the network knows the actual states of the model during the training phase. The target vector is the actual state vector.
- the network tries to minimize the square error between the current output and the target vector.
- The training data set is produced by running the system equations. The training set consists from 100 input/output pairs (x(k), z(k)). The test set consists also of a sequence of 100 data points. The test record is produced separately from the training.
- the training procedure is terminated if the training error tolerance is less than 0.01 or if the number of iterations of the training set is more than 50000.

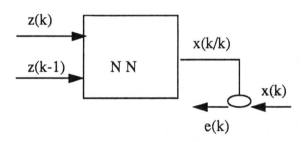

Fig1. Input recurrent Neural Network

In order to assess the performance of the above estimators, the mean square error, averaged over 50 Monte Carlo runs, is used:

$$MSE = \frac{1}{mc} \cdot \sum_{i=1}^{mc} \left[x(k) - \hat{x}(k/k) \right]^2$$

(6)

The simulation results are shown in Figs. 2-12. From the graphs the following can be concluded:

- The Kalman Filter is the optimal estimator for a linear state-space model with gaussian noises. In Model I with the additive non gaussian noise its estimates are no more optimal. However since it knows the exact statistic of the bias term it provides reliable estimates. On the other hand the second Kalman filter provides suboptimal estimates of the system states, due to the uncertainty regarding the statistics of the additive bias term.

- The Adaptive Lainiotis Filter can easily handle the uncertainty regarding the statistics of the model. The Adaptive filter first uses its nonlinear decision mechanism to detect the appropriate model, and then the best filter from its bank to provide the required estimates [6].

- The neural estimator performs satisfactorily, although the network is a highly nonlinear structure applied to a linear model. It can be easily seen that the recurrent network has almost the same performance, as the Adaptive filter. However the neural estimator does not require any specific knowledge about alternative measurement statistics, and therefor can handle the uncertainty using less information.

III. CONCLUSIONS

The problem of heave motion estimation was considered in this paper. A comparative evaluation of conventional statistical estimators and new neural estimators was made. The results can be summarized as follows:

- The neural estimator provides a very reliable solution to the estimation problem

- When the model which describes the physical phenomenon is completely known statistical filters like the Kalman Filter, provide the optimal solution

- In more realistic situations where the actual model is not completely known the neural estimator outperforms the conventional estimators. However, advanced statistical filters like the Adaptive Lainiotis Filter (ALF) can be used successfully in this

case, with a performance similar to this of a recurrent neural estimator

In conclusion, the ability of the neural network based estimator to provide accurate solutions to the heave compensation problem under more practical conditions, and its massively parallel structure and high speed, makes it the preferable choice for real time signal processing applications.

REFERENCES

[1] D.G. Lainiotis, S.K. Katsikas, S.D. Likothanassis, *"Adaptive Deconvolution of Seismic Signals - Performance, Computational Analysis, Parallelism"*, IEEE Transactions on ASSP-36, pp. 1715-1735, Nov. 1988.

[2] *J.C. Hassab, "Contact localization and motion analysis in the ocean environment"*, IEEE Journal of Oceanic Engineering, OE-8, pp. 136-147, July 1983.

[3] R.L. Moose, T.E. Dailey, *"Adaptive underwater target tracking using passive multi-path time delay measurements"*, IEEE Transactions on ASSP-33, pp. 777-787, August 1985.

[4] F. El-Hawary, *"Applications of dynamic heave compensation in the underwater environment and approaches to its solution"*, Proceedings of Oceans 1992, pp. 254-259, Newport, Rhode Island.

[5] D.G. Lainiotis, K.N. Plataniotis, C.J. Charalampous, *"Adaptive Filter applications to heave compensation"*, Proceedings of Oceans, 1992, pp. 277-282, Newport, Rhode Island.

[6] D.G. Lainiotis, *"Optimal adaptive estimation: Structure and parameter adaptation"*, IEEE Transactions on Automatic Control, pp. 160-170, 1971.

[7] D.G. Lainiotis, *"Partitioning: A unifying framework*

for adaptive systems, I- Estimation", Proceedings of the IEEE, Vol. 64, No. 8, pp. 1126-1142, 1976.

[8] D.G. Lainiotis, K.N. Plataniotis, C.J. Charalampous, "*Distributed computing filters: Multisensor marine applications*", Proceedings of Oceans, 1992, pp.265-270, Newport, Rhode Island.

[9] J.P. De Gruyenaece, H.M. Haffer, "*A comparison between Kalman Filters and Recurrent Neural Networks*", Proceedings of IJCNN-92, Vol. IV, pp. 247-251, 1992.

[10] A.J. Kanekar, A. Feliachi, "*State estimation using artificial neural networks*", Proceedings of IEEE Conference on Systems Engineering, pp. 552-556, 1990.

[11] Y.H. Pao, G.H. Park, D.J. Sobajic, "*System identification and noise cancellation: A quantitative comparative study of Kalman filtering and neural network approaches*", Proceedings of Automatic Control Conference, 1991, pp. 1408-1411.

[12] D.E. Rumelhart, J.L. McClelland (eds.), "*Parallel distributed processing: Explorations in the Microstructure of Cognition, Vol. I*", M.I.T. Press, 1986.

[13] D.G. Lainiotis, C.J. Charalampous, K.N. Plataniotis, S.K. Katsikas "Adaptive multi-initialized neural network training algorithm." Proc. of Artificial Neural Networks in Engineering, ANNIE 93, Missouri 1993

[14] D.G. Lainiotis, K.N. Plataniotis, Dinesh Menon, C.J. Charalampous "Heave compensation via Neural networks." Proc. of Artificial Neural Networks in Engineering, ANNIE 93, Missouri 1993

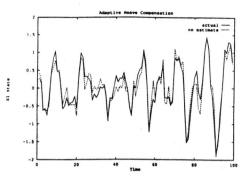

Fig. 2 Heave compensation: state X1, neural estimator

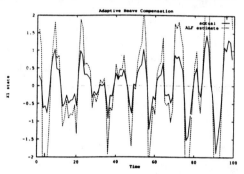

Fig. 3 Heave compensation: state X1, ALF filter

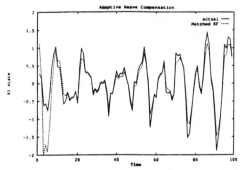

Fig. 4 Heave compensation: state X1, matched Kalman filter

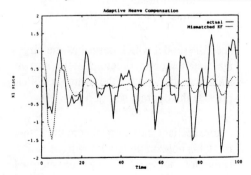

Fig. 5 Heave compensation: state X1, mismatched Kalman filter

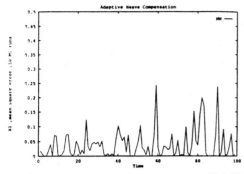

Fig. 6 Neural estimator, state X1: Mean square error, 50 MCR

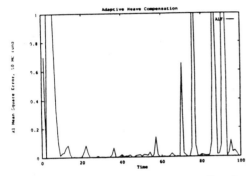

Fig. 7 ALF filter, state X1: Mean square error, 50 MCR

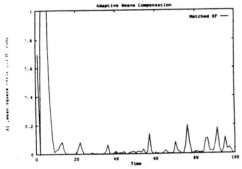

Fig. 8 Kalman filter (matched), state X1: Mean square error, 50 MCR

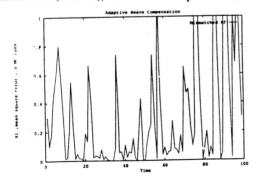

Fig. 9 Kalman filter (mismatched), state X1: Mean square error, 50 MCR

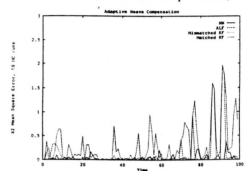

Fig. 10 Comparative evaluation State X1: Mean Square Error, 50 MCR

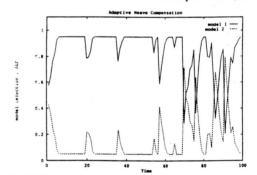

Fig. 11 Comparative evaluation State X2: Mean Square Error, 50 MCR

Fig. 12 Heave compensation : ALF model selection

The final chapter in Part One describes different applications of neural networks to voltage control. Although there is obvious crossover between this chapter and the papers included in Part Two (Power Systems), the nature of the papers upon closer examination did tend to align more closely with the papers found in Part One.

Four papers are included in this chapter. **Paper 6.1** applies the multilayer perceptron (MLP) neural network to the regulation of DC/DC buck converters. **Paper 6.2** applies the MLP neural network to power inversion in electronics. **Paper 6.3** uses neural networks to optimize the operation of power generation units. **Paper 6.4** uses MLP neural networks to control photovoltaic/diesel hybrid power generation systems.

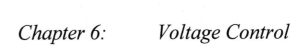

Chapter 6:   Voltage Control

A NEURAL NETWORK BASED APPROACH TO THE REGULATION OF DC/DC BUCK CONVERTERS

Allan Insleay   Géza Joós

Department of Electrical and Computer Engineering
Concordia University
1455 de Maisonneuve Blvd., West
Montreal, Quebec H3G 1M8
tel:(514) 848-3116

Abstract - This paper proposes the neural network controller as a viable alternative to the PI controller used in dc/dc converters of the buck type for voltage regulation. The PI controller, although robust and simple, requires a priori knowledge of the system characteristics and once designed for a specific load, its parameters remain fixed. The neural controller, in the on line mode has the ability to learn from experience, thus eliminating the need for a priori knowledge of the system dynamics. The neural network can adapt to variations in the load, and still allow the system to track a specific reference without redesign. Performance comparisons made with the standard PI regulator clearly bring out the superior performance of the neural network regulator.

I. INTRODUCTION

Neural networks (NN) have learning and self-organizing abilities allowing them to adapt to changes in data. Many attempts have been made to apply NN to the control field where it may be used to deal with non-linearities and any uncertainties that may develop in the system[1,2,3,4,5].

In [1], an on line NN is used to control the tracking of an industrial drive. The controller consists of four units, a preprocessor, a classifier, a look-up table, and a servo drive unit. Measurements of output and input values, once classified by the NN are used to generate the appropriate signals for the proper control of the drive.

A NN consisting of time delay elements and a fuzzy logic learning method was employed as a robotic motion controller in [2]. This technique sported increased learning speed and improved convergence when dealing with non-linear dynamical systems.

Another approach uses a NN as an emulator that identifies the system's dynamics and one as a controller that tracks the dynamical process [3]. The parameters of both the emulator and the controller were determined via the inherent learning properties of the NN.

Recently a NN controller was used in [4] to control the operation of an inverter. An on-line training technique using sinusoidal currents as references forces the output current of the inverter to track these references. It was found

that the NN controller exhibited good characteristics when compared with the conventional fixed-band and hysteresis current control methods.

This paper proposes a NN regulator for a dc to dc buck converter as a viable alternative to the traditional PI controller shown in Fig. 1.

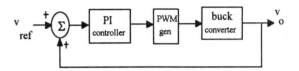

Fig. 1 Buck converter with PI controller

The remainder of this paper will be organized in the following manner. Section II will provide a description of the backpropagation neural network (bpn). Section III details the two types of NN regulator implementations and their training techniques. Section IV gives the simulated results of the topologies described in III. Finally, conclusions are summarized in Section V.

II NEURAL NETWORK BASICS

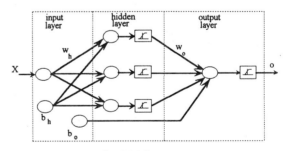

Fig. 2 NN structure

The bpn has the structure shown Fig. 2. The basic building block of the above structure is the NN model of the neuron. Each neuron has multiple inputs and one output. Each input flows through a connection weight. The neurons output is a function of the input, the weights, a bias term and a node non-linearity. The NN is built from three distinct layers. The input layer is really a fictitious layer used to establish connection points transferring the input signal to each node in the hidden layer. Once the signal flows through the connection weights (w_h) it gets combined with a bias (b_h) and awaits processing. The neuron processes each of these signals according to the following equation

$$i_j = F\left(\sum_{j=1} W_{h_j} * X_j + B_{h_j}\right) \qquad (1)$$

where,

X_j = input signal to the input layer
W_{hj} = connection weight for hidden layer
B_{hj} = bias weight for the hidden layer
$F(.)$ = sigmoid non linearity

The signal generated at the output layer uses equation (1) as its input signal. This signal then flows through connection weights (w_0) to get combined with a bias (b_0) and await processing. The output neuron processes all of these signals according to the following equation

$$O = F\left(\sum_{j=1} W_{o_j} * I_j + B_o\right) \qquad (2)$$

where

I_j = input signal to the output layer
W_0 = connection weight for output layer
B_0 = bias weight for the output layer
$F(.)$ = sigmoid non linearity

At this point we have a feed forward system, since each layer receives only signals from the previous layer. The NN has not yet begun to learn the desired mapping since for learning to occur, the NN's weights on both the hidden layer and the output layer must be adapted. It is through this adaptation that the notion of bpn arises.

The bpn uses the error between the output O, of the NN and a desired target, to adjust the weights on the output layer. There is no way to specify a desired target for the hidden layers. Therefore a portion of the error at the output is propagated back through to the hidden layer to adjust the weights. Both the on-line and the off-line techniques use an error signal (e) to adjust the weights and biases as the NN learns to generate an appropriate output from a specific input. However, they are trained in different manners.

III TRAINING

The two training techniques that will be examined are the off-line and the on-line training methods. The off-line technique requires the acquisition of a sample data set. The data set is obtained from the system shown in Fig 3.

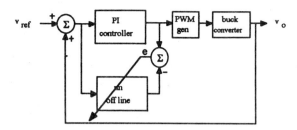

Fig. 3 Off-line training method

The data set must be sufficiently rich to ensure stable operation, since no additional learning will take place after training. The off-line training technique is a very accurate method based on gradient type minimization. The accuracy arises from the minimization of the square error of the following cost function

$$e = \frac{1}{2} \cdot \sum (output - \text{target})^2 \qquad (3)$$

In general backpropagation networks have a slow convergence speed which is dependent upon the nature of the data set. The bpn will not extrapolate well. Thus for the network to learn to emulate the system the data set must cover the entire input space. Thus armed with the data set, the Matlab NN toolbox for Sun station was employed to compute values for weights and biases. These parameters are inserted into the NN and then used in the recall mode shown in Fig 4.

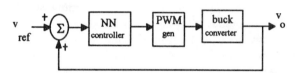

Fig. 4 Off-line NN in recall mode

One of the salient features of on-line training is its ability to learn with little or no a priori knowledge of the system that it will control shown in Fig.5. Under this assumption the bpn will attempt to minimize the error between the output voltage of the buck system and a reference.

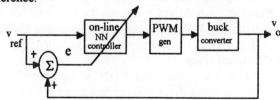

Fig. 5 On-line NN regulator

The bpn shown in Fig 3 will perform the least square minimization based on equation (3). From this performance index the following update rules for the weights may be defined. The steepest descent gradient search will be applied to (3) to compute an update rule for the output layer weights.

$$E = \frac{1}{2} \cdot \left(v_{ref} - v_{out}\right)^2 \qquad (3)$$

$$\frac{\partial E}{\partial w_o} = -\left(v_{ref} - v_{out}\right) \cdot \frac{\partial v_{out}}{\partial w_o} \qquad (4)$$

but

$$\frac{\partial v_{out}}{\partial w_o} = \frac{\partial v_{out}}{\partial O} \cdot \frac{\partial O}{\partial net} \cdot \frac{\partial net}{\partial w_o} \qquad (5)$$

and

$$\frac{\partial E}{\partial w} = \left(v_{ref} - v_o\right) \cdot \frac{Es}{v_{carrier}} \cdot F'(net) \cdot i_j \qquad (6)$$

which gives the following update rule for the output weights.

$$w_{o\,j}(t+1) = w_{o\,j}(t) + \frac{\partial E}{\partial w_{o\,j}} \qquad (7)$$

A similar rule for the hidden layer is now presented

$$E = \frac{1}{2} \cdot \left(v_{ref} - O \cdot \frac{Es}{v_{carrrier}}\right)^2 \qquad (8)$$

thus,

$$\frac{\partial O}{\partial w_h} = \frac{\partial O}{\partial neto} \cdot \frac{\partial neto}{\partial i_j} \cdot \frac{\partial i_j}{\partial neth} \cdot \frac{\partial neth}{\partial w_h} \qquad (10)$$

and

$$\frac{\partial E}{\partial w_h} = F'(net) \cdot x_j \cdot \sum_j \partial o_j \cdot w_{o\,j} \qquad (11)$$

Hence the weights on the hidden layer are updated based on the following

$$w_{h\,j}(t+1) = w_{h\,j}(t) + \frac{\partial E}{\partial w_{h\,j}} \qquad (12)$$

These equations show that some knowledge of the system is needed for the weight update rules to be defined.

IV RESULTS

A typical DC to DC buck topology was designed to operate at a frequency of 2 kHz a DC bus of 380 V and rated power of 8 kW into a 0.8 Ω load. The converter was controlled in turn by each of the three previously discussed regulators. The three controllers were subjected to step changes in the reference voltage shown in Fig. 6. It can be observed that the PI controller always exhibits similar overshoot response for each step change in the reference. The off-line trained NN has similar characteristics, whereas the on-line NN controller has minimal overshoot and fast dynamic response.

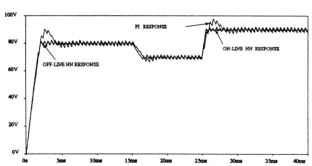

Fig. 6 Response to step changes in the reference voltage

TABLE I
PERFORMANCE INDICES EVALUATION

CONTROLLER TYPE	overshoot start up %	overshoot at 70V %	overshoot at 90V %
PI	5	9.71	4.79
off-line NN	2	8.9	2.35
on-line NN	1.68	0.7	1.6

Each regulator performed to the best of its ability however, their physical limitations were reached when the load was dropped from its initial value of 0.8Ω to a value of 0.1Ω and then increased to double its original value. Their responses are shown in Fig.7.

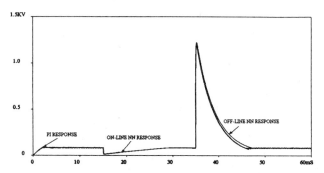

Fig. 7 Step change in load resistance

The system with the on-line NN in place was tested with the natural frequency held constant while the damping ratio was varied. The training time is defined as the settling time of the output response. It may be observed from Fig.8 and table II that once the on-line NN has acquired a base value for its weights during start up, its response to subsequent variations in the reference is rapid and dependent of the load connected.

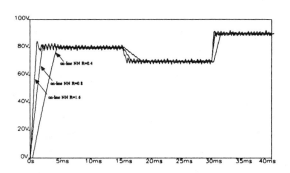

Fig. 8 Training times

TABLE II
TRAINING TIME EVALUATION FOR ON-LINE NN

	load r = 0.4Ω	load r = 0.8Ω	load r = 1.6Ω
start up	3.2mS	2.3mS	1.8mS
11% step down	3.4mS	2.4mS	2.3mS
25% step up	1.4mS	1.3mS	1mS

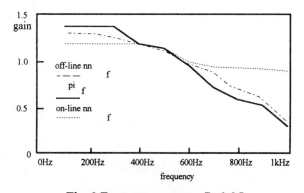

Fig. 9 Frequency response R=0.8Ω

The bandwidth of each system was tested and their response is shown in Fig.9. They were fed with a reference upon which a sinusoidal signal was overlaid. The frequency of the sinusoid was varied from 100Hz to 1kHz. The bandwidth of the PI controller in general is restrained by the cut-off frequency of the design which is dependent on the resonant frequency of the system. The off-line trained NN has a bandwidth similar to that of the PI controller. Whereas the gain of the on-line NN is near unity throughout all the test frequencies. Furthermore, these bandwidth figures change substantially with load for the PI and the off-line NN but not for the on-line NN.

V CONCLUSIONS

The simulation results show that the NN controllers offer stable response and good output regulation. The buck system is linearized about a single operating point to complete a PI controller design. The training set for the of the off-line NN was based on this design. Its training was lengthy and dependent upon the size and the quality of the data set. However good results were obtained. The on-line NN required the least effort in terms of design time and provided the most accurate and uniform results under changing load conditions. Finally, the NN offers fast dynamic response and enhances the performance of DC/DC buck converters over the conventional PI regulated converters.

REFERENCES

1. Heng-Ming Tai, Junli Wang and Kaveh Ashenayi,"A Neural Network -Based Tracking Control System", *IEEE Trans. Ind. Elect.*, vol.39,no. 6, pp. 504-510, Dec. 1992

2. Toshio Fukuda, Takanori Shibata, Masatoshi Tokita, and Toyokazu Mitsuoka, "Neuromorphic Control: Adaptation and Learning", *IEEE Trans. Ind. Elect.*, vol.39,no. 6, pp. 497-503, Dec. 1992

3. Julio Tanomaru and Sigeru Omatu,"Process Control by On-Line Trained Neural Controllers", *IEEE Trans. Ind. Elect.*, vol.39,no. 6, pp. 511-521, Dec. 1992

4. H. Nguyen and B.Widrow,"Neural Networks for Self-Learning Control Systems",*Control Systems Magazine*, pp.18-23, April 1990

5. Bor-Ren Lin and Richard G. Hoft,"Power Electronics Inverter Control with Neural Networks",*APEC Conf. Rec.*, pp. 128-134, 1993

6. V. K. Sood, N. Kandil, R. V. Patel, K. Khorasani, "Comparative Evaluation of Neural Network Based and PI Current Controllers for HVDC Transmission", *PESC Conf. Rec.*, pp.553-560, 1992

7. James A. Freeman and David M. Skapura, "Neural Networks Algorithms, Applications, and Programming Techniques", Addison-Wesley Publishing Company, I

POWER ELECTRONICS INVERTER CONTROL WITH NEURAL NETWORKS

Bor - Ren Lin and Richard G. Hoft
Power Electronics Research Center
University of Missouri - Columbia

ABSTRACT

Current - controlled voltage source inverters offer substantial advantages in improving motor system dynamics in high-performance ac drive systems. The controller switches follow a set of reference current waveforms. Fixed-band hysteresis and sinusoidal-band hysteresis controllers have been studied. This paper develops a neural network-based current-controlled voltage source inverter. The modes and learning techniques have been investigated by simulation. The implementation of neural networks are described and simulation results are presented.

INTRODUCTION

One of the main areas of interest in power electronics as applied to modern drive systems is the supply of ac machines from a dc voltage link via a current-controlled inverter. A variety of current control methods have been studied and reported in the literature [1]. Among the various current control methods, hysteresis current control is the simplest and most extensively used method. However, a current controller with fixed hysteresis bands has two disadvantages. First, the switching frequency varies during the fundamental period, resulting in irregular operation of the inverter. Second, the ripple current is relatively large. As a result of these disadvantages, the load current contains harmonics that cause additional machine heating. Recently B. K. Bose [2] proposed an instantaneous feedback controlled PWM inverter with adaptive hysteresis control technique. However, the shortcoming of that method is that the operation is achieved at the expense of implementation complexity. Some researchers studied a sinusoidal-band hysteresis current controller. In this method, the ripple can be varied and reduced with the current magnitude so that the load current contains lower harmonic content.

Neural network techniques have grown rapidly in recent years. Extensive research has been carried out on the application of artificial intelligence. Artificial neural network technology has the potential to provide an improved method of deriving non-linear models which is complementary to conventional techniques. Neural networks are instrinsically non-linear and the actual algorithmic relevant set of training examples is required which can be derived from operating plant data. In contrast to other

machine learning techniques, neural networks can modify their behavior in response to the environment, have the flexibility of easily handling different problem sizes, and have the potential for hardware implementation.

FIXED-BAND AND SINUSOIDAL-BAND CURRENT CONTROL

The inverter ac motor drive has many advantages over the conventional dc motor drive and, therefore, high-performance ac servo motor drives have increased in popularity. It is well known that precise current control is a key technology to realize high-performance ac drives. In the existing current controls for a voltage-fed inverter, the current hysteresis-controlled PWM and the subharmonic PWM shown in Figure 1 are widely used.

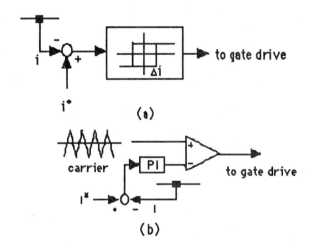

Figure 1. Conventional current controls
(a) Current hysteresis-controlled PWM
(b) subharmonic PWM

In the current hysteresis-controlled PWM, hysteresis comparators are used to impose a dead band or hysteresis band in a small range from the reference current. The hysteresis control scheme provides excellent dynamic performance because it acts quickly. The disadvantage of this method is that the switching frequency changes according to the operating condition of the motor. The subharmonic PWM has no problem associated with the switching frequency, but the steady state phase lag is a problem for high frequency operation. Recently several researchers use a sinusoidal-band hysteresis current controller where the hysteresis bands vary sinusoidally over a fundamental period rather than being fixed. Figure 2 shows the fixed-band current control and sinusoidal-band current control.

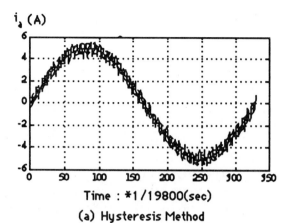

(a) Hysteresis Method

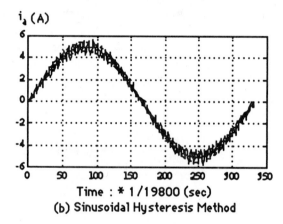

Time : * 1/19800 (sec)
(b) Sinusoidal Hysteresis Method

Figure 2. (a) Fixed-band hysteresis current control
(b) Sinusoidal-band hysteresis current control

The principle of hysteresis current control is very simple. Consider Figure 3, which shows a simple single phase voltage source inverter (VSI). Here, the switches (S1,S4) and (S2,S3) are switched as switch-pairs 1 and 2 respectively. The load voltage can be described by the following differential equation

$$V_{DC} = i_{ab}*R + L(di_{ab}/dt) \qquad (1)$$

For the hysteresis control the load current is feedback to be compared with the reference current. When the actual current is greater than the upper reference band (S1,S4) turn off and (S2,S3) turn on. When the actual current is lower than the lower reference band (S1,S4) turn on and (S2,S3) turn off.

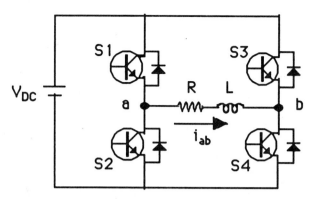

Figure 3. Single phase VSI

The actual current is thus forced to track the sinusoidal reference wave within the desired hysteresis.

1) Fixed-band hysteresis control

The algorithm for this scheme is

$$i_{ref}(t) = I_{ref}\sin(wt)$$

upper band $\qquad i_u = i_{ref}(t) + \Delta i$

lower band $\qquad i_l = i_{ref}(t) - \Delta i$

where Δi = hysteresis band limit

if $i_{ab} > i_u$, $V_{ab} = -V_{dc}$

if $i_{ab} < i_l$, $V_{ab} = V_{dc}$

2) Sinusoidal-band hysteresis control

The algorithm is

$$i_{ref}(t) = I_{ref}\sin(wt)$$

upper band $\qquad i_u = (I_{ref} + \Delta i)\sin(wt)$

lower band $\qquad i_l = (I_{ref} - \Delta i)\sin(wt)$

for $\qquad i_{ref}(t) > 0 :$

if $i_{ab} > i_u$, $V_{ab} = -V_{dc}$

if $i_{ab} < i_l$, $V_{ab} = V_{dc}$

for $i_{ref}(t) < 0 :$

if $i_{ab} < i_u$, $V_{ab} = V_{dc}$

if $i_{ab} > i_l$, $V_{ab} = -V_{dc}$

The load voltage, V_{ab}, obtained is used to solve (1).

NEURAL NETWORK CONCEPTS

There are many artificial neural network architectures that have been proposed. One architecture has been predominant; that is the feedforward neural network (FNN). The standard neuron structure illustrated in Figure 4 is adopted which is comprised of a summer and a logistic function f(net $_{p,i}$) that can be either a sigmoid or a linear function. The equation for the i-th neuron of the p-th layer structure is

$$\text{net}_{p,i} = \sum_{k=1}^{n} w_{p,i,k} O_{p-1,k} + \theta_{p,i} \qquad (2)$$

$O_{p,i} = f(\text{net}_{p,i})$ （3）

where $O_{p,i}$ is the output

$O_{p-1,k}$ is the k-th output at the (p-1)-th layer

$w_{p,i,k}$ is the weight from the k-th input of (p-1)-th

layer to the i-th output of the p-th layer

$\theta_{p,i}$ is the bias

These neurons are organized in layers as shown in Figure 5. Scaled data enters the network at neurons of the input layer and is propagated to the output through

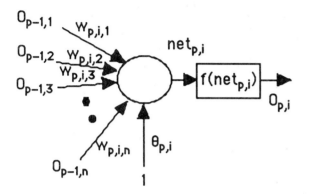

Figure 4. Structure of an elementary neuron

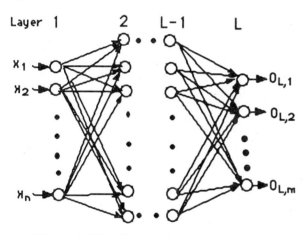

Figure 5. Feedforward neural network architecture

intermediate layers. Each connection has associated with it a weighting which acts to modify the signal strength. There are various techniques for optimizing criterion functions to train the neural network. One important characteristic of neural network classifiers is that their training usually requires iterative techniques. The backpropagation classifier is the most popular technique trained by using the gradient descent method. The advantage of this method is that it is simple and easy to understand, but the disadvantage is that convergent speed is slow. One way of overcoming these limitations is to use numerical analysis and stochastic methods. The RLS (recursive least square) method [3] - [5] uses extended Kalman estimation to optimize a function which is only known through random samples. This approach can be applied to linear or nonlinear problems. The power of RLS is obtained at the price of a fairly large amount of computation $O(N^2)$ for every update where N is the dimensionality of the input vector. The conjugate gradient algorithm [6] - [8] optimizes a criterion function by assuming that it is locally quadratic. This algorithm requires $O(N)$ computations per iteration. Although the backpropagation classifier is not so robust, it is easy to understand.

The backpropagation algorithm is now introduced. In the training phase, the weights are updated using the standard backward error propagation algorithm, also known as the generalized delta rule. The system first uses the input vector to produce its own output vector and then compares this with the desired output, or target vector. If there is no difference, no learning takes place. Otherwise the weights are changed to reduce the difference. Now the problem is to minimize the total mean-squared error E given by

$$E = 1/2 * \sum_{k=1}^{n} (t_{L,k} - O_{L,k})^2$$ （4）

where $t_{L,k}$ is the k-th target output at the output layer, $O_{L,k}$ is the k-th actual output at the output layer. This error can be minimized by taking partial derivatives of E with respect to each weight. In Rumelhart [9], the generalized delta rule used is

$$w_{p,j,i} = w_{p,j,i} + \Delta w_{p,j,i}$$ （5）

$$\delta_{p,j} = (t_{p,j} - O_{p,j}) * f'(\text{net}_{p,j}), \text{for output layer} \quad (p=L)$$

$$\text{or} \sum_{k=1}^{n} (\delta_{p+1,k} w_{p+1,k,j}) * f'(\text{net}_{p,j})$$ （6）

,for hidden layer (p≠L)

where $\Delta w_{p,j,i}$ is the weight change between the j-th neuron at the p-th layer and the i-th neuron at the (p-1)-th layer. To get the correct generalization of the delta rule, $\Delta w_{p,j,i}$ is propotional to $-\partial E/\partial w_{p,j,i}$. In order to implement gradient descent for E, weight changes should be made according to

$$\Delta w_{p,j,i} = \eta \, \delta_{p,j} \, O_{p-1,i}$$ （7）

where η is the learning rate. For practical purposes, η is chosen as large as possible without leading to oscillation. One way to increase the learning rate without leading to oscillation is to modify the generalized delta rule to include a momentum term. This can be accomplished by the following rule

$$\Delta w_{p,j,i}(k+1) = \eta \delta_{p,j} O_{p-1,i} + \alpha \Delta w_{p,j,i}(k) \qquad (8)$$

where η is the learning rate and α is a constant which determines the effect of past weight changes on the current direction of movement in the weight space. If $f(.)$ is a logistic function,

i.e., $f(net_{p,j}) = 1/(1+\exp(-net_{p,j}))$,
then $f'(net_{p,j}) = f(net_{p,j}) * (1 - f(net_{p,j}))$
$$= O_{p,j} * (1 - O_{p,j}) \qquad (9)$$

The above generalized delta rule is used to update the neural network weights until the total output error is less than a defined small value.

NEURAL NETWORK INVERTER CONTROL

The voltage source inverter (VSI) is illustrated in Figure 6. The input signal to the inverter is an analog signal such as current error or voltage error. The output signal of the inverter is a binary signal. Therefore, the controller has the properties of a nonlinear function to map the analog input into binary output. Neural network architectures have the capacity to learn nonlinear system models. They can perform collective processing and learning and provide powerful processing capabilities with great potential for highly parallel computation. Figure 7 shows the seven discrete voltage vectors resulting from the control of the inverter switching.

The hysteresis and neural network controls both have to find an algorithm for the nonlinear mapping function. In the neural network method, training is required to learn something about the plant behavior. The inputs to the neural network are three phase current errors and the outputs are the voltage vectors. Current errors can be randomly generated at the neural network input and the backpropagation method is used to update the weights so as to decrease the current errors. Since the hysteresis current control for the VSI is known, the neural network must learn the dynamic behavior of the hysteresis current control. It can be on-line or off-line learning. In on-line learning, the learning rule is

$|i^* - i_{ab}| < \varepsilon \Rightarrow$ keep the switches at the same state
$i^* - i_{ab} > \varepsilon \Rightarrow$ (S1 , S4) turn on , (S2 , S3) turn off.

$i^* - i_{ab} < -\varepsilon \Rightarrow$ (S1 , S4) turn off , (S2 , S3) turn on.
$$(10)$$

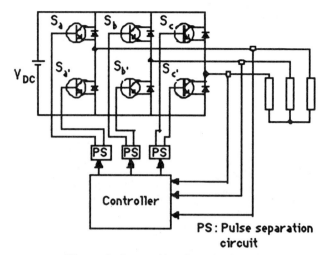

PS : Pulse separation circuit

Figure 6. Conventional control method

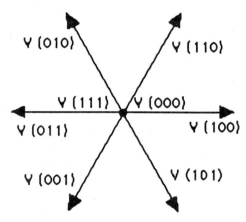

Figure 7. Voltage vector

where i^* is the sinusoidal reference current, i_{ab} is the output current from point a to b in Figure 3, ε is a small error value, such as 0.02. If i_{ab} is less than $i^* - \varepsilon$, then (S1 , S4) turn on and (S2 , S3) turn off which will increase i_{ab}. If i_{ab} is larger than $i^* + \varepsilon$, then (S1 , S4) turn off and (S2 , S3) turn on which will decrease i_{ab}.

Figure 8 shows the neural network inverter control. The three sinusoidal reference currents are $i_{a,ref}$, $i_{b,ref}$, $i_{c,ref}$. Reference currents $i_{b,ref}$ and $i_{c,ref}$ are phase shifted $120°$ and $240°$ respectively from $i_{a,ref}$. First , the three phase currents from the VSI are measured and compared with the three reference currents. The error signals are multiplied by given coefficient, G, and then input to the neural network.

The neural network is trained to have minimum output error. The training rule is

if $|\,i_{m,ref} - i_m\,| < \varepsilon \quad \Rightarrow$ keep O_m at the same state
if $\;i_{m,ref} - i_m \; > \varepsilon \quad \Rightarrow$ let $O_m = 1$
if $\;i_{m,ref} - i_m \; < -\varepsilon \quad \Rightarrow$ let $O_m = 0 \qquad$ (11)

where m = a, b, c, O_m is the output of the neural network. PS is the pulse separation circuit that will keep two output waveforms of PS from overlapping. If the two output waveforms from PS overlap, the upper and lower transistors in one inverter leg will conduct at the time, which will damage the transistors. Finally, as expected, the three current output waveforms of the VSI will follow the three sinusoidal reference currents.

SIMULATION RESULTS

To perform a comparative evaluation of fixed-band hysteresis, sinusoidal-band hysteresis and neural network methods, a simulation model is developed. The system parameters in Figure 8 are

DC bus voltage V = 75 volts
Inductance L = 0.01 mH
Resistance R = 2 Ω
Switching frequency = 19.8 kHz

Simulation results for the output currents of the VSI controlled by fixed-band, sinusoidal-band hysteresis and neural network methods are shown in Figure 9 with G=1 and the hysteresis band, $\Delta i = 0.06$A. From the simulation, the peak to peak current error of phase A is 0.6012 A, the ratio of the number of actual device switchings to the number of possible switchings is about 63.5%, and the variance of current error

$$\sigma = \sqrt{\dfrac{\sum\limits_{k=1}^{n}(\Delta i_k)^2}{n}} \qquad (12)$$

where Δi_k = current error during k-th interval
n = total number of intervals per cycle

is 0.1241 A in the fixed-band hysteresis control method. In the sinusoidal-band hysteresis control method, the peak to peak current error of phase A is 0.5892 A, the ratio of the number of actual device switchings to the number of possible switchings is about 74.85%, and the variance of current error is 0.1103 A. In the neural network control method, the peak to peak current error of phase A is 0.5541 A, the ratio of the

number of actual device switchings to the number of possible switchings is about 64.85%, the variance of current error is 0.1214 A. The neural network control method has lower variance and peak to peak current error than the other two methods. Figure 10 show comparisons of the variance of the current error. The variance of the current error for the fixed-band and sinusoidal-band hysteresis methods increased as the hysteresis band increased, but the variance did not change too much for the neural network method. Figure 11 shows comparisons of the peak to peak current error. The peak to peak current error of the fixed-band and sinusoidal-band hysteresis methods also increased as the hysteresis band increased, but it did not change much with the neural network method. In summary, the sinusoidal-band hysteresis method has less variance and peak to peak current error than that of the fixed-band hysteresis method. The harmonic content of the sinusoidal-band hysteresis method is also lower than that of the fixed-band hysteresis method. The neural network control method has both lower variance and peak to peak current error than that of the fixed-band and sinusoidal-band hysteresis methods.

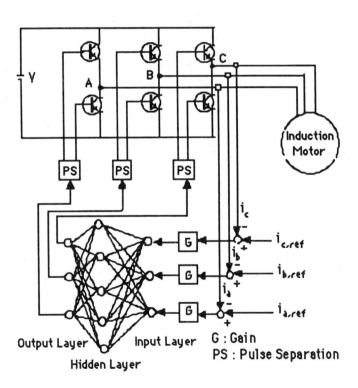

Figure 8. Neural network inverter control

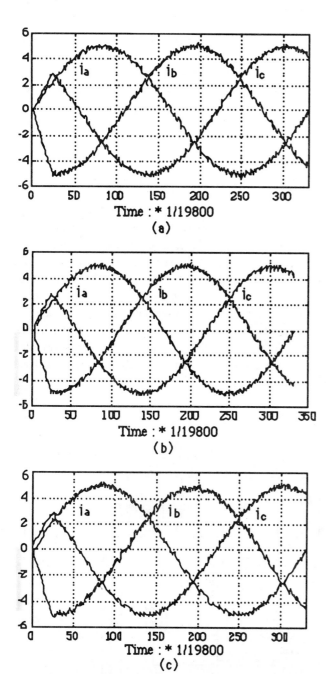

Figure 9. Three phase load current ia, ib, ic
(a) Fixed-band hysteresis method
(b)Sinusoidal-band hysteresis method
(c) Neural network method

Figure 12 shows comparisons of the VSI output current waveforms for a change in frequency command. Figure 13 shows the comparisons of the total harmonic distortion of these three methods.

CONCLUSION

Neural network control of a sinusoidal current controlled VSI is presented in this report. Three different controller structures are considered; first, the fixed-band hysteresis controller; second, the sinusoidal-band hysteresis controller and finally a neural network controller. Simulation results are presented for all the three types of controllers and comparison shows that the neural network control has good characteristics compared to conventional fixed-band and sinusoidal-band hysteresis current control methods. The neural network also has fast processing speed and fault tolerance. The fault tolerance property will allow the neural network to work well even if one of three current sensors failed. Thus, neural networks appear to have significant advantages in power electronic applications.

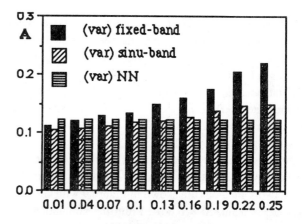

Figure 10. Comparisons of the variance of the current error

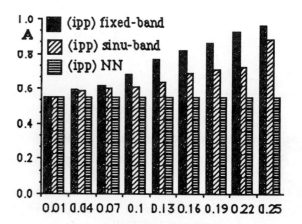

Figure 11. Comparisons of the peak to peak current error

216

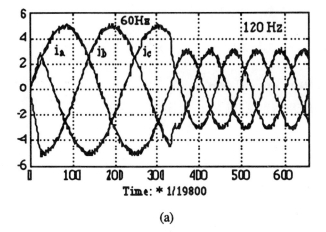

(a)

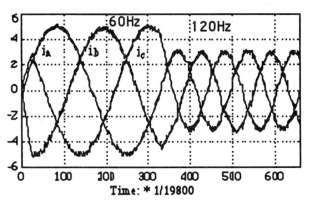

(b)

Figure 12. Inverter output current waveforms for change in frequency command (a) hysteresis control method (b) neural network method.

REFERENCES

[1] D. M. Brod and D. W. Novotny, " Current Control of VSI-PWM Inverters ", IEEE / IAS 1984 Annual Meeting p.418-425

[2] B. K. Bose " An Adaptive Hysteresis-Band Current Control Technique of a Voltage Fed PWM Inverter for Machine Drive System ", IECON 1988 p.684-690

[3] M. R. Azimi-Sadjadi and R. J. Liou " Fast Learning Process of Multilayer Neural Networks Using Recursive Least Squares Method ", IEEE Transactions on Signal Processing Feb. 1992.

[4] G. V. Pushorius and L. A. Feldkamp " Decoupled Extended Kalman Filter Training of Feedforward Layered Networks ", IJCNN 1991 Volume 2, p.771 - 777.

[5] S. Kollias and D. Anastassion ," An Adaptive Least Squares Algorithm For the Efficient Training of Artificial Neural Networks ", IEEE Transactions on Circuits and Systems, 1989, 36, p.1092 - 1101.

[6] W. H. Press B. P. Flannery, S. A. Teukolsky and W. T. Vetterling ," Numerical Recipes in C ", p.317 - 323. 1988 Cambridge.

[7] G. H. Golub and C. F. Vanloan ," Matrix Compulations ", p.516 - 537. 1989, Johns Hopkins.

[8] M. J. D. Powell ," Restart Procedures for the Conjugate Gradient Method ", Mathematical Programming , Vol 12, p.241 - 254, April 1977

[9] David E. Rumelhart , Parallel Distributed Processing , MIT Press, 1986.

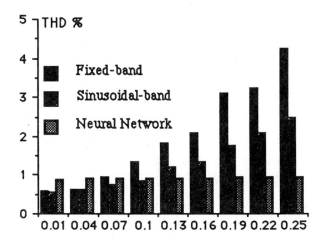

hysteresis band (Δ)

Figure 13. Comparisons of the total harmonic distortion

Application of Neural Network to Operation of Power Generating Units

Kazuo Nishimura*, Haruhiko Iida*,
Hideki Hayashi**, and Toshiaki Asano**

(Toshiba Corporation)

ABSTRACT

This paper proposes a new method based on neural network technology to optimize the operation of generating units. The iterative use of a neural network permits less accuracy of learning and makes the method applicable to larger power systems. Simulations of transmission loss reduction and steady-state stability improvement have demonstrated the effectiveness of the proposed method.

1. INTRODUCTION

Just as Economic Load Dispatch minimizes the operating cost of a power system, proper adjustment of generating unit outputs can realize some objectives of optimization. Some of the objectives such as stability improvement and environmental acceptance are hard to describe in mathematics. A neural network, because of its learning ability, can utilize human experts' heuristics to realize these objectives and provides an effective and generalized means to determine the generating unit outputs.

Some attempts to apply neural networks to optimization of the generating unit operation have been reported[1]-[3] and they have shown the potential advantages of neural networks. However, those studies have been restricted to small scale power system models because the neural networks in those studies have to compute the generating unit outputs accurately. It becomes difficult for neural networks to learn the training data accurately as their scales become larger. The requirement of accurate learning makes some of real world applications very difficult.

(*) R&D Center, Systems & Software Eng. Lab.
70 Yanagi-cho, Saiwai-ku, Kawasaki,
Kanagawa 210, Japan
(**)Fuchu Works
1 Toshiba-cho, Fuchu-shi, Tokyo 183, Japan

In this paper, a new method has been proposed to apply a neural network to determination of generating unit outputs. The proposed method employs the iterative use of a neural network and this scheme permits less accuracy of learning.

The effectiveness of this method has been demonstrated by the simulations of transmission loss reduction on a small scale power system model. The minimized transmission loss has been compared to that obtained through a number of load flow computations. Maximization of steady-state stability has been also employed as an objective of optimization to show that the proposed method copes with another kind of optimization. Finally, the method has been applied to the realistic scale power system model to show its feasibility.

2. METHOD TO DETERMINE OUTPUTS OF POWER GENERATING UNITS

Fig.1 shows the proposed method. The neural network is iteratively used in the computation loop to determine the generating unit outputs. In the i-th iteration (i=1,2...), the neural network computes the desirable direction of generating unit output changes $\{\Delta P_n^{(i+1)}\}$ (n=1,2,...) for the given values of the generating unit outputs $\{P_n^{(i)}\}$ (n=1,2,...) and the system loads $\{L_m\}$ (m=1,2,...). The system loads are assumed to be constant during the computation. As $\{\Delta P^{(i)}\}$ include errors depending on degree of learning, $\{P_n^{(i)}\}$ are updated by the refrained increments $\{\varepsilon \Delta P_n^{(i)}\}$ as follows.

$$P_n^{(i+1)} \leftarrow P_n^{(i)} + \varepsilon \Delta P_n^{(i)} \quad (0 < \varepsilon < 1.0) \quad \ldots (1)$$

The coefficient ε should be smaller when the power system becomes larger. The neural network receives this updated outputs $\{P_n^{(i+1)}\}$, and the direction vector $\{\Delta P_n^{(i+1)}\}$ is computed. The same process is iterated untill the direction vector $\{\Delta P_n\}$ becomes very small. The final updated outputs $\{P_n\}$ are employed to change the unit outputs. In this

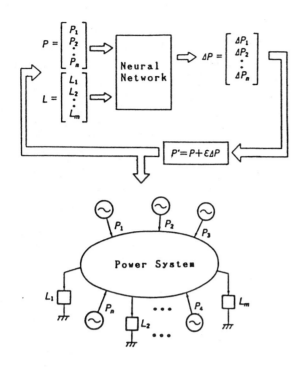

Fig.1 Proposed Method to Determine Generating
Unit Outputs by Iterative Use of
Neural Network

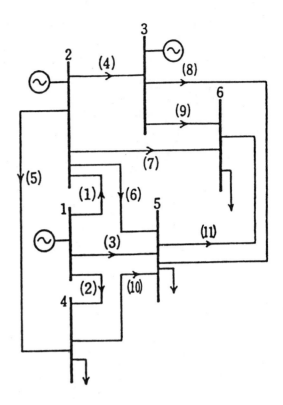

Fig.2 Small Scale Power System Model

scheme, the effect of error in {Pn} is supressed so long as the {Pn} is not far from the power output vectors in the training data.

Once the vector {Pn} is updated, it becomes an unknown vector for the neural network whether the initial vector is included in the training set or not. Then, the interpolation ability of the neural network is very important in this method.

3. SIMULATION ON SMALL SCALE POWER SYSTEM MODEL

The power system model employed here is shown in Fig.2. It consists of 3 machines and 3 system loads[4]. The neural network has 6 input, 10 hidden, and 3 output units. The output unit for the slack node is redundant. It has learnt 35 training patterns. Backpropagation has been employed for the training. The training patterns are composed of 7 system load conditions and 5 variations of generating unit outputs for each of the system load conditions. The totals of the system loads are all 2.1 [pu] in this trainig data. Another load level has been used to check the robustness of this method in the following simulations.

3.1 TRANSMISSION LOSS REDUCTION

The employment of a neural network would be meaningless if the objective of operation is solely to reduce transmission loss because the objective

can be described mathematically. The advantages of neural networks will be obtained when the operation has to depend on human experts' heuristics. Transmission loss reduction is employed here because the effect of the proposed method can be quantitatively evaluated by its comparison to the exact solution.

The investigation here assumes that the training data are almost ideal;that is, the training data have been made by load flow computations so that the data are consistent. When the operation must be based on heuristics, the training data would be made more or less by intuition.

Fig.3 shows transmission loss reductions by the neural network that has learnt the 35 training data. The instruction of 35 patterns is counted as one learning trial. The initial input vector consisting of {Pn} and {Lm} (n,m=1,2,3) is an unknown pattern for the neural network. The total of the system loads is 2.3[pu] and heavier than 2.1 [pu] of the training data. The network leads to substantial loss reductions not only when fully trained (2500 trials) but also when trained poorly(500 and 250 trials). Even the very poor learning(100 trials) results in a certain amount of loss reduction. This result suggests that the learning accuracy is not so critical in the proposed method.

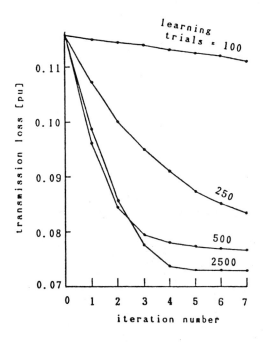

Fig.3 Transmission Loss Reduction
(Small Scale Power System Model)

Table 1 compares the transmission loss minimized by the neural network and that obtained by a number of load flow computations. They are in good agreement. This result suggests that the proposed neural network method is comparable to the exact computation so long as the consistent training data are obtainable. It is more difficult to prepare consistent training data for larger power systems.

Table 1 Comparison of Transmission Losses Minimized by Neural Network to Those Obtained by Load Flow Computations

System Loads [pu]			Minimum Transmission Losses [pu]	
L_1	L_2	L_3	Neural Network(•)	Load Flow Computations
0.7	0.7	0.7	0.067	0.067
0.5	0.6	1.0	0.065	0.065
1.0	0.6	0.5	0.073	0.072
0.9	0.6	0.6	0.070	0.069
0.6	0.9	0.6	0.071	0.070
0.6	0.6	0.9	0.065	0.065
0.55	1.0	0.55	0.074	0.073

(•) values at 7th iteration

3.2 STEADY-STATE STABILITY IMPROVEMENT

While transmission loss is a real value and uniquely determined, steady-state stability is more qualitative. However, as the performance of the neural network should be evaluated quantitatively, the following index has been used for convenience.

$$I = \Sigma_k \mid \delta i^{(k)} - \delta j^{(k)} \mid \quad ...(2)$$

where, $\delta i^{(k)}$ and $\delta j^{(k)}$ are the voltage angles of the sending and receiving ends, respectively, of the k-th transmission line. The lower value of this index indicates the higher stability. The trainig data have been made to lower the index. The other conditions are the same as in the above section. Fig.4 shows that the neural network leads to augmentation of steady-state stability.

One of the advantages of the proposed method is that the same scheme can deal with different objectives of optimization. The operating modes of the generating units can be switched by changing the weight coefficients of the neural network. For example, an energy saving mode may be used for ordinary operation and it may be switched to a high stability mode when the system loads become heavy.

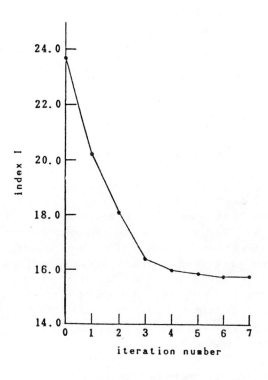

Fig.4 Steady-State Stability Improvement

4. SIMULATION ON REALISTIC SCALE POWER SYSTEM MODEL

The simulation of transmission loss reduction on the small scale power system model has shown that the proposed method permits less accuracy of learning. As a result, the proposed method is applicable to a larger power system although the final state of the power system may not be the optimal but the better one. However, it is difficult to prepare training data for a larger power system even if the objective of optimization can be described mathematically. Intuition will be necessary to prepare the training data.

The proposed method has been applied to the power system model consisting of 70 nodes, 16 machines, and 26 system loads. This model has been developed based on some real power system, although they are not identical. The neural network has 42 input, 10 hidden, and 16 output units. The training data have been made by intuition. For example, for an increase of some system load, the supervising data have been made to increase the outputs of the units near the load. As the purpose of this investigation is to show that the proposed method can be applied to a realistic scale power system model, the number of system states are limited to make the investigation easy. The neural network has learnt the 14 training data by Backpropagation. The learning trials are 10000 when the instruction of 14 patterns is counted as one learning trial.

Transmission loss is again used here to show the effect of the proposed method quantitatively. Although the quality of the training data is poor, the neural network still leads to a considerable reduction of transmission loss as shown in Fig.5. It turns out from this result that the training data by intuition can be effective if the intuition is based on proper heuristics.

5. CONCLUSIONS

The new method to determine the generating unit outputs based on a neural network has been proposed. The neural network is iteratively used for modifications of generating unit outputs in computation loop. This scheme permits looser learning accuracy and enables the application of a neural network not only to small scale power system models but also to realistic scale power system models.

The simulation of transmission loss reduction on the small scale power system model has shown that the proposed method is comparable to the exact solution in terms of optimizing performance so long as the training data are almost ideal.

The simulation of steady-state stability improvement on the small scale power system model has suggested that the proposed scheme can be applicable to different objectives of optimization. The different operating modes of generating units will be selected by changing the weight coefficients of the neural network.

The simulation on the realistic scale power system model has shown that the training data obtained by intuition can be effective. This result indicates the feasibility of the generating unit operation based on human experts' heuristics for realistic scale power systems.

REFERENCES

(1) S.Matsuda and Y.Akimoto,"The Representation of Large Numbers in Neural Networks and Its Application to Economical Load Dispatching of Electric Power",IJCNN89, Washington D.C., I-587 - I-592, June, 1989

(2) Y.Uekl and Y.Fukuyama,"Application of Neural Network to Dynamic ELD", National Convention, JIEE, no.1044, 1990

(3) K.Saito and J.Toyoda,"Application of Neural Network to Load Dispatch", National Convention, JIEE, no.1190, 1991.

(4) A.J.Wood and B.F.Wollenberg,"Power Generation, Operation, and Control",pp.413, John Willey & Son, 1984

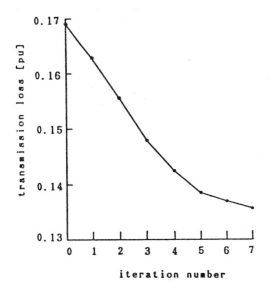

Fig.5 Transmission Loss Reduction
(Realistic Scale Power System Model)

Optimal Operation of Photovoltaic/Diesel Power Generation System by Neural Network

Yasuharu Ohsawa, Shin-ichi Emura and Kenji Arai
Dept. of Electrical and Electronics Eng.
Kobe University
Kobe, 657 Japan

Abstract

In this paper an artificial neural network is applied to the operation control of the photovoltaic/diesel hybrid power generation system. The optimal operation patterns of the diesel generator are calculated by dynamic programming (DP) under the known insolation and load demand, which minimize the fuel consumption of the diesel generator. These optimal patterns are learned by the three layers neural network, and it is tested for the different insolation and demand data from those used in the learning. Two kinds of neural networks are examined, and the results are compared with each other.

1 Introduction

Many isolated islands in Japan are supplied electric power mainly by diesel generators. But diesel generation has some problems, e.g. bad maintainability, unreliable fuel supply and high generation cost. One method in order to alleviate these problems is a photovoltaic/diesel hybrid generation system, which consists of solar cells (SCs), storage batteries (Batt.s) and diesel generators (DGs). In this system, diesel generators are used as a supplementary power supply for charging the storage battery, and is operated near the full output point as long as possible in order to attain the highest generation efficiency and reduce the fuel consumption.

The operation of the photovoltaic/diesel hybrid system should be determined according to the output power of the solar cell, the load demand power, the stored energy of the battery and the capacity of the diesel generator. Although empirical operation rules have been proposed so far, and they can be said reasonable, they are not the optimal operation rules with regard to the fuel consumption. If the insolation and the load demand are known, it is possible to obtain the optimal operation. However, it is difficult to operate the hybrid system optimally under the uncertain insolation and load demand.

This paper examines the possibility of using an artificial neural network for the operation control of the photovoltaic/diesel hybrid system. First, under the known insolation and load demand, the optimal operation pattern of the diesel generators are calculated by dynamic programming (DP) method, which minimize the fuel consumption without causing power supply interruption. Next, the neural network (NN) learns this optimal operation, and the neural network can operate the hybrid system under a new insolation and demand condition. Two kinds of neural networks are examined, and the results of the computer simulation of the learning are presented. The obtained neural network is tested for the different insolation and demand data from those used in the learning, and its validity is examined.

2 Photovoltaic/Diesel Hybrid System

A photovoltaic/diesel hybrid system consists of solar cells, batteries and diesel generators. As shown in Fig.1, two types of hybrid system can be considered, that is, dc connected type and ac connected type[1]. In either type, the output from the solar cell first supplys the load demand, and the remainder is stored in the battery. The diesel generator is used to charge the battery or to supply the load in case of the shortage of the solar power.

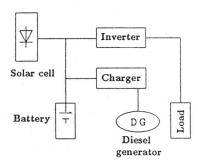

(a) dc connected type

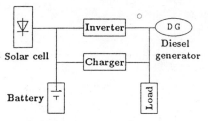

(b) ac connected type

Figure 1: Two types of hybrid system.

In the dc connected system, the output of the solar cell and the output of the diesel generator are connected on dc, and the dc power is supplied to the load after the dc-ac conversion. The control of this type is rather simple, since the connection is done on the dc side. The efficiency is low, however, because the output of the diesel generator is converted as ac-dc-ac. In order to improve the efficiency, it is necessary to make the operation time of the diesel generator short. Hence, dc connected type is suitable for the system with high solar percent. In the high solar percent system, a large portion of the load demand is supplied from the solar cell and the battery, and more than 50% of the solar power is supplied to the load through the battery. Since the charge-discharge efficiency of the battery is not high (60-80%), the overall efficiency becomes low.

In the ac connected type, the solar cell and the diesel generator are connected on the ac side, and the ac power is supplied to the load directly. Although the control of this type is more complex than the dc connected type, the drop of the efficiency due to the power conversion is elliminated, since the output power from the diesel generator is directly supplied to the load. Also, flexible operation of the photovoltaic generation and diesel generator is possible. In this paper we suppose the ac connected system.

When the insolation is high, the load is supplied from the solar cell, and the surplus power is stored in the battery as shown in Fig.2(a). If the insolation becomes low, the battery supplies the load (Fig.2(b)). If the stored energy of the battery becomes lower than the limit value, the diesel generator is started up and the load is supplied from the diesel generator, and also, the battery is charged by the generator (Fig.2(c)).

A small isolated island whose daily load demand averaged for a year is about 30kW is chosen as a model site of the photovoltaic/diesel hybrid system. The optimal operation of the hybrid system is calculated, and the learning of the results by neural network is examined. The monthly average daily load curve is given for every hour. The rating of the solar cell, the battery and the diesel generator are 130kWp, 130kWh and 45kW, respectively, which are the adequate values for the load assumed. The energy conversion efficiency of the solar cell and the charge-discharge efficiency of the battery are assumed to be 10% and 80%, respectively. The fuel consumption rate versus output power of the diesel generator is taken from measured data at an island. The efficiency of the inverter (Inv.) and the battery charger are assumed 100%.

3 Calculation of Optimal Operation by Dynamic Programming

For the hybrid system mentioned in the preceding section, the optimal operation, which is used as the training data for the neural net-

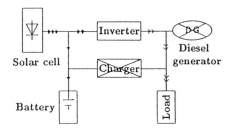

(a) high insolation

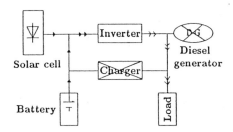

(b) low insolation

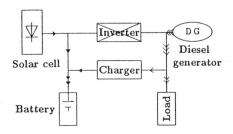

(c) low insolation and low Batt.SOC

× : not in operation
→ : flow of dc power
⇒ : flow of ac power

Figure 2: Operation modes of hybrid system.

work, is calculated by dynamic programming method[2]. The insolation data are given for every hour every day in a year. They are the values measured in Kochi Prefecture; the southern area in Japan. The solar cell array is installed facing the south and its inclination angle is equal to the latitude at the installed site. The battery can be discharged until the depth of discharge of 0.7. Since the objective of the optimal operation is to minimize the fuel consumption without causing power supply interruption, the performance index to be minimized is chosen as the fuel consumption with the large penalty in case of supply interruption. Furthermore, in order to avoid frequent start and stop of the diesel generator, start-up cost is added to the performance index.

Time is sampled every one hour, and the state of charge of the battery (batt.SOC) between 0.3 and 1.0 is digitized into 100 steps (Fig.3). Both the initial value and the final value of the battery state of charge are set 65 kWh.

223

Batt. SOC

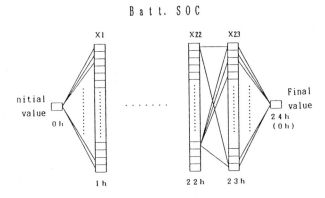

Figure 3: Solution by dynamic programming.

4 Learning of Optimal Operation by Neural Network

The learning by NN of the optimal operations obtained in the preceding section is examined. The NN used is a multilayer type (3 layers) NN. One NN has four input units and one output unit. As shown in Fig.4, the inputs are the battery state of charge, the solar cell output (or equivalently the insolation power), the load, the present time of the day and the one for threshold value. The number of the hidden layer units is 12, and the output is the output power of the diesel generator. The other NN has 13 inputs; three inputs in Fig.4 (Batt.SOC, SC output and load) are given not only the present value, but the values for three hours; the value for three hours ago, two hours ago and one hour ago. The input-output function of each unit is the sigmoid function. Error back propagation algorithm is used for the learning, where the learning rate and the coefficient of momentum term are 0.1 and 0.9, respectively. Data for 15 days in May are chosen as the training data.

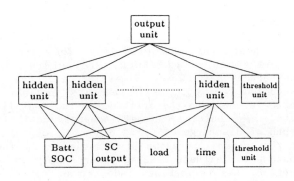

Figure 4: Construction of neural network.

Fig.5 shows the learning characteristics for two NNs. The learning converges faster for the NN with 13 inputs than for the one with 4 inputs. The oeration by NN with 13 inputs is shown in Fig.6(a) for one day. The optimal control by DP and the controls by NNs are compared with each other in Fig.6(b). Although the optimal

control is learned fairly well by either NN for this day, the results by NN with 13 inputs is better than those by NN with 4 inputs. By the NN with 4 inputs, several days could not be learned properly. One example from them is shown in Fig.7. Using the NN with 13 inputs the same data could be learned better as shown in Fig.7(b).

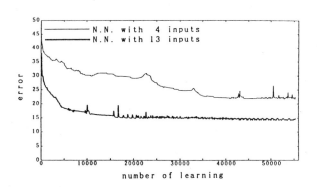

Figure 5: Convergence of learning.

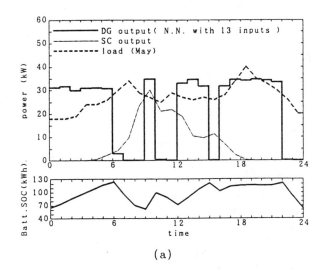

(a)

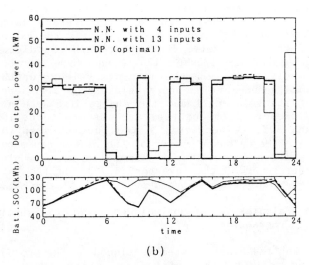

(b)

Figure 6: Operation by NN for training data.

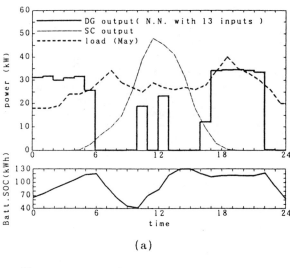

(a)

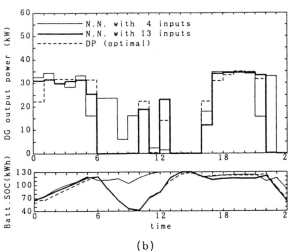

(b)

Figure 7: Operation by NN for training data.

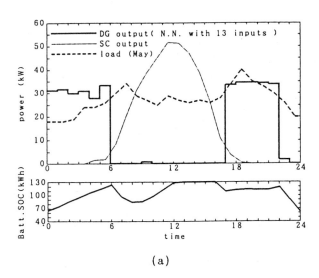

(a)

Fig.8(a) and Fig.9(a) show the control by NN with 13 inputs for untrained fine day and cloudy day in May, respectively. For either day, the stored energy in the battery remains above the lower limit, and the power supply interruption does not occur. The comparison of the results

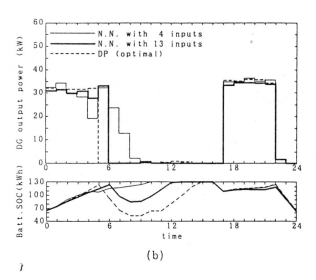

(b)

Figure 8: Operation by NN for untrained data.
(fine day in May)

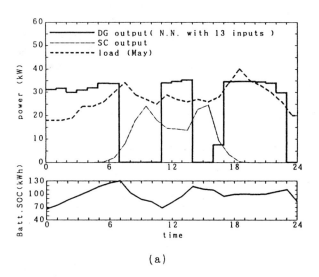

(a)

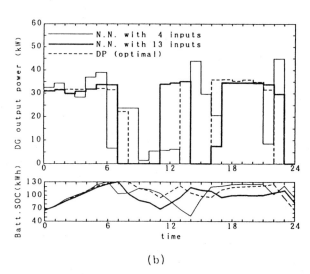

(b)

Figure 9: Operation by NN for untrained data.
(cloudy day in May)

for the same day by NN with 4 inputs, by NN with 13 inputs and by DP is shown in Fig.8(b) and Fig.9(b). The results for another load demand curve (the load demand for February) are shown in Fig.10.

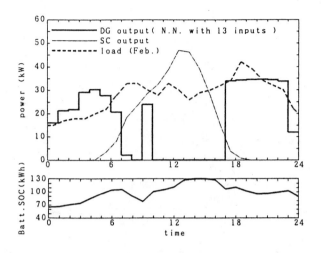

Figure 10: Operation by NN for untrained data. (load demand curve for Feb.)

5 Conclusions

The application of artificial neural network to the operation control of photovoltaic/diesel hybrid generation system was examined. Two kinds of NNs are compared with each other, and the performance of the one with larger number of input units is better than the other. The results can be said encouraging. In order to improve the results further, utilization of another type of NN suitable for learning time series data, e.g. recurrent network, is to be examined.

References

[1] M. Tsukamoto, et al.,"Optimization of Equipments Size of Photovoltaic Power System with Diesel Generator," Energy and Resources, Vol.10, No.4, pp.372-378, 1989.(in Japanese)

[2] Y. Ohsawa, et al.,"Operation of Photovoltaic Power Generation Systems by Neural Network," Proc. of IEEE Int. Conf. on Systems Eng., pp.491-494, 1992.

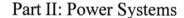

Part II: Power Systems

The power industry has both supported and successfully employed neural networks in several different areas since the early 1990's. Work in this area spans the globe, with a great deal of activity in the United States, Japan, and India. Because of the sheer pervasiveness of electric power, even small improvements can lead to tremendous savings and increased profits. To date, there have been two highly successful conferences dedicated to this topic entitled the *International Forum on Applications of Neural Networks to Power Systems (ANNPS)*.

This part of the book covers the three most active power application areas: fault detection (Chapter 7), load forecasting (Chapter 8), and security assessment (Chapter 9). Power system applications that fall outside of these three areas have been combined into a fourth chapter entitled other power applications areas (Chapter 10).

Power System Fault Detection

Abnormality diagnosis of power equipment before a fatal crash occurs is vital to the reliability of power generation facilities. A large number of data streams must be monitored continually to detect small changes that could lead to catastrophic failures. Neural networks have been repeatedly demonstrated to be excellent candidates for such applications. The five papers in this chapter illustrate unique neural network approaches to the power system fault detection problem. **Paper 7.1** applies adaptive resonance theory (ART) neural networks to abnormality diagnosis in Gas Insulated Switchgear (GIS). **Paper 7.2** uses the Boltzmann Machine neural network to estimate the fault section in a power system. **Paper 7.3** employs multilayer perceptron (MLP) neural networks to locate faults in power transmission lines. **Paper 7.4** combines neural networks and knowledge-based systems to understand the underlying cause of a detected fault. **Paper 7.5** uses the MLP to detect Corona discharge in power cables.

Chapter 7:   *Fault Detection*

ABNORMALITY DIAGNOSIS OF GIS USING ADAPTIVE RESONANCE THEORY

Hiromi OGI   Hideo TANAKA
Yoshiakira AKIMOTO
Computer & Communication Research Center
Tokyo Electric Power Company (TEPCO)
1-4-10, Irifune, Chuo-ku, Tokyo 104 JAPAN
ogi@aisun.tepco.co.jp

Yoshio IZUI
Industrial Systems Laboratory
Mitsubishi Electric Corporation
8-1-1,Tsukaguchi Honmachi,Amagasaki
Hyogo,661 JAPAN
izui@soc.sdl.melco.co.jp

Abstract

The paper presents an artificial neural network(ANN) approach using ART2(Adaptive Resonance Theory 2) to a diagnostic system for a Gas Insulated Switchgear(GIS). To begin with, we will show the background of abnormality diagnosis of GISs from the view point of predictive maintenance of them. Then, we will discuss the necessity of ART-type ANNs, as an unsupervised learning method, in which neuron(s) are self-organized and self-created when detecting unexpected signals even if un-trained by ANNs through a sensor. Finally, we will present our brief simulation results and their evaluation.

Keywords : Gas Insulated Switchgear, Adaptive Resonance Theory, Artificial Neural Network, Abnormality Diagnosis

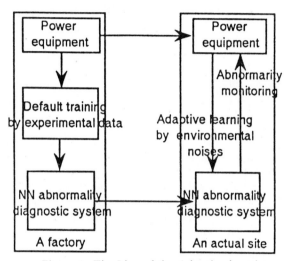

Figure 1: The Idea of the Adaptive learning

1   Introduction

Abnormality diagnosis of power equipment such as GISs, before a fatal fault occurs in a power system in particular, is playing an important role in keeping the reliability of electricity supply. It requires the advanced information processing technologies either to process analog signals attached to the equipment or to identify the abnormality more quickly. There have been a lot of sensing devices or systems developed and attached to power equipment so far. The principle of them, however, is a kind of level-detection method, by which a monitoring system only catches the magnitude of a signal and transfers it to a maintenance personnel at the control center. Such a diagnostic system has little abilities of noise tolerance, location and cause of abnormality as well as precise and quick identification.

On the other hand, ANNs that simulate human nervous system may have new abilities such as learning, adaptation, self-organization that have big potential in abnormality diagnosis. Among the variety of ANN architectures, the need for self-organized and self-enhanced ANNs like ART2 arises as a function of the diagnostic system to adapt ANN itself to the equipment variations, actual environmental variations and unexpected abnormalities.

As power equipment under operation in an actual site has very little fault possibilities, we have no way obtaining abnormality data for ANN training except through factory experiments. As for the equipment variations, we have several kinds of types of GISs that each training set may be

required for every type of GIS. However, if we can assume a typical GIS and make the diagnostic system adapt to the other GISs, no training data for them may be needed any more.

As for the actual environmental variations, the environment in which GISs are equipped is different from the one in the factory. In addition, seasons and weather make the environmental variations. Unless the diagnostic system adapts itself to the environmental variations, it may misclassify an environmental noise as an abnormal status. The diagnostic system must adapt itself to the actual environment through self-training the external noises under operation of equipment.

As for the unexpected abnormality problem, this means that there may not be included in the already-trained abnormality-cause set of data. Even in this situation we require the diagnostic system that can classify the unexpected abnormality as not abnormal status but unusual status. In the paper the abnormal status means just abnormal identified by inspection of the equipment, and the no-normal status means the one including whether an abnormality or a noise.

We call the concepts above adaptability of the diagnostic system in the paper. ANNs that have static characteristics never resolve those problems, because they learn only pre-obtained training set and lack the adaptability. ART2-type ANNs, however, may have the potential of the adaptability to resolve those problems because of its self-organization and self-enhancement capabilities.

2 Predictive Maintenance for GISs

2.1 Predictive Maintenance

The fundamental idea of predictive maintenance is that detecting signals through sensors as symptoms of an abnormality before a fatal damage of equipment happen, allows us to keep the normal operation for the equipment. Even if a small signal of the symptom is found in the equipment, with the signal magnitude of the phenomena becoming larger, that may lead to a fatal damage of the equipment. That is, it is important for the predictive maintenance system that it has to detect smaller symptoms before a fatal fault. To get better performance of diagnosis, we have to consider both sensing devices and signal processing technologies.

2.2 Sensing devices for GISs

It is popular to catch the symptoms from the partial discharge phenomena in order to detect abnormalities of GISs. The symptoms include sound, flush, heat, gas contamination, electro-magnetic waves and leakage current etc. occurred inside an enclosure of the GIS. Sensing devices must catch these physical signals out of the enclosure. There are some devices such as acceleration sensor detecting mechanical vibration, supersonic sensor, differential voltage sensor, gas checker detecting dissolved insulation gas, and so on. It is said that sensing devices themselves have higher performance.

2.3 Signal Processing of Sensor Output

The principle of conventional method was level-detection of signal magnitude. That is, if the output of a sensor is over a threshold level set in advance, the judgement is abnormal. On the other hand, if it is under the threshold, the judgement is considered as normal. Only whether normal or abnormal can be identified by the method. Precise judgement is also very difficult in the method. We have a premise that abnormal conditions has always bigger signals than threshold level manufacturers usually decided. Sometime, misclassification may happen because an environmental noise makes the signal output distorted.

3 Adaptive Learning

3.1 Why Adaptive Learning?

There are problems discussed so far in developing GIS diagnostic system even if ANN technologies are employed. The problems are related to;

- Unexpected abnormality

- Environmental noise variations

- Equipment structure variations

The problems above may be expected to be resolve by the adaptive learning of self-organized and self-enhanced ANNs.

3.1.1 Unexpected Abnormality

Generally speaking, few abnormality in the equipment has been found out in its operation. Imaginary abnormal conditions have been pre-defined and experimented to obtain some abnormal data for NN training in a manufacturer's factory of GISs.[5] If these abnormal data are trained by an ANN, whether supervised-training or unsupervised-training, correct classifications would be provided according to their abnormality-cause training set. Unexpected abnormality or no-normal status, however, would not be guaranteed to identify the cause of it even if any conventional technology is used. Although ANN may not identify what the cause is, ANN is expected to classify it as the other abnormality-cause pattern which has not been trained so far.

3.1.2 Environmental Noise

The data for training have been acquired in a manufacturer's factory, where several experiments are conducted on the target equipment with some sensing devices and under better condition in general than an actual site. The training data are obtained with some noises in factory environment, which may not be the same as the ones in a site environment. To solve the problem training data should be directly measured in the site, after that, additional abnormality-cause data set should be trained to the ANN. The actual environment, however, varies from hour to hour, for example, weather variation such as fine and rainy, calm and windy. Some are the sounds of circuit breakers and disconnecting switches, Some are the vibrations from steps of inspection personnel and from collisions between the enclosure and rainfalls. We can not obtain data of all those variations for ANN training. One of the compromising approaches is the combination of default training in the factory and self-training during a certain period in the site, where a new pattern not including the default training patterns, is regarded as normal status temporally.

3.1.3 Equipment Variation

ANN approaches require sufficient and non-partial data for training, which come from a fixed-object environment. The fixed-object means that training data obtained from a specified GIS are available to the very GIS which has the same specifications on its physical structures. It is expected that typical GISs should be experimented with an ANN for the default training, the ANN trained should be built in the other GISs.

3.2 Method for Adaptive Learning

Figure 1 shows the method for the default training and adaptive learning. In the manufacturer's factory, a diagnostic with an ANN is trained by artificially-generated abnormality data from a standard equipment (Default training). In a site of a power company, the equipment is transported to the site and equipped with an environment under operation, the diagnostic system is also attached to the equipment, and monitoring the external noises for certain period as well as the internal status of the equipment.

3.3 Constraints for Adaptive Learning

One of the easiest way of adaptive learning is to continue to re-train on-line data which are obtained and restored in memories as comparing them with already-stored data. The way has at least two constraints, there are;

- As the way has to restore the past training data, a large amount of memories will be required and that lineally increased according to time in the diagnostic system.

- Strictly speaking, the way has no supervised signal of training, so that a human has to teach what the signal means and why it comes from after the system detected an unexpected data.

3.4 Behavior of Adaptive Learning NN

We considered that the current training data are only used in the default training stage without storing the past-trained data. The diagnostic system should be able to identify either the abnormality cause which was already-trained during default training or no-abnormal status that is unexpected abnormality which was no alternative in the training pairs.

If the hierarchical NN is used in the diagnostic system, it may judge the identification well for well-trained pairs, but a large amount of memory may be required in the case of hierarchical NN, because all the training data in the past must be restored. In order to cope with the constraints above, the output neurons of the adaptive learning NN should be labeled, when one of them is already-trained as default training is invoked, the label of the neuron is displayed, when there happens an input pattern which is not included in the default learning pairs, an additional neuron of the output will be generated with a label of input signal or pattern not already-trained so far. As in this stage it is difficult for the system to identify the abnormality-cause of the generated neuron, a human expert may have to teach the cause of no-normality to the system.

4 Basis of ART2

4.1 Why ART2?

To meet the constraints with NN architectures, ART2(Adaptive Resonance Theory 2) with analog data is examined in the beginning of the study, because it has features of self-organization for unexpected changes in an external environment and that autonomously and in real-time. In the basic idea of ART2, a bottom-up information is focused on an expectation based on a top-down information, so that past memory would not be erased by new learning events. If a learning event is not stored in a database, the data will be stored in the database without inconsistency.

4.2 Outline of ART2

ART2 was proposed by Carpenter&Grossberg of Boston University in 1986.[6, 7, 8] There are some versions like ART1 for binary data, ART2 for analogous data and ART3 refined by biological findings. The ART2 features sensory system for creatures which can simulate to autonomously learn and identify patterns from the continuous signals including noise input under on-line and real-time conditions. The structure of the ART2 is two-layered network which consists of input neurons and output neurons labeled by invoked patterns. The ART2 is one of the unsupervised and feedback-type NNs which means that information of output neurons affects the input neurons. We focus on the features capable of on-line, real-time and self-trained pattern classifier.

The learning algorithm of ART2 is based on the Hebbian learning rule which is the connections of neurons enhanced each other when they are excited at the same time. The ART2 is a self-created neural network model, which uses a clustering algorithm. The algorithm is that the similarity of input patterns is compared with already-learned LTM(Long term Memory)s, the most similar LTM is revised by the input pattern. If the degree of the similarity is less than the pre-defined threshold, that is the input pattern is not similar than any other past-trained patterns, then the new input pattern will be stored in the LTMs. There are two differences between the ART2 and conventional clustering. In the conventional clustering, clustering center and input pattern are normalized by unit vector, on the other hand, in the ART2, they are not always normalized because of biological findings. The ART2 takes the approach of resonance between an input pattern and the LTM, which means the ART2 revises the input pattern based on the LTM after it remembers the most similar LTM.

4.3 Dynamics of ART2

Figure 2 illustrates some ART2 dynamics features. There are two principal fields of ART2, one is an attentional subsystem which contains an input representation field F_1 and a category representation field F_2, and an orienting subsystem which interacts with the attentional subsystem. The two fields are linked by both a bottom-up adaptive filter and a top-down adaptive filter. A path from the ith F_1 node to the jth F_2 node contains a long term memory(LTM) trace, or adaptive weight z_{ij}. The $\mathbf{I}$ is an input vector of a signal, the vector $\mathbf{w}$ is the sum of the input vector $\mathbf{I}$.

Each rectangle shows a short term memory(STM), in which internal feedback signal vector $a\mathbf{u_i}$ and activity vector $\mathbf{x_i}$ are calculated.

$$\mathbf{w_i} = \mathbf{I_i} + a\mathbf{u_i} \qquad (1)$$

$$\mathbf{u_i} = \frac{\mathbf{v_i}}{\|\mathbf{v}\|} \qquad (2)$$

$$\mathbf{x_i} = \frac{\mathbf{w_i}}{\|\mathbf{w}\|} \qquad (3)$$

At the top F_1 layer $\mathbf{p}$ sums both the internal F_1 signal $\mathbf{u}$ and all the $F_2 \rightarrow F_1$ filtered signals. That is,

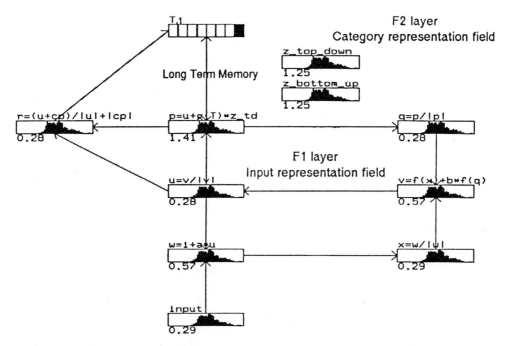

Figure 2: Dynamics of ART2

$$\mathbf{P_i} = \mathbf{u_i} + \sum_j g(\mathbf{y_i})\mathbf{z_{ji}} \qquad (4)$$

where $g(\mathbf{y_i})$ is the output signal from the $\mathbf{j}$th F_2 node and $\mathbf{z_{ji}}$ is the LTM trace in the path from the $\mathbf{j}$th F_2 node to the $\mathbf{i}$th F_1 node.

$$\mathbf{q_i} = \frac{\mathbf{P_i}}{\|\mathbf{p}\|} \qquad (5)$$

$$\mathbf{v_i} = f(\mathbf{x_i}) + bf(\mathbf{q_i}) \qquad (6)$$

$$f(x) = \begin{cases} 0 & if \quad 0 \le x \le \theta \\ \theta & if \quad x \ge \theta \end{cases} \qquad (7)$$

There is a resonance in the LTM between $\mathbf{T_j}$ and p. The vector $\mathbf{r}$ monitors the degree of match between F_1 bottom-up input $\mathbf{I}$ and the top-down input $d\mathbf{z_j}$. System reset occurs if $\|\mathbf{r}\| < \rho$, where ρ is a dimensionless vigilance parameter between 0 and 1. Vector $\mathbf{r}$ obeys the following equation.

$$\mathbf{r_i} = \frac{\mathbf{u_i} + c\mathbf{p_i}}{\|\mathbf{u}\| + \|c\mathbf{p}\|} \qquad (8)$$

$$\rho > \|\mathbf{r}\| \qquad (9)$$

Suffix shows the number of a neuron(the element number of vectors), $\| * \|$ is a norm and a, b, c, d are appropriate parameters.

$$\frac{dz\mathbf{ij}}{dt} = g(\mathbf{y_j})[\mathbf{p_i} - \mathbf{z_{ji}}] \qquad (10)$$

$$\frac{dz\mathbf{ji}}{dt} = g(\mathbf{y_j})[\mathbf{p_i} - \mathbf{z_{ji}}] \qquad (11)$$

$$g(\mathbf{y_j}) = \begin{cases} d & if \quad \mathbf{T_j} = max_j \mathbf{T_j} \\ 0 & otherwise \end{cases} \qquad (12)$$

$$\mathbf{T_j} = \sum_i \mathbf{p_i} \mathbf{z_{ij}} \qquad (13)$$

In the short term memory, although we have to note that differential equations(8) and (9) should be calculated as well as LTM, so that we can get calculation time shorten by calculating the stable status. Equation(7) means the value less than θ is regard as noise, there is no problem even if it is ignored.

In the long term memory, $\mathbf{z_{ij}}$ or $\mathbf{z_{ji}}$ is equivalent to a kind of template or prototype. Equation(10) and (11) are learning equations. The most similar template is selected by equation(12) and (13). After the template is compared with the evaluation function $\mathbf{r}$, a new neuron is generated in the long term memory if the value is less than ρ.

In the actual ART2 diagnostic system implementation, abnormality-cause label should be assigned to the neuron $\mathbf{T_j}$ in the LTM when the cause is already known.

5 Simulation

5.1 Data Acquisition

We had conducted a field experiment for data acquisition from the 275kV GCB(Gas-insulated Circuit Breaker) to evaluate the methodology of identifying abnormalities during April 19— April 28,1991 at the TAMAHARA Power-station in TEPCO. The result showed that there was no abnormality during the experiment. The data were acquired from one acceleration sensor fixed by metallic enclosure and protected out of external vibrations, so that in fact only data we got during the period was the ON/OFF switching signal from the circuit breaker.

On the other hand, we have also carried out a prelimi-nary test generating abnormal conditions at the factory of the GIS Manufacturer during November — December,1992 to get continuous signal of two kinds of sensors which were

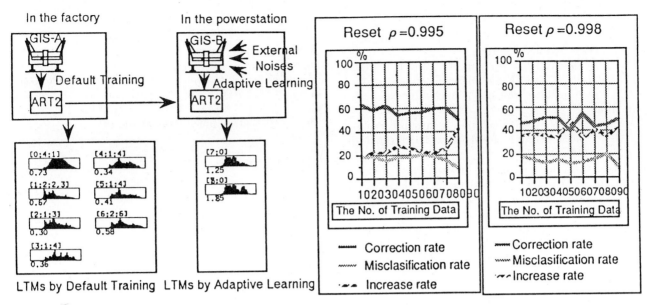

In the factory   In the powerstation

LTMs by Default Training   LTMs by Adaptive Learning

Figure 3: Default training and Adaptive training

Figure 4: Reset threshold

originally mounted on the enclosure of GIS, that is, an acceleration sensor and a differential voltage sensor.

In the first step we assumed six patterns of experimental conditions of abnormalities which include particles inside an enclosure of GIS and bad contacts modeled by a small gap between conductors and a loose-coupled ring around a conductor. A particle made of a thin aluminum wire of 1mm diameter and a ring around a conductor were used in the experiment. The abnormalities caused by particles were modeled by particle fixed on the conductor, the one fixed on the enclosure and floating one within the enclosure. These particles and bad contacts make partial discharge inside the enclosure under high voltage, which vibrates the insulated gas of SF_6 and the enclosure itself. The acceleration sensor mounted on the outside of the enclosure detects the acceleration change of the vibration.

An example of the conditions were set in the test as follows:

- Insulated gas used: SF_6 $4kg/cm^2$

- Test voltage: $0 - 2\times$ nominal voltage

- Particle model: A thin aluminum wire

- The length of a particle: X=28 mm, Y=40 mm

- Abnormal conditions tested:

  1. No particle(i.e. normal status)
  2. Fixed particle on the conductor
  3. Fixed particle on the enclosure
  4. Floating particle within the enclosure
  5. A small gap between conductors
  6. An insufficiently-fixed metal fitting

5.2 Outline of the Experiment

In the application of ART2 to abnormality diagnosis of GISs: learning stages are separated from default training and adaptive learning. GIS-A in the factory and GIS-B in the powerstation have been experimented by the ART system, they have almost same specifications.

1. Default training in the factory
   In the manufacturer's factory shown in left in Figure 3, we have obtained approximately 100 data for training including the six abnormalities above from the GIS-A. Then the ART2 was trained by the data as varying the number of them to check the dependency of relations between correction rate and the number of training data. ART2 learns the abnormality status with little noises derived from pre-assumed abnormal causes so that it predicts perfectly pre-assumed abnormalities.

2. Adaptive learning in the Powerstation
   In the stage of adaptive learning shown right in Figure 3, ART2 system was put in the GIS site of a powerstation, and had been collected the environmental noises so that it performed classifications of them. If one of them is classified to one of pre-assumed abnormal causes, ART2 modifies a LTM in the already-learned LTMs in the system. If it is not classified to any LTM, ART2 creates one more new neuron and classifies it as a new no-normal status. In fact, the ART2 system trained by default six abnormality-cause pairs were implemented at the Protective Relay Room in the TAMAHARA Powerstation, where an output cable from an acceleration sensor mounted on the enclosure of GCB(GIS-B) was connected to the system. The system had been monitoring the GCB during almost 10 days. For the convenience after analysis of the experiment, raw signals from the sensor were also recorded by DAT(Digital Audio Tape)s.

6 Evaluation

The sample data of the spectrum patterns were selected in random under nominal voltage to train the ART2 by data out of about 100 samples. Both correction rate and misclassification rate were evaluated in the GIS-A.

6.1 Default training in the factory

Figure 4 show the correction rate and misclassification rate. 10% to 90% out of the 100 data were selected, each percentage of the data was trained on the ART2, rest of the data were input to the ART2 to evaluate the correction rate and misclassification rate, that is considered trained data as assumed abnormalities, rest of the data as unexpected abnormalities.

The correction rate means that when a pattern is input to the ART2, the cause of it is already trained and is equivalent to the LTM invoked.

The misclassification rate means that the cause of it is already trained but is not equivalent to the LTM invoked. Increase rate means that the cause of it was not trained by the training data. The left hand figure is a threshold of the Reset as $\rho = 0.995$, the right hand one is that as $\rho = 0.998$ which is tighter than the left, in other word, it is difficult to classify the unexpected abnormalities correctly, so that right one shows there are more neurons self-generated than the left one.

6.2 Adaptive learning in the Powerstation

Figure 3 show the LTMs stored by default training in GIS-A and that of by adaptive learning in GIS-B. After the diagnostic system with the ART2 was trained by data from the GIS-A, the system was provided with the GIS-B in the TAMAHARA Powerstation and input by on-line signals from the acceleration sensor mounted on the GIS-B. Adaptive learning was conducted for several days in the site, that is in a new environment. In fact, in the actual field, there was no abnormality except environmental noise. The pattern of the right hand figure shows FFT patterns come from abnormal status with the environmental noise and switching status of the circuit breaker of the GIS-B.

7 Conclusion

We have applied ART2 as self-trained NN, on-line and in real-time, to abnormality diagnosis of GISs. It is considered that signal processing technologies in the power industry are now less under development than sensor technologies are.

GISs have been operated for over 20 years in the past, and its rate of faults and malfunctions are fairly lower than those in the other conventional equipment partly because of the protection of charged section against external environment. But invisibility inside GISs prevents us from inspecting them easily through daily patrol or quick-locating an abnormality before fatal damage occurs. We believe that gas-insulated substations bring their power facilities maintenance-free out of weathering and contamination problems and reduced size of equipment and devices, but locating (of faults and malfunctions) problems such as internal corona activity or any breakdown of the insulation system, have been unsatisfactory. Therefore further R&D improvement for predictive diagnostic technologies should be done including interpreting online signal data from single or multiple sensors. We expect that pattern classification capability of ANNs with learning function might bring one of the solutions in the near future. We will investigate any other adaptive type ANNs as well as the ART2 and develop the prototype of diagnostic system with adaptive type NN in a couple of years.

Acknowledgement

The authors wish to express gratitude to those who works in the ITAMI WORKS of Mitsubishi Electric Corporation and in the TAMAHARA Powerstation of the TEPCO for their great contributions to the approaches.

References

[1] L.Lundgaad et al., "Acoustic Diagnoses of Gas Insulated Substations; A Theoretical and Experimental Basis", *IEEE PES Winter Meeting*, Paper no.90 WM 133-9 PWRD, Atlanta, 1990

[2] T.Yamagiwa et al., "Development of Preventive Maintenance System for Highly Reliable Gas Insulated Switchgear", *IEEE PES Winter Meeting*, 90 WM 160-2 PWRD, Feb.1990.

[3] H.Tanaka,et al., "Design and Evaluation of Neural Network for Fault Diagnosis", *Proc. of ESAP'89*, pp.378-384, July 1989.

[4] D.E.Rumelhart et al., "Learning representations by back-propagating errors", *Nature*, Vol.323,9, pp.533-536, Oct. 1986.

[5] H.Ogi et al., "Preventive Maintenance System for Gas Insulated Switchgear Using an Artificial Neural Network", *Proc. of ESAP'91*, pp.627-633, April 1991.

[6] G.A.Carpenter and S.Grossberg, "ART2: self-organization of stable category recognition codes for analog input patterns", *Applied Optics*, vol.26, No.23, pp.4919-4930, 1987.

[7] G.A.Carpenter and S.Grossberg, "A Massively Parallel Architecture for a Self-Oeganizing Neural Pattern Recognition Machine", *Computer Vision Graphics Image Processing*, vol.37, No.54, 1987.

[8] G.A.Carpenter and S.Grossberg, "ART3: Hierarchical Search Using Chemical Transmitters in Self-Organizing Pattern Recognition Architectures", *Neural Networks*, Vol.3, No.2, pp.129-152, 1990.

[9] D.L.Lubkeman et al., "Unsupervised Learning Strategies for the Detection and Classification of Transient Phenomena on Electric Power Distribution Systems", *IEEE Applications of Neural Networks to Power Systems(ANNPS91)*, p.107-p.111, July 1991.

[10] H.Ogi et al., "Fault Diagnosis System for GIS using an Artificial Neural Network", *IEEE Applications of Neural Networks to Power Systems(ANNPS91)*, p.112-p.116, July 1991.

[11] Mori et al., "Power System Voltage Diagnosis by an Artificial Neural Network", *IEE Electric&Energy*, 138, 1992.

Fault Section Estimation in Power System Using Boltzmann Machine

Tsutomu Oyama
Division of Electrical and Computer Engineering
Yokohama National University
Yokohama 240, Japan

Abstract

The fault section estimation problem can be formulated as a non-linear integer optimization problem. In this paper, the Boltzmann machine is applied to solve the problem. Since the objective function for the problem has the form of high order polynomial expression, an approximation is made so that the Boltzmann machine can be easily used for the problem. Another problem is to find out all solutions that have equal probability. The objective function is modified for solving the problem. As a result, for single and double fault cases, the Boltzmann machine with modified objective function works very well.

1. Introduction

Once a fault occurs in the power system, the fault section must be estimated from inadequate information on protective relays and circuit breakers. There have been several researches to develop an automatic estimation method. Knowledge engineerings, three layered perceptron type neural network, etc., have been used.

The fault section estimation problem can be formulated as a non-linear integer optimization problem. It is well known that the Hopfield network and the Boltzmann machine are suitable to solve the non-linear integer optimization problem. In this paper, the Boltzmann machine is applied to solve the fault section estimation problem.

First, the formulation of the fault section estimation problem is described. The problem is treated as the error minimization problem (probability maximization problem). Since the objective function can be formulated in the quadratic form, it is easily implemented on the Hopfield network and Boltzmann machine. The relationship between objective function and the network constants (weights and thresholds) is explained.

Using the objective function, the most probable solution may sometimes be the case with no fault; i.e., false operations of the protective relays. It is considered to be a trivial solution. In order to suppress this kind of trivial solution, the objective function is modified so that the cases with one or more faults become more probable.

Another problem is to find out all solutions that have equal probability. In case if several solutions have equal probability (the number of solutions is not known), it is very difficult to collect all of them. Since the result of the Boltzmann machine has probabilistic nature, all the cases may be or may not be collected after hundreds of trials. If the cases that have already been chosen can be suppressed, all the probable cases are easily obtained. In order to suppress the cases, again, the objective function is modified.

2. Fault Section Estimation Problem

Fault section estimation problem can be formulated as the probability maximization problem.

$$\text{Prob}(x) \to \max. \qquad (1)$$
subject to
$$F(x) = O, \qquad x \in H \qquad (2)$$
where,
- x: state vector of system condition
- H: set of possible hypotheses
- F: alarm function
- O: alarm information

In other word, the fault section estimation problem is to find the most probable hypothesis that can explain the alarm information.

Since it is difficult to define the probability function Prob(x), the error function E(x) is used to represent the probability in this paper.

$$E(x) = \text{(the number of fault sections in } x) + \text{(the number of malfunctioning protective devices)} \qquad (3)$$

239

If $E(x)$ becomes smaller, $\text{Prob}(x)$ becomes larger. Therefore, the problem can be rewritten as follows:

$$E(x) \rightarrow \min. \tag{4}$$
subject to
$$F(x) = 0, \qquad x \in H \tag{2'}$$

The error function $E(x)$ has the form.

$$E(x) = \Sigma |s_i| + \Sigma |c_j - c_j^*(r)| + \Sigma |r_k - r_k^*(x)| \tag{5}$$

where,
  $x = [s^t, c^t, r^t]^t$: state vector of system condition
  s_j: condition of the section j (0: normal, 1: fault)
  c_j: condition of the CBj (0: non-operational state, 1: operational state)
  r_k: condition of the relay k (0: non-operational state, 1: operational state)
  c^*: circuit breaker function (1: if it should operate, 0: otherwise)
  r^*: relay function (1: if it should operate, 0: otherwise)

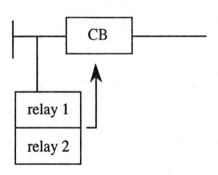

Fig. 1. Operation of circuit breaker

For example, circuit breaker function of the CB in fig. 1 is as follows.

$$c^*(r) = 1 - (1 - r_1)(1 - r_2) \tag{6}$$
where,
  r_1: condition of the relay 1
  r_2: condition of the relay 2

The relay function of the main protection relay (relay 1) is as follows.

$$r_1^*(x) = s \tag{7}$$
where, s: condition of the protected line

The relay function of the backup protection relay

(relay 2) is as follows.

$$r_2^*(x) = s(1 - r_1) \tag{8}$$

Since every variable in this problem has the value of 1 or 0, the fault section estimation problem is formulated as the integer optimization problem.

3. Application of Boltzmann Machine to Fault Section Estimation

In the Hopfield type neural network and the Boltzmann machine, the energy of the network is given as follows.

$$e(t) = -\frac{1}{2} \sum_i \sum_j w_{ij} U_i(t) U_j(t) - \sum \theta_i U_i(t) \tag{9}$$

The energy of the network gradually decreases. If the Boltzmann machine is used, the network finally reaches the global minimum energy point.

In the fault section estimation problem described above, every variable takes either one or zero. Following replacement can be done.

$$x_i^2 = x_i \tag{10}$$

Therefore, the error function (3) can be changed to the form.

$$\begin{aligned} E(x) &= \Sigma |s_i| + \Sigma |c_j - c_j^*(r)| + \Sigma |r_k - r_k^*(x)| \\ &= \Sigma s_i + \Sigma (c_j - c_j^*(r))^2 + \Sigma (r_k - r_k^*(x))^2 \\ &= \Sigma s_i + \Sigma \left(c_j - 2c_j \cdot c_j^* + c_j^{*2} \right) + \Sigma \left(r_k - 2r_k \cdot r_k^* + r_k^{*2} \right) \end{aligned} \tag{11}$$

In this expression, since circuit breaker function c^* is the function of relay condition r only, the second term can be calculated directly from the alarm information. The first term of the third term, r_k, is also included in the alarm information. Given the alarm information, they can be considered as the constants. The error function is changed to the following form.

$$E(x) = f(x) + \text{const.} \tag{12}$$
$$f(x) = \Sigma s_i + \Sigma \left(-2r_k \cdot r_k^* + r_k^{*2} \right) \tag{13}$$

The fault section estimation problem can be rewritten as:

$$f(x) \to \min. \qquad (14)$$

subject to

$$F(x) = O, \qquad x \in H \qquad (2'')$$

The relay function r* is a polynomial expression of conditions of sections. If the number of protected areas of each relay is less than or equal to two, the relay function is the second order (or the first order) polynomial expression. The objective function f(x) also becomes the second order polynomial function. It can be written as follows.

$$f(x) = f(s) = \Sigma A_i s_i + \Sigma B_{ij} s_i s_j \qquad (15)$$

It has the same form as eq. (9) with the replacement given below.

$$
\begin{aligned}
s_i &\to U_i \\
A_i &\to -h_i \\
B_{ij} &\to -w_{ij}
\end{aligned}
$$

The objective function is translated to the energy of the network.

4. Example of Fault Section Estimation

Using the model system shown in fig. 2, the fault section estimation is demonstrated. The objective function f(x) for the system is as follows.

$$
\begin{aligned}
f(s) =\ & (1-2r_1)s_1 + (1-2r_2)s_3 + (1-2r_3)s_5 + (1-2r_4)s_2 \\
& + (1-2r_5)s_2 + (1-2r_6)s_4 + (1-2r_7)s_4 \\
& + (1-2r_8)s_2(1-r_4) + (1-2r_9)s_2(1-r_5) \\
& + (1-2r_{10})s_4(1-r_6) + (1-2r_{11})s_4(1-r_7) \\
& + (1-2r_{12})[1-\{1-s_3(1-c_2)\}\{1-s_4(1-c_3)(1-c_2)\}] \\
& + (1-2r_{13})s_1(1-c_1) + (1-2r_{14})s_5(1-c_4) \\
& + (1-2r_{15})[1-\{1-s_3(1-c_3)\}\{1-s_2(1-c_2)(1-c_3)\}] \\
& + s_1 + s_2 + s_3 + s_4 + s_5
\end{aligned}
$$
$$(16)$$

where,

$r_1 - r_{15}$: conditions of relays Am, Bm, Cm, L1Am, L1Bm, L2Bm, L2Cm, L1Ap, L1Bp, L2Bp, L2Cp, L1As, L1Bs, L2Bs, and L2Cs, respectively

$c_1 - c_5$: conditions of circuit breakers CB1, CB2, CB3, and CB4, respectively.

$s_1 - s_5$: conditions of sections A, L1, B, L2, and C, respectively

Using the Boltzmann machine, several case studies are made.

In the first case, protective devices in opera-

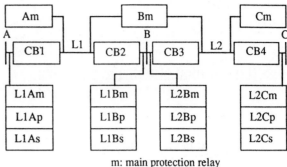

m: main protection relay
p: primary backup protection relay
s: secondary backup protection relay

Fig. 2. Model system

tional states are as follows.

(L1Am, L1Bm, CB1, and CB2)

The output of the Boltzmann machine is the section L1. The value of the objective function is -1. In this case, L1 is the most probable fault section. The output of the Boltzmann machine is considered to be reasonable.

In the second case, protective devices in operational states are as follows.

(L1Am, L1Bp, CB1, and CB2)

No fault section is selected by the Boltzmann machine. It means this case is caused by the false operation of protective devices. The value of the objective function is 0.

Searching every possible fault case, it is found that the value of objective function is also 0 if a fault occurs at section L1. Two of the candidates (fault at L1 and no fault) have the same probability. It should be noted that no fault case is a trivial solution. The Boltzmann machine should be modified to exclude it.

In the third case, protective devices in operational states are as follows.

(L1Am, L1Bm, L2Bm, L2Cp, CB1, CB2, CB3, and CB4)

The output of the Boltzmann machine is double fault case (L1 and L2). The value of objective function is -1.

Searching every possible fault case, it is found that a single fault at L1 also has the same objective function value. In this case, there are two candidates that have same probability. The Boltzmann machine should list all candidates that have the same probability.

5. Modification of Boltzmann Machine

5.1 Exclusion of trivial solution

As described in the previous section, the trivial solution (no fault case) should be exclude from the output of Boltzmann machine. If the objective function of the cases with at least one fault can be decreased, the trivial solution can be excluded (fig. 3).

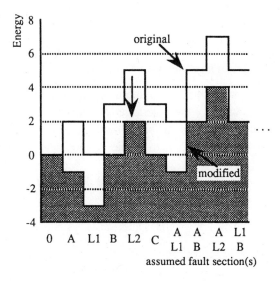

Fig. 3. Exclusion of Trivial Solution

Consider the function that has the value one if there is one or more fault.

$$D(s) = 1 - \Pi(1 - s_i) \qquad (17)$$

If the objective function is modified as follows,

$$f(x) = f(x) - \alpha D(s) \qquad (18)$$

The trivial solution is excluded with arbitrary constant α.

The function $D(s)$ has the form.

$$D(s) = \Sigma s_i - \Sigma s_i s_j + \Sigma s_i s_j s_k - .... \qquad (19)$$

Since the section si is assigned to each neuron in the implementation of Boltzmann machine, however, it is impossible to include third or higher order term. Therefore, the approximation is made and the function is modified as follows.

$$D(s) = \Sigma s_i - \Sigma s_i s_j \qquad (20)$$

This approximation has the effect on triple or more multiple fault cases. On the triple fault cases, the values of objective function are unchanged. On more multiple cases, the values become even larger. The values of objective function (energy of the network) are shown in fig. 4.

Since triple or more multiple fault hardly occurs, the approximation is expected to have no effect on the result usually. However, this modification should be used only in the case the output of Boltzmann machine is the trivial solution.

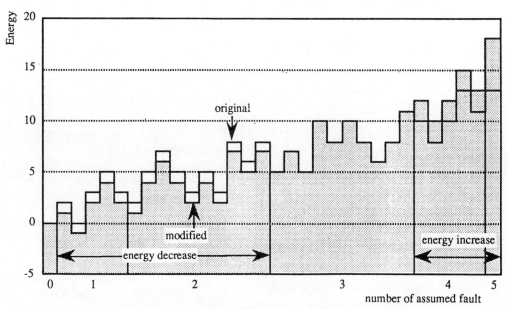

Fig. 4. The effect of the modification on objective function

5.2 Collection of all probable cases

It is well known that the result of the Boltzmann machine has the probabilistic nature. If several solutions have the same energy, even after hundreds of trials, there is no guarantee that all of them are collected.

Since fault section estimation is formulated as the integer optimization problem, it is possible that

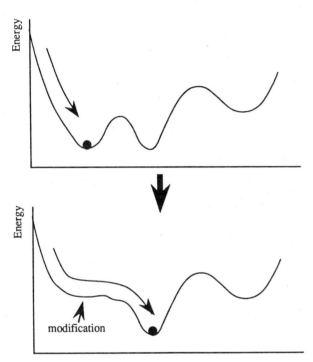

Fig. 5. Modification of objective function

there are several solutions that have same objective function (energy). The objective function should be modified so that all of them can be collected systematically.

If the objective function of the solution that is already obtained can be increased, it is guaranteed that other solution(s) can be collected (fig. 5).

In order to increase the value of objective function, following modification is made.

1) Single fault case
In case if the single fault at section s_i is selected, the modification is as follows.

$$\theta_i = \theta_i + C$$
$$w_{ij} = w_{ij} - C \quad \text{all } j, j \neq i \tag{21}$$
$$\text{where, } C: \text{arbitrary constant}$$

2) Double fault case
In case if the double fault at s_i and s_j is selected, the modification is as follows.

$$w_{ij} = w_{ij} + C \tag{22}$$

After two cases (one is single fault case, another is double fault case) are selected, the objective function for each case is changed as fig. 6. It is shown that the objective function of the cases that are already selected increase as expected. Some of the cases that have three or more faults, however, are influenced.

The objective function decreases in some cases. There is a possibility that triple or more multiple fault case that is not likely to occur may be collected

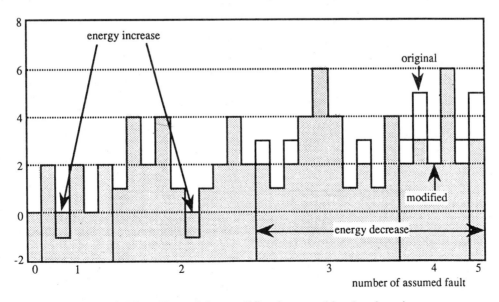

Fig. 6. The effect of the modification on objective function

243

after the modification. The objective function of collected cases should be checked somehow afterward.

6. Study on Large Model System

The proposed method is applied to the large model system shown in fig. 7. The result obtained is very reasonable. The calculation time for selecting one case is less than 20 seconds using NEC-PC (80286 + 80287) and BASIC interpreter.

The calculation time can be reduced, if fast processor is used. Farther, since neural network is easily implemented on parallel processing system, huge reduction on calculation time is expected.

7. Conclusion

Fault section estimation problem can be formulated as the non-linear optimization problem. Since Boltzmann machine is suitable to solve the non-linear optimization problem, it is applied to the fault section estimation.

In order to collect all probable solutions, the objective function must be modified. The modification method is described and the effect of the approximation is evaluated. The result obtained is reasonable and it is expected that the calculation time can be made very short.

References

[1] C. Fukui and J. Kawakami, "An expert System for Fault Section Estimation Using Information from Protective Relays and Circuit Breakers," IEEE Trans. on Power Delivery, Vol. PWRD-1, No. 4, 1986.

[2] H. Okamoto, A. Yokoyama, and Y. Sekine, "A Real-Time Expert System for Fault Section Estimation Using Cause-Effect Network," 10th Power Systems Computation Conference, Graz, Austria, 1990.

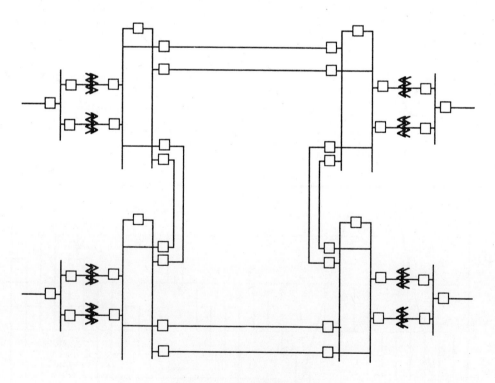

Fig. 7. Large model system

A Study on Practical Fault Location System for Power Transmission Lines using Neural Networks

H. Kanoh, K. Kanemaru, M. Kaneta, M. Nishiura

Hitachi Cable, Ltd.
5-1-1 Hitaka-cho, Hitachi-shi,
Ibaraki-ken, 319-14 JAPAN

Abstract

For the efficient operation of power transmission facilities, the authors have developed a new fault location (FL) system and put it to practical use. This system uses neural networks (NNs) to analyze the distribution pattern of the current induced in overhead ground wires (GWs) along the power line. Improved reliability results from the introduction of fuzzy operation of input data, a fault-type decision method and an index expressing the reliability of the fault location result. These FL systems are installed in eight commercial lines, and run normally, one of which experienced a fault due to lightning and successfully located the fault point.

1 Introduction

Since power transmission lines are indispensable to supply electric power, they are equipped with various protection systems. It is almost impossible, however, to avoid all the problems from the lines that are installed in wide areas and that are subjected to severe environments. Therefore, it is important to be able to promptly locate malfunctions so that repairs can be made quickly.

The authors have previously proposed a new fault location (FL) method that transmits distributed fault information along the power line using composite fiber-optic overhead ground wire (OPGW) [1,2]. This system uses neural networks (NNs) to analyze the distribution pattern of the current induced in overhead ground wires (GWs) along the power line. This method has several distinctive features in contrast with conventional methods that use the values of power line current and voltage obtained at the line end, such as digital FL equipment [3]. It is capable of locating fault sections with high reliability even for secondary power lines with complicated configurations. The range resolution can also be selected in advance, as it is decided by the distance between the sensors.

Previous reports have shown that the successful location ratio and range resolution can be reached to practical levels. In putting the NN system to practical use, however, it is most important to further improve reliability. Specifically, previous proposals have not addressed how to deal with unexpected input data to NNs.

This paper introduces fuzzy operation of input data, a fault-type decision method and an index expressing the reliability of the fault location result to improve reliability. First, the features of measured GW current and the problems in conducting fault location are clarified. Then, countermeasures and a practical system outline are described. Finally an example is presented of a successful location result in a commercial power line. The total performance of the NN method is also discussed in comparison with the expert system that has been previously developed and put into practice [4].

2 Problems and Countermeasures

2.1 GW current in commercial power lines

When an electrical fault occurs, current is induced in the GW due to electromagnetic coupling and bypass flow to the ground. This GW current is simultaneously detected with current sensors using current transformers (CTs) in several towers along the line. The output from the CTs is converted from electric to optical signals and transmitted to the central processing station through optical fibers with OPGW. These systems have been installed in 13 commercial lines, and provide substantial GWs current data under fault conditions [5]. Figure 1 shows examples of these data. This FL system analyzes the pattern, such as Fig. 1, and locates a fault point with the installation sections of these sensors as a unit for location. In the following, the sensor installation section will be referred to simply as "section" and the section that includes the fault point among these sections as "fault section".

Figure 1(a) shows an example of a current distribution pattern under fault conditions on the primary power system with a simple configuration [6]. Figure 1(b) and (c) show the patterns on the complicated secondary power system. In Fig. 1, measured current values (r.m.s. values) and current phase angles are shown by circles and crosses, respectively. Calculated values using EMTP (Electro-Magnetic Transients Program) are also shown by solid and dotted lines [7]. The accuracy of the measurement was 10 percent for current value and 10 degrees for phase angle. Fig. 1 shows the following:
(1) The whole pattern of measured current value is very similar to the calculated one. However the values of these data have been found to have deviations up to 20 or 30 percent near the fault section and 10 percent in other sections from the calculated values.
(2) A close agreement between measured and calculated values is obtained for the phase angle.

The GW current distributions of the actual lines are affected largely by: (a) the grounding resistance of towers; (b) the arc resistance; (c) the distance between the ground wire and the transmission lines; (d) the resistivity of the earth; and (e) the short-circuit capacity of the power source. The fact that these values cannot be grasped accurately causes ambiguity in the measured GW current distributions. Among these, (a), (c) and (e) are the causes of random deviations in the line direction and (b) and (d) are the causes of the uniform deviations.

245

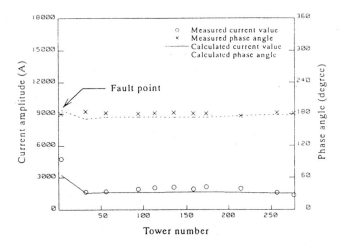

(a) Pattern on a primary power system

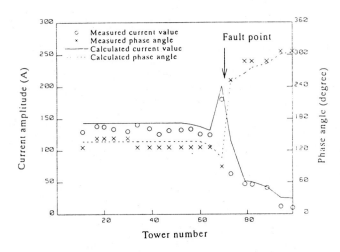

(b) Pattern on a secondary power system

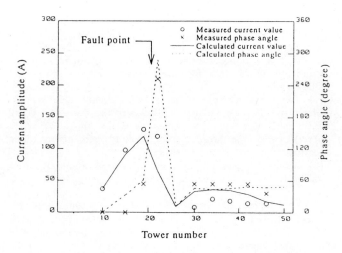

(c) Pattern on a secondary power system

Fig. 1 Examples of Current Distribution
Pattern under Fault Condition

2.2 Problems in reliability improvement

The fault location method utilizes the relationship between the GW current distribution pattern and the fault section by learning in advance the NNs with EMTP-calculated values. The above deviations, however, are larger than expected and thus higher generalization performance should be required for NNs for unexpected input data that were not used in the NN learning. In addition to the above deviations, it was found from various measurements that the data include many other uncertainties. The most annoying factor is the influence from other power lines connected to the same bus tie or installed close to the system. Also, it is necessary to deal with current sensor malfunctions and unexpected changes of the power system configuration.

2.3 Policies

There are three policies for improving reliability.
(1) It is effective to reduce the possibility of local minimums for improving the reliability of NNs. That is to say, the input data are devised so that NNs learning will make smooth progress. The measured data are feature-extracted using fuzzy sets and transformed by fuzzy operation based on experiential rules, before applying to NNs. For the following rule, for example, the fuzzy description is considered better than direct NN-learning;
[Rule]
"If the phase angle difference is large in the section, and the line is regarded as uniform, then there is a possibility that a grounding fault to tower structure occurred in its vicinity. If the current value is very small, however, then this possibility turns out to be low."
(2) It was noticed that a human expert uses the result of fault-type estimation to locate the fault point. If the fault type can be decided with higher confidence than the result of fault location, then reliability improvement is expected by using different NNs corresponding to the fault types. The fault-type decision is also useful for quick restoration work of power lines.
(3) Still, it will be impossible to eliminate all the factors impairing reliability of the fault location result. In this system, indices expressing the degree of deterioration are introduced to evaluate the reliability of the whole system.

3 Practical Improvement

3.1 Preprocessing by fuzzy operation

The rule shown in section 2.3 is expressed by the following logical expression.
　IF
　　(line is regarded as uniform) and
　　(the phase angle difference is large) and
　　(the current value is large)
　THEN
　　(possibility of occurring fault is high)　　　　(1)
The authors have previously developed a knowledge base with rules such as Eq. (1) for a practical FL system. From this experience, it was found that "both phase angle difference and current value are large" was an important guiding fact of fault location. Our policy for Eq. (1) is that the guiding fact should be described by the fuzzy set while the other factors are obtained by the NNs learning.

The transmission line is divided into small sections by the towers where the current sensors are installed. Fuzzy sets then are considered in these sections as follows. These are decided intuitively by power transmission engineering experts upon crossing the A.C. theory. and are not derived by unsophisticated pure theory.

$$A_n = \begin{cases} 1 & (\Delta\phi_n \geq \Delta\phi_0) \\ (\Delta\phi_n/\Delta\phi_0)^2 & (\Delta\phi_n < \Delta\phi_0) \end{cases}$$

$$B_n = \begin{cases} 1 & (I_n \geq I_0) \\ (I_n/I_0)^2 & (I_n < I_0) \end{cases}$$

$$\Delta\phi_n = \phi_{n+1} - \phi_n$$
$$\Delta\phi_0 = \text{constant}$$
$$I_0 = \text{constant}$$

where $\phi_n (n=2,...,m)$ is a phase angle that is measured by n-th current sensor while the first sensor is the angle origin, and m is the total number of sensors, $I_n(n=1,...,m)$ is the current value measured by the n-th sensor. A_n and B_n are membership values of fuzzy sets for "phase angle is large" and "current value is large", respectively. Using A_n and B_n the fact "both phase angle difference and current value are large" can be written as "$A_n \times B_n$ is large". NN1, in which $A_n \times B_n$ are added to input data, and NN2 with only measured values as input data, are shown in Fig. 2.

Fault location simulation was executed for five real systems shown in Table 1 to confirm the effect of fuzzy operations. About 300 to 4000 cases of GW current distributions for each system during the fault are calculated using EMTP. The results are put into the NNs to perform the learning by back-propagation method. Then the calculated data are superimposed with 30 percent random deviations in the line direction and 30 percent uniform deviations for the evaluation of learned NNs. The result of this evaluation is shown in Table 2. The fuzzy operation effect is confirmed, since a successful location ratio of NN1 is better than NN2's on all the systems in Table 2.

3.2 Fault-type decision

Power line faults can be classified into two types as viewed from the cause of occurrence. One is with the single-line grounding faults or the short-circuit faults through grounding, both due to lightning flashing over to the tower structure. Many power line faults belong to this type. The other is the phase-to-phase short-circuit fault due to flying objects or direct earth-grounding fault due to the contact of trees, etc. There is a fear of facility damages although the occurrences of the foregoing fault type is low. These are called type-1 and the type-2, respectively.

Table 3 shows the results of fault-type decisions obtained by the same learning experiment as shown in section 3.1. Fuzzy

Table 1 Parameters for Practical Systems

System	A	B	C	D	E
Rated Voltage[kV]	500	66	66	275	154
Short Circuit Capacity [MVA]	21840	1800	2112	9800	3704
Neutral Grounding Resistance [Ω]	direct	65	63.5	direct	78.2
Length [km]	175	34.9	12.8	21.3	46
No. of Circuits	2	2	2	2	2
No. of Sensors	11	18	13	13	5

Table 2 Fault Location Results (Success Ratio in %)

System	A	B	C	D	E
N N 1	98.8	91.3	94.7	92.8	95.0
N N 2	97.4	83.6	92.2	81.7	90.5

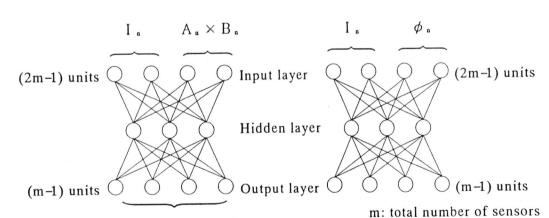

I_n $A_n \times B_n$ I_n ϕ_n

(2m–1) units — Input layer — (2m–1) units

Hidden layer

(m–1) units — Output layer — (m–1) units

m: total number of sensors

corresponding to sections divided by sensors

(a) NN1
input: measured values and fuzzy operation results

(b) NN2
input: only measured values

Fig. 2 Neural Networks configurations

operation was performed to input data in this experiment. A high success ratio is achieved in systems A, C and D. In these systems, fault location tests were performed for each fault type. Table 4 shows these results. The first and the second line in Table 4 is the fault location results by the NNs for type-1 and type-2, respectively. The weighted average of these two results with respect to the total number of simulation cases is shown on the third line. A weighted average value multiplied by a success ratio of fault type is the final success ratio shown on the 4th line. In Table 3, the successful fault location ratio for type-1 with all systems is 100 percent, and the final success ratios are better than Table 2 with systems A and D.

Since most of the faults in practical transmission lines are type-1, it is thought that fault type consideration is expected to be more useful than the results of this experiment.

Table 3 Results of Fault Type Estimation
(Success Ratio in %)

System	A	B	C	D	E
Estimation	100.	73.7	97.7	99.4	62.7

Table 4 Fault Location Results for Individual Fault Type
(Success Ratio in %)

System	A	C	D
Type-1 (No. of Faults)	100. (3312)	100. (492)	100. (68)
Type-2 (No. of Faults)	97.1 (1104)	89.5 (492)	91.4 (173)
Weighted Average	99.3	94.8	93.8
Overall Result	99.3	92.2	93.3

3.3 Introduction of Reliability Index

The factors impairing the reliability in the FL method using GW current are as follows;
(a) The change of the grounding resistance of towers and the distance between conductors.
(b) Noises caused by transient current under fault conditions.
(c) Trouble with sensors or data transmission equipments installed on towers.
(d) When the fault current value is almost the same as the ordinary current.
(e) When the fault type is type-2.
In this system, the degree of these factors was decided as the output value of NN for (a), the current waveform distortion value shown in chapter 4(1) for (b), the number of sensors in trouble for (c), the maximum value of measured current for (d), and the fault type for (e).

4   Fault Location System

Figure 3 shows an example of the operation procedure of the practical FL system. Under fault conditions, the GW current is measured for 256 msec by current sensors installed at each sensing tower. Then these data are transmitted to the central processing station through optical fibers. The central processing equipment is composed of a personal computer, and the fault section is decided there by the following procedure.

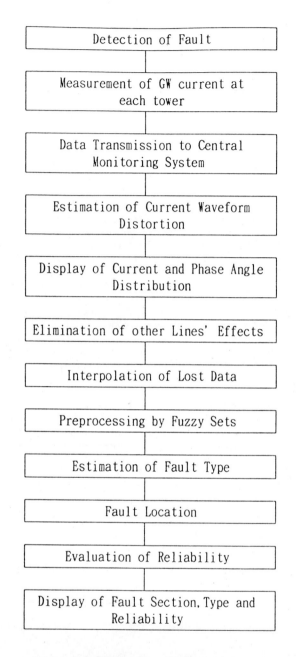

Fig. 3 An Example of Fault Location
Process in Practical System

(1) Estimation of current waveform distortion
In general, current under fault conditions is the superposition of the fundamental wave with commercial frequency and higher harmonics component and D.C. component that decreases slowly with time. Also, the current waveform is distorted from the sinusoidal wave due to the nonlinearity of CT and LED. This current waveform is compared with a standard one that has already been memorized to estimate the degree of distortion.

(2) Display of current distribution figures
Current values and phase angles are displayed on the CRT, in a form similar to Fig. 1, and recorded onto a hard-disk unit as a database.

(3) Elimination of other lines' effects

It is then decided whether or not the fault is in the line in which the system is installed. In case of other lines' faults, the current waveform distortion is very large and the current values have very large deviations from the calculated ones in all cases. In this case, the following procedures are omitted.

(4) Interpolation of data

Defective data caused by sensor malfunctions or transmission errors are linearly interpolated with the data on both sides.

(5) Fault location

The fault section is decided using 3 NNs for the power lines where the simulated success ratio of fault type is very high. First NN decides the fault type, then the other NN corresponding to each fault type decides the fault section.

It has already been shown in previous reports that both successful location ratio and range resolution can be improved using an inference model NN, and separate-type NNs.

5 Evaluation

5.1 Practical evaluation

Fault location systems using NNs have been installed and run normally in eight commercial lines. Five secondary power line systems are included in these eight lines. One of them experienced a fault due to lightning and successfully located the fault section. Current distribution at this fault has already been shown in Fig. 1(a).

More than 20 current distribution patterns have been obtained by the systems as mentioned in section 2.1 up to now. These actual fault data were applied to offline fault location processes and all offered successful fault location results.

5.2 Comparison with expert system

An expert system (ES) and NN are generally useful as an automated analyzing method of patterns that need domain-specific knowledge. In our method, successful location ratio, range resolution and reliability can be improved by reflecting experiential rules to the input data and the structure of NNs. Table 5 shows a general comparison of NN characteristics used in the FL system and ES that have already had 17 cases of successful fault location results. The NN system is superior to expert systems with respect to the above performance, as well as computing speed, program size, and overall economy.

Table 5   Comparison of NN and ES

Item	NN	ES
Execution Environment	PC C-lang.	PC C-lang. prolog
Design Period [day]	15	80
Program Size [kB]	10	250
Execution Time [sec]	1	20

6 Conclusion

The authors have developed a new fault location system using NNs. Features of the GW current in commercial power lines were shown, and the method to improve the reliability and the operation procedure of the practical system were discussed in this paper.

It has been said that power transmission engineering experts can estimate fault points by analyzing the GW current distribution patterns. However, any systematic studies have not yet been made. This point was clarified in this paper, and the authors' study will contribute to the reliability considerations for fault location systems.

AI techniques (NN, ES, Fuzzy, etc.) are said to be useful for automated operation of power facilities, since there are many occasions that need expert's intuition and experience. The technique in getting high reliability using fuzzy sets and NNs described in this paper is expected to be applied widely to other systems.

Acknowledgment

The authors wish to thank Professor Yuzo Hirai of the Institute of Information Sciences and Electronics, University of Tsukuba, for his guidance and discussions in carrying out this research. Also, we wish to thank Katsuya Ohtomo and Masao Takahashi of Hitachi Cable, Ltd., for their cooperation.

References

[1] H. Kanoh, M. Kaneta and K. Kanemaru, "Fault location for Transmission Line using Inference Model Neural Network", Trans. IEE Japan, Vol. 110-C, No. 7, pp. 420, 1990.

[2] H. Kanoh, M. Kaneta and K. Kanemaru, "Improvement of Fault Location for Transmission Lines using Neural Network", Trans. IEE Japan, Vol. 111-B, No. 11, pp. 1215, 1991.

[3] T. Takagi, M. Yamaura, R. Kondow and T. Matsushima, "Development of a new type fault locator using the one-terminal voltage and current data", IEEE Trans. Power Apparatus Syst., PAS-101, pp. 2892, 1982.

[4] K. Urasawa, H. Kanoh, K. Kanemaru, and K. Sugiyama, "Fault Location System for Electric Power Transmission Lines Based on Fuzzy Knowledge Base", Trans. IEE Japan, Vol. 110-C, No. 2, pp. 70, 1990.

[5] K. Kanemaru, H. Kanoh and M. Nishiura, "Application of OPGW-utilized Fault Location System for Power Transmission Lines and its Experience in Commercial Lines", The Hitachi Densen, No. 9, pp. 19, 1990.

[6] M. Isozaki, K. Ohtomo, R. Matubara, M. Nishiura and J. Kaito, "Maintenance and Monitoring System for UHV Power Transmission Line using OPGW", The Hitachi Densen, No.12, 1993.

[7] Ametani, Murotani and Asano, "On the Aplicability of Electromagnetic Transients Program (EMTP), Nisshin Denki Giho, 27, pp.53, Jan. 1982.

AN ARTIFICIAL NEURAL NETWORK AND KNOWLEDGE-BASED METHOD FOR REASONING CAUSES OF POWER NETWORK FAULTS

Y. Shimakura,   J. Inagaki

Hokuriku Electric Power Company
15-1, Ushijima-cho, Toyama
Toyama, Japan

S. Fukui,   S. Hori

Mitsubishi Electric Corporation
1-1-2, Wadasaki-cho, Hyogo-ku
Kobe, Japan

ABSTRACT — Understanding the cause of a fault in an electric power system in the system operation is essential for quick and adequate recovery actions such as the determination of the propriety of carrying out forced line charging and the necessity of network switching, and an efficient patrolling.

In this paper, the authors will discuss a technique using artificial neural network and knowledge-based for reasoning causes of power network faults and the result obtained from a verification in which this technique was applied to a prototype system.

Keywords: Artificial Neural Network, expert system, reasoning causes, power network faults

1. INTRODUCTION

In the past, the determination of the causes of power network faults have been done by its operators based on data about the operating relay condition, weather, season, time, geography and other factors involved.

However, it is often difficult to narrow the possible causes down to a single culprit because all the necessary data cannot always be obtained and different types of fault rarely present characteristics unique to them. This is why there has not been realized a fault causes reasoning system.

In this paper we will give an outline explanation of the prototype system we have developed and discuss in detail the operations of the expert system and artificial neural network employed in the system. Then we will present the result of evaluation of the system using actual data, which demonstrated its effectiveness.

2. OUTLINE OF PROTOTYPE SYSTEM

In the event of a power network fault, it is difficult to pinpoint its cause as explained above. We discussed the possibility of using an artificial neural network to help address the problem. However, this approach also involves a problem: the neural net itself can become a black box, making it difficult to give a well-grounding reasoning for the output data. Table 1 gives a comparison between the operations of an artificial neural network and an expert system in guessing the cause of a fault.

To permit identifying the cause of a fault properly, therefore, we employed a combination of an artificial neural network and an expert system in our prototype system. The system also uses the result of oscillograph data analysis to improve the accuracy of fault cause determination.

In addition, the reasons for the judgment made are given based on the fault cause estimation rules applied, making it possible for the operator to see if the result of the estimation is reasonable.

2.1 Flow of processing

Figure 1 illustrates the flow of the processing with the prototype system.

Both the expert system and artificial neural network are run in parallel to process the fault information entered. By judging the information obtained from the two system, the cause of the fault can be identified.

Table.1 Comparison between Expert System and Artificial Neural Network

	Expert System	Artificial Neural Network
(1) Processing time	○Small	◎Very small
	Symbolic calculation is needed.	Only simple calculation is needed.
(2) Learning time	○Nothing	×Very large
		Learning data are needed, and convergence is not experienced in some cases.
(3) Expansibility	△Not high (Rule addition)	○High (Repeated learning)
	It's necessary to add new rules and examine them.	New learning data can be added to learned data.
(4) Accuracy	△Low	○High
	For using only implemented rules, and it's difficult to deduce causes in some cases.	It can always reason not only learned data, but also not learned data.
(5) Lack of fault information	×Cannot be considered	○Can be considered
	It's difficult to deduce causes in some cases.	It's possible to obtain satisfactory solutions.
(6) Explanation for results	○Easy	×Difficult
	Tracing fired rules can provide explanations.	The artificial neural net is a black box, making it difficult to provide explanations.

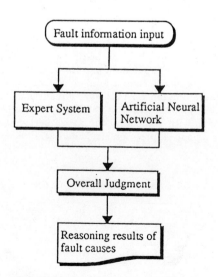

Fig.1 Processing flow of prototype system

2.2 Fault information

Information obtainable at the time of a fault includes the date of the fault, weather, the name of the affected transmission line, the operating relay condition and the phase of the fault. The size and voltage class of the affected line and the geographical data of the fault site can be used as fault information by retrieving the transmission line database. The accuracy of estimation can be improved by using the results of oscillograph data analysis showing the characteristics of the fault.

2.3 Type of fault cause

For our prototype system, we employed six types of fault cause: lightning stoke, construction equipment bumping, tree contact, bird/animal dashing, galloping, and sleet jump. These are the most frequent causes identified through the analysis of the past fault reported.

3. EXPERT SYSTEM

In estimating the cause of a fault, based on the past experience of operators, it is possible to eliminate unlikely possibilities. e.g.: there may not arise a fault due to construction equipment bumping in a stormy weather; there can arise no sleet jump or galloping in any season other than winter; or there may not arise a fault due to tree contact in a plain area.

In this manner, it is possible to narrow the scope of possible causes of the fault to some extent. An expert system can therefore be built by making operators' experience rules.

3.1 Base of rules

Table 2 gives a matrix of rules for use to narrow down the possible causes of a fault. In the table, those that do not correspond to a particular fault type are marked with a cross (x). For example, the table gives a rule: if the season is not winter, the fault cannot be a galloping or sleet jump.

3.2 Method of judgment

With the expert system, based on the narrowing down rules(3.1), it is possible to set judgment levels by the type of fault for specific input information in the following manner:
(1) Level A: There exists no corresponding rule, that is, this is the possible cause of the fault.
(2) Level B: There exists the corresponding rule, that is, this is unlikely to be the cause of the fault.

In this manner, judgment levels can be set for each fault type, providing reference information for overall judgment.

4. ARTIFICIAL NEURAL NETWORK

It is possible to build input/output relations, which cannot be described with specific rules, on an artificial neural network by having the artificial neural network learn the past fault data. Since the artificial neural network is not badly affected by a data loss, it is possible to obtain a satisfactory solution even if part of the input data is lost.

4.1 Model structure of Artificial Neural Network

We used an artificial neural network of the generally employed three-layer structure comprising an input layer, a hidden layer and an output layer. The artificial neural network has 27, 100 and one neurons in the input, hidden and output layers, respectively.

Figure 2 gives the model structure of artificial neural network.

Table 2 Rule matrix

	Rule	*1	*2	*3	*4	*5	*6
(1) Season	if not winter					×	×
(2) Time	if not from 8 to 18		×				
	if not from 3 to 20				×		
(3) Weather	if not lightning	×					
	if not snow						×
	if not snow or strong wind					×	
	if not fine or cloudy or rain		×		×		
(4) Voltage class	if not 77kv or lower				×		
(5) Wire size	if not thick					×	
	if not thin						×
(6) Geography	if not plain		×				
(7) Ry type	if not groundfault		×	×	×		
	if not short-circuiting					×	×
(8) Fault phase	if not single phase			×	×	×	
	if not double phase					×	×
	if not inclusive phase		×				
(9) Oscillogram	if not with higher harmonics	×	×	×	×		
	if not long continuation of higher harmonics				×		
	if not short continuation of higher harmonics	×	×	×			

*1 lightning stoke   *2 construction equipment bumping
*3 tree contact   *4 bird/animal dashing
*5 galloping   *6 sleet jump

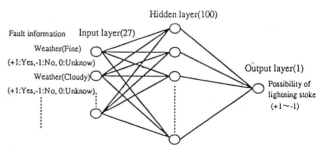

Fig.2 The model structure of Artificial Neural Network

4.2 Structure of Artificial Neural Network

To obtain accurate data while reducing the learning time, we built an artificial neural network for each fault type. For example, the artificial neural network for faults due to lightning learns that particular faults can be caused by lightning based on the learning data entered. If actual fault information is input, the artificial neural network outputs the possibility of whether the cause of the fault is lightning.

Figure 3 gives the artificial neural network structure.

4.3 Input/output data

Show below are the nine input types and twenty seven input items used in our system to classify fault information (cf. 2.2).

(1) Season   : Spring   (March to June)
              : Summer   (June to September)
              : Autumn   (September to December)
              : Winter   (November to March)
(2) Time   : Morning   (4:00 to 7:00)
              : Daytime   (7:00 to 16:00)
              : Evening   (16:00 to 18:00)
              : Nighttime (18:00 to 4:00)
(3) Weather   : Fine
              : Cloudy
              : Rain
              : Snow
              : Lightning
              : Strong Wind
(4) Voltage class : 275kv
              : 154kv
              : 77kv or lower
(5) Wire size : Thick
              : Thin
(6) Geography : Plain
              : Mountain
              : River
(7) Relay type : Short-circuiting/Ground fault
(8) Fault phase : Fault phase number:single phase
              : Inclusive of low line
(9) Oscillogram : With higher harmonics
              : Long continuation of higher harmonics

The input data is assigned the value 1.0 to -1.0 depending on whether it corresponds to the item concerned. Also, the intermediate value 0.0 is assigned for items for which no information is obtained.

In the case of a fault occurring in April, for example, the value 1.0 is given to the input item "Spring" in the input type "Season" while the value -0.1 to the remaining input items "Summer", "Autumn" and "Winter". In like manner, there may be a case in which input information relates to more than one input items.

Input information is given to all artificial neural networks, allowing each artificial neural network for a specific fault type to output the possibility of whether the corresponding item is the cause of the fault concerned. The output values are used to make estimation by fault type.

In this manner, each artificial neural network gives an estimated value for each possible cause of fault. These values are used as reference data for overall judgment.

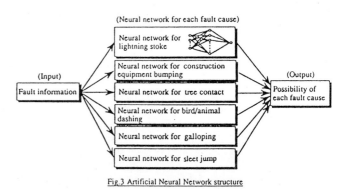

Fig.3 Artificial Neural Network structure

4.4 Learning data

A total of 192 past fault records were used as learning data.

Specifically, the values entered for the input items discussed abobe were used as input data. The value 1.0 was given to the artificial neural network for the possible cause of the fault for the learning data concerned and the value -1.0 to the other artificial neural networks for use as output data.

4.5 Learning method

In our artificial neural network placing emphasis on positive items (cause of fault) alone, it seems unnecessary to strictly bring the value of negative items (non-cause of fault) close to the learning value -1.0. The generally employed learning method is to keep the value of negative items, which are output items, within the set value of convergence norm (currently set at 0.1), that is, less than -0.9. Thinking that this makes convergence difficult, we used a learning method that allows the output value of negative items to be less than 0.0. In this way, we assigned a range (0.0 to -1.0) for the learning values of output data for negative items, resulting in a shorter learning time and improved convergence. It must however, be noted that with respect to the output at the time of estimation, output values of less than 0.0 is meaningless within the range. (For example, it is meaningless to compare the output value -0.3 and -0.7.)

5. OVERALL JUDGMENT

5.1 Judgment method

Levels for overall judgment are set for each cause of fault based on the estimation values obtained from the artificial neural networks as well as the judgement levels obtained from the expert system.

(1) Level 1 : Level A with expert system, and estimated
              possibility of 50% or more with artificial
              neural network.
(2) Level 2 : Level A with expert system, and estimated
              possibility of less than 50% artificial neural
              network.
(3) Level 3 : Level B with expert system.

5.2 Display of result

The results of estimation are displayed in the descending order of judgment levels for the possible causes of the fault concerned, together with the content of each estimation and the reason therefor.

(1) Message for the cause of the fault judged to be level 1 in overall judgment:

- Fault cause A was judged to be a highly possible cause of the fault.

  Reason:

  Ground of judgment by expert system ..... ‡‡‡, ‡‡‡[*1]

  Value estimated by neural net ..... XX %

(2) Message for the cause of the fault judged to be level 2 in overall judgment:

- Fault cause B was judged to be a possible cause of the fault.

  Reason:

  Ground of judgment by expert system ..... ‡‡‡, ‡‡‡[*1]

  Value estimated by neural net ..... XX %

(3) Message for the cause of the fault judged to be level 3 in overall judgment:

- Fault cause C was judged to have nothing to do with the fault.

  Reason:

  Ground of judgment by expert system ..... ‡‡‡, ‡‡‡[*2]

  Value estimated by neural net ..... XX %

(Note)

‡1 This gives the fault information on which the judgment was made.

  If a rule that corresponds to the cause of the fault is found in the narrowing rule (3.1), the related fault information is displayed.

‡2 This gives the fault information on which the judgment was made.

  If the fault information corresponds to one of the narrowing rule (3.1), the unrelated information is displayed.

Table.3 Result of judgment made with the Expert System and Artificial Neural network individually (without oscillograph data)

Causes of faults	Result of judgment (Expert System / Artificial Neural Network)				Total	Probability of the correct case (%)
	Number of the correct case (‡1)	Number of the correct case (‡2)	Number of the correct case (‡3)	Number of the incorrect case		
Lightning stoke	30/50	35/5	0/0	0/10	65/65	100/85
Construction equipment bumping	0/2	1/1	2/0	2/2	5/5	60/60
Tree contact	15/3	0/0	0/0	0/12	15/15	100/20
Bird/Animal dashing	0/2	8/3	3/0	2/8	13/13	85/38
Galloping	2/0	1/2	0/0	1/2	4/4	75/50
Sleet jump	4/8	2/0	0/0	4/2	10/10	60/80
Total	51/65	47/11	5/0	9/36	112/112	92/68
	(46/58%)	(42/10%)	(4/0%)	(8/32%)	(100/100%)	

(Note)

‡1 : Number of the correct case, it was possible to narrow down the possible causes to one correct cause.

‡2 : Number of the correct case, it was possible to narrow down the possible causes to two causes including correct cause.

‡3 : Number of the correct case, it was possible to narrow down the possible causes to tree causes including correct cause.

Table.4 Result of overall judgment

Causes of faults	Result of overall judgment (without oscillograph data / with oscillograph data)				Total	Probability of the correct case (%)
	Number of the correct case (‡1)	Number of the correct case (‡2)	Number of the correct case (‡3)	Number of the incorrect case		
Lightning stoke	58/58	7/7	0/0	0/0	65/65	100/100
Construction equipment bumping	2/3	1/0	0/0	2/2	5/5	60/60
Tree contact	15/15	0/0	0/0	0/0	15/15	100/100
Bird/Animal dashing	5/10	3/0	1/0	4/3	13/13	69/77
Galloping	2/2	0/0	0/0	2/2	4/4	50/50
Sleet jump	5/5	1/1	0/0	4/4	10/10	60/60
Total	87/93	12/8	1/0	12/11	112/112	89/90
	(77/83%)	(11/7%)	(1/0%)	(11/10%)	(100/100%)	

(Note)

‡1 : Number of the correct case, it was possible to narrow down the possible causes to one correct cause.

‡2 : Number of the correct case, it was possible to narrow down the possible causes to two causes including correct cause.

‡3 : Number of the correct case, it was possible to narrow down the possible causes to tree causes including correct cause.

6. TESTING WITH PROTOTYPE SYSTEM

The prototype system is intended to cover fault on the transmission lines (101 lines), under control of one control station.

To test the prototype system, we used the data of 112 faults reported in the past one year, including 65 cases of lightning, 5 cases of construction equipment bumping, 15 cases of tree contact, 13 cases of bird/animal dashing, 4 cases of galloping, and 10 cases of sleet jump. Table 3 gives the result of judgment made with the expert system and artificial neural networks individually, and Table 4 gives the result of overall judgment.

6.1 Overall judgment without oscillograph data

The testing showed that the probability of estimating the correct causes of faults was 89%. In 77% of the test cases, it was possible to narrow down the possible causes to one correct cause.

These levels are substantially higher than the correct data estimation rate (68%) with an artificial neural network alone and also the probability (46%) of selecting one correct cause with expert system alone. This is, a combination of expert system and an artificial neural network can give better results than those obtained through expert system or an artificial neural network individually.

253

6.2 Overall judgment with oscillograph data

Since the test data did not include oscillograph data. we also tested the prototype system by including the following data which seem reasonable:

(1)   High harmonics (cases of lightning. construction equipment bumping. tree contact. bird/animal dashing)

(2)   Long continuation of high harmonics (a case of bird/animal dashing)

The results of our testing showed that while the rate of estimating the correct causes was almost the same as with the case without oscillograph data but the probability of estimating one correct cause was 83% as against the latter case (77%). It is likely that including oscillograph data as a factor in estimating the cause of a fault would result in improved estimation accuracy.

7. CONCLUSION

In this paper we have discussed in detail the development of a prototype system using an artificial neural network and expert system for the purpose of estimating the cause of a fault based on information obtained at the time of the fault, such as the weather condition. geographic data and operating relay. Our testing with actual data demonstrated the effectiveness of the system.

We plan to improve the accuracy of estimation and discuss the possibility of expanding the scope of possible causes of fault that can be covered by the system to make it much more practical. For this purpose. we need to add to our pool of fault data. We also expect that by incorporating this system into a SCADA system. it will be possible to respond to power network faults for prompt recovery.

BIOGRAPHY

Yasuharu Shimakura, born in 1937. received the B.S. degree in Electrical Engineering from Tokyo Denki University, Tokyo. Japan in 1960.
He joined the Hokuriku Electric Power Company(HEPCO) in 1960. and is presently Deputy General Manager of Power System Operation Department. Mr. Shimakura is a member of the Institute of Electrical Engineers of Japan(IEEJ) and the Artificial Intelligence Society of Japan.

Jun Inagaki, born in 1955. graduated from the Department of Electricity of Tsuruga Technical High School. Fukui, Japan in 1974. and joined HEPCO in 1974. Mr. Inagaki is a member of IEEJ.

Shinta Fukui, born in 1958. recieved the B.S. degree in Electrical Engineering from Tokyo University, Tokyo. Japan in 1980. and joined Mitsubishi Electric Corporation (MELCO) in 1980. Mr. Fukui is a member of IEEJ. the Information Processing Society of Japan, and the IEEE.

Seiichiro Hori, born in 1964. graduated with the B.S. degree in Electrical Engineering from Kansai University in 1988. and joined MELCO in 1988. Mr. Hori is a Member of IEEJ.

Application of the Neural Network to Detecting Corona Discharge Occurring in Power Cables

T. Hara   A. Itoh
Dept. of Electrical Engineering
Kyoto University
Kyoto, 606, Japan

K.Yatsuka   K. Kishi   K.Hirotsu
Sumitomo Electric Industries, Ltd.
Osaka, 554, Japan

Abstract

In this paper, the system of detecting corona discharges automatically with an artificial neural network is examined and a network which can distinguish between corona and noise patterns occurring in power cables is investigated. A feed-forward type of a neural network with three layers, i.e., input, hidden and output layers is used. It is found that the network which learns only corona and no noise patterns does not show a good performance. This means that the network should learn both corona and noise patterns even for recognizing only corona discharges. The network which uses frequency spectra of the waveforms obtained by fast fourier transform (FFT) method as input patterns is also investigated. The network with FFT pretreatment is found to show a better performance than the one without FFT pretreatment.

1   Introduction

Recently, as power cables have come into wide use, maintenance of them have been more and more important. There have been proposed several methods of finding the extraordinary voltages of power cables.[1]~[3] One of them is detecting corona discharges occurring before full breakdowns. But, in this case, it is difficult to distinguish between corona discharges and noises comming from the outer of cable.

In this paper, the system of detecting corona discharge automatically with an artificial neural network have been examined. A feed-forward type of a neural network with three layers, i.e., input, hidden and output layers have been used. The input, hidden and output layers include 50, 8 and 2 neurons, respectively (we call it "2 output model"). Connection weights of the network are self-organized through back-propagation learning with data of corona and noise waveforms. Two neurons in the output layer are for judging corona and for judging noise respectively and have been made to judge "corona" or "noise" for each input. Because of so many patterns of noise

waveforms in real system, it is difficult for the neural network to learn all of those noise patterns. Therefore, we newly made the neural network including only 1 neuron in the output layer (we call it "1 output model") and made the network learn only corona waveforms. We examined whether this network could judge corona waveform "corona" and judge all the other "noise".

The methods of inputting frequency spectra of the waveforms obtained by using FFT (fast fourier transform) into the network were also examined. The reason why we apply the frequency spectrum data to the network is that the feed-forward type of a neural network, self-organized through back-propagation learning, needs normalization or elimination of offset of input data to raise the correct rate and is not tolerant to the influence of temporal shifts in input waveforms. So, this time, we use FFT method and input the frequency spectra of the wave forms into the network.

2   Construction of the Neural Network

2.1   Construction of the neural network

Figure 1 shows the feed-forward type of the neural network used in this research. The elements of the neural network are neurons and these neurons are assembled into three layers (i.e.,input, hidden and output layer) include 50, 8, 1(or 2) neurons respectively. As a function of the neuron in the hidden and the output layer, we use the sigmoid function. So, the output of the neurons is from 0 to 1. It is seen from Fig.1 the neurons are connected each other and these connections are called "synapse". Connection weights are initialized by random numbers and are adjusted by the neural network through back-propagation learning method. When the difference between output patterns and the teacher signals become less than 0.001, we make the network stop learning. But if the difference is still more than 0.001 after learning training data 1000 times, we change the initial values of connection weights and make the network learn them again. Two output model judges a input pat-

255

and the neuron for judging noise ignites in the output layer. One output model judges a input pattern "corona" if the neuron ignites in the output layer.

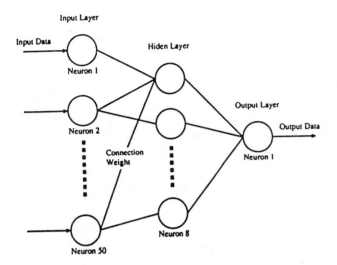

Fig.1 The neural network with three layers.

2.2 Corona waveforms and noise waveforms

We obtained 14 corona waveforms and 56 noise waveforms from a measurement circuit shown in figure 2. The corona discharges occur at the A point, where there is a void made artificially, near the insulated joint of cables . On the other hand, noises are occurred at B point where is the outer of the cable. Such corona discharges and noises are surveyed by the digital oscilloscope.

Figure 3 shows examples of waveforms surveyed. As input patterns to the neural network, we use "sampling data" that are sampled at 50 points every 10 nsec from the surveyed waveforms. So, one sampling data consists of 50 numerical values and each values are respectively inputed into the neurons in the input layer. We divided these sampling data into 2 sets. The one is "training data set" that is used when the network adjust connection weights through backpropagation. The other is "testing data set" that is used for us to calculate "the correct rate" of the neural network. Training data consists of 6 coronas and several noises whose number are changed from 0 to 16 on the purpose of making a comparison between the performance of the neural network learned only coronas and the network learned both coronas and noises.

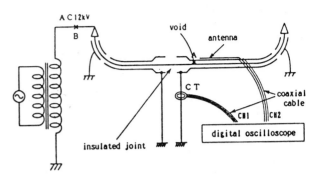

Fig.2 The measurement circuit.

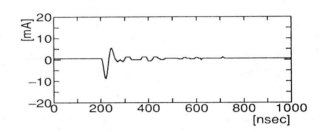

Fig.3.(a) Examples of corona waveforms.

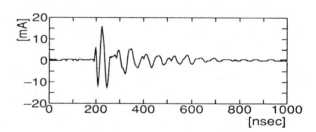

Fig.3.(b) Examples of corona waveforms.

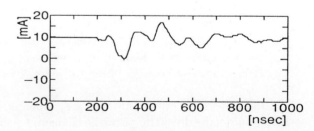

Fig.3.(c) Examples of noise waveforms.

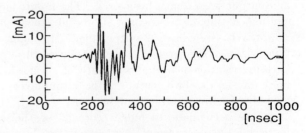

Fig.3.(d) Examples of noise waveforms.

3 The Performances of the Network

3.1 The comparison between one output and two output model

Here, we compare the correct rate of one output model with that of two output model which we have been used up to now. The results are shown in Figure 4. Fig.4.(a) and Fig.4.(b) respectively indicate the correct rate that the neural network show after learning 6 corona waveforms, and in addition, 2, 4, 8, 16 noise waveforms. The thing that varied between the two cases is the set of the initial values of connection weights. The reason why we change the set of initial values is that it may be not founded the differences of the two if we examine only one case.

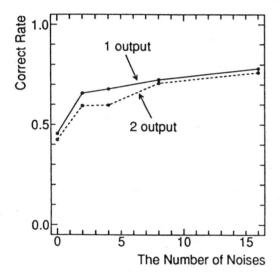

Fig.4.(a) The comparison of one output model with two output model.

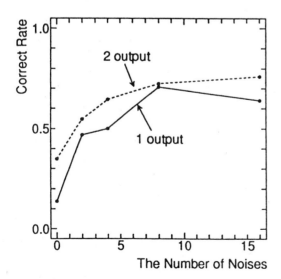

Fig.4.(b) The comparison of one output model with two output model.

In Fig.4.(a), though the difference between the values is small, the correct rate of one output model is higher than that of two output model regardless of the number of noise waveforms that the network learned. But we see the opposite facts in Fig.4.(b). The correct rate of two output model is higher than that of one output model. Because we cannot find the much difference in Fig.4, we changed the initial values of connection weights and recomputed more five times. The result is shown in Table 1. But we can not find the difference between the two here either.

Table 1 The correct rate obtained by a repetition of initializing the initial values of connection weights and learning five times.

	1 output	2 output
1	86.2%	84.5%
2	81.0%	62.0%
3	72.4%	79.3%
4	77.6%	87.9%
5	84.5%	70.0%

From the above results, we can conclude that there is not so much difference between the performance of one output model and that of two output model. Therefore we use one output model after this which becomes easy for us to analyze. Also, the time one output model takes for learning is less than that two outpout model takes.

3.2 The neural network without learning noise waveforms

In this section, we examine whether the neural network learned only corona waveforms performs as well as that learned both corona and noise waveforms. From the result of the section 3.1, one output model is used. Changing the initial value of connection weights five times, we examine the performance of the neural network learned only corona waveforms. The result is shown in Table 2. It is seen from this table that the correct rate is very low which is 45% at maximum. But it is found from Fig.4 that the more noises the network had learned, the higher the correct rate becomes.

Table 2 The correct rate of the neural network that learned only corona waveforms. The rate is obtained by changing the initial value of connection weights and making the network learn five times.

	Correct rate
1	45.1%
2	13.6%
3	19.7%
4	27.3%
5	36.4%

Next we examine the reason, why the network learned only coronas doesn't perform well, by examining the value of connection weights between the hidden layer and the output layer. Figure 5 shows the value of connection weights after learning the six corona waveforms 0 and sixteen noise waveforms, the horizontal axis indicates the number of the neuron in the hidden layer(the ninth shows the threshold value of the neuron in the output layer) and the vertical axis indicates a value of the connection weight. The neuron of a certain number reacts to the corona when the value is positive and reacts to the noise when negative. So, under the condition as shown in Fig.5.(a), it is difficult for the neural network to recognize noise, because the negative values are small and relatively smaller than the absolute value of the threshold. Therefore, the potential of the neuron in the output layer is apt to ignite from the following equations that are used through back-propagation:

$$U_j = \sum_j W_{kj} H_j - \theta_k \qquad (1)$$

$$O_k = f(U_j) \qquad (2)$$

where j and k are respectively the number of the neuron in the hidden and the output layer and H_j and O_k are respectively output of the neurons in the hidden and the output layer. θ_k is the threshold of a neuron in the output layer. f is the sigmoid function. From Eqs.(1), (2), it is clear that when the difference between positive value of weights and threshold value is large, the neuron is apt to ignite.

This situation occurs regardless of the initial values of connection weights because during learning only coronas the connection weight values are reduced as follows:

$$\Delta W_{kj} = \eta \delta_k H_j \quad (\eta > 0) \qquad (3)$$

$$\delta_k = (T_k - O_k) O_k (1 - O_k) \qquad (4)$$

where ΔW_{kj} is the correction factor of the connection weight. T_k is the teacher signal. η is the coefficient of weight update. Here, because the teacher signal is a value 1 during the network learning only coronas and the value of H_j or O_k is from 0 to 1, δ_k is positive and ΔW_{kj} is positive absolutely. Therefore, as the network learn only coronas, the negative values become smaller than the positive values relatively. As the same way, the threshold is always adjusted to negative.

From the above facts, the neural network learned only corona waveforms is found to difficult to recognize noise waveforms. On the contrary, it is found from Fig.4 that the neural network learned four or sixteen noises can recognize the noise and correct rate increases.

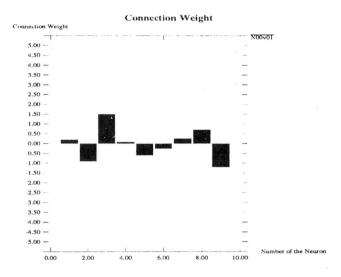

Fig.5.(a) The connection weight after learning only 6 coronas.

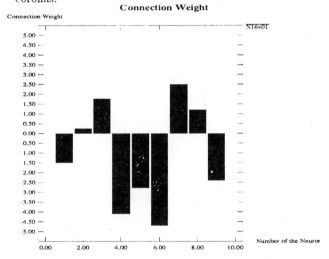

Fig.5.(b) The connection weight after learning 6 coronas and 16 noises.

4 FFT Pretreatment

4.1 The comparison of the neural network between with FFT pretreatment and without pretreatment

In the above sections, the sampling data of waveforms are used as the input data to the neural network. In this section, the result of using frequency spectra of the waveforms obtained by FFT as input patterns are investigated. Figure 6 shows the comparison of the cases using no pretreatment to the input patterns and using FFT pretreatment. It is found that the correct rate doesn't increase much in spite of increasing the number of noises that the network learned for the case without FFT pretreatment, but the rate increases much for the case with pretreatment. Particularly after learning 6 coronas and 16 noises, the rate archives 100%.

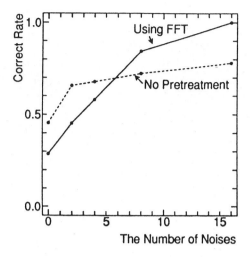

Fig.6 The comparison of the correct rate of using no FFT pretreatment with that of using pretreatment.

States of neurons in the hidden layer are shown in Figure 7. It shows the states of neurons for testing data that includes 8 coronas and 40 noises. The horizontal axis indicates the number of the neuron in the hidden layer and the vertical axis indicates the number of testing data. The number 0 to 8 correspond to coronas and 9 to 50 to noises. It is found that many state patterns exist in the hidden layer for testing data in the case of using no pretreatment. Therefore it seems to be difficult for the neuron in the output layer to classify these patterns into two patterns. The one is for coronas and the other is for noises. On the other hand, only two states patterns exist in the case of using FFT. The first, third, seventh and ninth neurons are reacting to coronas and the other neurons are reacting to noises. From these facts, FFT pretreatment is thought to play a role of classifying the input.

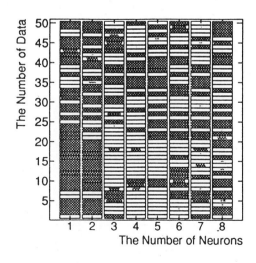

Fig.7.(a) States of neurons for the testing data for the case without FFT pretreatment.

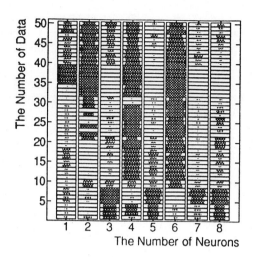

Fig.7.(b) States of neurons for testing data for the case of with FFT pretreatment.

4.2 The influence of the initial values of the connection weights

The initial value of connection weights are chosen randomly. Here, influences of the initial values are examined. We computed for four sets of the initial value of connection weights. From Table 3 it is found that the influence of the initial values of connection weights are less for the case with FFT pretreatment than without pretreatment. For example, when the network learned the training data set including 6 coronas and 8 noises for the case with FFT pretreatment, the correct rate fluctuates between 83% and 85%, on the other hand, for the case without pretreatment, the correct rate fluctuates between 59% and 72%. From the above facts, it is clear that the influences of changing the initial values of the connection weights of the network is small when FFT pretreatment is used.

Table 3.(a) The correct rate for the case without FFT pretreatment.

	No.1	No.2	No.3	No.4
8 noises	72.4	60.3	70.7	58.6
16 noises	78.0	82.2	64.3	80.1

Table 3.(b) The correct rate for the case with FFT pretreatment.

	No.1	No.2	No.3	No.4
8 noises	84.8	82.8	84.5	84.5
16 noises	100.0	100.0	100.0	100.0

4.3 The influence of changing the starting sampling point of the input waveforms.

The influence of changing the starting sampling point of the input waveforms are investigated and the result is shown in Figure 8. For example, for the case without pretreatment, the correct rate varies between 60% and 80% according to the shifts of initial sampling point, while it is almost constant for the case of using FFT pretreatment. So we conclude that the neural network becomes influenced by temporal shifts of sampling point by inputting the frequency spectrum data.

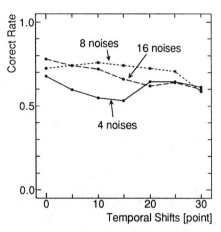

Fig.8.(a) The influence of changing the starting sampling point of the input waveforms for the case without FFT pretreatment.

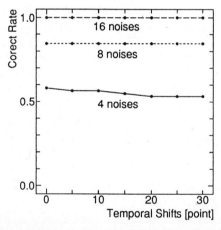

Fig.8.(a) The influence of changing the starting sampling point of the input waveforms for the case with FFT pretreatment.

5   Conclusions

(1) There is no difference between the performance of "1 out put model" and "2 output model". The neural network should learn both corona and noise data in any case for obtaining the higher network performances.

(2) By using FFT pretreatment of the input data, the neural network is found to improve the correct rate, and less influenced by the temporal shifts of sampling point of the input waveforms.

References

[1] H.Suzuki and T.Endoh, "Pattern Recognition of Partial Discharge in XLPE Cables Using a Neural Network" , IEEE Transactions on Electrical Insulation, Vol. 27 No. 3, pp. 549, June 1992.

[2] N.Hozumi, T.Okamoto and T.Imajo, "Discrimination of Partial Discharge Patterns Using a Neural Network", IEEE Transaction on Electrical Insulation, Vol. 27 No. 3, pp. 556, June 1992.

[3] M.Seki, K.Aihara, S.Kitai and K.Hirotsu, "Fault Diagnosis of Power Cables by Neural Network", T.IEE Japan, Vol. 110-D, pp. 273-280, March 1990, (in Japanese).

Power System Load Forecasting

Power systems have vastly different loads over the period of a year. From extreme cold to extreme heat, the weather can create varying demands for power. Holidays such as Christmas create varying fluctuations on power. Other factors can also influence the demand for power. For power systems to be most economically efficient, they must have just enough power available during each day. Too little means that power must be purchased to meet the demand. Too much means power is being wasted. Because of their ability to learn nonlinear functions from historical data, neural networks have been applied to the load forecasting problem. This chapter contains five papers that reflect different neural network approaches to various aspects of load forecasting. **Paper 8.1** employs the multilayer perceptron (MLP) neural network to forecast daily and hourly load requirements. **Paper 8.2** also uses the MLP neural network, but replaces the gradient descent learning algorithm with the faster conjugate gradient learning algorithm. **Paper 8.3** analyzes the performance of a recurrent neural network that is used for short-term load forecasting. **Paper 8.4** utilizes a fuzzy neural network to perform load forecasts two days in advance. **Paper 8.5** applies the learning vector quantization (LVQ) neural network to classify electric payloads.

Chapter 8:   Load Forecasting

Data Partitioning for Training a Layered Perceptron to Forecast Electric Load

M.A. El-Sharkawi, R.J. Marks II, S. Oh

Department of Electrical Engineering, FT-10

University of Washington

Seattle, WA 98195

C.M. Brace

Puget Sound Power and Light Company

Bellevue, WA 98009-9734

U. S. A.

Abstract

The multi-layered perceptron (MLP) artificial neural network has been shown to be an effective tool for load forecasting. Little attention, though, has been paid to the manner in which data is partitioned prior to training. The manner in which the data is partitioned dictates much of the structure of the corresponding neural network. In many neural network forecasters, a different neural network is used for each day. We compare the performance of a daily partitioned neural network and hourly partitioned neural network. In our experiments, the hourly partitioned neural network forecaster has better performance than the daily partitioned neural network forecaster.

I. Introduction

Load forecasting using the multilayered perceptron (MLP) artificial neural networks has been shown to be quite effective [1-4]. Load forecasting data contains numerous stationary and cyclostationary components. There exists, for example, a daily pseudo-cyclostationary. The expected profile of the load from weekday to weekday is similarly cyclostationary. In many neural network load forecasters, one neural network is trained to forecast the load over a single cycle of a weekday. (Statistics for weekends and holidays are different and required separate neural networks.) Training data in most previously proposed load forecasting neural networks, was partitioned by days.

Alternatively, the data can be partitioned into loads at 8AM, 9PM, etc. and a separate neural network trained for each time. One advantage of such an approach is that the resulting statistics for each neural network are pseudo stationary. One expects, in general, that a feed forward MLP can predict stationary processes better than nonstationary (*e.g.* cyclostationary) processes. In this paper, we compare the results of neural networks trained in each way. We demonstrate that the autocovariance of the load data is maximum every 24 hours, thus

suggesting that hour partitioning should give better results. This, indeed, is the case.

II. Problem Description

The electric load of Puget Power is forecasted at 9:00 AM of the previous day. For example, Tuesday forecasting is done on Monday at 9:00 AM. The exceptions are Saturday, Sunday, and Monday where forecasting is done on Friday at 9:00 AM. The available data is the true hourly temperature at Seattle/Tacoma airport, forecasted hourly temperature at Seattle/Tacoma airport, and the current hourly load. We forecast the hourly load based on the above available data.

III. Comparison between Daily Partitioned and Hourly Partitioned Neural Network Forecasters

1. Daily Partitioned Neural Network

We elected to use five neural networks. The neural network are for Monday, Tuesday, Wednesday through Friday, Saturday, and Sunday. The input data is

- Hour of the forecast (k).

- Forecasted temperature.

- Actual temperature and load 48 hours earlier (k-48).

- Actual temperature and load 49 hours earlier (k-49).

- Actual temperature and load 50 hours earlier (k-50).

- Actual temperature and load one week earlier (k-168).

In this simulation, we use the single hidden layer with 8 neurons. This is the manner by which the load was forecast in [3].

2. Hourly Partitioned Neural Network

Here, one neural network is used for each hour regardless of the day of the week. The input data for this structure is

- Forecast year.

- T(k) : Forecasted temperature at hour k.

- $[T(k)-60]^2$: The square of the difference between the forecasted temperature and the average indoor temperature.

- T_{max} : Maximum temperature of the forecast day.

- $[T_{max} - 60]^2$.

- T_{max2} : Maximum temperature of two days before.

- $[T_{max2} - 60]^2$.

- T_{min} : Minimum temperature from the forecast day.

- $[T_{min} - 60]^2$.

- T_{min2} : Minimum temperature of two days before.

- $[T_{min2} - 60]^2$.

- Sum of temperature at hour k of previous 7 days.

- Sum of loads at hour k of the previous 7 days.

- Load at hour k of previous day.

- Load at hour k two days earlier.

- Load at 9:00 AM of the current day.

In this simulation, we use the single hidden layer with 8 neurons.

3. Results

For training, we use the winter data from 1986-1987 to 1989-1990 in the Seattle/Tacoma area. The testing is done from November 7, 1990 to March 31, 1991. Figure 1 shows the relative error of the forecasting and the actual load from test data. As can be seen in Figure 1, the performance of the hourly partitioned neural network is better than that of the daily partitioned neural network. Figure 2 shows the autocovariance of the load.

The autocovariance is defined as

$$COV(n) = NUM(n) / DEM \qquad (1)$$

where

$$NUM(n) = E[\{L(m+n)-E(L)\}\{L(m)-E(L)\}],$$

$$DEM = E[\{L(m) - E(L)\}^2]$$

and $E(\cdot)$ indicates the mean value. As can be seen in Figure 2, the autocovariance is maximum every 24 hours. This means that the functional relationship of the hourly partitioned neural network is more smooth than that of the daily partitioned neural network. This is why neural

networks trained on hourly partitioned data perform better than those trained on daily partitioned data.

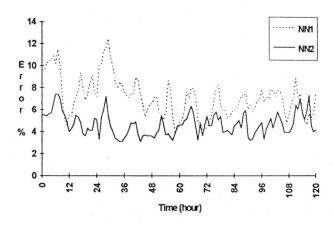

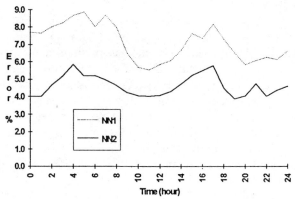

Figure 1: Comparison for the error of two structures. The solid line is for an hourly partitioned network and the broken line is for a daily partitioned network.

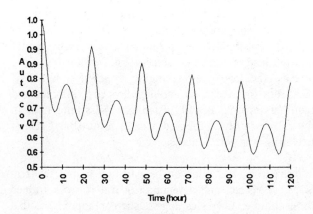

Figure 2: The autocovariance of the load after normalization by the maximum and minimum load of each hour. The peak occurs every 24 hours.

IV. Forecast Temperature Bias Effect

The performance of load forecasting depends highly on the accuracy of the forecasted temperature. One might expect that the error between the forecast temperature and the true temperature is unbiased. This, however, is not the case. The error is biased for certain time intervals. One solution to adjust for this bias is to train the neural network on the forecasted and the true temperature. In the data base available to us, however, the forecasted temperature data is not included. Another method is use of a correction term to augment the forecasted load. We choose the linear fit

$$L = C_1*NN + C_2*(T_f - T_a) + C_3 \qquad (2)$$

where L is forecast load, NN is neural network forecasted load, T_f is forecast temperature, and T_a is actual temperature. The coefficient values, C_1, C_2 and C_3 are determined by minimum mean square error. In the adaptive training mode, we used the above equation. In the testing mode, however, we do not have knowledge of the actual temperature. The second term of the above equation is therefore dropped.

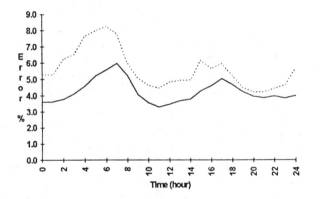

Figure 3: The error of the temperature compensating network. Solid line is for compensated network and broken line is for normal hourly partitioned network.

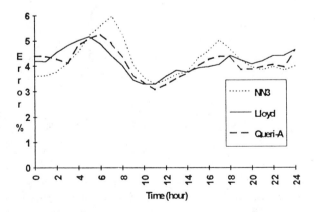

Figure 4: Forecasting contest (Courtesy of Puget Sound Power and Light Company).

Figure 3 and 4 show the comparison of the error between the forecast and actual load with this consideration and without this consideration in the period of November 7, 1991 to November 30, 1992. The results using (2) are clearly better. This forecast was placed into competition

with other techniques in competition coordinated by the Puget Sound Power and Light Company. It did quite well. The interested reader is refereed to Brace et.al. [5] for details. Figure 4 shows the performance of the NN as compared to human forecaster (Lloyd) and a comprehensive regression method (Queri-A). These tests are reported in reference [5]

V. Conclusion

We compared the daily partitioned neural network and hourly partitioned neural network. The hourly partitioned neural network forecaster had better performance than the daily partitioned neural network forecaster. In addition, we demonstrated a technique whereby the effect of the forecasted and actual temperature can be corrected.

Acknowledgments

The authors would like thank to the Puget Sound Power and Light Company to provide the data and the Washington Technology Center.

References

[1] D.C. Park, M.A. El-Sharkawi, R.J. Marks II, L.E. Atlas, and M.J. Damborg, "Electric Load Forecasting Using An Artificial Neural Network," *IEEE Transactions on Power Systems*, pp.442-449, May 1991.

[2] M.A. El-Sharkawi, S. Oh, R.J. Marks II, M.J. Damborg, and C.M. Brace, "Short Term Load Forecasting Using An Adaptively Trained Layered Perceptron," *Fist International Forum on Application of Neural Networks to Power Systems*, Seattle, July 23-26, 1991, pp.3-6.

[3] C.M. Brace, "A Comparison of the Forecasting Accuracy of Neural Networks with Other Established Techniques," *Fist International Forum on Application of Neural Networks to Power Systems*, Seattle, July 23-26, 1991.

[4] D.C. Park, O. Mohammed, M.A. El-Sharkawi, and R.J. Marks II, "Adaptively Trained Neural Networks and Their Application to Electric Load Forecasting," *IEEE International Symposium on Circuits and Systems*, Singapore, June 11-14, 1991.

[5] C.M. Brace, J. Schmidt and V. Bui-Nguyen "Another look at forecast accuracy of neural networks," to appear in *Second International Forum on Application of Neural Networks to Power Systems*, Nagoya, Japan , 1993.

Artificial Neural Network for Forecasting Daily Loads of A Canadian Electric Utility

B.S. Kermanshahi   C.H. Poskar   G. Swift
P. McLaren   W. Pedrycz

University of Manitoba
Dept. of Electrical and Computer Engineering
Winnipeg, Manitoba, R3T2N2, Canada

W. Buhr   A. Silk

Manitoba Hydro
System Operation Department
Winnipeg, Manitoba, R3C2P4, Canada

Abstract – This paper describes the application of an artificial neural network to short term load forecasting. One of the most popular artificial neural network models, the 3–layer back–propagation model, is used to learn the relationship between 86 inputs, which are believed to have significant effects on the loads, and 24 outputs: one for each hourly load of the day. Historical data collected over a period of 2 years (e.g. calendar years 1989 and 1990) is used to train the proposed ANN network. In the testing stage, data of the same nature collected over 1 year (e.g. calendar year 1991) is used. Based on the known differences among the load responses for the days of the week, a separate ANN is used for each day of the week: seven ANN's in all. In the forecasting stage, the ANN network is supplied with only the input data for the forecasted day and the network presents a 24 hour load forecast for that day at one time. A one year sliding window is used to continually re–train the ANN. Very accurate results have been obtained for all days of the week. The results of the proposed ANN networks have been compared to those of the present system (multiple linear regression) and show an improved forecast capability.

Keywords : Short–Term Load Forecasting, Artificial Neural Networks, Back–Propagation, Conjugate Gradient.

Introduction

The primary reason for forecasting daily loads, one day in advance, is to allow the utility to match its generation capabilities to the expected requirements. This is particularly important if a steam generating station is needed to meet the requirement. Adequate notice must be given to the operators of the steam plant to ensure that the plant is fully operational by the time its power is needed. A predictable load pattern is also needed to schedule maintenance and export power to other utilities. Work or inspection of parts of a power system may cause decreased generation for the duration of the intended work. However this maintenance could be scheduled so as not to occur during times of peak requirements.

Manitoba Hydro (a provincial utility) has been using a multiple linear regression method for short term (tomorrow) load forecasting and sought to find a more accurate and less time–consuming method, if such were possible. Since artificial neural networks (ANN) have been used or proposed for load forecasting by several groups, it was decided to try this approach. Basically several researches have been done for short–term load forecasting in the last 30 years. Most of these researches have been concerned about application of different models based on different behavioral assumptions about the load shape such as: regression [1], Box–Jenkins time series models [2], state space models [3], expert system based models [4]. Alternatively, some work has been done on application of artificial neural networks for short–term load forecasting [5], [6].

One of the unique things about this part of the world is the extremes of temperature. Even in average years the temperature drops to –40C in the winter and rises to +35C in the summer. The electric heating load is therefore significant at one part of the year, and the air–conditioning load is significant at another part of the year. In other words weather plays a major role in short term load forecasting. It is then hypothesized that the weather components: temperature, wind speed, and amount of sky cover will govern the amount of change in peak load from one week to the next. (These were chosen for their apparent relationship to changes in the daily loads and for the availability of reliable forecasts of these weather components. The latter is crucial for reliable load forecasting.)

Some published ANN architectures were tried and found to give poor results for local data which, incidentally, were available in detail for the years 1989, 1990 and 1991. Therefore, some new approaches were developed by the authors, resulting in some ideas that other researchers may find useful:

(1)   Contrary to conventional methods, no "reference day" is used because a poor choice of reference day was the primary reason for large prediction errors with conventional methods. Instead, the Tuesday ANN (for example) is trained entirely on historical Tuesday data.

(2)   There are three weather–related inputs: temperature, wind speed and sky cover. Twenty–four–point forecasts for these inputs are derived by a pre–processing algorithm, based on official weather predictions for 4 distinct times of the forecasted day.

(3)   Since the "months" input neurons are so dominant, they are connected directly to the output neurons – that is, they bypass the single hidden layer through which the other variables pass.

The Traditional Approach to Short–Term Load Forecasting

The present method of short term load forecasting used by Manitoba Hydro is based on the premise that there is a linear relationship between changes in load and changes in weather. The basic relationship is given by:

$$\Delta L = K_T \Delta T + K_W \Delta W + K_S \Delta S \qquad (1)$$

where ΔL is the change in load from a given reference day to the forecast day. Similarly, ΔT is the change in temperature, ΔW the change in wind speed (wind direction is neglected), and ΔS the change in the sky cover, from the given reference day to the forecast day. This can be summarized as:

$$\Delta L = L_F - L_R \qquad (2)$$
$$\Delta T = T_F - T_R \qquad (3)$$
$$\Delta W = W_F - W_R \qquad (4)$$
$$\Delta S = S_F - S_R \qquad (5)$$

where
L_F is the forecast day load,

L_R is the reference day load.

T_F is the forecast day temperature,

T_R is the reference day temperature.

W_F is the forecast day wind speed,

W_R is the reference day wind speed.

S_F is the forecast day sky cover,

S_R is the reference day sky cover.

The coefficients K_T, K_W and K_S are calculated using a linear regression analysis of historical weather and load data. The forecasted load for a particular day is then given by (2):

$$L_F = L_R + \Delta L$$

where ΔL is calculated using (1). The coefficient set K_T, K_W, and K_S are actually three sets of coefficients which vary throughout the year in regular patterns, and vary from year to year with system load growth (or decay). To remove any anomalous data, the linear regression analysis requires data over a sufficiently long period of time. However a balance must be struck so as not to average out the effect of system load growth over this time. It was found experimentally that at least three to four years worth of data was required as a minimum, but that when approaching ten years of data the growth factor could not keep up. For this reason seven years of data was chosen.

Due to this annual regularity and the computational time required to perform the linear regression, it was decided to calculate only one coefficient set of K_T, K_W, and K_S for each month of the year, and to use nonlinear smoothing to develop an annual curve of points for each coefficient. The coefficients are therefore updated once annually for a period beginning in July of the present year, and ending in June of the following year.

Once the coefficients have been developed, the actual operation is quite simple. The forecast day is chosen as the next day. A weather forecast for this day is supplied from an outside source, at a time as close to the forecast day as still useful to the person doing the forecasting. This data is then entered into a program along with advance knowledge of industrial load site changes (such as a 200 MW smelter shutting down for a month), and the forecast date. The user is then prompted to choose a **reference day** from the historical data base. A reference day is chosen to have the following characteristics*:

(1)   the same day of the week as the forecast day,

(2)   to be from the recent past (usually no more then one year),

(3)   to have similar weather patterns as the forecast day.

(* Note: These characteristics do not hold for holidays.)

The user is then provided with the 24 hour load forecast, by means of equations (1) – (5). This system has been developed and used for the past several decades. In that time it has been found that while in general performing adequately, there are several areas where improvement could be made.

(A)   The area of greatest error using this system is the accuracy of the weather forecast. While the accuracy of the forecast cannot be improved, a system which would not rely on this accuracy so greatly would be an improvement.

(B)   A second drawback to this system is that it heavily relies on having expert users. The user is required to choose an appropriate reference day before evaluating the load forecast, correcting it or even replacing it with one of his own. Choosing the reference day is key to this system, as the basic assumption is made that there is only a change of load due to the weather from the reference day to the forecast day. For making this choice, the simple guidelines above often lead to several choices for reference day, but not all of them are good ones (a common problem in an environment with many extremes of weather and changes in weather). As for correcting the load forecasts the error can still range to over 20% even after the experienced user has corrected it. Therefore a system which could lower the dependency on the ability of the user would also be advantageous.

(C)   Lastly there are the basic assumptions used to devise this method to begin with. Is the relationship between load and weather linear? Does the change in load depend on only one reference day (the problem of erratic weather changes)? To investigate these questions a nonlinear system could be developed with various input data schemes. This system could then model both linear and nonlinear relationships, and would therefore be an improved system.

Therefore, a better method of forecasting would be one that could find nonlinear relationships between load and weather variables and is adaptable to changes. A methodology that best suits these requirements is the use of artificial neural networks.

The Artificial Neural Networks Approach

Our objective in the development of the neural network is to provide a forecasting method which performs at least as well as the conventional methods without using either the reference day or expert users and also without requiring an extensive amount of calculation such as that needed to determine the coefficients in regression techniques. The proposed method has the advantages of saving time and being inexpensive while accomplishing the same task with equal reliability. The technique lends itself well to **automatic fine–tuning** over the long term.

Back–Propagation Neural Networks

Artificial neural networks using the back–propagation algorithm perform supervised learning. The network is supplied with both a set of patterns to be learned and the desired system response for each pattern. The advantages for using such a network center around some of their properties. Firstly, they automatically generalize their knowledge enabling them to recognize patterns which are similar to those with which they have had experience. Secondly, they are robust enough to recognize patterns that have been obscured by noise. Lastly, once they have been trained on the initial set of patterns, their recognition of similar patterns is accomplished very quickly.

Back–propagation training has also two more key advantages for applications which other network paradigms do not possess. The first advantage is that back–propagation training is mathematically designed to minimize the mean squared aggregate error across all training patterns. The other advantage is that it is a supervised training technique. This means that the network designer can dictate the exact results he or she wants the network to achieve, and the network's performance can always be measured against those results. Supervised training is efficient, easy to use, and predictable, and thus, it is prime favorite for our application.

Back–Propagation Learning Algorithm

The back–propagation learning algorithm was developed independently by several researchers. However, it was brought to a bigger audience by Rumelhart, McClelland, and the PDP group through their publication in 1986 [7]. This model is well known for its practical use in solving many mapping problems. It has been proved that a 3–layer back–propagation network can approximate many arbitrary continuous mappings [8]. During the training stage, the back–propagation calculates the differences (errors) between the actual outputs and the target samples, and then it propagates back these errors from the output layer down to the input layer. The total squared error can be described as

$$E = \frac{1}{2}\sum_{h}^{M} E_h = \frac{1}{2}\sum_{h}^{M}\sum_{i}^{N}(t_{hi} - O_{hi})^2 \qquad (6)$$

where the index h ranges over the set of input and target pattern pair, i refers to the ith output neuron, t_{hi} is the hth target pattern for the ith component, O_{hi} is the actual output value of the ith component for pattern h, E_h represents the error on pattern h, and E is the total error of the entire set of patterns. The network uses this error informations to organize its weights. Thus, the training's objective is to minimize the total squared error between the actual outputs and the targets by modifying the weights. The learning rule employs the so called LMS (Least Mean Square) procedure to change the weights. The learning rule is defined as

$$\delta_{hi} = (t_{hi} - O_{hi})O_{hi}(1 - O_{hi}) \qquad (7)$$

$$\delta_{hi} = O_{hi}(1 - O_{hi})\sum_{k}^{N}\delta_{hk}w_{jk} \qquad (8)$$

$$\Delta w_{ij}(n + 1) = \epsilon\ (\delta_{hi}O_{hj}) + \alpha\ \Delta w_{ij}(n) \qquad (9)$$

where Δw_{ij} is the change in the weight between neuron i and j, n is the index of the training cycle, and δ_{hi} is the error signal of neuron i for pattern h. Eq. (7) calculates the error for an output neuron, Eq. (8) calculates the error signal for an arbitrary hidden neuron, Eq. (9) calculates the weight change. The ϵ and α in Eq. (9) are the learning rate and the momentum parameters respectively. The samples are presented several times to the network while training, until the total squared error is equal or less than a certain tolerable error. Therefore, the training on back–propagation is an iterative process. It usually takes many cycles before it converges to a solution, if that solution exists. The network topologies, the learning parameters, and the initial weights used are some of the important factors for back–propagation to find the solution.

Simulation Results

In this paper, the development of a neural network tool has been facilitated by the use of an existing powerful software package, the Xerion neural network simulator, and by the existence of a large data–base of raw data that is used to train and test the network.

Data Samples

Historical data (actual hourly weather and load data) collected by Manitoba Hydro over a period of 2 years is used to train the proposed ANN network. In the forecasting stage, data of the same nature with training collected over 1 year is used. Based on the known differences among the load responses for the days of the week, a separate ANN is used for each day of the week: seven ANN's in all. All data are *normalized* into real values between 0.0 and 1.0. This is necessary since every neuron in the hidden and output layers of the back–propagation employs a **sigmoid** function which has the range from 0.0 to 1.0. The normalization is done using the following equation

$$Normalized\ Input = \frac{raw\ data - (upper\ value - lower\ value)}{upper\ value - lower\ value}$$

$$(10)$$

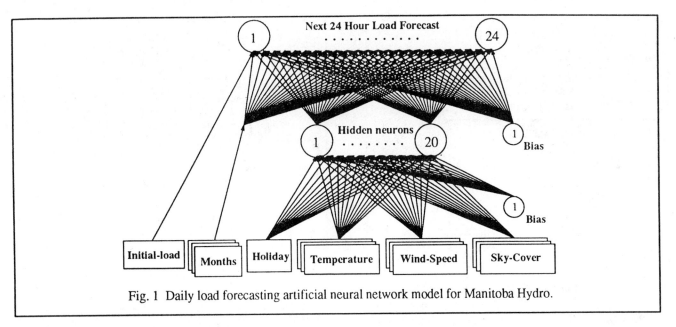

Fig. 1 Daily load forecasting artificial neural network model for Manitoba Hydro.

Table 1 Input characteristics.

Inputs	Lower value Upper value	Number of neurons
Month	Binary	12
Holiday	Binary	1
Initial load	1000–5000 MW	1
Temperature	–45 – +45 C	24
Wind speed	0 – 110 km/h	24
Sky cover	0 – 10	24

3–layer back–propagation networks with 24 neurons as the output, 86 neurons as the input, and 20 hidden neurons are selected in the experiment (Fig.1). The 86 input neurons with their specifications are given in Table 1. For the output load, the following values were used for normalization: (5000, 1000 MW). The selection of the neurons is based on the assumption that these neurons influence the 24 hours load. The initial load in Table 1 is the predicted load of 00:00 tomorrow. It is taken from another ANN network used for today's re–forecast.

The 86 input vectors and 24 target vectors was used as the training set. The format of the example files in training data was:

Training data
$$\begin{cases} iiii.....i\,, \\ tttt.....t\,; \\ \quad . \\ \quad . \\ \quad . \\ iiii.....i\,, \\ tttt.....t\,; \end{cases}$$

where i are the input values (binary and/or floating point) to be presented to the input units, and t are the target values (floating point) to be presented to the output units. The number of neurons in the hidden layer, however, was varied from 6, 12, 18, 20, 24, and 86. The experiment using various numbers of hidden neurons is necessary since, as far as the author's are aware, there is no known technique to determine the exact number of hidden neurons beforehand that leads to an optimal solution. Therefore, the empirical approach was preferable for this experiment. In our case 20 neurons for the hidden layer showed very reasonable results in almost all of the training and testing. Therefore, we fixed the number of hidden neurons at 20 for all of our experiments. Every neuron in the hidden and output layers has a *bias* and employs a *sigmoid* transfer function. The bias acts like another neuron in the layer below with a constant output, which is connected to the hidden and output layer. It usually has an adjustable value. It also provides a means of adding a constant value to the summed input, which can be used to scale the average input into a useful range The network is fully connected. except for months of the year and initial load, which bypass the hidden layer and are directly connected to the output neurons.

Training the Net

Once the example sets have been added to the net, it can be trained. If the load is to be forecasted for a Tuesday, then the example sets in the Tuesday historical data are selected for the training cases. A one year **sliding window** is used here which represents continuous updating of the learning phase. (Fig.2). As an example, in order to forecast the load for a day in May 1991 our sliding window period will become from May 1990 to April 1991. In order to incorporate this, we have broken up the data into blocks of months (this could be changed to blocks of days or weeks).

Forecasting the Load

After the neural network is trained on the pattern associations of input and output factors for the historical data,

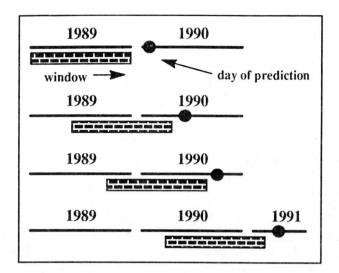

Fig. 2 Sliding window for re-training.

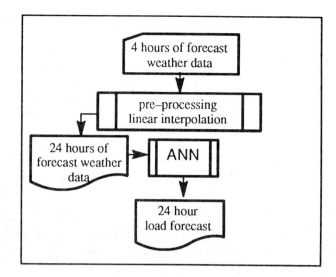

Fig. 3 The forecasting procedure.

it generates output patterns when presented with input patterns. In this way, the trained neural network predicts future daily load based on new sets of input factors.

In the forecasting stage, weather forecast data is used. The temperature, wind speed, and sky cover forecast for the forecast day are given for 9:00, 12:00, 17:00, and 22:00. These

forecasts are provided from the Prairie Weather Center, between 11:00 and 12:00 daily. Since predictions of these weather components are made only for 4 particular hours, and 24 hour weather data is required as input to our ANN, we need to take these data and feed them into a pre-processing program. This program uses linear interpolation and yields 24-point forecast weather data. (Fig.3)

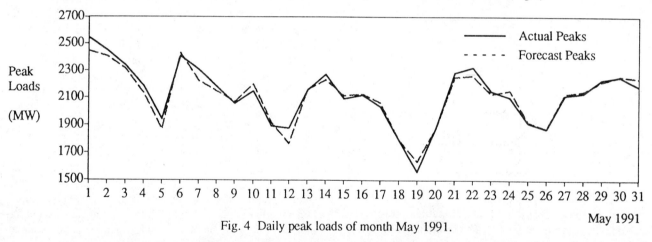

Fig. 4 Daily peak loads of month May 1991.

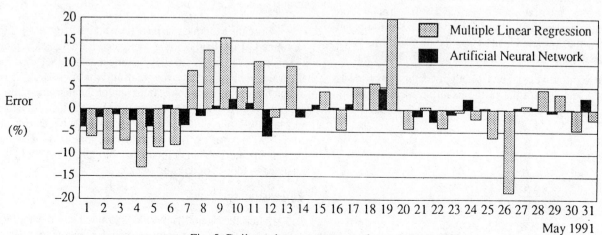

Fig. 5 Daily peaks percent error of month May 1991.

The forecasting using ANN has been run on actual load and weather data obtained from Manitoba Hydro. The results of a simulation of a period of one month (May 1991) are given in Fig. 4 where the actual peak loads are plotted, along with their forecasts as made one day ahead. Forecasts were performed for daily peaks. We then compare how close the ANN can forecast the actual peaks. Fig. 5 illustrates the forecast accuracy by comparing the performance of the present system (multiple linear regression) with the forecasts produced by the ANN. For the one month forecasted period, an absolute average percentage error (AAPE) is shown to be 1.68 % for May 1991. This error is defined by Eq. 11.

$$AAPE = \frac{\sum_{i=1}^{n} |(Actual - load)_i - (Forecast - load)_i|}{n} \times 100(\%)$$

n : number of forecasted days **(11)**

Conclusions

An artificial neural network for short–term load forecasting has been developed in this paper. The obtained results show an improvement over the present linear regression technique. It allows operators to plan the system loading without exceeding the system capacity. The application of neural networks in short–term forecasting will not change his/her functions. The neural network is transparent to the operator. The operator will be required to provide a set of input data and receive forecasting load as the output data much as is required with present method. There is no requirement to chose a reference day and thereby a major source of possible error is removed. Using a typical month (May 1991) as an example, the linear regression method yields an absolute average percentage error of 13.84 %, where the corresponding error for the new ANN method is 1.68 %. The big advantage with this method compare to traditional approaches is that no prior knowledge of how load relates to weather is needed. To generate more accurate results, more elaborate neural networks e.g. a recursive type of network, could be considered employing additional load and weather data such as illumination level, humidity, wind direction, wind chill, onset of darkness, daylight–saving time, and industrial load.

References

[1] N. Hubele and C. Cheng, "Identification of Seasonal Short–Term Load Forecasting Models Using Statistical Decision Functions", IEEE Power Engineering Society, Summer Meeting (1989).

[2] P. Bolzern and G. Fronza, "Role of Weather Inputs in Short–Term Forecasting of Electric Load", Electric Power and Energy Systems, Vol. 8, No. 1, pp 42–46 (1986).

[3] J. Toyoda, M. Chen, and Y. Inoue, "An Application of State Estimation Short–Term Load Forecasting, Part 1: Forecasting Modeling", IEEE Transactions on Power Apparatus and Systems, Vol. PAS–89, NO. 7, PP 1678–1682 (1970).

[4] S. Rahman and R. Bhatnagar, "An Expert System Based Algorithm for Short–Term Load Forecast", IEEE Transactions on Power Systems, Vol. 3, NO. 2, PP 392–399 (1988).

[5] T.M. Peng, N.F. Hubele, and G.G. Karady, "Advancement in the Application of Neural Networks for Short–Term Load Forecasting, ", IEEE Power Engineering Society, Summer Meeting (1991).

[6] D.C. Park, M.A. El–Sharkawi, R.J. Marks II, L.E. Atlas, and M.J. Damborg, "Electric Load Forecasting Using An Artificial Neural Network", IEEE Transactions on Power Systems, Vol. 6, NO. 2, PP 442–449 (1991).

[7] D.Rumelhart, J.McClelland and the PDP group, Parallel Distributed Processing. Explorations in the Microstructure of Cognition, Vol. 1: Foundations. Cambridge, MA: The MIT Press, pp. 568 (1986).

[8] R.Hecht–Nielsen, Neurocomputing. Menlo Park, CA; Addison–Wesley, pp. 433 (1989).

B.S. Kermanshahi was educated at the Tokyo Metropolitan University. Dr. Kermanshahi is a Chief Researcher in the Computer Software Development Company of Japan and is now a Visiting Scientist in the Electrical and Computer Engineering Department of the University of Manitoba.

C.H. Poskar was educated at the University of Winnipeg, the Hebrew University, and the University of Manitoba. Currently he is a graduate student in the Electrical and Computer Engineering Department of the University of Manitoba.

G.W. Swift was educated at the University of Alberta and the Illinois Institute of Technology. He is a senior member of the IEEE, and a Professional engineer in the Province of Manitoba. He is presently a Professor in the Electrical and Computer Engineering Department of the University of Manitoba.

P.G. McLaren was educated at the Universities of St. Andrews, Dundee and Cambridge in the U.K. He is a senior member of the IEEE, a Fellow of the IEE, a Euro. Eng and a Professional engineer in the Province of Manitoba. He is presently the NSERC Chair in Power Systems at the University of Manitoba.

W. Pedrycz was educated at the University of Gliwice. He is a member of the IEEE. He is presently an Associate Head of the Electrical and Computer Engineering Department of the University of Manitoba.

W.D. Buhr was educated at the University of Manitoba. He is a member of the IEEE and a Professional engineer in the Province of Manitoba. He is presently the Integrated Network Performance engineer in the System Performance Department of Manitoba Hydro.

A. Silk was educated at the University of Manitoba. He is a Professional engineer in the Province of Manitoba. He is presently an AC Studies engineer in the System Performance Department of Manitoba Hydro.

Short-Term Load Forecasting Using Diagonal Recurrent Neural Network

K.Y.Lee, T.I.Choi, C.C.Ku

Department of Electrical and Computer Engineering

The Pennsylvania State University

University Park, PA 16802

J. H. Park

Department of Electrical Engineering

Pusan National University

Pusan 609-735, Korea

Abstract-This paper presents a new approach for short term load forecasting using a Diagonal Recurrent Neural Network with a adaptive learning rate. The fully connected recurrent neural network(FRNN), where all neurons are coupled to one another, is difficult to train and to converge in a short time. The DRNN is a modified model of FRNN. It requires fewer weights than FRNN and rapid convergence has been demonstrated. A dynamic Backpropagation Algorithm coupled with adaptive learning rate guarantees even faster convergence. To consider the effect of seasonal load variation on the accuracy of the proposed forecasting model, forecasting accuracy is evaluated throughout a whole year. Simulation results show that the forecast accuracy is improved.

Keywords: Load Forecasting, Diagonal Recurrent Neural Networks

1. INTRODUCTION

One of the most promising application areas of ANN is the load forecasting. There are many classes of load forecasting models reported in literature [1]. Some load models which use no weather information have been presented by time sequence [2]. The other load models have included the effects of weather variables on the power system load [3]. The former is based on the extrapolation and the load behavior is represented by fourier series or trend curves in terms of time functions. The weather sensitive load is mostly predicted using the correlation techniques and the non-weather sensitive load is modeled by the method mentioned above. Each load component is predicted separately and the sum gives the forecast of the total load. Recently, a new method of adaptively identifying the load model was developed, which reflects the stochastic behavior without the aid of weather variables [4]. They decomposed the load model into three components: the nominal load, the residual load and the type load. The parameters of the model are adapted to the load variations.

Several authors have attempted to apply the backpropagation learning algorithm to train ANNs for forecasting time series. Both the backpropagation algorithm for the training of feedforward ANN [5] and dynamic backpropagation algorithm for the training of recurrent ANN are proposed [6] as methodologies for electric load forecasting. A nonlinear load model is suggested and the parameters of the nonlinear load model are estimated using backpropagation and dynamic backpropagation algorithms. Although the ANN is a very promising tool for load forecasting, several key issues must be addressed before it can be effectively used. The load profile is dynamic in nature with temporal, seasonal and annual variations. During the course of this study, several attempts were made to enhance the accuracy of the forecast by selecting different structures of neural networks. As a matter of fact, a simple ANN can outperform several complex and extensive forecasting systems.

The load has two distinct patterns; weekday and weekend patterns. The weekend pattern includes Saturday, Sunday, and Monday loads. Comparing weekday loads with Saturday loads, the level of Saturday loads is relatively low during p.m.. The level of Monday loads during a.m. influenced by Sunday loads is also low. The weekday loads at the same hours are similar to each other due to daily periodic patterns of the customers, but vary slowly during the year. Factors changing loads are economical, sociological, seasonal and meteorological effects. However, since load variations are slow, loads are sufficiently predicted by the appropriate technique in prediction algorithm.

2. ARTIFICIAL NEURAL NETWORKS

A generic feedforward neural network (FNN) is shown in Fig. 1. Processing elements in an ANN are also known as *neurons*. These neurons are interconnected by means of information channels called interconnections. Each neuron can have multiple inputs, while there can only be one output. Inputs to a neuron could be from external stimuli or could be from output of the other neurons. Copies of the single output that comes from a neuron could be input to many other neurons in the network. It is also possible that one of the copies of the neuron's output could be input to itself as a feedback. In this case, the network is called recurrent neural network (RNN). There is a connection strength, *synapses*, or weight associated with each connection.

When the weighted sum of the inputs to the neuron exceeds a certain threshold, the neuron is fired and an output signal is produced. The network can recognize input patterns once the weights are adjusted or tuned via some kind of learning process. The *backpropagation* learning algorithm is the most frequently used method in training the feedforward neural networks (FNN). In order to train the recurrent neural networks (RNN), a modified learning algorithm called *dynamic backpropagation* learning algorithm [6] is used.

3. DYNAMIC BACKPROPAGATION ALGORITHM

The error function is defined as

$$E_p = \frac{1}{2}\sum_j (t_{pj} - o_{pj})^2. \tag{1}$$

let $E = \sum_p E_p$ be the overall measure of the error, where t_{pj} is the target output for j-th component of the output pattern for pattern p and o_{pj} is the corresponding network output. The diagonal recurrent neural network is specified as

$$o_{pj} = f_j(net_{pj}), \tag{2}$$

$$net_{pj} = \sum_k w_{jk}o_{pk} + w_{jd}z^{-1}(o_{pj}), \tag{3}$$

where w_{jd} is the weight for the delayed feedback and z^{-1} is a unit delay operator.

To obtain a rule for adjusting weights, the gradient of E_p with respect to w_{ji} is used and it is represented as follows:

$$-\frac{\partial E_p}{\partial w_{ji}} = \delta_{pj}(o_{pi} + w_{jd}z^{-1}\frac{\partial o_{pj}}{\partial w_{ji}}), \tag{4}$$

where δ_{pj} is defined for the output layer as

$$\delta_{pj} = (t_{pj} - o_{pj})f_j'(net_{pj}), \tag{5}$$

and for a unit in an arbitrary hidden layer as

$$\delta_{pj} = f_j'(net_{pj})\sum_k \delta_{pk}w_{kj}. \tag{6}$$

The output gradient is generated by the dynamic or recurrent equation as follows:

$$\frac{\partial o_{pj}}{\partial w_{ji}} = f_j'(net_{pj})(o_{pi} + w_{jd}z^{-1}\frac{\partial o_{pj}}{\partial w_{ji}}). \tag{7}$$

For the hidden and output layer, o_{pi} is the i-th component of the input, which can be the output from the previous layer.

For the recurrent weight, the error gradient is represented as follows:

$$-\frac{\partial E_p}{\partial w_{jd}} = \delta_{pj}(z^{-1}(o_{pj}) + w_{jd}z^{-1}\frac{\partial o_{pj}}{\partial w_{jd}}) \tag{8}$$

where δ_{pj} is defined as

$$\delta_{pj} = (t_{pj} - o_{pj})f_j'(net_j) \tag{9}$$

and the output gradient is generated by the dynamic or recurrent equation

$$\frac{\partial o_{pj}}{\partial w_{jd}} = f_j'(net_j)(z^{-1}(o_{pj}) + w_{jd}z^{-1}\frac{\partial o_{pj}}{\partial w_{jd}}). \tag{10}$$

Thus the rule of adjusting weights is defined as

$$\Delta w_{ji}(n+1) = \eta(-\frac{\partial E_p}{\partial w_{ji}}) + \alpha\Delta w_{ji}(n). \tag{11}$$

4. LOAD FORECASTING USING ANN

Two different methods of application of ANN are presented for the short-term load forecasting. The first method is a *static mapping* in the sense that the 24-hour load vector is forecasted simultaneously using the previous load patterns. The second method is a *dynamic approach* in the sense that the 24-hour load is forecasted sequentially using the previous-time forecasts. However, when the recurrent neural network is used to the second method, the current state memorizes the previous state, which makes this approach truly a *dynamic approach*.

4.1 Simultaneous Forecasting

In general, the load model for one-day ahead forecasting can be represented as a nonlinear mapping of previous loads in each pattern:

$$y(i) = F_p(W_i, Y(i-1)), \quad p = 1, 2, \ldots, P \tag{12}$$

where
$y(i) = \{y(i, t) : t = 1, 2, \ldots, 24\}$: the actual load vector for day i
$y(i, t)$: the actual load at day i, time t
$Y(i-1) = [y(i-1)^T, y(i-2)^T, \ldots, y(i-k)^T]^T$
k: index for data length
W_i: the weight vector for day i
$F_p(\cdot, \cdot)$: nonlinear vector function representing ANN for pattern p
P: the number of patterns

In contrast to conventional approaches, the nonlinear function is used with the weight vector to represent the load model. The weight vector W_i can be thought of as the storage that contains a certain load pattern, and $F_p(\cdot, \cdot)$ is the general nonlinear function that can comprise all loads in each pattern.

(a) Training

To estimate the load for day i, a number of latest loads can be used to adjust the weight as following:

$$y(i-1) = F_p(\hat{W}_i, Y(i-2)), \; p = 1, 2, \ldots, P, \quad (13)$$

where the output data $y(i-1)$ is the load for day $(i-1)$, $Y(i-2) = [y(i-2)^T, y(i-3)^T, \ldots, y(i-k-1)^T]^T$ is the load vector for the next k latest days, and $\hat{W}_i$ is the estimated weight vector using these input and output data. Both weekday and weekend patterns can be trained using this model. Often, the forecasting errors in weekend are higher than those in weekdays. To improve the forecasting accuracy, additional inputs such as temperature can be added, or the Functional-Link Net mapping can be utilized [7]. In adjusting the weight vector, the backpropagation algorithm can be used to decrease the error, for example,

$$E_p = (y(i-1) - F_p(\hat{W}_i, Y(i-2)))^T (y(i-1) - F_p(\hat{W}_i, Y(i-2)))$$
$$(14)$$

is minimized following the rule, eqn. (11), until the error decreases to a predetermined tolerance.

(b) Forecasting

Once the weight vector for day i is estimated, the load is forecasted using the estimated weights as:

$$\hat{y}(i) = F_p(\hat{W}_i, Y(i-1)), \; p = 1, 2, \ldots, P, \quad (15)$$

where $\hat{y}(i)$ indicates the load forecast for day i.

The above scheme worked well when enough number of patterns are classified and the results were fairly good except at peak time hours [5].

4.2 Sequential Forecasting

The autocorrelation function of the load shows peaks at the multiples of 24 hour lags, which indicates that the loads at the same hours have strong correlation with each other independent of the day of the week including weekend [5]. Thus the following sequential load model is proposed:

$$\begin{aligned} y(i,t) = & \; F_p(W(i,t), y(i,t-1), y(i,t-2), \ldots, y(i,t-m), \\ & \; y(i-1,t), y(i-1,t-1), \ldots, y(i-1,t-m), \\ & \; \vdots \\ & \; y(i-n,t), y(i-n,t-1), \ldots, y(i-n,t-m)), \\ & \; p = 1, 2, \ldots, P, \end{aligned}$$

where n and m indicate the data length.

Note that this model differs from the usual time-series model. Since it includes loads for both previous times and previous days, it better represents the daily and hourly variations than the first model. Another advantage of this model is that training is easier since it has a single output, as compared to the first model which has the 24×1 vector output. The load patterns can be classified into weekday pattern and weekend pattern. The weight vector $W(i,t)$ can be estimated at each time using previous load data for each pattern in a similar way as the first model, i.e., i is replaced by $i-1$ for training.

After the weight vector for day i, time t is estimated, the load is forecasted with the load data of previous days as well as the forecasted load data for the same day, day i, at previous time steps as follows:

$$\begin{aligned} \hat{y}(i,t) = & \; F_p(\hat{W}(i,t), \hat{y}(i,t-1), \hat{y}(i,t-2), \ldots, \hat{y}(i,t-m), \\ & \; y(i-1,t), y(i-1,t-1), \ldots, y(i-1,t-m), \\ & \; \vdots \\ & \; y(i-n,t), y(i-n,t-1), \ldots, y(i-n,t-m)), \\ & \; p = 1, 2, \ldots, P, \end{aligned}$$

where $\hat{y}(i,t)$ indicates the load forecast for day i, time t. It should be noted that the estimate $\hat{y}(i,t-1), \ldots, \hat{y}(i,t-m)$ are used as inputs to the model to obtain $\hat{y}(i,t)$. This is because we need to forecast the entire 24 hour loads for the one-day-ahead forecasting problem. The first model is a *static* mapping while the second is a *dynamic* model. The feedforward neural network can be used for both models. However, when the recurrent neural network is used, the internal states memorize previous states, and, thus, less neurons can be used to capture the dynamic behavior than the feedforward neural network. This will be demonstrated numerically in the following section.

5. SIMULATION RESULTS

Case studies for the proposed method were carried out for a one-day ahead forecasting of hourly electric loads using historical data of Puget Sound Power and Light Company. The results were analyzed based on the following indices:

Standard deviation

$$\sigma = \sqrt{\frac{1}{N} \sum_{i=1}^{N} [y(i,t) - \hat{y}(i,t)]^2} \quad (16)$$

Percent relative error

$$\epsilon = \frac{1}{N} \sum_{i=1}^{N} |y(i,t) - \hat{y}(i,t)| \cdot 100/y(i,t) \quad (17)$$

5.1 Comparison between FFNN and DRNN

Several structures of ANN with the backpropagation and dynamic backpropagation learning algorithms were tested. The learning rate η and the momentum constant α in eqn. (11) were fixed to 0.5 and 0.01, respectively. The tolerance of adjusting the weight vector was 0.005. One hidden layer was used with various numbers of neurons. The data lengths m and n were changed to compare the result. For example, if m is 1 and n is 3, inputs to the ANN are load for time t and $t-1$ of three previous days, and the forecasted load for time $t-1$ of the future forecasting day, totalling 7 inputs. The neural network with one hidden layer was simulated and 7, 15, and 1 neurons were used in the input, hidden, and output layers, respectively. The results were analyzed in detail on an hourly base and presented in Table 1 for one day (July 31, 1991). Both FFNN and DRNN resulted in small percentage error, where DRNN shows the smaller error of 0.867% compared to 0.982% for FFNN. The average iteration number is also smaller for DRNN, 99 compared to 115 for FFNN. The results for one week (July 22 - July 28, 1991) and one month (July 1991) are compared. DRNN shows better results of 1.624% for one week compared to 1.674% for FFNN, and 1.911% for one month compared to 1.954% for FFNN. The iteration numbers to converge into the given error reference are compared and DRNN converges faster than FFNN. For convenience, the maximum iteration number is set to 200. Fig. 2 shows the comparison of actual load and forecasted load for two weeks (July 8-21, 1991). Different structures for input and neurons are compared for one month by using DRNN and FFNN, respectively (July 1991). The DRNN shows better results than FFNN, and the input structure with m=1 and n=3 shows the best result. Therefore the DRNN is used throughout the following experiment.

5.2 Different Structures for Input and Neurons

Since it is known that two hidden layers are sufficient for any kind of nonlinear mapping, two hidden layers with DRNN are tested with various numbers of inputs and neurons. The learning rate η, the momentum constant α, and the tolerance are the same as in the previous method. With two hidden layers of $15-15-15-1$ neuron structure, the input structure of m=1 and n=7 shows a good result comparable with the input structure of m=1 and n=3 for the one hidden layer. Both structures are tested for a one-day-ahead load forecasting for one year from September 1990 to August 1991. The percent relative error is 2.251% and 2.274%, for one and two hidden layer, respectively. Test results shows that one hidden layer is enough. Thus, the results from one hidden layer are used to examine the seasonal effects for four representative months in four seasons. These months are February, May, July and October for Winter, Spring, Summer and Fall, respectively. The minimum values of the standard deviation

and percent relative error are found in Summer, which are 50.21[MW] and 1.726%, respectively, and the maximum values are found in Fall, which are 81.84[MW] and 2.642%, respectively.

5.3 Weekday and Weekend Models

As mentioned before, the load behavior for weekdays (Tuesday through Friday) shows the same pattern and is different from the weekend load pattern. Most classic approaches used several different models according to the load pattern. For example, in [5,6] the load model is divided into weekday and weekend models. The weekend model is further classified into several load types.

Table 2 shows the comparison between the use of one model and the use of two models, one for weekday and another for weekend. It can be concluded that two different models can be used to improve the forecasting accuracy for weekend load and the total accuracy for one month (July 1991) can also be improved. However, this results in a slight increase in error for weekday.

5.4 Temperature Effects and Functional-Link Net mapping

Weather variables are playing an important rule in changing the load patterns. Thus, often loads are classified as weather sensitive load and non-weather sensitive load. Temperature data is obviously a very important factor affecting the load. However, its value is often limited to the confidence level on weather forecasting. Therefore, unless the weather forecasting is very accurate, much care should be made on the use of temperature data. Additional inputs using temperature or Functional-Link Net mapping are experimented to improve the forecasting and Table 4 shows the results. With the structure of m=1 and n=0, two temperatures for time t and $t-1$ of the future forecasting day are added to the inputs and with the structure of m=1 and n=1, four temperatures for time t and $t-1$ of previous day and future forecasting day are added. But the results are not improved. For the use of Functional-Link Net mapping, three inputs of $L(1)^2$, $L(2)^2$, $L(1) \times L(2)$ are added to the inputs, where $L(1)$ is the the load for time $t-1$ of the future forecasting day and $L(2)$ is the load for time t of the previous day. Only the accuracy of the weekend forecasting is slightly improved.

5.5 Adaptive Learning Rate

A large learning rate may make the forecast inaccurate while a small learning rate makes the training process too slow. To guarantee convergence and for faster learning, an approach that uses adaptive learning rates was developed [8-10]. Fig. 3 shows the comparison of the iteration numbers for one day (July 31, 1991), and shows that the adaptive learning rate approach converges faster than fixed learning rate approach. The forecasting results for one month (July 1991) is 1.811%, which is better than 1.911% for the fixed learning rate .

6. CONCLUSION

Artificial neural network method is applied to the short-term load forecasting of one-day ahead hourly electric loads in several different ways. A nonlinear load model is proposed and the weights are estimated using dynamic backpropagation learning algorithms for the diagonal recurrent neural network (DRNN). Several structures for input and neurons are tested with one hidden layer to compare between the DRNN and FFNN. The dynamic approach using DRNN performs better than FFNN in the sense that it uses less number of neurons and weights, converges faster, and gives better results. One hidden layer is shown to be enough to get the comparable result compared with two hidden layers. Each power system has its own load characteristics. Since the load profile is dynamic in nature with temporal, seasonal and annual variations, many structures for inputs and neurons need to be tested experimentally to get the best forecasting result. The forecasting accuracy for weekend load is improved by using two different models (weekday and weekend). Additional inputs using temperature and Functional-Link Net mapping can be used to improve the forecasting results with careful investigation. The forecasting error is about 2% for the percent relative error and thus shows a promise for the use of artificial neural network method in load forecasting.

ACKNOWLEDGEMENTS

The work is supported in parts by grants from Allegheny Power System and Korea Electric Power Corporation. However, any findings, conclusions, or recommendation expressed herein are those of the authors and do not necessarily reflect the views of APS or KEPCO.

REFERENCES

[1] IEEE Committee Report, "Load forecasting bibliography phase I, " *IEEE Trans. on Power Appr. and Sys.*, vol. PAS-99, pp. 53-58, 1980.

[2] W. R. Christiaanse, "Short-term load forecasting using general exponential smoothing," *IEEE Trans. on Power Appr. and Sys.*, vol. PAS-90, pp. 900-910, 1971.

[3] M. Nakamura, "Short term load forecasting using weekday load models and bias models," *Proc. PICA Conference*, pp. 37-42, 1984.

[4] J. H. Park, Y. M. Park and K. Y. Lee, "Composite modeling for adaptive short-term load forecasting", *IEEE Trans. on Power Sys.*, vol. 6, pp. 450-457, May 1991.

[5] K. Y. Lee, Y. T. Cha and J. H. Park, "Short-term load forecasting using an artificial neural network", *IEEE Trans. on Power Sys.*, vol. 7, pp. 124-132, Febuary 1992.

[6] K. Y. Lee, Y. T. Cha and C. C. Ku, "A Study on Neural Networks for Short-Term Load Forecasting", *Proc. of ANNPS '91*, pp. 26-30, Seattle, WA, July 1991.

[7] Y. H. Pao, "Adaptive Pattern Recognition and Neural Networks", Addison-Wesley, Reading, MA, 1989.

[8] C. C. Ku and K. Y. Lee, "Diagonal Recurrent Neural Network Based Control Using Adaptive Learning Rates", *Proc. 31st IEEE Conf. on Decision and Control*, Tucson, Arizona, Dec. 16-18, 1992.

[9] C. C. Ku and K. Y. Lee, "Diagonal Recurrent Neural Networks for Dynamic System Control", *accepted for publication in the IEEE Transactions on Neural Networks*.

[10] C. C. Ku and K. Y. Lee, "Diagonal Recurrent Neural Networks for Controller Designs", *Proc. of ANNPS '92*, April 19-22, 1993, Yokohama, Japan.

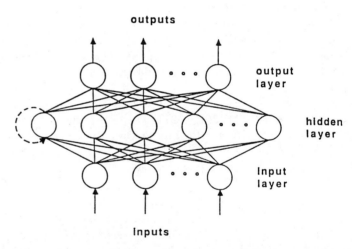

Figure 1: Artificial Neural Network (with recurrent neurons)

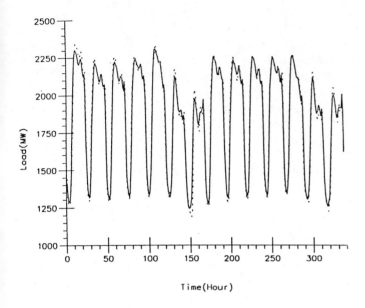

Figure 2: Comparison of actual load and forecasted load using DRNN for July 8-21, 1991. (solid:actual load; dot:forecasted load)

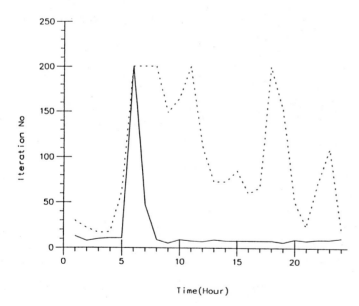

Figure 3: Comparison of Iteration number for convergence for July 31, 1991. (solid:adaptive learning rate; dot:fixed learning rate)

Table 1: Comparison of forecasting results for one day

	FFNN		DRNN	
hour	p.err	iter.no	p.err	iter.no
1	0.174	38	-0.790	30
2	1.244	23	0.724	22
3	0.916	24	0.896	17
4	1.555	25	1.235	18
5	0.669	83	0.481	62
6	-1.067	201	-1.122	201
7	-1.582	201	-1.763	201
8	-0.519	201	-0.892	201
9	0.620	173	0.614	149
10	0.501	201	0.604	165
11	-0.310	201	-0.086	201
12	0.110	180	0.799	112
13	0.245	78	0.514	73
14	0.247	89	0.295	73
15	-0.929	110	-0.847	85
16	0.599	80	0.519	60
17	0.902	90	0.593	67
18	-0.030	201	0.012	201
19	-2.054	201	-1.762	153
20	-1.188	72	-1.140	51
21	1.497	31	1.015	23
22	-0.973	97	-1.307	72
23	-3.272	121	0.822	110
24	-2.366	29	-1.972	20
total	0.982	115	0.867	99

Table 2: Comparison between one model and two models for one month

model	one model		two model	
index	s.dev	p.err	s.dev	p.err
weekday	40.52	1.498	47.42	1.689
weekend	68.81	2.487	63.00	2.173
one month total	54.17	1.911	54.64	1.896

Table 3: Additional inputs using temperature and Functional-Link Net mapping

model	weekday		weekend	
index	s.dev	p.err	s.dev	p.err
w/o add.input	47.42	1.689	63.00	2.173
2 temp. m=1 n=0	48.26	1.729	64.06	2.200
4 temp. m=1 n=1	71.61	2.076	64.33	2.241
3 F-L.N.M.	68.32	1.986	61.96	2.169

A FUZZY ADAPTIVE CORRECTION SCHEME FOR SHORT TERM LOAD FORECASTING USING FUZZY LAYERED NEURAL NETWORK

P.K.Dash & S. Dash
Energy Research Centre
Regional Engineering College
Rourkela, INDIA

S.Rahman
Virginia Polytechnic Institute
& State University
Blacksburg, U.S.A.

Abstract - *A hybrid neural network-fuzzy expert system is developed to forecast one hour to forty-eight hour ahead electric load accurately. The fuzzy membership values of load and other weather variables are the inputs to the neural network and the output comprises the membership value of the predicted load. An adaptive fuzzy correction scheme is used to forecast the final load by using a fuzzy rule base and fuzzy inference mechanism. The paper also presents a fuzzy pattern classification approach for identifying the day-type from the historical load database to be used for training the neural network.Extensive studies have been performed for all seasons, although the results for a typical winter day are given in the paper to demonstrate the powerfulness of this technique.*

1. INTRODUCTION

Short term forecasting of electricity and power demand is important for optimum operation planning of power generation facilities, as it affects both system reliability and fuel consumption. Accurate forecasting of energy demand determines the type of facilities required, and provides the basis for assessing future revenues. Power demand forecasting, on the other hand facilitates the day to day operation of generating plants, ensuring a reliable supply of electricity all the time. Adequate planning should take into account the effect of various factors on the load, such as, weather conditions, day of the week records of historical data.

The current techniques for load forecasting use conventional smoothing techniques, regression methods and statistical analysis. These methods fail to give an accurate forecast because of their inherent limitations. Although much effort has also gone into the attempt to develop knowledge based expert systems to adequately forecast the future demand of electricity, entirely successful results have remained elusive. Recent research in the area of neural network technology [1-5] has shown that neural network possess the properties required for such applications, such as, nonlinear and smooth interpolation, ability to learn complex non-linear mappings, and adapting themselves to different statistical distributions. In addition, they can improve their performance by learning from past experiences and making generalizations of their knowledge for novel scenarios. With the standard multi layered neural network problem, learning algorithm such as the error backpropagation requires rather a large training time and results in not too accurate prediction due to the nonstationary nature of the data, and its dependence on temporal seasonal and annual variations.

Thus to obtain an accurate power demand forecast based on the multilayer perceptron using backpropagation algorithm and a fuzzy expert system for error correction are used in this paper.

The approach taken in this paper is to produce the load forecast in two steps. In the first step the inputs to the neural network are classified into overlapping regions like low, medium and high categories using nonlinear membership functions. The neural network produces a forecast of the power demand at the output node. In the second step, a fuzzy expert system is used to manipulate the forecasted value by using a fuzzy rule base and inference mechanism pertaining to load and weather parameters to determine the final forecast .

2.FUZZY-LAYERED MODEL NEURAL NETWORK FOR INITIAL FORECAST

Artificial neural networks are a massively parallel interconnection of simple neurons that function as a collective system. Their high computation rate enables real-time processing of huge data sets and the redundancy of their interconnections ensures robustness.

The utility of fuzzy sets lies in their capability in modelling ambiguous data so often encountered in real life. Fuzzy concepts have already been incorporated into neural nets in control problems [6-7] and to model possibility distributions.

The present work attempts to develop a fuzzy model of the multilayer perceptron using the gradient-descent based backpropagation algorithm by incorporating concepts from fuzzy sets at various stages. The proposed model is capable of producing an initial load forecast and also classification of fuzzy patterns of the day types.

Broadly the network passes through two phases, i.e., training and testing. During training supervised learning is used to assign class membership values to the output nodes for each training vector. The backpropagated error is computed with respect to each such desired output. After a number of cycles the neural net converges to a minimum error solution.

This error is minimized by using a gradient descent algorithm by starting with any set of weights and repeatedly updating each weight by an amount

$$\Delta W_{ji}^{h}(n+1) = -\eta \frac{\partial E^{(h+1)}}{\partial W_{ji}} + \alpha \Delta_{ji} W(n) + \beta \Delta W_{ji}(n-1) \quad (1)$$

where η is the learning rate and α and β are momentum coefficients. A large η would speed up the convergence initially but oscillations tend to occur as the error progressively becomes small and thus it has to be reduced. The value of η is fixed at .001 and once oscillations occur η is reduced to .0001. However, α and β are fixed at 0.8, -0.15, respectively. Training is stopped in each case, once the error does not reduce by less than .001% over 1000 iterations.

3. FUZZY LOGIC AND PATTERN REPRESENTATION IN LINGUISTIC FORM

We use the modified π - function to assign membership values for the input features corresponding to the linguistic

properties low, medium and high. Let x = $\{x_1, x_2, \ldots, x_L\}$ be a set of L pattern points in an N-dimensional feature space. The fuzzy set associated with X is defined as

$$X(a,b,\lambda) = \{\mu_{x(a,b,c)}(x_i), x_i\},$$

for i = 1,2, ... , L $\qquad$ (2)

where $\mu_{x(a,b,c)}(x_i) = \pi(x_i, a, b, \lambda,)$
Hear $X(a,b,\lambda)$ is a fuzzy set of points such that $\mu_{x(a,b,c)}(x_i)$ devotes the degree of belongingness of x_i to this set.

For example, the load, temperature, humidity, etc. can be classified into three categories, i.e., small, medium and large and the membership function of each is obtained as

$$\mu_i = 1/[1+(x_i/b_i-a_i/b_i)^{\lambda}] \qquad (3)$$

where μ_i : membership of the quantity x and category i

x_i:load/temp./humidity,etc.in category i

a_i, b_i : coefficients corresponding to category i

λ_i: a suitable index based on experiment for category i

The values of a_i and b_i for load, temperature, humidity, wind speed and sky cover are shown in Table 1. Here λ_i is taken as 4. Further Fig.2 shows the membership function associated with each of the above variables for a typical forecasting problem on a winter day. In the fuzzy neural network model under consideration, each input feature F_j (in quantitative and/or linguistic form) can be expressed in term of membership values indicating a measure of belongingness to each of the linguistic properties, small, medium and large. Therefore, an n-dimensional pattern X_l = $[F_1, F_2, \ldots, F_n]$ may be represented as a 3n-dimensional vector:

$$X_l = [\mu_{small(F_1)}(X_l), \mu_{medium(F_1)}(X_l),$$

$$\mu_{high(F_1)}(X_l), \ldots \mu_{high(F_n)}(X_l) \qquad (4)$$

Hence in trying to express an imprecise input X_l through its linguistic properties, we are effectively dividing the dynamic region of each feature into three overlapping patterns.

4. NEURAL NETWORK TRAINING

During training the input patterns to backpropagation neural network comprise several features like past load at hour (t-1), temperature at hour t, temperature at hour (t-1), humidity at hour t, humidity at hour (t-1), etc. Thus input pattern is used for producing 1 to 6 hours ahead forecast. However, for 24 or 48 hours ahead forecast, the load 24-hours back at hour t, temperature and humidity 24-hours back at hour t and t-1, respectively, are used as inputs to the neural network. These features are normalized by using their maximum and minimum values.

After the data initialisation is done, the membership functions of the data belonging to the categories Small(S), Medium(M) and Large(L) are found out. For example, the past temperature at hour t is represented to the neural network as

1.00S   0.15M   0.00L

To illustrate the learning procedure for 1 to 2 hours and 24 hours ahead forecasting, the following case studies are repeated. To predict the load on January 20th at hours 10 onwards (for 6 to 14 hours), a four week data base having the maximum correlation (as presented in the preceding section) is scanned. Assuming it to be a week day, the previous 24 hours data is used for training and producing a forecast on the required day. Thus for the 10th hour prediction on January 20th, the inputs to the ANN during training are (data pertains to January 19th)

P(9),T(9),H(9),T(10),H(10)

where P,T,H stand for load, temperature, humidity respectively and bracketed numeric quantity indicates the hours. Each of this feature has 3-categories and thus the input layer of the ANN comprises 15 inputs. The hidden layer has 17 neurons and the output layer consists of 3 neurons corresponding to the predicted load P(10).

The error between the predicted load and the actual load at hour 10 on January 19th is

$$e(10) = A(10) - P(10) \qquad (5)$$

Similar error values are computed for the entire 24 hour period on January 19th.

After the initial prediction is obtained from the ANN, a fuzzy expert system is designed to handle this error and the errors of the weather parameters like temperature and humidity and produce corrections to the predicted load for hour 10 on the January 20th. (Fig.1).

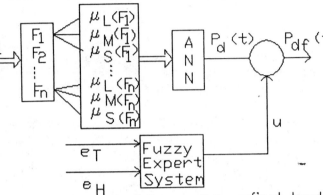

L=large, M=medium, S=small, P_{df}=final load forecast

Fig.1 Block diagram for Load forecasting using ANN & Fuzzy Expert System

5. FUZZY EXPERT SYSTEM

Zadeh [4] proposed fuzzy logic and fuzzy sets theory to make a rapprochement between the precision of classical mathematics and imprecise information from the real world. The fuzzy set theory works with grades of membership of x in A, i.e., $\mu_A(x)$, taken from the set M=[0,1]. If $\mu_A(x)$ and $\mu_B(x)$ represents grades of membership of an object in fuzzy sets A and B, respectively, then these logics are defined as:

ZADEH LOGIC:

AND $(\mu_A(x),\mu_B(x))$=min $(\mu_A(x),\mu_B(x))$

OR $(\mu_A(x),\mu_B(x))$=max $(\mu_A(x), \mu_B(x))$ (6)

NOT $(\mu_A(x))$ = 1 - $\mu_A(x)$

For load forecasting the load, temperature and humidity errors for the training example (i.e.24 hours before the day of forecast) are found out as

$$e_L = A(t) - P(t)$$

$$e_T = T(t) - T(t-1)$$

$$e_H = H(t) - H(t-1) \qquad (7)$$

For these errors the corresponding membership $\mu(e_L),\mu(e_T)$ and $\mu(e_H)$ values

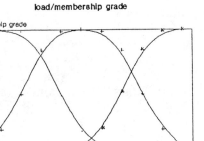

load/membership grade

— small   —+— medium   —*— large

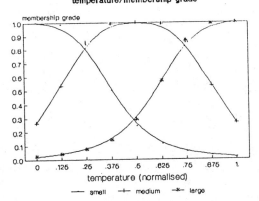

temperature/membership grade

— small   —+— medium   —*— large

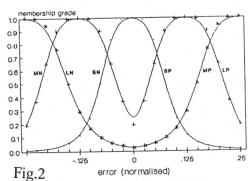

error/membership grade

Fig.2

— small   —+— medium   —*— large

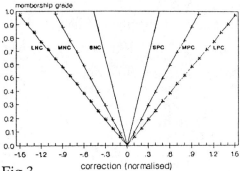

correction/membership grade

Fig.3

— small   —+— medium   —*— large

The value of ΔC_{max} is a function of the maximum error bound which can be adaptively changed for 24, 48 or 72 hours ahead predictions respectively. Fig.3 shows the load correction membership function and its adaptive version is shown in Fig.4. The value of ΔC_{max} is quantitatively obtained (Fig.5) as

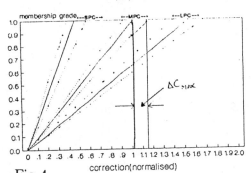

correction/membership grade
(adaptive)

Fig.4

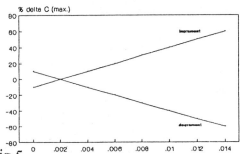

delta C/error(max)
(linear adaptive)

Fig.5

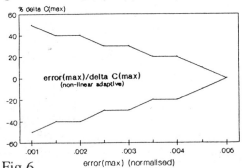

Fig.6

are calculated using equation (3).

Fig.2 depicts the membership functions associated with each of these errors. The membership value of the load error correction is

$$\mu(e_{LC}) = (1/C_{max}).e_{LC} \qquad (8)$$

e_{LC} = Actual load (t) - Predicted load (t) and C_{max} is the slope of the load correction and is shown in Fig 3.

For small errors e_{LC} for one hour ahead prediction equation, is adequate. However, for large errors occurring for load forecast 24, 48 or 72 hours ahead, the membership function for the load error correction is

$$\mu(e_{LC}) = (1/C_{max} \pm \Delta C_{max})].e_{LC} \qquad (9)$$

$$\Delta C_{max} = f_1 \{e_{max} \text{ or } \hat{e}(t+1|t)\} \quad (10)$$

In this arrangement change in e_{max} will change ΔC_{max}. However, by changing the effective slope in Fig.4, the model can be made sensitive to error.

5.1 FUZZY RULE BASE

For forming the rule base for the fuzzy expert system, the six categories, like SP(small positive), MP(medium positive), LP(large positive), SN(small negative), MN(medium negative), LN(large negative) are used for all the features like load error, temperature error, humidity error, etc. and is thus used for forming the rule base for error correction. The following five sample rules in the knowledge base of the fuzzy expert system are used for load error correction:

<u>Rule 1.</u> IF e_T is SP AND e_H is SP THEN correction to the load is SP.

<u>Rule 2.</u> IF e_T is SP AND e_H is MP THEN correction to the load is MP.

<u>Rule 3.</u> IF e_T is SP AND e_H is LP THEN correction to the load is LP.

<u>Rule 4.</u> IF e_T is MP AND e_H is SP THEN correction to the load is MP.

<u>Rule 5.</u> IF e_T is MP AND e_H is MP THEN correction to the load is MP.

For the case considered here, the total number of production rules is 36.

From the above rules the load correction required for a given hour in the above example is found out at the defuzzification stage using the Centre of Gravity method as

$$u = \sum_{k=1}^{L} \mu(e_{LC}).e_{LC} \Big/ \sum_{k=1}^{L} \mu(e_{LC}) \quad (11)$$

Where L is the set of load corrections for a pair of temperature and humidity errors.

6. RESULTS

To demonstrate the effectiveness of the proposed hybrid ANN and Fuzzy Expert System based approach, load forecasting is performed on the data base of an electric utility.

Figs.7 and 8 show the forecasted errors for hourly prediction on a typical summer day and winter day, respectively. Increasing lead time from hourly predictions to 24 hours and 48 hours, respectively the maximum %age errors are 0.78 (78 MW) and 1.19 (119 MW). Figs.9 and 10 show the 24-hour lead time % error curve over a period of twenty four hours for summer and winter days. The increase in error necessitates the use of adaptive fuzzy correction.

The results of hourly load forecast for a typical winter day we shown in Table-2. After fuzzy corrections, the maximum percentage error after the ANN prediction reduces from 1.58 (158 MW) to 0.18 (MW) for one-hour ahead forecast. However, in case of 24-hour ahead forecast this error reduces from 2.36 (236 MW) to 0.69 (69 MW) with fuzzy correction.

By employing adaptive fuzzy correction it is, however, seen that the maximum percentage error for one hour ahead forecast reduces to 0.06 (6 MW) and 0.02 (2 MW) for linear adaptive and non-linear adaptive corrections, respectively. For 24-hour ahead forecast it is 0.26 (26 MW) and 0.21 (21 MW) for linear and non-linear adaptive corrections, respectively.

7. CONCLUSION

A new methodology (hybridizing neural network and fuzzy expert system) is developed for calculating one-hour to forty eight-hour ahead prediction of hourly electric load. This approach uses backpropagation technique for an initial forecast and then a fuzzy expert system ia used for error minimization and the final forecast. Moreover, an adaptive approach has been employed to minimize the error more precisely. The results obtained from this study are highly encouraging as the adaptive hybrid expert system produces a very correct estimate of short term load magnitudes. Further the fuzzy neural net model is applicable for all seasons as it categorizes the uncertain data into a set of fuzzy variable taking values between 0 and 1.

ACKNOWLEDGEMENT

The authors acknowledge the funds from the National Science Foundation (NSF Grant No. INT-9209103), U.S.A. for undertaking this research.

REFERENCES:
[1] M.A.El-Sharkawi, S.Oh, R.J.Marks, M.J.Damborg and C.M.Brace, "Short Term

Electric Load Forecasting using an Adaptively Trained Layered Perceptron", First Int. Forum on Applications of Neural Networks to Power Systems, Seattle, Washington, July 23-26, 1991, pp. 3-6.

[2] D.C.Park, M.A.El-Sharkawi and R.J.Marks, "Adaptively Trained Neural Network", IEEE Trans. on Neural Networks, May 1991, pp. 334-345.

[3] M.C.Brace, "A Comparison of the Forecasting Accuracy of Neural Networks with other Established Techniques", First Int. Forum on Applications of Neural Networks to Power Systems, Seattle, July 23-26,1991.

[4] L.A.Zadeh, "Fuzzy Sets", Information & Control, vol.8, 1965, pp. 338-358.

[5] S.K.Pal, and D.Dutta Majumdar, Fuzzy mathematical approach to pattern recognition (book), Wiley (Halsted Press), New York, 1986.

TABLE-1

Coefficients of a and b.

Category		a	b
Load	small	6054	650
	medium	7964	700
	large	9873	750
Temperature	small	32	4
	meium	44	4.5
	large	56	5
Humidity	small	30	3
	medium	65	4
	large	100	5

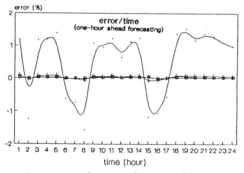

error/time
(one-hour ahead forecasting)

— neural + fuzzy * linear -□- non-lin.

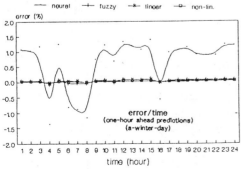

error/time
(one-hour ahead predictions)
(a-winter-day)

— neural + fuzzy * lin. adpt. -○- non-lin. adpt.

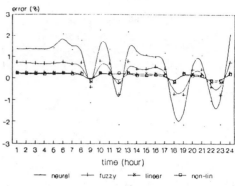

error/time
(24-hour ahead predictions)

— neural + fuzzy * linear -□- non-lin

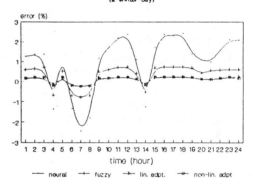

error/time
(24-hour ahead predictions)
(a-winter-day)

— neural + fuzzy * lin. adpt. -○- non-lin. adpt.

Table 2 (one-hour ahead predictions)
(a-winter-day)

Hour	Actual load(KW)	Linear adpt. error(%)	Non-lin adpt error(%)
1	22556.40	+0.03	+0.01
2	20793.77	+0.03	+0.01
3	19809.84	+0.05	+0.01
4	19435.59	-0.07	-0.02
5	19485.99	+0.05	+0.01
6	20320.76	+0.03	+0.01
7	22167.88	+0.04	+0.01
8	26448.05	-0.03	-0.01
9	30317.06	+0.03	+0.01
10	31605.94	+0.04	+0.02
11	31276.87	+0.03	+0.01
12	30847.45	+0.07	+0.02
13	30356.89	+0.07	+0.02
14	29581.29	+0.06	+0.02
15	29168.89	+0.09	+0.03
16	29116.26	-0.03	-0.01
17	28887.12	+0.03	+0.01
18	28028.98	+0.03	+0.01
19	28322.02	+0.04	+0.02
20	27346.63	+0.04	+0.02
21	26857.33	+0.04	+0.02
22	26122.78	0.04	+0.02
23	25766.18	+0.05	+0.02
24	24589.54	+0.04	+0.02

Application of the Kohonen Network to Short-Term Load Forecasting

Thomas Baumann
SIEMENS AG Austria
Vienna, Austria

Alain J. Germond
Laboratoire de Réseaux d'Energie Electrique
Swiss Federal Institute of Technology
Lausanne, Switzerland

Abstract - This paper analyses the application of Kohonen's self-organizing feature map to short-term forecasting of daily electrical load. The aim of the paper is to study the feasibility of the Kohonen's self-organizing feature maps for the classification of electrical loads. The network not only "learns" similarities of load patterns in a unsupervised manner, but it uses the information stored in the weight vectors of the Kohonen network to forecast the future load. The results are evaluated by using several months of hourly load data of a real system to train the network, and forecasting the daily loads for two periods of one month. The method is then improved by adding a second type of neural network for weather sensitive correction of the load previously calculated with the Kohonen network. This second type of network is a one-layered linear delta rule network.

Keywords: Short-term load forecasting, Artificial neural networks, Kohonen network

1 INTRODUCTION

The problem of short-term load forecasting of electrical load has been addressed for many years with methods such as extrapolation, correlation, temporal series and regression [1].

Today's computer technology is mainly based on sequential von Neumann machines. Unfortunately, due to the deterministic nature of these machines, many important tasks where the basic laws are not known, as e.g. the pattern recognition of noisy data, are difficult to solve. Due to their fault tolerant capabilities, Artificial Neural Networks (ANN) can overcome these problems.

An ANN is a collection of simple processing units or neurons interconnected by a weight. The processing units operate independently from each other, thus realizing an architecture that is parallel and distributed, resulting in high speed information processing and potential fault tolerance. The connection weights that determine the way in which neurons interact can be modified during the networks operation, providing a high degree of adaptability. This adaptation process is the so-called learning.

In contrast to classical software algorithms, which are programmed by a succession of instructions, the ANNs work with a training process. In other words, an algorithm is not programmed anymore, but the ANN is trained by a succession of examples (Input / Output pairs). Therefore, this approach is useful for tasks where the basic laws are not or poorly known, which is typically the case for load forecasting.

At present there exist a great number of different architectures of ANN. Among them, the best adapted one must be found for a particular task.

There are different ways to create a taxonomy of ANN's. We use the character of the training phase to separate the ANN in two main groups, supervised and self-organized learning (Fig. 1).

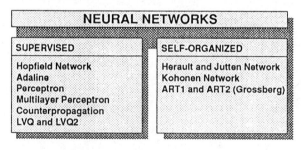

Fig. 1 Taxonomy of ANN

Supervised learning needs the correct desired output for a controlled adaptation of the weights in order to minimize a certain energy function (e.g. error between neural output and desired output).

In contrast to the supervised learning, self-organized ANNs organize themselves only as a function of their inputs. This type of ANN can e.g. be used for principal component analysis or for quantification of an input vector space. A number of input vectors are presented to the ANN, which has to find the proper characteristics of the inputs.

Although the first use of unsupervised learning for treating the electric load forecasting problem dates back to 1975 [2], most of the applications of neural networks to load forecasting use multilayer feedforward networks with supervised learning [3], [4] and [5]. Improvements such as non fully connected model [6] have been proposed to improve the learning efficiency.

A strategy of the concept of minimum distance to historical patterns was proposed for selecting the training cases [7]. Unsupervised learning with Kohonen's self-organizing feature maps [8] was recently used for classifying the type of load [9], whereas the prediction itself was made with a multilayer perceptron.

The originality of our approach is to use a Kohonen map to classify data representing load patterns and to use directly the information stored in the weight vectors of the Kohonen map to predict the load [10].

2 THE KOHONEN NETWORK

In 1982, Teuvo Kohonen proposed a new neural network architecture, which implements a self organizing algorithm [8].

As noted above, an ANN can be characterized as a collection of processing elements (PE), also called neurons, which can all perform the same task in parallel. The information to be treated is distributed through one-directional connections (weights) to all PE's.

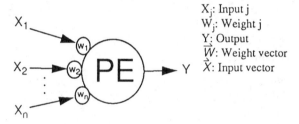

X_j: Input j
W_j: Weight j
Y: Output
$\vec{W}$: Weight vector
$\vec{X}$: Input vector

Fig. 2   The processing element or artificial neuron

Fig. 2 shows a schema of a PE where each input X_j is connected to the PE through a synaptic weight W_j. $\vec{X} = (X_1, X_2, .. X_n)$ is called input vector and on the other hand the $\vec{W} = (W_1, W_2, .. W_n)$ is called weight vector.

For most ANN the basic operation between $\vec{X}$ and $\vec{W}$ to calculate the output Y is the scalar product. For the Kohonen network, the basic operation is the Euclidian distance:

$$Y = D_{Eucl} = \sqrt{\sum_{j=1}^{N} (X_j - W_j)^2}$$

where N is the number of components of the input vector.

The basic architecture of the Kohonen network is composed of an input layer with N inputs followed by a layer with M * M neurons, arranged in a two-dimensional lattice. Each input is connected through a weight W_{ij} to all neurons of the second layer.

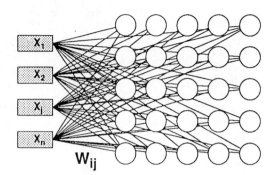

Fig. 3   Basic architecture of the Kohonen network. (Connections are only shown partially)

The training of an ANN is done by a continual modification of the weights W_{ij}, following an internal law which differs from network to network. This needs a repeated presentation of input vectors until the ANN is organized.

A singular learning step can be summarized by the two following phases:

1. Find the neuron c whose weight vector is nearest to the input vector. (Find the best-matching neuron c)

An input vector $\vec{X}$ is presented to the map and the Euclidian distance between this input vector and all the weight vectors $\vec{W_i}$ (i = 1.. M^2) is calculated. Therefore an Euclidian distance is calculated for each neuron. The neuron with the smallest distance is the winner (also called active neuron). This neuron gets the index c. The weight vector $\vec{W_c}$ is consequently the nearest to the input vector $\vec{X}$. This phase can be summarized by:

$$D_{Eucl}(\vec{W_c}, \vec{X}) = min(D_{Eucl}(\vec{W_i}, \vec{X})) \quad for \ i = 1 ... M^2$$

2. Update the unit c and its neighbours.

Once the winner has been located, unsupervised learning proceeds by updating the weights of neurons within a neighbourhood N_c defined around winner neuron c (Fig. 4).

Fig. 4   Neighbourhood around the winner neuron

All other weight vectors are not modified. In the beginning, the radius of the neighbourhood N_c is big (approximately half of the network size) but then decreases with the learning step until it reaches zero. If the radius is zero, only the neuron c is updated. Updating is done as follows:

$$\vec{W_i}(t+1) = \vec{W_i}(t) + \alpha(t) \times (\vec{X}(t) - \vec{W_i}(t)) \qquad i \in N_c$$

$$\vec{W_i}(t+1) = \vec{W_i}(t) \qquad i \notin N_c$$

where $\alpha(t)$ is the gain term $(0 < \alpha(t) < 1)$ which decreases in function of the training iteration step, as well as the neighbourhood.

One can notice that the training law brings the weight vectors inside the neighbourhood N_c closer to the input vector.

The self-organization and the topology preserving of Kohonen maps results from the fact that not only the winner neuron is modified, but also its neighbours.

Briefly, the algorithm performs a reduction of dimensionality. In our case the dimension of the input vector space is reduced to two, arranging vectors on a self-organizing feature map.

Kohonen maps partition the input vector space into M^2 sub-spaces, also called "receptive fields", which are determined by the set of inputs selecting the same neuron. This mapping is done, conserving the topology of the input vectors. In other words, if two partitions of the input vector space are "neighbours", then the two corresponding units of the Kohonen map are topological neighbours, too.

The choice of the learning gain α and of the radius of neighbourhood N_c are dominant for a topologically correct organization of a Kohonen map. Our simulations showed that the initial learning gain α should be between 0.2 and 0.5 and the initial radius of the neighbourhood must be about half the size of the maximal dimension of the Kohonen map.

The decrease of the two parameters with the discrete time index is very important. A slow decrease leads to better organization but needs also more learning time. In all our simulations both parameters decrease with the inverse of the number of iteration steps.

2.1 Application of the Kohonen network to auto-associative memory

Once the training is done, it is possible to apply a vector with missing components and the Kohonen network can again complete the vector. This is called auto-associative memory. Example: When the Kohonen network has been trained with binary images and only a part of an image is presented to the Kohonen network, it will reconstruct the whole binary image.

This method consists of ignoring the missing components of the input vector and calculating the Euclidian distance with the known components only. As in the normal case, the nearest neuron to the (incomplete) input vector is computed. The weights between this selected neuron and

all the ignored input components are then the missing values of the input vector. In Fig. 5 the Kohonen network is trained with four consecutive load values, L(t-2) until L(t+1), and the recall is done with three load values and the load L(t+1) is missing

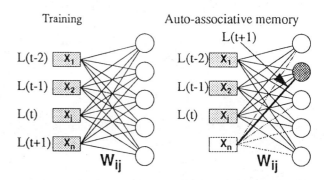

Fig. 5   Principle of auto-associative memory

3 THE LOAD-FORECASTING METHOD

The proposed method consists of two phases: the basic load-forecast and the weather dependent load correction (Fig. 6). In phase 1, the load is calculated without weather data influence using the Kohonen ANN (see section 2.1).

In Phase 2, a one layered ANN is trained to produce a weather dependent correction of the loads obtained in phase 1 (see section 3.4).

3.1   The data

For all our simulations, real load and weather data of a European electric utility has been used. The time range is from 1. January 89 until 11. February 92. The maximal load is approximately 1500 MW. The special holidays (Christmas, Easter, etc.) are excluded from the data.

3.2   Application of auto-associative memory to load forecasting (Phase 1)

An application of auto-associative memory with the Kohonen network to one day term load forecasting is described. If needed, the results of the forecast can be used again as input data to the ANN and therefore more than one day can be forecasted (up to 7 days).

This type of ANN is well suited for the task of load forecasting due to its characteristic of feature extraction of input vectors.

During this feature extraction, the Kohonen network creates (= self-organization) a fixed number of reference vectors corresponding each to a day of the year (reference day). Each neuron stores a reference day in its weights.

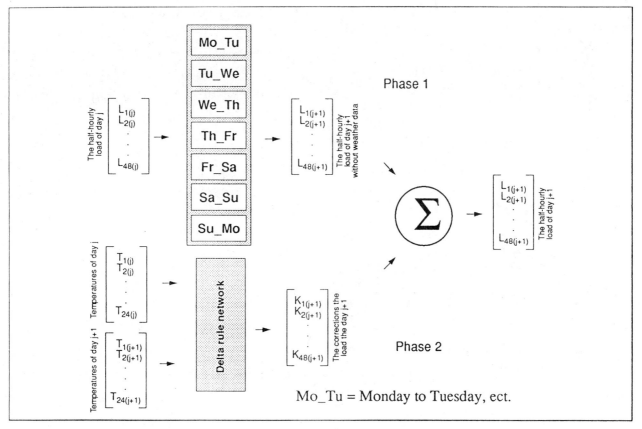

Fig. 6   The data flow of the forecasting method.

Therefore, the number of reference days is fixed by the number of neurons in a Kohonen map. We used 100 neurons networks for all our simulations.

Due to the different load shapes of the seven days in a week, we used seven Kohonen maps, too. The day type could also be introduced as input to the neural network, but our experience gave better results by choosing one Kohonen map for each day type. The inputs, the desired outputs after learning as well as the seven Kohonen maps are shown as phase 1 in Fig. 6.

The seven ANN's are trained with one to three years of load data, depending on the availability of data. During training the input vector to the Kohonen maps is composed of 96 inputs (48 loads of day j + 48 loads of day j+1). When forecasting, only the first 48 inputs are presented and the Kohonen network finds the missing 48 loads of the next day by auto-associative recall.

During training each neuron is specialized to a certain profile of the load. Fig. 7 shows for what period during the year all the neurons are specialized in a 6 *6 Kohonen network. From the top left corner to the lower right corner the days which are mapped in the ANN become gradually colder and colder. Two neighbour neurons will also contain two days with similar load profiles. The spring and autumn neurons are mapped in the same region due to similar temperatures of the two periods.

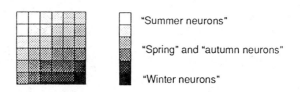

Fig. 7   Organization of one Kohonen Network after training

3.3   Trend correction

If the seven Kohonen networks are trained with periods of one to three years, the produced reference days, which are stored in the neurons of the Kohonen maps will statistically contain too small load values, due to the growing load over years. The bigger the data period to train the ANN's, the more this statistical effect will be important.

We propose a simple trend correction method to overcome this problem.

The difference between the load input to the ANN and the 48 weights of the best-matching neuron c is added to the intermediate output Y_j (calculated with auto-association) of the ANN. This can be summarized by:

$$Y_j^{phase1} = Y_j + \delta \cdot (X_{j-48} - W_{c,j-48}) \quad \text{for } j = 49 \ldots 96$$

where δ is a factor between 0 and 1. With $\delta = 0.75$ we obtained best results. In Fig. 6 the calculation of trend corrected loads is included in phase 1.

This method is also useful, if rapid load profile changes occur (e.g. summer vacation). After one day, the method adapts the output to the new circumstances.

3.4 Introduction of weather data (Phase 2)

Phase 1 with trend correction performs already well. But the forecast of days with important temperature changes between two days gives very bad results. Now a second neural network is introduced to correct the forecasted load as a function of weather data. The basic idea is to relate the errors produced with phase 1 to weather data. So an ANN is trained to predict the errors of phase 1 as a function of weather data and then add it to the output of phase 1 (Fig. 6, phase 2). Therefore, the input to the ANN is the weather data and the desired outputs are the load errors produced by phase 1. The weather data is composed of the temperature of today and the predicted temperature of the day to be forecasted. Intuitively, the ANN should learn a zero correction, if the temperature of the following days does not change in comparison with today.

For that purpose we used a one-layered linear ANN, trained with the delta rule [12]:

$$o_i^{net} = \sum_{j=1}^{N} x_j \cdot w_{ij} \qquad \text{recall}$$

$$\Delta w_{ij} = \eta \cdot (o_i^{desired} - o_i^{net}) \cdot x_j \qquad \text{learning rule}$$

where o_i^{net} is the network output of unit i, x_j the jth input, Δw_{ij} the changes of weights between two learning steps, $o_i^{desired}$ the desired output and η the learning rate. Note that the weights w_{ij} are different from the weights in the Kohonen maps.

At present, only one ANN is used for the seven days. In the future it will be tested, if the use of more ANN's will increase the performance. Our simulations showed that the training data should be composed of the one or two last months of the actual and last year.

4 RESULTS

The results are demonstrated using the half-hourly loads and the corresponding weather data of an european electric utility between the 1. January 89 and 11. February 92.

The following error definitions are used:

Relative error
$$e_i^{rel} = \frac{load_i^{desired} - load_i}{load_i^{desired}}$$

Mean Abs Deviation
$$\mu_{Abs}^{rel} = \frac{1}{N} \cdot \sum_i Abs(e_i^{rel})$$

Root Mean Square Error
$$RMS = \sqrt{\frac{1}{N} \cdot \sum_i (e_i^{rel})^2}$$

We present results of two different forecasting periods of four weeks, one period in summer, one in winter. The two periods are:

Summer: 1. July - 28. July 1992

Winter: 15. Jan - 11. Feb 1992

For the two periods, the training was performed with recorded data from the 1.1.89 until one day before the concerned period. The forecasting of the four weeks is then performed with the previously trained ANNs. The following tables give an overview of the performance of the forecasting method based on ANN over the two periods. The different performances are calculated with the whole period and with 48 loads for one day.

Table 1:

Summer	MAD [%]	RMS [%]
Phase 1	1.55	2.18
Phase 1 + 2	1.53	2.15

Table 2:

Winter	MAD [%]	RMS [%]
Phase 1	2.21	3.30
Phase 1 + 2	1.66	2.14

In summer, the introduction of the weather data does almost not influence the errors, but in winter we notice a considerable improvement of the performance. This statement may only be true for the examined power company, but not necessarily for companies in other climate zones.

In Fig. 8 two diagrams are shown, one containing the effective and forecasted load after phase 1 (without weather data) on the 15. Jan. 92 and the other containing the corresponding errors. This day is particularly difficult to forecast, because the temperature increased 6 degrees Celsius from the 14th to 15th of January. The diagrams are hard copies of our forecasting tool.

By adding the correction with weather data (phase 2), the errors decreased as shown in Fig. 9.

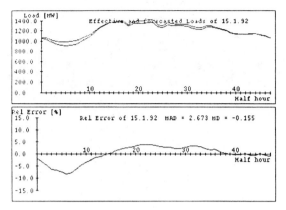

Fig. 8 Forecasted load, effective load, and forecasting error on the 15.1 92 after phase 1.

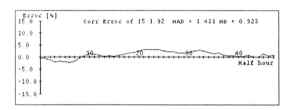

Fig. 9 Error on the 15.1 92 with phase 1 and 2

5 CONCLUSION

In this paper we presented a new forecasting method based on Kohonen's self-organizing feature maps and a one layered linear delta-rule ANN. The method includes three parts: First, the self-organized arrangement of reference days in Kohonen maps, second the auto-associative memory part with trend correction and third the weather dependent load correction. The errors (MAD), calculated over one month vary between 1.5% and 1.7%, depending on season.

In the future, the one-layered ANN will be replaced by a multi-layered ANN with backpropagation learning.

The proposed method has been compared to other forecasting methods [13]. The method proved to be the most appropriate for fast environment changes (e.g. summertime -> wintertime, summer holidays).

6 REFERENCES

1) Brace, M.C., Schmidt, J., Haldin, M., "Comparison of the Forecasting Accuracy of Neural Networks with other Established Techniques", IEEE, Proc. First International Forum on Applications of Neural Networks to Power Systems, Seatle, Washington, pp. 31-35, July 23-26, 1991.

2) Dillon, T.S., Morsztyn, K., Phua, K., Short Term Load Forecasting Using Adaptive Pattern Recognition and Self-Organizing Techniques, Proc. of Fifth Power Systems Computation Conference, Cambridge, Paper 2.4/3, pp. 1-16, 1975.

3) Park, D.C., El-Sharkawi, M.A., Marks II, R.J., "Electric Load Forecasting Using An Artificial Neural Network", IEEE Transactions on Power Systems, Vol 6, No. 2, pp. 442-448, may, 1992.

4) Lee, K.Y., Cha, Y.T.,Park, J.H. , "Short-Term Load Forecasting using an Artificial Neural Network", IEEE Transactions on Power Systems, Vol 7, No. 1, pp. 124-130, February, 1992.

5) Ho, K.L., Hsu, Y.Y., Yang, C.C., "Short Term Load Forecasting using a Multilayer Neural Network with an Adaptive Learning Algorithm", IEEE, Transactions on Power Systems, Vol 7, No. 1, February, 1992.

6) Chen, S-T, Yu, D.C., Moghaddamjo, A.R., "Weather Sensitive Short-Term Load Forecasting Using Nonfully Connected Artificial Neural Network", IEEE Transactions on Power Systems, Vol. 7, No. 3, pp. 1098-1105, August 1992.

7) Peng, T.M., Hubele, N.F., Karady, G.G., "Advancement in the Application of Neural Networks for Short-Term Load Forecasting", IEEE Transactions on Power Systems, Vol 7, No. 1, pp. 250-257, February, 1992.

8) Kohonen, T., "Self-Organization and Associative Memory", 3rd edition, Springer Verlag, Berlin, 1989.

9) Hsu, Y.Y., Yang, C.C., "Design of Artificial Neural Networks for Short-Term Load Forecasting. Part 1: Self-Organizing Feature Maps for Day Type Identification. Part II: Multilayer Feedforward Networks for Peak Load and Valley Load Forecasting", IEE Proceedings-C, Vol. 138, No. 5, September 1991.

10) Germond, A.J., Macabrey, N., Baumann, T., "Application of Artificial Neural Networks to Load Forecasting", INNS:Workshop on Neural Network Computing for the Electric Power Industry, Stanford University, Stanford, California, August 17-19, 1992.

11) Kohonen, T., "Self-Organized Formation of Topological Correct Feature Map", Biological Cybernetics, vol. 43, pp. 59-69, 1982.

12) Rumelhart, D.E., Hinton, G.E., Williams, R.J., "Learning Internal Representations by Error Propagation", In Parallel Distributed Processing, chap 8, pp. 318-362, MIT Press, Cambridge, 1986.

13) Baumann, T., Strasser, H., Landrichter, H., "Short-Term Load Forecasting Methods in Comparison: Kohonen Learning, Backpropagation Learning, Multiple Regression Analysis and Kalman Filters",- Submitted to PSCC in Avignon, France, 1993.

Power system security is defined as the ability to reach an operating state within the specified safety and supply quality in the event of a contingency. Restated, when an unexpected power demand is required, can the power system safely meet that demand. Neural networks have been applied as pattern classifiers to the security assessment problem because the large number of variables often interact in a nonlinear fashion. This chapter includes three papers on power system security assessment. **Paper 9.1** applies the learning vector quantization (LVQ) neural network to static security assessment. **Paper 9.2** utilizes multilayer perceptron (MLP) neural networks for determining the degree of system security and follows this with a neural optimization neural network to determine the critical clearing times of the power system. **Paper 9.3** employs both MLP and LVQ neural networks to monitor voltage instability in power systems.

Chapter 9:   Security Assessment

Static Security Assessment of Power System Using Kohonen Neural Network

M. A. El-Sharkawi   Rajasekhar Atteri

Department of Electrical Engineering
University of Washington
Seattle, WA 98195

ABSTRACT

Static security assessment of power systems is a time-intensive task involving repetitive solutions of power flow equations. The issue addressed in this paper is how to substantially reduce the amount of off-line security assessment simulations used for NN training. A Kohonen-based classifier is developed for this purpose. With the proposed scheme, the status of the system security is not needed for all training patterns. Only a selected sample of the training patterns needs to be assessed through simulations. Once the network is adequately trained, neurons that respond to secure or insecure states are self organized in clusters. In the testing stage, the pattern security status is determined by correlating the test pattern with a cluster of a known security status.

The proposed scheme also provides information on the degree of system insecurity, and the range of the operation violation.

INTRODUCTION

Static security of power system is defined as the ability of the system, following a contingency, to reach an operating state within the specified safety and supply quality. The assessment is based on the fact that the fast acting automatic control devices have restored the system load balance, but the slow acting controls and human decisions have not yet responded.

The static security assessment of a large power system is a computationally demanding task. It involves the solution of several nonlinear models (AC power flow) containing a large number of variables and constraints that define the feasible region of operation. In addition, the amount of memory required to store the massive data for different system configurations and contingencies is equally prohibitive. These considerations seriously undermine the application of static security assessment, in real-time, without the support of large computing capability.

Because of its ability to classify patterns, layered perceptron NN's have been proposed for static security. In earlier research, the inputs to the NN were typically the pre-contingency system attributes while the output was the post-contingency security status [1-6]. But layered perceptron is still suffering from the need for massive off-line simulations to generate a good representative data set for NN training. The training data set should span the entire demand space including the hourly, daily and weekly variations of system loads. The effects of different contingencies that can occur have to be taken into account as well. The successful full-scale implementation of this scheme will of course depend heavily upon the availability of neural network hardware. A software implementation is ruled out due to the size and the combinatorial complexity of the problem at hand.

The methods used to reduce the computational burden include Fast decoupled load flow [7] and contingency selection and ranking [8,9]. The computational time of system security using such methods is substantially reduced. Nevertheless, it still exponentially growing when the number of contingencies increases. Expert system has also been proposed for security assessment. The technique incorporates the knowledge of operators at the control centers in the form of rules that are then processed by an inference engine [10]. The technique may also suffer from the curse of dimensionality due to the large number of cases to be evaluated.

The main issue addressed in this paper is how to substantially reduce the amount of off-line security assessment simulations used for NN training. A Kohonen-based classifier [11,12] is developed for this purpose. With the proposed scheme, the status of the system security is not needed for all training patterns. Only a selected sample of the training patterns needs to be assessed through simulations. Once the network is adequately trained, neurons that respond to secure or insecure states are self organized in clusters. In the testing stage, the pattern security status is determined by correlating the test pattern with a cluster of a known security status.

The proposed scheme also provides information on the degree of system insecurity, and the range of the operation violation.

KOHONEN NEURAL NETWORK:

The Kohonen network [13] is a two-dimensional array of neurons. Each input is connected to every neuron in the array. A weight vector $\underline{W_i}$ with length equal to the number of inputs is associated with each neuron.

The distance between two neurons is expressed in terms of the "neighborhood order." For example, in Fig. 1, the neurons adjacent to neuron 6 are 1,2,3,5,7,9,10 and 11. They are labeled neighbors of the first order. Neurons 13,14,15,16,12,8 and 4 are thus neighbors of 2nd order.

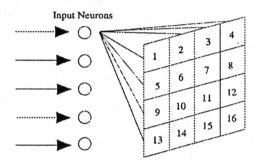

Fig 1 Kohonen Neural Network

The output of the ith neuron O_i is the distance between its weight vector and the input vector.

$$O_i = \Sigma (W_i^k - I^k)^2 \qquad k = 1..n \qquad (1)$$

Where n is the length of the vector k. The neuron with the least output is termed "excited" neuron. Once the training is completed, data of *certain* type will excite a neuron in a *clustered* region of the array.

The training patterns are fed iteratively to the network until it "learns" to classify the input patterns into distinct types. During training, the weights of the excited neurons, and those in their neighborhoods, are updated. The size of the neighborhood decreases as the iteration progresses. The strength of the updates is also decreased during convergence.

The classification of the network can be evaluated by the neighborhood order function β given in equation (2). In the equation, the variable t is for the iteration step. The time constant τ_k determines the rate of decaying of β. The constant c represents the maximum neighborhood order based on the topology of the net. β specifies the maximum neighborhood order of neurons to be updated

during the training process. Because of its exponentially decreasing value with respect to the number of iterations, β controls the size of the neighborhood.

$$\beta = c \, e^{(\frac{-t}{\tau_k})} \qquad (2)$$

The function (α) is the step size of weights update. It is also an exponentially decreasing function and is dependent on the order of neighborhood d. Neurons of a lower neighborhood order, with respect to a centroid of a cluster, are updated using larger step size as compared to the more distant neurons. The neurons that have an order of neighborhood greater than the β are not updated at all.

$$\alpha = \frac{\alpha_o \exp(\frac{-t}{\tau_\alpha})}{1+d} \qquad (3)$$

The training algorithm can be explained as follows:

1. Initialize all weights randomly

2. Feed in the input patterns

3. Find a neuron whose output is minimum. This neuron is selected to be a centroid of a cluster.

4. Calculate α

5. Calculate the size of the neighborhood β

6. The weight of the neurons are updated as follows:

$$\underline{W_j} = \underline{W_j} + \alpha * (I - \underline{W_j})$$

for neighborhood order of neuron j $< \beta$

7. Stop if alpha is too small else go to step 2

Once the training is completed, the clusters must be classified. Selected samples of secure and insecure patterns are fed to the network. The neurons that are excited for each class are combined in a cluster.

During the testing stage, a test pattern is fed to the network. The cluster of the excited neuron determines the security status of the pattern.

TEST CASE 1

The IEEE 30-bus system was used in this study. The load pattern was generated by a correlated load model. Three contingencies were analyzed. First two were single line contingencies while the third was a double line contingency. They were selected from a lower part of a list of 27 contingencies ranked according to the number of voltage violations based on a set of heuristic rules [14]. This is because there is greater uncertainty among the lower ranked contingencies causing violations. Heuristics alone may not be adequate to resolve the ambiguity. Neural network classifiers can help improve the screening process.

125	123	42	82
68	71	107	132
176	134	0	0
160	115	0	165

Fig 2 Classification of training pattern

The combined Class-Mean-Selection (C-M-S) and Karhunen-Loe've Expansion (K-L) algorithms were used for features extraction [1,4]. 1500 patterns were used for training.

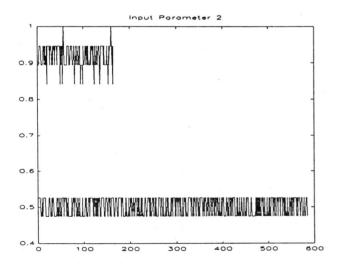

Fig 3 Voltage at bus #7

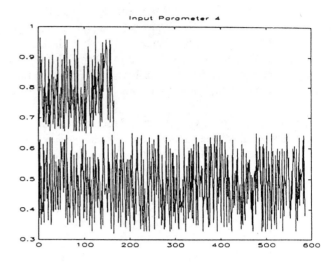

Fig 4 Real Power at bus # 7

Fig 2 shows the classification of the training patterns. The numbers represent how many patterns the particular neuron responded to. The darkened region represents the secure region.

The figure shows that the secure region was divided into two very distinct sub regions (neuron 16 and neurons 9,10,13,14). On further inspection of the training patterns, a clear distinction was observed between the patterns exciting the two sub regions. For example, Figures 2 and 3 show the normalized values of the voltage at bus 2 and the real power demand at bus 7. The pattern of the upper curve was found to excite neuron 16. The lower curve excited neurons 9,10,13 and 14.

32	52	19	32
23	25	34	33
54	40	0	0
51	45	0	60

Fig 5 Classification of testing patterns

The network actually classified the patterns into a total of three classes: one insecure and two secure. The network was able to not only classify the patterns as secure/insecure, but also to point out certain key distinguishing characteristics of the patterns within the same class. For example, Figure 3 and 4 shows the voltage and real power at bus 7 respectively. The voltage in Figure 3 is normalized for the reange between 0.95 to 1.05 pu. During the training process, the patterns related to the upper curves excited neuron #16, while the lower curves exited neurons 9, 10, 13 and 14. The NN divided the secure patterns into two subclasses based on the loading condition and system voltage.

After training, 500 new patterns were used for testing the NN. The result of the testing process is shown in Figure 5. In this test no misclassification was reported.

TEST CASE 2

In this test, different 400 training patterns were used. In this case, only the C-M-S feature extraction was used. Each pattern consisted of 18 variables (real power, reactive power and voltage magnitude at six neighboring buses). After training, two clear clusters emerged. The training results are shown in Fig 6.

In addition, the network was able to distinguish between dominant and subordinate variables within training patterns. Inputs like voltages at generator buses or P & Q at buses without load/generation had no influence on the NN weights.

44	42	0	48
25	0	0	44
23	32	0	35
27	37	0	45

Fig 6. Classification in test case 2

The rightmost column of the net of Figure 6 shows the secure cases. The 3rd column is unexcited and the first 2 columns represent the insecure cases.

A closer examination of the patterns revealed an interesting phenomenon. The training patterns were arrangement in the net according to their degree of security/insecurity. The neurons in the upper left corner (1, 2 & 5) were excited for patterns with more severe degree of insecurity. Similarly, the degree of security is higher going down column 4. Thus neuron 4 responded to patterns that were most secure.

Fig 7 illustrates this fact. The figure shows the real power of the load at bus 7. The load patterns are for insecure cases. The upper curve in the figure is for higher load demand as compared to the lower portion. A greater demand at a load bus would mean greater insecurity. During training, neurons 1,2 & 5 responded to this high load demand of the training patterns. The rest of the insecure neurons were activated by the lower load pattern.

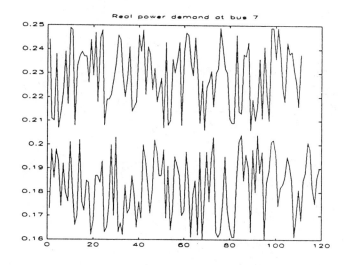

Fig 7. Real power demand at bus 7.

CONCLUSIONS

The results show how Kohonen net is successful in accurately classifying unseen test patterns. The net, once adequately designed, can form sub clusters indicating common features within the subclass such as the degree of system insecurity.

REFERENCES

[1]   S. Weerasooriya, M. A. El-Sharkawi, M. Damborg and R. Marks, "Towards Static Security Assessment of a Large Scale Power System Using Neural Networks," IEE Prceedings-C, pp.64-70, January 1992.

[2]   M. E. Aggoune, L. E. Atlas, D. A. Cohn, M. A. El-Sharkawi and R. J. Marks, "Artificial Neural Networks for Power System Static Security Assessment," IEEE International Symposium on Circuits and Systems, Portland, Oregon, May 9 - 11, 1989, pp. 490-494.

[3]   M. A. El-Sharkawi R. J. Marks, M. J. Damborg, L. E. Atlas, D. A. Cohn and M. Aggoune, "Artificial Neural Networks as Operator Aid for On-Line Static Security Assessment of Power Systems,"

Power Systems Computation Conference, Graz, Austria, August 19-24, 1990, pp. 895 - 901.

[4] Siri Weerasooriya and M. A. El-Sharkawi, "Use of Karhunen-Loe've Expansion in Training Neural Networks for Static Security Assessment," First International Forum on Applications of Neural Networks to Power Systems, Seattle, July 23 - 26, 1991, pp. 59-64.

[5] S. Weerasooriya and M. A. El-Sharkawi, "Feature Selection for Static Security Assessment Using Neural Networks," IEEE International Symposium on Circuits and Systems, San Diego, California, May 10-13, 1992, pp. 1693-1696.

[6] M. A. El-Sharkawi, R, J. Marks and Siri Weerasooriya "Neural Networks and Their Application to Power Engineering,"Analysis and Control System Techniques for Electric Power Systems, Academic Press, 1991, Volume 41, pp. 359 - 461.

[7] Wu, F.F and Kumagai, S., "Steady-State Security Regions of Power Systems", IEEE Trans. on Circuit and Systems, vol. CAS-29, no.11, no.v 1982, pp. 712-723.

[8] Scott B., "Review of Load-Flow Calculation Methods", Proceedings of the IEEE, vol. 62, no 7, July 1974, pp. 916-929

[9] Ejebe, G. C. and Wollenberg, B. F., " Automatic Contingency Selection", IEEE Trans. on Power, Apparatus and Systems, vol PAS-98, no. 1 Jan/Feb 1979.

[10] Sobajic, D. J. and Pao Y. H., "An Artificial Intelligence System for Power System Contingency Screening", Proceedings of the IEEE-PICA Conference, Montreal, May 87, pp. 107 ff.

[11] Dagmar Niebur, Alain J. Germond, "Power System Static Security Assesment Using The Kohonen Neural Network Classifier", IEEE transactions on Power Delivery, May 1992, pp. 865 - 871.

[12] D. Niebur and A. Germond, "Power Flow Classification for Static Security Assessment," First International Forum on Applications of Neural Networks to Power Systems, Seattle, July 23 - 26, 1991, pp. 83-88.

[13] Kohonen T., "Self-Organized Formation of Topologically Correct Feature Maps", Biol. Cybernetics no. 43, pp 59-69,1982.

[14] J.W. Cote and C-C. Liu, "Voltage security assessment using generalized operational planning knowledge," *IEEE-PES Winter meeting*, #92WM303-1PWRS, New York, NY, January, 1992.

APPLICATION OF NEURAL NETWORKS
TO DIRECT STABILITY ANALYSIS OF POWER SYSTEMS

D.B. Klapper and H.A. Othman
General Electric Co.
Power Systems Engineering Dept.

Y. Akimoto, H. Tanaka, and J. Yoshizawa
Tokyo Electric Power Company
Computer & Communication Research Center

ABSTRACT

The feasibility of designing neural networks capable of computing the critical clearing times of power system faults is explored. Two distinct approaches are investigated, the pattern recognition approach and the optimization approach. The theory of direct stability analysis of power systems is utilized in designing the input features of the pattern recognition approach, and the structure of the Hopfield optimization approach.

I. INTRODUCTION

The pioneering technical research presented here has the objective of blending together the unique features of neural networks as either general adaptive classifiers or optimization networks with the in-depth understanding of direct stability analysis theory. Of particular interest is the improvement of the speed of computations and the accuracy of the direct methods.

Direct methods (i.e., do not require time simulations) based on Lyapunov stability theory have been studied for decades and applied to the computation of critical clearing times of power system faults. They have not yet been accepted widely in the power industry due to their limited accuracy under some operating conditions, and the lack of familiarity of practicing power engineers with these direct methods. However, direct methods have the distinct advantage of speed over time simulations, which makes them a strong candidate for real-time on-line security assessment. Several direct methods have emerged over the years and many refinements to these methods have also been reported. A common theme among all the direct methods is the association of an energy level with the location of power system states along the fault-on trajectory. These states are the rotor angle separations between the generators, the machine speeds, the level of fluxes in various windings, ... etc. The second common theme is existence of a maximum level of energy, called the critical energy, that the system can absorb and still maintain its stability. All methods differ in their computation of the critical energy.

Interest in neural networks has surged in recent years and various applications have been reported in the literature. The ability of feed forward neural networks to be trained in order to extract patterns from sets of data is very appealing. In particular, our research aimed at training neural networks to identify the critical energy associated with a given fault and to compute the closeness of a system state to the stability boundary. Neural networks hold the promise of enhancing the accuracy of existing direct stability methods and the possibility of discovering new general methods that apply universally to all power systems. The ability of Hopfield neural networks to identify quickly the correct solution of a problem from a large number of solution possibilities is also desirable. We designed a Hopfield neural network to mimic one of the direct stability methods, namely the Controlling Unstable Equilibrium Method (Controlling u.e.p.). This neural network holds the promise of enhancing the speed of existing direct stability methods.

A brief exposition of direct stability methods is presented in Section II. In Section III, the pattern recognition capability of feed forward neural networks is utilized to predict the critical energy associated with a fault trajectory. The optimization capability of Hopfield neural networks is utilized in Section IV to design a neural network capable of mimicking the Controlling u.e.p. method in its search for the critical energy at a small fraction of the computation time. The Conclusions reached in this project are presented in Section V.

II. Direct Stability Methods

Many direct stability methods of varying degrees of speed and accuracy have emerged over the past two decades. Two of these methods have shown promise for large scale power system applications, namely the Potential Energy Boundary Surface method (PEBS) and the Controlling Unstable Equilibrium Point method (Controlling u.e.p.).

Both methods view the system operating point as a stable equilibrium point which is surrounded by a region in the state space, called the region of stability. If the power system is initialized inside the region of stability, the system will eventually return to the stable operating point. However, if the system state is initialized outside the stability region, the system will stay outside the region of stability and never approach its stable operating point. Direct stability analysis methods probe the depth of the region of stability in the direction of the fault-on trajectory. The length of time required by a fault to drive the system state outside the region of stability is called the critical clearing time (c.c.t.) .

The PEBS method views the region of stability as a bowl with the stable operating point residing at the bottom of the bowl. System state is viewed as a ball rolling on the inner walls of the bowl. The ridge of the bowl is of uneven height. Therefore, the level of energy needed to climb over the ridge of the bowl differs with the direction of the fault-on trajectory. This method assumes that the critical energy equals the maximum potential energy along the fault-on trajectory.

The Controlling u.e.p. method is based on the following facts :

1. Each fault drives the system state out of the region of stability in a unique direction in the state space which is different from other faults.

2. The boundary of the region of stability can be divided into segments connected between saddle type unstable equilibrium points.

3. Motion along each segment will converge to one of these saddle points. Hence there is a controlling unstable equilibrium point u.e.p. associated with each segment of the stability boundary.

4. Since each fault-on trajectory crosses the boundary of the region of stability at a unique point on only one segment, then each fault is associated with a controlling u.e.p.

5. The energy level at the controlling u.e.p. is the critical energy. This provides an accurate result provided the system is conservative.

III. PATTERN RECOGNITION APPROACH

The ability of trained feed forward neural networks to classify information not previously presented is crucial to this application. A specific objective of the pattern recognition approach to power system stability analysis is to establish a functional relationship between selected features on the fault-on trajectory and the location of system state relative to the boundary of the region of stability. From a theoretical stand point, this approach suggests that the region of stability of a power system operating point can be uniquely determined based on the selected neural network input features. In application, we wish to utilize only a small number of features taken along the fault-on trajectory to make a determination about the stability.

The relative energy margin of the system was chosen as a targeted output of the neural network. The relative energy margin is defined as the difference between system energy at a point on the fault-on trajectory and the critical energy of the associated fault, per unitized on the critical energy. This choice is made because it provides a continuous monitor of the relative location of the system state to the point on the boundary of the region of stability where the fault-on trajectory exits.

After some initial experimentation, the following input features were selected:

1. Potential energy
2. Kinetic energy
3. Derivative of potential energy

SIMULATION RESULTS

A fictitious, 3-plant, 8-load, power system was used in validating the feasibility of the pattern recognition approach. A one-line diagram of the system is shown in Figure 1. The three plants are modeled by classic generator models. The system was heavily loaded. Three-phase-to-ground faults at buses 20,10,7,11,12,15, and 16 were applied separately and the fault-on system trajectories were computed. The three selected input features of the neural network were computed along the fault-on trajectories and used for training.

Our major objective in this study is to assess the ability of the trained neural network to interpolate and extrapolate. Interpolation refers to the ability to predict the energy margin along a fault-on trajectory which lies between trajectories used for training. The extrapolation refers to the ability to predict the energy margin along a fault-on trajectory which lies outside the band of trajectories used for training.

The system was divided into two regions for the purposes of classification and training. The Eastern region included buses 1,20,10,7,11, and 14; while the Western region included buses 12,13,15,16,3, and 2. Two loading levels were used for training, 60% and 90%, while two other loading levels were used for classification, 80% and 100%. The loading is expressed as a percentage of the initial heavy system loading.

Three neural networks were trained:

1. Global Neural Network : the training set included faults at buses 20,10,7,11,12,15, and 16 when the loading level was 60% and 90%.

2. Eastern Region Neural Network : the training set included faults at buses 20,10,7, and 11 when the loading level was 60% and 90%.

3. Western Region Neural Network : the training set included faults at buses 12,15, and 16 when the loading level was 60% and 90%.

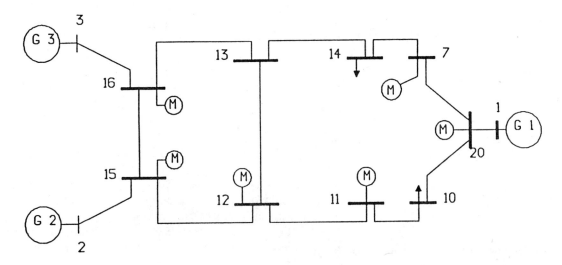

THREE GENERATOR TEST SYSTEM

BUS	1	2	3	7	10	11	12	14	15	16	20
GEN (MW)	26092	10000	3000								
LOAD (MW)	1500	600	0	3000	2000	3000	4500	3100	7300	3400	10600

Figure 1: One Line Diagram of the Three Machine Power System.

The ability of each of the three neural networks to predict the stability along a fault-on trajectory was tested using three-phase-to-ground faults at buses 12,15,16,20,10,11, and 7 when the loading level was 80% and 100%. The 80% loading level tested the interpolating capability of the neural networks while the 100% loading level tested the extrapolating capability. The classification results are summarized in Table 1.

Table 1 : Classification Results

		Critical Clearing Time (sec)		
Bus	Load	Actual	By Region	Global
12	80%	0.28	0.26	0.28
15	80%	0.20	0.19	0.14
16	80%	0.24	0.24	0.25
20	80%	0.10	0.10	0.12
10	80%	0.17	0.17	0.13
11	80%	0.26	0.27	0.29
7	80%	0.20	0.19	0.15
12	100%	0.11	0.16	0.13
15	100%	0.13	0.12	0.17
16	100%	0.17	0.17	0.13
20	100%	0.03	0.06	0.05
10	100%	0.05	0.08	0.08
11	100%	0.09	0.14	0.14
7	100%	0.07	0.10	0.10

Based on the results in Table 1, the pattern recognition approach seems to provide good estimates of the critical clearing times of faults. The neural networks are capable of distinguishing between faults and determining the closeness to the boundary of the region of stability for a wide range of operating points.

The interpolating capability of the neural networks is higher than the extrapolating capability. Also, it appears that training neural networks on small regions in the system is superior to training one global neural network on all the faults in the system.

IV. THE OPTIMIZATION APPROACH

The capability of Hopfield neural networks to search for the minimum of a function is used to search for the Controlling u.e.p. This search is an essential step in the Controlling u.e.p. method for predicting the critical clearing times of faults.

Hopfield neural networks are designed to minimize an objective function. The time evolution of the states of the neural network are in the direction of the gradient of the objective function. Hopfield networks are used successfully, as in the traveling salesman problem, to minimize quadratic functions because they allow the Hopfield network to be almost linear and thus require basically weighted summation operations. Our objective here was to search for the unstable equilibrium points of a power system. This task is complicated by the fact that these points are not readily available but rather are the solution of a set of nonlinear algebraic equations, which are the load flow equations. Consequently, the search for the controlling u.e.p. was formulated as a non-linear optimization problem. A neural network was designed to have global minima at the location of all u.e.p. Each u.e.p. is characterized by the rotor angles of all the generators in the system, and consequently, the state space of the neural network is the rotor angle space. This implies that the search is carried in N-dimensional space, where N is the number of generators in the system.

A significant problem with minimizing non-linear, non-quadratic, functions is that spurious local minima are usually created, which might lead the Hopfield network to converge to a local minimum which is not a u.e.p.

An important factor in the ability of the Hopfield network to converge to the correct controlling u.e.p., is the choice of the initial conditions of the Hopfield network. We used the rotor angles at the critical clearing time estimate provided by the PEBS method to initialize the Hopfield network. This approach has been used by others in the direct stability literature.

In order to avoid the need for any special hardware in the construction of the Hopfield neural network, we invented a new network called ADJOINT neural network. A feed forward neural network is first trained to emulate the non-linear function to be minimized. The feed forward network should have only one hidden nonlinear layer and one linear output layer. Then the partial derivatives of the non-linear function can themselves be obtained from the output a new feed forward neural network called the ADJOINT network. The weights and biases of the ADJOINT network are readily available from the original feed forward network. Standard neural network components could be used to construct such a network, such as operational amplifiers, resistors, and capacitors.

SIMULATION RESULTS

A two-plant test system was selected to evaluate the optimization approach. A one-line diagram is shown in Figure 2. Both generators were modeled using classical machine models. The following steps were taken :

1. A feed forward neural network was designed to take the rotor angles as inputs, and to give as output the squared sum of the power mismatches corresponding to these angles.

2. An ADJOINT neural network was designed using the weights and biases from step 1, to calculate the vector of partial derivatives of the squared power mismatches with respect to the generator rotor angles.

3. A fault was simulated and the rotor angles, potential energy, and total energy, were evaluated on the fault-on trajectory.

4. The output of the adjoint network was integrated and fed back to its inputs. This created a Hopfield network capable of searching for unstable equilibrium points.

5. The potential energy at the u.e.p. is the critical energy and is used to predict the critical clearing times.

Two operating conditions were simulated, the nominal condition as shown in Figure 2, and the off-nominal condition where the inertias and damping coefficients of both machines were doubled. Faults at buses 1,2,3, and 4 were used to test the optimization approach. Table 2 compares the critical clearing time estimates obtained from the Hopfield neural networks, against the exact critical clearing times.

Table 2 : Results of the Optimization Approach

Fault Location	System Condition	Critical Clearing Times (sec)	
		Actual	Hopfield
1	Nominal	0.33	0.35
2	Nominal	0.33	0.34
3	Nominal	0.26	0.26
4	Nominal	0.47	0.47
1	Off-Nominal	0.47	0.51
2	Off-Nominal	0.46	0.48
3	Off-Nominal	0.38	0.37
4	Off-Nominal	0.69	0.67

In the 2-plant test system, the optimization approach estimated very closely the critical clearing times, within approximately 5%, of 8 fault scenarios.

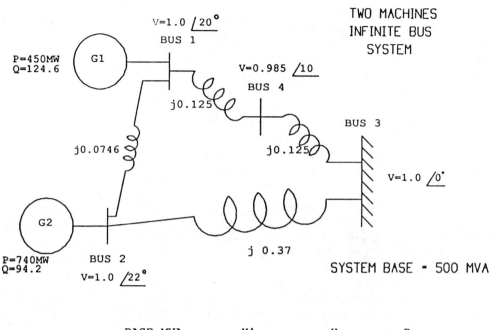

Figure 2: One Line Diagram of the Two Machine Power System.

V. CONCLUSIONS

Neural networks have the potential to estimate the critical clearing times of power system faults. System energies along the fault-on trajectories are good input features for feed forward neural networks. Adjoint neural networks provide a good approach for Hopfield network implementation. Further study on large power systems is still needed to further quantify the performance benefits of neural networks in assessing the stability of power systems.

A Decentralized Scheme for Voltage Instability Monitoring with Hybrid Artificial Neural Networks

Hiroyuki Mori
Dept. of Electrical Eng.
Meiji University
Kawasaki 214
Japan

Yoshihito Tamaru
Tokyo Electric Power Co.
Chiyoda-ku, Tokyo 100
Japan

Abstract -This paper addresses a method for voltage stability monitoring with hybrid artificial neural networks. A hybrid neural network is presented to estimate the index for voltage instability and capture the feature extraction of the power system transition. In this paper, a decentralized neural network scheme is proposed to handle a large scale power systems so that the curse of dimensionality is alleviated. The proposed method is demonstrated in a sample system.

Keywords: voltage instability, hybrid neural networks, multiple load flow solutions

I. INTRODUCTION

In recent years, voltage stability problem is one of key issues in power system operation and planning. Several aspects such as analysis, control, monitoring, and planning have been studied. The main research topics are qualitative analysis, development of indices, evaluation of critical points, load characteristics, etc. Since the problem is related to the nonlinearity of power systems, it is not sufficient to relay on only one index in either parameter or state space. The voltage instability problem is influenced by two aspects of state and parameter space. The two indices are based on the margin to critical conditions with a pair of multiple load flow solutions. They are expressed by the angle between the operational conditions and the nearest singular point. One is expressed in state space which corresponds to the nodal voltage solution while the other is in parameter space which implies the nodal specified value of the load flow calculation.

Neural net computing is useful for complicated problems. Neural net based approaches have been developed in power system problems:

1) security assessment [4], [5], [13] [14], [17]
2) forecasting [12], [15]
3) identification[6], [9]
4) analysis[7], [10], [11],
5) control problems[8], [16]

This paper deals with item 1) to take preventive control with an artificial neural network based approach. Evaluation of the indices is important in understanding how close the power system to be studied is voltage instability. The indices serve as the operator's guideline for monitoring voltage instability. In this paper, the idea of VIPI [2] is employed to evaluate the margin. Since calculation of VIPI is a sort of combinatorial problems, it is time-consuming. In order to calculate the indices efficiently, artificial neural networks are used. This paper makes use of both a three-layered perceptron and a Kohonen net in order to proceed the voltage security assessment. The three layered perceptron is employed to estimate two indices so that the fast estimation of the indices is achieved. Indeed, the conventional method is quite time-consuming due to a kind of the exhaustive search for finding out the nearest solution to the operational point. At present, more

generalized methods for evaluating the counterpart of the operating point are not available. We have to rely on finding out the solutions with trial and error. However, the calculation takes a lot of CPU time. The artificial neural network expressed with the three-layered perceptron is effective for estimation problems in terms of accuracy and computational time. On the other hand, the Kohonen net is used to provide an insight into the security assessment. The artificial neural net has characteristics that a set of input data is arranged in a two-dimensional way by feature extraction called "feature mapping" and the meaningful self-organization is processed. Even though a power system has the same value in the indices, the system might have different situation in terms of security margin. That implies that the power system may drastically change and the behavior is not monotonous due to the nonlinearity of the voltage stability problem. Using the feature mapping, it is easily understood which conditions the power system is heading for. Also, tracing a series of trajectory of the power system on the feature mapping at each interval, it is easy to detect how the power system conditions are normal or not. Also, in this paper, a decentralized scheme for monitoring is proposed to cope with lager systems. It is quite hard to apply a neural network to larger power systems due to a large amount of variables In order to overcome the problems, power systems are decomposed into subsystems so that each subsystem independently carries out voltage instability monitoring. The proposed method is demonstrated in a sample systems.

II. ASSESSMENT OF VOLTAGE INSTABILITY

This section describes a method for evaluating voltage instability. Specifically, the idea of VIPI [2] is used to measure the margin in the nodal voltage and specified value space. As power system conditions become heavy-loaded, the index approaches zero. The problem is related to the nonlinearity of the load flow calculation. In general, the load flow calculation may be written as

$$y_s = y(x) \tag{1}$$

where
y_s: specified value of load flow calculation
$y(\cdot)$: nonlinear load flow equation
x: nodal voltage vector

Thus, it is not enough to relay on only one index [3]. It is influenced by two aspects of state and parameter space. The two indices are based on the margin to critical conditions with a pair of multiple load flow solutions. They are expressed by the angle between the operational conditions and the nearest singular point. One is expressed in state space corresponding to the nodal voltage solution while the other is in parameter space corresponding to the specified value of the load flow calculation.

Fig. 1 shows the singular vectors in both state and parameter space. As power system conditions become heavy-loaded, x_1 and x_2 approach singular vector a in x-space. Therefore, indices for static voltage instability in state and parameter space can be

307

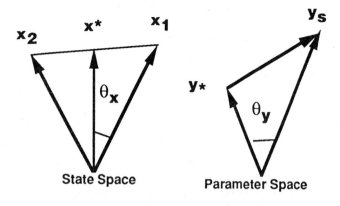

State Space   **Parameter Space**

Fig. 1   Singular Vectors in State and Parameter Space

written by Eqns. (2) and (3), respectively.

$$\theta_x := \cos^{-1} \frac{x_1^T x^*}{\| x_1 \| \cdot \| x^* \|} \quad \text{[deg.]} \quad (2)$$

or

$$\theta_y := \cos^{-1} \frac{y_s^T y^*}{\| y_s \| \cdot \| y^* \|} \quad \text{[deg.]} \quad (3)$$

where

x_1, x_2: a pair of the multiple load flow solutions such that

$$x_1 := x^* + b \quad (4)$$

$$x_2 := x^* - b \quad (5)$$

(x^*: singular vector in x-space)

$$y_s = y^* + y_b \quad (6)$$

$$y^* := y(a) \quad (7)$$

$$y_b := y(b) \quad (8)$$

(y^*: a singular vector in y-space)

The indices have an advantage that they are easily understood in a sense that they are expressed in degree. If the counterpart of the load flow solution obtained with the flat start is calculated by a method for finding multiple load flow solutions, the above indices are obtained.

III. HYBRID NEURAL NETWORKS

This section describes a hybrid neural networks which consists of a multi-layer perceptron and the Kohonen neural net. The proposed method has a couple of the following functions: a multi-layer perceptron (MLP) is used to to estimate indices for voltage instability; the Kohonen net is employed to understand power system conditions with the feature extraction thought the self-organization. Fig. 2 shows the concept of the proposed method.

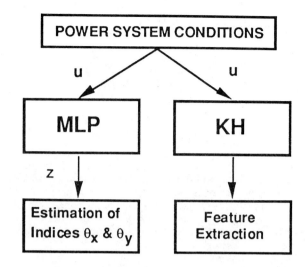

Fig. 2 Hybrid Neural Networks for Voltage Instability
        Monitoring

3.1 Estimation of Indices with Multi-layer Perceptron

The indices for voltage instability are estimated by the multi-layer perceptron. Since the neural network is based on the supervised learning, it is expected that the multi-layer perceptron provides more rigorous estimates than the Kohonen net. That is because the Kohonen net is involved in the category of the unsupervised learning. Concerning the multi-layer perceptron, input vector u is the power system conditions while output vector z is indices in space and parameter space, namely, θ_x and θ_y. In other words, these vectors may be written as

$$u = (V_1, P_2, Q_2, P_3, Q_3, \ldots, P_n, Q_n, 1)^T \quad (9)$$

$$z = (\theta_x, \theta_y)^T \quad (10)$$

3.2 Feature Extraction of Power System Conditions with the Kohonen Net

The Kohonen net is effective for the pattern classification problems. Using the function, the Kohonen is used to estimate the indices. However, this paper focuses on the feature extraction of input vector. Fig. 6 illustrates two-dimensional rectangular grid that represents output neurons. The mapping from input to output patterns with the self-organization can reflect the ordering of input patterns. In other words, input patterns with similar features are allocated to output neurons close to each other. Using the function, voltage instability monitoring is carried out by understanding bird's-eye view of power system conditions in terms of voltage instability. Power systems might encounter voltage instability if small changes of power system conditions trigger the voltage instability phenomena. In the sense, it is meaningful to investigate the neighbourhood of the operating point with respect to voltage instability margin. The feature mapping of the Kohonen allows us to understand where power system conditions to be studied exist on the output neuron grid.

IV. DECENTRALIZED SCHEME FOR VOLTAGE INSTABILITY MONITORING

A decentralized scheme for voltage stability monitoring is proposed with artificial neural networks. The centralized scheme

$$u'^M = 1.20\, y_s \tag{14}$$

$$u'^m = 0.80\, y_s \tag{15}$$

where, $M(m)$ denotes the upper (lower) bound.

Also, the slack voltage $e_1(k)$ has the following range:

$$e_1(k)^M = 1.02\, e_1 \tag{16}$$

$$e_1(k)^m = 0.98\, e_1 \tag{17}$$

For 6000 power system conditions, voltage instability indices θ_x, θ_y were calculated by the simplified exhaustive search method.

(b) The criterion of the convergence is 1000 iteration counts for MLP while it is 40 iteration counts for the Kohonen net.

(c) Output neurons were arrayed on the two-dimensional grid consists of 30×30 output neurons. The grid is expressed as rectangular lattice.

The estimation errors of the indices for MLP are 1.9 and 3.2[%] for θ_x and θ_y, respectively. On the other hand, those for the Kohonen net are 3.1 and 6.5 [%] for θ_x and θ_y, respectively. It can be seen that compared with the Kohonen net, MLP provides better estimates. Also, errors in the estimate of θ_x is smaller than those in estimate of θ_y. It seems that changes in parameter give more significant changes in voltage instability index θ_y.

Figs. 4 and 5 show voltage stability indecis θ_x and θ_y on the self-organization feature mapping of the Kohonen net. In those figures, the darker areas represents secure power system conditions. Noting that the assignments of the output neurons in Fig. 7 is the same as that in Fig. 8, it can be seen that securer areas in state space (x) do not correspond to those in parameter space (y). That is because of the nonlinearity of the load flow equation. This mapping can advise power system operators if power system conditions approach the critical conditions. Thus, it is expected that the representation is displayed on the CRT as an operator's guideline for voltage instability monitoring.

V. CONCLUSIONS

This paper has proposed a method for voltage instability monitoring with a hybrid artificial neural network. Voltage instability problem was considered from both state space and parameter space. As a hybrid neural network, two kinds of neural networks were used to deal with the evaluation of indices for voltage instability. One is the multi-layer perceptron to estimate voltage instability indices while the other is the Kohonen self-organization feature mapping to trace the trajectories of power system conditions.

REFERENCES

[1]   Y. Tamura, H. Mori and S. Iwamoto, "Relationship between Voltage Instability and Multiple Load Flow Solutions in Electric Power Systems ", IEEE Trans. on Power App. and Syst., Vol. PAS-102, No.5, pp.1115-1125, May 1983.

[2]   H. Mori and Y. Tamura, "On Voltage Security On-Line Index in Electric Power Systems ", Power System Engineering Committee of IEE of Japan, Paper No. PE85-41, June 1985 (in Japanese).

[3]   H. Mori and S. Tsuzuki, "Estimation of Critical Points on Static Voltage Stability in Electric Power Systems", IFAC Proc. of 1990 Symp. on Power Systems and Power Plant Control, pp. 550-554, Seoul, Korea Aug. 1990.

[4]   D.J. Sobajic and Y.-H. Pao, "Artificial Neural-Net Based Dynamic Security Assessment for Electric Power Systems", IEEE Trans. on Power Systems, Vol. 4, No. 1, pp. 220-224, Feb. 1989.

[5]   M. Aggoune, M.A. El-Sharkawi, D.C. Park, M.J. Damborg, and R.J. Marks II, "Preliminary Results on Using Artificial Neural Networks for Security Assessment", IEEE Proc. of 1989 PICA, pp. 252-258, Seattle, WA, May 1989.

[6]   H. Mori, H. Uematsu, S. Tsuzuki, T. Sakurai, Y. Kojima, K. Suzuki, "Identification of Harmonic Loads in Power Systems Using an Artificial Neural Networks", Proc. of Second Symposium on Expert Systems Application to Power Systems", pp. 371-378, Seattle, WA, July 1989.

[7]   H. Mori and S. Tsuzuki, "Power System Topological Observability Analysis Using a Neural Network Model", Proc. of Second Symposium on Expert Systems Application to Power Systems", pp. 385-391, Seattle, WA, July 1989.

[8]   N. Iwan Santoso and O.T. Tan, "Neural-Net Based Real-Time Control of Capacitors Installed on Distribution Systems", IEEE Trans. on Power Delivery, Vol. 5, No. 1, pp. 266-272, Jan. 1990.

[9]   R.K. Hartana and G.G. Richards, "Harmonic Source Monitoring and Identification Using Neural Networks", IEEE PES 1990 Winter Meeting, Paper No. 90 WM 238-6 PWRS, Atlanta, GA, Feb. 1990.

[10] S. Ebron, D. Lubkeman and M. White, "A Neural Network Approach to the Detection of Incipient Faults on Power Distribution Feeders", IEEE Trans. on Power Delivery, Vol. 5, No. 2, pp. 905-914, April 1990.

[11] H. Mori and S. Tsuzuki, "Determination of Power System Topological Observability Using the Boltzmann Machine", IEEE Proc. of 1990 ISCAS, pp. 2938-2941, New Orleans, LA, May 1990.

[12] D.C. Park, M.A. El-Sharkawi, R.J. Marks, M.E. Aggoune, L.E. Atlas and M.J. Damborg, "Electric Load Forecasting Using an Artificial Neural Network", IEEE PES 1990 Summer Meeting, Paper No. 90 SM 377-2 PWRS, Minneapolis, MN, July 1990.

[13] H. Mori, Y. Tamaru and S. Tsuzuki, "An Artificial Neural-Net Based Technique for Power System Dynamic Stability with the Kohonen Model", IEEE Proc. of 1991 PICA, pp. 293-301, Baltimore, Maryland, U.S.A., May 1991.

[14] H. Mori, and Y. Tamaru, "An Artificial Neural-Net Based Approach to Monitoring Power System Voltage Stability ", Proc. of Nulk Power System Voltage Phenomena II: Voltage Stability and Security, pp. 347-358, Deep Creek Lake, Maryland, U.S.A., Aug. 1991.

[15] H. Mori, K. Itou, H. Uematsu, and S. Tsuzuki, "An Artificial Neural Net Based Method for Predicting Power System Voltage Harmonics", IEEE Trans. on Power Delivery, Vol. 7, No.1, pp.402-409, Jan. 1982.

[16] H. Mori, "Decentralized Power System Voltage Control Using Artificial Neural Networks", Proc. of 1992 IEEE ISCAS, pp. 1701-1704, San Diego, CA, U.S.A., May 1992.

[17] H. Mori, "Monitoring and Control of Power System Voltage Stability Using an Artificial Neural Networks", Preprints of 1992 IFAC/IFIP/IMACS International Symposium on Artificial Intelligence in Real Time Control, pp. 433-438, Delft, the Netherlands, June 1992.

mentioned is inclined to increase the number of input variables as power systems are larger. It is well-known that the voltage problem has significant local characteristics. Therefore, a decentralized scheme is presented to estimate the estimates of the indices and carry out the self-organization of input patterns. Fig. 3 shows a decentralized voltage monitoring scheme with m subnetworks. The indices at each subnetwork are evaluated by local quantities such as nodal and branch power variables. Namely,

$$\theta_{xk} := \cos^{-1} \frac{x_{1k}^T x^*_k}{\| x_{1k} \| \cdot \| x^*_k \|} \quad [\text{deg.}] \quad (11)$$

or

$$\theta_{yk} := \cos^{-1} \frac{y_{sk}^T y^*_k}{\| y_{sk} \| \cdot \| y^*_k \|} \quad [\text{deg.}] \quad (12)$$

where

θ_{xk}: index in state space for subnetwork k

θ_{yk}: index in parameter space for subnetwork k

x_{1k}: element of voltage vector x_1 corresponding to subnetwork k

x^*_k: element of voltage vector x^* corresponding to subnetwork k

y_{1k}: element of voltage vector y_1 corresponding to subnetwork k

y^*_k: element of voltage vector y^* corresponding to subnetwork k

Hence, it is expected that the decentralized scheme is less time-consuming than the centralized one.

Concerning the decomposition of systems, a stochastic method such as the simulated annealing is used to determine the optimal decomposition.

IV. SIMULATION

In the previous section, decentralized neural networks ware given to voltage stability monitoring. Thus, real-size power systems are decomposed into subnetworks and a hybrid neural network is constructed for each subnetwork. Namely, it does not lack the generality that a small-size hybrid neural network is examined. The proposed method was applied to a five bus system. The following conditions are used:

(a) The input vector representing power system conditions is given by

$$u'(k) = (e_1(k), P_2(k), Q_2(k),..., P_5(k), Q_5(k), 1)^T \quad (13)$$

Since the input vector has ten elements, there are ten input neurons. In this paper, 6000 power system conditions were created by the uniform random number generator in which 5000 power system conditions were the learning data and 1000 system conditions were the test data. The upper and lower bounds of the specified value y_s were set as follows:

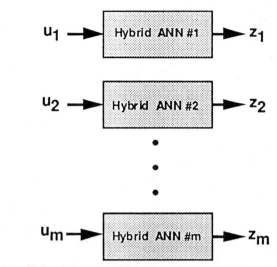

Fig. 3 Decentralized Neural Networks for Voltage Stability Monitoring

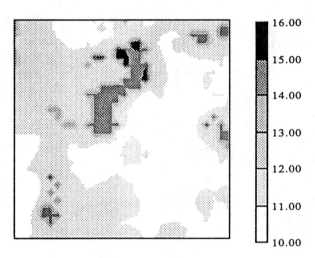

Fig. 4 Voltage Instability Index θ_x on Self-Organization Feature Mapping

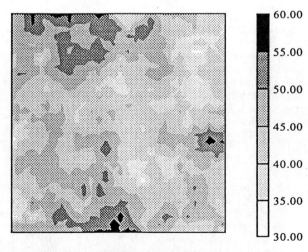

Fig. 5 Voltage Instability Index θ_y on Self-Organization Feature Mapping

Other Power System Applications

The preceding three chapters emphasized the major neural network application areas within power systems. This chapter includes three papers that did not fit into one of the preceding chapters, yet still defines a meritous power system application. **Paper 10.1** presents the use of McCulloch-Pitts binary-valued neural networks (threshold logic units) to implement interlocking schemes within power systems. **Paper 10.2** uses multilayer perceptron (MLP) neural networks to forecast flow rates in hydroelectric facilities. **Paper 10.3** proposes the use of neural networks to estimate the level of electric pollution present in a certain class of power systems.

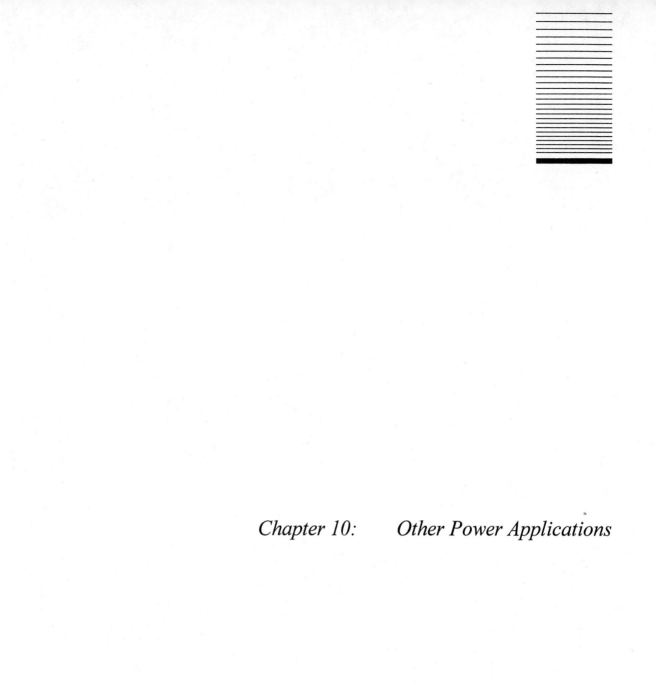

Chapter 10:   Other Power Applications

APPLICATION OF ARTIFICIAL NEURAL NETWORKS IN ADAPTIVE INTERLOCKING SYSTEMS

S.H. Agarwal, V.N. Prabhu
Computer Group, Testing Dept.
Tata Electric Companies.
Trombay Thermal Stn.
Chembur. Bombay. 400074 INDIA.

Abstract: Interlocks have been in use ever since the protective relaying schemes were implemented for power devices like generators, transformers, transmission lines, etc. Although the science of protective relaying has undergone marked changes and improvements, the interlocking philosophy has not changed much. Recently with the availability of Programmable Logic Controllers (PLCs), interlocking schemes have been implemented by means of these devices with basic philosophy of logic remaining the same. This paper suggests the implementation of interlocking schemes with Artificial Neural Networks employing Threshold Logic Unit (TLU) elements. It is demonstrated that while the basic hardware required is same as that of any common PLC, the suggested system will have added flexibility, adaptability to various switchyard modifications, electrical topology changes and equipment/switchyard conditions as well as network complexity.

Keywords: Neural Networks, Threshold Logic, PLCs, Interlocks.

I. Introduction

1.1 Propositional Logic and Interlocks:

Logical propositions can be realized by means of relay contacts (Normally Open or Normally Closed). It has been demonstrated that a logical proposition, no matter how complex, can be realized by means of logical elements like 'AND', 'OR', 'NOT' gates. Any logical proposition can also be implemented by repeatedly using two input 'NAND' gates.[1]

Interlocking schemes can be considered as basic and built-in protection mechanisms for power system equipments. Following requirements can be listed about any interlocking mechanism:

. Ensures safety of station equipment and operation/maintenance personnel.
. Prevents the operator from making incorrect operation.
. Ensures correct operating sequence (e.g. Start-up/Shutdown Sequence).

. Are hardware/software realization of predefined logic.
. Coexists with Protection Devices.
. Ensures that no equipment is stressed beyond the designed limit.

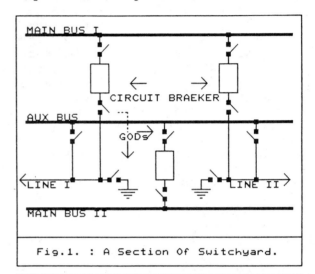

Fig.1. : A Section Of Switchyard.

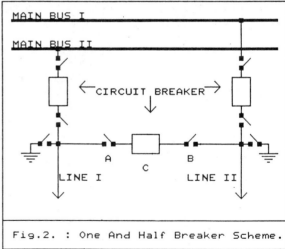

Fig.2. : One And Half Breaker Scheme.

Fig. 1 and 2 show sections of a typical switchyard. The operation of closing and opening of circuit breakers and GODs (Group Operating Disconnects) have to follow a predefined sequence of operation with permitted state of other devices in order to ensure safe and non-destructive operation. A typical interlocking condition for closing or opening of any GOD is that the GODs ('A' or 'B' for example in Fig. 2) can not be operated (opened or closed) if the associated circuit breaker ('C') is closed. Any wrong operation of the GODs may result in severe damage to the equipment. Similarly circuit breakers also have to be closed or opened in accordance to a predefined logic as these affect the fault levels of the switchyard.

1.2 Implementation of Interlocks in Power Systems:

Interlocking schemes thus implement boolean switching functions whose inputs are the equipment field status contacts (Digital Inputs). One of the function of an interlock is to generate a field permissive output which is either an enabling/disabling input for operating some power device (a circuit breaker for example) or a digital input to some other interlocking scheme. Interlocking systems are used to prevent wrong operation or operating sequence and may generate an alarm when a wrong operation is attempted. It is interesting to note that the present interlocking schemes are similar to the schemes 20 years ago, even though the protective relaying schemes have become complex and new technology (Microprocessor based) has replaced the older electro-mechanical relays. A detailed discussion of various current interlocking practices can be found in Ref. [6].

Conventional interlocking logic used relay/equipment operating contacts directly wired in series/parallel combination in such a way as to realize the desired logical proposition (Interlock). With the advent of high speed micro computers having high reliability and low cost, PLCs (Programmable Logic Controllers) have found widespread use in interlocking systems. These implement a logical switching function by continuously testing the validity of operation by means of running pre-programmed logic modules for the micro-computers.

The conventional relay/equipment contact based interlock logic worked well and was highly reliable. However, such a hard wired system left very little room for quick or automatic alterations of the logical propositions arising due to switchyard topology change or due to system conditions. Such a system also severely limited the choice and complexity of the switching function. A contact based interlocking system was bulky thus discouraging very complex switching functions. Another disadvantage with the

conventional interlocking schemes was that additional contacts were required to implement more complex logic or to take care of expansion/changes of the switchyard's electrical topology. This was normally achieved by adding auxiliary relays to multiply the number of available contacts in order to realize the desired switching function. However, such an arrangement usually leads to a reduced reliability of the interlocking scheme. The PLCs had a definite upper edge over the conventional contact based logic as these catered for high degree of complexity, ease of logical function realization, and redefinition with virtually no change of wiring and offered compact size with low power consumption.

The conventional contact or PLC based interlocking system also could not handle incomplete or conflicting (fuzzy) digital inputs (commonly known as bad D/I) which are frequent in real practice (e.g. Normally Open and Normally Closed contact status having equal value). While conventional contact based interlock logic is unable to handle such a situation, a manually entered 'Forced Digital Input' by the operator is required in case of a PLC based interlocking mechanism via a keyboard.

II. Artificial Neural Networks

2.1 Neural Networks:

The term 'Neural Network' (sometimes also referred to as 'Wetware') is derived from the study of how the human and animal nervous system work. Much of the earlier work in this area was concerned with explaining the activity of the living brain and to create "Brainlike Machines" with capabilities like vision, learning, pattern recognition, scene understanding etc. to mention a few. As reasoning and logic can be attributed to man's intelligent behavior, it also could be viewed as a process created due to the particular connections and inter communication of neurons in the living brain. As is known about the neurons, these are nerve cells which operate on "All Or None" principle, i.e. they are either active or not active. A neuron can contribute to excitation or inhibition of other neurons which may be in contact with the neuron's output, called 'Axon'. The junction where an axon makes contact with some other neuron is known as 'Synapse'. A neuron's output is active when the weighted sum of all inputs (from other neurons) exceeds a value called the "Threshold" of the neuron. A number of neural network models assume that the neurons are binary in nature. Such a model of neural network is often easier and more convenient to analyze. Although such a model in no way truly represents a real neuron and network, it is interesting to investigate how we can benefit from such devices in power systems. This paper suggests the use of neural networks with threshold logic devices for interlocking applications.

2.2 Threshold Logic:

The origin of Threshold Logic can be traced back upto 1960's when this subject attracted considerable attention of researchers [4,5]. Fig. 3 depicts a threshold logic gate element. As shown in the figure, the inputs are summed after weighing and the result is compared against a threshold value.

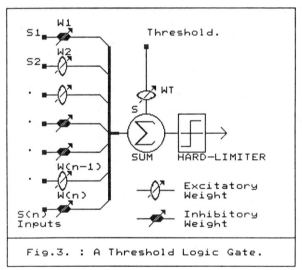

Fig.3. : A Threshold Logic Gate.

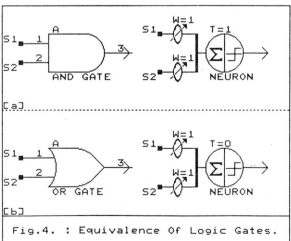

Fig.4. : Equivalence Of Logic Gates.

The weights can either be excitatory or inhibitory in nature (similar to synap-

tic junctions of neurons). If the output of this comparison is positive then output of the gate is a '1' or else a '0'. The non-linearity shown inside the box is a 'Hard Limiter'. Mathematically we could describe this weighing/decision process as follows:

$$\text{If} \quad \sum_{i=1}^{n} S(i).W(i) > S(t).W(t) \quad \text{then output} = 1$$

$$\text{If} \quad \sum_{i=1}^{n} S(i).W(i) < S(t).W(t) \quad \text{then output} = 0$$

where $S(i)$ s are inputs (generally binary), and $W(i)$ s are weights associated with the inputs, and $S(t)$ and $W(t)$ are threshold input and weight.

It can be demonstrated [3] that logical propositions of any complexity can be realized by suitably interconnecting several neural threshold elements and assigning a threshold value to each. Early works of Mc-Culloch, Pitts, and Minsky [2,3] have considered in details the use of neurons for realizing logical switching functions. Such a network can be realized either by direct synthesis or by various training algorithms [7]. An interesting property observed is network's ability to alter the switching function by means of changing the threshold value or by altering the weights. Fig. 4 demonstrates this property. Fig. 4 (a) shows an 'AND' gate which has a threshold value of 1. Fig. 4 (b) shows the effect of 'Relaxing' the threshold value to 0 which causes the gate to behave as an 'OR' gate.

2.3 Handling Incomplete or Conflicting Inputs with Neural Nets:

Incomplete or conflicting data is very common in practice and most systems (contact or PLC based) fail to deal with such a situation. In the event of conflicting inputs being simultaneously present (e.g. Auto/Manual, Raise/Lower, Start/Stop) a priority has to be preassigned or manual intervention is called for. On many occasions a particular logic criterion is not fulfilled due to contact or sensor failure or due to bad communication channels although actual equipment's status qualifies. In some instances, the required process status inputs are conflicting (i.e. Closed and Open or Start and Stop inputs are active at the same time). In such a case the process logic flow gets suspended as the logic device can not distinguish between a genuine missing criterion

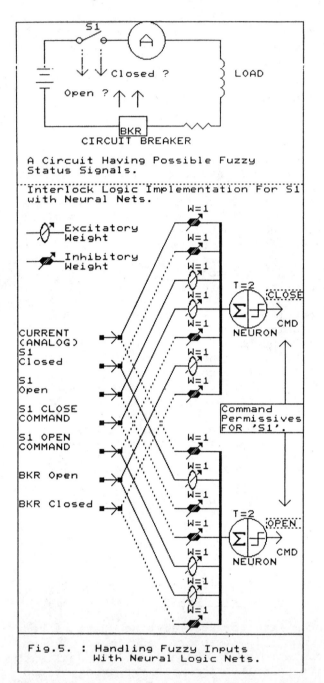

A Circuit Having Possible Fuzzy Status Signals.

Interlock Logic Implementation For S1 with Neural Nets.

Fig.5. : Handling Fuzzy Inputs With Neural Logic Nets.

and a criterion that is not fulfilled. In such a case a "Criteria Over-ride" input has to be imposed manually. Such an operation has to be done by the operator with utmost caution and responsibility. Any incorrect operation due to wrong judgement or overlooking important data can lead to major faults in the power station. This situation can be handled by means of including several correlated (or supporting) inputs in the decision network of neurons. This is demonstrated in Fig. 5, in which a

remote command to open/close the switch 'S1' is to be issued by a remote operator or by another interlocking system. The operating condition for the switch 'S1' is that it can neither make or break the circuit on load. The circuit breaker (BKR) is meant to make or break the load current. The switch 'S1' and the Circuit Breaker BKR each have two status signals (Open and Closed) and two command inputs (CLOSE and OPEN). If both Open and Closed status inputs of the switch are active, there is no way of knowing whether the switch is actually closed. Similar confusion can arise for the circuit breaker status contacts. Only way to decide the status of the switch is to study other related supporting parameters (such as load current) before arriving upon a conclusion. A simple neural network for achieving the desired switching logic to take care of such a conflicting situation is shown in the Fig. 5. The network can decide upon the current state of the switch or circuit breaker by a weighted evidence of existence of current. Higher the current, stronger is the evidence of 'S1' being closed. The dependence on any evidence can be adjusted by varying the associated weights. Such an adjustment may be a mere result of experience of the system operation. It can also be noticed that the network of Fig. 5 functions as a 'Vote Taker'. This endows the network with higher reliability and fool proof operation.

2.4 Neurons as 'Smart' Logic Elements:

From the above discussions it is clear that neural nets can directly replace the logic gates, namely the 'AND', 'OR', 'NOT' or any other conventional gate elements. As was demonstrated above, neurons with adjustable threshold can modify the logical switching function. In other words, a neuron can view an 'OR' gate as a relaxed condition of an 'AND' gate (with a lower threshold value). It can also be noticed that the decision process of logical nets made up of neurons have a queer resemblance to the IF-THEN-ELSE rules which are common in rule based systems. By means of having an adjustable threshold/weights, it is possible to have a desired switching function according to the requirement. Similarly, the switching function can be dynamically be altered by means of changing the threshold input. By suitably interconnecting neurons, a wide spectrum of switching functions could be realized. Some important properties of

318

logic nets using neurons can be listed as follows:

. These are made up of simple units which can be interconnected to form very complex networks.
. Capable of performing high speed parallel processing when interconnected suitably, even with slow and simple units.
. Self learning capability.
. Capability of generalization for unknown inputs based on previous learning/training.
. Logical proposition of any complexity can be realized by means of TLUs.
. Device (Gate) count is lower even with increasingly complex switching function.
. Alterable switching functions can be realized with suitable interconnections.
. Capability of handling 'Fuzzy Inputs'.
. Highly rugged and fault tolerant.

III. Applications of ANNs in Adaptive Interlocking Systems

3.1 Hardware Implementation of Neural Logic Nets in Interlocks:

The present work proposes the use of neural networks in order to implement interlocking systems for power equipment protection schemes and the same can be extended to other applications such as sequence control for other station equipment including process control. The advantages of the suggested scheme is as follows:

- Interlocking mechanisms can be implemented while retaining the framework of microprocessor based PLCs.
- The network can be made to have intelligence in order to slightly modify the interlocking schemes in case of emergencies to achieve the desired operations while protecting the equipment.
- Due to neural Network's ability to adaptively select the switching function depending on the situation, interlocking schemes can be made to be arbitrarily strict and automatically be flexible under emergency conditions.
- Such a system can also be extended to give a clue on the nature of fault and do alarm analysis, when suitable device flags/alarm contacts are wired in.

The present work employs multilayered ADALINE [8] model to achieve the desired interlocking function. As can be seen from the block diagram of Fig. 6 below

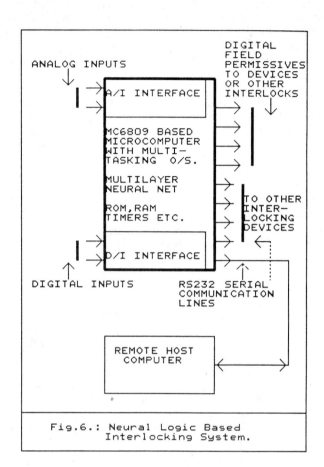

Fig.6.: Neural Logic Based Interlocking System.

the hardware required is basically same as that of any common PLC. The system uses Motorola MC6809 microprocessor and an in-house developed multitasking operating system for MC6809 [9]. The interlock boolean parameters can either be directly wired-in or communicated via RS232 C channels. The neuron models are run simultaneously on the machine taking advantage of multitasking. The relevant analog parameters can also be wired to the system in order to deal with bad digital inputs as discussed in Section 2.3. The neural logic network can be downloaded from a host machine or can be fixed in ROM based firmware. The system has capability to communicate with other similar devices over RS232 C lines in order to send or receive supporting parameters to resolve conflicting/missing inputs. The system can also be made to reinforce/weaken the weights associated with an input and thus adapt the switching function dynamically. This will endow the system with self learning capability.

3.2 Adaptive Interlocks:

In general, an interlock logic is fixed for a particular protective system. However, as the switchyard topology changes due to maintenance and operation requirements, the interlock logic schemes may need to adapt the situation in hand. This may be due to the changes in the fault level conditions, equipment outage constraints, faulty/noisy or unknown measurements of various parameters, equipment design ratings and tolerances, condition of equipment at that instance (e.g. transformer temperature or effectiveness of cooling system), ambient conditions etc. The altered electrical topology due to outages in the switchyard often require the modification of relay settings temporarily and automatic of the same when the equipments are taken into service. The contact or PLC based logic provides no such facility of accounting crucial operating parameters in the switching function or to generate an alarm in order to alert the operator. Such an operation has to presently performed manually. Manual methods are prone to mistakes and important data is likely to be overlooked by the operator under stress (e.g. failure to restore the relay settings back to normal). As discussed in previous sections the neural logic based system has capability of handling these shortcomings.

IV. Conclusions and Scope of Further Work

The implementation of such a system is under development as per the diagram of Fig. 6. Initial studies in this area indicate good potential of application of Artificial Neural Networks in adaptive interlocking systems.

With the availability of commercial neural chips from several semiconductor manufacturers, the interlocking system can be integrated in the power device itself (e.g. Relays, Breakers, GODs etc.). It has been demonstrated that neural nets can be successfully used in protective relaying also [10]. The interlocks and protection can thus be integrated in a power device and by means of a communication network between such distributed neural nets inside the power devices, different devices can be made to communicate with each other in order to evaluate the interlocking switching function and protective scheme, final permissive could be issued

to the device. As is known about the neural logic devices, these have high immunity to noise and are highly fault tolerant which qualifies them as ideal for such an application. Such an integration of interlocks and protection devices could open new dimensions in power system protection and control.

References:

1. Shannon, C.E.: "A Symbolic Analysis of Relay and Switching Circuits", AIEE Trans. Vol 57, p713-723. (1938).

2. Mc-Culloch, Warren S; Pitts, Walter,: "A Logical Calculus of the Ideas Immanent in Nervous Activity". Bulletin of Mathematical Biophysics 5, (1943).

3. Minsky, Marvin L.: "Computations: Finite and Infinite Machines". Prentice Hall N.Y. (1967).

4. Lewis, P.M., and Coates, C.L.: "Threshold Logic", Wiley N.Y. (1967).

5. Winder R.O: "Fundamentals of Threshold Logic" in Applied Automata Theory, J.T. Tou ed., Academic Press. N.Y. (1967).

6. British Electricity International: 'Modern Power Station Practices'. Vol D. p70-83,1992.

7. Rumelhart, D.E.; Mc-Clelland, J.L.: "Parallel Distributed Processing". Vol 1, MIT Press (1989).

8. Widrow, B.,and Hoff, M.E. Jr.: "Adaptive Switching Circuits", IRE WESCON Convention Record. Pt 4, p96-104, September. (1960).

9. Agarwal, S.H., et al. : "Multitasking/Multiprocessing On 8 Bit Microprocessors: An Application in Front End processing", Internal Report, Tata Electric Companies. August. (1990).

10. Khaparde, S.A., Kale, P., Agarwal, S.H. :" Application of Artificial Neural Network in Protective Relaying of Transmission Lines", 1st Int. Forum on ANNPS, Seattle, Washington, U.S.A. July (1991).

Application of Artificial Neural Network to Forecasting Methods of Time Variation of the Flow rate into a Dam for a Hydro-Power Plant

K. Ichiyanagi and H. Kobayashi
Dept. of Electrical Engineering
Aichi Institute of Technology
Toyota, Japan

T. Matsumura and Y. Kito
Dept. of Electrical Engineering
Faculty of Engineering
Nagoya University
Nagoya, Japan

Abstract

This paper describes an attempt to apply a neural network method to forecast river flow rate following a fall of rain. We use a perceptron-type network comprised of three layers. The input data to the neural network are rainfall amounts and subsequent river flow rates. Further the predicted total volume and duration of the spell of rainfall in question are taken as additional input data. The output from the neural network is forecasted river flow rate. It is found from our investigations that the forecasting accuracy of the neural network is improved by utilization of the linear input-output relations of neurons.

1 INTRODUCTION

It is widely feared at present that the global environment is being damaged by acid rain and by the greenhouse effects of CO_2 and other gases released by the excess consumption of fossil fuels such as an oil. Therefore it is desirable that the cleaner energy stored in water reservoirs should be converted into electric energy as effectively as possible in hydro-power plants.

Time variations of river flow rate following rainfall in the district upstream of a dam have been forecasted for actual use in electric power system operations by using various methods: the unit-graph method [1], the runoff transfer function method [2], the tank model method [3], the storage function method [4] and so on. The authors have previously proposed a practical forecasting method for river flow rate based on a concept of runoff transfer functions classified broadly into two groups according to the rainfall duration [5]. However, prior to obtaining a prediction of the river flow rate, the runoff transfer functions for the river concerned have to be numerically determined through vast and complicated computations.

In cases such as this one, in which the input-output functional relationships are neither well defined nor easily computable, artificial neural networks are found to be useful. Moreover, neural networks are able to compute results easily and speedily by learning from previous experience. Recently, various attempts have been made to apply neural networks to electric power system operations[6]- [11]. However, few papers have been published on the prediction of river flow rate by means of neural networks.

This paper describes an attempt to apply a neural network method to forecast river flow rate following a fall of rain. A neural network system for this purpose is developed through a case study on the Hatanagi-Daiichi Dam which feeds a hydro-power plant located on the upper section of the Oi-River in Central Japan.

The neural network used comprises three layers; an input layer, a hidden layer and an output layer. The input layer has 14 nodes for a forecast at time t. The input data to the neural network are rainfall amounts and subseqent river flow rates. Further, the predicted total volume and duration of the spell of rainfall in question are taken as additional input data. These values are previously obtained by a rainfall forecasting method which has been developed by the authors for typical Japanese rainfall moving from west to east [12]. A set of six nodes is adopted for the hidden layer. The output layer has a single node. The output from the neural network is the forecasted river flow rate. The forecasted river flow rate derived as an output from the neural network at time t is recurrently reused as an input datum at the next forecasting step for time $t + \Delta t$.

The training of the neural network is performed by using data of time variations of the rainfall amount and the river flow rate for 10 cases of rainfall from 1980 to early 1981. Then, the time variations of the river flow rate are forecasted for other 15 cases of rainfall from 1981 to 1983 using the trained neural network.

In the proposed neural network, a linear function is adopted to represent the relationship between the input and output of neurons. The prediction accuracy of this linear-function-based neural network is compared with that of a sigmoid-function-based neural network commonly used. When the input-output relation of neurons is represented by a sigmoid function, the neural network cannot successfully forecast rapid and large variations in the river flow rate. It is found from our investigations that the forecasting accuracy of the neural network is improved by the utilization of the linear input-output relationship of neurons. A linear-function-based neural network is able to forecast not only time variations of the flow rate displaying a single high and sharp peak but also ones with multiple peaks.

2 FORECASTING SYSTEM FOR TIME VARIATION OF RIVER FLOW RATE USING ARTIFICIAL NEURAL NETWORK

2.1 Mathematical Model for Runoff Mechanism in District Upstream of Dam

In the authers' previous paper[5], the nth order pulse-transfer-function was adopted to represent the runoff mechanism in the district upstream of a dam as shown in Fig. 1, where the rainfall amount is taken as the input datum and the river flow rate as the output data. The runoff transfer function can be represented by the following difference equation.

$$q(t) = -a_1 q(t - \Delta t) - \cdots - a_n q(t - n\Delta t) \\ + b_0 r(t) + b_1 r(t - \Delta t) + \cdots + b_n r(t - n\Delta t) \quad (1)$$

where t is the present time, Δt is sampling time (= 1 hour), $r(t)$ and $q(t)$ are rainfall amount and flow rate into the dam respectively, which are obtained discretely, $a_1 \sim a_n$ and $b_0 \sim b_n$ are coefficients, n is the order of the pulse-transfer-function.

The authors have investigated the simulation accuracy of Eq. (1) for $n = 1, \cdots, 8$. It has been found that for n values of 5 and below, the accuracy is improved with each increase of n, while for n values greater than 5, there is no significant difference in the simulated results[5]. Thus, $n = 5$ has been adopted in the present model.

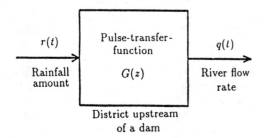

Fig. 1 Mathematical model for runoff mechanism

2.2 Neural Network Model for Forecasting Time Variation of River Flow Rate

Eq. (1) represents the fact that the flow rate $q(t)$ at time t is obtained from rainfall amount $r(t - l\Delta t)$ $(l = 0, 1, \cdots, 5)$ and flow rate $q(t - m\Delta t)$ $(m = 1, 2, \cdots, 5)$ which are previously observed up to the present time. Based on this composite nature of the runoff-transfer function, we propose a neural network which consists of three layers; an input layer, a hidden layer and an output layer, as illustrated in Fig. 2. The input data to the neural network are six magnitudes of rainfall amount $r(t - l\Delta t)$ $(l = 0, 1, 2, \cdots, 5, \Delta t = 1\text{hour})$ and 5 values of river flow rate $q(t - m\Delta t)$ $(m = 1, 2, \cdots, 5)$. Further, the following three items are taken as additional input data; the base flow rate $q(0)$, the predicted total volume of rainfall R_{total} and the predicted rainfall duration T_d. Thus, the input layer has 14 nodes in total.

The reason for including R_{total} and $q(0)$ in the input layer is that the runoff ratio is regarded as being very significantly affected by the total volume of rainfall and the base flow rate[13] [14]. The rainfall duration T_d is also added because the parameters of Eq. 1 are classified by rainfall duration [5]. R_{total} and T_d can be derived from the rainfall forecasting method developed by the authors for typical Japanese rainfall moving from west to east [12].

The output layer has a single node. The output from the neural network is the forecasted river flow rate $q(t)$. The predicted river flow rate derived as an output from the neural network at each time t is recurrently reused as an input datum at the next forecasting step for time $t + \Delta t$.

The accuracy of the river flow rate prediction depends on the number of hidden nodes k. Several cases are investigated for $k = 1, 2, \cdots, 8$. It is found that for k values of six and below the prediction accuracy is improved with each increase of k, while for k greater than six there is no significant improvement

in the prediction accuracy. Therefore $k = 6$ is adopted for the calculation.

The auther' neural network adopts the linear function instead of the sigmoid function commonly used to present the relationship between the input and output of neurons. The justification for this is discussed in section 5.2.

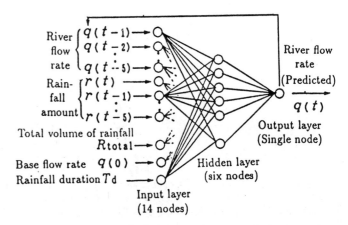

Fig. 2 Configuration of proposed neural network to forecast time variations of river flow rate

3 TRAINING OF THE NEURAL NETWORK

The operation of the neural network model is tested by using actual data obtained from rainfall upstream of the Hatanagi-Daiichi Dam feeding a hydro-power plant located on the upper section of the Oi-River in Central Japan. The training of the neural network is carried out with the aid of data for time variations of rainfall amount and river flow rate for 10 falls of rain from 1980 to early 1981. These falls of rain are shown as Nos.1 ~ 10 in Table 1. The following data are provided in each case: the date when the rain started, the total volume of rain, the duration, the base flow rate and the peak flow rate.

From the viewpoint of practical power system operations, it is desired that the time variation of the river flow rate up to its

Table 1 Rainfall data used in training of neural network

$\left(\begin{array}{c} \text{Hatanagi-Daiichi Dam located on the upper} \\ \text{section of the Oi-River in Central Japan} \end{array}\right)$

Fall of rain No.	Date [month.day.year]	Total volume of rain [mm]	Rain Dura- tion [h]	Base flow rate [m³/s]	Peak flow rate [m³/s]
1	04.06.1980	102	20	17.6	278
2	04.12.1980	148	46	25.2	356
3	05.15.1980	145	32	35.0	213
4	05.25.1980	122	30	35.0	272
5	09.10.1980	197	52	17.4	316
6	10.19.1980	120	54	24.3	122
7	05.11.1981	91	30	41.0	259
8	05.17.1981	44	21	38.0	92
9	06.21.1981	103	39	18.2	173
10	06.25.1981	117	71	40.2	124

Table 2 Rainfall data adopted in prediction of time variation of River flow rate

(Hatanagi-Daiichi Dam located on the upper section of the Oi-River in Central Japan)

Fall of rain No.	Date [month.day.year]	Total volume of rain [mm]	Rain Dura-tion [h]	Base flow rate [m³/s]	Peak flow rate [m³/s]
11	07.02.1981	127	74	39.1	186
12	09.03.1981	53	35	22.5	118
13	10.08.1981	205	38	24.1	380
14	10.22.1981	97	20	20.0	136
15	05.02.1982	84	46	19.0	141
16	05.14.1982	71	18	31.6	148
17	08.26.1982	123	34	20.6	238
18	09.24.1982	52	29	40.8	107
19	04.15.1983	230	63	26.7	425
20	05.06.1983	109	24	37.2	311
21	05.15.1983	207	38	43.0	504
22	06.20.1983	160	28	12.5	438
23	07.20.1983	159	72	70.9	215
24	09.26.1983	347	68	24.9	958
25	10.08.1983	154	70	34.0	187

peak should be forecasted as accurately as possible. Therefore, the data used for the training of the neural network cover the observed rainfall and flow rate during the period from the start of the rain up to a time 10 hours after the flow rate shows its peak value. That is, the training of the neural network relates only to the period when considerable variations occur in the river flow rate. The training does not cover the tailing-off period when the flow rate gradually subsides back to the base flow rate.

4 FORECASTING OF TIME VARIATION OF RIVER FLOW RATE

By using the trained neural network, the time variations of the river flow rate for other 15 falls of rain from 1981 to 1983 are forecasted. These are shown in Table 2.

Four examples of the forecasts are shown in Figs. 3 ~ 6. The upper part(a) in the each figure gives the time variation of the rainfall amount represented by a bar graph. The lower part (b) shows the time variation of the river flow rate, the solid line and small circles indicating the forecasted results and the actually observed ones, respectively. So far as these figures are concerned, the time variations of the river flow rate are forecasted with relatively little error except in the Fig. 6.

5 DISCUSSION

5.1 Errors in Prediction of the Flow Rate

It is of prime importance in power system operations that the peak value of the flow rate and the total volume of the flow should be forecasted as accurately as possible. Therefore the accuracy of the forecasts of these two values is discussed in this section. The peak flow rate error ε_{peak} is defined as the ratio of the difference between the forecasted peak value and the actually observed one to the latter. The total volume error ε_{total} is defined similarly with respect to the total volume of the river

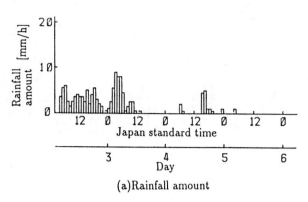

(a)Rainfall amount

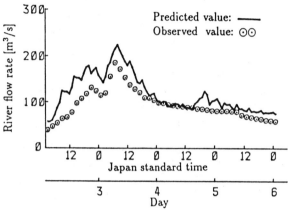

(b) Flow rate into the dam

Fig. 3 Forecasted result of flow rate into the dam on July 2, 1981 (Fall of rain No.11)

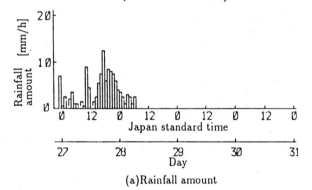

(a)Rainfall amount

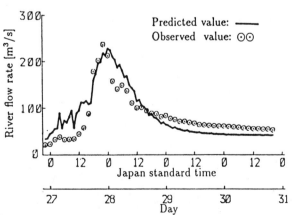

(b) Flow rate into the dam

Fig. 4 Forecasted result of flow rate into the dam on August 26, 1982 (Fall of rain No.17)

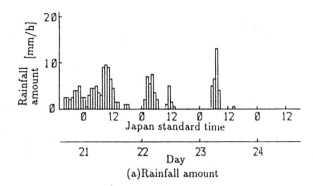

(a)Rainfall amount

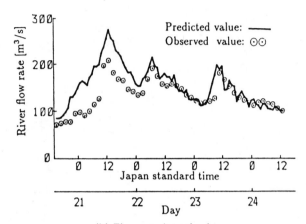

(b) Flow rate into the dam

Fig. 5 Forecasted result of flow rate
into the dam on July 20, 1983
(Fall of rain No.23)

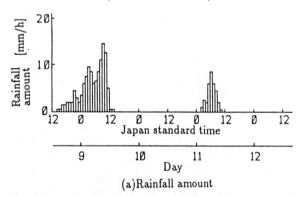

(a)Rainfall amount

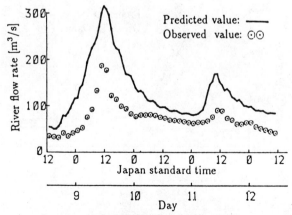

(b) Flow rate into the dam

Fig. 6 Forecasted result of flow rate
into the dam on October 8, 1983
(Fall of rain No.25)

flow. The mean absolute error of an instantaneous value of the flow rate ε_{abs} is also estimated by using the following equation.

$$\varepsilon_{abs} = \frac{\int_{t_0}^{t_2} |q_{fore}(t) - q_{real}(t)| dt}{\int_{t_0}^{t_2} q_{real}(t) dt} \qquad (2)$$

where $q_{fore}(t)$ and $q_{real}(t)$ are the forecasted and the actual river flow rates at time t.

Table 3 shows these three types of errors with respect to the forecasted flow rate. Both the peak flow rate error ε_{peak} and total volume error ε_{total} are within $\pm 30\%$ for 12 cases out of 15. In other words, only three cases of rainfall, Nos. 14, 24 and 25, have errors over $\pm 30\%$.

Our investigation shows that the total volume error ε_{total} is positive for 10 cases out of 15. Therefore it may be inferred that this neural network system tends to forecast a total volume of flow larger than the actual one. However, this tendency does not appear with respect to the forecasted peak flow rate.

The mean absolute error ε_{abs} tends to be larger than ε_{peak} and ε_{total}, because ε_{abs} is calculated every hour as the absolute difference between the forecasted flow rate and the actually observed one. However, there are only four cases in which the mean absolute errors are over $\pm 30\%$. Consequently, it is found that the time variation of the river flow rate is forecasted with less error in most cases by using our neural network.

Table 3 Three types of error in the forecasted flow
rate into the Hatanagi-Daiichi-Dam

Fall of rain No.	Date [month.day.year]	Prediction error (%)		
		ε_{peak}	ε_{total}	ε_{abs}
11	07.02.1981	20	24	24
12	09.03.1981	16	27	30
13	10.08.1981	− 11	21	27
14	10.22.1981	63	31	47
15	05.02.1982	17	25	29
16	05.14.1982	25	5	24
17	08.26.1982	− 4	2	26
18	09.24.1982	9	− 17	25
19	04.15.1983	− 27	− 4	30
20	05.06.1983	− 20	− 28	35
21	05.15.1983	− 26	− 17	28
22	06.20.1983	− 24	− 7	23
23	07.20.1983	28	16	19
24	09.26.1983	− 37	34	57
25	10.08.1983	68	77	76

ε_{peak}: Peak flow rate error

ε_{total}: Total volume error

ε_{abs}: Mean absolute error of instantaneous value of flow rate

5.2 Input-Output Relation of Neurons

In our neural network, the relationships between the input and output of neurons are represented by a linear function as shown in Fig. 7 (a). In most neural network systems, a sigmoid function is adopted for this purpose as shown in Fig.7 (b).

In this section, the time variations of the river flow rate are forecasted again, this time using a neural network with a sigmoid function. When the input-output relation of neurons is

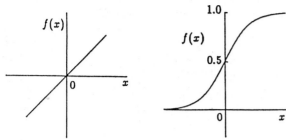

(a) Linear function adopted　　(b) a sigmoid function
    in this paper

Fig.7　Input-output relationships of neurons

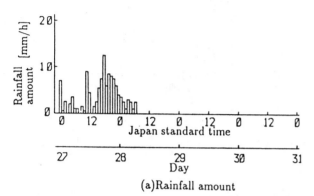

(a)Rainfall amount

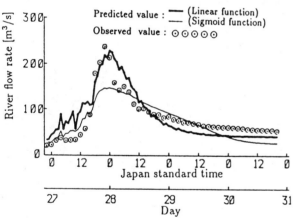

Predicted value : —— (Linear function)
　　　　　　　　　—— (Sigmoid function)
Observed value : ⊙⊙⊙⊙⊙

(b) Flow rate into the dam

Fig.8　Forecasted results obtained by using linear-
and sigmoid-function-based neural networks,
August 26,1982(Fall of rain, No.17)

represented by means of the kind of sigmoid function commonly used, the neural network gives good results only for the small and gradual increases in the river flow rate. However, large and rapid variations are not successfully forecasted with a sigmoid-function-based neural network. The forecast for the rainfall on August 26, 1982 (Fall of rain No.17) is illustrated by way of example in Fig. 8 (b). In this figure, the thin line shows the result derived from the sigmoid-function-based neural network, while the thick line represents the results obtained by the linear-function-based neural network. This is the same case of rainfall as shown in Fig. 4. The circles show the actual values. It is found from this figure that the thick line curve obtained by using a

linear function is located significantly closer to the actual values than the thin line curve is.

It is concluded from several such investigations that the forecasting accuracy of the neural network is improved by the utilization of a linear function for the input-output relationship of neurons. The linear-function-based neural network is able to forecast not only time variations with a single high and sharp peak but also ones with multi-peaks.

5.3　Effect of the Input Data on the Forecasted Results

The base flow rate $q(0)$, the predicted total volume of the rainfall R_{total} and the predicted rainfall duration T_d are taken as input data in our neural networks. In this section, in order to discuss the relative importance of these three data in the input layer for the forecasting of the flow rate, the input layer of the proposed neural network is modified as follows;

Original-neural-network(ONN) : with all 14 uints of data in the input layer.

Modified-neural-network-1(MNN1) : removing the data unit corresponding to the total volume of rainfall from the original input layer.

Modified-neural-network-2(MNN2) : removing the data unit corresponding to the base flow from the original input layer.

Modified-neural-network-3(MNN3) : removing the data unit corresponding to the rainfall duration from the original input layer.

The time variations of the river flow rate for 15 falls of rain are simulated again by using these three new neural networks. The mean absolute errors ε_{abs} are calculated and are shown with thin broken lines in Fig. 9, while the results derived from the original-neural-network are shown with a thick solid line. The mean absolute errors obtained by using the original-neural-network and modified-neural-network-2 are relatively smaller than those obtained by using the other two neural networks.

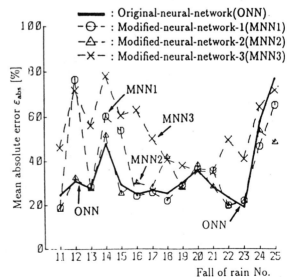

Fig.9　Relative influence of three additional input data on the mean absolute error

Therefore it may be inferred that the node corresponding to the base flow rate $q(0)$ is not entirely necessary to the input layer in our neural network. The reason for this lies in the nature of the recurrent type neural network, as "recurrence" implies that the history of the time sequence data can be learned. The base flow rate is included in the input data of each neural network as the flow rate at the time the rain starts.

On the other hand, the mean absolute error is increased by removing either the total volume of rain R_{total} or the rain duration T_d from the input data. Thus, it may be said that these two data are necessary for the neural network's forecast of the river flow rate and are required to be estimated as accurately as possible by an appropriate rainfall prediction method. As mentioned above, the authors have developed a prediction method for the total volume and duration of a for typical occurence of Japanese rain moving from west to east [12].

6 CONCLUSIONS

In conventional methods of forecasting a river flow rate, parameters of the river system concerned, such as the runoff ratio, have to be numerically determined through vast and complicated computation procedures, prior to the prediction. In contrast to this, it is found that a forecasting system based on a neural network readily yields good results for the time variations of the river flow rate by simply training the neural network on the previously observed data of amount of rain and river flow rate. It should be possible to improve this forecasting system automatically by reiterating the training in accordance with the patterns of change in the natural environment. Therefore the neural network proposed in this paper is useful as a practical system for forecasting the time variations of a river flow rate.

References

[1] Sherman,L.K. : "Streamflow from rainfall by the unit-graph method", *Eng. News Record*,108, 501 ~ 505 (1932)

[2] Powell,S.M. & Cluckie,I.D. : "On the sampling interval of discrete transfer function models of the rainfall-runoff process", *IFAC Identification and System Parameter Estimation* 1985, 1119-1124 (1985)

[3] Sugawara,M. : "Ryushutsukaisekiho"(in Japanese), (1972) Kyoritsu-Shuppan

[4] Prasad,R. : "A nonlinear hydrologic system response model", *Proc. ASCE.*, Vol.93, No.HY-4, pp.202-221 (1967)

[5] Ichiyanagi,K., Kobayashi,H., Mizuno,S., Matsumura,T. & Kito,Y. : "A Forecasting Method of Time Variation of the Flow Rate into the Dams for Hydro-Power Plants by means of the Runoff Transfer Functions Classfied by the Rainfall Pattern"(in Japanese), *Trans.IEE of Japan*, Vol.108-B, No.1, pp.32-38 (1988)

[6] Park,D., El-Sharkawi,M., Marks II,R., Atlas,L. & Damborg,M. : "Electric Load Forecasting Using An Artificial Neural Network", *IEEE Trans. Power Syst.*, 6, 2, 442 (1991)

[7] Sobajic,D. & Pao,Y. : "Artificial Neural-Net Based Dynamic Security Assessment", *IEEE Trans. Power Syst.*, 4, 1, 220 (1989)

[8] Aggoune,A., El-Sharkawi,M., Park,D., Damborg,M. & Marks II,K. : "Preliminary Result on Using, Artificial Neural Network for Security Assessment", *IEEE Trans. Power Syst.*, 6, 2, 890 (1991)

[9] Hartana,R. & Richards,G. : "Harmonic Source Monitoring and Identification using Neural Networks", *IEEE Trans. Power Syst.*, 5, 4, 1098 (1990)

[10] Ebron,S., Lubkemans,D. & White,M. : "A Neural Network Approach to the Detection of Incipient Faults on Power Distribution Feeders", *IEEE Trans. Power Delivery.*, 5, 2, 905 (1990)

[11] Niebur,D. & Germond,A. : "Unsupervised Neural Net Classification of Power System Static Security State", *Proc. 3rd Symp. on Expert Systems Application to Power Systems*, 336 (1991)

[12] Ichiyanagi,K., Kobayashi,H., Shinoda,A., Matsumura,T. & Kito,Y. : "A Forecasting Method of Time Variation of Rainfall in Upper District of Dams for Hydro-Power Plants by AMeDAS Data Processing" (in Japanese), *Trans.IEE of Japan*, Vol.106-B, No.9, pp.73-80 (1986)

[13] Ichiyanagi,K., Kobayashi,H., Takeuchi,D., Matsumura,T. & Kito,Y. : "Estimation of Runoff Ratio of Rainfall on Upper District of Dams for Hydro-Power Generation Taking into Account the Base Flow Rate" (in Japanese), *Trans.IEE of Japan*, Vol.105-B, No.8, pp.691-697 (1985)

[14] Hino,M. & Hasebe,M. : "Relation between Runoff Ratio and Antecedent Discharge as an Index of the Humidity of a Basin"(in Japanese), *Trans. SCE of Japan*, Vol.328, pp.41-46 (1982)

ELECTRIC POLLUTION STUDIES IN MESH TYPE MTDC SYSTEM USING NEURAL NETWORK

K.G.Narendra   H.S.Chandrasekharaiah
Department of High Voltage Engineering
INDIAN INSTITUTE OF SCIENCE
BANGALORE,INDIA

ABSTRACT

In this paper we are proposing a Neural Network identifier to estimate the electric pollution (harmonics) contents present in the voltage and current signals of a mesh type Multi Terminal Direct Current (MTDC) system under dynamic conditions. A digital computer program has been developed to implement the Neural Network and a modified form of Fourier series representation which improves the accuracy of the results is discussed.

Key Words: MTDC system, Neural Network, Harmonics

1 INTRODUCTION

The purpose of this paper is to conduct electric pollution studies in a mesh type MTDC system using Neural Network. This work was formulated since many two terminal HVDC stations are being converted into MTDC systems and a study of the dynamic interaction of harmonics in such systems is very helpful for designing of filters, whose cost affect significantly the economy of the overall system. Limited literature is available on the electric pollution analysis in MTDC systems [1]. In India also, MTDC system has potential future in meeting the growing power transmission requirements.

A digital computer program has been developed for dynamic analysis of a four terminal MTDC system with long DC lines connected in mesh with two inverters and two rectifiers transmitting 500MW power at 500kV potential[4]. The results obtained are fed to the Neural Network for estimation of the harmonic content (electric pollution) present in the signal. The concept used here is that a given signal can be represented by a finite number of sinusoids in the form of trignometric polynomial over the fundamental range. This yields a set of simultaneous linear equations. A matrix method has been developed to convert the overdetermined equations to a well defined positive definite matrix. A general *steep gradient* approach is used to express the matrix differential equation whose steady state solution yields the required harmonic coefficient of the polluted signal. The advantage of the method is that the concept developed can be applied for real time studies under various operating conditions of the system.

2 NEURAL NETWORK (NN) DEVELOPMENT

The Fourier series representation to approximate a given function, which satisfies the Dirichlet's conditions is a series with trignometric polynomials which are orthogonal over the fundamental range. This can be expressed as:

$$b(t) = X_0 + \sum_{r=1}^{q}(X_r.sin(\omega rt) + Y_r.cos(\omega rt)) \quad (1)$$

Over one fundamental period, equation (1) can be written for different time intervals can be written in the matrix notation as

$$[A]_{nx(2q+1)}.x]_{(2q+1)x1} = b]_{nx1} \qquad (2)$$

where, $[A]$ is the matrix of sinusoids (sine and cosine terms) , x] is the coefficient vector which is the unknown, and b] is the actual signal.

By pre-multiplying the equation(2) by $[A^T]$, it is reduced to,

$$[G].x] = d] \qquad (3)$$

where $[G] = [A^T].[A]$, and $d] = [A^T].b]$. Equation (3) is the *normal form* of representing the overdetermined set of linear equations into a *pseudo invertable* matrix. It is shown in reference [2] that matrix $[G]$ can be reduced to a *diagonal* matrix which is symmetric and positive definite. For analog representations which can give parallel solution in real time *neural optimization* principle is used which allows us to represent the matrix differential equation as:

$$d[x]/dt = -h.([G].x] - d]) \qquad (4)$$

with $x(0) = x^0$ and h is a scalar.
As described in [3] with $[G]$ positive definite and symmetric, equation (4) is equivalent to the unconstrained quadratic programming problem which gives *global minimum* solution of the energy function.

3 COMPUTATIONAL ANALYSIS

The required harmonic components can be calculated selectively because $[G]$ is diagonal.
The differential equation (4) is reduced to the *standard state space* form as:

$$\dot{y} = [H].y + [B].u] \qquad (5)$$

where,$[H]=[G]$, $y]=x]$, $[B]=diag(1)$ and $u] = [A^T].b]$. The steady state solution of (5) gives the required harmonic component. After evaluating the coefficients X_0, X_1 and Y_1, as discussed in [2], the Fourier series is described as:
$b(t) - X_0 - X_1.sin(\omega t) - Y_1.cos(\omega t) =$

$$\sum_{r=2}^{q}(X_r.sin(\omega rt) + Y_r.cos(\omega rt)) \qquad (6)$$

which can be written as:

$$b(t)_{-1} = \sum_{r=2}^{q}(X_r.sin(\omega rt) + Y_r.cos(\omega rt)) \qquad (7)$$

and $b(t)_{-1} = b(t) - X_0 - X_1.sin(\omega t) - Y_1.cos(\omega t)$ is the modified representation of the function by filtering the fundamental and dc harmonic contents from the signal. Similarly , while calculating the 3rd harmonic component,

$$b(t)_{-2} = \sum_{r=3}^{q}(X_r.sin(\omega rt) + Y_r.cos(\omega rt)) \qquad (8)$$

is used. In general, for finding p^{th} harmonic component the equation is written as:

$$b(t)_{-(p-1)} = \sum_{r=p}^{q}(X_r.sin(\omega rt) + Y_r.cos(\omega rt)) \qquad (9)$$

This representation has improved the numerical results to a great extent because the neural method matches only the un-calculated coefficients with that of the signal which does not contain the calculated harmonics [2].

4 BRIEF DETAILS OF THE MTDC SYSTEM

Four terminal dc system considered for the study is shown in fig.(A). It consists of mesh type parallel monopolar dc system connecting four ac systems by means of long dc lines of two 400, 600 and 800kM length. The converter system comprises of two rectifier and two inverter station, each is a 12-pulse bridge operating as two 6-pulse bridges in series. The dc power transmitted by each station is 500MW at 1kA current and 500kV potential. Each ac system consists of tuned filters ($5^{th}, 7^{th}, 11^{th}, 13^{th}$ and HP) and a static load (15%). Conventional PI current controller is used at each rectifier station and Minimum Extinction Angle (MEA) controller is used at each inverter station. For overall current order coordination, a Constant Current Margin (CCM) controller is employed. The fundamental frequency of operation is at 50Hz. The sampling rate is considered at 10kHz which is sufficient for the dynamic analysis. The simulation of the MTDC system is done by the method as explained in reference [4].

5 NUMERICAL RESULTS AND DISCUSSION

Digital simulation of the MTDC system described is carried out and the variables are then fed to the Neural Network to detect the required harmonic component from the electrically polluted wave form. In the fig. 1, the electric pollution studies of the source current under various system contingencies is shown. Harmonics present in the source current of the 'a' phase of a rectifier1 under steady state condition is depicted in fig 1a. It can be observed that, the convergence of all the harmonics(1-20) is achieved in only two steps in almost *super real time* (0.1microsecond). Phase variation under this condition is shown in fig. 1b. Following case studies were carried out:
1) Change in the system frequency from 50Hz to 48.5Hz after the two cycles from the steady state.
2) The transformer reactance of the upper bridge of the rectifier1 and inverter2 were increased by about 5%.
3) A 5% negative sequence voltage was added to

all the ac-sources.

The variation of harmonic magnitude and phase is illustrated in figs 1c,1d,1e,1f,1g,1h respectively for the three cases stated. The mark '*' in all the figures represents the 1% magnitude barrier of the fundamental. Only the 11th harmonic current is above this barrier. But significant *phase pollution* can be observed in all the cases. In fig.2 , the dc-side harmonic spectrum is depicted in which fig. 2a correspond to steady state condition and fig. 2.1b correspond to case 1. Higher order harmonics are significantly damped out in the case 1 which.can be due to the shift in the crossover point which has decreased firing angle and hence smoother response is observed (see fig. 2.1a from 0.02 to 0.04 second).

Further, a solid ground fault is created on the ac side of 'a' phase bus at the inverter2 (fig. 3a) from 0.015 to 0.02 second. The wave form is polluted after the system starts recovering and significant 10th harmonic is observed. In fig. 3b the magnitude spectrum for 20 harmonics over five cycles is illustrated which shows the presence of the uncharacteristic 10th harmonic, whose magnitude decreases with time.

For the same case on the dc side, electric pollution chrateristics of the rectifier1 dc voltage over four cycles is shown in fig. 4. In all these figures, '6p' represents the charateristic harmonic, plotted from 0 to 10 on the x-axis, uncharateristic harmonics '6p+1' is plotted from 11 to 20 and '6p-1' from 20 to 30, with p an integer varying from 1 to 10. As shown the uncharateristic 10th harmonic on the ac side, as discussed has now appeared on the dc-side as 11th harmonic with significant magnitude.

6   CONCLUSIONS

A Neural Network for *fast-evaluation* of the harmonic components present in the eletrically polluted signal of MTDC system is developed. From the studies it is observed that the *phase pollution* is more significant even under small disturbances which is normally ignored. Uncharateristic harmonics of significant magnitude play a dominant role over few cycles under the fault condition. It can be said that the knowledge of both the magnitude and phase of harmonic is a better criteria than taking only the magnitude for designing of filters and control parameters.

7   ACKNOWLEDGEMENTS

The authors would like to thank Prof. G.R. Nagabhushana, Chairman , department of High Voltage Engineering for his encouragement in this work.

8   REFERENCES

1 Melvod, D.J., T.Endo, and H.P. Lips, "Effects of operating configurations of Multiterminal HVDC Systems on DC filter performance",IEEE Trans., PWRD, Jul-91, p 924-930.

2 K. G. Narendra, H. S. Chandrasekahraiah, "A novel neural architecture for harmonic identification in an integrated ac-dc power system", (paper submitted for IEEE, P.E.S., SM.)

3 A. Cichocki and R. Unbehauen,"Neural Networks for Solving Systems of Linear Equations and Related Problems", IEEE Trans. Cir-Sys-1: Fundamental Theory and Applications, Vol. 39, No. 2, Feb-92, p 124-138.

4 Manohar P. and H.S. Chandrasekharaih,"Artificial commutation for inversion into weak ac system in multiterminal HVDC system", J. EPSR, (U.K.), Vol. 19, 1990, p 95-104.

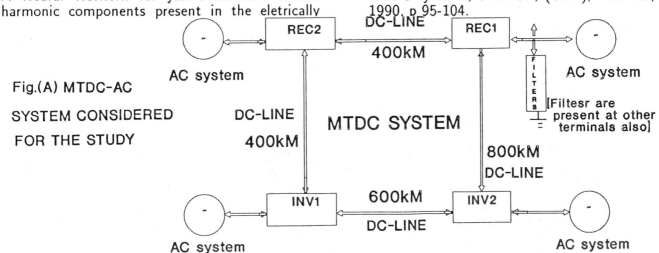

Fig.(A) MTDC-AC SYSTEM CONSIDERED FOR THE STUDY

MTDC SYSTEM

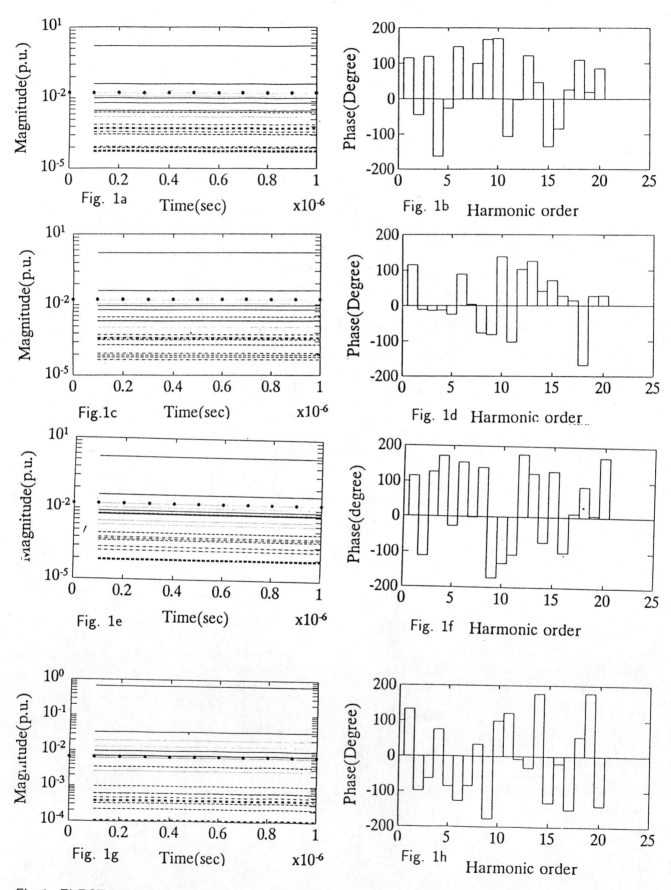

Fig. 1a

Fig. 1b   Harmonic order

Fig.1c

Fig. 1d   Harmonic order

Fig. 1e

Fig. 1f   Harmonic order

Fig. 1g

Fig. 1h   Harmonic order

Fig 1. ELECTRIC POLLUTION STUDIES OF THE SOURCE CURRENT OF RECTIFIER1

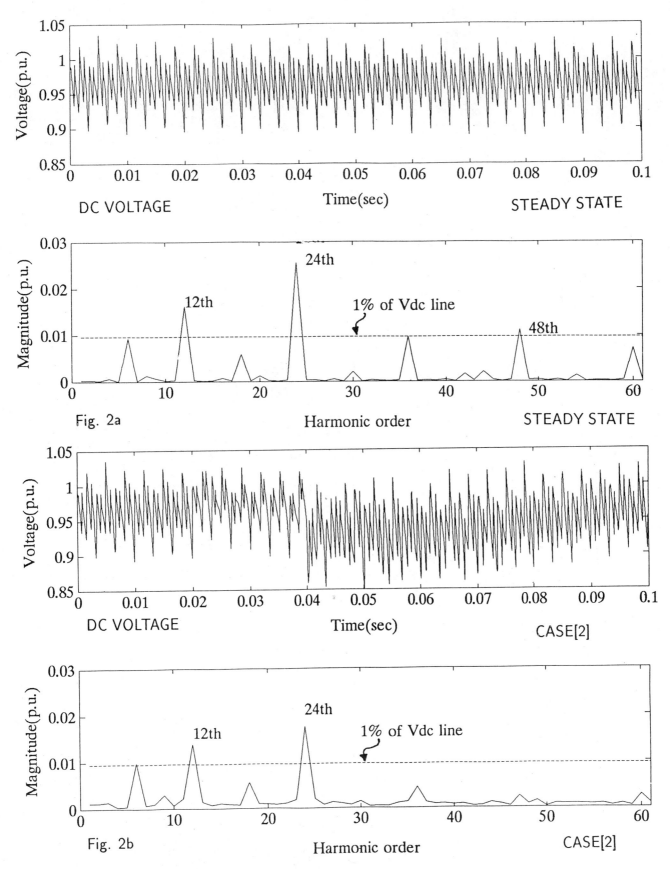

Fig. 2a

Fig. 2b

Fig. 2. HARMONIC SPECTRA OF DC VOLTAGE OF RECTIFIER1.

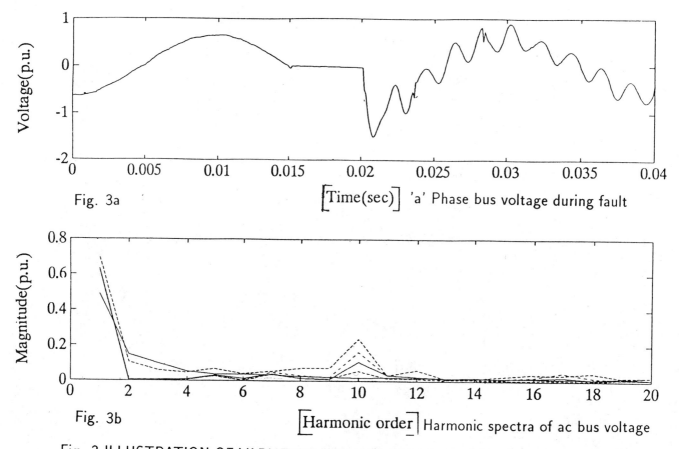

Fig. 3a   [Time(sec)] 'a' Phase bus voltage during fault

Fig. 3b   [Harmonic order] Harmonic spectra of ac bus voltage

Fig. 3 ILLUSTRATION OF VARIATION OF HARMONICS WITH TIME DURING FAULT.

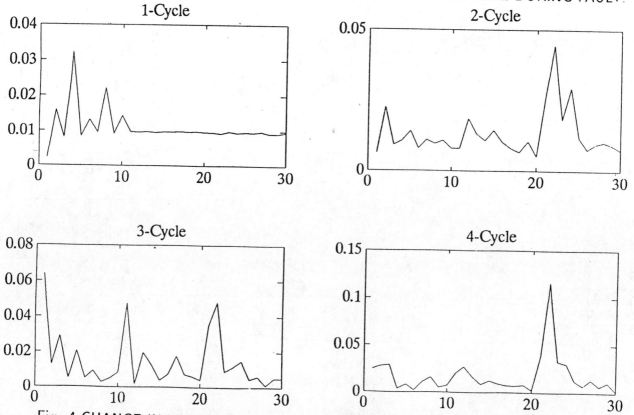

Fig. 4 CHANGE IN THE HARMONIC SPECTRA ON THE DC SIDE DURING FAULT.

Part III: Medical Systems

The seemingly exponential increase in health care costs has intensified the need for reliable low-cost health care tools that can increase the health-care provider's ability to administer to all sectors. Neural networks can improve diagnostic efficiency, reduce the time required to perform analysis of multi-sensor data, and automate many tasks that heretofore have required human processing.

The papers in this part are organized into three chapters. Chapter 11 includes papers that emphasize the diagnostic aspects of medicine, such as classification of disorders and prediction of disease progression. Chapter 12 looks at how neural networks can be used to process the massive amount of diverse signal data generated from diagnostic sensors such as electrocardiogram (ECG), electromiogram (EMG), and electroencephalograms (EEG). Chapter 13 focuses on the processing of image data produced from medical sensors such as X-rays, echocardiograms, and magnetic resonance imaging (MRI).

Medical Diagnosis

Medicine is a data intensive domain. Medical histories, diagnostic tests, physician evaluations, and many other data sets represent a rich set opportunity for neural networks. Neural networks can build models from historical data that can be used to diagnose diseases, detect medical problems, and forecast outcomes. The six papers found in this chapter represent several different applications of neural networks to diagnose medical problems. **Paper 11.1** applies several multilayer perceptron (MLP) neural networks to the classification of chromosomes. **Paper 11.2** describes the processing of cerebral blood flow measurements with an MLP to aide in the diagnosis of Alzheimer's disease. **Paper 11.3** compares Learning Vector Quantization (LVQ) and k-nearest neighbors for the classification of microorganisms that are used to predict Septicaemia. **Paper 11.4** utilizes the MLP and Boltzmann Machine neural networks to examine the relationship between occupational exposure and cancer. **Paper 11.5** compares multiple linear regression and LVQ at the classification of Parkinson rating-scale-date. **Paper 11.6** describes the application of an MLP neural network to the prediction of stenosis in patients who have already experienced myocardial infarction.

Chapter 11:   Medical Diagnosis

Classification of Chromosomes using a Combination of Neural Networks

Phil A. Errington and Jim Graham.

Department of Medical Biophysics,
University of Manchester, Oxford Road,
Manchester, M13 9PT, UK

Abstract– Visual analysis of microscope images containing chromosomes is an important clinical task in pre–natal diagnosis and cancer monitoring. In developing computer vision systems for analysing chromosomes images, a central task is the classification of the 46 chromosomes into 24 groups. We describe a combination of multi–layer–perceptrons for classifying isolated chromosomes and demonstrate that these perform as well as, or significantly better than a well developed statistical classifier. We suggest a method for using a competitive network to take advantage of constraints on the assignment of chromosomes to groups as a means of improving the classification rate.

I. INTRODUCTION.

The genetic material of all higher organisms is contained in a number of constituent parts of the organism's cell nuclei called chromosomes. At certain parts of the cell cycle these chromosomes exist as separate bodies which, appropriately stained, may be made visible under high resolution microscopy. Fig. 1 shows the appearance of a cell at the metaphase stage in which the chromosomes have been stained so that each exhibits a series of bands along its length (G–banding). The banding pattern, together with the chromosome length and centromere position (Fig. 2) can be used to assign the 46 chromosomes of a normal human cell into 24 groups (22 pairs of "autosomes" and two sex chromosomes: a pair of X chromosomes in the case of a female or an X and a Y chromosome in the case of a male) [15]. This classification by inspection (karyotyping) is a skilled and important task in pre–natal diagnosis of genetic abnormality and in diagnosis and monitoring of cancer. There has been considerable interest over many years in automating the analysis of chromosome images by computer vision [2], [5], [12], [13], [14]. A central issue in the development of automated systems is the specification of measurable features representing the banding pattern which cope with the considerable variability in banding appearance between cells. A range of features have been used for this purpose [2], [6], [7], [8], [12], [13], [16], [17], [21], usually derived intuitively and consequently lacking robustness to changes in preparation techniques.

An artificial neural network offers the possibility of an adaptable classifier for chromosomes [10]. Of particular interest are the feature extraction properties such models exhibit, which allow unrefined information to be presented to the classifier rather than specific intuitively defined features. This is reflected in our classification approach, as we use an artificial neural network to extract features from the raw grey level banding profile taken along the length of the chromosome. This profile is relatively easy to extract from chromosome images (Fig. 2). Additionally we use two other features representing the chromosome length and the position of its centromere (a characteristic constriction in the chromosome, see Fig. 2). This paper presents and compares the performance of an artificial neural network with a statistical classifier and discuses how the performance of the network classifier may be enhanced with the use of further neural networks.

Three extensive data sets of annotated measurements from G-banded chromosomes are used in our study, originating in Copenhagen, Edinburgh and Philadelphia. These have been used in previous classification studies using statistical methods [7], [16], [17], [21]. They cover a range of data quality, each set consisting of a large number

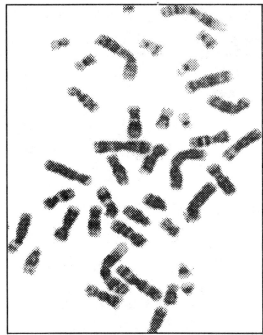

Fig. 1. An image of a metaphase cell showing G–banded chromosomes.

This work is supported by the UK Science and Engineering Research Council, Grant 90310105.

TABLE I

DETAILS OF THE THREE CHROMOSOME DATA SETS USED.

Dataset	Tissue of Origin	Digitization method	No. in set	Data quality
Copenhagen	Peripheral blood	Densitometry from photographic negatives	8106	Good
Edinburgh	Peripheral blood	T. V. Camera	5469	Fair
Philadelphia	Chorionic villus	CCD line scanner	5817	Poor

of chromosome density profiles extracted from images of cells in the metaphase stage of cell division.

Of the three data sets the Copenhagen set is considered the highest visual quality, as its chromosomes were carefully measured by densitometry of photographic negatives from selected cells of high quality. The other two data sets were taken from routine material with no attempt to remove measurements errors arising from overlapped or bent chromosomes. The Philadelphia set is considered the poorer of these two, as the nature of the slide preparation method results in direct chorionic villus samples providing cells of significantly poorer visual quality than in the case of peripheral blood. Details of the three data sets appear in Table I. It should be noted that the chromosomes are all from normal human cells and not from those exhibiting abnormalities. Such cells are expected to contain 46 chromosomes of 24 classes. These 46 chromosomes consist of 22 pairs of classes 1 to 22, with either one X and one Y chromosome (in male cells) or a pair of X chromosomes (in female cells).

II. CLASSIFICATION OF CHROMOSOMES

In our approach, classification takes place in two stages. The first involves classification of a chromosome independent of other chromosomes in a cell. For this task the Multi-Layer Perceptron (MLP) was selected. The bulk

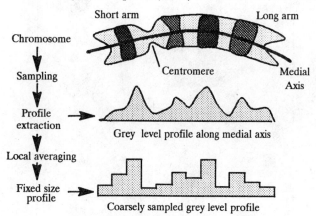

Fig. 2. An example of an extraction of a fixed length profile from a chromosome

of our work has been to modify and optimise classifiers built from this design of neural network.

During all classification experiments we use both a training and test set of data. Each of these sets is selected from approximately half of the data set under study. Two experiments are conducted, one with one half of the full data set as training data and then in a subsequent experiment as test data. Similarly the role of the other half of the data set is reversed. The classification rates we present are the mean classification rates over the two experiments.

III. FIRST STAGE CLASSIFICATION USING A MLP

A. Network Training Algorithm.

Preliminary work had shown the MLP to be a promising classifier for chromosome data [10] compared with other network topologies. For training our MLPs we chose a modification of the back–error propagation algorithm of Rummelhart, Hinton and Williams [19]. Our modification of the standard algorithm as described in [19] involves the use of a gradual reduction in gain (or learning rate). Initially the gain value in our network is set at a standard value (e.g. 0.1). As training proceeds two measures are monitored to select when a decrease in the gain term is required. These measures are the network classification error rate for the training data and the sum of the output node error signals for all of the training examples. The gain term is halved if the classification error rate does not decrease after 4 passes of the training data through the network. The gain is also halved if the sum of error signals increases by 10% over that observed on the previous pass of the training data set. This second measure (which is a scaled measure of the r.m.s. error between desired and actual outputs) prevents the network weights oscillating wildly with too high an original gain value, it is unlikely that such increases in the summed error signal will occur after the first few training passes.

The gain reduction mechanism permits larger values of gain to be initially used to allow considerable alteration in network weights, while allowing smaller more refined adjustments later in training for optimal classification performance. Fig. 3 shows a typical training curve for network error and classification performance using Copenhagen data.

Other algorithms (reviewed in [4]) have not yet been investigated for our MLP training, if training time becomes an issue it may be necessary to adopt one of these.

B. Use of the MLP for Chromosome Classification.

The number of samples in the banding profile of individual chromosomes in the data sets varies considerably. Profiles with up to 140 samples are present,

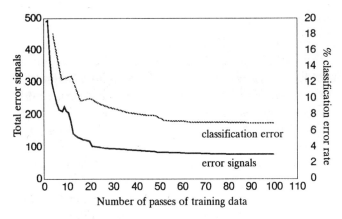

Fig. 3. The reduction in total error signals and classification error rate with training

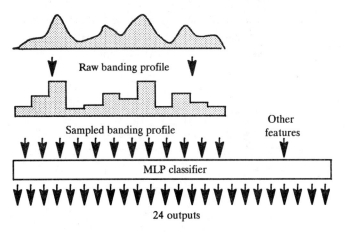

Fig. 4. Presentation of classification features to the MLP

although most profiles have approximately 90 samples. To maintain consistent inputs to the MLP the chromosome profiles are scaled to a constant length and local averaging used to produce a fixed number of averaged samples along the chromosome length (Fig. 4). These averaged inputs are presented to the MLP input nodes. If extra features are used these are presented alongside the banding profile at extra input nodes.

The network is trained so that the highest output denotes the category of the input pattern. As there are 24 classes of chromosome, 24 output nodes are required. A variable number of hidden nodes are used in one or two layers (see below).

C. Optimisation of the MLP Classifiers.

We have conducted a number of experiments to optimise our MLPs, using banding samples as the only inputs. The first stage of the optimisation involved testing the sensitivity of a particular network topology to changes in the value of the gain and momentum parameters. After varying the values of these parameters between 0.1 and 0.9 (involving 81 separate experiments in two halves) it was discovered that

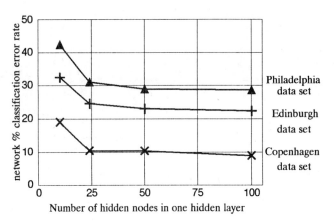

Fig. 5. The variation in classification performance of networks with different numbers of hidden nodes in one hidden layer

medium and high values of gain (greater than 0.6) and high momentum (e.g. 0.8, 0.9) resulted in unstable classifiers, while if the gain value was initially low (0.1) near optimal classification performance could be achieved with the entire range of momentum values. The result of the experiment was to select the best combination, in terms of training time efficiency, of gain and momentum which produces optimal classification performance. This combination was found to be an initial gain of 0.1 and a constant momentum value of 0.7.

Selection of an optimal topology for our problem was the next task. Although there are theoretical guide-lines to the number of hidden nodes required for a classification problem [1], [9], [20], these involve knowing something about the expected variability of the input data. As chromosome classification requires the network to cope with highly variable data, we selected the optimal topology for the MLP by experimentation.

Topology testing was performed with a fixed number of input nodes accepting banding inputs and 24 output nodes, one for each class of chromosome. Fifteen input samples were presented to the inputs as these had proved effective at representing the banding profile information in a preliminary study [10]. A variety of topology combinations of hidden nodes were tried. Initially a single hidden layer of nodes was used, with topologies involving 10, 24, 50 and 100 hidden nodes. The performance of these classifiers is shown in Fig. 5, which shows that the classification performance increases with increasing network complexity. Experiments with a second layer of hidden nodes were also conducted to evaluate the effect of their extra discriminating ability. The number of nodes in the first layer was set at 100 to reflect the best performing single hidden layer network. The results of trying 10, 24, 50 and 100 nodes in a second hidden layer is shown in Fig. 6. This

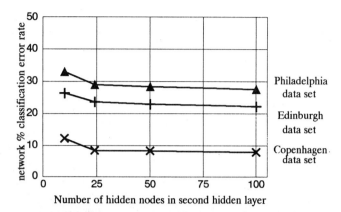

Fig. 6. The variation in classification performance of networks with a first hidden layer of 100 nodes and different numbers of nodes in a second hidden layer..

shows that there is very little variation in performance with increasing numbers of second hidden layer nodes. This is interesting as the training and classification times of the larger nets are far greater than those with fewer hidden nodes.

D. Classification Performance.

Once a good choice of topology and network parameters were made, the main advance in the performance of the classifier was achieved by including two extra features representing the length and centromere position. The centromere divides the chromosome into a long 'arm' and a short 'arm'. The ratio of the length of the short arm to that of the whole chromosome is called the centromeric index, and can be used as a representation of the centromere position, which varies depending on chromosome class. Length values are normalised to remove the effects of considerable inter-cell variation.

Three methods of including the centromeric index and length features were tried. The first involved each feature as an extra input along with banding inputs in a large MLP. The second used both features along with the banding information, but by far the most effective method was the use of an MLP pre-classifier (see Fig. 7).

Using the centromere position and chromosome length alone it is possible to classify the chromosomes into 7 broader groups, corresponding to the 'Denver' classification [3]. The pre-classifier was built to perform this broader classification, accepting the two features as inputs and producing likelihoods of membership of the 7 broader groups as outputs. This 7 group information was passed, together with the banding inputs, to a second MLP trained to produce the 24 class classification.

The optimisation of the MLP pre-classifier was performed in a similar manner to that discussed above; a number of topologies involving 2 inputs and 7 outputs were tried. The best performing of these topologies and their performance at classifying the 24 chromosome classes into the corresponding 7 Denver groups is shown in Table II.

The performances of the three inclusion methods for the centromere position and length features are shown in Table III, which indicates that a succession of two MLPs, the first performing a broad classification, later refined by a second using extra data, can out perform a single large MLP working on all the data.

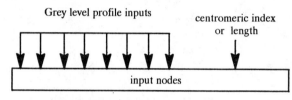

Method 1 : Profile plus single feature

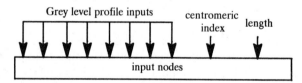

Method 2 : Profile plus pair of features

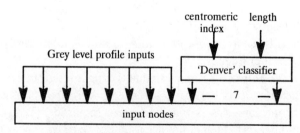

Method 3 : Profile plus pre-classified features

Fig. 7. Different methods of inclusion of the centromeric index and length features.

TABLE II
CLASSIFICATION ERROR RATES FOR THE BEST DENVER CLASSIFIERS USED
FOR PRE-CLASSIFICATION

Data set	Network Topology	Error rate for classifying into 7 groups
Copenhagen	2–14–7	5.4%
Edinburgh	2–14–7	10.1%
Philadelphia	2–14–7	14.6%

TABLE III
CLASSIFICATION ERROR RATES OF NETWORKS USING 15 GREY LEVEL
BANDING INPUTS WITH DIFFERENT REPRESENTATIONS OF CENTROMERE
AND LENGTH FEATURES.

Features Used	Data set		
	Cop.	Edi.	Phi.
Banding pattern alone	8.8%	22.3%	28.6%
Banding and normalised length	8.4%	19.4%	27.6%
Banding and centromeric index	7.7%	21.0%	26.5%
Banding, length and centromeric index	6.9%	18.6%	24.6%
Banding, and 'Denver' groups	5.8%	17.0%	22.5%

Using this combination of classifiers, chromosomes are classified according to the highest MLP output, and the overall performance compares favourably with statistical classifiers. Table IV compares the error rates for the three data sets we use with those of the best statistical classifier working under context free conditions on the same data [17]. As can be seen the neural network classifier outperforms this statistical classifier.

IV. SECOND STAGE CLASSIFICATION USING A COMPETITIVE NETWORK

The first classification stage works on individual chromosomes classified in isolation; no contextual information is used. The approach also relies on the highest MLP output representing the correct class of chromosome; information contained in the other MLP outputs is not considered. We propose to use a second stage of classification where the other MLP outputs are examined and used. Also in the second stage of classification we wish to apply context in the form of the number of chromosomes expected in each class when a cell of chromosomes is

TABLE IV
COMPARISON OF CLASSIFICATION ERROR RATES FOR A NEURAL
NETWORK CLASSIFIER USING BOTH BANDING AND DENVER GROUP
INPUTS WITH A HIGHLY OPTIMISED PARAMETRIC CLASSIFIER.

Data set	Classification error rate.		Significance of Improvement
	Network	Parametric [17]	
Copenhagen	5.8%	6.5%	2% level
Edinburgh	17.0%	18.3%	5% level
Philadelphia	22.5%	22.8%	Non significant

classified. We are investigating the application of a competitive network to both of these tasks.

From an MLP's output vector it is possible to select not only the most likely class, but secondary and less likely classes, using the second highest output, the third highest etc [18]. By considering all the MLP outputs, it may be possible to correctly classify chromosomes mis-classified on the basis of highest MLP output alone. To test the feasibility of this approach we have trained a competitive network using chromosomes mis-classified by the MLP and used it as a post-classifier for a separate test set of mis-classified chromosomes.

The competitive network we chose to use is a single layer topology of competitive nodes trained using a 'Winner Take All' algorithm. Each node receives the same input vector and compares this to its pattern of weights (which initially are random). The node with a pattern of weights closest to the input pattern is designated the winner. During training, winning nodes alter their weight values so that they are closer to their inputs. After a period of training each node has specialised to represent a class of similar input vectors (those for which it 'won'), and can be labelled with the class(es) of these vectors. The nodes can then be used to classify input vectors, the class of each vector being decided by the label of the winning node. The vectors we use are those produced at the 24 output nodes from the MLP first stage classifier. At present no lateral inhibition or Kohonen neighbourhoods [11] are used, each winning node updating only its own weights. It may be necessary to introduce some form of refinement near class boundaries as it becomes clear how the subclasses lie in weight space.

The results of classifying mis-classified chromosomes from the Copenhagen, Edinburgh and Philadelphia data sets, using a competitive network are presented in Table V.

The performance of this classifier is encouraging. It shows that, even when the highest value in the MLP output vector does not correspond to the true class, the entire vector contains information which allows classification to be made. However the classifier is not attempting to classify all chromosomes, only those mis-classified by the MLP. It is possible to train other competitive nodes to classify

TABLE V
PERCENTAGE OF CHROMOSOMES MIS-CLASSIFIED ON THE BASIS OF
MLP OUTPUT WHICH ARE CORRECTLY CLASSIFIED BY A COMPETI-
TIVE NETWORK TRAINED ON MIS-CLASSIFIED CHROMOSOMES.

Data set	Percentage of chromosomes correctly classified	
	Training data	Unseen data
Copenhagen	48.0%	23.1%
Edinburgh	42.1%	30.4%
Philadelphia	43.4%	31.7%

chromosomes correctly classified by the MLP. The nodes classifying these may then be included with nodes classifying mis-classified chromosomes. Combining 'correct' trained and 'error' trained competitive nodes in this manner, we have so far only managed to achieve a classification performance equivalent to selecting the highest MLP output as the correct class.

Our experiments involving the application of context to the classification of chromosomes also make use of a competitive network. The contextual constraint is that a cell of 46 chromosomes will possess 2 chromosomes each of classes 1 to 22, with either one X and one Y chromosome or a pair of X chromosomes. Application of this constraint has been shown to effect an improvement in the performance of statistical classifiers, [22].

We are currently investigating methods of applying this constraint using a competitive network. One method currently under consideration is to to classify all the chromosomes in a cell using a competitive network pre-trained to recognise MLP output vectors. A mechanism of penalising and rewarding competitive nodes according to how well they match the contextual constraints is applied in the winner take all competition. Nodes winning too few chromosomes in classification should therefore receive more, while those winning too many chromosomes should receive less.

V. CONCLUSIONS

Overall the application of trainable neural networks for chromosome classification has proved effective. The first stage of classification involving 2 MLPs out-performs a highly optimised statistical classifier working with the same data and splitting mechanisms [17]. We have begun investigations into the use of competitive networks in a second classification stage, with emphasis on applying contextual constraints for classifying all the chromosomes in a cell. Results so far are equivocal.

ACKNOWLEDGMENTS

This work was greatly facilitated by the exchange of materials and ideas available within the Concerted Action of Automated Cytogenetics Groups supported by the European Community, Project No. II.1.1/13. We are grateful to Jim Piper of the MRC Human Genetics Unit, Edinburgh for permission to reproduce some of his results.

REFERENCES

[1] E. B. Baum. "On the capabilities of multilayer perceptrons." *Journal Complexity* Vol 4 pp 193–215, 1988.

[2] K. R. Castleman and J. Melnyk. "An automated system for chromosome analysis– final report." *Internal document* No. 5040-30. Jet Propulsion Laboratory, Pasedena, Texas 1976.

[3] "Denver Conference. A proposed standard system of nomenclature of human mitotic chromosomes." *Lancet* Vol 1 pp. 1063–1065, 1960.

[4] S. E. Fahlman. "Faster learning variations on back-propagation: an empirical study." in *Proceedings Connectionist Models Summer School*, 1988, pp 38–51.

[5] J. Graham. "Automation of routine clinical chromosome analysis I, Karyotyping by machine." *Analytical and Quantitative Cytology and Histology*, Vol. 9 pp. 383–390, 1987.

[6] G. H. Granlund. "Identification of human chromosomes using integrated density profiles." *IEEE Trans. Biomed. Eng.* Vol. 23 pp. 183–192 1976.

[7] E. Granum. "Application of statistical and syntactical methods of analysis to classification of chromosome data." in *Pattern Recognition Theory and Application*, Kittler J. Fu KS, Pau LF, eds. NATO ASI (Oxford), Reidel, Dordreht, 1982, pp 373–398.

[8] F. C. A. Groen, T. K. Ten Kate, A. W. M. Smeulders and I. T. Young. "Human chromosome classification based on local band descriptors." *Pattern Recognition Letters* Vol. 9. pp. 211–222, 1989.

[9] S.C. Huang and Y. F. Huang. "Bounds on number of hidden neurons in multilayer perceptrons." *IEEE Trans on Neural Networks*, Vol. 2 pp. 47–55. 1991.

[10] A. M. Jennings. "Chromosome Classification Using Neural Nets," *MSc Thesis*, University of Manchester, U.K. 1990.

[11] T. Kohonen. "Self-Organisation and Associative Memory," *Series in Information Sciences*, Vol 8. Springer-Verlag, Berlin-New York-Tokyo, 1984. 2nd ed. 1988.

[12] R. S. Ledley, P. S. Ing and H. A. Lubs. "Human chromosome classification using discriminant analysis and Bayesian probability." *Comput. Biol. Med.* 10:209–218, 1980.

[13] C. Lundsteen, T. Gredes, E. Granum and J. Philip. "Automatic chromosome analysis II. Karyotyping of banded human chromosomes using band transition sequences." *Clin. Genet.* Vol. 19 pp. 26–36 1981.

[14] C. Lundsteen, T. Gerdes and J. Maahr. "Automatic classification of chromosomes as part of a routine system for clinical analysis." *Cytometry* Vol. 7 pp. 1–7, 1986.

[15] Paris Conference (1971), "Standardization in Human Cytogenetics." *Original Article series*, 8:7. The National Foundation, New York 1972.

[16] J. Piper and E. Granum. "On fully automatic feature measurement for banded chromosome classification." *Cytometry* 10:242–255, 1989.

[17] J. Piper. "Aspects of chromosome class size classification constraint," *CAACG Interlab meeting and Topical Workshop on High-level Classification and Karyotyping, Approaches and Tests*, University of Aalborg, 13–14 March 1991.

[18] D. W. Ruck, S. K. Roggers, M. Kabrisky, M. E. Oxley and B. W. Suter. "The Multilayer perceptron as an approximation to a Bayes Optimal Discriminant Function," *IEEE Trans Neural Networks*, Vol. 1 pp. 296–297. 1990.

[19] D. E. Rummelhart, G. E. Hinton and R. J. Williams. "Learning Internal Representations by Error Propagation." in *Parallel Distributed Processing: Explorations in the Microstructures of Cognition*. Rummelhart DE and McCelland JL (eds.), Vol. 1 Foundations, MIT Press, Cambridge, MA, 1986, pp. 318–362.

[20] M. A. Sartori and P. J. Antsaklis. "A Simple Method to Derive Bounds on the Size and to Train Multilayer Neural Networks." *IEEE Trans on Neural Networks*, Vol. 2 pp. 467–471, 1991.

[21] M. G. Thomason and E. Granum. "Dynamically programmed inference of Markov networks from finite sets of sample strings." *IEEE Trans. PAMI* Vol 8 pp. 491–501, 1986.

[22] M. K. S. Tso, P. Kleinschmidt, I. Mitterreiter and J. Graham. "An efficient transportation algorithm for automatic chromosome karyotyping." *Pattern Recognition Letters* Vol. 12 pp. 117–126, 1991.

Incremental Learning in a Multilayer Neural Network as an Aid to Alzheimer's Disease Diagnosis

Marie Chan[+*], Bernard André[*], Armando Herrera[*], Pierre Celsis[+]

*LAAS - CNRS 7 Avenue du Colonel ROCHE 31077 TOULOUSE Cedex - FRANCE
+U230 INSERM CHU Purpan Service de neurologie 31052 TOULOUSE Cedex - FRANCE

Abstract In the seventies and eighties, Expert Systems were developed as an aid to medical diagnosis. Despite some interesting and successful results, significant shortcomings were encountered, due to an inherent risk of errors, the complexity of the problems considered, and the difficulty of accessing the expert knowledge held by physicians. More recently, many techniques have been proposed in the field of Artificial Neural Networks (ANNs) allowing knowledge to be directly learned from experimental results and medical practice. In this paper an aid to Alzheimer's disease diagnosis is suggested using Cerebral Blood Flow (CBF) measurements from Single Photon Emission Computed Tomography (SPECT) which facilitate ANN training. An incremental learning technique is presented to memorize new input-output associations without necessarily starting the learning phase all over again. Two steps are proposed: 1) Off-line learning of the overall features that remain unchanged during any implementation, based on the patient's CBF measurements studied in the laboratory. 2) In-situ learning of each site's features: The physician can enter new input-output associations. In case of failure, a constructing procedure adds and trains new unit designed to represent new associations. Thus, learning is being added incrementally. This approach turns out to be more particularly useful for medical diagnosis in which the system designer does not possess the complete learning set right from the start. Indeed pieces of information are added as they become available, thus allowing for a man-machine dialogue to take place.

I. INTRODUCTION

Up to the eighties, the models used in computer science and medical diagnosis, were based on decision theory and probabilistic or statistical methods. Artificial Intelligence methods were developed to overcome some limitations associated with purely statistical methods based on a more structured representation of therapeutic or diagnosis problems [2] [10] [12] [6]. The techniques used aimed at clarifying deduction rules through use of a lot of information about a specific area. However given the complexity of Expert Systems involving combinatory explosions, and the difficulty in accessing the expert

Manuscript received July 15, 1993.

knowledge held by physicians, ANNs have been employed [1] [11] and allow direct learning of knowledge from experimental results and medical practice.

In this paper, ANN training is proposed in two steps: Off-line learning with well-known, validated samples completed by in-situ learning based on samples chosen by medical practice to diagnose Alzheimer's disease. Our software makes use of CBF measurements obtained from SPECT:

1) off-line learning: This phase concerns well-known diagnosis characteristics. It remains unchanged in any implementations. We select the set of subjects to train the ANN in two steps:

A) unsupervised learning: To point out the similarity properties of raw data and to obtain a partition of the subject space.

B) expert knowledge: A reliable criteria based on some symmetrical properties of the mean CBF values of pairs of regions of interest (ROIs) is used to distinguish subjects inside a class.

2) in-situ learning of the features specific to each site: This approach requires an incremental learning strategy. Incremental learning refers to learning samples added to the learning set towards which the network has previously converged.

Conventional learning algorithms based on gradient descent are not suitable for the incremental procedure, primarily because the network archictecture is selected by means of an error procedure on learning data. In addition the error surface may exhibit one or more local minimum. To circumvent these shortcomings, a new method suitable for incremental learning is proposed. The weights of a given ANN are adjusted so as to allow memorization of new input-output associations. In the case where convergence cannot be achieved for some associations, new units are then added. The incremental procedure relies on two separate learning processes:

- The so-called "Offset" procedure [7] which builds up a network operating as a parity machine.
- A learning algorithm for a fixed architecture, namely a parity machine, similar to the "least action" algorithm developed in [8].

In Section II the selection of data for an off-line learning of the diagnosis characteristics are presented, including the unsupervised learning algorithm and some expert knowledge on CBF measurement properties that allows to distinguish the subjects inside a class. The "Offset" algorithm and its extension to incremental learning are also presented. Section III deals with the results. Section IV draws the conclusion.

II. DATA AND METHOD

A group of subjects, in which 96 were probably affected by Alzheimer's disease and 30 were normal, was studied based on transverse slices of CBF measurements obtained from SPECT [3]. In particular 16 ROIs in the middle slice were considered. The set of subjects was then partitioned into two disjoint subsets and a software was constructed to help physicians in medical diagnosis of Alzheimer 's disease. First we analyzed multidimensional input measurement data. An unsupervised learning process [9] yielded two classes of subjects characterized by the similarity or proximity properties of the input data. Then specific subjects were selected inside each class based on criteria of symmetrical properties of mean CBF values of pairs of ROIs. The two classes of subjects were used for training the ANN using the "Offset" algorithm which dynamically builds layered network as a parity machine. The expert physician can add new input-output associations by means of incremental learning, assuming that the sofware is developed while the physician gives his opinion on difficult subjects or in the case where all subjects are not available at that time.

A. Multidimensional unsupervised learning algorithm

As previously developed in [9], Learning Algorithms for Multivariate Data Analysis (LAMDA) have been chosen because they do not need previous information about the number of classes and several similarity measures can be investigated easily to adjust the selectivity of the algorithms. The LAMDA classification method relies on an iterative algorithm that sequentially studies the items, represented by N-dimension vectors, and evaluates their membership with respect to all the existing classes: $C_1, C_2, ... C_m$, plus an empty class C_0. Then a decision procedure assigns the current analyzed item to the maximum membership class. The membership is computed from the observed values of the vector components and using the description parameters of each class. The contribution of each component is combined using "connective functions" related to the logical connectives in Boolean algebra, i.e. union or intersection. This method yields a partition of the subject space.

B. Expert knowledge

Large ROIs were defined by physicians [4], and from the mean CBF values obtained in pairs of ROIs, normalized indexes of asymmetry can be calculated according to the following formula:

$$I = (\chi - \mu)/\sigma \qquad (1)$$

$$\chi = 2(\phi_1 - \phi_2)/(\phi_1 + \phi_2) \qquad (2)$$

Where μ is the mean and σ the standard deviation of the weighted difference between the mean CBFs $\phi 1$ and $\phi 2$ observed in normals in a pair of ROIs.

By varying the ROIs considered, as shown in Fig. 1, we obtained indexes of anterior-posterior asymmetry (1,9; 2,10; 3,11;...right hemisphere, left hemisphere), of anterior-posterior asymmetry (3,4; 2,5; 1,6;...in both hemispheres), of cortical-subcortical asymmetry (1,8; 2,8; 3,8;...for both sides). We had the following formula for I:

$$-\alpha <= I <= +\alpha \qquad (3)$$

$$|I| > +\alpha \qquad (4)$$

Significant asymmetry properties were considered when the index absolute value was higher than 2, with the site of the predominant hypoperfusion being determined according to the index sign.

Each subject has 28 parameters that can take one of these binary values: (-1-1,-11,1-1), according to (3) or (4). Each subject corresponds to 56 binary inputs. In the class where the majority of subjects has a high number of symmetries, we suggest to keep only those subjects having the following criteria: *the number of symmetries are higher than or equal to 26,* and, for the class where the number of symmetries is smaller, we keep the subjects having: *the number of symmetries lower than or equal to 13.*

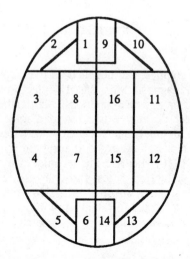

Fig. 1. The regions of interest in the middle slice of the brain.

This criteria chosen by the expert allows to have "reliable" learning data which remain unchanged in any implementation.

C. "Offset" algorithm

The "Offset" algorithm dynamically builds layered networks. The input space is partitioned so that units are added as they are needed during the learning phase [7]. The weight w and bias θ of each unit are determined by a perceptron-based algorithm which minimizes a classification error. Explicitly, when a new unit κ is added, the weights of the previously added units are frozen and the new desired outputs v_κ^* are computed by:

$$v_\kappa^* = v_{\kappa-1}^* \oplus v_{\kappa-1} \qquad (5)$$

Where $v_{\kappa-1}^*$ and $v_{\kappa-1}$ are respectively the target and the output of the previously added unit, $\oplus$ is the exclusive disjunction function (xor). Hence the κ-th unit is active only for the subjects misclassified by the $(\kappa-1)$-th unit and inactive for the well-classified subjects. The growth process terminates with unit n if it does not produce any error ($v_n = v_n^*$). Then, given that the desired output for the first added unit is the desired output for the network $v_1^* = v^*$, we can write:

$$v^* = v_1 \oplus v_2 \oplus v_3 \oplus \cdots \oplus v_n \qquad (6)$$

The network output is therefore the parity of the internal representation built by the growth process. Note that the parity function can be implemented by constructing another hidden layer with fixed weights determined by a geometrical construction procedure. Hence the first layer of n units maps any arbitrary d-dimensional dichotomy onto an n-parity problem and the second layer solves the n-parity problem.

D. Incremental learning

Incremental learning refers to the ability to learn additional examples without necessarily starting the learning phase all over again. To do this, the network must be capable of lengthening its size if it cannot accommodate all the new input-output samples. An incremental learning process can be done in two steps:

1) Adaptive step: The weights of the existing network are ajusted for new learning sample. A "least action" learning algorithm is used and weight modifications are made by the "thermal" perceptron rule developed by Frean for training individual units [5]. The weight corrections

made with this rule are biased exponentially towards correcting errors for which $|A|$ is close to zero:

$$\Delta\omega_i = \eta X_i e^{-|A|/T} \text{ for a negative response}$$
$$\Delta\omega_i = -\eta X_i e^{-|A|/T} \text{ for a positive response.}$$

2) Constructing step: In case the previous step fails, new units are added and trained to memorize the new samples. The "Offset" algorithm is particularly helpful for incremental learning because, in order to memorize new associations, it is able to increase the size of the network. New associations can be learned by training the newly added unit with targets computed by equation (5). In this case, "Offset" can be used in the construction step of the incremental learning process.

III. RESULTS

According to the flowchart of the learning procedure of Fig. 2 and following unsupervised learning of the raw data (mean CBF values of 16 ROIs for each subject), we obtain

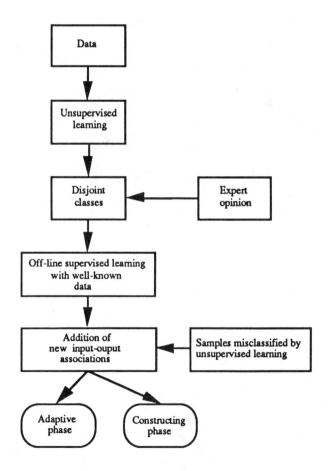

Fig. 2. The flowchart of the learning procedure

TABLE I
UNSUPERVISED LEARNING RESULTS

classes	C_1	C_2
patient	84	12
normal	21	9

the results given in table I. These results show that certain patients regarded as sick by the physician fall into the healthy category and vice-versa. However using the asymmetry properties of mean CBF values of pairs of ROIs allow certain patients to be discarded to keep only those known, through learning, to belong to either category (individual whose number of symmetries is less than or equal to 13 or higher than or equal to 26, meaning that he belongs either to the sick or the healthy class).

Then the constructing step involves the 47 subjects selected out of 126 according to an unsupervised learning and asymmetry property of mean CBF values of pairs of ROIs). The ANN can be derived using the "Offset" algorithm. Because of the limited number of cases available, we employ the "leaving-one-out" procedure of training. We train 47 networks, each network is trained on a subset of 46 of the 47 subjects and tested on the remaining one. This method enables us to determine the generalization performance for each network. In this case, 41 examples belong to the sick class and 6 examples belong to the healthy class. 6 subjects fail in the wrong class. 35 are well classed in the sick class and 6 in the healthy class. However the incremental procedure is always successful and includes all the remaining input-output samples not previously learned by the network in the construction phase. A network of 22 hidden neurons is built up to memorize the 126 input-output raw data.

IV. CONCLUSION

Building up a software to help the physician carry out his diagnosis is a challenging task, particularly in view of the reduced number of subjects enrolled in the study. Partitioning the individuals with the unsupervised learning is an alternative to the control of classification problems. Then selecting a criterion based on data properties makes it possible to keep only those subjects that definitely belong to a class. Following this, the off-line learning phase carried out in the laboratory can be initiated and remains unchanged in all cases. In situ, the physician is able to enter new input-output associations, providing there is no contradiction between associations. In other words, two subjects belonging to two different classes need to be different. The selection of 47 subjects enables us to build up the network. Then, a generalization test based on the "leaving-one-out" procedure yields 15 percent of errors, as certain pattern are not known to the learning phase. This error rate may be diminished by adding the simulated sick patient patterns to the learning data. The physician is also able to enter those input-output associations that he deems pertinent with incremental learning. Also the system's reliability could be enhanced by entering new measurement parameters. The use of ANN can be interesting in a software provided it can learn from examples correctly interpreted by a "teacher": the expert. We propose a global approach that relies on an unsupervised learning phase - combined with the selection of a criterion warrantying the exact determination of a subject to a class - for the off-line learning phase of the neural network and an in-situ learning phase wherein the expert physician can exploit the network through generalization or keep entering new cases through incremental learning. The approach is applied to a set of CBF measurements related to Alzheimer patients and healthy individuals. The generalization yields errors due to small set of data tested relative to the number of binary inputs. Other data from other apparatus, or other psychological tests, seem needed to improve the results.

ACKNOWLEDGMENT

A. Herrera would like to thank CONACyT for his support.

REFERENCES

[1] M. Akay, "Noninvasive diagnosis of coronary artery disease using a neural network algorithm," Biol. Cybern., vol. 67, pp. 361-367, 1992.

[2] B. G. Buchanan, "Issues on representation in conveying the scope limitations of the intelligent assistant programs," Machine Intelligence, vol. 9, pp. 407-425, 1979.

[3] P. Celsis, T. Goldman, L. Henriksen, N. A. Lassen, "A method for calculating regional cerebral blood flow from emission computed tomography of inert gas concentrations," J. Comput. Assist. Tomogr., vol. 5, PP. 641-645, 1981.

[4] P. Celsis, A. Agniel, M. Puel, J. F. Démonet, A. Rascol, J. P. Marc-Vergnes, "Hemodynamic subtypes of dementia of the Alzheimer type: Clinical and neurophsychological characteristics," in Imaging, Cerebral topography and Alzheimer's disease, S. R. Rapoport, H. Petit, D. Leys, Y. Christen Eds. Berlin Heidelberg: Springer verlag, pp. 145-157, 1990.

[5] M. Frean, "A "Thermal" perceptron learning rule," Neural Comp., vol. 4, pp. 946-957, 1992.

[6] C. A. Kulikowski, S. M. Weiss, "Representation of expert knowledge for consultation: The CASNET and EXPERT projects," in Artificial Intelligence in Medicine, P. Szolovits Ed AAAS Selected, symposium 51, 1982.

[7] D. Martinez, D. Estève, "The Offset algorithm: Building and learning method for multilayer neural networks," Europhys. Lett., vol. 18, (2), pp. 95-100, 1992.

[8] G. J. Mitchinson, R. M. Durbin, "Bounds on the learning capacity of some multi-layer networks," Biol. Cybern., vol. 60, pp. 345-356, 1989.

[9] N. Piera Carreté, J. Aguilar-Martin, "Controlling selectivity in non standard subject recognition algorithms," IEEE Trans. Syst. Sci. Cybern., vol. 21, (1), pp. 71-82, 1991.

[10] H. A. Jr. Pople, J. D. Myers, R. A. Miller, "DIALOG: A model of diagnosis logic for internal medicine," 4th IJCAI Tbilissi, 1975.

[11] D. E. Rumelhart, J. L. MCleland, Parallel distributed processing; Explorations in the microstructure of cognition: Foundation, vol. 1, Cambridge, MA, MIT Press, 1986.

[12] E. H. Shortliffe, "Computer based medical consultations: MYCIN," New-York, American Elsevier, 1976.

Comparison of Learning Vector Quantization and k-Nearest Neighbour For Prediction of Microorganisms Associated With Septicaemia

P.J.Worthy[1], R.Dybowski[2], W.R.Gransden[2], R.Summers[1].

1, Centre for Measurement and Information in Medicine,
Department of Systems Science, City University, London EC1V OHB, UK.

2, Department of Microbiology, UMDS, St Thomas' Hospital, London SE1 7EH, UK.

Abstract - **This paper describes the application of an artificial neural network technique (Learning Vector Quantization) and a statistical technique (k-nearest neighbour) to predict the most likely microorganism causing septicaemia given a set of measured patient variables. This objective, data-based approach contrasts with a subjective knowledge based system (MYCIN).**

I. INTRODUCTION

Septicaemia is the clinically significant occurrence of microorganisms in the blood stream. Successful management of patients with septicaemia requires, as a minimum, the prompt administration of appropriate antibiotic therapy. Inappropriate initial therapy significantly increases the mortality rate [1]. The appropriateness of the initial therapy is determined, in part, by the infecting organisms. Since the identification of the organisms usually takes 18-24 hours, it would be advantageous to have the ability to predict the most likely microorganisms prior to identification.

MYCIN [2] was designed in the 1970s to assist clinicians in the management of patients with septicaemia. The system was based on knowledge acquired from domain experts. Inference under uncertainty was conducted by the use of certainty factors and not by direct use of probability theory, however, the use of certainty factors is not entirely satisfactory [3].

Since the development of MYCIN, a database of past episodes of septicaemia has been compiled at St Thomas' Hospital comprising over 4000 episodes [4]. This has led to consideration of an alternative decision-support system [5], namely, one using *objective, data-based methods* instead of one centred on a subjective, knowledge-based approach.

II. DATA-BASED CLASSIFICATION METHODS

Statistical pattern recognition aims to classify a vector of measurements using vectors that are representative of the classes of interest. This classifies the object from which the measurements were taken. Here, "classification" is being used in a statistical sense and not in a taxonomic sense. The *k-nearest neighbours (k-NN)* algorithm has been chosen for this study. This algorithm is a commonly used non-parametric method for pattern recognition. A vector x is assigned to class c if out of the k (where $k \geq 1$) class-representative vectors nearest to x (measured by the Euclidean metric) most belong to class c. This decision rule can be derived from Bayes' theorem [6].

Artificial Neural Networks (ANN's) is a field that encompasses a range of machine learning paradigms that have emerged at a rapid rate since the early 1980s. *Learning Vector Quantization (LVQ)* developed by Kohonen [7] is an architecture that is notably different to other ANN paradigms. LVQ differs in that there are no interconnections and no transformation of input values.   The network organises its own representation of the data set by spanning the input space with category representative nodes which model the probability distribution of the training data. The learning algorithm dictates how these vectors are actually placed in input space and in the recall phase the nearest (again by the Euclidean metric) category vector to the input vector is deemed to be the 'winning' category.   A graphical representation of the two techniques is given below in Fig.1 and 2.

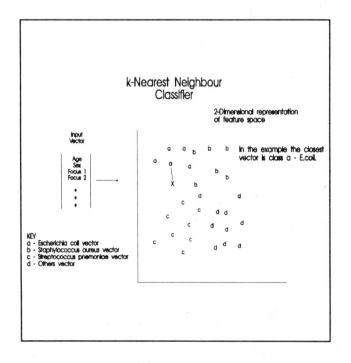

Figure 1 - k Nearest Neighbour (k-NN)

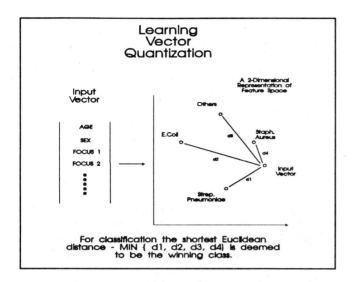

Figure 2 - Learning Vector Quantization

III. PROGRESS

Exploration of the techniques has been with full-size data sets, that is, statistical techniques such as Principle Components Analysis or Canonical Variance Analysis have not been used to reduce the number of measured parameters for classification (as suggested by Hand [6]). The 51 elements of the input vector were (a) year, (b) age, (c) sex, (d) whether the infection was acquired in the hospital, (e) whether the patient is already on antibiotics, and binary dummy variables for the following categories: (f) medical speciality of the ward, (g) the underlying diseases (if any), and (h) the anatomical site of the infection. The 'training' or 'derivation' data were generated by random sampling from the database and totalled 1664 examples. Similarly the testing data set contained 1664 examples.

The k-NN algorithm was tested with k set to unity. The LVQ algorithm was tested with 1 and 2 vectors to represent each category (Escherichia coli, Staphylococcus aureus, Streptococcus pnemoniae and Other microorganism) giving 4 vectors in total.

Fig.3 below shows the percentage correct classification rates (on the test set) obtained with the different techniques.

Figure 3 - Classification rates

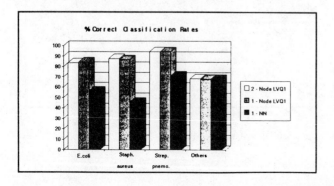

For the microorganism categories E.coli, S.aureus and S.pnemoniae the LVQ algorithms give a 23-28% higher correct classification rate compared to k-NN. For the large category of 'Other microorganisms' the performance is not significantly different.

Further work is required on the use of different numbers of vectors per category (for example proportional to a priori probability of categories) and extensions to the LVQ1 algorithm (LVQ2 and LVQ3) which are capable (in theory) of improving the decision surface.

IV. SUMMARY

Initial experimentation with the LVQ algorithm has yielded classification results of a higher accuracy (23-28%) than that of the established statistical technique, k-nearest neighbours. It is envisaged that further work on reducing dimensionality of the input vector (as suggested by Hand) will lead to a further increase in the classification accuracy of both the LVQ and k-NN algorithms

REFERENCES

[1] J.H.Gatell, A.Trilla, X.Lattore, et al, "Nosocomial bacteremia in a large Spanish teaching hospital: Analysis of factors influencing prognosis", *Review of Infectious Diseases*, 10 (1988) pp203-210.

[2] E.H. Shortliffe, *Computer-based medical consultations: MYCIN* , 1976, Elsevier, New York,.

[3] J.B. Adams, "A probability model of medical reasoning and the MYCIN model", *Mathematical Biosciences*, 32, 1976, pp177-186.

[4] W.R.Gransden, S.J. Eykyn and I.Phillips, "The computerized documentation of septicaemia", *Journal of Antimicrobial Chemotherapy, Supplement C* , 25, 1990, pp31-39.

[5] R.Dybowski, W.R.Gransden and I.Phillips, "Towards a statistically-oriented decision-support system for the management of septicaemia", *Artificial Intelligence in Medicine,* In press 1993.

[6] D.J. Hand, *Discrimination and Classification* , 1981, John Wiley, Chichester.

[7] T.Kohonen, *Self-Organisation and Associative Memory*, Third Edition, 1989, Springer-Verlag, Berlin.

Pattern Recognition of Occupational Cancer Using Neural Networks

Vincent Ng,[1] Raymond Fang,[1] Joel Bert,[2] Pierre Band,[1]
Laurence Svirchev[1] and Anya Keefe[1]
[1] Division of Epidemiology, British Columbia Cancer Agency,
[2] Department of Chemical Engineering, University of British Columbia,
Vancouver, British Columbia, Canada

ABSTRACT

This paper presents an application of multi-layered neural networks to occupational epidemiology for the Pulp and Paper industry. Various architectures of Feedforward Networks with and without hidden layers have been tested to examine the relationships between occupational exposure and cancer. The inputs to the networks consist of chemical exposures derived from epidemiological studies. The outputs are the cancer types of the patients. The results of the classification performances demonstrate that an appropriate network architecture with some pre-processing of the exposures might lead to more efficient results.

1 Introduction

The relationship between cancer and occupation was first suggested in 1775, when an English surgeon, Percival Pott, reported an increased incidence of scrotal cancers among London chimney sweeps[1]. Subsequently, in the 19th century, workers exposed to tar, paraffin oils, and inorganic arsenic were observed to have higher rates of skin cancer, and occupational exposure to certain dyes was reported to be a risk factor for bladder cancer[1]. More than 50% of the chemicals classified by the International Agency for Research on Cancer (IARC) as proven human carcinogens are present in the occupational environment. Estimates of the proportions of human cancers attributable to workplace exposure range from 2-8%[2] to as high as 20%[3].

A Job Exposure Matrix (JEM) is an exposure classification system linking occupation- and industry-specific job titles with the chemical agents to which individuals are occupationally exposed. The use of JEMs holds promise as an effective strategy by which occupational exposure can be related to the incidence of disease (e.g. cancer). The National Institute of Occupational Safety and Health (NIOSH) has recently produced a JEM consisting of over 8000 potentially hazardous chemicals cross-referenced by occupation and industry. This JEM is based on the exposure data collected by 20 engineers during the 1972-1974 National Occupation Hazard Survey (NOHS), a field survey of 4636 industrial facilities across the United States[4]. In 1987, an independent JEM of the pulp and paper industry in British Columbia was developed by the British Columbia Cancer Agency, in collaboration with the Department of Chemical Engineering at the University of British Columbia[5].

To utilize the JEMs in cancer risk assessments, we have used an occupational database with cancer information[6]. The joining of all these data represents a large volume of information. Traditional statistical methods are difficult to use and to interpret due to the size of the database and the underlying statistical assumptions. Non-linearity among different etiological factors and possible incomplete information contribute to additional difficulties. Neural Networks, which can be used as classifiers, provide an alternative approach to the traditional statistical analysis. Neural networks have been widely studied and been used in the statistics communities[7]. Over the last few years, neural network software has become publicly available and the networks have grown in popularity. It has been used in psychiatry[8], pediatric radiology[9], breast cancer[10] and ocular tumor[11]. In this paper, we report initial findings of our work which applies neural networks to occupational cancers.

2 Data

In 1982, the Division of Epidemiology in British Columbia Cancer Agency initiated a comprehensive occupational cancer research program aimed at iden-

Feedwater Engineer	carbon dioxide
	sulfur dioxide
	benzo-pyrene
	sodium hydroxide
	monosodium phosphates
	......
Bleach Operator	chlorine
	sodium hydrosulfite
	sodium hydroxide
	sodium silicates
	sulfur dioxide
	......

Figure 1: Occupational Chemical Exposure

Environmentally Related	Non-Environmentally Related
Liver	Esophagus
Lung	Stomach
Bladder	Colon
Kidney	Rectum
Brain	Nose
Leukemia	Prostate
...	...

Figure 2: Cancer Types

tifying occupational cancer risk factors in the work place. An occupational database, including lifetime work history for 15,463 cancer patients, has been developed. From this database, we have selected to study the risk of cancer for occupations in the pulp and paper industry with the exception of administrative and clerical staff. To take into account the latency period between exposure and the development of cancer, only patients who have worked more than 10 years in the industry were selected.

Two separate Job Exposure Matrices(JEMs) were used: the NIOSH JEM and the PP JEM we developed for the pulp and paper industry. In the NIOSH matrix, each job title has a specific exposure profile. Additionally, there is information about the number of active and full-time employees in the industries for each job title; however, there is no information about the level nor the frequency of exposure. For the pulp and paper industry, we have identified 888 unique exposures(i.e. materials and/or energies) for job titles applicable to this study. It is difficult to process a neural network with such a large number of exposures. Therefore, to make this preliminary study tractable, we have excluded trade name exposures and those materials used infrequently in the industry. Following these exclusions, 243 chemicals remained.

In the PP matrix, a list of chemical exposures and their probable levels in the work environment(i.e. concentration and frequency) have been assigned to each particular job title. However, the additional information relating to concentration and frequency was not used in this study. There are 257 unique exposures in the matrix initially. After repeating the exclusion process, 151 chemicals remained. To illustrate, Figure 1 contains a list of some chemical exposures for two different occupations from the PP matrix.

Of the many cancer sites, we are interested in cancers which have a possible correlation with occupational exposures. Based on the work report of the Action Plan on Health and the Environment [12], we divided cancer sites into two main types: *environmentally related* and *non-environmentally related*. In Figure 2, we have listed some of the cancer sites in each type.

The NIOSH and PP matrices were merged separately with the occupational database. For each merge, we randomly selected 150 subjects. For each subject, we have obtained the cancer site, age, smoking history, work duration and ethnic information, as well as the exposures related to the subject's usual occupation. The input vector to the neural networks contains all the information except the cancer site whereas the output vector contains only the cancer site. To further simplify the input data, all information has been transformed into binary values. If a subject is exposed to a chemical, it will have the value 1 in the specific entry for that chemical in the input vector; otherwise the value is 0. The cancer type has a value of 1 if it is environmentally related; otherwise the value is 0. The subjects are divided into two groups. The first group has 100 subjects and is used to train the network. The second group has 50 subjects and is used to validate the trained networks.

3 Artificial Neural Networks

For this study, we have experimented with two types of networks. The first type of network is the Boltzmann Machine[13] with no hidden layer as shown in Figure 3. The network in this figure contains 3 input nodes and 1 output target. It represents a recurring network in which input vectors are fed to the input nodes and the output of each node is fed back to the nodes. The actual network we used has the same architecture but

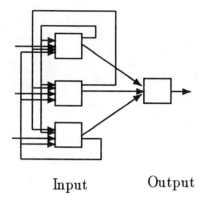

Input   Output

Figure 3: Type I Network with no hidden layer

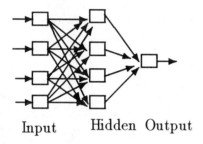

Input   Hidden Output

Figure 4: Type II Network with a hidden layer

	$Data_1$	$Data_2$	$Data_3$	$Data_4$
Type I	A	-	B	-
Type II	C	D	E	F

Figure 5: Different Network/Input Configurations

independent variables in the PP data. As a result, two new data sets were formed by removing those dependent variables in each matrix. Altogether, four data sets of input exposures were investigated:

- $Data_1$:= PP matrix with 155 inputs.

- $Data_2$:= PP matrix with 22 inputs after removal of linear dependencies.

- $Data_3$:= NIOSH matrix with 247 inputs.

- $Data_4$:= NIOSH matrix with 24 inputs after removal of linear dependencies.

With the four data sets, we investigated the 6 combinations of networks and data sets as shown in Figure 5.

We have used Aspirin/Migraines[14] and Xerion[15] to build, to train and to test the neural networks. The Aspirin/Migraines system is developed by the Mitre Corporation to streamline the constructions of different neural network paradigms and to execute large networks efficiently. It has been used to construct all the type II networks in this work. Xerion is a collection of C routines on which different neural network simulators can be built. It is a research development project of the Computer Science Department of the University of Toronto. We have used the Boltzmann machine module to construct the type I networks. The two software packages have been installed in a Sun SparcStation 2 which has 64 Megabytes of RAM.

4 Results

The results presented here have been selected from many training and validation sessions. At the beginning of each training session, the connection weights were randomized. Various training tolerances, learning coefficients, and numbers of hidden nodes were investigated.

The Boltzmann networks took more than 100 CPU hours in the Sun workstation to converge and did not perform as well as the backpropagation networks. We have chosen an error tolerance at 50%(i.e. a patient's cancer is classified as environmentally related if the

many more input nodes.

The second type of network is the commonly used backpropagation network comprising an input layer, a hidden layer and an output layer as shown in Figure 4. Input signals fed to the input layer are modified by weighting factors before being distributed to the nodes in the hidden layer. In the hidden layer the sum of signals to each node are further processed before the hidden layer's outputs are distributed to the output layer. The input and output layers are not connected directly. The network has a full connection topology for which every input node is connected to every hidden node, and every hidden node is connected to every output node. The number of nodes in the hidden layer has to be determined before training. When there are n nodes for the input layer, we have experimented with networks containing a number of hidden nodes ranging from $n + 1$ to $2n + 1$.

For the NIOSH and PP job exposure matrices, we have prepared separate sets of data. In addition, we checked for collinearity (linear relation) in the input vector. In the NIOSH matrix there were only 24 independent inputs; all others could be expressed as a linear combination of those 24 inputs. There were 22

	Type I	Type II
$Data_1$	55% (A)	81% (C)
$Data_2$	-	85% (D)
$Data_3$	52% (B)	73% (E)
$Data_4$	-	77% (F)

Figure 6: Correct Classification of Training Groups

	Type I	Type II
$Data_1$	52% (A)	46% (C)
$Data_2$	-	68% (D)
$Data_3$	72% (B)	48% (E)
$Data_4$	-	88% (F)

Figure 7: Correct Classification of Testing Groups

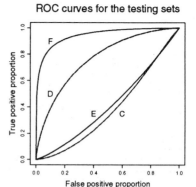

ROC curves for the testing sets

Figure 8: ROC Analysis

output node fired at >0.5). When the type I networks were applied to the training group, they only achieved about 50% accuracy(see Figure 6). The testing group of 50 patients with known cancer types was used to validate the performance of the networks. The correct classifications of the testing groups are shown in Figure 7. Network A is a Boltzmann network using data in $Data_1$. It classified 26 patients in the testing group correctly, whereas network B classified 36 patients in the same group correctly.

For the type II or backpropagation networks, we have experimented with different numbers of hidden nodes. For each data set, we have chosen to present results for the network with the best performance in the testing group. When applied to the training group, the networks had >70% accuracy as shown in Figure 6. For the two networks with data from the PP matrix, network D performed better than network C. Network C had 250 hidden nodes, 155 input nodes and it correctly classified 23 patients in the testing group. Network D had 45 hidden nodes and 22 input nodes, and predicted 34 correct classifications. Network E had 360 hidden nodes and 247 input nodes; it classified 24 patients in the testing group correctly. Network F had the best performance and correctly classified 44 patients; it had 40 hidden nodes and 24 input nodes.

To acquire a better understanding of the power of discrimination of the networks, we used the Relative Operating Characteristic(ROC) analysis [16, 17]. In general, the performance of neural networks is measured by the proportion of accurate classifications, but it relies heavily on the selection of cutoff value of out-

puts. The ROC technique removes the arbitrary nature of cutoff value selection. It has been shown that the area(A_{ROC}) under an ROC curve ($A_{ROC} = 1$ for perfect network performance) equals the probability of separation between two populations [17]. The method had been applied to the outputs of the testing groups. Figure 8 shows the ROC curves for Network C, D, E, and F. It shows that Network F(A_{ROC}=0.9447) has the best classification performance of the four networks. Overall, when collinear inputs were removed from Network C and E, the resulting two networks(D and F), had better performance.

5 Discussion

Because of the complexity and quantity of information concerning chemical exposures in the work place, it is difficult to identify cancer-causing agents in different occupations. This study demonstrates the use of neural networks on pattern recognition of cancer related to occupational exposure. Although the results obtained from the networks are preliminary, they are encouraging.

However, there are some problems identified in the study which demand further work. We have not included the frequencies nor the level of exposures in the inputs to the networks. Furthermore, since the types and levels of exposures may vary over time [18], the networks should be extended to include temporal information.

The second potential problem is related to the restriction of the number of exposures. Only selected exposures have been included as inputs to the networks. Those chemicals excluded from the input vector may have high correlations with cancers.

Despite these problems, the study demonstrates that neural networks can be used to classify cancers based on occupational information which may not be treated easily with traditional multivariate methods. Interestingly, networks D and F performed better than the corresponding networks with full inputs. These backpropagation networks have been simplified by removing collinear inputs, and a significant saving in training time was realized. However, when we wanted to study the networks based on the weights of the inter-nodal connections, they are more difficult to interpret. Further work, such as grouping chemicals into chemical families, should be attempted. It is our intention to continue the investigation of the use of neural networks with occupational databases to provide further insights of the subtle correlation between chemical exposures and cancers. In particular, we intend to obtain more detailed job exposure information, to work with larger data sets and to explore further different network architectures.

References

[1] A.M. Bernard , R.R. Lauwerys. *Relationship Between Cancer and Occupational Exposure to Chemicals: An Overview of the Evidence*, Recent Results in Cancer Research, Vol. 122 (1991), pp. 52-59.

[2] R. Doll, R. Peto. *The Causes of Cancer: Quantitative Estimates of Avoidable Risk of Cancer in the United States today*, JNCI, Vol. 66 (1981), pp. 1191-1308.

[3] K. Bridbord, P. Deciufle, J.F. Fraumeni, D. Hoch, R. Hoover, D. Rall, U. Saffioti, M. Schneiderman, A. Upton. *Estimation of the fraction of cancer in the United States related to occupational factors*, Report by the NCI, NIHHS, NIOSH, Bethesda, 1978.

[4] W.K. Sieber Jr., D.S. Sundin, T.M. Frazier and C.F. Robinson. *Development, Use and Availability of a Job Exposure Matrix Based on National Occupational Hazard Survey Data*, American Journal of Industrial Medicine, Vol. 20 (1991), pp. 163-174.

[5] Internal Report. Division of Epidemiology, Biometry and Occupational Oncology, British Columbia Cancer Agency, 1989.

[6] P.R. Band, J.J. Spinelli, R.P. Gallagher, W.J. Threlfall, V.T.Y. Ng, J. Moody, D. Raynor, L.M. Svirchev, D. Kan, and M. Wong. *Identification of Occupational Cancer Risks Using a Population-Base Cancer Registry*, Recent Results in Cancer Research, Vol. 120 (1990), pp. 181-189.

[7] B.D. Ripley. *Statistical Aspects of Neural Networks*, Invited lectures for SemStat, Sandbjerg, Denmark, April 25-30, 1992.

[8] B.H. Mulsant. *A neural network as an approach to clinical diagnosis*, MD. Computing, Vol. 7 (1990), pp. 25-36.

[9] J.M. Boone, G.W. Gross, V. Greco-Hunt. *Neural networks in radiologic diagnosis. I. Introduction and illustration*, Invest. Radiology, Vol. 25 (1990), pp. 1012-1016.

[10] M.L. Astion and P. Wilding. *Application of Neural Networks to the Interpretation of Laboratory Data in Cancer Diagnosis*, Clinical Chemistry, Vol. 38, No. 1 (1992), pp. 34-38.

[11] R.H. Silverman. *Ultrasonic Pattern Recognition and Classification of Ocular tumors by use of Neural Networks*, Ph.D. Dissertation, Polytechnic University, Dissertation Abstracts International, Vol. 51, No. 5 (Nov. 1990), pp. 2467-B.

[12] Internal Progress Report. Laboratory of Control Disease Center, Ottawa. 1993.

[13] D.H. Ackley, G.E. Hinton and T.J. Sjnowski. *A learning algorithm for Boltzmann machines*, Cognitive Science, Vol. 9, pp. 147-169.

[14] R.R. Leighton. *The Aspirin/MIGRAINES Software Tools: User's Manual*, MP-91W00050, The Mitre Corporation.

[15] D. van Camp. *A Users Guide for the Xerion Neural Network Simulator*, Department of Computer Science, University of Toronto.

[16] J.A. Swets and R.M. Peckett. *Evaluation of Diagnostic Systems: Methods from Signal Detection Theory*, Academic Press, New York, 1982.

[17] R. Fang. *Simultaneous and Sequential ROC Analyses for Diagnostic Tests*, Master Thesis, Department of Statistics, The University of British Columbia, 1991.

[18] G.M. Svanson. *Cancer prevention in the workplace and natural environment. A review of etiology research design and methods of risk reduction*, Cancer, Vol. 62 (1988), pp. 1725-1746.

Classification of Parkinson Rating-Scale-Data Using a Self-Organizing Neural Net

T. Fritsch[1], P.H. Kraus[2], H. Przuntek[2], P. Tran-Gia[1]

[1]Institute of Computer Science, University of Würzburg, Am Hubland, D-8700 Würzburg, F. R. Germany
[2]Department of Neurology, University of Bochum, Gudrunstr. 56, D-4630 Bochum 1, F. R. Germany
[1] Tel.: +49-931-8885513, Fax: +49-931-8884601,
e-mail: [fritsch-trangia]@informatik.uni-wuerzburg.dbp.de
[2] Tel.: +49-234-5093925, Fax: +49-234-5092414

Abstract—The overall score of assessment of clinical stages with rating scales is problematic. The unknown weights of the items and the non-linearity of the interrelation between real expression of the symptoms and rated values cause only weak correlation between sum-scores and an integrative assessment by an expert.

In this paper we present an application of a self-organizing neural net of Kohonen type to the data of 666 de-novo Parkinsonian patients of a multi-center study. The data to be learned are the 10 items of the Webster rating scale and one additional item with 4 stages, following the classification by Hoehn and Yahr. For reasons of comparison multivariate linear statistical methods have been applied to the data, yielding linear models, which are able to derive the Hoehn and Yahr staging from the staging of the Webster rating scale. The methods succeeded with a quote of correct classification of about 50 %. In contrast to these unsatisfying results, a Kohonen net with 40x40 neurons achieved a surprisingly high classification rate of approximately 90 % for the 4 stages of Hoehn and Yahr. The patients, which could not be classified correctly, can be identified as outliers. Further experiments on generalization, variation of net dimensions and single feature representation have been carried out, producing different results. For practical purposes, a similar proceeding with an integrative expert rating as 'predictor' can yield a better alternative to the assessment of sum-scores.

I. INTRODUCTION

In medical diagnosis a number of problems occur concerning the correct assignment of symptoms or combinations of symptoms to a specific form of expression of a disease. It is very difficult to diagnose the specific form, if the mechanisms of the disease are un-known. Furthermore, the expert generally has to validate data, which stem from patient self-observation. It is obvious, that this kind of classification is rather vague or in technical terms, the data are superimposed with "noise". Therefore non-linear classification methods are required, which take into account the uncertainty of this type of data. Up to now only sum-scores of the rating-scale values are used, which do not regard the correlations between the different real expressions of the symptoms and the rated values.

II. PROBLEM STATEMENT

In our study [1], whose medical implications still have been discussed at the annual meeting of the German Society of Neurology, we investigated data of 666 de-novo Parkinsonian patients of a multicenter study at the University of Bochum [3] concerning the question how different scores reflect the same clinical state. The rating scale used was that of Webster [6], consisting of ten items, which are the following ones: bradykinesia, rigidity, posture, swinging arms, walking, tremor, gesture, seborrhea, speech, and independence. Each of these 10 items possesses 4 stages. More integrative is the rating of Hoehn and Yahr [2], which puts main emphasis on different symptoms. Due to the detected weak symptoms of the patients, we found only Hoehn and Yahr stages from 1 to 4 (129 patients stage 1, 265 patients stage 2, 231 patients stage 3 and 41 patients stage 4.) All 10 items of the Webster rating scale and the Hoehn and Yahr rating were analysed with multivariate linear statistical methods like multiple regression and discriminant analysis in an explorative way. It should be estimated, to what degree the results of both scales represent the same information. Both proceedings yielded linear models which are used to "predict" the Hoehn and Yahr stages from the staging of the Webster rating scale items. Multiple regression as well as discriminant analysis yielded a quote of correct classification of about 50 %. Discriminant analysis was superior to multiple regression for extreme ratings (Hoehn and Yahr stage 1 and 4.) For reasons of comparison, it should be noticed that random classification would deliver values of 25 % for the 4 stages of the Hoehn and Yahr scale.

III. Application of a neural net

Since these results are very unsatisfactory, a non-standard kind of non-linear classification is proposed. Generally it is the aim of diagnosis to recognize the expression of a specific type of the Parkinson syndrom in an early state of its evolution. This aim can only be reached, if the vagueness of the input data can be separated from their characteristics. Therefore the idea is, to use an artificial neural net which is capable to extract characteristic features from data though having only human-made observations of the Parkinson syndrom. These observations are blotted out by individual self-assessments which can possibly be wrong and cause uncertainties. They can be interpreted as an abstract kind of noise. The task of classification the Hoehn and Yahr stages from learned input vectors, whose components are equivalent to the items of the Webster rating scale was performed by a neural net of Kohonen type, following the application of H.Ritter and T.Kohonen on semantic relationships between abstract entitities like words or sentences [4]. In this application the semantic relationships in the data are reflected by the relative distances of corresponding neuron clusters in the topologically ordered map, which represent different semantic entities. As the self-organizing feature map algorithm of Kohonen is well-known in the neural net literature we refer for detailed information to [4] or [5]. A brief description of the algorithm is given to outline the process of non-linear classification.

The net consists of 2 layers of neurons, which are fully interconnected. Each neuron of the input layer is connected with each neuron of the mapping array. The number of input neurons is determined by the dimension of the input vectors, 10 components

for the Webster items and 4 for the Hoehn and Yahr stages. The number of neurons in the mapping array has to be chosen suitably. Some experiments will soon show, which problem-dependent number of neurons will suffice, since further increasing of the neuron number would not improve the classification quality.

A. Algorithm

The algorithm can be characterized by the following steps:

1. Presentation of a new input vector $\mathbf{v(t)}$

2. Computation of the distance d_j between all input neurons and all mapping array neurons j according to

$$d_j = \sum_{i=1}^{N} (v_i(t) - w_{i,j}(t))^2$$

   with $v_i(t)$ as the i-th component of the N-dimensional input vector and $w_{i,j}(t)$ as the connection strength between input neuron i and mapping array neuron j at time t corresponding to the Euclidean metric.

3. Choosing the mapping array neuron j^* with minimal distance d_{j^*}

4. Update of all weights, restricted to the actual topological neighbourhood $N_{j^*}(t)$

   $$w_{i,j}(t+1) = w_{i,j}(t) + \eta(t)(v_i(t) - w_{i,j}(t))$$

   for $j \in N_{j^*}(t)$ and $1 \leq i \leq N$. Here $\eta(t)$ represents a monotonically decreasing function of the actual environment of the winner neuron.

5. Iteration of the steps above until a predetermined error criterion is met.

In our application the 14-dimensional input vectors consist of 10 Webster items with values lying in the interval between 1 and 4 and 4 <u>additional</u> components for the stages of Hoehn and Yahr, each having values either 1 or 0. This coding scheme is similar to that one in Ritter [4]. In this application the input vector, say $\mathbf{v}$, is assumed to be the concatenation of two or more fields, one specifying a symbol code, denoted by $\mathbf{v_s}$, and the other one an attribute set, denoted by $\mathbf{v_a}$, respectively. The input vectors used in this paper are constructed in a similar way. The following equation illustrates in a vector notation that the encodings of the Webster items, denoted by $\mathbf{v_W}$, and the Hoehn and Yahr stages, denoted by $\mathbf{v_H}$, form a vector sum of two orthogonal components.

$$\mathbf{v} = \begin{bmatrix} v_W \\ v_H \end{bmatrix} = \begin{bmatrix} v_W \\ 0 \end{bmatrix} + \begin{bmatrix} 0 \\ v_H \end{bmatrix}$$

The main idea of this symbolic mapping is that the two parts are weighted adequately. This must be done such that the weighted Hoehn and Yahr part or the weighted Webster part can predominate each other, depending on which relationship is to be examined. As usual for the class of Kohonen nets, the entire input vector is normalized to an Euclidean length of one and the Gaussian function is used as neighborhood function.

B. Net dimension and weighting of components

The experiments we carried out focus on the following questions:

1. Which net dimension is appropriate?

2. Which weighting of the components is suitable?

3. Is the net capable to generalize the features, i.e. to predict an unknown second data set from the learned data set?

4. Does the net show generalization capability when learning and prediction are restricted to an unique data set?

5. Can outliers be determined?

6. How does the net represent items of the Webster rating-scale, which are weakly correlated?

For reasons of computing time we started with nets of dimension 20x20 neurons with fixed learning rate $\eta = 0.8$ and varied the weighting of the Hoehn and Yahr (HY)- components between 0.001 and 10. Although the recognition rate was low (about 50 %), it turned out that the weighting with 1 led to the best results, but high weighting resulted in a map dominated by the 4 HY-components. The recognition rate was only about 15 % in this case. Weights lower than 1 did not reduce the recognition rate seriously.

Neural net with 30 x 30 neurons			
type	*# patients*	*# recognitions*	*percent*
1	129	98	76.0
2	265	170	64.2
3	231	141	61.0
4	41	35	85.4
total	666	444	66.7

Table 1: Results for neural net with 30 x 30 neurons

Neural net with 40 x 40 neurons			
type	*# patients*	*# recognitions*	*percent*
1	129	104	80.6
2	265	224	84.5
3	231	203	87.9
4	41	40	97.6
total	666	571	85.7

Table 2: Results for neural net with 40 x 40 neurons

The net size was then increased by steps of 10 neurons in each direction starting with 30x30 neurons. The experiments varying the net dimensions between 20x20 and 80x80 neurons by steps of 10x10 have shown that nets both with 40x40 and 60x60 neurons delivered good results. Further increasing of the number of neurons up to 80x80 neurons did not achieve effective improvements. The results are shown accordingly in Tab. 1 and Tab. 2.

C. Generalization

The generalization capability of the net was tested in two cases:

i) The first task was the prediction of an unknown data set, consisting of 520 input vectors obtained by data of the same patients half a year later. The data of those patients, having finished the medical treatment were not included in the data set used. The aim was to find out, whether the net had represented common features of the data sets. The values of the data changed according to the influence of the medication process, so we expected the recognition rate to be reduced. The results of the tests confirmed this assumption, as can be seen in Tab. 3.

ii) As a second experiment another neural net learned the new data separately. It delivered results similar to those above. A further test should show whether a better generalization can be achieved if

Neural net with 40 x 40 neurons			
type	# patients	# recognitions	percent
1	168	66	39.3
2	248	103	41.5
3	89	45	50.6
4	15	7	46.7
total	520	221	42.5

Table 3: Generalization results for neural net with 40 x 40 neurons

Neural net with 60 x 60 neurons			
type	# patients	# recognitions	percent
1	129	106	82.2
2	265	238	89.8
3	231	216	93.5
4	41	40	97.6
total	666	600	90.1

Table 4: Results for neural net with 60 x 60 neurons

the same old data set would randomly be splitted in two or three parts. One of these parts should be learned by the self-organizing feature map and the others should be used as unknown data, serving as test vectors. In this experiments the recognition rate further reduced down to 40 % in the average.

The conclusion we obtain from this case study is that the neural net shows low generalization capability and can be described as a "specialist" for a given distribution of input vectors. Nevertheless the net shows optimal results when it is applied to the set of remaining input vectors. Therefore it can serve as a tool to discover outliers i.e. those patients which cannot definitely be assigned to one of the 4 Hoehn and Yahr stages. In our case only 10 % of outliers are detectable.

D. Representation of single features

Since the items of the Webster rating-scale are highly correlated except two of them, tremor and seborrhea, we put emphasis on the question how the net represented these items, especially tremor. The net we used consisted of 60x60 neurons with a recognition rate according to Tab. 4.

The final mapping of the neural net is shown in Fig. 1, where the bestmatching neurons for the different HY-types are represented by 4 symbols, where

bestmatching means that those neurons are depicted by a special symbol, whose HY-component is 1.

The assignment of the 4 different HY-types to the 10 level gray-scale picture representation of item 6 (tremor) is shown in Figs. 2- 5. The gray scale levels vary between 0 (low) and 9 (high), represented by white and black pixels.

It can be deduced that larger connected areas in the mapping array of neurons in Fig. 1 represent local subgroups, whereas in mixed areas no definite interpretation can be made.

From a clinical point of view it is comprehensible that in Figs. 2- 5 the areas with high responsibility for tremor can be assigned to HY- types 1 and 2, whereas for HY-types 3 and 4 no significant intersection is visible.

IV. Conclusions

Applying a self-organizing neural net to Parkinson data shows significant improvements of the recognition rate, comparing with linear predicting models. The application of the neural net to unknown data is less promising. The neural net appears to be a specialist for the learned data set. Patients which cannot be represented by the neural net can be interpreted as outliers. Regarding the feature "tremor" it is shown, that local subgroups of neurons exist, which are comprehensible from clinical viewpoint. The results justified a combination of an expert assessment with a proper evaluation of rating-scores.

Acknowledgment: The authors would like to thank V. Heuveline and J. Wolf for their emphasized help in the implementation of the simulators.

References

[1] **Kraus P.H., Fritsch T., Tran-Gia P., Przuntek H.,** Classification of rating-scale-data using an artificial neural net, 65. Annual meeting of the German Society of Neurology, Sep. 1992, extended abstract published in Journal of Neurology

[2] **Hoehn, M.M., Yahr M. D.,** Parkinsonism: onset, progression and mortality, Neurology 17, pp 427-442, 1967

[3] **Przuntek H., Welzel D., Schwarzmann D., Letzel H., Kraus P.H.,** Primary combination therapy of early Parkinson's disease, European Neurology 32 (suppl.1), p. 36-45, 1992

[4] **Ritter H, Kohonen, T.,** Self-Organizing Semantic Maps, Biological Cybernetics 61, p. 241-254, 1989

[5] **Ritter H., Martinetz T., Schulten, K.,** AN IN-
TRODUCTION TO THE NEURAL INFORMATION PROCESS OF
SELF-ORGANIZED NETWORKS , Addison-Wesley, 1991

[6] **Webster D. D.,** CLINICAL ANALYSIS OF THE DISABILITY
IN PARKINSON'S DISEASE, Modern treatment, Vol. 5, pp.
257-282, 1968

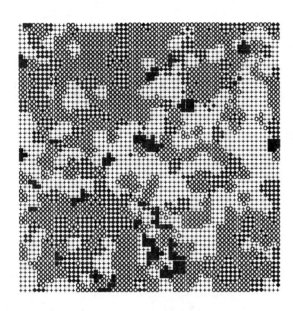

Figure 1: *Final mapping of HY-types in self organi-
sing feature map*

    Type 1: Representation by solid ◇

    Type 2: Representation by ○

    Type 3: Representation by +

    Type 4: Representation by solid □

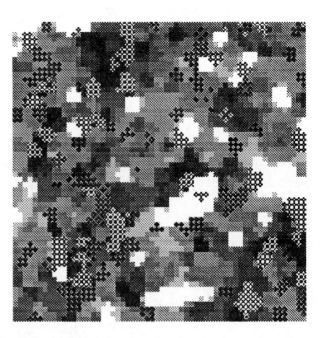

Figure 2: feature 6 map, overlapped with bestmatching neurons for type 1

Figure 3: feature 6 map, overlapped with bestmatching neurons for type 2

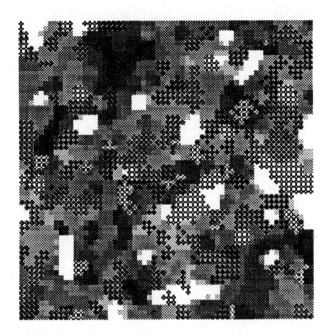

Figure 4: feature 6 map, overlapped with bestmatching neurons for type 3

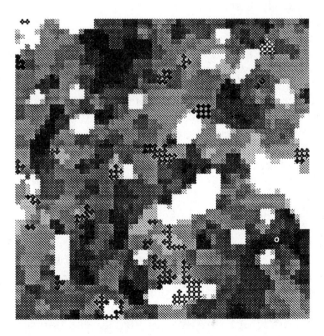

Figure 5: feature 6 map, overlapped with bestmatching neurons for type 4

A NEURAL NETWORK MODEL FOR PREDICTION OF PROGRESSION OF LEFT ANTERIOR DESCENDING CORONARY ARTERY STENOSIS IN HYPERLIPIDEMIC PATIENTS AFTER A FIRST MYOCARDIAL INFARCTION

Gary T. Anderson*, Ju Zheng*, Murray R. Clark*, Richard P. Wyeth†, and the POSCH Group

*Department of Electronics & Instrumentation, University of Arkansas at Little Rock
Little Rock, AR 72204

†Division of Cardiology, University of Arkansas for Medical Sciences

Abstract

A neural network model to predict the progression of stenosis in the left anterior descending coronary artery (LAD) was developed. The model has inputs from 27 physiologic parameters, and can handle missing data on up to 8 of the inputs. The network is 77% successful in predicting progression of coronary artery disease in the LAD with a sensitivity of 82% and a specificity of 73%. KEYWORDS: neural network, coronary artery disease, stenosis, prognosis.

Introduction

Study of factors that predict progression of coronary artery disease have produced contradictory results. Some authors suggest that the degree of stenosis at the time of the initial angiogram is an important factor [1,2], while others indicate that it is not [3]. Part of the problem may be in the selection of patients used for each analysis [2]. Whatever the cause, these contradictory investigations have hampered physicians in their prognosis of and planned management for patients with coronary artery disease, i.e., how aggressively should these patients be treated.

The "Program On the Surgical Control of Hyperlipidemia" (POSCH) was organized to determine if partial ileal bypass surgery could modify lipid risk factors associated with the progression of coronary atherosclerosis in post myocardial infarction (MI) patients with hyperlipidemia [2]. POSCH also found that in the control population (patients not undergoing partial ileal bypass surgery) high percentages of some cholesterol fractions and triglyceride levels upon entry to the study were associated with progression to total occlusion of coronary arteries both by three and five years of follow up.

In addition to identifying serum lipid fractions associated with progression to total occlusion in coronary arteries, it is also desirable to predict which patients will have a subtotal progression of the stenosis in their arteries. This too may add information that assists physicians in deciding how aggressively they need to treat such individuals. The Left Anterior Descending (LAD) coronary artery is sometimes called the "widow maker" because its occlusion frequently results in the death of the patient. In order to assess the likely progression of the degree of blockage or stenosis in the LAD within three years, a back propagation neural network model was developed and trained on data obtained from the POSCH group study. Because of their capability to perform nonlinear mappings, neural network techniques are well suited to make predictions based on exemplars [4, 5].

Neural Network Model

Twenty-seven parameters were selected as potentially important in predicting the progression of stenosis in the LAD. These factors include patient age, weight, sex, smoking history, type of MI, initial percentage stenosis, serum glucose level, triglyceride level, total cholesterol, and cholesterol subfractions. The percent stenosis in the LAD was independently assessed by two readers from coronary angiograms. Data from 397 control patients was obtained for the study. Of these, 246 (62%) patients had a complete set of input parameters, and 151 (38%) had data for at least one of the parameters missing.

Missing data poses two problems. The first difficulty concerns obtaining sufficient data to train the network to make reliable predictions, while the second involves making predictions for patients who do not have the complete medical profile required by the network. In order to address both these difficulties, it was decided to use data sets with missing inputs for both the training and testing of the neural network. Missing data was handled in the following manner [5, 6]: 1) Twenty-seven input nodes were created for the network, one for each input parameter. 2) The number of network inputs was doubled so that each input node was paired with a complimentary node. 3) The input value of the complimentary node was set to the negative of its paired node. 4) All inputs were normalized so that the smallest value over the training or testing set was set to 0, while the most positive value for a given input was set to 1. 5) Input nodes with missing data had both the original input and its compliment set to 0. The above procedure allowed the hidden layer of the network to learn whether data was missing or not. If real data were present, the sum of an input plus its compliment always added up to +1, whereas if the data was missing the sum was always equal to 0.

The network used three layers, with 54 nodes in the input layer and 14 nodes in the hidden layer. The output layer had two nodes, one to represent a positive response and the other to represent a negative response. For each node, an output value of 1 represented a false and a 2 represented a true. The outputs would then "vote" and the node with the greatest value would carry the decision. The network was trained on 100 facts, 50 having a yes decision (i.e., a progression of stenosis) and 50 having a no decision. In order to help the network generalize, a small amplitude random noise signal was added to the network inputs during training. With the small amount of training data available, the network still had a tendency to overtrain, or memorize the training facts. Because of this, the network was periodically tested on 26 facts that were not part of the training set. These 26 facts included 13 that showed progression of disease and 13 that showed no progression. The trained network that tested best on this set of data was selected as the best network.

The network correctly predicted 9 out of 13 cases where coronary disease did progress and correctly predicted 11 out of 13 cases where it did not (sensitivity = 82% and specificity = 73%). Logistic regression was used to construct a mathematical model of the data in [2] and [7]. The logistic model was constructed from patients with complete data sets (that is, no missing data was allowed), and the model was constructed from the same data variables used to construct the neural network. The sensitivity of the logistic model was 60% and specificity was 77%. Although the predictive results of the logistic model could not be directly compared to the network predictions, it did provide a useful benchmark to judge network performance. The logistic model made correct predictions 81% of the time while the neural network was correct 77% of the time.

Conclusions

The neural network model developed has good sensitivity in its predictions of the progression of stenosis, but does less well at predicting which stenoses will not progress. This means that if the model predicts progression for a particular patient, an aggressive intervention strategy such as change of diet and/or drug intervention to reduce triglyceride and serum cholesterol levels may be indicated. However, caution must still be exercised in making predictions for patients that the model predicts will not progress due to the large number of false negative results.

One difficulty in modeling medical pathologies with neural networks is in getting enough training data to allow the network to develop a generalized model of the system. The current model is interesting because it makes predictions in the case of missing input data, thus increasing the set of allowable training data that is available.

References
[1] AVG Bruschke, TS Wijers, K Kolsters and J Landmann, "The Anatomic Evolution of Coronary Artery Disease Demonstrated by Coronary Angiography in 256 Nonoperated Patients. *Circulation.*, vol. 63, pp. 527-536, 1981.
[2] JK Bisset, WL Ngo, RP Wyeth and JP Matts, "Angiographic Progression to Total Coronary Occlusion in Hyperlipidemic Patients After Acute Myocardial Infarction", *Am J Cardiology*, vol. 66, pp. 1293-1297, 1990.
[3] C Shub, *et al.*, "The Unpredictable Progression of Symptomatic Coronary Artery Disease: a Serial Clinical-Angiographic Analysis", *Mayo Clin Proc*, vol. 56, pp. 155-160, 1981.
[4] WG Baxt, "Use of an Artificial Neural Network for the Diagnosis of Myocardial Infarction," *Ann of Int Medi*, vol. 115, number 11, pp. 843, 1991.
[5] JM Collins and MR Clark, "An Application of the Theory of Neural Computation to the Prediction of Workplace Behavior: An Illustration and Assessment of Network Analysis," *Personnel Psychology*, in press.
[6] California Scientific Software, private communication.
[7] JK Bisset, RP Wyeth, JP Matts and JW Johnson, "Plasma Lipid Concentrations and Subsequent Coronary Occlusion After a First Myocardial Infarction," *Am J Med Sci*, vol. 305, pp 139-144, 1993.

Chapter 12
Medical Signal Processing

New medical sensors seem to be produced on a daily basis, and with them comes the need to process and interpret their measurements. In addition, proven sensors have been used for such a long period of time that they can now be reliably moved to automation to reduce human intervention. Finally, medicine is rapidly developing more sophisticated artificial systems that require complex sensing and control. All of these areas are excellent candidates for neural network application. This chapter includes twelve papers that address various aspects of medical signal processing. **Paper 12.1** uses the Learning Vector Quantization (LVQ) neural network to classify blood pressure time series data. The next three papers emphasize different aspects of electrocardiogram (ECG) processing. **Paper 12.2** compares time-delay neural networks and radial basis function (RBF) networks for a series of ECG classification tasks. **Paper 12.3** utilizes the multilayer perceptron (MLP) neural network to classify heart vessel disease using ECG data. The next two papers in this chapter address electroencephalogram (EEG) processing. **Paper 12.4** analyzes the affect of network size on classification performance. In this paper, EEG data is used to determine the depth of anesthesia. **Paper 12.5** describes the use of both the MLP and LVQ to classify the brain maturation in children from EEG data. **Paper 12.6** applies the MLP to electromyographic (EMG) data processing for prosthetic control. **Paper 12.7** presents the results of a fuzzy neural network classifier that is used to predict the presence of metastasis from chromatographic analysis of urine data. **Paper 12.8** describes a noninvasive neural network approach to identifying gastric contractions from surface electrogastrograms (EGG). **Paper 12.9** applies neural networks to total artificial heart modeling in which a MLP neural network simulates the activities of a heart. **Paper 12.10** employs the MLP neural network to detect patient motion artifacts from blood volume changes. **Paper 12.11** describes how a radial basis function (RBF) network is used to classify different models when processing biomagnetic fields.

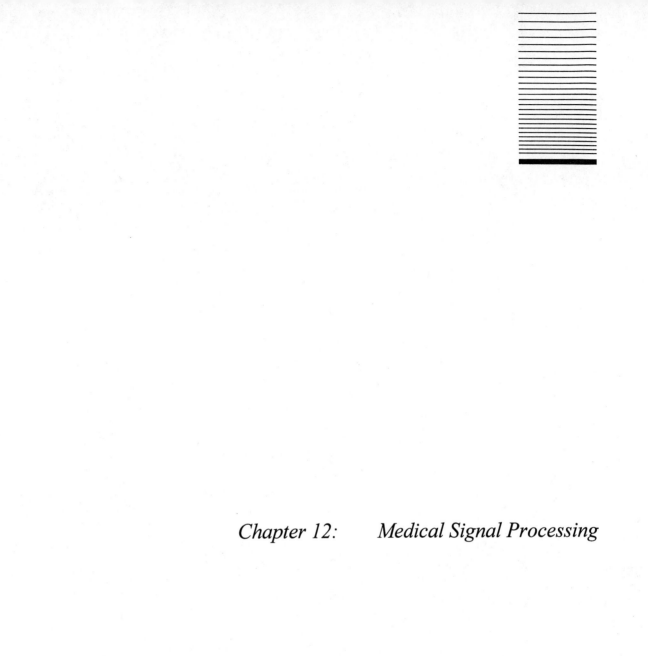

Chapter 12:   Medical Signal Processing

USE OF UNSUPERVISED NEURAL NETWORKS FOR CLASSIFICATION OF BLOOD PRESSURE TIME SERIES

María José Rodríguez, Francisco del Pozo, María Teresa Arredondo and Enrique Gómez
Grupo de Bioingeniería, ETSI Telecomunicación, Univ. Politécnica Madrid, 28040 Madrid, España

Abstract: This paper describes a method to classify blood pressure time profiles using artificial neural networks with unsupervised learning. Kohonen's Topology Preserving Maps were used to identify similar characteristics in 100 profiles from different subjects. Obtained classifier was validated using another group of 142 blood pressure profiles.

INTRODUCTION

The design of methods for automatically classifying subjects using time series of clinical data constitute an important part of medical research. Numerous methods have already been tested and used to classify blood pressure (BP) time series, but they don't offer good results when large amount of classification features have to be used. Artificial neural networks appear to be a useful technique for this purpose.

In this paper, a series of computer simulations of an unsupervised learning neural network is described to classify individuals as a function of their daily blood pressure profile. The Kohonen self-organizing neural network was chosen for this purpose. Our study aims to test its behaviour and usefulness for blood pressure time series classification tasks.

MATERIAL AND METHODS

During 24 hours, a total of 242 subjects measured their systolic (SBP) and diastolic (DBP) blood pressure using portable ambulatory Spacelabs monitors (90202 or 90207 models) which employ the oscillometric method. Blood pressure data were collected at 15-minute interval during the daytime (from 6 am to 12 pm) and at 20-minute interval during the nighttime (from 0 am to 6 am), so, a total of 90 samples were obtained for each subject [1].

BP profiles were divided in two subsets: the learning group (100 subjects) was used to define the network size and structure and to calculate the weights between inputs and outputs; a test group (142 subjects) was used to validate the obtained results.

An open problem nowadays is to classify BP profiles according to their morphology using only the information that we can obtain from the data, without the supervision of blood pressure classification criteria that do not take into account the temporal characteristics of the BP time series. Due to the signal characteristics of this application, we have to use a neural network that allows continued-value inputs.

There are some neural networks that are useful for classification tasks and allow unsupervised learning and analogue inputs: Kohonen's Topology Preserving Maps, Counterpropagation network, Adaptive Resonance Theory 2, etc ([2], [3]). After an extensive study, Kohonen's network was chosen because of the simplicity of its implementation, its capacity to classify similar patterns in clusters and the capacity of the weights to approximate the distribution of the input vectors, that is, the weight values of an output are equal to the mean value of all BP profiles classified in that output.

Kohonen's algorithm is applied to an architecture were there are N continuous-valued inputs (x_i), and M outputs arranged in an array (one- or two- dimensional). The outputs are fully connected to the inputs via the weights (w_{ij}). A competitive learning rule is used, choosing the winner (i^*) as the output unit with a weight vector closest to the current input.

The learning rule need a neighbourhood function that falls with the distance between units i and i^* in the output array, and a gain term that should start with a value close to the unit and decrease monotonically thereafter. The learning phase stops when the gain term is zero.

A software was developed that allows to assess the optimal size and structure (one- or two- dimensional array) of the output array and also the gain, neighbourhood and number of iterations during the learning phase.

Once the optimal conditions were chosen, the test data set was used to validate the results obtained during the learning phase.

RESULTS

As inputs to the neural network we used the time specified SBP and DBP values. To make the neural network learning phase practical is mandatory to reduce the number of inputs. Then, in a previous step, we calculate the average value within each hour interval of the SBP and DBP samples, in this way the input dimension is reduced from 180 to 48 (24 SBP and 24 DBP values). Normalized values (subtracting the individual mean value and dividing by the individual standard deviation) were used. Also, the sex, age and SBP and DBP daily time average for each subject can be used as inputs to the network.

The outputs are limited by practical reasons to a number

smaller than twelve; they can be distributed in a linear or planar array. All of these options were tested to select that one with better classification performance.

After some trials, a Gaussian curve was chosen as the neighbourhood function; this curve has its maximum value in the winner output and decrease as the distance between the winner and the other outputs increases. During the learning phase, the statistical deviation of the curve is decreased, so the number of neurons that change its weight diminish in each iteration. At the end of this phase, only the winner neuron weight should change.

In the learning phase, there are two steps that have a slightly different nature: initial formation of the correct order of the patterns and final convergence of the map into an asymptotic form. These two steps can be distinguished by the gain term used in each one. The time dependence of the gain factor that we have chosen take the form of a-bt. In the ordering phase, it starts with a value near to the unit (0.9) and ends with a value near to 0.01. In the convergence phase, the gain starts with this last value and ends with a value of 0. At that moment, the learning process automatically stops.

Results obtained using different sizes in the output array show that maximum classification power is obtained when using a 1x8 linear array. Figures 1a,b represent the different BP characteristic profiles for each output (each one of them representing a different cluster) when using as inputs the 24 SBP and 24 DBP values for each subject. Figure 1a represents the SBP values of each subject in mmHg in an 24-h interval and figure 1b represents the DBP values in the same interval.

It was realized that profiles with different morphologies belong to different clusters, showing a negligible dependence with SBP and DBP mean values; that is, normotensive and hypertensive people can be classified in the same cluster if they have the same kind of BP profile.

If the SBP and DBP mean values are used as inputs, another different classification is obtained. In this case, BP profiles are classified in different groups, more as a function of their SBP and DBP mean values than by their similar morphologies. In this way, it is possible to distinguish between normotensive and hypertensive people, defined according to the current criteria in use worldwide.

In both cases, results were validated using the test data set.

CONCLUSIONS

The main conclusion is that it is possible to use artificial neural network to classify BP time series without external supervision. Depending on the kind of inputs that are used, a different classification is obtained.

If only the normalized SBP and DBP values are used, Kohonen's Topology Preserving Maps can be used to detect different morphologies in the BP time series. If SBP and DBP mean values are added, the network is able to separate hypertensive and normotensive people in different levels.

REFERENCES

[1]   J.L. Palma: "Control ambulatorio continuo de la presión arterial". In: *Avances en Electrocardiología*. A. Bayés de Luna Ed. Barcelona: Doyma 1981, 177-182.

[2]   T. Kohonen: "The Self-Organizing Map", *Proceedings of the IEEE* 1990; 78: 1464-1480.

[3]   R.P. Lippmann: "An Introduction to Computing with Neural Nets", *IEEE ASSP Magazine*; April 1987: 4-22.

ACKNOWLEDGMENT

This work has been supported by the Spanish CICYT Grant No. TIC-271/92, and also by the European Program AIM: EPIC, project number A.2007 and IREP, project number A.2018.

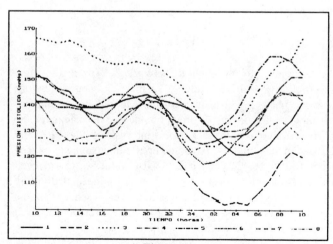

Figure 1a

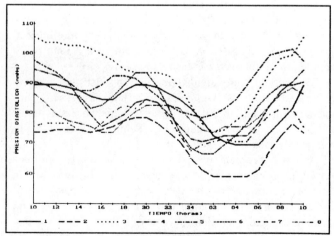

Figure 1b

Prediction-Based Networks with ECG Application*

J.S. Taur and S.Y. Kung
Princeton University

Abstract— A new class of prediction-based independent training (PBIT) networks for temporal patterns classification is proposed. Our approach combines the universal NN approximator and TDNN. The input vectors of PBIT are consecutively created by the time-delayed segment of a pattern. The network is robust since all input segments contribute in equal share to the classification result. To demonstrate the feasibility of PBIT, extensive simulations on ECG classification have been conducted. They have all reported respectable training performance and relatively good generalization accuracy. IIR filters can be adopted as preprocessors to extract information out of the time sequence so that smaller networks will suffice. For a comparative study, we have included another independent training classifier - hidden Markov model(HMM) - for temporal patterns. We have also included in the study some mutually training (MT) models, e.g. the (static) decision-based neural network(DBNN)[4]. Hybrid IT and MT techniques are also proposed to further improve classification accuracy.

I. PREDICTION-BASED INDEPENDENT TRAINING MODEL

The temporal dynamic models must be designed according to the specific application needs. Typical temporal processings, such as differentiation, integration, prediction, smoothing, or harmonic analysis, all require specially tailored model structures. In this paper, we propose a prediction-based neural model, for analysis of transient behaviors, and analyze its performance in the ECG recognition applications.

The prediction-based classifier has the same theoretical basis as the linear predictive classifier(LPC). The limitation of the LPC is that the linear constraint often renders it ineffective to approximate a nonlinear model. Neural networks can be adopted to remedy this problem. Since it is nonlinear, it offers a much more effective means to model nonlinear behaviors. Also it adopts the independent training scheme, i.e. each subnet is trained by positive examples only. So it is named *prediction-based independent training* (PBIT) model. According to the OCON structure, one PBIT net is assigned to each class. Referring to Figure 1, the PBIT model combines a time-delay neural network and a (two-layer) back-propagation model, making it very similar to the NETtalk configuration.

A long sequence x with length $\bar{N}$ is input through a tapped-delay line, cf. Figure 1(a), from which a set of N-dimensional vectors ($N << \bar{N}$) are consecutively extracted:

$$\mathbf{x}_j = [x(j+1)\ldots x(j+N)] \qquad (1)$$

where $x(n)$ denotes the n-th sample value of the signal sequence x. These N-dimensional vectors serve as the inputs to the back-propagation network. Each vector is processed to yield a best prediction for its immediate future sample $x(j+N+1)$. The prediction function is represented by $f_a(\mathbf{x}_j) = f(\mathbf{x}_j, \mathbf{w})$ — a function of the current input vector $\mathbf{x}_j$ and the weight vector w. The function is usually either sigmoid LBF or Gaussian RBF.

Cybenko[1] and Funahashi[2] have provided a useful approximation theorem showing that any input-output mapping can be approximately realized by a two-layer network with linear basis function. An RBF approximation theorem can be easily obtained from the classic Stone-Weierstrass theorem[5].

For each training pattern, the discriminant function ϕ is defined as the (negative) squared prediction error,

$$\phi = -\sum_{j=0}^{\bar{N}-N-1} (f_a(\mathbf{x}_j) - x(j+N+1))^2 \qquad (2)$$

In the **retrieving phase** a pattern is input to *all* the PBIT subnets and is classified into the subnet which yields the largest discriminant function, (i.e., the smallest prediction error). In the **training phase**, the objective is to minimize the sum of the squared prediction errors of all the M training patterns in the same class,

*This research was supported in part by Air Force Office of Scientific Research under Grant AFOSR-89-0501A.

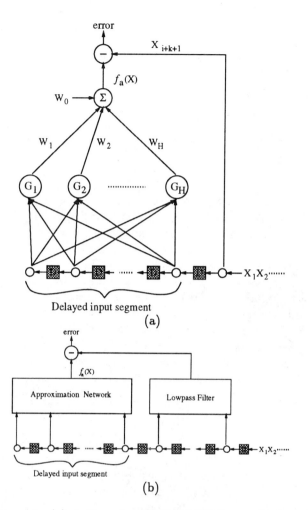

Figure 1: (a) A Gaussian RBF TDNN for prediction of a future sample. (b) Using output of a low-pass filter to replace the sample to be predicted.

$$E = \sum_{m=1}^{M} \sum_{j=1}^{\bar{N}-N} \left(f_a(x_j) - x(j+N+1) \right)^2 \qquad (3)$$

(This complies with the independent training principle.)In this formulation, the classifier is tolerant not only to shift but also to the length of the signal. The gradient-type updating rule can be adopted:

$$\triangle \mathbf{w} = -\eta \frac{\partial E}{\partial \mathbf{w}}$$

As shown in Figure 1(a), the tapped-delay line is followed by a multi-layer network. For the latter net, a Gaussian RBF classifier is favored. It offers a natural clustering capability, which is good for approximation/generalization in many applications. (The initial centroids of the hidden nodes can be estimated by the K-mean or VQ clustering algorithm, which usually yields a fast convergence

in the subsequent BP learning.) More importantly, the centroids of the Gaussian function can be trained to reflect the salient features in the signal. For example, some sample ECG waveforms are shown in Figure 2. It can be demonstrated that (cf. Figure 3) the centroids of the hidden nodes in the RBF networks actually capture the key segments in the original waveform. All but 2 of the 15 centroids represent the meaningful curves inherently embedded in the training ECG waveforms. When a test signal from the same class is presented, the trained centroids would be able to produce a close match and, therefore, a minimum prediction error.

We note that the window size for the PBIT model should be properly chosen so that it is robust with respect to time misalignments and uncertainty of the waveform length. Obviously, the window size must be adequate so that the information in each segment is sufficient to facilitate prediction. If the size is too large, it might hamper the network's ability to cope with temporal variations.

II. COMPARE STATIC AND TEMPORAL MODELS FOR ECG ANALYSIS

In this ECG classification experiment, there are 10 different classes. Each class has 10 sample waveforms, 5 used for training and the remaining, for testing. Some samples of the ECG pulses are shown in Figures 2(a) and (b). Both static and temporal networks are evaluated. Their generalization performance and tolerance to time misalignments are studied.

A. Static Models for ECG Analysis

In static models, the entire input waveform is treated as a long static input vector. For comparison, both decision and approximation based models are tried.

1. For the *approximation-based networks*, the teacher value is set to be 1 when the input sequence is in the class represented by the network; otherwise it is 0. Both the ACON (All-Class-in-One-Net) and OCON (One-Class-in-One-Net) models, with the conjugate-gradient algorithm, are adopted. The ACON model, using LBF, has 60 input neurons, 20 hidden neurons, and 10 output neurons. The OCON model has 10 subnets each using 4 (RBF) hidden neurons. Under the approximation-based formulation, the OCON and ACON models have very compatible performance, cf. Table 1.

2. For the *decision-based networks*[4], we adopt subcluster DBNNs with 10 subnets. Similar performances are reported for the DBNN(EBF), with 2 subclusters per subnet; and for the DBNN(RBF), with 4 subclusters per subnet. According to

	Model	Performance
Approximation-Based	LBF-ACON(20)	78%
Static Models	RBF-OCON(4)	80%
Decision-Based	DBNN(E_s)(2)	90%
Static Models	DBNN(R_s)(4)	90%

Table 1: Comparison of ECG classification by various static models. *All models reach 100% training accuracies.* For the DBNN(E_s)(2), a noise tolerance of 0.5 is adopted.

Algorithm	Noise Tolerance	Original	Shifted
DBNN(E_s)	0 (5 sweeps)	96%	93.6%
DBNN(E_s)	2.25	96%	96.8%
DBNN(R_h)	1.76	96%	97.2%
RBF-OCON	NA	96%	94%

Table 2: Networks are trained with right/left-shifted ECG data. In this simulation, the original set (50 patterns) and shifted data(250 patterns), respectively, are used to test the generalization capability of the network. The classification rates of the training set are 100% for all models. The number of subnodes is 4 for each subnet.

the ECG classification experiments summarized in Table 1, decision-based models outperform approximation-based models in convergence speed and training/generalization accuracy.

Tolerance to Temporal Misalignment Since the ECG segments are extracted from an original long waveform, it is likely that signal segments may be misaligned by an unknown time interval. It is critical that the neural model be made somewhat shift-tolerant. The static models are, unfortunately, not very tolerant. To enhance this, a special training procedure is adopted. All the (100) ECG waveforms are shifted forward or backward by one or two time steps. Samples of the shifted ECG waveforms are shown in Figure 2(c). Thus, the original data set is expanded by 5 fold. Half of the expanded set is randomly chosen as the training set. In the generalization experiments, both the original and shifted signals are used as test sets. The radial basis model DBNN(R_s) and the elliptic basis model DBNN(E_s) have very close generalization accuracies. For comparison, hidden-node DBNN(R_h) models are also experimented with. The results in Table 2 show that generalization performance is indeed improved by using shifted training data.

B. Temporal Models for ECG Analysis

In both training and retrieving phases, in order to smooth the noise in the signal, a small segment of signal is passed through a fixed-weight lowpass filter, and the output of the filter is used as teacher for the prediction network. The modified configuration is shown in Figure 1(b). In the ECG analysis, a 4-th order moving average low-pass filter appears to be adequate. To make the classifier tolerant to the DC level of the ECG segment, the values of the input segment and the output of the lowpass filter are both readjusted to have 0 DC-level. For both PBIT(LBF) and PBIT(RBF) networks, a window size of around 20 is found to be adequate. (In fact, the two networks have very similar accuracies.) All input segments contribute in equal share to the cost-criterion in Eq. 3, so the models are fairly robust. As expected, temporal models consistently outperform static models, cf. Table 3. In comparison with the HMM, the PBIT nets have either comparable or slightly better performance. However, more exhaustive experiments are needed before a more definitive conclusion can be reached. In a separate experiment, temporal models (based on sigmoid LBF net with a short window) were successfully applied to model nonlinear time-varying background noise in a ECG QRS detection application [3].

Tolerance to Temporal Misalignment It can be demonstrated by experiments, that the PBIT nets were inherently tolerant of temporal misalignment of waveforms. They were trained by the original unshifted patterns, and there is no need to use time-shifted patterns in the training set. (This is in contrast to the approach previously adopted for the static models.) Only the 50 original waveforms are used as the training set. By waveform time-shift, the original data set is expanded to a total of 500 patterns. Among them, 450 patterns were used as the test patterns. (Those used in the training set are excluded from the testing set.) The results of the experiment are summarized in Table 4. It appears that the PBIT nets have high generalization accuracy and were very shift-tolerant. Note that the linear predictive classifier (LPC) is somewhat intolerant to time-shift, although it has a very respectable generalization accuracy without time-shift. In comparison, PBIT(LBF) and PBIT(RBF) were more tolerant to shift. As predicted, the static DBNN(E_s) shows the least tolerance.

Hierarchical Training Strategy The design hierarchy is purposely divided into two stages. In the independent training rule, each model is trained by patterns from its own category. This is very appealing to temporal pattern recognition and offers cost-effective learning in the initial phase. If further training is needed, the mutual training

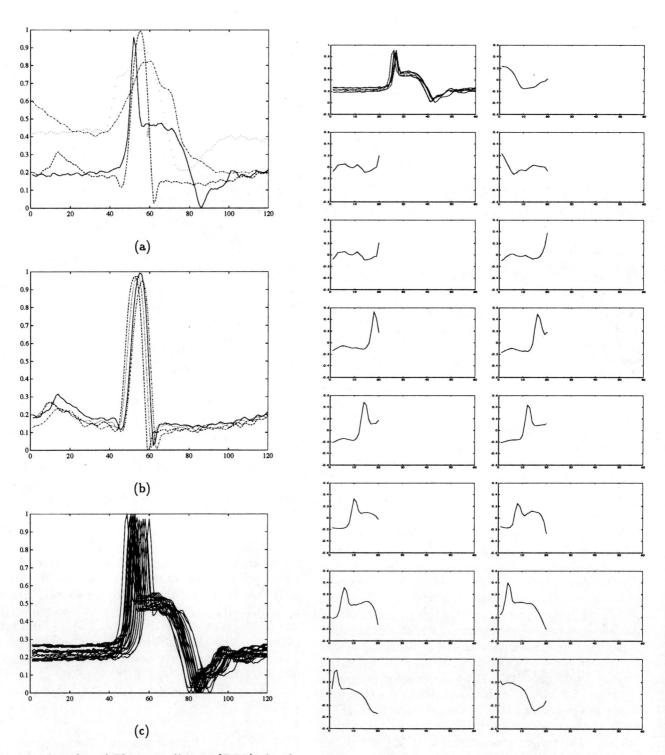

Figure 2: Samples of Electrocardiogram(ECG) signals: (a) original ECG waveforms from 4 different classes; (b) four ECG waveforms from the same class; and (c) time-shifted waveforms for the same class.

Figure 3: The centroids obtained for ECG Class No. 1. The training sequences are shown in the upper-left figure.

	Window Size	Hidden Units	Training	Test
(1)	30	NA	94%	94%
	40	NA	100%	94%
	45	NA	100%	76%
(2)	20	10	100%	98%
	20	15	98%	98%
	20	20	100%	94%
(3)	20	10	100%	94%
	20	15	100%	98%
	20	20	100%	96%
(4)	NA	30 states	0%	8%

Table 3: Training/generalization accuracies of several temporal models, including (1)LPC, (2)PBIT(LBF), (3)PBIT(RBF), and (4)HMM.

Classifier	Original Test Set	Shifted Test Set
DBNN(E_s)	90%	85.2%
LPC	94%	90%
PBIT(LBF)	98%	98%
PBIT(RBF)	98%	98.45%

Table 4: Comparison of the shift-tolerance of different static and temporal models. The models were trained by the original data but tested (mostly) by the shifted data.

scheme can always follow. Either DBNN or FDNN [4, 6] may be adopted to fine-tune the classifier. In this case, the prediction error becomes a discriminant function in those models.

III. ON-GOING WORK: IIR FILTER AS PREPROCESSOR

In general, it is not obvious how to select a proper window size. It is useful to design a model which is less sensitive to the window size. In a general configuration shown in Figure 4, the first part involves a linear or a nonlinear adaptive filter and the second part can be a feedforward (LBF or RBF) two-layer net. The weights in the feedforward network can be trained by the back-propagation algorithm. The back-propagation error signal for the interface neuron values (between the two parts) can be used for the training of the adaptive filter.

There are many ways to implement the adaptive filters. One example of the adaptive filter is the cascaded first-order IIR filter [7] in Figure 5. The parameter μ controls the memory depth of filter. The effective window size of the filter is N/μ, where N is the number of stages in

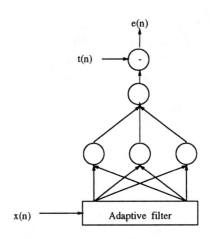

Figure 4: An overall system includes a multi-layer non-linear approximation net and an adaptive preprocessing filter.

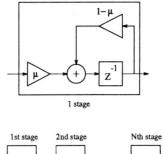

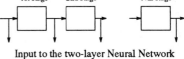

Figure 5: Cascaded First-Order IIR Filter.

	Window Size	No. of Weights	Training	Test
(1)	20	221	100%	98%
(2)	10	121	100%	96%
(3)	5	71	96%	98%

Table 5: Training/generalization accuracies of several temporal models, including (1)best PBIT(LBF), (2) PBIT(LBF) with a 10-stage filter and (3) PBIT(LBF) with a 5-stage filter.

the filter. The stability of the network requires only that $0 < \mu < 2$.

The simplest structure of the filter is the tapped delay line when $\mu = 1$. There are some disadvantages of it, for example, the performance might be sensitive to the window size of the tapped delay line. This is a genetic problem for every TDNN with a fixed window size.

By changing the value μ in the structure, we can adjust the window size to include enough information easily. For a smaller μ, the effective window size is larger but the resolution is coarser. The value μ can be trained by applying gradient-descent algorithm to the prediction error. Usually IIR filters can achieve the same performance with less parameters because of the redundant information in the time sequence. When the redundancy is high, a small number of stages and a small μ can be adopted. In this way, the training time and the number of parameters in the network can be greatly reduced.

From the previous experiments, we know that the best window size for the ECG classification application is around 20. We tried two different PBIT(LBF) configurations: a 10-stage filter with $\mu = 0.5$ and a 5-stage filter with $\mu = 0.25$. The results are listed in Table 5. The number of parameters in the network can be reduced from 221 to 71 while the performance remains about the same. Some other filter structures, e.g. lattice filter, are under investigation.

REFERENCES

[1] G. Cybenko. Approximation by superpositions of a sigmoidal function. *Mathematics of Control, Signals and Systems*, 2:303–314, 1989.

[2] K. Funahashi. On the approximate realization of continuous mappings by neural networks. *Neural Networks*, pages 183–192, 1989.

[3] Y. H. Hu, W. J. Tompkins, and Q. Xue. Artificial neural networks for ECG arryhthmia monitoring. In S. Y. Kung, F. Fallside, J. A. Sorensen, and C. A. Kamm, editors, *Neural Networks for Signal Processing, II*, pages 350–359. Proceedings of the 1992 IEEE Workshop, Helsingoer, Denmark, 1992.

[4] S. Y. Kung and J. S. Taur. Hierarchical Perceptron (hiper) networks for classifications. In S. Y. Kung, F. Fallside, J. A. Sorensen, and C. A. Kamm, editors, *Neural Networks for Signal Processing, II*. Proceedings of the 1992 IEEE Workshop, Helsingoer, Denmark, 1992.

[5] H. L. Royden. *Real Analysis*. Macmillan, New York, second edition, 1968.

[6] J. S. Taur and S. Y. Kung. Fuzzy-decision neural networks. Proceedings, IEEE International Conference on Acoustics, Speech, and Signal Processing, April 1993.

[7] B.D. Vries, J.C. Principe, and P.G.D. Oliveira. Adaline with adaptive recursive memory. In B. H. Juang, S. Y. Kung, and C. A. Kamm, editors, *Neural Networks for Signal Processing*, pages 101–110. Proceedings of the 1991 IEEE Workshop, Princeton, NJ, 1991.

Neural Net Analysis of Exercise ECG Waveforms

Tom Brotherton and Tom Pollard
The ORINCON Corp.
9363 Towne Centre Dr.
San Diego, CA 92121

Jeff Froning
Sunnyside Biomedical
2911 State St., Suite 'N'
Carlsbad, CA 92008

Victor Froelicher
Palo Alto VA Hospital
3801 Miranda Ave.
Palo Alto, CA 94305

A problem of current interst is the automated diagnosis of Exercise ECG waveforms. Traditional techniques parse the waveform to extract parameters which are then used by a rule based classifier to make a diagnosis. This method is prone to errors due to incorrect assumptions in the modeling and the loss of potentially important information in the ECG waveform.

Described here is a neural-network solution to this problem. The processing assumes no underlying model for the events of interest in the ECG data. Rather, the system "learns" to detect and diagnose significant events by examination of raw ECG waveform training data which have known cardiac conditions. The system functions more closely to how a trained human would interpret the raw waveforms than prior computer approaches.

1. INTRODUCTION

Current systems which perform automated diagnosis of Exercise ECG waveforms first parse the waveform into significant events. Parameters describing the duration, time intervals, and shapes of these events are then estimated from the parsed waveforms. Classification is performed using a rule base. The method is prone to errors due to incorrect assumptions in the models used to parse the waveform and the loss of potentially important information in the ECG waveform.

We introduce here a neural network solution to the problem. The system examines the raw Exercise ECG waveforms to make a diagnosis. The system functions more closely to how a human would interpret the Exercise ECG waveforms. The technique is being developed to include additional data representations - multiple neural network fusion solution to the problem. That approach has been used successfully to solve detection and classification problems in other medical applications, underwater acoustics, and mechanical system fault diagnosis[1],[2][3]. Here we concentrate on a single representation.

2. METHOD

Figure 1 shows a high level processing flow diagram used for the analysis of Exercise ECG waveforms. Initial processing determines where beats occur in the waveforms. Several waveforms are then time aligned and averaged so as to reduce noise and enhance cardiac events. The raw data and multiple representations are then entered into a hierarchy of neural nets to perform the detection and classification of cardiac events. Here we concentrate on the processing of the raw ECG waveforms (solid line boxes in figure 1). The alternative representation fusion (dotted line boxes) are

currently under investigation. All of the neural nets used are three layer perceptrons. For the example presented here, there are only two outputs. They are 'normal' heart beat and 'Depressed ST Segment' with in the heartbeat. The approach is general and a variety of other events / cardiac conditions can be included in the output set of classes.

Figure 2 shows an example of an averaged set of waveforms found over a 30 minute Exercise test. Each scan in the data contains 250 points. There are a total of 40 scans in figure. The start of the test is at the top of the figure. The peak in the Exercise test occurs about a third of the way into the data set. The second half of the data corresponds to recovery. Figure 3 shows the results of processing the raw Exercise ECG waveform with the system. The input is the averaged Exercise ECG waveform. The set of 40 scans is repeated several times in the figure. The inputs are shown on the left half of the figure. The actual display images are in color and show more detail. However in figure 3 the peaks of the QRS and T complexes are clearly visible. The input to the neural net is a two dimensional set of 1320 pixels which include 12 time scans and 110 points per scan. The retina is roughly centered around the ST segment in the data.

The right side of the figure shows the output from the neural net. There are two columns present. The output from the network is encoded by intensity. A 'white' column corresponds to high activation while a 'black' column corresponds to low activation. The two columns correspond to the two classes indicated. The column which has the brightest intensity is the output class from the system. Training is perfromed by presenting examples of data both with and without depressed ST segments. There is never any explicit measurement of the depression. In figure 3, the depressed ST segment when it appears is correctly identified. The system was tested with 4 patients all with depressed ST segments. The system worked equally well on all those patients.

4. CONCLUSIONS

We have presented preliminary results for a system designed to perform the diagnosis of Exercise ECG waveforms. The approach can be applied to a wide variety of medical processing problems. For the data sets processed to date, which contain depressed ST segments, the system appears to works well. Future development will fuse alternative representations of the data with the raw waveforms. The multiple representations of the waveforms are being developed to visually highlight salient features in the data. The fusion of multiple representations should lead

0-7803-2566-4/96 $5.00 © 1996 IEEE

377

to a gain in both the detection and classification performance while at the same time reducing the false alarm rate [1].

5. REFERENCES

[1] T. Brotherton and E. Mears, "Application of Neural Nets to Feature Fusion," Proc. of the 26th Asilomar Conf. on Signals, Systems, & Computers, Oct. 1992, Pacific Grove, CA.

[2] T. Brotherton, T. Pollard, and D. Jones, "Application of Time-Frequency and Time-Scale Representations to Fault Detection and Classification," Proc. of the IEEE-SP Int'l. Symposium on Time-Frequency and Time-Scale Analysis, Oct. 1992, Victoria, B.C.

[3] M.Wiederhold, T.Brotherton, T.Pollard, and R.Rickard, Artificial Neural Network Evaluation of Acoustic Doppler ULtrsound, The 37th Annual Conv. of the American Inst. of Ultrasound in Medicine, March 1993, Honolulu, HI .

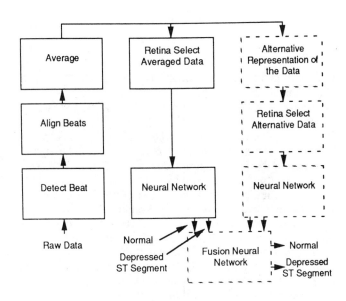

Figure 1 - Processing Flow Diagram

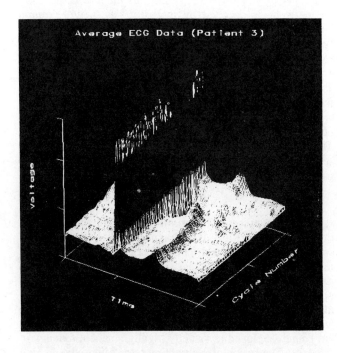

Figure 2 - 3D Exercise ECG Waveform

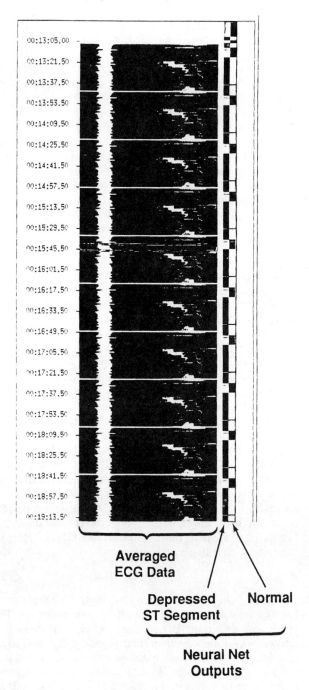

Figure 3 - Neural Net Processing Example

ANALYSIS OF HIDDEN NODES IN A NEURAL NETWORK TRAINED FOR PATTERN CLASSIFICATION OF EEG DATA

Ashutosh Sharma, M.S., and Rob J. Roy, M.D., D.Eng. Sc.
Department of Biomedical Engineering
Rensselaer Polytechnic Institute, Troy, NY 12180

Abstract – This paper discusses the effect of network size on the performance of a neural network design. The neural network discussed is part of computer-based EEG recognition system to measure the anesthetic depth. A four layer perceptron feedforward type of network was used in designing the recognition system. Clustering analysis was performed to determine the number of neurons in the second hidden layer. The number of neurons in the first hidden layer was dependent on the input space dimension. Addition of noise to the input neurons during training made the network more robust to external disturbances and improved the performance of the network significantly. An upper bound on the number of boundary samples needed for generalization of the network performance is also presented. The optimum network size for the depth of anesthesia recognition system was found to be 43-43-6-1.

INTRODUCTION

Artificial Neural Networks (ANN) have been used successfully in a wide range of applications in the field of pattern recognition. In recent years the ANN's have been used to predict the depth of anesthesia through the analysis of the electroencephalograms (EEG) [1]. The recognition system for estimating the depth of anesthesia has been developed at Rensselaer Polytechnic Institute. It uses the autoregressive (AR) parameters of the EEG along with the hemodynamic parameters blood pressure (BP) and heart rate (HR), as input to the ANN. The output of the neural network is the depth of anesthesia. The neural network is trained on the training data set and then tested on the testing data set. One of the important steps in neural network training is the selection of the network size and the number of input samples required for the network to be able to perform correctly with new sets of data. The requirement for successful training is that the network be supplied with adequate number of examples in the training set and that there be enough hidden neurons. Too small a number of hidden neurons may not allow the network to train at all, conversely too many hidden neurons could require excessive computer time and prevent the network from generalizing. In practice, the size of the neural network and the number of training samples required is solved through trial and error.

In recent years significant research has been done in this field to find the bounds on the number of samples needed for neural learning and also the optimum number of hidden neurons required [2-3]. The maximum number of separable regions (R) in the input space is a function of the number of hidden neurons (L), and the input space dimension (d). It has been shown by Mehrotra et al [2], that the number of samples needed for effective learning is related to the number of hidden layer nodes (L) and the complexity of a multiclass discrimination problem (the input dimension d). The number of boundary samples required for successful classification of C clusters of samples using a two hidden layer network, with d dimensional inputs and L nodes in the first hidden layer is given by $O(min(d,L).C)$. This was used to compute the bounds on the number of samples required for training the network, in predicting the depth of anesthesia from the electroencephalographic data.

METHODS

Anesthesia was induced in thirteen dogs with Methohexital sodium (16.5 mg/Kg) at the start of the experiment. The animals were placed on a closed circuit anesthesia system [4] at an anesthetic level high enough for the placement of monitors without animal movement. Arterial pressure, ECG and end-tidal CO_2 were monitored during the entire period of the experiment. The anesthesia was varied between 0.2% and 1.4% in increments of 0.2 at 20 minute intervals. Four channels of EEG data was recorded from L_f-L_o , R_f-R_o , F_z - O_z , and V - R_T , using subdermal needle electrodes. Tail clamping was used as the stimulus to elicit a positive response, in order to test the depth of anesthesia. A positive response was considered to be a gross purposeful movement of the head or extremities. The EEG data was prefiltered using a 20Hz second order Butterworth filter to avoid aliasing, and sampled at 150 Hz. A tenth order AR model was used to extract AR parameters from 2 sec. EEG segments. The AR parameters obtained before the tail clamp and the hemodynamic parameters recorded at that time instance were used as input to the neural network. The response obtained during the tail clamp was used as the output pattern of the network. The depth was graded from zero to one in increments of 0.5. A total of 129 input-output pairs were obtained, out of which 97 (75%) were used for training the network and 32 (25%) for testing.

RESULTS

A four layer perceptron feedforward type of network was used to design the recognition system. The number of hidden nodes in the first layer were varied over a range from 30 to 55 in case of complete data set (AR parameters + hemodynamic data) to test the performance of the network corresponding to different network sizes. The number of hidden nodes in the second layer was set equal to the number of clusters in the input space, which was determined using the PFS clustering method [5]. The number of clusters C was found to be 5, 6 or 7 depending on whether the input space comprised of hemodynamic data, complete data set, or AR parameters respectively. The training tolerance was set equal to 0.1 and the testing tolerance was set equal to 0.2, where the tolerance is defined as the percentage error between the desired output and actual output of the network. The results of the network performance for different network sizes are shown in Table I. For each case the network was trained with and without addition of the input noise. The number of cycles required for training for different network sizes are shown in Fig. 1. The % correct classification obtained when the input space was comprised of AR parameters only was 86% (network size 40-40-7-1) and in case of hemodynamic data only was 64% (network size 3-10-5-1).

DISCUSSION

The performance of the network is significantly improved in all the cases when the noise was added to the inputs during training. This improvement is achieved at the cost of longer time required for training, as shown in Fig. 1. The addition of the noise to the input neurons during the training phase makes the network robust. The problems due to sensor noise and external disturbances which can affect the input to the network can be overcome using this approach. From Table I, the optimum size of the network to be used in designing the recognition system is 43-43-6-1, which gives a classification rate of 94%. The number of boundary samples required corresponding to this size will be $O(\sim 250)$, in order for the network to generalize. The number of boundary samples actually obtained out of the 97 samples used for training was 80. Time required for training was also lowest for the network with the best performance, when noise was added to the inputs.

REFERENCES

[1] R. Watt, E. Maslana, and M. Navabi, " EEG spectral features provide basis for artificial neural network comparison of anesthetics," *Proc 14th Ann Int Conf IEEE Eng in Med and Bio Soc*, Paris, pp. 2407-2408, 1992.

[2] K. G. Mehrotra, C. K. Mohan, and S. Ranka, " Bounds on the number of samples needed for neural learning," *IEEE Trans. Neural Networks*, vol. 2, pp. 548-558, 1991.

[3] E. B. Baum and D. Haussler, " What size net gives valid generalization ?," *Neural Computation*, vol. 1, pp. 151-160, 1989.

[4] R. Vishnoi and R. J. Roy, " Adaptive control of closed circuit anesthesia," *IEEE Trans. Biomed. Eng.*, vol. 38, pp. 39-47, 1991.

[5] M. A. Vogel and A. K. C. Wong, " PFS clustering method," *IEEE Trans. Pattern Analysis and Machine Intelligence*, vol. PAMI-1, pp. 237-245, 1979.

TABLE I - CLASSIFICATION RESULTS

Network Size	% Correctly Classified (No noise added)	% Correctly Classified (Noise added)
43-30-6-1	66%	75%
43-35-6-1	75%	84%
43-40-6-1	75%	87%
43-43-6-1	84%	94%
43-46-6-1	78%	90%
43-50-6-1	66%	87%
43-55-6-1	81%	87%

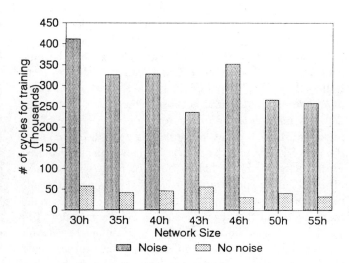

Fig 1. Training cycles used for different network sizes. (Noise⇒ noise was added to the inputs during training)

A SYSTEM FOR AUTOMATED BRAIN SIGNAL ANALYSIS: APPLICATION TO BRAIN MATURATION STUDY

L. Moreno, J. D. Piñeiro, J. L. Sánchez, *S. Mañas, J. Merino, L. Acosta, A. Hamilton.
Dept. of Applied Physics. University of La Laguna. Tenerife. Canary Islands. Spain.
*"Nuestra Señora de la Candelaria" Hospital, Dept. of Neurophysiology.
La Laguna. Tenerife. Spain

Abstract- **A system for computer-aided brain signal diagnosis (Quantitative EEG) and its application to the study of brain maturation in a sample of children are presented.**

The system is conceived as an intelligent assistant, organized in three layers of abstraction. This system provides a set of tools such as data acquisition (EEG and Evoked Potentials) with on-line computation and display of topographic maps, generic signal processing, artificial neural networks and statistical classifiers. Real-time capabilities are obtained exploiting the parallelism of Digital Signal Processing (DSP) and Transputer boards in a 486 PC microcomputer.

I. INTRODUCTION

Quantitative electroencephalographic (EEG) signal analysis has revealed as an important diagnostic tool in the last few years [1]. It allows rigorous assessments of patient data by means of powerful methods of displaying EEG-related information and makes easy the automated comparison of this data with normative databases. Our aim in this paper is to present an integrated system for computer-aided diagnosis of EEG signals that exploits this techniques. This system consists of a great variety of tools, that include acquisition and on-line display, graphic visualization, signal processing, and temporal waveform editing [2], [3]. The objective is that this system be used in automating the traditional way of brain diagnosis and that also serve as a research environment. A necessary requirement of such a complex system is that it be easy to use. For this purpose, it is necessary to apply Artificial Intelligence methods that isolate the user from the detailed technical knowledge of multidisciplinary nature built into the system. This way the user is free to express himself in his own field of expertise and does not become forced to be acquainted with, for example, signal processing techniques.

The brain maturation prediction in a group of children has been the first problem we have tackled with this system. This problem consists in reproducing the classification (maturation levels) carried out by an expert. The expert knowledge about maturation, acquired mainly with experience and not easily represented in explicit rules, is based on multiple criteria obtained from the EEG record.

We have chosen for the implementation of this system a low-cost and widely available platform, a 486DX PC with ISA bus. If we want to include in this system real-time monitorization tasks, then we must add some kind of parallelism to the machine chosen.

II. SYSTEM STRUCTURE

A. Organization

The system is organized in three layers as depicted in Fig.1. The lower layer (Level I) is formed by all the Signal Processing and Pattern Recognition knowledge both in terms of algorithms and embodied in Artificial Neural Networks (ANN). The middle layer (Level II) consists in abstract pattern descriptions (events) that serves as an interface between the lower and upper layers. The last layer (Level III) contains the pathology specifications defined in terms of the events of the middle layer. This structure preserves the independence between the Signal Processing and the interpretation (diagnosis) knowledge bases. The aim of this modular organization is that the system be modifiable by the proper specialist in each layer and also to provide easy extension.

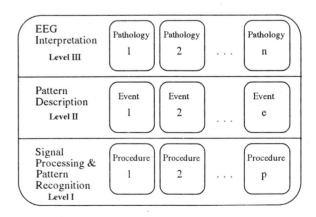

Fig. 1. System organization.

B. Hardware Implementation

The basic hardware used in the system is a low-cost and versatile platform, a standard 486 ISA microcomputer with a Direct Memory Access (DMA) data acquisition board for the capture of EEG and Evoked Potentials. In addition to this tasks, the system carries out on-line procedures as the display of time and frequency domain data with several display formats, one of which is topographic mapping of the signals. These last specifications require the extension of the standard PC architecture with parallelism. To evaluate the real-time capabilities of different architectures we have designed a set of parallel tasks (topographic mapping, multichannel power spectral density and waveform display) as a benchmark. Therefore, we are adding parallelism to the basic PC architecture with Digital Signal Processor (DSP) and Transputer cards that work concurrently with the main processor, its associated coprocessor and the DMA mechanism.

III. BRAIN MATURATION APPLICATION

Our goal is to capture the expert knowledge about maturation in a classifier system that would predict the degree of brain maturation relative to age (low or normal/high levels, as given by the expert). To this end, we have available a sample of EEG data (20 s., taken at rest with eyes closed) obtained from 130 healthy children. In first place, it is necessary to select a set of parameters relevant for the problem from the raw EEG data (feature extraction). Through close collaboration with the specialist we agreed to take as this set relative and total powers in all standard frequency bands from the occipital channels. Due to non-stationarity of the signals we took these parameters in the time instants where each power band presented its absolute maximum. This adds up to a high number of strongly correlated variables. The Principal Component Analysis tool is adequate in this situation to reduce the dimensionality of the feature vector while keeping its information content. The last step consists in determining the best classifier system from the set included in the tools [4]. Our performance criterion is to choose the classifier that generalizes better using data from a training group to a unknown set of new data (test group). The performances of the classifiers tried appear in Table 1. The best results are obtained with a Multilayer Perceptron trained with the popular backpropagation algorithm [5].

IV. CONCLUSION

In this work a system for the automated analysis of brain signals is described. It was designed modularly to allow its easy extension and updating. The system has been applied in a brain maturation analysis. The relevance of these studies lies in the possibility of explaining conduct or schooling problems in children with maturational lag. Now , we are analyzing some pathologies related to alterations in brain background rhythms.

REFERENCES

[1] E.R. John et al., "Validity, Utility and Limitations of Neurometric Evaluations in Children", in *Event-Related Potentials in Children*, A. Rothenberger (Ed.), Elsevier Biomedical Press, 1982.
[2] L. Moreno, J. L. Sánchez, L. Acosta, G. Vera, "A Software Package for Signal Processing: Application to EEG Signals", *Proc. of the ISMM International Conference (MICRO'90)*, Montreal, 1990
[3] L. Moreno, J. L. Sánchez, S. Mañas, J. D. Piñeiro, J. Merino, L. Acosta, A. Hamilton, "Multivariate Analysis and Mapping of EEG", *Clinical Neurophysiology Vol. 22/Suppl 1, September 1992 Abstracts of 6th European Congress of Clinical Neurophysiology, Lisbon 1992.*
[4] ————, "Application of Neural Networks to Automated Brain Maturation Study", in *Artificial Neural Nets and Genetic Algorithms*, R.F.Albrecht, C.R.Reeves, N.C.Steele (Eds.), Springer Verlag 1993, pp 125-130.
[5] D.E. Rumelhart et al, *'Parallel Distributed Processing'*, vol. 1. Cambridge, MA: MIT Press, 1988.

	Test % correct $x \pm \sigma$	Training % correct $x \pm \sigma$	Low level % correct $x \pm \sigma$	Norm/High level % correct $x \pm \sigma$
LVQ Network	63 ± 6	83 ± 5	61 ± 10	65 ± 9
Euclidean Distance	65 ± 7	67 ± 4	64 ± 11	65 ± 10
Linear Discriminant	75 ± 6	80 ± 4	70 ± 11	78 ± 9
Quadratic Discrimin.	75 ± 6	80 ± 3	71 ± 11	78 ± 8
MLP Network	81 ± 6	85 ± 2	78 ± 9	82 ± 6

Table 1. Performance of the classifiers.
LVQ Network: Learning Vector Quantization Network. Statistical methods: Euclidean Distance, Linear and Quadratic Discriminants. MLP Network: Multilayer Perceptron Neural Network trained with Backpropagation algorithm.

A DISCRIMINATION SYSTEM USING NEURAL NETWORK
FOR EMG-CONTROLLED PROSTHESES
~ INTEGRAL TYPE OF EMG SIGNAL PROCESSING ~

Katsutoshi Kuribayashi, Seiji Shimizu, Koji Okimura and Takao Taniguchi

Faculty of engineering, Yamaguchi University
Tokiwadai, Ube, Yamaguchi, 755 JAPAN
TEL(JAPAN)836-31-5100
FAX(JAPAN)836-35-9412

Abstract - The electromyographic (=EMG) signal from active muscle is observed on the surface of the living body. It has been considered one of the most effective signals to control externally powered upper extremity prostheses [1][2][3][4]. However, the EMG signal depends on physical condition, the state of mind and so on. So, it is difficult that the original EMG signal could be used as a command for controlling an externally powered upper extremity prosthesis directly.

In this paper, using an integral type of EMG signal processing and a neural network, a discrimination system for generating commands to control EMG controlled externally powered upper extremity prostheses is proposed. The neural network, in this system, is used to learn the relation between the integral values of the EMG signals and the performances desired by the physical handicapped. It was cleared that total discrimination time could become shorter than Fourier transform processing and the discrimination system could discriminate the seven performances from the EMG signals with the probability of 95.5(%), using integral processing of EMG signal.

INTRODUCTION

The number of the physical handicapped has increased due to accidents in the workshops, traffic accidents and diseases. Though many extremity prostheses have been developed, they are less satisfactory in daily works for the handicapped due to their less degrees of freedom. Recent advancements in technology of mechatronics have helped us develop the mechanism of the externally powered extremity prostheses (=EPUP) close to that of natural extremity. In order to develop EPUP, it is one of the most important problems that how the physical handicapped would communicate with the prosthesis according to their desires.

Recently, the use of the electromyographic (=EMG) signal has received wide attention [3][4]. The EMG signal is an electrical manifestation of neuromuscular activation associated with a contracting muscle. If the EMG signal of the remaining contracting muscles were used to accommodate the desire of the physical handicapped, EPUP could easily be controlled.

So far, the discrimination system for the EMG-Controlled externally powered extremity prostheses (=EMG-C-EPUP) 1 with three degree-of-freedom using neural network was reported in 1991 as shown in Fig. 1(a) [5]. In this system, the power spectra of the EMG signals detected by two electrodes are calculated by FFT algorithm, and these power spectra are defined as input vector to a neural network which has already learned the relation the EMG signals and the performances desired by the handicapped. The neural network can discriminate the EMG signals of the performances desired by the handicapped. In this discrimination system for EMG-C-EPUP 1, the discrimination ratio was about 61(%), which was not satisfactory for EMG-C-EPUP. The defect is due to few electrodes for detecting the EMG signals. The EMG signals detected by two electrodes didn't have enough information to detect the desirable performances.

To improve the discrimination ratio, in 1992, the discrimination system using four electrodes for EMG-C-EPUP 2 was reported as shown in Fig. 1(b) [6]. The discrimination ratio was about 80.7(%). In this system, there are two problems, that is, low discrimination ratio and long discrimination time. The former shows that EMG signals have a little information of desirable performances in frequency domain. The later is caused by FFT calculation which takes long time. Thus, this system is not appropriated to for the real EMG-C-EPUP.

In this paper, we propose a new discrimination system for EMG-C-EPUP using the integral values of the EMG signal in spite of the power spectra to improve the discrimination ratios and discrimination time. Fig. 2 shows the proposed discrimination system. The discrimination time in proposed system would be much shorter than that in old systems as shown in Fig. 1(a) and (b).

To verify the usefulness of the proposed system and the need of training to detect the EMG signals, we will carry out each experiment of three objects, that is, the subject A, B and C.

Moreover, we propose the usage of a neural network board, to shorten the learning processing time for neural network and aiming the practical application to the real EMG-C-EPUP.

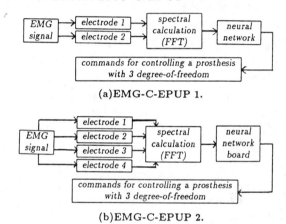

(a)EMG-C-EPUP 1.

(b)EMG-C-EPUP 2.

Fig. 1 Schematic block diagrams of control system for EMG-C-EPUP.

A NEW DISCRIMINATION SYSTEM USING A NEURAL NETWORK

A new discrimination system using a neural network for EMG-controlled prostheses is described. The schematic diagram of proposed discrimination system for EMG-C-EPUP is shown in Fig. 2. This system is composed of detective part, calculation part and discrimination part.

Detective Part

Detective part consists of four electrodes including differential amplifier and A/D converter. The electrodes detect the EMG signals, and the differential amplifier filters the noise from the EMG signal and amplifies the EMG signal.

Calculation Part

Fig. 3 shows the process in the calculation part. The EMG signals (A/D values) given from detective part are changed into absolute value and are integrated. This value is defined as the integral value of the EMG signal. Moreover, the integral values of all electrodes are defined as the components of input vector to the neural network of the discrimination part.

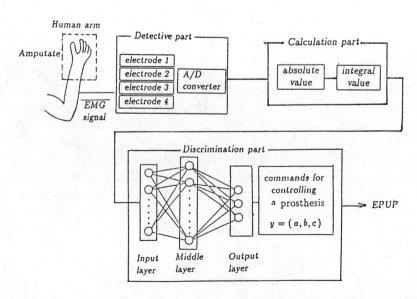

Fig. 2 The proposed system (Experimental system).

Discrimination Part

The neural network which has already learned the relation between the EMG signal and the performance desired by the handicapped can discriminate the desirable performances from the EMG signals. The schematic diagram of the neural network is shown in Fig.2. The neural network has three layers, that is, the input layer, the middle layer and the output layer. The input layer is composed of the number of cells as many as the number of surface electrodes. The output layer is composed of the number of cells as many as the number of pairs of opposite performance, for instance, a combination of hand opening and closing. A cell in the output layer delivers the value between 0 and 1. Output vector y is defined as

$$\mathbf{y} = (\,a, b, c\,)$$

The components are defined as,
$a = 0.0$: Hand closing,
$a = 1.0$: Hand opening,
$b = 0.0$: Palmar flexion,
$b = 1.0$: Palmar dorsiflexion,
$c = 0.0$: Wrist pronation,
$c = 1.0$: Wrist supination,
$a, b, c = 0.5$: relaxation.

This definition prevents the miss discrimination between opposite performances. The learning process for a neural network is shown in Fig. 4. The learning process will be described as follows.

Step 1 : A neural network learns the teaching data, that is, the EMG signals from desired performances by using a backpropagation algorithm [7]. One of a teaching data consists of a pair of an input vector and an output vector which shows performance desired by the handicapped.

Step 2 : After off-line teaching the neural network, on-line experimental discrimination to test the effectiveness of the discrimination system are carried out.

Step 3 : If the experimental discrimination ratio is lower than a probability given prior, Step 1 to Step 3 are repeated until acquiring the discrimination system which discriminates the desired performances with the probability given.

EXPERIMENTAL METHODS

Experiments were carried out in order to show the effectiveness of this system. The experimental method, the desirable performances, the measurement conditions and the experimental system will be presented.

The desirable performances are the seven performances which are defined as "Relaxation", "Hand opening and closing", "Palmar flexion and dorsiflexion", "Wrist pronation and supination".

The subjects, who are objects, are three persons in healthy condition. The subject A, who is a 23-year-old male, is trained to detect the EMG signals for one and half years, so he is trained enough. The subject B, who is a 23-year-old male, and the subject C, who is a 21-year-old male, are trained to detect the EMG signals for twenty or thirty minutes, so they are not trained enough.

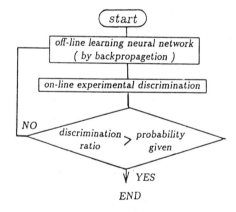

Fig. 4 The flow chart learning process.

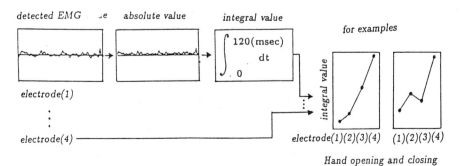

Fig.3 Calculation part

The EMG signals are detected on their left arm by surface electrodes. In the experiments, they hold the arm as shown in Fig. 5. Since a poor contact must be avoided, four surface electrodes are fastened by tightening bands on the surface of the forearm. As different position of the electrodes causes different EMG signals, the position of the electrodes should be kept same. The position of the electrodes are decided as shown in Fig. 6.

The specifications of the experimental devices are described in Table 1. While a subject makes one of the performances with maintaining constant force, the EMG signals are detected by the four surface electrodes and taken into the computer through A/D converter. The sampling time of the EMG is 0.20 milliseconds, the sampling number is 600. Thus, the sampling data length is 120 milliseconds.

After the sampling data are collected, the integral values of the EMG signals are calculated by the computer at calculation part and the integral values are sent to the neural network as input vector. Then, the learning process are performed by using a neural network board installed in a computer (PC-9801). The output vectors used as teaching data are shown in Table 2.

EXPERIMENTAL RESULTS

After learning process of the neural network in the neural network board, on-line experimental discriminations of the neural network were carried out. In the proposed discrimination system, the neural network is composed of 4 cells of input layer corresponding to the four surface electrodes, 50 cells of middle layer and 3 cells of output layer corresponding to three opposite performances.

The discrimination ratio was calculated by using the allowance shown in Table 3 for judging that discriminations were successful.

Learning Process of Neural Network

Fig.7 shows examples of experimental leaning processes of the neural network. The ordinate show errors which are differences between output vector and teaching data. The abscissa shows learning cycles. Fig. 7(a) shows the results by old discrimination system whose calculation part is FFT calculation type. Fig. 7(b) shows the results by proposed discrimination system whose calculation part is integral calculation type.

Fig. 5 The figure of the subject (left arm).

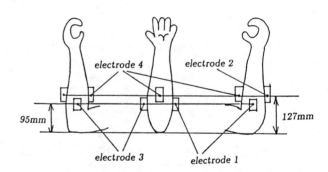

Fig. 6 The position of the surface electrodes (left arm).

Table 2 Teaching Data

performance	a	b	c
relaxation	0.5	0.5	0.5
wrist pronation	0.0	0.5	0.5
wrist supination	1.0	0.5	0.5
palmar flextion	0.5	0.0	0.5
palmar dorsiflextion	0.5	0.5	0.5
hand opening	0.5	0.5	0.0
hand closing	0.5	0.5	1.0

Table 3 The allowance for judging output value

allowance	reference output value y=(a, b, c)
0.00~0.25	0.0
0.25~0.75	0.5
0.75~1.00	1.0

Table 1 The specifications of the experimental devices

computer	NEC PC-9801 DS/U2 (CPU 386SX clock 16MHz)
A/D converter	ATEC AB-05 (12bit , 8channel)
electrodes	Imasen Electric Industrial Co. Ltd. surface electrode
neural network	MITEC INK. 24bit undicided decimal point DSP ×4 (Fujitsu MB86220) average 10M CPS(connections/second) data and memory capacity of 798KB~3.1MB SRAM

The total discrimination time using proposed discrimination system was about 0.13 seconds for 0.12 seconds of the sampling length.

Discrimination Ratio of Experimental Results

Table 4 shows relation between performance number and performance. Table 5 shows discrimination ratio of experimental results in case of the subject A, B and C. In Table 5, the colums on diagonal line between trial performance and discriminated performance show correct discrimination and the other colums show miss discrimination.

The average discrimination ratio of the subject A is 95.5(%), that of the subject B is 85.5(%) and that of the subject C is 90.4(%). The discrimination system for the subject A can discriminate the seven performances from the EMG signals correctly, comparing to the subject B and C. The subject A is well trained to detect the EMG signals and the subject B and C are poor trained. The difference of discrimination ratios between the well trained and the poor trained results in that the average discrimination ratio become low about 5~7(%). The difference of discrimination ratios between the poor trained, that is, the subject B and C, results in about 2(%) of individual difference.

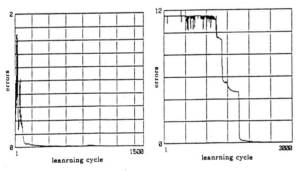

(a) The learning process of the old system.
cells of middle layer : 100
teachiing data : 21
learning time : 223(s)

(b) The learning process of the proposed system.
cells of middle layer : 50
teachiing data : 28
learning time : 443(s)

Fig. 7 The learning processes of the old system and the proposed system.

Table 4 Performance number

number	performance
No.1	relaxation
No.2	wrist pronation
No.3	wrist suspination
No.4	palmar flexion
No.5	palmar dorsiflexion
No.6	hand opening
No.7	hand closing

DISCUSSIONS

It was shown that the proposed system using integral values of the EMG signals and a neural network can discriminate the seven performances from the EMG signals with the high probability of 95.5(%), which is the best of the all experiments. The total discrimination time is about 0.13 seconds for 0.12 seconds of the sampling length, which suggests the potential of its practical application to the prostheses.

The level of how much the subject is trained to detect the EMG signals, that is, the difference between the subject well trained A and the subject B or C, causes a little difference of the discrimination ratios, 5~7(%). On the other hand, the difference between the subjects B and C is 2(%), which is negligible.

Table 5(a) Discrimination ratio (%) of experimental results of the subject A

		No.1	No.2	No.3	No.4	No.5	No.6	No.7	the others
Trial performances	No.1	100							
	No.2		100						
	No.3			85.3		4.2	2.1		8.4
	No.4				95.8		2.1		2.1
	No.5					95.8			4.2
	No.6			2.1			97.9		
	No.7	2.1						93.7	4.2

The average discrimination ratio is 95.5(%).

Table 5(b) Discrimination ratio (%) of experimental results of the subject B

		No.1	No.2	No.3	No.4	No.5	No.6	No.7	the others
Trial performances	No.1	100							
	No.2	1.2	78.1	7.3				1.2	12.2
	No.3			98.0					2.0
	No.4				89.8				10.2
	No.5	1.8				89.3			8.9
	No.6	4.2	2.8				79.2		13.8
	No.7							84.8	15.2

The average discrimination ratio is 88.5(%).

Table 5(c) Discrimination ratio (%) of experimental results of the subject C

		No.1	No.2	No.3	No.4	No.5	No.6	No.7	the others
Trial performances	No.1	100							
	No.2		92.0						8.0
	No.3	8.0		87.0		5.0			
	No.4				100				
	No.5			2.3		94.4		2.3	
	No.6	3.7					77.8		18.5
	No.7	3.4					5.1	81.5	

The average discrimination ratio is 90.4(%).

As shown in Fig. 8 and Table 6, comparing to the old discrimination system whose calculation part is FFT with the total discrimination ratio 80.7(%) and with the total discrimination time 2.35 seconds, both the discrimination ratios and the total discrimination time by using the proposed system get better.

Therefore, the proposed system is more excellent than the old system as a real-time discrimination system for EMG-C-EPUP.

CONCLUSIONS

The discrimination system using the integral value of the EMG signal and neural network for EMG-controlled prostheses was proposed.

The experimental result shows that the proposed discrimination system with neural network could discriminate the seven performances from the EMG signal with the high discrimination ratio 95.5(%). The total discrimination time was about 0.13 seconds which suggests the potential of its practical application to prostheses.

There is 5~7(%) difference of discrimination ratios between the well trained subject and the poor trained subject. There is negligible difference about 2(%) of discrimination ratios between the poor trained subject B and C.

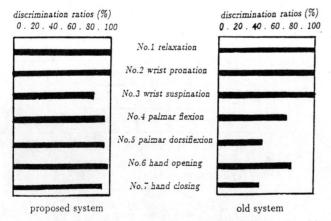

Fig. 9 Discrimination ratios of each performance in the old system and the proposed system.

In addition, we used neural network board installed in a personal computer. The learning times are about 443 seconds. Thus, the neural network board is very useful for a real-time EMG-controlled Prostheses.

ACKNOWLEDGEMENT

We would like acknowledge a part of financial support by the Support Center for Advanced Telecommunications Technology Research (=SCAT).

REFERENCES

[1]K. Tanie et al. , "The Analysis of the EMG signal", Biomechanism 3, Todai shuppankai, pp.73-78(1975)(in Japanese).

[2]H. Sakakibara et al. , "The Control of Multifunctional Powered Prostheses with Information of Frequency of the EMG Signal", Biomechanisms 4, Todai shuppankai, pp.131-138(1978)(in Japanese).

[3]A. Hiraiwa et al. , "EMG Pattern Recognition by Artificial Neural Network for Hand Control", Proc. of BME on the 6th Fall Conference the Japan Society of Medical Electronics and Biological Engineering, '92[Kitakyushu], p.187(1992).

[4]K. Ito et al. , "EMG Pattern Classification for a Prosthetic Forearm with Three Degrees of Freedom", Proc. of IEEE International Workshop on Robot and Human Communication '92[Tokyo], pp.69-74(1992)

[5]K. Nishikawa, K. Kuribayashi, "Neural Network Application to a Discrimination System for EMG-Controlled Prostheses", Proc. of IEEE/RSJ Int. Workshop on Intelligent Robots and System '91[Osaka], pp.231-236(1991).

[6]K. Kuribayashi, K. Okimura, T. Taniguchi, "A Discrimination System Using Neural Network for EMG-Controlled Prostheses", Proc. of IEEE International Workshop on Robot and Human Communication '92[Tokyo], pp.63-68(1992).

[7]NEURO TURBO MANUAL ver. 1.0 for a neural network board, MITEC INC., (1990).

Table 6 Discrimination time of old system and proposed system

	data length	calculation time	neural network	total time for discrimination
old system	102(ms)	2(s) (FFT)	250(ms)	2.352(s)
proposed system	120(ms)	a few millisec. (integration)	10(ms)	0.130(s)

Use of Fractional Powers to Moderate Neuronal Contributions

Donna L. Hudson
Section on Biomedical Informatics
University of California, San Francisco
2615 E. Clinton Avenue, Fresno, CA 93703

Maurice E. Cohen
Department of Mathematics
California State University, Fresno, CA 93740

Abstract—Numerous different approaches to neural network modeling have been tried, including modification of learning algorithms and variations in network design. In this paper, a learning algorithm is described which permits the incorporation of nodes in the network which may contribute to fractional powers, rather than at full strength. This approach has implications for the implementation of fuzzy neural networks in which membership functions can be used to determined the appropriate fractional exponents. In turn, this structure leads to the possibility of a variety of network architectures, where each layer can be viewed as a specific fractional layer. The method is illustrated in a medical application in which a decision model is developed for the analysis of time series data obtained through chromatographic analysis of urine taken from patients with melanoma. The resulting model shows good results in its ability to predict the presence of metastasis in these patients.

I. INTRODUCTION

In the past decade, neural network research has expanded in numerous areas, both theoretical and practical [1,2]. Medical decision making has been a prime area of application [3], since no previous tools tried in this domain, including knowledge-based systems and pattern classification systems, have proved entirely satisfactory. Major applications of neural networks in medicine have fallen into two categories: models which attempt to mimic the human information processing capabilities [4], and those which take what is currently known about the nervous system, and apply it in the creation of decision support tools [5-8]. In the latter category, a number of methods have been tried, including back-propagation [9], Kohonen networks and associative memories [10], Hebbian learning [11], and in fact virtually all theoretical approaches so far developed [12]. In addition, a number of researchers have developed fuzzy neural network models which rely on a number of techniques, including pre-processing of fuzzy input [13-15], learning algorithms for interval data [16-18], and analog models [19]. Another approach is the development of hybrid systems which combine neural networks with other decision making tools to produce practical decision aids [20,21].

In this paper, a learning algorithm developed by the authors based on an extension of the potential function learning algorithm is described [22], including the important feature which allows the development of networks in which nodes can contribute not only as linear or quadratic contributions, but can also be present with fractional powers [23]. A generalized orthogonal function developed by Cohen is used as the potential function, replacing the normal use of polynomials for this purpose. A special case of this function reduces to the polynomial case. Use of this general function permits one to view the contribution of nodes, or neurons, in a different light. One can compare this to a thresholding effect, but rather than being implemented as either an all or nothing firing, a partial contribution of the node can be considered, allowing the impact of a analog model. This approach also has possible implications for fuzzy neural networks in which a membership function could be derived to determine the degree of contribution of each node.

Although this method is general in nature, it will be illustrated as applied to time series data. The data used in this case are chromatograms of urine samples taken from patients with malignant melanoma versus a control set of normal patients. The resulting network is seen to be useful in developing a decision model for the determination of possible metastases in these patients [24].

389

II. THEORETICAL MODEL

A. Learning Algorithm

The learning algorithm utilizes supervised learning techniques. The basis of the technique is generalized vector spaces which permits the development of multidimensional non-linear decision surfaces. It is a modification of the potential function approach to pattern recognition. This learning algorithm has a number of advantages [25]:

- Dependent features are easily handled;
- Missing information can be accommodated;
- Convergence of the system is assured.

In many applications, a number of the input nodes will represent dependent information. Although statistically-based systems can accommodate dependent features, great care must be taken in handling them. The model described here is also quite robust in handling missing information. The last point concerning convergence is especially important. Work in the last decade with recursive systems has shown not only that such systems can propagate error, but under some circumstances, the systems will produce chaotic behavior. It can be shown theoretically that the method used here will not result in divergence or chaos.

The basic learning algorithm is:

Read in values for input nodes;
Compute value P_1.

Until no changes
Compute P_i
IF $P_i > 0$ and class 1, no change
IF $P_i < 0$ and class 2, no change
IF $P_i > 0$ and class 2, or $P_i < 0$ and class 1,
THEN Adjust P_i

Output decision hypersurface equation with weighting factors, $D(x) = P_i(x)$.

The method used is a modification of the potential function approach to pattern recognition. The potential function is defined by

$$P(x,x_k) = \sum_{i=1}^{\infty} \lambda_i \psi_i(x) \psi_i(x_k) \qquad (1)$$

for $k = 1,2,...n$ where $\psi_i(x)$, $i=1,2,3...$ are orthonormal functions and λ_i are non-zero real numbers. P_1 is computed by substituting the values from the first feature vector for case 1, x_1. Subsequent values for P_k are then computed by

$$P_k = P_{k-1} + r_k P(x,x_k) \qquad (2)$$

where

$$r_k = \begin{array}{ll} 1 & \text{if } P_i < 0 \text{ and class 2} \\ -1 & \text{if } P_i > 0 \text{ and class 2} \\ 0 & \text{if } P_i > 0 \text{ and class 2,} \\ & \text{or } P_i < 0 \text{ and class 1} \end{array}$$

The orthonormal functions can in fact be replaced by orthogonal functions, since multiplication by a normalizing factor does not affect the final relative outcome. These functions are chosen from the new set of multidimensional orthogonal functions developed by Cohen. These functions are represented by the general class:

$$F_n(m,a_t;s) = \sum_{k=0}^{n} \frac{\prod_{i=0}^{n-1} (m+a_i+a_k) \, x^{a_k}}{\prod_{j=0}^{k-1} (a_j-a_k) \prod_{s=1}^{n-k} (a_{k+s}-a_k)} \qquad (3)$$

where

$$\prod_{j=0}^{k-1} (a_j-a_k) = (a_0-a_k)(a_1-a_k)...(a_{k-1}-a_k) \; k \geq 1$$

$$\prod_{s=1}^{n-k} (a_{k+s}-a_k) = (a_{k+1}-a_k)(a_{k+2}-a_k)...(a_n-a_k) \; n \geq k$$

A number of special cases can be derived from this orthogonal series. In order to obtain orthogonal polynomials, the series a_k must be chosen to assume integral values. However, it should be noted that this function is capable of generating non-integral series, which can be used to develop networks in which nodal values contribute to fractional powers.

The general form of the decision function is

$$D_i(x) = \sum_{i=1}^{n} w_i x_i^a \sum_{i=1}^{n} \sum_{\substack{j=1 \\ i \neq j}}^{n} w_i w_j x_i^b x_j^c \qquad (4)$$

where n is the number of input nodes. The is the simplest non-linear case. It should be noted that higher order equations can also be generated, but more importantly, fractional nodal contributions are possible using this approach, an illustration of which is given below.

B. Multi-Layered Networks with Fractional Powers

The use of the method described above can result in multiple-layered networks, depending upon which fractional powers are included. The model permits wide flexibility in designing the structure of the network depending on existing knowledge regarding the application at hand. Both integer and fractional powers can be included in the same network. The importance of each node is of course determined by weighting factors derived from running the algorithm on data of known classification. Fig. 1 shows one possible network configuration using this structure, containing two different fractional powers, as well as a direct connection from the input layer to the output layer, which corresponds to a power of 1 for each variable x_i.

III. EXAMPLE

A. Analysis of Time Series Data

Chromatographic analysis of physiological fluids is a useful tool in medical applications to detect chemical constituents that may serve as markers for the presence and level of disease, or its absence. In these types of analyses, the objective is to classify the chromatographic results into categories. In the simplest case, this is a two-category problem, indicating either presence or absence of a particular disease, although it may be multi-category, such as determination of one disease out of two or more possibilities. A general problem in the management of cancer patients is the detection of occult metastatic disease. It has long been recognized clinically that some patients with advanced melanoma void a urine that is dark or that darkens upon standing. Chromatographic analysis is a useful tool in medical applications for the possible determination of presence or absence of disease which is exhibited by the occurrence of certain chemical compounds in the sera or urine of patients.

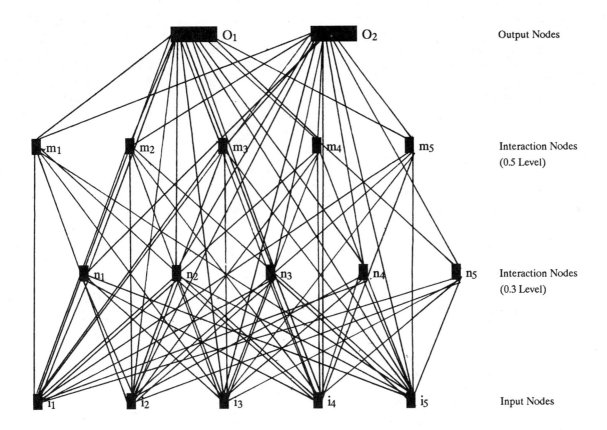

Figure 1: Network with Two Fractional Interaction Levels

High performance liquid chromatography (HPLC) is a technique for detecting chemical constituents of a physiologic fluid. The sample is injected into a machine called a chromatograph which produces a time series plot. Each peak on the plot represents a particular chemical constituent, which appears on the graph at a specific time (denoted the elution time). In these types of analyses, the objective is to classify the chromatographic results into categories.

In all, 144 urine samples were analyzed. These included a set of 66 normal controls. The melanoma patients were divided into two groups: those with no current evidence of the disease and those with clear evidence of metastasis. The following group assignments were made:

Class 1: Normal controls
Class 2: Melanoma patients with no evidence of disease
Class 3: Melanoma patients with metastasis

The maximum peak area was determined for each peak for the 144 samples. Each peak was then divided by the corresponding maximum, leaving a data set ranging between 0 and 1, inclusive, with 0 indicating no peak present for that constituent, and 1 indicating the maximum value. Thus the values between 0 and 1 represent a degree of presence for that peak. Uncertainty analysis is again required here, since the exact elution time varies from one run to another, so a window around the elution time is established, attaching a fuzzy number to the occurrence of that peak.

Once the data had been pre-analyzed to accommodate these complications, the neural network model was then run to determine the relative importance of each peak in separating samples with the following comparisons:

1: Group 1 versus Group 3
2: Group 2 versus Group 3
3: Group 1 versus Group 2

The first comparison considered was group 1 (normals) versus group 3 (melanoma patients with metastatic disease). For this case, the model selected four variables: x_1, x_2, x_3, x_4. Classification results are shown in Table I. The use of these four variables produces very good separation in these cases. The second comparison was group 2 (melanoma patients with no signs of metastatic disease) versus group 3. For this case, 5 variables were selected, including the four variables from above, as well as x_5. These results are shown in Table II. As might be expected, while these results are still quite good, the separation is not as strong as in groups 1 versus 3. There is the possibility that some metastatic disease is present in group 2 which is not clinically detectable. This comparison is particularly important for the potential detection of occult metastatic disease. Comparisons between groups 1 and 2 showed little separation, as would be expected if group 2 are clinically normal at this point in time, although there were some differences in these groups. A sample decision equation for this application takes the form:

$$D(\mathbf{x}) = 19.2 - 45.0x_1^{.3} - 18.8x_2^{.3} - 15.0x_3^{.3} - 8.5x_4^{.3} + 27.1x_1^{.5}$$
$$+ \cdots + 7.1x_4^{.5} + -3.9x_1^{.3}x_2^{.5} + \ldots - 19.6x_1^{.5}x_2^{.3} \qquad (5)$$

TABLE I
NORMALS VERSUS METASTATIC MELANOMA

	Correctly Classified	Incorrectly Classified	Percentage Correct
Normal Controls	62	4	93.9
Metastatic Disease	14	2	87.5
Total	76	6	92.7
Sensitivity			87.5
Specificity			93.9

IV. CONCLUSION

The use of the general algorithm described here permits the development of numerous neural network models with different characteristics. The fact that all the models can be generated from the algorithm simplifies the process for the user. As illustrated in the example, this method results in decision making aids which can easily be implemented as usable tools in practical applications.

The above algorithm has been incorporated into an overall system which performs automatic generation of training sets for the supervised learning, and test sets for verification of results. The algorithm is implemented on a SUN SPARCserver 470 computer. Because of the speed of this computer, it is feasible to run fairly large networks in the sequential implementation. Because of the parallel nature of many aspects of the algorithm, it can also be run on a parallel computer, if available. Work is continuing in refinement of the algorithm, and testing on additional data sets.

TABLE II
METASTATIC VERSUS NON-METASTATIC DISEASE

	Correctly Classified	Incorrectly Classified	Percentage Correct
Disease, No Metastasis	20	4	83.3
Metastatic Disease	12	4	75.0
Total	32	8	80.0
Sensitivity			75.0
Specificity			83.3

TABLE III
IDENTITIES OF VARIABLES, CHROMATOGRAPHIC ANALYSIS

Variable	Chemical Compound	Used in Table I Classification	Used in Table II Classification
x_1	Dihydroxyphenylacetic acid	x	x
x_2	Vanillactic acid	x	x
x_3	Homovanillic acid	x	x
x_4	2-S-cysteinyl-DOPA	x	x
x_5	Dihydroxyphenylalanine		x

REFERENCES

[1] B. Widrow, R. Winter, Neural nets for adaptive filtering and adaptive pattern recognition, *Computer*, 21, 3, 1988, 25-39.

[2] G. Carpenter, S. Grossberg, The art of adaptive pattern recognition by a self-organizing network, *Computer*, 21, 3, 1988, 77-88.

[3] Sabbatini, R.M.E., Applications of connectionist systems in biomedicine, in MEDINFO 92, K.C. Lun et al. Eds., Elsevier Science Publishers, Amsterdam, 1992, pp. 418-425.

[4] R.J. MacGregor, *Neural and Brain Modeling*, Academic Press, San Diego, 1987.

[5] Poli, R., Cagnoni, S., Livi, R., Coppini, G., Valli, G., A neural network expert system for diagnosing and treating hypertension, *Computer*, March 1991, pp. 64-71.

[6] Asada, N., Doi, K., MacMahon, H. Montner, S.M., Giger, M.L., Abe, C., Wu, Y., Potential usefulness of an artificial neural network for differential diagnosis of interstitial lung diseases: Pilot study, *Radiology*, December 1990, 857-860.

[7] Baxt, W.G., Use of an artificial neural network for the diagnosis of myocardial infarction, *Annals of Internal Medicine*, 1991, 115, pp. 843-848.

[8] Eberhart, R.C., Dobbins, R.W., Webber, W.R.S., - CASENET: a neural network tool for EEG waveform classification, in *Proc. II Ann. IEEE Symp. on Computer-Based Medical Systems*, IEEE Computer Society Press, 1989, pp. 60-68.

[9] D.E. Rummelhart, J.L. McClelland, and the PDP Research Group, *Parallel Distributed Processing*, vols. 1 and 2, MIT Press, Cambridge, 1986.

[10] Kohonen, T., *Self-Organization and Associative Memory*, Springer-Verlag, Berlin, 1984.

[11] B. Kosko, Differential Hebbian learning, *Proc. American Institute of Physics: Neural Networks for Computing*, 1986, 277-282.

[12] Grossberg, S., Ed., *Neural Networks and Natural Intelligence*, MIT Press, Cambridge, MA, 1988.

[13] E. Sanchez, Fuzzy logic neural networks in artificial intelligence and pattern recognition, *Int. Conf. on Stochastic and Neural Methods in Signal Processing, Image Processing and Computer Vision*, 1991.

[14] R.R. Yager, Modeling and formulating fuzzy knowledge bases using neural networks, *Iona College Machine Intelligence Institute*, Report #MII-1111, 1-29, 1991.

[15] M. M. Gupta, M. B. Gorzalczany, *Proceedings, IFSA*, R. Lowen, M. Roubens, eds., 46- 49, 1991.

[16] R. Fujioka, H. Ishibuchi, H. Tanaka, M. Omae, Learning algorithm of neural networks for interval-valued data, *Proceedings, IFSA*, R. Lowen, M. Roubens, eds., 37-40, 1991.

[17] T. Saito, M. Mukaidono, A learning algorithm for max-min network and its application to solve fuzzy relation equations, *Proceedings, IFSA*, R. Lowen, M. Roubens, eds., 184-187, 1991.

[18] Cohen, M.E., Hudson, D.L., Approaches to the handling of fuzzy input data in neural networks, *IEEE First Annual Conference on Fuzzy Systems*, 1992, pp. 93-100.

[19] A. Maeda, R. Someya, M. Funabashi, A self-tuning algorithm for fuzzy membership functions using computational flow network, *Proceedings, IFSA*, 1991, pp. 129-136.

[20] Eberhart, R.C., Dobbins, R.W., Using neural networks in hybrid medical diagnostic systems, in *Proc. IEEE Engineering in Medicine and Biology*, IEEE Computer Society Press, 1991, pp. 1470-1471.

[21] Hudson, D.L., Cohen, M.E., Banda, P.W., Blois, M.S., Medical diagnosis and treatment plans derived from a hybrid expert system, in *Hybrid Architectures for Intelligent Systems*, A. Kandel, G. Langholz, Eds., CRC Press, Boca Raton, Florida, 1992, pp. 329-344.

[22] D. L. Hudson, M. E. Cohen, M.F. Anderson, Use of neural network techniques in a medical expert system, *Int. J. of Intelligent Systems*, 6,2, 213-223, 1991.

[23] M.E. Cohen, , D.L. Hudson, M.F. Anderson, A neural network learning algorithm with medical applications, in *Computer Applications in Medical Care*, 13, IEEE Computer Society Press, 1989, pp. 307-311.

[24] Cohen, M.E., Hudson, D.L., Banda, P.W., Blois, M.S., Neural network approach to detection of metastatic melanoma from chromatographic analysis of urine, in *Computer Applications in Medical Care*, 15, P.D. Clayton, Ed., McGraw Hill, New York, 1991, pp. 295-299.

[25] Cohen, M.E., Hudson, D.L., Integration of neural network techniques with approximate reasoning in knowledge-based systems, in *Hybrid Architectures for Intelligent Systems*, A. Kandel, G. Langholz, Eds., CRC Press, Boca Raton, Florida, 1992, pp. 71-86.

NEURAL NETWORKS FOR IDENTIFICATION OF GASTRIC CONTRACTIONS USING ABDOMINAL ELECTRODES

Zhiyue Lin and Jian De Z Chen

Box 145, University of Virginia Health Science Center Charlottesville, VA 22908

Abstract - The established method for the measurement of gastric contractions is invasive by intubating a manometric probe in the stomach. A noninvasive method is developed in this paper for the identification of gastric contractions from the surface electrogastrogram (EGG) using neural networks. Using the EGG data in five subjects as the training set and the EGG data in another five subjects as the testing set, an accuracy of 92% for the identification of gastric contractions from the EGG was achieved using a three-layer back-propagation neural network.

INTRODUCTION

Gastric contractions can be measured mechanically by intubating a probe with pressure sensors into the stomach or myoelectrically by placing electrodes on the mucosal or serosal surface of the stomach [1]. However, all these methods are invasive and their uses are limited in patients.

It is known that gastric contractions are controlled by myoelectrical activity of the stomach which consists of two components: omni-present slow waves and spike potentials . Gastric myoelectrical activity can be measured by placing surface electrodes on the epigastric area in the abdomen and the cutaneous recording is called the electrogastrogram (EGG) [2]. Previous studies [3] have shown that the EGG is an accurate measure of the frequency of the gastric slow wave and the relative amplitude change of the EGG reflects the contractility of the stomach. Although the EGG may have different characteristics during motor quiescence and gastric contractions, no mathematical algorithms or 'if-then' statements can be made to distinguish the EGG because it is imprecise. However, a large amount of EGG data can be easily made available due to the noninvasive nature of the electrogastrographic technique. Therefore, the problems of the EGG in clinical applications are perfect candidates for the artificial neural networks (ANN).

The aim of this paper was to explore a noninvasive method for the identification of the gastric contractions based on the EGG using the ANN.

METHODS

The position of the stomach was localized by ultrasonography and surface electrodes were placed on the abdominal skin right over the distal stomach in an overnight study in ten health volunteers. Gastric contractions were simultaneously recorded using an intraluminal manometric probe consisting of 6 solid-sate pressure transducers, 3 in the antrum and 3 in the small intestine. Recordings were obtained for 2 hours in the fasting state. Two 20-min EGGs in each subject were selected, digitized at a sampling frequency of 2 Hz and subjected to computerized data analysis. These included 20-min EGGs during fasting motor quiescence and during fasting motor activity, respectively.

The running windowed exponential distribution (RWE) [4] was applied for the time-frequency representation of the EGG signal. The performance of the exponential distribution method for the time-frequency analysis of the EGG was thoroughly investigated in [5]. The previous study has shown that the RWE method is quite effective in suppressing interferences while retaining high resolution and provides an accurate estimation for both the frequency and the amplitude of the EGG. The parameters derived in [5] were used in this study.

The back-propagation neural networks [6] with one hidden layer were designed. The number of hidden nodes in the hidden layer, learning rate and momentum factor were optimized based on numerous experiments. The output of the network has two nodes, standing for gastric contractions and gastric motor quiescence, respectively. The EGG recording was divided to segments, each with 512 samples (4.27 min). Each segment of the EGG data was labeled as 1 if one or more contractions were present in the simultaneous manometric recording, otherwise it was labeled as 0. The spectral data (first 64 points) of each segment were presented to the ANN. The ANN was trained in such a way that it was adjusted to give an output of 1 if the input was labeled 1, and output of 0 if the input was labeled 0. The training process was completed when all EGG data from five subjects were presented. And then the EGG data from another five subjects were presented to the trained ANN and the ANN provided an output of either 1 or 0, i.e., classification of gastric contractions or quiescence, respectively. The output of the ANN was compared with the label of the input data to determine whether the ANN provided a correct classification.

RESULTS

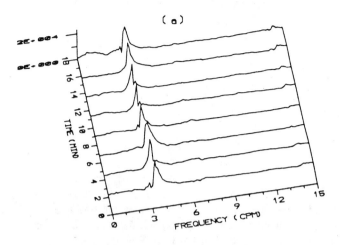

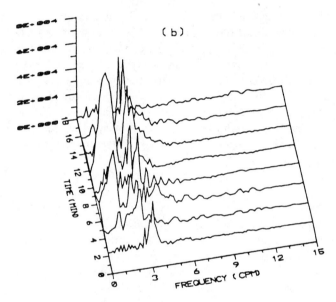

Fig. 1. Time-frequency representation of the EGG. (a) During motor quiescence. (b) During gastric contractions.

Table 1: Effects of the number of hidden nodes on the performance of the network (testing results). (learning rate=0.05, momentum factor=0.9, number of iterations=1000)

hidden nodes	accuracy (quiescence)	accuracy (contractions)
5	84%	91%
10	90%	94%
20	90%	94%
30	90%	94%

The time-frequency representation of the typical EGG signals is presented in Fig.1. Fig.1(a) is the time-frequency representation of a portion (20-min) of the EGG during motor quiescence and Fig.1(b) is that of the EGG during gastric contractions. It is seen that the EGG during gastric contractions has higher power and more low frequency components between 0 to 3 cycles min^{-1} (cpm).

The effect of the number of the hidden nodes on the

performance of the back-propagation ANN with three layers is presented in Table 1. It is seen that with a fixed number of iterations, ten hidden nodes resulted in better performance than five hidden nodes, whereas no further improvement was observed with the number of hidden nodes more than 10. With the optimized values of the learning rate (0.05) and momentum factor (0.9), the network with a structure of 64:10:2 (the number of nodes for input:hidden:output layers) recognized the EGG during gastric motor quiescence with an accuracy of 90% and the EGG during gastric contractions with an accuracy of 94%.

CONCLUSION

This paper presents a noninvasive method for identification of the gastric contractions of the stomach from the surface EGG using the back-propagation neural network. This noninvasive method has a great clinical potential and may be used to study whether a patient has a normal occurrence of cyclical gastric contractions in the fasting state and/or a normal postprandial pattern of gastric contractions after a solid meal.

ACKNOWLEDGEMENT

Acknowledgement is made to the Thomas F. and Kate Miller Jeffress Memorial Trust for the partial support of this research. The authors would like to thank Dr. Qiang Wu for his technical assistance.

REFERENCES

[1]   J. H. Szurszewski, "Electrophysiological basis of gastrointestinal motility," In Physiology of the gastrointestinal tract. Johnson L. R. (Ed.) Raven Press, New York, pp.383-422, 1987.

[2]   W. C. Alvarez, "The electrogastrogram and what it shows," Journal of Am. Med. Ass., Vol.78, pp.1116-1118, 1922.

[3]   A.J.P.M. Smout, E.J. van der Schee and J.L Grashuis, "What is measured in electrogastrography?" Dig. Dis. Sci., Vol.25, pp.179-187, 1980.

[4]   H-I. Choi and W. J. Williams, "Improved time-frequency representation of multicomponent signals using exponential distribution," IEEE Trans. on ASSP, Vol.37, pp.862-871, 1989.

[5]   Z.Y. Lin and J.D.Z. Chen, "Time-frequency representation of the electrogastrogram - application of the exponential distribution," submitted for publication.

[6]   R. C. Eberhart and R. W. Dobbins, Neural network PC tools, Academic Press Inc., San Diego, 1990.

A CARDIAC OUTPUT ESTIMATION MODEL WITH A NEURAL NETWORK -TOWARD TOTAL ARTIFICIAL HEART CONTROL-

Toru Masuzawa, Yoshiyuki Taenaka, Masayuki Kinoshita, Takeshi Nakatani,
Haruhiko Akagi, Hisateru Takano and Yasuhiro Fukui*
National Cardiovascular Center Research Institute
5-7-1 Fujishirodai, Suita, OSAKA 565 JAPAN
*Tokyo Denki University, JAPAN

ABSTRACT

A computer neural network model to estimate cardiac output from physiological data during exercise was developed toward studying total artificial heart (TAH) control. Treadmill exercise test was given to two normal goats to obtain the physiological data during exercise. Heart rate, mean arterial blood pressure, mixed venous oxygen saturation and physical activity were adopted in the neural network as input variables and cardiac output was used as an output variable. A three layer back-propagation network was used to construct the model. Feasibility of the neural network for modeling was evaluated by comparing estimated cardiac output and real data. Estimated cardiac output agreed well with real cardiac output with the individual data. The neural network technique should be a useful tool to develop control algorithm of TAH.

INTRODUCTION

Modeling of the cardiovascular system is a useful way to develop a control algorithm of a total artificial heart (TAH) [1],[2]. The neural network technique is expected to be a useful to establish a model that incorporates multiple input and output variables. In this study, a computer neural network model to estimate cardiac output from physiological data during exercise was developed and evaluated for feasibility of the modeling technique.

METHODS

1. Data sampling in the treadmill exercise experiment

Treadmill exercise experiment with two goats was performed to obtain the physiological data and to determine which data were useful for the model. Blood pressure catheters and a electromagnetic flow probe were implanted surgically to goats and the exercise tests were performed seventeen times with two goats after two weeks. The exercise test was composed of five minutes walking with speed of two miles/h and five minutes resting after walking. Left and right atrial pressure, arterial pressure, pulmonary arterial pressure, heart rate, pulmonary arterial flow rate as cardiac output, mixed venous oxygen saturation, and physical activity which was calculated from acceleration signal were sampled during the exercise and the average of these data for each ten seconds were digitized and recorded. The correlation between cardiac output and other data was evaluated to determine which data were useful to produce cardiac output estimation model.

2. Neural network configuration

The model to estimate cardiac output from other data was constructed based on a neural network technique. A three layer back-propagation neural network [3], which has the input layer with fifty-six cells, the hidden layer with thirty-two cells and the output layer with twelve cells, was used to organize the model (figure 1). The relative values, which were calculated as difference ratio against the control data before exercise, were used for the network. Each data was classified discretely to relate to each cell of the network. For example, if difference ratio of heart rate was 94%, the cell classified as from 90% to 100% would be fired.

3. Feasibility examination

Five hundred and ninety-eight sets and five hundred and thirty-six sets of data were obtained from each goat. Five hundred and thirty-three sets and four hundred and seventy-two sets of data of each goat were used for learning process of the neural network, and sixty-five sets and sixty-four sets of data of each goat were used for cardiac output estimation test. In this study, the correlation coefficient between estimated cardiac output and that of real data, CC, was used to evaluate the performance of modeling by the neural network. Following subjects were studied to evaluate the model.

1) Feasibility of the model by individual data

Data of a goat were used for the network. Seventy sets of the learning data and sixty-six sets of non-learning data were used to evaluate the accuracy of the cardiac output estimation of the model in individual data.

2) Feasibility of the model applied in different individual

Two kinds of cardiac output estimation were performed to study the influence of individual differences on the model..

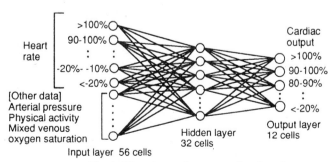

Fig.1 Structure of a neural network

(1) The cardiac output was estimated by the neural network that was learned by data of different goat. (2) The neural network was learned by data of both goats. Same data with the individual data study were used for cardiac output estimation to clarify the effect of individual differences to the model.

RESULTS

1. Evaluation of data in the treadmill exercise experiments

The correlation coefficient between cardiac output and other data is shown in Table 1. Heart rate, mean arterial pressure, mixed venous oxygen saturation and physical activity had better correlative relationship with cardiac output. These four variables and cardiac output were used to construct the neural network.

Table 1 Correlation coefficient between cardiac output and other data

Heart rate	0.85
left atrial pressure	0.03
right atrial pressure	0.0
arterial pressure	0.48
pulmonary arterial pressure	0.36
mixed venous oxygen saturation	0.85
physical activity	0.73

2. Feasibility examination

1) Feasibility of the model by using individual data

Figure 2 shows a result of the cardiac output estimation. The CC for the learning data was 0.975 (p<0.001) and that for the non-learning data was 0.881(p<0.001).

2) Feasibility of the model applied in different individual

(1)The CC based on different goat model was 0.826 (p<0.001). (2) The CC for the learning data was 0.677 (p<0.001) and that for the non-learning data was 0.789(p<0.001).

DISCUSSION

The cardiac output estimated by the neural network of individual data agreed well with real cardiac output. The neural network technique should be a useful technique to model mechanism of cardiovascular system regulation. However, the performance of the developed model decreased because of the influence of individual differences. Because, the structure of the neural network was too simple and had not enough ability to absorb the influence of individual differences. Further improvement of the network structure will be needed to overcome this problem.

CONCLUSION

A neural network model to estimate cardiac output from physiological data during exercise was developed toward studying total artificial heart control. Treadmill exercise test was given to two normal goats to obtain the physiological data during exercise. Feasibility of the neural network for modeling was evaluated by using exercise data. Estimated cardiac output agreed well with real cardiac output with the individual data. This technique should be useful for development of the total artificial heart control algorithm.

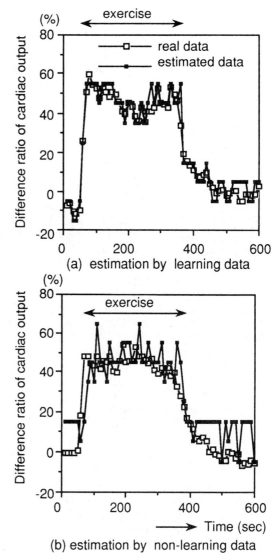

(a) estimation by learning data

(b) estimation by non-learning data

Fig.2 Results of cardiac output estimation

REFERENCES

[1]T. Masuzawa, Y. Taenaka, M. Kinoshita,T. Nakatani, H. Akagi, H. Takano, Y. Fukui, H. Sasagawa, and K. Takahashi, "A motor integrated regenerative pump as the actuator of an electrohydraulic totally implantable artificial heart," *ASIOA transaction*, vol. 38, no. 3, pp. M232-M236, 1992.

[2]T. Masuzawa, Y. Taenaka, M. Kinoshita, T. Nakatani, H. Takano, and Y. Fukui, "An electrohydraulic totally implantable artificial heart with a motor-integrated regenerative pump and its computer control," *Proceedings of the Fifth Annual IEEE Symposium on Computer-based Medical systems,* Durham, U.S.A., June 14-17, 1992, pp. 673-680.

[3]D.E. Rumelhart, G.E. Hilton, and R.J. Williams, "Learning representations by back propagating error," *Nature,* vol. 323, no. 9, pp. 533-536, 1986.

Detection of Motion Artifacts in Electrical Impedance Plethysmography Signals using Neural Networks

Dinesh G. Haryadi, Sastry K.L.A., Ramnath Boreda,
William D. Timmons, and Bruce C. Taylor
Department of Biomedical Engineering
The University of Akron, Akron, OH 44325

Abstract

An artificial neural network was developed to detect patient motion artifacts in electrical impedance plethysmography signals. The network was trained using back propagation, and could differentiate between motion free waveforms and waveforms corrupted by motion artifacts. The use of such a network in a continuous data acquisition system may result in considerable savings in physician's time and computer memory.

Introduction

Electrical Impedance Plethysmography (EIP) involves the study of blood volume changes in a body segment. Since blood is a conductor, the impedance across a body segment changes with each heart beat. To record this variation, a high frequency current (1ma at 100kHz) is passed into the limb or arm segment and the corresponding voltage changes are monitored. A typical signal comprises a systolic rise, a gradual diastolic fall, and a prominent dicrotic notch. See Fig.1.

For diagnosis, the peak amplitude, the ratio of peaks, and the area under the curve are computed and averaged over several cycles[1]. Errors in these measures may arise from baseline wander, motion artifacts, and high frequency noise. Baseline wander and high frequency noise can be eliminated using a band pass filter[2]. Motion artifacts, however, usually cannot be eliminated since their frequency components overlap those of the impedance signal. Instead, signals corrupted with motion artifact should be discarded. Automation of this process would save considerable time and energy for the physician, since, typically, motion artifacts are detected by visual inspection of the data record. In this paper, we therefore develop an artificial neural network to detect motion artifacts. Furthermore, this network can be used to eliminate motion corrupted signals during data collection, thus reducing the amount of media needed for data storage.

Data collection and Preprocessing

An EIP system was connected across the arm of a healthy subject to continuously record the signal. Motion artifacts in the signal similar to those found in clinical practice were created by sudden movement of the arm during data collection (Fig 1.) Data were collected at a sampling rate of 500Hz using an IBM data acquisition system with 12 bit resolution and band pass filtered (0.5 Hz to 20Hz) to eliminate low and high frequency noise.

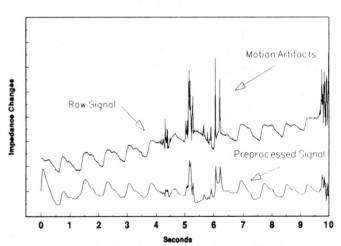

Fig 1: EIP signals before and after filtering.

The data set was then segmented so that it could be presented to the network in a consistent manner. The filtered EIP signal was differentiated using a band limited differentiator and the zero crossings were used to obtain the peak values in the signal. From the peak value, a set number of points on either side were used to form each segment, resulting in 71 points per segment. The segments were then visually classified as either "motion free" or "motion present".

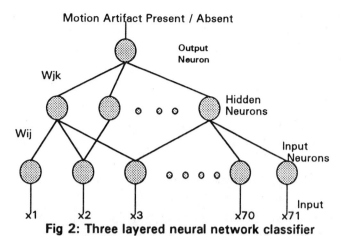

Fig 2: Three layered neural network classifier

The Neural Network

A three layer feed-forward neural network was used (Fig 2). The input layer consisted of 71 nodes corresponding to the 71 data points per segment. The hidden layer consisted of 10 nodes and was selected by trial and error. The output layer consisted of 1 node. Values less than 0.2 at the output node corresponded to a classification as "motion present" and values greater than 0.8 corresponded to "motion free."

The network was trained using backpropogation[3]. Ten segments, six "motion free" and four "motion present," were used for training. A learning coefficient of 0.25 and an epoch of 16 was used[4]. Weights were initially randomized between ±0.1 and the network was trained until the root mean square error was less than 0.05. On average, the network took 1500 iterations to reach this threshold.

Table 1: Network classifier results

Desired Output	Network Output	Classification
0	0.10	Motion Present
0	0.06	Motion Present
1	0.93	Motion Free
1	0.96	Motion Free
1	0.96	Motion Free
1	0.96	Motion Free
1	0.96	Motion Free
1	0.95	Motion Free
0	0.03	Motion Present
0	0.03	Motion Present

Results

The neural network was tested on a separate set of ten signals, the results of which are summarized in Table 1. From the table it can be seen that the trained network was able to successfully classify all the ten test signals.

Discussion

Once trained, feed-forward networks are very fast and can be used on-line. When such a network is used on-line to eliminate segments with motion artifacts from EIP signals, it can save both physician's time and storage space. At the least, this network can be used off-line to automate the elimination of signals with motion artifacts. In addition, this network can be adapted to individual patients' EIP signals. In summary, the feasibility of using an artificial neural network to detect motion artifacts in EIP signals has been studied and the results have been found to be encouraging.

References

[1] Penney B. C., "Theory and cardiac applications of electrical impedance measurements," *CRC Critical Reviews in Biomedical Engineering*, Vol. 13, Issue 3, pp. 227-229, 1986.
[2] Tarassenko L., *et al.*, " Use of digital techniques to process cerebral electrical impedance signals in the newborn," *Med. & Biol. Eng. & Comput.*, 22, 55-62, 1984.
[3] Lippmann R. P., "An introduction to computing with neural networks," *IEEE ASSP*, pp. 4-22, April 1987.
[4] *Neural Computing*, NeuralWorks Professional II/Plus and NeuralWorks Explorer, NeuralWare, Inc., pp. NC-141,1991.

This work was supported in part by the Lois Sisler McFawn Foundation and the William H. Falor Foundation.

CLASSIFICATION OF BIOMAGNETIC FIELD PATTERNS BY NEURAL NETWORKS

Martin F. Schlang[1], Ralph Neuneier
Siemens AG, Corporate Research and Development, Otto-Hahn-Ring 6, D-8000
München 83, Germany

Klaus Abraham-Fuchs, Johann Uebler
Siemens AG, Medical Engineering Group, D-8520 Erlangen, Germany

ABSTRACT

When analyzing biomagnetic fields, 3-dimensional source reconstruction plays an important role. We present a method which facilitates preprocessing for such a reconstruction: a neural net classifier decides whether from a given magnetoencephalographic map a localization using a given source model can be carried through. The performance in practical applications is compared for various types of networks. Some new information about the properties of the biomagnetic inverse problem is obtained by extracting rules from the trained nets.

INTRODUCTION

In the human body information is transmitted in nerves and muscles by electric impulses. The resulting electric currents create -according to Maxwell's equations- a magnetic field outside of the body. The KRENIKON®, a 37 channels measuring device, is able to record these very small magnetic fields using SQUIDs (superconducting quantum interference devices) /SHR 90/. Typically, the fields are 6 to 8 orders of magnitude smaller than the magnetic field of the earth. The electric processes that occur in the human body can be reconstructed by the measured external field distribution. A main advantage of the method is that it is a noninvasive and passive measurement, and therefore absolutely save for the patient.

Typical measurements produce an enormous amount of data owing to the great number of the SQUID magnetometers and high number of samples in time. Not all these data are of medical relevance. In /TLS 92/, /STA 92/ the authors showed how the data can be automatically filtered, segmented and clustered with neural nets. The aim of this previous study was to detect pathologic extrasystolic (out-of-order-) heart beats in the magnetocardiogram (MCG). This paper investigates the

---

1. Phone: +49/89/636-49408, FAX: +49/89/636-3320, e-mail: ms@leonce.zfe.-siemens.de

401

segmentation of measured biomagnetic data of the brain: the magnetoencephalogram (MEG).

A magnetoencephalogram is the magnetic analogy to the electroencephalogram.
It is a trace of the processes which take place in the human brain. In an epileptic
seizure or in repeated artificial stimulation with subsequential triggered averaging, one of these processes dominates considerably. In this case it is possible to
reconstruct 3-dimensionally the processes that take place in the brain from the
measured distribution of the magnetic fields.

In this paper, equivalent current dipoles (ECD) are assumed as fieldproducing
processes /SSA 90/. Under the condition that one of the active current dipoles
dominates very strongly, a reconstruction of this current source can be carried out
with the help of an arithmetical procedure. This procedure reveals the location,
orientation and strength of this electric dipole. The reconstruction of the dipoles is
carried out iteratively and requires very great computing power. Therefore, in
practical applications, it is not possible to calculate the source reconstruction for
all measured data.

It is the task of an operator or physician -as an expert on his subject- to track
down particular periods of time in which a source reconstruction is possible and
of diagnostic value. This is a very time consuming and tiring task. With the help
of neural nets we succeeded in finding a quick and reliable classifier for magnetic
field patterns, indicating where a localization of an equivalent current dipole is
promising. This predictor highly reduces the necessary interactive scanning time
for the operator. The physiological and clinical background for this pattern classification task is discussed in more detail in /ASU 92/.

THE PROBLEM

The task of our algorithm is to examine a measured MEG or MCG and to decide
whether a source reconstruction is possible and useful. This classification must be
carried out separately at any point in time. Human experts solve this task by judging the accompanying biomagnetic map for each time slice. Such a map can be
visualized e.g. by using isocontour lines (Fig. 1a). Even for an expert this task is
not easy. It must be considered that at a sampling rate of 1000 Hz and a measuring
time of five minutes a datafile contains about 300 000 maps. This was the motivation to use a neural net as a classifier with the hope that it can solve this problem
quickly and reliably. The network's output predicts a measure for the probability
P that an equivalent current dipole is the generator of a given magnetic map (Fig.
1b).

MODEL ASSUMPTIONS

The calculation of the magnetic field and the source reconstruction are only possible under restricted model assumptions. As sources we assume equivalent current
dipoles which are situated in a model of the part of the human body under investigation, e.g. the head or torso. In biomagnetism computationally simple models
are sufficient in most applications: for the human head we assume a homogeneous

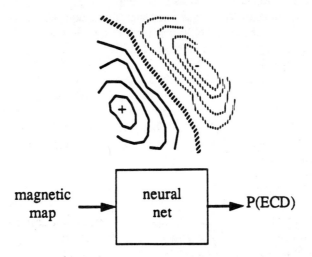

Fig. 1: The task: a) example of a magnetical map; b) the neural net approach: prediction of the probability that an electric current dipole (ECD) is the generator of the field map.

conductive sphere, for the human body we assume an infinite half space /SSA 90/ . Using these models, analytical expressions for the corresponding magnetic field at the location of the sensor array can be derived for a presumed current source (place, orientation and strength of a dipole in three-dimensional space), taking also into account the contribution of the secondary volume currents to the measured magnetic field. For physical reasons, the inverse of this problem -the calculation of the characteristics of the dipole source in dependence of a given magnetic field- has a unique solution only in case of simple point-like sources, such as an ECD.

PRODUCTION OF TRAINING DATA

Prior to the application to real measurements we train a neural net to predict the probability that a current dipole can be localized with a supervised training procedure using simulated data. For this purpose corresponding input/output patterns must be supplied. Using our software simulation tools, any desired amount of patterns can be produced.

First, dipoles with random strength, orientation and location are simulated. Then the corresponding magnetic field at the sensor array is calculated by a so called forward calculation under the presumed model assumptions (Fig. 2). Three different classes of field patterns are used in the training stage: a focal brain activity is modeled by a single ECD, multifocal brain processes by the simultaneous activity of three random dipoles, and brain background activity by random field patterns.

Gaussian noise at different noise levels may then be added to theses simulated field patterns. Subsequently, an inverse source reconstruction is carried out. If the reconstructed sources correspond to the dipoles within given bounds of tolerance, the corresponding magnetic map is marked as localizable (electrical current dipole probability $P = 1$).

As an example, the results of a subproblem of the general map classification task is discussed in detail here: the network is trained only with 3000 examples of very similar patterns which are difficult to distinguish. Further 2000 patterns are used for testing the generalization capability. These patterns are monopolar maps (i.e. showing only a section of the field pattern with uniform signal polarity), and having a signal to noise ratio of three.

PREPROCESSING

Appropriate preprocessing of the magnetic maps prior to classification can increase the recognition rate. First a normalization to constant energy of the map is carried out. This is possible because the field pattern depends on the dipole strength linearly and uniformly. Thus the manifoldness of possible field patterns is reduced.

Furthermore we investigated suitable transformations which may be summarized under the term 'feature vector extraction'. It can be shown that the ECD probability of a field map is invariant with respect to translation and rotation of the specific KRENIKON® sensor array relative to the ECD position.

First investigations with a Fourier Mellin transform in polar coordinates -such a transformation is variant to rotation- showed a slight decrease of recognition rates. The reason for this may be the necessity of an interpolation: for the Fourier transform, the magnetic field must be given on a polar grid but the KRENIKON® sensors are arranged on a hexagonal grid. According to our calculations at the edge of the sensor array errors in interpolation cannot be ignored. An even stronger decrease of the recognition rate was observed when moments were used as feature vectors. On the training set and recognition set the network achieved significantly worse recognition rates.

The best method for preprocessing is a rotation of the measured data without interpolation: first, the centre of gravity i. e. the first order moment, is calculated. Then, given by the symmetries of the sensor array, the map is rotated into a standard position modulo 60 degrees. The manifoldness of possible field patterns at the input of the neural net is highly reduced by this preprocessing step.

PROBABILISTIC BACKGROUND

The task is to classify correctly a given magnetoencephalogram (MEG) to the class ECD or not ECD ($\overline{ECD}$). In the training phase we have simulated examples of the MEG for both classes ECD and $\overline{ECD}$. The likelihood of a measured MEG

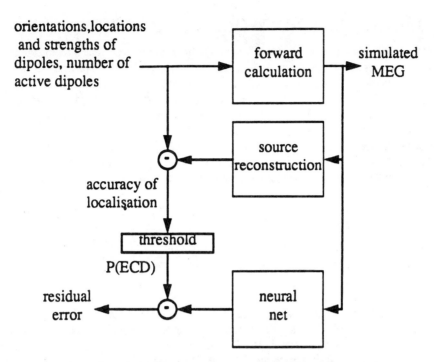

Fig. 2: The error function, which is minimized in the training phase.

given the class ECD is $P\,(MEG|\,ECD)$. In the recognition phase we need the posterior classification probability $P\,(ECD|\,MEG)$ i.e. the probability whether a given magnetic map (MEG) is an electric current dipole or not. The likelihood and the a posteriori probability are related through the Bayes rule

(EQ 1)

$$P\,(ECD|\,MEG)\,P\,(MEG)\,=\,P\,(MEG|\,ECD)\,P\,(ECD)$$

It can be shown that the output activity of the neural net will approximate $P\,(ECD|\,MEG)$ if the target values are unity for the localizable class and zero for the not localizable class.

Eq.1 shows that the frequency of the occurrence of the two different classes has to be considered for optimal classification results. In the following example we use the same amount of examples of the MEG for the class ECD and $\overline{ECD}$.

For the evaluation of the recognition results we select the class with the maximum a posteriori probability: each probability P(ECD) and P($\overline{ECD}$) is represented by an output node of the network. The output node which fires stronger is considered to be the winner.

THE NEURAL NETWORK TOPOLOGIES

In this paper we compare three different classification approaches: a feed forward net with sigmoidal nonlinearities as described in /ASU 92/, a neural net with gaussian radial basis functions and a conventional k-nearest neighbor classifier.

First we describe the approach using the "Gaussian Mixtures" based architecture proposed by Tresp et al. in /THA 93/. The network responds to an input according to the one-of-k-classes classification; i. e. there is one output per class and the strength of the output activity specifies the reliability of the networks decision. The kth output sums up the normalized responses of some basis functions b_i^k where index k specifies the class to which the unit i belongs

(EQ 2)

$$y_k(x) = NN_k(x) = \frac{\sum_i w_i^k b_i^k(x)}{\sum_l b_l(x)}$$

while the output weights w_i^k are originally fixed to one. Note that the sum in the denominator of eq. 2 runs over all units l assigned to any class, the sum in the numerator over the units assigned to class k. This means that the outputs are always positive and sum up to one. If we use as basis functions

(EQ 3)

$$b_i(x) = \kappa_i exp\left\{-\frac{1}{2}(x-\mu_i)'\Sigma_i^{-1}(x-\mu_i)\right\},$$

where the off-diagonal elements σ_{ij} of the correlation matrix Σ_i are zero we obtain a Gaussian classifier (fig 3).

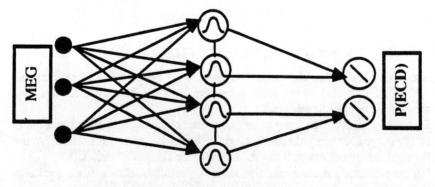

Fig. 3: Gaussian classifier for two classes.

There are three main advantages of investigating classification problems using this approach. **First**, the network has a probabilistic interpretation. Identify the sum $\Sigma_i \; b_i^k(x)$ of the basis functions assigned to class k with $P(x| class_k) P(class_k)$. Then we get the evidence

(EQ 4)

$$P(class_k| x) \; = \; \frac{P(x| class_k) P(class_k)}{\sum_l P(x| class_l) P(class_l)}$$

that input vector x belongs to class k which is equivalent to equation 2.

Second, there are a variety of prestructuring methods applicable. The obvious and most common used technique is the distribution of the centers μ via k-means clustering /DH73/, /MD90/ to minimize the total euclidean distances of the data points to the centers. This algorithm can be extended by including information of the output space: the clustering of the centers m_{ij}^k of the basis functions b_i^k is done only on the portion of the training data which belongs to class k. We obtain a more accurate distribution of the centers with respect to the class specific data points.

After the clustering of the centers the width σ_{ij} can be initialized by the P-nearest-neighbor method /MD90/. The individual σ_{ij} is determined as the average of the distance from center μ_{ij} to the nearest P centers. In this step, we use a threshold which limits the σ_{ij} to values higher than 0.1, to avoid an overlocalized modelling of the data. As above, we incorporate class-specific information by looking for those nearest centers μ_{ij}^k whose basis functions b_i^k belong to the same class.

Table 1 shows the performance of the different algorithms after prestructuring prior to any supervised learning. The values are the percentage of correct classified patterns for the training respectively test data. Obviously, the methods including class-specific information, class-k-means and class-P-nearest gave the best recognition rates.

Table 1: RECOGNITION RATES AFTER INITIALIZATION T: training set; G: generalization.

	fixed σ_{ij}	P-nearest	class-P-nearest
k-means	56% T / 53% G	53% T / 52% G	51% T / 48% G
class-k-means	75% T / 72% G	75% T / 70% G	75% T / 72% G

The **third** advantage of this architecture is that it is possible to reduce the complexity of the network with the iterative strategy proposed by Tresp /THA 93/. Also, these methods are applicable to avoid overfitting. Evaluating the relative importance of each basis function at its center, $\phi_i = b_i(\mu_i) / \Sigma_i b_i(\mu_i)$, gives a hint which units should be pruned. Successively removing the basis function with the smallest ϕ_i and retraining the network eventually yielded the performance results in table 2.

Table 2: RECOGNITION RATES AFTER TRAINING (BEST GENERALIZATION).

	Training	Generalisation	units	epochs
fixed output weights	78	74	40	400
learned output weights	80	75	40	550
sigmoidal network	81	76	50	1000
conventional k-nearest neighbor classifier[a]	68%	51%	3000	-

a. Due to a larger database the recognition results are not directly comparable with the others in this paper

If we allow w_i^k to take values different from one the performance can be improved, but we loose a probabilistic interpretation.

The conventional k-nearest neighbor classifier uses $K = 11$ neighbors. Due to the large amount of distance calculations, the classifier cannot be used in practical applications except using special algorithms like bump trees.

KNOWLEDGE EXTRACTION

When using networks with radial basis functions, rules about the modelled system can be extracted from the weight matrices of the trained net /HT 92/. Fig. 4 on the left shows the distribution of the variances σ_{ij}. Each row contains the variances of one basis function, ordered according to input dimensions (columns). Large σ_{ij}, which represent less dominant connections, are shown in a bright code. Small σ_{ij}, indicating a very local restricted information are coded black. The vertical bright stripes marked by arrows are remarkable. The magnetic sensors in the KRENI-KON®, which belong to these input nodes are all situated in the middle of the sensor array (see the circle in Fig. 4 on the right side). We can conclude that the SQUID's within this circle are less important for the map classification task than the sensors which are found further away of the center.

CONCLUSION

We have shown that neural nets can be applied very successfully to solve nontrivial classification problems. Their performance is better than a conventional k-nearest-neighbor classifier. We could improve the recognition rates by suitable preprocessing.

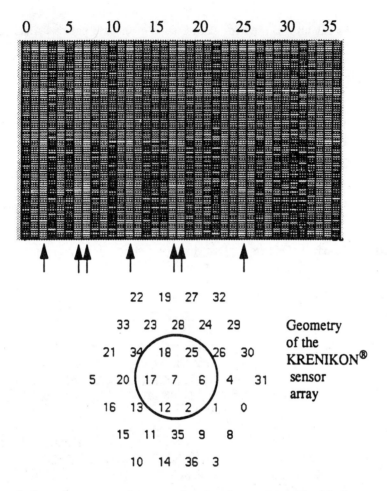

Fig. 4: Less important input nodes (top) correspond with the magnetic sensors within the
marked circle in center of the sensor array (bottom).

Currently our results indicate that the network with radial basis functions gives similar performance as a sigmoidal feed-forward net. The net with the radial basis functions has the advantage that further background knowledge about the physically underlying processes can be collected. This can be obtained by analyzing the covariance matrices of the basis functions, e.g. the weight matrices of the trained network. Another advantage of this architecture is the possibility of pre-structuring (table 1) the net parameters which accelerates the training phase.

Our method for the classification of magnetic maps will soon be implemented for the use in practical applications. Work in progress includes the investigation how these networks can also be used for classification of electric potentials and for source reconstruction itself.

REFERENCES

/ASU 92/   Abraham-Fuchs, K.; Schlang, M.; Übler, J.; Hellstrand, E.; Stefan H.: Map Classification in the Magnetoencephalogram by Neural Networks, Proc. 14. Ann. Int. Conf. IEEE Eng. in Med. & Biol. Soc, Lyon, 1992.

/DH 73/   Duda, R. O.;Hart, P. E.: Pattern Classification and Scene Analysis, Wiley-Interscience, 1973.

/HT 92/   Hollatz, J.; Tresp, V.: A Rule-based Network Architecture, Artifical Neural Network II, I. Aleksander, J. Taylor,eds., Elsevier, Amsterdam, 1992.

/MD 90/   Moody, J.; Darken, C.: Fast adaptive k-means clustering: Some emperical Results, Proc. Int. Joint Conf. on Neural Networks, San Diego, 1990.

/TLS 92/   Tresp, V.; Leuthäusser, I.; Schlang, M.; Neuneier, R.; Abraham-Fuchs, K.; Härer, W.: The Neural Impulse Response Filter, Artifical Neural Networks II, Elsevier, 1992.

/SHR 90/   Schneider, S.; Hoenig, E.; Reichenberger, H.; Abraham-Fuchs, K.; Daalmans, G.; Moshage, W.; Oppelt, A.; Röhrlein, G. Stefan, H.; Vieth, J.; Weikl, A.; Wirth, A.: A Multichannel Biomagnetic System for High Resolution Functional Studies of Brain and Heart, Radiology, Vol. 176, pp 825 - 830, 1990.

/SSA 90/   Stefan, H.; Schneider, S.; Abraham-Fuchs, K.; Bauer, J.; Feistel, H.; Pawlik, G.; Neubauer, U.; Röhrlein, G.; Huk, H. J.: Magnetic source localisation in focal epilepsy: Multichannel magnetoencephalography correlated with magnetic resonance brain imaging, Brain, 113, 1990.

/STA 92/   Schlang, M.F.; Tresp, V.; Abraham-Fuchs, K.; Härer, W.; Weismüller, P.: Neural Networks for Segmentation and Clustering of Biomagnetic Signals, Proc. IEEE Workshop on Neural Networks for Signal Processing, Copenhagen, 1992.

/THA 93/   Tresp, V.; Hollatz, J.; Ahmad, S.: Network Structuring and Training using Rule-based Knowledge, to appear in Advances in Neural Information Processing System 5, C. L. Giles, S. J. Hanson, J. D. Cowan, eds., Morgan Kaufmann, San Mateo, CA, 1993.

Chapter 13
Medical Image Processing

Like medical signal processing, where time series data is processed to assist in making health care decisions, medical image processing with neural networks can present several advantages. In this chapter are five papers that emphasize how neural networks are being used to process different types of medical image data. **Paper 13.1** describes how lung nodules can be detected in X-rays using multilayer perceptron (MLP) neural networks. **Paper 13.2** describes a classification system that combines fuzzy min-max neural networks and MLP neural networks to identify different cardiac tissue types in echocardiograms. **Paper 13.3** explains a linear neural network (ADALINE) reconstruction technique for electrical impedance tomography images. **Paper 13.4** explores the application of MLP neural networks for liver differentiation from echocardiographic images. **Paper 13.5** describes a neural network-based approach to segmenting magnetic resonance brain images.

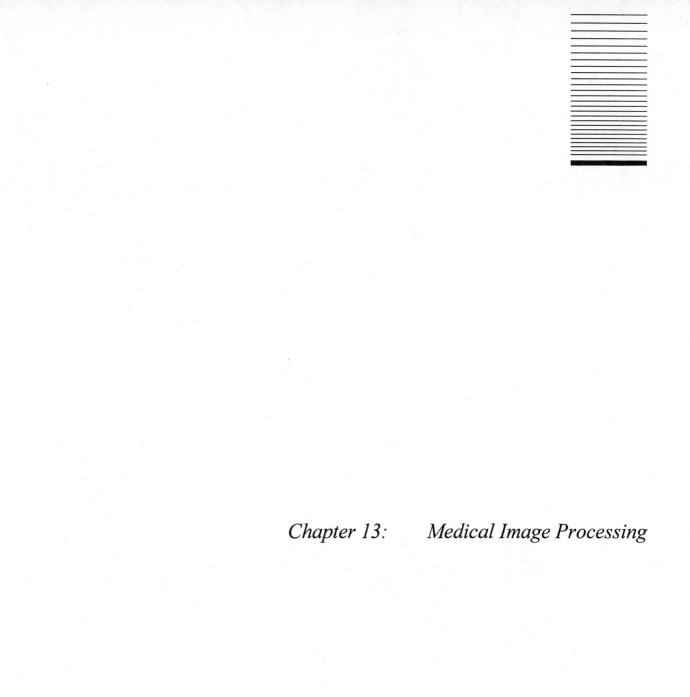

Chapter 13:   *Medical Image Processing*

Application of Neural Network Based Hybrid System for Lung Nodule Detection

Yun-Shu P. Chiou[S], Y. M. Fleming Lure[S], Matthew T. Freedman[#], and Steve Fritz[u]

[S]Caelum Research Corporation, Silver Spring, MD 20901, (TEL) (301) 593-1748, (FAX) (301) 593-3951

[*]Cybernetics Research Lab., E.E. Department, University of Maryland, College Park, MD 20742,

[#]Radiology Department, Georgetown University Medical Center Washington, D.C. 20007

[u]Radiology Department, University of Maryland Baltimore County, MD

Abstract

A Hybrid Lung Nodule Detection (HLND) system based on artificial neural network architectures is developed for improving diagnostic accuracy and speed for lung cancerous pulmonary radiology. The configuration of the HLND system includes the following processing phases: (1) data acquisition and pre-processing, in order to reduce and to enhance the figure-background contrast; (2) quick selection of nodule suspects based upon the most prominent feature of nodules, the disc shape; and (3) complete feature space determination and neural classification of nodules. Nodule suspects are captured and stored in 32 x 32 images after first two processing phases. Eight categories including true nodule, rib-crossing, rib-vessel crossing, end vessel, vessel cluster, bone, rib edge, and vessel are identified for further neural analysis and classification. Extraction of shape features is performed through edge enhancement, self-organized Kohonen feature map, histogram equalization, and evaluation of marginal distribution curves. A supervised back-propagation-trained neural network is developed for recognition of the derived feature curve, a normalized marginal distribution curve. Preliminary results show that this feature set is able to identify true nodule at accuracy up to 93% with false detection reduced down to 7%.

1: Introduction

Lung cancer, next to the heart disease, is the second highest cause of death in the United States. Successful detection of early-stage cancer tumors is able to bring up the cure rate. Detection of lung nodules by using digital image processing techniques has been investigated and demonstrated good results [1, 3, 4, 5, 6, 7, 11]. In spite of the accomplishments of digital computer-based automatic lung nodule detection, differentiation between true and false nodules still remains a challenging problem in terms of achieving high rate of success and fast processing. Application of artificial neural network (ANN) for nodule detection has been successfully used [9] since its superior properties including fault tolerance, generalization, and the capability of learning from training data. Integration of ANNs with digital signal/image processing techniques in a single system for shape feature analysis in diagnostic radiology provides robust recognition performance in the presence of noise and object-to-background sensory uncertainty [2]. Effective differentiation between true and false nodules, primarily due to the anatomic background, by using ANNs still needs further investigated. This paper presents a hybrid computational system called "Hybrid Lung Nodule Detection (HLND) System" for improvement of the performance of detection which includes several processing phases: data acquisition and pre-processing, quick selection of nodule suspects, image analysis of signal-ehnahced image, feature parameter extraction, and neural classification. In this paper, we describe the Hybrid Lung Nodule Detection (HLND) System, discuss feature extraction, image analysis by using self-organized Kohonen feature map, and supervised neural network detection approaches. Summary will also be presented.

2: Hybrid lung nodule detection (HLND) system

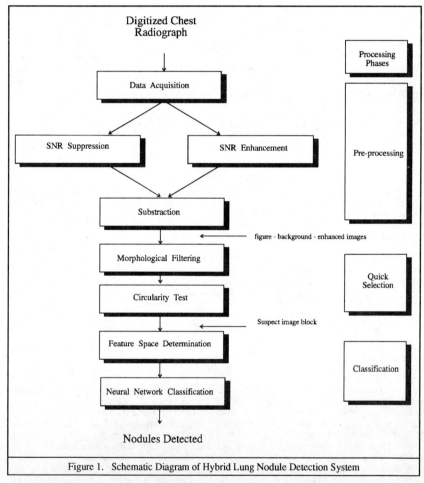

Figure 1. Schematic Diagram of Hybrid Lung Nodule Detection System

The Hybrid Lung Nodule Detection (HLND) System based on artificial neural network (ANN) architectures includes the following process phases: (1) data acquisition and pre-processing, (2) quick selection of nodule suspects, and (3) complete feature space determination and neural detection, as demonstrated in Figure 1.

2.1: Data acquisition and pre-processing

The digital chest images were obtained from Georgetown University Medical Hospital and University of Maryland Medical Hospital. Each pulmonary radiograph was digitized and stored in 500x512x12 bits and contains at least one nodule confirmed by radiologists. Potential nodule information in a pulmonary radiograph is enhanced by a differential technique which subtracts a nodule suppressed image (through a median filter) from a signal enhanced image (through a Laplacian matched filter with a spherical profile) [1, 3, 4, 5, 6, 7, 8]. A difference image, containing nodule-enhanced signal, is used for quick selection processing phase.

2.2: Quick selection

An algorithm is applied for quick (pre-) selection of all possible nodule suspects based mainly upon the most prominent feature of nodule - the disc shape. The difference image is processed by locally-adaptively area extraction process using edge and gray value tracking with different gray values for thresholding [5] and morphological operations [7]. It provides an initial determination of features, arising from nodules and arising from anatomic background. Circularity and effective radius of the segmented image block are evaluated at different thresholding levels to determine the location and the size of the nodule suspects. All the suspect areas (blocks) with dense area (high gray values) equivalent to 3 mm of diameter or less are captured for further evaluation.

2.3: Feature determination and neural classification

Beside the disk shape (including circularity and effective radius), the suspected nodule is analyzed to derive additional relevant parametric measures and characteristic patterns. Analysis of the features between true nodule and false positive nodules in 32x32 image provides several feature vectors for the neural processing. The function of our feature determination and ANN-based classifier architecture in the HLND System is a multistage platform involving a unsupervised self-adaptive output stage (such as Kohonen net [8]), followed by supervised learning processing stage (for example, back propagation ANN [12]). More detailed implementation and results are given in the following sections.

3: Image feature extraction

Anatomic Class								
	RX	RV	VC	EV	RE	BO	VS	TN
No. of samples	96	40	41	43	28	42	15	87
Total suspect image blocks: 392								
Table 1. Eight Types of Anatomic Classes								

After first two processing phases (pre-processing and quick selection), nodule suspect image blocks are determined from each image. Typically, there are 15-30 objects on a radiograph. The nodule suspect is extracted into a 32x32 pixel image (larger than 9 mm in diameter) sufficient for the ANN-based development. After processing 31 radiographs, more than 380 nodule suspects in **original** and **difference** image blocks (32x32 pixel) are obtained for further development of the ANN classification. Among the nodule suspects, 22.2% of them are true positive nodules. Since sufficient data base for various anatomic structures are required for analysis, many false positive nodules are included for further investigation. With properly adjustment of parameters, the success rate in detection of nodule can achieve 70% after first two phases. The suspect image blocks are first classified into 8 classes: true nodule (TN), rib crossing (RX), rib-vessel crossing (RV), vessel cluster (VC), end-vessel (EV), rib edge (RE), bone (BO), and vessel (VS), based on our experience and previous related works [6, 7, 11]. Most of the time, the suspect image blocks contains more than one class of information. It is found that among 392 images 24.5% are rib crossing and 22.2% are true, as shown in Table 1. Since eight (8) categories of anatomic classes are obtained from real radiographs, overlapping of several phenomenon in single image block is quite common. The classification is primarily based on the most dominant anatomic structure in the image. Based on these image blocks, several features are analyzed and extracted.

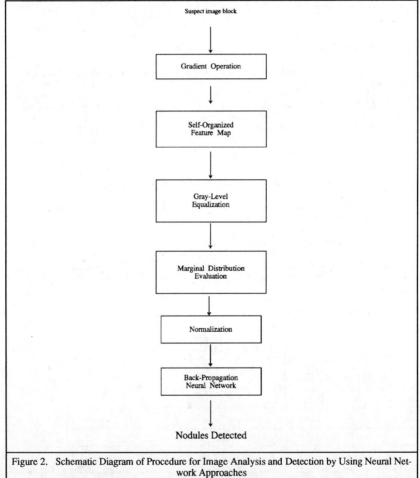

Figure 2. Schematic Diagram of Procedure for Image Analysis and Detection by Using Neural Network Approaches

The computing procedure for this feature estraction and classification include gradient operation, self-organized neural net processing, gray-level equalization, marginal distribution computation, and supervised back-propagation learning and classification, as depicted in Fig. 2. A 1-D histogram of gradient component (either amplitude or orientation) has been applied by Matsumoto et al., [11] for analysis of subtracted image block. In this analysis, we investigated both elements of gradient vector (amplitude and orientation) from original image block. A 3x3 Sobel operator for image edge enhancement is applied to the original image block to obtained two 32 x 32 images: one is amplitude image and another one is orientation image. The orientation angles are within the range between 0 and 360 degree, whereas the amplitude varies from 0 to 1024. Gradient vector pairs are generated within the center area from one image because it was found that most nodules exist in the center of the image blocks. The gradient vectors have long been used for shape identification, edge detection, and other image segmentation tasks.

A self-organized feature map implemented by Kohonen Net [8] is used to analyze the feature vectors. There are 10 x 10 nodes used as output neurons. Output nodes are extensively interconnected with many local connections. For gradient vector components, continuous-values input vectors from each class are presented sequentially in time without specifying the desired output. In the trained feature map of gradient vectors, each weight matrix demonstrates its own patterns similar to a 2-D histogram distribution of amplitude and orientation. The feature map will also guarantee the degree of separability and ensure the trainability of supervised neural network. Each cluster is then identified as certain class for the application of classification and detection. Final trained weights are then processed by using histogram equalization technique to transfer the gray level range into 0-4095 to interpolate amplitude and orientation axis into 32 equally-spaced bins. A typical set of weights (interconnections) of trained Kohonen net containing 8 different classes form a 2-D matrix. Vertical axis corresponds to orientation angles and horizontal axis corresponds to amplitude. By performing the integration with respect to each parameter, two sets of marginal distribution curves are obtained: one for orientation distribution and another one for amplitude distribution. Each distribution is normalized by performing substraction from its DC values, division by its spread from DC, and followed by taking its square. These curves are then used for development of supervised neural classifier in this study.

4: Neural network classification

A supervised back-propagation (BP) neural network classifier is developed for detection of each anatomic structure. The BP ANN classifier contains four layers. Input layer consists of 64 neurons corresponding to combination of both amplitude and orientation bins of marginal distribution. Two hidden layers contains 128 and 64 neurons, which are chosen as multiple of eight (pre-determined anatomic structure classes) since the properties of each class are desired to be coded evenly within the network. Finally a two-neuron output layer is used to classify either true positive or false positive nodules. More than half of the data set are used as training set depending on the results of image shape feature analysis [2]. It takes around 130 epoches to train the BP ANN classifier to learn up to 100% accuracy of the training data set. With a fully-trained BP ANN, the overall classification accuracy reaches up to 97.5%, as shown in Table 2. It is found that the trained BP ANN increases the detection accuracy of true nodule up to 93% with around 7% false detection. By examining the weight matrix, the effect due to different feature (either amplitude or orientation) can be determined. Such implementation can also be easily implemented in a highly parallel, reconfigurable, and scalable, neural network co-processor called MNR [13] for fast and real time processing.

		Actual Structure	
		True Nodule	False Nodule
Classified	True Nodule	93.3%	6.7%
	False Nodule	1.3%	98.7%
Overall Accuracy		97.5%	
Table 2. Classification Accuracy for Nodule Detection			

5: Summary

A neural network-based analysis and detection algorithms are developed for improvement of the performance of Hybrid Lung Nodule Detection (HLND) system. The configuration of the proposed system includes the following processing phases: (1) data acquisition and pre-processing, in order to reduce and to enhance the figure-background contrast; (2) quick selection of nodule suspects based upon the most prominent feature of nodules, the disc shape; and (3) complete feature space determination and neural classification of nodules. After first processing phases, several suspect image blocks are captured. Features extraction and classification are performed through edge enhancement, self-organized Kohonen feature map, gray-level equalization, evaluation of marginal distribution curves, normalization, and supervised back-propagation classification. Preliminary results show that this feature set is able to identify most true nodule at accuracy of 93% with around 7% false detection. More data set are still needed for further improvement of the HLND system.

6: Acknowledgement

This work is supported by grant number 1 R43 CA58116-01 from the National Cancer Institute, National Institute of Health. Its contents are solely the responsibility of the authors and do not necessarily represent the official view of the NCI/NIH.

7: References

1. Chan, H.P., Doi, K., Vyborny, C.J., et al.: "Improvement in Radiologists' Detection of Clustered Microcalcification Mammograms: The Potential of Computer- Aided Diagnosis," Inves. Radio., Vol. 25, 1990, pp. 1102-1110.

2. Chiou, Y.-S. P., Lure, Y.-M. F., P. A. Ligomenides, M. T. Freedman, and S. Fritz, "Shape Feature Analysis Using Artificial Neural Networks for Improvements of Hybrid Lung Nodule Detection (HLND) System ", SPIE Medical Imaging 1993 Symposium, Newport Beach, CA.

3. Doi, K.: "Feasibility of Computer-Aided Diagnosis in Digital Radiography," Jap. J. Radio. Technol. Vol. 45, 1989, pp. 653-663.

4. Doi, K., Giger, M.L., MacMahon, H., et al.: "Clinical Radiology and Computer- Aided Diagnosis: Potential Partner in Medical Diagnosis?," RSNA 1990, Scientific Exhibit, Space 129.

5. Giger, M.L., Doi, K., and MacMahon H.: "Image Feature Analysis and Computer-Aided Diagnosis in Digital Radiography. 3. Automated Detection of Nodules in Peripheral Lung Field," Med. Phy. Vol. 15, 1988, pp. 158-166.

6. Giger, M.L., Doi, K., and MacMahon, H., et al.: "Pulmonary Nodules: Computer- Aided Detection in Digital Chest Images," RadioGraphics, Vol. 10, 1990, pp. 41- 51.

7. Giger, M.L., Ahn, N., Doi, K., MacMahon, H., Metz, C.E.: "Computerized Detection of Pulmonary Nodules in Digital Chest Images: Use of Morphological Filters in Reducing False-Positive Detec-tions" Med. Phys., Vol. 17, 1990, pp. 861-865.

8. Kohonen, T., "Self-Organization and Associative Memory", Spring-Verlag, Berlin, 1984.

9. Lin, J.S., Ligomenides, P.A., Lure, Y.M.F., Lo, B.S. and Freedman, M.T.: "Application of Artificial Neural Networks for Improvements of Lung Nodule Detection," Proc. Symposium for Computer Assisted Radiology, S/CAR '92, SCAR, Baltimore, June 14-17, 1992.

10. Matsumto, T., H. Yoshimura, K. Doi, M. L. Giger, A. Kano, H. MacMahon, K. Abe, and S. Montner, "Image Feature Analysis of False-Positive Diagnosis Produced by Automated Detection of Lung Nodules", Investigative Radiology, 1992, pp. 587-597.

11. Montain, C.F.: "Value of the New TNM Staging System for Lung Cancer," 5th World Conference on Lung Cancer, CHEST:96/1, 1989, pp. 47s-49s.

12. Rumelhart, D.E., McClelland, J.L., Parallel Distributed Processing: Explorations in the Micro-structure of Cognition, MIT Press, 1986.

13. Ligomenides, P.A., Jump, L. B. and Chiou, Y-S: "A Reconfigurable Ring Architecture for Large Scale Neural Networks," Conf. Fuzzy and Neual System and Vehi. Appli., 1991, Tokyo, Japan.

Echocardiogram Structure and Tissue Classification Using Hierarchical Neural Networks

Tom Brotherton, Tom Pollard, and Karen Haines
ORINCON Corp.
9363 Towne Centre Dr.
San Diego, CA 92121

Anthony DeMaria
UCSD Medical Center
200 West Arbor Dr.
San Diego, CA 92103

A system to automatically classify structures and tissues in echocardiogram images is presented. Structure classification is the first step required for any system that is designed to measure cardiac parameters. Described here is a multiple feature, hierarchical neural network fusion solution to the problem. The system 'learns' to classify tissue types by examination of image training data. Classification assigns each image pixel a fuzzy membership measure for each structure or tissue type. Final hard classification, if required, is delayed until the system's output stage. This allows important "fuzzy" information to be retained throughout the system. The first layer in the hierarchy of networks determines gross cardiac structures. The second layer accounts for spatial dependence and fuses other useful information, such as motion and local texture measurements to make the final classifications. Here we focus on the processing to identify structures with in the images.

1. INTRODUCTION

A problem of interest is the automated classification of structures and tissue types in echocardiogram images. This processing is the first step required for any system that is designed to measure cardiac parameters such as volume, wall thickness, and ejection efficiency. Current state-of-the-art requires human expertise. For example, to measure ejection efficiency, a technician is required to outline a ventricular cavity in order to identify its approximate location. Edge detection is then used with in this outline to determine ventricular parameters.

We introduce here a multiple feature, hierarchical neural network fusion solution to the problem. This approach has been used successfully to solve detection and classification problems in other medical applications, underwater acoustics, and mechanical system fault diagnosis[1],[2][3]. The system functions more closely to how a human would interpret the images.

2. METHOD

Figure 1 shows a high level processing flow diagram used for the tissue classification system. Inputs to the system are sets of pixels that contain the raw image as well as motion and texture features [4]. There are two layers of processing in the system. The first layer is designed to determine gross cardiac structures. Each of the first layer feature extractors / neural nets is optimized to detect and classify a single structure type. The second layer of the network fuses the outputs from the first layer along with texture information to make a final classification decision. The second layer accounts for the spatial relationship between the gross

structures. Each of the networks used is a fuzzy min-max neural network developed by Simpson [5],[6]. The fuzzy neural net in essence assigns a fuzzy membership value to the pixel to be classified. Thus no hard tissue or structure class decision need to be made until the final system output.

3. RESULTS

Described here is the structure classification portion of the system. Thus we identify gross regions in the image. For example, we identify those regions where valves will be present, but do no track the moving valve. Future systems will perform that tracking. The four chamber apical echocardiogram view was used. Data from 8 patients was collected. The patient data was divided into testing and training sets (4 patients each). Images were digitized at 5 frames a second. Approximately one full heart beat cycle was used. Each of the images was then ground truthed as to structure and tissue type. There were 20 images used for training and 20 images used for testing.

Inputs to the first layer structure nets were compressed (64:1) images. Compression was done using simple pixel averaging. There were 9 structures identified (shown in table I). For identification of cardiac structures, two dimensional subset of pixels were selected from the reduced image as input to the neural net. Each of the extractor / neural nets in the first layer is looking for a single structure type. The size of the 2-D pixel subsets were selected to give the best classification performance for each structure to be identified.

Figure 2 shows an example input image. Figure 3 shows the results of parsing that image to identify cardiac structures with our approach. It can be seen that all of the structural regions of the image have been correctly classified. Table I is a confusion matrix that indicates the performance of the system over all the test samples. The worst classification performance is 67% correct classification for the tricuspid valve. The addition of full resolution texture and motion information will improve the valve classification.

4. CONCLUSIONS

We have presented a general approach to perform classification of structure and tissue types in echocardiogram images. The approach can be applied to a wide variety of medical image processing problems. The system works well for classifying gross cardiac structures in echocardiogram images. Future development will fuse motion and texture information with the structure information to give fine level structure and tissue classification.

5. REFERENCES

[1] T. Brotherton and E. Mears, "Application of Neural Nets to Feature Fusion," *Proc. of the 26th Asilomar Conf. on Signals, Systems, & Computers*, Oct. 1992, Pacific Grove, CA.

[2] T. Brotherton, T. Pollard, and D. Jones, "Application of Time-Frequency and Time-Scale Representations to Fault Detection and Classification," *Proc. of the IEEE-SP Int'l. Symposium on Time-Frequency and Time-Scale Analysis*, Oct. 1992, Victoria, B.C.

[3] M.Wiederhold, T.Brotherton, T.Pollard, and T.Rickard, "Artificial Neural Network Evaluation of Acoustic Doppler ULtrsound", *The 37th Annual Conv. of the American Inst. of Ultrasound in Medicine*, March 1993, Honolulu, HI .

[4] R.M.Haralick, "Statistical and Structural Approaches to Texture", *Proc. of the IEEE*, Vol. 67, No. 5, May 1979.

[5] P.K.Simpson, "Fuzzy Min-Max Neural Networks - Part 1: Classification", *IEEE Trans. on Neural Networks*, Vol. 3, No. 5, Sept. 1992.

[6] P.K.Simpson, "Fuzzy Min-Max Neural Networks - Part 2: Clustering", *IEEE Trans. on Fuzzy Systems*, Vol. 1 No. 1, Feb. 1993.

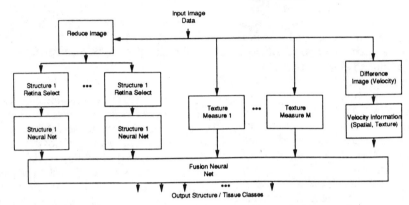

Figure 1 - Processing Flow Diagram

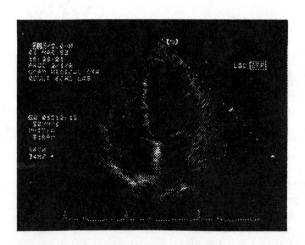

Figure 2 - Input Image

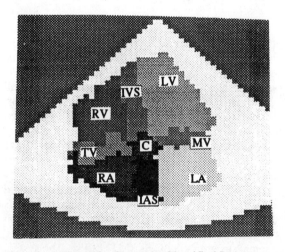

Figure 3 - Structure Classified Image

	Label	IAS	IVS	LV	C	RV	LA	RA	MV	TV	Other
Interatrial Septum	IAS	.94			.07		.17	.09			.09
Interventricular Septum	IVS		.74	.01	.03	.09				.09	.06
Left Ventricle	LV		.02	.90	.01		.01	.05	.04	.09	.03
Crux	C	.05	.04		.71		.04	.02	.01	.03	.04
Right Ventricle	RV		.02	.01		.85		.03		.09	.04
Let Atrium	LA	.01		.02	.06		.91		.19		
Right Atrium	RA				.02	.02		.83		.17	.01
Mitral Valve	MV			.03	.01		.02		.72		
Tricuspid Valve	TV				.02	.05			.09	.67	
Other	Other	.01	.18	.02	.07	.07	.01	.03	.04	.02	.80

Table I Confusion Matrix

IMAGE RECONSTRUCTION IN ELECTRICAL IMPEDANCE TOMOGRAPHY: A NEURAL NETWORK APPROACH

Andy ADLER, Robert GUARDO, Greg SHAW
Institut de Génie Biomédical
Ecole Polytechnique et Université de Montréal
Montréal, Québec, CANADA, H3C 3A7

ABSTRACT - **Reconstruction of images in electrical impedance tomography requires the solution of an inverse problem which is typically ill-conditioned due to the effects of noise and therefore requires regularisation based on a priori knowledge. This paper presents a linear reconstruction technique using neural networks which adapts the solution to the noise level used during the training phase. Results show a significantly improved resolution compared to the weighted equipotential backprojection method.**

INTRODUCTION

Electrical Impedance Tomography estimates the conductivity distribution of a medium from potential measurements produced by injected currents on the medium boundary. We are interested in dynamic imaging, which estimates conductivity changes in the medium from changes in these measurements, because these changes in measurements are much more stable than the measurements themselves to variations in electrode position, resistance, and amplifier gain.

The best image reconstruction techniques are based on fitting the measured voltages to finite element models (FEMs) of tissue conductivity. This inverse problem, however, is ill-posed for any reasonable number of elements (>50) in noisy data. Regularization, based on a priori knowledge of the problem is typically necessary. The neural network approach, however, can be used to calculate a linear inverse to the problem without any need of a priori knowledge.

FORWARD PROBLEM

Using the FEM, we simulate the voltage measurement vector by

$$v = F(r_h + r) = \frac{1}{\exp(r_h)} F(r) \qquad (1)$$

where r_h is the uniform homogenous log conductivity, r is a vector of the M element log conductivity changes, and F is a linear function of the injected current and a non-linear function of r. The voltage measurements are obtained from a 16 electrode system, using 16 current injection patterns, resulting in $N=256$ differential voltage readings. From (1) we calculate our dynamic measurement vector f by

$$f_i = \frac{[v_{inhom}]_i - [v_{hom}]_i}{[v_{hom}]_i} = \frac{F(r)_i}{F(0)_i} - 1 , \text{ for } 1 \le i \le N \qquad (2)$$

where $[v_{hom}]_i$ and $[v_{inhom}]_i$ represent the ith element of the voltage measurement vector before and after, respectively, a conductivity change.

We look for a linear approximation to this problem, in order to simplify the design and reduce the training time of the neural network. Linearizing about r = 0 results in:

$$f = Yr \quad \text{where,} \quad Y_{ij} = \frac{1}{F(0)} \frac{\partial F_i}{\partial r_j} . \qquad (3)$$

INVERSE PROBLEM

This inverse problem may be stated as finding the matrix Z which, in the presence of noise n, best approximates,

$$r \approx Z(f + n) \qquad (4)$$

in the least squared error sense. The neural network model considered here is the "adaptive linear element", or ADALINE[2]. One ADALINE corresponds to each value of r and sums each value of f by the corresponding row in Z. The values of Z are calculated or "trained" by the Widrow-Hoff learning rule, using a set of input vectors f_k and their (known) desired responses from the network d_k. Training aims to reduce the error ϕ for all training sets k.

$$\phi = \sum_k (d_k - Zf_k)^t (d_k - Zf_k) \qquad (5)$$

We choose the desired responses to be individual objects in each element, i.e. the column vectors of $I_{n \times n}$, and we obtain the input vectors from the direct problem, $f = YI = Y$. In order to train the network to deal with noise, we must include the expected noise in the input. Using this training set we carry out the following algorithm:

- Initially, all weights are set to zero.

- The training vectors are presented to the current network weights, outputting: $O = Z_k(Y + n)$

- The error $E = O - D$ is defined as the difference between the output, O, and the desired response, $D = I_{n \times n}$

- Network weights are updated by the learning rule:
$$Z_{k+1} = Z_k - \alpha E O^t \qquad (6)$$

In-Vivo Ultrasound Liver Differentiation using Artificial Neural Network

D. Zatari and N. Botros
Department of Electrical Engineering, Southern Illinois University
Carbondale,
Illinois 62901

Abstract

This paper presents a pattern recognition algorithm and describes required instrumentation for in-vivo ultrasound human liver differentiation. A 50-MHz microprocessor-based data acquisition and analysis system is designed and constructed to capture, digitize and store the ultrasound backscattered signal. The algorithm is based on a multilayer perceptron neural network using the backpropagation training procedure. The network is implemented to differentiate between normal and abnormal liver. The acoustic attenuation coefficient is calculated using the log spectral difference technique over the frequency range from 1.5 to 4.5 MHz. The change of speed of sound with frequency (dispersion) is estimated over the 3 MHz bandwidth. The attenuation and velocity dispersion are used as differentiation features. The results show that out of 30 cases, the system differentiated correctly 27 and 28 using the attenuation and the velocity dispersion, respectively.

Keywords: In-vivo ultrasound differentiation   Attenuation coefficient
        Velocity dispersion   Artificial neural networks

1: Introduction

Ultrasound imaging has proved to be a powerful tool in characterizing the state of soft tissues such as human liver for medical diagnostic purposes. Most conventional ultrasound imaging instruments present two dimensional images based mainly upon the amplitude of the returned rf signal [1],[2]. The brightness of the pixels comprising the image is a function of the amplitude of the backscattered signal. By observing the brightness and the texture of the image, the radiologist can determine whether or not the tissue is normal. However, in some cases it may be difficult to diagnose the tissue from this image alone, and a biopsy examination must be conducted. This image, moreover, may not provide definitive information about the type of abnormality present. Quantitative analysis often includes feature extraction from the signal followed by a pattern recognition algorithm to diagnose the tissue. The pattern recognition algorithms employed are mainly Bayes and nearest neighbor statistical classifiers. The goal of the present study is to enhance the capability of diagnosing disorders of tissues and organs. The approach taken involves analyzing quantitatively the backscattered signal and applying a powerful pattern recognition technique based on artificial neural networks. This method of interrogating the tissue is believed to be easier than visual interpretation of the time domain B-Scan image. Accurate results may preclude the need for biopsy examination.

2: Theoretical Analysis

2.1: Estimation of the attenuation coefficient for human liver

A theoretical model is developed to determine the features that can be extracted from the backscattered signal. The model is represented as

$$E_r(f) = H(f) \cdot E_t(f) \qquad (1)$$

where $E_r(f)$ is the power spectrum of the backscattered signal from a selected region of the liver, $E_t(f)$ is the power spectrum of the transmitted pulse from the ultrasound transducer, and $H(f)$ is the transfer function of the liver. Based on the model, and the scattering geometry given by [2], the attenuation coefficient can be expressed as

$$\alpha(f) = \frac{1}{2dx} \cdot \ln\left(\frac{E_r(x_1, f)}{E_r(x_2, f)}\right) \qquad (2)$$

where $E_r(x_1, f)$ and $E_r(x_2, f)$ represent the power spectra of the backscattered signal from depths x_1 and x_2, respectively, and $dx = x_2 - x_1$.

2.2: Estimation of velocity dispersion in human liver

Ultrasonic dispersion is difficult to measure accurately in soft tissue, because of its relatively small value and because methods of high accuracy are generally not available. However, dispersion can be estimated from knowledge of the attenuation coefficient using Kramers-Kronig relationships [3]. It can be shown that the dispersion can be written as

$$\delta c(\omega) = \frac{2c_0^2}{2\pi dx \omega^2} \cdot \sum_{\omega_0}^{\omega} \ln\left(\frac{E_r(x_1, f)}{E_r(x_2, f)}\right) \cdot \Delta\omega \qquad (3)$$

with $\delta c(\omega) = c(\omega) - c_0$ and $c(\omega)$ is the phase velocity at a convenient reference frequency ω_0 and speed c_0, and ω is the maximum frequency encountered.

3: Data acquisition system

The power spectrum of the ultrasound backscattered signal should be measured to determine the attenuation coefficient. A high speed data acquisition and analysis system was designed and constructed to capture, digitize and store the signal from different depths of the liver specimen. The digitized data is transferred to a personal computer for processing. The system was coupled to an ultrasound diagnostic machine. A block diagram of the system is shown in Fig.1.

4: Data collection and processing

In order to test the hypotheses culminating in equations 2 and 3, of the data of Ref. 1 were employed. These data were collected from 18 normal liver subjects and 12 abnormal liver subjects. The normality and abnormality were determined using an ATL (Advanced Technology Laboratory) ultrasound diagnostic machine MK-500 B-scanner, with a 3 MHz center frequency, and abnormality was confirmed by biopsy examination. Data were collected from different depths of 5 , 6.5 , and 8 cm. A sampling window, predetermined to be 32 (approximately equivalent to 4.8 cm of liver tissue), allowed the digital data to be gathered during this time interval. At each depth, and for every collection cycle, the backscattered signal was sampled eight times and stored in eight files on the microcomputer under names given by the operator. A Fast Fourier Transform (FFT) is applied to the 512 data points, and the power spectrum is calculated. Digital filtering and frequency histograms techniques are employed. This process reduced the data points of each file to 33. The attenuation coefficient and velocity dispersion (see Fig. 2) are calculated using equations 2 and 3 respectively.

5: Differentiation algorithm using the artificial neural network

A computer program was written to perform the analysis described in sections 2 and 3. The algorithm is primarily based on the use of the neural network as a pattern classifier (see Figs. 3 and 4). A feedforward network with one hidden layer of size 15 nodes was chosen for its relative simplicity and power. The network is used to differentiate among the states of liver, which would be normal or abnormal. The input to the network is a continuous valued vector

$$y_j = f\left(\sum w_{ij} - \theta_j\right) \quad \text{with} \quad f(\alpha) = \frac{1}{1 + e^{-\alpha}} \quad (4)$$

where θ_j is the offset (bias) of node j , w_{ij} is the weight of the connection between node j and node i , and the function is the sigmoid non linearity. The network is trained using the delta rule with momentum. The weights and offsets are adjusted recursively using the formulas

$$w_{ij}^{new} = w_{ij}^{old} + \mu\varepsilon_j x_i \quad \text{and} \quad \theta_j^{new} = \theta_j^{old} + \mu\varepsilon_j^{'} \quad (5)$$

where μ is the gain factor and is assumed to be 0.5 and ε_j is the error. The weights are considered stabilized if the value of each new weight is 99% of its previous value. If node j is an output node, then

$$\varepsilon_j = y_j\left(1 - y_j\right)\left(d_j - y_j\right) \quad (6)$$

where d_j is the desired output of node j, and y_j is the actual output. The desired output for all output nodes is set to either 0 or 1. If node j is a hidden node, then

$$\varepsilon_j = y_j\left(1 - y_j\right)\sum_k \varepsilon_k w_{jk} \quad (7)$$

where k is over all nodes in the layers above node j. After training is completed, any arbitrary vector, either for the attenuation or for velocity dispersion , can be applied as an input to the network for differentiation purposes.

6: Results

Twenty four files per case at depths 5 , 6.5 , and 8 cm of known classes (regions) were taken as a test set. Data stored in these files were processed, and the two classes (normal and abnormal) determined by the network. The results show that out of 30 cases the system diagnosed correctly 27 and 28 using attenuation and dispersion, respectively. The reasons for the failed cases may be due to noise generated by the system and/ or interference of the examiner by shaking his/her hand while holding the transducer, etc. However, the results of differentiation indicate that the system is working satisfactorily. The average dispersion in normal liver was found to be 0.7 m/s/MHz and in the abnormal cases is 1 m/s/MHz. These findings are in agreement with other investigators including [3].

7: Concluding remarks

It can be claimed that dispersive effects on liver are correspondingly negligible. This conclusion is also supported by [3]. The calculated quantities of attenuation and dispersion are used to identify liver pathologies. Despite the fact of small dispersion, it has been shown in this study that the magnitude of dispersion can be used as a useful discriminator. The results obtained for the estimated attenuation coefficient and the dispersion using this scheme and for the cases examined, suggest that in-vivo human liver differentiation for normal and abnormal cases can be achieved.

8: References

[1] N. M. Botros,"A PC-Based Tissue Classification System using Artificial Neural Networks,"
    IEEE Trans. on Measurement, vol.41, no. 5. pp. 12-18, Oct. 1992.
[2] A. Shumulewitz, "Ultrasonic Multifeature Maps of Liver Based on an Amplitude Loss Technique and Conventional B-Scan,"IEEE Trans. on Biomed. Eng., vol. 39, no. 5, May 1992.
[3] M. O'Donnell, E. T. Jaynes, and J. G. Miller, "Kramers-Kronig relationship between ultrasonic attenuation and phase velocity," J. Acoust. Soc. Am. vol. 69, pp. 12-18, 1981.

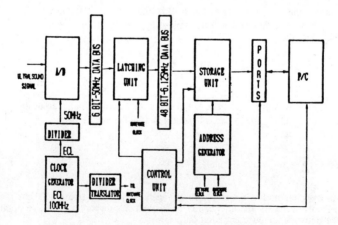

Figure 1: A block diagram of the system

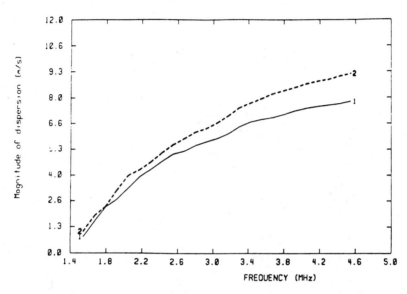

Figure 2 : Average ultrasound velocity dispersion vs frequency for (1)normal and (2)abnormal liver specimens

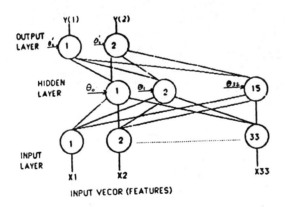

Figure 3: The artificial neural network

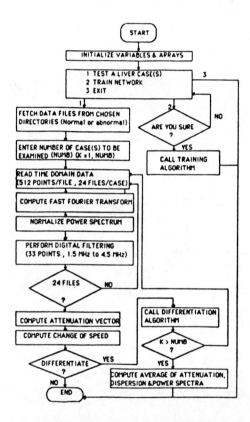

Figure 4: Overall differentiation algorithm

NEURAL NETWORKS FOR MODEL–BASED SEGMENTATION
OF MR BRAIN IMAGES

Gene Gindi
Department of Radiology
SUNY at Stony Brook
Stony Brook, NY 11794-8460

Anand Rangarajan
Department of Computer Science
Yale University
New Haven, CT 06520-2158

I. George Zubal
Department of Diagnostic Radiology
Yale University School of Medicine
New Haven, CT 06510-3333

ABSTRACT

Automated segmentation of magnetic resonance (MR) brain imagery into anatomical regions is a complex task that needs contextual guidance to overcome problems associated with noise, missing data, and the overlap of features associated with different anatomical regions. In this work, the contextual information is provided as an anatomical brain atlas. The matching of atlas to image data is represented by a set of deformable contours that seek compromise fits between expected model information and image data.

INTRODUCTION

There has been considerable interest in recent years in the possibility of segmenting anatomical structures as seen in magnetic resonance (MR) scans. By "segment", we imply the labelling of the image at every voxel with the correct anatomical descriptor(s). For example, a given voxel may be labelled with the symbol "caudate". There are many possible applications for a successful segmentation. In surgical planning, the identification and display of specific anatomial structures enables a surgeon to target or avoid such a structure in a surgical approach. A similar situation obtains in radiation therapy, where high-intensity beams of radiation must pass through the least damaging path of normal tissue in order to deposit dose in the target lesion. In many areas of psychiatric research, current hypotheses regarding forms of mental illness are posed in terms of morphometric measurements of brain structures. In such projects, the intended structure must currently be segmented by laborious and expensive human labor. If the patient database is large and the measurements subtle, then an automated or even semi-automated method could be attractive in its repeatibility, possible accuracy, and time savings. Automated segmentation may also find a use as a teaching tool.

METHODS

In this work, we attack a reduced version of the problem. The atlas contour of a single structure (striatum) in a selected transverse slice is obtained from an atlas [1]. The image contour of the same structure is obtained from a transverse MR slice of a given patient. Rather than consider all possible transformations, we have taken an atlas contour that is roughly registered to the image contour.

The atlas, image and deformable contours are represented as lists of coordinates. In our representation, we have taken the number of atlas and deformable contour points to be the same. The image, deformable, and atlas contour points are specified by $\mathbf{x}_i$, $\mathbf{y}_a$, and $\mathbf{z}_a$ respectively. The atlas and deformable contour points share the same index a since they are always in correspondence. We have considerable experience in dealing with the coupled problems of segmentation and correspondence as they arise in object recognition [2]. We now present the energy function for fitting a deformable contour to both atlas and image contours while establishing correspondence.

$$E\left(\{\mathbf{y}_a\}, \{M_{ai}\}\right) = \frac{1}{2}\sum_a \|\mathbf{z}_a - \mathbf{y}_a\|^2 + \frac{\delta}{2}\sum_a \|\mathbf{y}_{a+1} - \mathbf{y}_a\|^2 + \frac{\gamma}{2}\sum_{ai} M_{ai}\|\mathbf{x}_i - \mathbf{y}_a\|^2 \qquad (1)$$

where

$$\sum_a M_{ai} = 1, \quad \sum_i M_{ai} \leq 1 \text{ and } M_{ai} \in \{0, 1\}, \ \forall\, a, i. \qquad (2)$$

In (1), the first term expresses the fact that the deformable contour point $\mathbf{y}_a$ should be close to the atlas contour point $\mathbf{z}_a$. The second term is a smoothness constraint on $\mathbf{y}_a$. The third term expresses the fact that $\mathbf{y}_{ai}$ should be close to its corresponding image point $\mathbf{x}_i$. The actual correspondence is represented by a binary matrix M_{ai} which equals unity when point $\mathbf{x}_i$ corresponds to the point $\mathbf{y}_a$. In our model, we take the number of atlas points to be greater than the number of image data points (factor of two). Then, M_{ai} expresses the fact that for every data point there is at least one corresponding deformable contour point but not vice-versa. This accounts for the constraints in (2).

It would seem that a binary correspondence matrix M_{ai} would be very brittle for this kind of problem since only one deformable contour point is ultimately associated with each image point. Since the number of deformable contour points $\mathbf{y}_a$ outnumber the image points, we could instead associate more than one $\mathbf{y}_a$ to each $\mathbf{x}_a$. The deformable points associated with the image point would all fall within a neighborhood of the image point.

It has been shown [3] that an effective energy function implicitly containing the effect of M_{ai} can be directly derived from statistical physics. The startling feature of this approach is that a correspondence matrix M_{ai} can be constructed for each setting of a control parameter, β. This constructed matrix has the feature of allowing multiple associations between the deformable contour points and the image points and the strength of these associations depends on the value of the parameter. The effective energy function is

$$F\left(\{\mathbf{y}_a\}\right) = \frac{1}{2}\sum_a \|\mathbf{z}_a - \mathbf{y}_a\|^2 + \frac{\delta}{2}\sum_a \|\mathbf{y}_{a+1} - \mathbf{y}_a\|^2 - \frac{1}{\beta}\sum_i \log \sum_a \exp\left(-\frac{\beta\gamma}{2}\|\mathbf{x}_i - \mathbf{y}_a\|^2\right) \qquad (3)$$

The only difference between (1) and (3) is in the third term. M_{ai} has been eliminated and instead we have the $\log\sum\exp(\cdot)$ expression. An immediate connection between (1) and (3) can be established by "running steepest descent" on our new energy function. This obtains:

$$\frac{d\mathbf{y}_a}{dt} = -\left(\mathbf{y}_a - \mathbf{z}_a\right) + \delta\left(\mathbf{y}_{a+1} - 2\mathbf{y}_a + \mathbf{y}_{a-1}\right) - \gamma\sum_i M_{ai}\left(\mathbf{y}_a - \mathbf{x}_i\right) \qquad (4)$$

where we have identified

$$M_{ai} = \frac{\exp\left(-\frac{\beta\gamma}{2}\|\mathbf{x}_i - \mathbf{y}_a\|^2\right)}{\sum_b \exp\left(-\frac{\beta\gamma}{2}\|\mathbf{x}_i - \mathbf{y}_b\|^2\right)}. \qquad (5)$$

This expression for M_{ai} exhibits the feature of multiple associations each of whose strengths depends on the value of the global parameter β.

The above formulation keeps the image data $\mathbf{x}_i$ fixed. Clearly, this is inadequate. We would like to extract a new image contour directly from the MR image after updating it with reference to an atlas. To achieve this, the deformable contour must interact directly with the MR image data and not merely with a possible incorrect initial contour estimate ($\mathbf{x}_i$). It is possible to couple a low-level contour extraction algorithm with the above energy function thereby achieving our goal of direct interaction with a gray-level image.

A new energy function that achieves this is

$$G\left(\{\mathbf{y}_i\}, \{M_{ai}\}\right) = \frac{1}{2}\sum_{ai} M_{ai}\|\mathbf{z}_a - \mathbf{y}_i\|^2 + \frac{\delta}{2}\sum_i \|\mathbf{y}_{i+1} - \mathbf{y}_i\|^2 - \frac{\gamma}{2}\sum_i \|\nabla I(\mathbf{y}_i)\|^2. \qquad (6)$$

In the above equation, the match matrix has been moved over to a correspondence between the deformable contour and the atlas. The remaining two terms correspond to a first order "snake" [4]. Snakes are deformable contours that move across the image under mathematical forces that seek to corral anatomical regions. Typically, the mathematical representation of a snake is that of a closed contour; the pixels inside the contour are then considered to be members of a given region. Snakes are driven by dynamics that seek to minimize an objective function. The objective function contains terms that seek consistency of the snake with image features along with a degree of smoothness of the contour. A typical data-consistency term seeks to position the snake over a locus of high magnitude intensity gradients in the image.

We now have all the elements in place to specify our algorithm. Once the atlas and image contours are approximately registered, we insert them into the energy function that is then minimized with respect to the deformable contour $\mathbf{y}_a$. The energy function is first minimized for low values of β and then β is increased. Any standard descent algorithm can be used to minimize the energy function (we used conjugate gradient) at a fixed value of β.

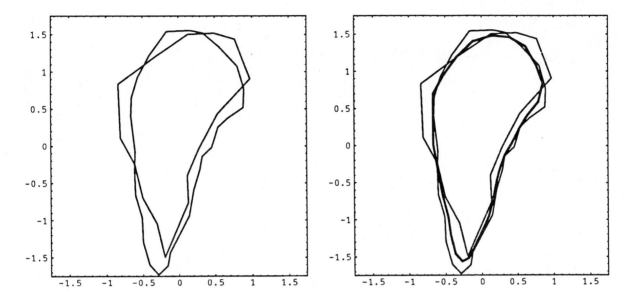

Figure 1: Left: Partially registered contours, Right: Deformable contour with $\delta = 1$ and $\gamma = 1$

RESULTS

Results are obtained for the case corresponding to (3). Currently, we are working on an implementation of (6) in which a snake is guided by the atlas data.

In Figure 1(a), an approximately registered version of the two contours is shown. Then in Figure 1(b), the results of running our network for the parameter settings of $\delta = 1$ and $\gamma = 1$ are shown. This is the choice for which no energy term in (1) is favored. In the figure, the deformable contour is displayed as a thick line. The deformable contour is relatively smooth and does not show excessive adherence to the atlas or image data.

DISCUSSION AND CONCLUSIONS

The segmentation of brain images into anatomical regions poses a complex task with potentially useful payoffs. While the problem is far from trivial, the fact that brain anatomy is topologically ordered and grossly similar in shape details from patient to patient makes the problem perhaps tractable. It appears that a variety of approaches may be needed to successfully segment the brain; for example, the grey – white matter boundaries may be difficult to model with an atlas as there is no "prototypical" boundary of this sort.

References

[1] J. Talairach and P. Tournoux, *"Co-Planar Stereotaxic Atlas of the Human Brain"*, Thieme Medical Publisher, Inc., New York, 1988.

[2] E. Mjolsness, G. Gindi, and P. Anandan, "Optimization in Model Matching and Perceptual Organization", *Neural Computation*, 1, pp. 218–229, 1989.

[3] P. D. Simic, "Statistical mechanics as the underlying theory of 'elastic' and 'neural' optimisations", *Network*, 1, pp. 89–103, 1990.

[4] D. Terzopoulos, J. Platt, A. Barr, and K. Fleischer, "Elastically Deformable Models", *Computer Graphics*, vol. 21(4), pp. 205–214, July 1987.

Part IV: Information Processing

It is estimated that the total amount of information produced since the beginning of recorded history is doubling every five years. Information processing, as defined within this context, is information that is not derived from sensors. The ability for humans to process this data has become impossible without the aide of computer-based automation. Neural networks are being employed in increasing numbers to assists humans with the daunting task of information processing. The following chapters describe four specific areas where neural networks are being applied to information processing. These areas include: Character Recognition (Chapter 14), Financial Processing (Chapter 15), Information Retrieval (Chapter 16), and Natural Language Processing (Chapter 17).

Character recognition has become a reality within many contexts. Ten top computers such as Apple's Newton have shown that handwritten data entry is possible. In addition, the U.S. Internal Revenue Service and the U.S. Postal Service have both initiated large programs for automated character recognition. In this chapter are several examples of how neural networks are being applied to different aspects of character recognition. The chapter opens up with a survey paper, **Paper 14.1,** that evaluates several different character recognition systems (neural network and others) using the National Institute of Standards and Technology's English character database. **Paper 14.2** describes the use of radial basis function (RBF) networks for recognizing degraded text. **Paper 14.3** presents the application of the hierarchical Neocognitron neural network for the difficult task of recognizing connected handwritten English characters. **Paper 14.4** reviews recent results in translation and scale invariant recognition of Tamil characters using the multilayer perceptron (MLP neural network. **Paper 14.5** also employs the MLP neural network, but here it is used for the automatic recognition of Arabic text. **Paper 14.6** applies the learning vector quantization (LVQ) neural network to printed Japanese characters. The last three papers focus on different aspects of Chinese character recognition. **Paper 14.7** describes the use of multiple convolution neural networks for the on-line character recognition. **Paper 14.8** presents the use of hybrid version of ARTMAP for shift invariant character recognition. **Paper 14.9** reviews a dynamic signature verification system that employs a Bayesian neural network.

Chapter 14:   *Character Recognition*

Evaluation of Character Recognition Systems

C. L. Wilson

National Institute of Standards and Technology
Gaithersburg. MD 20899

Abstract

At the first Census Optical Character Recognition Systems (COCRS) Conference, National Institute of Standards and Technology (NIST) produced accuracy data for more than 40 character recognition systems. The recognition experiments were performed on sample sizes of 58.000 digits. and 12.000 upper and lower case alphabetic characters. The algorithms used by the 26 conference participants included rule-based methods. image-based methods. statistical methods. and neural networks. The neural network methods included Multi-Layer Perceptron's, Learned Vector Quantization, Neocognitrons. and cascaded neural networks.

In this paper 11 different COCRS systems are evaluated using correlations between the answers of different systems. comparing the decrease in error rate as a function of confidence of recognition. and comparing the writer dependence of recognition. This comparison shows that methods that used different algorithms for feature extraction and recognition performed with very high levels of correlation. Subsquent experiments were performed by NIST to compare the OCR accuracy of various neural network and statistical classification systems. For each neural network system a statistical system of comparable accuracy was developed. These experiments tested seven different classifiers using 11 different feature sets and obtained OCR error levels between 2.5% and 5.1% for the best feature set sizes. This similarity in accuracy is true for neural network systems and statistically based systems and leads to the conclusion that neural networks have *not* yet demonstrated a clear superiority to more conventional statistical methods in either the COCRS test or in independent tests at NIST.

1 Introduction

At the first COCRS Conference a large number of systems (40 for digits) were used to recognize the same sample of characters [1]. A summary of these results is given in Table 1. Neural network systems. systems combining neural network methods with other methods (hybrid system). and systems based entirely on statistical pattern recognition methods were submitted to the COCRS conference. This provides a large test sample which can be used to detect differences between these various methods. In addition. subsequent test at NIST [2] using a seven different neural network (NN) and statistical classifiers confirmed that using a fixed set of features both types of methods have similar accuracies.

In this paper 11 different COCRS conference systems are discussed in some detail. These system are itemized by type in Table 2. These systems are broken into NN based systems, hybrid systems, and non-NN systems. The author realizes that this distinction is subject to interpretation, but it does allow some useful comparisons to be made. The COCRS conference systems were all designed to use different methods of feature extraction. In order to seperate feature extraction and classification, the image recognition group at NIST performed classification experiments using seven methods of classification and a common set of Karhunen-Loève (KL) based features [3]. The results of these tests are shown in Table 3.

In the past few years NN's have become important as a possible method for constructing computer programs that can solve problems, such as speech and character recognition, where "human-like" response or artificial intelligence is needed. The most useful characteristics of NN's are their ability to learn from examples, their ability to operate in parallel, and their ability to perform well using data that are noisy or incomplete. Many of these characteristics are shared by various statistical pattern recognition methods. These characteristics of pattern recognition systems are important for solving real problems from the field of character recognition exemplified by this paper.

It is important to understand that the accuracy of the trained OCR system produced will be strongly dependent on both the size and the quality of the training data. Many common test examples used to demonstrate the properties of pattern recognition system contain on the order of 10^2 examples. These examples show the basic characteristics of the system but provide only an approximate idea of the system accuracy.

As an example, the first version of an OCR system was built at NIST using 1024 characters for training and testing. This system has an accuracy of 94%. As the sample size was increased the accuracy initially dropped as more difficult cases were included. As the test and training sample reached 10000 characters the accuracy began to slowly improve. The poorest accuracy achieved was with sample sizes near 10^4 and was 85%. The 58.000 digit sample discussed in this paper is well below the 10^5 character sample size which we have estimated is necessary to saturate the learning process of the NIST system [3]. The best system developed by NIST uses probabalistic NNs (PNN) [13] and achieved an accuracy of 2.5% when trained on 7480 digits.

The goal of this paper is to discuss the different kinds of methods used at the COCRS Conference in a way that will illustrate why NN's and statistical methods achieved similar levels of performance. The various methods used are summarized in Figure 1 for classification and

Entered	Percentage Classification Error		
System	Digits	Uppers	Lowers
AEG	3.43 ± 0.23	3.74 ± 0.82	12.74 ± 0.75
ASOL	8.91 ± 0.39	11.16 ± 1.05	21.25 ± 1.36
ATT_1	3.16 ± 0.29	6.55 ± 0.66	13.78 ± 0.90
ATT_2	3.67 ± 0.23	5.63 ± 0.63	14.06 ± 0.95
ATT_3	4.84 ± 0.24	6.83 ± 0.86	16.34 ± 1.11
ATT_4	4.10 ± 0.16	5.00 ± 0.79	14.28 ± 0.98
COMCOM	4.56 ± 0.91	16.94 ± 0.99	48.00 ± 1.87
ELSAGB_1	5.07 ± 0.32		
ELSAGB_2	3.38 ± 0.20		
ELSAGB_3	3.35 ± 0.21		
ERIM_1	3.88 ± 0.20	5.18 ± 0.67	13.79 ± 0.80
ERIM_2	3.92 ± 0.24		
GMD_1	8.73 ± 0.35	14.04 ± 1.00	22.54 ± 1.22
GMD_2	15.45 ± 0.64	24.57 ± 0.91	28.61 ± 1.25
GMD_3	8.13 ± 0.39	14.22 ± 1.09	20.85 ± 1.25
GMD_4	10.16 ± 0.35	15.85 ± 0.95	22.54 ± 1.22
GTESS_1	6.59 ± 0.18	8.01 ± 0.59	17.53 ± 0.75
GTESS_2	6.75 ± 0.30	8.14 ± 0.59	18.42 ± 1.09
HUGHES_1	4.84 ± 0.38	6.46 ± 0.52	15.39 ± 1.10
HUGHES_2	4.86 ± 0.35	6.73 ± 0.64	15.59 ± 1.08
IBM	3.49 ± 0.12	6.41 ± 0.80	15.42 ± 0.95
IFAX	17.07 ± 0.34	19.60 ± 1.26	
KAMAN_1	11.46 ± 0.41	15.03 ± 0.79	31.11 ± 1.15
KAMAN_2	13.38 ± 0.49	20.74 ± 0.88	35.11 ± 1.09
KAMAN_3	13.13 ± 0.45	19.78 ± 0.60	33.55 ± 1.37
KAMAN_4	20.72 ± 0.44	27.28 ± 1.30	46.25 ± 1.23
KAMAN_5	15.13 ± 0.41	33.95 ± 1.22	42.20 ± 0.96
KODAK_1	4.74 ± 0.37	6.92 ± 0.78	14.49 ± 0.77
KODAK_2	4.08 ± 0.26		
MIME	8.57 ± 0.34	10.07 ± 0.81	
NESTOR	4.53 ± 0.20	5.90 ± 0.68	15.39 ± 0.90
NIST_1	7.74 ± 0.31	13.85 ± 0.83	18.58 ± 1.12
NIST_2	9.19 ± 0.32	23.10 ± 0.88	31.20 ± 1.16
NIST_3	9.73 ± 0.29	16.93 ± 0.90	20.29 ± 0.99
NIST_4	4.97 ± 0.30	10.37 ± 1.28	20.01 ± 1.06
NYNEX	4.32 ± 0.22	4.91 ± 0.79	14.03 ± 0.96
OCRSYS	1.56 ± 0.19	5.73 ± 0.63	13.70 ± 0.93
REI	4.01 ± 0.26	11.74 ± 0.90	
RISO	10.55 ± 0.43	14.14 ± 0.88	21.72 ± 0.98
SYMBUS	4.71 ± 0.38	7.29 ± 1.07	
THINK_1	4.89 ± 0.24		
THINK_2	3.85 ± 0.33		
UBOL	4.35 ± 0.20	6.24 ± 0.66	15.48 ± 0.81
UMICH_1		5.11 ± 0.94	15.08 ± 0.92
UPENN	9.08 ± 0.37		
VALEN_1	17.95 ± 0.59	24.18 ± 1.00	31.60 ± 1.33
VALEN_2	15.75 ± 0.32		

Table 1: Mean zero-rejection-rate error rates and standard deviations in percent calculated over 10 partitions of the COCRS conference test data. See [1] for details

feature extraction. Most of the systems presented at the Conference used separate methods of feature extraction and classification. In the discussion presented here any image processing which preceded the feature extraction is combined with feature extraction. The results of these comparisons are presented in sections 2 by algorithm type and in section 3 for NN and statistical algorithms.

Since the results of the COCRS conference were different than was originally expected, NIST conducted a set of pattern classification experiments using KL features sets of different sizes and using seven different classification methods. These experiments confirm the COCRS conference results. These results are discussed in section 5.

2 Types of Algorithms Used

The discriminant function and classification sections of the systems are of two types: adaptive learning based and rule-based. The most common approach to machine learning based systems used at the Conference was NNs. The neural approach to machine learning was originally devised by Rosenblat [4] by connecting together a layer of artificial neurons [5] on a perceptron network. The observations which were present in this approach were analyzed by Minski and Papert [6]. The results of this Conference suggest that many of these weaknesses are still relevant. The advent of new methods for network construction and training during the last ten years led to rapid expansions in NN research in the late 1980s. Many of the methods referred to in Figure 1 were developed in this period. Adaptive learning is further subdivided into two types, supervised learning and self-organization. The material presented in this paper does not cover the mathematical detail of these methods, but the bibliographic references provided with many of the systems [1] discuss these methods in detail.

The principal difference between NN methods and rule-based methods is that the former attempt to simulate intelligent behavior by using adaptive learning and the latter use logical symbol manipulation. The two most common rule-based approaches at the Conference were those derived from mathematical image processing and those derived from statistics. Image based methods are usually used for feature extraction while statistical methods are usually used for classification.

Most of the OCR implementations discussed in this report combine several methods to carry out preprocessing (filtering) and feature extraction. Many of the filtering methods used are based on methods described in texts on image processing such as [7] and on methods based on KL transforms [3]. In these methods, the recognition is done using features extracted from the primary image by rule based techniques. The filtering and feature extraction processes start with an image of a character.

The features produced are then used as the input for classification.

In a self-organizing method, such as [8], data is applied directly to the NN and any filtering is learned as features are extracted. In a supervised method, the features are extracted using either rule-based or adaptive methods and classification is carried out using either type of method.

In Figure 1, rules based on mathematical image processing are distinguished from rules based on statistics. These two types of rules are similar in that they both derive features based on a model of the images. Statistical rules derive these model parameters based on the data presented. For example, typical model parameters might be sample means and variances. Mathematical rules operate on the data based on external model parameters or on the specific data being analyzed. The model parameters might be designed to detect strokes, curvature, holes, or concave or convex surfaces.

All of the methods shown in Figure 1 can also be categorized broadly into linear methods, such as LVQ [9], and nonlinear methods, such as Multi-Layer Perceptrons (MLPs) [10]. This separation into linear and non-linear algorithms also extends to mathematical and statistical methods. Many of the convolution and transform methods, such as combinations of Gabor transforms [11] are linear. Other methods start with linear operations such as correlation matrices and become non-linear by removing information with low statistical significance: KL transforms [7] and principal component analysis (PCA) [12] are examples of this.

When training data is used to adjust statistical model parameters to train MLPs, certain methods may be classified as either NN or statistical methods. The PNN [13] is an example of this type of method. In another context PNN methods can be regarded as one class of a radial basis function (RBF) method [14]. The information in Figure 1 classifies methods of this kind in an arbitrary way when statistical accumulation or NN models of a given method are equivalent.

System	Features	Classification
Neural Net		
ATT_2	receptor fields	MLP
Hughes_1	neocognitron	
Nestor	necognitron	MLP
Symbus	raw	self-Org. NN
Hybrid		
ERIM_1	morophological	MLP
Kodak_2	Gabor	MLP
NYNEX	model	MLP
NIST_4	K-L	PNN
Non Neural Net		
Think_1	template	distance maps
UBOL	rule based	KNN
Elsagb_1	shape func.	KNN

Table 2: Feature extraction and classification methods used for the 11 system cussed.

System	24	28	32	36	40	44	48	52	56	60	64
KNN:1	2.9	2.7	2.7	2.7	**2.6**	2.6	2.6	2.7	2.7	2.7	2.7
KNN:3	2.8	2.7	2.7	2.7	**2.6**	2.7	2.7	2.7	2.7	2.8	2.7
KNN:5	2.9	2.8	2.8	**2.7**	2.8	2.8	2.8	2.8	2.8	2.8	2.8
WSNN:1.1	2.8	2.7	2.6	2.6	**2.5**	2.6	2.6	2.6	2.6	2.5	2.6
PNN:3.0	2.7	2.7	2.6	2.6	**2.5**	2.6	2.6	2.6	2.6	2.5	2.5
MLP:32	5.8	5.6	5.7	5.5	5.6	5.5	**5.3**	5.4	5.4	5.3	5.4
MLP:48	5.2	5.2	5.0	4.7	4.9	5.0	4.7	**4.6**	4.9	5.0	4.9
MLP:64	4.6	4.5	4.6	4.5	4.5	4.5	4.5	**4.3**	4.5	4.4	4.5
RBF1:1	13.2	13.1	13.9	13.0	**12.6**	13.4	12.6	13.2	13.3	13.2	13.2
RBF1:2	8.5	8.5	8.4	8.2	8.4	8.2	8.1	8.3	8.1	**7.9**	7.9
RBF1:3	6.7	6.6	6.5	6.5	6.5	6.4	6.4	**6.2**	6.4	6.2	6.3
RBF1:4	5.7	5.5	5.5	5.5	5.4	5.5	5.4	5.4	**5.3**	5.3	5.4
RBF1:5	5.0	4.7	4.9	5.0	4.9	4.8	4.7	4.9	4.9	4.7	**4.6**
RBF1:6	4.6	4.4	4.3	4.5	4.3	4.3	**4.2**	4.2	4.4	4.3	4.4
RBF2:1	8.7	9.5	9.1	9.1	9.2	**8.6**	8.8	8.8	8.9	8.9	8.9
RBF2:2	6.7	6.4	**6.1**	6.1	6.3	6.3	6.2	6.3	6.2	6.2	6.5
RBF2:3	5.6	5.5	5.0	6.0	5.4	**4.9**	5.7	4.9	5.0	5.6	5.0
RBF2:4	4.4	5.6	5.0	**4.3**	4.5	4.6	4.6	4.5	4.4	4.8	4.7
RBF2:5	4.5	4.6	4.4	4.6	4.4	4.4	4.4	4.2	4.1	4.1	**4.0**
RBF2:6	4.3	4.5	4.0	4.0	4.2	**3.9**	4.2	4.0	3.9	4.0	4.0
EMD:1	15.2	15.1	15.0	15.0	14.9	14.9	**14.8**	14.8	14.8	14.8	14.8
EMD:2	11.0	10.8	10.7	10.7	10.7	10.7	10.7	**10.6**	10.6	10.6	10.6
EMD:3	8.8	8.8	8.7	**8.6**	8.6	8.7	8.7	8.7	8.7	8.7	8.7
EMD:4	7.3	7.3	7.4	7.3	**7.1**	7.2	7.1	7.1	7.1	7.1	7.1
EMD:5	6.7	6.6	6.6	6.5	6.3	6.7	6.6	**6.2**	6.2	6.2	6.3
EMD:6	6.1	5.9	6.1	6.0	**5.7**	6.0	5.8	5.9	6.0	5.9	6.1
EMD:7	5.6	5.3	5.5	5.3	5.2	5.4	**5.1**	5.2	5.4	5.4	5.6
QMD:1	**4.8**	4.9	5.1	5.1	5.2	5.3	5.6	5.6	5.8	5.8	5.9
QMD:2	**4.7**	4.9	4.9	5.0	5.2	5.3	5.5	5.6	5.7	5.8	5.9
QMD:3	**4.0**	4.5	4.7	4.9	5.1	5.3	5.4	5.6	5.9	6.0	6.3
QMD:4	**4.5**	4.9	5.0	5.3	5.5	6.1	6.3	6.5	6.9	7.2	7.6
NRML	**4.8**	4.9	5.0	5.0	5.2	5.3	5.5	5.6	5.5	5.5	5.6

Table 3: Dependence of Classification Error on KL Transform Feature Set Dimensionality. Given with the classifier acronym are: For k-NN the value of k, for WSNN the value of α, for PNN the value of σ, for MLP networks the number of hiddens units, for RBF networks the number of centers per class, and for EMD and QMD classifiers the number of clusters per class. Bold type indicates the dimensionality yielding minimum error for each classifier. See [2] for more detailed discussion.

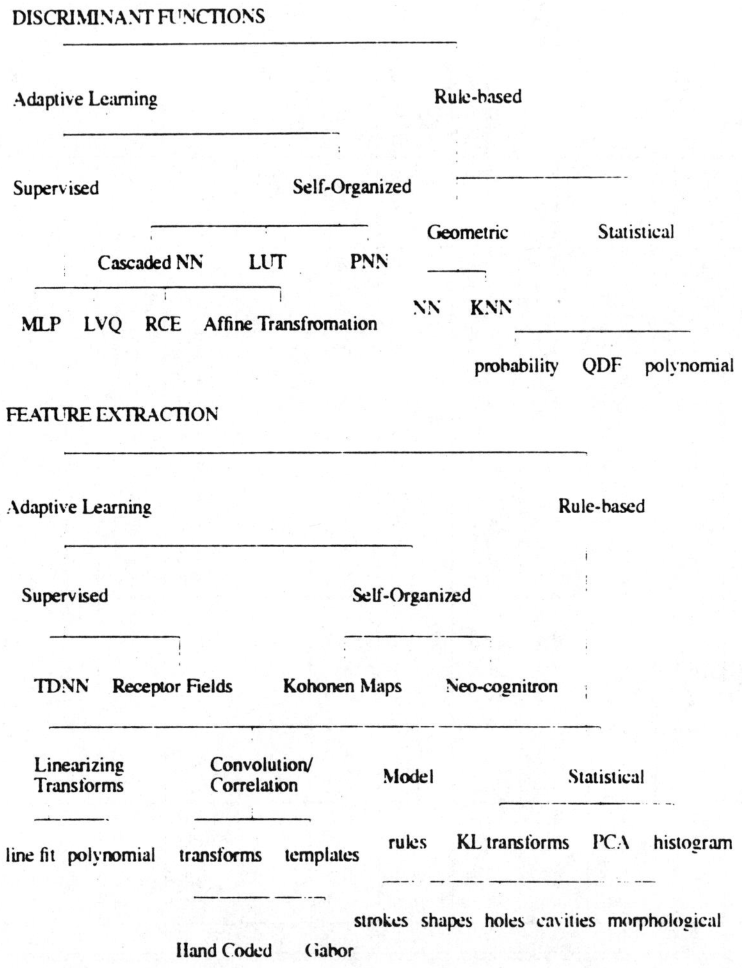

DISCRIMINANT FUNCTIONS

Adaptive Learning   Rule-based

Supervised   Self-Organized

                                    Geometric   Statistical

        Cascaded NN   LUT   PNN

MLP LVQ RCE Affine Transfromation   NN   KNN

                                      probability   QDF   polynomial

FEATURE EXTRACTION

Adaptive Learning   Rule-based

Supervised   Self-Organized

TDNN   Receptor Fields   Kohonen Maps   Neo-cognitron

Linearizing   Convolution/   Model   Statistical
Transforms   Correlation

line fit polynomial   transforms   templates   rules   KL transforms   PCA   histogram

                                            strokes shapes holes cavities morphological

             Hand Coded   Gabor

Figure 1: Types of methods used for feature extraction and classification.

Two types of data will be used to compare the neural and non-neural recognition systems. First the recognition accuracy as a function of reject rate is used and second the writer dependence as a function of reject rate is used.

Comparison of NN and statistical systems shows that with no rejection the neural and hybrid systems have errors between 3.67% (ATT_2) and 4.84% (HUGHES_1). The statistical systems have errors between 4.35% (UBOL) and 5.07% (ELSAGB_1). Since the standard deviations on these numbers is typically ±0.3% a significant overlap in performance exists. The best and worst neural systems are 4 standard deviations apart and the statistical system are about 2 standard deviations apart. Across the range of measured performance, the statistical systems can not be distinguished from each other. Across this same range of performance the neural systems can be distinguished form each other. As the fraction of characters rejected increases, the variation in accuracy increases for the NN system while the statistical systems remain tightly grouped. At 30% rejection the best NN system has an error of 0.15% (ATT_2) and the worst NN system has an error of 0.52% (SYMBUS). At the same rejection rate THINK_1 has an error of 0.27% and NIST_4 has an error rate of 0.21%. At high reject rates the statistical systems are nearing the performance of better NN systems and are significantly better than the worst NN system. For further details see [1],[15].

For the writer dependence of NN and statistical systems, the greatest writer differentiation, 50 writers, occurs at a reject rate of 5%. The best systems in terms of error have the least writer sensitivity. This is not because these systems get more writer correct at zero reject but because no system from either group gets over 80 writers correct at zero rejection. This separation of systems exists because when the worst characters from each writer are removed the best system from each group obtains a 50 writer advantage as the first 5% of the characters are rejected. Writer dependence is less significant in distinguishing systems than error performance. For further details see [1],[15].

3   NIST Classification Experiments

NIST evaluated four statistical classifiers and three NN classifiers. The statistical classifiers are Euclidean Minimum Distance (EMD), Quadratic Minimum Distance (QMD), Normal (NRML), and k-Nearest Neighbor (k-NN). The three neural classifiers included in the evaluation are the MLP, RBF, and PNN. For a given application, all the classifiers were given the same feature sets. Misclassification errors using a 23140 dataset are tabulated as a function of feature dimension and classifier parameters such as the number of prototypes. Table 3 shows for each classifier the estimated probabilities of *error*, expressed as percentages.

for increasing dimensionality of the KL feature set. Note that the optimal number of features yielding lowest classification error (shown in bold) is not the same for all classifiers, the parametric classifiers, QMD and NRML, being noticeably more parsimonious in the number of features required. It is also apparent that most of the classifiers essentially attain a plateau as the number of features reaches approximately 32 thereafter only gaining several tenths of a percent. The best classifiers are the computationally expensive nearest neighbor classifiers and the related PNN. They achieve one third less errors than the NNs and parametric classifiers. The optimum value of $\alpha = 1.1$ for WSNN corresponds to a 1-NN scheme for most test patterns. Accordingly, k-NN is seen to have a higher error rate for increasing k.

Two caveats should be made about the table. First, the MLP and RBF results depend on the initial guesses for the parameters. Often a number of different random guesses are tried assess the effect of the initial guess; for this table, because of the magnitude of the calculation necessary, only one initial guess was used.

These results show that for character classification accuracy NN methods and statistical methods have comparable accuracies confirming the COCR results.

4   Conclusions

Examination of the results of 11 OCR systems using a wide variety of recognition algorithms has shown that in accuracy and writer independence NN systems have not demonstrated a clear cut superiority over statistical methods. Some neural system have higher accuracy than statistical methods; other have lower accuracy. The performance of statistical methods is more closely grouped and is approximately the same as the performance of an average NN system considered here. One area where NN's may have an advantage is in speed of implementation and recognition.

Examination of Table 3 show that on OCR classification the ranking of the methods is similar. The neighbor-based methods are the most accurate with PNN being the best of these. The comparison of MLP and RBF methods show that RBF is usually the better method. When MLP and RBF methods are compared to multicluster EMD and QMD methods the NN methods are more straightforward to implement but do not show a clear accuracy advantage. All of the experiments presented here also suggest that the training set sizes used, although large, are not sufficient to fully saturate most of the machine learning methods studied here.

Acknowledgement

The author would like to acknowledge Patrick Grother for providing tables 1 and 3, Jon Geist for assistance in interpretation of results of classifier comparisons, and Rama Chellappa for help in designing the comparison experiments.

References

[1] R. A. Wilkinson, J. Geist, S. Janet, P. J. Grother, C. J. C. Burges, R. Creecy, B. Hammond, J. J. Hull, N. J. Larsen, T. P. Vogl, and C. L. Wilson. The First Optical Character Recognition Systems Confernce. Technical Report NISTIR 4912, National Institute of Standards and Technology, August 1992.

[2] Patrick J. Grother and Gerald T. Candela. Comparison of Handprinted Digit Classifiers. Technical Report NISTIR 51??, National Institute of Standards and Technology, June 1993.

[3] P. J. Grother. Karhunen Loève feature extraction for neural handwritten character recognition. In *Proceedings: Applications of Artificial Neural Networks III*. Orlando, SPIE, April 1992.

[4] F. Rosenblatt. The perceptron: a probabilistic model for information storage and organization in the brain. *Psychological Review*, 65:386–408, 1958.

[5] W. S. McCulloch and W. Pitts. A logical calculus of the ideas immanent in nervous activity. *Bull. Math. Biophysics*, 9:115–133, 1943.

[6] M. Minsky and S. Papert. *Perceptrons*. MIT Press, Cambridge, MA, 1969.

[7] Anil K. Jain. *Fundamentals of Digital Image Processing*, chapter 5.11, pages 163–174. Prentice Hall Inc., prentice hall international edition, 1989.

[8] K. Fukushima. Neocognitron: A self-organizing neural network model for mechanism of pattern recognition unaffected by shift in position. *Biological Cybernetics*, 36:193–202, 1980.

[9] T. Kohonen. *Self-Organization and Associative Memory*. Springer-Verlag, Berlin, second edition, 1988.

[10] D. E. Rumelhart, G. E. Hinton, and R. J. Williams. Learning internal representations by error propagation. In D. E. Rumelhart and J. L. McClelland, et al., editors, *Parallel Distributed Processing: Explorations in the Microstructure of Cognition. Volume 1: Foundations*, chapter 8, pages 318–362. MIT Press, Cambridge, MA, 1986.

[11] J. G. Daugman. Complete discrete 2-d Gabor transform by neural networks for image analysis and compression. *IEEE Trans. on Acoustics. Speech. and Signal Processing*, 36:1169–1179. 1988.

[12] T. P. Vogl, K. L. Blackwell. S. D. Hyman, G. S. Barbour, and D. L. Alkon. Classification of Japanese Kanji using principal component analysis as a preprocessor to an artificial neural etwork. In *International Joint Conference on Neural Networks*, volume 1. pages 233–238. IEEE and International Neural Network Society. 7 1991.

[13] Donald F. Specht. Probabilistic neural networks. *Neural Networks*. 3(1):109–118, 1990.

[14] T. Poggio and F. Girosi. Networks for approximation and learning. *Proceedings of the IEEE*. 78(9):1481–1497, 1990.

[15] Charles L. Wilson. Effectiveness of Feature and Classifier Algorithms in Character Recognition Systems. In D. P. D'Amato. editor, , volume 1906. SPIE. San Jose. 1993.

Design of an Elliptical Neural Network
with Application to
Degraded Character Classification

Michael C. Moed   Chih-Ping Lee*
Research Scientist Research Scientist

United Parcel Service
Research and Development
51–53 Kenosia Ave
Danbury, CT 06810

Abstract—

This paper describes a novel neural network architecture that is used to classify a set of patterns into one of a set of known classes. The network is comprised of a set of trainable neural processing units (neurons) that have an elliptical activation function and a set of adaptable connections. A fast training algorithm is provided for the network that guarantees that all elements of an arbitrary training set can be correctly learned by the network in finite time. To demonstrate the network's ability to train, and its ability to quickly generalize and classify noisy test data, a network is developed to classify degraded omnifont alphanumeric machine printed characters. Using a training set of over 69,000 characters and a separate test set of over 36,000 characters, classification accuracy of 97.5 percent with average network throughput of 211 characters per second is achieved.

I. Introduction

Artificial neural networks (ANNs) have been widely applied to the task of pattern classification. They function as a powerful computational tool whose benefits include adaptability, parallel computation, and robustness to noise. For the task of pattern classification, ANNs are able to form non-linear decision boundaries that can accurately represent training data and can generalize this data to classify novel, noisy patterns.

One of the most popular ANNs used for pattern classification is a feedforward network employing the Backpropagation training algorithm [1]. Using a set of non-linear processing neurons with sigmoid activation functions, the Backpropagation network can form arbitrarily-shaped decision regions in a hyperspace [2]. Using each neuron to compute a hyperplane decision boundary, decision regions are formed by training the weighted connections between neurons, thereby altering the hyperplane locations in the decision space.

Though extremely powerful and useful, from a pattern classification viewpoint the Backpropagation network suffers in two areas. First, the training technique is slow, and has difficulty in globally minimizing the difference between desired and actual classification outputs. This implies that there is no guarantee that a Backpropagation network can learn to correctly classify the training set in a reasonable amount of time. Second, if a trained network misclassifies a test patten, it is very difficult to determine which neuron, or set of neurons, led to the misclassification, and how to retrain and correct the error.

Another ANN that has been used for pattern classification is named the Restricted Coulumb Energy network (RCE) [3, 4]. The neuron activation function for the RCE is a hypersphere. Each neuron maintains a set of weights that represents the center of the hypersphere in the decision space, and a threshold value that represents the radius. In certain implementations, each hypersphere is associated with a particular pattern class. For these implementations, if a test pattern falls within the boundary of a hypersphere, the pattern is classified as the class associated with the hypersphere. Through training, the neurons of the RCE network adapt to determine the location and size of the hypersphere decision boundaries. By clustering hypersphere of different sizes, it is possible to represent arbitrarily complex classification regions in the decision space.

The RCE network eliminates the two Backpropagation problems mentioned above. First, the training technique forces the network to converge to a set of neurons that cor-

---

*Current address: Emhart Glass, 123 Day Hill Rd., Windsor, CT 06095

rectly classify all training sets. Second, if a test pattern is misclassified, one can determine exactly which neuron(s) were activated incorrectly, and modifications can be made to correct this problem. The RCE network, however, may require large computational resources or a large storage space to represent arbitrariliy shaped decision regions.

Refer to Figure 1 for an illustrative example. In this figure, we see a two dimensional decision space, so a pattern to be classified is represented by the vector (f_0, f_1). As shown in the figure, we have two possible decision classes, A and B, with corresponding decision regions. The decision region for **A** can be represented by just a few circular neurons (a 2D hypersphere is a circle) without much error. However, the decision region for **B** requires many hypersphere neurons due to its oblong shape. Using a reduced number of neurons for **B** would lead to large error regions. The large number of neurons needed for **B** leads to a large processing time and storage requirement, compared to the amount required for **A**. The argument easily can be extended for a decision space of any dimension greater than 2.

To eliminate the problems that the RCE network has with decision regions shaped similar to **B**, one may employ a network with neurons that can form more adaptable decision boundaries. The focus of this paper is on the design one such ANN, with neurons that have hyperellipsoidal decision boundaries [5, 6, 7]. This ANN is called an *Elliptical* neural network. As demonstrated in Figure 2, hyperellipsoids can represent arbitrary shapes (such as a narrow band or plane) much more easily than hyperspheres, and are guaranteed to be at least as efficient. This is guaranteed because a hyperellipsoid can default to a hypersphere if required. The ease of shape adaptation should reduce the amount of processing time and storage required by a network, when compared to the RCE model.

The paper proceeds as follows. Section II presents the architecture of the Elliptical neural network and governing equations. Section III presents a training algorithm that is guaranteed to converge in a finite number of iterations, and to correctly classify all training set data. Section IV describes the application of this network to the task of degraded alphanumeric machine printed character classification. Section V presents conclusions and describes plans for future work.

II. Architecture of an Elliptical Neural Network

The Elliptical neural network is comprised of several layers of neurons. As described below, each layer performs a specialized function. For reference, a diagram is presented in Figure 3. Without loss of generality, we assume that the network is classifying an input pattern vector **F** of k real values into one of s possible output classes.

The first layer of neurons **I** is called the *Input Layer* and functions as a set of broadcast elements. Each neuron $i_j \in \mathbf{I}$ receives as input one component of the pattern vector **F** to be classified, and broadcasts this value to all neurons in the *Processing Layer* **E**.

The neurons in **E** form the hyperellipsoidal decision boundaries in the input space. Each neuron $e_x \in \mathbf{E}$ receives input from every neuron in **I**, and maintains two sets of trainable parameter vectors $\mathbf{C_X}$ and $\mathbf{B_X}$. The first vector, $\mathbf{C_X} = (c_x^0, c_x^1, \ldots, c_x^{k-1})$, represents the center of the hyperellipsoid e_x in a k dimensional decision space. The second vector, $\mathbf{B_X} = (b_x^0, b_x^1, \ldots, b_x^{k-1})$, represents the axes of e_x. The number of neurons in **E**, labeled *Enum*, is also determined through the training technique. An example of a neuron with $k = 2$ is presented in Figure 3.

Each neuron e_x computes a preliminary value e_x^{pre} according to the equation:

$$e_x^{pre} = \sum_{j=0}^{k-1} \frac{(c_x^j - f^j)^2}{(b_x^j)^2} \tag{1}$$

where f^j is the jth element of the input pattern vector **F**. From this equation one can see that if a feature vector **F** falls within or on a hyperellipsoid decision boundary for a neuron e_x, then $e_x^{pre} \leq 1$; else, $e_x^{pre} > 1$. For computational convenience, each neuron then inverse thresholds this value to generate is final output e_x^{out} according to the equation:

$$e_x^{out} = \begin{cases} 0 & \text{if } e_x^{pre} > 1 \\ 1 & \text{if } e_x^{pre} \leq 1 \end{cases} \tag{2}$$

The neuron now outputs a 1 (state = *asserted*) if the feature vector lies within or on its decision boundaries, else it outputs a 0 (state = *non-asserted*).

Neurons in the next level, called the *Output Layer*, determine the amount of support provided to each of s output classes by the Processing Layer neurons. To determine the support, the Output Layer **O** contains a set of s neurons $(o_0, o_1, \ldots, o_{s-1})$, each of which corresponds to one of the s output classes. Each neuron o_i receives as input a set of weighted final output values from the Processing Layer neurons. The set of weights, developed through training, is called **W** and is of dimension (s x *Enum*).

Each neuron o_i in **O** computes its output value according to the equation:

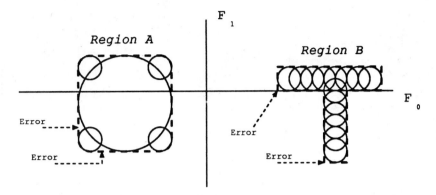

Figure 1: Decision space coverage using hyperspheres.

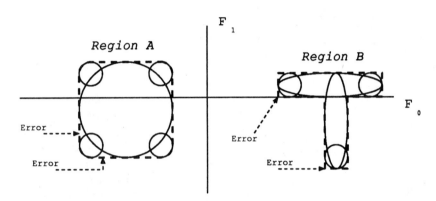

Figure 2: Decision space coverage using hyperellipsoids.

$$o_i = \sum_{j=0}^{Enum-1} \mathbf{W}_{ij} e_j^{out} \qquad (3)$$

Final classification is performed by determining the Output Layer neuron o_i that outputs the largest value. The input pattern $\mathbf{F}$ is then classified as the output class corresponding to this output layer neuron. If no output class has a value greater than 0, the input pattern is rejected.

There are several natural extensions to this architecture. For a given input pattern, one can use the values of the Output Layer neurons to compute a confidence value for the selected output class. This would allow a user to reject a classification if the class' support did not exceed a user-defined threshold. This is important when pattern misclassification is more costly then pattern rejection. Using the support values, the network can also provide alternative classifications and their relative ranks. This is helpful when combined with a postprocessing context database, which provides a secondary aid in classification. Also, when combining this network with other classification techniques, several output class alternatives is important to implement a voting strategy between the classifiers.

One may also extend this architecture to reduce input pattern rejection. If an input pattern vector is rejected on the first pass, one can alter the inverse thresholding setpoint of the Processing Neurons to allow each neuron to become asserted if the pattern vector is "just outside" the boundary of a decision region. The setpoint can be adjusted to maintain a user-defined acceptable misclassification rate, and will in turn reduce the rejection rate.

III. A Training Technique for an Elliptical Neural Network

Training the Elliptical network involves specializing the network architecture and parameters for a particular pattern classification task. There are four items that are modified during this training procedure. These items are:

1. The number of Processing Layer neurons.

2. The value of $\mathbf{C_X}$ for each Processing Layer neuron e_x. This value represents the center of the hyperellipsoidal decision boundary for that neuron.

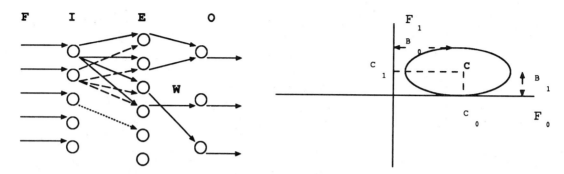

Figure 3: Left: Network Diagram. Right: Neuron Example

3. The value of $\mathbf{B_x}$ for each Processing Layer neuron e_x. This value represents the axes of the hyperellipsoidal decision boundary for that neuron.

4. The matrix $\mathbf{W}$ which contains weighted connection values between the Processing Layer and the Output Layer.

The training procedure presented below specializes the four above items using a technique that guarantees the following:

- All training patterns will be correctly classified.

- The training time is finite and of order $\mathbf{O}(n^3)$ where n is the size of the training set.

The nature of the training technique is an iterative growth and shrink process of Processing Layer neurons. The general idea is to create new Processing Layer neurons whose hyperellipsoids cover training set patterns of a particular output class, and shrink them so they don't overlap training set patterns of a different class (which will be covered by other hyperellipsoids). The algorithm is presented below.

Training Algorithm

Given a set $\Omega = (\omega_0, \omega_2, \ldots, \omega_{s-1})$ of s output classes. and a training set $\mathbf{T} = (t_0, t_1, \ldots, t_{n-1})$ of size n, where each element t_i has a pattern vector t_i^F and an output class t_i^ω ($\omega \in \Omega$), perform the following.

1. Set $Enum = 0$, $\mathbf{E} = \text{NULL}$, $\mathbf{W} = [0]$. There are no Processing Layer neurons currently in the network.

2. Repeat until all training set patterns are correctly classified (max $= n$ iterations):

    (a) Repeat for all j: $0 \leq j \leq n-1$:

        i. Let $\mathbf{F}'$ equal the training pattern $t_j^F \in \mathbf{T}$. Let $\omega' = t_j^\omega$.

        ii. Provide $\mathbf{F}'$ to the Input Layer neurons as input to the network. Observe the set of asserted Output Layer neurons.

        iii. For every asserted Output Layer neuron o_h that corresponds to a different output class than ω' determine the set of asserted, supporting Processing Layer neurons for o_h.

        iv. For each asserted, supporting Processing Layer neuron in this set, SHRINK the (incorrectly) asserted neuron so that $\mathbf{F}'$ falls outside its decision boundary. The maximum number of SHRINK operations is n for this step.

        v. If no asserted Output Layer neuron o_h corresponds to output class ω' then perform the following:

            A. Let $Enum = Enum + 1$. Create a new Processing Layer neuron e_{Enum}. Add e_{Enum} to the set $\mathbf{E}$.

            B. Set $\mathbf{C_j} = \mathbf{F}'$. The new neuron is centered at the training pattern location.

            C. Set $\mathbf{B_j} = \Lambda$, a vector of constant values. The initial axes are all the same size, so the decision surface for e_{Enum} is initially a hypersphere.

            D. For each training set element t_m: $0 \leq m \leq j$, SHRINK e_{Enum} so it does not misclassify these training set elements.

            E. Set $\mathbf{W}_{\omega', Enum} = 1$

3. Now, update support matrix $\mathbf{W}$. Repeat for all j: $0 \leq j \leq n-1$:

    (a) Let $\mathbf{F}'$ equal the training pattern $t_j^F \in \mathbf{T}$. Let $\omega' = t_j^\omega$.

    (b) Provide $\mathbf{F}'$ to the Input Layer neurons as input to the network. Let $\mathbf{E}'$ equal the set of asserted Processing Layer neurons.

(c) For each $e_x \in \mathbf{E}'$, let $\mathbf{W}_{\omega' x} = \mathbf{W}_{\omega' x} + 1$.

One can see from the above algorithm that the support that a Processing Layer neuron provides to an Output Layer neuron is the number of training patterns that fall within the Processing Layer neuron. We reason that a decision region that contains a cluster of same-class training patterns is more likely to be able to classify a same-class noisy test pattern than a region with few training patterns. Thus, a Processing Layer neuron that contains multiple training patterns may be considered to have "better" classification capabilities than one that contains fewer training patterns, and should provide a larger degree of support for an output class.

It is also evident that if a misclassification occurs when testing the network, one can readily determine which processing neuron(s) provided support to the incorrectly asserted Output Layer neuron. If desired, one can alter the size of the Processing Layer neuron to exclude this test vector using the SHRINK algorithm below. As noted earlier, this ability is one of the strengths of this architecture.

The SHRINK algorithm reduces the size of a hyperellipsoidal decision region for a neuron e_x when a training pattern vector $\mathbf{F}$ lies inside e_x and is incorrectly classified by e_x. The goal of SHRINK is to find a new hyperellipsoidal boundary (maintaining the same center $\mathbf{C_X}$) within the old boundary such that the new hyperellipsoid has the largest possible volume, yet $\mathbf{F}$ is outside the boundary. The proposition is given by the following:

Given a hyperellipsoidal decision region computed by e_x, with center $\mathbf{C_X}$, axes $\mathbf{B_X}$, and Volume V_x, determine a new set of axes $\mathbf{\Gamma_X} = (\gamma_x^0, \gamma_x^1, \ldots, \gamma_x^{k-1})$ to maximize $V_x(\mathbf{\Gamma_X})$, where:

$$V_x(\mathbf{\Gamma_X}) = \rho \prod_{j=0}^{k-1} \gamma_x^j \qquad (4)$$

subject to:

$$\gamma_x^j \leq b_x^j, \text{ for all } j: 0 \leq j \leq k-1$$

and

$$\sum_{j=0}^{k-1} \frac{(c_x^j - f^j)^2}{(\gamma_x^j)^2} \geq 1$$

where ρ is a volumetric constant.

Using the method of Lagrange multipliers, one can determine that the Γ_x that satisfies this proposition can be found by using the following method:

SHRINK Algorithm

1. For any j $(0 \leq j \leq k-1)$ such that $f^j = c_x^j$, set $\gamma_x^j = b_x^j$.

2. For the all other j,

$$\eta = argmax(j) \left[\frac{(\prod_{h=0, h \neq j}^{k-1} b_x^h)|c_x^j - f^j|}{\sqrt{1 - \sum_{h=0, h \neq j}^{k-1} \{(c_x^h - f^h)^2/(b_x^h)^2\}}} \right] \qquad (5)$$

3. Set:

$$\begin{cases} \gamma_x^\eta = \dfrac{|c_x^\eta - f^\eta|}{\sqrt{1 - \sum_{h=0, h \neq \eta}^{k-1} \{(c_x^h - f^h)^2/(b_x^h)^2\}}} - \epsilon \\[2em] \gamma_x^j = b_x^j \text{ for all other } j, \ 0 \leq j \leq k-1 \end{cases} \qquad (6)$$

In equation (6), ϵ is a small positive constant. From the description of the SHRINK algorithm it is evident that only one axis need be reduced to maximize the size of the reduced hyperellipsoid volume.

The training algorithm provides the following guarantees:

1. Each Processing Layer neuron corresponds to only one output class.

2. Several training patterns may lie within the decision boundary of the same Processing Layer neuron if each pattern has the same output class.

3. Several Processing Layer neurons can have the same output class.

4. Training patterns with different output classes will be covered by different Processing Layer neurons.

5. All training set patterns will lie within the boundary of at least one Processing Layer Neuron.

Other training methods for elliptical networks do not provide such guarantees. In [5], the proposed training method requires the placement of hyperellipsoidal neurons at preclustered data centers. Given this fixed number of neurons, the method then adjusts the size of each neurons hyperellipsoidal "bounding box" based on assumed information about the distribution of data in the region. This method does not provide above guarantees 4 and 5. In [6], an LVQ algorithm based on the Mahalanobis distance metric is used to alter the shape and center of a fixed number of hyperellipsoidal decision boundaries. Unfortunately, this method may violate guarantees 4 and 5 as well.

IV. Application of an Elliptical Neural Network to Character Classification

Character recognition is a classic pattern classification problem to which ANNs have been applied. In most character recognition applications, a feature vector is derived from the bitmap of an imaged alphanumeric character, and this vector is provided to the network as input. The network then processes the vector and outputs a value representing the "closest" character class, according to some metric.

At UPS Research and Development, we have assembled a database of over 105,000 machine printed characters from package labels that have been shipped by UPS. The labels have been optically scanned using a CCD-based scanner with a resolution of 250 dots-per-inch (dpi). A segmented bitmap image of every character on each of these labels and associated key-entered truth value have been stored in the database.

Due to the nature of the package labels, machine printed characters vary greatly from label to label. Almost any printing technique, including laser print, typewriter, dot-matrix, and carbon copy may appear on the label. Also, any machine printed font may be present. The size of the characters is also variable, although for this experiment, we limited the allowed font sizes to be between 8 and 18pt. Finally, many of the machine printed characters tend to be degraded due to printing technique, tape, poor contrast or marks and blurs introduced through shipping. It is sufficient to say that a large proportion of these characters cannot be recognized using simple template matching techniques.

A system consisting of seven Elliptical neural networks was constructed to classify the degraded machine print characters. The combined system was evaluated using four criteria:

- Accuracy rate (percent correct classification).

- Substitution rate (percent misclassification).

- Rejection rate (percent no classification).

- Speed.

There were 64 characters that our system was designed to classify. These were the upper case alphas (A-Z), the lower case alphas (a-z) the ten digits (0-9), "&", and "#". The 64 characters were divided into seven sets based on similarity of shape. The sets are: S1: OD0oCcQadge; S2: 1lIi7; S3: WwVvUuYyTtr; S4: EBFPp2Zz; S5: 35Ss8f9qg&Jj; S6: 4#ARKkXx; and S7: 6LbMNHhmn. In total, there were over 69,000 characters in the training set and over 36,000 characters in a separate test set. Unfortunately, we did not have an even distribution of character instances, e.g. there were many more "s" than "j" in the database.

If a single network was used for all 64 characters, the number of Processing Layer neurons would be large, resulting in a large execution time. Instead, we trained

seven networks each on a separate character set. A pre-processing nearest mean classifier is employed as a rough classifier. It determines to which set a particular input bitmap belongs, and routes the input to the appropriate network.

Two sets of features vectors are extracted from each bitmap. The first feature vector is obtained through a Hadamard Transform, and yields a feature vector of 66 elements. The second feature vector is obtained through a *Grid Transform*. The Grid Transform divides the input bitmap into 64 separate square regions and sums the number of black pixels in each region. This yields a feature vector of 64 elements. A Discriminant Transformation is applied to both feature vectors to increase feature discrimination and reduce vector size.

Table 1: Results of Machine Print Experiments

Set	Num	Acc.	Sub.	Rej.	Speed
S1	8237	98.3	1.4	0.3	77.7
S2	3246	88.5	11.2	0.3	180.4
S3	4531	98.0	1.7	0.3	167.8
S4	5299	99.2	0.6	0.2	441.6
S5	4958	97.4	1.7	0.9	115.3
S6	4888	99.2	0.6	0.2	444.4
S7	5658	98.1	1.2	0.7	176.8

The results are presented in Table 1. The number column is the number of characters in the test set. Accuracy, substitution, and reject are all percentage values. Speed is in characters per second on a SPARC II running Unix. The speed value only reflects the Elliptical network processing time, and does not reflect feature extraction time, or the time for rough classification. The average speed for all networks was 211 cps with an accuracy of 97.5%. One can see from the results that the network performed with high accuracy and with very high speed. Given the nature of the data set, this justifies the claim that the Elliptical network can efficiently generalize training information to correctly classify noisy data.

V. Conclusions and Discussion

This paper discussed the design of an artificial neural network architecture based on a neuron that has a hyper-ellipsoidal activation function. A training algorithm was provided that guarantees correct classification of training data. Experimental evidence demonstrated the classification abilities and speed that this architecture can provide.

We are currently improving upon the design of the pre-processing classifier, in order to increase the reliability of feature vector routing. Experiments have shown that by allowing a few characters to be members of more than one set, we can get preprocessing accuracy of over 99%.

We are also developing machine print databases for training that we believe will lead to better classification results. The proposed database will have more uniform representation of each of the 64 character classes. The database will combine live package images of characters with computer generated characters. The computer generated characters will represent over 40 font types and 8-18 point sizes. We will also develop a set of distortion filters similar to [8] that can be applied to the font sets to generate characters with defects representative of our package labels.

Finally, we are looking at ways to further improve the efficiency of the network, including methods to segment the decision space. This would restrict the number of Processing Layer neurons that need to process input, and reduce processing time.

References

[1] D. E. Rumelhart, G. E. Hinton, and R. J. Williams, "Learning internal representations by error propagation," in *Parallel Distributed Processing Volume I* (D. E. Rumelhart and J. L. McClelland, eds.), pp. 318–362, Cambridge, MA: The MIT Press, 1986.

[2] R. P. Lippmann, "An introduction to computing with neural nets," *IEEE ASSP Magazine*, pp. 4–22, April 1987.

[3] D. L. Reilly, C. Scofield, C. Elbaum, and L. N. Cooper, "Learning system architectures composed of multiple learning modules," in *IEEE First International Conference on Neural Networks*, vol. II, pp. 495–503, 1987.

[4] L. N. Cooper, C. Elbaum, and D. L. Reilly, "Self organizing general pattern class separator and identifier," *US Patent Number 4326259*, 1982.

[5] S. N. Kavuri and V. Venkatasubramanian, "Solving the hidden node problem in networks with ellipsoidal units and related issues," in *International Joint Conference on Neural Networks*, vol. I, (Baltimore), pp. 775–780, 1992.

[6] P. M. Kelly, D. R. Hush, and J. M. White, "An adaptive algorithm for modifying hyperellipsoidal decision surfaces," in *International Joint Conference on Neural Networks*, vol. IV, (Baltimore), pp. 196–201, 1992.

[7] M. C. Moed, "An elliptical neuron-based network for character classification," tech. rep., United Parcel Service, Research and Development, Danbury, CT, January 1992.

[8] H. S. Baird, "Document image defect models," in *Proceedings IAPR Workshop on Syntactic and Structural Pattern Recognition*, (Murray Hill, NJ), pp. 38–46, 1990.

Connected Character Recognition with a Neural Network

Kunihiko Fukushima

Department of Biophysical Engineering, Faculty of Engineering Science

Osaka University

Toyonaka, Osaka 560, Japan

Abstract

The "selective attention model" proposed by the author is a neural network model which has the ability to segment patterns, as well as the function of recognizing them. The principles of this selective attention model has been extended for the recognition and segmentation of connected characters.

1 Introduction

Machine recognition of connected characters in cursive handwriting of English words is a difficult problem. It cannot be successfully performed by a simple pattern matching method because the same character can be scripted differently when it appears in different words, in order to be connected smoothly with the characters in front of it and following it.

The "selective attention model" proposed by the author [1],[3] is a neural network model which has the ability to segment patterns, as well as the function of recognizing them. The principles of this selective attention model has been extended for the recognition and segmentation of connected characters.

2 Connected character recognition system

2.1 Network architecture

The selective attention model used for connected character recognition is a hierarchical multilayered network, which has backward (i.e., top-down) as well as forward (i.e., bottom-up) connections between layers. Figure 1 illustrates how the cell layers are connected in the network. Each rectangle in the figure represents a group of cells arranged in a two-dimensional array.

Figure 2 shows how the different types of cells, such as u_S, u_C, w_S and w_C, are interconnected in the network. Each circle in the figure represents a cell. The notation u is used to represent cells in the forward paths, and w, cells in the backward paths. Although the figure shows only one of each type of cell in each stage, numerous cells actually exist, arranged in a two-dimensional array. We will use the notation u_{Cl}, for example, to denote a u_C-cell in the lth stage, and U_{Cl} to denote the layer of u_{Cl}-cells. The highest stage of the network is the Lth stage ($L = 4$ in this example).

2.2 Pattern recognition

The signals through the forward paths manage the function of pattern recognition. If we consider the for-

ward paths only, the model has almost the same architecture and function as the neocognitron [2], which can recognize input patterns robustly, with little effect from deformation, changes in size, or shifts in position.

Cells u_S are feature-extracting cells, which correspond to the S-cells in the neocognitron. Cells u_C correspond to the C-cells and have the function of tolerating positional errors of the features extracted by the u_S cells. Each u_C-cell has fixed excitatory connections from a group of u_S-cells which extract the same feature, but from slightly different positions. Therefore, the u_C-cell's response is less sensitive to shifts in position of the input patterns.

The process of feature extraction by u_S-cells and the toleration of positional shift by u_C-cells are thus repeated in the hierarchical network. During this process, local features extracted in the lower stages are gradually integrated into more global features. This is effective for endowing the network with robustness against deformation in the patterns during recognition. Since errors in the relative position of local features are tolerated in the process of extracting and integrating features, the same u_C-cell in the layer at the highest stage responds, even if the input pattern is deformed, changed in size, or shifted in position. Thus, the u_C-cells at the highest stage work as the recognition cells.

2.3 Segmentation

The signals through the backward paths manage the function of selective attention, segmentation and associative recall. The cells and connections in the backward paths of the network are arranged in a mirror image of those in the forward paths.

The output signal of the recognition layer U_{CL} is sent through the backward paths, and reaches the recall layer W_{C0} at the lowest stage. The routes of the backward signals are controlled by gate signals, which are given to the w_S-cells in the backward paths from the corresponding u_S-cells in the forward paths. Guided by the gate signals, the backward signals reach exactly the same positions at which the input pattern is being presented.

When two patterns or more are simultaneously presented to the input layer U_{C0}, usually only one cell corresponding to the category of one of the patterns is active in the recognition layer U_{CL}. Since the backward signals are sent only from the active recognition cell, only the signals corresponding to the recognized

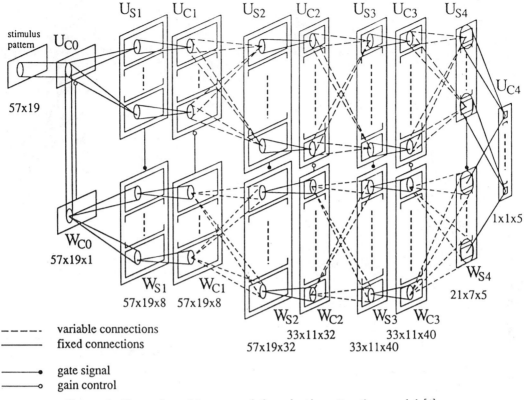

Figure 1: Network architecture of the selective attention model [4].

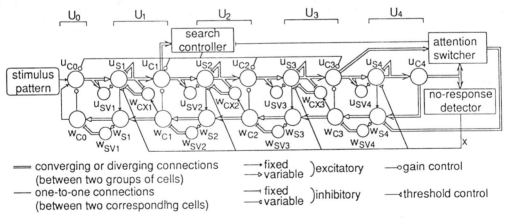

Figure 2: Hierarchical network architecture illustrating the interconnections between different types of cells [4].

pattern reach the recall layer W_{C0}. Therefore, the recognized pattern is segmented from the other patterns and appears in the recall layer W_{C0}. Even if the input pattern, which is now recognized, is a deformed version of a training pattern, the deformed pattern is segmented and emerges with its deformed shape.

2.4 Repairing imperfect patterns

If it is detected that some part of the input pattern is missing and a feature which is supposed to exist there fails to be extracted in the forward paths,

the thresholds for feature-extracting cells around that area are automatically decreased. Thus, the system is forced to extract even faint traces of the undetected feature. Once a feature is thus extracted in the forward paths, the backward signals are now guided by the gate signal from the feature-extracting cell. Therefore, even if the input pattern is an imperfect one, a complete pattern, in which defective parts are interpolated, emerges in the recall layer W_{C0}.

A threshold-control signal is sent also from the no-response detector shown at far right in Figure 2. If all the recognition cells are silent, the no-response detector sends the threshold-control signal to the feature-extracting cells in all stages, and lowers their thresholds until at least one recognition cell responds.

2.5 Attention focusing

When a backward cell w_C is active, it sends a gain control signal to the corresponding forward cell and increases the gain of the cell. Thus, only the forward signal flow in the paths in which backward signals are flowing is facilitated. This has the effect of focusing attention on only one of the patterns in the stimulus, because the backward signals are sent from only the active recognition cell.

2.6 Search control

A search controller is introduced in order to restrict the number of patterns to be processed simultaneously. The system mainly processes the input patterns contained in a small "search area", which is moved by the search controller. The gain control signal from the search controller produces the search area by decreasing the gain of the forward cells situated outside the search area.

The position of the search area is shifted to the place in which a larger number of line-extracting cells are active. The search area has a size somewhat larger than the size of one character. It is not necessary to control the position and the size of the area accurately, because the original selective attention model has the ability to segment and recognize patterns by itself, provided the number of patterns present is small. The only requirement is that the search area covers at least one pattern. It does not matter if it covers a couple of patterns simultaneously.

2.7 Attention switching

Once a pattern has been recognized and segmented, the attention is automatically switched to recognize another pattern. To be more exact, a detector in the network determines the timing of attention switching. When the detector becomes active, the backward signal flow is cut off for a short period. This causes the gain control signal from the backward cells to disappear. The fatigue of the forward cells is used by the system for attention switching. A forward cell is fatigued if it receives a strong gain control signal. It cannot maintain a high gain without receiving a large gain control signal. Once the gain control signal disappears, the gain of the forward cell decreases rapidly, and cannot recover for a long time. This is effective in preventing the system from recognizing the same character twice.

The search controller again seeks a place in which a larger number of line-extracting cells are active, and shifts the search area to the new place. If the responses of all line-extracting cells are small because of cell fatigue, however, the system stops, assuming that all characters in the input string have been processed.

2.8 Size and position information

In the recognition of cursive handwriting, the information of the height or vertical position of characters sometimes becomes important. For instance, the

character 'ℓ' in script style can be interpreted as a deformed version of character 'e'. They differ only in their heights. Since our selective attention model has the ability of deformation-resistant pattern recognition, both of them might be recognized as the same pattern (see Fig 3 below). In order to discriminate between them, we have introduced a mechanism to measure the height and vertical position of the segmented character.

2.9 Computer simulation

It has been shown by computer simulation that individual characters in connected character strings can be recognized and segmented correctly, even if the

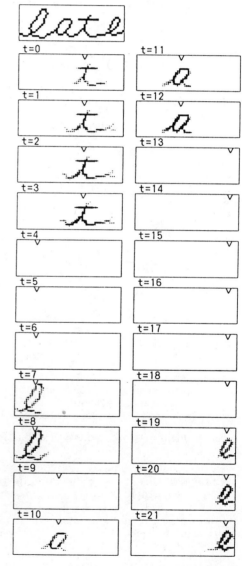

Figure 3: Time course of the response of layer W_{C0}, in which the result of segmentation appears. A character string presented to the input layer is shown at the top [4].

462

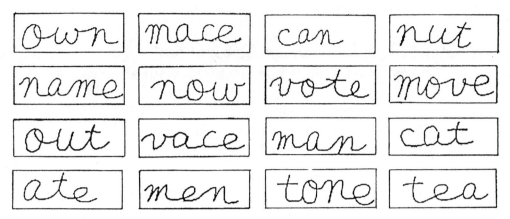

Figure 4: Some examples of input character strings which have been successfully recognized and segmented.

characters are deformed from the training patterns [4].

Figure 3 shows how the response of the recall layer W_{C0}, in which the result of segmentation appears, changed with time when a handwritten character string 'ℓate', shown at the top of the figure, was presented to the input layer U_{C0}. Time t after the first presentation of the character string is indicated in the figure. The mark $^{\vee}$ indicates the position where the center of the search area is moved. It can be seen from this figure that character 't' was recognized first and segmented, then followed by 'ℓ', 'a', and 'e'. Attention was switched just after $t = 3$, 8, and 12. The model stopped working just after $t = 21$, when all the characters in the input string had been completely recognized and segmented.

3 Improvement of the system using bend detectors

From previous work on the neocognitron, we found that the introduction of bend-detecting cells greatly improves its generalization ability for pattern recognition. The neocognitron with bend-detecting cells can easily be trained to robustly recognize deformed patterns [5].

Therefore, we have tried to introduce bend-detecting cells in the connected character recognition system [6]. Following the introduction of the bend-detecting cells in the forward paths, an identical network is added to the backward path, through which the backward signals are made to flow, retracing the same route as the forward signals.

The ability to segment each individual character has been improved by the introduction of the bend-detecting cells, and the error rate for word recognition has been reduced. Figure 4 shows some examples of input character strings which have been successfully recognized and segmented.

Acknowledgments

The author would like to thank T. Imagawa and H. Shouno for their significant contributions to this work. This work was supported in part by Grant-in-Aid #02402035 and #05267103 for Scientific Research from the Ministry of Education, Science and Culture of Japan; and by the grant for Frontier Research Project in Telecommunications from the Ministry of Posts and Telecommunications of Japan.

References

[1] K. Fukushima: "A neural network model for selective attention in visual pattern recognition and associative recall", *Applied Optics*, **26**[23], pp. 4985–4992, Dec. 1987.

[2] K. Fukushima: "Neocognitron: A hierarchical neural network capable of visual pattern recognition", *Neural Networks*, **1**[2], pp. 119–130, 1988.

[3] K. Fukushima: "A neural network for visual pattern recognition", *IEEE Computer*, **21**[3], pp. 65–75, March 1988.

[4] K. Fukushima, T. Imagawa: "Recognition and segmentation of connected characters with selective attention", *Neural Networks*, **6**[1], pp. 33–41, 1993.

[5] K. Fukushima, N. Wake: "Improved neocognitron with bend-detecting cells", *IJCNN'92-Baltimore*, Baltimore, MD, U.S.A., Vol. IV, pp. 190–195, June 1992.

[6] H. Shouno, K. Fukushima: "Character recognition in cursive handwriting using selective attention model with bend detectors", (in Japanese), *Tech. Report IEICE*, No. **NC92**-105, Mar. 1993.

Translation and Scale Invariant Recognition of Handwritten Tamil Characters Using a Hierarchical Neural Network

T.Paulpandian and V.Ganapathy
School of Computer Science and Engineering
College of Engineering, Anna University
Madras - 600 025, India

Abstract- A hierarchical neural network which can recognize handwritten Tamil characters independently of their position and size is described. A character is input as a pattern of (x,y) coordinates, subjected to very simple preprocessing. The network is trained by using the backpropagation learning algorithm. The performance of the hierarchical neural network is compared with and found superior to the performance of two other classifiers, namely,a single neural network approach and the method of moments in conjunction with a feedforward network.

I INTRODUCTION

The problem of recognizing handwritten characters invariant under translation and scale transformations is of enormous practical and theoretical interest. Neural networks have been constructed which recognize handwritten digits [1], complex handprinted Chinese characters [2], handwritten alphanumeric characters [3], and handwritten Kanji characters [4]. This paper describes a hierarchical neural network that recognizes handwritten characters of Tamil (which is one of the ancient langauages of India and more than 5000 years old) robustly, with little effect from changes in size, or shifts in position.

In practical applications, translation and scale invariant pattern recognition is usually achieved by a two-stage process: conventional feature extraction methods are used to obtain appropriate invariant features from the patterns;this step is then followed by a trainable classifier which assigns a class label to the input pattern according to the extracted features. The proposed method for Tamil character recognition has exploited the hierarchical structure of the Tamil characters for feature extraction. There exists a similar substructure for a group of Tamil characters. "Good" features which safisfy the following two requirements can be easily obtained for Tamil characters: (i) small intraclass invariance - slightly different shapes with similar general characteristics should have numerically close values, and (ii) large interclass separation - features from different classes should be quite different numerically. The extracted features are presented to a hierarchical neural network (HNN) classifier to recognize each character. The performance of the HNN approach is compared to those of two other classifiers, namely, a single neural network (SNN) approach and the method of moments in conjunction with a neural network classifier [5].

II INPUT PATTERN, FEATURE EXTRACTION AND NETWORK STRUCTURE

Each group of Tamil characters is composed of substructures which are similar. The twelve Tamil characters used in our experiment are shown in Fig.1. The group of characters shown in Fig.1(a) have a similar substructure of " க ". Similarly, each group of characters is composed of common substructures. In order to utilise the similar substructures, a modified crossing counting technique [6] is used.

To make the features invariant to translation and scale distortions, the characters are centered and rescaled [7]. The origin is set at the center of a character:

$$x_0 = (x_{max} + x_{min})/2 \ \text{ and } \ y_0 = (y_{max} + y_{min})/2$$

and the character is rescaled according to the factors:

$$f_x = (x_{max} - x_{min})/2$$
$$f_y = (y_{max} - y_{min})/2$$

The new coordinates:

$$(x-x_0)/f_x \ \text{ and } \ (y-y_0)/f_y$$

are such that both x and y vary between -1 and +1.

The character is placed in a square box. In Fig.2, the point 0 is the centre of the character, and a, b, .., h are

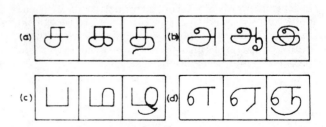

Fig.1.   Examples of the four group of characters

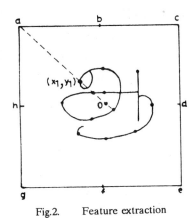

Fig.2.   Feature extraction

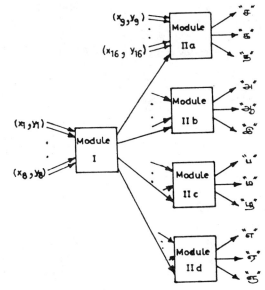

Fig.3.   Architecture of hierarchical neural network

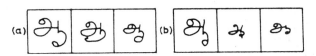

Fig.4.   Two sets of a handwritten character. The characters in (a) are used for training. The characters in (b) are used for testing.

arbitrary points on the edge of the box. The point (x_1,y_1) is the point where the line ao first meets black during the first phase of writing the character. The points $(x_2,y_2)...(x_8,y_8)$ define the first set of features. The points $(x_9,y_9)....(x_{16}, y_{16})$ which are obtained during the second phase of writing the character define the second set of features. The features so captured define topological features along the curve of the character.

The architecture of the HNN is inspired by the hierarchical structure of the Tamil characters. The first set of eight features satisfy the requirements of the "good" features for classifying the four different groups of characters. Similarly, the second set of eight features are utilized to classify characters in each group. The HNN architecture is shown in Fig.3. Each module is a two-layer feed-forward network with one hidden layer and one output layer. Each module is trained using backpropagation learning algorithm [8]. The module I in the first level of HNN is trained to classify the four groups using the first set of features of all the twelve characters. Each module in the second level of HNN is trained to classify the three characters in each group using the second set of features of the corresponding characters.

III SIMULATION RESULTS

The results of applying neural network classifier to twelve Tamil characters are reported. Training has been performed with a set of 3 examples of each character (for a total of 36) produced by a variety of writers. Testing has been carried out with another set of 36 examples produced by different set of writers. Three of the examples of the character ' ஜ ' used for training and testing are shown in Fig. 4(a) and Fig.4(b) respectively. Three sets of experiments are carried out. The HNN is used in the first set of experiments. The other two classifiers utilized are the SNN and the method of moments. The classifiers are simulated on a 80386 based PC/AT. Backpropagation

algorithm has been used to train each of the neural network classifiers. The selected parameters for the classifiers are as follows: initial weight assignment from -0.5 to 0.5, learning rate 0.7, momentum coefficient 0.7, and the stopping criterion for the algorithm a sum squared error value of 0.1.The classification accuracy is estimated by finding the ratio of the number of the correctly classified test samples to the total number of test samples.

A. Experiments with HNN

In the first set of experiments, the HNN as described in section II is used. The number of output nodes is four for the first level module and three for each of the second level modules. The number of nodes used in the input layer is 16 for each module. The number of hidden layer nodes is varied from 4 to 32. Fig.5(a) and (b) show the results of the experiments with the HNN classifier when the number of hidden nodes is varied.

B.Experiments with SNN

We have also investigated the performance of the SNN with one hidden layer. All the sixteen features extracted from the character as described in section II are applied as inputs to SNN. The number of output nodes is 12. Sixty samples are required for satisfactory training of the network. The corresponding results are presented in Fig.5(a) and (b).

C. Experiments with Moment-Invariant Features

To compare the HNN approach with other state-of-the art classifiers, we have examined the performance of a neural network classifier in conjunction with classical moment invariants[5]. Moment invariants are a set of nonlinear functions which are invariant to translation, scale and orientation and are defined on the geometrical moments of the image. Details of the method of moments can be found in the literature [5]. Khotanzad and Lu[5] utilized them for classification of English characters. We therefore adopt this scheme for comparison with HNN. The data base consists of 64x64 binary image of the 12 Tamil characters. A set of six nonliner functions ϕ_1 through ϕ_6 obtained from each of the three images per character are used as the features for training a mulitlayer neural network with one hidden layer. The number of output nodes is 12 and the hidden layer has 32 nodes. The speed of convergence of this classifier is very slow since some of the characters have similar features due to structural resemblance. The training is stopped after 3000 passes over the training data. The results are summarized in Table I for comparison.

TABLE I
PERFORMANCE COMPARISON AMONG HNN,
SNN AND MOMENT INVARIANTS METHODS

Method	Training Time (s)	Classification Accuracy(%)	No.of Hidden Nodes
HNN	420	94.4	4
SNN	1800	72.2	20
Moment Invariants	5400	72.2	32

IV CONCLUSIONS

A hierarchical neural network for the recognition of handwritten Tamil characters independently of their position and size has been implemented. A feature extraction method based on the structural properties of the Tamil characters has been introduced which is found to be suitable for neural network classifier. The performance of the HNN classifier is compared with and found superior to the performance of two other classifiers, namely the SNN classifier and the method of moments followed by a conventional neural network classifier in terms of less training time and high classification accuracy. The HNN method leads to ecomomical networks with a relatively small number of hidden nodes because of modularity compared to other classifiers. Further research is under progress toward recognition of a large character set.

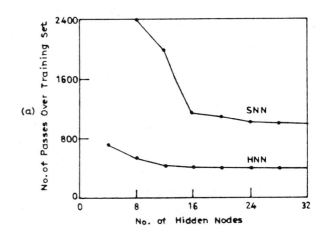

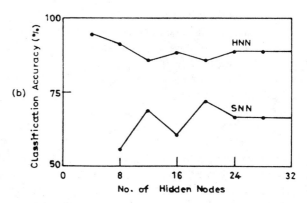

Fig.5. Comparative performance of hierarchical and single neural networks using varying number of hidden nodes: (a) classification accuracy and (b) number of passes over training set.

REFERENCES

[1] D.J.Burr,"A neural network digit recognizer," IEEE-SMC,1621-1625,1986.

[2] Yong Yao, "A neural network model of CAAM and its application to handprinted Chinese character recognition," Proceedings ofthe IEEE First Intern. Con. on Neural Networks,California,1987.

[3] K.Fukushima and N.Wake,"Handwritten alphanumeric character recognition by the neocognitron," IEEE Trans.on Neural Networks,vol.2, pp.355-365,1991.

[4] Y.Mori and K.Yokosava,"Neural networks that learn to discriminate similar Kanji characters," Advances in Neural Information Processing Systems 1,(ed)D.S.Touretzky, Morgan Kaufmann Publishers,1989,pp.332-339.

[5] A.Khotanzad and J.Lu," Classification of invariant representations using a neural network," IEEE Trans.on ASSP, vol.18,pp.1028-1038,1990.

[6] J.R.Ullman, Pattern Recognition Techniques, London Butterworths, 1973.

[7] I.Guyon,P.Albrecht,Y.Le Cun,J.Denker and W.Hubbard,"Design of a neural network character recognizer for a touch terminal," Pattern Recognition,vol.24,pp.105-119, 1991.

[8] D.E.Rumelhart and J.L.McClelland, Parallel Distributed Processing: Explorations in the Microstructure of Cognition. Vol.1, Foundations. Cambridge, MA: MIT Press, 1986.

An Automatic Text Reader Using Neural Networks

Gasser Auda and Hazem Raafat
Computer science Department, University of Regina,
Regina, Saskatchewan, Canada

Abstract __ This paper proposes an Arabic typewritten text reader using Neural Networks. The idea is based on the way by which humans read. The system's input is real newspaper texts written in the most common Arabic font (Naskh). The system predicts the size of the font, and uses it in separating lines, words and sub-words. Then, it scans the text to recognize its individual characters using a set of nine Neural Networks according to a certain procedure. The whole text is then rebuilt and stored to be used by any application. Using Neural Networks in segmentation results in an accurate and fast performance. Some enhancements are proposed in order to reach a more powerful and general version of this system.

INTRODUCTION

An automatic text reader can be used in many important applications [1]. For example, document editing, archiving, and analysis. Moreover, it can be of great help to the blind when integrated with a speech synthesis system. There are several commercial English Optical Character Recognizers (OCRs). However, to our knowledge, there is no commercial Arabic OCR so far although the Arabic characters are used in writing several languages [1]. However, there are several research efforts in this direction [2-6]. In fact, the Arabic text recognition problem is very complicated due to some special characteristics: Arabic words are written cursively, a word may consist of two or more separated sub-words, many different characters are very similar in shape, there are odd combinations between some pairs of characters, some characters allows vertical overlapping with other near characters, each character has up to four shapes according to its place in the word, and finally, there are "hundreds" of Arabic fonts [2].

In this paper an Arabic typewritten text reader is proposed using Neural Networks in a way reminding us with the human way of reading. The system scans the text line by line from right to left (the writing and reading direction of Arabic texts), and recognizes characters before segmenting them. A simplified block diagram appears in figure 1.

SEPARATING LINES, WORDS, AND SUB-WORDS

Horizontal and vertical projection profiles [1] are used in these experiments:

$$\text{Horizontal prof(i)} = \sum_j P(i,j), \quad \text{Vertical prof(i)} = \sum_i P(i,j)$$

where $P(i,j)$ is a pixel value (0 or 1), and i and j are the vertical and horizontal coordinates of the pixel (figure 2).

Horizontal projection profile: In many real typewritten samples, a small overlapping of two successive lines may occur and appear in the horizontal profile as non-zero values in the regions separating lines. Taking the local minima of the profile does not always work because there may be more than one local minima between lines due to random occurrences of the large characters and those carrying dots (figure 2). Passing the profile through a low pass filter solved the problem. The undesirable tiny segments which may appear after cutting will not affect the system due to the robustness of the Neural Network (NN) classifier used.
Different sizes of the same "Naskh" font are allowed. From the orientations of line slices, the system detects the size of the font used, and defines, accordingly, different character widths, and sub-words' threshold.

Vertical projection profile: A vertical projection profile is drawn for every line where its zeros represent spaces. Sub-words inter-spaces are separated from those of the whole words by the threshold defined above.

RECOGNITION BEFORE SEGMENTATION

There are three main approaches for the recognition of cursive words. Sometimes every word is recognized as a unique grid-pattern without applying any kind of segmentation. This approach is suitable only for limited dictionary problems, however, it may be useful in many real applications. To solve the general recognition problem, i.e. dealing with any word, not dedicated to a certain dictionary,

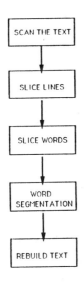

Figure 1. Block diagram
for the main orpeations

Figure 2. Horizontal projection profile.

467

words have to be segmented. One approach here is to detect predefined simple shapes (sometimes called primaries or strokes) where every character is formed of one or more of these shapes [4], [5]. There should be a procedure to rebuild characters from strokes after recognition. The third approach is to segment complete characters. Recognizing characters may be before [7] or after segmentation. If it is after segmentation, a certain segmentation technique is defined and its output is passed to the classifier to recognize characters [2,3]. In our experiments, every character is captured by a moving window, transfered to a separate 50x50 grid, normalized, represented by a feature vector, recognized by the NN classifier, and finally, segmented according to the procedure described later.

Preprocessing and feature extraction of characters: It is impractical to manipulate a huge NN by assigning every pixel of the 50x50 grid to an input node [7]. Therefore, characters should be represented by a numerical feature vector which possesses the useful information, in the sense of discrimination between characters. To prepare the characters for feature extraction, the following preprocessing stages are performed: Geometrical moments of the characters are used to "normalize" the character with respect to scaling and translation variations [8,9]. Translation invariance is achieved by moving the centroid (and of course the whole character too) to the origin of the grid. Scale invariance is accomplished by changing the number of pixels of each character (the zero order moment component) to be equal to a constant value [9].

The following "topological features" are applied after normalization and concatenated to form a 46 element feature vector [8]:

1.Shadow features: Sixteen masks are defined (figure 3). Each point on the grid is projected onto the nearest vertical, horizontal, and diagonal bar mask. The percentage of each "shadow" to the whole mask length is the feature element.

2.Circles-and-sectors features: The grid is subdivided into ten sectors and ten concentric circles around the origin. A feature element is the number of object pixels that fall in one circle or sector of them.

3. Mean distance features: Using the ten sectors, the distances between the centroid of the character and the centroid of each sector contents form the feature element.

Neural Network classifier: The training data of the NN is around 1300 samples of the Arabic characters representing all their shapes and variations. The period, Arabic comma (،), "hamza" (ء), and the famous combination of ل and ا (لا) are also considered.

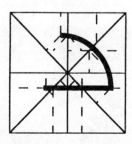

a. Shadow features: object pixels are projected to the nearest mask.

b. Grid is divided into 10 Sectors to be used by mean distance and sector feature vectors.

Figure 3

The utilized NN in these experiments is the three layer, analog input/output, supervised, adaptive Backpropagation network (BP). The BP NN showed, in many experiments, a better recognition accuracy than traditional classifiers [8,9]. The NN also enhances the system's speed substantially when implemented in hardware.

SEGMENTATION PROCEDURE

The NN's job is to classify the whole set of different shapes of characters. A huge NN was tried to do the whole classification job but resulted in a weak performance. This is due to the big number of categories and the resemblance between many groups of them. In order to facilitate the job of the NN classifier, the set of characters is divided into smaller groups. One NN is trained to classify each group separately. At first, three groups are formed: separated characters (S group), characters at the end of a word (E group), and characters at the beginning or the middle of a word (B group). Using the following procedure, there will be no difference between the beginning and middle shapes of the characters, except و , ر ز , and لا , where the beginning and middle shapes are simply considered two different characters.

These groups are further divided into more groups according to their width. It is noticed that characters of every group have approximately three distinct widths. This resulted in nine groups and nine NNs are required to do the segmentation work (figure 4).

The right side of the window is fixed, and the left side is moved to capture a number of slices (according to the procedure). The captured slices will be passed (after feature extraction) to the right NNs. According to the chosen networks' response, it is decided which one of them will be used in recognizing and "slicing" the character. Then, the left side moves to a new position to repeat recognition and segmentation.

The BP takes a classification decision by passing the input feature vector through its layers and weights to produce some analog numbers at the outputs. The BP node transfer

Figure 4. The Arabic alphabet is divide into 9 groups according to their width: The first three are the S group, then the B group, and finally the E group (each group is sorted assendingly to width).

function is: $x_j[s] = f\{ \sum_i (w_{ji}[s] * x_i[s-1]) \}$

where $x_i[s]$ is the current output state of $j\underline{th}$ neuron in layer s, $w_{ji}[s]$ is the wieght between layers [s-1] and [s] from neuron i to j, and f can be any differentiable non-linear function, chosen here to be the segmoid function: $f\{\partial\} = (1 + e^{-\partial})^{-1}$

Ideally, according to the training samples, the output which represents the correct category should be 1 and the others should be zeroes. What happens is that the outputs are always slightly under 1 and above zero. The correct output gets away from 1 as the subjected input is more deviated from the learned samples, and when the output gets lower, this means the network is less "sure" about its decision. When the NN is tested by a category which does not belong to the learned categories at all, the highest output is expected to point to the closest learned category to the subjected sample, and with a far value from 1.

The procedure begins by loading a subword and detecting its width. If it is too small, it is considered noise and skipped. If it is larger than the largest separate character, three nets only are used for detecting the first character (the B group). Note that group E is not considered because we are still at the beginning of the word or subword.

According to the example shown in figure 5, three "slices" are cut and three networks are used for detection (NN4, NN5, and NN6). The character is considered ـس as NN6 was "more sure" about its decision. The left side of the window is now shifted to the left by the width of ـس and the procedure continues. If there is a possibility of being a separate character, then NN2 is included, NN3 is used if not too large to be considered. NN4, NN5, and/or NN6 is used in case its width + the least width of the end groups is comparable to W. This is because there should be enough room for an end character (at least the narrowest one) before the word or subword terminates. It cannot be terminated by a B group character. Then, the rest of the word or subword is calculated, and a similar sequence of steps is held. Note that we are now considering group E (end forms) with group B (middle forms) instead of group S (separate forms).

CONSIDERED WIDTH=W4
MAXIMUM OUTPUT OF NN4=0.71
REFERING TO "ﻼ"

CONSIDERED WIDTH=W5
MAXIMUM OUTPUT OF NN5=0.25
REFERING TO "ـہ"

CONSIDERED WIDTH=W6
MAXIMUM OUTPUT OF NN6=0.98
REFERING TO "ـس"
CORRECT RECOGNITION AND
SEGMENTATION

Figure 5. An example of segmenting a subword.
The decision was taken according to NN6.

The right side of the window should skip the constant part of the vertical projection profile, if any, and begin a next cut just at the beginning of a new change. This eliminates the constant thickness dashes put sometimes between connected characters for matters of justification.

The problem of vertical overlapping is solved by considering the characters: ﻻ , ز , ر , و in the middle forms group as well as the separate and the end form groups. In the middle form learning samples, some noise was put, on purpose, in the place of overlapping. Hence, although a part of the next character is wrongly cut with the slice, the NN is still able to recognize those characters perfectly. The procedure in this case defines a beginning of a subword before proceeding.

EXPERIMENTAL RESULTS

The average correct recognition rate of the utilized networks is 95%. The problem with a single recognition error is that it may cause more than one segmentation error; if the wrong decision is different in width from the correct one, the segmentation of the rest of the subword may be corrupted. The efficiency of our segmentation procedure tested on 4 sample paragraphs is 83%. On the 486-66 M. Hz PC, processing rate is 10 characters/minute. However, we do not consider this to be the final system's rate; the NNs are substantially faster when implemented in hardware. This system is in its early stages, and we are currently working on enhancing these performance rates. However, the main idea seems to be working. Our future plan for the next version of this system to: Enlarge the training data set in order to enhance the correct recognition rate of the NNs, use a different feature vector and another set of networks to take a final decision in case of ambiguous decisions (small difference between the networks' outputs), use a dictionary for error correction, implement the procedure and the NNs in hardware, and to consider different odd combinations of the connected characters, and teaching them to the NNs as separate characters. In these experiments we only considered the ﻻ and it was successfully recognized as a separate character.

CONCLUSION

In this paper, we proposed an Arabic text reader using NN, the main idea is working, and using NNs will result in a fast system when implemented in hardware. Recognition and segmentation correct rates are 95% and 83%, respectively. Some enhancements to the system are proposed in order to achieve better results.

ACKNOWLEDGMENT

This research is supported in part by the Natural Sciences and Engineering Research Council of Canada (NSERC), research grant 8154.

469

REFERENCES

[1] T. Akiyama et al., "Automated entry system for printed documents",Pattern Recognition, Vol. 23, No.11, pp.1141-1145, 1990.

[2] H. Al-Yousefi and S. S. Udpa, "Recognition of Arabic characters", IEEE Transactions on Pattern Analysis and Machine Intelligence,Vol.14, No.8, pp. 853-857, Aug. 1992.

[3] T. S. El-Sheikh and R. M. Guindi, "Computer recognition of Arabic cursive scripts", Pattern Recognition, Vol. 21, No. 4, pp. 293-302, 1988.

[4] F. El-Khaly and M. Sid-Ahmed, "Machine recognition of optically captured machine printed Arabic text", Pattern Recognition, Vol. 23, No. 11, pp. 1207-1214, 1990.

[5] H. Abdel-Azim, "Text recognition: Theory and application", Ph.D. Thesis, Cairo University, Jan. 1989.

[6] S. S. El-Dabi et al., "Arabic character recognition system", Pattern Recognition,Vol.23,No.5,pp.485-495, 1990.

[7] K. Joe et al., "Construction of a large-scale neural network: simulation of handwritten Japanese character recognition on NCUBE", Concurrency: Practice and Experience, Vol. 2(2), pp.79-107, June 1990.

[8] G. Auda, "Performance criteria for Neural Network evaluation", M.Sc. Thesis, Electronics and Communications Department, Cairo University, Nov. 1992.

[9] A. Khotanzad and Y. Hong, " Classification of invariant image representations using a Neural Network", IEEE Transactions on Pattern Analysis and Machine Intelligence, Vol. 38, No.6, 1990.

Printed Japanese Character Recognition Based on Multiple Modified LVQ Neural Network

Kageyasu Miyahara   Fumio Yoda

Personal–use Electronics Laboratory

Mitsubishi Electric Corporation

5-1-1, Ofuna, Kamakura 247, Japan

Abstract

In this paper, we propose a multiple modified LVQ neural network model that can recognize Japanese characters over 3,000 categories with high performance both in accuracy and speed. Multiple modified LVQ network is based on LVQ (Learning Vector Quantization) neural network and a large scale of network can be implemented easily because of its simple structure. This network has a training function of fast convergence and of easy modification without disturbing past trained weights for Japanese character recognition.

This paper also describes an experiment system using a neuro-computer with four digital neuro-chips and experiment results. With the experiment system it takes 18 minutes to learn 35,000 samples by 20 training cycles, while it takes more than one week with a workstation. Moreover it can recognize about 350 characters a second for 3,584 categories. High recognition rate of 100 % for training fonts and of over 99 % for testing fonts were achieved with 49,500 samples.

1 Introduction

Character recognition is one of the interesting tasks in the field of pattern recognition, and several neural network models have been applied to a character recognition with good results[1]-[4]. However most of these neural networks are used to recognize a small scale of characters, such as alphabets and numerals. And it is difficult to apply these network models to a Japanese (Kanji) character recognition application, because their scales of network size are limited while Japanese character is composed of more than 3,000. To apply a neural network model to a Japanese character recognition, it is necessary for a network to have a training function of fast convergence and of easy modification without disturbing past trained weights.

In this paper, we propose a neural network model (multiple modified LVQ neural network) that can recognize Japanese characters over 3,000 categories with high performance, and report the recognition result with an experiment system using digital neural chips. Multiple modified LVQ neural network is based on LVQ neural network model[5], and has a very simple structure so that the large scale network can be implemented easily. Though this structure is very simple, the performance is proved to be fairly high.

2 Multiple modified LVQ neural network model

Multiple modified LVQ neural network is composed of plural modified LVQ networks that process different kinds of feature vectors independently. This network find the final class that an input pattern may belong to by using the output activation of the each modified network. The modified LVQ network and the multiple modified LVQ neural network are discussed in this section.

2.1 Modified LVQ network

LVQ2 (Learning Vector Quantization 2)[5] is a kind of training algorithm for multi templates classification method of KNN (K-nearest-neighbour) algorithm. The LVQ2 network is reported to have a high clustering performances, though its structure is very simple. However we cannot get enough performance to recognize Japanese characters with LVQ2 network itself. To achieve high performance in recognition accuracy we have developed a modified LVQ neural network model by improving LVQ2 network. Fig.1 shows the structure of the modified LVQ neural network.

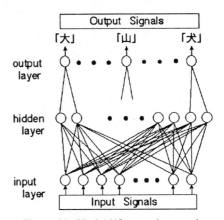

Fig.1: Modified LVQ neural network

Modified LVQ neural network is composed of three layers, an input layer, a hidden layer and an output layer. An input node in the input layer receives each value from a corresponding element of input feature vector X. Each hidden node in the hidden layer is connected with all input nodes through weights and output a value corresponding to a sub-class of each category. In this network a similarity of inner products is used to calculate activity value of a hidden node, while original LVQ2 neural network uses a Euclidean distance. The output layer has output nodes, one output node for each category to be recognized. Output node is selectively connected with hidden nodes corresponding to a sub-class that belongs to a category of the output node through fixed weight. An output node selects the greatest value of activity values in hidden nodes connected to the output node.

A training algorithm of this network is performed as followings. Here we assume that an input feature vector X belongs to a category class Cj and a class Ci is the nearest class of all classes but class Cj. And let Wci be the weight vector connected to a hidden node that outputs value O(X, Ci). Likewise let Wcj be the weight vector connected to a hidden node that outputs value O(X, Cj).

The weight vector Wci and Wcj are updated according to the following rule:

$$Wci(t+1) = Wci(t) - a(t)\{X - Wci(t)\}$$
$$Wcj(t+1) = Wcj(t) + a(t)\{X - Wcj(t)\} \quad (1)$$

if $O(X,Cj) > O(X,Ci)$ and $O(X,Cj) - O(X,Ci) \leq \beta 1$,

$$Wci(t+1) = Wci(t) - a(t)\{X - Wci(t)\}$$
$$Wcj(t+1) = Wcj(t) + a(t)\{X - Wcj(t)\} \quad (2)$$

if $O(X,Cj) \leq O(X,Ci)$ and $O(X,Ci) - O(X,Cj) \leq \beta 2$,

$$Wcj(t+1) = Wcj(t) + a(t)\{X - Wcj(t)\} \quad (3)$$

if $O(X,Ci) - O(X,Cj) > \beta 2$,

where $a(t)$ is a sufficiently small positive constant which is decreasing monotonically in time. The constant $\beta 1$ and $\beta 2$ are predetermined positive threshold. If a node of the Cj does not exist in the output layer, a new node is added into the hidden layer and the output layer.

2.2 Multiple modified LVQ neural network applied to Kanji recognition

In general, it is difficult to achieve high recognition accuracy only using a single kind of feature vector, thus using plural kinds of feature vector to get high ability. In these cases, feature vectors to be used are selected to have far correlation among them. This means that large memory size and calculation time are required if plural kinds of features are inputted to a single network. To solve this problem, we developed a new neural network model, multiple modified LVQ neural network. This network unifies outputs value of plural modified LVQ networks that process each feature vector respectively, and determines the final estimated class of an input pattern. Processing each feature vector by an independent sub-network can save many memory space and time so as to improve total performance. Fig.2 shows a configuration of character recognition system that uses multiple modified

LVQ neural network. First this system normalizes inputted binary pattern, then extracts two kinds of feature vectors from a normalized pattern, one is a blurred image of 8 x 8 gray level pixel of 64 elements (MESH feature vector) and the other is contour direction code distribution of 64 elements (CDC feature vector). Two kinds of feature vector are fed into each modified LVQ network respectively, and recognition and training processes are performed.

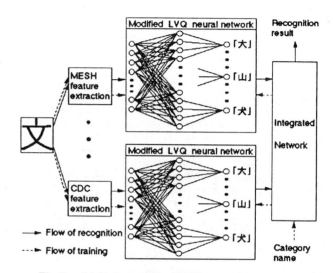

Fig.2: Multiple modified LVQ neural network

In the recognition phase, after each modified LVQ network calculates its output activity value in the output layer, an integrated network received all the output values from each modified LVQ network at the class corresponding nodes for each class, providing integrated output value for each category by summing the values received from output nodes in the output layer of each modified LVQ network through fixed weights. The category class that has the greatest integrated output value is determined as a recognition result.

In the training phase, weights in a modified LVQ network are updated according to the learning rules described in section 2.1.

2.3 Feature vectors

We use two kinds of feature vector, a MESH feature and a CDC feature vector described above, for multiple modified LVQ network.

To extract a MESH feature vector, an input pattern is divided into 8x8 sections. Then the amount of black pixels is counted in every section. Totally 64 elements of MESH feature vector are extracted by this process.

To extract a CDC feature vector, first each contour pixel direction is detected by scanning the mask pattern of 3x3 range. The kinds of 3x3 mask are 256 and each mask has an attribute of each direction. We define 4 codes as directions, horizontal, vertical, right-up and left-up. Secondly the pattern is divided into 4x4 sections. The amount of each direction code pixel within a section is summed and totally 64 elements (4 directions codes x 16 sections) are obtained as a CDC feature vector.

3 Basic experiments using alphabetic and numeral database

In this section, we present a simulation experiments that are aimed to evaluate three kinds of neural network models and KNN (K-nearest neighbour) method to recognize multi-font printed alphabets (uppercase letters and lowercase letters) and numerals. A database is composed of 62 categories, 100 samples for each category. One hundred samples are all different fonts, and 50 samples of them are used for training data and the remaining 50 samples for unknown testing data.

In first experiment, a MESH and a CDC feature vector is used for each model independently. Table 1 shows the results of this experiment.

Table 1: Results of experiments using a single feature

Algorithm	MESH	CDC
KNN	91.23 %	94.61 %
LVQ2	95.45 %	95.84 %
BP	95.84 %	96.16 %
Modified LVQ	96.58 %	97.45 %

In the experiment, we set 4 output nodes a category in LVQ2 network, where a window size is set to a very large positive value. Likewise we use 4 hidden nodes a category in modified LVQ network, where 0.03 and 0.1 is used for the constant $\beta1$ and $\beta2$. BP network[6] here is composed of 3 layers, 64 input nodes, 100 hidden nodes and 62 output nodes, where learning constant was set to 0.02 and the momentum constant was set to 0.7. For KNN method, we used 4 templates each category, which is created by k-means methods. When a MESH feature was used, it took 322 training cycles before the training completed with BP network, while it took only 20 cycles with the modified LVQ network. Also recognition rate of the modified LVQ network is largely improved compared with other algorithm.

In second experiment, we evaluated a multiple modified LVQ network that is composed of two modified LVQ networks using a MESH and CDC feature vector respectively. Table 2 shows the result of this experiment with a comparison between multiple modified LVQ network and KNN method. The condition of parameters is the same as that of first experiment. From the result shown in Table 2, the recognition rate of multiple modified LVQ network is improved by 2.42 % than that of KNN method.

Table 2: Result of multiple modified LVQ

Algorithm	MESH + CDC
KNN	96.00 %
Multiple modified LVQ	98.42 %

4 Experiment system

We have developed an experiment system so as to evaluate multiple modified LVQ network with a large scale of Japanese characters. This system is composed of a workstation and a neuro-computer that has digital neuro-chips[7] in it. The neuro-chip used here has 64 digital signal processor like PNs (Processor Nodes) operating in a SIMD (Single Instruction stream Multiple Data stream) configuration at 15 MHz. A single PN is shown in Fig.3.

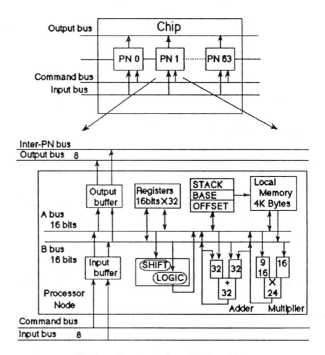

Fig.3: Construction of the Chip

Each PN has 4K bytes local memory and is composed of registers, an adder, a multiplier, a logical unit, and so forth. Each PN is located in a linear array and connected to three global buses, a data input bus of 8 bits, an output bus of 8 bits and a command bus of 32 bits.

This experiment system let 256 PNs run in parallel using four neuro-chips. Once a binary pattern in 64x64 pixels is inputted into this system, 64 PNs normalize the input pattern to 48x48 pattern using linear mapping, where each PN processes pixels in a column. Mesh and CDC feature vectors are extracted from the normalized pattern in parallel, using 48 PNs. Two hundreds and fifty six PNs are assigned to calculate integrated output values of multiple modified LVQ network and determine a category corresponding an input pattern. One PN calculates output values of 28 hidden nodes and 14 outputs nodes, and all 256 PNs can run in parallel. Table 3 shows processing time in this system. The result of the Table 3 shows that this system can recognize about 350 characters a second for a recognition target of 3,584 categories.

Table 3: Recognition time

Processing	Time
Normalization & Feature extraction	1,601 usec
Signal flow through networks	1,126 usec
Sorting	196 usec
Total	2.9 msec

5 Result with experiment system

We evaluate a recognition rate and speed with the experiment system using 49,500 samples (15 different fonts x 3,300 kinds) of printed Japanese characters including the first level of JIS Kanji, Hiragana, Katakana, symbols, alphabets and numerical characters. The different 11 fonts are used as training data, and the remaining 4 fonts as unknown testing data. We have compared the performance of multiple modified LVQ network with KNN method in a recognition accuracy. Templates of KNN are created by K-means clustering algorithm. Weights of each modified LVQ network are also initialized by K-means clustering algorithm. Multiple modified LVQ network is trained by 20 cycles using training data (about 35,000 patterns). It takes 18 minutes with this experiment system to train the data, while it takes over a week with a Sun SPARC station 2. Table 4 shows the recognition results for Japanese characters. For training data the recognition rate of 100 % is achieved. For testing data multiple modified LVQ network give better result than that of KNN method and the recognition rate of over 99.0 % is obtained.

Table 4: Recognition result with Japanese character set

		KNN	Multiple modified LVQ
Training data (11 fonts)		99.08 %	100 %
Unkown data	Font 1	99.53 %	99.63 %
	Font 2	98.73 %	99.16 %
	Font 3	99.20 %	99.51 %
	Font 4	98.20 %	99.17 %

Fig.4 shows an example of weight vector connected from input nodes to a hidden node, one of representative hidden nodes of a category "大", in modified LVQ network for MESH feature. The size of black square indicates a positive strength of a weight value, and the size of white square indicates a negative strength of a weight value. Fig.4 shows that positive elements of a weight vector are formed by training process for classifying categories "大" ,"大" and "太" as similar groups in shape, and negative elements of a weight vector are formed for distinguishing "大" from other similar categories "犬" and "太".

Fig.4: Example of weight vector connected to category "大"

6 Conclusion

The authors have proposed a neural network model for printed Japanese characters including more than 3,000 characters. It is very easy to apply this network to Japanese character recognition, nevertheless high performance is achieved. The recognition rate of over 99.0 % is obtained for unknown fonts data. Furthermore 350 characters can be recognized in a second by this experiment system with digital neuro-chips.

Most traditional Japanese character recognition algorithm adopts a hierarchal classification method, which selects 100 to 300 categories from 3,000 categories by pre-classification method. However this pre-classification cause a problem that pre-classification error will not be corrected by any detailed classification algorithm. Not to use pre-classification algorithm and directly to classify an input pattern in this network also gives us a good recognition results, besides a benefit of training mechanism.

References

[1] K. Fukushima, "A neural network model for selective attention", Proceeding IEEE First Annual International Conference on Neural Networks, 1987.

[2] Y.Le Cun, B.Boser, J.S.Denker, D.Henderson, R.E.Howard, W.Hubbard, L.D.Jackel: "Handwritten Digit Recognition with a Back-Propagation Network", Neural Information Processing Systems 2, 396-404,1989

[3] Keiji Yamada, Hiroyuki Kami, Jun Tsukumo, Tsutomu Temma, "Handwritten Numeral Recognition by Multi-layered Neural Network with Improved Learning Algorithm", Proceeding of IJCNN'89, Vol.2, pp. 259-266 ,1989

[4] Akira Iwata, Yoshihisa Suwa, Yutaka Ino and Nobuo Suzumura, "Hand-Written Alpha-Numeric Recognition By A Self-Growing Neural Network CombNET-II", Proceeding of IJCNN'92, Vol.4, pp. 228-234 ,1992

[5] Teuvo Kohonen, "The Self-Organizing Map", Proceeding IEEE, Vol.78, No.9, pp. 1464-1480, September 1990.

[6] D.E. Rumelhart, J.L. McCleland and the PDP Research Group, "Parallel Distributed Processing", Vol.1, MIT Press, 1986

[7] Dan Hammerstrom, "A VLSI Architecture for High-performance, Low-cost, On-Chip Learning", Proceeding of IJCNN'90, Vol.2, pp. 537-544 ,1990

ON-LINE RECOGNITION OF LIMITED-VOCABULARY CHINESE CHARACTER USING MULTIPLE CONVOLUTIONAL NEURAL NETWORKS

Quen-Zong Wu*, Yann Le Cun**, Larry D. Jackel**, Bor-Shenn Jeng*

*Telecommunication Laboratories, Taiwan, R.O.C.
**AT&T Bell Laboratories, Holmdel, NJ 07733, U.S.A.

ABSTRACT

This paper presents a new feature extraction method together with neural network recognition for on-line Chinese characters. A Chinese character can be represented by a three-dimensional 12x12x4 array of numbers. Multiple convolutional neural networks are used for on-line small vocabulary Chinese character recognition based on this feature extraction method. We choose one hundred character classes as an example for recognition. Simulation result shows that 98.8% and 94.2% of training examples and test examples are correctly recognized respectively.

1. INTRODUCTION

The most popular input device for data processing machines is the keyboard. However, in many applications, such as the ones that involve Chinese text, keyboards are neither convenient, nor easy to use. Chinese is one of the most widespread languages in the world, yet no fully satisfactory text input device exist for it. A system that could recognize handwritten Chinese characters as they are written on "electronic paper" would be an ideal solution to the input problem.

Among the many methods that have been proposed for on-line handwritten character recognition [1, 2], two broad categories can be identified: memory-based techniques in which incoming characters are matched to a (usually large) dictionary of templates, and parameter-based methods in which preprocessed characters are sent to a trainable classifier such as a neural network [3].

Two characteristics differentiate Chinese character recognition from, say, Roman character recognition: the large number of classes, and the richness, and potentially complex internal structure of each character. Many papers [4, 5, 6] have addressed the problem of on-line Chinese character recognition. However, most of them are memory-based and make strong assumptions about the order in which the strokes are drawn.

A better long-term strategy would be to base the recognizer on *shape* information rather than dynamic information. In this paper, we introduce a small-vocabulary Chinese character recognizer which combines a shape-based preprocessor, and a neural network. The main advantage of this approach is its independence with respect to the writer, the writing speed, the stroke order, and the pen lifts.

2. PREPROCESSING

The preprocessing stage transforms the pen trajectory information into a three-dimensional 12x12x4 array of numbers using the following procedure:

(1) a rectangular grid of 12x12 points (called center points) is created so as to uniformly cover the bounding rectangle of the character. To each of these points, we associate a four-dimensional vector.

(2) Two connected adjacent points that are read by the digitizer constitute a microsegment. For each microsegment we

475

determine the center point which is closest to it. Components 0, 1, 2, 3 of the 4D vector associated with the center point are respectively incremented by an amount proportional to the projection of the microsegment onto the North-South, NE-SW, East-West, SE-NW directions, and weighted by a decreasing function of the distance from the microsegment to the center point.

The character is therefore represented by a 12x12 spatial map in which each location represents the density of microsegments around that location for each of the four main orientations.

3. THE NEURAL NETWORK

The classification is performed by a multiple convolutional neural network [7] trained with the backpropagation algorithm. The term "convolutional" means that some layers of the neural network are composed of several groups of units called feature maps. Units within a particular feature map are connected to a limited neighborhood in the previous layer, and are constrained to have identical weights, thereby performing the same operation on different parts of the input.

The four 12x12 feature maps are expanded to four 16x16 feature maps by adding blank boundary locations to the original feature maps. These four 16x16 feature maps are used as the input to the neural network. Each 16x16 feature map is convolutionally connected to two H1 14x14-unit groups. Every 2x2 units of all H1 groups are then locally connected to the corresponding units of both two H2 7x7-unit groups. H2 groups are then fully-connected to the 100 units in the output layer.

4. PERFORMANCE TESTING

A set of one hundred Chinese characters shown in Figure 1 was chosen to test the system. Seventeen writers were asked to write each character once. The characters produced by the first 12 writers were used for training the neural network, and the remaining 5 were used for testing. Figure 2 shows an example of unit activations in the neural network.

The performance data for training set and test set are listed in Table 1. These include the percentages that the scores of the desired class are within top 1, 2 and 3 highest scores. We also simulate the performance for recognition by using 1-layer fully connected neural network and 2-layer fully connected neural network. These performance data are listed in Table 2. Table 3 lists the comparison on numbers of weights for these three kinds of neural networks.

According to the above tables, we know that multiple convolutional neural network is superior to 1-layer fully connected network and 2-layer fully connected network.

Table 1. Performance for multiple convolutional N. N.

Set / Top	Training	Test
1	98.8%	94.2%
2	99.2%	98.4%
3	99.4%	98.8%

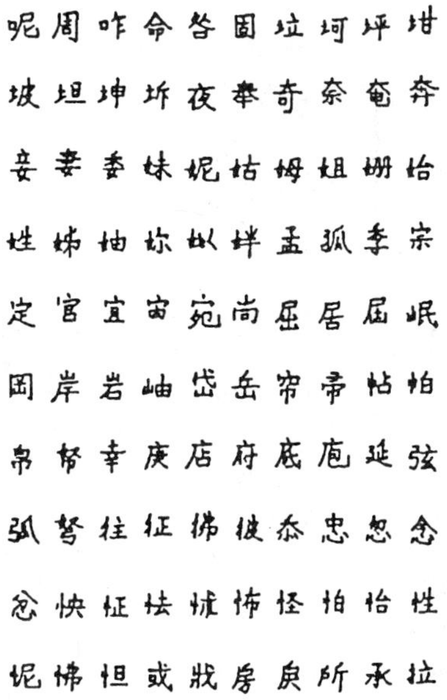

呢周咋命各固垃坷坪坩
坡坦坤圻夜舉奇奈奄奔
妾妻委妹妮姑姆姐姍怡
姓姊抽㭠㕛坪孟孤季宗
定官宜宙宛尚屈居屈岷
岡岸岩岫岱岳帘帝帖帕
帛帑幸庚店府底庖延弦
弧弩往征佛彼忝忠忽念
念快征祛㞛怖怪怕怡性
妮佛怛或戕房良所承拉

Figure 1: A subset of on-line handwritten Chinese characters.

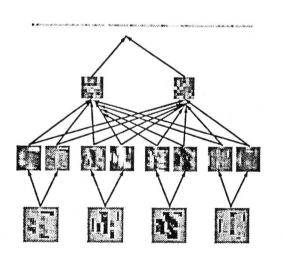

Figure 2: Neural network architecture.

output layer   2 H2 groups   8 H1 groups   4 Input groups

Table 2. Performance for 1-layer fully connected N. N. and 2-layer fully connected N. N.

N. N. \ Set	Training	Test
1-layer fully connected	99.9%	80.6%
2-layer fully connected	99.9%	91.8%

Table 3. Comparison on numbers of weights

multiple convolutional N. N.	13214
1-layer fully connected N. N.	57700
2-layer fully connected N. N.	135500

5. CONCLUSION

This handwritten Chinese character recognizer can be used for limited-vocabulary applications. The high recognition rate for the training set shows that it is excellent for multiple writer applications. The recognition rate for test set depicts that it is also suitable for writer independent applications. In addition, this recognizer can be extended for large-vocabulary Chinese character recognition by introducing a preclassifier into it.

REFERENCES

[1]   C. Y. Suen, M. Berthod and S. Mori, *Automatic Recognition of Handwritten Characters - the State of the Art, Proc. IEEE*, Vol. 68, pp. 469-487, 1980.

[2]   J. Mantas, *Methodologies in Pattern Recognition and Image Analysis - a Brief Survey, Pattern Recognition*, Vol. 20, pp. 1-6, 1987.

[3]   I. Guyon, P. Albrecht, Y. Le Cun, J. S. Denker and W. Hubbard, *Design of a Neural Network Character Recognizer for a Touch Terminal, Pattern Recognition*, Vol. 24, pp. 105-119, 1990.

[4]   S. I. Hanaki and T. Yamazake, *On-Line Recognition of Handprinted Kanji Characters, Pattern Recognition*, Vol. 12, pp. 421-429, 1980.

[5]   *K. Ikeda et al., On-Line Recognition of Handwritten Characters Utilizing Positional and Stroke Vector Sequences, Pattern Recognition*, Vol. 13, pp. 191-206, 1981.

[6]   K. Odata, H. Arakawa and I. Masuda, *On-Line Recognition of Handwritten Characters by Approximating Each Stroke with Several Points, IEEE Trans. Syst., Man., Cybern.*, Vol. 12, pp. 898-903, 1982.

[7]   Y. Le Cun, O. Matan, B. Boser, J. S. Denker, D. Henderson, R. E. Howard, W. Hubbard, L. D. Jackel, H. S. Baird, *Handwritten Zip Code Recognition with Multilayer Networks, Proc. of the International Conference on Pattern Recognition*, 1990.

An ARTMAP based Hybrid Neural Network for Shift Invariant Chinese Character Recognition

Cheng-An Hung and Sheng-Fuu Lin*

Department of Control Engineering

National Chiao Tung University.

1001 Ta Hsueh Rd, Hsinchu, Taiwan 30050, R.O.C.

Abstract—In this paper, we propose an ARTMAP based hybrid neural network to recognize position-shifted Chinese characters. Faster learning speed of a hybrid architecture makes practical the use of neural network in large scale neural computation. Four translation-invariant transformations were used to extract features of two-dimensional patterns. Results of experimentation with three different hybrid neural networks are also presented.

I. Introduction

Supervised learning neural network classifiers with high accuracy and robust performance provide a new direction for adaptive pattern recognition. But a large set of output codes require increasing amounts of training time and patterns, the computational complexity of the learning process quickly reaches unmanageable proportions [1]. Hecht-Nielsen [2] used a counterpropagation network to improve learning speed. The counterpropagation is a hybrid neural network which combines supervised and unsupervised learning in the same network. Since the hybrid neural network architecture is fixed; that is, the number of nodes and its interconnectivity are specified before learning begins. Hence it is necessary to retrain the network after adding a new pattern. This problem can be solved by using a self-growing neural network [3]. One feature of a self-growing architecture is that the nodes and connections may be added during learning. Model families of Adaptive Resonance Theory (ART) and its variations [3,4,5,6] are self-growing neural networks.

In this paper, we intend to combine a unsupervised self-growing neural network and an inter-ART module for position-shifted Chinese characters. The hybrid neural network uses fast initial learning with a slower rate of forgetting to classify unnormalized input patterns. If the memory capacity could be chosen arbitrarily large, the network would achieve 100% recognition for a fixed training set.

II. An ARTMAP Based Hybrid Neural Network (AHNN)

The principal elements of an ARTMAP based hybrid neural network are shown in Fig. 1. This supervised learning system includes a self-growing module, a inter-ART module, and a target field module. The self-growing network can rapidly learn to cluster input patterns without supervision. Any ART module can be used to replace this network for different applications. The inter-ART module consists of a map field, a map field gain control, and a map field orienting subsystem. It links the F_2 field of a self-growing neural network and the target field module. In classification problems, the target field requires all target values to be set to 0 except for the node that is marked to correspond to the class the input is from. That target value is 1. As described above, the system can be applied to identify the corresponding category for an input pattern.

In this remainder of this section, we will describe the main computations of the hybrid network. The algorithm is given below:

1. Input

    Given a M-dimensional input vector $I \equiv [I_0, ..., I_M]$ to F_1.

2. F_2 activation

    The initial choice at F_2 field is one node with index J satisfying

    $$J = Arg \min_{j \in N_c} \|I - Z_j\|, \qquad (1)$$

    where N_c is a set of committed nodes, $Z_j \equiv [z_{1j}, ..., z_{Mj}]$, and $\|I - Z_j\| \equiv \sqrt{\sum_{i=1}^{M}(I_i - z_{ij})^2}$. When F_2 makes a choice, the F_2 may be characterized as $y_J = 1$ and $y_j = 0$ if $j \neq J$.

---

*Please address all correspondence to the second author.

3. Map field activation

The activity of the map field is defined as

$$b_k = \begin{cases} 1 & \text{if } d_k + G + \sum_j y_j u_{jk} > 1 + \bar{u} \\ 0 & \text{otherwise,} \end{cases} \quad (2)$$

where d_k is the target value, $k = 1, ..., P$; u_{jk} is an adaptive weight in the pathway from the jth F_2 node to the kth map field node, and $\bar{u}$ is a critical weight strength such that $0 < \bar{u} < 1$. The map field gain control signal G obeys the equation

$$G = \begin{cases} 0 & \text{if } F_2 \text{ and } F_3 \text{ are both active} \\ 1 & \text{otherwise.} \end{cases} \quad (3)$$

This rule for map field activation is called the 2/3 *Rule* [3].

4. Reset or resonance

Two mismatch events can trigger a reset signal r to the orienting subsystem of a self-growing neural network. One is determined by R_1, and the other is determined by R_2. As illustrated in Fig. 1, the matching signal R_1 is defined by

$$R_1 = \begin{cases} 1 & \text{if } \|I - \hat{Z}_J\| > \rho \\ 0 & \text{otherwise,} \end{cases} \quad (4)$$

where ρ is a distance threshold. If the effective radius ρ is chosen large enough, the network can carry out learning with the minimum necessary number of F_2 nodes. The map field matching signal R_2 is determined by

$$R_2 = \begin{cases} 1 & \text{if } |d| - |b| > 0 \\ 0 & \text{otherwise,} \end{cases} \quad (5)$$

where $|d| \equiv \sum_{k=1}^{P} d_k$ and $|b| \equiv \sum_{k=1}^{P} b_k$.

The binary reset signal r satisfies the equation

$$r = \begin{cases} 1 & \text{if } R_1 + R_2 > 0 \\ 0 & \text{otherwise.} \end{cases} \quad (6)$$

When the signal is one, J is reset to the index of an arbitrary uncommitted node. Otherwise, node J remains active until an input pattern I shuts off. This state is called *resonance*.

5. Learning

When resonance occurs, the hybrid neural network either refines its weights or learns a new category. Here, we consider two learning processes, called *map field learning* and *long-term memory (LTM) learning*.

- Map field learning
  The adaptive weights u_{jk} initially satisfy

$$u_{jk}(0) = 1. \quad (7)$$

When an input I activates an F_2 category node J and resonance is established,

$$u_{Jk} = b_k. \quad (8)$$

It implies that node J can learn to predict the corresponding class for an input pattern I.

If the target field receives no input vector $d \equiv (d_1, ..., d_P)$, then all u_{jk} remain equal to 1 by (2).

- LTM learning During resonance with the F_2 category J is active, the LTM traces is set to be

$$\hat{z}_{Ji}^{new} = z_{iJ}^{new}$$
$$= \begin{cases} z_{iJ}^{old} + \beta y_J [\min(I_i, z_{iJ}) - z_{iJ}^{old}] & \text{if } J \in N_c \\ I & \text{if } J \in N_u, \end{cases} \quad (9)$$

where N_u is a set of uncommitted F_2 nodes. The learning rate $\beta \in [0, 1]$.

The learning rule (9) is the same as the Cluster Unidirectional algorithm used by [7].

6. Retrieving

When the target values are absent, the input pattern I could retrieve a recognition code based on previous learning or make no prediction. If the F_2 node J is active and it only activates one node k in the map field, then we say that I retrieves a class k. If all map field nodes are inactive, then we say that I makes no prediction.

□

III. Translation-invariant feature extraction

Most of pattern recognition techniques, especially template matching methods, are sensitive to shifts in position. The position-shifting problem can be overcome by using translation-invariant features. Some well-known techniques such as the Fourier transform, Rapid transform [8], M-transform [9], and two-dimensional moments [10,11] are used to extract features of one- or two-dimensional patterns which are invariant under translation. These transformations may be applied to the problem of recognizing position-shifted Chinese characters.

A two-dimensional image $f(n_1, n_2)$ of $N_1 \times N_2$ pixels with each pixel represented by 1 or 0 is dependent on whether it is black or white. The methods used to extract features of a character image are described as follows.

A. Fourier Transform

The Fourier transform representation of signals plays a important role in both one-dimensional (1-D) and two-dimensional (2-D) signal processing. We discuss the idea of invariant transforms by starting with the discrete Fourier transform (DFT) for a 2-D image $f(n_1, n_2)$:

$$F(k_1, k_2) = \sum_{n_1=0}^{N_1-1} \sum_{n_2=0}^{N_2-1} f(n_1, n_2) W_{N_1}^{-k_1 n_1} W_{N_2}^{-k_2 n_2}, \quad (10)$$

where $W_N \equiv e^{2\pi j/N}$, $j = \sqrt{-1}$, $k_1 = 0, 1, ..., N_1 - 1$, and $k_2 = 0, 1, ..., N_2 - 1$.

Translation of a character is reflected as a phase change in frequency domain. The magnitude component of the DFT is relatively stable. In general, the magnitude features are translation invariant.

B. Rapid Transform

The rapid transform (R-transform) is a class of fast translation-invariant transforms for position independent pattern recognition problems. It is faster than the fast Fourier transform (FFT) since the arithmetic computation involves only summation and absolute difference.

The R-transform is similar to Walsh-Hadamard transform (WHT) except for the absolute difference operation. If the input pixels are binary, the summation and absolute difference operations can be replaced with the operations logical AND and OR. The generalization of R-transform is called the M-transform.

C. Moment-Invariant Features

Two-dimensional moments are a set of nonlinear functions which are invariant to translation, sacle, and rotation and are defined on geometrical moments of the image. A set of feature vectors called *moment invariants* which are useful for recognizing rotated, shifted, and scaled patterns can be found in [10,11].

IV. Experiments

A database consisting of 100 printed Chinese characters is used in our experiments. Each character in the data set has 50 samples with different positions and different levels of noise. In most experiments, we use one clean smaple to train the classifiers and the remaining noisy samples to test them. Fig. 2 (a) shows a set of noiseless patterns and Fig. 2 (b) shows a set of 15% noise patterns. The noisy pattern is done by randomly selecting some of the pixels of a noiseless binary image and reversing their values from 0 to 1 or vice versa.

A. ARTMAP: Binary Pattern Recognition

There are two training schemes for ARTMAP, which are described as fast learning and slow learning. The ARTMAP simulations in the section were all carried out in fast learning conditions. Using fast learning the weight values are modified to update the category to a perfect match in just one presentation of the input. Any subsequent learning will refine these categories by incorportating more features found in the training patterns.

Since a binary pattern match can be computed by counting the number of matching bits, the most critical parameter of ARTMAP is the baseline vigilance threshold. It controls the resolution of the classification process. Lower vigilance parameters ($\rho < 0.5$) will produce coarser categories. Conversely, higher vigilance parameters (tending to 1) will produce finer categories.

The ARTMAP network can learn to classify printed Chinese characters rapidly and accurately. In our simulations, recognition is achieved by finding a category whose match function meets the vigilance criterion. The resonant state is nonadaptive since the LTM traces are fixed. If the match function is below the vigilance parameter, the character is classified as unknown.

For recognizing noisy patterns, the network is trained with noiseless patterns and tested with the noisy ones. The experimental results obtained from our simulations show that the better choice of vigilance parameter is 0.8. If the vigilance parameter is set too large, the rejection rate will increase.

First-order similarity measure of ARTMAP leads to a loss of higher-order information about the input pattern. Therefore it is not invariant under translation, rotation, or scaling. These invariances can be achieved by incorporating additional processing stages. In our simulations, the M-transform is applied to extract features of printed Chinese characters which are invariant under translation.

The recognition results of shifted patterns via M-transform are shown in Fig. 3. A recognition rate of 100 percent can be achieved for noiseless patterns, while the recognition rates are very low for noisy patterns. As the above results indicate, the performance of M-transform is sensitive to noise.

B. Hybrid Neural Networks: Analog Pattern Recognition

After describing the binary pattern recognition, we will apply two hybrid neural networks which are designed for continuous-valued inputs to recognize the position-shifted and noisy Chinese characters. One is our proposed hybrid neural network and the other is a hybrid neural network whose self-growing neural network is replaced by ART 2-A. The major difference of two hybrid neural networks is that the former codes unnormalized inputs and the latter codes normalized inputs. Three sets of experiments are carried out. The 2-D Fouier transform, the R-transform, and the 2-D moments are utilized in our experiments.

(1). 2-D Fourier transform:

In the first set of experiments, 2-D Fourier transform was used in our character recognition task. Fig. 4 graphically display the performance of ART 2-A classifier using the first 35 magnitude features. As the above results indicate, the performance significantly worsened when the threshold θ is made larger than zero. It implies that the noise suppression/contrast enhancement may be inappropriate for the feature space.

In order to reduce the number of features efficiently, we choose features according to the larger ordering of their standard deviations. Fig. 5 shows the recognition results of AHNN and a linear STM feedback ART 2-A. The classifier with a small size of features can perform as well as the previous experiment with larger number of features.

(2). R-transform:

In the second set of experiments, the R-transform was used to extract features of printed Chinese characters which are invariant under translation. One of the most attractive properties of R-transform is its simple computation. As the technique used in 2-D FFT features, we can also choose features according to the standard deviations scheme. The performance of two classifiers using fifteen features is plotted in Fig. 6.

(3). 2-D moments:

Finally, eight central moments and six moment-invariant features were chosen to train our classifiers to recognize noisy and shifted Chinese characters. Because the numerical values of moment-invariant features are very small, we use the logarithms of the absolute values of these six functions to train the AHNN classifier. The moment-invariant features are all negative, they are not appropriate for ART 2-A. The experimental results are shown in Fig. 7. We find that the moment features are very sensitive to noise.

To summarize the results of the previous three sets of experiments, we can find that the performance of AHNN using fifteen critical FFT features is the best. In our experiments, the learning phase of the hybrid neural network runs approximately several minutes on an 80386-based computer.

V. Conclusions

In this paper, we propose a hybrid neural network to recognize printed Chinese characters. Shorter learning time is obtained in our experiments. Because we use a self-growing architecture and an inter-ART module to

classify patterns, the problem of distance vigilance selection can be overcome. If the vigilance parameter is set large, the network can carry out learning with the minimum necessary number of category representation nodes.

We also compare the performance of four transformations for recognizing position-shifted Chinese characters. As the above experiments indicate, the performance of classifiers using fifteen critical FFT features is better than that using other features. Future works include the modification of the feature extractor and the classifier for recognizing the rotated, scaled, and multi-font printed Chinese characters. Further work also includes the recognition of handwritten Chinese characters.

References

[1] S.B. Cho and J.H. Kim, "Hierarchically structured neural networks for printed Hangul character recognition," *IEEE IJCNN*, Vol.1, pp.265-270, 1990.

[2] R. Hecht-Nielsen, "Counterpropagation networks," *Applied Optics*, Vol. 26, No.23, pp.4979-4985, 1987.

[3] G.A. Carpenter and S. Grossberg, "A massively parallel architecture for a self-organizing neural pattern recognition machine," *Computer Vision , Graphics, and Image Processing*, Vol.37, pp.54-115, 1987.

[4] G.A. Carpenter and S. Grossberg, "ART2: stable self-organization of category recognition codes for analog input patterns," *Applied Optics*, Vol.26, No.23, pp.4919-4930, 1987.

[5] G.A. Carpenter, S. Grossberg and D. Brosen, "ART 2-A: an adaptive resonance algorithm for rapid category learning and recognition," *Neural Networks*, Vol.4, pp.493-504, 1991.

[6] G.A. Carpenter, S. Grossberg and J.H. Reynolds, "ARTMAP: supervied real-time learning and classification of nonstationary data by a self-organizing neural network," *Neural Networks*, Vol.4, pp.565-588, 1991.

[7] B. Morre, "ART 1 and pattern clustering," in *Proceedings of the 1988 Connectionist Models Summer School*, D. Touretzky, G. Hinton, and T. Sejnowski, Eds. San Mateo, CA:Morgan Kaufmann Publishers, pp.174-185, 1989.

[8] P.P. Wang and R.C. Shiau, "Machine recognition of printed Chinese character via transformation algorithms," *Pattern Recognition*, Vol.5, pp.303-321, 1973.

[9] H. Burkhardt and X. Müller, "On invariant sets of a certain class of fast translation-invariant transforms," *IEEE Trans. ASSP*, Vol.28, No.5, pp.517-523, October 1980.

[10] G.L. Cash and M. Hatamian, "Optical character recognition by the method of moments," *Computer Vision , Graphics, and Image Processing*, Vol.39, pp.291-310, 1987.

[11] A. Khotanzad and J.H. Lu, "Classification of invariant image representations using a neural network",*IEEE Trans. ASSP*, Vol.38, No.6, pp.1028-1038, June 1990.

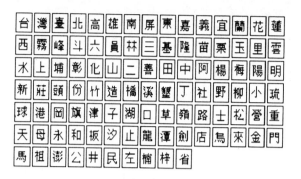

(a)

(b)

Fig 2: (a) A set of noiseless Chinese characters. (b) A set of 15 % noise Chinese characters.

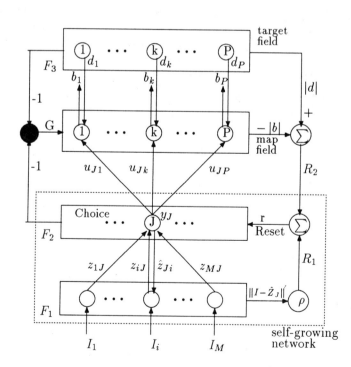

Fig 1: An ARTMAP based hybrid neural network architecture.

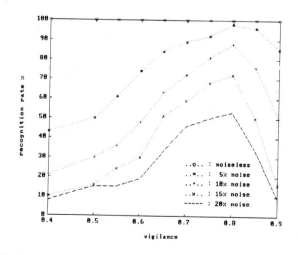

Fig 3: Performance of the ARTMAP via M-transform.

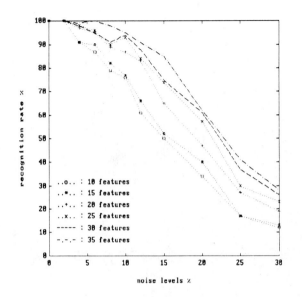

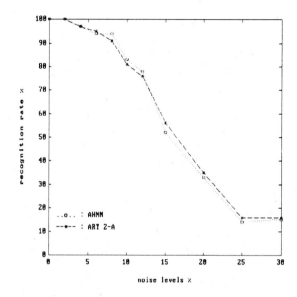

Fig 4: Classification results of ART 2-A using the first 35 FFT features.

Fig 6: Recognition results of the linear STM feedback ART 2-A and the AHNN classifiers using 15 critical R-transform features.

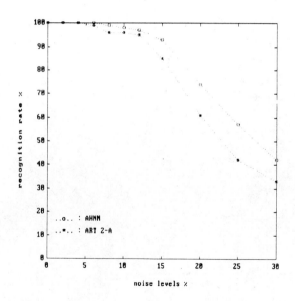

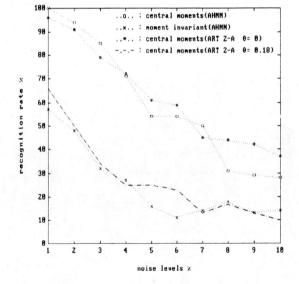

Fig 5: Classification results of the linear STM feedback ART 2-A and the AHNN classifiers using 15 critical FFT features.

Fig 7: Recognition results using eight central moments and six moment invariants.

Dynamic Handwritten Chinese Signature Verification

Hong-De Chang[*], Jhing-Fa Wang[†] and Hong-Ming Suen[†]

[*]Department of Electrical Engineering,[†]Institute of Information Engineering,
National Cheng Kung University, Tainan, Taiwan, R.O.C.

Abstract

--- In this paper, A dynamic handwritten Chinese signature verification system based upon a Bayesian neural network is presented. Due to a great deal of variability of handwritten Chinese signatures, the proposed Bayesian neural network is trained by an incremental learning vector quantization (ILVQ) algorithm, which endows this system with incremental learning ability, and outputs a posteriori probability to give a more reliable distance estimation. The performance analysis was based upon a set of signature data consisting of 800 true specimens, 200 "simple" forgeries and 200 "skilled" forgeries. The experimental results show the type I error is about 2% and the type II error rates are about 0.1% and 2.5% for "simple" and "skilled" forgeries respectively.

Keywords: Handwritten Chinese Signature; Preprocessing; Feature Extraction; Verification; Bayesian Neural Network.

1.Introduction

The handwritten Chinese signatures (HCS) have been the primary form of legal attestation and are commonly used in daily life. Due to the complex structures of the Chinese characters, the handwritten Chinese signatures are usually very complex, while the signatures are constructed by two or more characters, and difficult to imitate. So the HCS is indeed a good personal attribute for identity verification. With the growing need for individual identification in many applications such as banking transactions and sensitive information access, the design of an automatic signature verification system has become a challenge. In general, the signature verification system needs a representation of the signature for computer processing. There are basically two ways to obtain such a representation. They are referred to as "DYNAMIC" (on-line) and "STATIC" (off-line) according to the acquisition process that occurs during the signing process itself or after writing. The information get by the way of "DYNAMIC" is more difficult to imitate than the information extracted by the "STATIC" way and many "DYNAMIC" signature verification systems[1] have been constructed. The features used in the dynamic signature verification can be classified in two types, functions and parameters. Functions (i.e. pressure, velocity, acceleration vs time, etc.) usually extract by some special acquisition equipments[2-5]. Due to the deficiency of these equipments, the presented system uses the commercial digitizer as an input device. It outputs the digitized position of the pentip as X,Y coordinate pairs at a constant rate. We derive 15 parameters from the acquired position signals for verification process.

In this paper, we propose a Bayesian neural network to do the work of decision process. Neural network approaches have been used in many classification problems[6-8]. They unlike traditional classifiers which tend to test competing hypotheses sequentially, neural networks test the competing hypotheses in parallel, thus providing high computation rates. Although the neural networks have the above merits, they also have the defects of being without incremental learning ability and taking too much training time. Here the proposed net is trained by an incremental learning vector quantization (ILVQ) algorithm, which endows this system with incremental learning ability and with fast training speed. Experimental results show the proposed approach is a fast and effective method for handwritten Chinese signature verification.

2. Feature Extraction

The diagram of Figure 1 depicts the configuration of the presented verification system. The digitizer output a position signal $ux,y(t)$ to represent the written signature. Figure 2b shows the digitizer output of specimen shown in Fig. 2a. The next step is referred to as the feature extraction. Since the name of the Chinese usually contain two, three, or four characters, these characters may be separated or connected together in signing due to her/his habits. Therefore we can detect the number of components (NC) according to the squarly characteristic of the Chinese characters. For each component, we extract some timing features such as the total time (TT), the average velocity (V), the number of segments (NS) and the average length in the eight directions (MDi) of the signature. The others are width/height ratio (W/H), left-part/right-part density ratio (L/R) and upper-part/lower-part density ratio (U/D). The set of features extracted from $ux,y(t)$ forms a feature vector for each component, as shown in Fig. 2c.

3. Verification via Bayesian Neural Network

After the feature vector of the observed signature being extracted, the comparison is the most straightforward. There are many techniques have been proposed for signature verification[5, 9-10]. In this paper, we use the neural network technique to do this work. The computer calls up the network corresponding to the signatory. The network has been trained by a set of true signatures. If the feature vector is close enough to trained specimens then the signature is regarded as a true signature; otherwise is regarded as an attempted forgery. The proposed Bayesian neural network and its training algorithm will be described in the following Sections.

3.1 Bayesian Neural Network Architecture

The fundamental architecture of a Bayesian neural network used in our approach contains three slabs: the input slab, the Gaussian slab and the mixture slab as shown in Fig.3. The input slab is broadcasted to all processing elements (PE) in the Gaussian slab and the weights between the input slab and Gaussian slab are all set to 1. In the Gaussian slab, there are M processing elements initially and each PE represents one sub-cluster of handwritten Chinese signatures. We use the K-means algorithm to classify the training specimens with the same NC into M sub-clusters according to their feature vectors. Then, we calculate the distribution of the feature vectors which belong to the same sub-cluster to form a multivariate normal distribution. Consequently, there are M multivariate normal distributions for the M sub-clusters individually in the Gaussian slab. The mixture slab contains one PE for one cluster and connects to each Gaussian PE by the weighted connections.

The operation of the Bayesian network, serving as a Bayesian classifier, can be separated into two phases, the ILVQ algorithm training phase and the verification phase. During the training phase, each PE calculates the Gaussian probability density between the input vector and its weight vector. These Gaussian probability densities are then used to select the PE with the closest weight vector if its density is above a threshold. Otherwise, a new PE is created based on the input vector. In the verification phase, the Gaussian probability densities are calculated between the test vector and each PE's weight vector on the Gaussian slab. The cluster conditional probability is approximated by a mixture of the Gaussian probabilities densities that are assigned to the same cluster. The cluster conditional probability is then weighted by *a priori* probability of the corresponding cluster to produce the *a posteriori* probability. Finally, the *a posteriori* probability is transformed into a log distance.

3.2. ILVQ Training Algorithm

Initially, we use the K-means algorithm to classify the training specimens of the enroment user j into M sub-clusters (M=3 in our system) according to their feature vectors. Each sub-cluster forms a multivariate normal distribution. For the successive training specimen S_j, we calculate the Gaussian probability density $P_{m;j}(S_j|W_i(m))$ between each sub-cluster $W_i(m)$ and the input vector according to

$$P_{m;j}(S_j|W_i(m)) = \frac{1}{(2\pi)^{N/2}(\prod_{n=1}^{N}\sigma_{i;m;n}^2)^{1/2}} \times \exp[-\sum_{n=1}^{N}\frac{(S_{j;n}-\mu_{i;m;n})^2}{2\sigma_{i;m;n}^2}] \quad , \quad m=1,2,...,M$$

where N is the dimension of the sub-cluster center and the input vector, $\mu_{i;m;n}$ is the mean of sub-cluster $W_i(m)$ and $\sigma_{i;m;n}$ represents the standard deviation in $W_i(m)$. Then we select the $P_{k;j}=\max(P_{m;j})$, m=1,2,....,M, and check whether the $P_{k;j}$ is larger than a threshold TH or not. If it is larger than TH then S_j is assigned to the **kth** sub-cluster and the mean and variance of the **kth** sub-cluster are adapted, according to

$$\mu_{i;k;n}^* = \frac{\mu_{i;k;n} \times NUM_k + S_{j;n}}{NUM_k + 1} \quad , \quad n=1,2,3,......,N$$

$$\sigma_{i;k;n}^{*2} = \frac{(\sigma_{i;k;n}^2 + \mu_{i;k;n}^2) \times NUM_k + S_{j;n}^2}{NUM_k + 1} - \mu_{i;k;n}^{*2}, \quad n=1,2,3,......,N$$

$$NUM_k^* = NUM_k + 1$$

where NUMk is the total number of the training specimens which belongs to the **kth** sub-cluster. Otherwise, a new sub-cluster is constructed and S_j stands for the sub-cluster center. The variance of the new sub-cluster is then defined as

$$\sigma_{i;M+1;n}^2 = \frac{\sum_{m=1}^{M}\sigma_{i;m;n}^2}{M} \quad , \quad n=1,2,3,......,N.$$

4. Experimental Results

The experiments are based on the database consisting of 800 true specimens, 200 "simple" forgeries and 200 "skilled" forgeries. True specimens were obtained from 80 persons. Every person signed his Chinese name 10 times as specimens. The "simple" forgeries were written by 20 different forgers who make no attempt to simulate the true signatures and the "skilled" forgeries were written by 10 different trained forgers who were given the opportunity to practice many times. According to the variability of handwritten Chinese signatures, each enroment user corresponds to a Bayesian neural network as shown in Fig. 4 which is constructed by the fundamental Bayesian neural network described previously and contains three parts. The part of neural network consists of 4 fundamental Bayesian neural networks and each fundamental Bayesian neural network represents a type of signatures with the same NC. The output of each fundamental Bayesian neural network is the distance between the observed signature S_j and the reference templates. Namely, if S_j is closest to the ith type of signatures in the network then the output of the ith fundamental Bayesian neural network will be the minimum one. The next part is an arbitration comparator. It uses the following formula

$$f_a(i) = \begin{cases} \alpha & \text{if } S_j(NC) \neq T_i(NC) \\ f_b(i) & \text{if otherwise} \end{cases} \quad \text{for } i = 1 \text{ to } 4,$$

to verify whether the S_j is the signature of the observed user, where $f_a(i)$ and $f_b(i)$ are outputs of the arbitration comparator i and fundamental Bayesian neural network i respectively. If the value of $f_a(i)$ is equal to $f_b(i)$ which means that the S_j has the same NC with the reference specimens represented by the ith fundamental Bayesian neural network; otherwise set the output of the arbitration comparator to be a very large value. The minimum selector selects the minimum one from the output of the arbitration comparators. If the $\min(f_b(i)) \leq T_{uj}$ (T_{uj} is the personalized threshold of the signer u_j), then the S_j is accepted otherwise S_j is rejected.

The experimental results show the type I error is about 2% and the type II error rates are about 0.1% and 2.5% for "simple" and "skilled" forgeries respectively.

5. Conclusions

In this paper, we introduce an dynamic handwritten Chinese signature verification system based upon neural network. The proposed ILVQ algorithm endows our system with incremental learning ability. The training time of the Bayesian neural network is very short and it can be incrementally trained while adding a new signature to the network. The experimental results show the proposed Bayesian net is effective and the selected features suit for discriminating HCS. For the database consisting of 800 true specimens, 200 "simple" forgeries and 200 "skilled" forgeries, the type I error is about 2% and the type II error rates are about 0.1% and 2.5% for "simple" and "skilled" forgeries respectively.

References

[1] Rejean Plamondon and Guy Lorette, "Automatic Signature Verification and Writer Identification --- The State of the Art", *Pattern Recognition*, Vol. 22 No. 2, pp. 107-131, 1989.

[2] Maarse, F.J., Janssen, H.J.J., and Dexel, F. "A special pen for an XY tablet", in *Computer in Psychology: Methods, Instrumentation and Psychodiagnostics*, F.J.Maarse, L.J.M. Mulder, WPB Sjouw and AEAkkerman (Eds.), Swets and Zeithlinger, Lisse, Netherlands 1988, pp. 133-139.

[3] Stuckert, P.E., "Magnetic pen and tablet", *IBM Tech. Disclosure Bull (USA)* **22**, no3, 1979, pp. 1245-1251.

[4] De Bruyne, P., "Dynamic signature verification using your own pen", *Proc. Carnahan Conf. on Crime Countermeasures*, 1988a.

[5] Hewitt D. Crane and John S. Ostrem, "Automatic Signature Verification Using a Three-Axis Force-Sensitive Pen", *IEEE Trans. Syst. Man, Cybern.*, vol. SMC-13, no. 3, pp.329-337, 1983.

[6] R. P. Lippmann, An Introduction to Computing with Neural Nets, *IEEE ASSP Mag.*, vol. 4, pp. 4-22, Apr 1987.

[7] Y. Yong, Handprinted Chinese Character Recognition via Neural Networks, *Pattern Recognition Letters*, 7, pp. 19-25, 1988.

[8] K. Fukushima, S. Miyake and T. Ito, Neocognitron: A Neural Network Model for a Mechanism of Visual Pattern Recognition, *IEEE Trans.on SMC* 13, pp.826-834, 1983.

[9] J. J. Brault and R. Plamondon, "Histogram classifier for characterization of handwritten signature dynamic", *Proc. 7th Int. Conf. Pattern Recognition*, Vol. 1, pp. 619-622, 1984.

[10] G. Lorette, "On-line handwritten signature recognition based on data analysis and clustering", *Proc. 7th Int. Conf. Pattern Recognition*, Vol. 2, pp. 1284-1287, 1984.

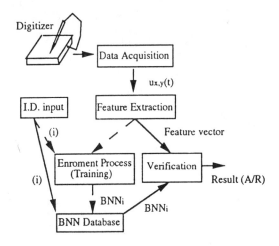

Fig. 1. The configuration of the presented system.

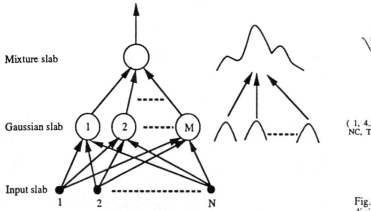

Mixture slab

Gaussian slab

Input slab

1   2   N

Fig. 3. The fundamental architecture of a Bayesian neural network.

(a)   (b)

(1, 4.51, 151.94, 1, 0.10, 0.12, 0.10, 0.30, 0.02, 0.02, 0.05, 0.30, 2.96, 1.94, 0.98)
NC, TT,   V, NS, MD1, 2, 3, 4, 5, 6, 7, 8, W/H, L/R, U/D

(c)

Fig. 2. (a) Handwritten Chinese signature specimen. (b) The digitizer output of the specimen (a). (c) The extracted feature vector of (a).

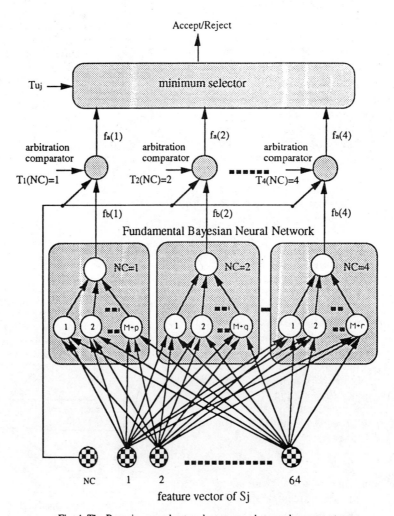

Fig. 4. The Bayesian neural network corresponds to each enroment user.

Neural networks have taken the financial world by storm. Neural networks are being used to forecast stocks, currency exchange rates, bonds, commodities, and a myriad of other finance products. The majority of this work has been going on quietly in almost every major financial institution with little or no public disclosure of the results. Recently, there has been a slight change in this posture. The *IEEE Computation Intelligence for Financial Engineering Conference (CIFEr)* was held for the first time in New York City during April 1995, and by all standards was considered a smashing success. The next CIFEr meeting is already being planned for the same location. This chapter contains three of the better papers written on the topic of financial applications of neural networks through the end of 1993. **Paper 15.1** compares the performance of the multilayer perceptron (MLP) neural network against the Black-Scholes formula for the estimation of market price options. **Paper 15.2** compares the performance of the MLP against ARIMA models for predicting the German Stock Index. **Paper 15.3** compares the performance of the MLP neural network against multiple linear regression for stock ranking.

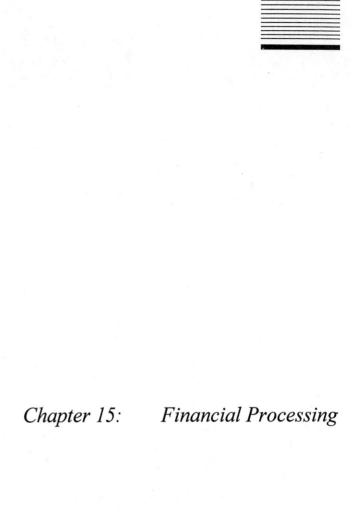

Chapter 15:   *Financial Processing*

Beating the Best: A Neural Network Challenges the Black-Scholes Formula

Mary Malliaris
Management Science Department
Loyola University Chicago
820 N. Michigan Ave.
Chicago, IL 60611

Linda Salchenberger
Management Science Department
Loyola University Chicago
820 N. Michigan Ave
Chicago, IL 60611

Abstract

A neural network model which processes financial input data is developed to estimate the market price of options. The network's ability to estimate option prices is compared to estimates generated by the Black-Scholes model, a traditional financial model. Comparisons reveal that the neural network outperforms the Black-Scholes model in about half of the cases examined.

AI Topic: Neural networks
Domain Area: Financial modelling
Language/Tool: NeuralWorks Professional II™
Status: Prototype has been successfully developed
Effort: Approximately 2 man-years of effort
Impact: Our results show that a neural network can successfully compete with a sophisticated, well-established mathematical model.

The Black-Scholes option pricing model

In 1973, Black and Scholes [1] proposed a model for computing the current market worth of an option. An option is an agreement giving the holder the right to purchase [a call] or sell [a put] some asset at an agreed upon future time, called the date of expiration. The price that will be paid at this future date is called the exercise price of the option. The market price of the option is the price you pay now for the privilege of buying or selling the underlying asset on or before the expiration date. The Black-Scholes model uses five input variables [exercise price of the option, volatility of the underlying asset, price of the underlying asset, number of days until the option expires, and interest rate] to estimate the price which should be charged for an option. The Black-Scholes option pricing formula for calculating the equilibrium price of call options is shown in (1)

$$C = S \cdot N(d_1) - X e^{-rT} \cdot N(d_2) \qquad \textbf{(1)}$$

where C is the market price to be charged for the option, N is the cumulative normal distribution, T is the number of days remaining until expiration of the option expressed as a fraction of a year, S is the price of the underlying asset, r is the risk-free interest rate prevailing at period t, X is the exercise price of the option and d_1 and d_2 are given by (2) and (3)

$$d_1 = \frac{\ln\left(\frac{S}{X}\right) + \left(r + \frac{\sigma^2}{2}\right) \cdot T}{\sigma\sqrt{T}} \qquad \textbf{(2)}$$

$$d_2 = d_1 - \sigma\sqrt{T} \qquad \textbf{(3)}$$

where σ^2 is the variance rate of return for the underlying asset. For any time interval [0,t] of length t, the return on the underlying asset is normally distributed with variance $\sigma^2 t$ [4].

One of the critical assumptions underlying this model is that the distribution of prices is log-normal and the volatility is constant [1], [3]. For a rigorous presentation of the derivation of the Black-Scholes model, see [5]. The exercise price, number of days to expiration, and closing price are observable. The volatility cannot be directly observed so it is computed implicitly. Most observers use the Implied Standard Deviation of observed option prices as an estimate of volatility [2]. We used at-the-money call options for this estimate and then used that estimate of volatility to calculate all the call options for that day.

Options with an exercise price equal to the closing price of the index are said to be at-the-money. In the pricing of calls, exercise prices less than the closing price are in-the-money, and exercise prices greater than the closing price are out-of-the-money.

Since its introduction in 1973, the Black-Scholes

options pricing model has performed better overall than any model. Empirical tests show that Black-Scholes remains superior among option pricing equilibrium models, with the possible exception of cases in which trades are made deep-in and deep-out-of-the-money. The volume of research which continues to proliferate related to the Black-Scholes model, even 20 years after its introduction, indicates there is considerable interest and value in developing a model which is more robust than Black-Scholes. In addition, there is some reason to believe that the trading process itself may reveal underlying strategies as well as analytical models and there is information to be gained from historical pricing data. Neural networks have been shown to be useful in modelling nonstationary processes and nonlinear dependencies and thus, may represent a channel of investigation in the search for another type of option pricing model.

Methodology

The data set used for this research was developed using option price transactions data published in the Wall Street Journal during the period from January 1, 1990 to June 30, 1990. The exercise price, market price of the option, and closing price of the S&P 100 index are reported for each trading day. The interest rate came from the results of the 3-month US Treasury Bill Monday auction, as reported each Tuesday in the Wall Street Journal. The data set selected for testing includes pricing data from April 23 to June 29, 1990 and includes in-the-money options and out-of-the-money options with time to expiration between 30 and 60 days. Typically, 6 different call prices per day are quoted.

The five variables selected to estimate the market price of the option are those used in the Black-Scholes model; exercise price, time to expiration, closing price, volatility, and interest rate. For the neural network, we added two lagged variables: yesterday's closing price, LAG CLOSE PRICE, and yesterday's market price of the option, LAG MARKET PRICE.

Preliminary data analysis revealed dependencies and relationships between the variables which were used to partition the data sets for the neural network. Experimentation with different training sets showed that better results could be obtained in the neural networks when the data was separated into in-the-money and out-of-the-money groups. Prices in-the-money vary from $60.00 to $0.75; prices out-of-the-money vary from $15.50 to $0.0625. A larger proportion of observations exist for out-of-the-money prices than for in-the-money prices. Correlations were also found between time to expiration

and market price of the option, and between the closing price and the market price of the option.

Under supervised learning, the feedforward, backpropagation neural network learns relationships between input and output variables during a training process, as data are presented to the network. One approach to testing the performance of the network is to check its accuracy in estimating values for a holdout sample generated from the training set. For evaluating the performance of the option price neural network, we selected a more realistic and more difficult performance measure. The network was trained using historical data and option price estimations for a future period were developed with the trained network and compared to actual prices.

To capture the volatile nature of the options market, a relatively short time frame was used for the training sets and testing sets. The testing sets were developed using a two-week time frame; this was a convenient choice because interest rate and volatility changed weekly and were relatively stable over a two-week period. Five two-week periods were selected for price estimation; the weeks beginning April 23, May 7, May 21, June 4, and June 18. To provide the neural network models with a variety of examples, each training set included as many observations as necessary to provide at least one full cycle (30 days prior to the estimation period) of pricing data.

The neural network model

Since feedforward, single hidden layer neural networks have been successfully used for classification and prediction, we selected this network model for our initial experiments and used the backpropagation training algorithm. A neural network consisting of 7 input nodes, 4 middle layer nodes, and 1 output node was developed. The input nodes represent the five financial variables used in the Black-Scholes model (EXER, DAYS, CLOSE PRICE, VOL, and INT) and two lag variables (LAG CLOSE PRICE and LAG MARKET PRICE), and the output node (MARKET PRICE) represents the market price of the option.

The network is fully connected, with a direct connection from exercise price (EXER) to the output node (MARKET PRICE). Better results were achieved with this additional connection because of the linear dependence between EXER and MARKET PRICE observed in the data set and verified with a series of regression models. All the connection weights were initially randomized, and were then determined during the training process.

The generalized Delta rule was used with the backpropagation of error to transfer values from internal nodes. (For a more detailed explanation of backpropagation learning and the generalized Delta rule, see [6].) The sigmoidal function is the activation function specified in this neural network and is used to adjust weights associated with each input node.

Supervised learning was conducted with training sets consisting of the seven predictor variables and the corresponding market price of the option for each exercise price, for each trading day. For the input nodes in which the data was not in ratio form, the values were scaled to be within a range of 0 to 1. This minimizes the effect of magnitude among the inputs and increases the effectiveness of the learning algorithm. The selection of the examples for the training set focused on quality and the degree to which the data set represented the population. The size of the training set is important since a larger training set may take longer to process computationally, but it may accelerate the rate of learning and reduce the number of iterations required for convergence.

The learning rate and momentum were set initially at 0.9 and 0.6, respectively and the learning rate was adjusted downward and the momentum was adjusted upward to improve performance. The training examples were presented to the network in random order to maximize performance and to minimize the introduction of bias. Training was halted after a minimum of 40,000 iterations. The network was implemented using the software package Neuralworks Explorer running on a 386-based microcomputer with a math co-processor.

Results

To compare the estimations made by each model, we compute and report the mean absolute deviation (MAD), mean absolute percent error (MAPE), and mean squared error (MSE) for each of the 5 two-week periods for both in-the-money and out-of-the-money prices. Option prices were estimated from the Black-Scholes model using a computer program based on equations (1)-(3). Neural network estimations were developed by inputting the estimation sets into a trained network.

The initial results showed that, compared to the actual prices, the neural network estimations had a lower MAPE than Black-Scholes for 4 of the 5 two-week periods for the out-of-the-money case, but Black-Scholes was superior for 4 of 5 two-week periods for in-the-money trades. These results are reported in Tables 2 and 3.

Paired sample comparisons tests were run on the Black-Scholes estimates and actual market prices and on the neural network estimates and actual market prices. These results show that the Black-Scholes consistently overprices the options, while the neural network underprices them. We also observe that the standard deviation of the differences is smaller in the neural network prices.

Results of the paired sample comparisons test for the in-the-money cases show that there is a statistically significant difference between the means of the sample of neural network predictions and the sample of actual market prices. The Black-Scholes however, did not show a significant difference from zero, hence it provides a better model for in-the-money, for this data set.

A few observations about the results can be made. First, although we have only presented summary statistics, one can observe similarities between the individual price estimates made by the two models. Each model has difficulty computing prices when the trades are deep in-the-money. This is expected for the neural network because the majority of trades are close to at-the-money and thus, there are insufficient examples to present to the network for these cases. Secondly, we would not expect to achieve results with the neural network which are significantly different than those of Black-Scholes if many traders are using the Black-Scholes model and the market prices reflect their strategies. The neural network is only capable of learning the relationships which are imbedded in the observations. The neural network exhibited a bias of underpricing the options and in fact, may be best utilized as input into another pricing mechanism.

Summary and conclusions

This empirical examination of the Black-Scholes option valuation model and the neural network option pricing model leads to some interesting conclusions. First, while the two modelling approaches differ fundamentally in their methodology to determining option prices, some common results emerge. While the neural network performs better than Black-Scholes on prices out-of-the money, estimations near the expiration date are accurate for both. The neural network may play a valuable role in some type of preliminary data analysis for in-the-money, rather than directly computing prices.

Second, are several limitations which may restrict the use of neural network models for estimation. There is no formal theory for determining optimal network topology and therefore, decisions like the appropriate number of layers and middle layer nodes must be determined using experimentation. The development and interpretation of neural network models requires more expertise from the user than traditional analytical models. Training a neural network can be computationally intensive and the results are sensitive to the selection of learning parameters, activation function, topology of the network, and the composition of the data set.

Thirdly, the paper illustrates that the neural network methodology offers a valuable alternative to estimating option prices to the traditional Black-Scholes model. The evidence reported here is encouraging, particularly in view of the essentially undisputed superiority of the Black-Scholes model. Analytically, it is remarkable, that the well-developed methodology of Black-Scholes, with its explicit formula for pricing options, derived using sophisticated financial arbitrage arguments and advanced stochastic calculus techniques, can actually be approximated by neural networks.

References

1. Black F and Scholes M (1973) The pricing of options and corporate liabilities. J. Pol. Econ. **81**, 637-654.

2. Chesney M and Scott L (1989) Pricing European currency options: a comparison of the modified Black-Scholes model and a random variance model. J. Fin. Quant. Anal. **24**, 267-284.

3. Chiras D and Manaster S (1978) The information content of option prices and a test of market efficiency. J. of Finl. Econ. **6**, 213-234.

4. Macbeth J and Merville L (1979) An empirical examination of the Black-Scholes call option pricing model. J. Fin. **34**(5), 1173-1186.

5. Malliaris A and Brock W (1982) Stochastic Methods in Economics and Finance, North-Holland, Amsterdam.

6. Rumelhart D E and McClelland J L (1986) Parallel Distributed Processing. MIT Press, Cambridge, MA.

Table 1.   Comparative analysis, actual prices with estimated prices, out-of-the-money

Week beginning	MAD	MAPE	MSE
April 23			
Black-Scholes	.598932	30.81731	.435342
Neural Network	.207702	12.74440	.074409
May 7			
Black-Scholes	.340729	16.23661	.160047
Neural Network	.382937	15.04892	.253373
May 21			
Black-Scholes	.378636	9.43207	.204219
Neural Network	.422369	12.30240	.253676
June 4			
Black-Scholes	.286645	9.104615	.245477
Neural Network	.312945	9.097162	.231779
June 18			
Black-Scholes	.660788	17.45452	1.250466
Neural Network	.447812	10.94668	.455352

Table 2.   Comparative analysis, actual prices with estimated prices, in-the-money

Week beginning	MAD	MAPE	MSE
April 23			
Black-Scholes	.676936	3.8057	1.05573
Neural Network	.82434	5.1689	1.175115
May 7			
Black-Scholes	.670291	2.7142	1.459724
Neural Network	1.289340	7.4727	3.127410
May 21			
Black-Scholes	.766019	2.8867	1.386018
Neural Network	.832762	4.6876	1.006885
June 4			
Black-Scholes	.784969	2.8864	1.771361
Neural Network	1.053282	5.2136	2.397112
June 18			
Black-Scholes	1.391258	7.2002	3.945318
Neural Network	.987918	6.6399	1.407175

Comparing Artificial Neural Networks with Statistical Methods within the Field of Stock Market Prediction

Prof. Dr. Matthias Schumann, Dipl.-Kfm. Thomas Lohrbach

University Goettingen, School of Management, Information Systems Department,
Platz der Goettinger Sieben 7, D-3400 Goettingen, Federal Republic of Germany,
Phone: +49-551/39-4433 and 39-4442, Fax: +49-551/39-9679

Abstract:

Within the field of stock market prediction a controversial discussion between technicians and fundamentalists concerning the qualification of these different methods has taken place. On the one hand, experts use so-called charts to extract those formations they regard to be significant for the future development of stock prices. On the other hand, the fundamentalists have to decide which information, even regarding other influences, they take into consideration. Therefore, it is intended to link both perspectives. ARIMA-Models and Artificial Neural Networks (ANN) are two problem-solving approaches that are investigated in this paper. Our intention for both approaches is a short-term prediction (the following day's stock price).

1 Characterization of the stock market prediction

For predicting stock market prices, it is necessary to discuss whether an influence exists between the information of the past and the prospective development of the prices. Presuming that the development of prices depends on the decisions of potential investors, who only can take those values of the past into their consideration, a certain slope must exist.

For a prediction it is necessary that the stock market is not an information-efficient market. Such a market is characterized by Fama in the following way: "A market in which prices always ´fully reflect´ available information is called efficient." As a result information influencing the market must not allow any profits because the market itself reacts on proclaimed ´news´ with an immediate adaptation of the prices. Various interpretations concerning the presence of information efficiency exist. Thus, analysing the possibilities of predicting stock market prices also implies the denial of information efficiency at a first glance. The next step will show which information is important for price changes. There are various issues that come into account such as overall economic development and situation on the capital market etc. or merely the course of the shares on their own respectively mathematical transformations of these.

On the one hand the technicians maintain that all factors which influence the price level are still considered in the quotation, since it represents the supply and demand on the stock market.

On the other hand the fundamentalists even regard external terms like interest rates and economic policy etc. separately. They argue that such influences are not implicitly regarded in the prices. Both ideas are investigated in this paper.

A period must be fixed for which the prognosis has to be investigated. Often one tries to identify a long-term trend (i.e. one year) for the price development. According to a fast reaction on changes in the stock market a shorter period (i.e. one day) may be more interesting.

2 Data material and methods for prognosis

Although quotations of various shares, indices and other so-called ´external´ information were available (period from 12-31-82 till 12-31-91), within this article it is only referred to the German Hochtief-share and Deutscher Aktienindex (DAX). The presentation is bounded to these two values, for the main conclusions of our

498

investigations, this limitation is of no significance. External information (daily quoted) according to:

the number of all traded shares, the number of shares that increased, remained at the same level and decreased in the Frankfurt stock market and Wall Street, Dow-Jones-, Nikkei-, Financial-Times- and Westbau-Index (index, referring to shares within the field of construction trade), money market rates, exchange rates, gold price as well as oil price was available.

The next question concerns methods, used for prediction. Because of the (supposed) influence of stochastic elements on those time-series, it is necessary to use a method which is able to filter such undesired elements.

One method with such filtering abilities is the ARIMA-method. The virtue of ARIMA is well characterized by Vandaele: "... can be viewed as an approach by which time-series data are sifted through a series of progressively finer sieves ...". The aim of sifting some components is to identify so-called ´white-noise-processes´ (merely stochastic influences on the time-series).

Another approach with such capabilities is ANN. ANN consist of many simple elements (units, neurons, processing elements, PE) which are interconnected. Their way of working can be described as the parallel interaction of these simple elements where several operations are performed at the same time. ANN are not programed but trained with a large amount of examples. ANN do not store their ´information´ locally but all units are responsible for working correctly. This results in a major advantage since the loss of some elements or incomplete input does not automatically lead to a wrong answer.

It is exactly these abilities which predetermine ANN for the prediction of stock price development.

3 Stock prediction with ANN

3.1 Describing of the ANN´s configuration

Within this investigation, a Counterpropagation Network (CPG) and the Software NWorks (using an IBM RS 6000) was used. The CPG consists of four layers (Input-, Normalization, Kohonen- and Output-Layer) and selects from a set of exemplars by allowing the neurons to compete amongst each other.

Some problems need consideration. No detailed instructions exist concerning the dimension of the Kohonen Layer. One might suggest utilizing two elements, since it deals with the prediction of whether a stock price increases or decreases. But it is the question if the complete data set only consists of two exactly defined classes. Various patterns might exist which are too different to be represented by a single neuron only. Thus, one can propose to place as many neurons in the Kohonen Layer as there are training examples. This would cause complex nets which might not be able to extract reliable information but merely memorize all training data. The configuration of the Kohonen Layer, in order to find a compromise between memorization and generalization, needs variation. One has to create stationary time-series, because when using original values, identified structures of the past can not be transposed into the future because of their different spread of values. Fig. 1 shows which output was investigated.

Output layer		Output	
PE		pos.	neg.
1	price increases the following day	1	0
2	price decreases the following day	1	0
3	price increases the following day significant (>0.5 %)	1	0
4	price decreases the following day significant (>0.5 %)	1	0

Fig. 1:   Description of the output

Because the output of the ANN is between 0 and 1, it must be interpreted. A result near to 0 or 1 will be regarded as price decreases or increases. Three methods for the interpretation are used (see fig. 2).

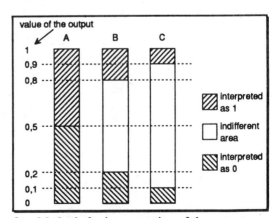

Fig. 2:   Methods for interpretation of the output

A statistical auxiliary means (cross-correlation analysis) should show which of the above-mentioned time-series is influential for the further development of the investigated shares and therefore was used as input data.

In addition, the question remains how long a once-trained net is able to predict. Testing various possibilities is necessary. First of all, two proportions (prop. 1: 2089 training data, 50 testing data and prop. 2: 209 training data, 50 testing data) were investigated.

With regard to the number of training steps, two different approaches are possible. The training volume might be determined by the user, but this procedure seems to be very arbitrary. Therefore, the error of the determined and existing output during the training is used as a convergence criterion. Training is to be terminated if this error reaches a very low level or if it does not change during a large number of training steps.

3.2 Results using ANN for prediction

The figures below show the results (in percent) of correctly classified output, according to each output neuron (PE 1-4, see fig. 1) refering to the three interpretation methods (see fig. 2). The notation pos./neg. explain the number of correctly recognized output values 1/0 (see fig. 1) with respect to the number of classified values. The notation class. describes the number of classified values (see fig. 2).

PE	1			2		
method	pos. in %	neg. in %	class. in %	pos. in %	neg. in %	class. in %
A	66.67	47.73	100	47.73	66.67	100
B	100	0	4	0	100	4
C	0	0	0	0	0	0

PE	3			4		
method	pos. in %	neg. in %	class. in %	pos. in %	neg. in %	class. in %
A	100	79.17	100	0	79.59	100
B	100	92.31	28	0	84.62	52
C	0	100	36	0	86.36	44

Fig. 3: Results and number of classifications in percent (DAX), 'pure' time-series, prop. 1

Such a spreading of the results seems to be necessary, since only one digit alone is not satisfactory for a differentiation. An example can illustrate this. Simply counting the 'correct' prognosis, without any reference whether it dealt with an in- or decreasing output, using PE1 attains 25 'correct' answers (50%) whereas PE3 makes 40 'correct' statements (80%). Choosing either PE1 or PE3, one has to interpret the results either as 'bad' or 'good'. Thus, a single digit does not allow exact conclusions concerning the ability for recognizing structures. At least i.e. the average for the four PE must be computed in order to get a clear statement.

The first tests used the last 40 quotations. Each was presented as the relative change of two following days (continuously coding) as the input for the ANN.

PE	1			2		
method	pos. in %	neg. in %	class. in %	pos. in %	neg. in %	class. in %
A	43.75	61.76	100	61.76	43.75	100
B	0	0	0	0	0	0
C	0	0	0	0	0	0

PE	3			4		
method	pos. in %	neg. in %	class. in %	pos. in %	neg. in %	class. in %
A	44.44	75.61	100	100	61.22	100
B	0	100	2	0	64.71	34
C	0	0	0	0	60	10

Fig. 4: Results and number of classifications in percent (Hochtief-share), 'pure' time-series, prop. 1

The high results of PE 3 and PE 4 for the Hochtief-share are remarkable. But it needs consideration that the networks mostly recognized decreasing developments with such high results. Although the main trend of prices also has been decreasing, it is questionable whether a sufficient generalization has been attained.

But in spite of the assumption, prop. 2 would improve the results because of the smaller temporal distance of training and testing data, the results arranged contrary.

Subsequently, so-called indicators are investigated. As opposed to the above-described procedure not only the time-series itself but transformations of these are used. Five of those indicators will be taken into consideration for this investigation:

- the Trend-Oscillator (TO),
- the Relative-Strongness (RS),
- the Momentum (MM),
- the Relative-Strongness-Index (RSI) and
- the Overbought/Oversold Indicator (OBOS).

A cross-correlation analysis showed the highest influence of: MM and OBOS for the DAX and of RS and RSI for the Hochtief-share.

Additionally, it is to allude that the correlation of all extracted indicators only was close-fitting the significance level.

PE	1			2		
method	pos. in %	neg. in %	class. in %	pos. in %	neg. in %	class. in %
A	58.62	57.14	100	55.56	59.38	100
B	71.43	61.54	54	60	68.75	52
C	100	75	20	100	87.5	18

PE	3			4		
method	pos. in %	neg. in %	class. in %	pos. in %	neg. in %	class. in %
A	18.75	76.47	100	25	78.57	100
B	33.33	72.73	56	33.33	75.76	72
C	25	85.71	22	25	73.68	38

Fig. 5: Results and number of classifications in percent (DAX), using indicators, prop. 1

PE	1			2		
method	pos. in %	neg. in %	class. in %	pos. in %	neg. in %	class. in %
A	45	63.33	100	66.67	51.43	100
B	44.44	84.62	44	100	50	34
C	100	85.71	16	100	66.67	14

PE	3			4		
method	pos. in %	neg. in %	class. in %	pos. in %	neg. in %	class. in %
A	38.89	81.25	100	45.45	61.54	100
B	60	81.3	56	66.67	57.89	44
C	100	85.71	30	0	60	20

Fig. 6: Results and number of classifications in percent (Hochtief-share), using indicators, prop. 1

The same investigation took place referring to prop. 2. For the DAX it leads to nearly the same results. The number of classifications concerning the hard criteria increased. Thus, only the results of the DAX are listed.

PE	1			2		
method	pos. in %	neg. in %	class. in %	pos. in %	neg. in %	class. in %
A	75	55.26	100	58.33	65.38	100
B	75	54.84	86	63.16	66.67	86
C	75	54.84	86	63.16	66.67	86

PE	3			4		
method	pos. in %	neg. in %	class. in %	pos. in %	neg. in %	class. in %
A	30	80	100	20	77.5	100
B	16.67	82.86	82	25	78.95	84
C	16.67	82.86	41	25	78.95	42

Fig. 7: Results and number of classifications in percent (DAX), using indicators, prop. 2

On the one hand, the results using indicators, referring to method A, neither seem to be worse nor improved significantly. On the other hand, there are differences in the case of the hard criteria method B and C (see fig. 2). At a first glance, a comparison between the results by using 'pure' time-series and the results by using indicators is difficult because the number of classifications is almost zero (using 'pure' time-series, method B and C, see fig. 3 and 4) and so no prognosis took place in the first case. Taking into account that in both series of tests (pure time-series vs. indicators) identical variations for determining the best number of neurons in the Kohonen Layer are used, one can draw the conclusion to prefer indicators. As mentioned in 3.1, only a hard criterion is able to identify relevant patterns. Thus, the results using indicators are regarded as being better because more 'hard selected' samples have been recognized.

An improvement in this case might be the usage of pruning during training. Pruning can be understood as a method that attempts minimizing both, network complexity and error over the learning data set. An ANN with minimal complexity which does well on a learning data set will generalize for the future better than a more complex network. The reduction of complexity will be attained by removing those small weights whose influence in gaining a good result is neglectable. Then, all relevant indicators could be identified because the

ANN itself judges whether a piece of information is necessary for classification or not. This will be our next topic of further research.

The next step consists of regarding the influences of so-called external information. For that purpose, the statistical auxiliary means (cross-correlation) was used again to investigate the influence between the above-mentioned shares and all daily available time-series. Those with the highest correlation were used as input. Doing so, the results turned out to be extremely worse. An analysis of the data material showed that the structure of the proportions, as opposed to the technical approach, is not suited for using fundamental information. An example may illustrate this. The Dow-Jones showed the highest correlation with the DAX. Whereas the development (prop. 1 and prop. 2) of the DAX followed that of the Dow-Jones in 60.49% with regard to the whole data material, the analysis of the testing data merely points to a quota of 52%. Therefore, a third prop. (prop. 3: 1.604 learning and 535 testing data) was built which beared this fact in mind.

PE	1			2		
method	pos. in %	neg. in %	class. in %	pos. in %	neg. in %	class. in %
A	49.8	55.94	100	55.43	56.41	100
B	87.5	68.18	8.6	55.56	91.67	7.85
C	55.56	66.67	5.05	55.56	77.78	5.05
PE	3			4		
method	pos. in %	neg. in %	class. in %	pos. in %	neg. in %	class. in %
A	53.85	72.08	100	65	72.04	100
B	83.33	79.41	26.54	66.67	71.21	25.23
C	100	86.67	5.98	66.67	86.21	5.98

Fig. 8: Results and number of classifications in percent (DAX), using fundamental information, prop. 3

At first the DAX will be regarded. Beginning with all daily available information as input (22 time-series), the results were not satisfying. Therefore, the input needed further analysis. 7 of the time-series refer to stock statistics, i.e. number of all increased/decreased/not-changed shares at Frankfurt Stock Market etc. Their influence is reduced, since it seems to be sufficient to regard only the number of increased shares. Decreased

shares i.e. will be correlated to the increased. An elimination of some exchange rates and money market rates took place, too. This leads to the remaining 13 time-series (see fig. 8).

Tests were much better than those of the bigger input vector. A further reduction of the information (only seven time-series) worsened the results. On the one hand, the change from 22 to 13 input elements showed that too much information can cause a fitting of the noise. On the other hand, the loss of relevant information produces bad results. This points out that such a ´manual´ pruning is not satisfactory because it is too inexact and therefore confirms again the importance of pruning. The same way was used for predicting the DAX as applied for the Hochtief-share (see fig. 9). The conclusions coincided with those of the DAX.

PE	1			2		
method	pos. in %	neg. in %	class. in %	pos. in %	neg. in %	class. in %
A	51.11	59.15	100	54.63	55.74	100
B	52.63	61.22	21.87	50	57.32	22.43
C	53.85	59.09	10.65	44.83	53.45	16.26
PE	3			4		
method	pos. in %	neg. in %	class. in %	pos. in %	neg. in %	class. in %
A	41.18	66.22	100	36.59	62.75	100
B	36.84	69.44	30.47	33.33	67.65	41.5
C	38.46	64.15	12.34	33.33	66.25	18.32

Fig. 9: Results and number of classifications in percent (Hochtief-share), using fundamental information, prop. 3

Overall, the outcome concerning the identification of relevant patterns did not improve when using fundamental information. Especially when one regards the DAX, using indicators, prop. 2, the results of the fundamental approach are to be considered worse. But one has to take into account that the number of classifications of prop. 3 refer to a higher number of testing data than i.e. those of prop. 2.

The probability that the relevant patterns were identified might therefore be higher for the greater proportion (prop. 3) than for the smaller one (prop. 2).

The next test consists of not only analyzing either technical or fundamental information but to combine both approaches. Indeed, only the best input concerning the technical as well as the fundamental approach has been combined, using prop. 3.

PE	1			2		
method	pos. in %	neg. in %	class. in %	pos. in %	neg. in %	class. in %
A	51.79	58.82	100	51.61	54.44	100
B	53.21	55.41	34	43.33	58.47	33
C	55.06	56.25	29	42.86	57.69	30
PE	3			4		
method	pos. in %	neg. in %	class. in %	pos. in %	neg. in %	class. in %
A	43.2	74.63	100	37.21	72.16	100
B	45.31	72.34	49	31.03	74.5	52
C	46.03	74.42	36	32.14	74.4	37

Fig. 10: Results and number of classifications in percent (DAX), fundamental and technical information, prop. 3

PE	1			2		
method	pos. in %	neg. in %	class. in %	pos. in %	neg. in %	class. in %
A	46.85	57.83	100	52.69	56.73	100
B	43.55	59.22	31	51.28	58.62	34
C	42	58.9	23	50	54.26	25
PE	3			4		
method	pos. in %	neg. in %	class. in %	pos. in %	neg. in %	class. in %
A	36	56.71	100	47.17	65.27	100
B	30.36	64.86	52	46.15	65.85	51
C	26.67	62.9	32	48	68.13	35

Fig. 11: Results and number of classifications in percent (Hochtief), fundamental and technical information, prop. 3

It was expected that the results improved significantly. But comparing the outcome for the DAX (see fig. 10) with that of the technical analyzis (see fig. 5 and 7) the results are worse. Regarding the neurons 3 and 4, the number of correct prognosis and number of hard criteria are often lower. In spite of that it is remarkable that the number of classifications in comparison to the fundamental approach increased (see fig. 8 and 10). The valuation of Hochtief coincides not exactly with that of the DAX (see fig. 11). The conclusion to be drawn must be that in this case there is all together a lower number of patterns within the training data which are significantly characterizing the further course. This can be explained by the fact that the selection of input data was very arbitrary. It can not be stated that input which separately leads to good results for either technical or fundamental approach, automatically leads to good results if it is added as a unified input vector.

At this place pruning must be mentioned again because it seems to be the only way to avoid manual preselection that sometimes causes worse results. It can also be criticized that even for a combination of technical and fundamental input, various combinations must have been tested. But with regard to the high number of combinations still existing for each single approach, this number increases exponentially when combining both. This can be seen considering that about 500 nets have been tested, each of these needs some hours (varying from 2 to 12 hours) for training.

4 Stock prediction with ARIMA-models

4.1 Describing the ARIMA configuration

Now a statistical approach is used for comparing the results of the ANN. Using ARIMA-models, at first a model needs identification with which a time-series can be best adapted. For that purpose parameters are determined to select the best model. As opposed to the usual way, with respect to the AR- (Autoregressive) and MA-components (Moving Average) all possibilities, so-called parameter-variations, were tested. Usually such a procedure would cause an enormous number of models. Therefore, it was referred to results of other investigations according to the prediction of time-series. Löderbusch stated that a parameter-variation with a limit of four degrees is sufficient with respect to the MA- and AR-components.

Each economic process can be transformed by double differences into a weak stationary process, which is necessary for ARIMA. These two reflections lead to 75 models to be tested, while only regarding non-seasonal models. An extension to seasonal models, providing that the identification of seasonal influences took place before, causes again a large amount (75 x 75 = 5625) of models. This number is reduced, assuming that a ´pure´ seasonal model is possible for identifying all seasonal, deterministic elements of a time-series. Besides the stochastic elements merely the non-seasonal components remain. Thus, a two-stage procedure is proposed, identifying the parameters of the best seasonal model in the first step. In the second step, based on the previous results, the non-seasonal parameters are determined. Using this approach, only 150 models (75 + 75) need to be tested.

Three auxiliary means for detecting seasonal influences exist: the Auto-Correlation-Function (ACF), the Partial Auto-Correlation-Function (PACF) and the Spectral-Analysis. The aim of using ACF and PACF is to recognize certain patterns visually. This is done by comparing the real course of dependencies with those of ´theoretic´ courses which can be created for each ARIMA-Process. This comparison is based on the idea that each data set contains influences which adulterate the correct ´course´. In spite of that, an experienced analyst should be able to identify the correct process. But in reality, it is very difficult to recognize dependencies. Therefore, the abilities of Spectral Analysis were tested. As opposed to the above-described methods, the Spectral Analysis does not refer to the time domain but is carried out in the frequency domain. But the usage of only the Spectral Analysis did not lead to satisfactory results, either. Thus, Autocorrelation and Spectral Analysis were combined. If both methods showed the same influences, it can be expected that the correct dependencies have been identified with high probability.

Beyond that, the coefficients of an ARIMA-model must be fixed. Box/Jenkins propose the maximum likelihood estimater. The coefficients are ascertained by the method of the smallest squares. Doing so, a complete model is described. Comparing both, the newly created and the origin time-series, the quality of the approximation can be determined.

To judge the quality, different units of measure exist. The mean squared error (MSE), the mean absolute percentage error (MAPE) and the TU (Theil´scher Un-gleichheitskoeffizient). All of these have in common that they refer to the level of the time-series. Such a pro-

cedure is not suited for this investigation because the tendency of stock development is of most interest. Thus, a better-suited criterion was created. The TTQ (Tendenz-Treffer-Quote) shows to what percentage the tendency of the predicted change corresponds with the tendency of the original change with regard to the entire time-series. Even here there exist two different alternatives. As well the real (Δx_t) as the prognosticated change ($\Delta \hat{x}_t$) refer to the last value (x_{t-1}) of the original time-series. In this case the level of the time-series would be taken into account. Eliminating this influence, it is necessary that the prognosticated change ($\Delta \hat{x}_t$) refers to the last value of the prognosticated time-series ($\hat{x}_{t-1}$). Then, only the tendency is regarded.

The great advantage can be regarded that i.e. a permanent overestimation of the level does not lead to an error as long as the tendency is recognized correctly. In our investigation a test of about 11.500 models (including the various time-spans etc.) was necessary. They were performed with the program SPSS+ 4.0.

4.2 Results using ARIMA-Models for prediction

Various time domains for identifying the best time-span, an ARIMA-model can be adapted to an original time-series, were investigated. The conclusions are demonstrated using the Hochtief-share as an example.

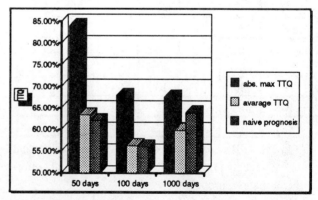

Fig. 14: Results of different spans of time for the Hochtief-share

The best results were pointed out within a span of 50 days, although it seems remarkable that the TTQ of the naive prognosis (the best estimator for the value of time $_t$

is the value of time $_{t-1}$) increased while using the biggest time-span. The following results always refer to the time-span of 50 days because the fig. 14 significantly demonstrates the advantage of that time-span.

In particular Hochtief had a maximum TTQ of 84%, an average TTQ of 63.35% and a naive prognosis of 62%. For the DAX the results run as follows: maximum TTQ of 68%, average TTQ of 50.71% and a naive prognosis of 48%. The following figure illustrates the structure of the results (for identifying the 'best suited' model). One can see how large the portion of models is that gains a certain TTQ. Especially Hochtief showed rather high performance. Thus, for the Hochtief-share similar to the DAX the 'best' model has been identified.

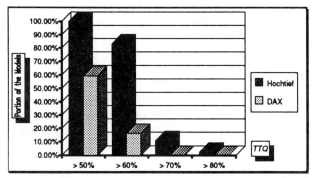

Fig. 15: Portion of models differentiated with various groups of results

Later on these are used for a 'real prognosis' of the future course of DAX and Hochtief. Even for the future a span of 50 days is regarded. ARIMA showed a TTQ of 64% for the DAX and 72% for Hochtief whereas the TTQ of the naive prognosis only had 46% for the DAX and 48% for Hochtief.

Additionally, another approach is presented. It is also very interesting to regard other influences than merely to look at the time-series itself. This leads to a multivariate procedure. Unfortunately, the tool we used does not allow a multivariate approach within ARIMA. But it is possible to build so-called intervention-models. These are able to take external 'disturbances' into consideration while using so-called binary 'dummy-variables' for describing such effects. According to the fundamental idea, external time-series are regarded as influences on the time-series. Thus, external time-series are considered as disturbances in this case. Doing this, an intervention-model is able to include such external information if the

values of the dummy-variables are extended from binary to real values. Therefore, the intervention-models seem to be well-suited for building multivariate models because more than one disturbance can be taken into account. But it should be mentioned that this procedure is an auxiliary means causing a 'simple' multivariate approach of an ARIMA-model. The means of identifying the parameters as well as the parameters theirselves coincide with those of the above-described univariate ARIMA-models.

The next step consists of the selection of external information influencing the course of a time-series. A Cross-Correlation-Analysis showed the following time-series with influences on Hochtief:

Westbau-Index, number of all increased shares at Frankfurt Stock Market, number of all unchanged shares at Frankfurt Stock Market, number of all traded shares at Wall Street, daily Money Rate and the moving average (100 days) of the Hochtief-share.

This combines fundamental as well as technical information.

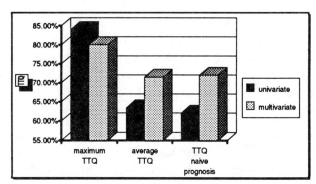

Fig. 16: Comparison of uni- and multivariate approach (Hochtief-share)

It can be demonstrated (see fig. 16) that the maximum TTQ of the univariate model is not reached using the multivariate approach. But it is much more interesting that nearly 75% of all adapted multivariate models point out a TTQ higher than 70% and with respect to this a high average TTQ. Even increasing naive prognosis TTQ about 10% states the assumption that extended information improve the quality of prognosis. For a 'real prognosis' ARIMA showed a TTQ of 58% for the DAX and 66% for Hochtief whereas the TTQ of the naive prognosis only had 46% for the DAX and 48% for Hochtief. This as well shows that ARIMA-models extract structures within the courses of a share because the results of the models are on a much higher level than those of the naive prognosis. The better results of the univariate model are caused by the higher TTQ of its best model that is used for prognosis. The question whether an univariate or the multivariate way has to be preferred can not be answered in a satisfactory manner. On the one hand, the univariate way has the highest maximum TTQ which also leads to the best 'real prognosis'. On the other hand, the multivariate way has a broader spread of results which may point to a higher probability for reaching good results.

5 Conclusions

First of all, the information-efficiency-hypothesis should be reflected upon. The number of correct prognosis using ANN as well as ARIMA proved to be higher (with respect to anticipated number of correctly prognosticated values) compared to a randomly estimation whether a share's price increases or decreases the next day. This might be an indication for the invalidity of the hypothesis concerning information-efficiency. In order to reject the information-efficiency-hypothesis with a greater security, it will be necessary to undertake further investigations. In spite of that, it must be considered that the daily prognosis is a rather difficult task.

For comparing both approaches it seems necessary to transform the percentage values of the different PE (see fig. 1) of the ANN results to one single digit by building the average of the four PE. Nevertheless, such a single digit is to be handled with care, as mentioned earlier.

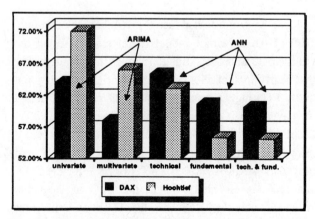

Fig. 17: Overall results of the different approaches

Nevertheless, the results of both ARIMA and ANN indicate that structures within the courses have been recognized, though the results of ARIMA are on a somewhat higher level. This may be caused by the fact that more detailed instructions, concerning the way how the best adapted model can be identified, are available for ARIMA-models. Particularly this problem has not yet been solved in a satisfactory manner with regard to the configuration of ANN. This can be seen regarding the way the configuration of ANN has been identified within this investigation. Using such a 'trial-and-error procedure', too much time has to be spent on tests that end up gaining no satisfactory results. Hence, in subsequent series of tests pruning must be inquired.

Another important conclusion resulting from this investigation touches upon the question whether a technical or a fundamental approach is to be preferred. Although neither all possible technical information nor all available fundamental information or combinations of both have been tested, the conclusion can be drawn that the results do not show a clear advantage of one or the other approach. Thus, in future both ideas have to be regarded.

Another question to be mentioned concerns the length of the time-span that is as well necessary for adapting an ARIMA-model as for determining the learning data set of an ANN. Often, for ARIMA the ACF is used to identify this period by choosing that one with the highest dependencies between the values of the time-series. The results were not satisfactory. Therefore, another procedure (using TTQ for best adaptation) was used. This can be explained when considering ACF only reflects linear dependencies. Of course even non-linear dependencies exist within the time-series. The ARIMA-models are only able to approximate these by linear equations.

According to the non-linear learning and smooth interpolation capabilities of ANN an improvement of the ANN results can be assumed when eliminating the above criticized weaknesses. A solution in the case referring to the time-span for adapting an ANN might be a so-called 'moving learning algorithm'. Its idea is not to state fix periods for learning and testing but rather immediately including prognosticated values within a new adaptation. This will also be examined in our further research. As mentioned above, there exist signs that the information efficiency hypothesis can be rejected because structures within the course of the time-series have been detected.

This leads to another interesting conclusion. The Random-Walk-Hypothesis states that share quotations fully reflect all relevant information without any time lag. Thus, a completely information-efficient market is presumed. Regarding all of the relevant information, the ´value´ of a share can be estimated. Varying quotations only arise from different interpretations of this information. This leads to an over-/under-estimation of the ´real´ quotation. Presuming, that the clues of information are highly independent from each other and actors are interpreting them isolated, the trends and altitudes of changes in the quotations must be random. As opposed to ARIMA, the changes in the quotations can not be seen as generated by a mechanism (that has to be detected), but merely behave as random changes (that can not be detected). With respect to the results of the short span of time (50 days), this hypothesis must be rejected, so that it can not be generally validated.

Summarizing, one can not prefer one of the two methods (ANN vs. ARIMA), because all identified conclusions are based on acting in unison depending on both approaches. Thus, also in the future both ideas must be pursued.

REFERENCES:

[1] Box, G. E. P. and Jenkins, G. M., Time-series Analysis - Forecasting and Control, 2. ed., San Francisco 1976.

[2] Brogsitter, B., Ableitung optimaler Strategien am Aktienmarkt, Köln 1977.

[3] Fama, E. F., Efficient Capital Markets: A Review of Theory and Empirical Work, in: Journal of Finance, 25(1970)2, pp. 383-417.

[4] Freeman, J. A. and Skapura, D. M., Neural Networks - Algorithms, Applications and Programming Techniques, Reading et al. 1991.

[5] Ginsberg, R., Möglichkeiten der Aktienkursprognose, Frankfurt 1975.

[6] Götze, E., Technische Aktienanalyse und die Effizienz des deutschen Kapitalmarktes, Heidelberg 1990.

[7] Granger, C. W. J. and Morgenstern, O., Predictability of Stock Market Prices, Lexington 1970.

[8] Herlitz, K., Kritische Analyse der Anwendung von Chart-Theorien zur Kursprognose deutscher Standardwerte, Berlin 1975.

[9] Hruby, P. W., Kritische Betrachtung der Chart-Analyse, Erlangen - Nürnberg 1991.

[10] Kitzig, T., chartHeft 2.0: PC-Software zur Aktienkursverfolgung, München 1990.

[11] Löderbusch, B., Modelle zur Aktienkursprognose auf Basis der Box/Jenkins-Verfahren - eine empirische Untersuchung, Krefeld 1981.

[12] Makridakis, S., Accuracy of Forecasting: An Empirical Investigation, in: Makridakis, S. (Ed.), The Forecasting Accuracy of Major Time-series Methods, Chichester 1984, pp. 35-103.

[13] Möller, H. P., Die Informationseffizienz des deutschen Aktienmarktes - eine Zusammenfassung und Analyse empirischer Untersuchungen, in: Zeitschrift für betriebswirtschaftliche Forschung 37(1985)6, pp. 500-518.

[14] Müller, B. and Reinhardt, J., Neural Networks, An Introduction, Berlin, Heidelberg and New York,1991.

[15] Neural Ware, Inc., Reference Guide, Neural Works Professional II Plus, Pittsburgh 1990.

[16] Pankratz. A., Forecasting with Univariate Box/Jenkins Models, New York 1983.

[17] Pfister, P., ARIMA-Methoden versus Ökonometrie - ein theoretischer und empirischer Vergleich, Basel 1984.

[18] Reilly, D. L. and Cooper, L. N., An Overview of Neural Networks: Early Models to Real World Systems, in: Zornetzer, S. F., Davis, J. L. and Lau, C. (Ed.), An Introduction to Neural and Electronic Networks, San Diego et al. 1990, pp. 227-248.

[19] Schlittgen, R. and Streitberg, B. H. J., Zeitreihenanalyse, München 1984.

[20] Schumann, M., Neuronale Netze zur Entscheidungsunterstützung in der Betriebswirtschaft, in: Biethahn, J., Bloech, J., Bogaschewski, R. and Hoppe, U. (Ed.), Wissensbasierte Systeme in der Wirtschaft, Wiesbaden 1991, pp. 23-50.

[21] Schwarze, J. Statistische Kenngrößen zur Ex-Post-Beurteilung von Prognosen (Prognosefehlermaß), in Schwarze, J. (Ed.), Angewandte Prognoseverfahren, Berlin 1980, pp. 317-344.

[22] SPSS+ 4.0 TRENDS for the IBM PC/XT/AT and PS/2, Chicago 1990.

[23] Thurnes, G. N., Expertensystemgestützte Aktienanalyse, Ulm 1990.

[24] Uhlir, H., Überprüfung der Random-Walk-Hypothese auf dem österreichischen Aktienmarkt, Wien 1979.

[25] Vandaele, W., Applied Time-series and Box-Jenkins Models, London 1983.

[26] Weigend, A. S., Hubermann, B. A. and Rummelhart, D. E., Predicting the Future: A Connectionist Approach, in: International Journal of Neural Systems, 1(1990)3, pp. 193-209.

STOCK RANKING: NEURAL NETWORKS Vs MULTIPLE LINEAR REGRESSION

A. N. REFENES, M. AZEMA-BARAC & A. D. ZAPRANIS
Department of Computer Science,
University College London,
Gower Street WC1 6BT,
London UK.

ABSTRACT

Modeling of the capital markets has traditionally been done in partial equilibrium. Such models have been very useful in expanding our understanding of the capital markets; nevertheless many empirical financial anomalies have remained unexplainable. Attempting to model financial markets in a general equilibrium framework still remains analytically intractable.

Because of their inductive nature, dynamical systems such as neural networks can bypass the step of theory formulation, and they can infer complex non-linear relationships between input and output variables. In this paper we examine the use of neural networks to replace classical statistical techniques for forecasting within the framework of the APT (Arbitrage Pricing Theory) model for stock ranking. We show that neural networks outperform these statistical techniques in forecasting accuracy terms by an average of 36 percentage points, and give better model fitness in-sample by one order of magnitude. We identify values for network parameters for which these figures are statistically stable.

1. INTRODUCTION

A great deal of effort has been devoted into developing systems for predicting stock returns in the capital markets. Limited success has been achieved. It is believed that the main reason for this is that the structural relationship between an asset price and its determinants changes over time. These changes can be abrupt. For example, one month a rise in interest rates will strengthen sterling, whilst the next month a rise will weaken sterling. This phenomenon of unstable structural parameters in asset price models is a special case of a general fundamental critique of econometric and statistical models. A relationship might be established, for example, between consumer spending and personal income. A tax cut could then be analysed via its effect on personal income. Critics, however, assert that this cannot be done, because a change in policy (the tax cut) will not only change the level of income, but will change the relationship between spending and income. Neural networks could in principle deal with the problem of structural instability.

Neural network architectures have drawn considerable attention in recent years because of their interesting learning abilities. Several researchers have reported exceptional results with the use of neural networks [1, 3, 4, 5, 6]. Neural networks are generally believed to be an effective modeling procedure when the mapping from input to output vectors contains both regularities and exceptions and they are, in principle capable of solving any non-linear classification problem, provided that the network contains a sufficiently large number of free parameters (i.e. hidden unit and/or connections).

In this paper we investigate the performance of neural networks in the non-trivial application of stock ranking. The problem consists of a universe of stocks whose returns are linked to three factors. The idea is to predict the relative outperformance of each stock in the universe, six months in advance given the current values of these three factors. The whole process is part of the **APT** model (Arbitrage Pricing Theory). Currently the prediction is done by linear regression. Our target is to outperform linear regression with respect to three metrics:

-   goodness of fit *in-sample* (convergence);

-   goodness of fit *out-of-sample* (generalisation);

-   stability of results with varying network parameters and different data sets.

We show that neural networks give better model fitness *in sample* by one order of magnitude and outperform linear regression in forecasting by 36 percentage points in terms of prediction accuracy in direction of change. We identify intervals of values for the parameters that influence network performance over which the results are stable, and show that the same performance figures persist across different training/test sets.

In section 2 of this paper we give a brief overview of the stock ranking application. In section 3 we discuss the neural network setup. We also define the metrics for evaluating the convergence and generalisation ability of different network configurations and comparing with multiple linear regression. In section 4 we discuss our results using as a benchmark the Multiple Linear Regression (**MLR**), and finally, in section 5 we give some brief concluding remarks.

2. STOCK VALUATION: THE APT MODEL

The Arbitrage Pricing Theory (APT) is widely used in portfolio management as an alternative to the the Capital Asset Pricing Model (CAPM). The APT has the benefit of being a more powerful theory; it requires less stringent assumptions than the CAPM, yet it produces similar results. The difficulty with the APT is that it shows that there is a way to forecast expected asset returns but it does not specify how to do it.

The key idea of the theory is that there exist a **set of factors** so that *expected returns* can be explained as a linear combination of each asset's exposure to these factors.

The APT is based on a *no-arbitrage* assumption that can be stated as requiring an upper limit on the ratio of the *expected-excess-return* so that any risk investment divided by the volatility of that same investment is bounded. If that ratio was not bounded then it would be possible to get positive expected-excess-returns for very low levels of risk. With the no-arbitrage assumption there always exist a portfolio that we call portfolio Q which is efficient and has the highest ratio of expected-excess-return to volatility. In this case any asset's (or portfolio's P) expected-excess-return will be proportional to their covariance with the portfolio Q. For portfolio P we have:

$$E(r(P)) = \gamma(n) E(r(Q)) \qquad (1)$$

where $\gamma(n)$ is the "beta" of the asset with respect to the portfolio Q, $E(r(P))$ is the expected excess return of the portfolio P, and $E(r(Q))$ is the expected excess return of the portfolio Q.

The advantage of this is that it does not require any special assumptions in order to arrive at the result. The disadvantage is that we do not know the portfolio Q. The effort to uncover the portfolio Q usually takes the form of searching for *attributes* of Q rather than the actual portfolio holdings. The idea is that the particular portfolio Q will depend on the universe of assets we are considering and the properties of those assets at that time.

Amongst the various techniques for putting the APT model to practical use DynIM is perhaps the most commonly used. According to the quantitative stock selection (DynIM) framework, three stages are necessary during the investment process:

- pre-processing of data to calculate relative values for the factors involved.

- ranking the stocks,

- constructing the portfolio.

The second stage of DynIM has so far been modeled by linear regression. However it is not always possible to estimate the exposure of an asset to the factors accurately using linear methods. In this paper we show that Neural Networks are an effective substitute for linear regression, and yield better accuracy both in fitting the model and predicting relative outperformance six months ahead.

3. EXPERIMENTAL SET-UP

3.1 The Stock Ranking Problem

The purpose of stock ranking is the construction of a portfolio. Stock ranking is defined as the task of assigning ratings to different stocks within a universe. This is actually a classification problem: *given a set of classes and a set of input data instances, each described by a suitable set of features, assign each input data instance to one of the classes.* In our case the different stocks form the set of input instances and the various ratings form the possible classes to which the input stocks can belong.

509

Table 3.1: Sample training data				
Y	A	B	C	STOCK CODE
-0.203553	+1.268286	-0.128681	+0.616215	6811.000000
-0.066618	-0.272814	-0.187851	-0.124382	6842.000000
+0.170599	+0.175118	+0.331097	+0.420197	6870.000000
-0.078946	-0.061965	-0.181817	+0.309313	6926.000000
+0.193520	-0.342653	+1.379686	+0.215267	8118.000000
+0.112259	+0.792553	-0.417726	+0.066999	8320.000000
-0.190763	+1.016654	+0.270754	+1.166889	8800.000000
-0.104398	-0.194282	+0.169641	-0.036239	8846.000000
-0.124752	-0.021836	+0.900211	+0.338135	9344.000000
-0.070049	-0.135540	-0.064680	+0.599856	9601.000000

Each stock instance can be described by a set of features which represent important financial information about the company which the stock represents.

More formally the problem statement is as follows : Let S represent the space of stocks, $S_1, S_2, S_3, ..., S_n$, and R be the set of possible (mutually exclusive) stock ratings, $R_1, R_2, R_3, ..., R_m$. Let F represent the k dimensional feature space, $F_1, F_2, F_3, ..., F_k$, describing each of the stocks. Each stock S_i can be considered as a k-tuple $(F_{1,S_i}, F_{2,S_i}, F_{3,S_i}, ..., F_{k,S_i})$ in the Cartesian space $F_1 x F_2 x F_3 x \cdots x F_k$. Rating the stocks involves finding the one-to-one mapping function f [1].

$$f : F_1 x F_2 x F_3 x \cdots x F_k \to R \qquad (2)$$

In this application we have 143 stocks updated on a monthly basis. Each stock is characterised by three factors (A, B, C) and the ranking is based on the predicted relative outperformance of each stock six months ahead.

3.2 Training and Test Sets

The training and test sets consist of data provided in a pre-processed form and presented as factor A, factor B, factor C and resultant outperformance Y. The factors A, B and C are parameters extracted from the balance sheets of the companies in the universe of the U.K. stocks. Details of these factors were not specified. **Table 3.1** gives an example of the training dataset we use in this application.

The rightmost column is a code for each stock in the universe. A, B, and C are the inputs to the network with Y being the target output (i.e. the outperformance of

the stock). The outperformance of the stock P in the tth month is the result of the application of an unknown function g on P_t / P_{t+6}, where P_t is the price of the stock P in the tth month, and P_{t+6} is the price of stock P after six months (in the $(t+6)^{th}$ month). More formally:

$$Y_t^P = g\left(\frac{P_t}{P_{t+6}}\right) \qquad (3)$$

where Y_t^P stands for the outperformance of the stock P in month t.

The dataset covers the period May 1985 to December 1991, and concerns 143 stocks. The overall size of the dataset therefore is given by: $143 \times m \times y = 143 \times 12 \times 6 - 36 = 10,260$ training vectors.

The networks are trained on 6 monthly batches of data and evaluated for the next six month period. Thus each training/test run consists of $143 \times 6 = 852$ training vectors. The intermediate size for each training run makes the problem non-trivial and allows for extensive tests on convergence and generalisation.

3.3 Performance Metrics

The main point of reference for evaluating the performance of the networks is by comparison to current "best practise" (i.e. multiple linear regression). The main measures of network performance that we are interested are the following:

- convergence: the *in-sample* performance of the network is important because it determines its convergence ability and sets a target of feasible *out-of-sample* performance which can be achieved by fine-tuning the network parameters and training discipline. The target here is to achieve good model fitness but without penalising generalisation.

- generalisation: is the main property that should be sought. The aim here is to achieve generalisation performance (i.e. prediction of relative stock out-performance) which is better than that of linear regression. We use two metrics to quantify prediction accuracy (see below).

- stability: neural networks have been known to produce wide variations in their predictive properties. This is to say that small changes in network design, learning times, initial conditions, etc may produce large changes in network behaviour. Our target here is to identify intervals of values for these parameters which give statistically stable results, and to demonstrate that these results persist across different training and test sets.

To quantify the convergence and generalisation performance of the two methods (i.e. linear regression and neural networks) we use two metrics. The first metric is the common Mean RMS Error. The Mean RMS Error, clearly is a measure of the correctness of prediction in terms of absolute values and can sometimes be misleading because of its averaging properties. Another metric that could be used instead is Percentage of Change in Direction (POCID for short).

In terms of stock ranking, POCID is a measure of the relative outperformance of the stock universe. It provides an approximation to the "shape" of one's portfolio six months ahead. If our stock universe were a time-series, then POCID would give a metric of the direction of change. The Percentage of Change in Direction is calculated by finding the differences $(t_2 - t_1)$, $(t_3 - t_2)$, ..., $(t_m - t_{m-1})$ and $(o_2 - o_1)$, $(o_3 - o_2)$, ..., $(o_m - o_{m-1})$, where t_i are the desired values and o_i are the predicted values of the outperformance and m is the total number of patterns in the training set, and then by comparing the pairs of differences $((t_i - t_{i-1}), (o_i - o_{i-1}))$ for each pair of adjacent training patterns one by one. The POCID metric is defined as the number of pairs $((t_i - t_{i-1}), (o_i - o_{i-1}))$ which have the same sign for both differences $(t_i - t_{i-1})$ and $(o_i - o_{i-1})$, expressed as a percentage of the total number of such pairs $(m - 1)$.

POCID to a certain extend, is sensitive to the order in which the training patterns are presented and therefore that order should be preserved. Furthermore, it cannot be regarded as a measure of correct prediction of the direction of change of the outperformance, but as an indication of how well the network predicts the shape of the universe of outperformances.

3.4 Network Set Up

The learning algorithm used is the standard backpropagation learning algorithm with a momentum term. All simulations run on SUN4 workstations; convergence is reached within 30,000 iterations typically requiring 3-4 days of CPU time.

The need for statistical stability in the results requires extensive experimentation with the parameters that influence network performance. Our target here is to identify intervals of values for these parameters which give statistically stable results, and to demonstrate that these results persist across different training and test sets. Below we give a list of these parameters and how they are varied in the performed simulations.

- Network Architecture: We examine layered, fully connected, feedforward networks. The number of neurons of the input and output layers are defined by the application and they are three for the input layer (one for each factor A, B and C) and one for the output layer (the representing the outperformance Y). The parameters in respect to network topology are the number of hidden layers and the number of neurons of each layer.

- Gradient Descent Terms: The parameters here are the learning rate and the momentum term. The epoch is kept always equal to one, so that the weights are updated after each presentation of a training pattern. This is the "on-line" or "stochastic" version of backpropagation, as opposed to the "batch" version. Also there is no offset added to the derivative of the transfer function. The objective is to find the ranges of momentum term and learning rate that yield stable performance for a given network architecture, as a function of the training time.

- Training Time: the number of presentations of the entire training set to the network (iterations).

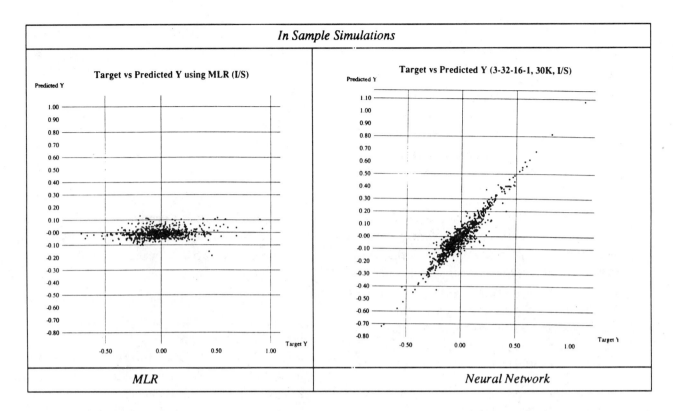

Figure 4.1: Target vs Predicted Outperformance, *in-sample* simulations (May '85 - Oct '85), with MLR and a 3-32-16-1 network with learning rate η = 0.3, momentum *m* = 0.7, trained for 30,000 iterations.

- This parameter is of great importance since the effect of any network configuration on network performance must be seen as a function of the training time. The aim is to identify the largest possible interval of network topologies for which the results show small standard deviation from the mean value.

- Transfer Function, Cost Function, and Initial conditions: these are not parameters; for all simulations we use the common asymmetric sigmoid, and the common quadratic error function. We test the stability of the results with varying initial conditions.

4. RESULTS

4.1 Overall Results: Comparison with MLR

The first performance target of this work is to show that the *in-sample* performance of the network gives a better fit than linear regression. The *in-sample* performance of the network is important because it determines its convergence ability and sets a target of feasible *out-of-*

sample performance which can be achieved by fine-tuning the network parameters and training discipline. Figure (4.1) shows two scattergrams depicting the target vs predicted outperformance for MLR and a neural network with topology 3-32-16-1, learning rate η = 0.3, momentum rate *m* = 0.3, trained for 30,000 iterations.

The ideal shape in both scattergrams in Figure (4.1) would be a straight line with a slope of 45 degrees, which crosses the origin. The reason is obvious; if the desired outperformance is, let's say 0.2 the ideal would be that the predicted is also 0.2; if the desired is -0.1 the predicted should be the same, and so on. The points (0.2, 0.2), (-0.1, -0.1) define the line we described above. We see in Fig. (4.1) that in the scattergram for MLR the dots are scattered all over the place; in contrast in the scattergram for the neural network they form a shape which resembles more of a line. The conclusion is evident: the neural network yields much better in-sample fitness than MLR.

The second network performance metric is generalisation. Our goal here was to achieve *out-of-sample* performance comparable to MLR.

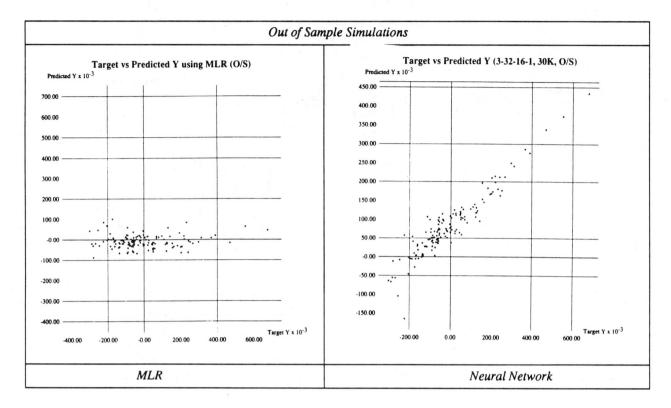

Figure 4.2: Target vs Predicted Outperformance; *out-of-sample* simulations (May '85 - Oct '85), with MLR and a 3-32-16-1 network with learning rate $\eta = 0.3$, momentum $m = 0.7$, trained for 30,000 iterations.

Figure (4.2) depicts again the target vs predicted outperformance for MLR and the same neural network as in Figure (4.1), but for *out-of-sample* testing. As we see in Figure (4.2) the results *out-of-sample* are much better than regression. The network clearly outperforms MLR in both cases.

Table 4.1 gives a summary of the values of the RMS and POCID metrics in and out of sample for both MLR and the neural network. It is interesting that out of sample the RMS for the neural network is marginally better than the RMS for MLR, while the POCID for the neural network is much better.

RMS is often a misleading metric of performance because of its averaging behaviour. The network performance *out-of-sample* in fact is far better than RMS implies. To illustrate this we depict in two graphs (see Figure (4.3)) the target and the predicted outperformance, for the stocks of the testing dataset (*out-of-sample*). We observe how much better the predicted line follows the shape of the target line in the case of the neural network. For this network configuration we have POCID of 85.2 against 51.4 for

the MLR, and RMS equal to 0.112 against 0.123 for the MLR. It is clear that both metrics, should be used in order to have a more exact indication of network performance.

METHOD	RMS(in-sample)	RMS(out-of-sample)
NN	0.044	0.112
MLR	0.138	0.123
	POCID(in-sample)	POCID(out-of-sample)
NN	85.5	85.2
MLR	54.9	51.4
	Table 4.1	

The results presented above far outperform MLR. However, for a real-life application such as the one described here it is important to examine how these results vary with network parameters. Our objective was to identify intervals of statistical stability for these parameters.

4.2 Stability with Network Architecture

We experimented with the architecture of the network, varying the number of hidden layers from one to three.

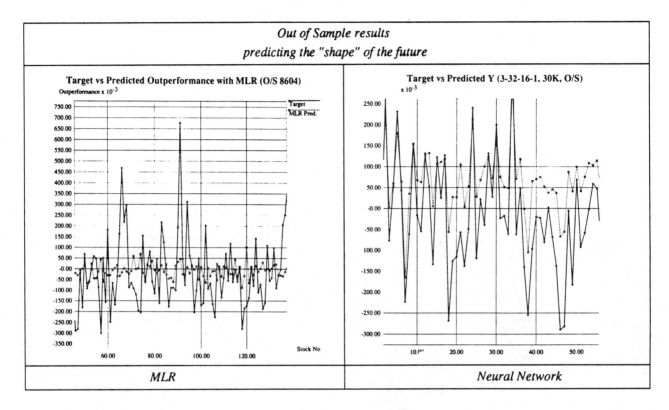

Figure 4.3: Target vs Predicted Outperformance for *out-of-sample* simulations (Nov '85 - Apr '86), with MLR and a 3-32-16-1 network with learning rate η = 0.3, momentum *m* = 0.7, trained for 30,000 iterations.

The number of neurons of each layer was also varied. For all these simulations the learning rate (η) and the momentum rate (*m*) were fixed (η = 0.3 and *m* = 0.7). The number of iterations varied from 500 to 30,000. At the high end of training times, the RMS error *in-sample* remains very stable varying from 0.044 to 0.072. Single layer networks give RMS outside this range. The *out-of-sample* performance also remains stable around 0.11 for networks with two hidden layers; the same is true for POCID which remains stable around 85% [7].

4.3 Stability with Gradient Descent Terms

In summary, learning rates in the range 0.2 to 0.4 when combined with a momentum term less than 0.7 yield better convergence ability. In general, one and two-layered networks with a learning rate η =0.2 and a momentum term $0.3 < m \le 0.5$ yield the best combination of convergence and generalisation [7].

4.4 Stability with Training Time

For simple networks with one hidden layer, 5,000 iterations were sufficient to stabilise the RMS to a virtually unchanged (with the number of iterations)

value. For more complicated networks with more than one hidden layers, even 25,000 iterations are not sufficient to reach that limit. The POCID metric behaves like the RMS, tending asymptotically to a maximum which is generally found after the 25,000 iterations limit, although the shape of the curve is more noisy.

For *out-of-sample* performance, although we have the best results for large numbers of iterations, there are ranges with temporary performance drop-offs (both in terms of increased RMS or decreased POCID). We do not think however that these can be interpreted as signs of *overtraining*, because they appear rather early (mainly between 5,000 and 10,000 iterations). Probably their existence implies that the network is still *undertrained*, and the better solutions are yet to come for larger numbers of iterations. This behaviour persists across different datasets.

4.5 Stability with Different Training Sets

All the simulations we mentioned so far, were performed for the same training and testing datasets. The training dataset contained monthly data for the period May '85 to October '85, and the testing dataset contained data for April '86. In order to examine the effect of the dataset on the performance of the network, we performed simulations for the topology 3-32-16-1, using the mean values for the learning and network parameters.

The convergence and generalisation performance of the network did not alter significantly. It appears that the performance of the network is slightly worse than the mean performance in the previous dataset but well within the range of the standard deviation.

4.6 Stability with Initial Conditions

Backpropagation is known to be sensitive to the values of initial conditions i.e., random weights values. It is always desirable to observe the mean and standard deviation of the network performance measures for a large number of different initial conditions. We have so far performed only two simulation runs for the same network but with different initial conditions.

In-sample the curves for the RMS are very much the same but for all other comparisons in and *out-of-sample* the first set of initial weights marginally outperforms the second one. Some adjustment to the network configuration, while using the second set of initial weights, might help to bridge that gap in performance. It is clear that the starting point of the training phase can make a difference (maybe not a great one) and it should be one of our considerations when training the network.

5. CONCLUSIONS & CURRENT WORK

Classical statistical techniques for prediction reach their limitations in applications with non-linearities in the dataset. Most forecasting methods are only capable of picking up trends and have difficulty in modeling cycles that are by no means repetitive in amplitude, period or shape. Despite their inadequacies techniques such as multiple linear regression have proven a useful tool in the Capital Markets and are used routinely.

We showed that even simple neural learning procedures such as the backpropagation algorithm far outperform current "best practise" in a typical application for stock ranking within the framework of the Arbitrage Pricing Model. Their smooth interpolation properties allow neural models to fit better models to the data and to

generalise significantly better.

We believe that the performance measures obtained here, can be improved further with careful network design and pre-processing of the data. As far as the data is concerned there is at least one obvious area of improvement. It concerns the existence of malicious vectors in the training set. These are vectors which lie close to the boarders between classes (i.e. one-to-many mappings) and which the quadratic cost function used here finds difficult to learn (at best it averages). We have developed an algorithm for detecting such malicious vectors [7] and applied it to the training set. We found that up to 13% of the training data were classified as such vectors, and we currently experiment with various strategies for removing such vectors.

6. REFERENCES

[1] Dutta Sumitra, and Shashi Shekkar, "Bond rating: a non-conservative application", Computer Science Division, University of California.

[2] Hinton Geoffrey, "Connectionist Learning Procedures", Computer Science Department, Carnegie-Melon University, December 1987.

[3] Refenes A. N., "Constructive Learning and its Application to Currency Exchange Rate Prediction", in "Neural Network Applications in Investment and Finance Services", eds. Turban E., and Trippi R., Chapter 27, Probus Publishing, USA, 1992.

[4] Refenes A. N., et al "Currency Exchange rate prediction and Neural Network Design Strategies", Neural computing & Applications Journal, Vol 1, no. 1., (1992).

[5] Refenes A. N., & Zaidi A., "Managing Exchange Rate Prediction Strategies with Neural Networks", Proc. Workshop on Neural Networks: techniques & Applications, Liverpool (Sept. 1992).

[6] Schoenenburg E., "Stock price prediction using neural networks: a project report", Neurocomputing 2, pp. 17-27, 1990

[7] Zapranis A. D., "Stock Ranking Using Neural Networks", Project Report, Department of Computer Science, University College London, (Sept. 92).

Information Retrieval

Information retrieval has only recently begun to apply neural networks to many of its problem areas. This chapter contains two papers on the subject. **Paper 16.1** describes the application of the multilayer perceptron (MLP) neural network to automatically classify natural language documents. **Paper 16.2** presents the application of the MLP neural network to adaptive information retrieval of documents in a large corpus.

Chapter 16:   *Information Retrieval*

Neural Networks and Document Classification

Jennifer Farkas
Communications Canada
Centre for Information Technologies Innovation (CITI)
1575 Chomedey Boulevard
Laval, Québec, Canada, H7V 2X2

Abstract— In this paper we discuss the relevance of neural networks to the problem of classifying electronic natural language documents. We show that such documents can be represented as numeric concept vectors in a semantically meaningful way, so that *AI* tools such as the back-propagation learning algorithm and self-organizing maps can be used to build efficient and effective automatic document classifying systems. We show that the neural networks concerned can be taught to classify natural language text according to predefined specifications within tolerable error bounds. The convergence properties of the prototype *NeuroZ* described in this paper show that neural networks provide a promising platform for the automatic classification of natural language documents and that a system can be built which distinguishes in a semantically consistent way between relatively complex distinct linguistic patterns.

INTRODUCTION

In order to manage and use the exponentially increasing volume of textual information accumulated in most research and administrative environments, it has become common practice to classify and cluster the information into semantically similar categories. These partitions of information often reduce the search time for information, while maintaining the integrity of the total information stored. According to [11], this approach is justified by the *cluster hypothesis* which states that closely associated documents tend to be relevant to the same requests. In addition, this approach ensures the consistency, uniformity, economy and speed of information classification and storage required for efficient and reliable data access. This paper shows that neural networks are well suited to this task since, as pointed out by Rothman [9], they possess "the ability to recognize and respond to patterns of information in the environment." The work described in this paper shows that they can be used with promising success to classify natural language documents for which similarity of patterns of information can be taken to mean *semantic similarity*.

One of the most widely used algorithms to build neural networks is the back-propagation algorithm. As pointed out in [5], this architecture has become "the standard network paradigm for modelling, forecasting, and classification." We therefore use this paradigm to develop an automatic textual pattern classification system, which we call *NeuroZ*. The system is designed to classify a variety of types of natural language documents whose topics involve the areas of *artificial intelligence, multimedia technology, database management*, and *operating system environments*.

The prototype *NeuroZ* was developed for the PC environment using the NeuralWorks Professional II software development tool (cf. [8]). The document preprocessing and the vector representation of concepts required were accomplished by means of system-specific C-routines, and by using the lexical pattern generator *Flex 2.3*.

DOCUMENTS AND CONCEPTS

The preprocessing of the documents required the extraction of an appropriate set of *keywords* occurring in the base documents, and the formation of equivalence classes of keywords. The documents were interpreted numerically as vectors whose coordinates consist of numerical representations of the equivalence classes of keywords. Each vector was then assigned one of the *topics* T_1 = *artificial intelligence*, T_2 = *multimedia technology*, T_3 = *database management*, and T_4 = *operating system environments*.

The document set underlying *NeuroZ* consists of scientific abstracts of documents from the *Inspec* database. The documents were studied for their semantic content and 191 characteristic terms were identified as *keywords*. These words were grouped into forty-four classes $C_1, \ldots, C_{44}$ according to their similarity of meaning. We think of these classes of keywords as *concepts*. Among the concepts upon which *NeuroZ* was built are such concepts as Cognition, Machine Learning, Memory Management, Multitasking, Neural Network, Parallel Processing, and Software Engineering. Some of the keywords which comprise the concepts Cognition, Machine Learning and Neural Network are shown below:

Cognition	=	{*cognition, cognitive model, cognitive process, cognitive science, cognitive task,...*}
Machine Learning	=	{*learning algorithm, learning law, learning system, machine learning, supervised learning,...*}
Neural Network	=	{*artificial neural network, back-propagation network, connectionism, connectionist model, neurocomputing, neural modelling, neural network, neuron, perceptron,...*}

For consistency and completeness, these concepts were validated against an *ISO*–type thesaurus using the Information Sciences and Technologies Thesaurus of the Centre for Information Technologies Innovation (CITI). The *concept vectors* required for the numerical representation of the documents were computed by the lexical pre-processor and specific numerical representation algorithms mentioned above. Each document D was interpreted as an input vector of the form

$$< D_1, \ldots, D_{44} > \qquad (1)$$

consisting of forty-four intries $D_i = \frac{c_i}{N}$, where N is the number of occurrences of keywords in D and c_i is the number of occurrences of keywords in D belonging to the concept C_i. For example, a document in which only the concepts Neural Network and Machine Learning occur, with three occurrences of *neurocomputing*, one occurrence of *connectionism*, five occurrences of *learning system*, and four occurrences of *learning algorithm*, was represented by the vector

$$< \ldots, \frac{4}{13}, \ldots, \frac{9}{13}, \ldots > \qquad (2)$$

with "..." denoting the appropriate strings of 0's.

The output vectors were taken to be vectors of the form

$$< v_1, v_2, v_3, v_4 > \qquad (3)$$

with $0 \leq v_i \leq 1$. They denote the degrees of membership in the topics *artificial intelligence, multimedia technology, database management*, and *operating system environments* which *NeuroZ* has assigned to a concept vector after a given number of training iterations. The value of v_i expresses the degree of certainty that an input document D belongs to the topic T_i.

ARCHITECTURE

NeuroZ consists of three layers and is made up of fifty-two processing elements and a bias. The input layer consists of forty-four processing elements, corresponding to the forty-four concepts C_i. The hidden layer contains four processing elements and the output layer consists of four processing elements corresponding to the topics T_j known to the system. Each processing element consists of a set of inputs representing the output of another processing element or a system input. Each input is multiplied by a corresponding weight and all of the weighted inputs are added and jointly determine the activation level of a processing element. If the inputs to a processing element are, for example, $x_1, x_2, \ldots, x_n$, and the corresponding weights are $w_1, w_2, \ldots, w_n$, then the excitation level of the processing element involved is the linear combination of the x_i and w_i, i.e.,

$$\lambda = x_1 w_1 + \cdots + x_n w_n \qquad (4)$$

A *transfer function* τ transmits an output signal of 1 or 0 depending on whether λ has or has not reached a locally determined *threshold value*. Thus

$$\tau(\lambda) = \begin{cases} 1 & \text{if } \lambda \text{ is greater than a threshold value} \\ 0 & \text{if } \lambda \text{ is less than a threshold value} \end{cases}$$

One of the most frequently used functions for the transfer of signals between processing elements, and the one used in *NeuroZ*, is the *sigmoid function*, defined by

$$\tau(\lambda) = (1 + e^{-\lambda})^{-1} \qquad (5)$$

NeuroZ uses the *delta learning rule* for the purpose of updating the weights of the connections between the processing elements and to reduce the difference (the delta) between the desired output value and the actual output value of a processing element during a training cycle. This rule is an iterative gradient learning algorithm designed to minimize the mean square error between the actual output of a multilayer feed-forward network and the desired output (cf. [10]).

TRAINING AND TESTING

The *Inspec* documents from which *NeuroZ* was developed, were divided into 382 *training documents* and 395 *test documents*. As the following figure shows, the separation into training and test documents was designed to achieve a balance between training and test documents for all four classification topics:

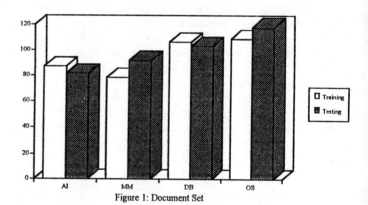

Figure 1: Document Set

The documents were grouped into the topics $T_1, \ldots, T_4$, i.e., into the groups *artificial intelligence* (AI), *multimedia technology* (MM), *database management* (DB), and *operating systems environments* (OS) by a classification specialist according to their similarity of meaning. The actual numbers of documents making up the different topics are given in the following table:

Table 1: Grouping of Documents

	AI	MM	DB	OS
Training	87	79	107	109
Testing	82	92	103	118

The quantitative relationship between the four topics is shown graphically in Figure 1 above.

In the training phase, each concept in a document was used to link the input and output layers of the network. A sequence of forward and backward passes through the entire training set constitutes a training cycle. After a certain number of iterations of the training cycle, the classification error reached a least mean square minimum. At this point, the network was considered to have *learned* the relationships between the input and output vectors corresponding to the training documents.

During each testing phase, the network was examined for its ability to use the information contained in the connection weights to assign the correct output vectors to the test documents, i.e., to assign the correct topic to a document.

Prior to the actual training of *NeuroZ*, the training set was presented to the network and after some initial experimentation with different training cycles, the system was set for a maximum of 50,000 training cycles.

The training period was divided into seven phases, and snapshots of the performance of the system were taken after 1,000, 2,000, 5,000, 10,000, 20,000, 25,000, and 50,000 iterations. At the end of each phase, the training was interrupted and the system was tested both on the training documents and on the test documents, whose textual patterns were unknown to the system. In order to be assigned to a topic T_i, a document had to receive a "membership" value of 0.85 or greater for that topic and a value of no more than 0.20 for the other topics. The following figures and tables show the decrease in the classification errors achieved through an increase in the length of the training cycles:

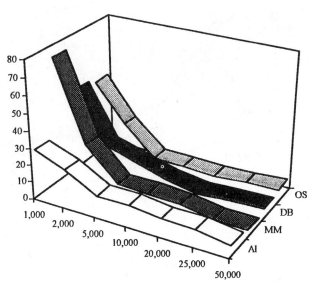

Figure 3: Test Results

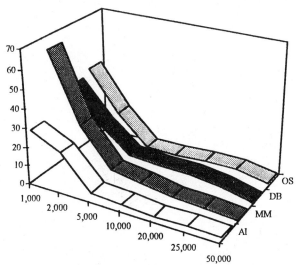

Figure 2: Training Results

Figure 2 represents graphically the number of documents which *NeuroZ* failed to classify at the various phases:

Table 2: Unclassified Training Documents

Iterations	AI	MM	DB	OS
1,000	28	63	38	41
2,000	20	27	20	19
5,000	3	7	7	4
10,000	2	5	6	4
20,000	1	2	6	5
25,000	1	1	4	5
50,000	1	0	0	2

At the end of each training phase, the test documents were used to examine the number of new documents which *NeuroZ* was able to classify correctly. The following figure shows the decrease in classification errors in the test results as the number of training cycles was increased:

The actual numbers of unclassified or incorrectly classified test documents after each training phase of *NeuroZ* can be gleaned from the following table:

Table 3: Unclassified Test Documents

Iterations	AI	MM	DB	OS
1,000	28	73	48	45
2,000	21	27	18	23
5,000	11	8	12	6
10,000	11	8	7	6
20,000	9	7	4	5
25,000	9	4	5	6
50,000	6	4	6	7

At approximately 50,000 iterations of the training process, *NeuroZ* converged to an average classification error of less than 1% on training documents and less than 6% on test documents. The precise values are the following:

Table 4: Average Classification Errors

Iterations	Training Phase	Testing Phase
1,000	44.50 %	49.11 %
2,000	22.51 %	22.53 %
5,000	5.50 %	9.38 %
10,000	4.45 %	8.10 %
20,000	3.66 %	6.33 %
25,000	2.88 %	6.08 %
50,000	0.79 %	5.82 %

Graphically, the improvement in the performance of *NeuroZ* can be seen in Figure 4 below:

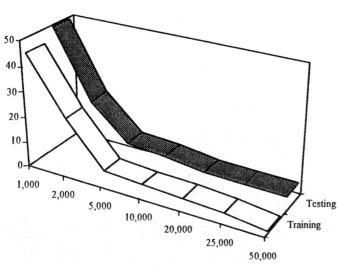

Figure 4: Average Classification Errors

Figures 2 and 3 show that the average performance of *NeuroZ* improved with every increase in the number of training cycles. After 50,000 iterations, *NeuroZ* had reached its optimal performance level and no improvement in the classification accuracy of the system could be achieved by a further increase in the number of training iterations. As was to be expected, *NeuroZ* performed less well on the test documents which had not been part of the training process. On the other hand, it performed well in relative terms since it achieved an average classification accuracy on these documents of over 94%.

CONCLUSION

It is clear from the performance accuracy achieved by a system such as *NeuroZ* that the neural network approach to conceptual pattern recognition and to document classification is promising and that this technology can be expected to provide certain advantages over traditional methods for the conceptual analysis and classification of clustered types of documents. At this stage, *NeuroZ* represents a proof-of-concept prototype and a more comprehensive system is under development. In particular the use of the self-organizing-map paradigm is being used as a tool for refining the document classes. Independently, a document retrieval component for *NeuroZ* is also being developed. In addition, new areas of application involving more extensive sets of concepts are being explored.

REFERENCES

[1] B. G. Batchelor, *Practical Approach to Pattern Classification*, New York: Plenum Press, 1974.

[2] J. S. Deogun and V. V. Raghavan, "Automatic Cluster Assignment of Documents," in: *Proceedings of the 7th IEEE Conference on Artificial Intelligence Applications*, Miami, Florida, 24-28 February 1991, pp. 25-28.

[3] J. Farkas, "IndeXpert: An Intelligent Indexing System with Geometric Document Ranking," In: *Avignon '92: Proceedings of the 12th International Conference*, Avignon, France, vol. 3, 1-6 June 1992, pp. 139-149.

[4] R. Hecht-Nelson, *Neurocomputing*, Reading, MA: Addison-Wesley, 1990.

[5] C. C. Klimasauskas, "Applying Neural Networks, Part II," *PC AI*, pp. 27-34, March/April 1991.

[6] R. P. Lippmann, "Pattern Classification Using Neural Networks," *IEEE Communications Magazine*, vol. 27, pp. 47-64, 1989.

[7] M. McCord Nelson and W. T. Illingworth, *A Practical Guide to Neural Nets*, Reading, MA: Addison-Wesley, 1991.

[8] Neural Computing: NeuralWorks Professional II/Plus Reference Manual, NeuralWare, Inc., 1991.

[9] P. Rothman, "Syntactic Pattern Recognition," *AI Expert*, vol. 7, pp. 41-51, 1992.

[10] D. E. Rumelhart, G. E. Hinton and R. J. Williams, "Learning Internal Representations by Error Propagation," in: *Parallel Distributed Processing: Explorations in the Microstructure of Cognition*, Cambridge, MA: MIT Press, vol. 1, 1986, Chapter 8.

[11] R. Sharma, "A Genetic Machine for Parallel Information Retrieval," *Information Processing & Management*, vol. 25, pp. 223-23, 1989.

An Application of Neural Networks in Adaptive Information Retrieval

S.K.M. Wong   **Y.J. Cai**

Department of Computer Science, University of Regina
Regina, Saskatchewan, Canada S4S 0A2

Y.Y. Yao

Department of Mathematical Sciences, Lakehead University
Thunder Bay, Ontario, Canada P7B 5E1

Abstract

This paper shows how a neural network can be used in the design of an adaptive information retrieval system. In particular, a two-layer neural network is used to implement a linear retrieval system; a three-layer neural network is used to implement a bilinear retrieval system. The results of this preliminary investigation strongly suggest that neural networks are useful tools for developing adaptive information retrieval systems.

I. INTRODUCTION

In a typical information retrieval environment, there exist a group of users and a set of *documents*. An information retrieval system is designed with the objective of providing, in response to a user query, documents that will contain the information desired by the user. More specifically, the system ranks the document representatives (surrogates) so that the user will obtain the required information by reading those documents being ranked at the top.

In information retrieval, one can represent documents and queries by vectors in a vector space [8].

This requires the application of an automatic or manual indexing procedure to identify from the individual text the keywords (index terms) and their occurrence frequencies, from which the document vector is constructed. Similarly, we can construct a vector to represent the query. In addition to the difficult task of indexing, one has to introduce an appropriate function to rank the document vectors according to the user's preference.

It is important to design a retrieval system with a learning capability in order to take advantage of the user's feedback. There are two kinds of adaptive models. In the single-query feedback method, the query vector is constructed by inductive learning [6, 10]. The multi-query feedback method, on the other hand, is designed to learn the term-association matrix [4, 5]. Although these methods have produced encouraging results [8], it remains necessary to develop a systematic method for estimating the required parameters.

In our preliminary work [10], we analyzed only the single-query feedback. In this study, we want to establish a common framework for both the single-query and multi-query feedback processes. First, we will show that the single-query feedback can be understood in term of a two-layer neural network, whereas the multi-query feedback can be implemented by a three-layer neural network with a linear threshold function [9]. We will demonstrate that the learning algorithms in neural networks provide effective methods for constructing suitable ranking functions.

II. ADAPTIVE INFORMATION RETRIEVAL SYSTEMS

Given a set of documents D, a user *preference* can be defined by a binary relation $\succ$ on D [10] as:

$$d \succ d' \text{ if the user prefers } d \text{ to } d'. \quad (1)$$

The preference relation $\succ$ describes the user's judgments on the usefulness of the documents. Suppose each document $d \in D$ is represented by a vector $\mathbf{d} = (d_1, d_2, ..., d_n)$ in a n-dimensional vector space V^n, namely:

$$\mathbf{d} = \sum_{i=1}^{n} d_i \mathbf{t}_i \quad (2)$$

where $\mathbf{t}_i$ is a *document term* vector. The set of vectors $\{\mathbf{t}_1, \mathbf{t}_2, ..., \mathbf{t}_n\}$ is assumed to be a basis of the vector space V^n. The relation $\succ$ on D can be mapped to a relation on the set $\mathbf{D}$ of document vectors. For convenience, we will denote the relation on $\mathbf{D}$ by the same symbol $\succ$.

It is clear that if documents are to be ranked in a manner beneficial to the user, the ranking should faithfully reflect the user's preference relation. Therefore, the primary objective of an information retrieval system is to find an *order-preserving* function f on $\mathbf{D}$, satisfying the following condition: for $\mathbf{d}, \mathbf{d}' \in \mathbf{D}$,

$$\mathbf{d} \succ \mathbf{d}' \Longrightarrow f(\mathbf{d}) > f(\mathbf{d}'). \quad (3)$$

This condition is equivalent to:

$$f(\mathbf{d}') \geq f(\mathbf{d}) \Longrightarrow \neg(\mathbf{d} \succ \mathbf{d}'). \quad (4)$$

That is, a function obeying condition (3) ensures that the less preferred documents will not be ranked ahead of the preferred. Such a function f is called an *acceptable* ranking function.

Let $\mathbf{q} = (q_1, q_2, ..., q_n)$ denote a query vector in V^n, namely:

$$\mathbf{q} = \sum_{j=1}^{n} q_j \mathbf{s}_j, \quad (5)$$

where $\mathbf{s}_j$ is a *query term* vector. Likewise, the set $\{\mathbf{s}_1, \mathbf{s}_2, ..., \mathbf{s}_n\}$ is assumed to be a basis of the vector space V^n. In the adaptive linear model for single-query feedback [10], the ranking function f is chosen to be: for all $\mathbf{d} \in \mathbf{D}$,

$$f(\mathbf{d}) = \mathbf{d} \cdot \mathbf{q} = \sum_{i,j} d_i q_j \mathbf{t}_i \cdot \mathbf{s}_j$$

$$= \sum_{i=1}^{n} d_i (\sum_{j=1}^{n} q_j \mathbf{t}_i \cdot \mathbf{s}_j) = \sum_{i=1}^{n} d_i w_i, \quad (6)$$

where $w_i = \sum_{j=1}^{n} q_j \mathbf{t}_i \cdot \mathbf{s}_j$ and $\mathbf{t}_i \cdot \mathbf{s}_j$ denotes a scalar product. According to the acceptable ranking criterion (3), the task is to construct a *solution* row matrix $\mathbf{w} = (w_1, w_2, ..., w_n)$ such that for any $\mathbf{d}, \mathbf{d}' \in \mathbf{D}$,

$$\mathbf{d} \succ \mathbf{d}' \Longrightarrow \mathbf{d}\mathbf{w}^{\mathrm{T}} > \mathbf{d}'\mathbf{w}^{\mathrm{T}}, \quad (7)$$

where $\mathbf{w}^{\mathrm{T}}$ denotes the transpose of $\mathbf{w}$. Of course, the *complete* preference relation is not known *a priori* unless the user has read all the documents. In practice, we may assume that the user is able to express his preference judgments on some document pairs. The problem is then reduced to constructing the matrix $\mathbf{w}$ from the preference information on a sample set of documents.

Let $\mathbf{Q}$ denote a set of query vectors. For multiple queries, the user preference can be defined by a binary relation $\succ$ on $\mathbf{D} \times \mathbf{Q}$ as follows:

$$(\mathbf{d}, \mathbf{q}) \succ (\mathbf{d}', \mathbf{q}) \Longleftrightarrow \text{ the user prefers } \mathbf{d} \text{ to } \mathbf{d}'$$
$$\text{with respect to query } \mathbf{q}. \quad (8)$$

We may use the following ranking function:

$$g(\mathbf{d}, \mathbf{q}) = \mathbf{d} \cdot \mathbf{q} = \sum_{i,j} d_i q_j \mathbf{t}_i \cdot \mathbf{s}_j$$

$$= \sum_{i=1}^{n} \sum_{j=1}^{m} d_i a_{ij} q_j = \mathbf{d}\mathbf{A}\mathbf{q}^{\mathrm{T}} \quad (9)$$

where $a_{ij} = \mathbf{t}_i \cdot \mathbf{s}_j$ measures the strength of association between document term t_i and query term s_j, and $\mathbf{A} = (a_{ij})$ is therefore called the *term-association matrix*. Then, the task in multi-query feedback is to construct a term-association matrix $\mathbf{A}$ such that for any two document-query pairs $(\mathbf{d}, \mathbf{q}), (\mathbf{d'}, \mathbf{q}) \in \mathbf{D} \times \mathbf{Q}$,

$$(\mathbf{d}, \mathbf{q}) \succ (\mathbf{d'}, \mathbf{q}) \implies g(\mathbf{d}, \mathbf{q}) > g(\mathbf{d'}, \mathbf{q})$$
$$\iff \mathbf{dAq}^\mathrm{T} > \mathbf{d'Aq}^\mathrm{T}. \quad (10)$$

This term-association matrix can be learned from the user's preference judgments on a sample set of document-query pairs.

In the next section, we will show how the feedback problems can be solved by the neural network learning algorithms.

III. NEURAL NETWORKS FOR RELEVANCE FEEDBACK

In information retrieval, the primary objective is to rank the documents according to the user's preference rather than to classify them. We therefore have to modify the standard neural network learning algorithms for the purpose of ranking [1, 2, 7].

A. *The single-query feedback*

The single-query feedback can be modeled by a two-layer neural network. Each document term forms one node in the input layer. Given a document vector $\mathbf{d} = (d_1, d_2, \ldots, d_n)$ as input, the network produces a weighted sum, $\sum_i d_i w_i$, as its output. We call $\mathbf{w} = (w_1, w_2, \ldots, w_n)$ a *solution* matrix. This means that the two-layer network generates an ordered list of documents by a linear ranking function.

Consider two document vectors $\mathbf{d}$ and $\mathbf{d'}$ with $\mathbf{d} \succ \mathbf{d'}$. We say that the neural network correctly ranks the two documents if $\mathbf{dw}^\mathrm{T} > \mathbf{d'w}^\mathrm{T}$; otherwise, an error occurs. This error can be corrected by adding $\mathbf{d}$ to $\mathbf{q}$ and subtracting $\mathbf{d'}$ from $\mathbf{q}$. The following modified learning algorithm can be used to construct a solution matrix [10]:

Algorithm FIND-SOLUTION-MATRIX

(i) Choose an initial $\mathbf{w}_0$ and let $k = 0$;

(ii) Let $\mathbf{w}_k$ be the row matrix in the $(k + 1)$th iteration; identify the set of incorrectly

ranked document vectors:

$$\Gamma(\mathbf{w}_k) = \{(\mathbf{d}, \mathbf{d'}) \mid \mathbf{dw}_k^\mathrm{T} \leq \mathbf{d'w}_k^\mathrm{T}\}; \quad (11)$$

If $\Gamma(\mathbf{w}_k) = \emptyset$, terminate the procedure;

(iii) Let

$$\mathbf{w}_{k+1} = \mathbf{w}_k + \sum_{(\mathbf{d}, \mathbf{d'}) \in \Gamma(\mathbf{w}_k)} (\mathbf{d} - \mathbf{d'}) ; \quad (12)$$

(iv) Let $k = k + 1$; go back to step (ii);

It can be proved that this procedure converges to a solution matrix satisfying equation (7) in a finite number of steps, provided that such a solution exists. Thus, this learning algorithm provides a systematic method for finding a solution to the single-query feedback problem.

B. *The multi-query feedback*

Here we suggest to use a three-layer neural network to implement the multi-query feedback. We use a linear threshold function $f = \alpha x$ in all layers [9], where α is a scaling factor that regulates the magnification of the processing element's activity x. Figure 1 shows the configuration of such a network. Document vectors are the input to the network. The nodes in the input layer represent the document terms. The nodes in the hidden layer are query terms. The weight a_{ij} between document term t_i and query term s_j represents the degree of their association. Since the value q_j represents the importance of term s_j in a query, it is used as the scaling factor. The output layer consists of only one node, which pools the input from all the query terms. For this neural network, we set the weights of all its input to 1. More precisely, we have:

Input layer: Given the input vector $(d_1, d_2, \ldots, d_n)$ with the scaling factor $\alpha^{(1)}$ and all connection weights $\beta_i^{(1)}$ being equal to 1, the activation of node t_i is:

$$g_i^{(1)} = \alpha^{(1)} d_i \beta_i^{(1)} = d_i.$$

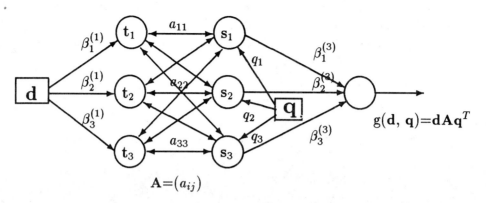

Figure 1: A Multi-Query Feedback Network Configuration

Hidden layer: With $g_i^{(1)}$ $(i = 1, 2, ..., n)$ as input, the activation of the node associated with query term s_j is:

$$g_j^{(2)} = \alpha_j^{(2)} \sum_i g_i^{(1)} a_{ij}$$

$$= q_j \sum_i d_i a_{ij} = \sum_i d_i a_{ij} q_j,$$

where a_{ij} is the strength of association between document term t_i and query term s_j, and $\alpha_j^{(2)} = q_j$.

Output layer: With $g_j^{(2)}$ $(j = 1, 2, ..., n)$ as input, the output is:

$$g = \alpha^{(3)} \sum_j g_j^{(2)} \beta_j^{(3)}$$

$$= \sum_j \sum_i d_i a_{ij} q_j = \mathbf{d} \mathbf{A} \mathbf{q}^{\mathrm{T}},$$

where all the input weights $\beta_j^{(3)}$ and scaling factor $\alpha^{(3)}$ are equal to 1.

The network configuration as shown in Figure 1 is similar to the Gamba perceptron [3] except that a) we use a linear threshold function instead of a step threshold function, and b) the weights of the input and output layers in this neural network are fixed. This makes the task of training the network much easier, because only the weights of the neural network in the hidden layer are adjustable. We suggest the following algorithm to construct a term-association matrix.

Algorithm FIND-ASSOCIATION-MATRIX

(i)   Choose an initial matrix $\mathbf{A}_0$ and let $k = 0$;

(ii)   Let $\mathbf{A}_k$ be the matrix in the $(k + 1)$th; iterationidentify the set of incorrectly ranked pairs :

$$\Gamma(\mathbf{A}_k) = \{[(\mathbf{d}, \mathbf{q}), (\mathbf{d}', \mathbf{q})] \mid \mathbf{d} \mathbf{A}_k \mathbf{q}^{\mathrm{T}} \leq \mathbf{d}' \mathbf{A}_k \mathbf{q}^{\mathrm{T}}\};$$

If $\Gamma(\mathbf{A}_k) = \emptyset$, terminate the procedure;

(iii)   Let

$$\mathbf{A}_{k+1} = \mathbf{A}_k + \left[\sum_{[(\mathbf{d},\mathbf{q}),(\mathbf{d}',\mathbf{q})] \in \Gamma(\mathbf{A}_k)} (\mathbf{d} - \mathbf{d}') \right]^{\mathrm{T}} \mathbf{q};$$

(iv)   Let $k = k + 1$; go back to step (ii);

One can show that this procedure converges to a term-association matrix satisfying equation (10) in a finite number of steps, provided that such a matrix exists.

We performed experiments on a number of document collections to test the effectiveness of the learning algorithms. The experimental results indicate that our approach compares favorably with the other feedback methods [4, 5].

IV. CONCLUSION

In this paper, we have shown how the problem of adaptive information retrieval can be transformed into a problem of learning in a neural network. In particular, we have demonstrated that a two-layer neural network is an effective tool to implement a linear adaptive retrieval system. Likewise, we can use a three-layer neural network to implement a bi-linear adaptive retrieval system. More importantly, this preliminary investigation suggests that a neural network provides a sound basis for designing an adaptive information retrieval system.

Although our discussion here focuses on information retrieval, the proposed approach can be used to design other decision support systems in which the primary objective is to rank decision alternatives.

REFERENCES

[1] M. A. Arbib, Brains, *Machines, and Mathematics*, New York: Springer-Verley, 1988.

[2] R. O. Duda and P. E. Hart, *Pattern Classification And Scene Analysis*, New York: Wiley, 1973.

[3] M. Minsky and S. Papert, *Perceptrons – An Introduction to Computational Geometry*, extended edition, Massachusetts: MIT Press, 1988.

[4] V. V. Raghavan and G. S. Jung, A machine learning approach to automatic pseudo-thesaurus construction. *Proceeding of the 4th International Symposium on Methodologies for Intelligent Systems: Poster Session Program*, 111-121, 1989.

[5] V. V. Raghavan and C. T. Yu, Experiments on the determination of the relationships between terms. *ACM Transactions on Database Systems*, *4*, 240-260, 1979.

[6] J. J. Jr. Rocchio, Relevance Feedback in Information Retrieval. In Salton, G. (ed.), *The SMART Retrieval System — Experiments in Automatic Document Processing*, Englewood Cliffs, NJ: Prentice-Hall, 313-323, 1971.

[7] Rumelhart, McClelland and the PDP Research Group, *Parallel Distributed Processing*, Volume 1: Foundations, The MIT Press, 1986.

[8] G. Salton and M. H. McGill, *Introduction to Modern Information Retrieval*. New York: McGraw-Hill, 1983.

[9] P. K. Simpson, *Artificial Neural Systems - Foundations, Paradigms, Applications, and Implementations*. New York: Pergamon Press, 1990.

[10] S. K. M. Wong and Y. Y. Yao, Query formulation in linear retrieval models, *Journal of the American Society for Information Science, 41*, 334-341, 1990.

Chapter 17
Natural Language

Natural language, like information retrieval, is an area where the number of neural network applications has been relatively sparse. Much of the work in this area is dominated by rule-based and grammar-based approaches. Nonetheless, this chapter does contain two papers that address critical issues in natural language processing. **Paper 17.1** proposes the application of neural networks to solve the algebraic formulation of the language acquisition problem. **Paper 17.2** describes the use of recurrent neural networks as discrete finite automata, hence providing the ability to learn new grammars (both from scratch and incrementally) and then decompose the resulting neural network into a set of rules.

Chapter 17:   Natural Language

ADAPTIVE LANGUAGE ACQUISITION USING INCREMENTAL LEARNING

K. Farrell[1], R.J. Mammone[1], and A.L. Gorin[2]

[1]CAIP Center, Rutgers University, Piscataway, New Jersey 08855
[2]AT&T Bell Laboratories, Murray Hill, New Jersey 07974

ABSTRACT

An incremental approach to solving an algebraic formulation of the language acquisition problem is presented. This problem consists of solving a system of linear equations, where each equation represents a sentence/action pair and each variable denotes a word/action association [1]. The algebraic model for language acquisition has been shown [1] to provide advantages over the relative frequency estimate models when dealing with small-sample statistics. In this paper, two incremental methods are investigated to solve the system of linear equations. The incremental methods provide a *regularized* solution that is shown experimentally to be advantageous over the pseudo-inverse solution for classifying test data. In addition, the methods are more efficient with respect to computational and memory requirements.

1 INTRODUCTION

The methods for adaptive language acquisition presented in [2, 3, 4] rely on mutual information estimates that represent word/action associations. The word/action associations can be computed using smoothed relative frequency estimates, i.e., using the number of occurrences of a given word and the number of times an action occurred for sentences containing that word. That method for determining word/action associations is *context independent*, meaning that the update of a word/action association for a given word is independent of the other words that occur along with it in the sentence. This trait is undesirable and leads one to formulate the problem of *focused learning* [1], referring to the ability to concentrate on words that convey most of the meaning of a sentence.

As an example of focused learning, consider two sentences from the Inward Call Manager database [2], which consists of requests to an operator in a department store that may be routed to the *furniture*, *clothing*, or *hardware* departments. The two example sentences are: "*I'm looking for a mauve sweater*", and "*I need a new etarge*", where the underline denotes a new vocabulary word. The smoothed mutual information method will tend to create an equal level of association of the words *mauve* and *etarge* with their corresponding classes, namely *clothing* and *furniture*. This is due to the algorithm only using the information that it has seen *mauve* occur once for the *clothing* category, and *etarge* occur once for *furniture* category. However, the desired response of an algorithm would be to create a relatively small association of *mauve* with clothing and a relatively large association of *etarge* with furniture. Intuitively, this motivates the use of an algorithm whose update for the word/action association is proportional to the error signal. In the above example the first sentence would probably be classified correctly, thus having a small error, whereas the second sentence would probably be misclassified, hence having a large error. Formulating the language acquisition problem as a system of linear equations [1], i.e., algebraic learning, is our proposed means of incorporating the error signal in the update for the word/action association.

Algebraic learning consists of modeling the language acquisition problem as a system of linear equations, where each equation represents a sentence/action pair and each variable denotes a word/action association. The pseudo-inverse solution for this system of linear equations has been found to provide connection weights that are less sensitive to small numbers of samples than are the smoothed relative frequency estimates. The pseudo-inverse solution in [1] was computed using a singular value decomposition (SVD). However, the direct computation of the pseudo-inverse has some limitations. It is costly to use for updating weights and is found to provide suboptimal performance for cross-validation.

In this paper, we present two methods of incremental learning to overcome the drawbacks of the pseudo-inverse solution. The following section reviews how the language acquisition problem can be formulated as a system of linear equations. The incremental methods for solving this system are then described in Section 3. Experimental results are provided for the text-based Inward Call Manager [2] system in Section 4 and in Section 5 the conclusions and summary of this paper are given.

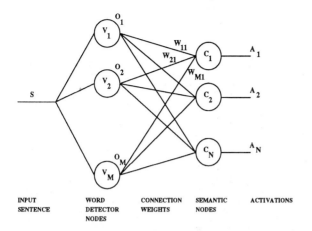

| INPUT SENTENCE | WORD DETECTOR NODES | CONNECTION WEIGHTS | SEMANTIC NODES | ACTIVATIONS |

Figure 1: Single layer neural network for sentence/action mapping

2 PROBLEM FORMULATION

Our most basic language acquisition model can be interpreted as a single layer neural network, as illustrated in Figure (1). The input nodes V_i are word detectors whose outputs O_i represent the probability that a word is in sentence s. In this text-based experiment, the output of the word detectors is either 0 or 1. Note that the number of input nodes M increases in time as the vocabulary grows. The connection weights w_{ij} represent the word/action association and was defined in [2] as the *mutual information* between words and actions. The output nodes C_j correspond to the set of N possible actions and are evaluated as the inner product of O and W_j. The action A is chosen according to which output node C_j has the largest value.

It was shown in [1] that the language acquisition model described above can be characterized as a set of linear equations. In particular, given a sentence/action pair for the jth sentence, define a vector λ_j as:

$$\lambda_j = < 00...0100...10 > \qquad (1)$$

where a one or zero in position i indicates the presence or absence of word i. A straight-forward generalization will use word probabilities in place of the 0s and 1s [5]. Note that the dimension of λ is equal to the number of words in the vocabulary, namely M, which grows over time. An equation derived for a sentence/action pair is thus:

$$< \lambda_j, W^k > = A_j^k = \left\{ \begin{array}{l} 1 \ if \ \lambda_j \in action \ k \\ 0 \ if \ \lambda_j \notin action \ k \end{array} \right\}. \qquad (2)$$

This equation is independent of word order in a sentence, and can thus be characterized as a "bag of words" model. In [1], it was shown how to extend this model to depend on word order. By using the formulation in equation (2) for each sentence in the

system, a system of linear equations can now be expressed as:

$$\Lambda W^k = A^k, \quad 1 \le k \le N. \qquad (3)$$

In equation (3), Λ is an M by P matrix, whose row vectors are that as given in equation (1). The variable P represents the number of sentences, which also grows over time, W^k is an M dimensional vector containing the connection weights for the kth action, and A^k is a P dimensional vector representing the labels for the kth action. In this experiment, we consider the case where the labels $A^k \in \{1, 0\}$ denote whether or not the sentence corresponds to the kth action.

The pseudo-inverse solution to equation (3) is denoted as:

$$W^{k\dagger} = \Lambda^\dagger A^k, \qquad (4)$$

where the pseudo-inverse matrix $\Lambda^\dagger$ for equation (4) can be computed using the SVD of Λ. For example, the SVD decomposes the Λ matrix as a product of unitary matrices and and a diagonal matrix containing the singular values of Λ. The pseudo-inverse matrix $\Lambda^\dagger$ is computed by inverting the nonzero singular values and letting the zero singular values stay zero. In practice, singular values below some threshold are considered zero and are not inverted.

3 INCREMENTAL METHODS

Two incremental methods are evaluated for solving the system of equations in (3) for W^k. The first method minimizes the quantity:

$$E_k^2 = \sum_{j=1}^{P} [A_j^k - < \lambda_j, W^k >]^2, \qquad (5)$$

where j is the sentence index. This quantity is minimized for each of the k systems, hence the superscript k is omitted in the remaining discussion for simplicity of notation. The method used to minimize the error quantity in equation (5) is known as the row-action projection (RAP) [6] algorithm, and can be used to incrementally calculate the pseudo-inverse solution of equation (3). The RAP algorithm for the system in equation (3) is implemented by using the update equation:

$$W^{(i+1)} = W^{(i)} + \mu \frac{\epsilon_j}{\|\lambda_j\|} \frac{\lambda_j^T}{\|\lambda_j\|} \qquad (6)$$

where

$$\epsilon_j = A_j - < \lambda_j, W^{(i)} >. \qquad (7)$$

In expressions (6) and (7), the superscript i denotes the iteration, the vector λ_j refers to the jth row vector of the matrix Λ, ϵ_j is called the error, and μ is a gain parameter, which is usually chosen between zero and two. Intuitively, the weight vector W in equation (6) is updated by projecting in the direction $\lambda_j^T / \|\lambda_j\|$, by an amount given by $\epsilon_j / \|\lambda_j\|$. The choice of μ contributes to the trade-off between rate of the convergence and the accuracy of the solution. The RAP method minimizes the error quantity E in equation (5) by cycling over the P equations until the error is below some threshold. Each cycle over the P equations will henceforth be referred to as an epoch.

Asymptotically, the RAP algorithm will converge to the pseudo-inverse solution of equation (4). However, in the short term, the RAP algorithm de-emphasizes the inversion of small singular values and provides a *regularized* inverse solution as described in [6]. The resulting singular value taper is given by:

$$\sigma_i = \frac{1}{\sigma_\Lambda}\left[1 - (1 - \frac{\lambda}{N}\sigma_\Lambda^2)^{l+1}\right], \qquad (8)$$

where σ_Λ and σ_i are the singular values of the data matrix and its inverse, N is the dimension of the solution, and l is the iteration index for the block of P equations. The regularized solution represented by equations (6) and (7) is more robust to noise than the pseudo-inverse solution [6]. This regularization tends to improve the classification of test data since the inversion of small eigenvalues, as performed in the SVD computation of the pseudoinverse solution, tends to overfit the training data.

A second approach is a nonlinear incremental method, which minimizes the error quantity:

$$E_k^2 = \sum_{j=0}^{P}[A_j^k - f(<\lambda_j, W^k>)]^2. \qquad (9)$$

The function $f()$ used in equation (9) is the sigmoid activation function [7]:

$$f(<\lambda_j, W>) = \frac{1}{1 + e^{-<\lambda_j, W>}} = y_j. \qquad (10)$$

The effect of the nonlinear activation is to replace the error term ϵ_j in equation (7) with $\tilde{\epsilon}_j$, which is given as:

$$\tilde{\epsilon}_j = y_j(1 - y_j)(A_j - y_j). \qquad (11)$$

In equation (9), since $A_j^k \in 0, 1$ and $0 < f() < 1$, the error for the jth sentence is bounded by $0 < |E_j| < 1$. Thus, large errors of the same sign are deemphasized. The use of the sigmoid activation function introduces a different error norm that is more robust to this type of error [8].

4 EXPERIMENTAL RESULTS

The two incremental methods were applied to the text-based Inward Call Manager [2] database. The database consists of requests to a department store that may fall under the three categories of *furniture*, *clothing*, or *hardware*. This system consists of 1105 sentences comprised of the first sentence in each dialogue of a natural language experiment. The vocabulary size of the 1105 sentences is 1356. All experiments reported in this paper use the first 800 sentences for training, which contains 1122 vocabulary words.

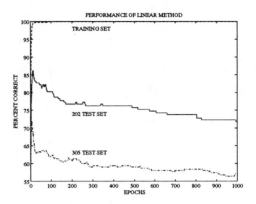

Figure 2: Linear Method

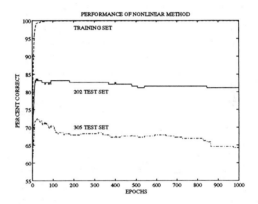

Figure 3: Nonlinear Method

Figures (2) and (3) show the learning curves for the two algorithms. These plots illustrate the performance when the system is trained on 800 sentences and tested with 1) the training set, 2) the test set (305 sentences), and 3) the subset of the test set (202 sentences) containing known *salient* words. For example, in the test sentence, *I'm looking for a table*, if *table* was encountered in the training set, then this sentence would be labeled as containing a known *salient* word.

The peak classification performance for both methods and test sets occurs at roughly 15 epochs. At the peak operating point, the linear method correctly classifies 99% of the training set, 85% of the 202 test set, and 72% of the 305 test set. The nonlinear method correctly classifies 98% of the training set, 84% of the 202 test set, and 72% of the 305 test set. The pseudoinverse as computed with an SVD (thresholding singular values less than 0.1) correctly classifies 99% of the training set, 69% of the 202 test set, and 57% of the 305 test set. These results are summarized in Table 1 along with the smoothed mutual information (SMI) estimates.

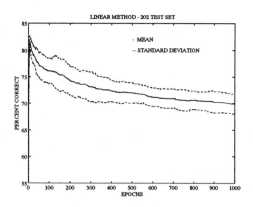

Figure 4: Linear Method - Random Training

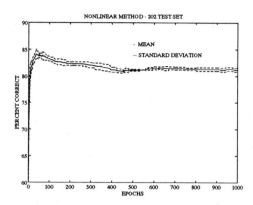

Figure 5: Nonlinear Method - Random Training

Table 1: Classification Performance

Method	Training	Test (305)	Test (202)
SMI	93%	73%	83%
SVD	99%	57%	69%
Linear-peak	99%	72%	85%
Nonlin-peak	98%	72%	84%
Linear-1000	99%	57%	72%
Nonlin-1000	99%	64%	81%

Though the peak performance of both incremental algorithms is roughly equal, the nonlinear method maintains its classification performance as opposed to the linear method, whose performance degrades after numerous iterations. An additional experiment was performed, where the 800 training sentences are randomly ordered prior to estimating the performance. Note that this does not change the final solution to the system of equations. However, the path that the weights take towards their optimum will be different and hence effect performance. Eight random orderings were tested, whose mean and one standard deviation for classification performance on the 202 test set are shown in Figures (4) and (5). The standard deviation at the 1000th epoch is 0.375 for the nonlinear method and 1.866 for the linear method. Hence, the nonlinear method is more robust than the linear method with respect to order sensitivity.

5 CONCLUSION

Two incremental methods have been evaluated on the adaptive language acquisition problem. For the 305 test set, the incremental methods correctly classify 72% of the test sentences at their peak operating point. When evaluated on a subset of the test set containing known salient words, the incremental methods correctly classify 84% of the test sentences. The nonlinear incremental method is found to maintain its level of generalization while the linear method is more vulnerable to overtraining. The non-

linear method is also less sensitive to equation ordering. Both methods perform significantly better than the pseudo-inverse, which correctly classifies about 57% and 69% of the sentences in the 305 and 202 test sets, respectively. The performance of the incremental methods is similar to that of the smoothed mutual information method for the test set, but yields better performance for the training set.

REFERENCES

[1] N. Tishby and A. Gorin. Algebraic learning of statistical associations for language acquisition. In *Neural Networks for Speech and Image Processing*. Chapman Hall, 1993.

[2] A.L. Gorin, S.E. Levinson, A.N. Gertner, and E.R. Goldman. On adaptive acquisition of language. *Computer, Speech, and Language*, pages 101–132, Apr. 1991.

[3] A.L. Gorin, S.E. Levinson, and A.N. Gertner. Adaptive acquisition of spoken language. In *Proceedings IEEE ICASSP 1991*, Toronto, May 1991.

[4] L.G. Miller and A.L. Gorin. A structured network architecture for adaptive language acquisition. In *Proceedings IEEE ICASSP 1992*, San Francisco, CA, Mar. 1992.

[5] A.L. Gorin, L.G. Miller, and S.E. Levinson. Some experiments in spoken language acquisition. In *Proceedings IEEE ICASSP 1993*, Minneapolis, Mn, Apr. 1993.

[6] R.J. Mammone. *Computational Methods of Signal Recovery and Recognition*. Wiley, New York, NY, 1992.

[7] D.E. Rumelhart and J.L. McClelland. *Parallel Distributed Processing*. MIT Cambridge Press, Cambridge, Ma, 1986.

[8] P.J. Huber. *Robust Statistics*. Wiley, New York, NY, 1981.

Rule Refinement with Recurrent Neural Networks

C. Lee Giles [a,b], Christian W. Omlin [a,c]

[a] NEC Research Institute, 4 Independence Way, Princeton, NJ 08540 USA

[b] Institute for Advanced Computer Studies, U. of Maryland, College Park, MD 20742 USA

[c] Computer Science Department, Rensselaer Polytechnic Institute, Troy, NY 12180 USA

Abstract— **Recurrent neural networks can be trained to behave like deterministic finite-state automata (DFA's) and methods have been developed for extracting grammatical rules from trained networks. Using a simple method for inserting prior knowledge of a subset of the DFA state transitions into recurrent neural networks, we show that recurrent neural networks are able to perform rule refinement. The results from training a recurrent neural network to recognize a known non-trivial, randomly generated regular grammar show that not only do the networks preserve correct prior knowledge, but that they are able to correct through training inserted prior knowledge which was wrong. (By wrong, we mean that the inserted rules were not the ones in the randomly generated grammar.)**

I. MOTIVATION

Refining rules in a rule-based system is a very important task. What if the input data disagrees with the rules; how can the rules be changed? The problem of changing incorrect rules has been addressed for rule-based systems ([10], [17], [16]). This work demonstrates that recurrent networks can be applied successfully to rule refinement; that is, once rules have been inserted into the network, they can be verified and even corrected!

Inserting *a priori* knowledge has been shown useful in training feed-forward neural networks (e.g. see [6], [1], [23], [22], [2], [12], [18], and [20]). The resulting networks usually performed better than networks that were trained without a priori knowledge. It has been shown that recurrent neural networks can be trained to behave like deterministic finite-state automata ([7] [19], [24], [8]). Methods for inserting prior knowledge into recurrent neural networks have

be discussed in [3], [4], [11], [14], and [9]. [14] and [9] demonstrated that prior knowledge can significantly reduce the amount of training necessary for a network to correctly classify a training set.

We refer to individual transitions between DFA states as *rules*; they correspond to production rules of the grammar generating a regular language. In the remainder of this paper, *prior knowledge* refers to all production rules that are known prior to training. Rule refinement consists of three stages: 1) insert all the available prior knowledge by programming some of the weights of a network; 2) the network is trained on the data set; 3) a deterministic finite-state automaton (DFA) is extracted from the trained network ([7, 8, 13]). We say a network is preserving a known rule if it appears in the inferred grammar. (Since we know the DFA that generated the training set, we can compare the original DFA with the extracted DFA. In general, the DFA that generated the training set is unknown.) The network is permitted to change the programmed weights. In order for a network to be a good tool for rule refinement, we expect a network to preserve previously inserted *genuine* initial rules and to correct wrong initial knowledge. For a testbed, we trained networks to recognize a regular language generated by a random, non-trivial 10-state DFA. We show that, as might be expected, networks are able to correct wrong prior information and to preserve genuine prior knowledge. Thus, they meet our criteria of good tools for rule refinement.

II. RECURRENT NETWORK

We use discrete-time, recurrent networks with weights W_{ijk} to learn regular grammars ([7], [19], [8], [24]). A network accepts a time-ordered sequence of inputs and evolves with dynamics defined by the following equations (Fig. 1):

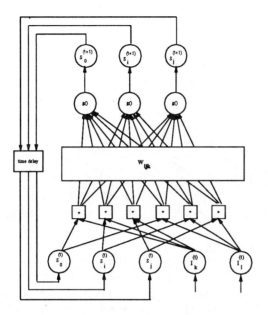

Figure 1: Recurrent network architecture. A second-order, single layer recurrent neural network consists of state neurons $S_i^{(t)}$, input neurons $I_k^{(t)}$ and second-order weights W_{ijk}.the operation $W_{ijk} \times S_j^{(t)} \times I_k^{(t)}$. $g()$ is the (sigmoidal) transfer function.

$$S_i^{(t+1)} = g(\Xi_i + b_i), \qquad \Xi_i \equiv \sum_{j,k} W_{ijk} S_j^{(t)} I_k^{(t)},$$

where g is a sigmoid discriminant function and b_i is the bias associated with hidden recurrent state neurons S_i. The weights W_{ijk} are updated according to a second-order form of the RTRL learning algorithm for recurrent neural networks ([25]). For more details see [7].

III. RULE INSERTION

The algorithm used here to insert rules into a second-order network is discussed in detail in [14] and [9]. For a method for inserting prior knowledge into first-order networks see [4] and [5]. Given some partial information about the DFA (states and transitions), rules are inserted into a second-order network which (partially) define a nearly orthonormal internal representation of the DFA states. By programming a subset of the weights to either $+H$ or $-H$ (where the rule strength H is an arbitrary value) and the biases to $-H/2$, the (untrained) network achieves the desired dynamics (state transitions).

IV. RULE EXTRACTION

We extract symbolic rules about the learned grammar in the form of DFA's. The extraction algorithm is based on the hypothesis that the outputs of the recurrent state neurons tend to cluster when the network is well-trained and that these clusters correspond to the states of the learned DFA ([7] and [8]). Thus, rule extraction is reduced to finding clusters in the output space of state neurons and transitions between clusters. Our algorithm employs a dynamical state space exploration along with pruning heuristics to make the extraction computationally feasible. The specific issues of the extraction algorithm and quality of the extracted rules are discussed in [13] and [15].

V. RULE REFINEMENT

A. Random Grammar

In order to explore the rule checking capability of recurrent neural networks, we used a non-trivial, randomly generated DFA with alphabet {0,1}(Fig. 2a). The networks we trained had 11 states neurons, one neuron for every state of the automaton and an additional output neuron. The training set consisted of 1,000 strings, alternating between positive and negative example strings in alphabetical order. The weights and biases were initialized to random values in the interval [-0.1, 0.1] and some weights were programmed to $+H$ or $-H$ as required by the rule insertion algorithm along with the biases.

We distinguished three different kinds of rules: 1) correct rules that partially define the DFA; training will provide the missing states and transitions. 2) partially correct rules, i.e. the state transitions have some resemblance with the state transitions of the true DFA. 3) rules which have no resemblance with the actual rules of the regular grammar to be learned. The rules extracted from the trained networks were not equal to the original DFA for all values of H for which the training converged within 5,000 epochs. However, the correct rules inserted were preserved in all cases and incorrect (malicious) rules were always corrected. We do not claim that our choice of noise methods is representative for any particular application; we are presenting preliminary results on rule refinement capabilities of recurrent neural networks. A quantitative approach must be taken to evaluate the potential and the limits of recurrent neural networks as tools for rule refinement.

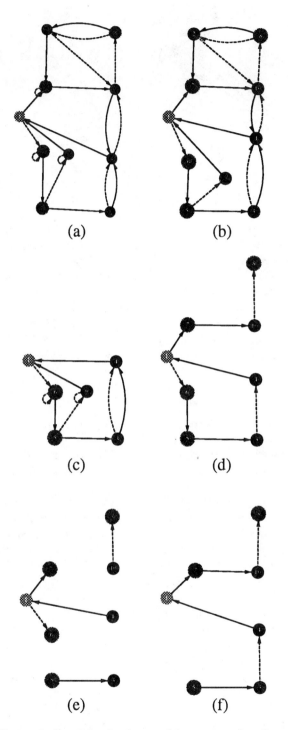

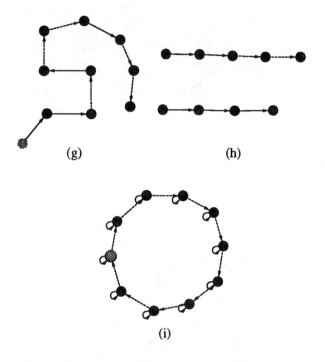

Figure 2: (continued) (g) rules for string '001011011' without programming loop (h) rules for strings '000' and '0011' but no transitions shared (i) rules for 10-parity

(a)

(b)

(c)

(d)

(e)

(f)

Figure 2: Partial rules inserted into networks. State 1 is the start state of the (partial) DFA. Accepting states are drawn with double circles. State transitions on input symbols '0' and '1' are shown as solid and dashed arcs, respectively. (a) all rules (entire DFA) (b) all rules except self-loops (c) partial DFA (d) rules for string '10010001' (e) rules for string '1(0)0(1)00(0)1' (f) rules for string '(10)010001'

B. Genuine Rules

We first investigated the ability of the recurrent neural networks to supplement incomplete rules by learning from a training data set. To demonstrate the effectiveness of our rule insertion technique, we inserted rules for the entire DFA (Fig. 2a), i.e. we programmed all the transitions and the accepting DFA states into the network. The learning curve 3a shows that the network did not need any training at all for large enough rule strength H. Self-loops, i.e. transitions from a state to itself (Fig. 2b), are easily learned in recurrent networks (graph 3b).

In order to demonstrate a network's capability to supplement correct, but incomplete prior knowledge other than the easy case of self-loops, we inserted the rules of a subset of all states and transitions (Fig. 2c). The network learned the training set and preserved the inserted rules (graph 3c). For some values of H, the extracted DFA was identical with the original DFA. In general, this was not the case, as shown in Fig. 4a. The network developed an internal representation of the DFA with more states, but the inserted rules were preserved.

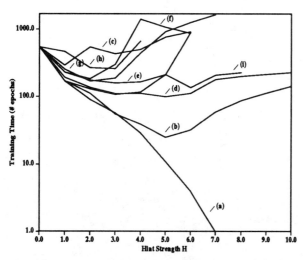

Figure 3: Training with known rules. Training times for learning with rules (number of epochs) as a function of the rule strength H on a logarithmic scale. The training time without rules is shown at $H = 0$. No training times are shown where a network failed to converge within 5,000 epochs. (a) all rules (b) all rules except self-loops (c) partial DFA (d) rules for string '10010001' (e) rules for string '1(0)0(1)00(0)1' (f) rules for string '(10)010001' (g) rules for string '001011011' without programming loop (h) rules for strings '000' and '0011' but no transitions shared (i) rules for 10-parity

Suppose we knew the state transitions for a single string in the training data set. How helpful is that information? We inserted the rules for a single string which visited almost all states of the DFA, but used only a small subset of all transitions (Fig. 2d). Information about the transitions of a single string can significantly improve the convergence time (graph 3d). (The effect of knowning the transitions of a single string on the training time depends on how many states of the entire DFA are known.)

Even partial information about the transitions occurring for a single string can be of help and the network is able to learn the remainder of the rules from the training data set. We inserted the rules '1(0)0(1)00(0)1' (Fig. 2e) and '(10)010001' (Fig. 2f) where parentheses mean that we do not know the transition for that particular symbol. The learning curves 3e and 3f support our hypothesis that knowing the transitions from the start state is more helpful than knowing state transitions deeper in the DFA.

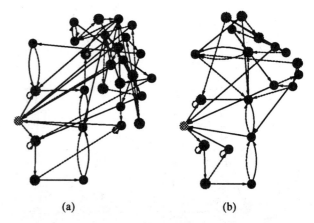

(a)   (b)

Figure 4: Rule preservation and correction. The extracted DFA's are not identical with the DFA that generated the training set, but they are consistent with the all example strings. (a) The rule 2c (partial DFA) was inserted into a network. The correct riles are preserved after training. (b) The rule 2g (no loops) was inserted into a network. The network recognized that the rules needed to be part of a loop in the DFA and corrected the wrong prior rules.

C. Incorrect Rules

We define incorrect rules as rules which correctly represent some aspects of the rules of the DFA, but which contain some error in the way the rules are represented.

Often, strings visit states several times when the DFA has loops. Suppose, we are given a string but we do not know that there is a loop. Is the network able to detect and correct that error? We inserted rules for the string '001011011' where the transitions on substring '101' form a loop in the DFA (Fig. 2g). We programmed the weights of the network as if there were no such loop, i.e. a new state is reached on every symbol of the string. The training times are shown in graph 3g. The extracted DFA demonstrates that the network recognized that the inserted rules were wrong and it corrected the error by forming the loop, although a DFA different from the original automaton was extracted for some values of H (Fig. 4b). Many strings of a given training data set share some of the transitions in the corresponding DFA. Two strings obviously share transitions if they have a common prefix and if the rules for two such strings were known, then the inserted rules would reflect this transition sharing. However, we wanted to test a network's ability to recognize that transitions were shared (Fig. 2h). Two separate paths with distinct states for the strings '0011' and '000' were programmed into a network. The network was able to merge the common parts of the paths through the DFA taken by the two strings (graph 3h).

D. Malicious Rules

It is difficult to give a precise definition of a malicious rule, because there are many ways in which a rule can convey wrong information such as wrong number of states, wrong accepting states, and wrong transitions. For the purpose of our investigation, we used the language 10-parity as a malicious rule (figure 2i) . This language consists of all strings in which the number of occurrences of the symbol '0' is a multiple of 10. We would have expected rule refinement to be difficult for a recurrent neural network in this case as the rules define a complete internal state representation, i.e. transitions for every possible input are accounted for. As the rule strength increases, the dynamics of the recurrent network become defined more rigidly which potentially makes the unlearning of the 10-parity DFA even more difficult. The simulation results show, however, that the network learns the unknown grammar rather easily (graph 3i).

VI. CONCLUSIONS

We have demonstrated that second-order recurrent neural networks can be applied to rule refinement. Given a set of rules about the unknown deterministic finite-state automaton (DFA) and a training data set, networks can be trained on the data set after the partial knowledge has been inserted into the networks. By comparing the rules extracted from the trained networks in the form of a DFA with the prior knowledge, the validity of this knowledge was established. We tested the networks' rule refinement cability by training them to behave like a non-trivial, random DFA with 10 states. Our simulation results show that recurrent networks meet our criterion of good tools for rule refinement, i.e. they preserve genuine knowledge and they correct wrong prior information. In some simulations, the extracted DFA was identical with the original, randomly generated automaton. In general, however, it is not required that the extracted DFA be identical with the unknown DFA and we consider a recurrent neural network to be a good tool for rule refinement as long as genuine rules are preserved and wrong rules are corrected. Rule refinement becomes more and more difficult with increasing rule strength H when wrong rules are inserted into networks. The results we obtained for rule refinement using second-order recurrent neural networks are promising. We are currently exploring a quantitative approach to evaluate the limits of re-

current network as tools for knowledge refinement.

Another research direction worth investigating is a combination of rule insertion and extraction *during* training ([21]). By continuously inserting and extracting rules from a network, starting with little or no prior knowledge, the size of the network would change after each rule insertion/network training/rule extraction cycle and be determined by the current partial knowledge of the DFA, i.e. the extracted symbolic knowledge would control the growth and decay of the network architecture. Furthermore, the symbolic knowledge may substitute for training samples, i.e. the network may select example strings for further training based on the extracted knowledge rather than using all strings for training. It is conceivable that this symbolically-guided training procedure could lead to faster training and better generalization performance.

VII. ACKNOWLEDGMENTS

We would like to acknowledge useful discussions with P.J. Hayes, C. Ji and G.Z. Sun.

REFERENCES

[1] Y.S. Abu-Mostafa, "Learning from Hints in Neural Networks", Journal of Complexity, Vol. 6, p. 192, 1990.

[2] H.R. Berenji, "Refinement of Approximate Reasoning-Based Controllers By Reinforcement Learning", *Proceedings of the Eighth International Machine Learning Workshop*, Evanston, IL, p. 475, 1991.

[3] S. Das, C.L. Giles, G.Z. Sun, "Learning Context-free Grammars: Limitations of a Recurrent Neural Network with an External Stack Memory", *Proceedings of The Fourteenth Annual Conference of the Cognitive Science Society*, Morgan Kaufmann Publishers, pp.791-795, 1992.

[4] P. Frasconi, M. Gori, M. Maggini, G. Soda, "An Unified Approach for Integrating Explicit Knowledge and Learning by Example in Recurrent Networks", *Proceedings of the International Joint Conference on Neural Networks* IJCNN-91-SEATTLE, Vol. I, p. 811, 1991.

[5] P. Frasconi, M. Gori, M. Maggini, G. Soda, "Unified Integration of Explicit Knowledge and Learning by Example in Recurrent Networks", *IEEE Transactions on Knowledge and Data Engineering*, to appear, 1992.

[6] C.L. Giles, T. Maxwell, "Learning, Invariance, and Generalization in High-Order Neural Networks", *Applied Optics*, Vol. 26, No. 23, p. 4972, 1987.

[7] C.L. Giles, D. Chen, C.B. Miller, H.H. Chen, G.Z. Sun, Y.C. Lee, "Second-Order Recurrent Neural Networks for Grammatical Inference", *Proceedings of the International Joint Conference on Neural Networks,* IJCNN-91-SEATTLE, Vol. II, p. 273, 1991.

[8] C.L. Giles, C.B. Miller, D. Chen, H.H. Chen, G.Z. Sun, Y.C. Lee, "Learning and Extracting Finite State Automata with Second-Order Recurrent Neural Networks", *Neural Computation*, Vol. 4, No. 3, p. 393, 1992.

[9] C.L. Giles, C.W. Omlin, "Inserting Rules Into Recurrent Neural Networks", *Neural Networks for Signal Processing II, Proceedings of The 1992 IEEE Workshop*, S.Y. Kung et al. (Eds), IEEE Press, pp.13-22, 1992.

[10] A. Ginsberg, "Theory Revision via Prior Operationalization", *Proceedings of the Sixth National Conference on Artificial Intelligence* , St. Paul, MN, p. 590, 1988.

[11] R. Maclin, J.W. Shavlik, "Refining Algorithms with Knowledge-Based Neural Networks: Improving the Chou-Fasman Algorithm for Protein Folding", S. Hanson, G. Drastal, R. Rivest (Eds), *Computational Learning Theory and Natural Learning Systems*, MIT Press, to appear, 1992.

[12] K.A. Al-Mashouq, I.S. Reed, "Including Hints in Training Neural Nets", *Neural Computation* , Vol. 3, No. 3, p. 418, 1991.

[13] C.W. Omlin, C.L. Giles, C.B. Miller, "Heuristics for the Extraction of Rules from Discrete-Time Recurrent Neural Networks", *Proceedings of the International Joint Conference on Neural Networks (IJCNN'92)*, Baltimore, MD, Vol. 1, p. 33, 1992.

[14] C.W. Omlin, C.L. Giles, "Training Second-Order Recurrent Neural Networks using Hints", *Machine Learning: Proceedings of the Ninth International Conference (ML92)*, D. Sleeman, P. Edwards (Eds), Morgan Kaufmann, San Mateo, CA, p. 363, 1992.

[15] C.W. Omlin, C.L. Giles, "Extraction of Rules from Discrete-Time Recurrent Neural Networks", submitted, 1992.

[16] D. Oursten, R.J. Mooney, "Changing Rules: A Comprehensive Approach to Theory Refinement", *Proceedings of the Eighth National Conference on Artificial Intelligence* , Boston, MA, p. 815, 1990.

[17] M.J. Pazzani, "Detecting and Correcting Errors of Omission after Explanation-Based Learning", *Proceedings of the Eleventh International Joint Conference on Artificial Intelligence* , Detroit, MI, p. 713, 1989.

[18] S.J. Perantonis, P.J.G. Lisboa, "Translation, Rotation, and Scale Invariant Pattern Recognition by Higher-Order Neural Networks and Moment Classifiers", *IEEE Transactions on Neural Networks*, Vol. 3, No. 2, p. 241, 1992.

[19] J.B. Pollack, "The Induction of Dynamical Recognizers", *Machine Learning*, Kluwer Academic Publishers, Boston, MA, Vol. 7, p. 227, 1991.

[20] L.Y. Pratt, "Non-Literal Transfer of Information among Inductive Learners", R.J. Mammone & Y.Y. Zeevi (Eds), *Neural Networks: Theory and Applications II*, Academic Press, to appear, 1992.

[21] J.W. Shavlik, "A Framework of Combining Symbolic and Neural Learning", TR 1123, Computer Sciences Department, University of Wisconsin - Madison, 1992.

[22] S. Suddarth, A. Holden, "Symbolic Neural Systems and the Use of Hints for Developing Complex Systems", *International Journal of Man-Machine Studies*, Vol. 35, p. 291, 1991.

[23] G.G. Towell, J.W. Shavlik, M.O. Noordewier, "Refinement of Approximately Correct Domain Theories by Knowledge-Based Neural Networks", *Proceedings of the Eighth National Conference on Artificial Intelligence* , Boston, MA, p. 861, 1990.

[24] R.L. Watrous, G.M. Kuhn, "Induction of Finite-State Languages Using Second-Order Recurrent Networks", *Neural Computation*, Vol. 4, No. 3, p. 406, 1992.

[25] R.J. Williams and D. Zipser, "A Learning Algorithm for Continually Running Fully Recurrent Neural Networks". *Neural Computation*, Vol. 1, pp.270-280, 1989.

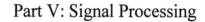

Part V: Signal Processing

Signal processing, especially digital signal processing, has become a mainstay of electrical engineering. Neural networks are one of many tools in the signal processing arsenal. The four chapters contained in this part represent areas within signal processing that have benefitted from the use of neural networks: communications (Chapter 18), remote sensing (Chapter 19), seismic processing (Chapter 20), and speech processing (Chapter 21). Related chapters, such as medical signal processing (Chapter 12) and automatic inspection (Chapter 22) could have been included in this part as well, but because of their stronger connections with medical processing and manufacturing, respectively, they were included in those parts of this book.

Communications has exploded in growth over the past decade. Pagers, cellular phones, Internet, and direct satellite television are only a few of the reasons. Adding fuel to this fire in the very near future will be ATM networks and personal communication systems. With these advances come a whole new set of challenges. There is a constant need to send more information over less bandwidth for longer distances with lower error rates. This chapter includes eleven papers that span a diverse set of communication applications ranging from meteor burst communications to data compression. **Paper 18.1** describes three applications of multilayer perceptron (MLP) neural networks to meteor burst communications (trail type classification, trail amplitude prediction, and trail type prediction). **Paper 18.2** introduces the neural tree network and applies it to the classification of modulation type for digitally modulated signals. The next two papers present two different applications to equalization. **Paper 18.3** describes the use of the MLP neural network to equalization, decoding, and intersymbol interference rejection. **Paper 18.4** reviews the use of the radial basis function (RBF) network for optimal blind equalization. **Paper 18.5** describes the application of RBF networks to spread spectrum multiple access demodulation. **Paper 18.6** propose the use of a hybrid fuzzy neural approach for frequency management in the VHF band. The next four papers present different applications of neural networks to different aspects of frequency management. **Paper 18.7** describes a neural optimization approach to rearranging switching networks. **Paper 18.8** proposes the application of self-organizing feature maps for the optimization of cellular communication base locations. **Paper 18.9** describes the application of the MLP neural networks to routing in telecommunication networks. **Paper 18.10** presents the application of the MLP neural network to traffic prediction in ATM networks. **Paper 18.11** presents a comprehensive examination of the learning vector quantization (LVQ) network's ability to perform still image compression.

Chapter 18:   *Communications*

Mind over Matter - Neural Networks and Meteor-Burst Communications

David D Fraser

Department of Electronic Engineering, University of Natal
King George V Avenue, Durban 4001, South Africa
E-mail: dfrase@elaine.ee.und.ac.za

Abstract

This paper discusses the reasoning behind neural networks and their applicability to meteor-burst communications. Details of data capture and processing, neural network structure, training and testing are given. The details of three neural networks for trail type classification, trail amplitude and trail type prediction are given. Conclusions on their application in adaptive data rate modems, and other uses of neural networks in meteor-burst communications are drawn.

1 Introduction

Meteor-burst systems follow the laws of physics and are deterministic, i.e. they are sufficiently quantifiable to allow statistical prediction and modelling on the macroscopic level. However, individual meteor trails are sufficiently stochastic to defy traditional methods of predicting their attributes on a trail-by-trail basis. This characteristic makes meteor-burst communications ideally suited to the application of artificial neural networks (NN's).

Neural networks are adept at generalizing the data with which they are presented and are thus able to interpolate results when presented with new and unseen data. This makes neural network decision-making extremely robust and insensitive to noise. Furthermore, the slight parametric changes that can be expected in data from a natural phenomenon are used constructively in the decision making process to refine predictions, rather than being considered as disturbances.

This paper considers the general applicability of neural networks to problem solving in the meteor-burst communications environment. It also considers three examples of actual neural networks used for trail type classification, trail peak amplitude prediction and trail type prediction.

2 Neural Network Background

Artificial Neural Networks (NN's hereafter) have evolved out of an attempt to emulate the functionality of the human mind from the bottom up [1]. That is, they attempt to model the cellular processing units of the brain which are then grouped into sub-systems called layers. These in turn are connected to form the neural network. Neural networks acquire knowledge through training and not through the codifying of explicit rules. A NN provides a level of abstraction which represents the interworking of many complicated and imprecisely defined facts. The methods used in learning and recall are thus critical to NN functionality.

Figure 1 shows a single cellular processing element called a neuron after its biological counterpart [2]. The neuron has several inputs X_n, each of which have a relative importance (called a weight W_n). This indicates the degree to which a neuron responds (or fires) to any particular input. The neuron responds to the weighted sum (I_j) of the neural input (X_n) multiplied by the strength of interconnection weight (W_n). For example a weight of +1 would not alter the input signal, +0.5 would reduce the significance of the input by a factor of 2, and -1 would inhibit the input signal.

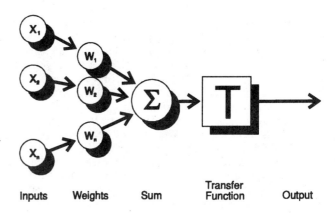

Figure 1 - Single processing element - (neuron)

Once the summation has been completed, the signal level is modified by a non-linear transfer function ($f(I_j)$), most frequently a sigmoid or hyperbolic tangent function. This allows the neuron to act in a non-linear and analogue fashion to data appearing at its inputs.

Many neurons form a layer or slab. There are typically 3 layers in most neural networks, viz. the input layer, the hidden (middle) layer and the output layer (Figure 2) [3]. The output of each neuron in a particular layer is connected to an input of every neuron in the suceeding layer. This is termed a fully connected network.

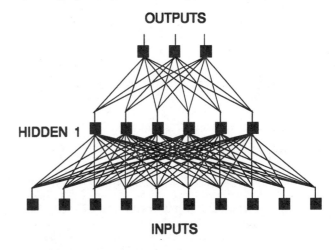

Figure 2 - Three-layer fully connected neural network

The network is now ready to be trained with data. Pairs of input-output data are gathered which describe a particular system implicitly. If the data used to train the network consists of coupled input-output pairs, the learning process is said to be supervised. Typically, the training data comprises 85-90% of the available data, the other 15-10% being used for testing [4]. It is important that the data pairs are ordered randomly. This reduces the possibility of learning trends associated with the data capture method rather than the actual data. The data must also be normalized and scaled relative to the maximum range of input/output values associated with the neuron transfer function [4].

When the input vector and the desired output vector are to be identical, the NN is called auto-associative. If the input vector is to be different to the desired output vector, (but associated by internalized rules), then the NN is called hetero-associative [5].

The training input vectors are presented to the input layer. Then the intermediate weights of all the connections are adjusted to make the output layer best represent the desired outputs. The process is repeated many times until the weights contained in the NN, are representative of the implicit rules contained in the data. By iterating through the training data many times, the NN is able to generalize the rules implicit in the data. A generalized NN is then robust in the presence of corrupt or noisy data (noise being used in the general sense of anything which taints data).

The method of adjusting weights is called the learning rule [5]. If the weights are incremented when the input vector corresponds well with the output vector, it is termed Hebbian learning. If the weights are adjusted to minimize the error between the input and output vectors, then it is called delta-rule learning.

The most commonly used type of NN is back-propagation (BP) [1]-[7]. BP is classically used for pattern recognition and classification tasks. In BP, the global NN error at the output is propagated back through the layers from the output to the input, hence the name. Each local error is adjusted to minimize the global error [5]. There are many variants on the standard BP algorithm allowing for faster convergence and more accurate representation. Inclusion of factors such as a momentum term [5] help prevent the learning process from becoming trapped in a local minima and help drive it towards the global minimim.

The trained NN may now be used in recall mode. When a new input proposition is made to the NN, it is able to provide a reasonable answer which best fits the input data. The data used to train the NN, appear as points in multi-dimensional state-space. When presented with novel data, the NN is able to interpolate between the discrete training points in the state-space and provide an answer which lies on the "surface contour" formed by the training points [8].

Thus the result of novel input data is a function of the generalized rules which were embedded in the NN by adjusting the weights. Once trained, the NN can be viewed as a functional representation of the system used to train it. It can be embedded in fast processing architectures, to outperform traditional classification and pattern recognition techniques both in speed and in accuracy.

3 Data Capture & Processing

3.1 Data Source

The data used to train the neural networks were gathered on a monitoring system developed by the Department of Electronic Engineering at the University of Natal, Durban, South Africa, which captures meteor trail reflection signals on a 24 hour a day basis [9]-[11]. Continuous-wave (CW) transmissions from Pretoria at 50 MHz are received, digitized (5 ms intervals) and stored on mass media at a remote monitoring site (eg. Arniston, Durban). The

variation in amplitude and phase of the received signal is due to the reflection coefficient of each meteor trail.

Two different monitoring systems were used as a source of data for the training of the NN's. These systems are briefly summarised in Table 1 below:

Table 1 - Data Capture Systems

Link	1100km Midpath ('C' system)	550km Midpath ('E' system)
Tx Site	Pretoria (26°S, 28°E)	Pretoria (26°S, 28°E)
Rx Site	Arniston (34°S, 20°E)	Durban (30°S, 31°E)
Tx Antenna	Stacked 5-element Yagis (9 dBi each)	11-element Yagi (12 dBi)
Tx Antenna Height	Lower 9m Upper 14m	3 m
Tx Power	350 W	350 W
Rx Antenna Height	Lower 9m Upper 14m	3 m
Rx Elevation	0°	0°

3.2 Preprocessing Phase

Different data preprocessing methods were used for each of the three neural networks constructed. The preprocessing stage produced the outputs assumed to be "correct" and the data extraction stage produced the input feature vectors for the NN's. Together they constitute the coupled input-output training and testing data:

- *NN 1. Trail type classification* - features extracted from the entire sampled trail envelope (inputs), expert system classification of entire trail (outputs).

- *NN 2. Trail amplitude prediction* - features extracted from the first 100 ms of the sampled trail envelope (inputs), peak trail amplitude of entire trail (outputs).

- *NN 3. Trail type prediction* - features extracted from the first 100, 150 and 200 ms of the sampled trail envelope (inputs), expert system classification of entire trail (outputs).

A rule-based expert system named TrailStar [12] was used to classify the entire trail into one of 29 distinct trail categories or classes. The classification is based on shape features of the trail amplitude envelope.

For NN 1 and NN 3, the decision of TrailStar was taken as the correct output of the data training pairs. A software preprocessor then classified each trail, for NN training purposes, as being of class 0, 1 or 2. Class 0 indicates the general overdense group, class 1 the general underdense group, and class 2 trails of types which cannot be conclusively determined to be in class 0 or class 1. This latter group includes the initial 'unknown' type (type 22), the 'mush' group of trails which consist of short duration trails which appear as straight lines of various inclinations on a time-amplitude axis, and the 'bell' group. These appear as bell-like shapes on a time-amplitude display. These trails initially seemed to exhibit underdense characteristics, but a matching study of trails received by two systems indicated that many of these bells are in fact the 'tops' of overdense trails. Thus it is still debatable whether these should be classified as underdense or overdense trails, and they were included in class 2 [13].

Class 2 trails were excluded from training and testing of the NN's, although it is expected that the NN's in their current form would have the same problem as humans do in deciding whether these trails were underdense or overdense.

For NN2, the peak trail amplitude was taken as the correct ouput of the data training pairs.

3.3 Relevant Data Extraction

For NN 1, NN 2, and NN 3, a number of numeric routines taken from the TrailStar expert system were employed to determine particular features of the trails. These features formed the training and testing input vectors to the NN's.

For NN 1, these routines used the entire trail sample length. For NN 2 and NN3 (truncated trails), these routines were used on the basis that feature descriptors which had been relevant in the classification of entire trails would have a high likelihood of being relevant in the classification of just one part of the trail, and knowing that irrelevant features would be discarded by the neural network. The feature and numeric routines involved are described below [12].

- B0 and B1 - the equation of the least squares line fit to the entire trail.

- The variance and standard deviation of the least squares line fit to the trail.

- The maximum and the minimum amplitude readings encountered in the trail.

- The presence or absence of an upper plateau in the trail, together with the length of such a plateau, if it exists. (This is determined by allowing a tolerance of 2 dBm, and asserting that an upper plateau exists if three or more consecutive samples are within this tolerance from the peak amplitude reading.)

- The number of minima (fades) in the trail. (A point is determined to be a minimum if it is the lowest encountered as the trail followed a downward slope, and a sample of 4 dBm or more greater than the lowest has been encountered, indicating that the trail is now on an upward slope. This approach allows for 'jittering' trails which have samples varying by one or two dBm up and down forming a straight line not seen as having a large number of fades.)

- The number of maxima (rises) in the trail. Determined in an analagous way to the previous minima feature..

- The B0 and B1 constants for the equation of the line fit to the fall section of the trail (the section from the peak amplitude position to the end of the trail).

- The variance and deviation associated with the line fit to the fall slope.

- The B0 and B1 constants for the equation of the line fit to the rise section of the trail (the section from the beginning of the trail to the peak amplitude position).

- The variance and deviation associated with the line fit to the rise slope.

- The sample at which the end of the rise is determined, and that at which the start of the fall is determined. (Note : not necessarily the peak amplitude position, as there could be an upper plateau between end of rise and start of fall.)

- The variance of the trail from the best parabola fit that could be applied to it.

4 Neural Networks for MBC

4.1 Neural Network for Trail Classification - NN 1

A neural network was developed to classify meteor trails into underdense and overdense trail categories based on data from the entire trail [14]-[15].

Several neural networks were implemented using California Scientific Software's *BrainMaker* software suite. *BrainMaker's* back-propagation algorithm is a slight adaptation of the standard layered feed-forward technique with continuously valued neurons. The standard sigmoidal neuron transfer function was used throughout the network and all initial weights randomized. The inputs consisted of 12 trail statistics (from the list in 3.3) and 20 normalized sample points corresponding to the first 100 milliseconds of the received signal amplitude. The number of hidden layers was varied between 1 and 2, and the number of neurons per hidden layer between 12 and 45. The number of hidden neurons was initially kept small to reduce memorization of the training facts and improve generalizing ability and gradually increased to enhance training. An increase in the number of hidden layers increased training time without a significant improvement in trained network performance.

The training tolerance, additive noise present during training and network learning rate we also varied. Training tolerance is the range of neuron output levels which are considered to be correct. A 10% tolerance was found to produce a good compromise between decision accuracy and the ability of the network to converge during training. Noise added to the connections during training led to poorer network performance under test and was thus set to zero. With the noise at zero, the training times were greatly shortened.

With a learning rate of 1, *BrainMaker* always converges during training if convergence is possible. With a learning rate of 4, training times were reduced by nearly 75%, though sometimes the network failed to converge at all. To ensure convergence, a learning rate of 1 was used until near the end of training after which a rate of more than 1 accelerated the completion of training.

Various subsets of training data were also tried, each requiring different numbers of input neurons. Training times varied from 5 minutes to over 1 hour corresponding to the number of facts used in the training file and the number of hidden neurons and layers employed.

4.2 Neural Network for Peak Trail Amplitude Prediction - NN 2

After developing some prototypes using the *BrainMaker* package, it was decided to implement the back-propagation NN using the superior *NeuralWorks Professional II+* package from Neural-Ware [16]-[17]. Predictions were based on the first 100 ms of trails data. As various feature descriptors had worked well in the TrailStar expert system which classified entire trails, it was decided to use these applied the first 100 ms of trails as preprocessed inputs to the NN. (A number of NN implementations have indicated that some preprocessing of inputs yields better results than merely using raw data as inputs [18].)

There are 26 inputs used. These include the features given in 3.3, but applied to 100 ms of trail only. Initially two hidden layers were used, one of thirty neurons and one of ten. Results obtained were disappointing. It was decided to instead design the NN with just a single hidden layer of 40 neurons, as research indicates that simpler one-hidden-layer designs are often more effective [19].

The NN has two outputs, one being the peak amplitude expected in the entire trail, the other being the expected duration of the entire trail.

The NN was trained on some eight hundred trail reflections, which had been recorded on a Pretoria-Durban link ('E' System.). It was then tested on fifty unseen trails from the E System, and on some two thousand seven hundred from the 'C' system (a Pretoria-Cape Town link). The NN was trained until both outputs returned RMS errors of under 0.021. The two systems have markedly different characteristics in a number of respects, including path length and antenna configurations.

Clearly if a NN trained on the one system could be a reasonable predictor for the other then NN implementation for purposes of adaptive data rates etc. would be a great deal simpler - the alternative being to train up a NN every time a new link is established. The earlier work on trail classification [12] had shown that the same trail types could be expected across a wide variety of systems, but was not able to determine whether or not the proportions of the various types would be the same across systems, so the question was still open as to whether a net trained on one system would be effective on another.

4.3 Neural Network for Trail Type Prediction - NN 3

It was decided to train the NN separately on portions of trails containing twenty, thirty and forty samples respectively (ie. first 100 ms, first 150 ms and first 200 ms) [20]. This would allow comparison of how pronounced an effect the added information gained by further information would effect the accuracy of the NN's predictions after training. To this end, the preprocessing package was used to truncate trails to appear as if they were only twenty, thirty or forty samples long, with their class (0 or 1, class 2 trails not considered st this stage) stored as the basis of 'correct' answers for training.

Again the back propagation algorithm was implemented using *NeuralWorks Professional II+*. The inputs consisted of the same 26 features used in NN 2 but adjusted for the 3 different trail truncation lengths.

A single hidden layer consisting of 40 neurons was used. The NN had two outputs, one giving the strength of its excitation for a class 0 trail, and one for a class 1 trail. The higher of these two has been used to make the decision of which class the neural net has decided upon ('winner takes all') in the results presented in this paper.

5 Results

5.1 Results - Trail Classification - NN 1

Testing was performed by presenting the network data with which it had not been trained, and verifying the corresponding outputs. The success rates for various network topologies ranged from 33 to 97% [14]-[15].

Table 2 - NN for Trail Classification

Network	Hidden layers	Neurons in 1st hidden layer	Neurons in 2nd hidden layer	Amplitude samples present	% correctly classified
A	1	12	-	NO	84%
B	1	40	-	YES	67%
C	2	40	20	YES	64%
D	1	32	-	YES	97%

It was found that the network which best discriminated between trail types (97% success rate), utilized 32 inputs, 32 hidden neurons in a single layer and two outputs representing the choice of underdense or overdense trail type.

5.2 Results - Peak Trail Amplitude Prediction - NN 2

The data used for testing the NN had not been presented to the NN during training. It consisted of data from both E and C systems. The results achieved for amplitude prediction and duration prediction differed markedly, with the former (and more critical for adaptive data rate optimization) yielding encouraging results and the latter disappointing results [16]-[17]. To discuss the duration results first, the coefficient of correlation (r) between predicted and actual duration was a mere 0.291 (29.1%) for the 50 E System trails, and 0.353 (35.3%) for the 2700 C System trails. While the fact that the NN actually performed better on trails from a system that it had not encountered during training might be of some interest, the low correlations clearly indicate that the current NN is not an effective duration predictor, and more work remains to be done here. However, the inability to predict trail duration correlates with findings on statistical analysis of factors influencing trail duration [21].

The prediction of peak amplitude was far more effective. Testing on the 50 E System trails yielded a 0.966 coefficient of correlation (96.6%) between predicted and actual peak amplitude, while a 0.858 correlation (85.8%) was found in the C System tests on 2700 trails.

The results clearly show that the NN can give a most useful indication of peak amplitude to be expected in an arriving trail on the basis of characteristics exhibited in the first 100 ms of its life.

5.3 Results - Trail Type Prediction - NN 3

The results of the 100, 150 and 200 ms sample case testing are given in the tables below. Once again, the NN was tested on trails that had not been included in the training set [20].

Table 3 - Trail Type Prediction

Trained on C, Tested on C				
Samples:	100 ms	150 ms	200 ms	Mean
Overdense correct	32%	28%	33%	33%
Overdense incorrect	13%	8%	6%	9%
Underdense correct	50%	56%	57%	54.3%
Underdense incorrect	5%	3%	4%	4%

Table 4 - Trail Type Prediction

Trained on E, Tested on C				
Samples:	100 ms	150 ms	200 ms	Mean
Overdense correct	50%	30%	39%	39.3%
Overdense incorrect	16%	10%	15%	13.6%
Underdense correct	23%	54%	36%	37.6%
Underdense incorrect	11%	6%	10%	9%

The results indicate that the NN is able to discriminate between underdense and overdense trails fairly well on the basis of initial samples received (ie. on the 'early' part of the trail) which is encouraging. It is interesting to note that there does not seem to be any statistically significant difference between the degree of discrimination when 40 samples are used and when 20 samples are used. This would indicate that the first 100 ms of a trail is sufficient to classify the trail. Despite being trained on a different system, the results for the E-system NN tested on C-system data are very good.

6 Conclusions

It has been demonstrated that a NN is able to perform the task of trail type classification with a high degree of accuracy (97%). This was based on data from the whole trail. The result is important since it indicates that a NN can perform the task of a rule-based expert system without explicit formalization of the rules.

The application of NN's to peak trail amplitude prediction was also shown (86-97% correlation between predicted and actual peak amplitudes). Prediction is a form of pattern recognition/classification except that only a limited period of trail sample was used (100 ms). The success of these NN's shows that sufficient features for prediction are present in the early trail samples.

The NN designed for trail type prediction used similarly truncated trail data to that used in peak trail amplitude prediction. When trained and tested on data from one system, it was able to correctly predict overdense trails 79% of the time and underdense trails 93% of the time. The significance of both these predictions is that for many trails they broadly predict the shape and amplitude of the coming trail, *before* the trail is completely formed. The distinct amplitude and duration characteristics of meteor trails, have a direct bearing on the data rate that can be supported on different trails, and at different times during the useable lifetime of any given trail. This implies that the throughput capacity of the channel can be greatly enhanced by the use of intelligent adaptive rates mechanisms [22]-[24]. Since the shape (type) of a trail can be distinguished early on in the trail's lifespan, a NN-based adaptive system could fully utilize the potential of each individual trail. This is particularly useful when operating in open-loop conditions where continuous MBC channel performance feedback is not available for adapting the data rate, eg. half-duplex or simplex low-cost remote units [25]-[26]. Furthermore, NN predictive techniques may be extended to include adaptive protocols and modulation techniques in higher performance systems.

Overdense trails generally have a larger reflection footprint than underdense trails. In a trucking/mobile application it is advantageous, to discriminate between overdense and underdense trail types to reduce interference to neighbouring units in a congested network. If a NN-based decision could be made sufficiently early in the trail lifetime, transmission could cease on overdense trails and only take place on underdense trails thus reducing the number of packet collisions.

Other uses of NN's in MBC may include communications network routing optimization [27]-[28] and data conditioning and compression [4]-[5]. Currently, research in both these areas is being conducted at the University of Natal.

References

[1] Wasserman, P. D., *Neural Computing - Theory and Practice*, Van Nostrand Reinholdt, 1989

[2] Hecht-Nielson, R., *Neurocomputing*, Addison-Wesley Publishing Company, 1990

[3] McCord Nelson, M. and Illingworth, W. T., *A Practical Guide to Neural Nets*, Addison-Wesley Publishing Company, 1991

[4] Maren, A., Hartson, C and Pap, R, *Handbook of Neural Computing Applications*, Academic Press Inc, 1990

[5] Handbook, *Neural Computing*, NeuralWare Inc, 1991

[6] Fahlmann, S. E., "An Empirical Study of Learning Speed in Back-Propagation Networks", *CMU Technical Report*, CMU-CS-88-162, June, 1988

[7] Rumelhart, D. E., and McClelland, J. L., "Parallel, Distributed Processing: Explorations in the Microstructure of Cognition", *Foundations*, Volume I, MIT Press, 1986

[8] Anderson, J, A, "Neural-Network Learning and Mark Twain's Cat", *IEEE Communications Magazine*, Vol. 30, No. 9, September, 1992

[9] Mawrey, R.S., "A Meteor-Scatter Measurement System", MSc thesis, University of Natal, 1988

[10] Fraser, D. D., "Phase Effects in Meteor-Burst Communications Systems", MSc thesis, University of Natal, 1991

[11] Larsen, J.D., Melville, S.W., Mawrey, R.S., Letschert, R.Y. and Goddard, W.D., "Throughput Capacity of Meteor-Burst Communications" in *Transactions of the SAIEE*, Vol 81, pp 20 - 30, 1990

[12] Melville, S.W., Larsen, J.D., Letschert, R.Y ., and Goddard, W.D., "The Classification of Meteor Trail Reflections by a Rule-based System", *Transactions of the SAIEE*, Vol 80, No 1, pp 116 - 132., 1989

[13] Melville, S.W., "A Practical Investigation of Meteor-Burst Communications", PhD Thesis, University of Natal, Durban, 1991

[14] Fraser, D.D., Khan, Z. and Levy, D.C.,"A Neural Network for Meteor Trail Classification" *Proceedings of the International Conference on Artificial Neural Networks (ICANN '92)*,pp. 1992

[15] Fraser, D.D., "Neural Networks and EFD in MBC Amplitude Prediction", Research Report, Salbu (Pty) Ltd, PO Box 109 Irene 1675 South Africa, February, 1992

[16] Goldstein, H., Melville, S. W., & Fraser, D. D., "A Neural Net for Meteor Trail Prediction", *Proceedings of the 3rd South African Workshop on Pattern Recognition*, Pretoria, South Africa, 26 November 1992

[17] Fraser, D. D., & Melville, S. W., "Artificial Neural Networks for MBC Amplitude Prediction", Research Report, Salbu (Pty) Ltd, PO Box 109 Irene 1675 South Africa, September, 1992

[18] Werbos, P.J., "Neurocontrol : Where is it Going and Why is it Crucial", *Proceedings of the International Conference on Artificial Neural Networks (ICANN '92)*, pp 61 - 68, 1992

[19] Widrow, B., "An Overview of Neural Systems", plenary address to the 1992 International Conference on Artificial Neural Networks, Brighton, 4 - 7 September, 1992

[20] Fraser, D. D., & Melville, S. W., "Artificial Neural Networks for MBC Trail Type Prediction" Research Report, Salbu (Pty) Ltd, PO Box 109 Irene 1675 South Africa, February, 1993

[21] Fraser, D.D., "Early Fast Doppler as an MBC Amplitude Predictor", Research Report, Salbu (Pty) Ltd, PO Box 109 Irene 1675 South Africa, July, 1991

[22] Larsen, J.D., Melville, S.W. and Mawrey, R.S., "Adaptive Data Rate Capacity of Meteor-Burst Communications", *Conference Record of the 1990 IEEE Conference on Military Communications*, Vol 2, pp 40.1.1 - 40.1.5, 1990

[23] Smith, D.K. and Donich, T.G., "Maximising Throughput Under Changing Channel Conditions", *Signal*, Vol 43, pp 173-178, 1989.

[24] Davidovici, S., and Kanterakis, E., "Performance of an MBC System Using Packet Messages with Variable Data Rates", *IEEE Trans. Commun.*, Vol. 37, No. 1, pp. 6-17, 1989

[25] Melville, S. W., & Fraser, D. D., "Meteor-Burst Communication: A Review", *Trans. SAIEE*, Vol. 84, No. 1, pp. in print, 1993

[26] Fraser, D. D., & Broadhurst, A. D., "Open-Loop Amplitude Prediction in Meteor-Burst Communications", *Trans. SAIEE*, Vol. 84, No. 1, pp. in print, 1993

[27] Funabiki, N., Takefuji, Y., Lee, K. C., Cho, Y. B., Kurokawa, Also, H., "A Neural Network Approach to Broadcasting in Multihop Packet Radio Networks", *Proc. of IJCNN-Singapore*, pp. 2515-2520, 1991

[28] Takefuji, Y., *Neural Network Parallel Computing*, Kluwer Academic Press, 1992

Acknowledgements

The author wishes to thank Salbu (Pty) Ltd and the University of Natal Electronic Engineering Department for funding and support. I also wish to thank Dr Stuart Melville for his invaluable software assistance and stimulating discussions, and Rod Radford for diligently maintaining the data capture site.

Author's Biography

David D Fraser was born in Florida, South Africa. He completed his BSc (Eng) and MSc (Eng) at the University of Natal, Durban. He is currently completing his PhD degree while employed as a lecturer in the Department of Electronic Engineering at the University of Natal, Durban, South Africa.

MODULATION CLASSIFICATION
USING A NEURAL TREE NETWORK

K.R. Farrell and R.J. Mammone

CAIP Center, Rutgers University
Piscataway, New Jersey 08855

1 Abstract

A new classifier is presented for estimating the modulation type for digitally modulated signals. The new classifier is known as the neural tree network (NTN). The NTN is a self-organizing, hierarchical classifier that implements a sequential linear decision strategy. The NTN does not require a statistical analysis of the features, as do Bayesian methods or decision trees. The NTN also allows for a more flexible partitioning of feature space than the prior classification methods. The features used for modulation classification are obtained from an autoregressive model of the signal. These features include the instantaneous frequency, bandwidth, and derivative of the instantaneous frequency. The modulation types to be estimated are continuous wave, binary and quadrature phase shift keying, and binary and quadrature frequency shift keying. The experiment results show the NTN to perform well for low carrier to noise ratio (CNR) input signals, in addition to outperforming the decision tree classifier.

2 Introduction

Signal interception consists of signal detection followed by estimation of modulation parameters and finally demodulation. Due to the increasing density of the frequency spectrum, the problem of signal interception is becoming more difficult. Previous systems have relied on manual identification of signal parameters, which would then be used for signal classification or demodulation. However, due to the increased activity in the frequency spectrum, manual identification methods are less practical and automated techniques for modulation classification are becoming desired.

Modulation classification can be accomplished by first extracting features from the signal that are characteristic of the modulation type. These features are then input to a classifier, which decides the modulation type. The modulation types considered here include continuous wave (CW), phase shift keying (PSK), and frequency shift keying (FSK). Several classifiers have been suggested for estimating modulation types, which include Bayesian discriminant analysis [1] and sequential decision-based methods [2].

This paper evaluates a new classifier for modulation classification. The new classifier is the neural tree network (NTN) [3]. The NTN is a self-organizing, hierarchical classifier that implements a sequential linear decision strategy. The NTN has several advantages over the traditional statistical and decision tree-based approaches for classification problems. These advantages include a more flexible partioning of the feature space, in addition to not requiring information regarding the feature statistics. The following section provides the problem formulation. Feature extraction is then discussed, where the features used are similar to those previously reported [2]. The NTN is then described. Experimental results are provided that compare the NTN to decision trees for estimating the modulation type within various carrier to noise ratios (CNRs). These results are followed by the conclusion of the paper.

3 Problem Formulation

This paper evaluates a new classifier for estimating the modulation type for a digital communications signal. Consider a signal $s(k)$ that is contaminated with additive white Guassian noise $n(k)$ to form the receiver input $x(k)$:

$$x(k) = s(k) + n(k). \quad (1)$$

An automated technique is desired for estimating the modulation type for the signal $s(k)$. The modulation types considered in this paper are continuous wave (CW), binary PSK (BPSK), quadrature PSK

(QPSK), binary FSK (BFSK), and quadrature FSK (QFSK). The general form of these signals is:

$$s(k) = A \, cos(\omega_c k + \phi(k) + \theta), \qquad (2)$$

where A is the amplitude (assumed here to be constant), ω_c is the carrier frequency, $\phi(k)$ corresponds to the modulation type, and θ is the phase at the receiver. The phase term $\phi(k)$ determines the modulation type as follows:

$$\phi(k) = \begin{cases} 0 & CW \\ 0, \pi & BPSK \\ 0, \pm\frac{\pi}{2}, \pi & QPSK \\ \pm\omega_d k & BFSK \\ \pm\frac{\omega_d}{2}k, \pm\omega_d k & QFSK \end{cases} . \qquad (3)$$

In equation (3), the ω_d represents the frequency deviation for the FSK modulation type. Methods for estimating the carrier frequency and the bit rate have been previously reported [2, 4, 5] and are not repeated here.

4   Feature Extraction

The features for determining the modulation types of equation (3) are typically derived from the instantaneous frequency. Several methods exist for computing the instantaneous frequency, such as the Hilbert transform [4], zero crossings [5], and autoregressive modeling [2]. This paper uses the autoregressive modeling approach.

Autoregressive modeling is an alternative to Fourier analysis for obtaining the frequency spectrum of a signal. The method used here for autoregressive modeling is known as the autocorrelation method. This method proceeds as follows. Given an input signal, $x(k)$, estimates of the autocorrelation terms $\hat{R}_{xx}(k)$ can be found via:

$$\hat{R}_{xx}(k) = \sum_{n=0}^{M} x(n)x(n+k). \qquad (4)$$

The M in equation (4) represents the number of samples in the analysis frame. The parametric model of the spectrum is obtained by solving the following system of equations:

$$\begin{bmatrix} \hat{R}_{xx}(0) & \hat{R}_{xx}(1) & \dots & \hat{R}_{xx}(N-1) \\ \hat{R}_{xx}(1) & \hat{R}_{xx}(0) & \dots & \hat{R}_{xx}(N-2) \\ \vdots & \vdots & \ddots & \vdots \\ \hat{R}_{xx}(N-1) & \hat{R}_{xx}(N-2) & \dots & \hat{R}_{xx}(0) \end{bmatrix}$$

$$\cdot \begin{bmatrix} a_1 \\ a_2 \\ \vdots \\ a_N \end{bmatrix} = \begin{bmatrix} \hat{R}_{xx}(1) \\ \hat{R}_{xx}(2) \\ \vdots \\ \hat{R}_{xx}(N) \end{bmatrix} . \qquad (5)$$

In equation (5), the a vector represents the coefficients for the polynomial whose inverse best fits the frequency spectrum. The Z-domain expression for this polynomial is:

$$1 - a_1 z^{-1} - a_2 z^{-2} - \dots - a_N z^{-N},$$

and the corresponding factored form is:

$$\Pi_{i=1}^{N/2}(1 - z_i z^{-1})(1 - z_i^* z^{-1}).$$

It is well-known [6] that the roots of this polynomial are related to the spectral peaks and their corresponding bandwidths. For a sampling frequency F_s, the exact relation can be obtained from equations:

$$F_i = \frac{F_s}{2\pi} tan^{-1} \left[\frac{Im(Z_i)}{Re(Z_i)} \right] \qquad (6)$$

and

$$BW_i = -\frac{F_s}{\pi} 10 \, log_{10} \left[\frac{1}{Im(Z_i)^2 + Re(Z_i)^2} \right]. \qquad (7)$$

The quantities F_i and BW_i provide measures for the frequency and bandwidth within the analysis frame. Hence, they are not actually "instantaneous", but are averaged over the analysis frame. Numerous frames are obtained and the statistics of these features are used for classification of modulation type. For example, given numerous instantaneous frequency (IF) measurements, it was found [2] that the standard deviation of the instantaneous frequency can be used to distinguish between FSK and non-FSK signals. The standard deviation of the instantaneous bandwidth (IB) can be used to separate CW and PSK signals. Also, the first order difference of the instantaneous frequency:

$$\Delta F(k) = F(k) - F(k-1) \qquad (8)$$

can be used as a feature. Here, the peaks of $\Delta F(k)$ are extracted and the mean is computed. This feature is useful for distinguishing between BPSK and QPSK signals and also BFSK and QFSK signals. Hence, the feature vector to be used by the classifiers is:

$$X = [\sigma_{IF}, \, \sigma_{IB}, \, \mu_{\Delta IF(peaks)}]. \qquad (9)$$

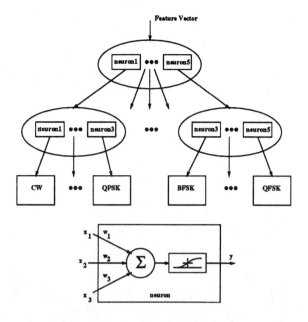

Figure 1: Neural Tree Network for Modulation Classification

5 Classification Algorithm

The neural tree network (NTN) [3] is a hierarchical classifier that combines properties of feed forward neural networks [7] and decision trees [8]. A NTN uses a tree architecture to implement a sequential linear decision strategy. Each node at every level of the NTN corresponds to a decision and uses an exclusive subset of the training data. The architecture of a NTN is illustrated in Figure 1.

In Figure 1, each node of the NTN consists of a number of neurons, where there is one neuron per class. Since the NTN is being used to distinguish between five modulation types, this is a five class problem and there are a maximum of five neurons per node. Given a trained NTN, the retrieval of the class for a feature vector proceeds as follows. First, the feature vector is applied to the root node of the NTN. The output of each neuron is computed and the path is selected corresponding to the neuron with the largest output. This process continues until the feature vector arrives at a leaf node where it will be assigned the label of that node.

An M-class NTN can be trained recursively as follows. Given a set of feature vectors, a node will first determine how many classes exist among these feature vectors. If there is only one class, then the node is labeled as a leaf with the class label of those vectors. Otherwise, a neuron is trained for each class. Each neuron is trained in a binary fashion, where the data for the class corresponding to that neuron is la-

beled as "one" and the data for all other classes is labeled as "zero". The training is accomplished with a gradient descent algorithm. For example, given the ith input pattern X_i, the output of a neuron is found as:

$$y_i = f(< W, X_i >), \qquad (10)$$

where $f()$ is the sigmoid function defined as:

$$f(x) = \frac{1}{1 + e^{-x}}. \qquad (11)$$

An error measure is obtained as:

$$\epsilon_i = t_i - y_i, \qquad (12)$$

where t_i is the target label, which is a zero or one. A weight update is found by evaluating the gradient of an error function with respect to the weights. The corresponding update equation is:

$$W^{k+1} = W^k - \lambda \frac{\partial E_i}{\partial W^k}, \qquad (13)$$

where λ is a scaling parameter and E_i is a function of the error. The function E_i used for the NTN is the L_1 norm:

$$E_i = |t_i - y_i|. \qquad (14)$$

The corresponding update equation for the weight vector is:

$$W^{k+1} = W^k - \lambda y_i (1 - y_i) sgn(\epsilon_i) X_i, \qquad (15)$$

where $sgn(\epsilon)$ outputs a +1 for a positive ϵ and -1 otherwise.

After all neurons within a node are trained, the training data for that node is applied to each neuron to obtain the sets of data partitioned by each neuron. A new node is formed for each neuron and the above procedure (starting from "determine how many classes...") is repeated. This process continues until the leaves of the tree completely partition the training data.

6 Experimental Results

The features considered in this paper were previously evaluated [2] with a decision tree. The prior classification algorithm is represented by the flowchart in Figure 2.

The corresponding decision tree for this flowchart is shown in Figure 3. To construct the decision tree, an analysis is first performed to find the discriminating features for each modulation type. The thresholds are then chosen to minimize the total probability of error for each feature.

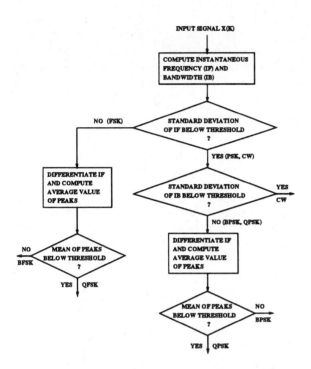

INPUT SIGNAL X(K)

COMPUTE INSTANTANEOUS
FREQUENCY (IF) AND
BANDWIDTH (IB)

STANDARD DEVIATION
OF IF BELOW THRESHOLD
?

NO (FSK)

YES (PSK, CW)

DIFFERENTIATE IF
AND COMPUTE
AVERAGE VALUE
OF PEAKS

STANDARD DEVIATION
OF IB BELOW THRESHOLD
?

YES
CW

NO (BPSK, QPSK)

MEAN OF PEAKS
BELOW THRESHOLD
?

NO
BFSK

YES   QFSK

DIFFERENTIATE IF
AND COMPUTE
AVERAGE VALUE
OF PEAKS

MEAN OF PEAKS
BELOW THRESHOLD
?

NO
BPSK

YES   QPSK

Figure 2: Flowchart for Modulation Classification

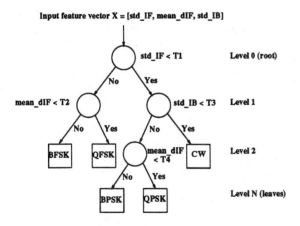

Input feature vector X = [std_IF, mean_dIF, std_IB]

std_IF < T1   Level 0 (root)

No   Yes

mean_dIF < T2   std_IB < T3   Level 1

No   Yes   No   Yes

BFSK   QFSK   mean_dIF
                     < T4   CW   Level 2

No   Yes

BPSK   QPSK   Level N (leaves)

Figure 3: Decision Tree for Modulation Classification

A weakness of the decision tree is that the discriminant boundaries must be perpendicular to the feature axes. For example, the root node checks if the standard deviation of the instantaneous frequency is below a threshold, $T1$. Hence, in feature space the discriminant will be perpendicular to the σ_{IF} axis at the point $T1$. This can hinder performance for problems that require a diagonal discriminant.

The NTN as outlined in the previous section is tested with a computer simulation. The simulation consists of signals having a carrier frequency of 10 KHz within an intermediate frequency of 20 KHz. The sampling rate is 40 KHz. The input signal is contaminated with bandlimited Gaussian noise to produce input CNRs ranging from 5 to 20 dB. The noise source consists of bandlimited white Gaussian noise. The symbol rate is chosen as 1200 symbols/second. The input $x(k)$ duration is 0.048 seconds, thus giving 60 symbols. The analysis frames consist of 0.4 *msec* segments overlapping by .2 *msec*. The frequency deviations used for FSK signals are 5 KHz for BFSK and 2.5 KHz for QFSK. One thousand random 60-symbol sequences were generated for each of the considered modulation types for both training and testing.

The classification results for a 10 decibel CNR are provided in the confusion matrices shown in Figures (4) and (5), for the decision tree and NTN, respectively.

The confusion matrices in Figures (4) and (5) show the NTN to perform at 97.8%, whereas the decision tree (DT) performs at 86.8%. This experiment is repeated for CNR levels ranging from 5 to 20 dB input CNR levels. For each CNR, an NTN is trained and thresholds are estimated for the decision tree. These results are summarized in Figure 6. The NTN consistently outperforms the decision tree for varying CNRs.

7   Conclusion

A new classifier is presented for estimating the modulation type for digitally modulated signals. The new classifier is the neural tree network. The neural tree network does not require prior knowledge regarding the statistical properties of the features. Also, the neural tree network is not constrained to creating discriminants perpendicular to the feature axes, as are decision trees. The NTN and decision tree are both applied to several experiments for classifying the modulation type of digitally modulated signals. The NTN performs well for CNRs as low as 10 dB in addition to consistently outperforming the decision tree classifier.

ACTUAL MODULATION	ESTIMATED MODULATION (DT)				
	CW	BPSK	QPSK	BFSK	QFSK
CW	1000	0	0	0	0
BPSK	0	822	178	0	0
QPSK	0	160	840	0	0
BFSK	0	0	0	841	159
QFSK	0	0	0	164	836

Figure 4: DT Confusion Matrix, CNR=10 dB

ACTUAL MODULATION	ESTIMATED MODULATION (NTN)				
	CW	BPSK	QPSK	BFSK	QFSK
CW	1000	0	0	0	0
BPSK	0	943	57	0	0
QPSK	0	38	962	0	0
BFSK	0	0	0	995	5
QFSK	1	0	0	10	989

Figure 5: NTN Confusion Matrix, CNR=10 dB

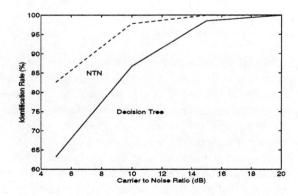

Figure 6: Identification % versus CNR

8 Acknowledgments

The research reported here was made possible through the support of the New Jersey Commission on Science and Technology and the Computer Aids for Industrial Productivity Center at Rutgers University. The authors wish to thank K.T. Assaleh for his assistance with the feature extracting software.

References

[1] J.E. Hipp. Modulation classification based on statistical moments. In *IEEE MILCOM 1986 Conference Proceedings*, Monterey, Ca, Oct 1986.

[2] K. Assaleh, K. Farrell, and R.J. Mammone. A new method of modulation classification for digitally modulated signals. In *IEEE MILCOM 1992 Conference Proceedings*, pages 712–716, 1992.

[3] A. Sankar and R.J. Mammone. Growing and pruning neural tree networks. *IEEE Trans. on Computers*, Mar. 1993.

[4] R.J. Mammone, R.J. Rothaker, and C.I. Podilchuk. Estimation of carrier frequency, modulation type and bit rate of an unknown modulated signal. In *Proceedings IEEE International Conference on Communications*, Seattle, Wa., Jun. 1987.

[5] S. Hsue and S. Soliman. Automatic modulation recognition of digitally modulated signals. In *IEEE MILCOM 1989 Conference Proceedings*, 1989.

[6] L.R. Rabiner and R.W. Schafer. *Digital Processing of Speech Signals*. Prentice-Hall, Englewood Cliffs, NJ, 1978.

[7] R. Lippmann. An introduction to computing with neural nets. *IEEE ASSP Magazine*, pages 4–22, Apr. 1987.

[8] L. Breiman, J.H. Friedman, R.A. Olshen, and C.J. Stone. *Classification and Regression Trees*. Wadsworth international group, Belmont, CA, 1984.

[9] H. Taub and D.L. Schilling. *Principles of Communications Systems*. McGraw Hill, New York, NY, 1986.

THE USE OF NEURAL NETS TO COMBINE EQUALIZATION WITH DECODING

Khalid A. Al-Mashouq
King Saud University, P.O.Box 800, Riyadh 11421, Saudi Arabia

Irving S. Reed
University of Southern California, Los Angeles, CA 90089,U.S.A.

ABSTRACT

Conventionally, equalization and decoding are performed independently in cascade. In this paper a multilayer neural net is proposed to perform these two tasks simultaneously. The proposed method is compared with the conventional ones in the case of severe inter-symbol-interference (ISI). It is shown that a remarkable improvement is achieved with the neural-net equalizer/decoder.

1. INTRODUCTION

Decoding is amenable to analysis in the presence of additive white Gaussian noise (AWGN). The optimal decoder can be derived under this condition. Nevertheless, suboptimal solutions are usually implemented to avoid the complexity of the optimal decoder.

If an additional source of interference is present, the problem becomes even more cumbersome. A practical example is the inter-symbol-interference (ISI) which is commonly encountered in bandlimited channels. In such a case an optimal decoder can be very difficult to realize.

Two suboptimal solutions are discussed here. The first one uses a conventional approach which is a direct extension of linear equalization. The second one is a novel approach which uses a neural net to combine equalization with decoding.

2. ERROR-CORRECTING CODES

The discussion in this paper is restricted to block codes [4]. Block codes are characterized by three parameters, $[n, k, d]$, where n is called a codeword length, k is a message length, and d is a minimum Hamming distance. Throughout this paper binary codes are used, which means that the number of codewords is 2^k.

Decoding

Decoding is necessary to restore the useful data bits from possibly noisy received samples. Three important decoding methods are reviewed here. The first method is bounded-distance (BD) decoding. In the BD decoding errors are corrected only if they are less than half the minimum Hamming distance. This method is by no means the optimal decoding strategy. Nevertheless it is widely used in algebraic decoders due to its simple implementation.

A better performance may be obtained by using the minimum Hamming distance (MHD) decoding. In such a decoder the received analog samples are hardlimited to be either 0 or 1. Then, the decoder compares the binary n-tuples with each codeword and chooses a codeword which is at a minimum Hamming distance from the input vector. This type of decoding is generally difficult to implement except with very special codes such as the first-order Reed-Muller code.

For an AWGN channel, it is well known that the optimal decoding is the minimum Euclidean-distance (MED) decoding if the codewords are equally probable [8]. For such a decoding method, the received continuous-valued vector is compared with all of the codewords, and the codeword with a minimum Euclidean distance is declared to be the most likely transmitted codeword. The implementation of this type of decoder is the most difficult and exhaustive of the three decoders.

Codes Used in Simulation

Two codes are used in the forthcoming simulations. A description of these codes follows.

Code H: [7,4,3] Hamming code

Hamming codes are described as "perfect" codes. This is due to the tight packing of the codewords in the n-dimensional binary space. Each n-tuple is either a

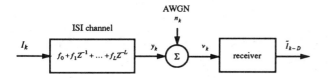

Figure 1: Block diagram of a discrete-time communication system which has both ISI and AWGN.

codeword, or at a unity distance from a codeword. In a [7,4,3] Hamming code a 4-bit message is mapped onto a 7-bit codeword. It has a minimum Hamming distance of 3. This makes it capable of correcting single errors. Each codeword is surrounded by 7 words, each of which is at a unity Hamming distance from the codeword.

Code RM: [8,4,4] Reed-Muller Code

Reed-Muller codes [6, 4], $RM(r, m)$, are a family of linear block codes which are characterized by an order r and degree m. For the purpose of simulation, the values $r = 1$ and $m = 3$ are chosen. This results in a code with a minimum Hamming distance of 4 and it is capable of correcting a single error.

3. EQUALIZATION AND DECODING

Figure 1 illustrates a block diagram of a discrete-time system which has both ISI and AWGN. The channel is modeled as a finite impulse response, FIR, discrete-time filter with an impulse response $\underline{f} = (f_0, f_1, \ldots, f_L)$. Let the input consist of a sequence of statistically independent symbols, $\{I_k\}$, which are passed through the channel. The AWGN has zero mean and a variance σ_n^2. The detector observes the received samples $\{v_k\}$ and produces a symbol, $\tilde{I}_k$, which is an estimate of the transmitted symbol I_k.

Often there are uncertainty about the ISI. For example in making a telephone call many possible paths might be taken. Each path introduces its own ISI. That is why it is important to "learn" the channel before establishing a reliable communication link.

A simple way to learn a channel is to use a linear equalizer [5]. The linear equalizer needs a training sequence in order to adapt to the channel in the hope of eliminating or at least reducing the ISI. Here the concern is about "severe" channels which cannot be simply equalized with a linear equalizer. Coding is useful to reduce the effect of ISI. To decode in such a difficult enviornment, two suboptimal methods are investigated next.

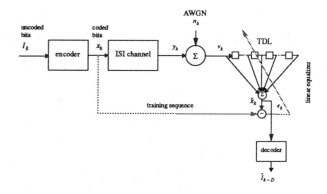

Figure 2: A conventional approach to perform equalization and decoding.

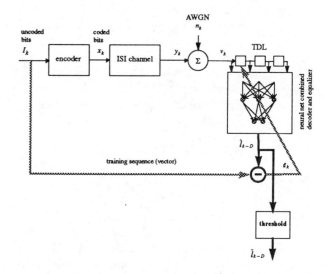

Figure 3: Neural net approach for combining equalization and decoding.

A Conventional Approach

Figure 2 explains the conventional [3] approach for combining equalization with decoding. In this approach the receiver operation is divided into two stages. The first stage is equalization in which a tapped delay line (TDL) equalizer is used to mitigate the effect of ISI. The equalizer weights can be learned from an initial training sequence.

The second stage could be any standard decoder such as a minimum Euclidean distance (MED) decoder, a minimum Hamming distance (MHD) decoder or a bounded distance (BD) decoder.

A Neural Net Approach

The neural net approach is depicted in Figure 3. Unlike the former technique, equalization and decoding are performed simultaneously. A multilayer net receives its input from a TDL. This input data is then passes through the consecutive layers of the net which ultimately produce an estimate $\hat{I}_k$ of the *uncoded* data symbol I_k. Such an estimate is quantized, or hardlimited in the $I_k = \pm 1$ case, to produce the output symbol, $\tilde{I}_k$.

With a net of "sufficient" size and training time, the net equalizer/decoder can learn a code from the received samples since they contain information about the code and about the ISI and AWGN. Training is performed using the back-propagation algorithm [7] with the uncoded data as the desired output. It is interesting to note that the receiver does not require knowledge about the utilized code. It requires knowledge only about the uncoded messages—from which the training sequence is generated. After the training is completed, the weights are fixed and the net is ready to provide estimates of the uncoded data.

Using a 3-layer neural net, one can always find a net that is equivalent to the conventional approach with a bounded distance, BD, decoder. The first layer serves as an equalizer and the two other layers can be made into a BD decoder [1]. However, due to the excess degrees of freedom of a neural net in the form of many levels of adjustable weights, and due to training, one might expect that the performance of such a multilayer-net equalizer/decoder would yield a substantial improvement.

4. EXPERIMENTAL RESULTS

Two channels are used in the following simulations. Both channels are severe in the sense that they have nulls in their spectra. The impulse response, $\underline{f}$, of the first channel (Channel 1) to be examined is given by

$$\underline{f} = (0.3, 0.5, 0.3)$$

Code H is used to mitigate the severe effect of the ISI and AWGN. A tapped delay line (TDL) of length 27 is used to feed a linear equalizer, and a similar TDL feeds a neural net.

Figure 4.a shows the probability of error when using a 27:19:2 (27 input, 19 hidden and 2 output nodes) neural net as a function of the SNR which is defined by

$$SNR = \frac{\underline{f} \cdot \underline{f}^T}{\sigma_n^2}.$$

Also it is compared with the use of a linear equalizer followed by one of three conventional decoders MED, MHD or BD. As a benchmark the performance of a linear equalizer without coding is also shown. It is clear that the neural net outperforms all of the other methods. The coded neural net system provides a coding gain, at $SNR = 10$ dB, of more than 8 dB over the uncoded linearly equalized system.

On the other hand, MED decoder provides only 3 dB in coding gain. This confirms the fact that in the presence of ISI, that the MED decoder is not an optimal decoder. The MHD decoder is substantially worse and differs by about 12 dB from the neural-net decoder. It is well-known that in the case of a Hamming code the MHD and BD decoders are identical.

Although this channel is severe, the neural-net equalizer/decoder results in a significantly improved performance. This is partially due to the low-rate code (Code H has a rate $r = 4/7$) which helps in decoupling the effects of ISI. However, these advantages of a code are not utilized properly by the decoders other than the neural net because the other decoders lack the capability of learning or adapting to the channel characteristics.

A similar experiment is run with another channel. This second channel (Channel 2) has the following impulse response

$$\begin{aligned} \underline{f} = \ & (3.842, 4.19, 0.53, -1.55, -1.756, -1.362, \\ & -0.955, -0.658, -0.452, -0.322, -0.232, \\ & -0.167, -0.129, -0.096, -0.077, -0.058). \end{aligned}$$

This channel is a very close model of a real magnetic recording channel [2]. Code RM is deployed to help combating the ISI/AWGN combination.

The TDL has 41 taps which is fed to a linear equalizer followed by a decoder, and a similar TDL is also fed to a 41:19:4 neural net. Figure 4.b illustrate the performance of the decoders due to Code RM. In this case, none of the conventional decoders achieve any positive gain, while the neural-net equalizer/decoder results in about a 2.5 dB gain at a $SNR = 12$ dB. The improvement is less than the previous case because Channel 2 in less severe (nulls are not very deep nulls) than Channel 2 as one can verify from the spectra of Channels 1 and 2.

5. CONCLUSIONS

A multilayer net is proposed here to replace the function of an equalizer and decoder. With a proper structure and training, the neural-net equalizer/decoder is shown to substantially outperform the more conventional decoders, including the MED decoder which is optimal for the AWGN case. This is because the optimality conditions are violated by the presence of ISI. Since the neural net and the MED decoders have a comparable burden of complexity, this should be considered to be an important success for the application of neural nets to a very practical problem.

Moreover, the coding gain achieved with the neural-net equalizer/decoder ranges from 2.5 dB to more than 8 dB, depending on the channel and code types. Such an improvement translates to a substantially greater transmission rate or throughput in communication systems and more capacity in magnetic-recording media. Moreover, a neural net performs its processing in parallel and its operations are simple (addition, multiplication and thresholding) which make the processing delay minimal. This property is essential in any high-rate data flow system.

It is expected that the complexity of the neural net depends on the size of the code and not on the channel. If this is to be true, then codes with a very large number of codewords should be avoided. This limitation, however, does not prevent the practicality of a neural net combined equalizer and decoder, since it is shown that a very simple code yields a dramatic improvement in the performance.

6. REFERENCES

[1] Al-Mashouq, K., Reed, I.S., "Including hints in training neural nets," *Neural Computation*, vol. 3(3), 1991.

[2] Bergmans, J.W.M., Rajput, S.A., and Van De Laar, F.A.M., "On the use of decision feedback for simplifying the Viterbi detector," *Philips J. Res.*, 42:399-428, 1987.

[3] Chevillat, P.R., and Eleftheriou, E., "Decoding of trellis-encoded signals in the presence of intersybol interference and noise," *IEEE Trans. on Communications,* vol. 37(7):669-676, 1989.

[4] Kumar, P.V. "Error-correcting codes." in Mohanty, N.C.(ed.), *Space Communications and Nuclear Scintillation*, Van Nostrand Reinhold, 1991.

[5] Proakis, J.G., *Digital Communications*, McGraw-Hill, 1983.

[6] Reed, I.S., "A class of multiple-error-correcting code and the decoding scheme," *IRE Trans. on Information Theory*, vol. 4:38-49, 1954.

[7] Rumelhart, D., and McCleland, J.L., *Parallel Distributed Processing: Exploration in the Microstructure of Cognition*, vol. 1, MIT Press, 1986.

[8] Wozencraft J.M., and Jacobs I.M., *Principles of Communication Engineering*, John Wiley and Sons, 1965.

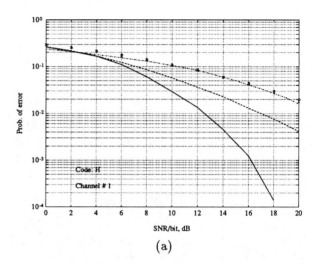

(a)

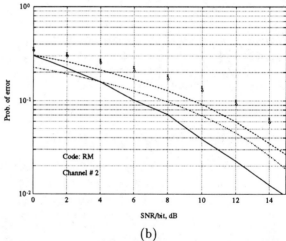

(b)

Figure 4: Performance curves of a neural net (solid curve) compared with a linear equalizer followed by: MED decoder (dashed curve), MHD decoder (oo) and BD decoder (x x) and also compared with a linear equalizer with no coding (dashdotted curve). The code name and the channel number are indicated on the graph.

RECURRENT RADIAL BASIS FUNCTION NETWORKS FOR OPTIMAL BLIND EQUALIZATION

Jesús Cid-Sueiro*, Aníbal R. Figueiras-Vidal

* ETSI Telecomunicación-UV, 47011, C/ Real de Burgos s/n, Valladolid, Spain
DSSR, ETSI Telecomunicación-UPM, Ciudad Universitaria, 28040 Madrid, Spain
E-mail cid@gtts.ssr.upm.es

Abstract. A recurrent version of a Radial Basis Function (RBF) network can compute optimal symbol-by-symbol decisions for equalizing Gaussian channels in digital communication systems, but the (linear or not) channel response and the noise variance must be known. Starting from theoretical considerations, a novel technique for learning the channel parameters in a non-supervised, non-decision directed way is proposed in this paper, providing a simple and fast algorithm that can be used for tracking in time variant environments or for blind equalization purposes.

INTRODUCTION

Neural Networks have been recently proposed as alternative structures for channel equalization in digital communications, to solve the low detection capabilities or the excessive complexity problems of classical schemes: linear equalizers, DFE or Viterbi detectors. Several schemes, as Multilayer Perceptrons [1], Radial Basis Function (RBF) networks [2], Pao networks [3] or Self-Organizing Maps [4] have been tested by means of computer simulations. Usually, these novel schemes get better detection capabilities than those of linear structures, but their training is several orders of magnitude slower.

The coefficients of a linear or quasi linear channel response and the statistics of a Gaussian noise distribution contain all the information that is necessary to make optimal decisions, and learning them is faster and easier than training the parameters of a non-linear structure, reducing local minima problems. However, there is not usually a direct conversion from channel to network parameters. The RBF network is just the exception.

If the channel is corrupted by additive Gaussian noise, an RBF network can compute optimal symbol-by-symbol decisions [2]. In [8] we show that a recurrent version of the RBF network can compute the optimal symbol-by-symbol decisions based on all the received samples till the detection instant (delayed decisions are also possible). The network can be trained by learning the channel response [5][6] and, after this, computing network parameters in a direct way.

Non-supervised learning with neural equalizers has been studied in [8] where it is shown that combined RBF-DFE equalizers outperform Viterbi detectors in time-

This work has been partially supported by CAICYT grant TIC 92 # 0800-C05-01

variant environments. However, a usual decision-directed LMS rule is used for updating the network parameters, resulting a bad performance in low signal-to-noise ratio channels.

This paper considers the problem of training recurrent RBF networks for blind equalization or tracking purposes. We follow the line initiated in [9], where a non-supervised non-decision-directed learning rule is proposed, taking advantage of an important feature of optimal RBF and RRBF equalizers: they make decisions by computing the probabilities of the possible states of the channel. The proposed rule is derived from theoretical considerations, and it is similar to a modified LMS algorithm, where the adaptation direction is not a vector of decisions, but another one that is computed as a linear function of these state probabilities.

RECURRENT RBF NETWORKS FOR OPTIMAL DETECTION

Consider a transmission of equally probable symbols belonging to a binary alphabet $X = \{+1, -1\}$ through some finite-memory communication channel corrupted by additive white $N(0, \sigma_n^2)$ noise. If $r(k)$ represents the received sample at time k, we can write

$$r(k) = y(k) + n(k) \tag{1}$$

where $n(k)$ is the noise sample and

$$y(k) = \mathbf{h}\{x(k),....,x(k-m)\} \tag{2}$$

where m is the channel memory and $\mathbf{h}\{.\}$ is a possibly non-linear function of the last m transmitted symbols, characterizing the channel response. A weight vector $\mathbf{h} = (h_0,....,h_m)^T$ defines the particular case of a linear FIR response, and then

$$y(k) = \mathbf{h}^T \mathbf{x}(k) \tag{3}$$

where vector $\mathbf{x}(k)$ is equal to $(x(k).....x(k-m))^T$.

The optimal symbol-by-symbol detector based on the information provided by all the received sequence till k has been derived in [10], (see Table I for a binary transmission case). As shown in Fig. 2, a recurrent RBF structure (RRBF) can implement it. Previous computations of the network are used as variable weights of the linear combiner ($g_{i,j}$·(k) in Table I), and the activation nodes, compute the noise probability density function f_n centered at each possible value of y.

NON-SUPERVISED TRAINING ALGORITHM FOR RRBF EQUALIZERS

An advantage of optimal RBF schemes is that they provide statistics of the channel states: the outputs of the $M = 2^{m+1}$ multipliers in Fig. 1 are proportional to the probabilities of $x(k)$ being equal to each possible combination of m transmitted symbols, x_i, $i = 0.....M-1$; i.e., if, at time k, the multiplier outputs are $g_i(k)$, $i = 0.....M-1$, then

1. Initialization:

$$g_j(0) = \begin{bmatrix} 1 & j = 00...0 \\ 0 & \text{otherwise} \end{bmatrix}$$

2. For $i = 0,1$, and $k > 0$;

$$g_{i,i'}(k) = f_n(r_k - y_{i,i',0})g_{i',0}(k-1) + f_n(r_k - y_{i,i',1})g_{i',1}(k-1)$$

$$G(k,i) = \sum_{j=i0...0}^{i1...1} g_j(k)$$

3. Decide $\hat{s}k = i$ maximizing $G(k,i)$

4. $k = k+1$

5. Return to 2.

Table I. Optimum symbol-by-symbol detection algorithm with zero delay for a binary transmission. f_n is the noise probability density function. The sub indexes of scalar centroids 'y' must be interpreted as a concatenation of binary sequences or values. For example, $y_{i,i',0}$ denotes the centroid with a sub index resulting from the concatenation of the binary values i, the sequence i' and "0".

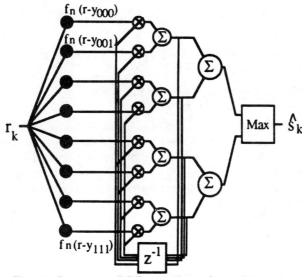

Fig. 1. Recurrent RBF equalizer, for a binary transmission in a channel with memory m=2.

$$\Pr\{x(k) = x_i | r(0), r(1),....r(k-1)\} = \frac{g_i(k)}{\sum_{j=0}^{M-1} g_j(k)} \qquad (4)$$

This information is essential in the non-supervised adaptive algorithm we propose. Now, let us define

$$p_i(k) = \Pr\{\mathbf{x}(k) = \mathbf{x}_i | r(0), r(1), \ldots, r(k-1)\} \tag{5}$$

Let us consider that everything is known, except the channel response (classical methods can be used for learning the noise variance). If at the k-th step of the adaptive algorithm we get the channel estimate $\mathbf{h}_e(k)$, we assume that $\mathbf{h}$ is a Gaussian random vector with mean $\mathbf{h}_e(k)$ and covariance matrix $S_h(k)$, i.e., by using the following notation for a m-dimensional Gaussian p.d.f.,

$$N(\mathbf{h}, S) = \frac{1}{\sqrt{(2\pi)^m \det(S)}} \exp\left(-\tfrac{1}{2}\mathbf{h}^T S^{-1}\mathbf{h}\right) \tag{6}$$

we can write

$$f_h(\mathbf{h}) = N\big(\mathbf{h} - \mathbf{h}_e(k), S_h(k)\big) \tag{7}$$

The information provided by r(k) modifies our lack of knowledge about $\mathbf{h}$. In the Appendix we show that the conditional probability density function of $\mathbf{h}$ based on r_k is given by

$$f_h(\mathbf{h}|r_k) = \sum_{i=0}^{M-1} p_i(k+1) N\big(\mathbf{h} - \mathbf{h}_{e,i}(k), S_{h,i}(k)\big) \tag{8}$$

where

$$\mathbf{h}_{e,i}(k) = \mathbf{h}_e(k) + \frac{1}{\sigma_n^2 + \mathbf{x}_i^T S_h(k)\mathbf{x}_i}\big(r_k - \mathbf{h}_e(k)^T \mathbf{x}_i\big) S_h(k)\mathbf{x}_i \tag{9}$$

$$S_{h,i}(k) = S_h(k) - \frac{1}{\sigma_n^2 + \mathbf{x}_i^T S_h(k)\mathbf{x}_i} S_h(k)\mathbf{x}_i\mathbf{x}_i^T S_h(k) \tag{10}$$

The conditional p.d.f. of $\mathbf{h}$ is a sum of M Gaussian functions, and it would be a sum of M^2 Gaussian functions, if we also include the information provided by r_{k+1}. Therefore, computing the theoretical evolution of the conditional p.d.f. of $\mathbf{h}$ would be impractical.

The mean vector and the covariance matrix of the conditional density $f(\mathbf{h}|r_k)$ are given, respectively, by

$$E\{\mathbf{h}|r_k\} = \sum_{i=0}^{M-1} p_i(k+1)\mathbf{h}_{e,i}(k) \tag{11}$$

$$\mathrm{Var}\{\mathbf{h}|r_k\} = \sum_{i=0}^{M-1} p_i(k+1)\big[S_{h,i}(k) + \mathbf{h}_{e,i}(k)\mathbf{h}_{e,i}(k)^T\big] - \mathbf{h}_e(k+1)\mathbf{h}_e(k+1)^T \tag{12}$$

At time k+1, the decision is taken by using the estimate of $\mathbf{h}$ given by

$$\mathbf{h}_e(k+1) = E\{\mathbf{h}|r_k\} \tag{13}$$

In the next iteration of the algorithm, $\mathbf{h}$ is considered a Gaussian random vector with mean $\mathbf{h}_e(k+1)$ and covariance matrix $S_h(k+1)$ given by

1. Initialization:

$$g_j(0) = \begin{bmatrix} 1 & j = 00\ldots0 \\ 0 & \text{otherwise} \end{bmatrix}$$

$$\mathbf{h}_e(1) = (0,\ldots,0)^T$$

$$S_h(1) = (\text{high positive value})I$$

2. For $i = 0,\ldots,M-1$,

$$\varepsilon_i(k) = r_k - \mathbf{h}_e(k)^T \mathbf{x}_i$$

$$\sigma_i^2(k) = \sigma_n^2 + \mathbf{x}_i^T S_h(k)\mathbf{x}_i$$

3. For $i = 0,1$, $i' = 0,\ldots,M/4-1$, and $i''=0,1$, the RRBF computes

$$f_{i,i',i''}(k) = N(\varepsilon_{i,i',i''}(k),\sigma_{i,i',i''}^2)g_{i',i''}(k-1)$$

$$g_{i,i'}(k) = f_{i,i',0}(k) + f_{i,i',1}(k)$$

$$G(k,i) = \sum_{j=0}^{M/4-1} g_{i,j}(k)$$

4. For $i = 0,\ldots,M-1$,

$$p_i(k+1) = \frac{f_i(k)}{G(k,0) + G(k,1)}$$

$$\mathbf{d}_i(k) = S_h(k)\mathbf{x}_i$$

$$\mathbf{h}_{e,i}(k) = \mathbf{h}_e(k) + \frac{1}{\sigma_i^2(k)}\varepsilon_i(k)\mathbf{d}_i(k)$$

$$S_{h,i}(k) = S_h(k) - \frac{1}{\sigma_i^2(k)}\mathbf{d}_i(k)\mathbf{d}_i^T(k)$$

$$\mathbf{h}_e(k+1) = \sum_{i=0}^{M-1} p_i(k+1)\mathbf{h}_{e,i}(k)$$

$$S_h(k+1) = \sum_{i=0}^{M-1} p_i(k+1)[S_{h,i}(k) + \mathbf{h}_{e,i}(k)\mathbf{h}_{e,i}(k)^T] - \mathbf{h}_e(k+1)\mathbf{h}_e(k+1)^T$$

5. Decide $\hat{s}_k = i$ maximizing $G(k,i)$
6. $k = k+1$
7. Return to 2

Table II. Blind RRBF equalization algorithm with zero delay for a binary transmission. $M=2^{m-1}$

$$S_h(k+1) = \text{Var}\{\mathbf{h}|r_k\} \tag{14}$$

In summary, a sum of Gaussian p.d.f.'s is approximated by a unique Gaussian function with identical mean and variance. Table II shows the final algorithm in a binary transmission case.

Note that, in a supervised mode, when a training sequence is available, we can take $p_i(k+1)$ equal to zero for all i except for that corresponding to the current training vector, and the algorithm of table II is still valid and equivalent to the RLS algorithm.

The complexity of the proposed algorithm is yet excessive for a practical application, unlike perhaps for detecting symbols in channels with short-length impulse response. In a general case, an excessive number of matrix products must be accomplished.

In order to reduce the computational burden, a diagonal approximation can be used, by forcing the covariance matrix to be zero outside the diagonal. With this assumption, vector and matrix operations in the algorithm of Table II are replaced by a set of scalar operations. However, this approach leads to an excessive number of fails in training, in which the algorithm is trapped in some local minima with error probabilities near 0.5, and a strong difference between predicted and true errors. We have found several ways to avoid this problem. Here, we consider the simplest one.

An interesting idea remains from the proposed algorithm. The channel estimate is updated as a function of 'a posteriori' probabilities of the different states of the channel, x_i. The classical decision-directed LMS rule is based on the false assumption of a perfect knowledge of the channel state, and the estimates are updated in the direction of the assumed state. However, if we just know statistics about it, we can construct the training vector as a linear combination of the states, weighted by its probabilities. The resulting algorithm can be seen as a simplified version of that of Table II, consisting on forcing the covariance matrix to be proportional to the identity matrix, or even as the stochastic gradient algorithm applied to this particular problem. It is shown in Table III and, working in a supervised mode, it is equivalent to the conventional decision-directed LMS rule.

SIMULATION RESULTS

For clearance purposes, let us call in the following PRLS to the learning algorithm of Table II, and PLMS to that of Table III.

In order to show the difference between decision-directed and non-decision-directed methods, we train an RRBF network in a supervised way, for equalizing the linear channel $h=(0.5,0.6,0.3)$ (noise variance 0.2) in a binary transmission case. After that, at each iteration, we change h by adding a random perturbation $n_p(k)$ with variance 10^{-6}. In 50 simulations 300 samples long each, the final symbol error probability was 0.10 using PRLS, 0.15 using PLMS, and 0.17 when a decision directed LMS rule is employed.

With the same channel (noise variance 0.08), an RRBF network was trained in a non-supervised way without any initial reference sequence. In this case, it is known that a phase ambiguity exists, and there are two global minima of the cost function. For experimental purposes, we consider successfully training when one of both minima is reached.

Fig. 2 averages the evolution of the quadratic distance between estimated and true vectors in 20 simulations. The continuous line shows that 200 samples are good enough to learn the channel impulse response with PRLS, and that its theoretical prediction (the trace of the covariance matrix, dotted line) follows experimental results. On the other hand, stochastic gradient methods (dashed lines), using an exponentially decaying adaptation step with a time constant 0.99, are much slower. No significant differences appear between LMS and PLMS in this case. By reducing the time constant, the convergence is faster, at the expense of a greater probability of wrong training, mainly using LMS.

1. Initialization:

$$g_j(0) = \begin{bmatrix} 1 & j = 00...0 \\ 0 & \text{otherwise} \end{bmatrix}$$

$$\mathbf{h_e}(1) = (0,...,0)^T$$

$$\sigma_h^2(1) = \text{(high positive value)}$$

2. For $i = 0,...,M-1$,

$$\varepsilon_i(k) = r_k - \mathbf{h_e}(k)^T \mathbf{x_l}$$

$$\sigma_{nh}^2(k) = \sigma_n^2 + (m+1)\sigma_h^2(k)$$

3. For $i=0,1$, $i'=0,.....M/4-1$, and $i''=0,1$, the RRBF computes

$$f_{i,i',i''}(k) = N(\varepsilon_{i,i',i''}(k), \sigma_{nh}^2(k))g_{i',i''}(k-1)$$

$$g_{i,i'}(k) = f_{i,i',0}(k) + f_{i,i',1}(k)$$

$$G(k,i) = \sum_{j=0}^{M/4-1} g_{i,j}(k)$$

4. For $i = 0,...,M-1$,

$$p_i(k+1) = \frac{f_i(k)}{G(k,0) + G(k,1)}$$

$$\mu(k) = \frac{\sigma_h^2(k)}{\sigma_{nh}^2(k)}$$

$$\mathbf{h_e}(k+1) = \mathbf{h_e}(k) + \mu(k)\sum_{i=0}^{M-1} p_i(k+1)\varepsilon_i(k)\mathbf{x_l}$$

$$\sigma_h^2(k+1) = \alpha\sigma_h^2(k)$$

5. Decide $\hat{s}_k = i$ maximizing $G(k,i)$
6. $k = k+1$
7. Return to 2

Table III. Stochastic Blind RRBF equalization algorithm with zero delay for a binary transmission. $M=2^{m-1}$

CONCLUSIONS

Optimal equalizers based on Radial Basis Functions have the exceptional advantage of providing 'a posteriori' probabilities of the channel being in each possible state. In this paper, we take advantage of this fact, providing non-supervised, non-decision-directed methods for learning the channel response, which outperforms classical decision-directed methods for blind equalization and tracking problems. Furthermore, these methods can be interpreted as generalizations of adaptive LMS and RLS algorithms, for cases in which there is some uncertainty in the training vector.

In spite of this, two important problems remain: first, convergence to bad solutions arises in some simulations, because of the simplifying assumptions of the theoretical derivation. As we have seen, this difficulty is partially solved at the expense of reducing the convergence speed.

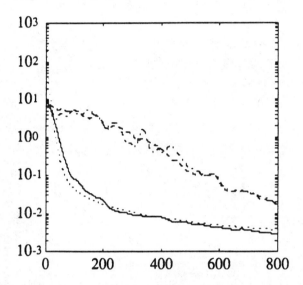

Fig. 2: RRBF blind equalizer. Evolution of the norm of the difference between the channel response and the estimations with PLMS and decision directed (dashed lines) rules and PRLS (continuous line) rules. The dotted line is the theoretical prediction for PRLS.

The second problem deals with the complexity of the RRBF structure, which grows exponentially with the size of the channel impulse response. In [7] and [11], we show that, when the symbol error probability is low enough, RRBF equalizers can be drastically simplified without severe performance loss. If a fairly good initial estimate of the channel is available, these conditions hold, and the proposed algorithms are expected to provide practical equalizers for detection in time variant environments. Simplified structures are, therefore, the topic of our future research.

APPENDIX

The p.d.f. of $\mathbf{h}$ conditioned by a given r_k can be written in the form

$$f_h\left(\mathbf{h}|r_k\right) = \frac{f_h(\mathbf{h})f_r\left(r_k|\mathbf{h}\right)}{f_r(r_k)} \tag{15}$$

Applying elemental probability theorems, we write

$$f_r(r_k|\mathbf{h}) = \sum_{i=1}^{N} \Pr\{\mathbf{x} = \mathbf{x_i}\} f_r(r_k|\mathbf{h}, \mathbf{x_i}) = \sum_{i=1}^{N} p_i(k) N(r_k - \mathbf{h}^T \mathbf{x_i}, \sigma_n^2) \tag{16}$$

$$f_r(r_k) = \sum_{i=1}^{N} p_i(k) f_r(r_k|\mathbf{x_i}) = \sum_{i=1}^{N} p_i(k) N(r_k - \mathbf{h_e}(k)^T \mathbf{x_i}, \sigma_i^2) \tag{17}$$

where

$$\sigma_i^2 = \sigma_n^2 + \mathbf{x_i}^T S_h(k) \mathbf{x_i} \tag{18}$$

Combining (15),(16) and (17), we get

$$f_h(\mathbf{h}|r_k) = \frac{1}{f_r(r_k)} \sum_{i=1}^{N} p_i(k) N(r_k - \mathbf{h}^T \mathbf{x_i}, \sigma_n^2) N(\mathbf{h} - \mathbf{h_e}(k), S_h(k)) \tag{19}$$

The product of two Gaussian functions is equal to a unique exponential with argument

$$\arg = -\frac{1}{2}(\mathbf{h} - \mathbf{h_e}(k))^T S_h^{-1}(k)(\mathbf{h} - \mathbf{h_e}(k)) - \frac{1}{2\sigma_n^2}(r_k - \mathbf{h}^T \mathbf{x_i})^2 \tag{20}$$

and, after some algebra including the application of the matrix inversion lemma in the equality

$$\left[S_h^{-1}(k) + \frac{1}{\sigma_n^2} \mathbf{x_i}^T \mathbf{x_i} \right]^{-1} = S_h(k) - \frac{1}{\sigma_i^2}(S_h(k)\mathbf{x_i})(S_h(k)\mathbf{x_i})^T \tag{21}$$

we can write (20) in the form

$$\arg = -\frac{1}{2}(\mathbf{h} - \mathbf{h_{e,i}}(k))^T S_{h,i}^{-1}(k)(\mathbf{h} - \mathbf{h_{e,i}}(k)) - \frac{1}{2\sigma_i^2}(r_k - \mathbf{h_{e,i}}^T \mathbf{x_i})^2 \tag{22}$$

Finally, by noting that the unique eigenvalue of

$$S_h^{-1}(k) S_{h,i}(k) = \left[I - \frac{1}{\sigma_n^2} \mathbf{x_i}^T \mathbf{x_i} S_h(k) \right] \tag{23}$$

that is different of 1 is equal to σ_n^2/σ_i^2, we can write

$$\det(S_{h,i}(k)) = \frac{\sigma_n^2}{\sigma_i^2} \det(S_h(k)) \tag{24}$$

By using (21), (22) and (24), it is easy to show that the product of two Gaussian functions in (19) is equal to

$$N(r_k - \mathbf{h_e}(k)^T \mathbf{x_i}, \sigma_i^2) N(\mathbf{h} - \mathbf{h_{e,i}}(k), S_{h,i}(k)) \tag{25}$$

and, finally

$$f_h(\mathbf{h}|r_k) = \sum_{i=1}^{N} \frac{p_i(k) N(r_k - \mathbf{h_e}(k)^T \mathbf{x_i}, \sigma_i^2)}{f_r(r_k)} N(\mathbf{h} - \mathbf{h_{e,i}}(k), S_{h,i}(k)) \tag{26}$$

The division in (26) is exactly the value of $p_i(k+1)$ computed by the RRBF network and, therefore, (8) holds.

REFERENCES

[1] S. Chen, G. J. Gibson, C.F.N. Cowan, "Adaptive Equalization of Finite Non-linear Channels Using Multilayer Perceptrons", Signal Processing, vol. 20, no. 2, pp. 107-119; 1990.

[2] G. J. Gibson, S. Siu, C.F.N. Cowan, "The Application of Nonlinear Structures to the Reconstruction of Binary Signals", IEEE Trans. Signal Processing, vol. 39, no. 8, pp. 1887-1884; 1991.

[3] S. Arcens, J. Cid-Sueiro, A. R. Figueiras-Vidal, "Pao Networks for Data Transmission Equalization"; in Proc. of the International Joint Conference on Neural Networks, vol. 2, pp. 963-967; Baltimore, MA, Jun. 1992.

[4] T. Kohonen et al, "Combining Linear Equalization and Self-Organizing Adaptation in Dinamic Discrete-Signal Detection", in Proc. of the Int. Joint Conf. on Neural Networks, vol. 1, pp. 223-228; San Diego, CA, Jun 1990.

[5] S.Haykin: Adaptive Filter Theory (2nd ed.). Englewood Cliffs, NJ: Prentice-Hall; 1991.

[6] L. Weruaga-Prieto, J. Cid-Sueiro, A. R. Figueiras-Vidal, "Optimal Variable-Step LMS Look-Up-Table Plus Transversal Filter Nonlinear Echo Cancellers"; in Proc. of the IEEE ICASSPP'92; vol. 4, pp.229-232; San Francisco (CA), March 1992.

[7] J. Cid-Sueiro, A. R. Figueiras-Vidal, "Igualación no Lineal Optima para Comunicaciones Digitales por Satélite", in Actas del II Congreso INTA, pp. 485-490; Madrid (Spain), Oct. 1992.

[8] S. Chen, B. Mulgrew, S. Mc Laughlin, P.M. Grant, "Adaptive Bayesian Equaliser with Feedback for Mobile Radio Channels"; presented at 2nd Cost #229 WG. 4 Workshop on Adaptive Algorithms in Communications; Bordeaux (France), Oct. 1992.

[9] J. Cid-Sueiro, L. Weruaga-Prieto, A.R. Figueiras-Vidal, "Optimal Blind Equalization of Gaussian Channels"; accepted for presentation at Int. Workshop on Artificial Neural Networks, Sitges (Spain), Jun. 1993.

[10] J. F. Hayes, T.M. Cover, J.B. Riera, "Optimal Sequence Detection and Optimal Symbol-by Symbol Detection: Similar Algorithms", IEEE Trans. on Communications, vol. COM-30, pp. 152-157, Jan. 1982.

[11] J. Cid-Sueiro, L. Weruaga-Prieto, A.R. Figueiras-Vidal, "Recurrent Radial Basis Function Networks for Optimal Symbol-by-Symbol Equalization"; accepted for presentation at Cost #229 WG. 1+2 2nd Vigo Workshop on Adaptive Methods and Emergent Techniques for Signal Processing and Communications; Vigo (Spain), Jun. 1993.

Neural Network Techniques for Multi-user Demodulation*

U. Mitra and H.V. Poor

Dept. of Electrical Engineering
Princeton University
Princeton, New Jersey, USA 08544

Abstract—

Adaptive methods for demodulating multi-user communication in a Direct-Sequence Spread-Spectrum Multiple-Access (DS/SSMA) environment are investigated. In this setting the noise is characterized as being the sum of the interfering users' signals and additive Gaussian noise. The optimal receiver for DS/SSMA systems has a complexity that is exponential in the number of users.

Adaptive Radial Basis Function (RBF) networks that operate with knowledge of only a subset of the system parameters are studied. This approach is further bolstered by the fact that the optimal detector in the synchronous case can be implemented by a RBF network when all of the system parameters are known.

The RBF network's performance is compared with other multi-user detectors. The centers of the RBF neurons, when the system parameters are not fully known, are determined using clustering techniques. This work shows that the adaptive RBF network obtains near optimal performance and is robust in realistic communication environments.

I. INTRODUCTION

There is a need for multi-user communication for computer networks, radio transmission, telephony, and satellite broadcast channels. In this work, we propose a Radial Basis Function (RBF) neural network as an alternative to the optimal multi-user detector. In Code Division Multiple-Access (CDMA) communication, each user is distinguished by a unique code (called a *spreading code*) which is used to modulate their binary antipodal data. The signal sent over the shared channel is the sum of the individual users' signals. Ambient channel noise is characterized as an additive, white Gaussian process.

CDMA communication, which is a form of spread spectrum communication, allows simultaneous and asynchronous communication; thus many more subscribers can

*This research was supported by the National Science Foundation under Grant NCR 90-02767.

share a frequency band which leads to more efficient use of that band. In other channel division modes, resources are commonly left unused.

II. PREVIOUS MULTI-USER RECEIVERS

In order to grasp the need for simple, robust and adaptive multi-user receivers, a review of the previously used multi-user receivers is presented. The conventional single user receiver is a filter matched to the code of the user. It is optimal, with respect to the probability of detection error, in the presence of additive Gaussian noise only. The matched filter suffers from the *near-far problem*, *i.e.* performance is severely degraded by the effects of a large received power for the interferers with respect to the desired user. The optimal receiver for multi-user detection uses maximum likelihood sequence detection [11] which is implemented by a dynamic programming algorithm. Such a detection scheme has a complexity that is exponential in the number of users. Due to this complexity, much attention is being devoted to the development of sub-optimal receivers with more moderate complexity. The *decorrelating detector* achieves near-optimum performance when the users' spreading codes form a linearly independent set and retains the near-far resistance of the optimal detector [5]. In the noiseless case, the decorrelating detector achieves perfect demodulation.

Whereas the optimal detector requires knowledge of the distinguishing codes of each of the users as well as their received power, the decorrelating detector needs only the codes. Neither of these receivers is adaptive and performance is diminished if a subset of the users is not communicating. There are several factors that motivate us to investigate the use of neural networks as multi-user receivers. First, in addition to computational efficiency, near-far resistance and near-optimal performance, we seek adaptivity. Secondly, the decision boundaries formed by the optimal receiver are non-linear in nature. And finally, the highly structured nature of multiple-access interference (it is cyclo-stationary and the users' spreading codes remain static during transmission) suggests that a neural network should be able to learn how to combat the multiple-access interference (MAI) with great facility. Aazhang, Paris, and Orsak [1] showed empirically that multi-layered perceptrons can perform as multi-user receivers. The authors have supplied further, theoretical evidence of the merit of these neural network receivers [7]. Here, we investigate an alternative neural network structure, the Radial Basis Function network, as a potential multi-user receiver.

III. RADIAL BASIS FUNCTIONS

Whereas a single layer perceptron network performs a non-linear operation on a linear combination of the components of the vector input data, Radial Basis Function (RBF) networks output a linear combination of non-linear functions, each of which is applied to the vector input data. Originally RBFs were used in the multi-dimensional data fitting arena where each data pair $(\underline{x}_{input}, y_{output})$ had a corresponding RBF neuron associated with it and the output weights were found by solving for the optimal weights to minimize an error criterion. Researchers noted that this interpolation activity was akin to the process of finding a function to meet pre-defined input and output associations which were described in the form of the data pairs previously mentioned.

The RBF network structure is defined by the equations given below:
$$y = \sum_{i=1}^{N} W_i \Phi_i(\underline{x} - \underline{c_i})/\sigma_i{}^2. \qquad (1)$$
$\Phi_i(\cdot)$ is a continuous, non-linear function from $R^+ \rightarrow R$. Other conditions which stem from regularization and approximation theory can be found in [8]. $\underline{x}$ is the input data vector, $\underline{c_i}$ is called the *center* of the RBF neuron, σ_i is the *spread* of the neuron and the W_i are the weights which optimize some error criterion. The methods by which the $\Phi_i(\cdot), c_i, \sigma_i$, and W_i are selected, constitute much of the current research on RBF networks. Traditionally, the centers were randomly chosen from the given data set, the spreads were then calculated by determining the minimum distance between centers using the appropriate distance metric and the weights could be solved for given a simple error criterion (e.g. minimum mean squared error) [4]. Particular applications of the RBF network can effectively circumscribe the gamut of practical methods used to find these network parameters.

Our investigation of RBF networks as multi-user receivers is inspired by the work of Chen, Mulgrew and McLaughlin [2] who used these networks and modifications thereof to perform equalization. Before we consider the RBF network as a multi-user receiver, we describe the communication model and discuss maximum likelihood detection for synchronous communication.

IV. COMMUNICATION MODEL

This paper addresses the analysis of an adaptive multi-user receiver for single user demodulation with moder-ate complexity. We consider this problem in the context of coherent, synchronous Direct-Sequence Spread-Spectrum Multiple-Access (DS/SSMA) signaling. After chip matched-filtering and chip-rate sampling, such a signal can be modeled in discrete time as,

$$\underline{r}_i = \sum_{j=1}^{K} \underline{s}_j^i + \underline{n}_i \qquad where \; \underline{s}_j^i = A_j b_j^i \underline{m}_j, \qquad (2)$$

and $\underline{r}_i$ is the received signal at time i, K is the number of active users, $\underline{s}_j^i$ is j'th user's signal at time i, $\underline{m}_j$ is the j'th user's spreading code, A_j the amplitude and b_j^i the bit value of the j'th user at time i. Note that the time index i is with respect to the symbols and not the chips. The additive Gaussian noise process is $\underline{n}_i$. It is assumed that all relevant timing and phase information is available. In addition, the receiver is assumed to have access to the desired user's spreading code, but not those of the interfering users.

V. HYPOTHESIS TESTING AND MAXIMUM LIKELIHOOD DETECTION

Our detection problem can easily be cast into one of *hypothesis testing* [9]. Effectively there exist two possibilities of interest: our desired user transmits a +1 or a −1. This desired bit is embedded in noise which consists of additive Gaussian noise and the MAI. When all of the system parameters are known (the number of users, all users' spreading codes, delays, transmitting powers), we can characterize the statistics of this noise. We shall be considering Bayesian hypothesis testing, which minimizes the average cost incurred by the decision rule. Let $\underline{r}$ be the observation of the desired signal in noise, $\underline{r} = \Theta + \underline{n}$, where Θ is the desired signal vector, i.e. $\Theta = A_1\underline{m_1}$ or $\Theta = -A_1\underline{m_1}$; n is the noise component. We denote the probability density of the observation r under the null hypothesis (H_0) by p_0, and similarly p_1 is the density under the alternative hypothesis, H_1. The likelihood ratio is then $L(\underline{r}) = \frac{p_1(\underline{r})}{p_0(\underline{r})}$. The Bayesian decision rule (δ_b) compares the likelihood ratio to a threshold, τ, which is determined by the cost function and the prior probabilities of Θ. For zero cost for a correct decision and a unit cost for an incorrect decision, and equal priors, $\tau = 1$. We assume that each user's data bit is independent of the other users' bits and each data bit is equally likely to be +1 or −1. This leads to the following distributions for our scenario,

$$p_l(\underline{r}) = \frac{1}{2^{K-1}} \sum_{i=1}^{2^{K-1}} \frac{1}{(2\pi)^{2^{K-2}}|\sigma^2 I|^2}$$
$$\exp \; -\{\frac{1}{2\sigma^2}\|\underline{r} - \Theta_l - \underline{\mu_i}\|^2\}, \qquad (3)$$

where K is the number of users, σ is the Gaussian noise variance, Θ_l is the desired signal vector given H_j and $\underline{\mu_i}$ is the i'th permutation of the sum of the interferer's signals. This results in the likelihood ratio,

$$L(\underline{r}) = \frac{\sum_{i=1}^{2^{K-1}} \exp -\{\frac{1}{2\sigma^2}\|\underline{r} - \underline{\Theta}_1 - \underline{\mu}_i\|^2\}}{\sum_{i=1}^{2^{K-1}} \exp -\{\frac{1}{2\sigma^2}\|\underline{r} - \underline{\Theta}_0 - \underline{\mu}_i\|^2\}}. \quad (4)$$

The resulting decision rule is,

$$
\begin{aligned}
\delta_b(\underline{r}) = \ & sgn(\sum_{i=1}^{2^{K-1}} \exp -\{\frac{1}{2\sigma^2}\|\underline{r} - \underline{\Theta}_1 - \underline{\mu}_i\|^2\} \\
& - \sum_{i=1}^{2^{K-1}} \exp -\{\frac{1}{2\sigma^2}\|\underline{r} - \underline{\Theta}_0 - \underline{\mu}_i\|^2\}), \quad (5)
\end{aligned}
$$

where the *sgn* function returns the sign of its operand.

Recalling (1), it is clear that the Bayesian decision rule can be implemented with a RBF network under the following conditions:

$$\Phi(\underline{x}) = \exp -\{\frac{1}{2}\|\underline{x} - \underline{c_i}\|^2\} \quad (6)$$

$$W_i = \begin{cases} 1 & \text{if } i \in I_1 \\ -1 & \text{if } i \in I_0 \end{cases} \quad (7)$$

where σ_i is the Gaussian noise variance, σ^2, $\underline{c_i}$ is equal to $\underline{\mu}_i$ from above, and I_j is the set of indices corresponding to hypothesis H_j.

It has been shown that the above maximum-likelihood detector is in fact the optimal one-shot detector for decentralized detection of a single user in the multi-user communication scenario [10]. So, if all the system parameters are known we can implement the optimum single user detector above. In practical communication systems, all system parameters are not known; in this investigation we focus on communication when only a subset of the parameters are known to the receiver.

VI. DETECTION WITH KNOWN SYSTEM PARAMETERS

Once the exact centers for the RBF neurons are known, one can determine exactly what the weights for the linear combiner should be [8]. In order investigate the dynamics of the system, however; we chose to use Least Mean Squares (LMS) adaptation techniques to see whether the optimal weights for the network could be learned given that the centers were known.

The LMS update equation for the weights is:

$$\underline{W}_{k+1} = \underline{W}_k + \eta(y_k - d_k)\underline{\Phi}(\underline{r_k}), \quad (8)$$

where η is the adaptation gain which controls the rate of change, $y_k (= W_k^T \underline{\Phi}(\underline{r_k}))$ is the output of the RBF network at time k, $\underline{\Phi}(\cdot)$ is the vector RBF non-linear functions applied to the input, d_k is the desired user's bit value at time k and $\underline{r}_k$ is the received multi-user signal. The LMS adaptive algorithm converges in the mean to the set of weights that minimize the mean squared error between the desired signal and the algorithm output. It can be shown that the mean weight values are numerically indistinguishable from those required for the optimal synchronous detector, i.e.

the two optimality criteria (minimum mean squared error and minimum probability of error) result in the same set of weights. This implies that even in the presence of additive Gaussian noise, our RBF network will yield the minimum probability of error demodulator in the mean.

Adaptation with the additive noise present still yields close to optimal performance (with nearly optimal weights) as is shown in Figs. 1 and 2 where the probability of error with respect to changing SNR (with respect to the desired user) or Near Far Ratio (NFR = E_2/E_1, where E_i is the received power of user i) is plotted. N is the length of the spreading codes used. The performance of the RBF network is compared to several other known detectors: the optimal detector described in (6) - (7), the decorrelating detector, the conventional matched filter, a linear filter that minimizes the mean squared error, and the single layer perceptron network studied in [7]. Convergence of the RBF network was effectively attained within 20 to 50 bit intervals when the weights were initialized with small random values.

Practically, one does not always have access to the exact centers for this network. We next investigate methods for determining the centers given a subset of parameter information.

VII. CLUSTERING TECHNIQUES FOR CENTER ESTIMATION

As was seen in Section V, the distribution of our observations, $\underline{r}$, is a Gaussian mixture. The goal of any clustering

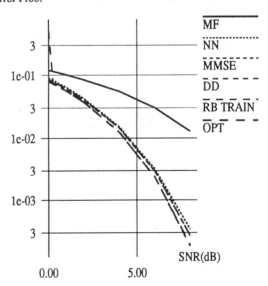

Figure 1: Probability of Error as a function of SNR1 for several detectors in a 2-user synchronous Gaussian channel (N=31) with NFR = 4.0.

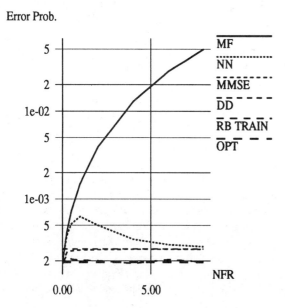

Error Prob.

MF
NN
MMSE
DD
RB TRAIN
OPT

NFR

Figure 2: Probability of Error as a function of NFR for several detectors in a 2-user synchronous Gaussian channel (N=31) with SNR1 = 8.0dB.

technique we use is to determine the modes of the distribution; these are the desired centers of the RBF network. Traditional clustering techniques are computationally intensive [3]. Most techniques operate on a *proximity map* which describes the distances between all the points in a data set, given an appropriate distance metric. Clustering involves iterating an algorithm over the map until the final set of clusters is achieved. Rather than using traditional clustering techniques which make no assumptions about the data to be clustered, we will exploit our knowledge of the system parameters and modify conventional methods.

A. Supervised Clustering

In the RBF network application to equalization [2], the authors suggest, among other techniques, supervised clustering for finding the centers. Supervised clustering for our application requires the knowledge of all of the users' bits. Note that the number of centers is exponential in the number of users. All the observations that stem from a particular combination of the K users' bits are averaged to yield the desired center. The distribution of the observation conditioned on a particular combination of the bits is simply a Gaussian distribution with the variance of the noise and a mean which is the sum of each of the user's signals given that bit combination. The Law of Large Numbers guarantees that averaging in this manner will yield the mean of the distribution, which is our desired center.

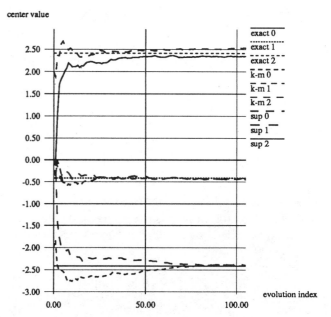

center value

exact 0
exact 1
exact 2
k-m 0
k-m 1
k-m 2
sup 0
sup 1
sup 2

evolution index

Figure 3: Comparison of the Supervised and K-Means Clustering Algorithms. The evolution of the three components of the first center is shown (N=3).

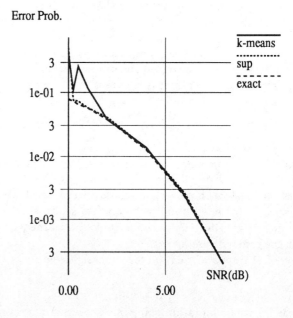

Error Prob.

k-means
sup
exact

SNR(dB)

Figure 4: Probability of Error as a function of SNR1 for the RBF network with the centers known exactly, and estimated by the Supervised and by the K-Means Clustering algorithms in a 2-user synchronous Gaussian channel (N=31) with NFR = 4.0.

B. Derivative of K-Means Clustering

In the previous clustering example, we assumed knowledge of each users' bit sequence only. In a communications system, this is an unlikely scenario. It is more conventional that we have access to the spreading codes, but not the bit sequence. We use the k-means clustering algorithm [6] which is initialized with centers which correspond to all possible bit combinations, but we assume that each user is transmitting with unit received power. The distance metric used was Euclidean. The convergence of this algorithm to the modes of the Gaussian mixture from which the observations are derived can be found in [6]. Each center has as many components as the length of the spreading code. The evolution of the first center is shown in Fig. 3. Notice that both clustering methods have similar convergence rates, though the rates may not be practical.

We next examine how well the RBF network performs with these centers estimated by the two different clustering methods. In moderate NFR (NFR=4.0), the clustering algorithms work adequately when the SNR1 is varied. This is shown in Fig. 4. We expect that the supervised method will better estimate the centers than the k-means method when the NFR is large or very small (i.e. less than unity). This is somewhat borne out by the performance simulations. When the NFR is extremely large, the k-means algorithm is initialized with values that are far away from the desired values. The supervised algorithm makes no assumptions about the initial values. Fig. 4 shows the performance of the two clustering methods' RBF networks. However, by increasing the amount of

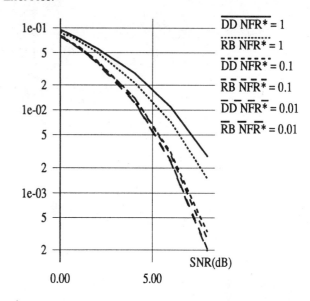

Figure 6: Probability of Error as a function of SNR1 for the decorrelating detector and the RBF network in a 3-user synchronous Gaussian channel (N=31) with NFR = 4.0, where the third user is spurious.

training time for the centers, we can improve the performance of the k-means algorithm, this is reflected in the plots in Fig. 4.

The two clustering techniques employed require knowledge of the number of users in the system. Since all users are transmitting with differing amounts of received power, it is the strong interferers that pose the largest problem to our detection system. Focusing only on mitigating the effects of the powerful interferers, would reduce the size of our RBF network. We next consider the robustness of the RBF network when we consider a subset of the interferers which are relatively more powerful than the rest of the interferers.

VIII. SMALL SPURIOUS USER IN KNOWN SYSTEM

A robust multi-user demodulator will be able to withstand the presence of small, unknown users. Generally in a multi-user environment, the MAI due to powerful users presents the most degrading noise factor. The next set of experiments determines how robust the RBF network is to the insertion of a relatively small, but unknown third user into a two user system. The RBF neuron centers are those for the two user system with total parameter knowledge and the linear weights are trained in the presence of the third user as well as the existing MAI and ambient channel noise. The performance of the RBF network was

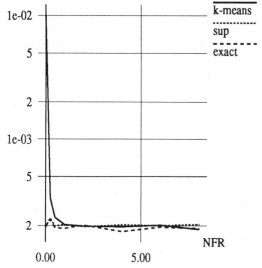

Figure 5: Probability of Error as a function of NFR for the RBF network with the centers known exactly, and estimated by the Supervised and by the K-Means Clustering algorithms in a 2-user synchronous Gaussian channel (N=31) with SNR1 = 8.0dB.

Error Prob.

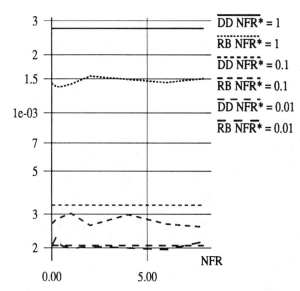

Figure 7: Probability of Error as a function of NFR for the decorrelating detector and the RBF network in a 3-user synchronous Gaussian channel (N=31) with SNR1 = 8.0dB, where the third user is spurious.

compared to the decorrelating detector for the two user system.

Figures 6 and 7 show the results of these simulations. Once again the RBF network outperforms the decorrelating detector. NFR* is the near far ratio between the spurious third user's received power and that of the desired user's. These findings imply that even in situations where we may know all of the system parameters, we can choose to ignore the smaller users and thus reduce the complexity of the RBF network detector. The knowledge of the number of strong interferers would allow us to also reduce the complexity of the clustering algorithms used to determine the centers of the RBF neurons.

IX. CONCLUSIONS

In this paper we have shown that the optimal multi-user receiver for synchronous detection of DS/SSMA signals can be implemented with a Radial Basis Function network. We have investigated several aspects of making this network adaptive: how to find the optimal weights, and the use of clustering methods to determine the centers of the RBF neurons. Simulations were performed to compare the performance of the RBF network and several previously derived multi-user receivers. These simulations show that the RBF network has the desirable properties of fast convergence and near-optimal performance in realistic communication environments.

Further areas of study will concentrate on faster methods for clustering the data and better exploitation of the known system parameters. In addition, the issue of RBF network size must be addressed. The current implementation has 2^K neurons when there are K users. A realistic communication system should be able to handle a few hundred users.

REFERENCES

[1] B. Aazhang, B.-P. Paris, and G. Orsak, "Neural networks for multi-user detection in CDMA communication," *IEEE Trans. on Comm.*, August 1991.

[2] S. Chen, B. Mulgrew, and S. McLaughlin, "Adaptive bayesian equaliser with decision feedback," to appear in *IEEE Signal Processing Magazine*, August 1991.

[3] A. K. Jain and R. C. Dubes, *Algorithms for Clustering Data.* Advanced Reference Series, New Jersey: Prentice Hall, 1988.

[4] D. Lowe, "Adaptive radial basis function nonlinearities, and the problem of generalisation," in *Proceedings of the 1st IEE International Conference on Artificial Neural Networks*, pp. 171 – 175, IEE, October 1989.

[5] R. Lupas and S. Verdu, "Linear multiuser detectors for synchronous code-division multiple-access channels," *IEEE Trans. on Info. Theory*, vol. 35, no. 1, pp. 123–136, January 1989.

[6] J. B. MacQueen, "Some methods of classification and analysis of multivariate observations," in *Proceedings of the Fifth Berkeley Symposium on Mathematical Statistics and Probability*, pp. 281–297, 1967.

[7] U. Mitra and H. V. Poor, "Adaptive receiver algorithms for near-far resistant CDMA," in *Proceedings of the 3rd Symposium on Personal, Indoor and Mobile Radio Communications*, IEEE, October 1992.

[8] T. Poggio and F. Girosi, "Networks for approximation and learning," *Proceedings of the IEEE*, vol. 78, no. 9, pp. 1481 –1497, 1990.

[9] H. V. Poor, *An Introduction to Signal Detection and Estimation.* New York: Springer-Verlag, 1988.

[10] H. V. Poor and S. Verdu, "Single-user detectors for multi-user channels," *IEEE Trans. on Comm.*, vol. 36, no. 1, pp. 50–60, January 1988.

[11] S. Verdu, "Minimum probability of error for asynchronous gaussian multiple-access channels," *IEEE Trans. on Info. Theory*, vol. 32, no. 1, pp. 85–96, January 1986.

A HYBRID NEURAL-FUZZY APPROACH
TO VHF FREQUENCY MANAGEMENT

Nancy H. Millström, Allen R. Bonde, Jr., and Michael J. Grimaldi
GTE Government Systems Corporation
Needham Heights, MA 02194
e-mail: nancy@rocky.ndhm.gtegsc.com

Abstract. A unique hybrid architecture for real-time monitoring and analysis of the VHF band is proposed. The design employs digital signal processing and neural network techniques for detection and classification, along with novel fuzzy logic enhancements and decision-making. The resulting hybrid solution is shown to provide significant performance improvements as compared to a binary logic-based system, and simplifies design and coding requirements.

INTRODUCTION

Of particular importance to the Army is the frequency management of the VHF band (30 - 88 MHz). On the battlefield, this band has a high ratio of users (emitters) to available frequencies (channels). As a result, extensive frequency reuse is required (see figure 1). Furthermore, interference, both friendly and non-friendly, poses a frustrating situation for users, especially at the battlefront where interference is greatest.

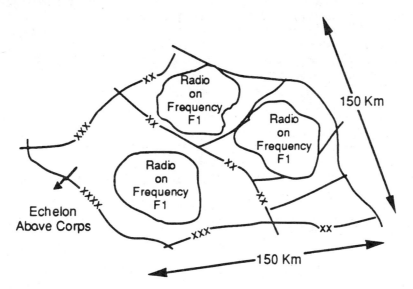

Figure 1: Frequency reuse on a corps-level deployment.

Prior to deployment, frequency plans for the MSE mobile subscribers and Combat Network Radios (CNRs) are generated by network planners. This is a time-consuming process not well suited to the dynamics of modern battlefield situations. Hence, there is a need for coupling real-time frequency management to the (re)planning process.

An experimental solution to the VHF frequency management problem has been developed at GTE. The solution involves real-time monitoring of the VHF band for interference and unauthorized usage. The work to date employs a combination of digital signal processing and neural networks for detection and classification followed by decision logic. The output of the decision logic is sent to remote planning sites, in the form of electronic reports, to aid the planners in adapting to critical situations.

The decision logic was first implemented using a set of rules based on hard thresholds. Later, fuzzy logic was investigated as an enhancement to the decision-making process.

Fuzzy Logic

Fuzzy logic is a departure from classical two-valued sets and logic, that uses "soft" linguistic (e.g. large, hot, tall) system variables and a continuous range of truth values in the interval $\{0, 1\}$. Fuzzy logic is based on Zadeh's fuzzy set theory [1], which provides a robust mathematical framework for dealing with "real-world" imprecision and non-statistical uncertainty. An excellent introduction to fuzzy systems is found in [2].

Fuzzy rule-based systems have proven effective in a number of application areas such as intelligent control [3], especially where a system is difficult to model and has strict implementation constraints. However, its true potential may lie in the integration of fuzzy logic with other machine intelligence methods such as artificial neural networks. For example, the emerging synthesis of fuzzy and neural algorithms offers powerful solutions to real-time system diagnosis [4], pattern recognition [5], and decision and control [6] problems.

A Hybrid Neural -Fuzzy Approach

The intent of this paper is to examine the actual decision-making components of GTE's VHF frequency management solution, and show how fuzzy logic is an integral addition to the process. The resulting hybrid solution incorporates a three-layer neural network, a frequency shift keying (FSK) detector, and now, fuzzy logic, as shown in figure 2.

The design and development of each of these components is described in the next three sections.

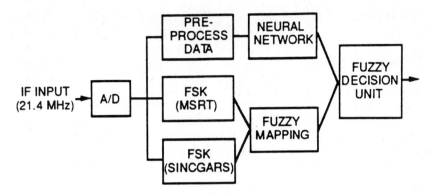

Figure 2: Block diagram of the Neural-Fuzzy approach.

FSK DETECTOR

A noncoherent detection of binary FSK was implemented using a pair of matched filters and envelope detectors [7, 8]. Because we have knowledge *a priori* of the specific bit rates for the known emitters, the demodulated signal can be compared to each rate and then a match/no-match can be determined (see figure 3). In this application two emitters were detected: MSRT (Mobile Subscriber Radio Transmitter) and SINCGARS (Single Channel Ground to Air Radio System).

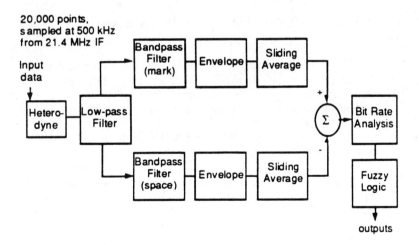

Figure 3: Block diagram for the FSK detector.

The bit rate analysis produces an estimate of the mean and an estimate of the standard deviation of the mean. If this estimate +/- the standard deviation falls within the range {+1, -1}, a match is detected. This strict threshold worked well for high signal-to-noise ratio cases. However, some noisier emitter cases failed to meet these requirements by just a fraction. The need for a soft and more gradual transition between "within" and "not within" range prompted a fuzzy logic approach.

Soft Thresholds

The fuzzy FSK membership function, shown in figure 4, describes the *degree* to which the output is considered "within". This truth value, μ, ranges in value from 0 to 1, depending on where the mean +/- the standard deviation of the estimate of the mean fall. In this way, an FSK value that lies within the range (+1,-1) is handled as before; however, a marginal case (e.g. 1.2) which was previously discarded, is now considered to be "mostly" (e.g. 0.8) within.

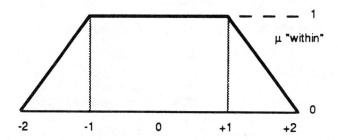

Figure 4: Membership function for the FSK detector.

Fuzzy Mapping

The fuzzy values from each FSK are combined using the following rules, where not within = 1 - within:

    1. if Sincgars is *not within* AND Msrt is *not within* then no-decision
    2. if Sincgars is *not within* AND Msrt is *within*   then msrt
    3. if Sincgars is *within*   AND Msrt is *not within* then sinc
    4. if Sincgars is *within*   AND Msrt is *within*   then both

In all of the fuzzy decision rules, AND and OR are implemented by taking the minimum and maximum, respectively, of the two truth values.

Each decision (msrt, sinc, etc.) has an associated truth value or "activation" for every pass of the system. This activation is carried forward and later combined with the neural network decision.

NEURAL NETWORK CLASSIFIER

Much of the artificial neural network (ANN) design effort and the success of the solution depended on developing effective and efficient preprocessing. For this application, all prototype designs were built and tested on a SUN 4 using the GTE-developed LAWS (LARS™ Automated Work Station) graphical development environment.

LAWS Development Environment

This icon-based environment includes math and signal processing libraries, vector processing, various neural network algorithms for training and testing, and digital filter [9, 10, 11] design. By using LAWS, the signal processing functions depicted in Figure 5 required parameter selection and testing by the engineer, but no formal programming.

In LAWS, the neural network was trained using the back propagation learning algorithm. The six network outputs were mapped between 0 and 1 in order to facilitate their integration with the FSK detector. A seventh output was added to indicate a "no decision" from the neural network.

ANN Outputs:
1. msrt - Mobile Subscriber Radio Transmitter
2. sincgars - Single Channel Ground to Air Radio System
3. sincgars synchronization - a beacon signal to establish a call
4. left - a signal with energy concentrated in left side of the band
5. right - a signal with energy concentrated in right side of band
6. other - an unknown signal that is not noise
7. no decision - a detection was not possible, where

$$\mu_{no\ decision} = 1 - MAXIMUM\ (\ of\ all\ six\ outputs)$$

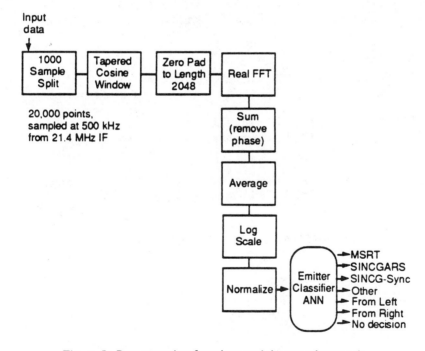

Figure 5: Preprocessing functions and the neural network.

FUZZY DECISION UNIT

The outputs of the mapped FSK detector and the neural network (representing fuzzy truth values) were integrated using a fuzzy decision unit. This type of "back-end" decision-making, and the interpretation of neural network outputs, is a natural role for fuzzy logic, and has been used in other neural-fuzzy applications, e.g. [4].

The actual fuzzy rules fell out of the design specifications, and naturally represent the decision-making process. Implementation simply required the computation of minimums and maximums to arrive at the final fuzzy output of the system. This application required only a few iterations before the final set of fuzzy rules were established.

Fuzzy Decision Rules:

<u>key to abbreviations</u>

ann	= artificial neural network		none	= no decision
left	= signal from left		othr	= any other type of emitter
both	= msrt and sincgars		rght	= signal from right
msrt	= msrt		sinc	= sincgars
mult	= multiple emitters		synch	= sincgars synchronization

<u>rules</u>

1. if ((FSK = sinc, OR msrt OR none) AND (ANN = synch))
$$\text{then decision = synch}$$

2. if ((FSK = sinc) AND (ANN = sinc OR othr OR left OR rght OR none))
   OR if ((FSK = none) AND (ANN = sinc))
$$\text{then decision = sinc}$$

3. if ((FSK = msrt) AND (ANN = msrt OR othr OR left OR rght OR none))
   OR if ((FSK = none) AND (ANN = msrt))
$$\text{then decision = msrt}$$

4. if ((FSK = none) AND (ANN = othr OR left OR rght))
$$\text{then decision = othr}$$

5. if (((FSK = sinc) AND (ANN = msrt)) OR
   if ((FSK = msrt) AND (ANN = sinc)) OR
   if ((FSK = none) AND (ANN = msrt AND sinc)) OR
   if (FSK = both))
$$\text{then decision = mult}$$

RESULTS AND CONCLUSIONS

Current results, although preliminary, have shown that the new hybrid solution has an advantage over previous methods in robustness, design time, coding tasks, and performance. Figure 6 compares classification results for the original binary logic- and new fuzzy logic-based decisions. For these experiments, "defuzzification" of the outputs was determined by simply taking the highest output (activation) as the final decision.

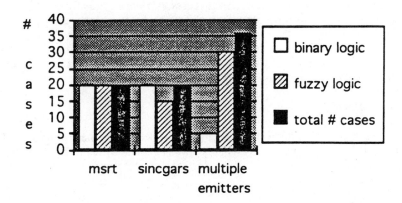

Figure 6: Number of correct classifications for binary vs. fuzzy decision logic.

As these results illustrate, the fuzzy approach does very well on the multiple emitter cases, and correctly recognizes 83 percent of the test cases vs. only 14 percent for the binary logic. Since one of the original goals for the fuzzy approach was to capture more multiple emitter cases (an inherently difficult problem due to a wide variance in relative signal levels), this is considered as an important and successful result. This improved performance did come at a small cost, namely a decrease from 100 percent to 75 percent in the number of sincgars cases correctly classified (current modifications address this sensitivity).

Discussion

There are several advantages to the fuzzy-neural hybrid approach presented in this paper. The neural network classifier provides a model-free approach that easily handles a wide spectrum of the data. The ANN is able to interpret 20,000 samples per data example in an efficient manner. Using the LAWS environment for neural network and preprocessing development provided us with rapid design and retraining capabilities.

The fuzzy logic enhancements allow significant gains over the original binary logic-based processing--with little extra effort or cost. The process of defining rules and membership mappings during the design stage aided in the actual coding effort. The number of lines of code required to adapt the previous ("classical" logic) software to the fuzzy solution was minimal. In fact, dealing with linguistic variables allows almost direct translation into C code, and required fewer rules than the original binary rule base. Furthermore, because fuzzy rules are naturally descriptive, translation of knowledge to code is almost direct, removing the margin for coding error. Any changes that were required were easily modified or inserted because the code exemplifies the design specifications.

The fuzzy decision-making techniques described in this paper provide continuous mapping of information and soft, gradual thresholds. These features allow the enhanced system to acquire many cases that were originally discarded by the classical design. In other words, in effect the fuzzy system allows one to "pipeline" decisions and their associated truth values until later in the process, when a well-informed or more complete decision can be made. Information is not lost during interim steps due to hard thresholds. The successful acquisition of most of the multiple emitter cases appears to confirm these benefits.

Acknowledgments

The authors gratefully acknowledge the following people for their work at GTE Government Systems on the VHF Frequency Management System: Burke Buntz, David Freeman, Tad Hofmeister, Rob Martin, Kari McHugh, Joe Musmanno, Robin Pappas.

REFERENCES

[1] L.A. Zadeh, "Fuzzy Sets," Information and Control, Vol. 8, pp. 338-353, 1965.

[2] B. Kosko, Neural Networks and Fuzzy Systems: A Dynamical Systems Approach to Machine Intelligence, Englewood Cliffs, NJ: Prentice-Hall, 1992.

[3] A. Bonde, Jr., "A Prototype Fuzzy Line-of-Sight Antenna Controller," presented at the First International Conference on Fuzzy Theory and Technology, Durham, N.C., Oct. 14-18, 1992.

[4] J.J. Choi, K.H. O'Keefe, and P.K. Baruah, "Non-linear Systems Diagnosis Using Neural Networks and Fuzzy Logic," in Proceedings of the IEEE International Conference on Fuzzy Systems, 1992, pp. 813-820.

[5] J.C. Bezdek, "Computing with Uncertainty," IEEE Communications Magazine, Vol. 30, No. 9, pp. 24-36, September 1992.

[6] C.T. Lin and C.S. Lee, "Neural-Network-based Fuzzy Control and Decision System," IEEE Transactions on Computers, Vol. 40, No. 12, pp. 1320-1336, December 1991.

[7] B. Sklar, Digital Communications Fundamentals and Applications, Englewood Cliffs, NJ: Prentice-Hall, 1988.

[8] A. B. Carlson, Communication Systems: An Introduction to Signals and Noise in Electrical Communication, New York: McGraw Hill, 1975.

[9] A.V. Oppenheim and R.W. Schafer, Discrete-Time Signal Processing, Englewood Cliffs, NJ: Prentice-Hall, 1989.

[10] L. S. Marple, Digital Spectral Analysis, Englewood Cliffs, NJ: Prentice-Hall, 1987.

[11] A.V. Oppenheim and R.W. Schafer, Digital Signal Processing, Englewood Cliffs, NJ: Prentice-Hall, 1975.

Neural Network Controller for Rearrangeable Switching Networks

Young-Keun Park* and Vladimir Cherkassky**
Department of Electrical Engineering,
University of Minnesota, Minneapolis, MN 55455
*email : park@ee.umn.edu, **email : cherkass@ee.umn.edu

Abstract—The rapid evolution in the field of communication networks requires high speed switching technologies. This involves a high degree of parallelism in switching control and routing performed at the hardware level. In this paper a neural network approach to controlling a three stage Clos network in real time is proposed. This controller provides optimal routing of communication traffic requests on a call-by-call basis by rearranging existing connections with a minimum length of rearrangement sequence so that a new blocked call request can be accommodated. The proposed neural network controller uses Paull's rearrangement algorithm, along with the special (least used) switch selection rule in order to minimize the length of rearrangement sequences. The functional behavior of our model is verified by simulations and it is shown that the convergence time required for finding an optimal solution is constant regardless of the switching network size. The performance is evaluated for random traffic with various traffic loads. Simulation results show that applying the least used switch selection rule increases the efficiency in switch rearrangements, reduces the network convergence time and also keeps the network from being trapped in local minima. The implementation aspects are also discussed to show the feasibility of the proposed approach.

Index terms — Constrained optimization, neural networks, rearrangeable switching networks.

I. INTRODUCTION : BACKGROUND AND MOTIVATION

Most communication systems contain a switching network as a basic functional unit. The controller for the switching network provides routing of communication traffic. Modern high performance communication channels support a port speed of more than 100 Mbits/sec. Hence, the switching speed must be fast enough in order to handle such a port speed without significant performance degradation. Switching functions of conventional packet switches are typically performed in software running on a general purpose computer. For large switching systems, implementation of routing algorithms on a sequential computer may not be effective since it requires a large amount of computation time. On the other hand, the neural network approach can offer a potential solution for fast switching due to its high degree of parallelism and rapid convergence. Advances in VLSI technology have made it possible to realize the neural networks on a single chip. In the rest of this section, we give a brief background on switching networks.

A connecting network is called a *rearrangeable switching network* if it can realize every connection between inputs and outputs and it can reconfigure existing connections to route a new call. There are two possible modes of operations : *synchronous* or *asynchronous*. In synchronous mode, all multiple input/output request pairs need to be routed simultaneously. On the other hand, in asynchronous mode, given a new call, the existing connection paths are reconfigured asynchronously on a call-by-call basis. For the rest of the paper, we only assume the asynchronous mode of operation. Such networks usually consist of several stages of crossbar switches.

In 1953, Clos[1] introduced three stage switching network(Fig.1). It consists of r input crossbar switches, m intermediate crossbar switches and r output crossbar switches. He showed that the total number of crosspoints required for three stages is minimized to $6N^{3/2} - 3N$, when $n = r = \sqrt{N}$ and $m = n$. A call request may be *blocked* when all available routes are occupied by other existing connections. However, since the switches are rearrangeable, it can perform all possible connections between inputs and outputs by rearranging its existing connections so that a connection path for a new input-output pair can always be established. Such a three stage rearrangeable network is called *nonblocking in the wide sense*.

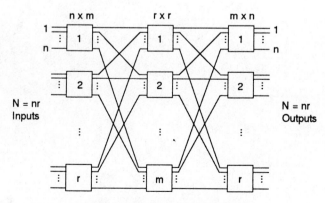

Figure 1. Three Stage Clos Network

Now, the problem is to rearrange the existing connections in order to accommodate the new call request that is blocked and how to achieve it in an optimal fashion, i.e. with the minimum number of rearrangements of existing connections. In the following sections, we give detailed descriptions of known approaches and our approach to rearrangements in Clos networks.

II. CONVENTIONAL AND NEURAL NETWORK APPROACHES TO REARRANGEMENT

A. Rearrangement Algorithm

In 1962, M.C. Paull proposed a rearrangement algorithm for the three stage Clos network[2]. He showed that if $m = n = r$, then at most $n-1$ existing calls need be rearranged in order to unblock a blocked call request. In general, for $m = 2n - j$ ($j = 1..n$), no more than $j-1$ rearrangements are required. Fig.2 illustrates an example of this algorithm. For simplicity, in the rest of the paper we assume $m = n = r = 4$ in our examples. The rows correspond to the input switches (first stage) and the columns correspond to the output switches (third stage). Each entry may contain from zero to m symbols which correspond to the m intermediate switches (second stage). A symbol "A" in entry (i,j) implies that a call originating from input switch i is routed through center switch "A" to output switch j. In Fig.2(a), notice that there are two calls between the input switch 3 and the output switch 2. One is routed through center switch "A", the other is routed through center switch "D". A new call request $(2,2)$ is blocked. The corresponding connection paths of a Clos network are shown in Fig.3.

Since the input/output switches are composed of strictly non-blocking crossbars, we do not distinguish between the n external connections of a particular input/output switch. Since the connections on the input/output switches are uniquely specified by the connections on the intermediate switches, only the connections within the intermediate switches are considered. Call requests are therefore simply denoted as (i,j), where i is the input switch number and j is the output switch number.

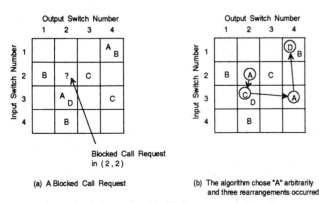

Figure 2. An Example of Paull's Rearrangement Algorithm

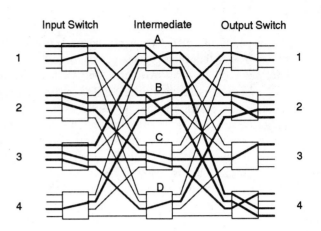

Figure 3. States of the switches

The following constraints must be considered:

1. There can be no more than m symbols in any row or column since the total number of intermediate switches is m.

2. No two symbols in any row (or column) may be the same.

3. Each entry (i,j) may contain up to m symbols depending on the number of calls.

When a call request arrives, determine whether it is *legal* or *illegal*. A call request (i,j) is called *illegal* if there are no available lines at the input switch i or at the output switch j. That is, if there are already m symbols in row i or m symbols in column j, it is not a legal call request. In this case, the call request is not accepted. If it is a legal call request, determine whether it is blocked or not. If there is any symbol Q that does not exist in row i and column j, it is not blocked. Then place a Q in entry (i,j) and no rearrangement is required. If it is blocked, we choose any symbol Q and place a Q in entry (i,j). Then there must be another row i' such that the entry (i',j) contains a Q also. Similarly, there may be another column j' such that the entry (i,j') has a Q. Then replace the Q in such entries with another symbol R. This procedure is successively continued until no two symbols appear in the same row or column. Paull proved that this algorithm could always find an unblocking rearrangement.

B. Conventional Approaches

Most of the conventional control algorithms are sequential and their computation complexities are $O(N\log_2 N)$ [8,9,10]. The processing time for the algorithms must be sufficiently short in order to handle high port speed. The performance of switching networks depends very much on the control overhead. Unfortunately, the conventional approaches are practical only for very small networks because the central control is the bottleneck of this approach. The

591

switching capacity of current conventional packet switches ranges from 1 to 4 thousand packets per second, with average nodal delay of 20 ~ 50 msec[16]. Due to this control overhead, the maximum throughput is less than 50 percent[15]. The network throughput is defined as the ratio of the number of successfully handled requests to the offered load. Much research has been done to improve the network throughput by queueing call requests using input/output buffers (or internal buffers). However such queueing solutions are not cost-effective since they have too much hardware overhead for just 10 percent of throughput improvement.

C. Neural Network Approaches

One way to reduce the control overhead and to improve the throughput is to distribute the control function by using a high degree of parallelism and the hardware level routing control. We can realize this by using neural network approaches due to their analog parallel processing and the fast convergence.

Brown proposed a neural network model for the multistage rearrangeable switches[4]. He applied Paull's algorithm to the rearrangement problem using a time delay trick to produce the desired behavior of rearrangements. He used two different kinds of neurons (primary neurons and memory neurons). The memory neurons have larger time delays than the primary neurons. Each memory neuron is attached to each primary neuron and it is used to distinguish a primary neuron that has been on for a long time from a primary neuron that has recently turned on. This difference helps the rearrangement proceed sequentially without oscillating. However, the total number of neurons used was doubled ($2r^2m$, where r is the number of input/output crossbar switches and m is the number of intermediate crossbar switches) and he didn't provide any empirical performance evaluation results to verify his approach.

Funabiki and Takefuji recently proposed a parallel control algorithm for multistage interconnection networks of a base-2 structure[6]. They described a neural network model with N^2 (i.e. r^2m^2) neurons. They solved small-sized network (32×32) problems by simulations. Their model requires hundreds of iterations to find an optimal solution. They also proposed a parallel control algorithm for three stage Clos networks using r^2m neurons[7]. From their simulation results, it is shown that the network converges within 120 iterations with the average 97 percent of accuracy under medium traffic load conditions. We have implemented their model in software and duplicated their results for medium traffic loads. However, we found that for heavy traffic loads their model does not provide good performance. Therefore, we developed a better approach in the following section.

III. NEURAL NETWORK CONTROLLER

The physical consequence of rearrangements is to momentarily disturb network connections and the time duration of this disturbance may result in serious degradation of throughput in high speed communication networks. Therefore it is desirable to minimize this disturbance. During the rearrangement procedure of Paull's algorithm, the switches are chosen arbitrarily and such an approach has been implemented in a neural network controller[7]. In our model, we suggest to use Paull's algorithm with a better strategy for choosing switches. Notice that in Fig.2(b), if a "C" were chosen for entry (2 , 2), only one rearrangement would occur. Unfortunately, in real time, we cannot predict which choice would provide the shortest rearrangements. Jajszczyk and Rajski[5] showed that the intermediate switches selection rules affect the rearrangement process and the computation time required for rearrangements can be decreased by choosing the least used switches. Their theorem states that the number of calls in progress that need to be rerouted in order to connect an idle pair of terminals is not greater than minimum(a , b), where a, b are the number of existing connection paths passing through the switches A, B, respectively. Empirical simulations in the next section show that applying this rule to our neural network model not only saves the processing time for rearrangements but also keeps the network from being trapped in local minima.

We use the neural network topology originally proposed in [7] but with a different energy function. The network consists of r^2m neurons where r represents the number of input/output crossbar switches and m represents the number of intermediate crossbar switches. An example is shown in Fig.4. This figure corresponds to the state matrix shown in Fig.2(a) and the corresponding connection paths of a Clos network are shown in Fig.3. The shaded neurons represent their ON-states. The actual connections among the neurons are not shown in this figure. The states of neurons represent the connection states of the intermediate crossbar switches.

The following constraints must be satisfied :

1. In each entry (i , j), as many neurons as the number of calls may be ON.

2. Within each entry, always select the least used intermediate switch.

   (Select the switch with the minimum number of connection paths.)

3. In each row (or column), no two neurons with the same label may both be ON.

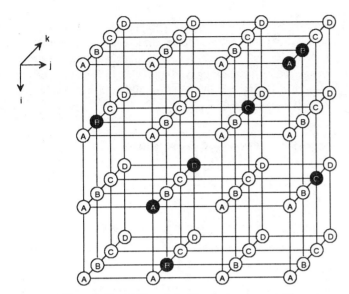

Figure 4. Neural Network Architecture ($m = n = r = 4$)

Notice that the least used intermediate switch is the switch "D" for the example in Fig.3. This neural network controller will offer fast solutions to the rearrangement problems provided that the network behavior and the appropriate set of connections and their weights between neurons are well defined.

Let U_{ijk} denote the total input of the ijk'th neuron where i, j, k represents i'th input switch, j'th output switch, k'th intermediate switch, respectively. Let V_{ijk} denote the output of the ijk'th neuron. The value of $V_{ijk} = 1$ means that the ijk'th neuron is ON and $V_{ijk} = 0$ means that the ijk'th neuron is OFF. For our model, we define V_{ijk} as suggested by Funabiki and Takefuji[6,7]:

$$V_{ijk}^{new} = \begin{cases} 0 & \text{if } U_{ijk} \leq -\alpha , \\ 1 & \text{if } U_{ijk} \geq \alpha , \\ V_{ijk}^{old} & \text{if } -\alpha < U_{ijk} < \alpha , \\ & \text{where } \alpha > 0. \end{cases}$$

The constant α is determined empirically for the fastest convergence. Our simulation experiments (described in the next section) use the value $\alpha = 5$. With the three constraints described above, the following equation represents the total input change of a neuron.

$$\frac{dU_{ijk}}{dt} = (a - \frac{c}{r} \sum_{p=1}^{r} \sum_{q=1}^{r} V_{pqk}) f(t_{ij} - \sum_{l=1}^{m} V_{ijl})$$
$$- b(\sum_{p=1,p\neq i}^{r} V_{pjk} + \sum_{q=1,q\neq j}^{r} V_{iqk})$$

where a, b, c are positive constants, t_{ij} denotes the number of call requests in entry (i , j), r the number of crossbar switches in the input/output stage and m the number of center stage switches.

The function $f(x)$ is 1 if $x > 0$, 0 if $x = 0$, -1 if $x < 0$.

The first term in the above equation represents the first and the second constraints previously discussed. The second term represents the third constraint. The first term initiates the rearrangement procedure in such a way that the least used switch selection rule is applied whenever a new call request arrives.

The first term is zero, positive or negative depending on the difference between the number of call requests in entry (i , j) and the number of neurons turned on in entry (i , j). If a new call request arrives in entry (i , j), then the first term is positive and it forces the ijk'th neuron to be turned on. The second term is zero if there is no other neuron turned on in row i or column j with the same k. Otherwise it forces the ijk'th neuron to be turned off.

The factor $(a - \frac{c}{r} \sum_{p=1}^{r} \sum_{q=1}^{r} V_{pqk})$ is related to the least used switch selection rule (i.e. the second constraint) and the constants a and c must be defined in such a way that this factor is always positive, the denominator r (the number of input/output crossbar switches) normalizes the value of the total number of neurons turned on within the k'th intermediate switch. Whenever a new call request arrives, the total number of neurons turned on within the k'th intermediate switch affects on the amount of input change of ijk'th neuron. Since every neuron in entry (i , j) has different value of this factor, the neuron with the largest input (i.e. the least used one) wins the competition and this difference accelerates the convergence speed. This is also true when an existing call is released. In this case, the least used switch is released. The constant a must be larger than the constants b and c so that the rearrangements can proceed without oscillations. These constants are determined empirically. With these proper values of constants a, b and c, each neuron tries to converge to either ON or OFF state based on the three constraints discussed before.

IV. SOFTWARE SIMULATIONS

We used the random traffic model as most previous studies on switching networks. Both the heavy load and the medium load cases were considered, where the traffic load is defined as the number of existing connections when a new call comes in. In the case of *medium* traffic load, existing calls occupy roughly half of maximum allowable connections, and in the case of *heavy* traffic load, most of the switches are being used for the existing calls. For various sizes of networks, the average number of iterations (i.e. average number of updates per neuron, corresponding to network convergence time), the average length of rearrangement sequences, blocking rates (i.e. the probability that a new call is blocked) and the success rates(i.e. the ratio of the number of successful convergence to total number of call requests) are shown in Fig.5, Fig.6, Fig.7 and Fig.8, respectively. When the network did not converge within a specified iteration limit, it was counted as a failure. The rearrangement sequences are counted only when the blocked call is unblocked successfully by rearrangements. For our model, we used $a = 5$, $b = 1$, $c = 3$, $\alpha = 5$, Iteration limit = 200. We also simulated our model without applying the least used switch selection rule (i.e. the second constraint). For every size of network, sequences of rm number of new calls were used, where rm represents the maximum number of connections in m number of $r \times r$ center stage switches. Simulations show that our model with the least used switch selection rule converges at least two times faster than the model with the random selection of intermediate switches. By applying the least used switch selection rule, the average number of iterations and the average length of rearrangement sequences are halved and the better performance is achieved even with the smaller value of iteration limit.

The reason why the random selection method does not provide good success rates for heavy traffic load is that it doesn't solve the rearrangement problems well in blocking situations. Therefore, we can conclude that applying the least used switch selection rule not only increases the efficiency in switch rearrangements, but also reduces the network convergence time since it keeps the network from being trapped in local minima. It is also shown that the network convergence time and the average length of rearrangement sequences do not depend on the network size, rather they depend on the traffic loads. We can also notice that the blocking rate (this implies the frequency of rearrangements) depends on the traffic load. Under heavy traffic load, the blocking rate is slightly larger than that of the random selection method. However, it is less than that of the random selection method under light load.

V. IMPLEMENTATION ASPECTS AND FEASIBILITY STUDY

Recent studies have shown that the Hopfield Network can be implemented with analog VLSI circuit technology[14] and a general purpose neural network system has been developed which can simulate the Hopfield-type networks, back-propagation networks and many others by using neurochips[12]. Most of recent studies have used analog circuits in hardware implementations[13,14]. Unfortunately, with the current technologies it is difficult to implement large networks by using analog circuits since the high-precision resisters are required and the circuits are easily affected by electrical noise and the power consumption is very high. It

is also shown that for large scale neural networks, digital circuits may be more suitable than analog circuits[11,12] since digital neurons can be easily integrated on a wafer by using CMOS technology and the neural functions can be mapped to digital circuits that are fully compatible with conventional computers.

Average Number of Iterations (Convergence Time)

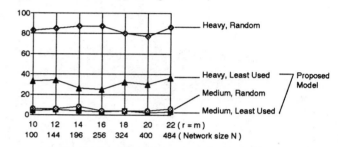

Figure 5. Average number of iterations

Average Rearrangement Sequences

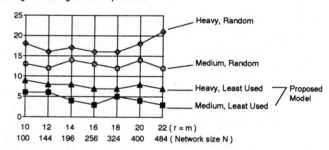

Figure 6. Average length of rearrangement sequences

Blocking Rates (%)

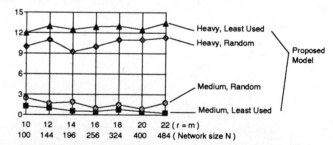

Figure 7. Blocking rates

Success Rates (%)

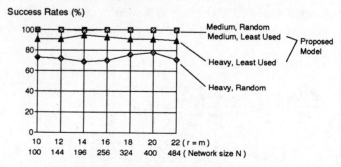

Figure 8. Success rates

Digital circuits also have some disadvantages : One digital neuron requires more transistors than one analog neuron, thus it requires much more chip area. Also in a digital implementation, the network convergence time is proportional to the number of neurons since they are using time sharing bus architecture in order to connect all neurons.

In our model for switch controller, all r^2m neurons are not fully interconnected but they are interconnected within each axis of the three dimensional grids (Fig.4). Therefore analog VLSI implementation would be more efficient than digital circuits provided that some technology-dependent limitations are overcome. This design may not be cost-effective with the current technology but the progress in modern analog VLSI technologies will enable the large VLSI implementation that was previously impossible. If this comes true, we can realize high speed switching networks without much throughput degradation that usually results from a low switching speed in conventional RAM controlled switching mechanism.

In a conventional RAM controlled switching mechanism, the processing time of the best algorithm is $7(N\log_2 N)$ cycle times (this includes the memory access time required to partition the memory and access times for the decomposition) for $N \times N$ switching networks[8]. For $N = 1000$ and the RAM with 50 nsec access time, and a 25 Mhz clock, on a 1-Mips machine, the processing time is about 60 msec. This means that the average nodal delay of the switching network is 60 msec which is too slow for a modern high speed channel with more than 100 Mbits/sec port speed. On the other hand, if the routing function is performed by the analog parallel processing, the average nodal delay lies in nano-second range. The performance of small size Hopfield type analog VLSI for a single crossbar control has already been evaluated[3]. The convergence time of such a network is 100 nsec. Hence, analog implementation of our neural network model can reduce the nodal delay to just 100 nsec, which is sufficient to support 100 Mbps port speeds.

Among design parameters, cost is another important factor. The hardware complexity of proposed model is $O(N\sqrt{N})$ (i.e. r^2m processing elements). Although the analog VLSI design is more costly than the digital single processor implementation, it does not suffer from time bottleneck ($O(N\log_2 N)$). Since the cost of integrated circuits is dropping exponentially and the transistor count on a chip is increasing by about 25 % per year, we expect to see cost-effective analog realizations of large neural networks in the near future.

VI. CONCLUSIONS

A lot of research has been done to compensate the mismatch between transmission speed and switching speed. As the transmission speed is getting faster and faster, new switching technologies are required to improve the performance in an efficient and cost-effective way. In this paper, a neural network approach to control a rearrangeable switching network is proposed. It is shown that the proposed neural network model converges in a constant time regardless of the switching network size. Success of the proposed model is due to incorporating conventional heuristic (least used switch selection rule) into the neural network controller. Based on our experience, we believe that successful neural network applications can be developed only by combining application-specific domain knowledge into neural network models. If the proposed model is implemented in analog VLSI, then apparently it would offer the maximum possible throughput with shorter nodal delays than other existing approaches.

REFERENCES

[1] C. Clos, "A study of non-blocking switching networks," Bell Syst. Tech. J., Vol. 32, pp. 406-424, March 1953.

[2] M. C. Paull, "Reswitching of connection networks," Bell Syst. Tech. J., Vol. 41, pp. 833-855, May 1962.

[3] A. Marrakchi and T. Troudet, "A neural net arbitrator for large crossbar packet-switches," IEEE Trans. on Circuits and Systems, Vol. 36, no. 7, pp. 1039-1041, July 1989.

[4] T. X. Brown, "Neural networks for switching," IEEE Communications Mag., pp. 72-81, Nov. 1989.

[5] A. Jajszczyk and J. Rajski, "The effect of choosing the switches for rearrangements in switching networks," IEEE Trans. on Communications, Vol. Com-28, NO. 10, pp. 1832-1834, Oct. 1980.

[6] N. Funabiki, Y. Takefuji, and K. C. Lee, "A neural network model for traffic controls in multistage interconnection networks," IJCNN 1991, Vol. II, pp. II A-898.

[7] N. Funabiki and Y. Takefuji, "A parallel algorithm for traffic control problems in three-stage connecting networks," Journal of Parallel and Distributed Computing, in press.

[8] D. C. Opferman and N. T. Tsao-Wu, "On a class of rearrangeable switching networks," Bell Syst. Tech. J., Vol. 50, pp. 1579-1618, May-June 1971.

[9] Nelson T. Tsao-wu, "On neiman's algorithm for the control of rearrangeable switching networks," IEEE Trans. on Communications, Vol. Com-22, NO. 6, pp. 737-742, June 1974.

[10] G. Colombo, C. Scarati and F. Settimo, "Asynchronous control algorithm for increasing the efficiency of three-stage connecting networks for multipoint services," IEEE Trans. on Communications, Vol. 38, NO. 6, pp. 898-905, June 1990.

[11] M. Yasunaga, N. Masuda, M. Yagyu, M. Asai, M.Yamada and A. Masaki, "Design, fabrication and evaluation of a 5-Inch wafer scale neural network LSI composed of 576 digital neurons," IJCNN 1990, Vol. II, pp. II-572 - II-535.

[12] Y. Hirai, K. Kamada, M. Yamada and M. Ooyama, "A digital neuro-chip with unlimited connectability for large scale neural networks," IJCNN 1989, Vol. II, pp. II-163 - II-169.

[13] J. Hopfield, "Neurons with graded response have collective computational properties like those of two-state neurons," Proc. Nat. Acad. Sci. USA, Vol.81, pp. 3088 - 3092, 1984.

[14] M. Sivilotti, M. Emerling and C. Mead, "VLSI architectures for implementation of neural networks," Conference on Neural Networks for Computing, AIP Conference Proceedings, pp. 408 - 413, 1896.

[15] H. Ahmadi and W. Denzel, "A survey of modern high-performance switching techniques," IEEE J. on Selected Areas in Communications, Vol.7, no.7, pp. 1091-1103, Sept. 1989.

[16] J. Huber and E. Mair, "A flexible architecture for small and large packet switching networks," in Proc. ISS'87, Phoenix, AZ, Mar. 1987, pp. B10.4.1-B10.4.6.

An Integrated Approach to Cellular Mobile Communication Planning Using Traffic Data Prestructured by a Self-Organizing Feature Map

Thomas Fritsch and Stefan Hanshans

Institute of Computer Science, University of Würzburg, Am Hubland, D-8700 Würzburg-F. R. Germany
Tel.: +49-931-8885518, Fax: +49-931-8884601, e-mail: fritsch@informatik.uni-wuerzburg.dbp.de

Abstract—The planning decision for the locations of the radio base stations in a cellular mobile communications network is the crucial point in the design phase of the network. Regular hexagonal cell lattices, equipped with the well known periodic frequency reuse pattern were the most used concepts in cellular radio network planning. However this simple model and its derivatives are not able to take into account the constraints resulting from the topography of the covering area and the corresponding traffic density. In this paper we present an algorithm, which determines the locations of the radio base stations using a set of sensory neurons, which detect the field strength of the radio wave propagation. The sensory neurons themselves are distributed according to the traffic density, which was learned by a self-organizing feature map. Under the assumption that there exist effective methods to estimate or measure the real traffic density in the covering area as well as to calculate the field strength at the different positions of the neurons, the presented approach provides a high-performance alternative to the existing concepts.

I. INTRODUCTION

An increasing number of subscribers of mobile communication radio networks like the analog C-Net in Germany and the recently introduced digital pan-European GSM-Net are very exacting for the design and planning of the radio network.

This concerns not only the geographical planning but also the optimal usage of the frequency spectrum and moreover, juridical questions. The first important task in designing a radio network is the choice of suitable locations for the base stations which are necessary to build up communication links in the radio network. These locations must be determined taking into consideration the morphological structure of the network's covering area. In reality the radio wave propagation is never homogeneous and isotropic, resulting of reflection, deflection and refraction caused by obstacles. The real covering area of the base stations is irregularly bounded, depending on the topography and the transmitting power.

The second task is the determination of the estimated traffic demand, i.e. the traffic density distribution in the affected region. To a certain degree the traffic distribution also depends on the topography. This problem is strongly related to the choice of the base station locations, but the time-varying characteristics of the traffic flow are usually not considered. Furthermore a realistic estimation of the traffic demand is essential for the planning of frequency reuse patterns. The concept of frequency reuse is crucial for an optimal usage of the existing radio spectrum. Briefly it means the reuse of a frequency in a spatially different region, where the distortion, caused by interferences is low. Since the regions have no regular form it is very complicated to reconstruct a new frequency reuse pattern, if dynamic channel allocation has been applied. This strategy can prove to be necessary, if traffic characteristics are time-dependent. Moreover juridical problems can influence the planning decisions too.

II. PROBLEM STATEMENT

Facing the problems described above, we looked for an appropriate neural net solution, which would be able to represent the radio field strength according to topographical information. At first the idea was to learn the topography of the chosen area by a self-organizing feature map [4] and then to propagate a simulated radio wave from a transmitting station, resulting in a covering area, where at all points a field strength beyond a critical value is detectable. The value of the field strength F is calculated following the formula in [2]

$$F/(dB(\mu V/m) = 74.8 + 10\, lg\,(P_s/W)$$
$$+ 10\, lg\,(G_s) - 20\, lg\,(d/km) \qquad (1)$$

with F as the field strength in dezibel(dB), P_s as the transmitting power in Watt(W), G_s the antenna gain and d as the distance to the transmitting station in km. The transmitting power P_s and the antenna gain values can vary to powers of ten, thus P_s and G_s are calculated in a logarithmical scale. For more details see [?].

First experiments showed to be promising. The Kohonen net learned artificial terrain data well, but learning of the field strength distribution caused several problems, since the rearrangement of transmitters was followed by a complete new learning process. Thus this approach was rejected and we were looking for a dynamic algorithm, which would need less computing time. The following integrated approach to radio network planning includes the consideration of the traffic density in the concerning covering area and in conjunction with some restrictions a quasi-optimal arrangement of the locations of the transmitting stations is developed. The restrictions refer to the radio wave propagation, which was simplified and the estimation of the traffic density. These two problems can be treated separately. Further details are available from the authors.

III. Determination of the traffic density with a selforganizing feature map

Most important for the determination of the locations of the transmitting stations is the traffic density in the covering area because supplying an area without any possible user of the radio network would be uneconomical. Normally the traffic density is obtained by measurements.

The method presented in this paper uses a fixed set of sensory neurons, which are spread over the covering area and whose distribution density effectively influences the positioning of the transmitting stations.

Consequently we need a method which associates the mean traffic density $E[V] = V^*$ with the dis-

tribution of sensory neurons, so that different traffic values are represented by a corresponding distribution of the sensory neurons. This implies, that high values must be represented by high density of sensory neurons and vice versa.

Kohonen nets [4] are well suited for those topological mappings. These nets reflect the topological relationships of the input space in their neighborhood structure. Moreover the dimension of input space and and image space may be different. We renounce to outline the Kohonen algorithm, assuming that it is well known in the neural net community. In our case the stimuli presented to the net are three-dimensional, but the weights of the neurons are two-dimensional. A stimulus v looks like this:

$$v = (x, y, V^*) \qquad (2)$$

where V^* is the mean traffic density at the point (x, y) in the covering area. The learning rate ϵ is now chosen proportional to V^*:

$$\epsilon(V^*) = c * V^*,\ c \text{ fixed} \qquad (3)$$

The selection probability of stimuli must be uniformly distributed. The modification of ϵ allows us to use two-dimensional weights, although we have three-dimensional input vectors. The choice of ϵ proportional to V^* results in very good mappings.

Lacking exact measurement of the real traffic we need an alternative method to achieve useful sensor distributions. Regarding a map of the covering area it is obvious that most of the traffic takes place on roads or highways or in towns. The location of highways or towns is dependent of the morphostructure. Most of them are located in lower terrain. So a modified stimulus v has the following form:

$$v = (x, y, h) \qquad (4)$$

where h now represents the topographical height at coordinates (x, y). Now we choose ϵ inversely proportional to h with the following constraint.
At the very lowest points of the area there is a river, where only low traffic density can be found. If such a point is chosen, ϵ will be set to a low value, so that

the corresponding distribution of the sensory neurons will be low. The weight vectors of the neurons are taken as the positions of the sensory neurons for the method outlined in the next section. A resulting sensory neuron density map of this modified learning phase is shown in Fig. 5.

IV. THE ALGORITHM

The algorithm takes advantage of "simulated annealing", which is well known from statistical physics [5]. In this algorithm a thermodynamic system is assigned an energy value for every state and a corresponding temperature, which is reduced slowly at each discrete time step. The goal is to reach equilibrium for the system, that means to be in a state with minimal energy. Transitions between states of the system take place with a certain probability, in our case

$$prob\{Z^{new} = Z^{act}\} = e^{-\frac{\Delta E}{\tau}} \qquad (5)$$

with Z as the system state and ΔE as the energy difference between the old state energy and the actual state energy with temperature τ.

The system consists of a set of transmitting stations, which are able to change their positions and transmitting power, and a set of sensory neurons, which are fixedly located according to a predefined distribution density.

Algorithm:

1. (a) Transmitting Stations
   A transmitting station T is defined by

   $$T := (Pos(T), P(T)) = (x, y, P) \qquad (6)$$

   with (x, y) representing the position and P the power of T.
   Additionally a vector $F(T) := (\Delta x, \Delta y)$ is introduced, called the position error of T. $F(T)$ is used to determine the direction of the next possible displacement of the transmitting station in the adaptation step. A variable $n(T)$ counts the number

of free sensory neurons which are added in the selection step. On the other hand the number of sensory neurons which were assigned to multiple transmitting station stations is subtracted from $n(T)$. The value of $n(T)$ delivers a criterion, how many sensory neurons are covered by a transmitting station station T. Furthermore this criterion and the values of $F(T)$ are used to decide whether the position or the power of the transmitting station station shall be changed. The set of all transmitting station stations is called **T**.

(b) Sensory Neurons
   A sensory neuron or "sensor" S is defined by

   $$S := (Pos(S), H) = (x, y, H) \qquad (7)$$

   with $H := (H_1, ..., H_k)$ as the field strength values detected from the transmitting stations $T_1, ..., T_k$ by sensor S.
   The set of all sensory neurons is called **S**.

2. Initial Conditions

   - Distribution of n sensory neurons $S \in$ **S** according to the traffic density learned by the self-organizing feature map.

   - Location of all base stations $T \in$ **T** with initially low transmitting power P_0. This initialization allows more flexible changing possibilities for the transmitting stations at the start of the algorithm.

   - Suitable choice of the temperature parameters τ_0 (initial value) and decrement parameter $\Delta \tau$.

   - Initialization of $\Delta x, \Delta y$ and n with zero for all transmitting stations.

3. Determination of the supplying areas $V(T_j)$ for all transmitting stations $T_j \in$ **T**.
   Let $H_{receive}$ be the minimal field strength underneath no satisfying reception is possible. The supplying area $V(T_j)$ of a transmitting station T_j is then defined by

$$V(T_j) := \{S_i \in \mathbf{S} : H_j(S_i) \geq H_{receive}\},$$
$$\forall i,j = 1\ldots k \quad \text{and} \quad \mathbf{V} := \bigcup_{T_j \in \mathbf{T}} V(T_j) \quad (8)$$

In the undistorted case all supplying areas are circular shaped. Irregular forms as well as disconnected regions originate from attenuations caused by obstacles.

4. Selection Step

Select a sensory neuron S_i randomly under the assumption of uniform distribution.

(a) S_i belongs to no supplying area

$$S_i \notin \mathbf{V}$$

- Find the transmitting station T_{next} with minimal spatial distance to S_i.

$$T_{next} := T_j \quad \text{with}$$

$$\|Pos(S_i) - Pos(T_j)\| \leq \|Pos(S_i) - Pos(T_k)\|$$
$$\forall T_k \in \mathbf{T} \; T_k \neq T_j \quad (9)$$

- Add to the position error $F(T_{next})$ of T_{next} the difference vector of the positions of S_i and T_{next}. This causes an attraction of T_{next} by S_i (see Fig. 1).

$$F^{(new)}(T_{next}) := F^{(old)}(T_{next})$$
$$+(Pos(S_i) - Pos(T_{next})) \quad (10)$$

- Increase $n(T_j)$

(b) S_i lies in exactly one supplying area

$$S_i \in V(T_j) \wedge S_i \notin V(T_l) \quad \forall T_l \neq T_j \quad (11)$$

In this case no changes take place.

(c) S_i is assigned to more than one supplying area of the transmitting stations

$$S_i \in V(T_{j_1}) \cap \ldots \cap V(T_{j_l}), \; 2 \leq l \leq k \quad (12)$$

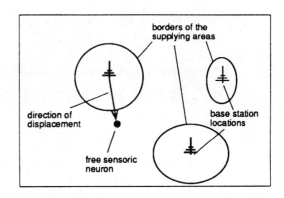

Figure 1: Case of attraction

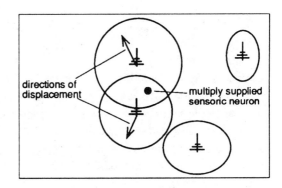

Figure 2: case of repellation

- Subtract the difference between the positions of S_i and T_{j_s} from the position error $\forall s = 1,..,l$. This causes a repellation of the transmitting stations from S_i (see Fig. 2).

$$F^{(new)}(T_{j_s}) := F^{(old)}(T_{j_s})$$
$$-(Pos(S) - Pos(T_{j_s})) \quad (13)$$
$$\forall T_{j_s} \quad \text{with} \quad S_i \in V(T_{j_s})$$

- Decrease $n(T_{j_s})$

5. Adaptation Step

A system state Z at time step (t) is characterized by the assignment of all sensory neurons S_i according to the actual distribution of the transmitting stations T_j and their corresponding supplying areas $V(T_j)$ to one of the following sets:

i. free sensory neurons

$$\mathbf{S_f} := \{S_i | S_i \notin \mathbf{V}\}$$

ii. multiply assigned sensory neurons

$$\mathbf{S_m} := \{S_i | S_i \in \bigcup_{l,j} \{V(T_j) \cap V(T_l)\}\},$$

$$\forall l, \forall j, \ l \neq j$$

iii. definitely assigned sensory neurons

$$\overline{(\mathbf{S_f} \cup \mathbf{S_m})}$$

(a) Determine T_{worst}, the transmitting station with maximum $\|F\|$
$T_{worst} := T_j$ with

$$\|F(T_j)\| > \|F(T_k)\|, \ \forall j, k, \ T_j \in \mathbf{T} \quad (14)$$

We now introduce the concept of the energy of a system state. We identify the order of the system by the magnitude of $(\mathbf{S_f} \cup \mathbf{S_m})$. The category of the system's energy which is decreasing with increasing order is introduced analogous. Therefore a minimization of $\overline{(\mathbf{S_f} \cup \mathbf{S_m})}$ corresponds to the minimization of the system's energy.

(b) Save the system's state before changing the position or the power of the transmitting station.
Let $E^{(old)}$ be the energy and $Z^{(old)}$ the system's state at time step t, that means before a change of T_{worst}.

(c) If $\|F(T_{worst})\|$ takes on values, which make a displacement necessary
$\|F(T_{worst})\| \geq t_{move}$
adapt the position:

$$Pos^{(new)}(T_{worst}) := \ Pos^{(old)}(T_{worst})$$
$$+ \ \epsilon * F(T_{worst}) \ (15)$$

The threshold t_{move} is won by experience and prevents displacements at positions with low $\|F\|$.
The transmitting station T_{worst} is moved into that direction, where many attracting sensory neurons are located, and in the opposite direction in the case of repellation. The parameter ϵ plays the role of a scaling factor also preventing extreme displacements.

(d) If $F(T_{worst}) < t_{move}$
adapt the transmission power

$$P^{(new)}(T_{worst}) := \ P^{(old)}(T_{worst})$$
$$+ \ n(T_{worst}) * p \ (16)$$

where p is a fixed value for the magnitude of change of power.

6. Optimization Step

(a) Determine the energy $E^{(act)}$ of the actual system state $Z^{(act)}$ at time step $(t+1)$

(b) Check, if a state transition can take place
   i. Determine $\Delta E := E^{(act)} - E^{(old)}$
   ii. If $\Delta E < 0$ set $\Delta E := 0$
   In this case the state transition shall happen with probability 1
   iii. A state transition into state $Z^{(new)}$ happens with probability

$$prob\{Z^{(new)} = Z^{(act)}\} = e^{-\frac{\Delta E}{\tau}} \quad (17)$$

Remaining in state $Z^{(old)}$ takes place with probability

$$prob\{Z^{(new)} = Z^{(old)}\} = 1 - e^{-\frac{\Delta E}{\tau}} \quad (18)$$

(c) Decrease the temperature τ

$$\tau^{(new)} := \tau^{(old)} - \Delta\tau \quad (19)$$

(d) Reset Δx, Δy and n for all transmitting stations

7. If $\tau^{(new)}$ reaches zero and ΔE is about zero this situation can be interpreted as a possible state of minimal disorder. Then finish, otherwise repeat from step 4.

V. EXPERIMENTAL RESULTS

In Fig. 3 we see the topographical terrain of a 10km x 10km area in the north of Würzburg. Dominating is the river Main on the left side. The resolution of the data of the digital terrain model, delivered by the Bavarian Departement of Surveying [1] is 100 meters. The figure is printed out with eight gray scales, where dark points are assigned to low terrain and light points to high terrain. In Fig. 4 we see the final arrangement of six transmitting stations, each region represented by a different symbol. Fig. 5 shows the final distribution of sensory neurons, reflecting the estimated traffic density in the area which was learned by a selforganizing feature map. The final placement of transmitting stations was plausible to a human expert. Nevertheless it is necessary to compare the algorithm to other existing methods, e.g. the fuzzy-logic-based program GRAND [3] which already yielded excellent results for highly complicated areas like in Switzerland. Furthermore, the problems concerning field strength prediction and traffic density measuring can influence the performance of the algorithm effectively. Further research shall clear the question how optimal the algorithm works.

VI. CONCLUSIONS

In this paper we presented an algorithm, which is able to arrange the locations of the transmitting stations of a cellular mobile communication network according to an existing traffic distribution, learned by a selforganizing neural net. With its help it is possible to contribute to the planning of radio networks in a more realistic way as it is provided by hexagonal concepts, if efficient methods for field strength prediction and traffic measurement are available. Alternative approaches like fuzzy logic could also be used to improve the quality of the achieved solution, since covering areas can be regarded as fuzzy cells with uncertain borders. Future research shall be concentrated on the combination of neural nets and fuzzy sets for the realistic mapping of the covering area and on the other hand, on the consideration of time-varying channel demand for dynamic channel allocation.

REFERENCES

[1] DIGITAL TERRAIN MODEL OF THE BAVARIAN DEPARTMENT OF SURVEYING, USING ALLOWED AT 9.4.92 WITH AZ.: VM 2280 B - 3115 (IN GERMAN)

[2] Lee W.C.Y., MOBILE COMMUNICATION DESIGN FUNDAMENTALS, Howard W. Sams, Indianapolis, 1986

[3] Krueger M., Beck R. GRAND - A PROGRAM SYSTEM FOR MOBILE RADIO COMMUNICATION PLANNING (IN GERMAN), PKI Tech. Mitt. 2/1990

[4] Kohonen, T., SELF-ORGANIZING FEATURE MAPS, tutorial at IJCNN-89, Washington, D.C. June 18-22, 1989

[5] Aarts E., Korst J., SIMULATED ANNEALING AND BOLTZMANN MACHINES, Wiley, New York, 1990

Figure 3: Digital terrain map in the north of Würzburg

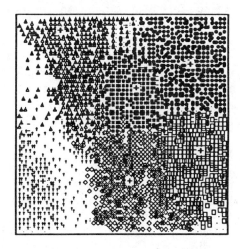

Figure 4: Assignment of the supplying areas to six base station locations indicated by '+'

Figure 5: Traffic density, learned by a self-organizing feature map

APPLICATION OF NEURAL NETWORKS FOR ROUTING IN TELECOMMUNICATIONS NETWORKS

Mark Collett and Witold Pedrycz

Mark Collett, Operational Systems Specialist, Manitoba Telephone System, Winnipeg, Canada
Witold Pedrycz, Professor and Associate Head (Computer Engineering), Department of Electrical and Computer Engineering, University of Manitoba, Winnipeg, Canada

Abstract

This article discusses the application of neural networks to routing in telecommunications networks under normal and abnormal conditions. Concepts related to optimal routing will be discussed from the theoretical and telecommunications networks perspective to define a translation to the neural network paradigm. A sample network is then used to determine optimal neural network parameters, which are then tested to determine routing accuracy and performance under normal and abnormal routing conditions. Following the analysis of the results, conclusions and recommendations on the results will be provided.

Introduction

The importance of network routing is increasing due to several factors: telecommunications companies are under pressure to become more efficient, requiring maximum network utilization; increased public and corporate dependence on networks requires improved network reliability and availability; and the introduction of new technology has made the network more complex. Routing methods must evolve to maximize network utilization under normal conditions, and adapt to and minimize the effects of abnormal network conditions. Conventional routing approaches are superior to older methods, but still have disadvantages in terms of speed and flexibility. By utilizing the adaptive properties of neural networks, advanced network routing methods could be created without the disadvantages of conventional ones.

Routing Theory

Network routing has been researched extensively from a theoretical perspective to determine efficient algorithms; for the purposes of this research, our study focused on shortest path (SP) problems. Several good sources classify the types of SP algorithms available. Deo and Pang [1] classified different algorithms based on a number of factors to identify suitable candidates for parallel implementation and computation; the majority of the material for this section was obtained (unless otherwise noted) from this source.

SP algorithms are dependent on a number of problem factors. One of these factors is the network topology, such as network node density, the directedness of the arcs between the nodes, the arc lengths and what these lengths are based on. In characterizing a telecommunications network, it can be represented as a sparsely connected, undirected graph with positive arc values based on a deterministic function related to euclidean distance between the nodes. While the pure euclidean distance can be used, several factors can be combined to come up with an effective cost function for a transport facility such as cost of use, type of equipment, and network delay factors.

The type of solution required is another factor in determining the desired SP algorithm. The solution type is governed by path selection constraints, whether the solution provides the shortest path only or defines K-th shortest paths, and whether the solution provides specific paths to a single node or an all nodes solution. In telecommunications networks the paths for restoration routing are typically unconstrained, but the other characteristics are not as clearly defined, allowing for a number of possible routing methods. For this study a K-th shortest path solution was desired to provide routing solutions involving multiple restoration paths, and an all nodes routing solution was desired to allow for routing solutions capable of adapting to network node failure conditions.

The last major factor that classifies SP algorithms is the technique used to determine the shortest path. Each algorithm can be described by its use of preprocessing and the method used to determine the solution, and can be further broken into combinatorial and algebraic techniques.

In considering the type of solution method desired, effort was focused on combinatorial methods, notably *graph traversal techniques*, where the arcs of a graph are traversed and information recorded as the optimal path is found. Several graph traversal techniques are available which have been mapped onto neural networks or applied to communications networks. In one application, Ephremides and Verdu [2] assert that distributed implementation of a label correcting algorithm (a type of graph traversal technique) is well suited to communications networks, where messages between nodes can be processed to determine the labels for each link. Using this method, the information is updated asynchronously, no network coordination is required, the nodes rely only on receiving information from adjacent nodes, and accurate knowledge of the network is maintained if the communication is continuous.

Neural networks and telecommunications routing

A search of neural network and telecommunications literature identified numerous cases where neural networks have been applied to this field. Most of this research involves some form of routing decision, but the specific applications, conditions, and methods vary. Brown [3] and Melsa et al [4] investigate neural network routing within digital telephone switches, where the priority is performing the maximum number of input/output connections. Other applications include Hiramatsu [5,6], Chugo at al [7] and Frisiani at al [8] where routing decisions for data networks are based on traffic levels within transport facilities, network delay times, and messages between nodes. Lastly, Rauch and Winarske [9] and Jensen et al [10] investigated performing routing decisions in the transport network under normal and abnormal conditions.

Attributes of an optimal routing method using neural networks

Based on the review of telecommunications, routing theory, and existing neural network applications, the list of attributes of a preferred network routing system using neural networks can be defined. These are:
- the method must perform routing decisions quickly,
- the method should be distributed to provide the fast decision times, for centralized methods incur decision or transmission delays

(Ephremides and Verdu and Jensen et al demonstrated or presented distributed routing,)
- the routing method should provide multiple route alternatives,
- the routing method should utilize information provided by adjacent nodes for performing routing decisions, and
- a neural network implementation should be easily scalable.

Description of routing method under study

The routing method studied performs distributed routing, with individual network nodes performing routing decisions. These routing decisions are based on the relationship between the originating node where the routing decision is performed, the desired destination node, and the links that connect the originating node to its adjacent nodes in the network. By limiting the routing decision to these links, the number of alternatives the neural network has to consider in performing the routing function is reduced.

Routes through the network consist of an originating node, a destination node, and a sequence of intervening links and nodes between them that define the route. One of the intervening links in the route is the link connecting the originating node to an adjacent node. There will always be at least one route that will connect any two nodes; in most cases there will be multiple routes between them. In order to make a routing decision, some type of criteria is required to allow for comparison of the multiple potential routes between the originating and destination nodes. One method of providing this criteria is by assigning a weight to the network's links and nodes; a route that is comprised of a sequence of links and nodes is then assigned a weight equal to the sum of these weights. By relating the weights of the multiple routes to the links that connect the originating node to its adjacent nodes, a pattern is defined that can be used as the criteria for performing routing decisions. To perform the routing decisions properly, the routes related to the adjacent links must comply with the following rules:
- the routing sequence from the originating to destination node through a specific adjacent link must be the best route using that link based on the criteria used for routing, and
- the routing sequence from the originating node to the destination node through a specific adjacent link must not reuse the originating node.

Single network node modelling

To study a neural network's ability to perform network routing decisions, a sample network was required to provide test data. The sample network used is shown in Figure 1. After defining the sample network, the relationships of the input and output layers of the neural networks were related to the sample network nodes. Each neural network is trained to determine routing results for a specific node in the sample network; the neurons in the neural network's input layer represent the nodes of the sample network and the neurons in the neural network's output layer represent the links of the specific node in the sample network to its adjacent nodes, as shown in Figure 2.

In considering the various neural network topologies, activation functions, and learning rules available, the following choices were made:
- the learning rule used was Back Propagation,
- the network topology was a four layer feed forward network consisting of an input, an output, and two hidden layers,
- the neural network activation function is the continuous sigmoid function given below, with
  - a(t+1)   is the activation value of a neuron,
  - w(t)   is the weighted sum of the neuron's inputs, and
  - T   is the network temperature.

$$a(t+1) \;=\; \frac{1}{1 \;+\; e^{-w(t)/T}}$$

Routing criteria were established by assigning weights to the network links and nodes, and using the sum of the weights of a sequence of links and nodes to determine the route weight. A time based weighting factor was chosen, for a time related factor can be used to model both the links and nodes of a telecommunications network. The weighted values were created by scaling the actual link lengths and dividing by a velocity factor to create a time based value. After determining some sample route weights, the individual link weights were scaled again to ensure that route weights would fit within the

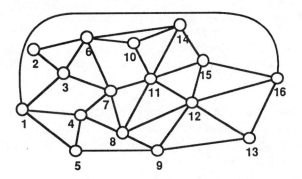

Figure 1:
Sample Network

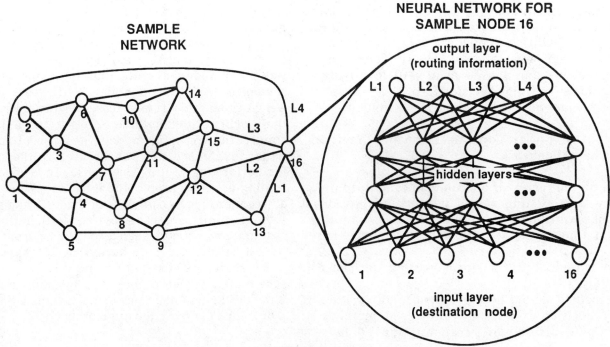

Figure 2:
Neural Network and its relation to the Sample Network

activiation function range. Pattern files containing route weights determined from the above method were then created.

With the basic neural network topology, activation function, learning rule and initial training sets defined, network training was performed. The simulations were performed using MacBrain 2.0 and 3.0 on an Apple Macintosh IIfx with 4MB RAM and an 80 MB hard drive. Instead of using the entire sample network to test the performance of different neural network topologies, three nodes were selected for initial testing. These nodes - nodes 2, 9, and 11 - have 2, 4, and 6 adjacent links respectively and provide a measure of the test network's ability to perform routing over a range of adjacent link values. The objective of these initial simulations was to determine the optimal parameters for the remainder of the testing. The parameters tested included:
- the optimal number of neurons in the neural network's two hidden layers; these layers were the only parts of the network not defined by external parameters. Three hidden layers topologies were tested, where both hidden layers would contain 6, 8, or 10 neurons,
- the method of training the neural networks,
- the format of the training set.

Test Results

The three neural network topologies (6,8, and 10 neurons/hidden layer) were tested with the three training sets and with three different training methods. The results were compared using the following information:
- the neural network Mean Squared Error values,
- the average of the absolute value of the difference of between the target and actual output values for each network,
- the distribution of difference values,
- direct comparison of the training results as a function of number of hidden layer neurons and training method,
- comparison of the routing rankings learned by the neural network to the actual routing rankings of the adjacent links connected to the originating node.

After comparing the various networks, the following results were found:
- No single network topology (6, 8, or 10 neurons/hidden layer) consistently outperformed the other topologies on the basis of numerical comparisons. However, the 8 neuron/hidden layer topology performed the best or close to the best for all output combinations.
- The best training results in the numerical comparisons were provided by a learning method that annealed the neural network at a point where the MSE curve reached a minimum during training, then held the temperature (T) of the activation function constant while allowing learning to continue.
- When the neural networks were compared on the basis of the routing rankings, the 8 neurons/hidden layer networks produced better output ranking results than the 6 or 10 neurons/hidden layer networks.

At this point, the best neural network topology was able to determine network routing rankings with a 90% accuracy. To improve this performance, the format of the training set was revisited. Analysis of incorrect routing results found that errors resulted from training values of different adjacent links that were very close in value; as a result, a small error in learning was sufficient to produce the incorrect result. To overcome this problem, the training set was quantized; the ranks of the initial training set were calculated and translated into discrete steps between the minimum and maximum activation values.

After modification of the three training sets, the 8 neurons/hidden layer topology was retested and compared to the original results. The new results demonstrated improved learning of the routing rankings, with a 99% routing accuracy. This accuracy was at the expense of poorer learning of the actual target values when compared to the original training results.

Full network routing simulation

Using the single node research results, the remaining nodes of the sample network were simulated and their routing performance studied. For each network node the routing information and rankings were determined, a neural network was created and trained, and the trained output values and routing rankings compared against the target values and routing rankings. Analysis of the results found eight routing ranking errors out of 990 possible routing rankings in the sample network, for a 99.19% routing accuracy. All the routing errors occured in network nodes with 5 or more adjacent links; nodes with 4 or less links learned the routing rankings without error. The occurrence of the routing errors suggests that neural networks with larger number of output neurons are more susceptible to errors; these networks had smaller quantization steps between the modified output values, and would be more sensitive to large learning errors. In addition, the errors occurred in the highest or lowest ranked outputs at the extremes of the output value range, where the slope of the sigmoid curve is smallest; at these extreme ranges a small input variation can map into a large output error. Table 1 details the routing performance for the complete sample network and for the sets of nodes with equal numbers of links.

Performing routing decisions

The trained neural networks contain output values representing routing rankings of a specific network node; these must be combined with information on availability of the node's adjacent links to perform a routing decision based on shortest time and link availability. To implement this function a winner-take-all circuit was added above each neural network's output layer, where the learned routing value is from a boolean value representing link availability. If a link was available, the availability value is set to 1, and the value into the winner-take-all circuit is 1 minus the learned value. If all links are available, then the highest input value into the circuit would be associated with the smallest learned routing value representing the shortest route time. If a link is unavailable, the availability value is 0, and the value into the winner-take-all

Table 1:
Comparison of routing performance for Sample Network
for the entire network and different valence values

Item	Number of Nodes	Number of routes	Number of mismatches	Error (Percent)	Accuracy (Percent)
2 link nodes	1	30	0	0%	100%
3 link nodes	3	135	0	0%	100%
4 link nodes	7	420	0	0%	100%
5 link nodes	3	225	4	1.78%	98.22%
6 link nodes	2	180	4	2.22%	97.78%
Full network	16	990	8	0.81%	99.19%

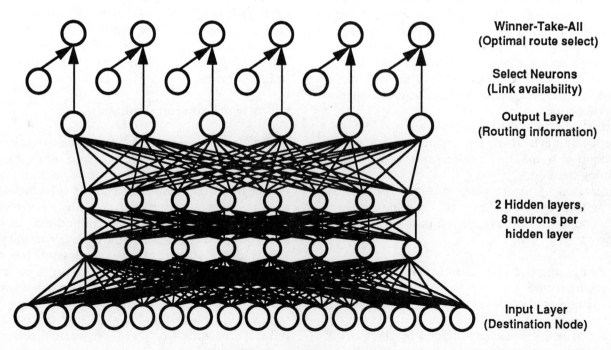

Winner-Take-All
(Optimal route select)

Select Neurons
(Link availability)

Output Layer
(Routing information)

2 Hidden layers,
8 neurons per
hidden layer

Input Layer
(Destination Node)

Figure 3:
Final Neural Network topology

circuit would be a negative number with all input values with available links will be larger in value. The complete neural network structure is shown in Figure 3.

To test the routing performance between two sample network nodes, the following steps are performed:
- The neural network representing the originating node is selected,
- The input layer neurons are all set to zero, except for the neuron representing the destination node, which is set to one,
- The availabilities of adjacent links are set (link available=1, link unavailable=0,)
- The inputs are propagated to the winner-take-all layer where a single output will be set to 1, selecting the adjacent link and related node on the shortest route to the destination.

The steps are then repeated with each selected node until the destination node is reached.

Network routing results

Under normal conditions, optimal routes were selected when decisions involved nodes that successfully learned routing rankings. Optimal routes were not determined if a ranking error involving the first choice route to the destination node occured in any network node between the originating and destination nodes.

In performing routing decisions involving an unavailable link along the optimal route, a shortest alternate route was selected except in the case where a node with a ranking error involving the first choice route to the destination node was on the alternate path to the destination node. The path of this alternate route was dependent on the routing decision performed when the unavailable link was encountered; a decision to directly route to the destination node produced new unique network routes, while a decision to route around the unavailable link found the shortest alternate route to the node at the far end of the unavailable link and reused the remaining links along the original route.

In performing routing decisions involving an unavailable node, an optimal route was always determined, except in the case of the originating or destination nodes being the unavailable node.

Conclusions and Recommendations

Based on the research performed, neural networks can be used to perform static and dynamic routing within telecommunications networks, and offer many opportunities for further study. There are many potential areas for optimization in the method studied, including investigation of other learning methods, activiation functions, and training sets. In addition, by studying the information learned by the neural networks, a better understanding of the routing process can be obtained. Furthermore, one can easily model different conditions in the system by assigning various weights to the nodes. Lastly, hardware implementation of the work performed through simulation could test the actual routing performance in real world conditions.

References

[1] N. Deo and C. Pang. Shortest path algorithms: Taxonomy and annotation. *Networks*, Volume 14, 1984, pp. 275-323.

[2] A. Ephremides and S. Verdu. Control and Optimization Methods in Communication Network Problems. *IEEE Transactions on Automatic Control*, Vol 34, No. 9, September 1989, pp. 930-941.

[3] T.X. Brown. Neural Networks for Switching. *IEEE Communications Magazine*, November 1989 pp. 72-81.

[4] P.J.W. Melsa, J.B. Kenney, and C.E. Rohrs. A neural network solution for call routing with preferential call placement. *IEEE Global Telecommunications Conference (Globecom) 1990*, pp. 1377-1381.

[5] A. Hiramatsu. ATM communications network control by neural network. *IEEE International Joint Conference on Neural Networks (IJCNN) 1989*, pp. I-259-266.

[6] A. Hiramatsu. Integration of ATM call admission control and link capacity control by distributed neural networks. *IEEE Global Telecommunications Conference (Globecom) 1990*, pp. 1382-1386.

[7] A. Chugo, W. Sotelo, and I. Iida. Holonic Routing Scheme based on Neural Computations. *IEEE Global Telecommunications Conference (Globecom) 1990*, pp. 1366-1370.

[8] G. Frisiani, T. Parisini, L. Siccardi, and R. Zoppoli. Team theory and back-propagation for dynamic routing in communication networks. *IEEE International Joint Conference on Neural Networks (IJCNN) 1991*, pp. I-325-334.

[9] H.E. Rausch and T. Winarske. Neural Networks for Routing Communications Traffic. *IEEE Control Systems Magazine*, Volume 8, Issue 2, April 1988, pp. 26-31.

[10] J.E. Jensen, M.A. Eshera, and S.C. Barash. Neural Network Controller for Adaptive R outing in Survivable Communications Networks. *IEEE International Joint Conference on Neural Networks (IJCNN) 1990*, pp.II 29-36.

ATM Multimedia Traffic Prediction Using Neural Networks

Ahmed A. Tarraf, Ibrahim W. Habib, Tarek N. Saadawi, and Samir A. Ahmed

City College of New York. Electrical Engineering Department

Abstract *Asynchronous transfer Mode (ATM) Broadband networks support a wide range of multimedia traffic (e.g. voice, video, image, and data). Accurate characterization of the multimedia traffic is essential, in ATM networks, in order to develop a robust set of traffic descriptors. Such set is required, by the Usage Parameter Control (UPC) algorithm, for traffic enforcement (policing). In this paper, we present a novel approach to characterize and model the multimedia traffic using Neural Networks (NNs). A backpropagation neural network is used to characterize and predict the statistical variations of the packet arrival process resulting from the superposition of N packetized video sources and M packetized voice sources. The accuracy of the results were verified by matching the Index of Dispersion for Counts (IDC), the variance, and the autocorrelation of the arrival process to those of the NN output. The reported results show that the NNs can be successfully utilized to characterize the complex non-renewal process with extreme accuracy.*

I. Introduction

Broadband Integrated Service Digital Networks (B-ISDN) are designed to provide multimedia traffic services (e.g. data, voice, video) over the same transport and switching systems. The Asynchronous Transfer Mode (ATM) technique has been recommended by the CCITT as the transport vehicle for B-ISDN [1]. In ATM-based networks, the multimedia information is packetized and transported in small size packets called "cells". (The cell size is 53 bytes, 5 of which is the header)

Variable Bit-Rate (VBR) video and voice sources produce multimedia traffic that possess high bit-rate fluctuations over relatively short time periods. This traffic is highly bursty and correlated in the sense that its interarrival time has a squared coefficient of variation C2 (which is the ratio of the variance to the square of the mean value) higher than that of the simple uncorrelated Poisson process. For example, it was shown in [2] that the value of C2 is 18.1 for the packet arrival process due to a single voice source, which is very large compared to that

of a Poisson process which has C2 = 1. It was also observed that over short time intervals, the superposition process of M voice sources does look like a Poisson process, however over longer time intervals, the cumulative effect of positive correlations among the successive packet interarrivals cause the process to substantially deviate from the Poisson process.

In general, the traffic can be charracterized by a complex non-renewal process [3]. It is essential, in ATM networks, to provide efficient admission control and traffic enforcement techniques in order to avoid serious congestion problems. These techniques require specific knowledge of the statistical-behavior of the input traffic declared via its traffic descriptors [4],[5]. Parameters such as peak bit-rate, average bit-rate, and burst length(which is the duration of the peak bit-rate) are often used as a simple set of parameters that can be used to characterize the multimedia traffic [5],[6]. More complicated second-order time domain parameters (e.g. IDC, IDI, ...etc.) are also used to fully capture the burstiness and the correlations properties of the arrival stochastic process especially those of VBR video and voice sources [7]. Mathematical models such as Continuous Time Markov Chain (CTMC), Semi Markov Modulated Process (SMMP), and Markov Modulated Poisson Process (MMPP) [8] are used to characterize and model the traffic with many approximations that limit their efficacious. Traffic characterization using simple parameters often ignores most of its important correlations and burstiness properties. Hence, leading to the definition of incorrect UPC parameters, that could seriously advert the network performance [9].

The performance of the UPC algorithm can be improved by using more sophisticated parameters that police the probability distribution function (PDF) of bit-rate of the source [10],[11]. Unfortunately in most cases, this probability distribution function can not be described by a known mathematical model. For example, the Gabarit policing mechanism [11] approximates the (PDF) by a mathematically well defined distribution (e.g. a Gaussian distribution). However, due to the complexity of its implementation, it is unfeasible to police the Gaussian envelope continuously over all points. Hence, a stair-case shape function is used to approximate the Gaussian envelope leading to errors in the estimation of UPC parameters.

In this paper, we adopt a novel approach to this problem by using NNs. NNs can predict the bit-rate variations of a complex stochastic process using simple parameters such as the instantaneous bit-rate which is measured by the number of packet arrivals within a certain time-period. The NN approach would, not only, best characterize (the bit-rate variations) of the multimedia arrival process but also predict these variations over a fixed time interval in the future. Hence, it can be used to dynamically allocate the bandwidth, to each call, and enforce the traffic subsequently. We believe that it is the only possible solution to actually avoid congestion in ATM networks before it occurs. The traffic prediction is achieved as the NN learns the actual (PDF) of the traffic. The results show that, with a proper NN architecture, the traffic can be accurately characterized and consequently described with simple parameters. The advantages of the NN approach over other computational algorithms (e.g. [7]-[9]) is the simplicity of implementing a UPC function that can characterize and predict the bit-rate variations of the traffic and hence police it. The motivation behind our selection of NNs is that it is very effective in learning, and hence predicting, non-linear complex functions, thus making it an ideal tool to employ in ATM networks.

Neural networks were proposed to solve some control problems [12],[13]. Applications to the communications networks control were reported in [14]-[17]. However NNs have not been used in the context of multimedia traffic modeling and characterization. Section II describes the NN architecture and the proposed model, section III reports simulation results and section IV contains numerical results whereas the conclusions are given in section V.

II. Neural Network Model For Traffic Characterization And Prediction

The main objective of this paper is to explore how a three-layered backpropagation NN can be used to characterize and predict non-renewal type processes. NNs based on backpropagation algorithm, can learn a nonlinear relation between many variables. These networks have been used in a number of deterministic and stochastic problems [18], [19]. It has been found that these networks perform well in most cases with accurate results.

Before we start the analysis of the NN model for traffic prediction , we briefly describe the video arrival process and the voice arrival process as follows:

Video Arrival Process: In this paper, the video traffic is generated by simulating a variable bit-rate (VBR) video source which comprise mainly head and shoulder video sequences types without scene changes. The picture sequences, produced by the video source, comprise a lot of redundant information, hence a suitable compression technique is employed to remove this redundancy, while maintaining a constant picture quality. A number of coding algorithms are employed to code the video signal such as interframe differential pulse code motion (DPCM), intraframe DPCM, conditional replenshiment (CR), motion compensation discrete cosine transfer (MC-DCT) [20]-[22]. In this paper, a simulation of a (VBR) source employing scene without abrupt movement is used.

The change in the coding bit rate process of a VBR video source is described by a number of mathematical models [23],[24], however, the burstiness of the (VBR) video source depends on the compression algorithm and the nature of the video scene. For a scene without abrupt movement (head and shoulders video type), it was proved in [23] that the bit-rate has a bell shaped stationary probability density and has exhibit significant correlations for an interval of several frames. Also, this burstiness depends on the time scale to evaluate the coded information variation. In this paper, the bit rate encoded information is evaluated frame by frame. Rate variation caused by the video signal line scanning is assumed to be smoothed out before packet assembly.

In this paper the simulation model used to generate the (VBR) video coded traffic is a continuous-state discrete-time stochastic process. A first order Autoregressive (AR) markov process X(n) that takes into consideration the autocorrelation of the sequence is used. The definition of the AR process is as follows [23]:

$$X(n) = aX(n) + bW(n) \qquad (1)$$

Where X(n) is the bit rate during the n th frame, W(n) is a sequence of independent Gaussian random variables where a and b are constants.

Voice Arrival Process: This process possesses correlations among the number of packets arrivals in adjacent time intervals. This complexity is due to the bursty nature of the packet arrival process from single voice source [8]. The ON/OFF periodic process is used to model the voice source, where both ON and OFF time periods are assumed to be exponentially distributed random variables with means $1/\alpha$ and $1/\beta$, respectively. During the ON period a fixed number of packets is generated, each of duration T. Backpropagation networks have basically three layers, the input layer, hidden layer(s), and an output layer. Each layer contains a number of processing elements (PE), and is fully connected to the next layer. The input data vector is presented via the input layer which fans out the input data without making calculations. The data flows along the connections toward the hidden layer(s) and the output layer. The final result of this operation is that the input data vector is transformed (mapped) into some corresponding output vector at the output layer. Each PE in a hidden or output layer has a connection from each PE in the preceding layer. Associated with each of these connections is an adaptive weight. The output of a PE in a hidden or output layer is calculated by applying an activation function to the weighted sum of the input to that PE. Various activation functions such as S-shaped functions (sigmoid) and bump function (Gaussian), [19] are available.

During the learning phase of the network, the actual output data vector is compared to the desired output data vector, and the errors between these two vectors are calculated. The error values are then used to calculate the new wights for all output and hidden layers PEs and thereby reduce the error in the network output. This process is repeated until the mapping from the input vector to the output vector has been trained to the desired accuracy. The idea is to find a set of weight values that result in maximum accuracy and minimum error. The error criterion used by backpropagation networks is the Mean Squared Error (MSE) [25].

The role of the NN, in this application, is to capture the unknown complex relation between the past and future values of the traffic. In other word, the NN is employed as an adaptive predictor that learns the stochastic properties of the traffic. Figure (1) illustrates the basic idea in training a NN to act as a predictor. The packet arrival process, from the source(s), is represented by the data vector [H(i+m)] which is the NN target output vector. [H(i+m)] provides the NN with the bit-rate information from which the predictions will be made. The NN predicts the bit-rate variations by exploiting the inherent correlations that exist among the arrivals in the packet arrival process. For training purpose, the input data vector [(H(i)] to the NN, is the delayed value of the data vector [H(i+m)]. The NN, then tries to match the target output data vector [H(i+m)] with its predicted output data vector [Ĥ(i+m)] by adjusting its weights. It, then, follows that when the input to the NN bypasses the delay unit, the output vector [Ĥ(i+m)] is a prediction of the values the traffic will have in the future. The delay unit, shown in figure (1), delays its input [H(i+m)] for m time steps. Assuming that the NN requires a negligible amount of time to compute its output from its input, then the NN, after training, provides estimates for the values of traffic [Ĥ(i+m)] m steps in the future. This approach to adaptive prediction rests on the assumption of a parameterized class of models for functional relationship between the current and past values of the traffic and its

later values, or equivalently between earlier values of the traffic and its current values.

Figure (2) Shows the backpropagation NN structures used in this paper. The offered traffic to the NN is the multimedia traffic resulting from superposition of N video sources and M voice sources. The NN model used is

$$[\hat{H}(i+m)] = NN_f\{[H(i)], [W]\} \qquad (2)$$

NN_f denotes neural network transfer function, where [W] presents the weight matrices of the hidden and output layers. The vector [H(i)] can be used to present the instantaneous values of bit-rate over the past measurement period (T_m) up to the present instant i. Alternatively, the same vector [H(i)] can be used to represent the count process N(0,t) which measures the number of packet arrivals in time (0,t). In this paper, the count process N(0,t) is used for traffic descripdor in ATM networks due to its robustness against the delay variability of the packets interarrival times. Thus, the vector [H(i)] consists of m samples of bit-rate process or m samples of the count process. These samples are obtained by sampling the arrival process at every sampling period (T_s). [$\hat{H}(i+m)$] is the output vector from the NN, presenting the expected traffic over the next measurement period (T_m), see figure (3). It then follows that,

$$T_m = m * T_s \qquad (3)$$

The Neural Network input traffic pattern [H(i)] is expressed as

$$[H(i)] = \begin{bmatrix} h(i) \\ h(i-1) \\ . \\ . \\ . \\ h(i-m-1) \end{bmatrix} \qquad (4)$$

where h(i) is the value of h(t) at the sampling instant i expressed in packets/sec. The target traffic pattern for the next m measurement intervals [H(i+m)] is expressed as

$$[H(i+m)] = \begin{bmatrix} h(i+m) \\ h(i+m-1) \\ . \\ . \\ . \\ h(i+1) \end{bmatrix} \qquad (5)$$

where m represents the number PEs in the NN input and output layers.

The measurement period T_m, and the sampling period T_s have a direct effect on the NN structure and complexity. The NN can characterize the traffic over an arbitrary length measurement interval T_m. However, increasing T_m while maintaining a small number of samples, within it, will give a poor prediction. Because, in this case, the number of samples in the input traffic pattern (equal to m) will not be sufficient to capture the fluctuations of the arrival process. On the other hand, increasing T_m and decreasing T_s (i.e., increasing number of samples) will give an excellent prediction, at the expense of a massive increase in the number of PEs in the NN. Increasing the number of PEs of the NN leads to a prolonged training time of the NN (the training time of the backpropagation is proportional to the number of PEs). Needless to mention, the complexity of the NN physical realization will be magnified by several orders of magnitude. So firstly, T_m should be selected to give a reasonable prediction window. For example, T_m is chosen to match the renewal period of 1 sec. for the voice traffic, whereas it could be set to one frame length for the video traffic. Secondly, T_s should be selected such that the input traffic vector [H(i)] would reveal the bit-rate fluctuations of the arrival process during the measurement interval. In the mean time, a reasonable number of PEs in the selected NN architecture is maintained.

In order to best select the sampling interval T_s, typical N video sources are simulated and their aggregate arrival process is observed at every T_s. We selected a (VBR) video source produces 30 frame/sec. Several experiments have been performed using different values for N and T_s

The power spectral density [26] for the sampled traffic was calculated for each experiment as shown in figure (4) and (5). It was found that the maximum frequency component of the autocorrelation function of the arrival process to be 15 Hz. In this paper, the sampling interval T_s , for the video traffic, was selected to be 1/30 sec. (1/number of frame per second). This result is expected since we choose a video source produces 30 frame/sec, and the coding information is taken to be constant during the frame. This means that observing the video traffic at every 1/30 sec will guarantee that the obtained sampled version of the video arrival process captures all correlations contained in the actual video traffic.

For the voice traffic it was shown in [27] that 10 msec. sampling interval is sufficient to capture all variations of the voice arrival process. For the multimedia traffic resulting from multiplexing of N video sources and M voice sources, it is clear that sampling interval of 1/30 sec will not be sufficient to capture the voice traffic fluctuations, however, taking the sampling interval $T_s = 10$ msec makes sure that the instantaneous variations for both

video traffic and voice traffic will be captured.

The proposed model was verified by matching the statistical characteristics of the arrival process to those of the proposed NN model. The arrival process is a correlated non-renewal process and can be characterized by several parameters such as the mean arrival rate, the variance of the number of packet arrivals, the index of dispersion for intervals (IDI), the index of dispersion for counts (IDC), the autocorrelation R(n) of the number of packet arrivals and the third moment of the number of packet arrivals. The variance of the number of packet arrivals in an interval t V(t), the IDC, and the R(n) were used to measure how well the output process, from the NN, matched the actual arrival process. These parameters were chosen since they could best capture the increase in the variance of the arrival process over the sum of consecutive intervals [5].

Let the count process N(0,t) denote the number of packet arrivals in interval (0,t). Let $M_i(t)$ be the ith moment of N(0,t), it then follows that:

$$M_i(t) = E[N^i(0, t)] \qquad (6)$$

where the variance of the number of arrivals in (0,t), V(t) is given by

$$V(t) = M_2(t) - M_1^2(t) \qquad (7)$$

The index of dispersion for counts satisfies

$$I(t) = \frac{V(t)}{M_1(t)} \qquad (8)$$

The autocorrelation R(n) is defined as follows:

$$R(n) = \frac{E[(x(m) - A)(x(n+m) - A]}{Var[x(m)]} \qquad (9)$$

where x(m) is the number of packets arrivals during the m th interval, E[.] is the expectation, var[.] is the variance, and A is the mean of x(m). A detailed calculation of V(t) , I(t), and R(n) is mentioned in the next section. In performing this verification, the NN is trained to predict the count process over the next measurement interval. The traffic descriptor used in this,case is the number of packets arrivals in a consecutive intervals of length T_s.

III. Simulation Results

Extensive simulations were performed to obtain the NN data set, for both training and production phases, and also to assess the performance of various NNs architectures.

The packet arrival process, resulting from superposition of N packetized video sources and M packetized voice sources, was simulated on a Sun Sparc station 330 using the C language.

In the simulation of the video source, the first order autoregressive mentioned in section II is used. The parameter used in this model are [23]: a=0.8781, b=0.1108, the mean of W(n) is 4.3 Mbps, and the variance of W(n) is unity.

In the simulation of the voice source, the packet generation process of each voice source is modeled exactly as in [27]. The parameter used in this model are: mean active duration $1/\alpha=350$ msec, mean silence duration $1/\beta=650$ msec, fixed packetization period T=16 msec. As mentioned in section II, the video arrival process is sampled every $T_s=1/30$ sec while the multimedia arrival process are sampled every $T_s=10$ msec.

To generate the NN data set, the simulation model were run for 30 min operating time and about 100 million packets were generated. In prediction of the video traffic, the sampling period T_s was chosen to be 1/30 sec. Whereas in prediction of the multimedia traffic we used $T_s=10$ msec.

Two simulation runs were performed. In the first one, [H(i)] and [H(i+m)] were generated by sampling the arrival stream, at every T_s, using the bit-rate as a traffic descriptor. Whereas in the second one, [H(i)] and [H(i+m)] were generated by sampling the count process N(0,t) at every T_s. Also, during the second run, the variance of the number of arrivals V(t), the IDC, and R(n) were calculated by dividing the simulation time into adjacent intervals each of length KT_s where (K=1,2,....). Let N_{KL} be the number of packet arrivals in the Lth interval. Then the variance $V(KT_s)$ is:

$$V(KT_s) = n_K^{-1} \sum_{L=1}^{n_k} N_{KL}^2 - \left(n_K^{-1} \sum_{L=1}^{n_k} N_{KL} \right)^2 \quad (10)$$

Where n_K is an integer division of the simulation time by K [2]. Whereas, the IDC is given by

$$I(KT_s) = \frac{V(KT_s)}{\left(n_k^{-1} \sum_{L=1}^{n_k} N_{KL} \right)} \quad (11)$$

The autocorrelation R(n) was calculated by forming a vector (V) such that the elements of this vector present the number of packets arrivals during the consecutive intervals (each of length T_s). The XCORR() and COV() functions of the MATLAB signal processing tools [28] were used to calculate R(n) as follows:

$$R(n) = \frac{XCORR(V, 'biased')}{COV(V)} \quad (12)$$

The NNs were simulated using HNC Inc. EXPLORENET 3001 package [29]. Several experiments were performed using various backpropagation NNs architectures. During the work-course of this paper, two NNs architecture were used, they are called NN-1 and NN-2. NN-1 has 1 PE in the input layer, two slabs in the hidden layer (the first slab has 10 PEs, and the second slab has 5 PEs), and 1 PE on the output layer. NN-1 is referred to as (1,{10,5},1) while NN-2 is referred to as (5,{10,5},5). The activation functions of these NNs were selected to be sigmoid where the steepness parameter (a factor determines the non-linearity of the sigmoid function) was selected by trial and error method to obtain good results (in the sense of V(t), IDC, and R(n)).

IV. Numerical Results

In this section, we demonstrate the validity of the proposed NN model by comparing the numerical results obtained from this model to those obtained from the simulation model. Three experiments were performed to produce the results.

Experiment (1):
In this experiment, we used N=10, M=0 (ten video sources and no voice sources). NN-1 was used to predict the homogenous superposition video count arrival process over the next frame interval (m=1, $T_s=1/30$ sec). Figures (6) and (7) show that the predicted traffic, output from NN-1 has the same statistical characteristics as those of the actual input traffic.

Experiment (2):
In this experiment, we used N=1, M=1 (one video source and one voice source). NN-1 was used to predict the multimedia (heterogenous superposition process) count arrival process over the next sampling period (m=1, $T_s=10$ msec). Figures (8) and (9) show that NN-1 characterized and predicted the multimedia traffic with extreme accuracy. It is interesting to observe that NN-1 performance in this experiment is better than that in experiment (1), where it was exposed to video traffic only. This can be explained as follows:

The statistics of the multimedia traffic, resulted from superposition of one video source and one voice source, are dominated by the statistics of the single video source traffic as shown in figure (10). Where it shows the autocorrelation function of the multimedia traffic compared with those of the single video source traffic and single voice source traffic. It is clear that autocorrelation function of the multimedia traffic is very close to that of the single video source traffic. Hence, when we attempt to predict heterogenous multimedia traffic composite of one video and one voice, we actually attempt to predict the video arrival process, and since in this experiment the prediction window size, (m=1 with T_s =10 msec), was smaller than that for experiment (1), NN-1 performed better in this case.

Experiment (3):

In this experiment, we used N=1, M=1 (one video source and one voice source). NN-2 was used to predict the multimedia (heterogenous superposition process) count arrival process over the next five sampling period (m=5, T_s =10 msec). Figure (11) shows that NN-2 characterized and predicted the multimedia traffic with good accuracy. Since the prediction window size has been increased in experiment, we get certain prediction error compared with the results obtained in experiment (2).

V.Conclusions

Based upon the above experiments, we conclude that a suitable NN architecture can be chosen to characterize a specific type of traffic. After completing the training phase of the NN, it learns the PDF of the offered traffic. Hence, the NN can be used as an effective traffic descriptor. It describes the traffic by its actual PDF (instead of the approximated simple parameters such as the peak and mean bit-rates). In ATM networks, traffic management techniques require traffic parameters that can capture the various traffic characteristics. Adaptability to changes in the traffic characteristics is also important for robustness. The proposed model using the NNs is suitable for implementing an effective ATM traffic descriptor (UPC), since it can adaptively predict the traffic by learning the relationship between the past and the future traffic variations. The potential of the proposed model is demonstrated by its efficacious to predict the packet arrival process of the superposition of N video sources and M voice sources. The results show that NNs can be trained to learn the PDF of the arrival process hence it can function as an adaptive predictor.

References

[1] CCITT Recommendations, I series (B-ISDN), July 1992.

[2] K. Siriram, and W. Whitt "Characterizing superposition arrival processes in packet multiplexers for voice and data,"IEEE JSAC, Vol. SAC-4. NO. 6, Sept 1986.

[3] H. Heffes, and D. Lucantoni, "A Markov Modulated characterization packetized voice and data traffic and related statistical multiplexer performance," IEEE JSAC, Vol. SAC-4, NO. 6, Sept.1986.

[4] H. Yamada, and S. Sumita "A traffic measurement method and its application for cell loss probability estimation in ATM networks," IEEE JSAC, Vol 9, NO. 3, April 1991.

[5] I. Habib, and T. Saadawi "Multimedia Traffic characteristics in broadband networks," IEEE Comm. Mag. July 1992.

[6] K. Siriram, and D. Lucantoni "Traffic smoothing effects of bit dropping in a packet voice multiplexer," IEEE Trans. Comm, Vol. 37, No. 7, July 1989.

[7] H. Satio, and H. Yamada "Analysis of statistical multiplexing in ATM transport network," IEEE JSAC Vol. 9, NO. 3, April 1991.

[8] J Diagle, and J Langford "Models for analysis packet voice communications systems," IEEE JSAC, Vol. SAC-4, NO. 6, Sept. 1986.

[9] A. Baiocchi et al "Loss performance analysis of an ATM multiplexer loaded with high-speed on-off sources," IEEE JSAC, Vol. 9, NO. 3, April 1991.

[10] E. Rathgeb "Modeling and performance comparison of policing mechanisms for ATM networks," IEEE JSAC, Vol. 9, No. 3, April 1991.

[11] F. Denissen, E. Desmet, and G. H. Petit "The policing function in an ATM network," in Proc. 1990 Int. Zurich Sem. Digit. Commun., Zurich, MAR. 1990, PP. 131-144.

[12] Special section on neural networks, IEEE control sys. Mag., Apr. 1988.

[13] Bronoko soucek "Neural and concurrent real-time systems," the six generation, John Wiley & sons, Inc., 1989.

[14] T. Takahashi and Hiramatsu, " Integrated ATM traffic control by distributed neural networks.", in Proc. ISS'90, Stockholm, Sweden, May 1990, vol. III, PP. 54-65.

[15] A. Hiramatsu, "ATM communications network control by neural networks," IEEE Trans. neural networks, vol 1, PP. 122-130, 1990.

[16] A. Hiramatsu, "Integration of ATM call admission control and link capacity control by distributed neural networks," IEEE JSAC, Vol. 9, No. 7, Sept. 1991.

[17] B. Aazhang et al "Neural networks for multiuser detection in code-division multiple access communications," IEEE Trans. Comm, Vol. 40, NO. 7, July 1992.

[18] R. Lippmann "An introduction to computing with neural nets," IEEE Assp Mag., April 1987.

[19] R. Nielsen "Neurocomputing," Addison wesly publishing comp., 1989.

[20] R. Grunenfelder et al "Characterization of video codecs as autoregressive moving average processes and related queuing system performance," IEEE JSAC, Vol 9, No. 3, april 1991.

[21] M. Nomura, T. Fujii, and N. Ohta "Basic characteristics of variable rate video coding in ATM environment," IEEE JSAC, Vol. 7, No. 5, June 1989.

[22] H. Soon et al "Statistics od video signals for viewphone-type pictures," IEEE JSAC, Vol 7, No. 5, June 1989.

[23] B. Maglaris et al "Performance models of statistical multiplexing in packet video communications," IEEE Trans. Comm, Vol. 36, No. 7, July 1988.

[24] P. Sen et al "Models for packet switching of variable-bit-rate video sources," IEEE JSAC, Vol. 7, No. 5, June 1989.

[25] D. E. Rumelhart, J. L. McClellend, and PDP Research Group, "Parallel Distributed Processing," Vol I. Cambridge, MA: M.I.T. Press, 1986.

[26] J. Proakis, and G. Manolakis "Introduction to digital signal processing," Macmillan publishing comp., 1990.

[27] A. Tarraf, I. Habib, and T. saadawi "Characterization of packetized voice traffic in ATM networks using neural networks," Globecom'93.

[28] J. Little and L. Shure "Signal Processing Toolbox, for use with MATLAB," The MathWork, Inc, August 1988.

[29] HNC Inc. "HNC ExploreNET release 2.0 operating manual," 1991.

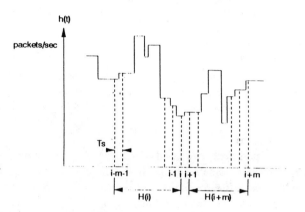

Fig. 3 The sampled superposition arrival process.

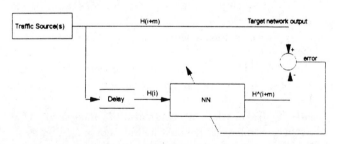

Fig.1 Using Neural Network for adaptive prediction

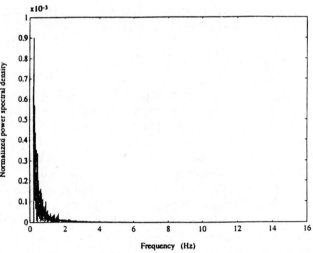

Fig. 4 The power spectral density of the video arrival process (N=10, Ts=1/30 sec)

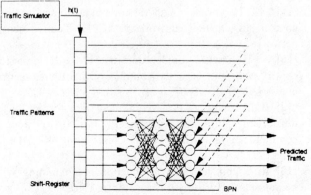

Fig. 2 Neural Network for traffic prediction.

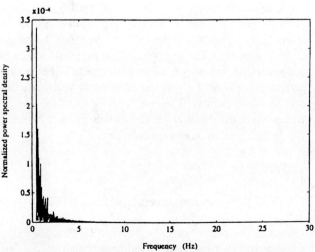

Fig. 5 The power spectral density of the video arrival process (N=10, Ts=1/60 sec)

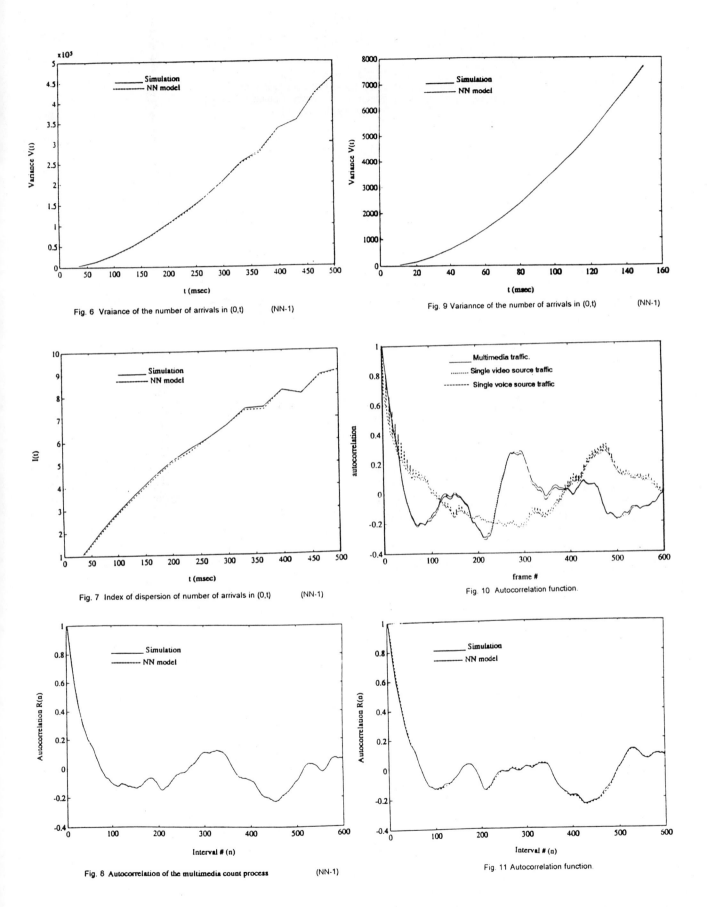

Fig. 6 Vraiance of the number of arrivals in (0,t) (NN-1)

Fig. 9 Variannce of the number of arrivals in (0,t) (NN-1)

Fig. 7 Index of dispersion of number of arrivals in (0,t) (NN-1)

Fig. 10 Autocorrelation function.

Fig. 8 Autocorrelation of the multimedia count process (NN-1)

Fig. 11 Autocorrelation function.

IMAGE COMPRESSION
USING LEARNED VECTOR QUANTIZATION

K. Ferens, W. Lehn, and W. Kinsner
Department of Electrical and Computer Engineering
University of Manitoba, Winnipeg, Manitoba, Canada R3T 2N2
E-Mail: ferens@ee.umanitoba.ca

ABSTRACT

This paper presents a study and implementation of still image compression using learned vector quantization. Grey scale, still images are compressed by 16:1 and transmitted at 0.5 bits per pixel, while maintaining a peak signal-to-noise ratio of 30 dB. The vector quantization is learned using Kohonen's self organizing feature map (SOFM). While not only being representative of the training set, the prototype vectors also serve as a basis for other histogram-similar images. Hence, these codebooks quantize other images not in the training set. Various optimization techniques are investigated. The effects of the uniform, linear, and cubic nested learning rate and neighborhood functions on rate of convergence are studied. Simulated annealing is applied to the SOFM network. By inserting impulses of high temperature at increasing time intervals, codebooks learn more quickly. Competitive learning, frequency sensitive competitive learning, and Kohonen's neighborhood learning are studied. An XView interface on the SUN SPARC Station 2 is built to facilitate a user interface, and to graphically illustrate the dynamic learning of the codebooks and vector-by-vector quantization and reconstruction of images.

I. INTRODUCTION

Image signal compression has attracted considerable attention, most notably in the field of multimedia communication [KFAG93, Kins91, Wall90]. The days of communicating ideas through text alone are coming to an end. People want to express themselves through text, graphics, sound, and moving images — everything and anything that will serve to get their message across more efficiently and effectively.

Communication via still images plays an important role in the graphics and moving images media. The use of images drastically improves the communication of ideas. But, with this improvement comes a very high and prohibitive price, data storage. For example, many universities, schools, and businesses carry a people database in which information on people is stored. This database is typically in the form of text only. If the database were enhanced with still images of head and shoulder pictures of people, the cost of storing this data would be prohibitively high. For instance, a university stores records on approximately 25, 000 students a year. If an 8-bit 256x256 image were taken of each individual, this would require $(25, 000)(256x256) = 1.6384$ GBytes of storage. Not only is the storage requirement unacceptable, but the cost of transmitting this data is also high. Transmitting large amounts of data through low bit-rate channels requires long periods of time. Finally, in this application, privacy and security are other problems associated with uncompressed data. Data compression can provide a natural source of data encryption.

Applications dealing with image identification do not require high quality. Human beings can identify facial patterns very effectively, especially in noisy circumstances. Some information in these images can be removed, while still maintaining sufficient quality for identification. This is an application of still image signal compression.

There are many data compression schemes available for data and signal compression. A taxonomy of the major data and signal compression techniques is given in [Kins91]. When selecting a particular data compression scheme, it is helpful to consider the type of data that is of interest. Images are inherently imperfect data. That is, minor losses of data (distortion or noise) in images are tolerable to the human eye. For example, it has been established that we cannot distinguish brightness levels less than 2% of 8-bit resolution [Lehn91]. Furthermore, our perception plays a major role in our visualization of the real world. When we observe images and store them in our memory, we are most likely performing some kind of compression. If we did not do such compression, the amount of data we would have to store in order to recall ordinary events would overflow our memory banks in a very short time.

Since images can be treated as imperfect data, we are free to choose a lossy compression scheme, i.e., the decompressed image will have some degree of distortion. Moreover, because of the inherent nature of the problem, we would tend to choose a compression scheme that mimics the compression that is involved in our, i.e., human, image processing system. This leads to a choice hereby called image compression using learned vector quantization (discussed in Section 2.1) incorporating the use of an artificial neural network (to mimic human data compression as discussed in Section 2.2).

II. VECTOR QUANTIZATION

Vector quantization is a non-uniform and many-to-one mapping, Ψ, of a vector space, V, into another vector space, S. Many elements of V are mapped into a single element of S. In this way, the space V is partitioned into a number of regions equal to the number of elements in S. There is a non-uniform number of elements of V that are assigned to a region. Each region generally contains a different number of elements from V. The mapping is referred to as an equivalence relation. Many vectors are mapped into a single region because they are equivalent in some sense. Information in V is removed in the mapping, and as such, the mapping is a lossy data or signal compression technique.

As a consequence of choosing a lossy compression scheme (vector quantization), we must consider the associated measurements of compression and distortion. The amount of compression of an image can be measured by a compression ratio or a compression rate. The *compression ratio* (CR) is defined as the number of pixels transmitted or stored divided by the actual number of pixels in the original image, as given by Eq. 2.1.

$$CR = \frac{\text{Pixels transmitted}}{\text{Original pixels}} \qquad (2.1)$$

In other words, the compression ratio gives the memory savings in that it tells us the size of the compressed file is CR (CR <= 1) times the original file. The *compression rate* (R) is defined as the number of pixels in a vector divided into the number of bits required to represent that vector (bits/pixel, bpp), as given by Eq. 2.2. For example, if each original vector consists of one byte and there were no compression, i.e., the original file were transmitted through the communications channel unmodified, then the compression rate, $R = 8$.

$$R = \frac{\text{Bits required to represent vector}}{\text{Pixels in a vector}} \qquad (2.2)$$

The quality of an image can be evaluated through a subjective evaluation and an objective evaluation. An objective evaluation involves a *peak signal-to-noise ratio* (PSNR), as given by Eq. 2.3, where MSE is defined as the point-wise Euclidean distance between original and reconstructed pixel.

$$PSNR = 10 \log_{10} \left\{ \frac{255^2}{MSE} \right\} \qquad (2.3)$$

Notice that the argument of the log function is the highest signal-to-noise ratio possible, since the original signal is assumed to be at maximum brightness throughout, thus the name peak SNR. The PSNR reduces variability between other experimenter's measurements. For example, two pairs of images (each consisting of an original and a decompressed version) may have the same MSE. However, one of the original images may be brighter than the other, and this would give a misleading SNR.

The *distortion measure* is the cost of representing an image vector by a prototype vector. While there are many metrics that can be used, perhaps the best choice is the Euclidean metric. When we view images, it is the intensity of the image that conveys most of the information. Intensity is related to energy, and the Euclidean metric measures energy. But the Euclidean metric can be deceiving sometimes. For these cases other measures can be taken [Kins91].

Having established the compression type and measurements of compression and distortion, the next section discusses how images, image vectors, regions, and prototype vectors apply to vector quantization.

2.1 Image Vector Quantization (VQ)

There are three stages to image VQ, i.e., prototype creation, image compression and transmission, and image reception and decompression. The image is defined as an m rows by n columns array of 8-bit pixels. Thus, the uncompressed image requires mn bytes of storage.

In the first step, the prototypes must be developed. Given an image, instead of representing the image in terms of m by n pixels, group together an array of local pixels, and call each array a vector IV_i, where the maximum value of i depends on the number of pixels, q, chosen to comprise a vector. Call the set of all such vectors, V:

$$V = \left\{ IV_i; \quad i = 1, 2, 3, \dots, \frac{mn}{q} \right\} \qquad (2.1)$$

where,

$$IV_i = (p_1, p_2, p_3, \cdots, p_q) \qquad (2.2)$$

Some of these vectors, $IV_i \in V$, will be similar in some respects. For example, many vectors may be extracted from a uniform area of an image. A statistically similar feature of these vectors may be very simply a correlation of their brightness levels, or it can be some unknown statistic. This leads to the following idea. From the set, V, that contains all such vectors from a certain image, determine r ($r \ll \frac{mn}{q}$) fundamental features exhibited by the set. The smaller the number of features (i.e., smaller r), the greater is the compression, because, to each feature, the vectors, IV_i, are assigned on the basis that they most closely exemplify that feature. In other words, the set of vectors, V, is partitioned into r distinct sets, S_i. Thus, each subset, S_i, represents a certain fundamental feature, that is exhibited by its member vectors.

$$\text{Partition of } V = \{ S_i; \quad i = 1, 2, 3, \dots, r \} \qquad (2.3)$$

Represent each subset, S_i, by a prototype vector, call it PV_i. The prototype vector, PV_i, is chosen in such a way as to optimally represent the image vectors, IV_i, that have been assigned to the feature denoted by the feature set, S_i. This prototype vector may or may not be an original member of the set, S_i. In this way each of the vectors in subset, S_i, is rounded off or quantized to a prototype

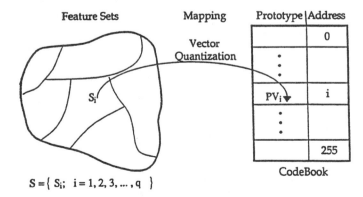

Fig. 2.1. Vector quantization. Statistically similar image vectors are collected into non-overlapping sets, S_i. Some function determines a representative vector, PV_i, a prototype vector for each set.

617

vector. In other words, the assignment acts as a many-to-one mapping of the image vectors.

The set of prototype vectors constitutes the codebook. This codebook contains r vectors, each of which has an address, $(1, 2, ... , r)$. Because the number of selected features is much smaller than the number of vectors in the image, the number of bits required to represent the address of a prototype vector is much smaller than the number of bits required to represent an image vector. For example, this paper presents a scheme where 128-bits are required to represent an image vector, ($q=16$ implies ($\Rightarrow$) $16 \times 8 = 128$ bits) while only 8-bits are required to represent an address of a prototype vector (256 selected features). This represents a compression ratio of 16-to-1. The codebook is resident at both the transmitter and receiver.

Now that the prototype vectors have been determined, the second step of VQ consists of image compression and transmission. Each vector in the original image is compared one-at-a-time to each of the prototype vectors in the codebook. The prototype that most closely resembles the input vector is selected, and its *address* is transmitted through the channel. A sequence of mn/q (8-bit) addresses is transmitted, because there are mn/q vectors in the image. Thus, the original image consisting of mn pixels is represented by $8mn/q$ bits rather than $8mn$ bits. The compression ratio is q.

The final step of VQ consists of receiving the compressed image, i.e., a sequence of mn/q addresses, and decompressing it. Each of the mn/q addresses one-at-a-time is used to look up the corresponding prototype vector in the codebook, and the sequence of these prototype vectors is used to reconstruct the image.

Note that the decompression at the receiving station does not undo exactly the compression performed at the transmitter. This is because of the many-to-one mapping. For each feature represented by set, S_i, there accumulates an error equivalent to the sum of the differences between the exemplar image vectors belonging to set, S_i, and the prototype vector. The total error for the entire image is the sum of all feature set errors. This error is called round off error or distortion. One of the main objectives in vector quantization is to use a codebook that minimizes the distortion.

This is more easily said than done, because the equivalence relation is unknown. The problem is determining the statistical properties of the input data. These statistics are generally not known. For example, this paper deals with compressing head and shoulder images of people. We cannot possibly obtain all images of people that have occupied this planet. Therefore, we cannot obtain exact statistics. Even if we were to find a statistical property correlating or clustering the vectors of an image in some sense, we are not guaranteed that this property is similar to one of the, perhaps, many properties we use when we perform image identification. This is the ultimate goal. We are trying to discover the features we use when we try to identify images. In our research, this amounts to applying an artificial neural network (ANN) to the task of prototype determination, as discussed in the next section.

2.2. Learning Prototypes Using Competitive ANNs

The prototypes in vector quantization can be *learned* by competitive artificial neural networks. There are a few variations of competitive learning networks, each of which were introduced in

order to solve a problem associated with the fundamental competitive network [Kins91, AKCM90, McAR90, NaFe88, TrMe90]. The most basic of these variations is hard Competitive Learning (CL). One problem associated with CL is underutilization of prototypes. This means, once learning is complete, not all codebook vectors are utilized equally. Now, if a so called prototype is used but once in quantizing an image, we would most likely not notice its presence in the image. Furthermore, if a codebook vector is used very little, then it hardly fits the definition of a prototype, that being of a vector that describes many patterns in an input image space. In this case the network is discriminating too much. The underutilized prototype is most likely specific to a certain image, not a common feature of many images. This is not very efficient use of the codebook.

There are two possible solutions. First, we could remove all of the codebook vectors that have a utilization frequency less than some threshold, say one. This means that the size of the codebook would decrease, the compression ratio would increase, and we would, perhaps, not even notice a change in the resulting quality. Second, we could incorporate a constraint into the network that ensured that all vectors in the codebook were being used equally and uniformly. This can be implemented by decreasing the probability that a currently frequent winner neuron wins in the future by weighting its subsequent metric calculations with a parameter reflecting the number of times it had won a decision in the past. This would tend to ensure that when an image is decompressed, all codebook vectors would be used with about the same frequency, so that the codebook can be said to be efficient in the utilization sense.

Frequency sensitive competitive learning (FSCL) and Kohonen's self-organizing-feature-map (SOFM) are networks that address the underutilization problem. FSCL uses a "frequency of winning" parameter in the similarity metric. This decreases the probability that a frequently winning neuron will win a competition in a future presentation of an image vector, and so increases the probability that a not so frequently winning neuron will win a competition. The SOFM network uses the idea of a neighborhood. One main difference between FSCL and SOFM is that the neighborhood method induces an organization in the output neuron space, while FSCL has no such organization. Since all of these networks architectures are basically equivalent, except for the frequency and neighborhood additions, only a detailed description of the SOFM is given here.

Figure 2.2 shows the architecture of the SOFM neural network. The input layer consists of 16 neurons, each of which has 8-bit resolution. These are the nodes through which the 8-bit image pixels are input. The input layer is connected to each output neuron through a weight vector. Thus, each output neuron has 16 weights connected to it. Each weight vector will train to become a prototype for a particular feature that is to be extracted from the image training data. The output layer is configured as a ring, and it consists of 256 neurons, each of which is also of 8-bit resolution. The placement of the output neuron in the physical ring determines the address that is transmitted through the communication channel after image compression.

The SOFM is trained using a sequence of image vectors. Each vector consists of sixteen 8-bit pixels extracted from a square patch of the image, as shown in the bottom of Fig. 2.2. During each presentation of an input vector, a net input to each output neuron is

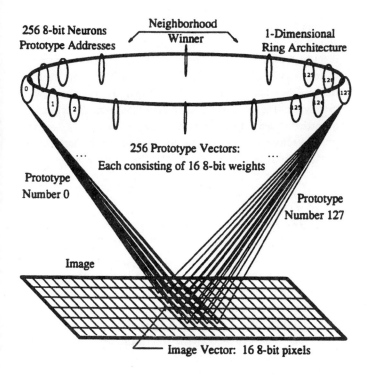

Fig. 2.2. Ring architecture of the competitive learning network.

calculated, and one winner is chosen based on a similarity measure, i.e., the winner is the neuron whose weight vector most closely resembles the input vector. The winner neuron along with its currently defined neighborhood become active. The winner's neighborhood is the set of neurons within the currently defined neighborhood distance from both the left side and right side on the ring (refer to Fig. 2.2). The weight vector connected to the winner and the weight vectors connected to the neighborhood neurons are updated by bringing their 8-bit values closer to the 8-bit value of the input vector. Many such input vectors are presented, and a corresponding amount of updates are made to the weights. Because there are far more input vectors than weight vectors, the weight vectors cannot fully satisfy all of the input vectors. Rather, the network is forced to extract higher order dimensional features of the input image. For each feature that is extracted, for each set of input vectors that are associated with a feature, the network learns a weight vector, i.e., the prototype of that feature.

Notice that the feature extraction is done in an organized way, because each extracted feature is mapped in a orderly fashion at the output of the network. All input vectors the network deems similar, i.e., belonging to the same feature, will activate a certain localized portion of the ring to a smooth degree of belongingness.

The following steps give a detailed description of the training procedure of the SOFM algorithm:

STEP 1: Initialize each weight in the weight matrix to the mean value of the pixels in the image plus some small random perturbation, *RP*.

STEP 2: Segment the image into 4x4 pixel square arrays and call each a vector of 16 pixels (elements). Randomly select one of the *mn*/16 vectors and present it to the network. *NTV* is a count of the number of training vectors that have been currently presented.

Alternatively, select a random number and use this as an index for forming a square vector from the input image. There are *mn* such vectors. Present this vector to the network. (The former method is implemented.)

STEP 3: Compute the distance between each weight vector and the input vector, as given by Eq. 2.4:

$$d_2 = \sum_{i=1}^{16} (IV_i - w_{ij})^2 \qquad \text{for } j = 1, \dots , 256 \qquad (2.4)$$

where IV_i is the ith pixel in the input vector, and w_{ij} is the connection strength impinging the jth output neuron and originating from the ith input pixel. w_j is the weight vector connecting the input vector, IV, to the jth output neuron.

STEP 4: Select as the Winner that output neuron whose weight vector w_{j^*} is closest to the input vector, IV.

$$\text{Winner} \Leftarrow w_{j^*} \Leftarrow d_2(min)_j = \min_{1 \leq j \leq 256} \left\{ \sum_{i=1}^{16} (IV_i - w_{ij})^2 \right\} \qquad (2.5)$$

where w_{j^*} is the weight vector yielding the minimum distance.

STEP 5: Update the weight vector w_{j^*} connected to the Winner and the weight vectors connected to the neighborhood neurons of the Winner according Eq. 2.6:

$$w_{ij}(new) = w_{ij}(old) + \alpha(n, NTV)[IV_i(t) - w_{ij}(old)] \qquad (2.6)$$

The learning rate function $\alpha(n, NTV)$ depends on both the (neighborhood) physical displacement of a neuron (n) in the ring from the Winner and the number of training vectors (NTV) presented so far, as shown in Fig. 2.3. w_{ij} is the weight vector connected to neuron n.

STEP 6: Update the neighborhood function as shown in Fig. 2.3. If NTV = EOT, (end-of-training) then stop; otherwise goto STEP 2.

2.3. Termination of Training Criterion

Notice that the above algorithm continues iteration until EOT, which is defined as a pre-specified number of presentations of image vectors. Kohonen has shown that the algorithm converges, but parameters governing the rate of convergence are not well understood. A way of determining the EOT could be to temporarily stop training at some point, and measure the total distortion. This would require performing the entire compression of the image and its decompression to measure the total distortion. If the total distortion is above a designed threshold, then training resumes, until at some other point when the calculation of the total distortion is below the threshold. But this would require prohibitively too much time. For example, a 512x512 images requires (512x512/16)x256 compares for a codebook of 256 prototypes. On a SPARC Station 2, this requires about 5 minutes of computing time.

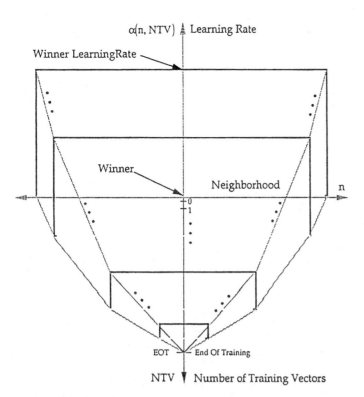

Fig. 2.3. Learning rate and neighborhood versus input vector.

A better way of determining approximately the total distortion is to take advantage of the training cycle. In the training cycle, distortions are already being calculated in order to determine the winner. We can choose a window whose width is equal to the number of vectors in the image. In this window the approximate total distortion is given by the sum of the distortions of a sequence of training vectors. Note that this does not give the exact total distortion, because the training vectors are presented randomly.

III. SYSTEM DESCRIPTION

The competitive learning neural networks were implemented on a SPARC 2 workstation incorporating a graphical user interface (GUI). The programs for the learning, compressing, decompressing, and other utilities were written in the C language, and the GUI was written using the XVIEW interface. Figure 3.1 shows the main window of the application. The left hand side displays the original image used for extracting vectors for training, or for quantizing, while the right hand side shows the quantized image. The rectangle image at the bottom of the window shows the prototypes. The two small boxes between the original image and the quantized image represent scaled versions of the currently extracted image vector from the original image, and the winner prototype extracted from the prototype rectangle. The small rectangles are 4x4 pixels, while the prototypes in the codebook are shown as 1x16 column vectors. This is done in order to display the continuous nature of the map.

There are basically three modes of operation, learning, quantizing, and decompression. However, decompression is incorporated as the last stage of both learning and quantizing. So, in the application, there are only two modes, learning and quantizing. In the learning mode, a 4x4 pixel square image vector is randomly extracted from the original image, and a scaled version is displayed in the left small box. This vector is then compared against all of the prototypes in the codebook. The winner prototype is determined, and it, as well as its neighborhood, are updated according to the algorithm described in Section 2.2. A scaled version of the winner neuron is displayed in the right small box. The prototype vector then is placed into the quantized image square at the same relative position from which the original image vector was extracted. This procedure is continued until all of the epochs are completed. During training the progressive nature of the learning is graphically displayed.

Various network parameters are selectable through the *Configuration* dialog panel. For example, the learning rate, winner threshold, number of training cycles, initial neighborhood can all be specified at the start of or during training.

For educational purposes, the learning speed, the display frequency, and the quantization speed can be controlled through the *Display* control panel. For example, the self organization of the codebook can be visually observed at any speed, from single stepping to full speed. This shows the dynamic behaviour of the network. One can study the effects of different neighborhood

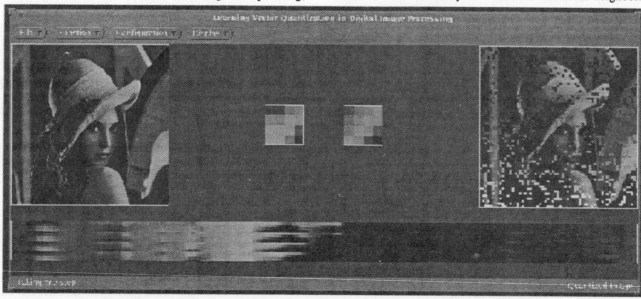

Fig. 3.1. Main window in the GUI for learning vector quantization of images. Training of the Lena image in progress.

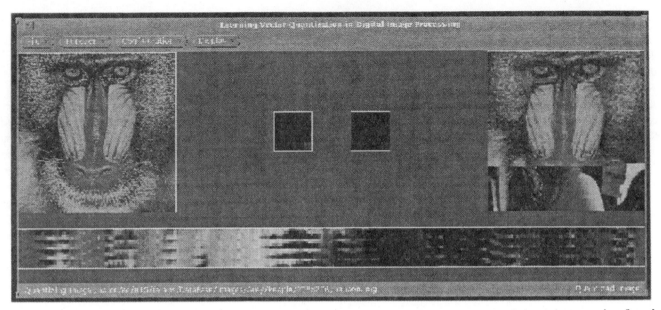

Fig. 3.2. Main window in the GUI for learning vector quantization of images. Quantization of the baboon image using Lena's codebook in progress.

reduction schemes, and of different learning rate schedules. The coarse tuning and fine tuning of the prototypes is obviously evident. Also, one can see the difference between the codebooks formed by FSCL and SOFM, the former being random, while the latter being a smooth transition of energy.

Once the network has learned on some training image, then other non-training images may be opened for quantization. For example, Fig. 3.2, shows the baboon being quantized with Lena's prototypes. With some theory of competitive learning networks discussed, and an application in which they may be implemented built, the next section discusses the experiments.

IV. IMAGE COMPRESSION EXPERIMENTS

The experiments part of this paper are intended to empirically substantiate and provide motivation for the ideas and methods described in the algorithm description of the LVQ technique of this report. The results are judged based on both objective and subjective criteria. The first experiment is aimed to establish validity of the procedure. The next experiment establishes a base level quantizer from which other quantizers can be judged. This is followed by discrimination and generalization experiments.

4.1 Memorization

If the size of the codebook of prototype vectors is exactly equal to the size of the original image, then it is reasonable to expect any compression algorithm to converge and be capable of reproducing the image exactly, i.e., reproduce the image exactly with no distortion. To show this, a 64x64x8 image (i.e., 64x64 pixel image, each pixel containing one of 256 grey levels) is learned by the codebook with a pixel size of 64x64x8. Each of the $64^2/16$ input image vectors consists of 16 pixels. Each vector is extracted from the image as a square array of 4x4 pixels. Each vector is presented once to the network; i.e., so that there are exactly $64^2/16$ presentations. The neighborhood is set to one. This type of learning is called hard competitive learning. Since each winner

weight vector is updated with a learning rate of 1.0, it exactly equals the input vector after being updated. The 8-bit address of this weight vector is transmitted. There are $64^2/16$ such addresses. Therefore, the resulting compression ratio is $64^2/16:64^2/16$ or 1:1, and the compression rate is $8/16 = 0.5$. The PSNR is infinite, i.e., the mean squared error is zero. The codebook has memorized the original image.

4.2 Linear Vector Quantization (VQ)

When the size of the codebook is smaller than the original image, it is reasonable to assume that distortion will be produced. The smaller the codebook the greater the amount of distortion. This is because the mapping from the original image to the codebook is many-to-one, and the "many" variable becomes increasingly larger for smaller codebooks. Hence, a main objective of any compression scheme is to minimize the distortion for a given compression ratio. To this end, it is useful to introduce a compression algorithm (i.e., a mapping) that utilizes the most straight forward, simplest, and fastest compression. While this primitive compression scheme does not produce very good results, it represents a starting point from which other techniques can be judged.

Perhaps one of the simplest many-to-one compression algorithms is the linear vector quantizer. The linear vector quantizer maps much like the linear scalar quantizer. In the linear scalar quantizer, each continuous analog sample ranging in value from –V to +V is quantized to a discrete digital number. We may say that the real signal is rounded off to the nearest integer determined by the resolution. In linear vector quantization, an entire vector consisting of generally different valued components is rounded off to a nearest vector consisting of equal valued components.

In particular, a codebook of size 256x8 is generated by assigning a number between 0 and 255 to the 256 vectors. Each vector consists of 16 pixels, each of which take on the grey level assigned to the vector, as shown in Fig. 4.2. This codebook is used to compress a 512×512×8 monochrome image of Lena

(Fig. A1). The compression scheme used is the same as that described in Section 4.2. Each extracted vector of 16 pixels from the original image is compared in the Euclidean distance sense to all vectors of the codebook. The index of the codebook vector most similar to the input vector is saved to a file. The compressed image is decompressed by a simple look up procedure as discussed in Section 4.3, and the result is shown in Fig. A2.

LINEAR VECTOR QUANTIZER CODEBOOK	
Vector	Values of the 16 pixels
0	(0, 0, 0, 0, 0, 0, 0, 0, 0, 0, 0 ,0, 0, 0, 0, 0)
1	(1, 1, 1, 1, 1, 1, 1, 1, 1, 1, 1, 1, 1, 1, 1, 1)
⋮	⋮
255	(255, 255, 255, ... , 255)

Fig. 4.2. Linear vector quantizer codebook.

The resulting image achieves a PSNR of 25.9db. Observing both images, it is noted that the smallest unit of information in the original image of Lena is a pixel (i.e., one 8-bit grey level), while the smallest building block of the decompressed image is a 4x4 pixel square. All smooth and uniform areas of the original image are mapped quite well in the decompressed image, while sharp lines and edges are approximated by a staircase function (coarse). This leads to a reasonable suggestion that this method would perhaps be best suited for large images that do not have too many sharp lines or edges. This does not include a wide variety of images. However, while this method has its definite limitations, its usefulness is the establishment of a starting point from which Kohonen's self organizing feature map of learning the codebook for vector quantization may be judged.

4.3 Codebook Learning Optimization

From the starting point established above (i.e., PSNR = 25.9db) we perform several experiments applying Kohonen's self organizing map to learn the codebook. We start from the simplest description of the procedure as described by Kohonen [Koho90] and continue by adding complexity in the form of modifying system parameters with the objective of improving the PSNR. The objective of this part of the experiments is to change certain system parameters and study how these changes affect the performance. This paper examines three such system parameters, the learning rate, neighborhood, and number of training cycles (epochs).

4.3.1 Learning Rate

In this paper the learning rate function of Kohonen's SOFM depends on two variables, namely, the number of vectors presented, k, and the neighborhood, n. The shape of the learning rate as a function of the neighborhood, n, with k held constant, represents short time learning or a nested learning rate. For each vector presented, each weight vector that is to be updated is done so with this nested learning rate function. The most basic way of doing this is as previously shown in Fig. 2.3, i.e., by updating all weight vectors connected to the neurons in the neighborhood by an equal amount. Alternatively, it seems reasonable and intuitive to assume that each weight vector associated with the neurons in the currently defined neighborhood should be updated in such a way as to reflect their distance from the winner neuron. In other words, the weight vector connected to the winner neuron should be updated with the maximum learning rate, while the weight vectors connected to neurons that are increasingly farther away from the winner neuron should be updated by proportionally decreasing amounts. The motivation for this idea is in part biological, i.e., in biological neuronal signals, when a central neuron is active, the weights connected to the neighboring neurons are affected by a characteristic function known as a "Mexican hat". This decreasing learning rate as a function of the distance from the winner neuron can be modelled different ways. In this paper, three nested learning rate schedules are compared.

As already mentioned the first learning rate function implemented is the nested step function. Figure 4.3 shows a plot of the step learning rate function.

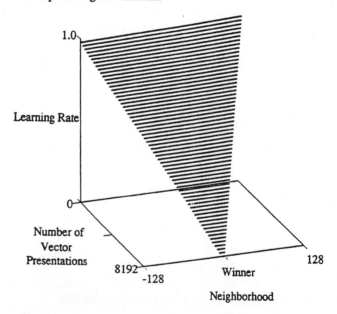

Fig. 4.3. Nested step learning rate. (1 epoch; 8192 TTVs; 26.49db.)

The second variation to the nested learning rate is a linear decrease from the winner neuron, as shown in Fig. 4.4, which is also constructed using run time data.

Finally, the third variation to the nested learning rate is a Mexican hat (approximated) decrease from the winner neuron, as shown in Fig. 4.5, which is also plotted using run time data. Note that this function is somewhat of a compromise between the step and the linear functions. For example, Fig. 4.5 shows a concave function, so that the learning rate drops very rapidly near the winner neuron, very much more so than the linear case. However, another possibility is a convex function, where the learning rate drops more

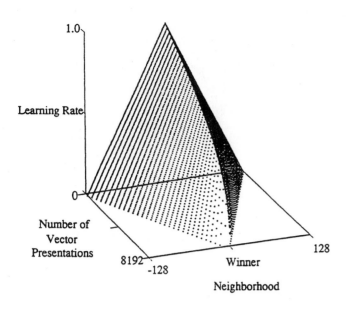

Fig. 4.4. Nested linear learning rate. (1 epoch; 8192 TTVs; 27.21db.)

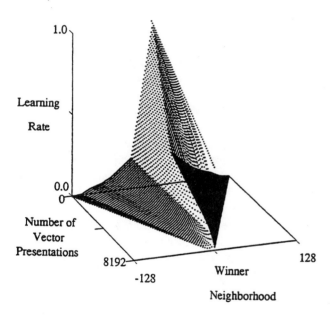

Fig. 4.5. Nested Mexican hat learning rate. (1 epoch; 8192 TTVs; 27.54db.)

Table 4.1. Nested learning rate optimization. Variables: *Initial training vectors* (ITV), *total training vectors* (TTV), *execution time* (XTime).

Training (1epoch; N)			PSNR(db)		
No. ITV	TTV	XTime (min)	Step	Linear	Mexican Hat
2048	2048	1/8	25.96	26.27	26.54
4096	4096	1/4	26.04	26.62	26.91
8192	8192	1/2	26.49	27.21	27.54
16384	32768	1	27.14	27.61	27.71
32768	32768	2	27.44	28.10	28.21

4.3.2 Neighborhood

In the previous three figures, the neighborhood function decreases linearly with the number of vectors presented. During the early stages of learning, when the number of vectors presented is less than the total number of vectors to be presented and the learning rate is large, the neighborhood should be large, since this is when each of the 256 weight vectors establishes a rough location in the feature map. Later on in training, when the learning rate is small, the neighborhood should decrease, since this is when fine tuning of the coarse map occurs. Since the fine tuning period is longer than the coarse formation, the neighborhood should decrease faster during fine tuning. Rather than a linear decrease, others, such as quadratic, cubic, and exponential decreases can be tried. Figure 4.6 shows the character of the linear learning rate utilizing a cubic

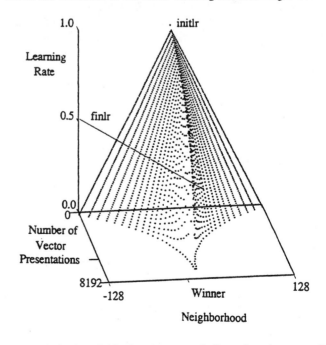

Fig. 4.6. Cubic neighborhood decrease in linear learning rate. (1 epoch; 8192 TTVs; N^3; 27.54db.)

slowly than the linear case near the winner neighborhood. This is implemented in Section 4.3.2.

The above three learning rate functions are implemented in learning the codebook for a 512×512×8 monochrome image of Lena, as shown in Fig. A1. The results are tabulated in Table 4.1. Note the consistent improvement of PSNR down each column (i.e., with increasing number of training vectors) and across each row from left to right (i.e., with the type of learning, namely, step, linear, and Mexican hat).

decrease in the neighborhood. This figure should be compared with Fig. 4.4, which is exactly the same as Fig. 4.6, except for the cubic decrease in the neighborhood.

Table 4.2 shows the effect of using a cubic decrease in the neighborhood. The results should be compared with Table 4.1, since the change from linear to cubic neighborhood decrease is the only difference between the two experiments. Note the consistent improvement in the PSNR point for point as compared with Table 5.1.

Table 4.2. Neighborhood function optimization. Variables: *Initial training vectors* (ITV), *total training vectors* (TTV), *execution time* (XTime).

Training (1epoch; N^3)			PSNR(db)		
No. ITV	TTV	XTime (min)	Step	Linear	Mexican Hat
2048	2048	1/8	27.50	27.80	27.89
4096	4096	1/4	28.10	28.24	28.35
8192	8192	1/2	28.41	28.59	28.68
16384	32768	1	28.77	28.83	28.95
32768	32768	2	28.80	28.92	29.05

4.3.3 Epochs

Another method can be used to increase the convergence rate of learning the codebook and to improve the PSNR. In the previous experiments, the VQ algorithm is implemented once, i.e., learning is complete when the predefined number of vectors have been presented to the network. The predefined number of vectors constitutes a training cycle or epoch. Note that learning begins with the initial learning rate, final learning, and neighborhood parameters set as follows: *initlr* = 1.0, *finlr* = 0.5, *initnei* = 128, and *finnei* = 0, respectively. More than one epoch can be applied with the learning rate and neighborhood parameters scaled down at the beginning of each subsequent epoch. In these experiments, *initlr* and *finlr* are scaled down by a factor of 1.25 and *initnei* and *finnei* are scaled down by a factor of 2.0. Recall that at the start of learning, the network establishes a coarse map, and near the end of a training cycle, the network fine tunes the feature map. By introducing another training cycle, this forces the network to perform coarse map formation after the fine tuning process of the previous epoch, and this is followed by another fine tuning, both done with scaled down parameters. For example, Fig. 4.7 shows a learning rate function over 7 epochs. The *initlr* at the beginning of the 6th epoch is 0.13 or 1/(6x1.25).

Note that at the start of each epoch the error increases, since coarse tuning is done after fine tuning. This is shown in Fig. 4.8, which shows a sliding error window over every *NIV* vector presentations. Increases in error can be seen at the beginning of each epoch, when the number of vectors presented is 1024, 3072, 7168, 15360, 31744, and 64512.

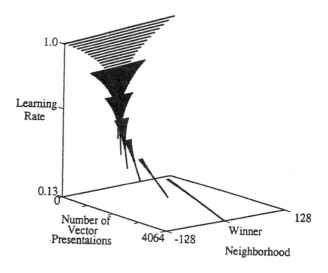

Fig. 4.7. Seven epoch learning. (7 epoch; 4064 TTVs; N^3; 28.82db.)

Forcing the network to learn over multiple epochs is a form of simulated annealing. When we observe sugar in a sugar bowl, we see sugar particles at rest in some position that is not the lowest possible energy state. They have attained this position as a result of a compromise between energy and entropy of the system. Entropy may be characterized as a state of a system where a large population of elements are located, even if this location does not represent the lowest possible energy. This location represents one of the many local minima of the system. When we tap the sugar bowl, we increase the temperature of the system, and this allows the sugar particles to escape the current local minimum and reach another minimum which is lower than the previous. Much in the same way, the minimum achieved by the VQ network after completion of a training cycle may be a local minimum. In order to move the system out of this local minimum, one possible method is to force it to perform coarse tuning of the feature map. This increases the temperature of the system, and when the temperature cools, the network performs fine tuning of the map once again. This repeats for each subsequent epoch.

Table 4.3 shows the results after training the codebook using 7 epochs. This table should be compared with Table 4.2, since the number of epochs is the only difference between the two

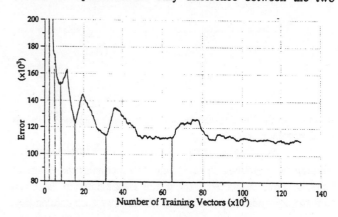

Fig. 4.8. Error window. (7 epoch; 32512 TTVs; N^3; MexHat; 29.74db.)

Table 4.3. Neighborhood function optimization. Variables: *Initial training vectors* (ITV), *total training vectors* (TTV), *execution time* (XTime).

Training (7 epoch; N^3)			PSNR(db)		
No. ITV	TTV	XTime (min)	Step	Linear	Mexican Hat
16	2032	1/8	27.50	27.61	28.99
32	4064	1/4	28.28	28.51	28.48
64	8128	1/2	28.89	29.19	28.99
128	16256	1	29.36	29.65	29.51
256	32512	2	29.75	29.84	29.74
512	65024	4	29.96	30.10	29.93
1024	130048	8	30.11	30.16	30.13
2048	260096	16	30.17	30.23	30.18

experiments. Note the consistent improvement in the PSNR as compared with Table 4.2. However, note also in Table 4.3 that the type of nested learning rate function is PSNR insignificant (read across each row) as the number of epochs increases. In fact, the linear learning rate function yields the best results for epoch number 7. The reason for this is that all three functions tend to approximate impulse functions centered at the winner neuron as the number of epochs increases and the initial neighborhood and initial learning rate diminish. While these functions start out with different character, they end up "looking" the same. Thus, different learning rate functions give different convergence rates for small number of epochs, but these differences vanish for large number of epochs. The 7-epoch version can also be compared with the single epoch version by observing Fig. 4.9, which shows the error window for both systems under similar conditions. Note that the coarse formation of the map is done much faster (greater slope) and reaches a lower error in the 7 epoch version. As a result, fine tuning begins at a lower error than in the single epoch version and, therefore, the system reaches an overall lower local minimum.

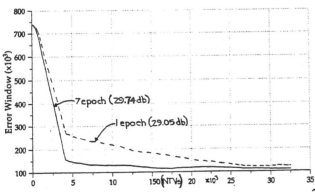

Fig. 4.9. 7-versus 1-epoch error window. (32512 TTVs; N^3; MexHat; 29.74db.)

4.4 Codebook Analysis

Having optimized learning of the codebook, a next step is to analyze how the codebook maps the features of the image. Figure 4.10 displays an image of the codebook along with the energy distribution.

As mentioned earlier, the output neurons are organized onto a one-dimensional ring. The image in Fig. 4.10 shows the brightness distribution of the weight vectors connected to the output neurons in the ring. There are 256 weight vectors each consisting of a 4×4 square array of pixels. Note that the two ends of the image should be connected to each other in order to form the circular ring. Note also that the envelope of the energy is a smooth function of the

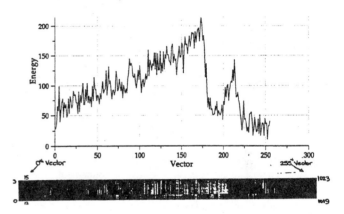

Fig. 4.10. Self organized feature map.

weight vector index, i.e., the location of the output neuron in the ring. Weight vectors with similar energy, i.e., similar mean brightness levels, are clustered in sets whose boundaries are fuzzy and continuous. The weight vectors are mapped in this way onto the ring because of the Euclidean metric used in determining the winner neuron and because of the chosen one-dimension topology (ring) of the output. Other methods of organizing the features onto a map are possible, and the visual display of a such a codebook would be different than the one displayed in Fig. 4.10. For example, we could apply the Euclidean distance metric in determining the winner, and we could use the a two-dimensional grid to define the organization of the feature map. In this case, we would expect the mean brightness levels to be mapped in a smooth two-dimensional function.

4.5 Generalization

Having optimized learning of the codebook for a specific image (i.e. Lena) and studied how the codebook maps features, the next question that should be asked is: How well does the codebook perform in quantizing other similar images? This question relates to the concept of generalization in artificial neural networks. The initial intention in learning a codebook for vector quantization is that the codebook vectors learn to represent higher order statistics of the original image. Our assumption is that these higher order statistics are not only characteristic of the original image, but they also characterize other similar images. The term "similar" is a fuzzy concept, but, in general, we mean head and shoulder images of people.

There are two types of generalization in learned vector quantization, autoassociative and heteroassociative. In autoassociative generalization, there is a great degree of resemblance between the test data and the training data. For example, in the application of interest, the test data consists of very similar head and shoulder pictures of people. In heteroassociative generalization, the resemblance may be very weak, or none.

4.5.1 Autoassociative Vector Quantization

The measurement of the degree of generalization is not straight forward since generalization is also a fuzzy concept. However, it can be judged by a simultaneous subjective and objective evaluation. We tend to characterize a codebook's ability to quantize images that it has not been trained on by visually comparing the original image with the decompressed image while noting the PSNR of the decompressed image. There are other factors that can be taken into consideration. For example, we can determine the significance of the correlation of the histograms between the trained image and the test images.

Figures A1-A9 show several images quantized by the 30.35db codebook trained using the 512x512x8 Lena original (Fig. A1). Overall, Lena's codebook performed well on these images, but there are some interesting characteristics that can be pointed out.

Lori (Fig. A4) achieves a PSNR of 31.6db, which is slightly higher than that achieved by the training image (Lena: 30.35db). We would not expect this unless the test image is a very close subset of the training image and contains more of the same type of redundancy that is contained in the original image. Indeed, in the image of Lori, we see that there exists a greater amount of the same type of redundancy in the image of Lena. For example, Lori's hat is mostly dark black. This dark black shape can be constructed exactly using a prototype vector extracted from the curved frame of the mirror in Lena's image. Similarly, the background in Lori's image appears to consist of one uniform grey level, whose prototype can be extracted from Lena's image. Also note, that Lori's earring decompresses quite well considering that Lena contains no similar macro object. Finally, note that the nail polish on Lori's finger nails has lost its original grey level.

Andrea (Fig. A5) achieves a PSNR of 33.44db, which is much higher than that achieved by the trained image (Lena: 30.35db). This seems peculiar from an objective point of view. One can agree that Lori's reproduction is better than Andrea's even though Andrea achieved almost 2db higher in PSNR. The objective reason for the high PSNR may be because of the large background area and the fact that the background is reconstructed quite well. The subjective reason for preferring Lori's decompressed image rather than Andrea's may be because the contrast between the background and the face of Andrea has diminished substantially. In the decompressed image of Andrea, the background seems to flow into the facial parts of Andrea, with out the sharp boundary evident in the original image of Andrea.

4.5.2 Heteroassociative Vector Quantization

The Renoit painting (Fig. A6) achieved a PSNR of 26db. While the image is recognizable to some extent, there are many details lost. The detailed design on the child's dress (neck, breast, and sleeve) has been lost; only faint remnants of the articulate design remain. The artist must have intended to rely on our perception of such shapes in order to communicate the image to us. As can be seen, such perception influenced images do not compress well using a compression scheme that does not take human perception into consideration. Finally, notice that the white boundary of the painting could not be reconstructed. Examining the original image, Lena, we cannot find a 4x4 pixel square, all of whose pixels have a 255 grey level.

4.5.2.1 Beauty and the Beast

In studying image compression algorithms, it is interesting to determine the limit of generalization and, perhaps, quantify, the applicability. Figure A7 shows the decompressed image of the Baboon image, quantized using Lena's 31.74db codebook. Lena's 31.74db codebook is the codebook learned from the Lena 512x512x8 image.

Figure A8 shows the decompressed image of the Lena image, quantized using the Baboon's 26db codebook. The Baboon's 26db codebook is the codebook learned from the Baboon 512x512x8 image. Note that the Baboon's reconstruction of Lena produced about the same PSNR as that achieved by the linear vector quantizer of Section 4.2, our starting point.

The reader should judge the resulting quality in these decompressed images, and, furthermore, determine the implications of such intermixing of prototypes.

The degree of generalization of images can be ascertained through an objective and subjective examination, as done above. However, an interesting question could be asked: Given a codebook trained on a certain image, can the suitability of quantizing other images be determined through a correlation between the histograms of the original image and the image to be compressed?

In general, the answer is no. To show this, a new image can be formed by randomizing the pixels of the 512x512x8 image of Lena. This new image still consists of exactly the same grey level distribution of Lena. When quantized, the decompressed image achieves a PSNR of only 17db. This shows that the VQ method extracts the features characteristic of the training image, and the codebook does not learn grey level distributions.

However, the histogram can be used to a limited extent in predicting the performance of a codebook in quantizing an image, provided that it is known a priori that the trained image and the test image are similar to some extent, as with the images experimented with above. In the images discussed above, with some exceptions, the histogram of each test images has a distribution that is a subset of the histogram of Lena, the training image. In other words, with some exceptions, all grey level and all frequencies of grey levels are contained in the histogram of Lena. If we are given an image that is subjectively similar to the training image, and if the histogram of the test image is a subset of the histogram of the training image, then we can say with a certain high probability that the quantization of the test image will produce results comparable with the PSNR achieved by the training image.

V. CONCLUSIONS

In this paper, Kohonen's SOFM has been used to compress several still monochrome images by a compression ratio of 16:1 at a compression rate of 0.5, while maintaining a PSNR of about 30db. C programs were written to implement learning, compressing, decompressing, analyzing error, and others for the VQ method. These programs were run on the SUN SPARC Station 2. Methods for optimizing learning have been presented. Given an image that is subjectively similar to the training image, and if the histogram of the test image is a subset of the histogram of the training image, then quantization of the test image will produce results comparable with the PSNR achieved by the training image.

ACKNOWLEDGEMENT

This work was supported in part by the Natural Sciences and Engineering Council (NSERC) of Canada.

REFERENCES

[AKCM90] S.C. Ahalt, A.K. Krishnamurthy, P.Chen, and D.E. Melton, "Competitive learning algorithms for vector quantization," *Neural Networks*, vol. 3, no. 3, pp. 277-290, 1990.

[KFAG93] W. Kinsner, K. Ferens, A. Langi, W. Grieder, L. Wall, G. Stacey, T. Tessier, and M. Kinsner, "Demos of data and signal compression for multimedai," InfoMedia '93 Symposium and Exhibition; Winnipeg, MB, March 9-10, 1993

[Kins91] W. Kinsner, "Review of data compression methods, including Shannon-Fano, Huffman, arithmetic, Storer, Lempel-Ziv-Welch, fractal, neural network, and wavelet algorithms," *Technical Report*, DEL91-1, Jan. 1991, 157 pp.

[Koho90] T. Kohonon, "The Self-Organizing Map," *Proc. IEEE*, vol. 78, no. 9, pp. 1464-80, Jan. 1990.

[Lehn91] W. Lehn, "Digital Image Processing," *Lecture Notes*. Winnipeg, MB; Department of Electrical and Computer Engineering, University of Manitoba, 1991.

[Wall90] G.K. Wallace, "Overview of the (ISO/CCITT) JPEG still image compression standard," Image Processing Algorithms and Techniques. In *Proc. SPIE*, vol. 1244, pp. 220-233, Feb. 1990.

[McAR90] J. McAuliffe, L. Atlas, and C. Rivera, "A comparison of the LBG algorithm and Kohonen neural network paradigm for image vector quantization," *Proc. IEEE Intern .Conf. Acoustics, Speech & Sign. Processing*, ICASSP90 (Albuquerque, NM; Apr. 3-6, 1990), IEEE Cat. no. 90CH2847-2, vol. 4, pp. 2293-96, 1990.

[NaFe88] N. Nasrabadi and R. Feng, "Vector quantization of images based on Kohonen's self-organizing feature map," *IEEE Intern .Conf. Neural Networks*, vol. 1, pp 101-8, June 1988.

[TrMe90] K. Truong and R. Mersereau, "Structural image codebooks and the self-organizing feature map algorithm," *Proc. IEEE Intern .Conf. Acoustics, Speech & Sign. Processing*; ICASSP90 (Albuquerque, NM; Apr. 3-6, 1990), IEEE Cat. no. 90CH2847-2, vol. 4, pp. 2289-92, 1990.

APPENDIX A

Fig. A1. Lena original (512×512 by 8 bpp).

Fig. A2. Lena (512×512 by 8 bpp) quantized using linear vector quantization. The PSNR is 26db. Note the smallest building block is a 4×4 array of pixels, each pixel having the same grey level.

627

Fig. A3. Lena (512×512 by 8 bpp) quantized using Lena's 30.35 db codebook. The PSNR is 30.35 db.

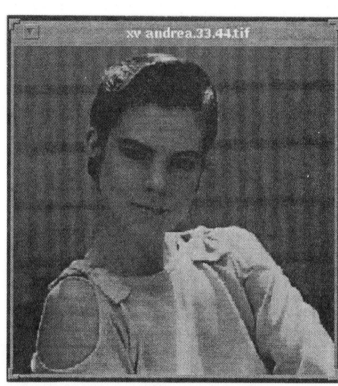

Fig. A5. Andrea (512×512 by 8 bpp) quantized using Lena's 30.35 db codebook. The PSNR is 33.44 db.

Fig. A4. Lori (512×512 by 8 bpp) quantized using Lena's 30.35 db codebook. The PSNR is 31.6 db.

Fig. A6. Renoit (512×512 by 8 bpp) quantized using Lena's 30.35 db codebook. The PSNR is 24.74 db.

Fig. A7. Baboon (512×512 by 8 bpp) quantized using Lena's 30.35 db codebook. The PSNR is 24 db, 2db lower than if Baboon's 26 db codebook is used.

Fig. A8. Lena (512×512 by 8 bpp) quantized using Baboon's 26 db codebook. The PSNR is 26.7 db, 3.65db lower than if Lena's 30.35 db codebook is used.

Remotely sensing the world continues to grow in importance with each passing year. Global trends, such as global warming, rely on remotely sensed data collected from satellites and in situ sensors to determine the level of health of the environment. Neural networks are playing a significant role in remote sensing in two areas: classification and clustering. The five papers included in this chapter provide examples of both types of processing. **Paper 19.1** describes the application of multilayer perceptron (MLP) neural networks to the classification of ice surfaces using data from special sensor microwave imager (SSMI) measurements. **Paper 19.2** describes the use of a learning vector quantization (LVQ) neural network for clustering followed by the MLP neural network for classification of land type from LANDSAT TM data. **Paper 19.3** presents the application of the MLP neural network to rainfall prediction from Geostationary Meteorological Satellite (GMS) image data. **Paper 19.4** describes the application of the MLP neural network to land cover classification from the fusion of SPOT HRV and LANDSAT TM data. **Paper 19.5** employs the Kalman filter training technique to an MLP neural network and applies the resulting system to landcover classification using SPOT HRV data.

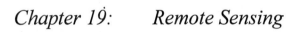

Chapter 19:   Remote Sensing

CLASSIFICATION OF REMOTE SENSING DATA USING
PARTIALLY TRAINED NEURAL NETWORK

Y.C. Rau, and Y.M.F. Lure
Caelum Research Corporation
11229 Lockwood Drive
Silver Spring, MD 20901, U.S.A.

ABSTRACT

The feasibility of a partially trained artificial neural network technique for classification of remote sensing ice coverage is presented. The neural network technique used is feed-forward back-propagation, and the sensing object is the ice coverage over Arctic region. This ice coverage information is obtained from the special sensor microwave imager (SSMI) microwave radiative measurements. Seven channels brightness temperature are used to identify six different surface classes. Different stages of partially trained feed-forward back-propagation artificial neural networks have been applied for the classification of ice coverage in order to investigate the performance of partial trained network at different training stages and to reduce the lengthy training time required by most BP ANN architectures.

Key words: neural network, remote sensing, brightness temperature, ice.

1. INTRODUCTION

The application of passive microwave satellite remote sensing to polar region ice coverage has been discussed since early 70's[5]. The classification of snow coverage and precipitation using multispectral passive microwave data without any ancillary information has been developed by Grody[6]. The microwave radiative aspect of different stages of Arctic ice are known to be quite different from others. The neural networks have been proved to be an effective tool as a classifier for terrain and pattern classification[3,4,8], due to its parallel processing ability, superior capability of supervised learning, graceful degradation of performance under conditions of ambiguity and noise, and easy to execute in realtime. It takes very lengthy time for an artificial neural network (ANN) to fully learn the desired features.

In this study, different stages of partially trained feed-forward back-propagation artificial neural networks (BP ANN) have been developed for the classification of remote sensing data in order to investigate the performance of the partial trained networks, and to reduce the lengthy training time required by most BP ANN architectures[7]. Various stages of partially trained BP ANN have been applied to obtain ice coverage information over the Arctic region from the special sensor microwave imager (SSMI) microwave radiative measurements. Preliminary results derived from the partially trained neural networks in Arctic region ice classification will be presented.

2. DATA SET DESCRIPTION

The multi-channel SSMI instrument, flown on board the Defence Meteorological Satellite Program polar orbiting satellite, is a seven-channel microwave radiometer measuring the surface brightness temperatures (radiance) at 19, 22, 37, and 85 GHz at both vertical and horizontal polarizations (only vertical polarization at 22 Ghz). The 19 and 22 GHz channels measurements mainly respond to variations in temperature and water vapor at large spatial scale. The 37 and 85 GHz channels measurements, due to scattering effects at high frequencies, respond to precipitation at smaller scale. Whereas, the detected brightness temperature data at 19, 37, and 85 GHz from SSMI satellite is very sensitive to the thickness of snow coverage[1]. Hence, these differences in radiative properties between different Earth's features, ice/snow coverage, open water, and land provide an unique signature for the identifying and monitoring the Arctic ice surface feature[2].

Six surface classes to be identified in the Arctic region include land, ocean (open-water), thin ice, thick ice, first year ice, and multi-year ice. The seven channels SSMI brightness temperature measurements used in this study were collected over the Arctic region in March 1988 and identified by human experts to provide the "ground truth" data for neural network developments and applications. The covered SSMI grid under study is 304 cells in horizontal dimension, 448 cells in vertical dimension with total 136,192 cells. Each grid cell is a 25 km * 25 km square area. There are totally 6,176 samples, with each class samples ranging from 775 to 1,089. Table I illustrates seven SSMI measurements frequencies and six class samples of surface features.

Table 1 SSMI Classification Characteristic and Surface Features							
SSMI	Channel Frequencies (GHz) and Polarization						
	19 H	19 V	22 V	37 H	37 V	85 H	85 V
Surface Features	Land	Ocean	Multiyear Ice	Thin Ice	Thick Ice	1st year Ice	
Samples	1089	1089	1088	1046	775	1089	
Total Sample Cases: 6176							

3. EXPERIMENT

Seven channels brightness temperature measurements are used to identify six different class of surface coverage features. A three-layer backpropagation artificial neural network (BP ANN) consisting of 7 input neurons in the input layer corresponding to seven channels SSMI brightness temperature measurement, 6 output neurons in the output layer corresponding to six surface classes, and 50 hidden neurons in the single hidden layer is developed experimentally to perform the ice classification. Although no specific rule for chosen the

635

number of neurons in hidden layers, it is found that 50 neurons provides better results thus far.

A back-propagation neural network supervised learning scheme is used to train layered feedforward network to become a pattern recognition engine. Through presenting the examples to a network repeatedly, the network is able to extract the features of the input examples. Training is performed by updating its interconnection strengths or weights through a graceful degradation as:

$$w_{ij}(t+1) = w_{ij} + \eta \delta_j x_i' + \alpha(w_{ij}(t) - w_{ij}(t-1)) \qquad (1)$$

where $w_{ij}(t)$ is the weight from node i to node j in different layer at time t, η is the learning rate or gain term, δ_j is an error term from node j, and α is momentum ratio (smooth factor). The network is said to be trained once the energy or error function between the desired and computed patterns reaches its minimum. There is no connection among the neurons of the same layers. A Sigmoid transfer function is used to modify the weighted sum of the input to a neuron. The output vectors are arranged in a mutually orthogonal form in order to enhance the performance of classification.

The classification is performed for each image pixel instead of the texture feature of the whole or subarea of the image. Totally 6,176 sample pixels used in this study, with number of sample pixels for each surface feature class ranging from 775 to 1,089 are selected in this study. Among 6176 sample pixels, 2.2 % of total sample pixels are chosen evenly from six classes as training set to avoid statistical bias. Rest of sample pixels are used to test the performance of the trained networks. The training of backpropagation neural network were continued until 2,200 epochs, with different early stage of partial trained networks been saved for the suitability study of partial trained network.

4. RESULTS

During the training courses, several partially trained neural networks have been obtained at different stage of iterations or epochs in the learning processes for further classification testing on remotely sensed SSMI radiance measurements data. After twenty iterations, the partially trained neural network classified 83 percent of total testing data successfully, as shown in Figure 1. The overall classification accuracy reaches 93.28 percent after sixty iterations, increases to 95.21 percent after three hundred and sixty iterations, and remains almost unchange afterward (the network testing accuracy is 95.5 percent after 2,000 epochs).

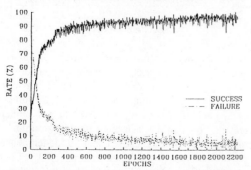

Figure 1 Polar ice classification performance using partially trained BP ANN.

The BP ANN networks have difference classification performance on different surface features, shown in Figure 2. Some surface features are easier to recognize than others. The features of ocean and multiyear ice are so unique, they can be recognized successfully at early iteration stages without any failure. Whereas the feature of land and thick ice are not that clear, land will be mis-identified as different features of ice coverage, and the thick ice will be mistaken as thin ice or first year ice, shown in Table 2. As the iterations increased, the miss detection and false alarm rates decreases dramatically, as from 20 to 60 iterations. The classification training process of all features reach stable state after 400 iterations. Based on the SSMI microwave measurements, all surface features can be recognized by the trained BP ANN network with accuracy over 90 % except land, which is 84 % after 360 iterations. The network training process on first year ice reaches local minimum between 200 to 400 runs, but overcome it after 400 runs.

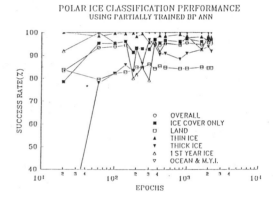

Figure 2 Ice classification performance at different stage of partially trained network.

Table 2 presents the surface classification accuracies of partially trained neural networks after 60 and 360 iterations. The uniqueness of multiyear ice and open water (ocean) radiance features are shown on column 4 and 5, with 100% classification accuracy. The feature of land will be miss-classified as the features of first year ice, thick ice, or open water, in that order shown in column 3. In some situations, thin ice, thick ice, and first year ice will be miss-classified among them but the occurrence of classification error is very limited.

Table 2. Surfaces Classification Accuracy						
Classified surfaces	Actual Surfaces					
	Iteration	Land	Ocean	M.Y.I.	Thin-Ice	Thick-Ice	1st Year
Land	60	79.4%	0	0	0.1%	1.4%	0
	360	84.1%	0	0	0	0.1%	0
Ocean	60	2.8%	100%	0	0	0	0
	360	0.9%	100%	0	0	0	0
M.Y.I	60	0	0	100%	0	0	0
	360	0	0	100%	0	0	0
Thin-Ice	60	6.5%	0	0	98.3%	8.6%	0
	360	4.2%	0	0	96.9%	4.3%	0
Thick-Ice	60	1.4%	0	0	1.6%	77.8%	0.1%
	360	1.7%	0	0	3.1%	94.1%	4.1%
1st Year	60	9.8%	0	0	0	12.1%	99.9%
	360	9%	0	0	0	1.5%	95.9%
Overall Accuracy: 93.28% after 60 iterations; 95.21% after 360 iterations						

Although the neural networks are only partially trained, the overall performance is quite promising on ice classification based on the SSMI microwave radiometer measurements. The overall accuracy of partially trained network on test samples reaches 93.28% after 60 iterations, and reaches 95.21% after 360 iterations. The testing accuracy of network is 95.53% after 2,000 iterations. An optimal number of iteration for partially trained BP ANN can be determined with reference to classification accuracy, miss detection and false alarm.

5. SUMMARY

This research effort presented the feasibility of the partially trained neural network on the Arctic ice classification based on the passive microwave satellite detections. Seven channels SSMI instrument measurements, flown on board the Air force polar-orbiting satellite, are used to classify six classes of Arctic surface features. These seven channel's measurements are brightness temperatures (radiance) at 19, 22, 37, and 85 GHz for H and V polarizations, except H for 22 Ghz. Six surface features to be classify include land, ocean, multiyear ice, thin ice, thick ice, and first year ice.
To avoid the sampling bias, we randomly and evenly selected 2.2 percent samples from six classes of total 6176 sample pixels to train the feedfoward backpropagation artificial network.

The partially trained neural network classification accuracy reaches 93.28% after sixty iterations. After three hundred and sixty iteration, the classification accuracy can reach as high as 95.21%. By employing a suitable partially trained neural network, we can save many hours of training time and still have a very satisfactory polar region surface features classification performance.

ACKNOWLEDGEMENTS

The authors are grateful for the discussion with Y. Chiou of Computer Systems and Architecture Group at Caelum Research Corporation.

REFERENCES:

[1] Cavalieri, D.J., and P. Gloersen, "Determination of Sea Ice Parameters with the NIMBUS 7 SSMR", *J. Geophys. Res.*, vol. 89, no. D4, pp. 5355-5369, June 30, 1984.

[2] Cosmiso, J.C., "Arctic Multiyear Ice Classification and Summer Ice Cover Using Passive Microwave Satellite Date", J. Geophy. Res., vol. 95, no. C8, pp. 13411-13422, Aug. 15, 1990.

[3] Dawson, M.S., A.K. Fung, and M.T. Manry, "Sea Ice Classification Using Fast Learning Neural Networks", in *Proc. of IGARSS 1992*, pp. 1070-1071.

[4] Decatur, S.E., "Application of Neural Networks to Terrain Classification", *Proceeding Int'l Conf. Neural Networks*, pp. 1284-1288, 1989.

[5] Gloersen, P., T.T. Wilheit, T.C. Chang, W. Nordberg, and W.J. Campbell, "Microwave maps of the polar ice of the earth", *Bull. Am. Meteorol. Soc.*, 55, pp. 1442-1448, 1974.

[6] Grody, N.C., "Classification of Snow Cover and Precipitation Using the Special Sensor Microwave Imager", *J. Geophy. Res.*, vol. 96, no. D5, 7423-7435, 1991.

[7] Lippmann, R.P., "An Introduction to Computing with Neural Nets"; *IEEE Acous. Spec. Signal Proc. Magazine*, pp. 4-22, 1987.

[8] Lure, Y.M.F., N.C. Grody, H.Y.M. Yeh, and J.S.J. Lin, "Neural Network Approaches to Classification of Snow Cover and Precipitation from Special Sensor Microwave Imager (SSMI)", *8th Interac. Info. Proc. Syst. (IIPS) for Meteo., Ocean., and Hydro.*, AMS, Atlanta, GA., 1992.

PATTERN CLASSIFICATION FOR REMOTE SENSING USING NEURAL NETWORK

Sigeru Omatu and Tomoji Yoshida

Department of Information Science and Intelligent Systems,
University of Tokushima, Tokushima, 770, Japan.

Abstract: We propose a pattern classification method for remote sensing data based on neural network theory. From Kohonen's self-organizing feature maps, training areas for each pattern are selected. Using the back propagation algorithm, layered neural network is trained such that the training patterns can be classified within a level. The experiments on LANDSAT TM data show that this approach produces excellent classification results compared with conventional Bayesian approach.

1. Introduction

It is well-known that neural network has strong power to classify various patterns as human brain can do [1]. Especially, the ability of image processing or speech recognition is excellent with that of conventional serial computers. Remote sensing has become important in pattern classification from the viewpoint of military and global environmental problems according to the progress of space technology. But pattern recognition method for remote sensing is mainly based on statistical methods such as maximum likelihood or Bayesian Methods. In this case classification is performed in a digital way under the Gaussian assumption and any pixel is classified into one of patterns. Hence, neighborhood relation of pixels cannot be taken into consideration and classification error probability is lower bounded [2]. In this paper, we propose a neural network classification method for remotely sensed data analysis in order to improve neighborhood relation between pixels and decrease error probability for pattern classification.

2. Remote Sensing Data Analysis

Remote sensing technique is to analysis the spectral information transmitted by electromagnetic energy reflected from objects. According to progress of space technology the remote sensing technique has become an important technology in image processing it can observe a wide range area at the same time in periodical way. Among many satellites for remote sensing, NOAA, SPOT, and LANDSAT are well-known in Japan.

In this Paper, we use LANDSAT TM data for remote sensing data analysis. It has seven bands from Band 1 to Band 7 and image resolution is 30m for all bands except for Band 6. Band 6 is thermal infrared spectral band and its resolution is 120m. We use Band 3 to Band 5 among LANDSAT TM data which were measured on October 8, 1984 by LANDSAT D satellite. The observation area is located at path 119 and row 36 where Tokushima City in Japan is Japan is Included.

3. Pattern Recognition by Neural Network

The present pattern algorithm by a neural network for remote sensing is described as follows: First we choose training patterns by using Kohonen's self-organization method. The training patterns are used to train a neural network based on the error back propagation algorithm. After training the neural network, we delete pixels in the training area is used to train the neural network. Finally, remote sensing data is used to be classified by the trained neural network.

4. Kohonen's Self-Organizing Feature Maps.

Kohonen's algorithm produces a vector quantizer by adjusting weights from common input nodes to M output nodes arranged in a two dimensional grid. Output nodes are mutually connected with many local connections. Analog input vectors are presented sequentially in time without specifying the desired output. After many input vectors have been presented, weights can produce cluster centers such that the density function of the cluster centers approximates the probability density function of the input vectors.

5. Error Back Propagation Algorithm.

After selecting the training areas by using Kohonen's self-organizing feature maps, we use three layered neural network. At input layer CCT levels of TM data from Band 3 to Band 5 are applied to each neuron. At output layer, neuron outputs are compared with desired values which represent a set of classification patterns selected by Kohonen's algorithm and geographical information. If there are some discrepancies between the desired values and neuron output, the error can be decreased by using the error back propagation algorithm. After training is complete, we delete erroneous pixels for pattern classification from the training areas determined by Kohonen's algorithm. The new training areas are learned until the lower limit of error function is obtained. The classification patterns

adopted here are dark part of forest(o_1), bare land (o_2), density inhabited district (o_3), forest or grassy place (o_4), river or sea (o_5), and farm (o_6). The three layered neural network has 3 neurons at the input layer, and 6 neurons at the output layer. At the hidden layer, number of neurons has been changed from 4 to 8.

For six patterns at the output layer, desired values y_j ($j=1,2,\cdots,6$) are settled as 1 at only one node and 0 except for that node. For example, for the dark part of forest the desired value is $(1,0,0,0,0)$ and for the bare land it is $(0,1,0,0,0,0)$.

6. Pattern Classification Results.

By using Kohonen's self-organizing feature maps and taking into consideration of the geographical information, six patterns have been extracted as typical patterns, which corresponds dark part of forest, bare land, density inhabited district, forest or grassy place, river or sea, and farm.

Table I shows the classification results by using Bayesian method and neural network method for various numbers N of neurons at the hidden layer, when the training areas are selected by Kohonen's algorithm and geographical information without deleting the erroneous pixels from the training areas. From the simulation results it is seen that classification errors cannot be decreased so small even if training is performed repeatedly. The remote sensing data does not include perfect information about the ground truth data and image data given by remote sensing is subject to noise such as path radiance or back scattering effect. Therefore, we delete some pixels from the training areas which cannot be correctly classified by the layered neural network and make new training areas. By using the new ones the neural network has been trained and classification error functions are illustrated by the circled number ② in Fig.4. In Table II the classification results based on the revised training areas. From this results we can see that the neural network approach gives an excellent classification results.

7. Conclusions

We have proposed the neural network approach to classify the remote sensing data into one of the patterns which have been determined by using Kohonen's self-organizing feature maps. From the data analysis by the proposed method it has been

shown that the present algorithm based on the neural network is more powerful than conventional Bayesian method in the sense that mean squared error is smaller.

References

[1] Y.H.Pao,"Adaptive Pattern Recognition and Neural Networks",Addison-Wesley,1989.

[2] W.K.Pratt,"Digital Image Processing",Wiley-Inter.Pub.,1978.

[3] R.P.Lippmann,"An introduction to computing with neural nets",IEEE ASSP Magazine,Vol.4,No.2,pp.4-22,1987.

Table I. Pattern recognition results and mean squared error where

I = dark part of forest, II = bare land, III = density inhabited district,

IV = forest or grassy place, V = river or sea, VI = farm, and VII = mean squared error.

			I	II	III	IV	V	VI	VII
Original image			12.30	24.02	6.00	10.56	5.71	41.41	
Bayesian method			8.85	25.32	5.11	36.12	4.39	20.21	1.19×10^{-1}
Neural networks	N	4	10.24	9.14	14.36	29.48	6.47	30.30	7.78×10^{-2}
		5	9.05	12.52	6.99	28.99	7.09	35.36	5.22×10^{-2}
		6	11.96	20.06	4.86	21.30	7.78	34.04	9.56×10^{-3}
		7	13.85	16.91	4.09	23.93	7.31	33.90	2.95×10^{-2}
		8	11.86	12.90	4.44	31.25	6.98	32.56	6.34×10^{-2}

Table II. Pattern recognition results for new training areas.

	I	II	III	IV	V	VI	VII
Original image	12.30	24.02	6.00	10.56	5.71	41.41	
Bayesian method	8.79	31.48	1.99	23.59	3.87	30.29	1.90×10^{-2}
Neural networks for N=6	12.50	21.54	7.06	12.80	6.52	39.57	8.19×10^{-4}

Rainfall Prediction Of Geostationary Meteorological Satellite Images Using Artificial Neural Network

Tao Chen   Mikio Takagi

Takagi Lab, Department of Electronics Engineering
Institute of Industrial Science, University of Tokyo
7-22-1 Roppongi, Minato-ku, Tokyo 106, Japan
email: tao@tkl.iis.u-tokyo.ac.jp, takagi@tkl.iis.u-tokyo.ac.jp

Abstract

Rainfall intensity calculation is an important research theme in rainfall precipitation forecast, navigation, weather prediction, etc.. In this paper, we propose a feature based neural network approach for rainfall prediction. We use a four-layer neural network to automatically learn the internal relationship between geostationary meteorological satellite GMS data and rainfall intensity distribution. The input data used are infrared and visible imagery of GMS Image. Back propagation learning algorithm is used. The experimental area is the open sea near Shikoku, Japan. The output layer has 4 outputs, indicating rain intensity levels. The ground truth radar data is used as expectation output during the training stage. Finally, the trained network is tested on the validation data set on the same image, and is used to classify rainfall intensity of other GMS image data.

1 Introduction

Rainfall intensity calculation plays an important role in GMS image analysis, navigation, rainfall precipitation forecast, weather prediction, etc.. Rainfall is also one of the most difficult elements to forecast because of the tremendous range of variability it displays temporally and spacially over a wide range of scales. Sevruk pointed in [1] that even rainfall measurement at a point by a single rain gauge is not an easy task. Browning and Collier [2, 3] estimate that half of the total error in short-range rainfall forecasting is due to measurement errors.

There are several available operational procedures for quantitative precipitation forecasting (QPF) [2, 4, 5]. The localization of the large-scale numerical model results can be attempted by the use of regression models, such as Model Output Statistics MOS [6] method used for the very short-term forecasting of severe local storms and thunderstorms. However, the use of statistical regression to partially bridge the gap between mesoscale and the scales resolved by large-scale numerical models specifically for precipitation involves difficulties such as

1. the identification of all the relevant meteorological variables that will be used as explanatory variables for each location;

2. the absence of high temporal correlation in the station precipitation records.

Apart from the numerical models, current QPF products are also prepared by forecasters based on experience and observed data and on the guidance of the numerical models. As much as subjective judgment can improve objective forecasts, local forecasters cannot quantify the uncertainty in the forecasts that they issue and generalization of a forecast procedure based on subjective judgment is practically impossible. The last point mainly results from the fact that success of local forecasters in predicting rainfall is based on a thorough understanding of local conditions.

Weather radar data currently comprise the major observation group in very short-term forecasting because of the ability of individual radars to detect and track severe weather and precipitation conditions that have life cycles of less than 6h. Satellite data provide the bridge from the larger scales and forecast periods of several hours to the convective storm scale and warning times of a few minutes. Thus, the combination of radar and satellite data appears most promising for increasing the effectiveness in mesoscale precipitation nowcasting. Several Countries, including Japan and the United States, are becoming increasingly involved in development of modern nowcasting systems.

It should be clear from the above discussion of forecasting techniques that rainfall forecasting is an extremely complex and difficult problem involving many variables which are interconnected in a very complicated way. Most of the realtionships describing the dynamical and spatial relations are non-linear. This complexity and non-linearity makes it attractive to try the neural network approach which is inherently suited to problems that are mathematically difficult to describe.

In this paper, we propose a novel image feature based approach to calculate automatically rainfall prediction by using neural network method. We employ a four-layer network to automatically learn the internal relationship between input data and rainfall intensities and types. The input data used are infrared and visible imagery of GMS Image. The experimental area is the near sea of Japan. The output layer has 4 outputs, representing 4 rain intensities levels. We are also careful in chosing appropriate data set that result in as unoverlapped decision boundaries in the input space as possible. The weather radar data are used as desired outputs during learning stage. Finally, we test the learning neural network on ground radar data (true value for rainfall intensity) of rainfall intensity of other GMS image data, and calculate their rainfall intensity distribution

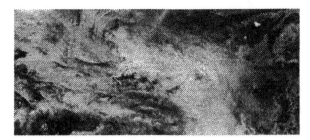

Fig 1: Visible Image for Training (700x300, March 18)

Fig 2: Visible Image for Validation (700x300, March 15)

maps.

2 Data Sets

The original data used are two GMS image sets of March 15 and 18 1992. The subject location is Open Sea near Shikoku, Japan. The image area is selected and divided into of 700×300 pixels (1 pixel is nominally 16 km^2). As a result of calibration, IR image represents brightness temperature image. The visible images of March 15 and 18 are shown in Figure 1 and Figure 2. In Figure 1 for each rainfall intensity level about 600 pixels are selected for training. The image of Figure 2 is reserved for validation.

In regression-based conventional rainfall prediction methods, only infrared temperature IR and visible image graylevel VIS are used as input data. Rainfall intensity P is calculated as follows (a_n: coefficients):

$$
\begin{aligned}
P \;=\; & a_0 + a_1 \times IR + a_2 \times VIS + a_3 \times IR^2 \\
& + a_4 \times IR \times VIS + a_5 \times VIS^2 + a_6 \times IR^3 \\
& + a_7 \times IR \times VIS^2 + a_8 \times IR^2 \times VIS + a_9 \times VIS^3
\end{aligned}
$$

The rainfall intensity P calculated by equation 1 is smaller than the true rainfall value while comparing with the ground radar value. Therefore, the following transformation in needed:

$$ SI \;=\; \alpha \times P + \beta $$

SI: the rainfall intensity index

α: the enlarge coefficience; β: the bias coefficience

Comparing with the ground radar value, the method based on the above equation was reported good in [7] when the rainfall intensity was at 20-30mm/h. The value calculated was larger than the true value within 4-16mm/h intensity, but smaller within more than 60mm/h intensity. Instead of IR and VIS, we also include the following two parameters T_{cov} and T_{mfd} as input data:

T_{cov} is derived from the division of variation and average of the $2°$ length region, centered at the current pixel.

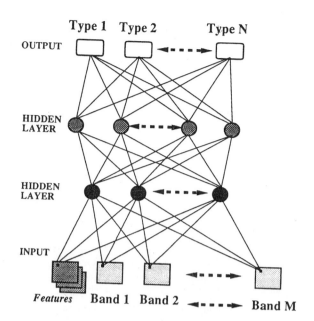

Fig 3: System Structure

T_{mfd} is calculated by averaging the difference of NW-SE and NE-SW ward in 3 grid distance.

T_{cov} represents the region uniformity centeren at the current pixel. T_{mfd} denotes direction-oriented image feature for the generally fixed direction of cloud flow. T_{mfd} is large when the region consists of the edges of cumulonimbus Cb and cirrus Ci; T_{mfd} becomes small when the variations of edges of Cb and Ci is small or the region is the sea. T_{mfd} value can used to recognize the existance of Ci and Cb. Therefore, larger the T_{mfd}, stronger the rainfall intensity. The T_{cov} parameter is the same as T_{mfd} parameter.

The whole data are seperated equally and randomly into two data sets: training data set and validation data set. The rainfall intensity measured by ground true radar is used as teacher signal during the training stage. The rainfall intensity in original radar data has 16 levels. At the very begin of the training, we simply set output units to 16, corresponding to the 16 intensity levels. However, learning procedure did not converge even after more than 100000 learning iterations. The reason is that data set of each intensity level overlappes with each other seriously. The neural network can not reach a stable stage (convergence) when there are too many input data belonging to different data set simultaneously. When we reduce the intensity level from 16 to 4, each data set seems to have different properties and features.

3 Four-Layer Network

Neural network is constructed by interconnecting many of simple neurons. The computation of these neurons is in parallel. The primary elements characterizing the neural network are the distributed representation of information, the local operations, and non-linear processing. These attributes emphasize the popular application areas of neural networks [8, 9, 10]:

1. situations where only a few decision are required from a massive amount of data, such as classification problem;

Fig 4: Distribution Map of Rainfall Intensity

2. applications involving large combinatorial optimization;

3. situation where a complex non-linear mapping must be learned, such as the task addressed in this work.

The ability of neural network to generalize to date not included in training data set depends on selecting a number of hidden nodes large enough to provide a means for sorting higher order relationships necessary for adequately abstracting the process. Increasing the number of training iterations alone, with no change in neural network structure, improves performance on the training data but does not necessarily improve performance on independent data. The four-layer neural network used in this project is shown in Figure 3. The GMS has two image bands, i.e. infrared and visible bands. The image features of current pixel in input data include IR and VIS and their combination, and T_{cov} and T_{mfd} parameters.

4 Result Analysis

The classification accuracy on validation data is 90.45 %. It is higher than the regression based conventional methods, because of the use of neural network and the addition of image features. The classification error may result from the measurement error and the rearrangement of rainfall intensity. The input data belonging to different rainfall intensity levels (esp. level 0 and 1) overlap with each other. The category boundaries between the input data is no clear enough. Most of the classification error is the misclassification of category 0 and category 1. The classification result of Figure 2 is shown in Figure 4. The dark graylevel denotes intensity level 0, and the brightest represents level 4. Table 1 is the individule classification accuracy for each intensity level after comparing with ground truth radar data of rainfall intensity level. Take level 1 for an example, the classication accuracy is 91.16 %, while 5.15 % pixels of level 1 are misclassified to level 0 and 3.68 % to level 2.

5 Further Works

The ability of neural network to learn the distribution of rainfall intensity has been illustrated. The classification accuracy is high and satisfactory. Two problems still exist, i.e. image feature contents and rainfall forecasting. In general, higher classification accuracy is exepcted when more image feature is used. Based on the current research and the analysis of series of images, well-trained neural network system to produce 1h lead or more time forecasts of rainfall is expected.

Level	0	1	2	3
0	78.91	21.09	0.00	0.00
1	5.15	91.16	3.69	0.00
2	0.00	3.08	92.94	3.98
3	0.00	0.00	6.12	93.88

Table 1: Calssification Accuracy (%) for Each Level

6 Conclusions

The rainfall intensity prediction method based on neural network method was represented. The comparision with ground-based radar data proved that the experiment result is satisfactory and reliable. The rainfall intensity categories can be expanded when different application requirement is proposed.

7 Acknowledgements

The authors would like to thank Japan meteorological administration for supplying the experiment data, and Mr. H.H.Lee, senior researcher at Korea meteorological administration, for kindly preparing the input data for this experiment research.

References

[1] B.Sevruk, Correction of Precipitation Measurements: Summary Report, Workshop on the Correction of Precipitation Measurements, April 1985, Zurich, pp13-23

[2] K.A.Browning, C.G.Collier, Nowcasting of Precipitation Systems, Rev.Geophys., Vol.27, No.3, pp345-370, 1989

[3] C.G.Collier, D.M.Golddard, and B.J.Conway, Real-Time Analysis of Precipitation Using Satellite Imagery, Ground-Based Radar, Conventional Observations and Numerical Model Output, Meteorological Magzine, 118, 1-8

[4] A.Bellocq, Operational Models of Quantitative Precipitation Forecasts for Hydrological Purposes and Possibilities of an Intercomparison, WMO, Geneva, pp6, 1980

[5] K.P.Georgakakos, M.D.Hudlow, Quantitative Precipitation Forecast Techniques for Use in Hydrologic Forecasting, Bull.Am.Meteor.Soc., Vol.65,No.11,pp1186-1200,1987

[6] National Weather Service, Meteorological Service Division, Two-to-Six Hour Probabilities of Thunderstorms and Severe Local Storms, National Weather Service, National Oceanic and Atmospheric Administration, Silver Spring, Maryland, Tech. Procedures Bull. Ser., No.295, pp13, 1981

[7] Y.Abe, K.Suzuki, Y.Yotsuya, T.Kurino, and T.Imaizumi, An Estimation Method of Precipitation Intensity Using Geostationary Meteorological Satellite Data - Satellite-Derived Index of Precipitation Intexsity, Monbusho Research Report, No. 63850119, March 1991

[8] D.Rogers,Weather Prediction Using Genetic Memory,Neural Networks,Concepts,Applications & Implementations,Vol.IV, pp275-289,Prentice Hall Advanced Reference Series,1991

[9] M.N.French, W.F.Krajewski, and R.R.Cuykendall, Rainfall Forecasting in Space and Time Using a Neural Network, Journal of Hydrology, Vol. 137, pp1-31, 1992

[10] D.W.McCann, A Neural Network short-term forecast of significant thunderstorms, Weather and Forecasting, Vol.7, pp525-534, 1992

A CLASSIFICATION METHOD USING SPATIAL INFORMATION EXTRACTED BY NEURAL NETWORK

Akira INOUE , Kiyonari FUKUE
Haruhisa SHIMODA , Toshibumi SAKATA

Tokai University Research and Information Center
2-28-4 Tomigaya , Shibuya-ku , Tokyo 151 , Japan

ABSTRACT

A land cover classification method using a neural network was applied for the purpose of utilizing spatial information. The adopted model of the neural network has three layered architecture, and the training method of network was the back-propagation algorithm. Co-occurrence matrices, which are extracted from original image data, were used for input pattern to the neural network. To evaluate this method, classification was conducted with this method for images of Landsat TM and SPOT HRV. Obtained classification accuracies were 7-12% higher than that of the conventional pixel-wise maximum likelihood method based on spectral information.

Key Words; landcover classification, co-occurrence matrix, neural network, texture, spatial information, Landsat TM, SPOT HRV

1.INTRODUCTION

Pixel-wise statistic classifiers using spectral information have been widely used for landcover classifications of satellite imagery. However, these classifiers do not present enough classification accuracy in many practices. One of the methods to improve the classification accuracy is to utilize spatial information contained in imageries. Though various studies on texture analysis for remotely sensed data have been done from this viewpoint, the results of these studies have not shown high classification accuracies as expected.

The most typical texture feature is expressed as a co-occurrence matrix, which is presented as a two dimensional array. Because of the difficulty to treat two dimensional arrays in conventional statistic classifiers like a maximum likelihood method, some scalar parameters, like energy, entropy, moment, etc, are extracted from co-occurrence matrix(Haralik,1979), and these features are used as a feature vector for classifier. However, these scalar parameters can contain only a part of texture information, hence it is desirable to utilize co-occurrence matrix itself.

On the other hand, it is easy to handle two dimensional data in neural networks. Therefore, classification using the original co-occurrence matrix can be carried out simply by using a neural network. In this paper, a classification method utilizing a neural network is proposed in order to use co-occurrence matrix as spatial information.

2. PROPOSED METHOD

The neural network model used in this study is a feedforward three layered network composed of the input, hidden and output layers. The proposed method is consisted of three phases, i.e., training of neural network, classification of each band of the image and final decision of classification categories.

At the training phase of neural network, co-occurrence matrices of each classification category are inputted to the input layer. Connection weights of each neuron are changed in a manner that the neuron at the output layer corresponding to the category should output the maximum score. This training method is called as a back-propagation algorithm. The co-occurrence matrices are generated from training samples which have the size of 5x5 pixels. Distance and direction of co-occurrence matrix is 1 pixel and 8 directions, respectively. This training is performed for each band individualy.

At the classification phase, co-occurrence matrix for a 5x5 pixel window, which moves pixel by pixel on the target image, is inputted to the input layer. Each neuron corresponding to each category at the output layer outputs a score as a recognition result to the inputted data. From these outputted scores, 1'st and 2'nd largest scores and categories corresponding to these scores were extracted as candidates of classified category. This second phase classification is performed for each band of the target image.

At the final decision phase, classification results for each band are combined and then the classification category for each pixel is decided. Two kinds of combining method, a maximum score method(MSM) and a maximum frequency method(MFM), are applied in our experiment. In the MSM, the final classification category is decided to the category in which sum of scores show the maximum value. In the MFM, it is decided to the category which shows the maximum frequency of candidate categories.

3. EXPERIMENT

In order to evaluate the proposed method, a Landsat TM(ch.1,2,3,4,5 and 7) image and a SPOT HRV(XS and P mode data) image were classified using the proposed method. Figure 1 shows the target image samples. The Sagami river basin in Japan was selected for the target area. This area includes the digital test site area which is already investigated and categorized to 52 landcover/use categories. It is easy to evaluate the accuracy of landcover classification using digital test site data. Table 1 shows 12 classification categories used in this experiments.

A personal computer with the neural network simulation board was used in the experiment. The maximum number of neurons at the input layer is limited to 1000 in this simulation board. Thus the maximum size of co-occurrence matrix is limited to 32x32, that means gray levels of target images should be 32 or less. From this reason, pixel data of target image were converted linearly from 8 bits to 5 bits.

Training samples were extracted randomly from the area overlayed with digital test site data. Training processes have converged to zero error after about 600 times of trainings. Figure 2 and Table 2 shows classified results and area weighting average of classification accuracies which is calculated by using digital test site data.

4. EVALUATION

A conventional pixel-wise maximum likelihood classification(MLC) using only spectral data was applied to those target images in order to compare the efficiency of the proposed method. This classification was done to 8 bits original image data. Classification accuracy of this method is shown in Table 2.

From Table 2, MSM and MFM showed similar performances as a combining method, though MSM showed a little higher classification accuracy. The proposed method using MSM achieves 7% and 12% higher accuracy for the images of Landsat TM and SPOT HRV, respectively compared to the classification results of MLC.

5. CONCLUSIONS

Co-occurrence matrix was used as a spatial information source for classification. In order to handle the co-occurrence matrix, a three layered neural network was utilized. Furthermore, two kinds of method

combining the classification result of each band were examined. Image data of Landsat TM and SPOT HRV were classified into 12 landcover categories and the classification accuracy is calculated by using digital test site data.

Although gray levels of target images were reduced from 256 levels to 32 levels, the proposed method improved accuracy of landcover classification for the test image data compared to the case of using conventional pixel-wise maximum likelihood classification method. Reduction of gray levels is caused from the limitation of the experiment system used. Utilization of a neural network is effective to adopt co-occurrence matrices in classification of satellite imagery.

REFERENCES

[1] Haralik, 1979. Statistical and structural approaches to texture. Proc. IEEE, vol.67, pp.786-804.

Table 1   Landcover categories.

		Major
1	coniferous tree	tree
2	broad leaved tree	
3	shadow of mountain	
4	paddy	paddy
5	high density area	urban
6	low density area	
7	factory	
8	sea	water
9	river	
10	grassland	other
11	sand	
12	bare ground	

(a)Landsat TM
(Nov.4,1984)

(b)SPOT HRV(XS+P)
(Jan.31,1989)

Fig.1 Target images.

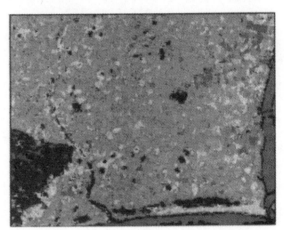

(a)Landsat TM

(b)SPOT HRV(XS+P)

Fig.2 Classified Results (combining method=MSM).

Table2 2 Classification accuracies.　　　　(%)

target image	combining method	major categories					weighting average
		tree	paddy	urban	water	other	
Landsat TM (ch.1-5,7)	MSM	43	50	75	59	48	62
	MFM	52	54	79	56	36	61
	MLM	58	72	70	66	20	55
SPOT HRV (XS+P)	MSM	32	33	78	62	20	62
	MFM	38	42	80	57	12	62
	MLM	47	26	52	78	33	50

Classification of Multispectral Imagery Using Dynamic Learning Neural Network

K.S. Chen, Y.C. Tzeng[+], C.F. Chen, W.L. Kao, and C.L. Ni

Center for Space and Remote Sensing Research
National Central University
Chung-Li, Taiwan, Republic of China

Abstract

This paper presents the results of classification of SPOT high resolution visible (RHV) multispectral imagery using neural network. The test site, located near Taoyuan county of the northern Taiwan, is an agriculture area containing small ponds, bare and barren soils, vegetation, built-up land, near shore sea, and man-made buildings. The classifier is a dynamic learning neural network (DL) using the Kalman filter technique as adaptation rule. The network architecture is the multi-layer perceptrons,i.e., feed-forward nets with one or more layers of nodes between the input and output nodes. Methodology of selection of training data sets is addressed. Then, accordingly, selected data sets from 512x512 pixels three-band image are used to train the neural nets to categorize different types of the land-cover. Both simulated and real images are used to test the classification performance. Results indicate that the DL substantially reduces the training time as compared to commonly used back-propagation (BP) trained neural network whose slow training process was shown to impede it from certain practical applications. As for the classification accuracy, the presented results also shown to be excellent. It is concluded that the use of dynamic learning network gives very promising classification results in terms of training time and classification accuracy. In particular, the proposed network significantly improves the practicality of the land-cover classification.

I. Introduction

The applications of the neural network to remote sensing is increasingly emerging in recent years and continues receiving attentions, although it is still in early stage, due to the following characteristics of a neural network[1,2,3]:(1) it has an intrinsic ability to generalize; (2) it makes a weaker assumptions about the statistics of the input data than a parametric Bayes classifier; and (3) it is capable of forming highly nonlinear decision boundaries in the feature space and therefore has the potential of outperforming a parametric Bayes classifier when a feature statistics deviate significantly from the assumed Gaussian statistics. The comparison of traditional statistical methods(such as k-nearest neighbor, and Gaussian classifier) made by Benediktsson et al[4] indicates that the neural network has the potential for processing multisource remote sensing data. Heermann and Khazenie[5] used a back-propagation neural network to classify the multispectral image data and concluded that neural network is a feasible classifier for very large volume images. Similar study was also carried out by Bischof et al [6] and showed that the neural network outperform the maximum likelihood classifier. In view of these studies, they all used back-propagation learning scheme which no doubt is the most popular one. Nevertheless, all these applications shows the drawback of slow learning process that inherently associated with back-propagation training scheme. In this paper, we shall use a newly developed dynamic learning neural network to perform the classification of SPOT HRV image. Two separated simulated images are constructed resembling a real image with known grey levels at each class; one is used for training the network and the other for classfication. The method of generation and simulation results are presented in Section 2. Section 3 illustrates the experimental result using a SPOT image where the ground truth was collected when it was imaged, to show the classifying capability of the presented network. Finally, a concluding remark is included.

II. Test of Network

A. Generation of Simulated Images

To test the performance of dynamic learning neural network developed in [7], we use the testing image with known parameters including mean and variance of grey level at three bands for each class such that the classification accuracy can be more easily evaluated. It should be noted that the simulated images should also be generated in such a way that they remain similar spatial and spectral complexity as the actual multispectral image, if it is so. The testing image thus designed has in fact ruled out the possibility of ideal situations where the neural network may perform extremely well while with little practical value. Two images are generated for the purpose of network test: one is used for training, and the other for testing the classification. In the following, we will describe the procedures on generating of such images. First, select an 512 x 512-pixel frame from an arbitrary SPOT image and then apply ISODATA clustering algorithm [8] to classify it into several classes (eight classes in this study). Next, we assume that the distribution of the grey level are normal with predetermined mean and variance. The assignments of the mean and variance at each class and each band are listed in Table 1. Noted that the variability of grey levels depends on the choice of variance; larger overlap with larger variance. Then, the image(Image I) is formed by randomly specifying grey level to each class at each band according the statistical distributions. In this study, we choose variance equal to 4 for all bands and classes. The resulting image is shown in Fig.1. It is seen that the boundaries thus generated are rather complex, making the classification using conventional statistical methods very difficult, if not impossible. The second image (Image II) is constructed from another SPOT image in the same procedure preserving similar properties but with different mean grey level values by one. Fig.2 shows the Image II which apprantly presents a different boundary pattern with Image I.

B. *Testing Results*

The arrangement of the inputs and outputs of the neural network is illustrated in Fig.3. To present the multispectral data to network, we first encode the input data sets. The purpose of encoding of a feature, a set of data, is to provide a mean to discriminate the similarity that diminishes the accuracy of the neural network during the classification stage. The detail discussions of the issue can be found in[10]. The training cycle for eight classes is now compared between DL and backpropagation using delta rule as given in Fig.3. It is obviously that the BP fails to reach a predetermined error threshold which is set to be 10^{-3} in this study, even after 200 training cycles. On the other hand, DL quickly achieves the required *rms* error in just a couple of iterations. Once the network has been trained using the training patterns from image I, generally, it should be able to classify images with statistically similar response without additional training process. To illustrate this statement, we now apply the network directly to classify image II. The resulting classification matrix is given in Table 2. As we can see, very high accuracy well over 95% for all classes under the consideration is obtained. It should be recalled that the mean grey level values of image II are all deviated from that of image I by one. The misclassfication rate is found to be dependent on the correlated properties of the related classes. In another word, higher overlapped may degrade the classification accuracy, which is in consistent with the fact under the practical situations. To resolve this problem, other information contents, such as texture and radar response, are helpful for the classification. This is beyond the scope of this study and will not be addressed further here.

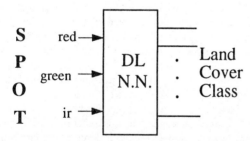

Fig. 3. Typical configuration of the neural nenetwork

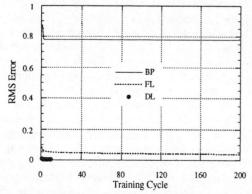

Fig. 4. Comparison of number of training cycle

Table 1: Mean assignments, variance = 4 in all cases

class	1	2	3	4	5	6	7	8
R	106	85	125	63	87	71	91	52
G	107	71	33	55	85	67	50	42
IR	99	73	48	61	83	69	59	51

Table 2: Classification Matrix for Image II using DL

class	1	2	3	4	5	6	7	8	u.c.	accur .%
1	22260	0	0	0	0	0	0	0	793	96.6
2	0	22286	0	0	0	24	0	0	286	98.6
3	0	0	16482	0	0	0	0	0	432	97.4
4	0	0	0	95023	0	3	0	1	546	99.4
5	0	2	0	0	32592	7	0	0	193	99.4
6	0	2	0·	14	0	34715	0	0	257	99.2
7	0	0	0	0	0	0	32071	0	76	99.8
8	0	0	0	0	0	44	0	3726	310	91.3

III. Experimental Results

In the previous section, we have demonstrated the excellent performance of the dynamic learning algorithm using two simulated images. Results indicate that the network training time is greatly reduced as compared to BP, while gives a very high classification accuracy. The application of DL to land-cover classification of SPOT high resolution imaginary data is now in order.

A. *Test Site*

The test site selected for classification in this study, located near Taoyuan county of the northern Taiwan, is an agriculture area containing small ponds, bare and barren soils, vegetation, built-up land, near shore sea, sea water wave, and man-made buildings. In this region, most areas were covered by the short vegetation within which several small ponds exist. Total of seven categories to be classified in this study based on the discriminating capability of the SPOT multi-spectral image: water, vegetation, bare soil, high reflection roof, barren land, sea wake, and built-up land. The false color imagery is shown in Fig.3 where The small in size but very bright area represented the highly reflective building roof. The correlation between different bands are computed to understand the correlated properties of different types of land-cover. High reflection roof is clearly the most distinguished one, while the bare land and building are not well discriminated. Also indicated is the fact that all types of land-cover are almost not discernible except high reflection roof and bare soil.

B. *Training Data Selection*

The neural network is trained by presenting a training data set of known category assignments. For the purpose of this study, we generate a set of training data by the aids of visualization and some of the ground truth, along with available base maps. The regions under these are selected as training data with total of 692 data points. The rest of the regions are then used for classification as will be presented in next section. Among them, high reflection roof and barren land have smallest percentage of training patterns due to a small regions they occupy in the feature space.

C. *Classification Results*

Fig.4 shows the classified image in which the major feature of the seven categories of interest can be identified. To asses in a more detail the performance of DL neural network classifier, a set of total 2000 pixels are randomly picked up from the image frame. Additional 1000 pixels are selected to aid the assessment of classification in the area of reflective roof and build-up land which are more difficulty to classify due to more complex decision boundaries, smaller occupied regions, and thus fewer representative training data sets. A simple random sampling scheme[9] is then applied to evaluate the classified map. Both 1:5000 and 1:25000 base maps, and field works are used as auxiliary data to assistant the performance evaluation. It is found that an overall 92% of accuracy is obtained. It should be emphasized at this point that in our previous test using the SPOT-like images, we have demonstrated the excellent performance of the proposed network.

IV. Conclusions

The significant reduction of the training time required and high accuracy of the presented neural network using dynamic learning algorithm based on the both simulated and real SPOT imaginary results have been demonstrated. The capability of the neural network to resolve the highly nonlinear and complex decision boundary problems, which usually are the cases of remotely-sensed data, is also illustrated. In comparison, the presented network outperforms Back-propagation network in that the newly developed learning algorithm has enhanced the practical uses in the land-cover classification from multispectral imagery. It should be emphasized that the use of Kalman filter enables the seasonal change detection from satellite images because the update equation which accounts for the change of states can be incorporated into the network. This should be of interested for further investigation.

V. References

[1]. R.P. Lippmann, "An introduction to computing with neural nets," *IEEE Acoustic, Speech and Signal processing Magazine*, 4(2):4-22, April 1987

[2]. D.R. Hush and B.G. Horne, "Progress in supervised neural networks," *IEEE Signal processing Magazine*, 10(1):8-39, Jan.1993

[3]. S. Haykin, W. Stehwien, C. Deng, P. Weber, and R. Mann, "Classification of radar clutter in an air traffic control environment," *Proc. IEEE*, 79(6):742-772, 1991.

[4]. J.A. Benediktsson, P.H. Swain, and O.K. Ersoy, "Neural network approaches versus statistical methods in classification of multisource remote sensing data," *IEEE Trans. Geosci and Remote Sensing*, 28:(4), 540-552,1990.

[5]. P.D. Heermann and N. Khazene, "Classification of multispectral remote sensing data using a back-propagation neural network," *IEEE Trans. Geosci and Remote Sensing*, 30:81-88, 1992

[6]. H. Bischof, et al, "Multispectral classification of Landsat images using neural networks," *IEEE Trans. Geosci and Remote Sensing*,28:482-489, 1992

[7]. Y.C. Tzeng and K.S. Chen, "A dynamic learning neural network using Kalman filtering technique," submitted paper, 1993.

[8]. G.H. Ball and D.J. Hall, "A clustering technique for summarizing multivariate data," *Behavioral Science*, 12, 153-155, 1967

[9]. R.G. Congalton, "A comparison of sampling schemes used in generating error matrices for assessing the accuracy of maps generated from remotely sensed data," *Photogrammetric Eng. & Remote Sensing*, 54(5): 593-600, 1988

[10].J.L.McCelland, D.E. Rumelhart, and G.E. Hinton, "The appeal of parallel distributed processing," in *Parallel Distributed Processing*, vol I, Rumelhart and McCelland, Eds, Cambridge, MA:MIT Press, 1986

Fig. 1. Simulated SPOT-like image (Image I)

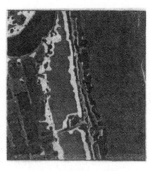
Fig. 2. Simulated SPOT-like image (Image II)

Fig. 5. False color SPOT HRV image of test site

Fig. 6. Classification results using DL network

Chapter 20
Seismic Signal Processing

Seismic signal processing deals with signals propagating through the Earth. Man-made signals are used to reveal the structure of the underlying ground. Natural signals are intercepted and processed to determine their origin. Seismic signal processing has not enjoyed as much attention as the other areas in this part, but the results are as impressive here as they are in the other areas. **Paper 20.1** addresses the discrimination of earthquake from explosion through passively received acoustic data. **Paper 20.2** compares the facie classification performance of the multilayer perceptron (MLP) network when trained on data collected by one company and tested with data collected by another.

Chapter 20:   *Seismic Signal Processing*

RECOGNITION OF EARTHQUAKES AND EXPLOSIONS USING A DATA COMPRESSION NEURAL NETWORK

Roy C. Hsu, Shelton S. Alexander
Electrical Engineering Department, Geosciences Department
The Pennsylvania State University, University Park, PA 16802
Tel.:814-863-7246; FAX: 814-863-7823
E-mail: hsu@geosc.psu.edu or shel@geosc.psu.edu

Abstract–The ability to reconstruct unlearned images using a neural network trained with a learned (known) image represents the generalization property of the network. Such a trained neural network should achieve significant data compression and give satisfactory reconstructions of both the original, learned image(s) and unlearned images belonging to the same class. The degradation of the reconstructed image compared to the original is expected to be least for the reconstructed, learned image, somewhat greater for a similar but unlearned image, and significantly greater for a dissimilar unlearned image. The method developed and tested in this study is based on the generalization properties of the trained image compression neural network and a measure of the degradation of the reconstructed image over the population of similar events and dissimilar events (i.e. explosions vs earthquakes).

INTRODUCTION

Image data compression and generalization capabilities are important for neural net models as learning machines. The data compression capability of neural networks has been investigated by various researchers in recent years [2, 6], and this study builds on these previous studies in developing a new method to distinguish explosion seismic signatures from earthquake signatures. The motivation for this particular application is the need to identify in near-real time any small, underground nuclear explosions that occur in a background of a large number of natural earthquakes; seismic monitoring in this context is one of the principal means of enforcing nuclear non-proliferation agreements among countries that have or may be trying to develop nuclear capabilities.

To implement the image compression neural network, the seismic signatures are first processed and transformed into 2-D frequency-velocity or frequency-slowness images to train the neural nets. The method developed for event identification is based on the generalization properties of the trained image compression neural network and a quantitative measure of the degradation of the reconstructed image over the population of similar events and dissimilar events (i.e. explosions vs earthquakes).

SIGNAL ANALYSIS AND PRE-PROCESSING

The distinctions between earthquake and explosive sources are manifested in the observed signals at any propagation distance through the relative excitation of compressional- and shear-wave signals. An explosive source generates only compressional waves, theoretically, whereas an earthquake source generates both compressional and shear waves. Propagation through a typical layered earth structure leads to very complicated seismic signatures resulting from multiple, different travel paths of each wave-type to the receiver, conversions from one wave-type to another at each boundary and constructive interference in the layers which produces dispersed surface wave modes in the waveguide. Despite the complexity of the signals and their variability as the source location and depth changes, explosions have a significant fraction of the total signal energy concentrated in the early, mostly compressional-wave portions of the signal whereas earthquakes have relatively more energy concentrated in the later portions comprised mostly of shear waves and surface waves.

In order to compare on a common basis signals that have travelled different distances and hence have different durations, it is desirable to transform from time to slowness or velocity. It is also desirable to compare the spectral distribution of signal energy present at common propagation velocities or slownesses. Therefore, the original time-domain signal for each event is transformed into a frequency-slowness or frequency-velocity image with the corresponding spectral amplitude assigned to each pixel. The transformation from time to slowness or to velocity is achieved by using the known distance to each event and the time that it occurred; the time point in the recorded signal corresponding to a given slowness or velocity is then easily determined. Determination of the spectrum of the signal present at that slowness or velocity completes the transformation to frequency-slowness or frequency-velocity. Events of the same type that are located at different distances will have closely matched images after this transformation.

To obtain the signal spectrum at a time corresponding to a given slowness or velocity, a moving window is centered on that time and the product of the signal and the window function is Fourier-transformed; the resulting spectrum is then assigned to the given slowness or velocity and used to construct the frequency-slowness or frequency-velocity image. In this study a moving box car window function with a cosine taper at both ends is applied to the seismic signal and the Fourier transform of each window is computed to perform the signal-to-image transformation. The length of the moving window used is 3 to 5 seconds (or 120 to 200 data points at the sampling rate of 0.025 sec^{-1} for NORESS array data) which encompasses at least three cycles of the lowest frequency comprising the seismic signal. The windowed signal is then padded with zeros to a total of 512 points and its FFT computed. The resulting 256 spectral amplitudes are assigned to the slowness or velocity of the center point of the window and used with spectra for other windows positions to construct the frequency-velocity or frequency-slowness seismic image.

To improve the signal-to-noise ratio of the images in this study, array stacking was performed over the 25 channels of vertical-component seismic signals at the NORESS array in Norway (Figure 1). In brief, the velocity-frequency or slowness-frequency seismic image is computed on each channel to include a noise window ahead of the first signal arrival (P_n). The seismic image for each channel is then corrected for noise by substraction and averaged across the array. To overcome the problem of different magnitude events, normalization with respect to the maximum value of the composite image is done after the array stacking procedure. Thus, a two-dimensional composite image with a maximum value of unity is obtained for each event.

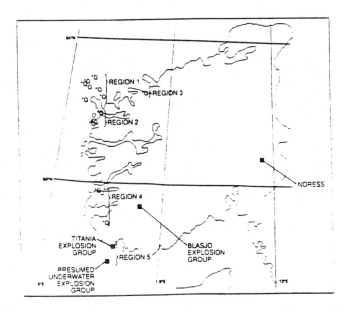

Figure 1. A set of known earthquakes (labeled as Q) and mining (chemical) explosions located in Scandanavia and recorded at a dense 2-dimensional seismic array (NORESS) in Norway. (Modified from [1])

657

Because a 256×256 pixel image is rather large to be used as the neural network input, the image was smoothed in both frequency and velocity to create a smaller decimated image of size 64×64; then the pixels below 1.25 and above 16.25 Hz (maximum frequency 20 Hz) were excluded in the input because of low signal to noise levels. Thus, the final size of the image compression neural network input and reconstructed output is 64×48.

METHOD DESCRIPTION

Figure 2 shows the image compression neural network for seismic signature recognition. The number of input and output nodes is the same (64×48),

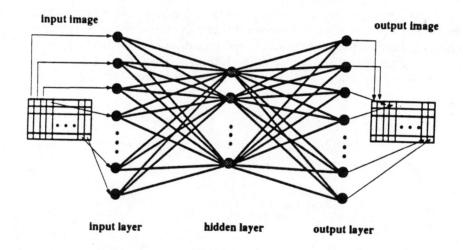

while the number of hidden nodes is selected as 64, significantly less than the number of the input and output nodes. The transmission channel in a traditional image compression neural network is eliminated for the task of seismic signature recognition. The algorithm used in the training of the neural network and adjustment of synaptic weights is error back-propagation learning [5], which gives a gradient-descent minimization of the overall error function in the output nodes. A momentum term is added in the calculation of incremental weight adjustment to speed up the convergence of the error back-propagation learning algorithm. Training of the neural network defines a composite weighting matrix to compress an image belonging to a particular class and a second composite weighting matrix to reconstruct approximately the corresponding complete image. The structure of this neural network is similar to a three-layered perceptron; however, it has the further advantage that the network not only can place an unknown event in the correct population but also identify the event(s) in the population most similar to the unknown one by comparing the variances calculated in the output layer. More detailed insight concerning within-class and opposite-class, diagnostic event features can be gained by examining the residual image constructed from the pixel by pixel difference between and input and reconstructed image. For example, portions of the input image that most closely match the composite class characteristics will have small residual values compared to other parts of the image.

The decimated 64×48 image calculated as described earlier is then used as the input to an image compression neural network to perform seismic event recognition. Application of this image compression neural network for seismic event recognition consists of the following steps:

1. Convert the two-dimensional training image (64×48 pixels in the example here) into an input vector to the neural network, which has an arbitrary number of hidden nodes (but significantly less than the input),

2. Train the neural network using images of events of the same type (i.e. explosions or earthquakes), stopping the iterations when the variance of the difference between the original and reconstructed image reaches a selected threshold or no longer decreases. The variances between the resulting reconstructed images and the true images are computed to establish the degradation expected over the population of each event type.

3. Train the neural network using images of events of the opposite type and repeat the procedures in step 2 to obtain another trained network. The variances between the resulting reconstructed and true input images are computed to establish the expected degradation over the population of this event type. We then have two trained networks which have the capability to generalize and reconstruct images representative of these two different types of events.

4. Process an unknown event through both the explosion and earthquake trained neural networks and compute the variance between the reconstructed and true image in each case.

5. The smaller of the two variances obtained in Step 4 indicates the population to which the unknown event belongs, thereby identifying it as an explosion or an earthquake.

6. Confidence estimates of the liklihood of correct classification can be found by comparing the observed variances with the distributions of variances for each type of events obtained in Steps 2 and 3.

The variance used in Step 2 and 3 is the Normalized Mean Square Error (NMSE) which gives both trained networks a comparable error criterion for the convergence of training. Note that a more complete use of known events would be to carry out Steps 1-3 above, training on each known event and for each obtain within- and opposite-population variances. Step 4 would be repeated using all of the trained neural networks and the resulting set of variances for the unknown event would be used for the classification. This approach has the further advantage that it would not only place an unknown event in the correct population but also identify the event(s) in the population most similar to the unknown one. In addition, a residual image can be constructed that shows which parts of the image are controlling the identification.

DATA SET

In the real situation, several known explosions and several known earthquakes may be available to use in applying this method in some geographic regions of interest, whereas for others very few or no known explosions and earthquakes may be available. In the case where only a few known events of each type are available with which to train the network the method would succeed, provided the true (but unknown) within- and opposite-population variance distributions do not overlap. If no observations of one or both types of events are available, synthetic signatures can be generated using models of the sources and models of the propagation media; in this case the training would be done treating the synthetic signals as known events.

To test the effectiveness of this neural network method, it was applied to a set of known earthquakes and mining (chemical) explosions located in Scandanavia and recorded at a dense 2-dimensional seismic array (NORESS) in Norway (Figure 1). Chemical explosions were used for this test because they share similar characteristics with underground nuclear explosions and several that were located near earthquakes were available for analysis [1].

EXPERIMENTAL RESULTS AND DISCUSSION

Figure 3a shows a sub-set of 4 of the 25 vertical-component seismic array recordings at NORESS for one of the known Scandanavian earthquakes.

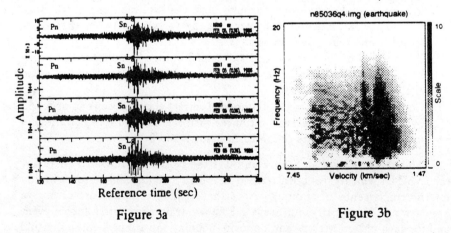

Figure 3a   Figure 3b

Figure 3. (a) A sub-set of 4 of 25 vertical-component seismic array recordings at NORESS for one of the known Scandanavian earthquakes. (b) Frequency-velocity image for the total time window shown in 3a.

Each of the 25 signals was transformed into a frequency-velocity image by calculating the Fourier power spectrum of a moving velocity window applied to the signal and plotting the resulting amplitude (or log amplitude) vs frequency at the velocity corresponding to where the window was centered in the signal. By making a noise correction to each individual image and summing the noise-corrected images over the 25-element array a composite image with greatly improved signal-to-noise levels were obtained for each event. These composite images were then used as the inputs to the neural network calculations described earlier. Figure 3b shows the composite frequency-velocity image computed in this manner for the event shown in Figure 3a; the gray-scale values correspond to the energy levels in the signal at any given velocity and frequency. Figure 4a shows a subset of 4 of the 25 NORESS array signals for a known mining explosion located in the same general area as the earthquake shown in Figure 3. Figure 4b shows the corresponding composite image for this explosion. (Note that the spectral modulation evident in this image is the consequence of ripple-firing where the source consists of a set of delayed explosive charges [1, 3, 4].)

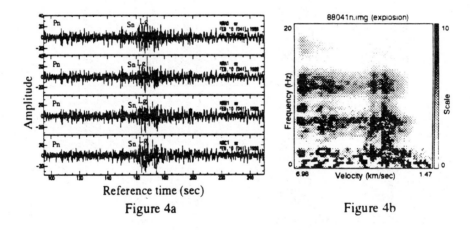

Figure 4a

Figure 4b

Figure 4. (a) A sub-set of 4 of 25 vertical-component seismic array recordings at NORESS for one of the known Scandanavian explosions. (b) Frequency-velocity image for the total time window shown in 4a.

A total of 11 natural earthquakes and 11 mining explosions recorded by the NORESS array were used in this study (Figure 1). Due to the small number of available known events in that area, a "leave-one-out" scheme was used in the neural network training. A particular known event is left out during the training phase and treated as unknown to test the trained networks; then a different known event is left out and the training done on the others, etc. Thus, the number of "unknown" events is 22, half earthquakes and half explosions. To maximize and preserve the generalization properties of the trained networks, every known event was re-ordered randomly in each training cycle. To halt the training process, the epoch NMSE was used and calculated until it reached a pre-selected threshold value (0.1 in this study). The epoch NMSE gives both trained networks a comparable criterion to use in a global sense for the convergence of training for the two populations of earthquake and explosions.

The identification results and the variances of the within- and opposite-population of earthquakes and explosions are shown in Table 1. All 11 "un-known" explosions and 10 "unknown" earthquakes are correctly identified,

Table 1. Identification results and the variances of the within- and opposite-population of earthquakes and explosions.

CLASSIFICATION OF EVENTS

"Unknown" Events	NMSE" (Earthquake NN Reconstruction)	NMSE" (Explosion NN Reconstruction)	Correct Identification (Y/N)
EQ1	0.0601	0.6481	Yes
EQ2	0.1481	0.8282	Yes
EQ3	0.1659	1.0454	Yes
EQ4	0.0672	0.1714	Yes
EQ5	0.0756	0.3460	Yes
EQ6	0.1045	0.1794	Yes
EQ7	0.0653	0.3805	Yes
EQ8	0.0697	0.6127	Yes
EQ9	0.0605	0.5518	Yes
EQ10	0.1431	0.6294	Yes
EQ11	0.3296	0.1765	No (?)
EXP1	0.6975	0.2574	Yes
EXP2	0.3773	0.3287	Yes
EXP3	0.5135	0.4455	Yes
EXP4	0.5173	0.1362	Yes
EXP5	0.9201	0.2985	Yes
EXP6	0.8376	0.1739	Yes
EXP7	0.4439	0.2505	Yes
EXP8	0.6966	0.4332	Yes
EXP9	0.4225	0.1911	Yes
EXP10	0.8023	0.5950	Yes
EXP11	2.4536	0.2266	Yes

** NMSE: Normalized Mean Square Error

while one event (EQ11) may be mis-identified. Except for EQ11 the within-population variances for the earthquakes are consistly smaller than those of the opposite-population. This result shows that the natural earthquakes from this area share similar frequency-velocity patterns. Even though all "unknown" explosions are correctly identified, the within- and opposite-population variances of two explosion events (labeled EXP2 and EXP3) differ only marginally. This indicates that the two events have different frequency-velocity patterns compared with the others of the same class. By looking at the frequency-velocity images, we found that both images exhibit scalloping effects along the velocity axis in certain frequency ranges, and both images have multiple spectral modulations (more than 4) which indicates longer than typical delay times for the explosive charges comprising the ripple-fired source.

The mis-identified event (which is labeled EQ11 and initially reported as a natural earthquake) is a questionable event (Baumgardt, personal communication). It was initially classified as natural earthquake, because no report existed indicating that there is a mining blast in the area where the event occured. It was later strongly suspected to be a mining blast due to the scalloping effect exhibited in the image in which case we have correctly identified it as an explosion. Another possibility is that it is a double earthquake source consisting of a mainshock-aftershock or a foreshock-mainshock pair of events closely spaced in time; this could produce the spectral modulation similar to that of a ripple-fired mining explosion.

Two residual images from the reconstruction of earthquakes and explosions by the earthquake trained neural network are shown in Figure 5. Figure 5a shows the residual image of a reconstructed earthquake; the residual differences are small and distributed relatively uniformly over the entire image, indicating that most parts of the image are contributing to the classification. However, the residual image of a reconstructed explosion using the same earthquake trained neural network (Figure 5b) exhibits relatively large residuals in portions of the image where the signal to noise in the input image is large. These large residuals identify the portions of the explosion image that are distinctly different from the earthquake population.

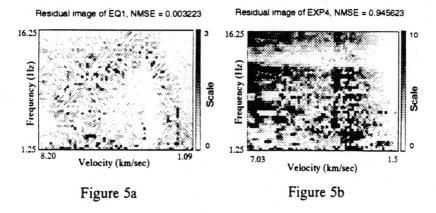

Figure 5a   Figure 5b

Figure 5. (a) A residual image of a reconstructed earthquake obtained from an earthquake trained neural network. (b) A residual image of a reconstructed explosion obtained using the same earthquake trained neural network.

SUMMARY AND CONCLUSIONS

In this paper, an image compression neural network architecture for seismic signal recognition is implemented and tested. The conclusions from the experimental results using this method are:

1. A data compression neural network trained on frequency-velocity seismic

images of the two event classes can correctly identify regional explosions and earthquakes.

2. Comparison of the NMSE from the reconstructed image using each of the trained neural networks on an unknown event provides an effective means of identification.

3. Stacking of individual, noise-corrected frequency-velocity images over an array of recording stations significantly improves the signal-to-noise of both the training set and unknown events, thereby enhancing the effectiveness of the compression neural network identification.

4. Smoothing and decimation of each initial 256×256 frequency-velocity image to a 64×48 pixel representation for input to the neural networks does not appear to seriously degrade the performance of the method.

5. This type of of image compression trained neural network can be applied in near-real time to enable large number of unknown events to be quickly identified.

ACKNOWLEDGEMENTS

The authors would like to thank Dr. Douglas R. Baumgardt of ENSCO Inc. for providing the data sets used in this study and for several very helpful discussions. Colleagues at the Pennsylvania State University also provided valuable comments and suggestions.

REFERENCES

[1] D. R. Baumgardt and G. B. Young, "Regional seismic waveform discriminants and case-based event identification using regional arrays," *Bull. Seism. Soc. Am.* vol. 80, No. 6, pp. 1874-1892, Dec. 1990.

[2] G. W. Cottrell and P. Munro, "Principal component analysis of images via back propagation," SPIE vol. 1001, *Visual Communications and Image Processing*, pp. 1070-1077, 1988.

[3] Z. A. Der and D. R. Baumgardt, "Automated seismic analysis using supervised machine learning," Technical Report, SAS-TR-TR-92-92, ENSCO, Inc., Springfield, Virginia, 1992.

[4] M. A. H. Hedlin, J. B. Minster, and J. A. Orcutt, "An automatic means to discriminate between earthquakes and quarry blasts," *Bull. Seism. Soc. Am.* Vol. 80, No. 6, pp. 2143-2160, Dec. 1990.

[5] D. E. Rumelhart, G. E. Hinton, and R. J. Williams. "Learninf internal representations by error propagation." In D. E. Rumlhart and J. L. McClelland (Eds.). *Parallel Distributed Processing, Vol. 1: Foundations* (p. 318). Cambridge, MA:MIT Press, 1986.

[6] N. K. Sonehara, M. Kawato, S. Miyake, and K. Nakane, "Image data compression using a neural network model," Proc. IJCNN, 1989, Washington DC, pp. II35-II41.

ON THE COMPARISON RESULTS OF THE NEURAL NETWORKS TRAINED USING WELL-LOGS FROM ONE SERVICE COMPANY AND TESTED ON ANOTHER SERVICE COMPANY'S DATA

Heidar A. Malki
University of Houston
Electrical-Electronics Technology
Houston, Texas 77204-4083

Jeffrey L. Baldwin
Mind & Vision Computer Systems
18627 North Lyford
Katy, Texas 77449

Abstract--This paper demonstrates the ability of neural networks to recognize facies logged by two different service companies on the same well. Two main tests were conducted: 1) Train the network with one service company and test it with another service company's data and 2) Train the network with both service company's data and test on each service company's data.

I. INTRODUCTION

The main goal of this paper is to compare the result of facies classification obtained from processing two different service company's data on the same well using neural networks. Specifically, if a neural network is trained on a set of training patterns extracted from one service company's well-log suite, then how well the network will perform on the log data obtained from another service company is of primary concern. This is a very important task which depends on several parameters such as resolution of the logging devices, noise, and human operator technique. It is a very difficult problem to address if conventional software packages are used for this comparison.

A geologist can classify facies from visual inspection of log data curves in combination with past experience. A geologist relies on experience and memory of what facies exist, and the appearance of log curves in various depositional environments when classifying facies from well logs. Neural networks can perform repetitious, mundane tasks involving pattern recognition faster and more efficiently than humans due to the parallel architecture of neural networks. It is worth mentioning that neural networks do not replace geologists. They will, however, allow more efficient utilization of the geologist's time and experience by performing repetitious facies identification from log profiles [1].

Neural networks have been successfully used to identify facies from well-log data. Lovenzetti [2] used neural networks to predict lithology from Vp and Vs acoustic data. Peck et. al. [3] applied neural networks for lithological interpretations. In [4] synthetic spontaneous potential (sp) and resistivity logs are used to train neural networks for lithology classification. All of this work has shown promising results in this field. To the best of our knowledge, no one has applied neural networks to train one service company's data and test it with another service company's well-log data. This has been a challenging task and an important problem for many geologists and log analysts using the conventional methods. In this paper, we have conducted this task with reasonable success.

II. GEOLOGY AND WELL LOG DATA

The geology of rocks used in this research is complex and multifaceted. This is a good test case because the complexity of these rocks matches that of most difficult-to-solve, real-world problems and because there is excellent control in this research well.

Most of the rocks in this well are comprised of silicon and aluminum-silicon crystalline structures called silicates and aluminosilicates. The rocks were formed by sedimentation in lagoons and near shore fronts, so these rocks are described geologically as siliciclastic. While a few limestone, dolomite, and coal formations are present, the overwhelming majority of rocks are of remarkably similar physical properties such as density, amount of void space (porosity), etc. This is due to the fact that most rocks are aluminosilicates and created by similar sedimentation mechanisms.

Subsurface formations are measured by various downhole devices lowered into wellbores after a hole has been drilled to a prespecified depth. The measurements are of three basic classes: electrical, nuclear, and acoustic. Each of these measurement classes has several different types of measurements (called logs because the recordings used to be written in log books) that can be made. For example, measuring the resistivity of formations with radio waves and recording the naturally occurring electrical potentials that exist downhole are both electrical measurements. Also, determining the rock density with gamma radiation, the rock void space space with neutron radiation, and recording naturally occurring levels of radiation in rocks are all three nuclear measurements. The physics of these measurements is well known but the interpretation of exactly what they mean is anything but clear.

The types of logs used in this research are short-spaced conductivity, natural gamma ray activity, bulk density, photoelectric effect, and neutron porosity recorded on a sandstone scale. Two service companies provided their versions of these measurements: Schlumberger (SWS) provided CLLS, GR, LDT RHOB, PEF, and CNL NPHI, while Welex - now Haliburton Logging Services (HLS) - provided SGRD, GR, SDL RHOB, PES (short-spaced), and DSN NPHI.

Even though the same well is logged by both service companies, there are differences between the two determinations of intrinsic formation characteristics. These differences are 1) Naturally-occurring borehole enlargement after the SWS logs and before the HLS were run has caused uncompensated environmental effects in the HLS logs, 2) Different fabrication and design of the two companies' measurement tools, and 3) Slightly different recording practices between the two companies (SWS has recorded one set of data at 1/2-foot increment and another set at 1/10-foot increment while HLS has recorded all data at 1/4-foot increments). These types of differences occur often and must routinely be dealt with in some manner by the petrophysicists who interpret log measurements. Since SWS and HLS logs in this well exhibit differences that are as similar as those observed in normal petrophysical data processing environments, then the data set used in this research will be representative of real-world requirements for neural network versatility if a successful interpretation is to be achieved.

Log measurements are utilized for a variety of tasks both quantitative and qualitative. Quantifying amount and type of hydrocarbons-in-place has obvious economic interests. Geologists often use log measurements to discover information about the geology and depositional environments of formations so as to predict location and size of reservoirs from data taken in a single well. The quantitative and qualitative relationships between log measurements and desired results are often highly non-linear, perturbed in varying degrees by white and non-white noise, only partially parameterized, and often overly simplistic. This is thus a field of science in need of technologies such as are afforded by neural networks.

III. RESULTS AND DISCUSSION

Several neural network training sets and structures were constructed for this segment of the research. The training set for the first segment performed and published [5] earlier this year was taken from a human's sequence stratigraphic interpretation. The training sets for the work reported here were obtained from a visual lithofacies description performed by a petrophysicist skilled in the art. In this work we have used multilayer neural networks based on the back-propagation training algorithm [6].

The practice of this research was to train on SWS and test on HLS data, and then train on the same HLS data and test on SWS data. Results were then contrasted for comparable network and data set configurations. The configuration alterations were of three types: 1) Changes to input log normalization ranges, 2) Increased curve filtering

by block average of the high resolution SWS data, and 3) Increased number of neurons in the hidden layer.

Results of training and testing the neural networks upon the two service companies' data sets are abstracted in this paper. A set of training procedures and parameter values established in the first segment of this research [5] was decided upon and this set of procedures and values was not significantly altered during this research work (e.g., number of training cycles=100000 always, Boltzmann Machine connection updates were always used, temperature annealing was always used). Thus, we were able to look separately at the effects of the three network and data set configuration alterations listed above.

Table I presents comparisons related to normalization effects. Column 1 lists the lithofacies number and column two shows the number of occurrences of each type in the test interval. Not every depth was assigned a lithofacies description and the total number of points in the test interval was about 10 times as large as this validation set. The remainder of the columns in this table present Percent-Correct-Classification (PCC) results for each of the neural network and data set configurations used. The bottom row in each table list totals of each column (the PCCs of individual lithofacies must be adjusted by the frequency of occurrence before computing the total PCC for each column). The top row of each table lists which network was used (numbered in arbitrary order), followed by which company's data was used for training (S=SWS, H=HLS) and then by which data was used for testing.

SWS input log data was normalized to some range before training and testing. When the HLS data utilized these same normalization ranges then the notation "H(U)" appears in the table to indicate that the HLS was data un-normalized to HLS ranges. When the HLS data utilized normalizations ranges that were derived for HLS data then the notation "H(N)" appears. If the SWS data utilized normalizations ranges derived from HLS data, then the notation "S(U)" is used. The notation "S" indicates that SWS data has been normalized to ranges derived for SWS data.

Table I clearly indicates that the best neural network performance is obtained by normalizing each data set to its own compatible range. Such ranges are discovered by crossplot of each input log datum from one company against the same log datum type from the other company. Effects of calibration error and to a lesser extent tool design and fabrication are thus normalized-out. The different neural networks appearing in Table I are for different degrees of block averaging on the SWS input data. In every case, using compatible normalization ranges produces the best results.

Notice, however, that training on SWS and testing on HLS data does not produce quite as good results as training on HLS and testing on SWS data. This is due to the uncorrected environmental effects in the HLS data. When a network trains on HLS data, it is able to produce correct results from erroneous and correct data (environmental effects are not present in every HLS log at every depth).

However, when a network trains on SWS data where the data is completely correct then it has no ability to compensate for incorrect data. This has implications for persons in the petroleum industry wishing to make use of this technology: be sure to train using both "perfect" data and some representations of problem data.

Table II presents comparisons of networks trained with differing degrees of averaging on the SWS data. The amounts of averaging correspond roughly to 14 levels, 22 levels, 32 levels, and 44 levels. Averaging of 32 levels produced input SWS curves of roughly equivalent resolution compared to the HLS curves. The 44 level average was included to test the hypothesis that training on HLS and testing on SWS data produced better results than vice versa because the higher frequency content of the SWS data appears to the network as "noise". This hypothesis is invalidated by over-averaging the SWS logs and repeating the tests (the last two columns in Table II). This table again has implications for persons in the petroleum industry wishing to make use of this technology: be certain that the resolution of the training set is either the lowest of all sets to be tested in the future, or include representations of low resolution data in the training sets.

Table III presents comparisons of networks with different hidden layer sizes (24, 30, and 35 neurons). The three sets of neural network structure sizes encompass changes in the amount of filtering on the SWS input log curves and change training sets to simultaneously include both SWS and HLS log data. Table 3 demonstrates that for all cases, 30 neurons in the hidden layer produces better results than 24 neurons, but not as good as for 35 neurons. Optimal network size for this problem is thus about 30 neurons. Also, it is apparent that better results are obtained when both service companies' data are used to produce training sets. The implications are clear: 1) test several neural network configurations to determine optimal network size, and 2) be certain to include in a training set representations of as many service company data sets as you plan to process in the future.

IV. CONCLUSIONS

Perusal of Table I clearly reveals that the best neural network performance is obtained by normalizing each data set to its own internally compatible range. Table 2 indicates that including low resolution data in the training sets increases the correct classification in the testing phase. Table 3 demonstrates that optimal network size for this problem is about 30 neurons. Finally, better results are obtained when both service companies' data are used to produce training sets.

ACKNOWLEDGMENT

The authors wish to thank Exxon Production Research Company for providing the data which this research is based on.

REFERENCES

[1] J. L. Baldwin, "Using a Simulated Bi-directional Associative Neural Network Memory with Incomplete Prototype Memories to Identify Facies from Intermittent Logging Data Acquired in a Siliciclastic Depositional Sequence: A Case Study," SPE #22843 presented at the 1991 Annual Technical Conference and Exhibition, Dallas, TX, October 6-9, 1991.

[2] Elizabeth A. Lovenzetti, "Predicting Lithology from Vp and Vs using Neural Networks," submitted to Society of Exploration Geophysicists Annual Meeting, October 24-27, 1992.

[3] M. D. Pollitt, J. Peck, and J. J. Scoble, "Lithological Interpretation Based on Monitored Drilling Performance Parameters," The Metal Mining Division of CIML, 1991.

[4] M. D. McCormack, "Neural Computing in Geophysics," Geophysics, January, 1991.

[5] Heidar A. Malki and Jeffrey L. Baldwin, "Well-Log Analysis using Multilayer Neural Networks to Classify Facies," IEEE International Conference on System Engineering, Kobe, Japan, September 17-19, 1992.

[6] D. E. Rumelhart, G. E. Hinton, and R. J. William, "Learning Internal Representation by Error Propagation," in D. E. Rumelhart and J. L. McClelland (eds.), Parallel Distributed Processing: Explorations in the Microstructure of Cognition. Vol. 1: Foundations, MIT Press, 1986.

TABLE I. EFFECTS OF NORMALIZATION RANGE CHANGES

FACIES #	FREQ	23 S H(U)	23 S H(N)	25 S H(U)	25 S H(N)	29 S H(U)	29 S H(N)	24 H(U) S(U)	24 H(U) S(N)	26 H(N) S(U)	26 H(N) S(N)
1	103	0	3	0	0	0	11	0	14	31	44
2	11	27	73	0	73	100	100	0	0	0	0
3	47	43	94	32	83	0	49	0	0	0	0
4	446	11	56	10	67	7	29	100	93	100	84
5	31	100	74	100	100	100	100	100	100	100	100
6	105	0	8	0	17	0	35	73	70	72	72
7	41	0	0	0	0	0	20	100	100	100	100
8	375	96	92	99	95	91	77	35	23	22	29
9	47	89	96	55	89	83	96	26	53	55	38
10	82	100	96	100	100	100	100	96	100	94	100
11	21	0	0	100	100	100	100	0	0	0	0
12	26	100	100	100	100	100	100	0	12	0	0
TOTAL	1,335	46	62	46	69	44	54	61	58	61	58

TABLE II. EFFECT OF AVERAGING SWS LOGS
(TRAINING AND TESTING)

FACIES #	FREQ	23 14 LEV S S	25 22 LEV S S	28 32 LEV S S	29 44 LEV S S	23 14 LEV S H(N)	25 22 LEV S H(N)	29 32 LEV S H(N)
1	103	24	36	28	40	3	0	11
2	11	100	100	100	100	73	73	100
3	47	81	100	100	70	94	83	100
4	446	92	92	94	93	56	67	29
5	31	100	100	90	100	74	100	100
6	105	62	67	69	89	8	17	35
7	41	100	85	100	100	0	0	20
8	375	83	87	88	86	92	95	77
9	47	94	83	96	100	96	89	96
10	82	100	100	100	99	96	100	100
11	21	100	100	100	100	0	100	100
12	26	65	92	100	100	100	100	100
TOTAL	1,335	82	85	86	87	62	69	54

TABLE III. EFFECT OF CHANGING NETWORK SIZE

FACIES #	FREQ	31A-1 S+H S 24N	32A-1 S+H S 30N	35A-1 S+H S 35N	29A-1 S S 24N	34A-1 S S 35N	29A-3 S H(N) 24N	34A-3 S H(.5) 35N	31A-3 S+H H(.5) 24N	32A-3 S+H H(.5) 30N
1	103	0	30	0	40	43	11	13	0	35
2	11	0	91	0	100	100	100	100	0	100
3	47	0	72	0	70	51	49	27	0	73
4	446	100	97	0	93	73	29	30	97	95
5	31	100	100	0	100	100	100	86	100	100
6	105	74	77	0	89	52	35	20	64	76
7	41	93	100	0	100	93	20	0	100	100
8	375	82	83	0	86	88	77	87	94	94
9	47	96	96	0	100	91	96	100	100	100
10	82	100	98	0	99	100	100	100	100	100
11	21	100	100	0	100	86	100	0	100	100
12	26	0	100	0	100	100	100	100	0	100
TOTAL	1,335	79	86	2	87	77	54	52	79	88

Chapter 21
Speech Processing

Like character recognition (Chapter Fourteen), speech recognition by machines has long been considered to be the ultimate method of interacting with computers. Closer examination of the problem reveals the complexity of the problem. As examples of this, speech is different for every person (accents, rate, volume), speech recognition by humans takes a great deal of context into account, and speech can be polluted with widely varying types of noise (including other speech). Because neural networks learn from historical data and they can generalize fairly well, they have been one of the key tools used in the speech processing toolbox. The eleven papers found in this chapter address several areas within speech processing. **Paper 21.1** describes the application of self-organizing feature map (SOFM) neural network and the time-delay neural network (TDNN) to the recognition of voiced-stop-consonants in speech. **Paper 21.2** presents a recurrent neural network entitled Memory Neuron Networks and applies the network to the classification of voiced explosives in speech. **Paper 21.3** presents a unique combination of lipreading and speech processing for the recognition of connected speech with a TDNN. **Paper 21.4** combines neural networks and fuzzy systems to create a fuzzy partition model for frame recognition. **Paper 21.5** describes the combination of neural networks and fuzzy systems for isolated word recognition. **Paper 21.6** reports the results of spoken word recognition with neural networks when the words are transmitted over a phone line with noise. **Paper 21.7** describes the application of a recurrent TDNN to speaker verification. **Paper 21.8** also focuses on speaker verification, but employs an auditory neural model of the cochlea in place of the TDNN. **Paper 21.9** addresses the removal of noise from speech using a TDNN. **Paper 21.10** presents a hybrid radial basis function (RBF) network and Hidden Markov Model approach to wordspotting. **Paper 21.11** proposes a recurrent MLP approach to normalizing the speech rate in an effort to make further speech processing simpler and more reliable.

Chapter 21:   Speech Processing

Speaker-Independent Voiced-Stop-Consonant Recognition Using a Block-Windowed Neural Network Architecture

Benjamin D. Bryant and John N. Gowdy

Electrical & Computer Engineering Department
Clemson University

Abstract

A critical problem in multi-speaker, continuous-speech recognition is the correct segmentation of an unknown speech signal into its component speech units. A phoneme recognition system would attempt to segment an input utterance into component phoneme tokens. Since the speech signal is a pseudo-random, dynamically-changing signal, the spectra produced for the same utterance by different speakers or by the same speaker at different instances of time will vary. Various connectionist architectures have been proposed to deal with the time and frequency variability of a given utterance produced by different speakers or different instances of the same utterance spoken by the same speaker. This research investigated some of the proposed connectionist architectures for their time and frequency shift-invariant properties.

1: Introduction

Because of the time and frequency shift-variability of speech spectra, many current connectionist models seem to be "less than robust" for modeling the complex interactions that must be taking place within the central auditory nervous systems (CANS) of human listeners upon speech perception. It is known from studies of the auditory periphery that nerve fibers going from the basilar membrane of the cochlea to the CANS encode information in at least three ways: place of innervation along the membrane, mean-firing rate, and interspike time-intervals [1]. To be considered as biologically accurate, therefore, a connectionist architecture is needed which can process at least these three types of auditory information encodings from the cochlea.

While this lack of robust connectionist models inhibits the complete modeling of the transmission and recognition mechanism in the peripheral auditory nervous system (PANS) and the CANS, current network models have performed quite well on the phoneme recognition task and others, given their limitations.

This research focused on the study of several of the more well-known connectionist models, and how they address the time and frequency variability of the multi-speaker, voiced-stop-consonant, recognition task. Among the network architectures reviewed or tested for this work were the Self-Organizing Feature Maps (SOFM) architecture by Kohonen [2], various derivaties of this architecture [3,4], the Time-Delay Neural Network (TDNN) architecture by Waibel et al. [5], various derivatives of this architecture [6,7], and the frequency and time shift-invariant architectures: Frequency-shift-invariant TDNN, and Block-Windowed Neural Network (FTDNN and BWNN) by Sawai [8].

Voiced-stop speech was extracted from up to four dialect regions of the TIMIT continuous speech corpus for subsequent preprocessing and training and testing of network instances. Various feature representations were tested for their robustness in representing the voiced-stop consonants [9].

After reviewing or testing the above listed architectures, it was decided to use the BWNN architecture by Sawai for all further studies [8]. This was due to its relatively simple implementation and small number of required parameters.

2: Feature Extraction

As mentioned above, feature representations were obtained from the extracted voiced-stop instances of TIMIT using various feature extraction techniques. For the sake of less variability among stop instances, only instances from the male speakers of up to the first four dialect regions of TIMIT were used to produce training and testing data. These extracted stop instances were preprocessed using an auditory model developed by Seneff [10], and a conglomerate mel-cepstral preprocessor developed by Bryant [9]. An important point to note concerning the extracted stop instances is that the instances extracted from TIMIT were variable-sample-length. This stop extraction procedure resulted in the production of a variable number of frames per training or testing token compared to the constant number of frames per token in the early work by Waibel et al. [5]. This variable number of frames per token produced worse results than could have been obtained using tokens of constant length, and is an area of ongoing research. The chosen feature extraction methods produced 40-dimensional representative frames at 10 ms frame intervals. A maximum of 15 frames were produced per token which corresponded to 150 ms of speech. For further information concerning the feature extraction algorithms used here, see the works by Seneff and Bryant [10, 9].

3: Evaluation of Architectures

Initially, the choice was made to investigate the SOFM architecture by Kohonen [2]. This architecture uses an unsupervised training rule to map feature vectors belonging to a given phoneme class to certain topographic regions of the network. In other words, certain regions of the network become "tuned" to "listen" for matching feature vectors. This process is very much like the traditional LVQ coding technique with the exceptions being that the training takes place according to a different training rule, and topographic regions of the net are mapped to certain classes after training. Upon presentation to the trained and calibrated net of an unclassified vector sequence, the network would hopefully create a series of trajectories which would indicate which phonemes were present in the sequence.

While the original SOFM performed well for cases in which the vector sequences were aligned for recognition, the architecture proved to be less robust for cases in which this alignment might be difficult or impossible to obtain. In these cases, adjustments were made to the original SOFM to give it a measure of robustness to temporal shift variability. Work by Kangas [3] and Torkkola and Kokkonen [4] attempted to take into account the time-shift variability of speech using the SOFM architecture by concatenating vector frames in the input or using the trajectories of the produced "neuron" firings to indicate which phonemes were being spoken during a given interval. In addition to this work, the work by McDermott et al. used the same input frame concatenation idea, but did not use the Kohonen learning rule for the updating of weight vectors attached to individual units [11]. An example of McDermott and Katagiri's LVQ-based shift-tolerant architecture is given in Figure 1 below.

The next series of evaluated architectures were the TDNN-based architectures, the first of which was originally designed by Waibel et al. to account for the time-shift variability of speech [5]. This architecture

originally used the backpropagation of errors training algorithm to obtain weight convergence.

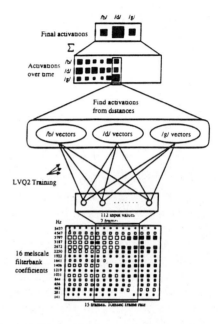

Figure 1. Linear-vector-quantization-based shift-tolerant architecture (Reproduced with permission of McDermott).

A large difference in the TDNN and a massively-connected FFNN, is the constraints on the weights for the TDNN and the sparse connectivity between subsequent layers. For more information concerning the weight constraints, see Bryant [9]. Figure 2 illustrates the TDNN architecture.

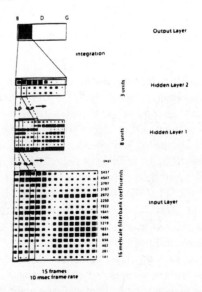

Figure 2. The Time-Delay Neural Network Architecture (Reproduced with permission of Waibel).

674

Various derivatives of the basic TDNN have been proposed. Among these architectures are the Linked-Predictive Neural Network architecture by Tebelskis et al. [12], the Meta-Pi architecture by Hampshire et al. [6], and the Integrated TDNN architecture by Hataoka et al. [7]. Each of these extensions to the TDNN architecture were attempts to scale the TDNN architecure to the multi-speaker or word recognition tasks. The Meta-Pi model and the Integrated TDNN architecture were of particular interest to this work, as they both attempted to scale the original TDNN to the multi-speaker, phoneme recognition task, and the integrated TDNN in particular was trained using the TIMIT continuous speech corpus.

The last set of networks evaluated for this work were those by Sawai [8]. The FTDNN and the BWNN architectures were attempts to handle the frequency-shift variance in addition to the time-shift variance of speech as will be encountered upon training networks using speech from different speakers. The BWNN architecture in particular was based on windowing each layer of the network with slideable time/frequency windows which make it possible to capture global features from upper layers and precise local features from lower layers. Illustrations of both the FTDNN and the BWNN are given in Figures 3 and 4 respectively.

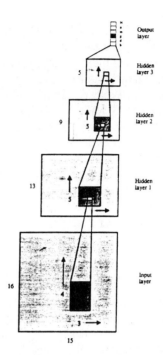

Figure 4. Block-windowed neural network architecture (Reproduced with permission of Sawai).

In some initial studies by Sawai concerning cross-speaker recognition ability of the FTDNN, BWNN, and original TDNN architectures, the BWNN was shown to give superior results compared with those of the other two architectures. This difference was amplified as the task went from the recognition of phonemes extracted from word speech to the recognition of phonemes extracted from continuous speech. Table 1 lists recognition results for the three architectures. It is notable that the BWNN architecture performed better than the other two architectures for all cases studied.

Table 1. Phoneme recognition results between different male speakers (%) (Reproduced with permission of Sawai).

Network	TDNN	FTDNN	BWNN
Word speech	59.8	75.2	80
Short phrase	60.3	63.2	69.1
Long phrase	65.9	68.5	72.8
Continuous	55.2	63.2	66.8

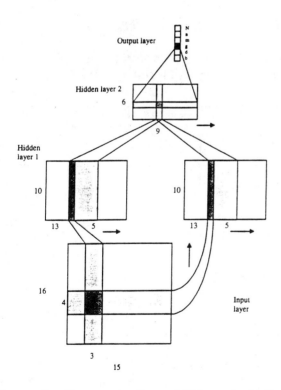

Figure 3. Frequency-time-shift-invariant time-delay neural network (Reproduced with permission of Sawai).

Based on the results of Sawai's testing which was illustrated in Table 1 comparing the performance of various architectures on a cross speaker recognition task, and because of the relatively small number of parameters and training time for these architectures compared with the Meta-Pi, Linked-Predictive, or Integrated TDNN architectures, the BWNN architecture was chosen for all following work. The BWNN or FTDNN architectures are thought to enable a lower error rate on the TIMIT multi-speaker corpus than the original TDNN. This hypothesis has some flaws. Among them are the fact that the BWNN will perform worse upon testing tokens as the tokens are time-shifted. This was communicated in a personal message from Sawai to Bryant earlier this year, and is due to the lack of weight constraints such as those found in TDNN training.

4: Results

After having chosen the BWNN architecture through some initial testing and evaluation of information, the first simulation task was designed to determine which network and window parameters for the BWNN architecture would give the best overall performance for the three-class, voiced-stop recognition task. This was determined by testing a total of 4 different network configurations and calculating an average recognition rate across all feature representations tested for each configuration (there were initially 4 types of feature representations tested per network configuration giving a total of 16 trained network instances). The network configuration that had the best average recognition score is shown in Figure 5. This network configuration was used for all subsequent simulations.

After determining the "best" configuration given the input and output layer size constraints, BWNN configuration #3 was trained using progressively more data to test network robustness as the training data set size increased. The training set size went from 386 training tokens to 2842 training tokens for data from one to four dialect regions data. The extracted stop instances were preprocessed into tokens as mentioned above, and the networks were trained using the representations obtained from three of the chosen feature extraction techniques (see Bryant [9]). Table 2 shows the results from the training set size scaling simulations. It is notable that the average recognition score rose with the addition of training data.

In a final series of simulations, the network was trained with data that had been corrupted with varying amounts of white Gaussian noise. This series of simulations was designed to test feature representation robustness and network generalizability to additive noise.

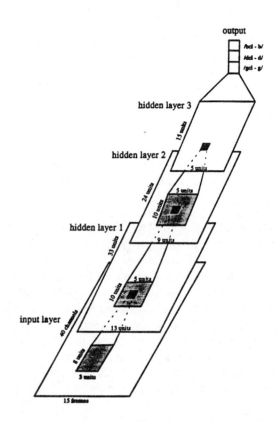

Figure 5. BWNN configuration #3.

Table 2. Percent correct recognition using various amounts of training data.

pre-processing method	One dialect region's data	Two dialect region's data	Four dialect region's data
mel-cepstral - pre-emphasis	59.8	66	67
auditory model synchrony resp.	67.3	67.8	71.3
auditory model mean-rate resp.	72.9	68.4	72
Recognition$_{Ave.}$	66.7	67.4	70.1

The equations governing the additive noise were given in Bryant [9], and will not be repeated here for the sake of space. The noise was added in 5 db SNR decrements from clean speech down to the 0 db SNR case. Figure 6 illustrates the effects that the additive noise had on the feature representation robustness and network generalization abilities.

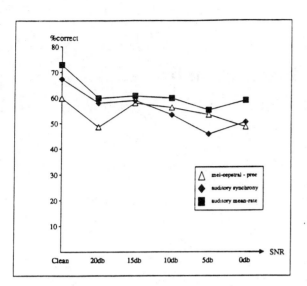

Figure 6. Recognition results obtained after training with data corrupted with varying amounts of additive Gaussian noise.

5: Conclusions

The results from the above simulations demonstrated the effectiveness of the chosen feature extraction techniques in representing the informational content of the voiced-stop instances. Additionally, the BWNN architecture is postulated to have contributed to a better recognition rate in the cross-speaker task than the TDNN or a massively-connected FFNN. This postulation remains to be determined experimentally.

6: Bibliography

[1] Yost, William A., and Donald W. Nielson. Fundamentals of Hearing: An Introduction. Holt, Rinehart, and Winston Publishers, New York, NY, 1977.

[2] Kohonen, Tuevo. "The Self-Organizing Map." Invited paper, Proceedings of the IEEE, volume 78, number 9, September, 1990.

[3] Kangas, Jari. "Phoneme Recognition Using Time-Dependent Versions of Self-Organizing Maps." Proceedings of ICASSP, volume 1, 1991.

[4] Torkkola, Kari, and Mikko Kokkonen. "Using the Topology-Preserving Properties of SOFMs in Speech Recognition." Proceedings of ICASSP, volume 1, 1991.

[5] Waibel, A., T. Hanazawa, G. Hinton, K. Shikano, and K. Lang. "Phoneme Recognition Using Time-Delay Neural Networks." IEEE Transactions on ASSP, volume 37, number 3, March, 1989.

[6] Hampshire, John B. II, and Alex H. Waibel. "The Meta-Pi Network: Connectionist Rapid Adaptation for High Performance Multi-Speaker Phoneme Recognition." Advances in Neural Information Processing, volume 2, Morgan Kaufman Publishers, San Diego, Cal., 1990.

[7] Hataoka, Nobuo, and Alex H. Waibel. "Speaker-Independent Phoneme Recognition on TIMIT Database Using Integrated Time-Delay Neural Networks (TDNNs)." Proceedings of IJCNN, 1990.

[8] Sawai, Hidefumi. "Frequency-Time-Shift-Invariant Time-Delay Neural Networks for Robust Continuous Speech Recognition." Proceedings of ICASSP, volume 1, 1991.

[9] Bryant, Benjamin D. Speaker-Independent Voiced-Stop-Consonant Recognition Using Various Feature Representations and a Block-Windowed Neural Network. M.S. Thesis, Clemson University, December, 1992.

[10] Seneff, Stephanie. "A Joint Synchrony/Mean-Rate Model of Auditory Speech Processing." Journal of Phonetics, volume 16, 1988.

[11] McDermott, E., and S. Katagiri. "Shift-Invariant Phoneme Recognition Using Kohonen Networks." Proceedings of the Acoustical Society of Japan, October, 1988.

[12] Tebelskis, Joe, Alex Waibel, Bojan Petek, and Otto Schmidbauer. "Continuous Speech Recognition Using Linked-Predictive Neural Networks." Proceedings of ICASSP, 1991.

Temporal Sequence Classification by Memory Neuron Networks

Pinaki Poddar & P.V.S.Rao
Computer Systems & Communications Group
Tata Institute of Fundamental Research
Bombay 400 005, INDIA
Email: poddar@TIFRVAX.BITNET

Abstract

A recurrent connectionist architecture, called Memory Neuron Network (MNN), has been applied for classification of temporal sequences. The network architecture allows a learnable, parametric representation of the activation history of the units. It had been shown that the network is generalized version of network with time-delays. The Learning protocol had been developed to train a collection of such networks as discriminant models for classes of temporal sequences. The design was tested in classification of voiced plosives /B/,/D/,/G/. Due to continuous movement of the articulators, the spectral characteristics of the speech signal change during transitions from one phoneme to the other. MNN had been used to model this dynamic behaviour during the transitions from plosive sounds to vowels.

1 Introduction

One of the major application areas for connectionist modeling is in classification of patterns into distinct categories. A canonical description of the pattern classification task can be made in terms of a set of scalar *discriminant functions*, $g_c(\mathbf{x}), c = 1, \dots, C$. Each discriminant function $g_c(\mathbf{x})$ maps the samples of class c such that $g_c(\mathbf{x}) > g_{c'}(\mathbf{x})$ for any $c' \neq c$ and for any $\mathbf{x} \in c$. In a sequential pattern classification paradigm, each input sample is represented by a temporally ordered set of observation vectors $\mathbf{X}_1^T = (\mathbf{x}_1, \dots, \mathbf{x}_T)$. The objective, in this case, is to estimate a set of *discriminant models*, $G_c(\mathbf{X}_1^T)$ which can map a sequence of arbitrary length into a scalar value for comparison.

In classification tasks, where the input observations are of fixed dimensionality and their order of occurance is immaterial, connectionist networks can be used to approximate non-linear discriminant functions [1]. This class of networks is called *static* because response of the network to the current input is independent of the past inputs or the previous history of the network. On the other hand, in sequence classification, where the temporal order of the input observation vectors would be a major consideration for categorization, a *dynamic* connectionist network that makes use of the the past activities of the network itself to generate the current response would be required.

In this paper, we study a recurrent connectionist network called the Memory Neuron Network (henceforth, MNN) [2] and its application as a discriminant model for classification of multivariate stochastic sequences. MNN offers a parametrized mechanism to *internally* represent the past states of the network. The internal representation is not determined *a priori* and is learnable for a particular task. In the first section, the architecture and learning rule of MNN are described. MNN can trained to be a predictive model of a class of stochastic sequences. A classifier system using a collection of MNN and trained in both discriminative and non-discriminative fashion had been described in the second section. The third section presents experimental results on performance of such classifier system for classification of speech spectral sequences of the burst to vowel transition for the voiced stops in a CV context (/B/,/D/,/G/).

2 Connectionist Architecture for Temporal Processing

In this section, we discuss the nature of connectionist architecture required for temporal processing and describe the architecture of MNN which is a modified version of the MultiLayer Perceptron (MLP), a classic form of static connectionist architecture [3]. A basic element or unit in an MLP receives its input from its neighbouring units through independent link-weights. The net input to an unit is transformed into an output activation by a (possibly non-linear) transfer function.

Dynamic connectionist networks implement sequential behaviour by allowing the current activity of an unit to be affected by the past activities of neighbouring units. The general formalism is to express the net input activation equation as a discrete convolution,

$$
\begin{aligned}
x_i(t) &= \sum_{j \in \mathcal{N}(i)} w_{ij}(t) * u_j(t) \\
&= \sum_{j \in \mathcal{N}(i)} \sum_{k=0}^{t} w_{ij}(k) * u_j(t-k)
\end{aligned}
\tag{1}
$$

To account for the entire past activity of $u_j(t)$, in a most general case, there should be t adaptable weights to represent the delay kernel. The linear increase in the length of the delay kernel with time is undesirable and infeasible in most applications. The basic aim of a parametric representation of the delay kernel is to find the conditions under which the kernel can be approximated by a fixed number (*i.e.* independent of t) of parameters.

2.1 Architecture of the Memory Neuron Network

The Memory Neuron Network incorporates a special set of *memory neurons* to store the past activities of each original neuron of a conventional static MLP network. Each original neuron is augmented with an array of neurons that store its past activations in a recursive structure. The original neuron representing the current activation is referred to as a *network neuron* and the associated neurons as *memory neurons*. We represent the activation of the augmented structure as $u_{ik}(t)$, where $k = 0$ would denote the network neuron and $k > 0$, the memory neurons. The dynamics of the system is described by the following set of equations,

$$x_i(t) = \sum_{j \in \mathcal{N}(i)} \sum_{k=0}^{K} w_{ijk} \cdot u_{jk}(t) \tag{2}$$

$$u_{i0}(t) = g_i(x_i(t)) \tag{3}$$

$$u_{ik}(t) = (1 - \mu_i)u_{ik}(t-1) + \mu_i u_{i,k-1}(t-1) \tag{4}$$

The weight w_{ijk} denotes the link to the i-th unit from the k-th memory neuron augmented to the j-th network neuron *i.e.* $u_{jk}(t)$. The adaptive coefficients, μ_i, referred subsequently as *memory coefficients*, determine the activations of the memory neurons. It would be shown later that the depth of the memory structure, K together with the memory coefficient describe the past activities of the each network neuron in a parametric form.

By proper choice of the memory coefficients and memory depth, the network can be configured in many ways. For example, for $\mu_i = 1$, the network reduces to a Time-Delay Neural Network architecture (TDNN) [4]. Because, then from (4),

$$u_{ik}(t) = u_{i,k-1}(t-1)$$
$$= u_{i0}(t-k)$$

So, the memory neurons are the delayed versions of the activities of the network neuron as in a TDNN. In another extreme example, for $\mu_i = 0$ or $K = 0$, the memory neurons do not contribute in the activation and the network behaves like a static MLP network.

2.2 Memory Neuron

The parameterization of the weight kernel provide an interpretation to the functionality of the memory neuron [5]. In this viewpoint, $w(t)$ can be expressed as a linear sum of a set of basis functions,

$$w(t) = \sum_j \sum_{k=1}^{K} a_k g_k(t) \tag{5}$$

where

$$g_k(t) = \frac{\mu}{(k-1)!} t^{k-1} \exp(-\mu t), \quad \mu > 0 \tag{6}$$

The set of basis functions $g_k(t)$ are known as *gamma kernel* because they are the integrands of normalized Γ-function. With appropriate choice of a_k and K, the approximation of $w(t)$ in terms of the basis functions $g_k(t)$ can be made as close as possible under L_2-norm [6]. Bert de Vries and Principe [5] showed that if the delay kernel $w(t)$ is parametrized as in (5) then the contribution of a single neuron to the net activation can be written as,

$$x_i(t) = \sum_j \sum_{k=1}^{K} a_k y_k(t) \tag{7}$$

where the variables $y_k(t)$ are computed from the recursive relation,

$$y_k(t) = (1-\mu) y_k(t-1) + \mu y_{k-1}(t-1) \tag{8}$$

Comparison with (4) shows that the variables $y_k(t)$ are identical to the memory neurons.

2.3 Learning in MNN

Learning, in the context of connectionist models, refers to the modification of the free variables of the network to optimize a given performance criterion defined over the output units. Conventional Back-Propagation (BP) algorithm for static MLP was extended for recurrent architecture by Werbos [7] and referred to as BackPropagation-Through-Time (BPTT). Learning rules for MNN had been derived using BPTT. In this method, the derivatives w.r.t. each free variable are computed recursively backwards in time starting at T, the end of the input sequence and ending at $t = 0$. Then, each free variable is modified by an amount proportional to the corresponding derivative.

3 Predictive Modeling using MNN

MNN can be trained as a generalized AutoRegressive (AR) model for a multivariate time series $\mathbf{X} = (\mathbf{x}_0, \ldots, \mathbf{x}_T)$ where the training input signal is the current sample $\mathcal{I}(t) = \mathbf{x}_t$ and the target output is the future observation $\mathcal{T}(t) = \mathbf{x}_{t+1}$ [9]. After learning to minimize the mean square error between the actual and desired output response, such a network would be similar to an AR model where the link-weights and the memory coefficients would characterize the model.

3.1 Classification by Prediction

The method of building predictive models of stochastic sequences can be extended to classification [8]. Let there be a set of sequences of arbitrary length each belonging to a particular class c. A MNN-based model for the sequences of the c-th class is denoted as $M_c(\mathbf{W}_c, \mu_c)$ where $\mathbf{W}_c, \mu_c$ are the set of weights and the memory coefficients that characterize the model. $E_{c,\mathbf{X}}$ is the prediction error when $M_c(\mathbf{W}_c, \mu_c)$ was used to predict $\mathbf{X}$. $E_{c,\mathbf{X}}$ is negatively monotonic with respect to the state-conditional probability $\Pr(\mathbf{X}|M_c)$ [10]. Hence, minimization of the prediction error would amount to maximization of the probability that $\mathbf{X}$ has been produced by the model M_c. Using Bayes rule, we can write,

$$
\begin{aligned}
\Pr(M_c|\mathbf{X}) &= \frac{\Pr(\mathbf{X}|M_c)\Pr(M_c)}{\sum_c \Pr(\mathbf{X}|M_c)\Pr(M_c)} \\
&= \frac{\Pr(\mathbf{X}|M_c)\Pr(M_c)}{\Pr(\mathbf{X}|M_c)\Pr(M_c) + \sum_{c' \neq c} \Pr(\mathbf{X}|M_c')\Pr(M_c')}
\end{aligned}
$$

Minimization of prediction error for a MNN separately would be equivalent to a Maximum Likelihood estimation of the model parameter from a Bayesian perspective. For purpose of classification, the quantity of interest is $\Pr(M_c|\mathbf{X})$, *i.e.* the a posteriori probability of model M_c given that $\mathbf{X}$ has been observed. So, in the maximum a posteriori estimate, the objective is to maximize $\Pr(\mathbf{X}|M_c)$ such that it is greater than $\Pr(\mathbf{X}|M_{c'})$ for all $c \neq c'$ and for $\mathbf{X} \in c$.

Two learning schemes were devised to train the collection of MNNs for sequential classification tasks from these two perspectives. In the first protocol, MNN for each class of sequence were trained separately. In the second protocol, for a sequence $\mathbf{X} \in c$, the parameters of the model M_c was trained to minimize the prediction error while the parameters of all $M_{c'}(c' \neq c)$ were adjusted to *increase* the prediction error such that $E_{c',\mathbf{X}} > E_{c,\mathbf{X}}$. The prediction error $E_{c',\mathbf{X}}$ can be increased using the same BackPropagation-through-time algorithm; only, in this case, the parameters should be changed *along* the direction of the gradient of the error surface instead in the opposite direction.

4 Classification of Voiced Stops

To study the learning behaviour of a collection of MNN, a set of speech spectral sequences were considered. The spectral sequences represented the transition regions of the three voiced stops (/B/,/D/,/G/) to back vowels. These were selected from manually labeled database of 200 sentences spoken by a single male speaker. The speech signal was sampled at 16 KHz and processed at 400 frames/sec with an analysis window of 160 samples. A set of 9 cepstral coefficients was computed as feature vector from 16-th order LPC analysis. There were 30 token sequences for each of the three voiced stops. These tokens were partitioned into the ratio to 2:1 into training and testing sets.

4.1 Performance Index

We compared the results of various experiments on the basis of performance indices which directly reflect the predictive accuracy of the models. The prediction accuracy of model M_c when operated on a sequence $\mathbf{X}$ was expressed as the logarithm of the normalized mean prediction error,

$$\epsilon_{c,\mathbf{X}} = 10 \log_{10} \sum_t \frac{\|\hat{\mathbf{x}}_t - \mathbf{x}_t\|}{\|\bar{\mathbf{X}} - \mathbf{x}_t\|} \tag{9}$$

where $\bar{\mathbf{X}}$ is the mean observation vector of the sequence, $\hat{\mathbf{x}}_t$ is the estimate of $\mathbf{x}_t$ by the predictive network and $\|\cdot\|$ denotes the Euclidean norm. The average class-to-class performance index between c and c' is expressed as,

$$J_{cc'} = \frac{1}{n_{c'}} \sum_{\mathbf{X} \in c'} \epsilon_{c,\mathbf{X}} \tag{10}$$

Note that, in general, $J_{cc'} \neq J_{c'c}$. The average intra-class and inter-class performance indices are defined as follows,

$$J_{\text{inter}} = \frac{1}{C} \sum_c J_{cc} \tag{11}$$

$$J_{\text{intra}} = \frac{1}{C(C-1)} \sum_c \sum_{c' \neq c} J_{cc'} \tag{12}$$

The *discrimination factor* is defined as the difference between the inter- and intra-class performance indices. In all the experiments, we report these performance indices for comparison of different learning protocols.

4.2 Simulation Results

A classifier system was a collection of three identical MNN, one for each class. In each learning epochs, all the sequences were trained in their corresponding MNN for a single update cycle of learning. The learning process was terminated after 100 epoch in a rather *ad hoc* fashion. In Table 1A and 1B, we summarize the results of the experiments in terms of the performance indices defined earlier and the classification accuracy over the training and test sets.

In fig. 1, we present the inter- and intra-class performance indices in successive epochs of two learning protocols. In MAP learning, the predictive model of a class was built with twin objectives of good predictive accuracy on the examples of its own class as well as poor prediction on members of the other classes. This objective was attained as the MAP

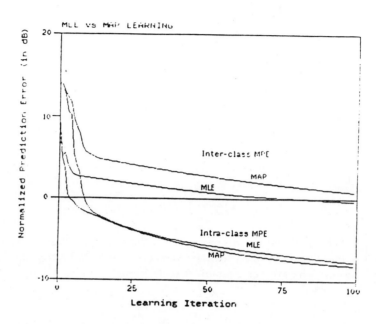

Fig 1: The intra-class and inter-class normalized mean squared prediction error (in dB) vs. learning iteration for MLE and MAP learning protocols. Effect of unlearning a negative exemplar sequence as compared to only learning the positive examples is manifested as an increased inter-class NMPE in MAP learning.

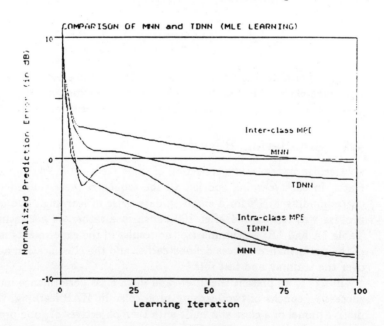

Fig 2: Comparative performance of two similar architectures: MNN and TDNN for predictive modeling. TDNN had an extra delay so that the number of free variables was the same for two architectures.

Table 1A : Performance Indices and Classification Accuracy (Train-set)

Network Model	Learning Protocol	J_{inter}	J_{intra}	Correct
MNN	MLE	-0.3	-8.2	60/60
	MAP	0.8	-7.8	60/60
TDNN	MLE	-1.2	-8.7	60/60

Table 1B : Performance Indices and Classification Accuracy (Test-set)

Network Model	Learning Protocol	J_{inter}	J_{intra}	Correct
MNN	MLE	0.7	-4.1	29/30
	MAP	1.6	-3.8	30/30
TDNN	MLE	1.2	-4.9	28/30

learning protocol achieves a higher value of J_{inter} compared to the MLE protocol.

As mentioned earlier, MNN provides a general form of time-delays and as a specific case, it can be reduced to TDNN architecture. In the second experiment, the memory coefficients were fixed to unity resulting in a TDNN model. Comparison of the performance of these two models shows that the discriminative power of MNN is better than that of TDNN, though both models are equally accurate in predicting the sequences belonging to its own class (fig. 2).

5 Conclusion

We have presented a prediction based discriminant model using Memory Neuron Network (MNN) for classification of multidimensional sequences. This architecture was employed in the classification of voiced stops with error rate of less than 5%. Despite of the limited dataset available with us, this result is promising because of the difficult nature of the task. The ability of MNN to model dynamic behaviour of speech sounds can be gainfully integrated into the recent approach of estimating the emission probabilities using connectionist networks in a Hidden Markov Model [11] or local probabilities in a Dynamic Time Warping search path [12]. The problem of poor discriminability using predictive network encountered by other researchers [13] can be avoided by more efficient modeling of MNN and employing the discriminant training methodology described here.

References

[1] K.Hornik, M.Stinchcombe and H.White, "Multilayer Feedforward Networks are Universal Approximators", *Neural Networks*, vol.2, pp.359-366, 1989.

[2] P.Poddar and K.P.Unnikrishnan, "Memory Neuron Networks: A Prolegmenon", Technical Report GMR-7493, General Motors Research Laboratory, Michigan, 1991.

[3] D.Rumelhart and J.McClelland, *Parallel Distributed Processing*, MIT Cambidge Press, 1986.

[4] A.Waibel et al, "Phoneme Recognition using Time-Delay Neural Network", *IEEE Trans. on ASSP*, vol.37, March 1989.

[5] Bert De Vries and J.C.Principe, "The Gamma Model - A New Neural Model for Temporal Processing", *Neural Networks*, (to appear).

[6] G.Szego, *Orthogonal Polynomials*, Colloquium Publications, vol.23, American Mathematical Society, Providence, RI, 1939.

[7] P.J.Werbos, "Backpropagation Through Time : What it does and How to do it", *Proc. of IEEE*, vol.78, no.10, October 1990.

[8] Kartikeyan and Sarkar, "Shape Description by Time Series", *IEEE Trans. on PAMI*, vol.11, no.9, September 1989.

[9] P.Poddar and K.P.Unnikrishnan, "Efficient Real-time Prediction and Recognition of Temporal Patterns", *IEEE Workshop on Neural Networks for Signal Processing*, Princeton, USA, October 1991.

[10] H.Boulard, N.Morgan and C.Wooters, "Connectionist approaches to the use of Markov Models for Speech Recognition", *Advances in Neural Information Processing Systems 3*, Morgan-Kaufmann, pp.213-218, 1991.

[11] H.Boulard and C.J.Wellkens, "Links between Markov Models and MultiLayer Perceptrons", *IEEE Trans. on PAMI*, vol.12, no.12, pp.1167-1178, October 1990.

[12] Ken-ichi Iso and Takao Watanbe, "Speech Recognition using Demi-Syllable Neural Prediction Model", *Advances in Neural Information Processing Systems 3*, Morgan-Kaufmann, 1991.

[13] J.Tebelskis et al, "Continuous Speech Recognition by Linked Predictive Neural Networks", *Advances in Neural Information Processing Systems 3*, Morgan-Kaufmann, 1991.

IMPROVING CONNECTED LETTER RECOGNITION BY LIPREADING

Christoph Bregler*, Hermann Hild, Stefan Manke, and Alex Waibel

University of Karlsruhe
Department of Computer Science
Am Fasanengarten 5
7500 Karlsruhe 1
Germany
bregler@ira.uka.de, manke@ira.uka.de

Carnegie Mellon University
School of Computer Science
Pittsburgh
Pennsylvania 15213
U.S.A.
hhild@cs.cmu.edu, ahw@cs.cmu.edu

ABSTRACT

In this paper we show how recognition performance in automated speech perception can be significantly improved by additional Lipreading, so called "Speech-reading". We show this on an extension of an existing state-of-the-art speech recognition system, a modular MS-TDNN. The acoustic and visual speech data is preclassified in two separate front-end phoneme TDNNs and combined to acoustic-visual hypotheses for the Dynamic Time Warping algorithm. This is shown on a connected word recognition problem, the notoriously difficult letter spelling task. With speechreading we could reduce the error rate up to half of the error rate of the pure acoustic recognition.

1. INTRODUCTION

Automated speech perception systems still perform poorly, when it comes to real world applications. Most approaches are very sensitive to background noise or fail totally when more than one speaker talks simultaneously (cocktail party effect), as it often happens in offices, cockpits, outdoors and other real world environments.

Humans deal with this distortions in considering additional sources. Very often misclassified acoustic signals can be corrected with the use of higher level context information. In recognition systems this is partly covered by language models or grammars. Psychological studies have shown [3], that on the lower level additional information contributes to human hearing as well. Besides the acoustic signal from both ears, visual information, mostly lipmovements, are subconsciously involved in the recognition process. This source is even more important for hearing impaired people, but also contributes significantly for normal hearing recognition.

We investigate this phenomena on the letter spelling

---

*The author is now with International Computer Science Institute, 1947 Center Street, Berkeley, CA 94704

task. No grammars or other higher level information are employed. If visual information is missing as well, even humans perform poorly. Just remember how hard it is to recognize spelled names at the telephone.

The spelling task is seen as a connected word recognition problem. As words we take the highly ambiguous 26 German letters. A test person in front of a microphone and video camera is spelling names and random letter sequences in German. We did not care about high quality recordings, we even degraded the acoustic signal with artificial noise to simulate some real world conditions.

As speech recognition system we present an extension of an existing Multi-State Time Delay Neural Network architecture (MS-TDNN) [6] for handling both modalities, acoustic and visual sensor input. It is shown how recognition performance with integrated acoustic and visual information achieves significant improvements over acoustic input only.

2. BIMODAL ACQUISITION AND PRE-PROCESSING

Our recording setup consists of a conventional NTSC camera and microphone. The video images are grabbed in real-time (30 fullframes/sec) into our workstation and are saved as 256x256 pixel images with 8bit grey-level information per pixel. This squared region covers the full face of the speaker. In parallel the acoustic data is sampled at a 16KHz rate and 12bit resolution. Also timestamps were saved, because the correct synchronization between audio and video signals is critical for later processing.

For acoustic preprocessing we follow the established approach to apply FFT on the Hamming windowed speech data in order to get 16 Melscale Fourier coefficients at a 10 msec frame rate. For visual preprocessing there is still the active discussion, how much preprocessing heuristics is appropriate before some connectionist classification schemes are applied to the data. We follow the idea to allow only transformations with fairly low information reduction. In other preprocessing algorithms like edge

687

detection, some "hard decisions" are made, which may hide useful information for the later learning scheme. In fact it has been reported [10] that such edge detectors are learned automatically in cases were it is necessary.

We apply two alternative preprocessing techniques: Histogram normalized grey-value coding, or 2 dimensional Fourier transformation. In both cases we just consider an area of interest (AOI) centered around the lips, and low pass filter these AOIs. The AOIs were initially segmented by hand, but an automatic procedure is now also available [11].

Grey-Value coding: We found that a 24x16 pixel resolution is enough to recognize lip shapes and movements (Figure 1). Each of these AOI pixels is the average grey-value of a small square in the original image (low pass filter). The grey-levels are rescaled in such a way that the darkest/brightest 5% in the histogram are coded with -1.0/1.0. The remaining 90% are scaled linear between -1.0 and 1.0.

2D-FFT: The AOI is rescaled to a 64x64 pixel image so that the 2 dimensional FFT results also with 64x64 coefficients. We just consider the log magnitudes of the first 13x13 FFT coefficients and rescale them to [-1.0, 1.0]. (After multiplying the complex FFT space with a 13x13 window and applying the inverse FFT, we could still recognize in the resulting low passed original image the distinct lip shapes and movements.) The motivation for considering the FFT is, that this coding is spatial shift invariant. It makes the recognition more stable against inaccurate AOI positioning.

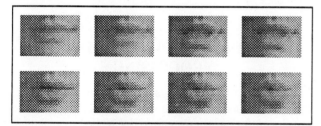

Figure 1: Typical AOIs

3. SYSTEM ARCHITECTURE

As recognition system we use a modular MS-TDNN [6]. Figure 2 shows the architecture. The preprocessed acoustic and visual data are fed into two front-end TDNNs [14], respectively. Each TDNN consists of an input layer, one hidden layer and the phone-state layer. Backpropagation was applied to train the networks in a bootstrapping phase, to fit phoneme targets.

Above the two phone-state layers, the Dynamic Time Warping algorithm [8] is applied (in the DTW layer) to find the optimal path of phone-hypotheses for the word models (German alphabet). In the letter layer the activa-

tions of the phone-state units along the optimal paths are accumulated. The highest score of the letter units represents the recognized letter. In a second phase the networks are trained to fit letter targets. The error derivatives are backpropagated from the letter units through the best path in the DTW layer down to the front-end TDNNs, ensuring that the network is optimized for the actual evaluation task, which is letter and not phoneme recognition. As before, the acoustic and visual subnets are trained individually.

In the final "combined mode" of the recognizer, a combined phone-state layer is included between the front-end TDNNs and the DTW layer. The activation of each combined phone-state unit is the weighted sum of the regarding acoustic phone-state unit and visual phone-state unit. We call these weights "entropy-weights", because their values are proportional to the relative entropy between all acoustic phone-state activations and all visual phone-state activations. Hypotheses with higher uncertainty (higher entropy) are weighted lower than hypotheses with lower uncertainty.

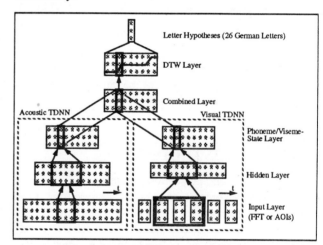

Figure 2: Neural Network Architecture

4. PHONEMES & VISEMES

For the acoustic classification we use a set of 65 phoneme-states (phoneme-to-phoneme transition states included). They represent a reasonable choice of smallest acoustic distinguishable units in German speech, and the TDNN architecture is very well suited to be trained as a classifier for them.

For visual features this will be different. Distinct sounds are generated by distinct vocal tract positions, and voiced/unvoiced excitations. External features of the vocal tract like the lips, part of the tongue and teeth, contribute only in part to the sound generation. I.e. /b/ and /p/ are generated by similar lip-movements, and cannot be distinguished with pure visual information. Training a TDNN to classify /b/ and /p/ based only on visual information would lead to recognition rates not better than guessing, or the net perhaps would get sensitive for features which are uncorelated to the produced speech. This leads to the design of a smaller set of visual distinguishable units in speech, so called "visemes". We investigate a new set of 42 visemes and a 1-to-n mapping from the viseme set to the phoneme set. The mapping is necessary for the combined layer, in order to calculate the combined acoustic and visual hypotheses for the DTW layer. For example the hypotheses for /b/ and /p/ are built out of the same viseme /b_or_p/ but the different phonemes /b/ and /p/ respectively.

5. SIMULATION RESULTS

Our database consists of 114 and 350 letter sequences spelled by two male speakers. They consist of names and random sequences. The first data set was split into 75 training and 39 test sequences (speaker msm). The second data set was split into 200 training and 150 test sequences (speaker mcb).

Best results were achieved with 15 hidden units in the acoustic subnet and 7 hidden units in the visual subnet. Obviously visual speech data contains less information than acoustic data. Therefore better generalization was achieved with as little as 7 hidden units.

Backpropagation was applied with a learning rate of 0.05 and momentum of 0.5. We applied different error functions to compute the error derivatives. For bootstrapping the McClelland error measure was applied, and for the global training on letter targets the Classification Figure of Merit [16] was applied.

	Acoustic	Visual	Combined
msm/clean	88.8%	31.6%	93.2%
msm/noisy	47.2%	31.6%	75.6%
mcb/clean	97.0%	46.9%	97.2%
mcb/noisy	59.0%	46.9%	69.6%

Table 1: Results in word accuracy (words correct minus insertion and deletion errors)

Table 1 summarizes the recognition performance results on the sentence level. Errors are misclassified words, insertion, and deletion errors. For speaker "msm", we get an error reduction on clean data from 11.2% (acoustic only) down to 6.8% with additional visual data. With noise added to the acoustic data, the error rate was 52.8%, and could be reduced down to 24.4% with lipread-

ing, which means an error reduction to less than half of the pure acoustic recognition. For speaker "mcb", we could not get the same error reduction. Obviously the pronunciation of speaker "mcb" was better, but doing that, he was not moving his lips so much.

It also should be noted that in the pure visual recognition a lot of the errors are caused by insertion and deletion errors. When we presented the letters with known boundaries, we came to visual recognition rates of up to 50.2%. The results of table 1 were achieved with histogram-normalized grey-value images. Experiments with 2D-FFT images are still in progress. In our initial 2D-FFT simulations we come to visual recognition errors, which are on average about 8% higher than the grey-level coding recognition errors.

We also took a closer look to the dynamic behavior of the entropy-weights. Figure 3 shows the weights from the acoustic and visual TDNN to the combined layer over time during the letter sequence M-I-E was spoken. The upper dots represent the acoustic weight A and the lower dots the visual weight V, where

$A=0.5+ (entropy(Visual\text{-}TDNN)\text{-}entropy(Acoustic\text{-}TDNN))/2K$

and

$V=1.0\text{-}A.$

Big white dots represent weights close to 1.0 and big black dots weights close to 0.0. K is the maximum entropy difference in the training set. At the end of the /m/-pho-

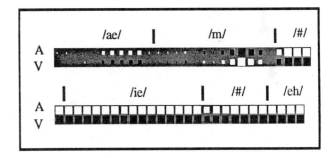

Figure 3: Entropy-Weights

neme when the lips are closed, V is higher than A. Obviously there the visual hypotheses are more certain than the acoustic ones. During the /ie/-phoneme the acoustic hypotheses are more certain than the visual ones, which also makes sense.

6. RELATED WORK

The interest in automated speechreading (or lipreading) is growing recently. As a non-connectionistic approach the work of Petajan et al. [9] should be mentioned. Yuhas et al. [15] did use a neural network for vowel recognition, working on static images. Stork et al. [13] used a conventional TDNN (without DTW) for speechreading. They limited the task to recognize 10 isolated letters and used artificial markers on the lips. No visual feature extraction was integrated into their model.

Also of interest are some psychological studies about human speechreading and their approach to describe the human performance. This measurements could also be applied to the performance analysis of automated speechreading systems. Dodd and Campbell [3], and Demorest and Bernstein [2] did some valuable work in this area.

7. CONCLUSION AND FUTURE WORK

We have shown how a state-of-the-art speech recognition system can be improved by considering additional visual information for the recognition process. This is true for optimal recording conditions but even more for non-optimal recording conditions as they usually exist in real world applications. Experiments were performed on the connected letter recognition task, but similar results can be expected for continuous speech recognition as well.

Work is in progress to integrate not only the time independent weight sharing but also position independent weight sharing for the visual TDNN, in order to locate and track the lips. We are also on the way to largely increase our database in order to achieve better recognition rates and to train speaker independently. Investigations of different approaches are still in progress in order to combine visual and acoustic features and to apply different preprocessing to the visual data.

ACKNOWLEDGEMENTS

We appreciate the help from the DEC on campus research center (CEC) for the initial data acquisition. This research is sponsored in part by the Land Baden Württemberg (Landesschwerpunktprogramm Neuroinformatik), and the National Science Foundation.

REFERENCES

[1] Christian Benoit, Tahar Lallouache, Tayeb Mohamadi, and Christian Abry. A Set of French Visemes for Visual Speech Synthesis. *Talking Machines: Theories, Models, and Designs*, 1992.

[2] M.E. Demorest and L.E. Bernstein. Computational Explorations of Speechreading. *In Submission.*

[3] B. Dodd and R. Campbell. Hearing by Eye: The Psychology fo Lipreading. *Lawrence Erlbaum Press*, 1987.

[4] C.G. Fischer. Confusion among visually perceived consonants. *J. Speech Hearing Res.*, 11, 1968.

[5] P. Haffner and A. Waibel. Multi-State Time Delay Neural Networks for Continuous Speech Recognition. In *Neural Information Processing Systems* (NIPS 4). Morgan Kaufmann, April 1992.

[6] H. Hild and A. Waibel. Connected Letter Recognition with a Multi-State Time Delay Neural Network. To appear in *Neural Information Processing Systems* (NIPS 5).

[7] K. Mase and A. Pentland. LIP READING: Automatic Visual Recognition of Spoken Words. *Proc. Image Understanding and Machine Vision, Optical Society of America*, June 1989.

[8] H. Ney. The Use of a One-Stage Dynamic Programming Algorithm for Connected Word Recognition. *IEEE International Conference on Acoustics, Speech, and Signal Processing*, April 1984.

[9] E. Petajan, B. Bischoff, D. Bodoff, and N.M. Brooke. An Improved Automatic Lipreading System to enhance Speech Recognition. In *ACM SIGCHI*, 1988.

[10] D.A. Pomerleau. Neural Network Perception for Mobile Robot Guidance. PhD Thesis, CMU. *CMU-CS-92-115*, February 1992.

[11] P.W. Rander. Facetracking Using a Template Based Approach. *Personal Communication.*

[12] D.E. Rumelhart, G.E. Hinton, and R.J. Williams. Learning Internal Representations by Error Propagation. *Parallel Distributed Processing Vol. 1*. MIT Press, 1986.

[13] David G. Stork, Greg Wolff, and Earl Levine. Neural Network Lipreading System for Improved Speech Recognition. In *IJCNN*, June 1992.

[14] A. Waibel, T. Hanazawa, G. Hinton, K. Shikano, and K. Lang. Phoneme Recognition Using Time-Delay Neural Networks. *IEEE Transactions on Acoustics, Speech, and Signal Processing*, 37(3):328-339, March 1989.

[15] B.P. Yuhas, M.H. Goldstein, and T.J. Sejnowski. Integration of Acoustic and Visual Speech Signals using Neural Networks. *IEEE Communications Magazine,*

[16] John B. Hampshire II and Alexander H. Waibel. A Novel Objective Function for Improved Phoneme Recognition Using Time-Delay Neural Networks. *IEEE Transactions on Neural Networks*, 1(2), June 1990.

SPEAKER-INDEPENDENT FEATURES EXTRACTED BY A NEURAL NETWORK

Y. Kato and M. Sugiyama

ATR Interpreting Telephony Research Laboratories
2-2 Hikaridai, Seika-cho, Soraku-gun, Kyoto 619-02 JAPAN

ABSTRACT

This paper proposes an algorithm using a neural network to normalize features that differ between speakers in speaker-independent speech recognition. The algorithm has three procedures: (1) initially train a neural network, (2) calculate the alignment function between the target signal and the network's output by Dynamic Time Warping, and (3) incrementally train the network for extracting speaker-independent features. The neural network is a Fuzzy Partition Model (FPM) with multiple input-output units to give a probabilistic formulation. The algorithm is evaluated in phrase recognition experiments by FPM-LR recognizers. The algorithm is compared with a conventional training algorithm in terms of recognition performances. The experimental results show that a neural network can be used as a new speaker-independent feature extractor.

1 Introduction

This paper proposes an algorithm using a neural network to normalize features that differ between speakers. A successful neural network approach for speaker-independent continuous speech recognition has already been reported[1]. The features extracted using the neural network can be considered as speaker-independent features. This is because the network's outputs correspond to phoneme classes and are calculated so that speech segments for all speakers belonging to the same phoneme class have the same vector. Feature mapping using a neural network[2] and speaker-independent codebooks[3] are studies related to feature extraction.

The proposed algorithm optimizes a neural network as a speaker-independent feature extractor. The algorithm includes two optimization procedures: the first procedure is non-linear time alignment between a vector in a speaker-independent space and a neural network output vector for any speaker. The second procedure is incremental neural network training up to the target signal given by the alignment. The network is combined with an LR parser for speaker-independent continuous speech recognition.

2 Neural network-based feature extractor

The network is designated so as to minimize the distance between the sequence of target signals in a speaker-independent feature space and the sequence of network outputs for any speaker.

2.1 Formulation of a neural network

Let f be a neural network for mapping,

$$f : \bigcup_A U^A \longrightarrow P, \tag{1}$$

$$F : U^S \longrightarrow P, \tag{2}$$

where U^A and U^S are sets of segments for arbitrary speakers and for a standard speaker, respectively. f and F represent the neural network for feature extraction and the function giving the network's target signal, respectively. Since various forms of F are possible, this paper uses either fuzzy membership functions (FMFs) or radial basis functions (RBFs). A bounded hyperplane P in R^M is defined as

$$P = \left\{ \boldsymbol{p} \in R^M \mid \boldsymbol{p} = (p_m), p_m \geq 0, \sum_{m=1}^{M} p_m = 1 \right\}. \tag{3}$$

P represents a speaker-independent feature space with probabilistic constraint. The network f is trained by the following criterion:

$$\min_f \min_{\sigma, \tau} \sum_{\boldsymbol{u}_{\tau(i)}^A \in U^A} d(F(\boldsymbol{u}_{\sigma(i)}^S), f(\boldsymbol{u}_{\tau(i)}^A)), \tag{4}$$

where σ and τ are alignment functions between sequential elements of $f(U^A)$ and $F(U^S)$; they are determined by Dynamic Time Warping (DTW). d is a distance function.

The criterion of conventional neural networks used for pattern classification is as follows:

$$\min_f \sum_{\boldsymbol{u}_i^A \in U^A} d(F(\boldsymbol{u}_i^A), f(\boldsymbol{u}_i^A)), \qquad (5)$$

where the target signal $F(\boldsymbol{u}_i^A)$ is given as

$$F(\boldsymbol{u}_i^A) = (\overset{1 \cdots}{0} \overset{j \cdots}{\cdots} \overset{M}{1 \cdots 0}) : \text{phoneme label}. \qquad (6)$$

σ and τ in Eq. (4) are identical to those in Eq. (5), and M is the number of phoneme classes. In the network using Eq. (5) each output is assumed to correspond to a phoneme class, and the target signal is a vector composed of zeros except for unity at the true class. The neural network trained by Eq. (5) is called a label-based (LB) neural network because $F(\boldsymbol{u}_i^A)$ is given by labels that indicate a phoneme class in speech. Human experts make efforts to label speech data and it is difficult to prepare the data for many speakers. The neural network in Eq. (4) is called an alignment-based (AB) neural network because $F(\boldsymbol{u}_{\sigma(i)}^S)$ is given by the time alignment function σ. A related study is the incremental training for speaker-dependent recognition[5]. The training procedure is a special case using Eq. (4) with $A = S$ and Eq. (6).

2.2 Target signal generation

The calculation of target signal generation requires a certain number of templates from a set of a standard speaker's speech segments. Neural-fuzzy training[6] is a related study to the generation and the target signal is calculated by using given all the training samples. Two approaches to obtain templates can be considered.

Category-dependent generation

Templates are generated *dependent* on phoneme classes. Although the number of outputs from a neural network depends on the number of phoneme classes, it is easy to merge target vectors *a posteriori*. A neural network supervised by such vectors serves as a phoneme classifier as well as a feature extractor because the network's outputs have acoustic meanings.

Category-independent generation

Templates are generated *independent* of phoneme classes. Any number of outputs from the neural network can be chosen *a priori*. A network trained by category-independent target vectors should be combined with a phoneme classifier, e.g. HMMs, because the network's outputs do not have a clear physical acoustic interpretation.

3 The algorithm

3.1 Initialization

The target vector for the standard speaker $F(\boldsymbol{u}^S)$ is calculated. Templates are generated from the set U^S

using the LBG algorithm. The templates can be generated either dependent on or independent of phoneme classes. When category-dependent generation is adopted, the fuzzy membership function F is defined as follows:

$$F(\boldsymbol{u}^S) = \boldsymbol{p} = (p_k) \in R^K, \qquad (7)$$

$$p_k = \sum_{l=1}^{L} \left[1 \Big/ \sum_{i=1}^{K} \sum_{j=1}^{L} \left\{ \frac{\|\boldsymbol{u}^S - \boldsymbol{c}_{kl}\|^2}{\|\boldsymbol{u}^S - \boldsymbol{c}_{ij}\|^2} \right\}^{1/(g-1)} \right], \qquad (8)$$

where $\boldsymbol{c}_{kl}, (k = 1, \cdots, K, l = 1, \cdots, L)$ is the lth template of the kth phoneme class. K, L are the number of phoneme classes and the number of templates per phoneme class, respectively. g is the fuzziness $(g > 1)$.

For the RBFs, F is defined as a normalized Gaussian expression:

$$p_k = \sum_{l=1}^{L} \frac{\exp\left\{\|\boldsymbol{u}^S - \boldsymbol{c}_{kl}\|^2 / 2V_{kl}^2\right\}}{\sum_{i=1}^{K} \sum_{j=1}^{L} \exp\left\{\|\boldsymbol{u}^S - \boldsymbol{c}_{ij}\|^2 / 2V_{ij}^2\right\}}, \qquad (9)$$

where V_{kl}^2 is the variance for the lth templates associated with the kth phoneme class. Eq. (9) assumes that the elements of $\boldsymbol{u}^S$ are uncorrelated. p_{ij} indicates the similarity between $\boldsymbol{u}^S$ and the kth phoneme class.

Let $A = S$ and $\sigma = \tau$. Then, initial training for the neural network is carried out according to Eq. (4).

$$\min_f \sum_{\boldsymbol{u}_i^S \in U^S} d(F(\boldsymbol{u}_i^S), f(\boldsymbol{u}_i^S))$$
$$= \min_f \sum_{\boldsymbol{u}_i^S \in U^S} d(\boldsymbol{p}, f(\boldsymbol{u}_i^S)). \qquad (10)$$

3.2 Alignment procedure using DTW

It is assumed that the qth sequence of vectors (for example words), $\boldsymbol{W}_q^A$ and $\boldsymbol{W}_q^S$, consist of

$$\boldsymbol{W}_q^A = (\boldsymbol{u}_1^A \cdots \boldsymbol{u}_i^A \cdots \boldsymbol{u}_I^A),$$
$$\boldsymbol{W}_q^S = (\boldsymbol{u}_1^S \cdots \boldsymbol{u}_j^S \cdots \boldsymbol{u}_J^S), \qquad (11)$$

where $\boldsymbol{W}_q^A$ and $\boldsymbol{W}_q^S$ are sequences for the arbitrary speaker A and the standard speaker S, and I and J denote the sequence lengths. The distance between $\boldsymbol{W}_q^A$ and $\boldsymbol{W}_q^S$ is calculated by

$$D = \frac{1}{Q} \sum_{q=1}^{Q} D(\boldsymbol{W}_q^S, \boldsymbol{W}_q^A), \qquad (12)$$

where Q is the total number of sequences. $D(\boldsymbol{W}_q^S, \boldsymbol{W}_q^A)$ is calculated by DTW as

Table 1. Experimental conditions for speaker-independent FPM training

Speaker	
Native male Japanese	
Number of speakers	Initial training: 1 Incremental training: 8
Acoustic Analysis	
Input pattern	16-channel FFT mel-scaled spectrum with 7 frames (70ms)
Frequency	12kHz
Frame rate	10ms
Window	256-point (21.3ms) Hamming
Neural Network Architecture	
4-layer Fuzzy Partition Model 25-phoneme classification type	
Target Signal	
Category-dependent generation	
Function	Fuzzy membership function ($g = 1.1$) Radial basis function
Training	
Initial training	2,620 isolated Japanese words 50,000 samples (1 speaker)
Incremental training	3,624 isolated Japanese words 50,000 samples (8 speakers) Includes initial training speaker

$$D(\boldsymbol{W}_q^S, \boldsymbol{W}_q^A) = \frac{1}{I+J} \min_{\sigma,\tau} \sum_{i=1}^{I+J} d(F(\boldsymbol{u}_{\sigma(i)}^S), f(\boldsymbol{u}_{\tau(i)}^A)). \tag{13}$$

The denominator of Eq. (13) is the normalizing factor of overall distance, and depends ont the matching path. In Eq. (13), a symmetrical path is selected. The distance function d is the Kullback divergence defined as

$$d(\boldsymbol{p}_1, \boldsymbol{p}_2) = \boldsymbol{p}_1 \log \frac{\boldsymbol{p}_1}{\boldsymbol{p}_2}, \tag{14}$$

where $\boldsymbol{p}_1$ and $\boldsymbol{p}_2$ satisfy Eq. (3). The alignment functions σ and τ are then determined from Eq. (13).

3.3 Training the neural network for extraction of speaker-independent features

The training sample element pairs of U^A and P are obtained by tracing back the σ and τ described in the previous subsection. The network f is trained incrementally by using the samples according to Eq. (4).

Table 2. Experimental conditions of phrase recognition

Task	278-phrase recognition
Recognizer	FPM-LR
LR parser	1672 rules

Open speaker: 2 male speakers

The procedures described in 3.2 and here are repeated until $D < \epsilon$, where ϵ is a positive threshold value. Segments for new speakers are then mapped to the feature space of the standard speaker, and the normalized features of the speakers can be extracted.

4 Phrase recognition experiments

4.1 Experimental conditions

The experimental conditions shown in Table 1 are used for speaker-independent phrase recognition. The neural network is a Fuzzy Partition Model (FPM)[4]. The FPM is a neural network architecture based on a probabilistic formulation. The distance function defined in Eq. (14) can therefore be used as the error function for FPM training. Each unit has multiple positive outputs whose sum is unity, unlike the conventional perceptron-type neural networks. The FPM has proven superior to TDNN approaches both in training speed and in speech recognition performance[1][5]. The 25 outputs correspond to the Japanese phoneme classes. Target signals are generated depending on the phoneme classes by using either FMFs or RBFs. The FPM is initially trained using one speaker. Then, the alignment in Eq. (13) is processed once using 8 speakers, including an initial speaker, and the FPM is incrementally trained.

Features extracted from the AB/FPM were evaluated by recognition of 278 phrases (Table 2). The FPM was directly combined with an LR parser. The recognition rate is evaluated for two open speakers that are never employed for FPM training.

4.2 Phrase recognition using a combination of the FPM and an LR parser

The phrase recognition results obtained using the proposed algorithms in the speaker-dependent mode and the speaker-independent mode are shown in Figs. 1 and 2, respectively. The results for the speaker-dependent mode are obtained before incremental training. Both figures show typical curves for recognition rate versus the number of templates per class. The recognition rates of the AB/FPM and the LB/FPM are shown in Table 3. The LB/FPM is trained using the criterion in Eq. (5). In the speaker-dependent mode, the recognition rate of the AB/FMF/FPM is better than that of the LB/FPM. In the speaker-independent mode, however, the recognition rate of the AB/FMF/FPM and

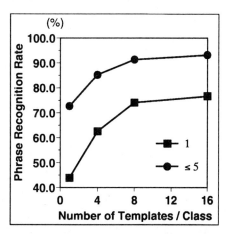

Figure 1. Speaker-dependent mode of 278-phrase recognition

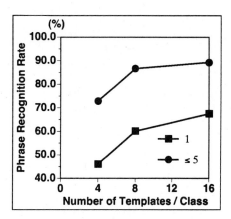

Figure 2. Speaker-independent mode of 278-phrase recognition

AB/RBF/FPM are worse than that of the LB-FPM. However, the results show that recognition rates of AB/FPM increase when larger numbers of tepmlates are used. A better recognition rate may be obtained by increasing the number of templates. v

5 Conclusion

This paper has proposed a neural network based method to normalize features that differ between speakers. The algorithm was shown to be useful for feature extraction by speaker-independent phrase recognition experiments. The results show that the phrase recognition rate of the alignment-based FPM is comparable with that of the label-based FPM. This algorithm is the first step toward obtaining better recognition performance. Two procedures (i.e. alignment procedure and the incremental neural network training procedure) must be optimized by using a global criterion, e.g. maximum likelihood or minimum error classification, not independently like with the present algorithm. Although a present phrase recognizer only

Table 3. FPM-LR phrase recognition

FPM architecture	Recognition rate (%)	
	Speaker-dep.	Speaker-indep.
LB	74.1 (91.4)	71.0 (87.9)
AB/FMF ($L = 16$)	76.3 (92.1)	67.5 (89.3)
AB/RBF ($L = 32$)	73.7 (91.4)	50.9 (78.5)

L: Number of templates/class,　(): rank ≤ 5

directly combines FPM with an LR parser, FPM will be combined with HMMs in the future. The combination is expected to use the advantages of both methods, i.e. the neural networks are highly accurate in recognizing static patterns and HMMs are better at treating time. Other future work is to apply the algorithm to speaker-independent language identification[7].

Acknowledgments

The authors would like to thank Dr. A. Kurematsu, President of ATR Interpreting Telephony Research Laboratories, for his support. They also wish to thank Mr. S. Sagayama, Head of the Speech Processing Department at ATR, and all other members of the department for their helpful discussions.

References

[1] K. Fukuzawa, Y. Kato, M. Sugiyama, "A Fuzzy Partition Model (FPM) neural network architecture for speaker-independent continuous speech recognition," Proc. ICSLP-92, pp.1383–1386, Oct. 1992.

[2] T. Kobayashi, Y. Uchiyama, J. Osada, K. Shirai, " Speaker adaptive phoneme recognition based on feature mapping from spectral domain to probabilistic domain," Proc. ICASSP-92, I, pp.457–460, Mar. 1992.

[3] T. Kawabata, "Predictor codebooks for speaker-independent speech recognition, " Trans. IEICE J75-D-II, pp.1770–1777, Nov. 1992 (in Japanese).

[4] Y. Tan T. Ejima, "A network with multipartitioning units," Proc. IJCNN-89, II, pp.439–442, June 1989.

[5] Y. Kato, M. Sugiyama, "Fuzzy Partition Models and their effect in continuous speech recognition," Proc. NNSP-92, pp.111–120, Aug. 1992.

[6] Y. Komori, "A neural fuzzy training aproach for continuous speech recognition improvement," Proc. ICASSP-92, I, pp.405–408, 1992.

[7] Y. Kato, I. Donescu, M. Sugiyama, "Language identification using speaker-independent features," to appear ASJ, Spring Meetings, Mar. 1993.

The Use of Fuzzy Membership in Network Training for Isolated Word Recognition

Yingyong Qi and Bobby R. Hunt
Department of Electrical and Computer Engineering

Ning Bi
Department of Speech and Hearing Sciences

University of Arizona
Tucson, AZ 85721

Abstract—We present a modification to the use of fuzzy membership in the training of an artificial neural network. The modified membership function can be applied to patterns that have a multi-center data structure in the feature space, and is used in network training for isolated word recognition. Results indicate that the network trained using this fuzzy membership function has better overall recognition rate than either the network trained by the conventional error back-propagation method or the classifier derived from vector quantization.

I. INTRODUCTION

The use of an artificial neural network for pattern classification involves a training phase and a classification phase. Here, training refers to the adaptive modification of the weight of each network link so that a known pattern of input will produce a pre-defined pattern of output. The process of network training is rather complicated, and an effective method was not available until the error back-propagation algorithm was developed. Through the use of this training method, a neural network can delineate an arbitrarily complicated pattern space that conventional methods of pattern classification may fail to partition. Once training is completed, pattern classification using neural network is a straightforward mapping from the input to the output pattern space, and only requires algebraic computations that can be implemented using simple circuit elements.

There are occasions when the ability to construct substantial complexity in the decision surface is a disadvantage. Consider the circumstance when the patterns to be classified occupy overlapping regions in the pattern space. It is possible to build a neural network which constructs a decision surface that completely "threads" through the *implied* boundary represented by the training patterns. However, this "tightly-tuned" fitting to the training patterns may not be an optimal choice for later pattern classification because some training patterns may represent outliers of the pattern ensemble.

One way of dealing with non-representative training patterns is to consider the collection of patterns as a fuzzy set where each pattern identifies itself with a continuous membership value. With these membership values, it is possible to modify the back-propagation algorithm so that training patterns with large membership values play a more crucial role than those with small membership values in modifying the weights of the network. As a result, the network will unlikely be degraded by a few possible outliers in the training set.

Hunt, Qi, and DeKruger [1] made a simple modification to the error back-propagation algorithm to allow the use of fuzzy membership in network training. The membership function was constructed based on geometric properties of the pattern space, and the membership value for each training pattern was computed as a non-linear function of the normalized distance from each pattern to the centroid of a pattern class. These membership values were used in network training for the spatial classification of synthetic data clusters and for the voiced-unvoiced classification of speech signals [2]. Results indicated that the use of fuzzy membership exhibited a number of desired properties for network training and classification [1].

The Hunt et al.'s method for computing fuzzy membership, however, is appropriate when each class of pattern constitutes a convex set, i.e, each class of pattern occupies a continuous area in the feature space. The method is not directly applicable when each class of pattern has a multi-center data structure, in which patterns of the same class may cluster around several centers and the space between these clusters may be occupied by patterns of a different class. A multi-center data structure is typical in many practical applications of pattern classification and the problem of isolated word recognition exemplifies the situation.

In this work, we modified the method for computing fuzzy membership so that it is equally applicable to simple convex and multi-center data sets. The modified method was applied to network training for isolated word recognition. Section I presents the modification of the fuzzy membership function. Section II describes the procedures and results of experiments using this membership function. Section III includes the discussions and conclusions.

II. THE MODIFIED FUZZY MEMBERSHIP FUNCTION

The original fuzzy membership function is defined as a nonlinear, monotonic-decreasing function of the normalized L_2 norm between each training vector and the cluster center. The function has the form

$$\phi_r(x_k) = \frac{2}{1 + exp(f_r(x_k)^p)} \qquad (1)$$

where x_k is the kth feature vector, $f_r(\cdot)$ is a function described below, p is a parameter that controls the rate of the exponential function, and $\phi_r(\cdot)$ is the membership for the rth class. The function f_r is the normalized distance from the centroid of the rth class, i.e.,

$$f_r(x_k) = (\bar{x}_r - x_k)^T C_r^{-1}(\bar{x}_r - x_k) \qquad (2)$$

where $\bar{x}_r$ and C_r are the centroid vector and covariance matrix of the rth class.

As mentioned earlier, this membership function is defined mainly for data sets that have a single center for each class of pattern. An extension of this definition for a multi-center data set could be made through replacing the $\bar{x}_r$ in equation 2 by the centroid of cluster i in class r, $\bar{x}_r^i$, and use the same equation 1 for computing the membership. This simple modification, however, is not appropriate when the number of vectors in each cluster is significantly unbalanced. For example, when a group of training vectors of the same class forms two clusters and one cluster has a large number of vectors and the other one has a few, the vectors in the small cluster will have membership values that are comparable to those in the large cluster based on equation 1. These membership values, however, contradict the fact that vectors in the small cluster should not be as representative as those in the large cluster for the particular pattern class.

In our modification of the membership function, we add a multiplicative factor to equation 1 so that the membership function not only depends on the normalized L_2 norm between the training vector and the centroid; but also depends on the relative number of vectors in each cluster. The modified membership function is

$$\phi_r(x_k) = (n/N)^\alpha \frac{2}{1 + exp(f_r(x_k)^p)} \qquad (3)$$

where n is the number of vector in cluster i, and N is the total number of vectors in class r. α controls the relative weight of this factor. $f_r(\cdot)$ now can be replaced by

$$f_r(x_k) = (\bar{x}_r^i - x_k)^T C_r^{-1}(\bar{x}_r^i - x_k) \qquad (4)$$

where $\bar{x}_r^i$ is the centroid of cluster i of class r. Equation 3 will be the same as equation 1 for a simple convex data set.

We note that the membership function so defined has the requisite property to be a membership function, i.e., it maps any vector in the pattern space into the interval $[0, +1]$. It also satisfies our geometric intuition since a vector near the centroid and within a large cluster should have a membership value that approaches one, and a vector either far away from the centroid or within a relatively small cluster should have a membership value that approaches zero.

We recognize that this membership function is data-defined. Information for constructing the membership function such as the number of vector in each cluster, the number of cluster in each class, and the centroid vector and covariance matrix of each cluster will be determined using statistical methods. Thus, parameters for constructing the membership function may not be available from a *priori* theoretical prescription. A more instructive discussion on data-defined, rather than linguistically defined, membership can be found in the article of Hunt et al. [1].

III. ISOLATED WORD RECOGNITION

In the following experiments, this modified membership function was applied to the problem of isolated word recognition. A few remarks about isolated word recognition are in order.

It is well-known that the vector quantization (VQ) method is extremely effective for the classification of patterns that have a multi-center data structure [3]. In the VQ method, the training of a classifier is accomplished by successively reorganizing the training data into a given number of clusters until each cluster possesses certain desired statistical properties [4]. A codebook is then generated from the training patterns based on the data clusters, and used as a dictionary for pattern recognition. Using the method of vector quantization, together with other techniques such as dynamic time warping and Hidden Markov Chain modeling, isolated word recognition can achieve an accuracy greater than 90% [5, 6]. It is not our intention here to compete with such a comprehensive word recognition system. Our focus is to see if the use of fuzzy membership in training could improve the performance of an artificial neural network in a limited word recognition problem. We used the straightforward vector quantization method here mainly for the following reasons:

1. The results obtained using VQ establishes a baseline where a comparison of performances between this classical pattern classification method and the neural network can be made.

2. The clustering process in vector quantization provides information on the structure of the data set and can be used for fuzzy membership computations.

A. Vocabulary

The database of this work consisted of isolated words produced by twenty female graduate students in the Department of Speech and Hearing Sciences of University of Arizona. Each subject read a word list consisting of eight repetitions of 10 digits, 26 alphabet letters, and 16 words (see appendix A). These words were recorded using a microphone and an audio tape recorder. The microphone was placed at about 10 cm from the lips of the speaker during recording and all recordings were made in a quiet room.

These recordings were digitized into the computer using a 10 kHz sampling rate and a 16 bit quantization level. The signal was passed through a lowpass filter with a cut-off frequency of 4.5 kHz prior to digitization. A waveform editor was used visually to label the silence space between words.

Two subsets of words from the labeled speech files were used in the experiments. One subset was the 10 numerical digits and the other was all the alphabet letters that contain the vowel /i/, i.e., the letter B, C, D, E, G, P, T, V, and Z. The first subset is a easy vocabulary set and the second subset is a difficult one for recognition [7]. For example, B and D only differ by one phoneme at the beginning of the word and there is little information to compensate for the small acoustical differences between them.

We assert that the use of vocabulary sets that have different degrees of possible pattern overlapping in the pattern space allows us to have a more complete examination of the advantages and limitations of using fuzzy membership in network training [1]. The similarity in size of these two data sets also allows for easy comparison of results.

B. Feature Vector

The feature vector for each word has sixty elements which include the normalized gain constant and cepstral coefficients of perceptual, linear predictive spectra [8]. The process of computing the feature vector is summarized as follows:

1. FFT short-term power spectra were computed for each word. A 25.6 ms Hamming window and a 12.8 ms window step size were used in the computation.

2. The short-term power spectra were warped in frequency based on the psychoacoustical bark scale and smoothed in amplitude by 16 weighting functions that simulate the critical bands of human auditory system.

3. This power spectra were time-normalized into a fixed (10) number of frames. The time normalization was made based on the relative spectral variation rate within each word. Only those spectral frames that produced a relatively large rate of spectral variation were kept.

4. Each frame of the time-normalized power spectra was approximated by a 5th order linear predictive (LP) model. The normalized

gain constant of the LP model and 5 cepstral coefficients, which were converted from the 5 LP coefficients, produced 6 elements for each frame.

5. The final feature vector for each word was a sequential concatenation of the 10 frames of feature elements.

In all the following experiments, the feature vectors were organized into 3 groups: the training set, the closed set, and the open set. Words in the training set were used for training exclusively. A word in the closed set means that other words from the speaker had been used for training before the recognition; whereas a word in the open set means that words from the speaker had never been used for training. There were 400 training vectors for digits and 360 training vectors for letters (4 repetitions of each word from 10 speakers). The number of vectors in the closed set was the same as the number of vectors in the training set (the other 4 repetitions of each word from the same 10 speakers). The number of vectors in the open set was 800 for digits and 720 for letters (8 repetitions of each word from the other 10 speakers). The division of feature vectors into these 3 sets was made randomly.

C. Word Recognition using Vector Quantization

The method of vector quantization was used first for the isolated word recognition. Training was accomplished using a modified LBG algorithm, in which only one cluster was split for each clustering cycle [4]. The number of clusters was a controlled parameter for the vector quantization algorithm and varied from 1 to 14 (at which the error rate for digit training set reached zero). Recognition was made based on the L_2 norm between the input and the cluster centers. Recognition error rates as a function of number of cluster can be summarized as the following.

1. The error rate is a decreasing function of the number of clusters for the training set.

2. The error rate for the closed set has a shallow minimum as the number of cluster increases.

3. The error rate for the open set behaves similarly to that for the closed set. The magnitude of error for the open set, however, is much larger than that for the closed set.

4. The error rate for letter recognition is much larger than that for digit recognition.

We noted that the best recognition rate do not result from minimizing the error rate for the training set, which is supportive to our claim that the decision surface should not fit all training patterns tightly in order to achieve an optimal recognition rate in pattern recognition.

D. Recognition Using Neural Network

The word recognition here was made by a neural network. The network was trained using the method of Hunt et al. for including fuzzy membership in the error back-propagation algorithm or the fuzzy back-propagation (FBP) algorithm [1]. For comparison, the network also was trained using the conventional back-propagation (BP) algorithm.

Fuzzy membership values were computed using the modified fuzzy membership function (equation 3) with $p = 1.5$ and $\alpha = 0.2$. All other necessary information for computing fuzzy membership, i.e., the centroid and covariance of each cluster, the number of vector in each cluster, and the number of cluster in each pattern class, was obtained from results of vector quantization.

The network architecture was a high-order, flat-net, due to the consideration that substantial reduction of acoustic information was made in the feature extraction process, and the final feature vector was approximately an uncorrelated or orthogonal representation of each word. In this network, the input nodes were inter-connected fully and directly with the output nodes. The number of nodes in the input layer was equal to the length of the feature vector (60), and the number of node in the output layer was equal to the number of output category which was 10 for digits and 9 for letters.

Network recognition was made by identifying the node that had the maximum output. If the maximum was not unique, one of the maxima was chosen randomly. A classification error was counted whenever the maximum of the output was located at a node other than the predesignated node for the particular word during training. Recognition error rates were computed for each training scheme (BP and FBP) in every 20 training iterations until a total of 4000 training iterations were exhausted. The classification error rates as a function of number of training iterations can be summarized as the following.

1. The error rate for the training set is a monotonic, decreasing function of the number of

training iterations.

2. The error rate for the closed set has a minimum as the number of training iteration increases.

3. The error rate for the open set also has a minimum. This minimum, however, does not occur simultaneously with the minimum for the closed set.

4. The magnitude of error for the open set is larger than that for the closed set. The error rate for letter recognition is much larger than that for digit recognition.

Here, we noted again that the best classification rates for the closed and open sets do not result from minimizing the error rate for the training set.

The classification error rate for network trained by the FBP algorithm was a function of the number of clusters used in the fuzzy membership computation. The best network performance was obtained when the number of clusters was around 5 and the worst network performance was obtained when the number of clusters was 1 for both digit and letter recognitions.

The classification error rates as a function of training iterations for digit and letter recognition indicate that the network trained by the FBP algorithm achieved a higher overall performance than that trained by the BP algorithm when the number of clusters was chosen properly for computing the fuzzy membership. To make a specific comparison, let us use the minimum error rate for the closed set recognition to determine weights for the network and compare the error rates for open set recognition, which are plotted in Fig. 1 together with error rates for vector quantization. As can be seen, the network trained by the FBP has the lowest error rates for both digit and letter recognitions. The difference in error rate between networks trained by BP and FBP algorithm is particularly significant for letters than for digits, which is consistent with our early findings that the use of fuzzy membership in network training increases the performance of the network more significantly for patterns that occupy partial overlapping regions in the feature space than for patterns that rarely overlap [1].

IV. DISCUSSIONS AND CONCLUSIONS

The relatively high error rates for the vector quantization method can be attributed, in part, to

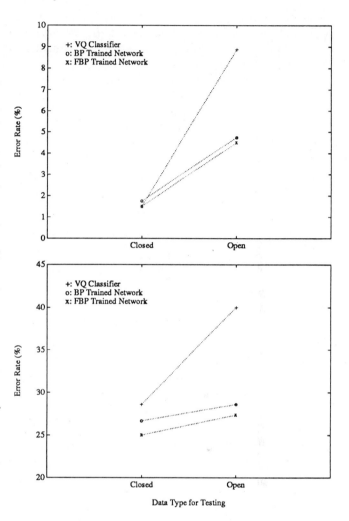

Figure 1: Error rates for digit recognition (top) and alphabet recognition (bottom)

the limited size of the training set. Typically, hundreds or thousands of training samples are needed in building a reliable VQ-classifier because of the statistical nature of the vector quantization method. When the size of training set is limited, as occurs in certain practical situations, the neural network could be a superior alternative, as has been demonstrated before [2].

The use of a flat-net seems to be an oversimplified approach for the word recognition task defined here. However, we have tried many network architectures with different degree of complexities; but none of them produces a recognition rate higher than that of the flat-net. Because the purpose of this work is to examine the effect of using of fuzzy membership function in network training, further extensive search of the best network architecture was not undertaken. It should be noted that the results obtained using the flatnet are quite reasonable.

In this work, we used the results of vector quantization to provide information for computing fuzzy membership. Interestingly, the best choice of number of clusters for vector quantization in terms of final classification error rate was not the same as that for the construction of membership function. Thus, before an optimal way for selecting the number of clusters for computing membership can be derived, this selection may have to be made on a *posteriori* basis. It is clear, however, that neither too few nor too many clusters for computing fuzzy membership are desirable. From informal inspections of the computed membership values, it seems that low error rates are associated with a skewed-Gaussian distribution of membership with the center of gravity biased toward larger membership.

Finally, we would like to point out that statistical methods for pattern classification and neural network use quite different approaches for the training of a classifier. Because of its simplicity and flexibility, the neural network has been increasingly used for pattern classification. The use of fuzzy membership in network training could function as a bridge between these two approaches.

In conclusion, we presented a modification to the use of fuzzy membership in the training of an artificial neural network. This modified method enables the computation of fuzzy membership for data that have a multi-center structure in the feature space. The method was applied to network training for isolated word recognition and an overall reduction of error rate was obtained.

REFERENCES

[1] B. Hunt, Y. Qi, and D. Dekruger, "Fuzzy classification using set membership functions in the back propagation algorithm," *Heuristics, Journal of Knowledge Engineering*, vol. 5, pp. 62–74, 1992.

[2] Y. Qi and B. Hunt, "Voiced-Unvoiced-Silence classifications of speech using hybrid features and a network classifier," *IEEE Trans. Acoust., Speech, Signal Processing*, vol. In Press, 1992.

[3] J. Makhoul, S. Roucos, and H. Gish, "Vector quantization in speech coding," *Proc. IEEE*, vol. 73, pp. 1551–1589, 1985.

[4] Y. Linde, A. Buzo, and R. Gray, "An algorithm for vector quantizer design," *IEEE Trans. Commun.*, vol. COM-28, pp. 84–95, Jan. 1980.

[5] B. Juang, "On the hidden markov model and dynamic-time warping for speech recognition – a unified view," *AT&T B.L.T.J.*, vol. 63, pp. 1213–1243, 1984.

[6] L. Morgan and S. Scofiled, *Neural Network and Speech Processing*. Englewood Cliffs, New Jersey: Prentice-Hall, 1991.

[7] R. Cole, K. Fanty, Y. Muthusamy, and M. Gopalakrishnan, "Speaker-independent rcognition of spoken english letters," in *IJCNN*, vol. 2, (San Diego, CA), pp. 45–51, 1990.

[8] Y. Qi and R. Fox, "Analysis of nasal consonants using perceptual linear prediction," *J. Acoust. Soc. Amer.*, vol. 91, pp. 1718–1726, 1992.

CITY NAME RECOGNITION OVER THE TELEPHONE

Mark Fanty   *Philipp Schmid*   *Ronald Cole*

Center for Spoken Language Understanding
Oregon Graduate Institute of Science & Technology
Beaverton, Oregon
97006 – 1999 USA

ABSTRACT

We present a neural-network-based speech recognition system for telephone speech. A neural network classifier provides phoneme probabilities for each frame of the utterance. A dynamic programming algorithm finds the most probable sequence of words. The classifier was trained on a spoken name corpus which contained the test vocabulary and many other words. The test set consisted of 262 utterances containing 44 cities and 2 states. The best result obtained on the test set was 92.9% word accuracy (90.1% on just the city names). Removing phoneme duration constraints reduced recognition accuracy to 82%. Performance fell to 82.4% using a network trained on a large vocabulary, fluent-speech corpus. Several other experiments are reported which did not produce significant changes in system performance.

1. INTRODUCTION

Our goal is to produce speaker-independent, rapidly-configurable (e.g. vocabulary-independent phoneme recognition), continuous speech systems for the telephone with sufficient accuracy to reliably perform tasks which require small to moderate vocabularies. The work reported here is a step in that direction. The task is city/state recognition; each utterance is either a single city name or a city/state pair. The utterances are from the Center for Spoken Language Understanding's telephone speech corpus of spelled and spoken names [1]. For this paper, we chose to test our system on 44 cities in Oregon and Washington.

We first describe the recognition system and give results for our test set. We then report several experiments which modify different aspects of the system:

- Same-task training data vs. different task.
- Phoneme duration models.
- Hand-tuned word pronunciations.
- Two-pass phoneme classification.
- Feature enhancement experiment.

2. SYSTEM OVERVIEW

In this section we describe the basic recognition algorithm. A neural network classifier provides phoneme probabilities for each frame of the utterance. A dynamic programming algorithm finds the most probable sequence of words—in this case either a city name or a city name followed by a state name.

2.1. Frame-Based Phonetic Classification.

Telephone speech is sampled at 8 kHz at 14-bit resolution. Signal processing routines perform a seventh order PLP (Perceptual Linear Predictive) analysis [2] every 6 msec using a 10 msec window, yielding eight coefficients per frame.

Frame-based phonetic classification provides estimates of phoneme probabilities. Classification is performed by a fully-connected three-layer feed-forward network that assigns 39 phonetic category scores to each 6 msec time frame. The input to the neural network classifier consists of 56 features representing PLP coefficients from 7 regions spanning a 174 msec window centered on the frame to be classified. The network is trained using backpropagation. The outputs of the network are divided by the corresponding prior probabilities of the category labels in the training set [3].

2.2. Broad-Phonetic Categories

In addition to the phonetic output from the classifier, we compute probabilities for ten broad-phonetic categories by summing the outputs of phonemes in the broad class. This sum is divided by the summed prior probabilities. Table 1 shows the broad category definitions.

2.3. Word Pronunciations

Each word in the vocabulary has a pronunciation model which is a finite-state grammar specifying all phoneme sequences which are valid pronunciations of the word. The word models were produced by an expert. All pronunciations were treated as equally likely.

2.4. Phoneme Durations

Phoneme durations are constrained to fall within certain limits during the name search. A penalty is applied to every frame which falls outside these limits. After experimenting on a development test set, we chose to set the duration limits at the fifth and ninety-fifth percentiles of durations for that phoneme in the TIMIT database, with separate stressed and unstressed values as determined by a pronunciation dictionary (i.e. lexical stress).

2.5. Noise and Extraneous Speech

In practical applications, it is necessary to recognize words in the recognition vocabulary in the context of out-of-vocabulary speech. We attempted to match out-of-vocabulary words with a word model called "ANY" which allows any sequence of broad phonetic categories. We used broad categories to reduce the number of states active in the search. Each between-state transition in the ANY word model was heavily penalized so the correct word model would have a higher score for within-vocabulary words.

2.6. Grammar

The allowed word sequences are specified by a finite-state grammar. The grammar used here allows initial noise (modeled by ANY), followed by any city name, followed optionally by either state name ("Oregon" or "Washington"), followed optionally by noise ("ANY"). All allowed words (except noise) are equally probable. There is no correspondence between the city and state name.

2.7. Search

The best scoring word sequence is found by a dynamic programming search which is essentially a Viterbi search with the following modification. It was observed that phoneme segments essential for the recognition of a word sometimes presented a barrier because the corresponding phoneme scored so low that, during the left-to-right search, no segment corresponding to that state would survive more than one frame. Because of the duration constraints, no path would exit the state and the correct word could not be matched no matter how well the other states scored.

This can be corrected by keeping a separate copy of each state in the active list for each possible starting time, but this slows the search considerably. We found that by noting which frames were likely boundaries and keeping a separate copy of each state only for these boundary frames, we could increase the performance with much less overhead. The likely boundaries were determined by taking the absolute difference, for each frame, of the phonetic output scores to the left of that frame and those to the right, and retaining frames with scores above a threshold as candidate boundaries.

3. TRAINING AND TEST CORPUSUS

We have collected a telephone speech corpus consisting of 3667 calls consisting mainly of spelled and spoken names [1]. For this study we used responses to the questions "What city are you calling from?", "What city and state did you grow up in?" and "What is your last name?" The phonetic classifier was trained on 910 hand-labeled responses—mostly city and state names. This is the "name" network.

For the test set, we chose 42 cities in Oregon and Washington plus these two state names. Although the training and test sets used different utterances produced by different speakers, about 1/3 of the words in the training set consisted of words in the test vocabulary, so networks trained on this corpus are not vocabulary independent.

A second network was trained on fluent telephone speech from 48 callers, each speaking for up to 50 seconds on any topic of their own choosing. This is the "story" network. There were more speakers in the name corpus, but less total speech. The total number of frames used to train the networks was about the same in each condition.

The test set consists of 262 new calls containing the 42 cities and two states. No single city occurs more than 20 times. Calls with extraneous speech and loud background noise (e.g. a screaming baby) were removed (about 10% of the potential test set). Poor connections, "normal" background noise, line noise, lip smacks and breath noise were left in.

4. PHONETIC LABELING

Both the name and story training sets were labeled phonetically in order to train neural network classifiers. The name corpus was labeled by hand.

The story corpus was labeled in two stages. First, a forced alignment was done using word boundaries provided by human transcribers and pronunciations provided by a dictionary. The recognition system described above was modified so that it would find the best phonetic alignment of the known word sequence given the known word boundaries (with a little slack for re-aligning the boundaries).

Each word was first converted to a phoneme network representing its possible pronunciations, then each phoneme in the network was mapped to a broad phonetic category by choosing the broadest possible category which did not include any neighboring segments. For example, an /ih/ between /m/ and /s/ would map to "son"; an /ih/ between /ow/ and /s/ (at a word boundary perhaps) would map to "front." We found that the alignment was more accurate when broad categories were used. Table 1 shows the broad phonetic hierarchy used.

front	iy ih ey y
round	w uw uh
owl	ow l
back	aw aa aor owl
mid	ah eh ae
ars	er r
son	ars mid back front round ay oy
stop	p k t d g b dh
fric	hh z f s th sh v
afric	jh ch
obs	fric stop afric
nasal	m n

Table 1. Broad-phonetic categories.

These automatic phoneme boundaries were then inspected manually and obvious corrections were made. This process is much faster than fully manual labeling and much more accurate than fully automatic labeling. In most cases, the dictionary provided only a single pronunciation of each word which we modified to allow for word-final stop deletion (no release). The automatic alignment should be improved substantially if likely alternate pronunciations are allowed.

5. EXPERIMENTAL RESULTS

Using the name network, we achieved a word accuracy (percentage correct minus insertions) of 92%. Ignoring the two state names, the word accuracy was 88.2%. All experiments were run on the same data. Statistical significance was determined using the McNemar's test.

5.1. Different-Task Training Data

Using the story network, which was trained on data from a different vocabulary and a different style of speaking but used roughly the same number of training frames, the word accuracy was 82.4% (80.2% on just cities—see table 2). This difference is significant (p = .0013).

training data	all words	just cities
same task (names)	92.0	88.2
different task (stories)	82.4	80.2

Table 2. Recognition for same task vs. different task.

5.2. Effect of Duration Models

The recognition system imposes duration constraints derived from the TIMIT database. When we used the name corpus to extract the fifth and ninety-fifth percentiles (although no longer separated by lexical stress), performance stayed essentially the same. We removed all duration constraints and got 82% accuracy (73.7% on just city names—see table 3). This difference is highly significant ($p < .01$).

duration constraints	all words	just cities
TIMIT w/stress	92.0	88.2
OGI names	91.5	88.9
None	82.0	73.7

Table 3. Recognition using different duration constraints.

5.3. Feature Enhancement

The neural network for the recognition system uses only PLP coefficients as input features. We tried one experiment with additional features. There was no improvement.

The slope (change) of each PLP coefficient was computed in a 36 msec window around each frame using linear regression. Peak-to-peak amplitudes (ptp: distance from minimum value in window to maximum value) and zero-crossing rates (zc) are computed for each frame. Finally, the slope of the ptp value was computed in a 36 msec window around each frame using linear regression.

The original PLP inputs to the neural network were supplemented with 8 features for PLP slope and 1 feature each for zc and ptp and ptp slope of the frame. The network was trained on the name corpus and evaluated under the same conditions as the original network. The word recognition accuracy actually fell to 90.2% (86.3% on just city names—see table 4). The difference was not significant (p = .24).

features	all words	just cities
Just PLP	92.0	88.2
Enhanced	90.2	86.3

Table 4. Recognition after enhancing the classifier inputs with zc, ptp, plp slope and ptp slope.

5.4. Hand-Tuned Pronunciations

On a separate development test set, it was observed that several cities had particularly poor performance. The pronunciation models for these cities were hand-tuned to match the behavior of the front-end (on the development set). When these pronunciations were used, the word accuracy increased to 92.9% (90.1% on just the city names—see table 5). This increase was not significant (p = .11); however we still feel that matching expected pronunciations to the behavior of the classifier is a promising approach. See [4] in these proceedings for a report on automatically-derived pronunciation models.

pronunciations	all words	just cities
expert	92.0	88.2
hand-tuned to net	92.9	90.1

Table 5. Effect of hand-tuning pronunciations to match the behavior of the classifier.

5.5. Two-Pass Classification

In an attempt to give the phoneme classifier information about the phonetic context of the current frame, we implemented a two-pass classifier. The second-pass neural network has as input a) the same PLP features used to train the first network and b) the average output of each phoneme from the first-pass net over the last 100 msec (an additional 39 features) [5]. The results were identical to the one-pass network.

5.6. "ANY" Models

While we don't have a suitable word spotting test set, we did test the word spotting capability of the ANY word models on a separate test set of 60 utterances each of which contained a city from the test vocabulary plus extraneous speech ranging from "uhh" to "I grew up in..." and "I am calling from..." The word recognition was 84.4% correct with 5.5% insertions. Note that each utterance contains a single city name and that the grammar allows at most one city name. We have noticed that the system does poorly when presented with whole utterances from outside the vocabulary.

Even with "clean" speech, the ANY models tend to help performance because they match lip smacks, breath and other noises. When the system was run without ANY words in the grammar, the performance dropped to 89.5% (83.6% on just city names—see table 6), but these results were not significant (p = .18).

6. DISCUSSION

Using a frame-based neural-network phoneme classifier trained on spoken names, we achieved 92.9% word ac-

	all words	just cities
ANY words	92.0	88.2
no ANY words	89.5	83.6

Table 6. Effect of removing the ANY noise-matching words.

curacy on a test set of 262 utterances containing 44 city names and 2 state names. Experiments showed a significant loss of performance for a network which was trained on fluent, out-of-vocabulary speech (82%). Since our goal is vocabulary independence, the difference represents a gap to be closed. We also showed significant loss of performance when we removed the duration constraints (82%). We believe more accurate modeling of duration probabilities based on context will yield large improvements in recognition accuracy.

This work is most similar to MIT's telephone city name system [6]. Using a vocabulary of 25 city names and data collected from real operator assistance calls, the authors achieved 93% performance when they trained on vocabulary words and 70.7% performance when they trained on out-of-vocabulary words [6]. They improved the algorithm in [7] and achieved a very low error rate of 3%, or less if they allow rejections. MIT uses a segment-based approach to phoneme classification. The work described here uses a frame-based approach and has a mixed in- and out-of vocabulary training set.

Lennig et al. achieve very impressive results of 96% speaker-independent word recognition over the telephone using a 1561 word vocabulary[8]. They trained context-independent phoneme HMMs on data from the same task, but with a different vocabulary than the test set.

Accurate speaker- and vocabulary-independent recognition of words in tasks which are not well constrained by language models (e.g., recognition of surnames, city names or company names from a large data base) requires accurate phoneme recognition. There is growing evidence that fine phonetic distinctions can be performed using a segment-then-classify approach [7, 9]. Previous work on recognition of spoken English letters, a task that requires many fine phonetic distinctions (e.g., B/D, T/G, M/N), has used a segment-then-classify approach to first locate segments then reclassify them using linguistically motivated features. This approach achieved 4% error rate on isolated letters using high quality speech (compared to 1% by human listeners)[10] and 11% error rate for isolated letters spoken over telephone lines (compared to 7% for human listeners)[9].

The recognition system described in this paper relied on phonetic categories derived from classification of individual frames of speech, using the same set of features for each frame. Recognition was not improved when additional features were added to the PLP coefficients, suggesting that we may have reached the performance limit for frame based classification for our training set. We expect that dramatic improvements in recognition performance will require extending phonetic classification to the design of classifiers based on the explicit location of segment boundaries.

7. ACKNOWLEDGEMENTS

Research supported by US West, Office of Naval Research and National Science Foundation.

REFERENCES

[1] R. Cole, K. Roginski, and M. Fanty. A telephone speech database of spelled and spoken names. In *Proceedings of the International Conference on Spoken Language Processing*, 1992.

[2] H. Hermansky. Perceptual Linear Predictive (PLP) analysis of speech. *J. Acoust. Soc. Am.*, 87(4):1738–1752, 1990.

[3] N. Morgan and H. Bourlard. Continuous speech recognition using multilayer perceptrons with hidden markov models. In *Proceedings IEEE International Conference on Acoustics, Speech, and Signal Processing*, pages 413–416, 1990.

[4] P. Schmid, R. Cole, and M. Fanty. Automatically generated pronunciation models for segment based speech recognition. submitted to ICASSP 92, 1992.

[5] R. D. T. Janssen, M. Fanty, and R. A. Cole. Speaker-independent phonetic classification in continuous English letters. In *Proceedings of the International Joint Conference on Neural Networks*, Seattle, 1991.

[6] I. Lee Hetherington, Hong C. Leung, and Victor W. Zue. Toward vocabulary-independent recognition of telephone speech. In *Proceedings of the Second European Conference on Speech Communication and Technology*, 1991.

[7] Hong C. Leung, I. Lee Hetherington, and Victor W. Zue. Speech recognition using stochastic segment neural networks. In *Proceedings IEEE International Conference on Acoustics, Speech, and Signal Processing*, pages I 613–616, 1992.

[8] Matthew Lennig, Douglas Sharp, Patrick Kenny, Vishwa Gupta, and Kristen Precoda. Flexible vocabulary recognition of speech. In *Proceedings International Conference on Spoken Language Processing*, pages 93–96, 1992.

[9] M. Fanty, R. A. Cole, and K. Roginski. English alphabet recognition with telephone speech. In J. E. Moody, S. J. Hanson, and R. P. Lippman, editors, *Advances in Neural Information Processing Systems 4*. San Mateo, CA: Morgan Kaufmann, 1992.

[10] R. A. Cole, M. Fanty, Y. Muthusamy, and M. Gopalakrishnan. Speaker-independent recognition of spoken English letters. In *Proceedings of the International Joint Conference on Neural Networks*, San Diego, CA, 1990.

Text–Dependent Speaker Verification Using Recurrent Time Delay Neural Networks for Feature Extraction

Xin Wang
Department of Electrical Engineering & Applied Physics
Oregon Graduate Institute of Science & Technology
19600 N. W. von Neumann Drive
Beaverton, Oregon 97006–1999, U. S. A.

Abstract — In this paper, the possible application of Time Delay Neural Networks(TDNN) to the text–dependent speaker verification problem is described and evaluated. Each person to be verified has a personalized neural network, which is trained to extract representative feature vector of the speaker by a particular utterance. Furthermore, a novel model called recurrent time delay neural networks, obtained through a local feedback connection at the first hidden layer level of the well–known architecture of TDNN is investigated. The training is carried out by backpropagation for sequence (BPS) — a variant of BP algorithm, which can be implemented just at the price of some additional variables computed in the forward stage and propagated forward in time. The modified structure is shown to outperform both a multilayer perceptron classifier and the original TDNN for feature extraction.

INTRODUCTION

The identity of a speaker is important for many applications such as access to secure information system, bank and credit authorization. It has received a great deal of considerable attention among speech researchers for many years.

TDNN is one of the well–known NN models, which was introduced by Waibel et. al[2] as a specific architecture that can take into account the dynamic nature of speech. Such a network is able to represent temporal relationship between successive acoustic frames, while providing some invariance under time translation. Only a few experiments have been reported on the use of TDNN models for speaker recognition problem[3]. In this paper, we extend previous work, and describe a modification to the architecture of TDNN through a feedback connection in the first hidden layer. We call the spatially–extended representation of NN model – recurrent time delay neural networks (RTDNN), and evaluate it to the problem of text–dependent speaker verification for feature extraction. Furthermore, feature extraction is performed together with desion making. This is another advantage of NN over the conventional speaker recognition approach. Also, experimental systems and results are provided.

RECURRENT TIME DELAY NEURAL NETWORKS

A Brief Review of TDNN

The basic TDNN is composed of an input layer, two hidden layer and an output layer. The input layer typically receives n_0 successive speech frames, represented by a m_0–dimensional vector of parameters; namely, the input pattern consists of m_0 rows * n_0 columns. By the same means, the first hidden layer is composed of a m_1 * n_1 matrix of units. The second hidden layer is a q * n_2 matrix, where q represents the number of classes in the output. Therefore, the output layer consists of q units.

Such a TDNN can be described by the following set of topological parameters :

$$m_0 \cdot n_0 / p_0 - m_1 \cdot n_1 / p_1 - m_2 \cdot n_2 / p_2 - q \cdot 1 \qquad (1)$$

where $n_1 = n_0 + p_0 - 1$, $n_2 = n_1 + p_1 - 1$, $m_2 = q$.

The typical input / output relationship of TDNN can be expressed by the following iterative equations (for $1 \leq l \leq 4$, $1 \leq p \leq P_l$) :

$$net^{(l)}_{k,j} = \sum_p \sum_i W^{(l)}_{p,i,j} \cdot O^{(l-1)}_{k+p-1,i}$$

$$O^{(l)}_{k,j} = f(net^{(l)}_{k,j}) \qquad (2)$$

where $net^{(l)}_{k,j}$, $O^{(l)}_{k,j}$ denotes the summation input and activation value of the neuron(k,j) in the lth layer, respectively; $W^{(l)}_{p,i,j}$ represents the connection weight linking the neuron(k,j) in the lth layer and the neuron(k+p-1,i) in the (l-1)th layer; p represents the time shift window; and f is the nonlinear activation function.

Architecture of RTDNN

The extraction of contextual information based on a wider window occurs in the upper layer of TDNN, where the extraction of low level acoustical features has already been achieved. In order to take into account the context to a greater extent, it would be useful that internal representation performed by the first hidden layer neurons is influenced by a wider portion of speech datas.

Recurrent network seems to be more natural to take into account a wider context information, meanwhile avoiding the problems related to the window increase. Our solution consists of using a high level memory, generated through a local feedback connection between the codified information resulting from the first hidden layer neuron at temporal coordinate "k", and the input of the same neuron at temporal coordinate "k+1".

The RTDNN in the first hidden layer operates according to the following equations :

$$net_{k,j}^{(l)} = W_{j,j} \cdot net_{k-1,j}^{(l)} + \sum_{p} \sum_{i} W_{p,i,j}^{(l)} \cdot O_{k+p-1,i}^{(l-1)} \tag{3}$$

where $W_{j,j}$ denotes the feedback connection. In the case of activation output feedback, (3) becomes :

$$net_{k,j}^{(l)} = W_{j,j} \cdot f(net_{k-1,j}^{(l)}) + \sum_{p} \sum_{i} W_{p,i,j}^{(l)} \cdot O_{k+p-1,i}^{(l-1)} \tag{4}$$

Unlike the original TDNN, the developed RTDNN has the advantage of coping better with the sequential nature of speech in the process of acoustic feature extraction, since the new model can explicitly exploit more information hidden in the temporal structure of speech.

Learning Algorithm of RTDNN

The learning method uesed for TDNN follows the conventional BP algorithm. In practice, we use an approach similar to the backpropagation for sequence (BPS) algorithm [4]. The method avoids the problem of backward path in time until the initial point during the backprogation stage, which is implemented at the price of some additional variables computed in the feedforward stage and propagated forward in time.

In our RTDNN, each output value of the network is the sum of the square of the activation value of several temporal replicated neurons in the second hidden layer. Plugging this into the defination of overall error function :

$$E = \frac{1}{2} \sum_i (O_i - d_i)^2 = \frac{1}{2} \sum_i (\sum_k o_{k,i}^{(3)\,2} - d_i)^2 \qquad (5)$$

And then, differentiating yeilds the partial derivative of error function with respect to the weight :

$$\frac{\partial E}{\partial W_{p,i,j}^{(l)}} = \frac{\partial E}{\partial net_{k,j}^{(l)}} \cdot \frac{\partial net_{k,j}^{(l)}}{\partial W_{p,i,j}^{(l)}} \qquad (6)$$

As can be observed in (6), the second factor can be calculated during the forward phase, whereas the first one can be exactly computed during the backward step as in BP algorithm. In comparison with BP, the error gradient with respect to weight connection of recurrent net in the second hidden layer, just requires the changing at the forward step :

$$Z_{i,j}(k) = \frac{\partial net_{k,j}}{\partial W_{i,j}} = W_{i,j} \cdot Z_{i,j}(k-1) + net_{k-1,j}$$

$$Z_{i,j}(0) = 0 \qquad (7)$$

If the local feedback connection provided for recurrent net by means of activation values, we adopt (4) and obtain :

$$Z_{i,j}(k) = W_{i,j} \cdot f'(net_{k-1,j}) \cdot Z_{i,j}(k-1) + f(net_{k-1,j}) \qquad (8)$$

Stability Analysis and Control

The feedback action of recurrent net considers the information not only limited to a finnite time interval determined by the topology of the network, but also extended backward in time in a way determined by the feedback weight magnitude. However, this consideration raises the problem of stability. The contributation of the past frames must actually decrease on going backward in time. Let "t" represents the temporal coordinate. We rewrite (3) as :

$$net_{k,j}^{(l)} = \sum_{t=1}^{k} W_{i,j}^{k-t} \cdot a_j(t)$$

$$a_j(k) = \sum_p \sum_i W_{p,i,j}^{(l)} \cdot O_{k+p-1,i}^{(l-1)} \qquad (9)$$

In order to estimate the influence of the signal window at $"k-t"$ to neuron at time $"t"$, we define :

$$\delta(k,t) = \frac{\partial net_{k,j}}{\partial a_j(k-t)} = W_{i,j}^t \qquad (10)$$

From (10), we can see that feedback weights must be constrained in the range of $[-1,1]$, in order to ensure the desired stability. Practically, the bond on the feedback weight can be implemented by introducing some control variables. We define the following relationship for each feedback connection :

$$W_{i,j}(d_{i,j}) = B \cdot \frac{1-e^{-d_{i,j}}}{1+e^{-d_{i,j}}} \qquad (11)$$

The variable $d_{i,j}$ is unconstrained, and thereby can be updated by the learning algorithm. The parameter B called decay bound constant allows to continuously vary the feedback amplitude in the range of value [0,1]. In so doing, the asymptotic stability of the network is automatically guaranteed. Therefore, for the learning algorithm, we can minimize error function with respect to the variable $d_{i,j}$ instead of $W_{j,j}$:

$$\frac{\partial E}{\partial d_{i,j}} = \frac{\partial E}{\partial net_{k,j}} \cdot \frac{\partial net_{k,j}}{\partial d_{i,j}} \qquad (12)$$

So the (7),(8) can be replaced with :

$$Z_{i,j}(k) = \frac{\partial net_{k,j}}{\partial d_{i,j}}$$

$$= W_{i,j} \cdot Z_{i,j}(k-1) + net_{k-1,j} \cdot W_{i,j}'(d_{i,j}) \qquad (13)$$

$$Z_{i,j}(k) = \frac{\partial net_{k,j}}{\partial d_{i,j}}$$

$$= W_{i,j} \cdot f'(net_{k-1,j}) \cdot Z_{i,j}(k-1) + f(net_{k-1,j}) \cdot W_{i,j}'(d_{i,j}) \qquad (14)$$

Actually, it is eaisly noted that by setting $B=0$, the described algorithm becomes the conventional BP algorithm, and the RTDNN is converted into original TDNN.

EXPERIMENTAL SYSTEMS AND RESULTS

Speech Database

The speech datas for the experiments were drawn from a 10 male speakers database, and consist of 480 utterances from the isolated words set. The database is divided into two parts. The first part for training the NN models to represent the speakers, and testing verification accuracy, contains 6 utterances of each speech text by 6 speakers. The other utterances are used for testing the imposter rejection capability of the approach. All experiments were carried out in Sun 4 / 260 work station.

Experimental Results

Table 1
Performance Comparison of RTDNN, TDNN, and MLP

	Number of Imposter Attempts	False Acceptances	Number of Admissible Attempts	False Rejections	Verification accuracy (%)	$\sqrt{FA \cdot FR}$ (%)
MLP	468	5(0.99%)	36	13(2.57%)	96.42%	1.59%
TDNN	468	4(0.79%)	36	10(1.98%)	97.22%	1.25%
RTDNN	468	2(0.39%)	36	7(1.38%)	98.21%	0.73%

Performance Comparison of RTDNN, TDNN, and MLP

This experiment was designed to compare the effectiveness of feature extraction with RTDNN architecture to that obtained by using MLP with one hidden layer, and original TDNN. The network weights were initialized with random values uniformly distributed in the range of [−0.05,0.05]. The experimental results in Table 1 show that structure of RTDNN outperforms both a MLP classifier and the original TDNN for feature extraction.

Performance Comparison of Different RTDNN Architecture

Different number of units in the first hidden layer and window length were also tested. Table 2 shows that 12 units in the first hidden layer and 128ms window length produces better generalization.

Table 2
Performance Comparison of Different RTDNN Architecture

	Number of Imposter Attempts	False Acceptances	Number of Admissible Attempts	False Rejections	Verification accuracy (%)	$\sqrt{FA \cdot FR}$ (%)
30·12/3—28·9/5—24·2-2	468	4(0.79%)	36	10(1.98%)	97.22%	1.56%
30·12/5—26·9/7—20·2-2	468	2(0.39%)	36	7(1.38%)	98.21%	0.73%
30·12/5—26·12/7—20·2-2	468	2(0.39%)	36	5(0.99%)	98.61%	0.62%

Performance Comparison of Different Amplitude of Feedback Connection

In order to investivigate the influence of different decay bound value to verification accuracy, 9 different experiments of this type were implemented, by fixing the same initial weights. The range of allowed bound value (the amplitude of the feedback) has been explored between 0.0 and 1.0 with the step 0.1. From the Table 3, in the case of B = 0 (TDNN), we have obtained the verification accuracy of 97.02% . However, the RTDNN instead exhibits a error treand, a reduction in relation to TDNN case. Performance improvement is particular marked for B = 0.5.

CONCLUSIONS

In this paper, we evaluated the ability of NN in text—dependent speaker verification problem. And, a novel NN structure − RTDNN is used for feature extraction of each speaker. This network was obtained through a feedback connection in the first hidden layer. Experimental results indicate the performance improvement of RTDNN model to extract feature vectors of each speaker due to the superior ability of recurrent net to treat the sequence nature of speech. Our future work will be devoted to extend the RTDNN model to the applications of other speech recognition problems.

Table 3
Performance Comparison of RTDNN with Different Feedback Amplitude

B	Number of Imposter Attempts	False Acceptances	Number of Admissible Attempts	False Rejections	Verification accuracy (%)	$\sqrt{FA \cdot FR}$ (%)
0.1	468	5(0.99%)	36	11(2.18%)	96.82%	1.46%
0.2	468	4(0.79%)	36	9(1.78%)	97.42%	1.18%
0.3	468	5(0.99%)	36	7(1.38%)	97.61%	1.16%
0.4	468	3(0.59%)	36	9(1.78%)	97.61%	1.02%
0.5	468	2(0.39%)	36	7(1.38%)	98.21%	0.73%
0.6	468	3(0.59%)	36	7(1.38%)	98.01%	0.90%
0.7	468	4(0.79%)	36	6(1.19%)	98.01%	0.96%
0.8	468	5(0.99%)	36	8(1.58%)	97.42%	1.25%
0.9	468	4(0.79%)	36	8(1.58%)	98.01%	1.28%

REFERENCE

[1] B.S. Atal, "Automatic recognition of speakers from their voices," Proc. of IEEE, Vol. 64, No. 4, pp.460−475, April 1976
[2] A. Waibel et. al. ,"Phoneme recognition using time−delay neural networks," IEEE Trans. on ASSP. , Vol. 37, No. 3, pp. 328−339, March

1989

[3] Y. Bennani and P. Gallinari, "On the use of TDNN-extracted features information in talker identification," Proc. of ICASSP 91, pp. 385-388,1991

[4] Gori M., Bengio Y.,and De Mori, "BPS : A learning algorithm for capturing the dynamic nature of speech," Proc. of IJCNN-89, Washington,1989

Auditory Model Representation and Comparison for Speaker Recognition

John M. Colombi[†], Timothy R. Anderson[‡], Steven K. Rogers[†],
Dennis W. Ruck[†], Gregory T. Warhola[†]
[†]AFIT, Wright-Patterson AFB, OH, 45433
[‡]AL/CFBA, Wright-Patterson AFB, OH, 45433

Abstract—The **TIMIT** and **KING** databases are used to compare proven spectral processing techniques to an auditory neural representation for speaker identification. The feature sets compared were **Linear Prediction Coding (LPC) cepstral coefficients** and **auditory nerve firing rates using the Payton model**. Two clustering algorithms, one statistically based and the other a neural approach, were used to generate speaker-specific codebook vectors. These algorithms are the **Linde-Buzo-Gray algorithm** and a **Kohonen self-organizing feature map**. The resulting vector-quantized distortion-based classification indicates the auditory model performs statistically equal to the LPC cepstral representation in clean environments and outperforms the LPC cepstral in noisy environments and in test data recorded over multiple sessions (greater intra-speaker distortions).

I. INTRODUCTION

Speech recognition and speaker recognition research traditionally use proven Linear Prediction Coding (LPC) cepstral coefficients and various weighted and transitional derivatives of the voice production model [1, 2]. These have been shown to be better feature sets than other spectral representations. However, auditory models which incorporate spectral analysis, automatic gain control, neural adaptation and saturation effects have demonstrated superior results for speech recognition [3, 4, 5]. Recently, it was shown that auditory models can be used effectively for speaker identification [6, 7].

Success has been reported on Vector Quantization (VQ) techniques for speaker recognition [8]. More recent research demonstrates successful classification with Hidden Markov Models, gaussian mixture methods and artificial neural classifiers; these often compare their results to VQ approaches.

This paper presents results using a physiologically motivated model together with a neural post processor for speaker recognition. Using speech utterances from both the TIMIT and KING databases, this paper specifically examines the performance of the Payton auditory mean-rate firing responses compared to LPC cepstral representations using speaker-dependent codebooks and minimum mean-squared error for classification.

II. PAYTON AUDITORY MODEL

The Payton model is a composite collection of stages each chosen based on physiological data [9]. The model accepts 16 KHz sampled data and provides predicted neural firing responses for 20 points along the basilar membrane, corresponding to center frequencies of 440 Hz to 6600 Hz. See Figure 1. The model incorporates low frequency filtering characteristics of the middle ear based on the circuit analysis of Guinan and Peake [9].

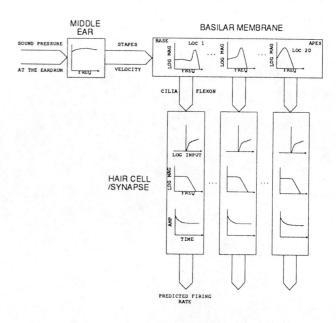

Figure 1: Payton Composite Model [9]

This model is unique in that displacement of the basilar membrane with respect to time and location is solved, using fluid dynamics and fixed plate equations. This section incorporates cochlea and cochlea partition physiological variables of fluid dynamics, tension, mass, size and shape of the membrane, using a method of solution by Sondhi and Allen [9]. A second filter is used to sharpen the basilar membrane responses to better approximate neural data. This modeling is theorized as effects due to inner and outer hair interactions with the tectorial membrane. The sharpening stage then feeds the non-linear transduction process of the inner hair cell/synapse. This stage provides half-wave rectification, amplitude compression, non-linear saturation, and time-varying adaptation. Due to shear caused by basilar membrane displacement, the potential of the inner hair cell changes, possibly, by the opening of ion channels. This potential change is phase selective for positive motion of the basilar membrane and subsequently triggers release of a neurotransmitter into the synapses of the auditory nerve. This phase selectivity is modeled by a half-wave rectification. To account for refractory properties of neural firing, amplitude compression and saturation effects of neural firing are provided by a static nonlinearity which introduces a "sloping saturation" for higher signal levels. Lastly, the cascade-reservoir model by Brachman [9] provides the correct temporal characteristics of adaptation, which is thought to be caused by depletion and replenishment rates of neurotransmitters or ions.

Other auditory models only approximate the auditory system response characteristics through a series of linear filterbanks [5, 10, 11]. However, as can be seen in Figure 2, nonlinear effects are evident at mid-to-high signal levels.

III. Databases

The narrowband portion of the KING Database contains 51 speakers collected in 10 sessions, speaking conversationally on several tasks for approximately one minute during each session. The speech is recorded over long distance telephone lines and sampled at 8 KHz. Typical evaluation on this database consists of training on the first 3 sessions, and testing on sessions 4 and 5.

The first 10 speakers of the KING database (sessions 1-5) were used in the comparison (all male). The data was framed using a 32 msec hamming window, stepped every 10.6 msecs. Tenth-order cepstral coefficients were derived from Tenth-order reflection coefficients calculated using the autocorrelation method. Each frame was tagged with a probability of voicing and a segment of 15 seconds was chosen per utterance which contained maximum voicing. These 15-second segments were used both for training (session 1 - 3) and testing (session 4 - 5). The calculated average signal-to-noise ratio (SNR), based on low voicing probability for noise power, was 14.75 dB over the first five sessions.

In sharp contrast, the DARPA TIMIT Acoustic Phonetic Database contains over 630 speakers, speaking 10 sentences (3 - 4 sec) recorded in a single session. The speech is studio quality sampled at 16 KHz. Again 10 speakers were chosen (7 male, 3 female) from various dialects. Similar signal processing was performed on the TIMIT utterances, however, this database is phonetically labeled, and thus a probability of voicing was not performed. The sentences are divided into three types: dialect sensitive (sa), random text (si) and phonetically balanced (sx). The sa and sx sentences were used in training and testing, respectively. The calculated average SNR, using silence as noise power, was 36.95 dB.

IV. Experimental Methods

The utterances were scaled appropriately to drive the auditory model to approximate conversational levels insuring not to saturate the neural responses. The Payton model references 0 dB with respect to a 1 KHz sinusoid, having adequate energy to drive firing of the 1 KHz Characteristic Frequency synapse to threshold, a firing level equal to 10% of its dynamic range. Scaling values of 4000 and 8000 were experimentally determined to provide adequate firing responses for the TIMIT and KING databases, respectively. These values correspond to model levels of approximately 52 dB for TIMIT and 43 dB for KING.

Typical values of codebook size tested in the literature range from 32 to 256 codewords. Computation time and storage often dictate codebook size for practical implementations; however, distortion improvements were insignificant above 64 codewords. Speaker-dependent codebooks were created, using the iterative Linde-Buzo-Gray (LBG) clustering algorithm with 64 codewords. Kohonen self-organizing feature maps were also used to create codebooks with 64 codewords (map size of 8 x 8). It was noted that Kohonen maps stabilized to a codebook configuration fairly quickly and improvements to overall SNR, using quantization error as noise, were small after 40 - 100 epochs. See Figure 3.

Classification was based on minimum average distortion defined over all speaker codebooks and N frames. For speaker s, the distortion, D_s, is

$$D_s = \frac{1}{N} \sum_{i=1}^{N} \min_{j \in k} \|x_i - m_{sj}\|^2$$

where the index over codewords is $k = 1, \ldots, 64$.

It was found that voiced speech carried more speaker-dependent information than all speech. This is shown in Figures 4 and 5 by relative distortions between speaker-dependent codebooks. Thus, all high ($\geq .9$) probability of voicing frames within the 15-second segments of KING were selected for quantization. TIMIT used all phonetically tagged vowels for quantization.

V. Discussion

A. KING

Results indicate that an auditory model provides improved features for speaker classification in degraded environments using the KING database. The auditory model provides an increase of 20% identification over cepstral features, as shown in Table 1. The Kohonen self-organizing feature map does not perform as well as the LBG algorithm with either representation. Although the self-organizing feature map does show a larger delta between the representations (25%) than does the LBG algorithm (20%).

It should be pointed out that in this experiment the classifiers were trained and tested in the noise and that the noise and channel effects were different for each session.

Table 1: KING Database: Speaker classification error. Trained on sessions 1 - 3, tested on sessions 4 and 5.

Classifier	LPC Cepstral	Payton Model
Kohonen	55%	80%
LBG	65%	85%

B. TIMIT

In this experiment the classifiers were trained with clean speech and tested with clean and noisy speech with a given signal to noise ratio. LPC cepstral coefficients performed as expected for this small subset of speakers on this quality of speech. With additive white gaussian noise (AWGN) the codebooks could not generalize, as seen in Tables 2 and 3. The auditory model closely matches the results of cepstral with slight improvements in noise. Since both quantizers non-parametrically approximate the underlying probability density function of the speakers' training samples, any significant difference in recognition results should be attributed to the clustering characteristics of the feature set. The auditory model as shown in Figure 3 allows better vector quantization.

A comparison of the quantization SNR, shows comparable levels of quantizer designs (Table 4). Since LBG is a gradient-descent algorithm, it often finds local minima of the distortion objective function. Kohonen's neighborhood may help "pull" nodes out of these local minima, during the competition process.

Table 2: TIMIT Database: Speaker classification using LBG designed speaker codebooks.

Using LGB	Clean	AWGN (SNR = 10dB)
LPC Cepstrum	100%	10%
Payton Model	96%	10%

Table 3: TIMIT Database: Speaker classification using Kohonen designed speaker codebooks.

Using Kohonen	Clean	AWGN (SNR = 10dB)
LPC Cepstrum	100%	16%
Payton Model	80%	28%

Table 4: Quantization Signal-to-Noise Ratios (SNR in dB) for the different quantizers. Kohonen provides a slightly improved quantizer over LBG.

	male		female	
	TRAIN	TEST	TRAIN	TEST
LBG	12.52	8.70	9.90	8.27
Kohonen	12.60	8.93	9.15	9.15

VI. SUMMARY

This initial examination of an auditory-model representation for speaker identification shows promise. Whereas distortion metrics and signal processing methods have been extensively developed for LPC and cepstral representations, these currently do not exist for neural data. Improvements in auditory modeling, often used for physiological understanding, should continue to be exploited for speech and speaker recognition.

Future work in this area will include the examination of temporal characteristics of the auditory-model firing patterns. It has been shown by Sachs and Young [12] that mean-rate firing patterns of synthetic vowels, presented to cats, saturate in noise and high stimulus levels. However, their proposed measure of synchrony (Average Localized Synchrony Rate) of interspike distributions provided a robust representation in these conditions. Similar results have been demonstrated by Ghitza's Ensemble Interval Histogram [10] and Seneff's Generalized Synchrony Detector [5].

Other classification schemes will also be investigated, such as Hidden Markov Models and recurrent neural networks. Each of these will be used to investigate the speaker-dependent temporal nature of speech for speaker recognition.

VII. ACKNOWLEDGEMENT

The authors would like to thank Janet Slifka, Systems Research Laboratories, Inc., for development of several Entropic ESPS utilities used throughout this work, and for valuable discussions and editorial comments.

REFERENCES

[1] Frank K. Soong and Aaron E. Rosenburg. On the use of instantaneous and transitional spectral information in speaker recognition. *IEEE Trans. ASSP*, 36(6):871–79, June 1988.

[2] Belle Tseng, Frank Soong, and Aaron Rosenburg. Continuous probabilistic acoustic map for speaker recognition. In *Proceedings of the 1992 International Conference on Acoustics, Speech and Signal Processing*, volume 2, pages 161–164, 1992.

[3] Timothy R. Anderson. A comparison of auditory models for speaker independent phoneme recognition. In *Proceedings of the 1993 International Conference on Acoustics, Speech and Signal Processing*, April 1993. In Press.

[4] Melvyn J. Hunt and Claude Lefebvre. Speaker dependent and independent speech recognition experiments with an auditory model. In *Proceedings of the 1988 International Conference on Acoustics, Speech, and Signal Processing*, pages 215–218, New York, 1988. IEEE Press.

[5] Stephanie Seneff. A joint synchrony/mean-rate model of auditory speech processing. *Journal of Phonetics*, 16:55 – 75, 1988.

[6] Hiroaki Hattori. Text-independent speaker recognition using neural networks. In *Proceedings of the 1992 International Conference on Acoustics, Speech and Signal Processing*, volume 2, pages 153–156, 1992.

[7] John M. Colombi, Timothy R. Anderson, Steven K. Rogers, et al. Auditory model representation for speaker recognition. In *Proceedings of the 1993 International Conference on Acoustics, Speech and Signal Processing*, April 1993. In Press.

[8] Soong, Rosenburg, Rabiner, and Juang. A vector quantization approach to speaker recognition. In *Proceedings of the 1985 International Conference on Acoustics, Speech and Signal Processing*, volume 1, pages 387–390, 1985.

[9] Karen L. Payton. Vowel processing by a model of the auditory periphery: A comparison to eighth-nerve responses. *J. Acoust. Soc. Amer.*, 83(1):145–162, 1988.

[10] Oded Ghitza. Auditory neural feedback as a basis for speech processing. In *Proceedings of the 1988 International Conference on Acoustics, Speech, and Signal Processing*, pages 91–94, New York, 1988. IEEE Press.

[11] Richard F. Lyon and Carver Mead. An analog electronic cochlea. *IEEE Trans. ASSP*, 36(7), 1988.

[12] Eric D. Young and Murray B. Sachs. Representation of steady-state vowels in the temporal aspects of the discharge patterns of populations of auditory nerve fibers. *J. Acoust. Soc. Amer.*, 66(5):1381–1403, November 1979.

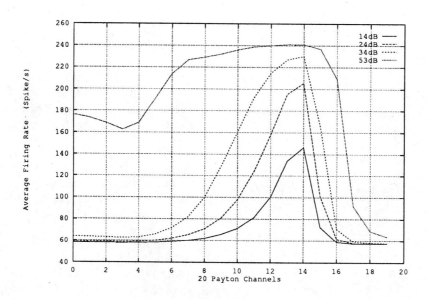

Figure 2: Model Neural Response. Channel 14 CF = 1133 Hz. Average response of the model to a 1 KHz sinusoid stimulus applied with varying energy levels. Note the non-linear response at mid-to-high stimulus levels.

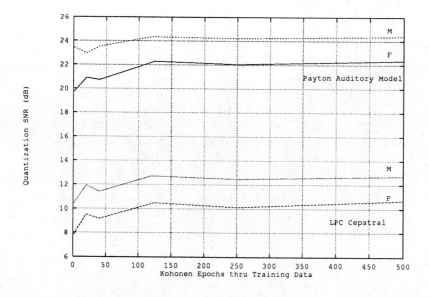

Figure 3: Kohonen learning for a TIMIT male(M) and female(F) speaker for varying iterations (epochs) for the two data sets examined. Quantizer "learns" in the first 100 epochs then stabilizes.

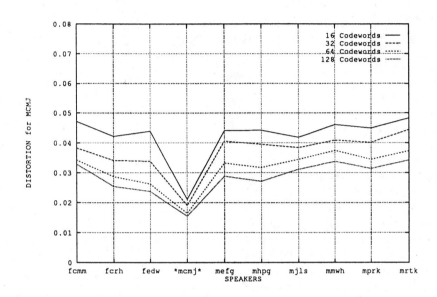

Figure 4: TIMIT speaker "mcmj" utterance showing distortions to all speaker dependent codebooks (LBG) using all speech. Note the low Figure of Merit for winning codebook.

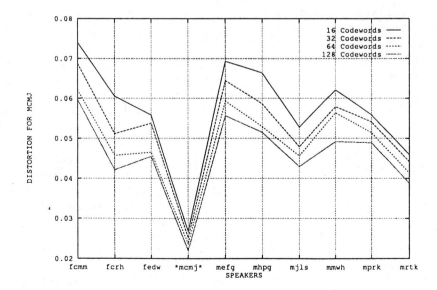

Figure 5: TIMIT speaker "mcmj" utterance showing distortions to all speaker dependent codebooks (LBG) using vowels. Note the higher Figure of Merit for winning codebook.

COORDINATED TRAINING OF NOISE REMOVING NETWORKS

Seokyong Moon,   *Jenq-Neng Hwang*

Information Processing Laboratory
Department of Elect. Engr., FT-10
University of Washington
Seattle, WA 98195, U.S.A.

ABSTRACT

When a recognition system designed with noise-free speech signal is deployed in the real world, it experiences severe performance degradation due to environmental acoustic ambient noise. An enhancement technique based on a *noise removing network* (NRN) which has recurrent connections is proposed in this paper. This NRN is trained in coordination with a *time delay neural network* (TDNN) which has been trained for noise-free speech recognition tasks. The proposed enhancement technique has favorable performance to white/colored Gaussian noisy speech when compared with the NRN without coordinated training and the classical linear Wiener filtering methods.

1 Introduction

In the real world, the speech signals to be processed are contaminated by environmental noise. Most speech recognition systems are designed either without considering the ambient condition of environment, or with strong assumption about the environmental condition in which the speech recognizer to be deployed. But the ever changing environment causes the condition mismatch for speech recognizer, hence the speech recognition system produces degraded performance [1]. Therefore, a speech enhancement system is essential to enable the existing speech recognizer for practical uses (see Figure 1).

Recently, artificial neural networks (ANNs) are used to tackle the problem of speech enhancement [2]. It is based on the assumption of the existence of a mapping $\mathcal{F}$ from k-th frame of noisy speech feature vectors $y(k)$ to noise-free speech feature vectors $z(k)$, i.e., $\mathcal{F}: z(k) = \mathcal{F}(y(k))$.

An ANN is used as a universal approximator $\tilde{\mathcal{F}}$ to approximate the unknown mapping function $\mathcal{F}$, which can be linear or nonlinear depending on speech contamination process by noise signal. It has also been shown that ANNs can form the arbitrary decision surface even for

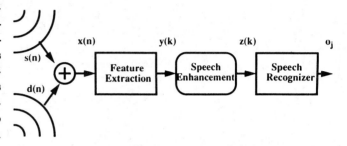

Figure 1: A typical noisy speech recognition system consists of a speech enhancement mechanism before the speech recognizer.

complex mapping from noisy feature vectors to noise-free feature vectors by training examples via a learning rule.

When used in the temporal signals with variable warping behaviors such as speech signals, the ANNs require dynamic properties (that is, recurrent connections) so that it is able to respond to the temporal behaviors. The Elman's simple recurrent network (SRN) was chosen as noise removing network (NRN), since it has been successful for temporal association of speech signal and can be easily trained with standard back-propagation (BP) algorithm [3]. Figure 2 shows the structure of Elman's SRN. Due to the recurrent connections, the Elman's network remembers cues from the past (i.e., contexts) and gives the dynamic properties for ANNs.

A coordinated training scheme for NRN is proposed in this paper. This scheme further takes advantage of the use of an ANN-based speech recognizer (e.g., a TDNN) for an efficient enhancement of the noisy speech features.

2 Speech and Noise Data

2.1 Speech Data

There are 4 sets of isolated E-set speech data (B, D, G only) sampled from the ISOLET database [4] used in our experiments. Each set consists of 15 females speakers, with each speaker speaking the (B, D, G) utterances twice (i.e., each set contains total of 90 tokens, 15 females × 6 utterances). In our experiments, 2 sets of speech were used for training the TDNN, 1 set was used for cross validation during the training, and the remaining set of speech was used for testing the performance. The LPC coefficients of orders 12 were used as features for each frame (256 samples) of speech data.

2.2 Noise Data

White or colored Gaussian noise $d(n)$ of n-th sample is added to the noise-free E-set speech $s(n)$ to generate different S/N levels of noisy training/testing speech $x(n) = s(n) + d(n)$. The S/N (dB) is calculated from

$$S/N = 10 \cdot log_{10} \frac{\sum_{n=1}^{L} s(n)^2}{\sum_{n=1}^{L} d(n)^2} \qquad (1)$$

where L is the length of each isolated speech utterance. The colored Gaussian noise is generated by a second order AR filtering process [1], i.e., $d(n) = 0.8018 \cdot d(n-1) - 0.3995 \cdot d(n-2) + w(n)$, where $w(n)$ is a white Gaussian noise.

3 TDNN for Noisy Recognition

A TDNN is a feed-forward type of network with a sigmoid activation for each units [5]. The TDNN employed in this paper has an input layer of 12 units (with 3 delays), a hidden layer of 8 units (with 5 delays), and an output layer of 3 units corresponding to each class of B, D, and G, respectively. Among a number of ANN-based speech recognizers, the TDNN was rather successful for isolated word recognition tasks. By explicitly delaying the speech of fixed amount of span at each layer during the training, it was able to cope with the time alignment problem implicitly.

Nevertheless, the TDNN is very sensitivity to ambient noise due to its deterministic nature of pattern matching. The performance degrades very quickly if speech patterns are corrupted by noise. Table 1 shows the recognition accuracies of a TDNN trained with 2 sets of noise-free (B, D, G) tokens (180 tokens in total) and tested with speech tokens of various S/N levels created from the the 4-th set of 90 tokens. For each S/N level, 900 white-noise and 900 colored-noise tokens are created for

testing (i.e., 10 noisy tokens for each isolated utterance). Note that the TDNN performance degrades rapidly when the noise level increases.

S/N (dB)	0	10	20	30	40
white	33.4	55.9	72.1	78.4	84.1
colored	44.8	62.6	80.0	84.0	84.6

Table 1: Recognition accuracies (in terms of %) of TDNNs when tested with white/colored Gaussian noisy speech.

Table 2 shows the recognition accuracies of TDNNs when the *implicit* Wiener filtering method [6] was used to enhance the noisy speech for TDNN classification. The observed noisy speech is passed through a filter, $H(w)$, in the time domain or frequency domain to get an estimate of the clean speech.

The implicit Wiener filtering method employs an iterative procedure for estimating $|S(w)|^2$ of speech, while the expected noise spectral magnitudes $E[|D(w)|^2]$ is obtained by averaging the spectral magnitudes of the background noise of 10 past neighboring frames.

S/N (dB)	0	10	20	30	40
white	46.4	63.3	75.2	82.3	84.4
colored	54.4	73.9	81.2	83.6	84.7

Table 2: Recognition accuracies of TDNNs when enhanced with an implicit Wiener filtering method.

4 A Noise Removing Network

When the signals (e.g., speech signals) exhibit temporal sequence behaviors, there are two commonly used input representation methods for ANN processing. The first method explicitly uses spatial metaphor to provide time information as part of the input. Specifically, it provides features of neighboring (past and future) frames as a windowed input to ANNs together with the features of the present input frame, i.e., $\mathcal{F} : \mathbf{z}(k) = \mathcal{F}(\cdots, \mathbf{y}(k-1), \mathbf{y}(k), \mathbf{y}(k+1), \cdots)$.

This spatial metaphor which parallelizes time converts the temporal processing problem to a static matching problem for which feed-forward ANNs are most suitable. The main drawback of fixed windowed input size approach is its inability to tackle the temporal signals of variable warping behavior such as speech signal. The second method, such as an Elman's SRN, which resorts the time information to be represented in the network feedback structure and in the course of learning gives dynamic properties to the ANNs, so that the ANNs are responsive to temporal sequences. The SRN produces noise-free speech feature vectors $z(k)$ from noisy speech features $y(k)$ and the feedback context units $c(k-1)$, i.e., $\mathcal{F} : s(k) = \mathcal{F}(y(k), c(k-1))$.

The NRN using a structure of SRN was also trained with E-set speech database described above. Among 4 sets of isolated speech, 2 sets were used for training the NRN, 1 set was used for cross-validation during the training, and the remaining set was used for testing purposes. Assuming the original E-set speech was degraded by additive white Gaussian noise and by additive colored Gaussian noise. Three NRNs were trained with 0dB, 10dB, 20dB S/N noisy speech respectively. Feature vectors of 12 LPC coefficients calculated frame-by-frame from noisy speech were provided as training data. The two-layer NRN network consists of 20 input units (12 noisy LPC inputs and 8 feedback context units), a hidden layer of 8 hidden units, and 12 output units to produce noise-free LPC coefficients. Twelve clean LPC coefficients, which were calculated from noise-free speech signals and were previously used in training the TDNN, were provided as training targets of NRNs.

Tables 3 and 4 show the recognition accuracies of TDNNs (trained with noise-free speech as discussed in Section 3) when tested with noisy speech features which have been enhanced by the trained NRNs.

S/N (dB)	0	10	20	30	40
0	64.9 †	63.7	58.7	60.0	62.2
10	58.2	71.0 †	74.4	72.0	69.6
20	49.1	66.8	72.2 †	70.0	65.8

Table 3: Recognition accuracies of TDNNs when tested with white Gaussian noisy speech with NRN enhancement.

S/N (dB)	0	10	20	30	40
0	71.4 †	74.7	69.0	64.6	62.3
10	64.2	74.8 †	76.2	71.1	68.3
20	53.0	76.7	82.2 †	82.2	80.6

Table 4: Recognition accuracies of TDNNs when tested with colored Gaussian noisy speech with NRN enhancement.

Note that the NRN enhancement before TDNN classification has very little help (maybe some help in very

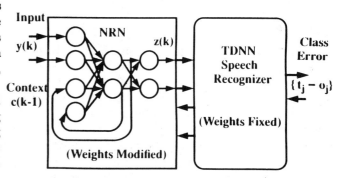

Figure 2: A coordinated training scheme for a NRN using a SRN with a trained TDNN.

low S/N levels) in improving the TDNN recognition accuracies. The intuition behind this poor performance is that the NRNs convert the noisy LPC features into some "noise-free" LPC features which do not correspond to any meaningful noise-free utterance, but simply correspond to some averaged form of several noise-free LPC features which can not be easily accepted by the trained TDNN.

5 Coordinated Training Scheme

As discussed in Section 4, a NRN, trained alone and cascaded to a trained TDNN in testing stage, cannot be always assumed that the outputs of a NRN will be well matched to the inputs of a TDNN which has been trained with (meaningful) noise-free speech features. A coordinated training scheme makes the outputs of a NRN to be constrained to the meaningful sets of inputs of a trained TDNN (see Figure 2).

This idea has a similar spirit as the neural network controller design [7], where the training of the controller is guided by the output error of the neural network representation of the plant rather than by mean-squared error of the controller itself.

In our proposed coordinated training, a NRN is cascaded to a trained TDNN before training stage and such a cascaded network is treated as one network with fixed connection weight set to 1 between the output units of a NRN and the input units of a TDNN. During training stage, only the weights of the NRN is modified while keeping the weights of the TDNN unchanged. A noisy-speech feature vector is presented as inputs to the NRN of this cascaded network to get a classification error from the TDNN outputs of the cascaded network. This classification error is back-propagated through the TDNN to the outputs of the NRN. When the gradient information appears at the output of the NRN, it is further back-propagated through the NRN to modify the weights of the NRN. This coordinated training ensures (constrains) the NRN to output meaningful noise-free speech features for TDNN to recognize.

Tables 5 and 6 show the recognition accuracies of TDNNs, when a coordinated training scheme is employed for the NRNs.

S/N (dB)	0	10	20	30	40
0	72.1 †	68.6	66.7	64.8	65.6
10	60.4	72.6 †	73.0	73.1	73.2
20	41.9	72.2	75.4 †	70.1	66.8

Table 5: Recognition accuracies of TDNNs for white Gaussian noisy speech with coordinated training of NRNs.

S/N (dB)	0	10	20	30	40
0	75.2 †	75.9	75.6	74.1	74.6
10	61.2	78.2 †	82.2	76.2	72.7
20	53.6	72.8	84.8 †	85.9	85.8

Table 6: Recognition accuracies of TDNNs for colored Gaussian noisy speech with coordinated training of NRNs.

Note that the proposed coordinated training scheme provides better recognition accuracies in general, when compared with those cascaded NRN systems without coordinated training. Simple indications (†) are shown in those values where the NRNs + TDNNs are trained and tested with the same S/N noisy speech features.

6 Conclusion

The 33.4% accuracy of TDNN for white Gaussian noisy speech at S/N of 0 dB can be increased to 64.9% by using an enhancing NRN trained without the coordination of the TDNN in presence of noisy speech data of the same 0 dB S/N level. The accuracy is further increased to 72.1% by using an enhancing NRN trained with the coordination of the TDNN in presence of noisy speech data of the same 0 dB S/N level. It is also worthwhile to mention that even though the implicit Wiener filtering enhancement method can produce very good performance in very high S/N levels, the NRN trained in coordination with TDNN outperforms the NRN trained

in no coordination with TDNN, as well as the Wiener filtering for most S/N levels. More specifically, the performance is less sensitive to the mismatched S/N levels in training and testing, which are usually the cases for most practical recognition environments.

References

[1] B. H. Juang. Hidden Markov models with first-order equalization for noisy speech recognition. IEEE Trans. on SP, 40(9):2136-2143, September 1992.

[2] Shin'ichi Tamura, Alex Waibel. Noise reduction using connectionist models. IEEE Int'l Conference on ASSP, pp. 553-556, 1988.

[3] J. L. Elman, D. Zipser. Learning the hidden structure of speech. J. Acoustic Soc. Am., Vol. 83, No. 4, pp. 1615-1626, April 1988.

[4] R. Cole, Y. Muthusamy, M. Fanty. The ISOLET Spoken Letter Database. Technical Report No. CSE 90-004, Dept. of Computer Science and Engr., Oregon Graduate Institute of Science & Technology, March 1990.

[5] A. Waibel, T. Hanazawa, G. Hinton, K. Shikano, K. J. Lang. Phoneme recognition using time-delay neural networks. IEEE Trans. on ASSP, 37(3):328-339, March 1989.

[6] J. S. Lim, A. V. Oppenheim. Enhancement and bandwidth compression of noisy speech (invited paper). Proceedings of the IEEE, 67(12):1586-1604, December 1979.

[7] M. I. Jordan, R. A. Jacobs. Learning to control an unstable system with forward modeling. Advances in NIPS'90, pp. 325-331, Denver CO., 1990.

HYBRID NEURAL-NETWORK/HMM APPROACHES TO WORDSPOTTING*

Richard P. Lippmann and Elliot Singer

Lincoln Laboratory, MIT
Lexington, MA 02173-9108

ABSTRACT

Two approaches to integrating neural network and hidden Markov model (HMM) algorithms into one hybrid wordspotter are being explored. One approach uses neural network secondary testing to analyze putative hits produced by a high-performance HMM wordspotter. This has provided consistent but small reductions in the number of false alarms required to obtain a given detection rate. In one set of experiments using the NIST Road Rally database, secondary testing reduced the false alarm rate by an average of 16.4%. A second approach uses radial basis function (RBF) neural networks to produce local matching scores for a Viterbi decoder. Network weights and RBF centers are trained at the word level to produce a "high" score for the correct keyword hits and a "low" score for false alarms generated by non-keyword speech. Preliminary experiments using this approach are exploring a constructive approach which adds RBF centers to model non-keyword near-misses and a cost function which attempts to directly maximize average detection accuracy over a specified range of false alarm rates.

1. INTRODUCTION

Two approaches to integrating neural networks into high performing hidden Markov model (HMM) wordspotters are presented. The goal of both approaches is to reduce the number of false alarms while maintaining keyword detection accuracy. One approach uses neural network secondary testing to analyze putative hits produced by a primary HMM wordspotter. Secondary testing would ideally reject all putative hits which were actually false alarms. A second approach uses radial basis function (RBF) neural networks to produce local matching scores for a Viterbi decoder. Network weights and RBF centers are trained at the word level to produce a "high" score for the correct keyword hits and a "low" score for non-keyword inputs. All experiments were performed using either the Road Rally or Switchboard talker-independent databases supplied by NIST.

*THIS WORK WAS SPONSORED BY THE DEFENSE ADVANCED RESEARCH PROJECTS AGENCY. THE VIEWS EXPRESSED ARE THOSE OF THE AUTHORS AND DO NOT REFLECT THE OFFICIAL POLICY OR POSITION OF THE U.S. GOVERNMENT.

2. USING NEURAL NETWORKS FOR SECONDARY TESTING

One approach to reducing false alarms is to perform a second stage of processing to evaluate the likelihood of each putative hit being either a true hit or a false alarm. This approach is motivated by the observation that false alarms are often easily distinguished from keywords by human listeners. A secondary testing classifier could focus on characteristics of individual words and could build complex models too computationally intensive for the primary wordspotter. Secondary testing techniques employed at other sites have included both statistical and neural network approaches [1,2,3]. Neural-network-based secondary testing has also been applied to the continuous speech recognition task [4].

The approach that we have taken uses neural networks as second stage classifiers, as shown in Figure 1. Input speech is fed to a primary HMM wordspotter which produces a stream of putative hits. The wordspotter used for this study is a continuous observation, tied Gaussian mixture, talker-independent HMM wordspotter developed at Lincoln Laboratory which uses filler models to represent non-keyword speech [5]. Putative hits produced by the wordspotter are separated by keyword and are processed by neural networks trained specifically to classify the putative hits for each keyword as either true hits or false alarms. Only those keywords with a high false alarm rate are subjected to secondary testing; putative hits from words which generate few false alarms are passed on unprocessed. The task of the neural network is to filter out the words incorrectly classified as hits (namely, the false alarms) without eliminating the true hits.

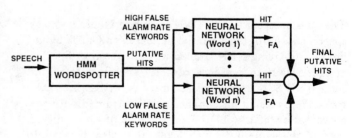

Figure 1: Secondary testing using neural networks.

Cross-validation testing was used to identify the input

feature set and to choose the neural network topology. Putative hits were transformed into fixed-length, static patterns by dividing each hit into three equal duration segments and representing each segment by its average cepstral and first difference cepstral vectors. The resulting 78 element patterns were too large for the amount of training data available so we used a combination of forward search, backward search, and trial and error to select a smaller subset of features to represent each putative hit. Using this reduced feature set, additional experiments evaluating several different types of neural networks suggested that multi-layer perceptrons, trained with back propagation and with one hidden layer of hidden units, provided the best performance. Further evaluation indicated that little improvement was obtained by using first difference cepstra or by performing a finer grain temporal analysis.

Secondary testing experiments were performed as part of the DARPA Speech Evaluation Workshop held on March 10-11, 1992. These experiments followed the training and testing guidelines developed by NIST which prescribed a training set (Waterloo male speakers), a test set (Stonehenge Male Test Set), additional training material (Stonehenge Augmented Male Training Set), and a 20-word vocabulary. Our evaluation procedure for both the primary wordspotter and the neural network postprocessors was conducted by training the primary Lincoln Laboratory wordspotter using all Waterloo male speakers and testing on the Stonehenge Male Test Set. Since the primary wordspotter uses a Viterbi decoder to produce putative hits, no *a posteriori* scores are available to rank order the hits. Thus, one run of the wordspotter with a specific value for the keyword transition probability produces one point on an ROC curve and multiple experiments must be performed to sweep out an entire ROC curve. Each point on the curve is the percentage of correctly detected keywords plotted against the false alarm rate expressed as false alarms per keyword per hour. The results of these runs at false alarm rates of approximately 2, 5, 7, 10, and 13 are shown in the bottom curve of Figure 2.

Neural network postprocessors were trained using the Stonehenge Augmented Male Training Set as the input to the primary wordspotter. This run produced a set of true hits and false alarms which were used to train the word-dependent neural network postprocessors which then reclassified the putative hits produced by the primary wordspotter on the test set. The results are shown in the top curve of Figure 2. Overall, the postprocessors reduced the false alarm rate by an average of 16.4% with most of the impact due to two words ("LOOK" and "MINUS"). This result suggested that neural networks can be used effectively as wordspotter postprocessors with little computational overhead. More test data, however, and evaluation with different keyword vocabularies is required to evaluate this approach thoroughly because the total number of putative hits processed was small (approximately 100 hits for one hour of speech at a false alarm rate of 5 false alarms per keyword per hour).

One drawback of applying neural networks to secondary testing is that very little task-dependent training data is generally available. Several techniques can be used to over-

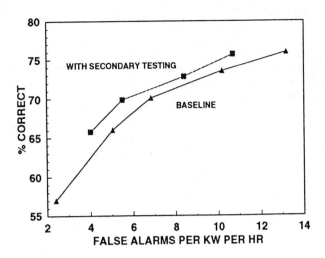

Figure 2: Wordspotting ROCs generated with and without secondary testing.

come this problem, such as using an N-best Viterbi decoder to generate additional true hits and false alarms. We explored another technique, which we refer to as cross-task training, which uses a supplementary database for the sole purpose of generating additional false alarms for neural network training. For this purpose we employed the Voyager database which consists of unprompted conversational queries directed at an interactive spoken language understanding system. We extracted a subset of the database which consisted of sentences from 49 male talkers for a total of two hours and seven minutes of speech. This data was spectrally normalized using blind deconvolution and fed to the primary wordspotter which produced 535 false alarms for 4 target keywords. Supplementing the Stonehenge false alarms with those obtained from the Voyager database yielded no additional improvement in overall wordspotter performance. We suspected that this result was due to the fact that the Voyager false alarms were not representative of Stonehenge false alarms. Further classification experiments which separated the training data into three classes (Stonehenge Hits, Stonehenge False Alarm, Voyager False Alarm) showed that the two false alarm classes could be separated perfectly, thus supporting our belief that the false alarm models from the two databases differ. For the cross-task training technique to be effective, the domains of the two false alarm models must overlap. With further consideration we conclude that the Voyager data is not representative of Stonehenge data because of its limited vocabulary and restricted syntax and that the use of cross-task training may still be useful, but that more care must be taken in the selection and use of the supplementary database.

3. HYBRID NEURAL NETWORK HMM/RBF WORDSPOTTING

Our experience with the primary HMM wordspotter in the secondary testing experiments and with a hybrid radial-basis-function (RBF)/HMM isolated word recognizer [6] suggests that better performance can be obtained by using neural networks within the primary wordspotter to provide word-level discrimination training. We have developed a hybrid RBF/HMM wordspotter designed to be trained at the word level to maximize the output score for the correct keyword and minimize scores for non-keyword speech. A block diagram of the wordspotter is shown in Figure 3. RBF networks produce local per-frame scores which are fed into Viterbi decoders, as in [6]. The alignment produced by these decoders is used to dynamically connect and disconnect RBF node outputs to nonlinear summing nodes for each word, as in the multi-stage time delay neural net described in [7]. This allows an overall keyword-level score to be computed for each keyword and an error signal to be back-propagated through the output weights in the RBF network.

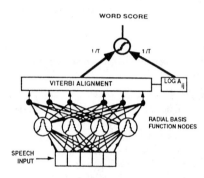

Figure 3: Hybrid wordspotter using radial basis function neural networks and Viterbi decoders.

During recognition, the RBF outputs are converted to log values and fed to a set of independent Viterbi decoders which align the speech to the keyword models and produce output scores for the words. The output of each Viterbi decoder is normalized by the length of the speech segment and fed to a sigmoid to produce the final word score of the wordspotter. Optionally, the sum of the log transition probabilities in the Viterbi path is added to the Viterbi score.

A new Viterbi path is started at every fourth speech frame and allowed to extend to a duration sufficient to accommodate the longest token expected for that keyword. The maximum normalized output of each decoder over the length of the speech segment identifies a score and a time interval for a keyword occurrence. This process results in a continuous stream of possibly overlapping hits which are fed to a simple postprocessing algorithm to perform overlap removal and peak-picking. The scores at the peaks, along with the associated time interval, are then recorded as the putative hits of the wordspotter.

The first wordspotter training pass occurs in two phases. In the bootstrap phase of training the RBF means and variances are set using k-means clustering on all the keyword tokens. Each token is uniformly segmented and the RBF weights are trained by presenting the token, a frame at a time, to the network and setting the desired output of the appropriate RBF node to 1 and the others to 0. In ad-

dition, a set of filler tokens, derived from randomly sampled segments of the training data, are also presented to the wordspotter and the weights are adapted with desired nodal outputs of 0. After the bootstrap phase, word level training is performed by presenting each keyword token to the network to produce a word score and Viterbi alignment path. Errors are back-propagated through the Viterbi path to train the RBF parameters.

In subsequent training passes, we run the wordspotter on the training conversations to generate a set of puative hits which correspond to either true hits or false alarms. We then continue the training process by training the network positively on the keyword tokens and negatively on the false alarms. We can also use the false alarms to add structure to the neural network by clustering the frames of the false alarms and adding hidden nodes to the RBF network using the cluster centers. The wordspotting and re-estimation procedure is repeated as many times as necessary to achieve the desired performance. This training procedure is illustrated in Figure 4.

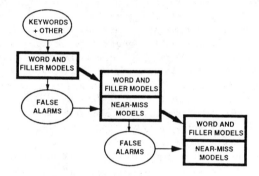

Figure 4: Constructive training for the neural network wordspotter.

3.1. Constructive RBF Training

Constructive training allows us to add structure to the network dynamically by adding explicit models of near misses. Near miss models can be added to the network by clustering the frames of false alarm tokens to form additional RBF hidden nodes. However, conventional RBF classifiers do not take full advantage of neural network disciminative training techniques because basis functions centers are positioned using non-discriminant clustering techniques such as k-means clustering. A new boundary hunting radial basis function classifier [8] was developed to correct this weakness by using a constructive algorithm to add RBF centers near class boundaries where confusions occur and corresponding RBF outputs are similar. Experiments performed on artificial and real-world data using this classifier demonstrated that error rates were equivalent to or lower than those obtained using conventional RBF classifiers. The approach used in the boundary hunting RBF classifier is also being explored using the hybrid wordspotter.

3.2. Figure of Merit (FOM) Back-Propagation

The wordspotter described above uses the conventional squared-error cost function to re-estimate network parameters using the back-propagation algorithm. For the wordspotting case, the squared-error cost function is not optimum since it minimizes the overall error from all the putative hits without regard to the effect of each putative hit on the overall figure of merit which is defined as the average detection rate for false alarm rates between 0 and 10 false alarms per keyword per hour. Thus, putative hits with low and high scores are treated equally. A better solution would be to use a cost function which maximizes the overall figure of merit directly.

Since the squared-error function can be described analytically, the error gradient for each input is easily computed. Unfortunately, this is not true for the figure of merit. However, we can calculate the gradient for the figure of merit by varying the score of each putative hit, either a true hit or a false alarm, and computing the derivative numerically. Using this result and the putative hit score, we can back-propagate a figure of merit gradient to re-estimate the parameters of the network. Note that while this procedure maximizes the figure of merit directly, it no longer allows the outputs of the network to be interpreted as Bayes probabilities.

4. RESULTS

The per-word figure of merit performance of the wordspotter for the three words "card," "credit" and "credit_card" is shown in Figure 5. Here the wordspotter was trained using data from 50 of the 70 talkers designated for training in the "Credit Card" portion of the Switchboard database and was evaluated on the remaining 20 talkers. In our first system ("BATCH") putative hits were generated by first wordspotting on all 50 talkers. The resulting false alarms and true occurrences were then used to re-estimate the RBF weights. In the next version ("PER_CONV") putative hits were generated by wordspotting on each talker. Weights were updated using true occurrences and false alarms after each talker's speech had been processed. A new set of false alarms was then generated by wordspotting on the next talker. Neither of these two systems employed filler tokens for training. In the system labeled "FILLER," filler tokens were clustered separately and the resulting centers were added to the RBF network. In the final system ("NEAR MISS") RBF centers were added by clustering the false alarm tokens. The training procedure for these systems was used to re-estimate only the RBF weights and the sigmoid parameters.

5. SUMMARY

This paper presented two approaches to integrating neural networks and hidden Markov models for wordspotting applications. In one approach neural networks were used to perform second-stage postprocessing on the putative hits produced by a high-performance, tied-mixture HMM wordspotter. Results on a standardized Road Rally database showed a modest improvement in performance at all false alarm rates. These results are encouraging, but the lack of sufficient training material prevents us from performing more extensive testing. A second approach combined radial basis function neural networks, Viterbi decoders, and word-level back-propagation training into an integrated pri-

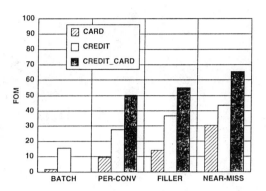

Figure 5: Neural network wordspotter performance improvements for three keywords.

mary wordspotter. This wordspotter is currently under development and will incorporate constructive RBF training and figure of merit back-propagation. Results to date have shown steady improvement in performance on a subset of the full 20 keyword vocabulary.

REFERENCES

[1] D.P. McCullough, "Secondary Testing Techniques for Word Recognition in Continuous Speech," in Proc. IEEE ICASSP-83, pp. 300–303.

[2] D.P. Morgan, C.I. Scofield, and J.E. Adcock, "Multiple Neural Network Topologies Applied to Keyword Spotting," in Proc. IEEE ICASSP-91, pp. 313–316.

[3] K.P. Li and J.A. Naylor, "A Whole Word Recurrent Neural Network for Keyword Spotting," in Proc. IEEE ICASSP-92, Vol. II, pp. 81–84.

[4] S. Austin, G. Zavaliagkos, J. Makhoul, and R. Schwartz, "Speech Recognition Using Segmental Neural Nets," in IEEE Proc. ICASSP-92, Vol. I, pp. 625–628.

[5] R.C. Rose and D.B. Paul, "A Hidden Markov Model Based Keyword Recognition System," in Proc. IEEE ICASSP-90, pp. 129–132.

[6] E. Singer and R.P. Lippmann, "A Speech Recognizer Using Radial Basis Function Neural Networks in an HMM Framework," in IEEE Proc. ICASSP-92, Vol. I, pp. 629–632.

[7] T. Zeppenfeld and A. Waibel, "A Hybrid Neural Network, Dynamic Programming Word Spotter," in IEEE Proc. ICASSP-92, Vol. II, pp. 77–80.

[8] E.I. Chang and R.P. Lippmann, "A Boundary Hunting Radial Basis Function Classifier which Allocates Centers Constructively," to appear in Neural Information Processing Systems 5, 1993, Morgan-Kaufmann: San Mateo, CA.

A Technique for Adapting to Speech Rate

Mai H. Nguyen   Garrison W. Cottrell
Department of Computer Science & Engineering
Institute for Neural Computation
University of California, San Diego
La Jolla, CA 92093-0114
mnguyen@cs.ucsd.edu

May 1993

Abstract. We propose a technique for automatically estimating and dynamically adapting to the rate of a speech signal. A recurrent network is first trained to predict the input signal at a "normal" rate. Once trained, the network essentially becomes a model of the signal. Then, with the weights fixed, the network's time constant is adapted using gradient descent as it receives the same signal at a different rate. The network's time constant thus becomes a measure of the rate of the signal and can be used to drive the recognition process. Processing speech signals in such a rate-dependent manner has several advantages: (1) it is an efficient way to handle rate changes without having to train on many different rates, (2) it provides global rate information to the recognition process for more robust classification, and (3) it represents a general approach that can be incorporated into any speech recognition system, regardless of the underlying technology. Our experiments show that on simple signals, the network adapts rapidly to new inputs of varying rates. The results suggest that rapid adaptation to speaking rate can be accomplished by this method.

Introduction

Accounting for acoustic variation is an essential element in speech recognition. Variation in the acoustic signal arises from physiological differences between talkers, coarticulatory effects in speech production, and external factors such as background noise and channel distortions. Another source of acoustic variation is speaking rate, which is the focus of this paper. Although speaking rate has received relatively little attention in the automatic speech recognition (ASR) literature, there is strong evidence that speaking rate varies substantially in conversational speech, and not only across speakers, but also in the speech of a single speaker. In fact, it has been shown that variation in rate during the course of a conversation averages about 31% [8] and can be as much as 60% [6]. Obviously, human listeners are not severely affected by such wide variations in speaking rate. Thus, it can be argued, there must be some process of adaptation by which the listener's rate of processing the conversation to which he/she is listening is adjusted to the rate of the incoming speech signal. This process of adapting to the speaking rate is of interest because we would like to incorporate a similar procedure in an ASR system to allow for increased robustness with respect to rate without having to train the system on data at many different rates. This paper describes a preliminary investigation of speaking rate adaptation using a connectionist approach, based on results obtained from studies on human perception of speech.

Rate-Dependent Processing

Several studies (e.g., [10] [4]) on human perception of speech have shown that speech rate, as determined from the surrounding context, biases interpretation of a phonetic segment. For example, a rapidly articulated long vowel is frequently interpretated as a short vowel if embedded in a sentence spoken at a slower rate [7]. Given the wide and frequent variation of speaking rate in conversational speech, this suggests that listeners must be sensitive to rate changes and process speech in a rate-dependent manner. It makes sense, then, that such rate-dependent processing is also necessary to produce good results in an automatic recognition system.

Conventional ASR techniques, such as Dynamic Time Warping (DTW) and Hidden Markov Models (HMM), have attempted to address the issue of acoustic changes caused by speaking rate variation. However, the solutions offered by these techniques do not take advantage of the additional information on rate provided by the surrounding context. DTW minimizes the effects of rate by normalizing each segment to its "normal," standard length by warping the time axis of a speech pattern so that, temporally, it matches the reference template, i.e., long versions of a word or phoneme are compressed, while short versions are stretched to a standard length. But in doing so, all timing information that may convey rate information is essentially eliminated. HMMs incorporate a statistical duration model which allows for some temporal differences between a test segment and its prototypical form. However, HMMs do not interpret any temporal differences such as duration *relative* to sentential rate. In fact, neither DTW nor HMM provides any mechanism for keeping track of global rate. Any variations in acoustic features that are manifestations of rate changes are interpreted segment by segment, without reference to the rate of the surrounding context. We claim that this rate-*independent* processing cannot yield 100% correct classification.

Some attempts (*e.g.*, [5]) have been made to build systems to recognize speech spoken under stress conditions, which includes speech at different rates. The approach is to use *multi-style training*, which simply means training the system on speech data produced using different styles of talking. Multi-style training does result in a system that can recognize speech of different styles. Since the system receives speech tokens produced under different talking styles during training, it is not surprising that multi-style training results in improved performance over training on just normal tokens. But this improvement is at the cost of more training data. The requirement of more training data is costly not only in terms of data generation and processing, but also in terms of training time and perhaps model complexity. Furthermore, such training data may not always be readily available. Many large, widely used databases exist that contain speech spoken only at one rate; to generate these data at other rates would be an expensive and time-consuming task. Thus, multi-style training is not an efficient solution to the speaking rate variation problem.

Dynamic Rate Adaptation

In contrast to the current approaches to handle rate effects, our approach is to treat variations caused by rate as additional information, and not as spurious noise, in the recognition process. The goal is to construct an ASR system that can detect rate changes, estimate rate from surrounding context, and use this information to effectively manage changes in the speech signal caused by variations in rate. The approach is to dynamically adapt to the rate of the speech input. Since the system will *adapt* to the rate of the input signal, it will not have to be trained on many different rates, thus, providing a more efficient solution to rate changes than multi-style training. And since the proposed technique of dynamic rate adaptation (DRA) makes use of global rate, more accurate classification should result. Furthermore, we believe that DRA is general enough so that it can be used to enhance the robustness of any ASR system, regardless of technology or paradigm, to speaking rate variations. Although the work described here is presented in a neural network (NN) paradigm, the technique for automatically estimating the rate of the speech input can be considered a separate process from the actual recognition task. This technique can thus be used to construct a rate-estimator module that can be incorporated into a NN-, DTW- or HMM-based recognition system to provide additional information for more robust recognition performance with respect to rate.

Recurrent Network for Rate Adaptation

Our technique for automatic rate estimation and adaptation is similar to the temporal auto-association technique [3]. A recurrent network is trained, using the real-time recurrent learning (RTRL) algorithm [12], to be a model of the input signal by predicting the signal at some delay. Rate estimation is accomplished as follows: The network receives, at time $t - \delta$, some input signal $S(t - \delta)$ and is trained to predict the same signal after some delay δ; that is, the network's output at time $t - \delta$ is its prediction of $S(t)$. The basic idea is to have the network adapt to the rate of the input based on the error between the network's prediction of $S(t)$ and the true value. In order to have a way to adjust the processing speed of the network, we use the Delta-Net technique [11]. The Delta-Net is simply a finite-difference approximation to a continuous-time network. The equations describing a continuous neural network are:

$$\tau_k \frac{dy_k(t)}{dt} = -y_k(t) + f(s_k(t)) \tag{1}$$

$$s_k(t) = \sum_j w_{kj} y_j(t),$$

where $s_k(t)$ is the net input to unit k at time t, $y_k(t)$ is the output of unit k at time t, w_{kj} are the weights from unit j to unit k, $f(\cdot)$ is the transfer function, and τ_k is the time constant of unit k. Time constants determine the time scale of the system. This can be easily seen by dividing both sides of (1) by τ_k. As τ_k increases, the right hand side of the equation decreases, which means that the network is changing more slowly. Analogously, as τ_k decreases, the opposite effect is achieved.

The equations for the Delta-Net are derived from a discretized version of the continuous network. One advantage of this approach is that the learning algorithm is simpler than the continuous versions, but the network still retains some essential characteristics of the continuous network [11]. The equations for the Delta-Net are

$$y_k(t + \Delta t) = (1 - \frac{1}{1 + \exp^{-a_k}}) \cdot y_k(t) + \frac{1}{1 + \exp^{-a_k}} \cdot f(s_k(t)) \tag{2}$$

$$s_k(t) = \sum_j w_{kj} y_j(t),$$

where, for a more stable implementation, we have replaced the time constant τ with $1 + \exp^{-a_k}$.

Note that (3) allows for one time constant per unit in the Delta-Net; however, in the following experiments, we have used only one time constant for the entire network to simplify the analysis. After the network has learned to predict $S(t)$, the weights are fixed. The network is then presented the same signal at a *different* rate as input. The time constant is then adjusted using the following update rule:

$$\Delta a_i(t) = -\eta \frac{\partial E}{\partial a_i(t)} = -\eta \sum_i \frac{\partial E}{\partial y_k(t)} \frac{\partial y_k(t)}{\partial a_i}. \qquad (3)$$

In this way, the network adapts its processing speed to the rate of the input signal, and the time constant's final value can be used as a measure of the rate of the input.

Application to Speech

The dynamic rate adaptation technique described above can be applied to speech input in the following way: A Delta-Net is used as a rate-estimation module. The input it receives is the acoustic energy computed from the speech signal. Vowels are the speech sounds with the strongest intensities [2]; thus, acoustic energy peaks can be used to indicate vocalic segments in the speech signal. Since the rate at which vocalic segments occur is comparable to the syllable rate in speech production [9], acoustic energy can be used to give a reasonable estimate of speaking rate.

The rate estimator is trained initially to predict the acoustic energy function for speech spoken at a normal rate. Then, when it receives energy values computed from speech spoken at a different rate, it adjusts its time constant to adapt its processing speed to the rate of the new input. We envision the incorporation of the rate estimation module and the recognizers into a complete system as follows: Each of the recognizers receives speech parameters as input, while the rate estimation module receives acoustic energy values. The rate estimator adapts to changes in the energy signal by adjusting its time constant. The adjusted time constant value is then transferred to the recognizers so that they can set their own time constants appropriately (e.g., each recognizer's time constant can be set to a function of the rate estimator's time constant). In this way, rate information is used to control processing speed of the recognizers as they process the speech input. The recognizer with the lowest error will then represent the system's classification decision of the target phoneme or word.

This rate adaptation technique can conceivably be incorporated into a non-neural network based system as well. For example, in a DTW-based system, rate information provided by the rate module can be used to dynamically alter the constraints on the slopes of the warping path during template matching. Similarly, an HMM-based system can make use of global rate information to modify the duration modeling parameters.

Experimental Results

Sine Waves

Our first set of experiments were to see if DRA would work for simple sine waves. We trained a network with two input units, four fully recurrent hidden units, and two output units (2-4-2) to predict two sine waves, $sin(x)$ and $sin(2x)$, with a phase delay of 36 degrees. Then, with the weights fixed, the time constant is allowed to change according to (3). We should note here that the problem posed to the system is exacerbated by the fact that we did not start the system at the original rate and slowly adjust it; we simply presented it with the fast signal abruptly. Nevertheless, the system adjusted to the rate of the input within three cycles, as shown in Figure 1. We had similar results with another network trained to predict four sine waves with four different phases. The four-phase network needed only a single cycle to adapt to the rate of the new input. The top graphs show that the system predicts the signal well, but not perfectly, after initial training. Nevertheless, this did not seem to hinder the system's ability to adapt to the rate during time constant learning.

Gait Data

To test DRA on a more complex signal, we used a 24-dimensional time-varying signal representing the average walking cycle for a seven-year-old. The data, produced at the Motion Analysis Laboratory at the Children's Hospital in San Diego, was extracted from free-speed, level-walking subjects. Each subject has twelve markers and four sticks precisely placed on their waist, legs, and feet as reference points. The pre-processed data is in the form of twelve joint rotation parameters from each side of the body, arranged in a gait cycle, defined as (for example) the time from heel-strike to heel-strike.

Each vector consists of 24 floating point numbers to represent the joint angles in both legs at each time step. Since we did not have data for children walking at different rates, we simulated different rates by sampling the signal at different intervals. The rate of the input is simulated as follows: normal rate refers to every other time step; fast rate refers to every third time step for a speedup of 1.5; and slow rate refers to every time step for a speedup of 0.5 relative to the normal rate.

The network architecture consists of 24 input lines, one for each of the 24 dimensions in the signal. The input layer is fully connected to a fully recurrent hidden layer of 10 units. The hidden layer is in turn fully connected to 24 output units. As with the sine wave experiments, results obtained here show that even though the system did not learn to predict the original signal perfectly, it was still able to adjust the time constant in order to adapt to the rate of the new signal. For the slow

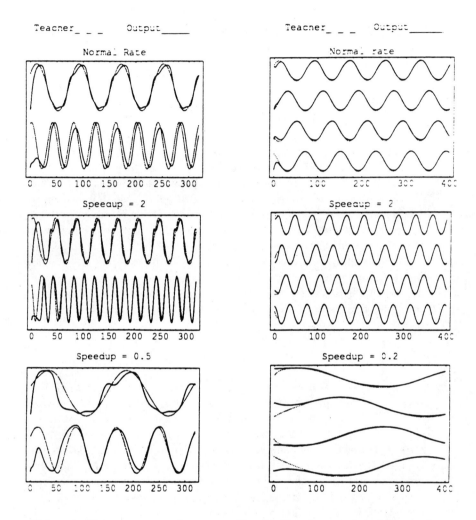

Figure 1: Sine wave experiments — Results for the two-frequency and four-phase are shown on the left and right, respectively. Top Row: Trained network on normal-rate input. Middle Row: Time constant adaptation to fast-rate input. Bottom Row: Time constant adaptation to slow-rate input. Number of updates is on the x-axis, and activation values is on the y-axis.

signal, rate adaptation was completed within four cycles; similar results were obtained for the fast signal.

Energy Contour

To apply our method of dynamic rate adaptation to speech, we used a similar network to predict the acoustic energy contour of a speech signal. This network had three input units ($E(t - \delta)$, $E(t - 2\delta)$, and $E(t - 3\delta)$), two hidden units, and one output unit for $E(t)$. The simple utterance "*ba ba...ba*" was used as data for this experiment. The utterance was recorded at three rates: 4 *ba*'s per second (fast), 3 *ba*'s per second (medium), and 2 *ba*'s per second (slow). The energy contour was computed for the utterance spoken by the same speaker at fast, medium, and slow rates, using 40-msec frames, 20 msec apart. The log_{10} of the energy function was taken, and the results were scaled to $[0, 1]$ and smoothed using a moving average for input to the recurrent network. Energy functions of the three different rates are shown in Figure 2.

For this experiment, we let time constant adapt along with the weights in the first training phase. The idea is allow time constant to settle to some optimal value for the medium rate before it was adapted to accommodate for other rates. As in previous experiments, the network was trained to predict the energy of the medium-rate utterance. To test how well the time constant can reflect rate changes, a "new" utterance was created by concatenating the three utterances in this order: medium, fast, medium, slow, medium. With the weights fixed, the network was given this concatenated utterance as input, and the time constant was adjusted. Figure 3 shows how the time constant changes to reflect rate variation for this test utterance. Five other test utterances were constructed in a similar fashion. For all six utterances, the time constant appropriately reflects the direction of rate change; that is, the time constant increases when the rate of the signal increases, and vice versa, for all rate transitions.

Conclusions

Motivations for incorporating rate-dependent processing into an automatic speech recognition system have been examined, and a technique has been proposed to implement it by having a system automatically estimate and dynamically adapt to the rate of the input signal. Our approach for rate adaptation has been shown to work on sine waves of different phases and frequencies, on complicated motion variables from human gait data, and on acoustic energy functions of a simple speech utterance.

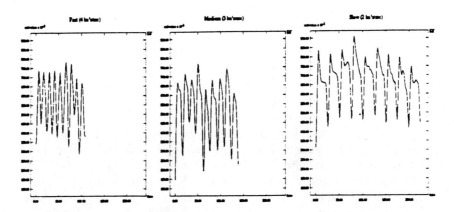

Figure 2: Energy contours of the utterance "ba ba ... ba," spoken by a single talker at three different rates: fast, medium, and slow.

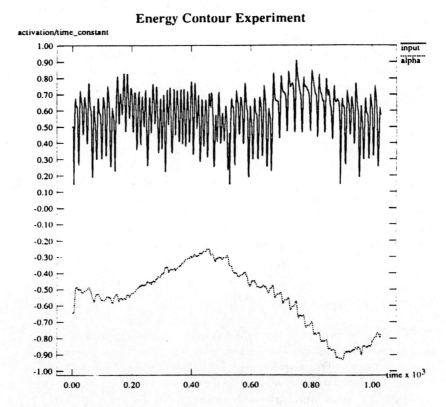

Figure 3: Energy contour experiment — The test utterance is a concatenation of medium-, fast-, medium-, slow-, and medium-rate utterances. The bottom curve illustrates how α changes along with the rate of the utterance.

Our plan is to apply it to speech by building phoneme recognizers and then adapting their rates to the signal dynamically, with the goal of providing the recognizers increased robustness with respect to rate.

References

[1] E. N. Biden D. H. Sutherland, R. A. Olshen and M. P. Wyatt. *The development of mature walking.* Oxford: Mac Keith, 1988.

[2] Peter B. Denes and Elliot N. Pinson. *The speech chain: the physics and biology of spoken language.* Bell Telephone Laboratories, 1963.

[3] Jeffrey L. Elman. Finding structure in time. *Cognitive Science,* 14:179–211, 1990.

[4] Terry L. Gottfried, Joanne L. Miller, and Paula E. Payton. Effect of speaking rate on the perception of vowels. *Phonetica,* 47:155–172, 1990.

[5] Richard P. Lippmann, Edward A. Martin, and Douglas B. Paul. Multi-style training for robust isolated-word speech recognition. *IEEE International Conference on Acoustics, Speech, and Signal Processing,* pages 705–708, 1987.

[6] Jacques Mehler, Emmanuel Dupoux, and Juan Segui. Constraining models of lexical access: the onset of word recognition. In Gerry T. M. Altmann, editor, *Cognitive models of speech processing.* MIT Press, 1990.

[7] Joanne L. Miller. Effects of speaking rate on segmental distinctions. In Peter D. Eimas and Joanne L. Miller, editors, *Perspectives on the study of speech.* Lawrence Erlbaum Associates, 1981.

[8] Joanne L. Miller, Francois Grosjean, and Concetta Lomanto. Articulation rate and its variability in spontaneous speech: a reanalysis and some implications. *Phonetica,* 41:215–225, 1984.

[9] Lawrence R. Rabiner and Ronald W. Schafer. *Digital processing of speech signals.* Prentice-Hall, 1978.

[10] Q. Summerfield, P.J. Bailey, J. Seton, and M. F. Dorman. Fricative envelope parameters and silent intervals in distinguishing 'slit' and 'split'. *Phonetica,* 38:181–192, 1981.

[11] Fu-Sheng Tsung. Learning in recurrent finite difference networks. In D. S. Touretzky, J. L. Elman, T. J. Sejnowski, and G. E. Hinton, editors, *Proceedings of the 1990 Connectionist Models Summer School.* Morgan Kaufmann, 1991.

[12] Ron Williams and Dave Zipser. A learning algorithm for continually running fully recurrent neural networks. *Neural Computation,* 1:270–280, 1989.

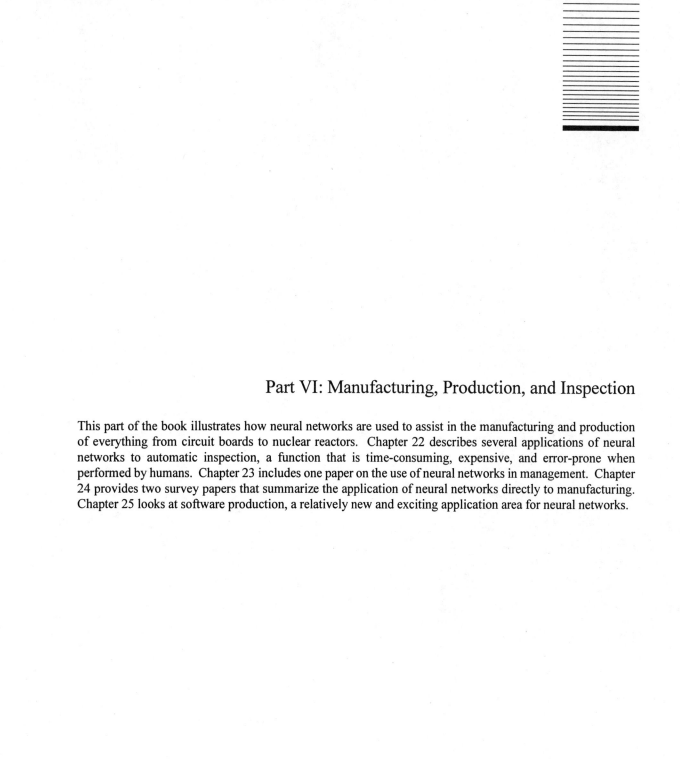

Part VI: Manufacturing, Production, and Inspection

This part of the book illustrates how neural networks are used to assist in the manufacturing and production of everything from circuit boards to nuclear reactors. Chapter 22 describes several applications of neural networks to automatic inspection, a function that is time-consuming, expensive, and error-prone when performed by humans. Chapter 23 includes one paper on the use of neural networks in management. Chapter 24 provides two survey papers that summarize the application of neural networks directly to manufacturing. Chapter 25 looks at software production, a relatively new and exciting application area for neural networks.

Chapter 22
Automatic Inspection

In any operation from the military to the household, the cost of repairing or replacing broken equipment immediately affects that operation's cash flow. It seems simple -- reduce repair costs and increase profits. The problem becomes how to identify when a repair is needed as soon as possible to eliminate further damage. This chapter focuses on the many different applications of neural networks for automatic inspection. The motivation is to produce low-cost inspection devices that can continually and accurately inspect a device. The first four papers in this chapter emphasize circuit board inspection. **Paper 22.1** describes the application of the multilayer perceptron (MLP) for detecting multiple faults in analog circuits. **Paper 22.2** presents an approach to automatically monitoring the production of integrated circuits and identifying potential fault areas before the board is used. **Paper 22.3** reports the application of MLP neural networks to printed circuit board inspection using image data produced from magnetic fields. **Paper 22.4** describes how neural networks can be used in combination with Built-In Test (BIT) systems in an aircraft environment. The remaining papers describe a wide variety of automatic inspection applications, including: reinforced concrete structures (**Paper 22.5**), drill wear (**Paper 22.6**), pneumatic control valves (**Paper 22.7**), helicopter transmissions (**Paper 22.8**), induction motors (**Paper 22.9**), oil-filled transformers (**Paper 22.10**), nuclear reactors (**Paper 22.11**), ocean water (**Paper 22.12**), and space shuttle engines (**Paper 22.13**).

Chapter 22:   Automatic Inspection

Neural Networks for Multiple Fault Diagnosis in Analog Circuits

Alessandra Fanni, Alessandro Giua, Enrico Sandoli

Istituto di Elettrotecnica, Università di Cagliari, P.zza d'Armi, 09123 Cagliari, Italy

email: fanni@elettro1.unica.it, giua@ecse.rpi.edu

Abstract

Fault diagnosis of analog circuits is a complex problem. The paper discusses how the features of neural networks of learning from examples and of generalizing may be used to solve this problem. In a detailed applicative example, we show how, given the voltages values in a set of test points, a network may be trained to recognize catastrophic single faults on a circuit part of a direct current motor drive. The network is then used to diagnose multiple faults on two and three components. In this case the network is generally able to detect at least one of the malfunctioning components, although less sharply than in the case of single faults.

1 Introduction

Fault diagnosis of analog circuits is a complex problem. Classical solutions require either a huge amount of calculation if parameter identification methods are used, or a great number of simulations of faulty conditions if fault dictionary methods are used [6,7].

Novel approaches based on Artificial Intelligence techniques have been developed in recent years to overcome the limitations of these classical methods. Among them, we recall qualitative reasoning and rule-based expert systems.

Systems based on qualitative reasoning [2,3,10] use a qualitative causal model of the device to diagnose. The model behavior is compared to the actual device behavior and the discrepancies trigger a diagnostic procedure. Although these methods suffer from lack of information that often leads to non unique solutions, they are able to handle incomplete knowledge of linear and non linear circuits. However, they need a model, albeit qualitative, of the system at hand, with consequent great computational cost if the system is very complex.

Rule based systems explicitly associate a symptom to a cause by means of heuristic rules. They are simple to use, but very difficult to create and maintain: knowledge formalization has proved to be the bottleneck of this technology.

The feature of the neural networks of learning from examples and of generalizing [12] has suggested their use in the fault diagnosis of electrical circuits. In this way it is possible to avoid many of the problems that affect other methods.

- The symptom-cause correspondence is derived automatically during the training of the net, without requiring an explicit formalization. Note that there is a small price to pay for this: while an expert system is generally able to justify its deductions, a neural network is not [13,14].

- Since the network is capable of generalizing, we may limit the number of fault simulations to a small set of accurately chosen faults. The network should be able to recognize fault configurations not explicitly comprised in the training set [5]. This is a clear advantage over fault dictionary methods.

- It is possible to avoid the problems connected with the calculation of circuit parameters and in general to the modelization, because the neural network does not need any circuital model or schema.

745

This paper reports on the results of our group at the University of Cagliari (see also [11]). Other approaches to the use of neural networks for circuit diagnosis have also been published recently.

Keagle *et al.* [5] discuss how networks trained to recognize single faults may be used to detect multiple faults. Tests are performed on a *digital* circuit consisting of nine logical gates affected by stuck-at 1 or stuck-at 0. The paper also presents results on the performance of the diagnostic system as a function of the network architecture.

Meador *et al.* [8] compare feedforward neural network performance with other classifiers: gaussian maximum likelihood and K-nearest neighbors. In each experiment a single parameter deviation fault on an operational amplifier circuit is considered. The classifiers must separate the input patterns corresponding to the correct behavior and to the faulty one. Results show that the neural network gives higher accuracy than the other classifiers.

Parten *et al.* [9] propose to use neural networks as part of a model-based expert system for diagnosing lumped parameter devices. The purpose of the net would be that of solving the equations ruling the behavior of the diagnosed device, modelled as a set of interconnected components.

Thompson *et al.* [13] consider the problem of diagnosing an IC board with approximately 60 components, both analog and digital. They use a backpropagation neural network with a modular structure, i.e., each part of the net recognizes a particular fault.

Totton and Limb [14] use neural networks to diagnose a high volume circuit board, part of a digital telephone exchange. They observed from historical data that failures on four types of components account for more than 85% of all faults. This led them to construct a network whose four outputs signal the presence of a faulty component of a given type, i.e., the network does not pinpoint the faulty component but simply detects what *type* of component is faulty.

In this paper we consider backpropagation neural networks. During a training process, based on single fault simulations, the network is able to associate the corresponding fault configuration to a generic configuration of test point voltage values, pointing out the malfunctioning component. Once the network has been trained, we have estimated the ability of the network to recognize multiple faults due to two and three simultaneously malfunctioning components. The voltage configurations corresponding to these multiple faults need not be presented to the network during the training.

We have restricted in the present investigation the class of faults considered. The faults in analog circuits may be *catastrophic faults*, that cause a large and sudden variation of the circuit parameter values, and *deviation faults*, associated to slight variations of the circuit parameter values from their nominal values [1]. Since statistics have shown that in the analog circuits 80-90% of faults are catastrophic [4], we chose to simulate faults of this kind, such as short circuits and open circuits between two terminals of a component.

2 Neural model

Consider a circuit with n components and a given set of m test points. We will use a three layer backpropagation neural net with m inputs and n outputs to diagnose the circuit.

The voltage of all test points is measured by an acquisition board during several simulations in the absence of faults, in the presence of an open circuit on a single bipolar component, and in the presence of a short circuit on a single bipolar component. Thus, for a circuit with n bipolar components it is necessary to run $2n+1$ simulations. We also simulated faults on components with more than two terminals. As an example, in the circuit shown in Section 4, there are trimmers and operational amplifiers. We considered two possible faults on a trimmer (cursor stuck up and cursor stuck down) and just one single fault on an operational amplifier (it was made inoperative by feeding with exceedingly high voltage). In general, let s be the number of the single faults taken into account; thus one needs to perform $s + 1$ simulations.

The voltage measured at a test point is a function of time during each simulation. In order to obtain a single meaningful value to represent it, we take its mean value. We have also considered the use of different indices, such as the root-mean-squared value. However, in the tests we performed the use of the mean value gave the best results. Thus, during the $i - th$ simulation we obtain the vector $\vec{x}_i = (x_i(1) \cdots x_i(m))^T$, where $x_i(j)$ is the mean value of the voltage of test point j.

We are now ready to construct the $s + 1$ input-output patterns that will be used to train the backpropagation neural network for the diagnosis of the circuit. Each pattern is given by a pair $(\vec{x}_i, \vec{y}_i)$. The vector $\vec{y}_i$ associated to each $\vec{x}_i$ is defined as follows:

$$y_i(k) = \begin{cases} 0 & \text{if component } k \text{ is short circuited during the } i-th \text{ simulation,} \\ 0.5 & \text{if component } k \text{ is not faulty during the } i-th \text{ simulation,} \\ 1 & \text{if component } k \text{ is an open circuit during the } i-th \text{ simulation,} \end{cases}$$

We modelled the faults on the trimmer as follows: a value 1 of the output node corresponds to a cursor stuck up fault, and a value 0 to a cursor stuck down fault. We modelled the fault on the operational amplifier assigning a value 0 to the corresponding output node.

Once the net has been trained, it may be used to perform the diagnosis of the circuit. One needs to give to the net as input vector $\vec{x}$ the mean values of the measured test point voltages. The net will produce an output vector $\vec{y}$; a value of $y(k)$ close to 0 (resp., 1) will pinpoint a short circuit (resp., open circuit) fault of component k; a value close to 0.5 will denote that the component is correctly functioning. Note that the value of $y(k)$ may be any number in the range $[0, 1]$ thus expressing a fuzzy membership of the component to one of the three states. This suggests that the network may be used to diagnose even parameter deviation faults [8].

It is also clear that although the net has been trained with the results of single fault simulations, it is potentially able to diagnose multiple faults. In this case, two or more elements of $\vec{y}$ will be close to 0 or 1.

This is the basic outline of our system. We now add a few remarks concerning the structure of the neural network and the training algorithm.

- We tested both linear and sigmoid functions as node transfer functions. The sigmoid gave the best results.

- The updating of the connection weights on backpropagation neural networks [12] depends on two coefficients: the learning coefficient η and the momentum term β. We obtained the best results using a value of β which decreased during the training from 0.6 to 0.05 and a value of η which decreased from 0.8 to 0.1.

- Networks with 2 layers are not capable of generalization and thus cannot be used to diagnose multiple faults.

- Networks with 3 layers and 4 layers are capable of generalization and their performance is improved if direct connections between input and output nodes are allowed. For the circuit discussed in Section 4, the best results were obtained using a 3-layer network with 45 nodes in the hidden layer. By increasing the number of hidden nodes, one slightly increases the capacity of the network but this considerably increases its complexity as well.

3 Data pre-processing

The data acquired from the circuit during the simulations are pre-processed before being used to construct the training patterns. This is a fundamental step that may dramatically increase the performance of the diagnostic system.

3.1 Filtering

Although the voltage measured at a test point is a function of time during each simulation, we used a single value (the mean value) to represent it. In a first approach we tried to keep the information on the shape of the voltage signal: we sampled it a few times during a period (say 7 times) and we gave the net 7 values per test point. Thus, the number of input nodes of the network was $7m$. Unfortunately, we realized that in these conditions the network behaves as a filter and its performance decreases.

The same problem of filtering was observed in the case where the distance between the input vectors of different patterns is small. To improve separability between training patterns we scaled the inputs in the interval $[-1, 1]$. For the test point j let $x_{\max}(j) = \max(x_0(j), \cdots x_s(j))$ and $x_{\min}(j) = \min(x_0(j), \cdots x_s(j))$. We associate a scaling function to test point j as follows:

$$f_j(x) = \frac{2x - x_{\max}(j) - x_{\min}(j)}{x_{\max}(j) - x_{\min}(j)}.$$

Finally, given a vector $\vec{x}$, we will transform it into a vector $\vec{x}'$ to be applied effectively to the net, where:

$$\vec{x}' = (f_1(x(1)), \cdots, f_m(x(m)))^T.$$

A similar approach is also used in [14].

Special care is required in all cases where $x_{\max}(j) - x_{\min}(j) < \varepsilon$ (here ε is a fixed tolerance), i.e., in all cases where $x_i(j)$ is constant for all i. This means that the reading of the test point j voltage is meaningless as far as regards the diagnosis. We may simply avoid considering it, thus decreasing the number of input nodes and simplifying the structure of the network.

3.2 Undistinguishable and undetectable faults

Another problem encountered was the following. Consider two (or more) components, say k and k' in parallel in the circuit. Let $(\vec{x}_i, \vec{y}_i)$ and $(\vec{x}_{i'}, \vec{y}_{i'})$ be the training patterns corresponding to the simulation of a short circuit on component k and k' respectively. Clearly $\vec{x}_i = \vec{x}_{i'}$. However, $\vec{y}_i \neq \vec{y}_{i'}$. In fact $y_i(k) = 0$ and all other elements of $\vec{y}_i$ are 0.5, while $y_{i'}(k') = 0$ and all other elements of $\vec{y}_{i'}$ are 0.5. Thus we train the net on a one-to-many correspondence, that is clearly not a suitable classification function [13]. The same problem appears when we consider the open circuit faults of series components, or more generally, when we have two or more *undistinguishable* single faults, i.e., faults that produce the same voltage configuration at the available test points.

A similar problem may arise when a fault is *undetectable*. In this case, the training patterns corresponding to the fault-free simulation and to the simulation of the undetectable fault have the same input vector but different output vectors. The presence of undetectable faults may have different causes.

- A component whose behavior is the same when faulty or functioning correctly. As an example, for all practical purposes the behavior of a reverse biased diode is the same when the diode is functioning well or when it is affected by an open circuit fault.

- The limited number of test points may not allow detection of an abnormal behavior of the circuit.

We point out that the ambiguity due to undistinguishable or undetectable faults does not depend on our diagnostic system but derives either from the behavior and topology of the circuit or from the choice of test points.

We chose to fix this problem in two steps.

A first coarse solution takes care of *topologically* undistinguishable faults. From an inspection of the circuit one makes a list of all sets of parallel components. Then, one needs to consider a single short circuit fault simulation for each set $\mathcal{C}_i$ of parallel components. There will be a single training pattern $(\vec{x}_i, \vec{y}_i)$ for such a fault. The vector $\vec{y}_i$ is such that $y_i(k) = 0$ for all $k \in \mathcal{C}_i$, while all other components have a 0.5 value. A dual procedure takes care of sets of series components.

There is a more general approach for removing from the training set conflicting patterns due to *behaviorally* undetectable and undistinguishable faults. The approach entails the pre-processing of all data acquired during fault simulation. We noticed that, due to measurement noise, different acquisitions for the same fault simulation produce different values of $\vec{x}$, all contained in a neighborhood of radius d. Thus, one may not distinguish between two different faults whose corresponding vectors $\vec{x}$ are closer than d. In this case one may proceed as follows.

1. Acquire q measurements during each of the $s + 1$ simulations. Let $\vec{x}_i^1, \ldots, \vec{x}_i^q$ be the q acquisitions for the simulation i ($i = 0$ in the absence of fault; $i > 0$ for all other faults).

2. Compute the averages: $\vec{x}_i = (\vec{x}_i^1 + \ldots + \vec{x}_i^q)/q$ for each simulation. Let $d = \max_{i,r}(|\vec{x}_i - \vec{x}_i^r|)$.

3. A fault i such that $|\vec{x}_0 - \vec{x}_i| \leq d$ will be considered *undetectable*. The corresponding patterns will be removed from the training set.

4. Any two (or more) faults i and i' such that $|\vec{x}_i - \vec{x}_{i'}| \leq d$ will be considered *undistinguishable* and will belong to the same fault class. A single pattern $(\vec{x}, \vec{y})$ will represent the class, where $\vec{x} = (\vec{x}_i + \vec{x}_{i'})/2$ and $\vec{y}$ will account for all faults in the class, as already shown for topologically undistinguishable faults.

4 Experimental results

We present the results obtained with our system on the circuit in Figure 1, part of a DC motor drive. The same circuit has also been diagnosed in [3]. In the figure, the $m = 12$ test points are marked by numbers within circles, while the $n = 36$ components are labeled by numbers in square brackets. Input nodes I_2 and I_3 are connected to DC voltage generators; input node I_1 is connected to a voltage generator which has a direct component and a sinusoidal component with a frequency of 10 Hz.

The measurements were collected through an "Analog Device" RTI-815-A acquisition board. The board has 32 channels in single ended mode and was controlled by a PC-486.

As explained in Section 2, there are 70 single faults to consider on this circuit. In fact, the circuit is composed of 36 components but only one fault is simulated for each of the two operational amplifiers. Thus, the overall training set should consist of 71 training patterns — the first being

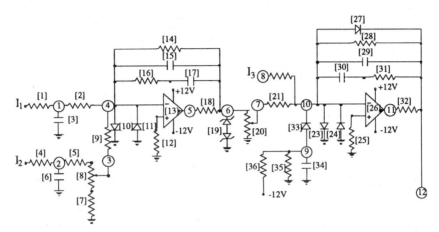

Figure 1: Test circuit.

related to the circuit behavior in absence of fault. However, due to the presence of conflicting patterns, the network performs poorly when all 71 patterns are presented for learning.

Pre-processing of the data gave the following results.

- The following sets contain topologically undistinguishable faults: { 10s, 11s }, { 14s, 15s }, { 23s, 24s }, { 27s, 28s, 29s }, { 34s, 35s }, { 16o, 17o }, { 30o, 31o }. Here 10s represents a short circuit fault on component 10, 16o represents an open circuit fault on component 16, etc.

- The set of behaviorally undetectable faults is: { 3o, 6o, 10o, 11o, 12s, 14o, 17s, 18s, 19o, 21o, 22o, 23o, 24o, 25s, 27o, 28o, 28s, 29o, 29s, 30o, 30s, 31o, 31s, 32s, 33o, 35o }.

- The following sets contain behaviorally undistinguishable faults: { 4o, 6s }, { 10s, 11s }, { 14s, 15s, 16o, 16s, 17o, 18o, 19s}, { 23s, 24s }, { 34s, 35s, 36o }, { 34o, 36s }.

The procedure shown in Section 3 gives a reduced training set consisting of 33 different patterns. We will present the results obtained with four different nets. Net N_1 was trained on the 33 patterns for 40.000 iterations. Net N_2 was trained on the 33 patterns for 120.000 iterations. Net N_3 was trained on 99 patterns (we have acquired three measurements for each simulation, thus increasing the number of training patterns) for 120.000 iterations. Net N_4 was trained on 99 patterns for 360.000 iterations.

We fixed two threshold values for the output nodes of the network. Outputs greater than 0.8 (less than 0.2) will certainly pinpoint an open (short) circuit on the corresponding component. We also consider two uncertainty bands; we say that an open (short) circuit on a component is *likely* if the corresponding output node has a value in the interval [0.7, 0.8] ([0.2, 0.3]).

As an example of diagnosis, Figure 2 and Figure 3 show the output obtained giving as input vector to the network the voltage configuration corresponding to an open circuit fault on component 2 and that corresponding to a short circuit fault on component 26, respectively. Finally, Figure 4 shows how the network behaves when its input vector is the voltage configuration corresponding to the presence of both faults previously considered. This shows that the network is not only capable of recalling a learned association but also of generalizing.

Table 1 shows the performances of the four networks when diagnosing single faults. Note that we have acquired new measurements for the same 33 simulations used to construct the training set. As can be seen, almost all single faults are correctly recognized. In a few cases the network shows a fault only as likely; this happens for faults whose input patterns are relatively close to the input pattern of the fault free simulation. No false alarms were ever detected in these cases.

Table 2 shows the performances of the four networks when diagnosing two simultaneous faults. We have considered 60 different pairs of faults (undetectable faults are not considered, of course).

Table 3 shows the performances of the four networks when diagnosing three simultaneous faults. We have considered 28 different sets of faults.

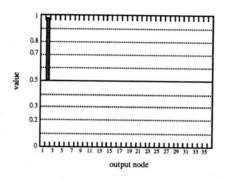

Figure 2: Network output when diagnosing an open circuit on component 2.

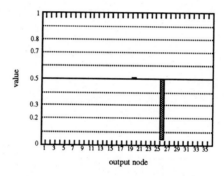

Figure 3: Network output when diagnosing a short circuit on component 26.

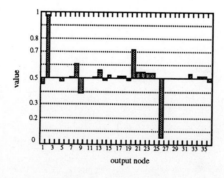

Figure 4: Network output when diagnosing a multiple fault: open circuit on component 2 and short circuit on component 26.

	N_1	N_2	N_3	N_4
Faults correctly detected				
without false alarms	26	31	30	30
with false alarms	0	0	0	0
Faults detected as likely				
without false alarms	3	2	3	3
with false alarms	0	0	0	0
Faults not detected				
without false alarms	4	0	0	0
with false alarms	0	0	0	0

Table 1: Diagnosis of single faults (33 simulations).

	N_1	N_2	N_3	N_4
Two faults correctly detected				
without false alarms	4	4	3	2
with false alarms	9	16	15	15
One fault correctly detected				
without false alarms	24	19	23	17
with false alarms	12	17	17	24
No fault correctly detected				
without false alarms	7	0	0	0
with false alarms	4	4	2	2

Table 2: Diagnosis of two simultaneous faults (60 simulations).

	N_1	N_2	N_3	N_4
Three faults correctly detected				
without false alarms	1	1	0	0
with false alarms	2	5	4	2
One or two faults correctly detected				
without false alarms	8	2	5	4
with false alarms	16	18	18	21
No fault correctly detected				
without false alarms	0	0	0	0
with false alarms	1	2	1	1

Table 3: Diagnosis of three simultaneous faults (28 simulations).

We could not obtain meaningful results when using the network to diagnose four or more simultaneous faults.

5 Conclusions

We have shown how a neural network, trained to recognize catastrophic single faults, may be used to diagnose multiple faults on analog circuits.

In general we observed that the network is always able to learn and recall the single fault patterns presented during the training. Multiple faults on two and three components may also be diagnosed, although less sharply than in the single fault case, due to the presence of false alarms. In this case, however, since the network is generally able to detect at least one of the malfunctioning components, we may use an incremental repair procedure, substituting the faulty components one by one.

We plan to increase the performance of the diagnostic system by appropriately choosing test points and voltage supplies in order to reduce the number of undetectable and undistinguishable faults.

The research will then continue in its attempt to verify the performance of the adopted technique in the case in which the training set is based on the simulation of deviation faults, i.e., percentile variation of the circuit parameters with respect to the nominal value.

References

[1] J.W. Bandler, A.E. Salama, "Fault Diagnosis of Analog Circuits," *Proc. IEEE*, Vol. 73, No. 8, pp. 1279–1325, August, 1985.

[2] Ph. Dague, O. Jehl, Ph. Devès, P. Luciani, P. Taillibert, "When Oscillators Stop Oscillating," *Proc. 12th Int. Joint Conf. on Artificial Intelligence* (Sydney, Australia), pp. 1109–1115, August, 1991.

[3] A. Fanni, P. Diana, A. Giua, M. Perezzani, "Qualitative Dynamic Diagnosis of Circuits," *Artificial Intelligence for Engineering Design, Analysis and Manufacturing*, Vol. 7, No. 1, pp. 53–64, 1993.

[4] W. Hochwald, J.D. Bastian, "A DC Approach for Analogue Fault Dictionary Determination," *IEEE Trans. Circuits and Systems*, Vol. CAS-26, No. 7, pp. 523–529, July, 1979.

[5] B.J. Kagle, J.H. Murphy, L.J. Koos, J.R. Reeder, "Multi-Fault Diagnosis of Electronic Circuit Boards Using Neural Networks," *Proc. Int. Joint Conf. on Neural Networks* (San Diego, California), pp. 197–202, June, 1990.

[6] R. Liu (Ed.), "Selected Papers on Analog Fault Diagnosis," *Advances in Circuits and Systems*, IEEE Circuits and Systems Society, IEEE Press, 1987.

[7] R. Liu (Ed.), *Testing and Diagnosis of Analog Circuits and Systems*, Van Nostrand Reinhold, 1991.

[8] J. Meador, A. Wu, C.T. Tseng, T.S. Lin, "Fast Diagnosis of Integrated Circuit Faults Using Feedforward Neural Networks," *Proc. Int. Joint Conf. on Neural Networks* (Seattle, Washington), pp. 269–273, July, 1991.

[9] C.R. Parten, R. Saeks, R. Pap, "Fault Diagnosis and Neural Networks," *Proc. 1991 IEEE Int. Conf. on Systems, Man and Cybernetics* (Charlottesville, Virginia), pp. 1517–1521, October, 1991.

[10] F. Pipitone, K. Dejong, W. Spears, "An Artificial Intelligence Approach to Analog Systems Diagnosis," in [7].

[11] E. Sandoli, "Neural Networks for Analog Circuits Fault Diagnosis" (in Italian), *Tesi di Laurea*, Istituto di Ingegneria Elettrotecnica, Università di Cagliari (Cagliari, Italy), December, 1991.

[12] P.K. Simpson, *Artificial Neural Systems*, Pergamon Press Inc., 1990.

[13] A.B. Thompson, J.C. Sutton, H.T. Nagle, "Diagnosis of Telephony Line Card Component Failures Using an Artificial Neural Network," *Proc. SOUTHEASTCON 91* (Raleigh, North Carolina), pp. 229–233, April, 1991.

[14] K.A.E. Totton, P.R. Limb, "Experience in Using Neural Networks for Electronic Diagnosis," *Proc. 2nd Int. Conf. on Artificial Neural Networks* (Bournemouth, England), pp. 115-118, November, 1991.

A Neural Network Based Approach for Surveillance and Diagnosis of Statistical Parameters in IC Manufacturing Process

W. Zhang and L. Milor
Electrical Engineering Department and Institute of Systems Research,
University of Maryland, College Park, MD 20742 USA

ABSTRACT

This paper presents a new approach for monitoring and diagnosing potential faults in the IC manufacturing process. A backpropagation neural network based diagnosing model is employed to synthesize the complicated mapping from process measurements to the unmeasurable process disturbances. This model is trained to detect significant shifts of the disturbances. Due to the inverse mapping diagnosis becomes very efficient and is quite promising to be done in real time. Several mathematical issues involved in this approach and an illustrative example are discussed.

1 Introduction

During the last decade, the feature size of VLSI devices has been scaled down significantly, and it is becoming even smaller. Despite advances in integrated circuit (IC) equipment and fabrication techniques, there still exist random fluctuations in any IC manufacturing facility. Due to the fact that devices and circuits are being designed with increasingly tighter parameters and performance margins, chip performance becomes even more sensitive to those statistical variations, which may adversely affect the production yield.

The random parametric variations or process faults that cause depreciation of IC process yield come from deviations in process conditions and the inevitable fluctuations inherent in the IC manufacturing process. The fabrication of integrated circuits requires multiple processing steps. If the elements in one or more of these steps exceed their tolerance margins, devices fabricated will either fail or not perform as intended. It has therefore become imperative to monitor the IC process continuously in order to take immediate corrective actions in case of a deviation.

Although many process parameters, such as temperature, gas flux and pressure can be measured and controlled accurately, some others like diffusivity of boron and arsenic, variance of implantation profile and surface state density are usually not directly measurable. A potential fault is created when one of these parameters shifts from its nominal value outside its tolerance limit. Therefore, monitoring these parameters, detecting and diagnosing process faults emerges as one of the important issues in stabilizing and improving yields of IC manufacturing. Some effort has been put into this issue in the literature [1][2].

Since the parameters of interest can not be directly measured, they have to be inferred by some of the in-line measurements that have been taken from the fabrication line. The relation between process faults and observable measurements can be modeled by a statistical process simulator[3]. We are using a neural network to map the measurements to the faults, the inverse of the process simulation model. In other words, the neural network is trained to detect large shifts in the parameters of interest based on the in-line measurements. This diagnosis process turns out to be efficient and can be done in a real time fashion.

The quantities of IC process parameters make it infeasible and uneconomical to monitor all to them. A more effective way is naturally to monitor those parameters that have a significant impact on the process yield. Because of complexity of the IC fabrication process, however, identifying those parameters to monitor is not a trivial task. In this paper, a rigorous algorithm is presented to determine fault observability for a given set of measurements. This algorithm proves to be straight forward and much less involved in computation than previous ones.

Another important issue in our neural network

based approach lies in the training procedure. A special sampling distribution is introduced to enhance the domain over which the neural network based model is valid. In an effort to speed up the learning rate, thresholding and coding techniques are employed to improve computational efficiency and handle higher dimensional problems.

2 Architecture of the Surveillance and Diagnosis Model

Depending on the designed performance margin, tolerance for fluctuations of process parameters varies. For a very small performance margin, a small variation may result in a considerable number of fabricated devices falling into defective categories. Therefore this small variation naturally becomes an target to be detected. While in most cases, small variations can usually be tolerated; what causes the emergence of a large number of defective devices is significant variations.

In the literature a methodology has been developed to diagnose small process variations [2] [4], in which polynomial models were established to approximate the map between process disturbances and measurable outputs. Actually in high dimensional cases, it is very difficult to build an accurate polynomial model at each operating point of a process, and in addition, it is very intensive in computation. Although this is a good approach to diagnose nominal values of the unmeasurable process disturbances and detect their usually small variations, real-time diagnosis is more difficult using this model than our approach.

A neural network based diagnosing model presented in this paper focuses on detection of relatively large variations of an IC process. The schematic of the diagnosing process is shown in Figure 1.

The neural network diagnosing model essentially consists of a multilayer backpropagation neural network. The number of input nodes of the network is determined by the given measurement set. The number of output nodes depends on the diagnosable set of process disturbances for the given measurement set. Simulated output measurements and process disturbances to be diagnosed come from a virtual IC fabrication process. The use of the virtual IC process stems from the fact that it is prohibitively expensive to do experiments on a real IC fabrication line. Essentially, an IC process simulator is employed as the virtual process.

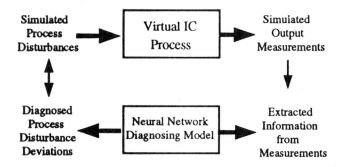

Figure 1: The neural network based diagnosing model

When the design and development stage of an IC process has been finished, a process simulator can be quite precisely tuned to this process. Then specially designed experiments are employed to input sets of simulation data to the tuned process simulator, and the corresponding outputs of the simulator are recorded. The next step is to generate training patterns for the neural network based on the simulation data. This is done by using a pair of output and input sets of data from the process simulator as the input and output of the neural network. In other words, the network uses the output measurements extracted from the IC process as its inputs, and it outputs the process disturbances to be monitored. These outputs will be analyzed to diagnose the significant shifts in the process disturbances.

When the learning procedure has been finished, the neural network is then ready to be used with the real IC fabrication line that has been simulated by the process simulator. As such it is possible to get a real time sampling of the process disturbances as long as a continuous sampling of the output measurements is available.

As mentioned before, the training patterns are generated from the data extracted from the virtual IC process, or a process simulator. It should be mentioned that training patterns based on the data extracted from the real IC fabrication line will improve the accuracy of the diagnosing model, since this can eliminate errors resulted from tuning of the process simulator. Therefore it is advantageous to use more data from a real fabrication process if possible to train the neural network while using it to monitor the process. This will make the diagnosing model more real-time oriented. However, since many process disturbances can not be observed or measured, the existence of simulated data is still quite necessary.

A distinguishing feature of this neural network based model is that diagnosing can be done within a very short time once the neural network has learned the mapping. This feature makes it practical to be applied to real time monitoring and diagnosing of process faults. Another advantage of the neural network model lies in its structural flexibility. It is very easy to add more input or output variables to the neural network model. Successful learning of the mapping can be achieved with high probability as long as a unique relation exists between variables which can be approximated. Thus the large number of output measurements and process disturbances inherent in IC process diagnosis becomes less of a severe problem in the neural network model than in the polynomial approximation model or other more mathematically involved models.

A simple reasoning suggests that computations increase approximately linearly with an increase in the input and output nodes of a neural network if the same number of hidden units are employed. This will significantly alleviate computational effort in high dimensional cases. Although the above reasoning is not strict mathematically, it can give us a feel for the computational complexity of the neural network method. A more detailed discussion on this topic can be found in [5].

3 Design of the Diagnosing Process

3.1 Fault Observability Algorithm

The statistical variations of an IC process arise from the existence of a set of low level, non-measurable, non-controllable, independently varying physical quantities, or process disturbances [2]. Each process disturbance can be represented by a random variable. Due to their physical nature, it is reasonable to assume that the random variables representing process disturbances are normally distributed according to the Central Limit Theorem in probability. With this assumption, we can completely specify process disturbances by identifying their means and standard deviations. Therefore what we actually deal with are statistics of disturbances.

It is known that highly nonlinear functions exist between process measurements and the disturbances. Diagnosing process disturbances using measurements of other variables, can be formalized as implementing a mapping from process measurements to the disturbances. To implement this nonlinear mapping, it should be assured that the process disturbances to be monitored are distinguishable and observable for a given set of measurements. A specific algorithm is devised to identify the distinguishable process disturbances for a given set of output measurements. The algorithm is briefly presented below.

Fault Observability Algorithm:

Step 1: Let the standardized normally distributed process disturbances be represented as $d_1, d_2, \cdots, d_n$, and the given set of standardized measurements as $y_1, y_2, \cdots, y_m$. Shift the ith disturbance d_i by a significant amount, say 3σ and find the shift, s_{ij}, in the jth measurement, y_j from its nominal value. If $|s_{ij}| > T_j$, a prescribed threshold, then set

$$f_{ij} = \begin{cases} 1 & \text{if } s_{ij} > T_j \\ -1 & \text{if } s_{ij} < -T_j \end{cases}$$

set $f_{ij} = 0$ if $|s_{ij}| < T_j$, where f_{ij} is an entry of a $n \times m$ matrix F, called the fault matrix.

Step 2: For each disturbance, $d_1, d_2, \cdots, d_n$, compute $\sum_{j=1}^{m} |f_{ij}|$. If

$$\sum_{j=1}^{m} |f_{ij}| = 0$$

then the ith disturbance, d_i is unobservable, given the measurement set. Eliminate d_i from the set of disturbances to be monitored or add additional measurements.

Step 3: Find out if there are two rows that are the same in the fault matrix. First compute:

$$r_{ij} = \sum_{k=1}^{m} |f_{ik} - f_{jk}|$$

If $r_{ij} = 0$, then rows i and j in the fault matrix are identical. This means that disturbances d_i and d_j are not guaranteed to be uniquely diagnosed, and are said to be in the same ambiguity group.

Step 4: Find out if there are two disturbances that have large and opposite effects on the measurements, since under these conditions they are also not uniquely diagnosable. To identify this situation. Compute:

$$r_{ij} = \sum_{k=1}^{m} |f_{ik} - (-1)f_{jk}|$$

If $r_{ij} = 0$, then disturbances d_i and d_j also belong to the same ambiguity group.

This algorithm is employed to examine sufficiency of a set of process measurements in detecting significant shifts in the disturbances that need to be monitored. Note that the determination of the threshold T used in Step 1 has a direct impact on size of the measurement set. It seems advantageous to select a small T so that more measurements could be included since extra measurements may provide more information, which may benefit fault diagnosing. On the other hand, using more measurements may also enlarge the possibility of redundancy and error, and this will unnecessarily further complicate the diagnosing system. Thus a compromise has to be made with regards to selection of the thresholds. This will be discussed in more detail in Section 4.2.

3.2 Control Charts, Thresholding and Coding

Since our objective is to detect large variations, such as on the order of 2σ or 3σ, the fault diagnosis problem can be greatly simplified by detecting in which range variations are likely to fall, instead of detecting the exact value of the variations. The statistical control chart technique has been applied in such circumstances [6].

Due to the statistical nature of the IC process, a few samples randomly taken from the fabrication line may hardly provide any meaningful information on process conditions. Statistical control techniques have to be employed to provide statistical inference. As the main tool of statistical inference, control charts can be used in monitoring and surveillance of the IC process with considerable effectiveness.

In the framework of statistical control, the type of control chart used in this project is referred to as a variable control chart. A typical variable control chart is shown in Figure 2. This type of control chart basically consists of a center line (CL) representing the nominal value, and several other lines that are parallel to the CL, which usually represent a $k\sigma$ departure from the CL. With mean μ and standard deviation σ known, the significance level of a process fault can be categorized. For example, if 3σ is the significance level, or control limit of interest, then a process fault may fall into one of three categories, namely outside $+3\sigma$, between $+3\sigma$ and -3σ, and outside -3σ. Measures have to be taken in the first and the third cases to correct the fault, while the second case suggests that no corrective action is

necessary.

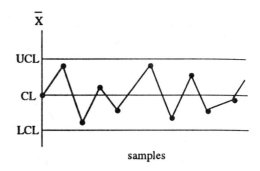

Figure 2: A typical variable control chart

Similar categorization can be done for the process measurements. The difference lies in that horizontal lines that are parallel to the CL, called thresholds in this context, may not be $k\sigma$ limits. Instead they are determined by a set of distinguishable process faults that have a significant impact on these measurements. This means that when none of this set of process faults occurs, the measurements will stay around their nominal values. If one or more of this set of process faults occurs, on the other hand, one or more of these measurements will depart from its nominal accordingly. The category into which one measurement falls may provide complete or partial information for diagnosing a specific process fault. In the case when a single measurement can provide only partial information, contributions from other measurements that have been affected by the same process fault will be incorporated to diagnose this fault.

This procedure is figuratively described in Figure 3. Figure 3(a) displays the corresponding relations between the control limits of the disturbances and the thresholds for the measurement. Figure 3(b) shows two control charts for disturbances and a corresponding measurement chart.

The determination of thresholds is critical in making the correct categories. This procedure, called thresholding, is carried out by a large number of simulations with different levels of simulated process faults. For a more detailed discussion on thresholding see [7].

In order to facilitate loading of inputs and outputs to the neural network and improve its computational efficiency, the inputs and outputs are encoded before being loaded to the network. A simple example is given in Figure 4 to show the coding procedure. Disturbances 1 and 2 in Figure 4 are encoded as a_2 and

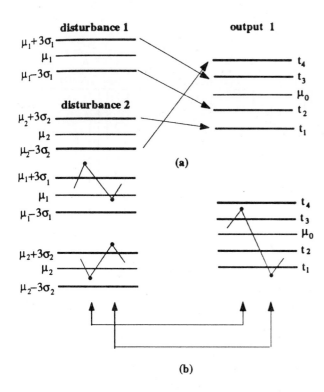

Figure 3: Generation of thresholds for a measurement affected by two disturbance

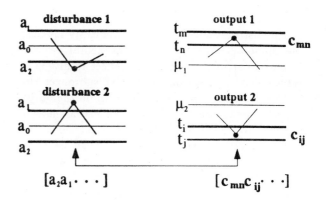

Figure 4: Generation of codes for disturbances and outputs

a_1 because of the ranges they fall in. Due to the significant shifts of disturbances 1 and 2, measurement 1 falls between the thresholds t_m and t_n. A unique code c_{mn} is then assigned to measurement 1. Similarly c_{ij} is assigned to measurement 2. By doing so, a unique pair of input-output patterns $[a_2 a_1 \cdots]$, $[c_{mn} c_{ij} \cdots]$ is produced.

Because of the utilization of coding, the patterns for the neural network are actually made up by sets of codes, or a limited number of discrete data, rather than numerical data obtained in manufacturing. The effectiveness associated with the coding method is reflected by a faster training session of the neural network.

3.3 Sampling Distribution Effects

As mentioned before, simulated data are used in the neural network's training patterns. Since the simulation data are generated by the Latin Hypercube Sampling (LHS) technique [8], which will be discussed below, the sampling distribution plays an important role in the quality of training patterns.

Simply speaking, LHS can be explained as weighted stratified sampling. Let the sample space S of X be partitioned into I disjoint strata S_i, and let $p_i = Pr(x \subset S_i)$ represent the size of S_i. Obtain a random sample $x_{ij}, j = 1, \cdots, n_i$ from S_i, where the sum of n_i for all samples is N, the total number of samples. If we wish to ensure also that each of the sample variables X_k has all portions of its distribution represented by sample values, we can divide the range of each X_k into N strata of equal marginal probability $1/N$, and sample once from each stratum. Let this sample be $x_{kj}, j = 1, \cdots, N$. These form the X_k components, $k = 1, \cdots, K$. Then components of the various X_k's are matched in a random fashion. Note that the strata are not necessarily of equal length, but each stratum contains the same probability $1/N$.

A distinct advantage of LHS appears when a model's output $Y(X)$ is dominated by only a few of the components of X, the model's input, which is exactly the case in the IC process. LHS ensures that each of those components is properly sampled.

In order to effectively apply LHS to IC process diagnosis, an important factor, namely the distribution effect has to be taken into consideration.

The discussion above implies that different distributions used with LHS have the effect of concentrating variable sampling in different subranges. As a result, a variable may be assessed as important when sampled in a specified range with one distribution and deemed unimportant when sampled in the same range but with a different distribution. Therefore it is important to determine the extent of the distribution effect on model output. If there is a significant distribution effect, selection of appropriate ranges and distributions for the simulated process disturbances is critical.

The distribution effect can significantly influence the mapping implemented by the neural network. In particular, if the distribution effect results in insufficient representation of variable subranges that happen to have important influences on the output measurements, the weights in the neural network can lead to erroneous dependency conclusions.

On the other hand, we can also make use of the distribution effect to serve a specific purpose. In fact when generating simulated process disturbances, the samples taken near the critical points $(k\sigma)$ dominate the determination of the thresholds for the measurements. The effect of random error in the process or the classification of output measurements is also most significant in these cases. Therefore it is preferable to take more samples in the area nearby the critical points of the process disturbances than in other areas.

A special distribution like that shown in Figure 5 can be constructed to serve this purpose.

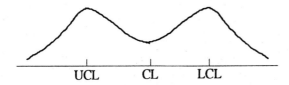

Figure 5: Probability distribution of sampling density

By using LHS, the area near UCL and LCL will be more heavily sampled than the area between them. From Figure 5, it is clear that the areas near the central line and far beyond the critical points are lightly sampled. This is exactly what we want because the samples from these areas have little effect on determining the thresholds of measurements. Figure 6 shows a sampling density distributions that has been used in our experiments.

4 Experimental Example

4.1 Experiment Model

A simple CMOS process model was used in this experiment. Since we focus on the manufacturing process, the circuit structure is of no concern. The 10 process faults, or disturbances monitored in this experiment are parameters relating to PMOS devices. They are listed in Table 1 with their definitions. Table 2 displays their nominal means and standard deviations.

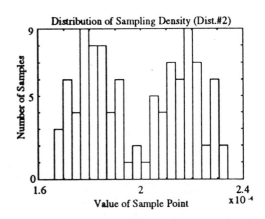

Figure 6: A typical example of distribution function of sampling density

Disturbance	Explanations
ΔW_p	nitride mask line-width variation
ΔL_p	poly mask line-width variation
Segcoefboron	segregation coefficient of boron
Diffoxboron	diffusivity of boron in oxide
Mlatarsen	lateral diffusion enhancement factor of arsenic
Diffphos	diffusivity of phosphorus
Parabolicwet	oxidation growth coeff parabolic wet
Speconres	specific contact resistivity intercept
Q_{ss}	surface state density
Coefucrit	coeff for hole mobility calculation

Table 1: Disturbances and their explanations

No.	Disturbance	μ(nominal)	σ(nominal)
1	ΔW_p (nitride mask)	2.605e-04	7.815e-06
2	ΔL_p (poly mask)	6.440e-05	1.932e-06
3	Segcoefboron	2.000e-03	6.000e-05
4	Diffoxboron	1.000e-01	3.000e-03
5	Mlatarsen	3.000e-01	9.000e-03
6	Diffphos	2.641e+01	7.923e-02
7	Parabolicwet	6.250e-02	1.875e-03
8	Speconres	1.400e+02	4.200e+00
9	Q_{ss}	7.489e+10	2.247e+09
10	Coefucrit	3.335e+03	1.000e+02

Table 2: Selected disturbances and their nominal values

The given set of measurements that have been used to determine the set of process disturbances, include physical and electrical parameters that are extracted from the simulated device. The measurement set used in this experiment is listed in Table 3. Here only their mean values are utilized.

No.	Name	μ^0
1	L [m]	2.354e-06
2	W [m]	8.439e-05
3	VTO [m]	0.000e-00
4	KP [A/V^2]	2.164e-05
5	GAMMA [$V^{1/2}$]	5.009e-01
6	PHI [v]	6.940e-01
7	PB [V]	9.201e-01
8	CGSO [F/m]	2.868e-10
9	CGDO [F/m]	2.868e-10
10	CGBO [F/m]	4.472e-10
11	RSH [Ω/□]	6.437e+01
12	CJ [F/m^2]	2.997e-04
13	MJ	5.000e-01
14	CJSW [F/m]	2.997e-06
15	MJSW	5.000e-01
16	JS [A/m^2]	4.476e-03
17	TOX [m]	2.809e-08
18	NSUB [/cm^3]	1.023e+16
19	NSS [/cm^2]	7.479e+10
20	NFS [/cm^2]	8.019e+10
21	XJ [m]	2.945e-07
22	LD [m]	2.394e-07
23	U0 [cm^2/Vs]	1.806e+02
24	UCRIT [V/cm]	0.000e+00

Table 3: Selected measurable output parameters

To build the training patterns, different combinations of 10 process faults are used to produce the output vectors of the neural network. An input vector consists of 24 measurements taken from the simulated fabrication process with the existence of a combination of process faults. Then a training pattern is formed by combining an input vector with its corresponding output vector. Usually a group of 50 to 60 patterns created this way are employed in a training phase. The training phase is carried out by presenting these patterns repeatedly to a neural network, which consists of 24 input nodes, 10 output nodes and 35 hidden units. Multiple training phases are often necessary to enhance the accuracy of diagnosing more combinations of process faults, although the generalization ability of the neural network has been fully utilized here to minimize this necessity.

Twenty testing sets are generated in a similar way, each of which includes 10 patterns. The results obtained by using these testing sets will be presented later.

4.2 Dependency of Measurements on Process Faults

In order to evaluate dependencies between disturbances and measurements, it is necessary to estimate the experimental error associated with the virtual fabrication process. To precisely define the impact of a process disturbance upon its relevant measurements, we must resort to statistical analysis. The analysis below is based on the assumption that the random variable under study is normally distributed.

Let us take a look at the difference between the effect of a non-shifted and shifted disturbance on its correlated outputs. This is actually a test of the hypothesis that the mean μ of an output equals its nominal value μ_0 when a disturbance has been shifted. The nominal of an output corresponds to the case when no shift has occured,

$$H_0 : \mu = \mu_0 \qquad (1)$$

$$H_1 : \mu \neq \mu_0 \qquad (2)$$

Since σ^2 is unknown, it is estimated by sample variance S^2. The test statistic is

$$t_0 = \frac{\bar{x} - \mu_0}{S/\sqrt{n}} \qquad (3)$$

where $\bar{x}$ is an average of all samples taken from a specific output measurement when a disturbance has been shifted. The null hypothesis $H_0 : \mu = \mu_0$ is rejected, or the hypothesis $H_1 : \mu \neq \mu_0$ holds if $|t_0| > t_{\alpha/2,n-1}$, where $t_{\alpha/2,n-1}$ denotes the upper $\alpha/2$ percentage point of the t distribution . This indicates that the output is dependent on the shifted disturbance.

In general, it is not just the statistics of the output when a disturbance is shifted that must be estimated by $\bar{x}_1$ and s_1^2, but also the statistics, $\bar{x}_0$ and s_0^2, of the output when a disturbance is not shifted must be estimated as well. Suppose n_0 and n_1 samples are taken of an output when a disturbance is at nominal and shifted respectively, the variances are pooled as follows

$$S_p^2 = \frac{(n_1 - 1)S_1^2 + (n_0 - 1)S_0^2}{n_1 + n_0 - 2} \qquad (4)$$

and the test to find out if a disturbance affects an output becomes a test if $|t_0| > t_{\alpha/2,n_1+n_0-2}$ where

$$t_0 = \frac{\bar{x}_1 - \bar{x}_0}{S_p \sqrt{\frac{1}{n_1} + \frac{1}{n_0}}} \qquad (5)$$

If $\bar{x}_1 - \bar{x}_0 = 0.2542$, $S_p = 3.0263 \times 10^{-3}$, and $n_0 = n_1 = 10$, then $t_0 = 188$, and $|t_0| > t_{0.0005,18} = 3.922$. This indicates that the hypothesis $H_1 : \mu_1 \neq \mu_0$ holds with $100(1 - \alpha)\% = 99.9\%$ confidence.

Next, suppose we choose a threshold T for a given output to determine if a disturbance affects that output, in order to construct the fault matrix F, where for the ith disturbance and the jth output

$$f_{ij} = \begin{cases} 1 & \text{if } \bar{x}_1 - \bar{x}_0 > T \\ -1 & \text{if } \bar{x}_1 - \bar{x}_0 < -T \\ 0 & \text{otherwise} \end{cases}$$

If we let $T = 5$ in our previous example, and if $\bar{x}_1 - \bar{x}_0 = 0.2542$, the shifted disturbance will produce a sample point outside of the threshold with more that 99.9% confidence.

Output measurements are not correlated with all process disturbances. Dependencies can be visualized in the following examples.

Example I: Control charts for correlated disturbances and measurements.

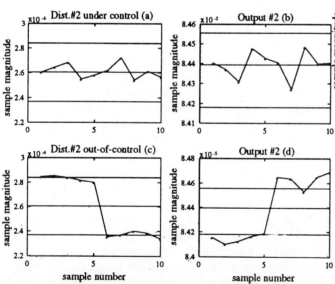

Figure 7: Control charts for a correlated disturbance and an output parameter

This set of control charts shows the dependency between process disturbance ΔW_p, the nitride mask misalignment and channel width W of the devices. Figure 7(a) displays the control chart for ΔW_p, which varies around its nominal value. The corresponding behavior of W has been drawn in Figure 7(b). It can be seen that W does not undergo

any significant shift as expected. When ΔW_p shifts outside its control limits, as shown in Figure 7(c), channel width W shifts significantly from its nominal value as indicated in Figure 7(d).

For comparison, control charts for another measurement parameter, channel length L in these two cases are shown in Figures 8(b) and 8(d), with ΔW_p in control and out of control in Figures 8(a) and 8(c), respectively. We can see that L does not shift significantly in either case. Thus the lack of correlation between these two parameters is readily identified.

Example II: Control charts for uncorrelated disturbance and output parameters.

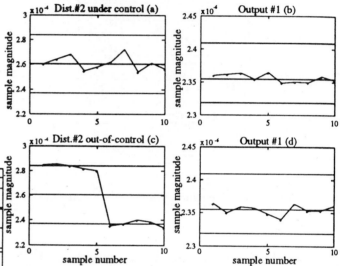

Figure 8: Control charts for a uncorrelated disturbance and an output parameter

Rigorously, the threshold T_j is used to say if the ith disturbance and the jth output are correlated, where $f_{ij} = 0$ indicates that there is no correlation. However, due to randomness in the process the probability that $f_{ij} = 0$ is less than one, even if the ith disturbance has no effect on the jth output. Let $\sigma_j{}^2$ be the variance of the jth output when all disturbances are nominal, then if $T_j = 3\frac{\sigma_j}{\sqrt{n}}$, where n is the sample size, the probability that $f_{ij} = 0$ is 0.9973. If T_j is increased, this probability will increase.

A set of measurements is said to be unable to detect the ith disturbance if

$$\sum_{j=1}^{m} |f_{ij}| = 0$$

However, suppose that the ith disturbance does not

affect any of the m measurements. Then the probability that $\sum_{j=1}^{m} |f_{ij}| = 0$ is

$$[prob(f_{ij} = 0)]^m$$

If $T_j = 3\frac{\sigma_j}{\sqrt{n}}$, $j = 1, \ldots, m$, and $m = 24$, for example, then the probability that the ith disturbance will be found to be unobservable is 93.7%. Similarly, for 24 measurements, a disturbance that has no effect on any output is found by the algorithm to be unobservable with $T_j = 2\frac{\sigma_j}{\sqrt{n}}$ to be 32.7% and with $T_j = 4\frac{\sigma_j}{\sqrt{n}}$ to be 99.93%. This analysis gives us a lower bound on the threshold T_j, which for $m = 24$ should be at least $3\frac{\sigma_j}{\sqrt{n}}$.

On the other hand, if T_j is set too large, it is not possible to distinguish a significant disturbance from an insignificant one. Figure 9 displays the probability density function of an output measurement in the presence of various disturbances. $Prob(f_{ij} = 0)$ is the area under the curve in the region maked $f_{ij} = 0$. In Figure 9(b), $Prob(f_{ij} = 0)$ is large because the disturbance has caused the output to shift by only a small amount compared to the threshold. Therefore it is hard to distinguish this disturbance from one that has had no effect on the output at all. As can be seen from Figure 9, the larger the shift of a disturbance with respect to the threshold, the smaller $Prob(f_{ij} = 0)$, and hence the higher the probability that it can be distinguished from an insignificant disturbance.

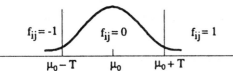

(a) pdf of an output when an insignificant disturbance is shifted

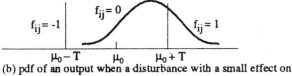

(b) pdf of an output when a disturbance with a small effect on the output is shifted

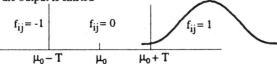

(c) pdf of an output when a significant disturbance is shifted

Figure 9: The effect of a shifted disturbance on the probability density function of an output

In order to find an optimal threshold for use in

defining ambiguity groups, it is useful to find the probability that an output that has undergone a shift by a certain amount is distinguishable from one that has been shifted by another amount. Assuming that $T_j = 3\frac{\sigma}{\sqrt{n}}$ and that output measurements are normally distributed, the probabilities that f_{ij} will be the same are plotted in Figure 10, in which $s = \frac{\sigma}{\sqrt{n}}$. Clearly shifts larger than $3\frac{\sigma_j}{\sqrt{n}}$ or less than $-3\frac{\sigma_j}{\sqrt{n}}$ can be distinguished from the case when the output has not been shifted. Furthermore when the shift is larger, it is easier to distinguish it. For instance the probability that an output that has shifted by $6\frac{\sigma_j}{\sqrt{n}}$ cannot be distinguished from one that has not been shifted is negligible. Hence it is best to choose the threshold to be as small as possible provided that requirements on $Prob(\sum_{j=1}^{m} |f_{ij}| = 0)$ are met.

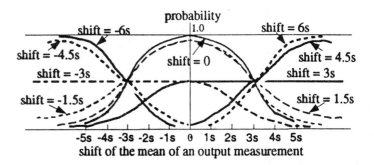

Figure 10: Probabilities that f_{ij} will be the same when an output is shifted by different amounts

Besides finding a set of measurements that are sufficient to detect large shifts in the disturbances, thresholding has also been used to encode the measurement data which is input to the neural network. These thresholds differ from the ones used to find a sufficient set of measurements since they can be used to distinguish between a disturbance that caused an output to shift by a large amount and one that caused a smaller shift. The generation of these thresholds has been described in Section 3.2.

4.3 Testing Procedure and Results

After a successful training of the neural network has been completed, it is then ready to be tested. The testing results are expressed in terms of number of matches between the output of the neural network and the target values. An illustrative example is given in Figure 11 to describe the testing procedure.

Note that a match occurs only when the output of

methodology can be readily applied to other complicated device models and other process parameters, where mathematical modeling may need to be applied to the virtual IC process in addition to the diagnosing model. We are currently looking into this problem as well as studying ways to improve the training of the neural network, especially relating to speeding up the rate of convergence and escaping from local minima. The distinguishing feature of our method is that its use in real time is feasible.

REFERENCES

1. A.J. Strojwas and S.W. Director, "A pattern recognition based method for IC failure analysis," *IEEE Trans. Computer-Aided Design*, Vol. CAD-4, No.1, pp.76-92, Jan. 1985.

2. C.J.B. Spanos, "Hippocrates: A methodology for IC process diagnosis," *Proc. ICCAD*, pp.513-516, Santa Clara, CA, 1986.

3. S. Nassif, A.J. Strojwas, and S.W. Director, "FABRICS II: A statistically based IC fabrication process simulator," *IEEE Trans. Computer-Aided Design*, Vol. CAD-3, No.1, pp.40-46, Jan. 1984.

4. C.J.B. Spanos, "Parameter extraction for statistical IC process characterization," *IEEE Trans. Computer-Aided Design*, Vol. CAD-5, pp.66-78, Jan. 1986.

5. I. Parberry, *Parallel Complexity Theory*, Wiley , New York, 1987.

6. D.C. Montgomery, *Introduction to Statistical Quality Control*, John Wiley & Sons, New York, 1991.

7. W. Zhang, "A neural network based approach for surveillance and diagnosis of statistical parameters in the IC manufacturing process," Master Thesis, University of Maryland, College Park, 1992.

8. R.L. Iman, et al, "Latin hypercube sampling," *Tech. Rep, SAND79-1473*, Sandia Lab, Albuquerque, NM, 1980.

PRINTED CIRCUIT BOARD DIAGNOSIS USING ARTIFICIAL NEURAL NETWORKS AND CIRCUIT MAGNETIC FIELDS

Hugh F. Spence, Ph.D.
Staff Engineer
Avionics and Support Systems
Southwest Research Institute

ABSTRACT

Testing of electronic systems using conventional testing methods has become more difficult and costly as these systems have become more complex and compact. Conventional testing methods and systems often require lengthy analysis to define testing strategies. These test systems may require lengthy test periods, complex stimulus and measurement instrumentation as well as complicated fixturing. The results are often ambiguous and require further interpretation. This paper presents an exploration of a "non-intrusive" test method based on interpreting changes in the magnetic field close to a Printed Circuit Board (PCB). Currents moving between devices on the PCB produce these magnetic fields. Changes of the PCB operational status due to faults cause changes in the associated magnetic field pattern that can be interpreted by Artificial Neural Networks (ANNs) for fault identification. An apparatus to collect magnetic field measurements is described along with some problems of collecting data. Typical magnetic field patterns for "known-good" and faulted PCBs are presented. Possible extensions of the method are discussed. This paper resulted from internally funded work at Southwest Research Institute (SwRI) concerning non-intrusive diagnostic techniques.

INTRODUCTION

Modern society is increasingly dependent on the electronic modules that control our household appliances, automobiles, workplaces, and military systems. Electronic circuits are becoming more complex, more expensive, and also more critical to the successful operation of the complete system. Printed Circuit Boards (PCBs) are critical components of electronic systems. As PCBs become increasingly sophisticated, they often become too costly to be considered throw away items. This is especially true in military applications. Manual techniques to detect and identify failures are no longer practical to use because of system diversity and complexity. To satisfy electronic testing needs, equipment manufacturers have developed Automatic Test Equipment (ATE) systems to make specified measurements on electronic circuits and interpret the results for failure identification. However, performing fault diagnosis on a PCB can often challenge even the best conventional ATE.

Both government and industry rely on ATE. The military uses ATE to repair weapon systems. Electronic manufacturers depend on ATE to test PCBs to ensure their functionality and isolate production defects. However, the failure diagnosis process using ATE is presently time consuming, complex, costly, and prone to inaccuracies. The increasingly widespread use of conformally coated PCBs, multilayer PCBs, and VLSI components will further complicate the diagnosis process. These and other technology innovations often make test points inaccessible to probing and generate the need for extremely complex test fixtures and software.

Conventional ATE systems based on probing of internal circuitry points, and the insertion and measurement of complex signals are inadequate for many diagnostic applications. New, cost effective, complementary approaches are needed to ease the task of maintaining electronic systems as they become more complex. An approach to solving this problem is the use of imaging techniques that consider infrared (IR) or other characteristics of a PCB or module. Through the analysis of these images combined with other data, failed or suspect components may be found more readily than by conventional ATE means. Infrared images of electronic PCBs have been used in previous programs to diagnose PCB problems[1,2]. A recent program[3] showed that changes in PCB infrared images compared to a "known good" PCB can be interpreted by Artificial Neural Networks (ANNs) to diagnose some types of faulted components. Changes in the power dissipated by PCB components due to altered PCB operational status cause these infrared image changes.

There are some drawbacks to the use of IR images including the cost of the equipment. Other information produced by the PCB, including other "images," could be used in a similar manner as infrared to diagnose circuit failures. These images include those produced by mapping the electric, magnetic or electromagnetic fields around a circuit. A diagnostic system may be possible using information obtained from the measurement and analysis of the PCB's magnetic fields. Electronic systems obviously require electrical power, and current paths through conductive traces on the printed circuit card deliver this power to devices. PCB traces also provide electrical current paths between devices for signals. Spatial measurement of the magnetic fields generated by these currents would produce an image that also may be used by a diagnostic system. The purpose of this paper is to present the concept of a PCB diagnostic tool based on magnetic mapping and preliminary results.

Magnetic Field Measurements

A review of literature preceding this effort indicated that although low level magnetic fields have been measured in biomedical and other applications, no applications for the diagnosis of printed circuits failures existed. The diagnostic use of the magnetic fields surrounding objects has been studied for applications in areas as varied as brain activity measurements and corrosion currents around rivets[4,5,6]. Some of this work attempted to map the currents producing the magnetic fields. However, for our diagnostic application, differences in the magnetic field images between a known good PCB and a defective PCB could be used directly and knowledge of the actual currents producing the fields is not needed. The ability to measure the magnetic image from a powered PCB is key to this approach.

The electrical currents of devices due to required power and associated signals produce complex varying magnetic fields. PCB trace currents, magnetic PCB components and the ambient magnetic field all combine to cause the resultant magnetic field pattern or image near the surface of the PCB. The magnetic field at any point is a vector that has both amplitude and direction, and varies in strength with varying current levels and with distance from the current paths. For any active circuit card there will be a complex magnetic field pattern.

The magnetic flux density generated by a straight conductor at a point in space varies proportionately with the ratio of the current carried to the distance from the conductor. In other words,

$$B = 2*10^{-7}\frac{I}{d}$$

where B is the magnetic flux density in Tesla, I is current in amperes, and d (distance from the conductor) is in meters. The factor $(2*10^{-7})$ is the permeability of free space (u_0). This formula is true for an infinitely long conductor and is only an approximation for any real conductor path. With this information, it is possible to calculate B for various currents and distances for simple conductors. The magnetic field at any position near a PCB is a complex function of all currents flowing on the PCB.

Table 1 provides a list of some of the sensors available to measure magnetic fields. The table lists sensor technologies and their sensitivity, based on the noise levels experienced with a 100 Hz bandwidth. The earth's magnetic field is approximately 50 pT.

TABLE 1. SENSITIVITIES OF MAGNETIC SENSOR TECHNOLOGY

Hall Effect Integrated Circuit	10 to 100 uT
Induction Coil	4 to 30 pT
Optically Pumped Magnetometer	1 pT to 1 nT
Shear Wave	approx. 10 nT
SQUID	30 to 100 fT
Fluxgate Magnetometer	3 to 200 pT

Of these devices, the fluxgate magnetometer is a sensor that combines high sensitivity, low cost and reasonable bandwidth. The fluxgate magnetometer in its simplest configuration is two coils wound around a highly permeable but saturable core. The first and second coils are wound such that they do not normally couple to one another. An alternating current waveform through the first coil rapidly drives the core into saturation, first in one direction and then in the other. The change in core permeability caused by saturation forces external magnetic field flux from the core. The second (or sensing) coil produces an output when the external flux through the core changes. Electronic circuitry drives the excitation winding, detects the sense winding signal, and linearizes the measurements.

The fluxgate magnetometer responds to low frequencies, can make quick measurements, uses inexpensive hardware, is sensitive, and works at room temperature. Small magnetometers can be constructed to increase spatial resolution. However, high spatial resolution and sensitivity could be difficult to achieve together since the fluxgate magnetometer loses sensitivity as the volume of the core decreases.

Our initial calculations to estimate magnetic field levels and patterns produced by typical PCBs indicated that the magnetic fields produced would be measurable by fluxgate magnetometers. Our early experiments using available fluxgate magnetometers confirmed that the spatial variations of PCB magnetic field currents are measurable and change with PCB operational status.

Figure 1 shows the overall concept for a diagnostic system based on the measurements of the spatial variation of PCB magnetic field. Measurements of the magnetic field over the PCB are made and could be represented as an image. Under normal operation, electrical currents flow in the traces of the PCB in some particular manner and produce an associated magnetic field pattern. Changes, such as faults, in the operational status of the PCB that cause changes in the pattern of current flow in turn cause changes in the associated magnetic field pattern. A classification mechanism or expert can be used to associate the magnetic field pattern changes with a PCB fault. The classification mechanism may involve a feature extraction step for information compression and an ANN.

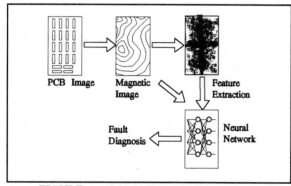

FIGURE 1. MAGNETIC FIELD BASED DIAGNOSTIC CONCEPT

Figure 2 shows components for a diagnostic system that uses the magnetic fields around a PCB. In this example, the PCB is held in a scanning fixture during magnetic field measurements. Magnetic shielding can reduce any effects of background fields on the environment around the PCB. A computer controls field measurements through a scanner and measurement interface. Measurements are first made of the spatial variations or "image" of the field of the unpowered PCB. Measurements of unpowered PCB's field information may compensate other active PCB field measurements. A computer controlled interface applies power and stimulus to the PCB and the spatial variations of the field around the PCB are again measured and recorded. The spatial field variations or "image" of a faulted PCB are compared with those obtained of a "known good" PCB. The

computer processing system performs the comparison and interprets or classifies the magnetic field information. The interpretation and classification algorithms can be ANN's, which can be trained with examples of data, or other classification techniques. Some information compaction method may be needed to reduce the volume of data. Unlike thermal images where components warm or cool, magnetic images may not have localized patterns changes. The magnetic images are summations of many contributors around the PCB and are not localized around PCB components. A possible technique useful for compacting the image would be a spatial Fast Fourier Transform (FFT) that converts the image into frequency components. These spatial frequency components could then be classified with the associated PCB fault.

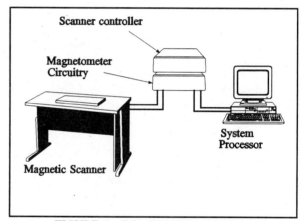

FIGURE 2. DIAGNOSTIC SYSTEM COMPONENTS

Early Results

Magnetic flux density measurements of a PCB were made using a system similar to that described above. We made measurements using mechanical scanning fixture with electronic position feedback and a small fluxgate magnetometer. The fixture scanned the PCB over the fluxgate sensor mounted with its axis perpendicular to the surface of the PCB. The fluxgate sensor measured only the vertical component of the PCB's magnetic field. The mounting of the magnetometer in a fixed position under a movable PCB and nulling the earth's magnetic field at the magnetometer circuit reduced the effects of background magnetic fields. The data acquisition system consisted of a '386 based Personnel Computer (PC) with an Analog to Digital (A/D) convertor interface.

We made measurements of an unpowered PCB, a powered PCB and a set of faulted PCBs using a PCB memory card from an LSI-11 computer. Because of the limited mechanical range of our magnetic scanner, the field over the entire surface of PCB was not measured.

The region used was approximately 3 inches by 3 inches and contained approximately 15 integrated circuits and several other components. Our initial measurements of an unpowered PCB indicated a low level magnetic field pattern due to magnetic materials used in the construction of the PCB. The magnetic materials were mounting screws and possibly some component leads. No currents were flowing on the PCB.

Power and stimulus were then applied to the PCB. The stimulus exercised the PCB's logic to insure all PCB devices were enabled during measurements. Figure 3a

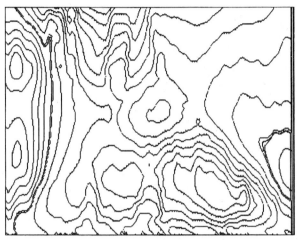

FIGURE 3a. MAGNETIC FIELD IMAGE OF "KNOWN GOOD" PCB

shows the measurements of this active "known good" PCB as a contour image. The field levels measured were much larger than for the unpowered PCB. Faults were inserted on the PCB and magnetic field measurements were made for each of these faults. Figure 3b gives the magnetic contour image for a lifted pin 18 on PCB device IC13. Table 2 lists other faults for which measurements were made.

TABLE 2. MAGNETIC IMAGE
MEASUREMENTS

Unpowered PCB
Powered PCB, no faults
Powered PCB, faulted IC13-18
Powered PCB, faulted IC14-1
Powered PCB, faulted IC14-14
Powered PCB, faulted IC17-18
Powered PCB, faulted IC21-18

The table lists the PCB integrated circuit number and the faulted pin number separated by a "-."

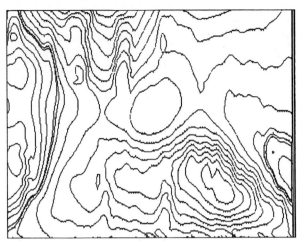

FIGURE 3b. MAGNETIC FIELD IMAGE OF
IC13-18 FAULTED PCB

FIGURE 3c. MAGNETIC DIFFERENCE IMAGE
FOR IC13-18 FAULTED PCB

There were significant differences among the images. Subtracting the magnetic measurements made of the "known good" PCB from those of each faulted PCB produced magnetic difference images. These difference images represent the changes produced in the PCB's magnetic field by the circuit fault. Figure 3c gives the contour plot of difference image for faulted IC18 pin 18 as an example.

The sensor used in this work was a single axis device and sensitive to the absolute field. Other sensor configurations could include multiaxis and gradient sensor configurations. Arrays of sensors to reduce the mechanical scanning requirements are possible.

SPATIAL FREQUENCIES

Although the pixels of the images could be directly used in some classification mechanism such as an ANN, preprocessing the data to reduce the volume of data normally lessens the pattern classification task. The spatial (2D) FFT[7] is a common preprocessing method and was used for each difference image. The magnitude of spatial frequencies in several bands was derived from the FFT. Difference band information computed for each of the difference images shows that the PCB faults could be classified from their associated spatial frequency patterns. Figure 4 shows the normalized frequency components for the difference images of several PCB faults.

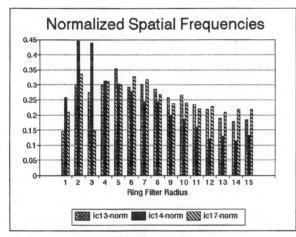

FIGURE 4. NORMALIZED SPATIAL FREQUENCIES FOR SEVERAL PCB FAULT MAGNETIC IMAGES

ARTIFICIAL NEURAL NETWORK CLASSIFICATION

ANNs had their origins about thirty years ago and have reappeared as a viable technique for the pattern classification[8,9]. Because of the present abundance of papers and other publications on the ANN subject, no attempt will be made here to explain their operation in detail. Basically an ANN is a collection of connected simple processing elements. They can be implemented in software or as hardware. They can be used to relate some input to some desired output. A major advantage they bring to applications is the ability to be trained to form these input/output associations through exposures to examples.

For our PCB diagnostic system using magnetic images, examples of the magnetic image pattern of a PCB along with knowledge of the associated fault would be presented to the ANN. The errors produced by the ANN during training would be used to correct the internal weights of the network. Once adequately trained, the ANN will produce the desired response when presented with a familiar pattern. Additional unfamiliar patterns can be used to improve the training of the ANN as they occur. An ANN can use subtle features of an input pattern for classification. An ANN would have little difficulty classifying the obvious differences apparent in our example magnetic images.

CONCLUSION

The objectives of this project were to demonstrate the feasibility of using magnetic measurements around PCBs for the diagnosis of circuit faults. The magnetic fields images of a printed circuit card are functions of the operational status of the circuit card. Changes in the PCB operational status, such as faults, that cause changes in the electrical current distribution on the PCB also cause changes in the magnetic field. The changes appear significant enough such that the pattern could be related to the associated fault. An ANN could be trained to form this association.

A diagnostic method based on the measurement and interpretation of PCB's magnetic fields would augment existing ATE techniques. The technique could be used to directly identify faults and to resolve the ambiguities that may occur with other ATE techniques. SwRI is continuing to explore the capabilities and limitations of this new magnetic filed diagnostic technique.

REFERENCES

[1] H.Kaplan, P. Hugo and R.Zelenka, " The Infrared Automatic Mass Screening (IRAMS) System for Printed Circuit Board Diagnostics," AutoTestCon '86 Symposium Proceedings, IEEE, pp 301-306.

[2] "Infrared Thermal Imaging Technology Study, Technical Report No. 90-1, June 1990, TMDE/ATE Branch, US Army Depot System Command, Chambersburg, PA 17201-4170

[3]. H. F. Spence et al., "An Artificial Neural Network Printed Circuit Board Diagnostic System Based On Infrared Energy Emissions," AutoTestCon '91 Symposium Proceedings, IEEE, pp 41-45.

[4] Granger, Susan, Letter dated 12/20/91, Brochure and Video Tape of HRSM-1 SQUID based scanning magnetometer by QUANTUM DESIGN

[5] Hari, Riitta and Lounasmaa, Olli V., "Recording and Interpretation of Cerebral Magnetic Fields," *Science* **244**, 432-436 (1989)

[6] Roth, Bradley J., Supulveda, Nestor G., and Wikswo, John P., "Using a Magnetometer to Image a Two Dimensional Current Distribution," *J. Applied Physics* **65**, 361-372 (1989)

[7] Press, William H. et al. *Numerical Recipes in C* Cambridge University Press, Cambridge, MA, 1988

[8] D. E. Rumelhart et. al., *Parallel Distributed Processing, Volume 1* The MIT Press, Cambridge, MA, 1986

[9] Hush, Don R. and Horne, Bill G., "Progress in Supervised Neural Networks," *IEEE Signal Processing Magazine*, April 1993, pp 8-39

OPTIMIZING NEURAL NETWORK TECHNOLOGY FOR BIT APPLICATIONS

Douglas C. Doskocil

Martin Marietta
Simulation & Automated Systems
Burlington MA   01803

ABSTRACT

Increased fault detection capability in airborne systems is needed to reduce system life-cycle maintenance cost and improve mission readiness. Neural network techniques have been used successfully in applications requiring capabilities similar to those required to cope with the Built In Test (BIT) false alarm problem, and have demonstrated flexibility for application to fault detection and diagnosis.

INTRODUCTION

False alarms in BIT systems are often caused by the inability to process measurement noise, and by with the limitations of fixed decision criteria that cannot adapt to operational and environmental variables. When implementing conventional BIT techniques, attempts to reduce false alarms also result in an undesired reduction in fault detection. In addition, Intermittent faults are often classified as false alarms since many BIT techniques cannot adequately corroborate measurements over time from multiple units and relate these to environmental and operational data, nor are they able to identify the conditions causing the fault so that it can be reproduced on the ground. Furthermore, existing techniques have limited ability to differentiate a true fault from system noise.

This paper defines the diagnostic false alarm problem, and bounds the solution with respect to applicable neural network technology. An approach is described which implements neural network techniques while avoiding some of their inherent drawbacks. Concepts of persistence, corroboration, and uncertainty processing are introduced. When incorporated into a federated BIT architecture the system takes on the characteristics of a neural network. A simulator is described which may be used to achieve both performance verification and learning through feedback in a manner consistent with configuration-managed, data-driven software.

DIAGNOSTIC FALSE ALARM REDUCTION

Improved fault detection capability in airborne systems is needed to reduce system life-cycle maintenance cost and improve mission readiness. A major problem impeding the achievement of increased capability is the occurrence of false alarms. False alarms are fault indications by BIT or other monitoring circuitry where no fault exists. Many BIT techniques are unable to properly detect transient faults, further reducing performance. False alarms represent the greatest weakness in fielded airborne systems. It is estimated. that 40% of all failure indications are false alarms, and 39% of real faults are transients. The result is often sufficiently disruptive that the operator is forced to disable his BIT warning light. In addition, no technology has been reduced to practice which controls false alarms while maintaining or increasing the fault detection effectiveness. Instead, an adjustment is usually made to test limits or other related factors when there is a perceived problem. Potential solutions using model-based reasoning or expert systems often require much more real-time processing than is available within the size and weight constraints of an airborne system. Additionally, the BIT software implementations in different aircraft subsystems have been developed independently, and are difficult to enhance or adjust. The test limits, sequences, and any associated filtering or averaging is usually embedded deep within the software code. In order for personnel to modify the characteristics of it they must understand the entire package of BIT software. Finally, there has been no effective method to verify the BIT performance requirements, other than by paper analysis or a maintainability demonstration. These BIT technology needs are summarized below:

- High Fault Detection Effectiveness

- Low False Alarm Rate

- Minimal/Integrated processing requirements

- Consistent BIT Software Architecture

- Verification of False Alarm Requirements

APPLICATION OF NEURAL NETWORKS

Neural network techniques have been used successfully in applications in which the technical problems are similar to those posed by of the needs stated above, and have been applied to fault detection and diagnosis. A top level view of a neural network is shown in Figure 1.

Neural networks are generally characterized by the following:

- Network of nodes linked by connections

- Information is passed from node to node over connections

- Nodes compute and communicate in parallel, can be synchronous or asynchronous

- Feedforward and feedback connections possible

- Can be fully or sparsely interconnected

- Number of layers and nodes may vary

Each node receives simple inputs using the connections from the other nodes, each of which may be weighted by a numerical "connection weight". The benefits of such techniques include:

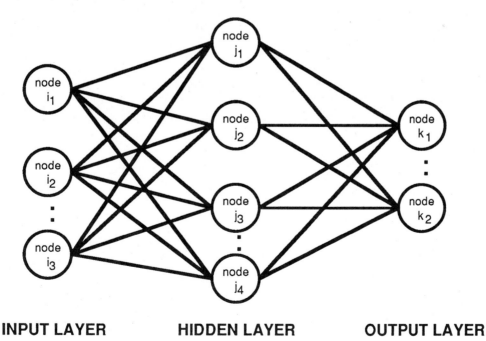

INPUT LAYER   **HIDDEN LAYER**   **OUTPUT LAYER**

Figure 1 - Neural Networks Structure

- Real-time computation and fault tolerance through massive parallelism

- Ability to handle large number of input features

- Can learn through parameter adjustment and topology modification.

To date, problems with actual application of the technology has been processing requirements, separation of neural networks from other operational functions, definition and bounding of the learning mechanisms, and verification. The large processing requirements to support an intermediate or large net presently make it undesirable for most BIT applications where such processing is simply not available. Additionally, most neural network applications have been autonomous, whereas a federated BIT system requires much interaction with the rest of the operational system at many of the normally hidden layers. This interaction is required for the BIT system to attain the data required for its processing, as well as to control the system when necessary for intrusive testing. The problem with classic neural network learning mechanisms is that such learning will ultimately result in modifying BIT parameters in flight. The result would be that each aircraft would have different thresholds and filtering, representing a severe configuration management problem. Finally, the uncertain nature of the processing which allows the functions to correctly process unpredicted situations in turn makes verification very difficult.

The proposed approach is to utilize neural network techniques without necessarily imposing the burdens of a full neural network system. This can be achieved by characterizing the technical content of the fault detection/false alarm problem, applying neural network techniques and concepts where they are applicable, and generating a solution which includes consistency with federated BIT architectures, controlled learning, and verification capability. Included in the approach is the definition of a BIT simulator for processing definition and performance verification during system development, and for system refinement during system operation and support.

CHARACTERIZATION OF BIT PROBLEM

As shown in Figure 2, the noise-induced BIT fault detection/false alarm problem is that simple thresholding alone is not sufficient to fault detect the high rates which are required while maintaining low false alarm rates. The figure depicts a histogram of BIT test results. The Gaussian distribution represents a correctly operating system. For example, a power supply's output measurements will most often be centered around its specified voltage when operating correctly. Certain factors, however, frequently cause measurements to be out of limits, even though the system is operating correctly. For example, a short voltage spike may be within the operating specification of the power supply, but it may be out of the specified DC range. The reason for the out of range measurements is noise, including characteristics of the system under test, noise in the stimulus or measurement signals, and inaccuracies in conversion or timing of the BIT software. The figure shows a single limit problem, only measuring for a failure on the low side of the measurement range.

The Rayleigh distribution within the histogram represents the BIT test of a failed system, including the associated noise. In general, the failure will result in a low measurement, however the measurement is often near the specified output of the system and may exhibit indications of a correctly operating system.

If thresholding alone is used to fault detect, then the threshold will be placed as shown in the figure. The result is that the higher test results of a failed system will appear as missed detections, and the lower shaded area will appear as false alarms. Any simple adjustment of the threshold will simply result in either increased false alarms with increased fault detections, or decreased false alarms with decreased fault detections, neither of which is desirable.

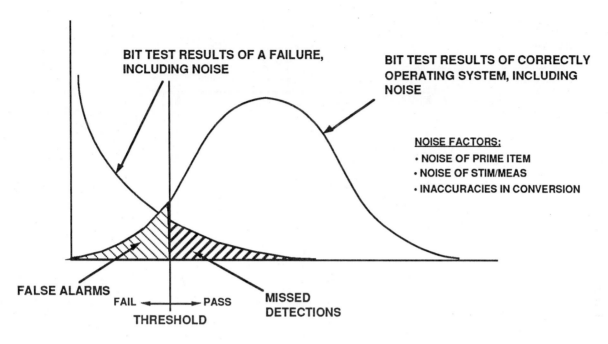

BIT TEST RESULTS OF A FAILURE, INCLUDING NOISE

BIT TEST RESULTS OF CORRECTLY OPERATING SYSTEM, INCLUDING NOISE

NOISE FACTORS:
• NOISE OF PRIME ITEM
• NOISE OF STIM/MEAS
• INACCURACIES IN CONVERSION

FALSE ALARMS

FAIL ◄——► PASS

THRESHOLD

MISSED DETECTIONS

Figure 2. BIT Results Using Thresholding Alone

FEDERATED BIT ARCHITECTURE

It is important to note that no single algorithm or equation will solve the ultimate problem, but that the solution instead lies in methods to process data and test results of a diagnostic system. The target diagnostic system is designed to be an integrated, multi-level system whose architecture is the same at all levels, such as in Figure 3. This is referred to as a federated BIT architecture.

The architecture is consistent with the overall system architecture, and at each level BIT there is some testing performed. Functions at any one level are divided into testing and managing BIT operations. "Test BIT" consists of those functions which are unique to the unit under test, while "manage BIT" performs the analysis of the test results and the BIT executive functions. Keeping the two functions separate minimizes the amount of unique code that must be written and changes which must be made when tests are changed.

APPROACH

The solution consists of table-driven software which allows persistence filtering of test results, corroboration of local results with other results and higher level tests, and uncertainty processing. Persistence is a serial evaluation of a sequence of test results from the same source. It is intended to process raw measurement samples, and uses the last "n" samples of one monitored signal to compensate for the noise level, and generate a confidence measure of the individual test result sequence. The confidence level depends upon the number of samples, the noise level, and the measurements' proximity to limits defined by the user. Corroboration is the parallel evaluation of health reports from different sources. It uses test results and their relationship to failure modes in order to evaluate parallel streams resulting from the persistence processing. Corroboration will result in the continuous evaluation of all failure modes to determine possible out-of-tolerance conditions, while simultaneously assuring that any reported fault is first verified. The uncertainty mechanisms allow for representation of graded results during the sequences associated with the processing. When implemented, the system is driven from tables at all levels of processing within the multilevel BIT system, and each table relates failure modes to test results. Each occurrence of "manage BIT" within the

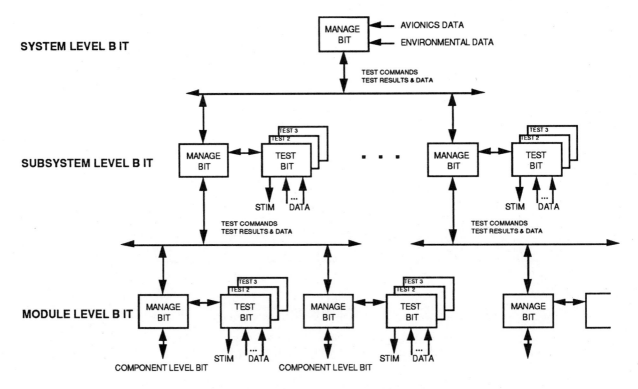

SYSTEM LEVEL B IT

SUBSYSTEM LEVEL B IT

MODULE LEVEL B IT

Figure 3 - Federated BIT Architecture

architecture corresponds to a neural node with connectivity weights represented as corroboration factors or uncertainty criteria.

Figure 4 exemplifies a table at one level. The left column lists the failure modes which may occur at that level, while the top row is the test results of the tests which operate at that

node. Note that these test results can also include failure mode conclusions sent up from a lower node. The fault verification equations represent the persistence and corroboration relationships as programmed by the test designer. The values within the table are dynamically updated as test results occur and failure modes are declared.

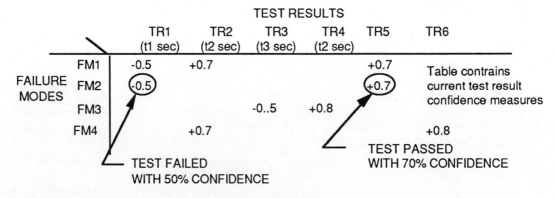

TEST RESULTS

	TR1 (t1 sec)	TR2 (t2 sec)	TR3 (t3 sec)	TR4 (t2 sec)	TR5	TR6
FM1	-0.5	+0.7			+0.7	Table contrains
FM2	(-0.5)				(+0.7)	current test result
FM3			-0..5	+0.8		confidence measures
FM4		+0.7			+0.8	

FAILURE MODES

TEST FAILED
WITH 50% CONFIDENCE

TEST PASSED
WITH 70% CONFIDENCE

CORROBORATION FAULT VERIFICATIONS EQUATIONS:

FM1 = (TR1 + (TR2 OR TR5/4))/2   > 0.6   (to verify a fault)

FM2 = (-TR1 + TR5)/2   > 0.8
FM3 = (TR3(t) - TR4(t-1))/2   < 0.7
FM4 =

Figure 4 - Test Result/Failure Mode Matrix - One node

One of the significant advantages to such an implementation is that it facilitates consistent usage of the BIT data, assuring that the testability analysis, hardware design, BIT software design, and TPS designs are consistent.

The designer populates the table with the persistence, corroboration, and uncertainty values which represent the signature of the failure modes, and programs the relative sequence of testing. When an anomaly is perceived within any subsystem, anyone who understands the table may adjust the system values, simulate the results if necessary, and then modify the data.

The development of the values for the tables is shown in Figure 5. In the first cycle, the mapping of tests to functional failure modes is made in support of initial BIT tradeoffs and MIL-STD-2165 analysis. During the hardware design phase, the allocated matrix is developed, as BIT functions are allocated to either hardware or software. The elements of the matrix then become part of the hardware requirements documentation. The tables are more fully optimized as the BIT and Automatic Test Equipment (ATE) software design is completed, and as such becomes part of the software documentation. This method allows a traceable handoff to other testing sites such as Factory or Depot via deliverables such as a Test Requirements Document (TRD). It should be noted that in a concurrent engineering environment, many of these developments are performed in parallel, but the task dependencies, deliverables, and associated documentation remain the same.

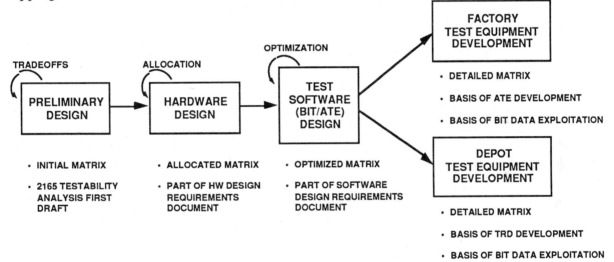

Figure 5. Table Driven BIT System

VERIFICATION AND LEARNING

Performance verification is currently a problem in the areas of artificial intelligence, expert systems, and neural networks. An element of the proposed approach is to use a simulator which will dynamically model the BIT system. This simulator is an off-line design tool used to define and evaluate the effectiveness of alternate nodal parameters.

Such a tool to simulate the BIT Fault Detection and False Alarm operation will generally function in accordance with the process diagram shown Figure 6. The libraries are files which specify parameters of a run, such as length of run, randomly occurring events such as transients, scheduled events, and user-initiated events. The system architecture defines the interconnectivity of the neural network nodes. The neural network process, as shown, is operating off of user -defined BIT parameters under evaluation. The timing and control function is required to allow system stepping, insight into the intermediate nodes, and to document the results of a run. The ultimate result is the output of the Process

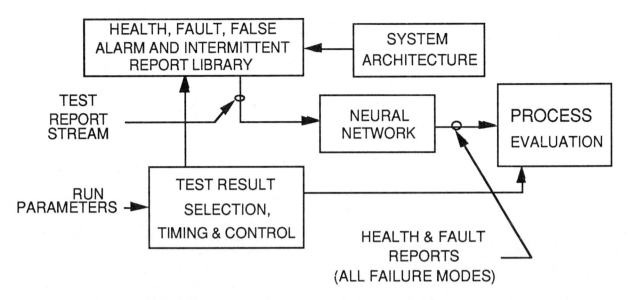

Figure 6 - Fault Detection/False Alarm Reduction Performance Verification

Evaluator, which compares and summarizes the appropriate Fault Detection, False Alarm Rate, and Latency data.

Such a tool has two uses: verifying via simulation the fault detection, false alarm rate, and latency performance of the system being designed; and future simulation during operation and support of the fielded system, to analyze anomalies and evaluate BIT implementations in conjunction with field updates and retrofits. It is via this simulator that the learning capability may be invoked. The BIT system collects the anomalies and other data necessary for a designer to update the parameters, but the actual update and associated analysis is performed on the ground with simulated results verified before fielding.

CONCLUSION

Many neural network techniques are applicable to optimizing BIT performance. Any implementations, however, must avoid drawbacks of neural networks such as processing requirements, real-time learning, and lack of effective verification means. An approach has been proposed which uses some of the techniques such as weighting and nodal connectivity, but suggests the need for simulators to verify and implement configuration controlled learning.

ASSESSMENT OF DETERIORATING REINFORCED CONCRETE STRUCTURES USING ARTIFICIAL NEURAL NETWORKS

N. Yasuda   T. Tsutsumi
Tokyo Electric Power Co., Tokyo, Japan

T. Kawamura
ToKyo Electric Power Services
Co. Ltd., Tokyo, Japan

S.Matsuho   W.Shiraki
Tottori University, Tottori, Japan

Abstract

A artificial neural network is used to model the damage assessment of reinforced concrete structures in thermal power plants along the coast of Tokyo Bay using periodical inspection data arranged by Tokyo Electric Power Company (TEPCO). Using a successfully trained neural networks, a sensitivity analysis to determine the influence of a change in each variable such as maximum crack width , area of peeling-off of concrete, exposure of reinforcement of reinforcement, etc., on the damage level.

keywords: neural network, damage assessment, reinforced concrete structures, thermal power plants, chloride-induced corrosion.

1. Introduction

Concrete structures have been long expected as permanent structures, and then they have been constructed without priory considering their maintenance. Recent years, however, they are suffered from severe damage such as alkali aggregate reaction and chloride-induced corrosion. The fields of maintenance, repair and durability assessment are growing in importance. In order to develop an efficient repair and maintenance program, the durability assessment of existing structures is very important. Hence, many researches have been performed on the damage evaluation, durability design and repair of concrete structures[1-3]. However, the shortage of data and the complex mechanism of structural deterioration limit the quantitative assessment of deteriorating structures.

In this paper, an artificial neural network is used to assess deteriorating reinforced concrete (RC) structures using periodical inspection data for thermal power plants along the coast of Tokyo Bay arranged by Tokyo Electric Power Company (TEPCO). In analysis, the attention is focused on chloride-induced corrosion damage of RC structures. 13 input variables such as crack width, crack direction, number of cracks, etc. are selected as the inputs to the artificial neural network, and 4 output variables are chosen as the desired damage levels. The model of the damage level assessment process is obtained using a neural network trained on a large number of sets of inputs as actual measurements and outputs as damage level estimated by experienced inspection engineers. The network is trained successfully with a very low system error. In order to find the important variables among 13 input variables that might strongly affect the damage level of deteriorating RC structures, a sensitivity analysis is then performed by calculating variations of the damage level with respect to each individual input. The results from the sensitivity study shows that the crack width, rust stains and exposure of reinforcement affect the damage levels II and III specified by TEPCO.

2. Neural Networks and Their Application to Damage Assessment of Reinforced Concrete Structures

2.1 Neural Networks

A network of artificial neurons, usually called an artificial neural network, is a data processing system consisting of a number of simple, highly interconnected processing elements in an architecture inspired the structure of the cerebral cortex portion of the brain. Hence, neural networks are often capable of doing things that humans do well but that conventional computers often do poorly. Neural networks exhibit characteristics and capabilities not provided by any other technology.

Neural networks approximate functions with raw sample data. An unknown function f produces the observed sample pairs of a set of input vectors $X=(x_1,x_2,\cdots,x_n)$ in n-dimensional space and a set of output vectors $Y=(y_1,y_2,\cdots,y_n)$ in m-dimensional space.

It can be expressed as $Y=f(X)$. The sample data modify parameters in the neural estimator such as weights on the connections between artificial neurons and bring the neural system's input-output responses closer to the input-output responses of the unknown estimand f. The approximation accuracy tends to increase as the sample size increase. In psychological terms, the neural system learns from experience.

Fig.1 shows the basic artificial neuron model. In Fig.1 x_i: inputs from other neurons; w_{ij}: weights on the connections between artificial neurons; θ_j: predetermined threshold level; $y_j=f(\sum_i w_{ij}x_i-\theta_j)$: output; f: adaptive modifier. The adaptive modifier is a nonlinear mapping operator which transforms the graded input into another graded value bounded over the interval[0,1]. In this study, a sigmoid transfer function expressed as Eq.(1) may be used.

$$f(z)=1/(1+\exp(-z/\delta)) \tag{1}$$

where δ is a sigmoid slope.

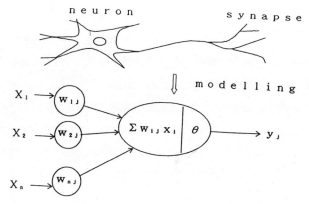

Fig.1 Basic Artifical Neural Model

2.2 Application Damage Assessment of Reinforced Concrete Structures

As it is pointed out in **Introduction** of this paper, the quantitative damage assessment of reinforced concrete structures has not been performed adequately for reasons of shortage of data, the diversity of damage patterns and the complexity of damage mechanism.

A degree of damage is usually indicated by four or five levels[4-6]. The judgement is performed by the experienced inspection engineers based on visual observations. The number of deteriorating structures increases year by year, and the increment of experts for damage assessment can not be expected. Hence, the adjustment of inspection data and the development of the expert system for damage assessment are pressing demands.

In this study, utilizing such important features of a neural network that it has an ability to model the input-output relationship of complex system, and that its training is efficiently performed using a large number of sets of inputs and outputs taken from actual observing data, an expert system for judgement of damage levels of reinforced concrete structures is developed. Furthermore, using a successfully trained neural networks, a sensitivity analysis to determine the influence of a change in each variable on the damage levels.

3. Damage Assessment System Using Neural Network

TEPCO has inspected concrete structures in thermal power plants along the coast of Tokyo Bay on their states of damage. The inspections has been carried out every half year since 1983. In order to utilize the obtained data efficiently, a research project has been started in which the developments of various computer-aided systems such as data base systems, statistical analysis systems, damage assessment systems, and damage prediction system are intended.

A damage assessment system proposed in this paper is a result obtained from the project.

3.1 Variables Selected for Neural Networks

Considering the environmental conditions at the construction sites of thermal power plants, the attention is focused on chloride-induced damage of RC structure. In order to find the important variables that might strongly affect the chloride-induced damage of RC structures, 13 variables were selected as the inputs to the artificial neural network, and 4 variables were chosen as the desired outputs. **Table 1** gives the list of the inputs. In the table (Y,N) means Yes or No. Table 2 shows the list of the outputs. In the table the damage levels were determined by experienced inspection engineers according to damage levels specified by

Table 1 Input Variables Selected for Neual Networks

1	maximum crack width	(mm)
2	rust stains	(Y,N)
3	exposure of reinforcement	(Y,N)
4	efflorescence	(Y,N)
5	leakage	(Y,N)
6	slip	(Y,N)
7	area of peeling-off of concrete	(m²)
8	area of delamination of concrete	(m²)
9	direction of crack perpendicular to axis of member	(Y,N)
10	direction of crack along the reinforcing	(Y,N)
11	direction of crack otherwise	(Y,N)
12	depth of crack (surface,intermediate depth,entire section)	
13	number of crack	(one,some)

Table 2   Output Variables Selected
for Neural Networks

1	Damage Level	I
2	Damage Level	II
3	Damage Level	III
4	Damage Level	IV

Table 3 Damage Levels of Concrete Structures for TEPCO

Damage Levels	Description
I	No Damage
II	Slight Damage •apperance of local cracks •maximum crack width:w<0.0035C° mm •area of peeling-off :S,<0.19m² •area of delimination:S₄<0.19m² •appearance of rust stains due to corrosion •appearance of exposure of reinforcement
III	Medium Damage •appearance of progressive cracks and serious crack pattern •maximum crack width:w≥0.0035C° mm •area of peeling-off :S,>0.19m² •area of delimination:S₄>0.19m² •appearance of rust stains over all member •appearance of serious exposure of reinforcement
IV	Severe Damage appearance of wider cracks and more serious peeling-off,delimination, rust strains and exposure of reinforcement than those of damage level III

C°=cover of reinforced concrete member

TEPCO as shown in Table 3 [6]. However, the actual judgements are very often different from those of by the specified damage levels. The judgement is performed based on the experiences and sense of inspection engineers. In this study their experiences and sense are modeled by neural networks.

3.2 Training for Neural Networks

The network used in this study is a four-layer backpropagation neural network[7]. From the data base arranged by TEPCO[8], 18 periodical inspection data on RC beams were selected as the training patterns. The backpropagation network was set up with 13 neurons in the input layer, each 15 in the two hidden layers, and 4 in the output layer.

The network was trained successfully with small error. The results of training are shown in **Table 4**. **Table 4** indicats that 18 patterns are all successfully trained. The values shown in **Table 4** are the output values which mean the confidence values of judgement for the damage levels.

In order to verify the usefulness of the neural network system developed above, another 14 data were chosen from TEPCO Data Base [8], and their damage levels were estimated by the use of this neural network system. The results is presented in **Table 5**. It is seen from the table that only two data such as Nos.K9 and K10 are misjudged.

Table 4 Results of Training

Data No	Actual Damage Level	Level I	Level II	Level III	Level IV
1	II	0.001	0.999	0	0.001
2	II	0	0.999	0	0
3	II	0	0.999	0	0.001
4	II	0	0.999	0	0
5	III	0.006	0.062	0.938	0.006
6	III	0.006	0.058	0.942	0.006
7	II	0	0.999	0	0
8	II	0	0.999	0	0.001
9	II	0.008	0.837	0.157	0.009
10	II	0	0.999	0	0
11	II	0.001	0.999	0	0.001
12	II	0.001	0.999	0	0.001
13	II	0	0.999	0	0.001
14	II	0.001	0.998	0.001	0.001
15	II	0.001	0.999	0	0.001
16	III	0.006	0.058	0.942	0.006
17	III	0.005	0.106	0.895	0.005
18	III	0.006	0.058	0.942	0.006

Table 5 Results of Estimation of Another Data Patterns

Data No	Actual Damage Level	Level I	Level II	Level III	Level IV
K1	III	0.012	0.086	0.913	0.021
K2	III	0.012	0.063	0.936	0.022
K3	III	0.014	0.070	0.929	0.025
K4	II	0.041	0.863	0.134	0.038
K5	III	0.009	0.147	0.854	0.015
K6	III	0.015	0.064	0.935	0.026
K7	III	0.008	0.084	0.916	0.014
K8	II	0.020	0.922	0.077	0.018
K9	III	0.012	0.948	0.052	0.011
K10	II	0.014	0.073	0.927	0.024
K11	III	0.016	0.051	0.948	0.029
K12	II	0.019	0.922	0.077	0.017
K13	III	0.012	0.060	0.939	0.022
K14	III	0.013	0.054	0.945	0.024

3.3 Sensitivity Analysis for Neural Modeling

A sensitivity analysis was performed to determine the important variables that could strongly affect the damage levels of RC structure. In sensitivity analysis, the successfully trained neural network was used as a mapping function which model the input-output relationships such as $Y=f(X)$ where $X=(x_1, x_2, \cdots, x_{13})$ is a set of input vectors with 13 components shown in **Table 1**, and $Y=(y_1, \cdots, y_4)$ is a set of output vectors with 4 components shown in Table 2.

For variations of each individual input, the confidence values of judgement for the damage levels were calculated by the use of the neural networks. The results from such a sensitivity analysis clarified that the maximum crack width, rust stains, exposure of reinforcement affected the damage levels II and III. Especially, the maximum crack width was the most important variable related to the damage levels II and III.

The results of the sensitivity analysis for the maximum crack width are shown in **Fig.2** and **Fig.3**. In these calculations each input variable except the maximum crack width was taken as the mean value for Damage Level III in **Fig.2**, and for Damage Level II in **Fig.3**. The two figures shows that the output variables, the confidence values of judgement for Level II and Level III, are strongly affected with respect to the variations of the maximum crack width. The judgement of Damage Level II and Level III is inversed with respect to variations of the maximum crack width.

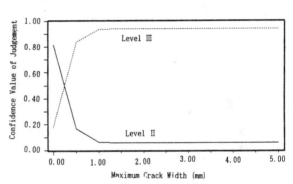

Fig.2 Results of Sensitivity Analysis for Damage Level III

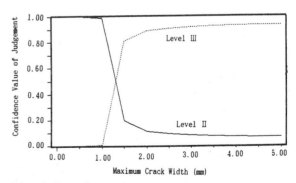

Fig.3 Results of Sensitivity Analysis for Damage Level II

4. Concluding Remarks

The damage assessment of RC structures has been depended on experienced inspection engineers. The judgement of damage levels has been very often performed based on their experiences and sense. It is difficult to analyze this type of problem which contains a personal view of inspection engineer by traditional analytical methods.

In this study, an artificial neural network was applied to the damage assessment of RC structures. A successfully trained neural network was set up, and was verified its usefulness. Using this neural network system, inexperienced engineers can determine the damage levels correctly. Furthermore, a successfully trained neural network was used to find the most important input variables which could strongly affect the damage level.

References

[1] Seki, H., Matsui, K., Matsushima, M. and Kaneko, Y., "Chloride-Induced Damage Evaluation of Concrete Bridges," Proc. of JSCE , No.402/V-10, 179-188, 1989.

[2] Furuta, H., Umano, M., Kawakami, K., Ohtani, H. and Shiraishi, N. , "A Fuzzy Expert System for Durability Assessment of Bridge Decks, " Proc. of ISUMA'90, 522-527, 1990.

[3] Miyagawa, T., "Durability Design and Repair of Concrete Structures: Chloride Corrosion of Reinforcing Steel and Alkali-Aggregate Reaction," Magazine of Concrete Research, Vol.43, No.156, 155-170, 1991.

[4] Hanshin Expressway Public Corporation, "Manual for Maintenance of Concrete Structures Damage by Alkali Aggregate Reaction(Tentative)," 1985

[5] Ministry of Construction, "Repair and Strengthening of Concrete Structures(Tentative)," 1986.

[6] Tokyo Electric Power Company, "Manual for Maintenance and Management of Civil Engineering Facilities in Thermal and Nuclear Power Plants," 1988.

[7] CRC Co. Ltd., "RHINE EX PC-9801 User's Manual," 1991.

[8] Tokyo Electric Power Company, " Data Base on Concrete Structures in Thermal Power Plants (Tentative)," 1992.

ON-LINE SENSING OF DRILL WEAR USING NEURAL NETWORK APPROACH

T.I. Liu
Department of Mechanical Engineering
California State University, Sacramento
Sacramento, California

K.S. Anantharaman
General Site Services
Intel Corporation
Folsom, California

ABSTRACT--A 9 X 14 X 1 neural network was used for on-line sensing of drill wear. The input vector of the neural network is obtained by processing the signals of the thrust and torque. Outputs are wear states and drill wear measurements. The learning process of the neural network can be performed by back propagation. The results of 9 X 14 X 1 neural network with and without adaptive activation - function slopes were compared. The 9 X 14 X 1 neural network with adaptive activation - function slopes can converge much faster than the conventional neural network. This modified neural network can achieve a success rate of 100% for on-line classification of drill wear even when the drilling condition has been changed. The neural network is also capable of measuring the drill wear accurately with an average error of 7.73%.

I. INTRODUCTION

On-line drill wear sensing system is crucial for a highly automated manufacturing system. Normally visual inspection of the cutting edge during machining operations is not feasible because the workpiece and chips obstruct the view. To overcome this difficulty indirect methods are required. For drill wear sensing many researchers use thrust and torque as indices for prediction of drill life [2,3].

In this work, whether the drill is usable or worn-out has been on-line determined using a modified 9 X 14 X 1 neural network. On-line measurement of drill wear has also been achieved accurately by the neural network. Furthermore, the performance of neural network with and without adaptive slopes has been compared.

II. EXPERIMENTAL SETUP AND DATA ACQUISITION

Drilling experiments was performed on a CNC milling machine. The work material used in this research was stainless steel 303. The drill material used was high speed steel (HSS). The drill size used in this work was 6.35mm (1/4").

Cutting forces were measured by a Kistler dynamometer. Signals were amplified using charge amplifiers and recorded with Nicolet digital oscilloscope. The outputs of the dynamometer are inputs to charge amplifiers. The outputs of charge amplifiers are then transmitted to the Nicolet oscilloscope. The experimental setup is shown in Fig. 1. Flank wear of the drill was measured off-line by a DoAll toolmaker's microscope.

III. FEATURE SELECTION

Eight features were selected. These features are described as follows :

1. Average of Thrust and Average of Torque - Average of thrust and torque were used by many researchers for on-line detection of tool wear conditions.

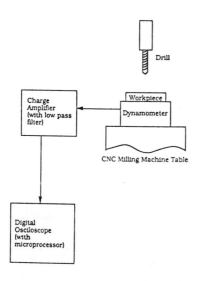

Fig. 1. Experimental setup

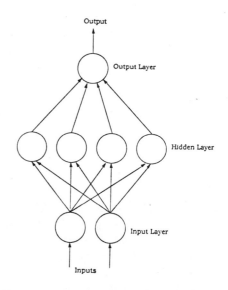

Fig. 2. Feedforward neural network
structure

2. Peak of Thrust and Peak of Torque –
Peak of thrust and torque are important
indices which are widely used.
3. RMS of Thrust and RMS of Torque – RMS
of thrust and torque are also very
important. These indices were used in
many research efforts. They indicate
the power consumption in the drilling
process.
4. Area under Thrust and Area under Torque
vs Time Curve – The two areas under
these curves are very sensitive to
drill wear during the drilling
operation and therefore were selected
as indirect indices.

All the above indices are chosen
because of the their previous successful
application for on-line monitoring and
diagnosis. Furthermore, these indices are
justified from our experimental
observations.

IV. ARTIFICIAL NEURAL NETWORK

Fig. 2 shows a typical feedforward
neural network having an input layer, a
hidden layer and an output layer. A
feedforward neural network must learn to
map the inputs to the outputs [5]. It takes
many iterations for conventional
feedforward neural networks with back

propagation to converge. Therefore, some
researchers try to modify this kind of
neural network. Activation functions with
adaptive slopes were used [1,4].

A. Activation Function with Adaptive Slopes

The technique of adaptive slopes for a
linear saturation soft limiter activation
function was proposed by Haves et al. and
Rezgui & Tepedelenlioglu, along with
results which indicate that adaptive slopes
can increase network performance [1,4].
The equations described below indicate a
new technique using the sigmoid activation
function. The derivation of the weight and
node offset adaptive formula remains
essentially unchanged from the conventional
back propagation algorithm. However, the
adaptive slopes allow the neural network an
additional degree of freedom in solving
nonlinear mapping problems.

$$Y_j = 1/\{1+\exp\ [-S_j(X_j + C_j)]\} \qquad (1)$$

$$X_j = \sum_j W_{ij}\ Y_i$$

where j stands for the current layer; i
stands for the preceding layer; W_{ij} is the
weight coefficient; C_j is the node offset

value; and S_j is the slope of the sigmoid function. From the above equations, all the node outputs would range between 0 and 1. Hence it is necessary to normalize all the input data between 0.1 to 0.9 before they are applied to the network. This is done by using the following equation:

$$X_n = [\{0.8/(P_{max} - P_{min})\}(P - P_{min})]$$
$$+ 0.1 \qquad (2)$$

where P_{max} and P_{min} are the maximum and minimum values of the data P respectively.

B. Learning Process

The generalized delta rule developed by Rumelhart and the parallel distributed processing group can work very efficiently for pattern recognition. This rule consists of presenting input patterns to the network and calculating the output patterns at the output nodes with the current set of offset values and weights. The actual output patterns is then compared with the required output patterns and the error is calculated. This procedure is then repeated for all input-output pairs in the training set and the total error is calculated. This is called the forward path. Next, the error is propagated backwards through the network to modify the slope, weight and node offset values. This is the modified back propagation technique with adaptive slopes. The slopes and weights preceding each output node are updated according to the following equations:

$$S_j(n+1) = S_j(n) + \epsilon_s \gamma_j$$
$$+ a_s[S_j(n) - S_j(n-1)] \qquad (3)$$

$$W_{ij}(n+1) = W_{ij}(n) + [\epsilon_w \delta_j Y_i]$$
$$a_w[W_{ij}(n) - W_{ij}(n-1)] \qquad (4)$$

where i and j are the previous and current node layers respectively. ϵ_s and ϵ_w are the learning rates and a_s and a_w are the momentum factors for slopes and weights respectively. S(n+1) and W(n+1) are the values for slopes and weights in the next iteration, S(n) and W(n) are the current

iteration values for slopes and weights, and S(n-1) and W(n-1) are the values for slopes and weights for the previous iteration respectively.

The correction factors, δ_j and τ_j for the nodes of the output layer are calculated as follows:

$$\delta_j = [S_j][Y_j][1-Y_j][D_j-Y_j] \qquad (5)$$

$$\tau_j = [X_j][Y_j][1-Y_j][D_j-Y_j] \qquad (6)$$

where j stands for the current layer.

The correction factors, δ_j and τ_j, are calculated for the nodes on the hidden layers as follows:

$$\delta_j = [S_j][Y_j][1-Y_j][\sum_k \delta_k W_{jk}] \qquad (7)$$

$$\tau_j = [X_j][Y_j][1-Y_j][\sum_k \delta_k W_{jk}] \qquad (8)$$

where j stands for the current layer and k stands for the succeeding layer.

The offset parameter C_j of each node is treated as an additional weight factor and updated as follows:

$$C_j(n+1) = C_j(n) + [\epsilon_c \delta_j] \qquad (9)$$

where ϵ_c is the learning rate for node offset value. The weights, slopes and offsets of the neural network are recalculated. The neural network repeats the calculation of the output values based on the same input data, compares them to the desired output values and readjusts the network parameters. This cycle is repeated until the calculated outputs have converged sufficiently close to the desired output or a preset iteration limit has been reached.

V. ON-LINE SENSING OF DRILL WEAR

A 9 X 14 X 1 neural network with adaptive-activation function slopes has been used for on-line classification and measurement of drill wear. The work was carried out in the following three stages:

Stage 1:   Comparison of Neural Network with and without Adaptive

Stage 2:   Activation-Function Slopes
            On-line   Classification   of
            Drill Wear
Stage 3:   On-Line Measurement of Drill
            Wear

A. Comparison of Neural Network with and without Adaptive Activation-Function Slopes

In the learning process, the experimental data with spindle speed 750 rpm, feedrates 3.3 mm/sec(7.8 in/min) were used for the training of artificial neural network. Linear interpolation program was used to obtain more data sets. Three points were interpolated between holes. No Interpolation was made between the last hole and next-to-last hole. There are 13 experimental data sets and 33 interpolated data sets, totalling 46 data sets.

The neural network used had 9 inputs and 1 output. Eight inputs were the selected features and the 9th input stands for drilling condition. In the learning process, the 9th input has a value of 0.1. However, for the on-line tests the 9th input is 0.9 since the spindle speed is increased. The output value was normalized to 0.3 for a usable drill and to 0.7 for a worn-out drill. The network was trained using this 46 sets of normalized data until an error of 0.01 was reached. The learning rate was 0.1 and the momentum learning rate was 0.5 for all networks. The trained artificial neural networks were used for on-line tests. For the 9 X 14 X 1 neural network, the network with adaptive slopes was able to converge to the desired error of 0.01 after 2008 iterations. The conventional neural networks can only converge to an error of 0.062 after 2008 iterations. The comparisons are shown in Fig. 3. It is very clear that the neural network with adaptive slopes can converge to the desired error much faster. Therefore, it is used for on-line classification and measurement of drill wear.

B. On-line Classification of Drill Wear

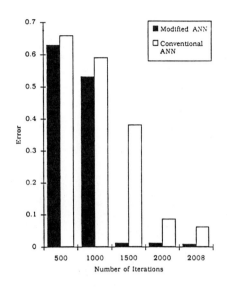

Fig. 3. Comparison of Conventional and Modified Neural Network Convergence

The trained artificial neural networks were used for on-line tests. On-line classification was conducted under different drilling condition so as to evaluate the capability of generalization of neural network and the flexibility of the on-line classification system.

The on-line tests were carried out with spindle speed 900 rpm and feedrate 3.3 mm/sec(7.8 in/min), 14 experimental data sets and 36 interpolated data sets, totally 50 data sets were tested. The drill wear conditions were classified into two categories based on the output of neural networks as follows:

Usable Drill - (.100 to .500)
Worn-out Drill - (.501 to .900)

The 9 X 14 X 1 neural network can distinguish a usable drill from a worn-out drill with a success rate of 100%.

C. On-Line Measurement of Drill Wear

In order to monitor the drill conditions continuously on a real time basis, the 9 X 14 X 1 neural network with adaptive activation function slopes was also used to measure the average flank wear for all the usable drills.

In the learning process, the data sets with spindle speed 750 rpm and feedrate 3.3 mm/sec(7.8 in/min) were used. A total of 45 data sets (12 experimental data sets and 33 interpolated data sets) were used for the training of neural networks. As before, linear interpolation was used to obtain more data points. Three points were interpolated between holes. The error limit used was 0.01. The learning rate was 0.1 and the momentum rate was 0.5 for weights, slopes and node offsets. The output was the measured flank wear. The neural network was trained until the error limit was reached.

For on-line tests, 49 data sets (13 experimental data sets and 36 interpolated data sets) with spindle speed 900 rpm and feedrate 3.3 mm/sec(7.8 in/min) were used. The results are very encouraging. The minimum error of the output was 0.4%, maximum error was 19% and mean error was 7.73%. The results are shown in Fig. 4.

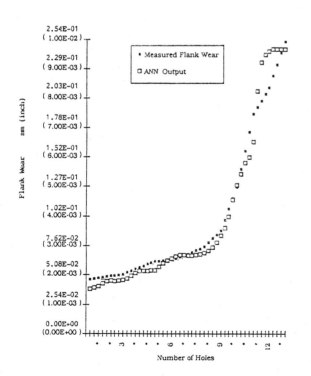

Fig. 4 Comparison of On-Line and Off-Line
Drill Wear Measurements

VI. CONCLUSIONS

From the above discussions, the performance of the modified neural network for on-line sensing is very successfully. This neural network with adaptive activation function slopes can converge much faster than the conventional neural network. Using a 9 X 14 X 1 modified neural network, the worn drill can be distinguished from the usable drill on-line with 100% reliability even under different drilling condition. This neural network can also measure the average flank wear on-line very accurately even under different drilling condition.

ACKNOWLEDGMENT

This work is partially sponsored by California State Funded Research, Scholarly and Creative Activity Grant.

REFERENCE

[1] M.D. Haves, S.C. Ahalt, K. Mirza, D.E. Orin, "Neural Network Control of Force Distribution for Power Grasp," Proceedings of the IEEE International Conference on Robotics and Automation, Sacramento, California, pp. 746-751, April 1991.

[2] T.I. Liu, E.J. Ko, "On-Line Recognition of Drill Wear Via Artificial Neural Networks," ASME Winter Annual Meeting Symposium on Monitoring and Control for Manufacturing Processes, Atlanta, Georgia, pp. 101-110, Nov 25-30, 1990.

[3] T.I. Liu, S.M. Wu, "On-Line Detection of Drill Wear," ASME Journal of Engineering for Industry, Vol. 112, pp. 299-302, August 1990.

[4] A. Rezgui, N. Tepedelenlioglu, "The Effect of the Slope of the Activation Function on the Back Propagation Algorithm," Proceedings of the International Joint Conference on Neural Networks, Washington, D.C., Vol.1, pp. 707-710, January 1990 .

[5] D. Rumelhart, J. McClelland, "Parallel Distributed Processing," MIT Press, Volume 1, 1986.

Failure Diagnosis System on Pneumatic Control Valves by Neural Network

Takeki Nogami

Shikoku Research Institute Inc.

2109-8, Yashimanishi-machi, Takamatsu-shi, Japan

Yoshihide Yokoi

The university of Tokushima

2-1, Minamijyosanjima-cho, Tokushima-shi, Japan

Masao Kasai, Katsunori Kawai and Katsuhisa Takaura

Mitsubishi Atomic Power Industries Inc.

4-1, Shibakouen 2-Chome Minato-ku, Tokyo, Japan

Abstract - A prototype failure diagnosis system has been developed using neural network technology for the actuators of pneumatic control valves. Because actual failure data was difficult to obtain, the data of 30 failure patterns were experimentally collected using more than 10 sensors. An FFT was carried out on the time series of the sensor signals. The data of the magnitude spectrum, phase difference and others are used as the characteristic parameters in our failure diagnosis. Appropriate failure diagnosis information was extracted from the data. Furthermore, similarities among the failure characteristics were established using fuzzy clustering and statistical analysis. The prototype that we developed consists of plural subnetworks and one main network. Each subnetwork is related to one specific sensor signal and deals with the magnitude spectra from the sensor signal. The main network makes the final decision according to the output from the sub-networks and other data. In our system, the number of network connections can be reduced by approximately 40% without degradation of the recognition capability in comparison with a conventional system where only one neural network is used.

I. INTRODUCTION

Generally, control valves are classified into 3 types by their actuator: pneumatic, electric, or oil hydraulic type. Our objective is to diagnose the actuators of pneumatic control valves which are frequently used in process control system of plants due to their easier isolation and quick response time properties. The failure of the actuator results in a shut down because of unstable control. There is a case of twin positioners at a control valve for keeping its reliability.[1] The diagnosis has been done intuitively and empirically by detecting the variability of the operational signal, open level, exhaust noise, pressure signal and so on by human experts. However the symptoms of failure and deterioration are subtle and it takes great skill to diagnose the problem. Therefore, research leading to a machine based diagnosis system seems worthwhile.

There are many ways for establishing such failure diagnosis systems. One way is the comparison of raw data with mathematical models of the pneumatic control valves. If the model was made, its diagnosability would be more reliable and universal. But the response characteristics of valves are non-liner and has also a time delay because of frictional force in the ground packing, mechanical slack etc. It is most difficult to diagnose the failure patterns when compared with the mathematical model simulating the normal or abnormal patterns.[2][3] A second approach is to employ an expert system based on empirical knowledge gleaned from the valves.[4] Unfortunately there are many valve components and at present it is not easy to summarize the knowledge of experts about the failure and wear of these individual parts. It is suggested that a neural network is suitable for solving problems involving pattern recognition and unalgorithmic diagnosis, because it is capable of being self-taught by teacher signals.[5][6]

For the purpose of establishing this new technology to diagnose actuator part failure, a prototype system has been developed using a neural network based on the premise that the pneumatic control valve is sinusoidally operated. The data of more than 10 sensors were experimentally collected for about 30 failure patterns. After extracting the useful characteristics with Fourier transformations and statistical analysis, similarities among the failure characteristics were revealed by using the fuzzy clustering. Furthermore, the usability of the plural sub-network was shown in comparison with using only one network.

II. EXPERIMENTAL EQUIPMENT

The experimental equipment is shown in Figure 1. It constitutes a valve, a diaphragm actuator and accessories (a booster relay, a positioner, an electric pneumatic transducer, pressure regulating valves etc).

When the valve receives an input signal to open wider, it operates as below: (1) Pressure increases in proportion to a input signal to an electric pneumatic transducer. (2) The balance beam moves up as the loading bellows in the positioner is pressurized. (3) The pilot valve stem top moves up and more air flows through the pilot valve, and the positioner output signal increases. (4) The positioner output signal is amplified by the booster to enhance the response, and pressure in the diaphragm increases. (5) The valve opens. At the same time, the drive lever moves up and the positioner cam rotates counterclockwise. (6) The spring beam moves

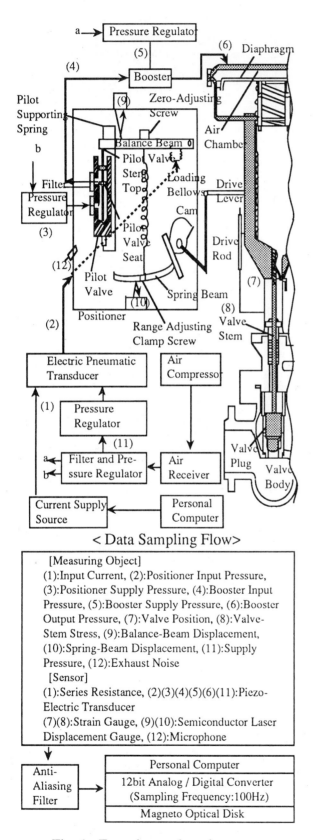

< Data Sampling Flow >

[Measuring Object]
(1):Input Current, (2):Positioner Input Pressure,
(3):Positioner Supply Pressure, (4):Booster Input
Pressure, (5):Booster Supply Pressure, (6):Booster
Output Pressure, (7):Valve Position, (8):Valve-
Stem Stress, (9):Balance-Beam Displacement,
(10):Spring-Beam Displacement, (11):Supply
Pressure, (12):Exhaust Noise
[Sensor]
(1):Series Resistance, (2)(3)(4)(5)(6)(11):Piezo-
Electric Transducer
(7)(8):Strain Gauge, (9)(10):Semiconductor Laser
Displacement Gauge, (12):Microphone

Anti-Aliasing Filter	Personal Computer
	12bit Analog / Digital Converter (Sampling Frequency:100Hz)
	Magneto Optical Disk

Fig. 1. Experimental equipment

down and the balance beam is pulled down. (7) An upward force on the loading bellows reaches a balance with the force on the spring beam by feedback. Therefore the valve reaches an open position to match any input signal.

After the output signals go through the anti-aliasing filter, they are converted into digital signals and sent to a personal computer at 100 Hz sampling frequency.

III. DATA COLLECTION

To establish a diagnosis system based on a neural network, it is necessary to collect a lot of failure pattern data. However it is not practical to collect data from new sensors attached to pneumatic control valves in a running plant in view of the cost and time involved. Furthermore valve failure is rare and the process control system must be shut down in order to attach many sensors. Accordingly the data of about 30 failure patterns were experimentally obtained from more than 10 sensors that are attached to a pneumatic control valve in our laboratory.

Any past failures that occurred in a plant were studied together with mechanical engineers and human experts. The failure patterns were selected as shown in Table I with

TABLE I.
LIST OF FAILURE MODES

[Single Failure]
P-1(S):Pilot-Valve Seat Abrasion
P-2(S)(M):Pilot-Valve Stem-Top Abrasion
P-3:Pilot-Supporting Spring Curvature
P-4:Looseness of Screw Linking Drive-Rod to Driver-Lever
P-5:Filter Clog(Output Side)
P-6:Filter Clog(Supply Side)
P-7(M)(L):Cam Abrasion
P-8:Looseness of Cam Lock-Nut
P-9:Failure of Zero-Adjusting Screw
P-10:Looseness of Range-Adjusting Clamp-Screw
P-11(S)(M):Air Leakage of Input Line
P-12(S)(M):Air Leakage of Output Line
P-13:Air Leakage of Supply Line
B-1(S)(M)(L):Abnormal High Sensitivity
B-2:Leakage by Parts Failure(Input Side)
B-3:Leakage by Parts Failure(Supply Side)
B-4:Imbalance between input and output pressure
D-1(S)(M)(L):Air Leakage of Input Line
[Compound Failure]
P-1(S)+P-2(L)
P-5+P-6
B-2+B-3
[Note] Failure Grade (S:Small, M:Medium, L:Large)
Failed Accessory
(P:Positioner, B:Booster, D:Diaphragm)

789

considerations given to the importance of the valve function and the occurrence frequency. The deterioration levels of a failure and compound failures were also considered. Moreover the sensor positions were determined on the basis of detectability and applicability in a plant.

The objective of our study is to diagnose the failure based on the sensor signals when the valve is sinusoidally operated. A valve with 50% open level (initial value) was operated by inputting a sine curve signal with 10% amplitude and 10 seconds frequency. And the sensor signals were obtained with sampling time of 100 Hz. The collection of failure data was done five times independently to derive the dispersion of the data and make both training data and non-training data for a neural network.

IV. SENSOR SIGNALS TRANFORMATION AND ITS CHARACTERRISTICS

The collected time series of sensor signals are shown in Figure 2.

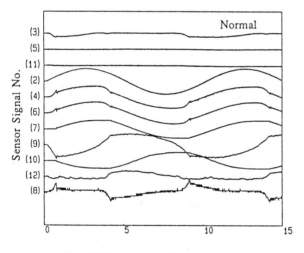

Fig. 2. Time series of sensor signal

Besides the wave pattern, these time series data include important information on wave phase, amplitude, initial value and so on. To analyze this information, an FFT was carried out because of the sinusoidal nature of the input signal curve and the cumulative probabilities were calculated.

The wave pattern frequency characteristics in the higher mode was about ten to fifteen times of the fundamental mode, hence the Fourier coefficients from the second to the sixteenth were used for diagnosis. The zero mode and first mode were not used, because the former is related to the initial value and the latter is related to the sinusoidal motion of a valve. Figure 3 shows the amplitude spectrum of a normal and a failure case. The characteristics of the failure case are seen in the higher modes. The number of modes is considered to be reasonable, because the coefficients above the fifteenth mode are relatively small. The phase differences between the input signal and each of the sensor signals were extracted. The mean and standard deviation were calculated. Supposing that the

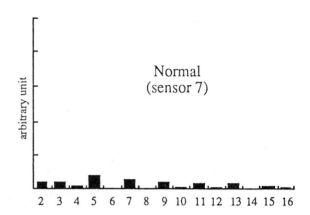

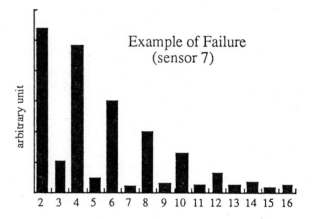

These spectra are obtained with Fourier transformation of time series data subtracted by ones averaged among 5 normal modes.

Fig. 3. Comparison of spectra

distribution is normal, the cumulative probabilities were inputted to a network. As to amplitudes and initial values the cumulative probabilities were calculated in the same way. Initial values were obtained by averaging the signals before inputting a sine curve. The characteristic of sensor signals is shown in Table II. The characteristic wave patterns, phase differences, amplitudes and initial values for each failure are easily seen. In the case of an actuator problem the valve stem stress signal (No.8) is important in diagnosing friction force and valve adhesion but the deviation of phase differences, amplitudes and initial values are large because of a residual stress in the valve stem. Therefore this signal is not useful because it was found that there are other signals to diagnose actuator problems instead of this sensor. There is also a case where the displacement sensor attached on a positioner was used to diagnose. A balance beam displacement sensor was tested experimentally to find it's sensitivity, and the balance beam was found to be useful. Also, the case of using a positioner displacement signal in diagnosis turned out to be quite useful as it is thought that a balance beam is highly sensitive to movement.

TABLE II.
CHARACTERISTIC OF SENSOR SIGNALS

Failure	\	Sensor Number Wave Pattern / Phase Difference / Amplitude / Initial Value									
	2	3	4	5	6	7	8	9	10	11	12
P-1 (S)		● ●	△		○△	●●△△	●	●△	△	○ ●●	●
P-1 (S)				△	○	○ △		○ ○			
P-2 (M)			△		○	○ ○				△ ●	
P-3		○	△△		○△	○○△△	△	○△△●			
P-4											
P-5								△		△	
P-6								△		△	
P-7 (M)		△				△ △		△			
P-7 (L)			○		●	● ○		●		△	
P-8								○			
P-9		○				△ ●△					
P-10		●○				●					
P-11 (S)	●	●●●				△ △					
P-11 (M)	●	△●△		△		● ○○			○	△	
P-12 (S)	●○●	●△			●●	●● △●		●●△○	○	○ ●●	△
P-12 (M)	●●○	●○			●●	●●○△●	●	●●●●	○	○ ●●	△
P-13	○ ○								●●●		
B-1 (S)		○○○			○	●△					
B-1 (M)		○●●	● ●		○△	●○		△●△		△	
B-1 (L)	△●○●	●●●	● ●		○●	●●	● ○			△	△
B-2					△	△				△	
B-3		△			○	△				△ △	
B-4	○○	●			●△	●△ △●	●○ △			○ ○○△	
D-1 (S)	○△●	●○			●△	●△ △●	●○ ○△			○ ●●△	
D-1 (M)	●○●	●●●	● ●		●●	●● ○●	●○ ○●			○ ●●△	
D-1 (L)	●●	●●●	● ●		●●	●●●△●	●	●●●●		○ ●●△	
P.1+P.2	○ ○		△		○△	○○ ○		○○ ●		○ ○●●	●
P.5+P.6					●						
B.2+B.3						●				△ △	

● :very characteristic   ○ :characteristic
△ :a little characteristic   no mark:characterless

TABLE III.
RESULT OF FUZZY CLUSTERING

Failure	Classification (Failure Mode)																		
	Normal	P-1	P-2	P-3	P-4	P-5	P-6	P-7	P-8	P-9	P-10	P-11	P-12	P-13	B-1	B-2	B-3	B-4	D-1
Normal			0.1		1.0	1.0	1.0		0.5	0.4						0.2			
P-1 (S)		1.0																	
P-2 (S)	0.3		0.5		0.3	0.3	0.3		0.6	1.0						0.1			
P-2 (M)			1.0							0.1									
P-3				1.0															
P-4	1.0				1.0	1.0	1.0		0.5	0.3						0.2			
P-5	1.0		0.1		1.0	1.0	1.0		0.5	0.4						0.3			
P-6	1.0				1.0	1.0	1.0		0.4	0.3						0.2			
P-7 (M)	0.7		0.1		0.7	0.7	0.7		1.0	0.7						0.2			
P-7 (L)								1.0											
P-8	0.7		0.3		0.7	0.7	0.7		1.0	0.8	0.1					0.2			
P-9	0.3		0.2		0.3	0.3	0.3		0.5	1.0						0.1			
P-10	0.1				0.1	0.1	0.1		0.1	0.1	1.0								
P-11 (S)	0.6		0.1	0.2	0.6	0.6	0.6	0.1	0.4	0.3		0.8		0.1	1.0	0.3			
P-11 (M)												1.0							
P-12 (S)													1.0					0.2	
P-12 (M)													1.0						
P-13														1.0					
B-1 (S)	0.9	0.1	0.4	0.1	0.9	0.9	0.9	0.2	1.0	0.8	0.2	0.1		0.1	0.2	0.7	0.5		
B-1 (M)															1.0	0.1			
B-1 (L)															1.0				
B-2	0.9				0.9	1.0	1.0		0.4	0.3						1.0	0.1		
B-3	0.2				0.2	0.2	0.2		0.1	0.1						1.0	1.0		
B-4																		1.0	
D-1 (S)																		1.0	
D-1 (M)												0.1							1.0
D-1 (L)																			1.0
P-1+P2	0.6	0.5	0.9	0.3	0.6	0.6	0.6	0.3	0.7	0.7	0.4	0.2		1.0	0.1	0.5	0.3	0.1	
P-5+P6	1.0		0.1	0.2	1.0	1.0	1.0		0.6	0.4						0.3	0.1		
B-2+B-3	0.1				0.1	0.1	0.1		0.1	0.1						1.0	0.9		

Maximum grade of membership is normalized to 1.0

In a running plant human experts diagnose using the open level, pressure, exhaust noise and so on. If time series data were collected without touching valves in a plant, they wouldn't be badly affected by the sensors. Non-touching sensors (7), (9) and (10) seem useful to detect the displacement because the characteristics are seen. The deviation of signals is used to diagnose the health of valves now. It is thought that the failures for which the characteristics are seen on Table II are detectable using those sensors in a plant.

This table shows that P-4,5,6,8, B-2,3 failures are not characteristic. To analyze a similarity between the failures, a fuzzy clustering was carried out.[8][9] The result is shown in Table III. These failures are similar to a normal case (particularly P-4,5,6). It is said that filter clogs and loose failures are not distinctive. Also a similarity between P-2(S) and P-9 is caused by a drift of a balance beam. Therefore, exactly identifying these failures requires either the use of a high efficiency sensor or the detection of a change in the actuating pattern (amplitude or frequency of sine wave, step signal).

V. PROTOTYPE OF FAILURE DIAGNOSIS

One way to input the time series data for each sensor into a neural network is to sample the arbitrary wave patterns; but a network becomes very large because a lot of data is required to input the pattern of higher modes. (Perhaps about 100 samples for each sensor will be needed.) Therefore, in our system the Fourier coefficients, phase differences, amplitudes and initial values were inputted.

Two prototypes were developed using a backpropagation algorithm [7] to diagnose eighteen kinds of failures and a normal case. In the first prototype (called system 1), all information is directly inputted into one neural network as shown Figure 4, but the problem is that in this structure the number of network connections is large and the information of the Fourier coefficients is much larger than that of phase differences and so on. Therefore, the other system with plural sub-networks (called system 2) was also developed as shown Figure 5. The recognition capability was compared between both systems.

The merit of system 2 is that if a sub-network is changed, only the new sub-network and the main neural network need to be re-trained. In system 2, the sub-networks processing the time series data send the reduced data based on the Fourier coefficients of each sensor to the main network. Phase differences, amplitudes and initial values are directly inputted to the main network. There is a problem in how to decide on the number of sub-network output units and the teacher signals, as it is difficult to intuitively identify the number of sub-network output units needed for the classification of wave patterns. Also, even if the number of them were decided, it would be difficult to make the teacher signals that could classify the wave patterns. Thus a non-subjective method must be considered.

By using the principal component analysis, the components that have above 5% contribution factors are selected for distinguishing the wave pattern. Namely, the number of sub-network output units is set by the number of eigen vectors that has above 5% contribution factors. The teacher signals are set to the correlation values between the eigen vectors and the Fourier coefficients.

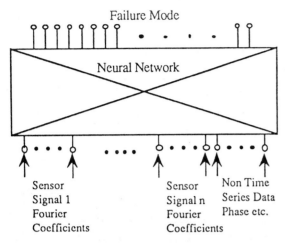

Fig. 4. Structure of System 1

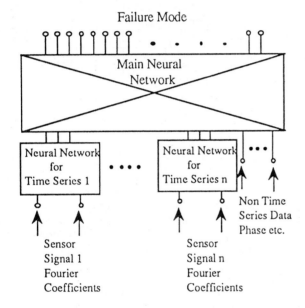

Fig. 5. Structure of System 2

TABLE IV.
RECOGNITION CAPABILITY NO.1

Failure	System1 Training 1	2	3	Non-training 4	5	System2 Training 1	2	3	Non-training 4	5
Normal	⊙	⊙	⊙	-	⊙	⊙	⊙	⊙	⊙	-
P-1 (S)	⊙	⊙	⊙	⊙	⊙	⊙	⊙	⊙	⊙	⊙
P-2 (M)	⊙	⊙	⊙	⊙	⊙	⊙	⊙	⊙	⊙	⊙
P - 3	⊙	⊙	⊙	⊙	⊙	⊙	⊙	⊙	⊙	P-6
P - 4	⊙	⊙	⊙	P-5	-	⊙	Δ	P-6	P-5	-
P - 5	⊙	⊙	⊙	O	P-6	⊙	⊙	O	O	P-6
P - 6	⊙	⊙	⊙	-	⊙	⊙	O	O	O	⊙
P - 7 (L)	⊙	⊙	⊙	⊙	⊙	⊙	⊙	⊙	⊙	⊙
P - 8	⊙	⊙	⊙	⊙	⊙	⊙	⊙	⊙	⊙	Nor
P - 9	⊙	⊙	⊙	⊙	⊙	⊙	⊙	⊙	⊙	P-2
P - 10	⊙	⊙	-	-	-	⊙	⊙	⊙	P-9	P-2
P -11 (M)	⊙	⊙	⊙	⊙	⊙	⊙	⊙	⊙	⊙	⊙
P -12 (M)	⊙	⊙	⊙	⊙	⊙	⊙	⊙	⊙	⊙	⊙
P - 13	⊙	⊙	⊙	⊙	⊙	⊙	⊙	⊙	⊙	⊙
B-1 (L)	⊙	⊙	⊙	⊙	⊙	⊙	⊙	⊙	⊙	⊙
B - 2	⊙	⊙	⊙	O	⊙	⊙	B-3	⊙	⊙	⊙
B - 3	⊙	⊙	⊙	Δ	B-2	⊙	O	⊙	-	⊙
B - 4	⊙	⊙	⊙	⊙	⊙	⊙	⊙	⊙	⊙	⊙
D-1 (L)	⊙	⊙	⊙	⊙	⊙	⊙	⊙	⊙	⊙	⊙
P-1+P-2	⊙	⊙	⊙	⊙	⊙	⊙	⊙	⊙	⊙	⊙
P-5+P-6	⊙	⊙	⊙	⊙	Δ	⊙	⊙	⊙	Δ	Δ
B-2+B-3	⊙	⊙	⊙	⊙	⊙	⊙	⊙	⊙	Δ	-

⊙ :give correct answer
O :give more than one answer,
    but correct failure mode first
Δ :give more than one answer,
    but correct failure mode after second
- :no answer
*-**:mistaken failure mode

TABLE V.
RECOGNITION CAPABILITY NO.2

Failure	System1 Non-training 1	2	3	4	5	System2 Non-trainig 1	2	3	4	5
P-2 (S)	⊙	⊙	-	⊙	⊙	⊙	⊙	⊙	⊙	⊙
P-7 (M)	⊙	-	-	⊙	-	P-10	-	-	P-8	-
P-11 (S)	-	⊙	⊙	⊙		⊙	O	⊙	O	⊙
P-12 (S)	-	-	-	-	-	⊙	-	⊙	-	⊙
B-1 (S)	-	-	-	P-5	-	⊙	B-3	B-3	B-3	B-3
B-1 (M)	⊙	-	-	-	-	⊙	⊙	⊙	⊙	⊙
D-1 (S)	B-4	B-4	B-4	B-4	B-4	B-4	B-4	B-4	B-4	B-4
D-1 (M)	⊙	⊙	-	-	-	⊙	⊙	⊙	⊙	O

VI. PERFORMANCE TEST

The five sets of data were collected for each failure. Three sets of them were used for training, the remainder were used for testing the detectability. Also some data was collected by changing the scale for the same failure. Tables IV and V show the recognition capability of both systems. In Table IV the recognition capability is tested using the same data as is used for training. In Table V it is tested using the small scale failure that is not used for training. In system 1 the recognition capability is near 100% using training data. In system 2 the recognition capability of some failures is inferior to system 1 because those failures P-4,5,6,B-2,3 are not characteristic and similar.

As to the non-training data, the recognition capability of both systems is identical. The recognition for normal, P-

4,5,6,8,9,10, B-2,3 and compound P5+P6 is not well. However, those failures are difficult to to be distinguished as the result of a fuzzy clustering. This result doesn't limit the neural network capability, but shows the difficulty including those failures.

For the non-training data, Table V shows a good recognition capability in p-2(S),P-11(S),B-11(M) and D-1(M) in system 2. This result can be predicted from a fuzzy clustering, but both systems couldn't recognize other failures.

There are some ideas to resolve this problem. A high efficiency sensor will be used for catching the patterns of difficult failures. Also, it is necessary to develop a neural network system that can list up all predictable failures with teacher signal determined by a fuzzy-clustering.

The number of network connections in system 2 is approximately 60% of those in system 1. Considering the same recognition capability in systems, it is said that system 2 with sub-networks is better.

VII. CONCLUSIIONS

The prototype of a failure diagnosis system has been developed using neural network technology for the actuators of pneumatic control valves. Because actual failure data was difficult to obtain, the data of 30 failure patterns were experimentally collected using more than 10 sensors. The data of magnitude spectrum, phase difference and others are used as the characteristic parameters in our failure diagnosis system. The results are given below: (1) Some sensors are unsuitable to use because of deviation, especially a valve stem stress signal because of deviation in the cause of residual stress. (2) Signals from displacement gauges in a positioner are effective for diagnosis. (3) Some failures are not characteristic and difficult to find.

As this system needs to diagnose using many sensors, a network tends to become large. When the hardware configuration is changed, the training must be carried out again. Therefore a system that consists of plural sub-network and one main network was developed to minimize the size of networks and the re-training. Each sub-network is related to one specific sensor signal and deals with the magnitude spectra from the sensor signals. The main network makes the final decision according to the outputs from the sub-networks and other data. A teacher signal in each sub-network is determined by a principal component analysis. Moreover, a conventional network system that doesn't have sub-networks was developed.

Both can easily recognize failure for the raining data. However, it is not easy to recognize the non-training data of uncharacteristic failures. In comparing both systems the recognition capability is same, but the number of network connections can be reduced by approximately 40% in a new layered network system.

In our future works, a fuzzy clustering analysis will be used to obtain the teacher data for our prototype system. This improved system will list up the candidate failures for uncharacteristic failure cases. Furthermore, another diagnostic system will be developed for step-wise valve movement which is one of the standard movements used currently for failure diagnosis.

ACKNOWLEDGEMNTS

Special thanks to Mr.Onoshita, an engineer in ABB Gaderius Inc., for technically supporting our experiments and Mr.Hayashi, our staff of Shikoku Research Institute Inc., for failure data collection.

REFERENCES

[1] T.Mizumoto, et al., "Redundant System for Feedwater Control Valve's Pneumatic Subcontrol System in PWR Plant", Mitsubishi Atomic Energy Technical Review, Vol.30, 1983, pp14-15.

[2] T.Asakura, M.Danno, H.Ohtake, "Improvement of Dynamical Characteristics of Electropneumatic Valve Positioner", Transactions of the Japan Society of Mechanical Engineers, 56-524, C,1990-4, pp 50-55.

[3] Bau.D.Y, Prezillon.P.J, "Model-Based Diagnosis of Power Station Control Systems", IEEE Expert, Vol.7,No.1,1992, pp36-44.

[4] Y.Sato, "Development of Maintenance Assistant Expert System for PWR Feedwater System", Mitsubishi Atomic Energy Technical Review, 52, 1989, pp13-15.

[5] Sorsa.T, Koivo.H.N, Koivisto.H,"Neural Networks in Process Fault Diagnosis", IEEE Transactions Syst Man Cybern, Vol. 21,No.4, 1991, pp815-825.

[6] S.Yoshihara, et al., "Many Components Monitoring System by Using Neural Network", Proc. Fall Meeting of the Atomic Energy Society of Japan, 1991, pp401

[7] Rumelhart, D. E.,Hinton, G. E. and Williams, R. J., "Parallel Distributed Processing", MIT Press, Vol. 1, 1986, pp 318-362.

[8] J.C.Bezdek,"Pattern Structures: A Tutorial in Analysis of Fuzzy Information", Vol.1,CRC Press, 1987, pp81-107

[9] J.C.Bezdek,"A Convergence Theorem for the Fuzzy ISODATA Clustering Algorithms:, IEEE Transactions on Pattern Analysis and Machine Intelligence,Vol.PAMI-2, No.1,1980, pp1-8.

NEURAL NETWORK-BASED HELICOPTER GEARBOX HEALTH MONITORING SYSTEM

Peter T. Kazlas, Peter T. Monsen, and Michael J. LeBlanc

Sensor and Communication Electronics Division
The Charles Stark Draper Laboratory
555 Technology Square, M/S 53
Cambridge, MA 02139

Abstract – This paper summarizes the results of two neural hardware implementations of a helicopter gearbox health monitoring system (HMS). Our first hybrid approach and implementation to fault diagnosis is outlined, and our results are summarized using three levels of fault characterization: fault detection (fault or no fault), classification (gear or bearing fault), and identification (fault sub-classes). Initial hardware results compare well with previously published software simulations. Our second all-analog implementation exploits the ability of analog neural hardware to compute the discrete Fourier transform (DFT) as a pre-processor to a neural classifier.

INTRODUCTION

One crucial mechanical component in a helicopter that is prone to mechanical failure is the main rotor gearbox. Currently, the standard method of controlling gearbox failure is to regularly overhaul the complete system, an expensive and time consuming process [1]. An alternative approach, explored here, would be to provide an on-board gearbox health monitoring system (HMS).

A helicopter gearbox, like any mechanical part, vibrates with a specific frequency characteristic, depending on its configuration and rotational speed. If a fault exists in the gearbox, this frequency characteristic will differ from the nominal case. The task of the HMS is to analyze the gearbox vibration data to determine if a fault exists in the gearbox, and, if so, the fault type. This application requires high computational throughput to decipher the continuous stream of vibration data, in order to display a timely report of the operational condition of the gearbox to the pilot.

794

In this paper, we describe a neural network-based system solution to the HMS problem, hosted on the first generation of Draper's Integrated Neurocomputing Architecture (INCA), INCA/1. While neural network researchers have previously addressed this problem, no neural network hardware-based solution has been implemented [2, 3].

We present two distinct hardware implementations, one hybrid (digital discrete Fourier transform (DFT) with analog classifier) and the other purely analog (analog DFT and classifier), and quantify the fault classification and detection performance of each.

INTEGRATED NEUROCOMPUTING ARCHITECTURE

The INCA/1 system is a stand alone, compact, real-time neural network hardware platform designed and developed by the Charles Stark Draper Laboratory. The neural network in INCA/1 is a large feedforward analog network constructed from devices designed by the Jet Propulsion Laboratory [4]. This compact system contains four layers of 64 analog neurons, supported by a VME-compatible digital shell. INCA/1 contains a Motorola MVME-147 processor board (25-MHz 68030), which hosts a real-time Unix-compatible operating system. The 4 x 64 analog network can perform up to 3.3 billion connections per second [5].

Currently, network training is performed by software. Circuit models of the neuron and synapse devices have been incorporated into a commercial workstation-based neural network simulator. Networks are constructed and trained on a workstation, using the sigmoidal models of the actual neuron circuits, and the resultant synapse matrix is downloaded to INCA/1.

GENERAL APPROACH

Gearbox vibration data from two accelerometers, mounted radially at the point indicated in Figure 1, were made available to us by the Naval Oceans System Center (NOSC). The data is a subset of the database generated by Mark Hollins at the Naval Air Test Center [6]. Originally, six accelerometer tracks were recorded. In generating the vibration data, faults were introduced under controlled conditions, to emulate the characteristics of actual in-flight faults. Approximately ten minutes of sample data were provided for each fault type. The six faults are defined as: No Fault, three Bearing Faults (Inner Race, Outer Race, and Rolling Element), and two Gear Faults (Gear Spall and Missing Half Tooth).

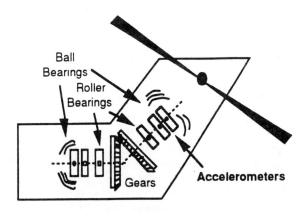

Figure 1: TH-1L Intermediate Helicopter Gearbox

There are three levels of fault diagnosis: Detection, Classification, and Identification. *Detection* is a simple fault/no-fault determination, but in many ways this is the most critical function. It is this level which determines whether or not a mission should be terminated. A missed fault could prove disastrous to both aircraft and pilot. However, false alarms are unacceptable in that they may require an unnecessary abort of mission. *Classification* is slightly more refined than detection. Here, the system determines whether a detected fault is a gear fault or bearing fault. *Identification*, the lowest level, attempts to localize the fault completely.

The inputs to the neural network are generated from the Fourier spectra. Only a subset of the available frequencies is used, as shown in Figure 2. Upon examination of the vibration spectra, the 4 to 11 kHz frequency range was selected, as it displays significant variation from fault to fault. Frequencies below 4 kHz are dominated by high energy noise, while frequencies above 11 kHz are negligible, since the response of both accelerometers drops off at approximately 10 kHz.

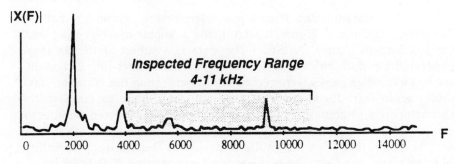

Figure 2: Fourier Spectrum Used to Generate Neural Network Inputs

The general approach to fault diagnosis is outlined in Figure 3: Samples are obtained from each channel, and Fourier transformed. The frequency samples for both channels are compressed, normalized, and concatenated to provide neural network inputs.

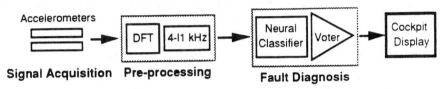

Figure 3: General Approach to a Neural Network-Based HMS

As stated previously, any false alarms are unacceptable, as are any missed faults. During normal operation, a variety of transients and intermittent unknowns can be seen, where the neural network, for an instant, misclassifies its input. In a real application, it would be unacceptable for an alarm to be sounded for each transient. By tracking the network output state over time, and majority-voting the results, intermittents are averaged out of the output of the overall system. The effect is that the overall system reports *trends* in network outputs, removing intermittent misclassifications. If the neural network *consistently* reports a gear fault, for instance, then the pilot may be alerted: spurious flickers in the Fourier spectra, however, are not reported, averting false alarms. In this way, the False Alarm Rate of the system is reduced, as is the Fault Miss rate, and the overall misclassification rate is reduced considerably.

The following sections describe two implementations, hybrid and purely analog, of a neural network-based HMS. In the first implementation, the DFT is computed on a digital processor, while in the second all-analog implementation, the DFT is computed by the first layer of the neural network.

HYBRID IMPLEMENTATION

In the hybrid implementation outlined in Figure 4, 256 samples are obtained from each channel, and the fast Fourier transform (FFT) of each is computed. The desired frequency range (4-11 kHz) is covered by 60 points of the 256-point FFT. These 60 points are compressed into 30 points through simple averaging, giving 30 spectral points for each channel. The two channels are then normalized and concatenated to give 60 neural network inputs.

A two-layer neural network with sixty inputs, sixty hidden units, and nine outputs, is used in this application. The nine outputs have been defined in such a way that they attempt to perform all three levels of classification at once: Two outputs indicate Fault/No-Fault status, two more indicate whether a fault is a Bearing or Gear fault, and the remaining five indicate exactly which fault type is present. The neural network is transparent to the application: The inputs are simply presented to INCA/1, and the outputs are then read. The output vector, indicating the neural network's fault classification, is reported on INCA/1's screen with each trial.

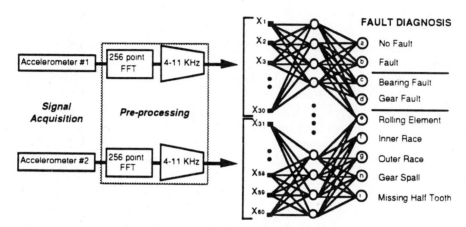

Figure 4: Hybrid Approach to Gearbox Fault Diagnosis

ALL-ANALOG IMPLEMENTATION

In an effort to provide a more compact and efficient system, an all-analog solution was investigated. Due to the limitations of the present hardware platform (i.e., 60 inputs) only one accelerometer channel could be used for fault detection. In an actual system, data from both accelerometers would be used, to maximize detection performance.

In place of calculating the Fourier transform digitally, we calculate the DFT using the first layer of our neural network. The all-analog implementation, shown in Figure 5, obtains 60 samples from the accelerometer, computes the DFT with the first neural network layer, and sends the inputs directly to the rest of the neural network for fault analysis. These inputs correspond to the magnitude of the frequency spectra from 4-11 kHz. The two outputs of the neural network (after voting) provide the desired fault detection.

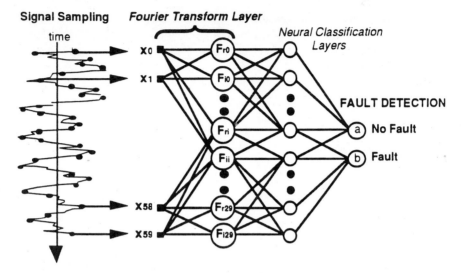

Figure 5: All-Analog Approach to Gearbox Fault Diagnosis

The discrete Fourier transform of an input vector, **x**, can be written as a matrix expression:

$$\mathbf{F} = (\mathbf{E} + j\,\mathbf{O}) \bullet \mathbf{x} \qquad (1)$$

where the **E** and **O** matrices contain the even and odd coefficients of the expanded Fourier integral:

$$E_{ij} = \frac{1}{N}\cos\left(\frac{2\pi i j}{N}\right) \qquad (2a)$$

$$O_{ij} = -\frac{1}{N}\sin\left(\frac{2\pi i j}{N}\right) \qquad (2b)$$

In a feedforward neural network, the ith neuron's input is simply the inner product of the neuron's weight vector ($\mathbf{w}_i$) and the corresponding neuron's input vector ($\mathbf{x}_i$), given by

$$\mathbf{w}_i \bullet \mathbf{x}_i \qquad (3)$$

The output of the neuron, y_i, is dependent on its activation function:

$$y_i = f(\mathbf{w} \bullet \mathbf{x}) \qquad (4)$$

By rewriting the Fourier multiplications in Equation (1) as two separate products,

$$\mathbf{F} = \mathbf{E} \bullet \mathbf{x} + j\,\mathbf{O} \bullet \mathbf{x} \qquad (5)$$

we can map the transformation in the first stage [7]. The weight matrix W is simply the interlacing of rows of the even and odd coefficients (i.e., the rows of E and O). As a result, the first layer as described by Equation (3) can be rewritten as

$$
W \cdot x =
\begin{bmatrix}
E_{0\,0} & E_{0\,1} & \cdot & \cdot & E_{0\,N-1} \\
O_{0\,0} & O_{0\,1} & \cdot & \cdot & O_{0\,N-1} \\
\cdot & \cdot & \cdot\cdot & \cdot \\
\cdot & \cdot & \cdot\cdot & \cdot \\
E_{\frac{N}{2}-1\,0} & E_{\frac{N}{2}-1\,1} & \cdot & \cdot & E_{\frac{N}{2}-1\,N-1} \\
O_{\frac{N}{2}-1\,0} & O_{\frac{N}{2}-1\,1} & \cdot & \cdot & O_{\frac{N}{2}-1\,N-1}
\end{bmatrix}
\begin{bmatrix}
x_0 \\
x_1 \\
\cdot \\
\cdot \\
\cdot \\
x_{N-2} \\
x_{N-1}
\end{bmatrix}
\tag{6}
$$

Note, since the inputs to the neural network are real, we may take advantage of the symmetry property of the Fourier transform and discard half of the coefficients. By substituting $N=60$ into Equation (6), we derive an equation for the first layer:

$$
\begin{bmatrix}
Fr_0 \\
Fi_0 \\
\cdot \\
\cdot \\
\cdot \\
Fr_{29} \\
Fi_{29}
\end{bmatrix}
=
\begin{bmatrix}
E_{0\,0} & E_{0\,1} & \cdot & \cdot & E_{0\,59} \\
O_{0\,0} & O_{0\,1} & \cdot & \cdot & O_{0\,59} \\
\cdot & \cdot & \cdot\cdot & \cdot \\
\cdot & \cdot & \cdot\cdot & \cdot \\
E_{29\,0} & E_{29\,1} & \cdot & \cdot & E_{29\,59} \\
O_{29\,0} & O_{29\,1} & \cdot & \cdot & O_{29\,59}
\end{bmatrix}
\begin{bmatrix}
x_0 \\
x_1 \\
\cdot \\
\cdot \\
\cdot \\
x_{59}
\end{bmatrix}
\tag{7}
$$

where Fr_0-Fr_{29} and Fi_0-Fi_{29} are the real and imaginary parts of the Fourier transform of the input vector x, respectively.

By setting the first-layer neuron's output function to equal the absolute value function (i.e., $f(w \cdot x) = abs(w \cdot x)$), a shift invariant time-frequency transformation is realized. If this first layer is then coupled with a neural classifier network, both acoustic preprocessing and classification can be accomplished in a single feedforward manner.

Using this method, a weight matrix can be generated for *any* neural network to perform an arbitrarily sized DFT. Presently, INCA/1 neurons can only implement a thresholding function with variable gain. Consequently, the absolute value function is computed off-line. Before the absolute value is taken, special care must be taken to *operate the neurons in their linear range*. Otherwise, the DFT output would be distorted by the nonlinear transfer functions of the neurons. With appropriate scaling and careful planning, this can be accomplished.

By transforming the analog data from the accelerometer via analog computation and adding a few simple analog circuits the entire system could be realized in analog hardware. This solution removes the unnecessary A/D and preprocessing delays found in digital solutions, and would considerably reduce the size of the HMS. In other words, the system would be extremely small and fast but would be only responsible for providing fault detection (i.e. make fault/ no fault determinations).

HYBRID IMPLEMENTATION FAULT DIAGNOSIS RESULTS

The hybrid implementation fault diagnosis was evaluated on three criteria: fault detection (fault/no fault), fault classification (bearing/gear), and fault identification (bearing and gear subclasses). The latter two criteria are important for maintenance reasons, while fault detection is most critical to the actual mission. INCA/1's classification performance is summarized in Tables 1 and 2.

TABLE 1: FAULT CLASSIFICATION CONFUSION MATRIX WITH VOTING

ESTIMATED CLASS

TRUE CLASS	No Fault	Bearing Fault	Gear Fault
No Fault	100%	0%	0%
Bearing Fault	0%	100%	0%
Gear Fault	0%	7%	93%

TABLE 2: FAULT IDENTIFICATION CONFUSION MATRIX WITHOUT VOTING

ESTIMATED CLASS

TRUE CLASS	Bearing Fault			Gear Fault	
	OR	IR	RE	GS	MHT
Outer Race	69%	24%	3%	4%	0%
Inner Race	2%	98%	0%	0%	0%
Rolling Element	49%	11%	29%	11%	0%
Gear Spall	5%	16%	3%	76%	0%
Missing Half Tooth	0%	0%	0%	0%	100%

Using the voting scheme described in the previously, the system is able to achieve 100% fault detection with a zero false alarm rate. Also, INCA/1 was able to classify faults (bearing or gear) with an average 97% success rate. Mixed results were observed in fault identification. The network was able to correctly identify the missing half tooth and inner race fault with a 100% and 98% success rate, respectively. The system had difficulty discriminating between two bearing faults, outer race and rolling element. This result is consistent with previous findings – both faults have nearly identical vibration spectra.

ALL-ANALOG IMPLEMENTATION RESULTS

For our all-analog implementation, we first demonstrated that a 60-point DFT of time-series data from a single accelerometer provides sufficient information for fault detection, by first computing the DFT with a 32-bit digital processor. The frequency components were then fed into INCA/1's neural network. Results show that a system using a 60-point DFT is capable of achieving 100% fault detection with a zero false alarm rate.

Preliminary hardware results for the all-analog approach (i.e. replacing the digital front end processor with analog computation) are encouraging. An 83% fault detection rate with a zero false alarm rate was realized using seven voted outputs. The amount of this degradation attributable to the nonlinearity of the first layer neuron transfer functions is still unclear. Work is continuing to address this issue, and to improve the performance of the all-analog solution. By designing a more suitable transfer function (i.e., $f = abs()$) for the first layer network elements, an increase in performance is expected.

CONCLUSIONS

This initial study has shown the feasibility of a helicopter gearbox HMS based on analog hardware neural networks. Neural network hardware has much to offer in a potential gearbox monitoring system: Small size, high throughput, and low power. Our results show that, using only two accelerometer channels and minimal majority-voting techniques, 100% fault detection can be achieved, with 93-100% correct fault classification. Preliminary results using the first layer of a neural network to generate the Fourier spectra are encouraging. Work is continuing, to improve the performance of this all-analog approach.

REFERENCES

[1] Mertaugh, Lawrence J., "U.S. Navy Vibration Analysis Evaluation Program for Helicopter Gearboxes," Proceedings of the National Specialists' Meeting, Bridgeport, CT, p. IV-1, 1988.

[2] Kuczewski, R. M. & Eames, D. R., "Helicopter Fault Detection and Classification with Neural Networks, " IJCNN, 1992, pp. II–947-956.

[3] Dellomo, M., "Helicopter Gearbox Fault Detection: A Neural Network Based Approach," MITRE, Code 535.

[4] T. Daud, T. Brown, M. Tran and A. Thakoor - JPL ; M. Dzwonczyk, M. Busa, M, LeBlanc and T. Sims - CSDL, "VLSI Implemented Building Block Neural Network Chips for Classification/Detection Applications," Neuro Nimes 92 - Neural Networks and Their Applications, November 1992.

[5] M. Dzwonczyk et al., "An Integrated Neurocomputing Architecture for Side-Scan Sonar Target Detection," presented at IEEE Conference on Neural Networks for Ocean Engineering, August, 1991.

[6] M. Hollins, "The Effects of Vibration Sensor Location in Detecting Gear and Bearing Defects," Report for Naval Air Test Center, Code RW82B, Patuxent, MD.

[7] A.D. Culhane, M.C. Peckerar, and C.R.K. Marrian, "A Neural Net Approach to Discrete Hartley and Fourier Transforms," IEEE Transactions on Circuits and Systems, Vol. 36, No. 5, pp. 695-703, 1989.

Neural/Fuzzy Systems for Incipient Fault Detection in Induction Motors

Paul V. Goode   Mo-yuen Chow

Student Member, IEEE   Senior Member, IEEE

Dept. of Electrical and Computer Engineering
North Carolina State University
Raleigh, NC 27695-7911
USA

Abstract

Industrial motors are subject to incipient faults which, if undetected, can lead to motor failure. The necessity of incipient fault detection can be justified by safety and economical reasons. The technology of artificial neural networks has been successfully used to solve the motor incipient fault detection problem. The artificial neural network, however, does not provide any heuristic knowledge of the fault detection procedure. This paper will introduce a hybrid neural network/fuzzy logic system that not only provides better performance on detecting motor faults, but also allows heuristic interpretation of the network fault detection process. The system will be applied to bearing faults in single phase induction motors. The paper will discuss how to extract heuristic information from the system to gain further insight into the motor fault detection procedure.

I. Introduction

The necessity of incipient fault detection can be justified by safety and economical reasons [1]. The induction motor, as with all rotating machines, is subject to the occurrence of incipient faults [1-6]. If these faults are left undetected, they will eventually degenerate into a machine failure. When a machine failure occurs, it has the potential to inflict injury on nearby personnel. Furthermore, there is generally a substantial cost associated with the down time and repair of the failed machine.

Artificial neural networks (ANNs) have proven to be capable of successfully performing motor fault detection [3,5,7-8]. Unlike other fault detection techniques such as frequency monitoring [9] and particle analysis, the ANN approach to incipient fault detection is inexpensive to implement while it can also perform fault detection on-line. The ability to detect incipient faults on-line with the use of inexpensive measurements while keeping the motor structure in tact makes this non-invasive fault detection technique attractive. The advantages of using ANN over other conventional fault detection techniques have been discussed in different literature [10-12] For example, the ANN does not require a rigorous mathematical model to perform motor incipient fault detection [1-6] and has the flexibility to learn and adapt itself to give the exact solution to a specific problem. These features, coupled with already proven satisfactory performance [3,5,7-8], indicate a promising role of ANNs in incipient fault detection.

However, although the ANN can provide the correct input-output fault detection relation, it is essentially a "black box" device; i.e., it does not provide heuristic reasoning about the fault detection process. If there is abnormal performance of the ANN fault detection, it will be difficult to diagnose which part of the fault detection process has trouble. Thus, we can not repair the ANN fault detector accordingly. Furthermore, if the correct fault detection process knowledge can be extracted in a heuristic manner, we can not only gain a better understanding of the fault detection process, but we can also further improve system fault detection knowledge and its design.

Fuzzy logic could be a solution to this problem. Fuzzy logic can easily and systematically transfer heuristic, linguistic, and qualitative knowledge preferred by humans to numbers and quantitative knowledge preferred by machines, and vice-versa. This provides a simple method to heuristically implement fault detection principles and to heuristically interpret and analyze their results. Based on the heuristics, fuzzy logic provides a general solution for a class of problems, thus making it insensitive to special cases or conditions. Unfortunately, the major drawback of fuzzy logic is that the technology is difficult to give an exact solution to the problems, while an exact solution is essential to motor fault detection.

By merging these two technologies, we can capitalize from the use of a simple non-invasive fault detection technique, the understanding and learning gained from the fault detection process, and the ability to diagnose the fault detection problems in a heuristic manner which may occur. The ANN can be constructed, in a modular fashion, based on fuzzy logic principles. Not only will this initialize the network with the general fault detection ability, but it will provide the network a better starting point to successfully learn the fault detection for a specific motor. Because the modular approach is based on fuzzy logic principles, the network can provide valuable information of the fault detection procedure in a heuristic manner. This information can be easily extracted from the network for easy diagnosis of any possible problems with the network. This information can also provide the engineers with a better understanding of the fault detection process and the motor in

804

question. This process will enable us to further improve the motor fault detection techniques.

This paper will discuss the methodology used to merge these two technologies to obtain a neural/fuzzy fault detection system. As an illustration, the neural/fuzzy fault detection network will be used to detect bearing faults in a single phase induction motor. The results obtained from this illustration will be evaluated heuristically by extracting the learned information from each module. This heuristic information will indicate if any incorrect assumptions were made when initializing the neural/fuzzy fault detection network. A procedure is also presented on how to interpret and correct these incorrect assumptions. The fault detection procedure proposed in this paper can be easily modified for some type of motor fault detection.

II. Motor Fault Detection Neural/Fuzzy System Structure

The overall motor fault detection neural/fuzzy system approach is shown in Fig 1. The bearing motor fault detection procedure is firstly implemented in fuzzy rules and membership functions. Then the neural/fuzzy system is configured based on these preliminary fuzzy rules and membership functions developed in modules. The output of the network provides three decision outputs $\in \{0, 1\}$ corresponding to GOOD, FAIR, or BAD.

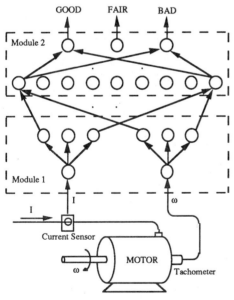

Figure 1. Neural/fuzzy system structure.

Module 1, the fuzzy membership function module, is comprised of layers 1 and 2 of the neural/fuzzy system. Layer 1 of the module provides the input measurements to the network. Motor current, I, and rotor speed, ω, measurements are used as inputs for bearing wear fault detection [7]. This is accomplished through the

use of an inexpensive current sensor and tachometer. Layer 2 of the module represents output nodes of "sub-networks" that are trained in advance. Each node corresponds to a membership function belonging to the fuzzy set for that input. The sub-networks contain the information for the fuzzy membership functions in their weights. These weights determine the shape of the membership functions of interest. The sub-networks allow representation of very complex membership functions [14] which are more flexible to adaptation for decision classification.

Module 1 is trained off-line before being inserted into the neural/fuzzy network. This is done by using vague heuristics of Low, Medium, and High to represent each of the inputs, I and ω. These heuristics are constructed into preliminary membership functions which build the universes of discourse X and Y corresponding to the input spaces of I and ω, respectively. The universes of discourse represent the normalized input data. For example, if the current data ranges in value from 3 amps to 14 amps, the universe of discourse represents a mapping of the data from the range of 3 to 14 to a range of 0 to 1. These are represented in the standard notation used in [16] :

$$X = [\, \mu_{low}(I\,), \mu_{medium}(I\,), \mu_{high}(I\,)\,], I \in X, \qquad (1)$$

$$Y = [\, \mu_{low}(\omega), \mu_{medium}(\omega), \mu_{high}(\omega)\,], \, \omega \in Y, \qquad (2)$$

where $\mu_i(\lambda\,)$ = the grade of membership of λ in $\mathcal{I} = \{\, i \in \mathcal{I} \mid low, medium, high\, \}$, $\lambda \in X, Y$

The actual values of the preliminary membership functions in (1) and (2) are shown below in Fig. 2.

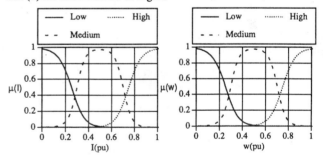

Figure 2. Preliminary membership functions.

These preliminary membership functions were chosen based upon heuristics of Low, Medium, and High. For example, the lowest current would be 0.0, which translates to 3 amps given the example above. This value for current would have the highest membership in the Low membership function for I. As seen in Fig. 2., this value is 1.0 (vertical axis). A value of 4 amps (approximately 0.2) would be *less Low* than would be the value 3 amps. As a result, its membership value in the Low set would be less (approximately 0.7), as is indicated in Fig. 2.

Module 2, the fuzzy rule base module, is also comprised of two layers. Layer 1 of the module (layer 3 of the network) provides the fuzzy rules (if-then statements) for the motor fault detection. Each node represents a rule in the fuzzy rule matrix. Each rule node should only have as many connections (weights) to it from the membership function module as there are inputs to the membership function module. These weights will not change since their only function is to pass fuzzy membership function values. Layer 2 of the module (layer 4 of the network) provides the output conditions of GOOD, FAIR, or BAD. The weights between these two layers are obtained by off-line training on a predetermined fuzzy rule base. This provides an initial rule base for the network.

For example, the bearing wear can affect many variables such as the motor damping coefficient, the motor current, and the rotor speed. As bearing wear increases, the coefficient of friction and motor current also increase while the rotor speed decreases. For example, bearing wear generally contributes five to ten percent of all rotational power (P) losses experienced by an average healthy motor. Considering this, a rule base for bearing wear can be easily constructed based upon the following heuristics:

Ploss = (Pstator loss + Protor loss + Protational loss)
IF Protational loss $\leq$ 0.05 (Ploss) THEN GOOD   (3)
IF 0.05 (Ploss) < Protational loss $\leq$ 0.10 (Ploss) THEN FAIR
IF 0.10 (Ploss) < Protational loss THEN BAD

Fig. 3 shows a conceptual diagram of bearing wear as a function of rotor speed and stator current, which is based on computer simulation.

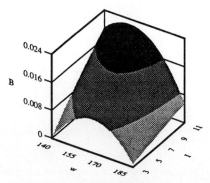

Figure 3. Surface plot of bearing wear as a function of motor current and rotor speed.

Based on the heuristics of (3), simulation results, and motor engineering experience, a preliminary rule base (for off-line training) of the neural/fuzzy fault detection system is constructed and shown in Table I. The inputs, I and ω, are evaluated in terms of a Low, Medium or High {L,M,H} linguistic description. The resulting rule

decision is classified in terms of either a Bad, Fair, or Good {B,F,G} linguistic description.

		ω		
		L	M	H
	L	G	F	G
I	M	F	F	G
	H	B	B	G

Table I. Fuzzy rule base for bearing wear.

III. Motor Fault Detection Neural/Fuzzy System Modification Procedure

Once the neural/fuzzy motor fault detection system has been initialized, it is to be trained for motor bearing faults by actual motor data. Through training, the system will modify the fuzzy membership functions and fuzzy rules based upon the input data and its initial fault detection heuristic knowledge through the neural/fuzzy motor fault detector network weights. These modifications made by the system will provide valuable heuristic information about the actual form of the fuzzy membership functions and the validity of the fuzzy rule base, as well as providing the exact fault detection results. The flowchart in Fig. 4 is used as a procedure for interpreting this heuristic information to modify the initial fault detection heuristics, if necessary.

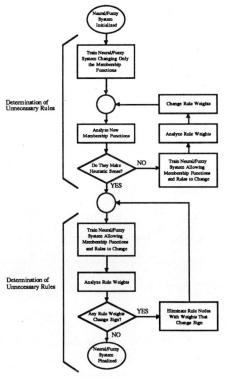

Figure 4. Flowchart for fuzzy membership function and rule modification.

IV. Motor Bearing Wear Fault Detection Example

The bearing wear in an induction motor problem is used to illustrate the procedure in Fig. 4. Using the initial membership functions of Fig. 2 and initial fuzzy rule base of Table I, the neural/fuzzy motor fault detector is trained. This first phase of training, as indicated in Fig. 4, is done while assuming the intial rule base is correct by not allowing the rule module weights to change. This is done to verify the validity of the initial rule base. Should one or more of the rules be incorrect, it will be manifested in the resulting membership functions because the membership function module is the only dynamic module at this point. Therefore, given an incorrect rule, after training the membership functions will violate heuristic reasoning; i.e., there may be a complete overlap of fuzzy sets, or maybe a fuzzy set will not be bounded between [0,1], etc.

If the resulting membership functions indicate an incorrect rule, the network is then trained again while allowing the rule module weights to change. From the changes made in the rule module weights and the new membership functions, the incorrect rule can be isolated. The physical interpretation of the rule weights is in the sign of the weight: a positive weight value indicates a valid rule, a negative weight value indicates an invalid rule. For example, the rule node $I=L$, $\omega=H$ should have a positive weight to the GOOD output node and negative weights to the FAIR and BAD output nodes (based on Table I). Through training, the value of the rule module weights should always increase in absolute value If they do not, then that indicates an incorrect or unnecessary rule (unnecessary rules will be addressed later). This can be verified mathematically [17]. For example, if the weight connecting the rule node $I=H$, $\omega=M$ to the output classification BAD changes from 12.2 to 9.3, then this rule is suspected as being incorrect.

Using these principles, the first phase of training yielded the following new membership functions and rules (the rule for $I=H$, $\omega=M$ was found to be incorrect):

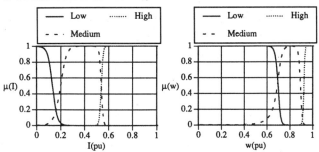

Figure 5. Membership functions after training with new rules constant.

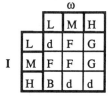

Table II. New fuzzy rule base for bearing wear.

This membership function module and rule base module proved to be very effective by properly classifying 100% of all testing data. A standard feedforward net with a configuration of two input nodes, eight hidden nodes, and two output nodes was only able to properly classify approximately 93% of all testing data. However, phase two of the training must still be implemented to determine if any rules are unnecessary. This phase is necessary because, even though 100% classification was achieved and the membership functions were heuristically correct, not all rule weights increased in absolute value. The procedure on the right side of Fig. 4 must now be followed. This is done by training the neural/fuzzy motor fault detector (initialized with the new fuzzy rule base) while allowing both modules to change their weights. Using the same principles of heuristically correct membership functions and positive rule module weight values, the unnecessary rule nodes can be isolated.

After training this phase, there were five suspect rules. By analyzing the training data with the new membership functions, it was found that three of these rule nodes had little or no training patterns. The rules module nodes representing the fuzzy rules of $I=H$ and $\omega=M$, and $I=H$ and $\omega=H$ were never activated (no training patterns). The rules module nodes representing the fuzzy rules of $I=L$ and $\omega=L$ had only one training pattern (node activation). Therefore, these rules were considered to be unnecessary for this motor. The new rule base of Table III was constructed and the neural/fuzzy motor fault detector was once again trained while allowing both modules to change their weights.

		ω	
	L	M	H
I L	d	F	G
I M	F	F	G
I H	B	d	d

Table III. Reduced fuzzy rule base for bearing wear (d = discarded).

This yielded the following membership functions shown below in Fig. 6. This network also classified all patterns correctly.

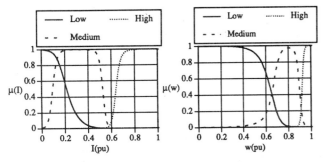

Figure 6. Membership functions after training with reduced rules changing.

As an illustration, the absolute value of the reduced fuzzy rule module weights, before and after training, are shown in Fig. 7. Notice that all weights increase in absolute value.

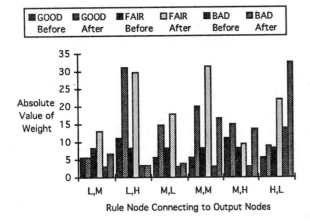

Figure 7. Reduced fuzzy rule base weights before and after training.

V. Conclusion

A neural/fuzzy motor fault detection system, using motor bearing wear detection as an illustration, was presented in this paper. The changes in the neural/fuzzy motor fault detection system were heuristically analyzed to determine the actual fuzzy membership functions and fuzzy rule base for properly detecting a motor bearing fault. These changes were easy to analyze because the system's modular structure, based upon fuzzy logic principles, allowed heuristic interpretation of the network dynamics and the motor dynamics. Furthermore, we found that the structure lends itself quite easily to diagnosis of any possible network problems, such as improper initialization. This heuristic knowledge of how the network classifies can lead to a better understanding of motor dynamics and fault detection procedures. With this knowledge, we can further our understanding of the motor fault detection process which may lead to more accurate fault detection systems.

VI.   Acknowledgments

The authors of this paper would like to acknowledge the support of National Science Foundation, for Grant No. ECS-8922727.

VI.   References

[1] Peter J. Tavner, James Penman, <u>Condition Monitoring of Electrical Machines</u>, Research Studies Press Ltd. John Wiley & Sons Inc.

[2] S. Cambrias and S.A. Rittenhouse, *Generic Guidelines for Life Extension of Plant Electrical Equipment*, Electric Power Research Institute Report EL-5885, July 1988.

[3] Mo-yuen Chow, Sui Oi Yee, "Application of Neural Networks to Incipient Fault Detection in Induction Motors," *Journal of Neural Network Computing*, Auerback, Vol. 2, No. 3, pp. 26-32, 1991.

[4] D.R. Boothman, E.C. Elgar, R.H. Rehder, and R.J. Woodall, "Thermal tracking-A rational approach to motor protection," *IEEE Transactions Power Apparatus and Systems*, Sept./Oct. 1974, pp. 1335-1344.

[5] Mo-yuen Chow, "Artificial Neural Network Methodology in Real-Time Incipient Fault Detection of Rotating Machines," in *Proc. National Science Foundation Workshop on Artificial Neural Network Methodology in Power Systems Engineering*, Clemson University (Clemson, SC), April 8-10, 1990, pp. 80-85.

[6] R.W. Smeaton, *Motor Application and Maintenance Handbook*, 2nd ed. New York: McGraw-Hill, 1987.

[7] Mo-yuen Chow, Peter M. Mangum, Sui Oi Yee, "A Neural Network Approach to Real-Time Condition Monitoring of Induction Motors," *IEEE Transactions on Industrial Electronics*, Vol. 38, No. 6, pp. 448-453, Dec. 1991.

[8] Mo-yuen Chow, Sui Oi Yee, "Methodology For On-Line Incipient Fault Detection in Single-Phase Squirrel-Cage Induction Motors Using Artificial Neural Networks," *IEEE Transactions on Energy Conversion*, Vol. 6, No. 3, pp. 536-545, Sept., 1991.

[9] James E. Timperly, "Incipient Fault Detection Through Neutral RF Monitoring of Large Rotating Machines," *IEEE Transaction on Power Apparatus and Systems*, Vol. PAS-102, No. 3, March 1983.

[10] Arun K. Sood, Ali Amin Fahs, Naeim A. Henein, "Engine Fault Analysis Part I: Statistical Methods," *IEEE Transaction on Industrial Electronics*, Vol. IE-32, No. 4, Nov. 1985.

[11] A. Keyhani, S.M. Miri, "Observers for Tracking of Synchronous Machine Parameters and Detection of Incipient Faults," *IEEE Transaction on Energy Conversion*, Vol. EC-1, No. 2, June 1986.

[12] James C. Hung, B.J. Doran, "High Reliability Strapdown Platforms Using Two-Degree-of-Freedom Gyros," *IEEE Transaction on Aerospace and Electronic Systems*, Vol. AES-9, no. 2, pp. 253-259, March 1973.

[14] C. Lin and C.S.G. Lee, "Neural-Network-Based Fuzzy Logic Control and Decision System," in *IEEE Transactions on Computers*, Vol. 40, No. 12, pp. 1320-1336, December, 1991.

[15] H. Okada, N. Watanabe, A. Kawamura, and K. Asakawa, "Initializing Multilayer Neural Networks with Fuzzy Logic," in *Proceeding of the International Joint Conference on Neural Networks*, 1992, Vol. 1, pp. 239-244.

[16] G.J. Klir and T.A. Folger, *Fuzzy Sets, Uncertainty, and Information*. New Jersey: Prentice Hall, 1988.

[17] Mo-yuen Chow, Paul Goode, "Adaptation of a Neural/Fuzzy Fault Detection System," in *Proceeding of the IEEE Conference on Decision and Control*, 1993.

Transformer Oil Diagnosis
Using Fuzzy Logic and Neural Networks

James J. Dukarm
Delta-X Research
Suite 222 - 2186 Oak Bay Avenue
Victoria BC Canada V8R 1G3

Abstract--Dissolved-gas analysis (DGA) is widely used for detection and diagnosis of incipient faults in large oil-filled transformers. Many factors contribute to extreme "noisiness" in the data and make early fault detection and diagnosis difficult. This paper shows how fuzzy logic and neural networks are being used to automate standard DGA methods and improve their usefulness for fault diagnosis. The use of neural networks for DGA--with or without fuzzy logic--is discussed, and some related work is described briefly.

INTRODUCTION

Most large power transformers use mineral oil as a dielectric fluid and coolant and have oil-impregnated kraft paper insulation between winding layers. Abnormal conditions can occur within a transformer because of severe overloading, lightning or switching transients, mechanical flaws, or chemical decomposition of oil or insulation, to name just a few possibilities. Such abnormalities usually manifest themselves by overheating of the oil or paper, by partial discharge, or by arcing. These symptoms are called "faults" in the context of electrical equipment maintenance. Because of the cost and economic importance of big transformers, it is necessary to detect and identify faults as early as possible.

Depending on the energy involved, the degree of localization, and intermittent or continuous occurrence, each fault type "cooks" the oil or paper in a different way, generating characteristic relative amounts of dissolved fault gases in the oil. For example, overheating of the oil tends to produce high levels of ethylene, while arcing in oil usually generates significant amounts of acetylene and hydrogen.

Periodic maintenance of large transformers includes chromatographic analysis of the insulating oil to measure concentrations (ppm by volume) of dissolved hydrogen (H_2), methane (CH_4), ethane (C_2H_6), ethylene (C_2H_4), acetylene (C_2H_2), carbon monoxide (CO), and carbon dioxide (CO_2). Differing operating conditions and structural peculiarities of transformers distort the chromatographic signatures of faults, making it advisable to apply several DGA methods to the data simultaneously to obtain a reliable diagnosis.

An ANSI/IEEE standard [1] describes three DGA methods--Key Gas Analysis, the Doernenberg Ratio Method, and the Rogers Ratio Method. These methods differ in several respects:

- Features upon which the diagnosis is based;
- Rules or computations for deriving a diagnosis from the features;
- What specific diagnoses are supported.

All three methods are computationally straightforward. When automated in a naive way, they tend to work well on diagnosing severe faults and to fall mute on subtle ones. Common to the three methods is the use of multiple numeric thresholds to classify features of the dissolved-gas data as to membership in various intervals. The interval membership information is used to infer a diagnosis. When a fault is intermittent or of low intensity, some of the input features may fall near but outside the expected intervals, with the result that no diagnosis is obtained.

If strict interval membership is replaced by fuzzy membership, the standard methods can be automated in a way that extends their usefulness while remaining faithful to their underlying technical basis.

KEY GAS ANALYSIS

Key Gas Analysis attempts to identify the following abnormalities:

> Overheated oil
> Overheated cellulose
> Partial discharge
> Arcing

The diagnosis is based on the predominant dissolved gases and their proportions relative to total dissolved combustible gas (TDCG). TDCG is the sum of the concentrations of hydrogen, methane, ethane, ethylene, acetylene, and carbon monoxide dissolved in the oil. The absolute dissolved-gas concentrations (in ppm) and generation rates (ppm/day) are used to judge the severity of any faults identified.

For example, according to [1] if the absolute level of TDCG is over 720 ppm and consists about 63% of ethylene, then there is an indication of overheated oil. Close monitoring is advised if the TDCG generation rate exceeds 10 ppm/day.

Key Gas Analysis with fuzzy logic

Key Gas Analysis is well-suited to implementation as a fuzzy logic expert system. A Key Gas Standard must be defined for each transformer or group of similar transformers. Such a standard is a set of thresholds:

- For TDCG and each gas, thresholds L1, L2, and L3 are defined as lower limits for Abnormal, High, and Very High levels, respectively.
- For each combustible gas, lower limits Q1 and Q2 are defined for High and Very High proportion of TDCG, respectively.
- For TDCG and each combustible gas, lower limits R1 and R2 are defined for High and Very High generation rates, respectively.

810

TDCG and the gases are each associated with several numeric input variables. For example, ppmAcet, incAcet, and pctAcet are, respectively, the concentration of dissolved acetylene, the acetylene generation rate (calculated with reference to an earlier oil sample), and the level of acetylene as a percentage of TDCG.

The first step in running the expert system is fuzzy classification of all the input variables. Classification consists of calculating each variable's degree of membership in fuzzy sets representing the applicable categories. Figure 1 shows the graphs of the membership functions representing ppmAcet=abnorm, ppmAcet=hi, and ppmAcet=vhi, defined in terms of acetylene's L1, L2, and L3 limits. Membership functions for incAcet=hi, incAcet=vhi, pctAcet=hi, and pctAcet=vhi are defined analogously, and similar membership functions are provided for classifying TDCG and all the gases.

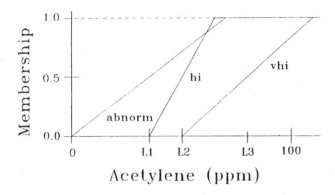

Fig. 1. Fuzzy membership functions for acetylene level.

The shapes of the membership function graphs are motivated by the requirement that the fuzzy classifications should correspond with intuitive classifications based on the thresholds. This is necessary in order for the rules to make intuitive sense and to ensure that apparently sensible rules have the intended meaning when interpreted by the fuzzy logic system. The correspondence must hold in two ways:

- Each threshold should mark the point where a classification's confidence factor (cf) reaches 0.50; and
- Intuitive relationships between the categories must be preserved. For example, a variable which is Very High with cf > 0.50 must also be High with cf > 0.50.

Each Key Gas Analysis rule shows how a diagnosis is derived from the classified input data. For example:

IF   ppmTDCG=abnorm AND pctEthy=hi
THEN   Cond=HotOil

When the expert system runs, all rules are applied. The cf of each rule's consequent is set equal to the minimum of the cf's of the rule's antecedents. Where the same diagnosis (such as Cond=HotOil) occurs as the consequent of several rules, the maximum of the cf's produced by those rules is returned as the cf of that diagnosis.

Examples of the use of this expert system are given in a later section of this paper.

GAS RATIO METHODS

The Rogers Ratio Method, as described in [1], uses three input features calculated from the chromatographic data to diagnose six conditions. The features are ratios of gas concentrations:

MH = methane / hydrogen
AE = acetylene / ethylene
EE = ethylene / ethane

These three features are each classified as low (low), medium (med), or high (hi) according to their membership in intervals as follows:

MH=low: Any value below 0.1.
MH=med: Between 0.1 and 1.0.
MH=hi : Above 1.0.
AE=low: Below 0.1.
AE=hi : Between 0.1 and 3.0.
EE=low: Below 1.0.
EE=med: Between 1.0 and 3.0.
EE=hi : Above 3.0.

The Rogers Ratio method matches certain combinations of input classifications with diagnostic outcomes as shown in Table I. The diagnoses are:

OK: Unit normal.
PD: Partial discharge.
TL: Low-temperature thermal.
TM: Medium-temperature thermal (below 700 C).
TH: High-temperature thermal (above 700 C).
ARC: Arcing.

TABLE I
ROGERS RATIO METHOD DIAGNOSIS

		EE=low	EE=med	EE=hi
MH=low	AE=low	PD	-	-
	AE=hi	-	-	-
MH=med	AE=low	OK	TL	-
	AE=hi	-	-	ARC
MH=hi	AE=low	-	TM	TH
	AE=hi	-	-	-

The Rogers Ratio method is regarded by maintenance engineers as accurate, but its usefulness is limited by the fact that it often fails to yield any diagnosis at all.

Fuzzy Rogers Ratio method

For the enhanced Rogers method, the input classifications MH=L, AE=H, and so on are given confidence factors calculated as the degree of membership of the gas ratio in fuzzy versions of the intervals shown above. Then the rules implicit in Table I are applied to derive confidence factors for all the Rogers diagnoses.

The fuzzy membership functions for Rogers Ratio input classifications are graphed in Figure 2 for MH, Figure 3 for AE, and Figure 4 for EE.

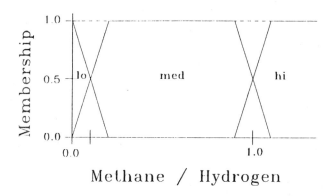

Fig. 2. Fuzzy membership functions for classifying Methane/Hydrogen ratio for the Rogers Ratio method.

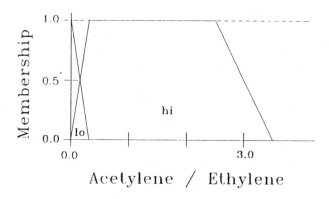

Fig. 3. Fuzzy membership functions for classifying Acetylene/Ethylene ratio for the Rogers Ratio method.

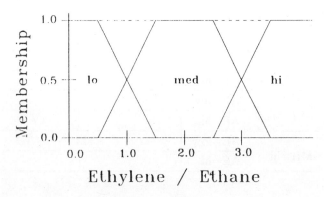

Fig. 4. Fuzzy membership functions for classifying Ethylene/Ethane ratio for the Rogers Ratio method.

To ensure consistency with the standard Rogers method, the membership functions of the fuzzy intervals are defined so that they equal 0.5 at the endpoints of the corresponding "crisp" intervals. This ensures that the cf of a diagnosis is greater than 0.5 if and only if the standard Rogers method produces that diagnosis. Since the cf is only a rough "strength of assertion" indicator and not a probability, the exact shape and width of the membership function graphs is not critical.

A similar treatment is used for the Doernenberg Ratio method, which uses four gas ratios to diagnose Thermal, Partial Discharge, and Arcing conditions.

DIAGNOSTIC EXAMPLES

The fuzzy systems described above were implemented in computer software and tested on historical examples supplied by industrial clients. A few of them are presented here.

Transformer 1

The first example is the one cited in the IEEE DGA standard [1], where several abnormal gas levels are observed. Here, all three methods show "Arcing." Rogers gives it a cf of 1.00, Key Gas Analysis gives it cf=0.46, and Doernenberg gives cf=0.32. Furthermore, Key Gas Analysis shows an almost-significant cf of 0.40 for "Overheated Cellulose," suggesting that paper insulation may be affected by the fault. According to [1], the problem was found to be arcing between an insulated tap-changer shaft pin and part of the drive mechanism.

Transformer 2

An oil sample showed an abnormal level of carbon monoxide, with a significant Key Gas diagnosis of "Overheated cellulose" (cf=0.54). Another oil sample eleven days later showed several high gas levels and high gas generation rates. Key Gas, Rogers, and Doernenberg all returned a diagnosis of "Arcing" with cf of 0.69, 1.00, and 0.99 respectively. The abnormal level of carbon monoxide was swamped by high levels of other gases, but Key Gas Analysis still showed "Overheated Cellulose" with cf=0.40, indicating that the abnormality involved paper insulation. Ten days later, the unit suffered a major internal flashover.

Transformer 3

In another case, an oil sample with several abnormal and high gas levels yielded a significant Key Gas result of "Overheated Cellulose" (cf=0.55) along with "Overheated Oil" (cf=0.44) and "Arcing" (cf=0.25). The latter by itself would not be meaningful, but in this case it supported a significant Rogers diagnosis of "Arcing" (cf=0.73). One month later, the unit failed with what the owner documented as a "core problem." An oil sample taken immediately after the failure showed three indications of "Arcing"--Rogers with cf=1.00, Doernenberg with cf=0.43, and Key Gas with cf=0.14.

DIAGNOSTIC NEURAL NETWORKS

Transformer oil DGA, which is essentially a pattern-recognition problem, should be a very good neural network application. Among the many possible approaches are:

- Neural network versions of the gas ratio methods discussed above, and some others;
- A new diagnostic method using a large network trained on many real fault examples;
- A new diagnostic method employing unsupervised learning and based an a very large volume of transformer oil data.

332

The Rogers Ratio Method enhanced with confidence factors can be simulated by a small 3-layer feedforward network (3 gas ratio inputs, 3 middle nodes, and 6 diagnostic cf outputs) trained by backpropagation (see [2]) to replicate Rogers Method diagnoses on real or simulated cases. When this is done, the practical effect is about the same as the fuzzy logic approach described above. An important difference is that the fuzzy logic implementation is faithful to the original Rogers method because the cf of a fuzzy Rogers diagnosis exceeds 0.50 if and only if the strict Rogers diagnosis would be the same. The relationship between the Rogers diagnosis and the corresponding cf returned by a neural network is not as clear.

A more complicated diagnostic method--the nomograph described in [3]--has been faithfully automated using fuzzy logic in combination with a simple neural network. The network was needed to overcome limitations of the rule-based logic described above in the Key Gas Analysis section. That work will be described in a separate paper.

The second approach listed above is to develop a neural network by supervised learning without any attempt to simulate an established diagnostic method. The author has experimented informally with a feedforward network with 10 gas ratios as inputs, a 6-node middle layer, and 3 outputs representing cf's for Thermal, Partial Discharge, and Arcing. When trained on 150 real and synthetic examples, the network seemed to perform well. The main obstacle to developing a real diagnostic tool this way is the lack of sufficient high-quality examples with which to train and validate a network of this type.

The third neural network approach mentioned above is to use a large body of gas-in-oil data, without any attached fault diagnosis, to train a self-organizing network such as Kohonen's (see [2]). The network would cluster the data in a way which might correspond to useful diagnostic categories. The success of this approach would depend on identifying a good set of input features to use (such as gas ratios) and on careful experimental and statistical work to identify the transformer abnormalities represented by the clusters.

CONCLUSION

Fuzzy logic can be used to automate standard methods of transformer oil DGA, providing enhanced information for the maintenance engineer while remaining faithful to the original methods. In some cases, neural networks can be used in combination with fuzzy logic to implement more complex diagnostic methods while maintaining a straightforward relationship between the enhanced method and the original one. Powerful new diagnostic methods based on large neural networks may be possible, but their development requires the assembly of a large database of examples for training and validation.

REFERENCES

[1] IEEE Std C57.104-1991, *IEEE Guide for the Interpretation of Gases Generated in Oil-Immersed Transformers*. New York: IEEE Press, 1992.

[2] J. A. Freeman and D. M. Skapura, *Neural Networks: Algorithms, Applications, and Programming Techniques*. Addison-Wesley, 1991, ch. 7, pp. 263-289.

[3] T. J. Haupert, F. Jakob, and E. J. Hubacher, "Application of a new technique for the interpretation of dissolved gas analysis data," *11th Annual Technical Conference of the International Electrical Testing Association*, 1989, pp. 43-51.

EVALUATION OF THE PERFORMANCE OF VARIOUS ARTIFICIAL NEURAL NETWORKS TO THE SIGNAL FAULT DIAGNOSIS IN NUCLEAR REACTOR SYSTEMS

Shahla Keyvan and Ajaya Durg
Nuclear Engineering Department
University of Missouri-Rolla
Rolla, MO 65401

Luis Carlos Rabelo
Department of Industrial
and Systems Engineering
Ohio University
Athens, OH 45701

Abstract--This is a study on the evaluation of the performance and comparison between various paradigms of artificial neural networks in nuclear reactor signal analysis for the purpose of developing a diagnostic monitoring system. Reactor signals from Experimental Breeder Reactor (EBR-II) are analyzed. The signals are both measured signals collected by Data Acquisition System (DAS) as well as simulated signals. ART2, ART2-A, Fuzzy Adaptive Resonance Theory (Fuzzy ART), and Fuzzy ARTMAP paradigms of the Adaptive Resonance Theory (ART) family, Standard Backpropagation, Cascade Correlation, and RCE networks are examined and compared in this study.

I. INTRODUCTION

The goal of this study is to develop a diagnostic monitoring system based on artificial neural networks and **ARMA** models for pattern recognition of faulty signals, identification of the faults, and prediction of the reactor condition. The system utilizes a hierarchy which combines unsupervised/supervised learning(See Figure 1). The first level of this hierarchy should have real time learning, degradation detection capabilities, and ability in qualitative classification. The second level of hierarchy is composed of several specialized supervised elements yielding a quantitative measure. Finally, third level based on an established database will forecast the progress of the wear. A comprehensive semi-benchmark tests have been performed, aimed at evaluating the performance of various paradigms to the application in the first level of hierarchy. ART2[3], ART2-A[5], Fuzzy Adaptive Resonance Theory (Fuzzy ART)[6], and Fuzzy ARTMAP[4,7,8] paradigms of the ART family, Standard Backpropagation[13], Cascade Correlation[9], and RCE networks[1,14] are examined and compared in this study.

This work is supported by National Science Foundation under reference number: ECS-9111145.

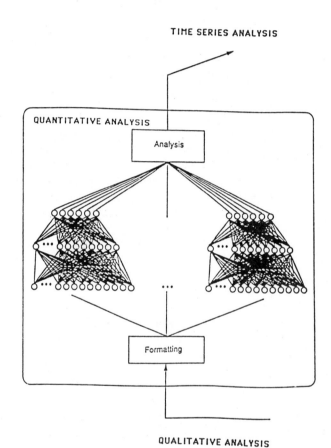

TIME SERIES ANALYSIS

QUANTITATIVE ANALYSIS

Analysis

Formatting

QUALITATIVE ANALYSIS

FIGURE 1. HIERARCHICAL SYSTEM SCHEME

ART2 is selected due to its powerful basic design characteristics. Fuzzy ART is selected because of its algorithm is developed based upon traditional neural network models such as ART 1, while incorporating fuzzy logic operators, hence enhancing the capabilities of ART 1 for analog input. Also, fuzzy ART includes two optional features (complement coding and slow recoding) which enables the network to overcome limitations associated with sequential data presentation. In addition, fuzzy ART is capable of retaining previously learned concepts in response to stochastic input fluctuations, while rapidly learning infrequent events. ART2-A is selected due to its speed and simplicity of the design. Fuzzy ARTMAP (based on hyper-rectangles) is selected because it has the capability to handle nonstationary stochastic signal and because of its supervised learning traits. RCE (based on hyper-sphere) is selected due to its unique design and speed. Standard Backpropagation is selected because of its popular utilization, hence a good reference for comparison with other selected paradigms. Cascade Correlation is selected because it represents a powerful network and contrary to Backpropagation, hidden units/layers are not pre-set in advance, rather each hidden unit/layer is added as needed. These selected schemes are are powerful paradigms which exhibit some desired properties for the quantitative level of hierarchical system.

II. SIGNAL DESCRIPTION

The signals utilized in this study are divided in two groups, the actual measured signals and the simulated signals. The measured signals are the pump power signals from pump number 1 of the EBR-II nuclear reactor. These samples are collected from sensors by plant data acquisition system(See Figure 2). Four sets of simulated signals were generated from the original signal representing the pump power simulated for four levels of degradation due to deposition of sodium oxide on the pump shaft using the system dynamics The system is based on noise analysis and utilizes Dynamic Data System (DDS) approach of Autoregressive Moving Average (ARMA) regression modeling. The mathematical representation of the model for a univariate system is:

$$(1- a_1 Z^{-1} - a_2 Z^{-2} ..... - a_n Z^{-n}) Y(k) =$$
$$(b_1 Z^{-1} - b_2 Z^{-2} .... - b_{n-1} Z^{-(n-1)}) R(k)$$

where,

$Y(k)$ = discrete signal data,
k = index of time interval,
$R(k)$ = white noise residual,
$Z^{-1} Y(k) = Y(k-1)$,
a,b = autoregressive, moving average parameters.

The autoregressive and moving average parameters are then decomposed into pairs of complex discrete roots (eigenvalues), i.e. for a second order dynamic :

$$r_{1,2} = a \pm b i$$

where,

$$a_1 = r_1 + r_2 \qquad a_2 = - r_1 r_2$$

similarly,

$$r^*_{1,2} = a^* \pm b^* i$$

where,

$$b_1 = r^*_1 + r^*_2 \qquad b_2 = - r^*_1 r^*_2$$

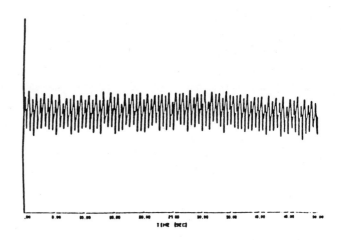

FIGURE 2. MEASURED PUMP POWER SIGNAL

The measure of wear progress in the system is achieved by introducing new parameters (representing an index of wear progress) which are based on the increase of the impact of the wear related dynamic on the signal fluctuation as degradation progresses [17,10]. The measured signals are referred to as category N. The four sets are classified as categories A, B, C, and D respectively. For the evaluation of the ART family, a specific time window from the measured signals (category N) is used to provide two sets of patterns, of 500 data points dimensionality representing first level of degradation. Similarly the two sets of simulated data for second level degradation are obtained from pattern B. In addition, to show the capability of Fuzzy Art in pattern recognition with less input dimensionality than is required for ART2 and ART2-A, twelve sets of data samples with a 250 input dimensionality were utilized.

For evaluation of the Fuzzy ARTMAP, RCE, Standard Backpropagation, and Cascade Correlation data of the five categories are used. This data is divided into various training and testing sets.

III. CASCADE CORRELATION PARADIGM

A major disadvantage with the Backpropagation algorithm is that it learns slowly. One of the reasons for this slowness is what is known as moving target problem [4]. Briefly stated, the problem is that all the units are trying to evolve into feature detectors simultaneously, complicating the problem faced by each individual unit. Cascade correlation scheme tries to overcome this moving target problem by adding just one hidden unit each time to the network. The hidden units are cascaded one after another until the network yields the desired performance. This architecture is termed as cascade architecture. For each new hidden unit, the correlation between the new unit's output and the residual error signal is maximized as defined below by:.

$$S = S_j |S_p (b - b_{ave}) (E_{p,j} - E_{ave})|$$

Where j is the network output at which the error is measured, p is the training pattern, b is the output of the candidate unit, Ej is the residual error at the output unit j. b_{ave} and E_{ave} are the values of b and Ej averaged over all the patterns. Hence the paradigm is termed as cascade correlation [4].

IV. FUZZY ARTMAP

Fuzzy ARTMAP [7,8] is a supervised learning paradigm. It incorporates two Fuzzy ART modules that are interlinked through a mapping field. The inputs to the Fuzzy ART modules are presented in complement form (i.e., A= (a,1,-a)). The symmetry achieved leads to the generation of hyper rectangles in multidimensional spaces. The process of learning increases the category resolution as a result of the growth of the rectangles and the decreasing value of weights. This increases the stability of the category formation process.

During training, at the start of each input presentation the vigilance factor of the first Fuzzy ART module equals the baseline vigilance of Fa, and the map field vigilance factor is set to 1. When a prediction by the first Fuzzy ART module is disconfirmed at the second Fuzzy ART module, match tracking is induced. The match tracking rule raises the vigilance factor of the first Fuzzy ART module enough to lead to activations of other categories. If the prediction of the first Fuzzy ART module is confirmed at second Fuzzy ART module, Map field learning takes place. This process implements a Maximum Learning Rule which maximizes code compression and enhances generalization

The neurodynamics of Fuzzy ARTMAP allows "incremental supervised learning of recognition categories and multidimensional maps in response to arbitrary sequences of analog or binary input vectors"[8]. In addition, architecture of the Fuzzy ARTMAP self organizes its internal structure as opposed to Standard Backpropagation.

V. ANALYSIS OF RESULTS

To evaluate and compare the learning and differentiation of patterns (N, A, and B) of the ART2, ART2-A, and Fuzzy ART networks several tests are performed. The result of this test is given in table I. The ART2 and ART2A networks are capable of distinguishing these patterns properly without any pre-processing of data. As shown in table I, the first two sets belonging to category N are assigned to category 0, the two sets of category A are in category 1, and category 2 is assigned to the two sets of category B. However, the Fuzzy ART network is not capable of proper classification of the 6 sets of raw (no pre-processing) data unless the normalization option is used. With the normalization pre-

processing, the fuzzy network is performs very well and classifies patterns properly as shown in table I[11,12].

TABLE I
Results of testing pattern classification for unsupervised paradigms of ART family

FILE	SIZE	NETWORK	PRE-PROCESSING	CATEGORY
NAB	500	ART2	NONE	001122
NAB	500	ART2A	NONE	001122
NAB	500	Fuzzy ART	L 1 NORMALIZATION	001122
NAB	250	Fuzzy ART	COMPLEMENT CODING	010123234545
NAB	250	ART2	NONE	010123214525
NAB	250	ART2A	NONE	010123214525

Next, another test is run to verify the fact that the Fuzzy ART networks is capable of proper classification when using its complement coding feature with much less input data than ART2 and ART2-A networks. Results of this test is shown in table I, with 250 input dimensionality in each set. Fuzzy ART is the only network among the ART networks tested here that is capable of properly distinguishing each pattern.

To evaluate and compare the performance of the selected supervised paradigms (RCE, Cascade, Backprop, and FUZZY ARTMAP) two separate Tests are performed. First only three categories(N,A, and B)are applied. Results are shown in table II.

TABLE II
Results of Fuzzy ARTMAP, RCE, Backprop, and Cascade for N, A, B based on three trials for testing

Trained on data	Tested on data	set size	number of patterns train test		Testing Performance (%) RCE	Cascade	Backprop	Fuzzy ARTMAP
File 1a	1b	55	7*	7	100	90	90	100
File 2a	2b	55	7	7	90	90	90	100
File 3a	3b	55	7	7	95	81	95	95

* This represents 7 sets of size 55 data for each pattern N, A, and B, hence 21 patterns in total.

Next, all supervised networks were trained and tested on five categories N, A, B, C and D. Results for each signal is listed in Table 3. Fuzzy ARTMAP gives the Best performance.

A. Order of Data Presentation

To observe the effect of data presentation,order was randomly changed to observe the effect on the performance. The networks were trained using data from different time windows, for the N,A,and B categories. Result show that performance does not seem to change with new order of presentation.

TABLE III
Network performance on signals N, A, B, and C D

NETWORK	N	A	B	C	D	TOTAL
RCE	6/7	6/7	5/7	7/7	5/7	83%
CASCADE	5/7	4/7	7/7	4/7	6/7	74%
BACKPROP	4/7	5/7	7/7	1/7	5/7	63%
FUZZY ARTMAP	5/7	6/7	7/7	6/7	6/7	86%

B. Fragmented/Noisy Data

To observe the effect of noisy data on the network pattern recognition performance, the above explained window corrected data sets were modified, and 1perturbations were introduced in each dataset. Even at low noise level of 10%, the performance of the networks are drastically reduced to 33% for RCE and Backprop, and to 0% for Cascade. However, Fuzzy ARTMAP was able to score 95%.

Training and recall speed are an important criteria for the development of real-time systems. For the purpose of network comparison, each paradigm was trained with same data set several times to get an average. For the supervised paradigms examined RCE and Fuzzy ARTMAP are the fastest networks. Cascade Correlation takes on the average, considerable less time than Backpropagation.

In the case of unsupervised paradigms, the ART family, all the tests were performed using fast learning trials. For ART2 the duration (on average) of one of these fast learning trials was two minutes using a simulator built in the C programming language for a Macintosh IIfx running under A/UX. The fast learning sessions required only one presentation of the input data set to provide stable results. Under the same condition a fast learning trial takes less than one second for both ART2A and Fuzzy ART, baring in mind that both have the same stabilization performance behavior.

V. CONCLUSIONS

RCE, Fuzzy ARTMAP, and Cascade Correlation networks determine their own network topology based on the input patterns. RCE performs better compared to Cascade Correlation network in the cases studied. Backpropogation gives performance close to Cascade Correlation but the latter seems to do better as number of patterns are increased.. RCE, Cascade, and Fuzzy ARTMAP are independent of presentation order in data patterns for the cases studied. In the case of Backprop input data are fed at random.

Noise as low as 10% of the data drastically affects the performance in all the three networks RCE, Cascade and backpropagation. Fuzzy ARTMAP was more robust in the presence of noise.

Several experiments are in progress to compare the plasticity and incremental learning capabilities of different artificial neural network paradigms. Nuclear reactor operations require systems capable of broadening their horizon, and evolving to cope with new information/situations. This is very important because the number of possible categories and new situations are unknown in several thousand hours of reactor operational time. Artificial neural networks might support the development of these systems.

REFERENCES

[1] Bachmann,C., Cooper, L., Dembo, A.,and Zeitiuni, O., "A relaxation model for memory with high storage density", Proceedings of the National Academy of Sciences, USA, 221, pp. 2088-3092.
[2] Carpenter, G. and Grossberg, S.,"A massively Parallel Architecture for a Self-Organizing Neural Pattern Recognition Machine", Computer Vision, Graphics, and Image Processing, 1987, vol. 37, pp. 54-117.
[3] Carpenter, G. and Grossberg, S.,"ART 2: Self-Organization of Stable Category Recognition Codes for Analog Input Patterns", Applied Optics, 1987, vol. 26, pp. 4919-4930.
[4] Carpenter, G. and Grossberg, S. and Reynolds, J.,"ARTMAP: Supervised Real-Time Learning and Classification of Nonstationary Data by a Self-Organizing Neural Network", PATTERN RECOGNITION By SELF-ORGANIZING NEURAL NETWORKS, G. Carpenter and S. Grossberg (EDs.), MIT Press, 1991, pp. 503-544.
[5] Carpenter, G. and Grossberg, S. and Rosen, D., "ART2-A: An adapdtive resonance algorithm for rapid category learning and recognition", CAS/CNS Technical Report, Boston University, CAS/CNS-91-011, 1991.
[6] Carpenter, G. and Grossberg, S. and Rosen, D., "Fuzzy ART", Poster paper presented at the Neural Networks for Vision and Image Processing Conference, Wang Institute of Boston University, May 10-12,1991.
[7] Carpenter, G. and Grossberg, S., Reynolds, J., and Rosen, D.,"Fuzzy ARTMAP: A Neural Network architecture for supervised Learning of Analog Multidimensional Maps",CAS/CNS Technical Report, CAS/CNS-91-016,1991.
[8] Carpenter, G. and Grossberg, S., Markuzon, N., Reynolds, J., and Rosen, D.,"Fuzzy ARTMAP: An Adaptive Resonance Architecture for incremental of Analog Multidimensional Maps", Proceedings of the International Joint Conference on Neural Networks, Baltimore, pp. III309-III314, 1992.
[9] Fahlman,S. and Lebiere,C.,"The Cascade Correlation learning Architecture", Technical Report CMU-CS-90-100, February 14,1990.

[10] Keyvan, S. , "Degradation Monitoring of Pump Components in a Nuclear Power Plant", American Neclear Society/ European Nuclear Society, Topical Meeting, July 31- August 3,1988 Snowbird, Utah.

[11] Keyvan, S. and Rabelo, L. C., "Sensor Signal Analysis by Neural Networks for Surveillance in Nuclear Reactors", IEEE Transactions on Nuclear Science, pp. 292-298, 1992.

[12] Keyvan, S., Rabelo, L. C. and Malkani, A., "Nuclear Reactor Condition Monitoring by Adaptive Resonance Theory", Proceedings of the International Joint Conference on Neural Networks, Baltimore, pp. III321-III328, 1992.

[13] Rumelhart, D., McClelland, J. and the PDP Research Group, PARALLEL DISTRIBUTED PROCESSING: Explorations in the Microstructure of Cognition, vol. 1:Foundations, Cambridge, Massachusetts: MIT Press, 1986.

[14] Scofield, C., Reilly, D., Elbaum, C. and Cooper, L., "Pattern Class Degeneracy in an unrestricted storage density memory", Nestor Inc., 1988.

Application of neural networks to fluorescent diagnostics of organic pollution in natural waters

Yuri V.Orlov, Igor G.Persiantsev, Sergey P.Rebrik
Microelectronics Department, Nuclear Physics Institute,
Moscow State University, Moscow, 119899, Russian Federation
E-mail on Internet: orlov@compnet.msu.su

Abstract—Use of a neural net allows one to build a sea water pollutant rapid diagnosis system. The neural net classifies sea water pollutant on the basis of its total luminescent spectroscopy (TLS) spectrum and is insensitive to the dissolved organic matter (DOM) spectrum variations. Gradual complication of task during learning is used to reach the minimal decision threshold value. The net gives an adequate answers to presentation of a mixture of pollutants spectra or spectra of unknown substances. Three-step determination of pollutant concentration comprises classification of a pollutant by basic net, its identification by auxiliary net, and concentration determination by linear neural net with a typical accuracy of 0.05 ppm. It is shown that use of a net with two hidden layers for classification of TLS-spectra of low resolution allows one to achieve classification thresholds close to those of standard TLS-spectra.

I. INTRODUCTION

Identification of a pollutant is a key problem in the field of rapid diagnosis of organic pollution of natural and technogeneous environment. In the total luminescent spectroscopy (TLS) method [1] every mixed condition of water environment corresponds to a two-dimensional TLS-spectrum (spectral signature), which is a matrix of emission intensity recorded in coordinates of excitation and emission wavelengths. For the fluorescent diagnostics of organic pollution an excitation range of 240-360 nm was used, and the spectral response was registered in the 200 nm wide window, red-shifted by 10 nm against the excitation wavelength. The standard size of the intensity matrix was 25 x 40 elements. The catalogue of potential natural water pollutants includes more than 50 samples (reference spectra of solutions and emulsions of pollutants in bidistilled water).

The pollutant samples classification made according to the similarity of their spectral images is given in Tables I–III. It turned out that such classification is in good correlation with the pollutant's physical and chemical properties. Fig.1 (a,b) presents spectra of substances from one class, while Fig.1 (c,d) demonstrates some typical spectra of substances, belonging to other classes.

In general the signature depends on the geographical region and is subject to seasonal change. In Figs.2a and 2b dissolved organic matter (DOM) spectra of the coastal zone of the Baltic and the North Sea are shown. The DOM type catalogue includes 7 samples mainly from the Baltic and the North Seas. The Raman Scattering Signal (RSS) of water molecules is dominant in fluorescence spectra of water with low DOM concentration (Fig.2c). The bidistilled water spectrum is shown in Fig.2d. Typical spectra of polluted sea water are shown in Fig.3.

Thus the recognition of a pollutant is hampered by the following: (a) camouflaging of the pollutant spectrum by the variable DOM spectrum and (b) the dependence of the TLS-spectrum shape on concentrations of the pollutant and DOM.

II. TRAINING PROCEDURE OF THE NEURAL NET

A well-known multi-layer feed forward neural net [2] and the backpropagation algorithm [3] were used.

To train the neural net we used 16 pollutant spectrum samples divided into 6 classes, different DOM spectra, and the RSS spectrum of water. The additive feature of the pollutant fluorescence signal, DOM fluorescence, and RSS allowed to synthesize the training spectrum for the concrete concentration of the pollutant just before presenting spectrum to the neural net. All spectra were normalized to unity at the point of maximum intensity.

The net was trained to determine the class of the pollutant. As spectra are normalized to unity in maximum, the spectrum for every mixture is determined only by the ratio of DOM and pollutant concentration (neglecting RSS of water). It is more convenient to use the pollutant's spectrum portion (PSP) in the overall spectrum instead of the pollutant's concentration. The resulting spectrum (without taking normalization into account) is given by:

$$S_i = PSP \cdot P_i + (1 - PSP) \cdot D_i,$$

where the i index corresponds to the i-th point in the spectrum and P_i and D_i are the intensities of the pollutant spectrum and DOM spectrum at that point.

Certain problem arises with the training process. The neural net must have a step-shaped dependence of the output neuron's activity on the PSP. It is clear that the PSP threshold value for which the pollutant's class determination is possible is not known beforehand. A too high threshold value will result in the underuse of the net's possibilities, and a too low value will confuse the net during the training process, as it will be expected to give an answer when necessary input information is absent. To solve this problem we introduced the following training schedule: at the beginning the net was trained on pure samples, including those of pure sea water, i.e. PSP = 1 or 0. At PSP = 0 all neurons should have zero activity; for PSP = 1 the activity of the neuron responsible for a given class is maximal (=1). After reaching a sufficiently high percentage of correct classifications (we had set a goal of 98% correct out of 100 presentations), the network weights are saved and the training set is modified : the net is given either the spectrum of pure water (PSP=0) or a spectrum of a randomly chosen pollutant, with a PSP also taken at random in the range 0.7-1. The learning goes on until the desired percentage of correct classification is reached. Then the lower PSP limit in the presented spectra is slightly decreased. Apparently, there exists the lowest PSP at which the percentage of correct classification can be maintained on the given level. The net weights obtained for this PSP are used for further data processing.

DOM spectra of the Baltic sea, the coastal North sea, the open water North sea, and spectrum of bidistilled water were used for training. This way the net was made insensitive to variations of DOM spectra.

III. CLASSIFICATION OF TLS-SPECTRA OF STANDARD SIZE

TLS-spectrum of standard size (SSS, 25x40 points) was presented to 1,000 input neurons; in the hidden layer there were 32 neurons, completely connected to the neurons of the input layer. In the output layer, that was completely connected to the hidden layer, the number of neurons corresponded to the number of classes into which the pollutant catalogue was divided.

Cumulative error was not used in the training process, the moment was equal to 0.9, training speed varied from 0.1 to 0.025. The number of single presentations after which decreasing the PSP did not allow the net to reach the desired percentage of correct classifications was about 4,000, and the lowest PSP limit was 0.2. The neural net was emulated on an IBM PC/AT-12MHz computer, equipped with a 80287 co-processor. A full training cycle required about 8 hours.

To test the neural net we used spectra, synthesized out of pollutants and DOM spectra that were not presented before (Table II), as well as real pollutant spectra recorded in sea water in the presence of DOM (Table III). When spectra of pure sea water (the first three spectra in Table II) were processed by neural net, the noise amplitude at the output layer did not exceed 0.1. This value was used to define threshold of the correct classification. A pollutant was considered to be correctly determined when the corresponding neuron's activity exceeded twice the maximum amplitude of the output noise, and exceeded the other neurons activity not less than two times. The threshold of correct classification, determined for the synthesized spectra, is shown in Tables I and II in the "Threshold for SSS" column. Typical value of the threshold is close to the lowest PSP limit reached in the training process.

All the test spectra from Table III, for which the pollutant's class is known, were classified by the neural net without mistakes. For other spectra from Table III, taken from a water body previously known to be polluted, the net classification indicates the possible presence of a pollutant. Unfortunately we had no alternative method to check the classification results.

To determine minimal detectable pollutant concentration, one needs DOM and pollutant spectra recorded at standard device sensitivity. The RSS can be used for the sensitivity standardization. Unfortunately, in many cases the pollutant's spectra and the RSS strongly overlap, and it is not possible to determine the RSS amplitude correctly. A high level of fluorescence signal also decreases the accuracy of normalization by the RSS.

As the pollutant detection threshold depends on the DOM concentration in water, two values of the threshold in concentration units are given in Tables I, II for the spectra that could be normalized to the RSS. The lower values correspond to the total absence of DOM, and the higher values were obtained for extremely high DOM concentrations (10 mg/l of organic carbon) typical for coastal zones of closed seas, i.e. in the most unfavorable conditions for diagnostics.

We tested the neuroclassifier on mixtures of pollutants and for all PSPs exceeding the threshold value the neural net did detect the presence of pollution. However, determination of the components classes is typically possible at higher PSP values and not in every case. Still, simultaneous activity of a number of output neurons can be used to detect situations where the system is responding to a complex signal.

At times it is necessary to know not only the class, but also the concentration of the pollutant. As each class contains a number of pollutants spectra with different fluorescence efficiencies, the identification of pollutant must precede the determination of concentration. This task can be solved by first classifying the pollutant by basic net. From a second, an auxiliary network, trained to identify the pollutants belonging to the determined class, is used. (We used a net similar to the one described above, but its hidden layer had from 4 to 8 neurons, and the size of output layer was equal to the number of pollutants in the given class.) Finally a neural net consisting of a single neuron with a linear output function determines concentration of the identified pollutant. Spectra in relative (i.e. normalized to the RSS) units were presented at the input of the neuron (the intensity was normalized to unity at the RSS maximum). Concentrations of the pollutant and DOM used to synthesize the spectrum were varied randomly in a wide range and the output neuron was trained to give the pollutant's concentration in ppm units (parts per million). Such nets were trained for a number of samples belonging to different classes. The training process took about 500 presentations. It was found

out that such a simple net can determine the concentration with the accuracy of $+/-$ 0.02 ppm.

IV. CLASSIFICATION OF TLS-SPECTRA OF DIMINISHED SIZE

Initially the registration of TLS-spectra of standard size was provided by a CCD. During further development of spectrometer it was suggested to use more efficient photo-electron multiplier with 20 channels of registration. So an important question arises - whether a neural network is able to classify spectra successfully if the amount of input information is significantly reduced (by one half in our case)?

TLS-spectra of diminished size (SDS, 25x20 points) were formed by averaging of adjacent points in SSS. We used different configurations of neural networks with one hidden layer (the number of hidden neurons varied from 32 to 64). In all cases thresholds of correct classification have increased 1.5-2.5 times (compared to those of SSS), while some of spectra of pure water were classified as polluted.

We also tried to use SDS formed from a left half of SSS (it is the most informative part of TLS-spectra of most pollutants), but the absence of its right half, where maximum of DOM fluorescence and total maximum at low pollutant concentration are located, does not allow to estimate the degree of water pollution, and all spectra of pure water were classified as polluted one.

As a next attempt to classify SDS we have used a net with two hidden layers of 32 neurons each. Every consequent layer was fully connected to the previous one. SDS were formed by averaging of SSS. Typical number of learning presentations increased from 4000 (for a net with one hidden layer) to 12000. As the computational cost of one presentation was approximately halved, the classification time also halved, so the learning time increased only 1.5 times. Thresholds of correct classification and limits of minimal detectable pollutant concentration for this net are presented in Tables I and II in the "Threshold for SDS" column. One can see, that this net has classification thresholds of SDS close to those of the net with one hidden layer in the case of SSS classification.

V. CONCLUSIONS

The neural net suggested in this paper is able to classify sea water pollution on the basis of its TLS (total luminescent spectroscopy) spectrum.

Learning is based on the gradual complication of classification task, what is attained by iterative decreasing of a pollutant concentration in presented mixtures. Also, during this procedure the minimal PSP (pollutant's spectrum portion) value for which the net can still be trained is reached.

The neural net is made insensitive to the DOM spectrum variations.

A typical minimal detectable PSP value is 0.2. This value corresponds to a pollutant concentration of 0.5-10 ppm for a high DOM concentration in water (10 mg/l of organic carbon), i.e. in a situation most difficult for diagnostics.

The net is capable of giving adequate answers when spectra corresponding to a mixture of two pollutants or spectra of unknown substances are presented. Simultaneous activity of a number of output neurons can be used to detect complex situations.

A three-step procedure is used for determination of pollutant concentration : at first basic net classifies a pollutant, then an auxiliary net corresponding to the determined class identifies a pollutant. Finally a linear neural net determines concentration of pollutant with a typical accuracy of 0.05 ppm; variations of the DOM spectrum shape and amplitude in reasonable limits do not affect the neural net's functioning.

It is shown that a net with one hidden layer can not classify TLS-spectra of low resolution, while addition of a second hidden layer allows to achieve classification thresholds close to those of standard TLS-spectra.

ACKNOWLEDGMENT

The authors would like to thank S.M.Babichenko and L.V.Poryvkina for providing the TLS-database and for helpful discussions of the work.

REFERENCES

1. A.E.Dudelzak, S.M.Babichenko, L.V.Poryvkina, K.U.Saar, "Total luminescent spectroscopy for remote laser diagnostics of natural water conditions", Appl. Opt., vol.30, no. 4, pp.453-458, 1991.

2. Lippmann R.P., "An Introduction to Computing with Neural Nets", IEEE ASSP Mag., vol.3, no.4, pp. 4-22, 1987.

3. Rumelhart D.E., Hinton G.E., and Williams R.J., "Learning Internal Representations by Error Propagation", *In: Parallel Distributed Processing: Explorations in the Microstructures of Cognition*, vol.1: Foundations, MIT Press, 1986, pp. 318-362.

TABLE 1. Training patterns

PATTERN	Classification	Threshold for SSS		Threshold for SDS	
		PSP	ppm*	PSP	ppm*
Baltic sea DOM	-	-	-	-	-
Bidistilled water	-	-	-	-	-
Pas - de - Kale DOM	-	-	-	-	-
Central part of North sea DOM	-	-	-	-	-
Belorussian crude oil Y-02	A	0.1	0.15-0.75	0.11	0.09-0.75
Perm crude oil O-73	A	0.11	0.13-0.5	0.14	0.1-0.65
Diesel oil LS-05	A	0.08	-	0.08	-
Compressor oil K-12-59	B	0.2	0.8-10.0	0.18	0.43-5.0
Transmission oil TEP-15-48	B	0.13	0.6-5.0	0.13	0.36-3.6
Residual oil	B	0.17	0.5-3.0	0.17	0.25-2.3
Unrefined machine oil SHF-68	C	0.14	0.5-4.0	0.11	0.25-3.5
Shale oil (medium fraction)	C	0.14	-	0.14	-
Diesel oil M-10B-67	C	0.14	0.5-2.5	0.07	0.12-1.6
Turbine oil T-30-66	D	0.13	0.08-0.75	0.14	0.04-0.9
Petrol fraction (oil-shale)	E	0.17	-	0.11	-
Gas turbine oil (oil-shale)	E	0.2	-	0.14	-
Timol	F	0.14	-	0.18	-
5-metil-2-etil-rezorcin	F	0.13	-	0.17	-
Rezorcin	F	0.11	-	0.14	-
Phenol	F	0.13	-	0.17	-

TABLE 2. Testing patterns

PATTERN	Classification	Threshold for SSS		Threshold for SDS	
		PSP	ppm*	PSP	ppm*
Baltic sea DOM	-	-	-	-	-
South of North sea DOM	-	-	-	-	-
Skagerrak DOM	-	-	-	-	-
Kaliningrad crude oil M-06	A	0.11	0.14-0.75	0.14	0.11-0.75
Siberian crude oil P-01	A	0.1	0.09-0.4	0.13	0.07-0.45
Diesel oil AV-87	A	0.1	-	0.13	-
Kerosene	A	0.13	0.75-3.0	0.18	0.55-4.2
Cylinder oil C-11-33	B	0.14	1.0-10.0	0.14	0.45-4.0
Industrial oil I20-A60	B	0.17	0.75-5.0	0.2	0.33-3.6
Shale oil (heavy fraction)	C	0.14	-	0.14	-
Transformer oil TF-31	D	0.13	0.05-0.5	0.14	0.03-0.6
Petrol AI-93	E	0.4	-	0.2	-
2-metil-rezorcin	F	0.13	-	0.17	-
5-geptil-rezorcin	F	0.14	-	0.18	-
4-geptil-rezorcin	F	0.2	-	0.26	-
5-metil-rezorcin	F	0.13	-	0.17	-
Stirol	F	0.13	-	0.17	-
Para-c-rezorcin	F	0.14	-	0.18	-

* The limits correspond to the DOM concentration variance in the range of 0.1-10 mg/l of organic carbon.

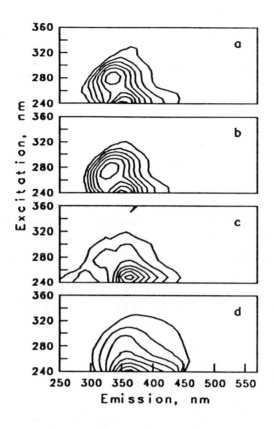

Fig.1.   Some examples from spectral catalog of pollutants:
         a— Siberian crude oil,
         b— Diesel oil,
         c— Turbine oil,
         d— Shale oil.

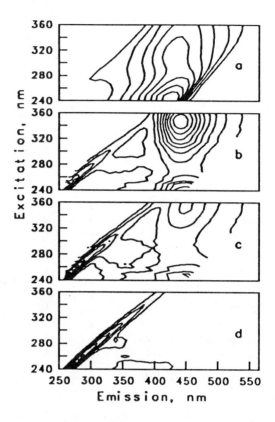

Fig.2   Spectra of Dissolved Organic Matter (DOM) :
         a—Gulf of Finland,
         b—central part of English Channel,
         c— central part of the North Sea,
         d— bidistilled water.

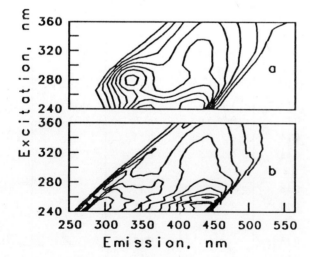

Fig.3   Typical spectra of polluted water of the Baltic Sea:
         a— water polluted by Siberian crude oil (see Fig.1a),
         b— water with unknown pollutant.

TABLE 3. Independent testing patterns

PATTERN	Classification
Siberian crude oil P-01	A
Perm crude oil 0-73	A
Turbine oil T-30-66	D
Petrol AI-93	E
	Network class
Baltic Sea (polluted water)	C
Baltic Sea (polluted water)	C
Baltic Sea (polluted water)	C
Baltic Sea (polluted water)	C
Baltic Sea (polluted water)	C
Kattegat (polluted water)	C

Genetic Algorithm based Input Selection for a Neural Network Function Approximator with Applications to SSME Health Monitoring[†]

Charles C. Peck and Atam P. Dhawan
Dept. of Electrical and Computer Engineering
University of Cincinnati
Cincinnati, OH 45221

Claudia M. Meyer
Sverdrup Technology, Inc.
NASA Lewis Research Center Group
Brook Park, OH 44142

Abstract— A genetic algorithm is used to select the inputs to a neural network function approximator. In the application considered, modeling critical parameters of the Space Shuttle Main Engine, the functional relationships among measured parameters is unknown and complex. Furthermore, the number of possible input parameters is quite large. Many approaches have been proposed for input selection, but they are either not possible due to insufficient instrumentation, are subjective, or they do not consider the complex multivariate relationships between parameters. Due to the optimization and space searching capabilities of genetic algorithms, they were employed in this study to systematize the input selection process. The results suggest that the genetic algorithm can generate parameter lists of high quality without the explicit use of problem domain knowledge. Suggestions for improving the performance of the input selection process are also provided.

I. INTRODUCTION

There is considerable interest within the space industry in improving the fault detection and isolation capabilities of rocket engine condition monitoring systems, both real-time and post-test. This requires developing accurate models of engine parameters based on other measured parameters. Developing accurate models is particularly difficult due to the highly complex, non-linear nature of rocket engines, the limited suite of measured parameters, and the large variability of behavior among engines of the same design.

It has been shown that neural networks with one hidden layer can uniformly approximate any continuous function [1, 2, 3]. Furthermore, neural networks are well-suited for problems in which the exact relationships between inputs and outputs are complex or unknown [4, 1]. These conclusions may be applied to dynamical systems if the system state is sufficiently represented in the inputs of the neural network. For these reasons, feedforward neural networks have been used to model critical parameters of the Space Shuttle Main Engine (SSME) during the start-up transient and they have been shown to be effective [4].

A task that is critical to the success of neural network modeling of complex, dynamical systems such as the SSME is the choice of input parameters. There are several constraints that complicate this task. First, while the instrumentation of the SSME is extensive, it is not complete. Therefore, it is unlikely that it will be possible to completely describe any subsystem input or output. This makes the use of characteristic equations particularly difficult [5]. Second, as was discussed above, it is necessary to provide enough state information to model the desired parameter. Finally, it is not practical to use a large number of inputs for the following reasons. First, large input sets make training the network considerably more difficult. In addition, the input set should be small to reduce the hardware and/or computational complexity and to reduce the processing delay. This last consideration is especially important if the system is to be used for real-time modeling.

The effect of the input size on the system performance is further exacerbated by the use of multiple past values (or time windows) of each input. A time window of each input parameter is typically used in order to provide time dependent information. The size of the window multiplies the number of inputs to the network. For example, if 10 parameters are chosen as network inputs and a time window of the past ten values is used for each parameter, then the effective number of inputs to the network is 100.

Many approaches for input selection have been proposed or used. These include characteristic equations, engine schematic analyses, correlations between candidate input parameters and the modeled parameter, and expert advice [5]. As suggested above, the use of some of these methods is limited due to the lack of sufficient instrumentation. Furthermore, some of these methods are subjective or they do not adequately measure the multivariate dependencies present in the system. For these reasons, a systematic approach for input selection under the existing

[†]This work was supported by a contract from the NASA Space Engineering Center for System Health Management Technology at the University of Cincinnati

constraints is desired.

The choice of inputs may be modeled as an optimization problem where the space of possible solutions is quite large. In fact, many hundreds of sensors are used for monitoring during test firings of the SSME. If only 100 sensors were used, then 2^{100} distinct input sets would exist. Since an exhaustive search through a space with this order of magnitude is clearly not possible, an alternative search method is required.

Genetic algorithms are well suited for searching in a large parameter space [6, 7]. Through the use of seeding (the process of providing an initial set of possible solutions), genetic algorithms search from a set of solutions or starting points, rather than a single starting point. Genetic algorithms are not derivative based, thus they can search spaces where methods such as conjugate descent fail. They work with both discrete and continuous parameters. They explore the parameter space and exploit the similarities between highly fit candidate solutions [6, 8]. Furthermore, through the use of elitism (a variant method in which the best solution of a generation is promoted unaltered to the next generation), a genetic algorithm can be guaranteed to perform at least as well the methods used to seed or initialize it. For these reasons, a genetic algorithm was used to select the inputs to a neural network that modeled an SSME parameter during the start-up transient.

This paper will first present the design issues and methodology applied to the selection of SSME input parameters. A presentation and discussion of results will follow. Finally, the conclusions and ideas for future work will be presented.

II. DESIGN ISSUES AND METHODOLOGY

There are three fundamental design requirements for applying genetic algorithms: encoding candidate solutions onto binary strings, decoding and evaluating a binary string, and developing a fitness function that will guide the genetic algorithm to produce the desired results.

For this application, encoding candidate solutions onto binary strings is trivial since a single bit is sufficient to indicate whether a particular parameter is to be included in the network input set. Accordingly, the string, or *chromosome,* has one bit for every candidate engine parameter. To reduce the size of the search space, redundant sensor measurements were eliminated and those parameters believed to be nearly independent of the modeled parameter were not included in the candidate parameter set. This reduced the size of the candidate parameter set to 49 parameters from the hundreds of parameters described above.

Decoding and evaluating a chromosome is also straightforward. First, the number of parameters encoded in the chromosome is determined. Then, a neural network with the proper number of inputs is created and the weights are randomly initialized. Each network is provided with ten hidden layer nodes. A training set is created using the parameters indicated in the chromosome. The input sets are expanded to include a time window of five past values for each parameter. Finally, the neural network is trained. To limit the computational requirements in training the neural networks, the QuickProp learning algorithm is used [9] and each network is trained for only 100 epochs, which was determined empirically to be sufficient to distinguish the performance of one network configuration from another. According to the analysis provided in [9], this should be comparable to 1000 epochs of training with standard backpropagation.

The fitness function must be able to guide the genetic algorithm to produce the smallest set of input parameters that are sufficient for a neural network function approximator to accurately predict a modeled parameter. Ideally, the resulting neural network function approximator should be able to learn and generalize the relationships between the input parameters and the output parameter such that the approximation is accurate even for test firings not encountered during training. Of these two network performance objectives, the determination of learning ability is the most straightforward and the only one considered in this paper. To provide the guidance described above, the fitness function must measure some properties of the candidate solution and compute a number that indicates the "fitness" of that solution. The properties considered in this paper include the performance of the generated neural network, the convergence properties of the training process, and the number of inputs. It should be noted prior to discussing fitness function implementation that, in this paper, the smaller the fitness function value, the better the evaluated solution is considered to be.

The performance of the neural network is determined by measuring the approximation error of the network on the training data. This provides a measure of how well a network is capable of learning the input/output relationships.

As mentioned above, the convergence properties of the training process are also considered in the fitness function. In this manner either early convergence or late convergence can be favored. This is important since, as described above, the neural networks are not fully trained during the genetic algorithm in order to reduce the computational requirements. To understand the relevance, consider two networks, one that has a low training error and early convergence, and another that has a higher training error and late convergence. It is not clear which network should be considered better. It may be argued that the first network is better since it converged to a stable condition rapidly. Conversely, it may be argued that the second network is better since it is still in a rapid learning phase

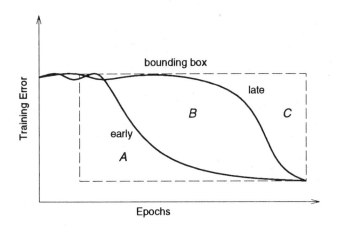

Figure 1: Early versus Late Training Error Convergence

and, with further training, its error performance may exceed the performance of the first network. Both of these cases were used in the overall system to evolve input parameter sets.

The method used to reflect the convergence properties exploits the observation that the training error of each neural network began on a high plateau and remained there, at least briefly, before falling rapidly, as shown in Figure 1. Since oscillations and unusual patterns in the training error were not observed, integration of the area bounded by the error curve and a bounding rectangle could be performed. To favor early convergence, the convergence term is computed by integrating this area of integration and normalizing it by the area of the bounding box. For example, if A, B, and C denote the normalized areas of their corresponding regions in Figure 1, the convergence term is A for the early training error curve and $A + B$ for the late training error curve. The convergence term favoring late convergence is simply the complement of the convergence term favoring early convergence. This corresponds to a convergence term of $B + C$ for the early training error curve and C for the late training error curve.

As described above, the fitness of a candidate solution is also related to the size of the input parameter set. Including the input set size constraint in the fitness function could be done simply by multiplying the training error by the number of parameters selected. This, however, results in a very strong constraint. The strength of the size constraint can be controlled by adding a constant to the number of parameters selected. A small offset created in this manner yields a strong size constraint, whereas a large offset yields a weak one. The fitness function may be further adjusted by squaring the size constraint term. This increases the strength of the constraint as the number of parameters increases.

The design of the size constraint term in the fitness function is further complicated by the size disparity between the chromosomes within the seeding population. The initial population of the genetic algorithm was seeded in two ways. First, four sets of input parameters were selected based on prior knowledge of SSME behavior. These seeding sets consist of approximately 10 parameters each. The remainder of the initial population was generated with the use of a random number generator, which selected each input parameter with a probability of 50%. Thus, the randomly selected seeding sets consist of approximately 25 parameters each. If all of the seeding sets were approximately the same size, a single offset could be chosen that would yield the desired input set size at the end of the evolution process. The size disparity, however, between the knowledge-based seeding sets and the randomly selected seeding sets results in either a strongly biased choice of input parameters or it results in input sets that are too large.

For the work presented in this paper, generation dependent offsets were used to avoid biasing the results while ensuring satisfaction of the size constraint. Initially, the offset was set very high to allow the candidate solutions to compete primarily on the basis of the training error. As the genetic algorithm proceeded, the size constraint was made progressively stronger. By the last generation the offset was small, yielding a strong bias for shorter lists. This change of offset with respect to the generation will be referred to as an offset progression. Two offset progressions were used: one yielding a generally weak size constraint, and another yielding a generally strong size constraint. The offset progression yielding the weaker size constraint ranged from 71 initially to 14 over 20 generations. The other ranged from 45 initially to 7 over 20 generations. The resulting fitness functions are shown in Equations 1 and 2, respectively:

$$f_{\text{weak}} = C \frac{(c + 71 - 3G)^2}{(71 - 3G)^2} \times \text{Training Error}, \quad (1)$$

$$f_{\text{strong}} = C \frac{(c + 45 - 2G)^2}{(45 - 2G)^2} \times \text{Training Error}, \quad (2)$$

where f is the fitness function value, C is the convergence term (which may be 1.0 if no convergence properties are considered), c is the number of parameters in the candidate input list, and G, which ranges from 0 to 19, is the generation number.

The process for selecting sets of input parameters proceeded in two stages. The first stage consisted of independently evolving three different populations of candidate solutions. One population was evolved using a fitness function without any training convergence bias. The other two were biased for early and late training convergence. Each of these populations was evolved with a weak size constraint to favor lower approximation error.

The ten most fit chromosomes from each of the three first stage populations were used along with 20 randomly generated chromosomes to seed the second stage genetic algorithm. The primary purposes of the second stage were to merge the three diverse and independent populations, and to further reduce the size of the parameter lists. To meet this last objective a fitness function with a strong size constraint and no convergence bias was used.

The use of three independent first stage populations increases diversity, robustness, and resistance to domination by "Super Individuals." "Super Individuals" are suboptimal solutions that are significantly more fit than other solutions early in the evolution process. This allows them to dominate a subsequent population after a few generations. The concept of "Super Individuals" should not be confused with elitism. Elitism only guarantees that the best string will be promoted to the next generation unaltered, it does not imply dominance.

Since the fitness functions described above are *noisy*, they provide less guidance than deterministic fitness functions. They are noisy because the approximation errors of a particular network will vary from the errors of other implementations of the same network. Implementations of a particular network vary because they are each initialized with random weights. Although different implementations perform similarly after training, they perform differently due to their generally unique final weight sets.

When noisy fitness functions are present, the *generational replacement* technique is typically used [7] to mitigate the undesirable effects of inaccurate fitness evaluations. Generational replacement is implemented by completely replacing the population each generation. In addition to using generational replacement in this study, each chromosome was reevaluated whenever it occurred in a population. Combined, these techniques "temporally" average the effects of fitness function variations on chromosomal representation in future populations.

III. RESULTS AND DISCUSSION

The fundamental output of the genetic algorithm consists of candidate parameter lists to be used as inputs to a neural network for modeling a particular parameter during start-up. The parameter that was modeled is the SSME's High Pressure Oxidizer Turbine (HPOT) discharge temperature, which has a Parameter IDentification (PID) number of 233. The three parameter lists generated by training-based fitness functions with the best fitness values from the last generation of the second stage are presented in Table 1. These three lists, labeled GA-1–GA-3, have been shown to be physically reasonable in the context of the SSME [10]. An additional list, labeled REF in Table 1, is also presented for the purpose of comparison. This "reference" list has been modified from the one presented in [4] to exclude autoregressive information. The PID's in each of these lists are described in Table 2.

It should be noted that the knowledge-based seeding lists were outperformed early in the process by genetic algorithm generated parameter lists. This may be explained by the larger number of input parameters included in the randomly selected seeding sets and the lack of a strong size constraint in the early generations. The larger sets of parameters had smaller training errors and they were not penalized for their size. While the behavior and results of the genetic algorithm were certainly affected by the knowledge-based seeding sets, the guidance provided by these sets did not appear to be strong.

To evaluate the performance of the parameter lists produced by the genetic algorithm and the reference list, feedforward neural networks were trained for 20,000 cycles using the standard backpropagation learning algorithm. Each network had one hidden layer with 10 hidden units and used a time window of five past values. The resulting networks were then used to approximate PID 233 using measured parameters from 12 actual SSME test firings. Four of the test firings were used for training the networks and eight were used to validate the resulting models. The results, as represented by the mean squared error (MSE), the normalized MSE, and the maximum percent error, are shown in Tables 3, 4, 5, and 6. A summary of these results is presented in Tables 7 and 8. The results are divided into two groups: one presenting the aggregate performance of the networks on the training data (Table 7), and the other presenting the aggregate performance of the networks on the validation data (Table 8). The first group measures the learning capabilities of the networks and the second group measures the generalization capabilities.

In considering the performance of the different networks, it should be recognized that even though the networks are fully trained, their final performance is still dependent on their weight initializations. Thus, the performance of another network implementation may differ. It is clear from the results that the parameter list GA-1 has the worst error performance of the four lists. This is compensated by the fact that this is the shortest parameter list. Even though the error performance of this parameter list is the worst, it is still close to the performance of the other lists, including the reference list.

The parameter lists GA-2 and GA-3 outperformed the reference list on the training data and performed only slightly worse than the reference list on the validation data. Due to the large standard deviations of validation data error, the differences in the error means between these two particular network implementations cannot be considered statistically significant. Thus, it can concluded that the parameter lists GA-2 and GA-3 perform approximately as well as the reference list.

IV. CONCLUSIONS AND FUTURE WORK

The results indicate that the error performance of the genetic algorithm generated parameter lists is roughly the

Table 1: Parameter Lists

Parameter List	Number of PIDs	Parameters
GA-1	6	21 58 209 734 951 1050
GA-2	7	21 58 209 327 734 951 1058
GA-3	8	21 52 58 209 327 734 951 1050
REF	9	40 42 59 231 480 1205 1212 O/Cs OPBs

Table 2: Parameter Descriptions

PID	Description
21	Main Combustion Chamber Oxidizer Injection Temperature
40	Oxidizer Preburner Oxidizer Valve Actuator Position
42	Fuel Preburner Oxidizer Valve Actuator Position
52	High Pressure Fuel Pump Discharge Pressure
58	Fuel Preburner Chamber Pressure
59	Preburner Boost Pump Discharge Pressure
209	High Pressure Oxidizer Pump Inlet Pressure
231	High Pressure Fuel Turbine Discharge Temperature
233[†]	High Pressure Oxidizer Turbine Discharge Temperature
327	High Pressure Oxidizer Pump Balance Cavity Pressure
480	Oxidizer Preburner Chamber Pressure
734	Low Pressure Oxidizer Pump Shaft Speed
951	High Pressure Oxidizer Pump Primary Seal Drain Pressure
1050	Oxidizer Tank Discharge Temperature
1058	Engine Oxidizer Inlet Temperature
1205	Facility Fuel Flow
1212	Facility Oxidizer Flow
O/Cs	Dummy Parameter indicating Open/Closed Loop Operation
OPBs	Dummy Parameter indicating Oxidizer Preburner Prime Time

[†] the modeled parameter

same as that of the reference list. Furthermore, in all cases, the genetic algorithm generated parameter lists are smaller than the reference list. Thus, the genetic algorithm was able to systematically generate physically reasonable parameter lists that performed well without the explicit use of problem domain knowledge.

Many improvements for the input selection process have been envisioned. One may, for example, modify the fitness evaluation function to be dependent on the error of a validation set instead of the training set. This would favor parameter lists that yield networks with superior generalizing capabilities instead of lists that yield rapid learning.

As demonstrated by the GA-1 list, smaller size can be overemphasized compared to the error performance. Instead of favoring a parameter list of the smallest size, a list of a particular size could be favored (e.g., the largest tolerable size). This would favor the inclusion of sufficient information while discouraging the use of parameters that

Table 3: Error Statistics from Parameter List GA-1

Test Firing	Training/ Validation	MSE	NMSE	Max. % Error
B1046	T	3.787033	0.000322	2.2330
B1060	T	14.743364	0.001223	4.8150
B1061	V	20.168583	0.001657	10.4348
B1062	V	34.029559	0.002832	9.6225
B1063	V	39.671779	0.003301	6.9063
B1066	V	30.608499	0.002532	7.5330
B1067	V	42.103255	0.003498	9.2189
B1070	T	11.699498	0.000945	3.1922
B1071	V	63.607371	0.005154	20.8187
B1072	V	23.816642	0.001898	8.3420
B1075	V	20.268258	0.001669	10.0018
B1077	T	12.931541	0.001045	5.3681

Table 4: Error Statistics from Parameter List GA-2

Test Firing	Training/ Validation	MSE	NMSE	Max. % Error
B1046	T	3.341027	0.000284	2.0253
B1060	T	6.059692	0.000503	3.1339
B1061	V	19.080619	0.001568	5.9461
B1062	V	37.601837	0.003129	9.9597
B1063	V	35.212338	0.002930	6.6999
B1066	V	33.799122	0.002796	7.3425
B1067	V	36.724494	0.003051	7.9440
B1070	T	10.692421	0.000864	3.6021
B1071	V	48.479267	0.003929	15.9965
B1072	V	17.781945	0.001417	5.1814
B1075	V	35.017457	0.002884	11.4959
B1077	T	7.973934	0.000644	2.6040

Table 5: Error Statistics from Parameter List GA-3

Test Firing	Training/Validation	MSE	NMSE	Max. % Error
B1046	T	4.015642	0.000341	1.7042
B1060	T	6.114787	0.000507	2.5343
B1061	V	20.477665	0.001682	6.2484
B1062	V	40.542411	0.003374	10.5837
B1063	V	38.320758	0.003188	7.1349
B1066	V	38.782970	0.003208	8.8021
B1067	V	39.245907	0.003261	8.4381
B1070	T	10.516996	0.000850	3.2462
B1071	V	53.008396	0.004296	18.9413
B1072	V	17.990471	0.001434	4.7040
B1075	V	33.172788	0.002732	12.0369
B1077	T	6.889614	0.000557	2.3684

Table 6: Error Statistics from Parameter List REF

Test Firing	Training/Validation	MSE	NMSE	Max. % Error
B1046	T	6.652181	0.000565	3.8462
B1060	T	7.375382	0.000612	3.0370
B1061	V	22.370471	0.001838	4.8509
B1062	V	23.747774	0.001976	7.2832
B1063	V	28.076726	0.002336	7.9618
B1066	V	16.538060	0.001368	7.6115
B1067	V	20.482848	0.001702	6.6011
B1070	T	6.588053	0.000532	3.8668
B1071	V	50.654580	0.004105	11.0878
B1072	V	42.897089	0.003419	6.7544
B1075	V	25.213499	0.002077	9.4449
B1077	T	7.809484	0.000631	4.5456

Table 7: Summary of Parameter List Performance on Training Data

Parm. List	MSE		NMSE		Max.	
	μ	σ	μ	σ	μ	σ
GA-1	10.790359	4.833357	0.000884	0.000392	3.902086	1.445958
GA-2	7.016768	3.101272	0.000574	0.000244	2.841333	0.679829
GA-3	6.884260	2.709112	0.000564	0.000212	2.463281	0.633292
REF	7.106275	0.589258	0.000585	0.000045	3.823920	0.617108

Table 8: Summary of Parameter List Performance on Validation Data

Parm. List	MSE		NMSE		Max.	
	μ	σ	μ	σ	μ	σ
GA-1	34.284241	14.485731	0.002818	0.001180	10.359750	4.397353
GA-2	32.962132	10.068242	0.002713	0.000832	8.820735	3.563816
GA-3	35.192673	11.349328	0.002897	0.000937	9.611175	4.430940
REF	28.747631	11.808645	0.002353	0.000932	7.699442	1.889502

do not significantly improve the error performance.

V. ACKNOWLEDGMENTS

The public domain genetic algorithm GENESIS Version 5.0, written by John J. Grefenstette, was used for the work described in this paper. Furthermore, the fitness evaluation function is a highly modified and optimized derivative of Terry Regier's implementation of the QuickProp training algorithm.

REFERENCES

[1] S. Chen, S. A. Billings, and P. M. Grant. Non-Linear Systems Identification Using Neural Networks. Research Report 370, University of Edinburgh, Mayfield Road, Edinburgh, Scotland, August 1989.

[2] G. Cybenko. Approximation by Superpositions of a Sigmoidal Function. *Mathematics of Control, Signals, and Systems*, 2:303–314, 1989.

[3] K. Funahashi. On the Approximate Realization of Continuous Mappings by Neural Networks. *Neural Networks*, 2:183–192, 1989.

[4] Claudia M. Meyer and William A. Maul. The Application of Neural Networks to the SSME Startup Transient. AIAA 91-2530, July 1991.

[5] D. K. Makel, W. H. Flaspohler, and T. W. Bickmore. Sensor Data Validation and Reconstruction, Phase 1: System Architecture Study. NASA CR 187122, 1991. Contract No. NAS3-25883.

[6] David E. Goldberg. *Genetic Algorithms in Search, Optimization, and Machine Learning.* Addison-Wesley Publishing Company, Inc., Reading, Massachusetts, 1989.

[7] Lawrence Davis. *Handbook of Genetic Algorithms.* Van Nostrand Reinhold, New York, 1991.

[8] David J. Powell, Michael M. Skolnick, and Siu Shing Tong. Interdigitation: A Hybrid Technique for Engineering Design Optimization Employing Genetic Algorithms, Expert Systems, and Numerical Optimization. In L. Davis, editor, *Handbook of Genetic Algorithms*, chapter 20, pages 312–331. Van Nostrand Reinhold, New York, 1991.

[9] Scott E. Fahlman. Faster-Learning Variations on Back-Propagation: An Empirical Study. In D. Touretzky, G. Hinton, and T. Sejnowski, editors, *Proceedings of the 1988 Connectionist Models Summer School*, pages 38–51, San Mateo, CA, June 1988. Carnegie Mellon University, Morgan Kaufmann Publishers.

[10] Charles C. Peck, Atam P. Dhawan, and Claudia M. Meyer. SSME Parameter Modeling using Neural networks and Genetic Algorithm based Input Selection. Technical Report TR_141/1/93/ECE, Dept. of Elect. and Comp. Eng., Univ. of Cincinnati, Dept. of Elect. and Comp. Eng., Univ. of Cincinnati, Cincinnati, OH 45221, January 1993.

Chapter 23:   Management

Chapter 23
Management

The notion of utilizing neural networks to assist managers is new. **Paper 23.1** describes a neural network that is used to determine the contractual parameters of incentive power contracts.

A NEURAL NETWORK APPROACH TO EVALUATE CONTRACTUAL PARAMETERS OF INCENTIVE POWER CONTRACTS

K.P. Wong   A.K. David
Department of Electrical Engineering
Hong Kong Polytechnic
HONG KONG

Abstract - This paper proposes a neural network approach to determining the contractual parameters of incentive power contracts. It describes the incentive power contract for a market in which the electricity supply industry has been largely privatized and suppliers compete to build plant and provide power supply. Since it is difficult to formulate and link practical decision factors such as management and technical factors with the parameters in terms of which a financial contract is usually formulated, neural networks appear to be a natural choice to solve the problem. A network will be set up and trained to solve this problem and to work out contractual parameters.

Keywords: Neural Networks, Incentive Power Contracts, Contractual Parameters

I. INTRODUCTION

In the new market driven competitive electricity supply scenario [1] that is emerging in several countries, power contracts need to be introduced to facilitate the functioning of the restructured power supply industry. The competitive electricity supply model adopted in this paper is as follows: "There exists a grid company which owns the common transmission grid, that is the electrical system of interconnected transmission lines and substations, and interconnects m market driven suppliers and n consumers. The grid company purchases power from the suppliers and performs system control facilities and resolves system emergency problems". In the following discussion, the terms buyer and seller will be used to refer to the grid company and competing suppliers, respectively.

To facilitate competition, some contractual mechanism, such as "bidding" for power investment and supply contracts, must be developed to link up the transmission grid system and the suppliers. As competition in the electricity supply industry increases, both power utilities and the regulators are recognizing that competitive bidding is the best approach for the acquisition of private power. Power sale, or purchase auctions, have already taken place in some places. Although the development and implementation of an electricity bidding system is a complicated business, a clearly defined power contract and its arrangement are needed to take into account the management, financial, technical and practical problems involved.

Incentive contracts [2] were first introduced by the Federal Government in USA, primarily the Department of Defense,

as an alternative to cost plus fixed fee contracts. Generally speaking, a procurement contract may be a fixed price contract, a fixed price incentive contract or a cost plus fixed fee contract. As the name implies, a fixed price contract is just that. If a cost overrun occurs, the losses are borne entirely by the seller while the super-profits of large cost underruns are also retained entirely by the seller. In the fixed fee contract the seller simply receives an agreed fee in addition to the cost price of service or goods. This cost price is computed according to some agreed procedures. The losses due to cost overruns and the benefits of underruns both accrue entirely to the buyer.

Since potential suppliers make their bids (set their prices and parameters) the contractual parameters of the bid determine a business strategy and define a contractual structure as will be described below. Apart from the basic contractual factors (price, cost and profit), decision factors such as management, financial, technical and practical factors greatly affect the outcome of a contract. A neural network approach is likely to be a convenient method to input the effect of some of these mathematically intangible factors into the decision making process.

The organization of this paper is as follows. The incentive power contract is briefly described in section 2 while section 3 investigates the determination of contractual parameters with a neural network approach . A conceptual illustration and the conclusions of this paper are presented in section 4 and 5 respectively.

II. INCENTIVE POWER CONTRACT

Let us assume that there is an opportunity to construct a power plant of some stipulated size and to supply electricity to the grid system for an agreed period. Let us further assume that the amount of energy to be purchased each year is agreed. Also, in the contracts that will be drawn up there are laid down procedures for estimating capital and plant operating costs. The contract is now open to competitive bidding. In the following discussion all formulae refer to annualized costs, payments, profits etc, the annualization to be done according to some standard methods.

The simple linear version of the incentive contract for a single transaction may be written as follows:

$$f_{contract} = \alpha b + \beta(b - c) + c$$

$f_{contract}$ is the actual payment which will be made to the winning bidder and b, which is hereafter called the price, is an amount which is bid by each potential contractor and is used as the basis for evaluating competitors. α, β are contract parameters which define the contract structure while c is the annualized *ex post* (i.e. final, or end of job completion) cost which will be worked out jointly by the buyer and the seller at the end of the contract in accordance with agreed rules and procedures.

If the contract parameters α and β are set by the buyer (purchasing utility or national grid), they will obviously remain constant for all bidders. This may be one way of setting up a "level playing field". Alternatively α, β and b may all be proposed by a bidder. In this case the buyer has to evaluate bids depending not only on the offered price b, but also depending on the different commissions (α) and risk sharing strategies (β) proposed by different sellers.

The bidder who offers the lowest b wins the contract in the common α, β case. c is initially unknown but its estimated value is specified. Therefore, the buyer only uses b as a criterion in awarding the contract. At the end of the contract if $b < c$, seller and buyer share the loss in the ratio $\beta : 1 - \beta$; if $b > c$, they share the benefit in the ratio $\beta : 1 - \beta$. Hence, β can be called the risk index or contractual risk parameter.

If $\alpha = 0$ and $\beta = 1$, the contract is a fixed price contract i.e. $f_{contract} = b$ in which case the winning company receives an amount b. $\beta = 0$ represents a cost plus a fixed fee contract i.e. $f_{contract} = \alpha b + c$ and therefore α is called a fee-related index. Viewed in this way these two limiting cases are special cases of the incentive contract. The cost plus a fixed fee contract has no incentive for the bidder to keep down production costs - note that c is evaluated *ex post*. The fixed price contract does not convey information to the buyer for evaluating which supplier is more efficient in implementing the project because the terms of the contract do not include the *ex post* cost at all and hence, the buyer cannot share in cost underrun benefits.

A proper incentive contract arises when $0 < \beta \leq 1$. If the price b exceeds the actual production cost, there will be a cost underrun (profit) which would be rewarded by a factor of β and paid to the seller. Otherwise, if the actual production cost turns out to be below the price, the penalty $\beta(c - b)$ will be suffered by the seller. Thus, the factor β, the risk-related index, determines the bidder's share of the risk connected with the uncertainty of production costs.

III. DISCUSSION OF CONTRACTUAL PARAMETERS α AND β

3.1 Spatial relationship between return & contractual parameters

Let us, initially, assume that investors behave as follows:-
i)   the investor estimates costs, decides what profit is desired and then sets a rough bid price
ii) a set of feasible solutions for contractual parameters are calculated to satisfy these requirements
iii) other decision factors such as management and financial level, technical and practical level are initially neglected

Let us call these estimates the deterministic return Z, the deterministic price b and the estimated production cost c. The value of α and β can now be determined by the relationship $Z = \alpha b + \beta(b - c)$ where $0 \leq \alpha \leq 1$ and $0 \leq \beta \leq 1$.

The relationship between the return and the contractual parameters α and β is depicted in Fig. 1 for some arbitrary b and c, $b > c$. The region of significance is contained by the four lines (OE, OG, EF, FG) where
line OE is $Z = \beta(b - c)$ with $\alpha = 0$ and $0 \leq \beta \leq 1$;
line OG is $Z = \alpha b$ with $\beta = 0$ and $0 \leq \alpha \leq 1$;
line EF is $Z = \alpha b + b - c$ with $\beta = 1$ and $0 \leq \alpha \leq 1$;
line FG is $Z = \beta(b - c) + b$ with $\alpha = 1$ and $0 \leq \beta \leq 1$.
Then, the practically relevant solution space { α, β } is enclosed by the vertical planes ABFG, BDEF, ODE, OAG and the two inclined planes OFG and OFE behind them in Fig.1. Let us define the following terms :-
i)   The **"no investment"** condition occurs when zero return occurs. That is the case when the bidding price b cannot cover the production cost c i.e. $c > b$ and for the α and β considered $Z \leq 0$. This does not satisfy the basic investment rule which is the same as in any other deregulated industry : Invest if net revenues (appropriately discounted and adjusted for taxes) are expected to be appreciably larger than building costs.
ii) The **"risk-free"** condition is when $Z = b - c$, note this is the same as $\alpha = 0$ and $\beta = 1$ (fixed price contract) or any other α, β value on the plane $Z = b - c$. Under the basic investment rule, the investor expects his investment to be profitable and also decides on some higher minimum expected profit (second investment rule) for risky cases. This base case ($Z = b - c$) is called "risk-free" as it is the reference level for the second investment rule.

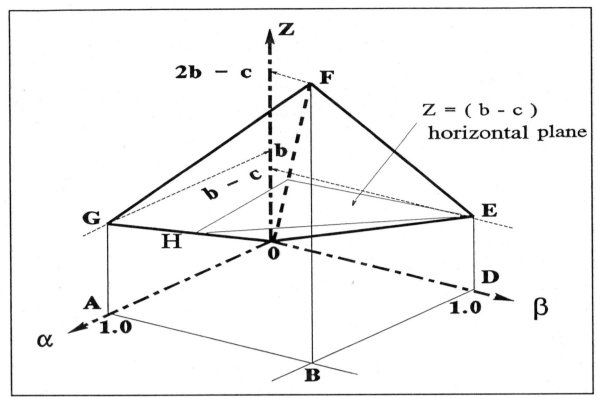

Figure 1 Spatial relationship between return (Z) and contractual parameters (α,β).

Note : The reason for not naming the plane OGA as the risk-free case, although this is the real simple risk-free case, is because only cases $\beta > 0$ (incentive contracts) are of interest to this paper.

iii) The "extreme risk" condition is the case when $\alpha = 1$ and $\beta = 1$ which is the maximum return condition $2b - c$.

In contractual bidding, the meaning of risk includes the consideration that if Z is high, risk is sure to be high because the contract may not be accepted. Risk Bounty RB is defined as the difference between the expected return $E(r)$ and the return on risk-free investment, where E is the expectation operator on the return r. The risk bounty RB therefore is

$$RB = \alpha b + \beta (b-c) - (b-c)$$
$$= \alpha b - (1-\beta)(b-c)$$

From this function, it is observed that the risk bounty is at a maximum when ($\alpha = 1$ and $\beta = 1$) or ($b = c$ and $\alpha = 1$). The first case is the maximum return condition with the maximum risk bounty b. The second case is when price is equal to the known production cost.

If an investor sets a price, knows the production cost and decides on a required return Z', he will in fact be setting out a horizontal plane Z' in which there are many sets of α and β value satisfying this condition. In making bidding decisions, he will choose a set of α and β which is favorable to him, has a low risk of loss of contract and which shares the uncertainty of production cost with the buyer.

3.2 Difficulty in presenting the relationship between contractual parameters and decision factors and in determining the contractual parameters

Power contracts are affected by the laws, regulations and compromises which strongly influence the decision-making of bidders (suppliers, grid companies and consumers). All power contracts between the bidders and the grid company which owns the whole of transmission grid will consist of three decision levels:

i) Management and Financial level
   (a) Identify the parties who are involved in the bidding contract
   (b) Rationale of contract
   (c) General agreements to be made during any negotiation
   (d) Rate of purchase and sale for unit power, wheeling rates
   (e) Billing periods and payment terms
   (f) Penalties and discounts

ii) Technical level
   (a) Delivery conditions including the point of delivery (voltage level), character of service (interruptible or uninterruptible power), power factor, continuity and reliability
   (b) Operating conditions including date of operation, operating procedure, sell-back condition and supervision of wheeling.

iii) Practical level
   (a) Control and protective apparatus
   (b) Meter provisions and metering arrangements

All these factors will lead to difficulties in deciding on values for contractual parameters and understanding their relationships. For instance, from the management and financial point of view, the contractual parameters (α and β) should be increased to allow for long billing periods or bad payment terms.

From the technical point of view, factors affecting the contractual terms are the delivery point of voltage level (extra high voltage EHV, high voltage HV, medium voltage MV, low voltage LV) suitability of the connection point on the grid and its ability to accept output of the power station, the power service (interruptible or uninterruptible electricity supply from the power companies), power factor (more than 0.8 or less than this value, for example) and reliability levels agreed upon.

At the practical level, for example, when all meter and metering arrangements and control plus protective apparatus are supported by the grid company, the parameters α, β can be made smaller.

Moreover, the value of α and β is affected by the investors's attitude towards risk which imposes an additional difficulty in this problem. For equal returns an investor regarded as a risk-averser will choose to set α high and β low if he thinks that the variance of production cost S_c is greater than some level. He may then find it desirable to collect the fixed fee from the target profit αb and reduce his sharing rate β with the buyer. However, this high α and low β set may not be accepted by the buyer who may respond by proposing another set of α and β values and negotiating with the seller until some compromise settings are agreed upon.

3.3 Neural network approach

Since there is no clear mathematical basis on which to formulate the relationship between decision factors such as management and financial, technical and practical levels with the contractual parameters in the incentive power contract, a neural network approach may be used to connect them. In this paper some initial studies of how this may be done are presented. These relationships are, as is usual in problems of this type, brought into the weight matrix which shows the connection strength between neurons. The objective is to try and obtain some suggestions for the contract parameters as the output of the neural network. The theory of neural network and relevant programming techniques may be found elsewhere [3,4].

IV.   CONCEPTUAL ILLUSTRATION

A three layer neural network is designed to work out the contractual parameters in the incentive power contract while bid price, cost, profit, the degree of aversion and decision factors are included as input neurons. The network can identify and connect the inputs, hidden and output layers by weight matrices which show the connection strength between layers and neurons.

For the sake of simplicity, we group each decision factor into three input neurons (i. inconsiderable, ii. considerable and iii. dominant). If we wish to analyze individual factors inside each decision factor, we must put more effort into recording the rating of this factor and add more input neurons into the network. A satisfactory and practical data base for doing this does not exist at the present time and therefore, a simple case is used to depict the problem in the initial form stated above. The information for this simple case is represented in table 1.

The contractual parameter determination network uses numeric input and output values. One neuron for each input item (13 total), and two neurons for the outputs will be assigned to work out the contractual parameters (α and β). The number of neurons in the hidden layer is initially set at half the total number in the input and output layers (6 or 7 in this example). During the learning process the number of neurons in the hidden layer as well as the weight matrix is updated until an acceptable degree of convergence is obtained.

Training is performed using, in a random order, the Training Facts File shown in Table 2. In a practical case this data would come from company internal reports, financial bureaus and available statistics. Here the File has been generated heuristically using a common sense approach to the matters discussed in Section 3.2.

The resulting weight matrix is shown in Table 4. In the upper portion of the table, W_{ij}, row i and column j, is the weight from input neuron j (note that these are rows in Table 1) to hidden neuron i. The last column (j=14) comes from a threshold neuron whose output is always deemed to be +1. It can also be seen that the program has generated 13 hidden neurons and the threshold neuron. The lower portion of table 4 are weights from these 13 hidden neurons to the α and β output neurons. The fourteenth column once again corresponds to a threshold neuron similar to the previous one.

Testing, after training, is done by picking 10% of the Facts in the Training File by a random method to form a Testing File. The results of the test are supplied in Table 3.

Table 1 Input & Output Information Representation

Information Representation - Input		
Neuron	Input	Typical values
1	Bid price b	1.0 to 3.0
2	Cost c	0.5 to 1.5
3	Profit Z	0.0 to 3.0
4	Degree of risk aversion λ	0.5 to 1.5
5	MFL_1 - i	0 or 1
6	MFL_2 - ii	0 or 1
7	MFL_3 - iii	0 or 1
8	TL_1 - i	0 or 1
9	TL_2 - ii	0 or 1
10	TL_3 - iii	0 or 1
11	PL_1 - i	0 or 1
12	PL_2 - ii	0 or 1
13	PL_3 - iii	0 or 1
Information Representation - Output		
Neuron	Output	Value range
1	Fee-related index α	$0 \leq \alpha \leq 1$
2	Risk-index β	$0 \leq \beta \leq 1$

Notes : *MFL*, *TL* and *PL* denote the factors of Management and Financial Level, Technical Level and Practical Level respectively. i, ii and iii represent inconsiderable, considerable and dominant respectively. For Instance, if i is true, i is 1 and then ii and iii must be 0. The degree of risk aversion λ is defined by the utility function $U(x) = x^\lambda$.

Table 2 Values of Facts in Training File

b	c	Z	λ	MFL			TL			PL			α	β
				i	ii	iii	i	ii	iii	i	ii	iii		
1.369	.750	.619	.8	0	1	0	0	1	0	0	1	0	.000	1.00
1.365	.760	.579	.8	0	1	0	0	1	0	0	1	0	.025	.900
1.359	.750	.582	.8	0	1	0	0	1	0	0	1	0	.025	.900
1.360	.755	.591	.9	0	0	1	0	1	0	0	1	0	.030	.910
1.358	.745	.607	.85	0	0	1	0	0	1	0	1	0	.032	.920*
1.375	.750	.625	1.0	0	1	0	0	1	0	0	1	0	.000	1.00
1.385	.760	.620	.95	0	0	1	0	0	1	0	0	1	.035	.915
1.390	.765	.620	1.15	0	0	1	0	0	1	0	0	1	.030	.925
1.365	.750	.588	1.0	0	1	0	0	1	0	0	1	0	.025	.900
1.365	.750	.587	.95	0	0	1	0	1	0	0	1	0	.020	.910
1.380	.755	.630	1.0	0	0	1	0	0	1	0	0	1	.040	.920
1.374	.760	.614	.8	0	1	0	0	1	0	0	1	0	.000	1.00
1.380	.765	.607	.9	0	0	1	0	0	1	0	0	1	.030	.920
1.375	.760	.594	1.0	0	0	1	0	0	1	0	1	0	.025	.910
1.370	.750	.592	1.2	0	1	0	0	1	0	0	1	0	.025	.900*
1.371	.751	.581	1.05	0	0	1	0	1	0	0	1	0	.010	.915
1.375	.749	.597	1.1	0	0	1	0	0	1	0	1	0	.015	.920
1.380	.750	.630	1.2	0	1	0	0	1	0	0	1	0	.000	1.00
1.385	.740	.613	1.15	0	0	1	0	1	0	0	1	0	.005	.940
1.378	.751	.597	1.0	0	1	0	0	1	0	0	1	0	.010	.930

Table 3 Output Results Tested by the Testing Fact File

b	c	Z	λ	MFL			TL			PL			α		β	
				i	ii	iii	i	ii	iii	i	ii	iii	Output	Pattern	Output	Pattern
1.358	.745	.607	.85	0	0	1	0	0	1	0	1	0	.027	.032	.921	.92
1.370	.750	.592	1.2	0	1	0	0	1	0	0	1	0	.012	.025	.906	.90

Table 4 Weight Matrices

From 13 input and one threshold to 13 hidden neurons													
0.478	-0.668	-2.122	0.025	1.312	-1.067	4.524	-0.334	-0.975	-0.588	1.14	1.513	-0.781	0.977
1.978	-1.353	-1.364	0.555	-1.034	-0.146	2.705	2.498	0.766	-1.226	0.613	-1.641	-0.776	1.286
-0.453	1.739	-0.323	-1.805	0.786	2.947	-1.146	-1.236	-1.123	-1.037	-0.623	1.564	-0.768	0.493
-0.741	-2.299	1.72	-1.42	-1.762	0.315	-1.692	-0.248	1.17	-1.204	0.011	-0.664	0.832	0.08
-0.379	-1.127	1.193	-0.033	-0.521	-1.427	0.402	0.777	-1.166	-2.121	-2.101	1.515	-0.017	2.407
-2.432	-0.94	-2.066	-0.723	2.125	2.447	0.048	-0.604	1.504	-0.321	-1.905	-1.54	1.308	0.364
1.513	1.919	1.8	-3.675	-0.567	1.74	-0.169	-1.088	-1.868	-0.933	-1.209	0.799	-0.138	0.991
2.093	1.311	0.034	-0.949	-1.488	1.09	-1.569	1.194	0.767	0.841	1.5	0.064	0.408	-1.644
2.739	-1.38	0.222	2.364	-0.23	1.964	3.106	0.828	1.025	-0.909	-0.125	1.571	-0.337	1.654
-0.435	0.64	1.889	0.023	0.426	-2.114	-0.306	-2.018	0.765	1.412	-0.759	-0.458	-0.989	-1.275
1.192	-2.239	0.179	0.76	2.027	-0.114	-0.749	-2.099	-0.896	-1.25	1.401	1.147	-0.836	0.458
-1.3	-0.731	-3.198	0.728	0.595	1.649	1.624	-0.284	0.556	2.453	0.123	0.447	2.751	-0.21
-2.333	2.536	2.729	-0.959	-0.52	1.917	2.361	1.295	-0.465	-2.496	0.689	1.679	-3.72	1.621
From 13 hidden and one threshold to 2 output neurons													
-0.052	-0.153	0.283	-1.954	1.384	3.899	0.971	-1.373	-0.629	2.119	-1.523	1.979	-2.693	-0.58
-2.691	0.001	-1.184	2.042	1.633	-1.855	1.253	0.259	-0.134	2.34	-0.626	-3.93	0.824	1.197

A threshold neuron is an extra neuron typically added to each layer of a network except the output layer for two reasons. The first reason is that the network works better with threshold neurons and second a layer will sometimes be given an input consisting of all zeros and asked to produce a non-zero output. The threshold neuron makes this possible.

V. CONCLUSIONS

This paper has introduced the concept of how the contractual parameters of the incentive power contract can be determined by the defined neural network. Not only the basic contractual factors (price, cost and profit) but also the role of important decision factors and the degree of risk aversion have been included. All factors can be thought of as neurons in the network while the contractual parameters are the output neurons. These relationship are inter-linked by the weight matrices. Its performance has also been tested satisfactorily by setting up a testing fact file. The results show that a neural network can be trained to determine the contractual parameters of the incentive power contract efficiently. This is due to the ability of neural networks to generalize the training set to cover unforeseen cases.

VI. ACKNOWLEDGEMENTS

A research grant from the Hong Kong Polytechnic as a stipend to one of the authors is gratefully acknowledged.

VII. REFERENCES

[1] A.K. David, Y.Z. Li,"Electricity Pricing With Competitive Supply Conditions", Electrical Power & Energy Systems, Vol 13 No 2 April 1991,pp.111-122

[2] Charles A. Holt, "Bayesian Analysis in Economic Theory and Time Series Analysis : Part I Bidding for Contracts", North-Holland Pub. Co., 1980

[3] J. Lawrence, "Introduction to Neural Networks and Expert Systems", California Scientific Software 1992

[4] "BrainMaker Professional: Neural Network Simulation Software User's Guide and Reference Manual", California Scientific Software 1990

BIOGRAPHIES

Wong kwok-po obtained his B.Eng. from Department of Electrical Engineering of the Hong Kong Polytechnic in 1991. He is currently pursuing a Ph.D. Degree at the Hong Kong Polytechnic. His research interests are power contracts, competitive bidding and planning in power system.

A.Kumar David obtained his B.Sc.(Eng.) from the University of Ceylon in 1963, and his Ph.D and D.I.C from Imperial College, University of London in 1969. He has worked in Sri Lanka, Zimbabwe, USA and Hong Kong and his research interests are in expert systems, planning, economics and reliability in power and in HVDC, and dynamic stability.

Chapter 24:   Manufacturing

Chapter 24
Manufacturing

Arguably, many of the papers contained in other chapters within this book could be considered manufacturing papers, specifically the chapters on automatic inspection (Chapter 22) and process control (Chapter 2). This chapter contains two survey papers that provide excellent summaries of the applications in these areas. **Paper 24.1** reviews the applications of neural networks to Computer Integrated Manufacturing. **Paper 24.2** provides a more comprehensive review of neural networks and manufacturing.

Neurally Inspired Models for Adaptive CIM Architectures

M. Calderini and M. Cantamessa

Dipartimento di Sistemi di Produzione e di Economia dell'Azienda

Politecnico di Torino, corso duca degli Abruzzi, 24, I - 10129 TORINO

Abstract A number of different CIM architectures have been proposed by several researchers, all aiming at the easiest and most efficient integration of different sectors of manufacturing activities. Allowing such architectures to adapt over time, following short and long-term modifications in information flow in the organization remains however an unaddressed (and very complex indeed) problem. In this paper the dynamic modelling and management of a network of decision-makers involved in manufacturing is attempted through the use of connectionist paradigms.

I. INTRODUCTION

Various definitions of CIM (Computer Integrated Manufacturing) have been proposed in previous years. A commonly accepted one [1] defines it as "a set of different manufacturing functions integrated through computers": hardware is viewed as an integrating factor for controlling the interaction of man and machines in creating the product from design to manufacturing. Such a definition puts the emphasis on technology, giving more relevance to the word "computer" than to the aspect of integration: integration is viewed as a function of computer technology. In this paper we will focus on the aspect of integration, which may be considered the crucial issue in modern manufacturing.

Several aspects of the manufacturing scenario have so dramatically changed during last years that relations existing in AMT (Advanced Manufacturing Technologies) between technology, integration and organisation must be widely reconsidered. In particular it might result of interest to point out how the way of conceiving technology and organisation has moved in totally diverting directions, resulting in architectures of extremely difficult integration.

Going back to the traditional Fordist model, characterised by scale economies of mass production, relevant aspects of manufacturing were a high degree of division of labour, extensive functional specialisation and most important, a strictly hierarchical organisation. Levy (et alii) in [2] consider that knowledge necessary was embodied in the system, using people as interchangeable parts, as they were designed and utilised to exploit scale economies of the production. This can be considered as a foreword to the consideration that one of the crucial features of modern manufacturing is the emergence, within the production flow, of "knowledge intensive" actors, be they human or technologies. In the modern enterprise, aside the production flow a new, ever more important flow is being generated: the information flow. The issue of

controlling it is central in most research work performed in the field of advanced manufacturing technologies.

The traditional approach to the management of information flow is definitely centralisation and hierarchy. CIM, at the time of its conception, had at least two good reasons to model itself under a hierarchical form [3]: formerly it was born in a strongly hierarchical context; secondly it implied the need to manage such a great amount of data to force systems designers to turn themselves towards hierarchical structures. Unfortunately, the evolution in market environment is pushing organisational structures towards dramatically different configurations. Several aspects of the new market scenario enforce the need of different approaches to production, since emphasis is now given on factors other than scale. Short product life cycle, product differentiation, low time to market, flexibility are only few of the new challenges cast on manufacturing in the nineties, which enforce pressure on the need for decentralisation. In order to concretise how modern approaches to manufacturing are moving towards a decentralisation, the example of JIT (Just in Time) and TQM (Total Quality Management) is often given [2]; the latter is in fact a typical management technique which shares responsibility of customer satisfaction through the whole organisational structure, implying a continuous and total refinement of knowledge and information; similarly, JIT is based on the strong hypothesis of multi-skilling, pointing out distributed responsibility in dispatching jobs within the network of the firm's processing resources.

The contrast between technology and organisational structure should appear quite clear, once stated these few considerations. Research has been done in order to point out a relation between technological change and organisational structure, but without achieving up to any consolidated result [2]. When trying to investigate the relation existing between technological changes related to CIM technologies and organisational structures a first tough challenge is proposed by interpretation given to the acronym itself. On one side computer communication seems to envisage a network structure which is at the basis of decentralisation; on the other side integration is often viewed as a synonymous for centralisation (although this statement has been counteracted by some authors [4]).

It is out of the scope of the paper to arise the debate between technological determinism and strategic choice, [2]. Our interest is here limited to the consideration that undoubtedly, whoever of the two is to influence the other, a good matching has to be found between technology and organisation; the question arising should be which is more

Manuscript received July 15, 1993. This work was partially supported by research funds of the II Faculty of Engineering of the Politecnico di Torino

likely to conform to the other. Since organisational structure in the nineties seems to be pushed towards heterarchy and decentralisation, it is our intention to investigate how technology, and in particular CIM, can be modelled in order to properly match the organisational structure. A problem arises of building models representing heterarchical and decentralised CIM architectures.

Modern manufacturing requires the joint co-operation of a very large number of decisions taken by several individuals and expert systems physically and cognitively independent. Decision making becomes a tough task, exacerbated by the fact that it is performed by local agents through utilisation of computers systems, but with a very poor capacity of effectively working together. In such a context the amount of information flowing through the system is so high that letting data freely flow from each decision making agent to the others would cause a flow of information sufficient to paralyse any activity; every individual would probably pass all of his time screening incoming data, without having the time to actually work on it. For this reason it is necessary to develop models both for describing the distributed decision making behaviour in networked manufacturing organisations and for controlling information flow so to guarantee on one side the required flexibility and to avoid chaos on the other side.

Such a view of the problem intrinsically refers to the concepts and approaches which are matter of research and debate in the field of Distributed Artificial Intelligence. DAI literature is fairly rich of models which may be considered suitable to be applied to our problem or, at least, extremely inspiring. Few examples are here reviewed, but many others would be worth of being mentioned.

Hewitt [5] models the problem solving structure of a society of experts to supplement the model of a single very intelligent human. The control structure emerges like a pattern of passing messages among the objects being modelled; the decomposition of the problem and the management of information flow is not directly tackled.

Davis and Smith [6] present an effective model for distributed problem solving, where each node with a task to be executed negotiates with idle nodes so to find an appropriate matching of tasks and nodes; this collection of nodes is referred to as the Contract Net, and has been proposed for developing heterarchical control systems in the field of shop-floor management [7-8]. The paper moves from the assumption that problem decomposition is part of the system's task, which is applicable to the modern manufacturing environment, whose complexity does not allow to start out with a predefined map of subproblems.

In [9] a framework for Networked Knowledge Based systems is presented; an interesting specification of the problem is outlined, identifying three crucial issues: the capabilities at each node, the basis on which networks should be organised and what knowledge should each node in the network own. The structure of the problem solving environment is hierarchical, thus not being directly applicable within the attempt of modelling a fully decentralised CIM environment.

In [10], which may be considered one of the first papers to explicitly point out a relation between CIM and DAI, a framework for enterprise integration is created; the underlying assumption is that complex enterprise activities can be subdivided into a collection of elementary tasks. The vision that emerges is a flood of information cruising over the enterprise. Individuals are screened from an excessive flow of information through "Intelligent Agents" able to autonomously dispatch ordinary matter. Neverthelesss, it is not specified how this could be actually performed.

As a starting point for our research we believe that the crucial matter at the present state of research in CIM modelling is to find an effective way to organise and dispatch the information flow throughout the enterprise's network. Experience in the field of manufacturing leads to suggest neural networks as an effective tool for facing the tough modelling problem described upon.

II. MOTIVATIONS FOR NEURAL MODELS OF DISTRIBUTED CIM ARCHITECTURES

The preceding paragraph has highlighted the need for modelling DAI applications in the development of innovative CIM systems. It is necessary to provide unified models, so to cope without substantial differences with agents of different nature that are present in the manufacturing environment, be they humans involved in a new-product development project, be they "intelligent machinery" involved in discrete or continuous shop-floor operations. The main issue (which isn't so evident in literature [9-10]) should be communication and global coordination, rather than the operative aspects of cooperation between agents of a specific kind.

This paper proposes to use the connectionist paradigm for developing these models; the motivations behind this idea are due to similarities existing between the properties of connectionist models, and the requirements cast by the manufacturing environment. Among these similarities we would like to point out some significant ones:

(1) *in connectionist models processing is distributed over a high number of processing elements.*
The complex and heterogeneous nature of the decision-making tasks involved in manufacturing has always called for some kind of decomposition (traditionally by separating functions, and by working them up into hierarchies)

(2) *in connectionist models the accent is cast on the processing capacity of the system as a whole, rather than on the performance of individual processing elements*
In all decompositions the crucial point is to make the performance of each element converge to a global optimum, rather than to its local one. Traditionally this is done with coordinating agents in higher levels of the hierarchy

(3) *In connectionist models, coordination between processing elements is distributed and performed with "learning rules" followed by each element.*

The traditional decomposition and coordination of decision-making tasks on hierarchical and functional principles in manufacturing is showing many limitations. These are due to the lack of flexibility and to the delays and distortions cast on communication between decision makers (quality of decision-making is known to depend closely upon the quality of communication). The idea of "managing by values" instead of issuing orders is now being more widely accepted in the field of manufacturing.

(4) *Connectionist models are adaptive*
Current approaches to CIM are scarcely flexible; the extreme instability of today's products, processes and demand volumes requires that the integration of agents involved in manufacturing allow the quick establishment of communication channels when required (and their rapid dismissal when the need for them ceases).

(5) *Connectionist models are robust*
Manufacturing systems have to face ever more stringent performance requirements in face of unexpected events (such as machine breakdown, or the illness of a domain expert). The distribution both of specific knowledge (or capability to perform actions) and of meta-knowledge (i.e. knowledge on "who knows - or is able to do - what") should make integrated manufacturing systems more robust.

(6) *Connectionist models are modular*
Manufacturing systems must not only perform well when crippled or downsized, but must also be easily upgraded and expanded without having to re-design the whole system. This is essential not only because of the variability of the manufacturing environment, but also because it allows investments to be distributed over successive time steps. The high investments typical of AMT may be more easy to justify and, often, this may be the only feasible way to make innovation affordable to the firm.

(7) *Connectionist models are able to generalize*
Manufacturing systems must be able to react to rapidly changing situations; this prevents them to be run by decision makers following a set of "hard-coded" rules, able to explicitly map the set of possible situations to the set of actions to be taken. Appropriate actions must be decided by working on patterns of known situations, and by comparing to a set of *values* which may be seen as constant over time.

With these point in mind, the traditional manufacturing system organization may change radically, as depicted (in a qualitative and rough way) in the following Fig.1, which shows examples of communication patterns in a typical action which occurs in manufacturing companies, with the joint involvement of different corporate functions: the product modifications which follow the detection of a design fault. The left part of Fig. 1 shows what happens in a traditional situation: field service staff detects the fault and reports to the function's responsible who, in turn, reports to the head of the manufacturing function. He then orders the head of the design function to do something about it (which is done by appointing a designer to the job). The process goes on with such up-down communication until the orders will be issued for manufacturing prototypes. The disadvantages and rigidity of such an approach are self-evident. The central part of Fig. 1 shows the approach which is currently taken by many companies trying to overcome the disadvantages shown before: the occurrence of a repeated problem brings to the appointment, by the heads of the various manufacturing-related functions, of a project team comprising people from each of the functions involved. This allows fast and direct communication among the people which are directly concerned with the design modification. It must be noted, though, that while communication and coordination *within* the group is horizontal, the assignment of the project group is due to communication and coordination which always follow the hierarchical scheme, and some rigidity remains in the system. A typical example of such rigidity is the following: no one will start thinking about changing the design until the board recognizes the problem and decides to appoint a team for dealing with it. Usually it takes time to get to this point and, to catch up, the board will tend to put the team on a tight schedule, during which designers won't have time to give good solutions. These would probably be found if they were given at least the awareness of the problem beforehand.

The right part of Fig. 1 shows what may happen in a distributed "neural" CIM environment: notice of the detected fault automatically reaches the designer whose experience best matches the case; he will start thinking and working on the problem and then issue the order of building prototypes directly to the shop floor, where a distributed production management will take care of it. It may be noted that now the communication links between operating agents and function responsibles change in nature. This vision may sound as hype, but it can be seen [11] as a way for manufacturing to achieve the flexibility goals cast by the market. In order to make it happen, research in manufacturing system integration should go in this direction (eventually by using neural-like paradigms).

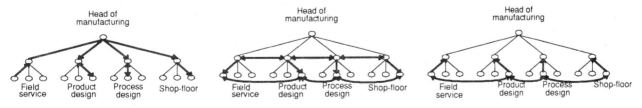

Fig.1. Different patterns of communication and control between corporate functions:
(a) strictly hierarchical, (b) hierarchical with project teams, (c) "neural"

III. THE DECISION MAKING PROCESS IN DISTRIBUTED CIM SYSTEMS

Let us now try to generalize the process that takes place with agents involved in a CIM system of the type depicted in the right part of Fig.1; such process is depicted in Fig. 2. There is a strong similarity, at this point, with assessed models of distributed decision making, such as the classical Actor model and, better still, to the Contract Net model.

In this proposed framework, each message exchanged between agents may be of two types, either a request message (RM), or an information message (IM). For clarity, we will now follow the process of RMs.

When an agent is appointed to execute some task, he checks whether he is able, or whether he needs to cooperate with other agents. In this second case, he "sets an auction" by broadcasting another RM, to which all other agents respond with a bid. The subtask is then assigned to the best offerer (dipending on the criteria adopted, such as speed, quality or whatsoever). After task completion, the agents report by broadcasting an "information message". Broadcasting to all agents is an expensive way of managing distributed systems of this kind. A few extremely approximate figures may help in illustrating this concept.

Let λ be the average rate with which each of n agents issues a request, and m be the average number of agents to whom requests are sent. The message exchange rate will be

$$T = n\lambda(2m+1) \qquad (1)$$

the term (2m+1) accounts for the auction announcement, the return of bids and the nomination to the best offerer. If $\alpha = m/n$ is the "selection ratio" which shows how each auction leader discriminates invitations to participate to the auction, it is

$$T = 2\lambda\alpha n^2 + \lambda n \qquad (2)$$

By plotting T against α for various values of n (Fig. 3) it is clear that to keep traffic at a reasonable level, and particularly for systems with many agents, some method for selecting recipients of RMs is essential. From the point of view of the single agent, the negotiation overhead may be estimated to be $O = n\lambda\alpha$ transactions per time unit. For high levels of α each agent would probably spend all of his time in the negotiation process, without actually carrying out any more processing.

The figures introduced are very rough indeed and have only been introduced so to state the need for some kind of selection when many agents are involved. In fact the rate λ is not constant, but depends on the negotiation overhead: any increase of the overhead (due to a high α, to problems with high need of cooperation, or to a high time needed for negotiating) will lower the number of processing tasks performed by each agent, and this decreases the number of RMs issued; an equilibrium in the negotiation communication and processing overhead could be found (although it is outside the scope of this paper).

Hierarchies and functional separations are the traditional way of dealing with this problem; another method is the establishment of a continuously updated knowledge by which each agent knows who ought to be addressed for carrying out sub-tasks it can't deal with. We will refer to such knowledge as *meta*knowledge.

It is now possible to explain the motivations which explain the addition of "information messages" to the Contract Nnet model. It is clear that metaknowledge should evolve over time, based on the past history of the bid assignments (RMs should be issued to the agents which have performed well in the past). But, if this mechanism alone is responsible for metaknowledge evolution, the motor which drives the system will be the past capacity of problem solving, which may be good for mechanistic processing tasks (e.g. job shop management), but not for tasks where human creativity is to be promoted; such creativity is an essential strategic element of manufacturing companies. Creativity has been viewed as the capacity to generate new associations between problems and solutions, starting from known patterns of such connections, both within and external to the actual problem domain. This may happen only if there is a distributed knowledge of the problem-solving activities which are going on in the organization [12]. In the example depicted in Fig. 1, the announcement that a product has a certain design fault doesn't reach the designer because he is looking for someone to help him (since he isn't even aware of the problem's existence). On the opposite, the field service staff is to give the news "to all that may be concerned with it", that there *is* a problem to be solved. The announcement isn't due to the fact that the field service staff is actually

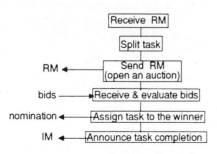

Fig. 2. Communication and coordination process between agents

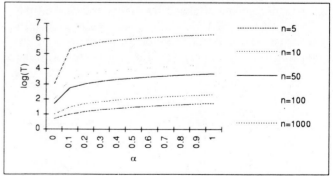

Fig. 3 - negotiation traffic as function of the selection ratio

trying to solve the *design* problem and asking someone for help, but is given either because they need help in simply fixing the products (it is therefore a RM), or because they have succeeded in the repair work by themselves, but want people to know (via an IM) about it.

Some kind of selection in IMs is also necessary so that they may reach only those agents which may actually benefit from receiving it. Alllowing some information on the global problem solving status of the system to be shared among agents may also be beneficial in more mechanistic tasks, since it may allow more sophisticated decision-making techniques to be implemented by each agent.

IV. A FRAMEWORK FOR THE DEVELOPMENT OF NEURAL MODELS FOR CIM ARCHITECTURES

Many connectionist models have been developed in recent years for covering an extremely wide range of applications. The aim of the following discussion is to point out which implications are cast by the behaviour of the manufacturing system's agents on the choice and establishment of connectionist paradigms to be used for modelling the communication and the coordination between them. The following formalism is therefore a working tool for discussion and for successive developments, rather than a conclusive proposal. In order to model manufacturing systems with neural networks, the main characteristics of the network itself have to be identified; at this purpose it is convenient to use the list of features given in [13].

1) *a set of processing units*
The set of the neural network's nodes will coincide with the set of the manufacturing system's agents $\{a_1...a_n\}$.

2) *a state of activation*
The agents' state of activation is to be closely related with their capacity of performing the tasks assigned to them. We will hereafter refer to this capacity as "skill". With skill we mean both the expertise and knowledge of an agent in problem-solving tasks, as well as the capacity of performing tasks of a more mechanistic nature (e.g., the processing speed of a machining cell). It must be noted, however, that the processing tasks that are carried out in a manufacturing system aren't related to a single subject, but are very different in nature and scope; the nature of each task is evidently to be explicitly taken into account when evaluating the ability of an agent to perform it. This may be done by using a set of K keywords $\{kw_1...kw_K\}$ over which to project both the skill of an agent, as well as the information content of RMs and IMs. The skill of agent ai may be given by a K-vector AK_i, whose component ak_{ik} will indicate the agent's skill on tasks relative to keyword kw_k. The skill of agents is limited, and therefore it will be convenient to have

$$\sum_k ak_{ik} = 1 \text{ for every } i \tag{3}$$

In other words, no agent can be an allround expert over all possible tasks, and each increase in skill over some kind of task will be obtained by loosing something elsewhere. A generic message RM or IM may also be seen as a point in the K-dimensioned space of keywords, where each coordinate rm_k or im_k will indicate how closely related the message is to keyword kw_k. It is convenient to normalize such information such that

$$\sum_k rm_k = 1 \tag{4}$$

3) *an output function for each unit*
For the sake of simplicity, the output function of each unit may be thought coincident with its internal state.

4) *a pattern of connectivity among units*
In neural networks the pattern of connectivity is generally given by a matrix containing the "connection weights" between processing units. These weights coincide with the "metaknowledge" that has been previously discussed, since they give a measure of how much each agent's skill is important to other agents it may cooperate with. It is necessary to introduce the further dimension given by the "nature" of the processing activity: in fact the set of agents to contact will depend both on the contacting agent and on the specific task to be performed. Connection weights may therefore be expressed by using a relation

$$M: N \times N \times K \rightarrow [0,1] \tag{5}$$

where m_{ijk} indicates the skill of agent a_i from the point of view of agent a_j, concerning tasks relative to keyword kw_k. Connection weights may, in principle, connect each agent to all the other ones, leaving to the learning rule the job of bringing to zero the useless ones. It is however possible to *a priori* set some weight values to a fixed desired value (such as zero); this will add a degree of unflexibility to the system but may reduce the size of the weight updating problem.

It is also necessary to model the reason which brought to the introduction of metaknowledge, that is the capacity of the agents in carrying out coordination and negotiation tasks, who limits both the number of agents to be contacted when issuing RMs and the number of agents issuing IMs to be heeded. This may be done by limiting the total sum of weight connections entering each agent; the sum of connection weights relative to a certain keyword should also be proportional to the skill on that subject. This brings to state

$$\sum_i m_{ijk} = ak_{jk} \text{ for every } j \text{ and } k \tag{6}$$

and, therefore

$$\sum_i \sum_k m_{ijk} = 1 \text{ for every } j \tag{7}$$

5) *a propagation rule*
The mechanism with which agents communicate is of the type shown in Fig. 2. It may be noted that such communication involves both RMs (which arise in an

asynchronous manner, but to which all participiants to the auction respond synchronously) and IMs (which arise in an asynchronous way). The coexistence of both synchronous and asynchronous phenomena in these networks certainly brings to some differences with respect to commonly used neural paradigms.

If the number of agents to contact in issuing RMs has been fixed to a number NA, when agent a_j has a RM to send he will deliver it only to the NA agents which rank best over a "contacting index"

$$CI_i = f(RM, M_{ij}) \quad (8),$$

where:

- CI_i gives the "utility" for agent j to contact agent i, given the message RM,
- M_{ij} is the vector of connections between agents i and j, over the different keywords.

Similarly, when an IM from agent a_i arrives to agent a_j, it will be taken into account if the index

$$CI_i = f(IM, M_{ij}) \quad (9)$$

overcomes a given threshold.

6) *an activation rule updating the activation level of units*

When agent a_j receives messages in response to a RM, he will have to evaluate the quality of the bids, and decide which of the responding agents wins the auction. To do this it is necessary to establish a "knowledge evaluating function" KEF able to give a measure of such quality. KEF will assume the generic form:

$$KEF(RM, V_j, B_i) \quad (10)$$

where

- V_j is the set of "values", or "evaluation criteria" that have been provided to the agent for this purpose,
- B_i is the bid sent by responding agent i.

An IM also will be evaluated by means of such KEF.

When an agent a_i wins the auction initiated by agent a_j and is assigned a task, he may update his own activation level so to take into account the increased skill it has achieved (or is achieving). A "knowledge updating function" KUF is to be introduced for calculating the new state. A generic form for KUF is:

$$AK_i(t+1) = KUF[AK_i(t), RM] \quad s.t. (3) \quad (11)$$

The assignment of a task does not, instead, change the internal state of the agent who has set the auction.

7) *a learning rule for modifying patterns of connectivity*

After the bids of an auction set by agent aj have been evaluated, the weights between the respondants and a_j have to be modified, depending on the quality assigned to each bid. It is necessary to introduce a "metaknowledge updating function" MUF which yields:

$$M_{ij}(t+1) = MUF[M_{ij}(t), KEF(RM, V_j, B_i)] \quad s.t.(7) \quad (12)$$

It may be noted that, having limited the total sum of weights of the connections entering a node, this calls for a form of competitive learning (all weight changes must sum up to zero). Function MUF may be very similar to the classical Hebbian rule, who states that weights between

nodes which are both highly active (in this case, the node who has set the auction and the ones whose bids were highly deemed by him) should be increased, while other weights should be decreased.

V. CONCLUSIONS

In this paper the problem, whose implications are of extreme importance in the field of manufacturing, of the dissonance existing between actual CIM architectures and emergent organisational models was at first discussed. A brief review of research work in the field of DAI has then been performed: such knowledge seems to give promising hints for further developments of innovative CIM architectures. Nevertheless, a lack of attention to the problem of information flow management was perceived; the authors suggest to use neural paradigms for modelling the systems, and a preliminary framework for the development of such models is proposed. This framework is intentionally general, so to allow to use the same modelling standard for agents of heterogeneous nature that cooperate in manufacturing environments. Research will continue with the implementation and experimentation of these models on different aspects of manufacturing enterprises.

REFERENCES

[1] U. Rembold, B. Nnanji, "The role of manufacturing models for the information technology of the factory of the 1990s", J. of Design and Manufacturing, vol.1 pp.67-87 (1991)

[2] P. Levy, J. Bessant, C. Levy, S. Smith, D. Tranfield, "Organizational strategy for CIM", Computer-integrated manufacturing systems, vol.4 n.2 (1991)

[3] H.R. Jorysz, F.B. Vernadat, "CIM-OSA part1: total enterprise modelling and function view", Int J. of Computer-Integrated Manufacturing, vol.3 nn.3-4 (1990)

[4] R. Boaden, "Organizing for CIM: project management, technology and integration", Computer-Integrated Manufacturing Systems, vol.4 n.2 (1991)

[5] C. Hewitt, "Viewing control structures as patterns of passing messages", Artificial Intelligence, vol.8 (1977), pp.323-364

[6] R. Davis, R.G. Smith, "Negotiation as a metaphor for distributed problem solving", Artificial Intelligence, vol.20 (1983), pp.63-109

[7] N.A. Duffie, R. Chitturi, J-I Mou, "Fault-tolerant heterarchical control of heterogeneous manufactuirng system entities", Journal of Manufacturing Systems, vol.7 n.4 (1988)

[8] D.M. Upton, M.M. Barash, A.M. Matheson, "Architectures and auctions in manufacturing", Int. J. of Computer-Integrated Manufacturing, vol.4 n.1 (1991)

[9] V.S. Jacob, H. Pirkul, "A framework for networked knowledge-based systems", IEEE Trans. on Systems, Man and Cybernetics, vol.20 n.1 (1990)

[10] J. Y.C. Pan, J.M. Tenenbaum, "An intelligent agent framework for enterprise integration", IEEE Trans. on Systems, Man and Cybernetics, vol.21 n.6, 1991

[11] R. Charan, "How networks reshape organizations", Harvard Business Review, Sept.-Oct. 1991

[12] I. Nonaka, "The knowledge-creating compay", Harvard Business Review, nov.-dec. 1991

[13] D.E. Rumelhart, G.E. Hinton, J.L. McClelland, "A general framework for parallel distributed processing", in D.E. Rumelhart, J.L. McClelland (eds.), Parallel distributed processing, MIT press, (1985)

Neural Networks in Manufacturing: A Survey

Samuel H. Huang and Hong-Chao Zhang
Department of Industrial Engineering
Texas Tech University

ABSTRACT: Artificial Intelligence (AI) has been claimed to yield revolutionary advances in manufacturing. AI technology is applicable to the entire range of manufacturing activities. As an AI technique, expert systems have been wildly used in manufacturing for over two decades. Recently, another AI technique, namely, neural networks, are gaining more and more visibility and have been successfully applied in manufacturing practices. While most of the survey papers about AI in manufacturing have been focused on expert systems application, fewer attentions have been paid to neural networks. However, expert systems are less effective in the ever-changing, complex, and open system environment of today's manufacturing systems. On the other hand, neural networks are able to learn, adapt to changes, and can mimic human thought processes with little human interventions. They could be of great help for the present Computer Integrated Manufacturing (CIM) and the future Intelligent Manufacturing Systems (IMS). Therefore, it is necessary to present the state-of-the-art of neural networks in manufacturing. The objective of this paper is to update information about neural networks in manufacturing, which will provide some guidelines and references for the research and implementation. In this paper, the basic concepts of neural networks are briefly introduced. Then, a survey of neural network applications in manufacturing is provided. Finally, the projection of future trends is given to help make decisions concerning neural networks implementation in manufacturing today and to aid in guiding research for tomorrow.

1. INTRODUCTION

Three major phases in the development of computer-aided manufacturing systems to the present time can be distinguished (IFAC 1984). The first phase was that of the direct computer control of groups of machine tools, first implemented in the late sixties. The second, that of the flexible manufacturing systems equipped with automatic workpiece transport and changing devices, automatic tool-changers and some form of online computer-based scheduling, was introduced in the seventies. The third phase, that of Computer Integrated Manufacturing (CIM), consists of systems that integrate the design, process planning, production control, assembly, quality control and stock optimization problems of the manufacturing process in a single, comprehensive, conceptual whole, is currently being implemented. It was proposed that the next phase would be that of *intelligent manufacturing systems* (IMS). Briefly, the systems belonging to this phase should be able to solve problems without either a detailed, explicit algorithm available for each solution procedure, or all the facts, mathematical relationships and models available in perfect arrangement and complete form for a deterministic answer to be found (IFAC 1984). Since the decision-making process in an advanced manufacturing systems environment is becoming increasingly difficult and overwhelming to humans, Artificial Intelligence (AI) is becoming widely adopted to assist human efforts. AI has been claimed to yield revolutionary advances in manufacturing. Since its emergence in the 1950s, AI has developed several techniques with applications in manufacturing, with expert systems being one of the most promising developments. Recently, neural networks are gaining more and more visibility, and have been successfully implemented in manufacturing (Udo 1992).

An outstanding analysis of the potential of AI techniques for automated manufacturing was provided by Hatvany (Hatvany and Nemes 1978, Hatvany 1987). Several papers about AI in manufacturing and expert systems in manufacturing also can be found in the literature (Gaines 1986, Soliman 1987, Valliere and Lee 1988, Badiru 1990). All these papers were focused on knowledge-based expert systems and few attentions have been paid to neural networks. However, expert systems are less effective in the ever-changing, complex, and open system environment of today's manufacturing systems (Udo 1992). On the other hand, neural networks have several advantages which are desirable in manufacturing practices, and could be of great help for Intelligent Manufacturing (Barschdorff and Monostori 1991). It is necessary to present the state-of-the-art of neural networks in manufacturing. The objective of this paper is to update information about neural networks in manufacturing, which will provide some guidelines and references for the research and implementation.

2. OVERVIEW OF NEURAL NETWORKS
2.1 Background

The year 1943 is often considered the initial year in the development of Artificial Neural Networks (ANN). At that year, McCulloch and Pitts (1943) outlined the first formal model of an elementary computing neuron. Their neuron model laid the groundwork for future development. Hebb (1949) first proposed a learning scheme for updating neuron's connections in the late 1940s. His learning rule made primary contributions to neural network theory. At 1954, Farley and Clark (1954) set up models for adaptive stimulus-response relations in random networks. Their theories were further elaborated by Rosenblatt (1958, 1959), Widrow and Hoff (1960), Caianiello (1961), and Steinbuch

(Steinbuch and Piske 1963). Many implementations of "neural computers" were realized in the 1960s. However, the existing machine learning theorems of that time were too weak to support more complex computational problem. In 1969, Minsky and Papert (1969) criticized existing neural network research as being worthless in their book entitled *Perceptrons*. It has been claimed that the pessimistic views presented by the book discouraged further funding for neural network research for several years. Instead, funding was diverted to further research of expert systems, which Minsky and Pappert favored.

It is only after mid-1980s that neural networks are beginning to make a strong comeback. The renaissance of neural networks is the result of rigorous works by a handful of researchers. The study of learning in networks of threshold elements and of the mathematical theory of neural networks was pursued by Amari (1972, 1977). Research on competitive learning and self-organization was performed by von der Malsburg (1973) and Grossberg (1976a, 1976b). Fukushima (1975, Fukushima and Miyaka 1980) explored related ideas with his biologically inspired *Cognitron* and *Neocognitron* models. Associative memory research was pursued by Kohonen (1977, 1984, 1987) and Anderson (Anderson et al. 1977). Unsupervised learning networks were developed for feature mapping into regular arrays of neurons by Kohonen (1982). Carpenter and Grossberg (1983, 1986, 1987, 1988, 1990) introduced a number of neural architectures and theories and developed Adaptive Resonance Theory (ART). Hopfield (1982, 1984) introduced a recurrent neural network architecture for associative memories in the early 1980s. More recently, Kosko (1987) extended some of the ideas of Hopfield and Grossberg to develop his adaptive Bidirectional Associative Memory (BAM) network. Other significant neural network models include probabilistic ones such as Boltzmann Machine developed by Hinton et al. (1984, 1986) In 1986, the publication of a two-volume set of books on parallel distributed processing, edited by Rumelhart and McClelland (1986), revitalized the field of neural networks. Beginning in 1986-87, many new research programs in neural networks were initiated. The intensity of research in neural networks can be measured by a quickly growing number of conferences and journals devoted to this field. Although the research in neural networks has had an interesting history, the field is still in its early stage of development.

2.2 Concepts and Models

Neural networks have been inspired both by biological nervous systems and mathematical theories of learning. Neural networks have the following main benefits (Barschdorff and Monostori 1991):
- processing speed through massive parallelism,
- learning and adapting ability by means of efficient knowledge acquisition and embedding,
- robustness with respect to fabrication defects and different failures, and

- compact processors for space- and power-constrained applications.

The definition of neural networks can be found in (Kohonen 1988a, Kohonen 1988b, Iyengar and kashyap 1991, Zurada, 1992). Generally speaking, neural networks are massively parallel interconnected networks that can acquire, store, and utilize experiential knowledge. Neural networks attempt to achieve good performance via dense mesh of computing nodes and connections. They also go by many names such as connectionist models, parallel distributed processing models, and neuromorphic systems. Figure 1 shows a neural network structure.

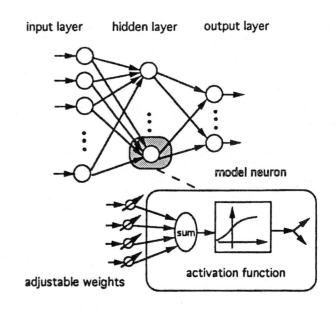

Figure 1. A neural network structure.

The basic components of a neural network are nodes (neurons) and weights (connections). The adjustable weights correspond to biological synapses. A positive weight represents an excitatory connection. A negative weight represents an inhibitory connection. The weighted inputs to a neuron are accumulated and then passed to an activation function which determines the neuron's response.

Neural networks may be distinguished on the basis of the directions in which signals flow. Basically, there are two types of network; feedforward network, and feedback networks. In a feedforward network, signals propagate in only one direction from an input stage through intermediate neurons to an output stage. While in a feedback network, signals may propagate from the output of any neuron to the input of any neuron (Zurada 1992). The neural network showed in Figure 1 is a feedforward network.

Neural networks also can be classified in terms of the amount of guidance that the learning process receives from an outside agent (Zeidenberg 1990). An *Unsupervised*

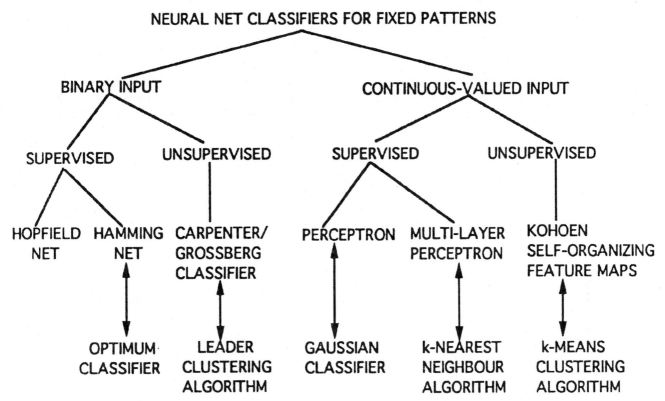

NEURAL NET CLASSIFIERS FOR FIXED PATTERNS

BINARY INPUT

CONTINUOUS-VALUED INPUT

SUPERVISED

UNSUPERVISED

SUPERVISED

UNSUPERVISED

HOPFIELD NET HAMMING NET CARPENTER/ GROSSBERG CLASSIFIER

PERCEPTRON MULTI-LAYER PERCEPTRON KOHOEN SELF-ORGANIZING FEATURE MAPS

OPTIMUM CLASSIFIER LEADER CLUSTERING ALGORITHM GAUSSIAN CLASSIFIER k-NEAREST NEIGHBOUR ALGORITHM k-MEANS CLUSTERING ALGORITHM

Figure 2. A taxonomy of neural network models (redrawn from Lippmann 1987).

learning network learns to classify the input into sets without being told anything. A *Supervised* learning network adjusts weights on the basis of the difference between the values of output units and the desired values given by the teacher, given an input pattern.

Neural network models, which depend on input data type (binary or continuous-value) and training methods (supervised or unsupervised), can be divided into six different categories (Lippmann 1987). The taxonomy is shown in Figure 2. Readers may refer to (Lippmann 1987) for more detail about different neural network models and learning algorithms.

Here we will briefly introduce three types of neural network models which are most frequently used in manufacturing practices. There are back-propagation networks, ART networks, and Hopfield networks.

- Back-propagation networks are multilayered feedforward neural networks that apply the back propagation procedure for learning (Rummlhart et al. 1986). The back-propagation procedure uses a gradient descent procedure which changes the weights in its original and simplest form by an amount proportional to the partial derivative of the error function with respect to the given weight. In a network without hidden layers, the computation of these derivatives is relatively easy, but for multilayered networks it is a harder task. The central idea of back-propagation is that these derivatives can be computed efficiently by starting with the output layer and working backwards through the layers. The back-propagation algorithm is a typical supervised learning

procedure. Back-propagation networks are applicable to almost every manufacturing domain.

- ART networks are neural networks based on the Adaptive Resonance Theory (ART) provided by Carpenter and Grossberg (1983, 1986, 1987, 1988, 1990). Carpenter and Grossberg's ART2 architectures, which work for analog and binary input pattern as well, embody solutions to a number of design principles, such as the stability-plasticity tradeoff and the search-direct access tradeoff. ART networks use an unsupervised learning procedure. They are stable because new input patterns do not wash away previously learned information. They are also adaptive because new information can be incorporated until the full capacity of the architectures is utilized. It seems the family of the ART structures can act as very valuable modules in intelligent systems, where real-time classification ability with self-learning and self-organizing capabilities are required (Barschdorff and Monostori 1991).

- Hopfield networks are feedback neural networks introduced by Hopfield (1982, 1984). The earliest Hopfield network, which employed two-state (on/off) neurons, is used for the design of neural Content-Addressable Memories (Hopfield 1982). Hopfield later introduced a modified version of his earlier model which employed a continuous nonlinear function to describe the output behavior of the neurons. A continuous Hopfield network can be characterized by its energy function (Hopfield and Tank 1986). The network will seek to minimize the energy function as it evolves to an equilibrium state. Therefore one may design a neural network for function minimization by associating variables in an optimization problem with variables in the energy function. Hopfield and Tank illustrated the use of the energy function to configure networks for several optimization applications including the travelling salesman problem (Hopfield and Tank 1985), a signal processing problem (Tank and Hopfield 1986), and a linear programming problem (Tank and Hopfield 1986).

2.3 Application Areas of Neural Networks

Neural networks have been applied in a fairly wide variety of practical problems. Pattern recognition, optimization, and control, are believed to be representative of the application areas of neural networks. However, the published technical references on applications of neural networks number well over a thousand papers and more than several hundred papers are printed every year. Among these publications, we can find that neural networks are being used in the field of database processing, decision making, medical diagnosis, language translation, and neural computers, etc. Since the area of neural networks is expanding very rapidly, there is no doubt that neural networks will be applied in areas beyond those mentioned in this paper.

2.3.1 Patten Recognition and Classification

The term "Pattern recognition" was introduced in the early 1960s, and it originally meant detection of simple forms such as handwritten characters, weather maps, and speech spectra. A more ambitious objective of patten recognition is to imitate the functions of the biological sensory systems in their most complete forms, that is, to implement *artificial perception* (Kohonen 1988a). The most important application areas for "neural patten recognition" could be the same as those for which conventional, heuristic methods have been developed during the past thirty years; (1) remote sensing, (2) medical image analysis, (3) industrial computer vision (especially for robotics), and (4) input devices for computers (Kohonen 1988a). We list some areas where neural patten recognition technique has been applied in the following.
- recognition of printed (or handwritten) characters and text (Chandra and Sudhakar 1988, Jackel et al. 1988, LeCun et al. 1989, Zurada et al. 1991),
- medical image analysis (Dayhoff and Dayhoff 1988),
- recognition of speech (Prager et al. 1989, Doutriaux and Zipser 1991, Laboissiere et al. 1991, Waibel and Hampshire 1991),
- segmentation and classification of regions from images (Cottrell 1991),
- machine vision (Koch 1987, Booth et al. 1989), and
- signal processing (Damarla et al. 1991, Chakrabarti and Bindal 1991, Shahani et al. 1991)

2.3.2 Optimization

The objective in optimization is to allocate a limited amount of resources to a set of certain partial tasks such that some objective or cost function is minimized (or maximized). In trying to solve such problems, we might proceed in what is called the deterministic manner, that is to try all configurations and find which configuration provides the best solutions. This is a naive approach and results in exponential-time solutions (Pao and Sobajic 1991). Neural networks, which can achieve high computation rates by employing a massive number of simple processing elements with a high degree of connectivity between the elements, provide a new approach for optimization problems. More specifically, feedback networks provide a computing model capable of exploiting fine-grained parallelism to solve a rich class of optimization problems (Tagliarini et al. 1991). The parameters of a feedback network can be explicitly computed, based upon problem specifications, to cause the network to converge to an equilibrium that represents a solution. Neural networks have been successfully applied for the solution of constrained optimization problems, such as linear programming and nonlinear programming problems (Tank and Hopfield 1986, Kennedy and Chua 1988, Maa et al. 1989).

2.3.3 Control

The basic objective of control is to provide the appropriate input signal to a given physical process to yield its desired response. Despite steady advances in control engineering, many complex processes continue to require human intelligence in the loop to ensure proper operation. Neural networks have several unique characteristics that allow them to perform some of the complex process control tasks that traditionally reserved for human. These characteristics include (Hall and Lu 1992):
- neural networks can be used to accurately represent response surface models of complex processes,
- neural networks can emulate the abilities of humans to incorporate new knowledge into existing models, providing the capability for self- improvement and adaptation,
- neural networks can emulate human abilities to reason from a general model to a specialized case, making human-like assumptions when faced with incomplete data, and
- neural networks can emulate human knowledge fusion capabilities by forming a single, coherent process model from a variety of partial knowledge sources.

The use of neural networks in control applications has recently experienced rapid growth. These applications include process control (Rehbein et al. 1992), robotics (Kawato et al. 1988, Sobajic et al. 1988), industrial manufacturing (Kooi and Khorasani 1991, Bozich and MacKay 1991), and aerospace (Meade et al. 1991), etc.

3. A SURVEY OF NEURAL NETWORKS APPLICATION IN MANUFACTURING

3.1 Group Technology

Group technology (GT) seeks to identify and exploit similarities of product design and manufacturing processes throughout the manufacturing cycle in order to achieve economies. The principle of GT has been applied in many fields including machining, part design, variant process planning, manufacturing cell design, facility layout, and scheduling, etc. (Hyer and Wemmerlöv 1989) By applying GT, many benefits, such as reduced setup times, lead times and work-in-process inventory in the shop floor, can be achieved.

Two engineering problems associated with implementing GT are part classification and part family formation. Kaparthi and Suresh (1991) propose a neural network system for shape-based classification and coding of rotational parts. A back-propagation neural network is trained to generate part geometry-related digits of the Optiz code from bitmaps of part drawings. A principal study shows that the network can generate codes accurately and promises to be a useful tool for the automatic generation of shape-based classes and codes. Although the examples used in their paper are rotational parts, Kaparthi and Suresh indicate that the neural network system also can be applied to non-rotational parts. They suggest that the trained network can be embedded in a Computer-Aided Design (CAD) system to facilitate the design procedure. For example, for the design of new parts, approximate or rough-cut designs can be used to retrieve parts within the same family. Prior designs could be used for new applications, or modified to fit the new application, resulting in standardization.

The use of neural networks for part family formation is also studied by a couple of researchers (Kao and Moon 1990, Moon and Roy 1991, Moon and Chi 1992). In their approach, a three-layer feedforward neural network is trained with the back-propagation algorithm. Each input unit of the network represents a part feature, and each output unit represents a part family. An operator plays the role of a teacher to the network by presenting each part in terms of part features, and by telling which family it belongs to. The trained network stores implicit discrimination rules through a set of connection weights, and exhibits consistent classification practice. The research demonstrates that neural network approach is capable of dealing with large part family formation problems efficiently.

The problems of part classification and part family formation are closely related, and usually the same approach is used for both problems. Regardless of the approach adopted for the formation and classification, a critical problem is how to maintain consistency. The consistency problem can be addressed most effectively if the classification and formation is a single procedure rather than two separate procedures. Kao and Moon (1991) present an approach for using the learning ability of neural networks to automate the process of part family formation during the part classification process. They divide the task into four phases; seeding phase, mapping phase, training phase, and assigning phase. In the seeding phase, three to five apparently distinctive parts are chosen from the part pool as part family representatives (seed parts). In the mapping phase, a code is assigned to each seed part. A neural network is also constructed. The number of input units is equivalent to the number of features contained in the classification code system used. In the training phase, a set of training pattern pairs are presented to the network. The network learns using the back-propagation algorithm. After training, the network is ready for the final task, classifying the rest of parts to the most appropriate part families. In the assigning phase, the network compares the presented part to the training set. If the features of the part are similar to the generalized features of any existing part family representative, the output of the network will be the same part family number. If there exist no significant similarities between the part and any of the part family representative, the output of the network will not indicate any existing family code. That means a new part family should be set up for this part.

Another GT problem is the machine-part cell formation problem. The assignment of a group of similar parts to a cell of machines having common processing characteristics greatly improves the efficiency of batch manufacturing. However, approaches to the problem of machine-part cell formation have been computationally inefficient for large machine-part matrices. Dagli and Huggahalli (1991) apply the binary ART network (ART-1) for machine-part cell formation. The columns and rows of the machine-part matrix are binary vectors that can be directly applied as inputs to an ART-1 network. Dagli and Huggahalli analyze the performance of the neural network classifier and find out that direct application of the basic ART-1 network does not provide very satisfactory result. They then reorder the input vectors derived from the machine-part matrix, and modify the original ART-1 paradigm. This produces drastic improvements over the performance of the basic ART-1. The result obtained compares favorably with popular algorithms proposed in the literature, such as the ROC2 algorithm provided by King and Nakornchai (1982).

Back-propagation networks and ART networks both can be used in solving GT problems. However, the learning results of a back-propagation network depend on the frequency of presenting a part. For example, if a network is trained three more times with a part A than with a part B, the network becomes biased toward A (Kao and Moon 1991). This problem is not so obvious when an ART network, which applies the unsupervised learning algorithm, is used. Since ART networks are both adaptive and stable, they are more suitable for solving GT problems than back-propagation networks. The use of ART networks to solve GT problems is a research topic that worth to be studied further.

3.2 Engineering Design

The application of neural networks in engineering design has been focused in two directions. The first is focused in configuring functionally complex systems built from standard systems or components. For example, design of a manufacturing system. The second is focused in the design of products based on design rules.

The design of manufacturing systems is often performed by means of simulation. Chryssolouris et al. (1990) develop a neural network approach for the design of manufacturing systems. A neural network is used to learn the inverse of the simulation function: given desired performance measure levels, the neural network outputs appropriate values for the system parameters. This approach is applied to the resource requirements design problem, that is, determining the appropriate number of resources for each work center of a job shop. Their results show that neural networks are capable of learning the mapping from desired performance measures to suitable designs.

Chen and Yan (1991) also apply neural network computing techniques in the design of an assembly planning system. The system they developed, CAAPS, which stands for Case Associative Assembly Planning System, integrates memory organization and neural networks computing techniques. The purpose of CAAPS is to provide an engineer with an environment in which he can think of assembly in terms of high level features and synthesize such assembly rapidly. At all stages of the design process he can consult the Case Associative Memory (CAM) to see what "experience" knows of similar assembly. Efficient use of prior experiences is emphasized. CAAPS remembers and recollects the assembly cases on the basis of internal similarity between cases. The precedence knowledge, constraints of operations are all stored as the contents of cases. Given design intentions, part names, and connection types among the parts, CAAPS will retrieve the past knowledge which is in the status of contents of particular cases, if exist.

Retrieval of old designs that meet current requirements on geometrical and/or technical information is a problem that is often encountered in batch manufacturing systems. Venugopal and Narendran (1992) model the design retrieval system as a human associative memory and apply a Hopfield net model to develop a design retrieval system. The system has been verified with test cases on rotational as well as non-rotational parts. The results show that neural network methodology is a promising tool for facilitating the development of practical design retrieval systems.

3.3 Monitoring and Diagnosis

The thrust in the present day factory environment is to automate the machining process. A key factor in achieving this objective is to monitor the machining process, tool condition, and machine condition. Govekar et al. (1989) apply a two layers neural network for the monitoring of a drilling process. Their result shows that Acoustic Emission

signals detected by a single sensor are applicable to recognition of operations like free run, drilling at different positions, and drilling with a worn drill. However, they also discover that the recognition ability is influenced not only by the neural network but also by the properties of the detected system. Later applications (Monostori and Nacsa 1990, Nacsa and Monostori 1990) show that neural networks can advantageously be used in real-time monitoring of manufacturing processes and other technical processes.

Kamarthi et al. (1991) investigate a new method for on-line measurement of flank wear through the synergy of vibration and force sensing. Their method uses a Kohonen's self-organizing feature map for correlating force and vibration signals with the tool wear levels. In the particular experiment, it is found that the trained feature map learned to detect the tool wear levels with a reliability close to 95%. Their results show that methods based on sensor data fusion using neural networks have potential to offer more reliable and robust methods for correlating tool wear levels with the signatures from force, vibration, and acoustic emission sensors for a wide range of process conditions.

Neural networks have been wildly used in machine monitoring and diagnosis. Elanayar and Shin (1991) apply neural network techniques to estimate the evolution of flank and crater wears using feed and cutting force measurements. Wasserman et al. (1991) use a neural network approach to detect and measure small cracks in the shafts of rotating machines. Guillot and El Ouafi (1991) apply a three-layer feed-forward neural network in the identification of tool breakage in metal cutting processes. Wu et al. (1991) present a neural network approach to diagnose processing damages in injection molding. Knapp and Wang (1992) apply a back-propagation neural network for machine fault diagnosis. Lin et al. (1991) use neural network techniques for sensor failure detection and data recovery.

3.4 Process Modeling and Control

For the control of machining processes, perhaps the greatest difficulty is that reliable models of the processes do not exist. Rangwala and Dornfeld (1989) suggest neural networks as learning structures for intelligent controllers that can model machining processes and use adaptive control. Andersen et al. (1990, 1991) apply a neural network approach for arc welding. The arc welding processes are viewed as multivariable systems, where a back-propagation neural network is used to model the systems off-line, as well as serving in closed-loop controllers. Any arc welding process is controlled by a number of parameters, and the ultimate objectives of the process are specified in terms of numerous parameters as well. As a result, any arc welding process can generally be viewed as a multiple-input/multiple-output system. The lack of reliable, general, and yet computationally fast, physical models of this multi-variable system, makes the design of a generalized real-time controller for arc welding nontrivial. One of the basic issues to be considered regarding the generalized control for arc welding is to determine what is to be controlled and which parameters are accessible to enact control actions on the process. The back-propagation networks are used for the modeling and control of the Gas Tungsten Arc Welding (GTAW). Various configurations, in terms of the number of layers and the number of network nodes, have been tested. For the application presented, two-layer networks consisting of a single hidden layer and an output layer have been proved to be adequate. Smartt et al. (1991) also apply a neural network approach in arc welding. Instead of using neural network to model the arc welding processes, they develop a new approach to quantify conditional logic rules and represented them in a neural network. The network is then used in place of a PI controller for a gas metal arc welding process.

The advantages of using neural network approaches in process modeling and control are indicated by Chryssolouris et al. (1992) The authors point out that while synthesis of multiple sensor information would provide better result, neural networks excell in dealing with situations in which process models do not adequately reflect the process complexity. A neural network's ability to learn a control algorithm without the benefit of a priori analysis or modeling can be of great help for difficult, complex, and nonlinear control applications. The same conclusion also can be found in (Bozich and Mackay 1991), in which Bozich and Mackay apply a neurocontroller in vibration cancellation.

3.5 Quality Control

Quality control is very important in modern manufacturing industry. Neural networks have been suggested and used for fulfilling different quality control tasks, mostly where high processing and classification capabilities are required.

Barschdorff (1990) report the application of neural network techniques for the quality control of electric drive motors. Daniels (1991) and Jayaraman et al. (1991) apply neural network approaches in power quality control. Smith (1991) uses back-propagation neural networks in quality control in an injection molding corporation. Back-propagation network handles both binary and continuous data well with little preprocessing and postprocessing, and is a supervised training technique. Supervision offers the advantage of teaching the network the desired classes explicitly. Neural networks are comparable to statistical techniques in goodness of output for process and quality control. An advantage of the network approach is the convenience of learning establishing the relationships directly, rather than through analysis and assumptions. Using a single network to monitor multiple products and/or quality parameters is an additional advantage. All of these quality control applications are somewhat related to monitoring and diagnosis, and the use of neural networks has been proved to be effective.

Neural network techniques also can be used in robust design, which is a cost-effective technique for achieving high quality and reliability. Schmerr et al. (1991)

describe a new approach for planning robust design experiments through the use of neural networks. The basis of their approach is to train a neural network on a set of tuples where each tuple corresponds to a Taguchi experiment along with its observed product response. Once trained, the neural network can probe the entire parameter space of design parameter settings, equivalent to performing a full factorial experimental design. Schmerr et al. discover that neural network had remarkable capabilities for generalization when trained on the same sparse array of experiments as used in complementary Taguchi analysis.

3.6 Robotics

Although neural networks applicable to the solution of robotics problems are, in fact, neurocontrollers, their function is specialized mainly to provide solutions to robot arm motion problems.

Neural network approaches in solving the forward kinematics problem for robots with two degrees of freedom has been studied by Nguyen et al. (1991) The authors design several network configurations for modeling of the manipulator kinematics. Their results show that neural networks can learn manipulator kinematics efficiently. Modeling of the desired trajectories or kinematic transformations can be achieved with a considerable degree of accuracy using a number of network architectures.

Sobajic et al. (1988) study the use of neurocontrollers in robot arm movement with two degrees of freedom and with a desired final end effector position. The results achieved demonstrate the unusual efficiency and potential of neurocontrollers for use in robot kinematics control systems.

Miller et al. (1990) use CMAC (Cerebellar Model Articulation Controller) neural networks to control a robot whose kinematics is unknown. After training, the neural network controller performs very well. The average error is always below the error of a fixed gain controller without learning.

The applications of neural network techniques in robot control are also addressed by Kawato et al. (1988), Shumsheruddin (1991), and many others. The objective of these studies is to investigate the feasibility of creating an intelligent robot control scheme in an unmanned working environment. Although all of the studies show that neural networks might be the solution of intelligent robot, there are still many works remain.

3.7 Scheduling

Scheduling is a resource allocation problem subjects to allocation and sequencing constraints. It belongs to the class of optimization problems and can be solved using neural networks.

Foo and Takefuji (1988) apply neural networks in job-shop scheduling problem. In a job-shop scheduling problem, the resources are typically machines and the jobs are the basic tasks that need to be accomplished using the machines. Each task may consist of several subtasks related by certain precedence restrictions. This problem can be formulated as a linear programming problem. The cost function to be minimized is defined as a sum of the starting times of all jobs subject to compliance with precedence constraints. The problem is solved using a linear programming network.

Most of the scheduling problems can be formulated as linear or non-linear programming problems and solved using an optimization network such as the Hopfield net (Sendaula et al. 1991, Fukuyama and Ueki 1991). However, a feedforward back-propagation network also can be used in scheduling problem. Yih et al. (1991) provide a hybrid method that combines back-propagation neural network, simulation, and semi-Markov optimization to solve the crane scheduling problem. The crane scheduling problem occurs in a circuit board production line where one overhead crane is used to transport jobs through a line of sequential chemical process tanks. Because chemical processes are involved in this production system, any mistiming or misplacing will result in defective jobs. The proposed method consists of three phases: data collection, optimization, and generalization. Training data are purified using operations research method (semi-Markov optimization). The neural network is used in building of the decision making model. The resulted system performs better than the human scheduler from whom the models were formulated.

4. FUTURE TRENDS

"*Artificial Intelligence is an unfortunate choice of title for an ill-defined technology that may, in the long run, be the single most important and most pervasive ingredient for the realization of true Computer Integrated Manufacturing (CIM).*" (Schaffer 1986). As a tool for AI, neural networks are applicable to the entire range of manufacturing activities, including design, machine monitoring and diagnosis, process modeling and control, quality control, process planning, scheduling, and robotics, etc.

Manufacturing is a highly knowledge-intensive domain. AI-based techniques are designed for capturing, representing, organizing, and utilizing knowledge on computers, and hence will be the key solutions to manufacturing problems. AI techniques can be classified into two categories (VerDuin 1990, Rose 1991): (1) the traditional "symbolic" approach (expert systems), and (2) the neurally-inspired "connectionist" approach (neural networks). In expert systems, knowledge is represented symbolically in some expressions or data structures, and can be understood easily. The situation is quite different in neural networks. According to Pao and Sobajic (1991), in neural networks, the processing is the knowledge representation. In other words, the very nature of the processing encodes the knowledge. There is no need for a separate body of global rules to be used

by the network for reasoning. If rules exist, they are in the nature of local processing steps carried out at individual processors in response to stimuli from other neurons.

Neural networks are models of the human nervous system. They have parallel distributed structures and a couple of advantages over traditional symbolic systems, which are desirable in manufacturing applications. It is becoming clear that symbolic systems alone are not adequate for solving manufacturing problems. As Valliere and Lee (1988) pointed out, "*to embody, the full expertise a human expert can have, expert systems may have to go beyond the rule based reasoning, or even the symbolic reasoning......they will function on computers using parallel architecture......*" Currently, there is an explosion of interests in neural networks. However, some of the expectations on neural networks are unreasonable. Feldman (1990) analyzed the advantages and problems with neural networks in manufacturing. He indicated that, "*We can be quite sure that neural networks will not replace conventional computers, eliminate programming, or unravel the mysteries of the mind. We can expect better understanding of massively parallel computation to have an important role in practical tasks and in the behavioral and brain sciences, but only through interaction with other approaches to these problems.*"

Neural networks are complementary to, rather than competitive with, traditional AI techniques. There is no doubt that neural networks will play an important role in the current Computer Integrated Manufacturing (CIM) and the future Intelligent Manufacturing Systems (IMS) development, but we must keep in mind that neural networks constitute an enhancing not a replacing technology. Many researchers in the neural network field are interested in merging the structures and functions of neural networks with those of symbolic systems. In the near future, we can foresee that neural network and expert system techniques will be integrated to solve manufacturing problems.

Expert systems have several advantages over traditional computerized methods. An expert system is able to handle symbolic information, use heuristic search as a means of reducing complexity of search, explain how it reached its conclusion, and accommodate new expertise whenever new knowledge is identified by a human expert. However, expert systems do have their weaknesses (Kokar 1989, Ben-David and Pao 1992). The building of an expert system usually requires both the efforts of a knowledge engineer and a domain expert. The knowledge engineer interviews the domain expert, extracts the domain expert's knowledge, and transfers the knowledge into an expert system. There are significant implementation challenges with this approach, known as the knowledge acquisition bottleneck (Hayes-Roth et al. 1983). The knowledge engineer, who designs the expert system, might totally ignorant with the domain expertise. The domain expert, who has actual experience and the domain expertise, might know little about computer technique. Although the knowledge engineer and the domain expert can cooperate well by getting know each other's domain, there are still serious problems.

Through years of experience, domain experts can easily provide appropriate responses to specific situations. However, it is far more difficult to create rules that are suitable for an expert system. Creation of useful rules requires clear identification of what factors are relevant in a situation, and exactly how they are related. Furthermore, even the best domain expert cannot think of every potential problem, especially as circumstances change over time. Thus, an expert system can only deal with a limited range of problems and circumstances, and cannot adapt to change (Kokar 1989, VerDuin 1992).

On the other hand, neural networks can acquire, store, and utilize experimental knowledge. By showing examples of input and desirable output, a neural network can be trained to perform a task. It can repeat all the training examples and, more importantly, generate appropriate outputs in response to new inputs. Another advantage of neural networks lies on their parallel distributed architecture. If realized in hardware, the computing speed of a neural network is much faster than an expert system. However, neural networks do have their deficiencies. The configuration of a neural network architecture usually requires trial-and-error method which is very time consuming. Although the processing of a neural network encodes knowledge (Pao and Sobajic 1991), the knowledge representation is vague and not easily understood. Unlike expert systems, neural networks cannot explicitly explain their results. For a neural network, it is very difficult to provide the end-user with convincing explanations about how a decision (recommendation) was made.

Neural networks and expert systems are complementary. The weaknesses of expert systems are offset by the strengths of neural networks, and vice versa. By combining expert system techniques and neural network techniques into a hybrid system, we can call upon the best features of each. Therefore, the integration of expert systems and neural networks is necessary and useful. Several papers discussed hybrid systems that combine expert systems and neural networks (Fu 1989, Sun and Waltz 1991, VerDuin 1991, Ben-David and Pao 1992, Lacher et al. 1992, Narazaki and Ralescu 1992). The advantages of such a hybrid system are:

1. The effort in knowledge acquisition is greatly reduced, since there are fewer rules need to be acquired in the system. Consequently, it is easier to maintain the system throughout its life cycle.

2. New knowledge can be updated to the system automatically by presenting new examples to the neural network.

3. The extraction of implicit knowledge (neural network learning) is relatively easy via the help of a certain amount of explicit knowledge (rules).

There are some applications in industry that exemplify the functionality and power of combining expert systems and neural networks in manufacturing environments (Hall and Lu 1991, Ben-David and Pao 1992, VerDuin 1992). All their results show that hybrid approach is feasible

and powerful. However, further research and implementation are still needed.

Currently, most of the neural network applications are simulated in the conventional computers. The next step will prospectively be, the application of special VLSI (Very-Large-Scale Integrated) neural chips to further accelerate the computation speed of neural networks. Neural network techniques can contribute to the further development of intelligent sensors, where sensing, preprocessing and decision making will be integrated into one unit. Neural networks are certainly the key technology for the future Intelligent Manufacturing Systems.

5. CONCLUSION

The development of computer-aided manufacturing systems has advanced into the CIM (Computer Integrated Manufacturing) phase. In this phase, the complicated machine tools, manufacturing cells and systems require systematic methods of control, monitoring, diagnosis and quick decision making. Neural networks, characterized by their learning and adapting ability, have been wildly used in today's manufacturing industry.

The application area of neural networks in manufacturing is surprisingly broad. It covers nearly all of the fields spreading from the design phase through control, monitoring, and scheduling to quality assurance. As the result of our survey, we believe that neural networks can be applied in any domain of manufacturing as expert systems do. It was found by most of the researchers that the neural network techniques can advantageously be used in the manufacturing domains for new solutions or as alternative of conventional methods. However, our survey also indicates that most of the approaches applied are restricted to the back-propagation neural network. While Hopfield net is used in solving optimization problem and ART net is used in group technology, back-propagation net has been applied in a variety of problems (including optimization and group technology). Although back-propagation is a useful technique, it usually requires trial-and-error method to determine the optimal network structure and a certain amount of training times are needed.

Neural networks have certain advantages (adaptability, learning from experience, and parallel distributed architecture, etc.) over traditional knowledge-based expert systems. However, the construction of a neural network structure is the key element to success. It is an unrealistic hope that a neural network can learn to perform any task using an initially uniform or random structure. Therefore, the construction of a network structure becomes the most important problem to be solved in neural network application. It is hoped that this problem can be solved by combining various AI techniques such as expert systems, machine learning, and fuzzy logic.

As a future trend, we can foresee that neural

networks will be integrated with symbolic systems (knowledge-based expert systems, etc.) in order to solve the current CIM and future IMS (Intelligent Manufacturing Systems) problems. While symbolic systems will remain playing an important part in high level manufacturing activities (global level factory management), neural networks will contribute a lot in low level manufacturing activities (multisensor fusion, adaptive controller, and process pattern recognizer).

REFERENCES:

Amari, S. I., 1972, "Learning Patterns and PatternSequences by Self-Organizing Nets of Threshold Elements," *IEEE Trans. Computers*, C-21, pp.1197-1206.

Amari, S. I., 1977, "Neural Theory of Association and Concept Formation," *Biol. Cybern.*, Vol. 26, pp.175-185.

Anderson, J. A., Silverstein, J. W., Rite, S. A., and Jones, R. S., 1977, "Distinctive Features, Categorical Perception, and Probability Learning: Some Applications of a Neural Model," *Psych. Rev.*, Vol. 84, pp.413-451.

Anderson, K., Cook, G. E., and Gabor, K., 1990, "Artificial Neural Networks Applied to Arc Welding Process Modeling and Control," *IEEE Transactions on Industry Applications*, Vol. 26, pp.824-830.

Anderson, K., Cook, G. E., Springfield, J. F., and Barnett, R. J., 1991, "Applications of Artificial Neural Networks for Arc Welding," in C. H. Dagli, S. R. T. Kumara, and Y. C. Shin, eds., *Intelligent Engineering Systems Through Artificial Neural Networks*, ASME Press, New York, pp.717-728.

Badiru, A. B., 1990, "Artificial Intelligence Applications in Manufacturing," in Cleland, David I., and Bopaya Bidanda, eds., *The Automated Factory Handbook: Technology and Management*, TAB Professional and Reference Book, New York, pp.496-526.

Barschdorff, D., 1990, "Case Studies in Adaptive Fault Diagnosis Using Neural Networks," *Proc. of the IMACS Annals on Computing and Applied Mathematics MIM-S2*, Brussels, Sept. 3-7.

Barschdorff, D., and Monostori, L., 1991, "Neural Networks: Their Applications and Perspectives in Intelligent Machining," *Computers in Industry*, Vol. 17, pp.101-119.

Ben-David, A., and Pao, Y.-H., 1992, "Self-Improving Expert Systems: An Architecture and Implementation," *Information & Management*, Vol. 22, pp.323-331.

Booth, R., Allen, C. R., and Adams, A. E., 1989, "A Neural Network Implementation for Real-Time Scene Analysis," *First IEE International Conference on Artificial Neural Networks*, London, UK, Oct. 16-18, pp. 71-75.

Bozich, D. J., and MacKay, H. B., 1991, "Vibration Cancellation Using Neural Controllers," in C. H. Dagli, S. R. T. Kumara, and Y. C. Shin, eds., *Intelligent Engineering Systems Through Artificial Neural Networks*, ASME Press, New York, pp.771-776.

Caianiello, E. R., 1961, "Outline of a Theory of Thought-Processes and Thinking Machines," *Journal of Theoretical Biology*, Vol. 2, pp.204-235.

Carpenter, G. A., and Grossberg, S., 1983, "A Massively Parallel Architecture for a Self-Organizing Neural Pattern Recognition Machine," *Computer Vision, Graphics, and Image Processing*, Vol. 37, pp.54-115.

Carpenter, G. A., and Grossberg, S., 1986, "Neural Dynamics of Category Learning and Recognition: Attention, Memory Consolidation, and Amnesia," in J. Davis, R. Newburgh, and E. Wegman, eds., *Brain Structure, Learning, and Memory*, AAAS Symposium Series.

Carpenter, G. A., and Grossberg, S., 1987, "ART 2: Self-Organization of Stable Category Recognition Codes for Analog Output Patterns," *Applied Optics*, Vol. 26, Dec., pp.4919-4930.

Carpenter, G. A., and Grossberg, S., 1988, "The ART of Adaptive Pattern Recognition by a Self-rganizing Neural Network," *Computer*, March, pp.77-88.

Carpenter, G. A., and Grossberg, S., 1990, "ART 3 Hierarchical Search: Chemical Transmitters in Self Organizing Pattern Recognition Architectures," *Proc. Int. Joint Conf. on Neural Networks*, Vol. 2, Wash. DC, Jan., pp.30-33.

Chakrabarti, A., and Bindal, N., 1991, "Radar Target Discrimination Using Artificial Neural Networks," in C. H. Dagli, S. R. T. Kumara, and Y. C. Shin, eds., *Intelligent Engineering Systems Through Artificial Neural Networks*, ASME Press, New York, pp.395-400.

Chandra, V., and Sudhakar, R., 1988, "Recent Developments in Artificial Neural Network Based haracter Recognition: A Performance Study," *Proc. IEEE Southeast Con.*, Knoxville, Tennessee, pp.633-637.

Chen, C. L. P., and Yan, Q.-W., 1991, "Design of a Case Associative Assembly Planning System," in C. H. Dagli, S. R. T. Kumara, and Y. C. Shin, eds., *Intelligent Engineering Systems Through Artificial Neural Networks*, ASME Press, New York, pp.757-762.

Chryssolouris, G., Lee, M., Pierce, J., and Domroese, M., 1990, "Use of Neural Networks for the Design of Manufacturing Systems,"*Manufacturing Review*, Vol. 3, No. 3, Sept., pp.187-194.

Chryssolouris, G., Lee, M., and Domroese, M., 1991, "The Use of Neural Networks in Determining Operational Policies for Manufacturing Systems," *Journal of Manufacturing Systems*, Vol. 10, No. 2, pp. 166-175.

Chryssolouris, G., Domroese, M., and Beaullieu, P., 1992, "Sensor Synthesis for Control of Manufacturing Processes," *Journal of Engineering for Industry*, Vol. 114, May, pp.158-174.

Cottrell, G. W., 1991, "Extracting Features from Faces Using Compression Networks: Face, Identity, Emotion, and Gender Recognition Using Holons," *Connectionist Models: Proceedings of the 1990 Summer School*, pp.328-337.

Dagli, C., and Huggahalli, R., 1991, "Neural Network Approach to Group Technology," in R. Sharda, J. Y. Cheung, and W. J. Cochran. eds., *Knowledge-Based Systems and Neural Networks: Techniques and Applications*, Elsevire, New York, pp.213-228.

Damarla, T. R., Ghosal, S., and Karpur, P., 1991, "Application of Neural Networks for Classification of Ultrasonic Signals," in C. H. Dagli, S. R. T. Kumara, and Y. C. Shin, eds., *Intelligent Engineering Systems Through Artificial Neural Networks*, ASME Press, New York, pp.377-382.

Daniels, R., 1991, "Power Quality Monitoring Using Neural Networks," in M. A. El-Sharkawi, and R. J. Marks, II, eds., *Proceedings of the first International Forum on Applications of Neural Networks to Power Systems*, Seattle, Washington, July 23-26, pp.195-197.

Dayhoff, R. E., and Dayhoff, J. E., 1988, "Neural Networks for Medical Image Processing," in *Proc. IEEE Symp. on Computer Applications in Medical Care*, Washington, D. C., pp.271-275.

Doutriaux, A., and Zipser, D., 1991, "Unsupervised Discovery of Speech Segments Using Recurrent Networks," *Connectionist Models: Proceedings of the 1990 Summer School*, pp.303-309.

Elanayar, S., and Shin, Y. C., 1991, "Tool Wear Estimation in Turning Operations Based on Radial Basis Functions," in C. H. Dagli, S. R. T. Kumara, and Y. C. Shin, eds., *Intelligent Engineering Systems Through Artificial Neural Networks*, ASME Press, New York, pp.685-692.

Farley, B. G., and Clark, W. A., 1954, "Simulation of Self-Organizing Systems by Digital Computer," *Institute of Radio Engineers - Transactions of Professional Group of Information Theory*, PGIT-4, pp.76-84.

Feldman, J. A., 1990, "Neural Networks, Artificial Intelligence and Computational Reality," *Computers in Industry*, Vol. 14, May, pp.145-148.

Foo, Y. P. S., and Takefuji, Y., 1988, "Integer Linear Programming Neural Networks for Job-Shop Scheduling," *Proceedings of 1988 International IEEE Conference on Neural Networks*, San Diego, CA.

Fu, L.-M., 1989, "Building Expert Systems on Neural Architecture," *First IEE InternationalConference on Artificial Neural Networks*, London, UK, Oct. 16-18, pp.221-225.

Fukushima, K., 1975, "Cognitron: A Self-Organizing Multilayered Neural Network," *Biol. Cybern.*, Vol. 20, pp. 121-136.

Fukushima, K., and Miyaka, S., 1980, "Neocognitron: A Self-Organizing Neural Network Model for a Mechanism of Pattern Recognition Unaffected by Shift in Position," *Biol. Cybern.*, Vol. 36, pp.193-202.

Fukuyama, Y., and Ueki, Y., 1991, "An Application of Artificial Neural Network to Dynamic Economic Load Dispatching," in M. A. El-Sharkawi, and R. j. Marks, II, eds., *Proceedings of the first International Forum on Applications of Neural Networks to Power Systems*, Seattle, Washington, July 23-26, pp.261-265.

Gaines, B. R., 1986, "Expert Systems in Manufacturing," *AUTOFACT 86*, November 12-14, Detroit, Michigan.

Govekar, E., Grabec, I., and Peklenik, J., 1989, "Monitoring of a Drilling Process by a Neural Network," *the 21st CIRP International Seminar on Manufacturing Systems*, Stockholm, Sweden, June 5-6.

Grossberg, S., 1976a, "Adaptive Pattern Classification and Universal Recording, I: Parallel Development and Coding of Neural Feature Detectors," *Biol. Cybern.*, Vol. 23, pp.121-134.

Grossberg, S., 1976b, "Adaptive Pattern Classification and Universal Recording, II: Feedback, Expectation, Olfaction, and Illusions," *biol. Cybern.*, Vol. 23, pp.187-202.

Guillot, M., and El Ouafi, A., 1991, "On-Line Identification of Tool Breakage in Metal Cutting Processes by Use of Neural Networks," in C. H. Dagli, S. R. T. Kumara, and Y. C. Shin, eds., *Intelligent Engineering Systems Through Artificial Neural Networks*, ASME Press, New York, pp.701-710.

Hall, J. W., Lu, S. C.-Y., 1991, "An Adaptive Machine Controller Utilizing Domain Knowledge and Quantitative Data," Knowledge-Based Engineering Systems Research Laboratory Annual Report, University of Illinois at Urbana-Champaign, pp.41-48.

Hall, J. W., and Lu S. C.-Y., 1992, "Emulating Human Process Control Functions with Neural Networks," Knowledge-Based Engineering Systems Research Laboratory Annual Report, University of Illinois at Urbana-Champaign, pp.145-152.

Hatvany J., and Nemes, L., 1978, "Intelligent Manufacturing Systems: A Tentative Forecast," in A. Niemi, B. Wahlstrom, and J. Virkunnen, eds., *A Link Between Science and Application of Automatic Control*, Proc. 7th World Congress of IFAC, Helsinki, Pergamon Press, Oxford, Vol. 2, pp.895-899.

Hatvany, J., 1987, "Matching AI Tools to Engineering Requirements," *Annals of the CIRP*, Vol. 36, No. 1, pp.311-315.

Hayes-Roth, F., Waterman, D., and Lenat, D. B., 1983, *Building Expert Systems*, Addison-Wesley, Reading, MA.

Hebb, D. O., 1949, *The Organization of Behavior: A Neuropsychological Theory*, John Wiley, New York.

Hinton, G. E., Sejnowski, T. J., and Ackley, D. H., 1984, "Boltzmann Machines: Constraint Satisfaction Networks That Learn," Technique Report, CMU-CS-84-119, Carnegie-Mellon University, Department of Computer Science.

Hinton, G. E., and Sejnowski, T. J., 1986, "Learning and Relearning in Boltzmann Machines," in T. L. McClelland, and D. E. Rumelhart eds., *Parallel Distributed Processing*, Vol. 1, Ch. 7, MIT Press, Cambridge, MA.

Hopfield, J. J., 1982, "Neural Networks and Physical Systems with Emergent Collective Computational Abilities," *Proc. Natl. Acad. Sci.*, Vol. 79, pp.2554-2558.

863

Hopfield, J. J., 1984, "Neurons with Graded Response Have Collective Computational Properties Like Those of Two State Neurons," *Proc. Natl. Acad. Sci.*, Vol. 81, pp.3088-3092.

Hopfield, J. J., and Tank, D. W., 1985, "Neural Computation of Decisions in Optimization Problem," *Biological Cybernetics*, Vol. 52, 1985, pp.141-152.

Hopfield, J. J., and Tank, D. W., 1986, "Computing with Neural Circuits: A Model," *Science*, Vol. 233, Aug., pp.625-633.

Hyer, N. L., and Wemmerlöv, U., 1989, "Group Technology in the US Manufacturing Industry: A Survey of Current Practices," *International Journal of Production Research*, Vol. 27, No. 8, pp.1287-1304.

IFAC, 1984, "Artificial Intelligence in Manufacturing," *Computers in Industry*, Vol. 5, pp.159-193.

Iyengar, S. S., and Kashyap, R. L., 1991, "Neural Networks: A Computational Perspective," in *Neural Networks: Concepts, Applications, and Implementations*, Prentice Hall, Englewood Cliffs, NJ, pp.1-30.

Jackel, L. D., Graf, H. P., Denker, J. S., and Henderson, D., 1988, "An Application of Neural Net Chips: Handwritten Digit Recognition," in *Proc. IEEE int. Conf. on Neural Networks*, Vol. 2, San Diego, CA., pp.107-115.

Jayaraman, B., Durham, M., Ashenayi, K., and Strattan, R., 1991, "Neural Net Based Correction of Power System Distortion Caused by Switching Power Supplies," in M. A. El-Sharkawi, and R. J. Marks, II, eds., *Proceedings of the first International Forum on Applications of Neural Networks to Power Systems*, Seattle, Washington, July 23-26, pp.198-202.

Kamarthi, S. V., Sankar, G. S., Cohen, P. H., and Kumara, S. R. T., 1991, "On-Line Tool Wear Monitoring using a Kohonen's Feature Map," in C. H. Dagli, S. R. T. Kumara, and Y. C. Shin, eds., *Intelligent Engineering Systems Through Artificial Neural Networks*, ASME Press, New York, pp.639-644.

Kao, Y., and Moon, Y. B., 1990, "Learning Part Families by the Backpropagation Rule of Neural Networks," *Proc. 1st Int. Conf. Automation Technology*, Hsinchu, Taiwan, July 4-6, pp.819-824.

Kao, Y., and Moon, Y. B., 1991, "A Unified Group Technology Implementation Using the Backpropagation Learning Rule of Neural Networks," *Computers and Industrial Engineering*, Vol. 20, No. 4, pp.425-437.

Kaparthi, S., and Suresh, N. C., 1991, "A neural network system for shape-based classification and coding of rotational parts," *International Journal of Production Research*, Vol. 29, No. 9, pp.1771-1784.

Kawato, M., Uno, Y., Isobe, M., and Suzuki, R., 1988, "Hierarchical Neural Network Model for Voluntary Movement with Application to Robotics," *IEEE Control Systems Magazine*, Vol. 8, No. 2, Apr., pp.8-16.

Kennedy, M. P., and Chua, L. O., 1988, "Neural Networks for Nonlinear Programming," *IEEE Trans. Circuits and Systems*, CAS-35, No. 5, pp.554-562.

King, J. R., and Nakornchai, V., 1982, "Machine-Component Group Formation in Group Technology: Review and Extension," *International Journal of Production Research*, Vol. 20, No. 2, pp.117-133.

Knapp, G. M., and Wang, H.-P., 1992, "Machine Fault Classification: A Neural Network Approach," *Int. J. Prod. Res.*, Vol. 30, No. 4, pp.81-823.

Koch, C., 1987, "Analog Neural Networks for Real-Time Vision System," *Proceedings of Workshop on Neural Network Devices and Applications*, Feb., Los Angeles, CA.

Kohonen, T., 1977, *Associative Memory: A System-Theoretical Approach*, Springer-Verlag, Berlin.

Kohonen, T., 1982, "Self-Organized Formation of Topologically Correct Feature Maps," *Biol. Cybern.*, Vol. 43, pp.59-69.

Kohonen, T., 1984, *Self-Organization and Associative Memory*, Springer-Verlag, Berlin.

Kohonen, T., 1987, "Adaptive, Associative, and Self-Organization Functions in Neural Computing," *Applied Optics*, Vol. 26, pp.4910-4918.

Kohonen, T., 1988a, "An Introduction to Neural Computing," *Neural Networks*, Vol. 1, pp.3-16.

Kohonen, T., 1988b, "State of the Art in Neural Computing," *Proceedings of IEEE First International Conference on Neural Networks*, pp.79-90.

Kokar, M. M., 1989, "Machine Learning," in A. Kusiak, eds., *Knowledge-based Systems in Manufacturing*, Taylor & Francis, Philadelphia, PA, pp.45-81.

Kooi, S. B. L., and Khorasani, K., 1991, "Control of Wood Chip Refiner Using Neural Networks," in C. H. Dagli, S. R. T. Kumara, and Y. C. Shin, eds., *Intelligent Engineering Systems Through Artificial Neural Networks*, ASME Press, New York, pp.567-572.

Kosko, B., 1987, "Adaptive Bidirectional Associative Memories," *Applied Optics*, Vol. 26, Dec., pp.4947-4960.

Laboissiere, R., Schwartz, J.-L., and Bailly, G., 1991, "Motor Control for Speech Skills: A Connecitionist Approach," *Connectionist Models: Proceedings of the 1990 Summer School*, pp.319-327.

Lacher, R. C., Hruska, S. I., and Kuncicky, S. C., 1992, "Back-Propagation Learning in Expert Networks," *IEEE Transactions on Neural Networks*, Vol. 3, No. 1, Jan., pp.62-72.

LeCun, Y., Boser, B., Denker, J. S., Henderson, D., Howard, R. E., Hubbard, W., and Jackel, L. D., 1989, "Backpropagation Applied to Handwritten Zip Code Recognition," *Neural Computation*, Vol. 1, pp.541-551.

Lin, C.-S., Wu, I.-C., and Guo, T. H., 1991, "Neural Networks for Sensor Failure Detection and Data Recovery," in C. H. Dagli, S. R. T. Kumara, and Y. C. Shin, eds., *Intelligent Engineering Systems Through Artificial Neural Networks*, ASME Press, New York, pp.735-740.

Lippmann, R. P, 1987, "An Introduction to Computing with Neural Nets," *Acoustics, Speech, and Signal Processing Magazine*, Vol. 4, No. 2, Apr., pp.4-22.

Maa, C. Y., Chin, C., and Shanblatt, M. A., 1989, "Improved Linear Programming Neural Networks," in *Proc. 31st Midwest Symp. on Circuits and Systems*, Urbana, IL., August, pp.748-751.

McCulloch, W. S., and Pitts, W. A., 1943, "A Logical Calculus of the Ideas Immanent in Nervous Activity," *Bulletin of Mathematics and Biophysics*, Vol. 5, pp.115-133.

Meade, A. J. Jr., Cheatham, J. B. Jr., and Adnan, S., 1991, "An Artificial Neural Network Application in Aerodynamics," in C. H. Dagli, S. R. T. Kumara, and Y. C. Shin, eds., *Intelligent Engineering Systems Through Artificial Neural Networks*, ASME Press, New York, pp.783-788.

Miller, W. T., Glanz, F. H., and Kraft, G., 1990, "CMAC: An Associative Neural Network Alternative to Backpropagation," *Proceedings of the IEEE*, Vol. 78, No. 10, Oct., pp.1581-1587.

Minsky, M., and Papert, S., 1969, *Perceptrons*, MIT Press, Cambridge, MA.

Monostori, L., and Nacsa, J., 1990, "On the Application of Neural Nets in Real-Time Monitoring of Machining Processes," *the 22nd CIRP Int. Seminar on Manufacturing Systems*, Enschede, Netherlands, June 11-12.

Moon, Y. B., and Roy, U., 1990, "Learning Group Technology Part Families from Solid Models by Parallel Distributed Processing," Technical Report MFE902, Department of Mechanical and Aerospace Engineering, Syracuse University.

Moon, Y. B., and Chi, S. C., 1992, "Generalized Part Family Formation Using Neural Network Techniques," *Journal of Manufacturing System*, Vol. 11, No. 3, pp.149-160.

Nacsa, J., and Monostori, L., 1990, "Real-Time Monitoring of Machining Processes," *Int. Conf. on Automatic Supervision, Monitoring, and Adaptive Control in Manufacturing*, Rydzyna, Poland, Sept. 3-5, pp.197-233.

Narazaki, H., and Ralescu, A. C., 1992, "A Connectionist Approach for Rule-Based Inference Using an Improved Relaxation Model," *IEEE Transactions on Neural Networks*, Vol. 3, No. 5, Sept., pp.741-751.

Nguyen, L., Patel, R. V., and Khorasani, K., 1991, "Neural Network Architectures for the Forward Kinematics Problem in Robotics," in *Proc. Joint IEEE Int. Neural Networks Conf.*, San Diego, CA., Vol. 3, pp.393-399.

Pao, Y.-H., and Sobajic, D. J., 1991, "Neural Networks and Knowledge Engineering," *IEEE Transactions on Knowledge and Data Engineering*, Vol. 3, No. 2, pp.185-192.

Prager, R. W., Clarke, T. J. W., and Fallside, F., 1989, "The Modified Kanerual Model: Results for Real Time Word Recognition," *First IEE International Conference on Artificial Neural Networks*, London, UK, Oct. 16-18, pp.105-109.

Rangwala, S. S., and Dornfeld, D. A., 1989, "Learning and Optimization of Machining Operations Using Computing Abilities of Neural Networks," *IEEE Trans. Syst., Man Cybern.*, Vol. 19, No. 2, pp.299-314.

Rehbein, D. A., Maze, S. M., and Havener, J. P., 1992, "The Application of Neural Networks in the Process Industry," *ISA Transactions*, Vol. 31, No. 4, pp.7-13.

Rose, D. E., 1991, "Appropriate Uses of Hybrid Systems," *Connectionist Models: Proceedings of the 1990 Summer School*, pp.277-286.

Rosenblatt, F., 1958, "The Perceptron: A Probalistic Model for Information Storage and Organization in the Brain," *Psychoanalytic Review*, Vol. 65, pp.386-408.

Rosenblatt, F., 1959, *Principles of Neurodynamics*, Spartan Books, New York.

Rumelhart, D. E., and McClelland, J. L., eds., 1986, *Parallel Distributed Processing: Explorations in the Microstructure of Cognition; Vol. 1: Foundations, Vol. 2: Psychological and Biological Models*, MIT Press and the PDP Research Group, Cambridge, MA.

Rumelhart, D. E., Hinton, G. E., and Williams, R. J., 1986, "Learning Internal Representations by Error Propagation," in D. E. Rumelhart, and J. L. McClelland, eds., *Parallel Distributed Processing: Explorations in the Microstructure of Cognition, Vol. 1: Foundations*, MIT Press, Cambridge, MA.

Schaffer, G. H., 1986, "Artificial Intelligence: A Tool For Smart Manufacturing," *American Machinist & Automated Manufacturing*, Vol. 130, No. 8, August, pp.83-94.

Schmerr, L. W., Nugen, S. M., and Forouraghi, B., 1991, "Planning Robust Design Experiments Using Neural Networks and Taguchi Methods," in C. H. Dagli, S. R. T. Kumara, and Y. C. Shin, eds., *Intelligent Engineering Systems Through Artificial Neural Networks*, ASME Press, New York, pp.829-834.

Sendaula, M. H., Biswas, S. K., Eltom, A., Parten, C., and Kazibwe, W., 1991, "Application of Artificial Neural Networks to Unit Commitment," in M. A. El-Sharkawi, and R. J. Marks, II, eds., *Proceedings of the first International Forum on Applications of Neural Networks to Power Systems*, Seattle, Washington, July 23-26, pp.256-260.

Shahani, K., Udpa, L., and Udpa, S. S., 1991, "Neural Networks for Classification of Ultrasonic NDE Signals," in C. H. Dagli, S. R. T. Kumara, and Y. C. Shin, eds., *Intelligent Engineering Systems Through Artificial Neural Networks*, ASME Press, New York, pp.407-412.

Shumsheruddin, D., 1991, "Neural Network Control of Robot Arm Tracking Movements," in J. G. Talor, eds., *Neural Network Applications*, Springer-Verlag, London, pp.129-139.

Smartt, H. B., Johnson, J. A., Einerson, C. J., and Cordes, G. A., 1991, "Development of a Connectionist Fuzzy Logic System for Control of Gas Metal Arc Welding," in C. H. Dagli, S. R. T. Kumara, and Y. C. Shin, eds., *Intelligent Engineering Systems Through Artificial Neural Networks*, ASME Press, New York, pp.711-716.

Smith, A. E., 1991, "Quality Control Using Backpropagation: An Injection Molding Application," in C. H. Dagli, S. R. T. Kumara, and Y. C. Shin, eds., *Intelligent*

Engineering Systems Through Artificial Neural Networks, ASME Press, New York, pp.729-734.

Sobajic, D. J., Lu, J. J., and Pao, Y.-H., 1988, "Intelligent Control for the Intelledex 605 T Robot Manipulator," *Proceedings of the 1988 IEEE International Neural Networks Conference*, San Diego, CA, Vol. 2, pp.613-640.

Soliman, J. T., 1987, "Expert Systems in Manufacturing," *Proceedings of The 17th ISATA Conference Keynote Speeches*, Munich, West Germany.

Steinbuch, K., and Piske, V. A. W., "Learning Matrices and Their Applications," *IEEE Trans. Electron. Comput.*, Vol. EC-12, 1963, pp. 846-862.

Sun, R., and Waltz, D., 1991, "A Neurally Inspired Massively Parallel Model of Rule-Based Reasoning," in *Neural and Intelligent Systems Integration: Fifth and Sixth Generation Integrated Reasoning Information Systems*, John Wiley & Sons, New York, pp.341-381.

Tagliarini, G. A., Christ, J. F., and Page, E. W., 1991, "Optimization Using Neural Networks," *IEEE Transactions on Computers*, Vol. 40, No. 12, Dec., pp.1347-1358.

TAI, 1991, "Are Neural Networks a Tool for AI," *Proc. of the 1991 IEEE Int. Conf. on Tools for AI*, San Jose, CA, Nov., pp.5-6.

Tank, D. W., and Hopfield, J. J., 1986, "Simple 'Neural' Optimization Networks: An A/D Converter, Signal Decision Circuit and a Linear Programming Circuit," *IEEE Trans. Circ. Syst.*, CAS-33, No. 5, pp.533-541.

Udo, G. J., 1992, "Neural Networks Applications in Manufacturing Processes," *Computers and Industrial Engineering*, Vol. 23, No. 1-4, pp.97-100.

Valliere, D., and Lee, J.-M., 1988, "Artificial Intelligence in Manufacturing," *Automation*, May, pp.40-44.

Venugopal, V., and Narendran, T. T., 1992, "Neural Network Model for Design Retrieval in Manufacturing systems," *Computers in Industry*, Vol. 20, pp.11-23.

VerDuin, W. H., 1990, "Solving Manufacturing Problems with Neural Nets," *Automation*, July, pp.54+.

VerDuin, W. H., 1991, "Neural Network Software Assists Expert System," *Control Engineering*, July, pp.37-40.

VerDuin, W. H., 1992, "The Role of Integrated AI Technologies in Product Formation," *ISA Transactions*, Vol. 31, No. 2, pp.151-157.

von der Malsburg, C., 1973, "Self-Organization of Orientation Sensitive Cells in the Striate Cortex," *Kybernetik*, Vol. 14, pp.85-100.

Waibel, A. H., and Hampshire, J. B., 1991, "Neural Network Applications to Speech," *Neural Networks: Concepts, Application, and Implementations*, vol. 1, Prentice Hall, Englewood Cliffs, NJ., pp.54-76.

Wasserman, P. D., Unal, A., and Haddad, S., 1991, "Neural Networks for On-line Machine Condition Monitoring," in C. H. Dagli, S. R. T. Kumara, and Y. C. Shin, eds., *Intelligent Engineering Systems Through Artificial Neural Networks*, ASME Press, New York, pp.693-700.

Widrow, B., and Hoff, M. E., 1960, "Adaptive Switching Circuits," *1960 WESCON Convention*, Record Part IV, 1960, pp.96-104.

Wu, H.-J., Liou, C.-S., and Pi, H.-H., 1991, "Fault Diagnosis of Processing Damage in Injection Molding Via Neural Network Approach," in C. H. Dagli, S. R. T. Kumara, and Y. C. Shin, eds., *Intelligent Engineering Systems Through Artificial Neural Networks*, ASME Press, New York, pp.645-650.

Yih, Y., Lian, T.-P., and Moskowitz, H., 1991, "A Hybrid Approach for Crane Scheduling Problems," in C. H. Dagli, S. R. T. Kumara, and Y. C. Shin, eds., *Intelligent Engineering Systems Through Artificial Neural Networks*, ASME Press, New York, pp.867-872.

Zeidenberg, M., 1990, *Neural Networks in Artificial Intelligence*, Ellis Horwood, New York.Zurada, J. M., 1992, *Introduction to Artificial Neural Systems*, West Publishing Company, St. Paul, MN.

Zurada, J. M., Zigoris, D. M., Aronhime, P. B., and Desai, M., 1991, "Multi-Layer Feedforward Networks for Printed Character Classification," in *Proc. 34th Midwest Symp. on Circuits and Systems*, Monterey, CA., May 14-16.

Chapter 25:   Software Production

Chapter 25
Software Production

One of the more unique applications of neural networks is in the area of software production. The papers found in this chapter represent some of the few that have been published in this area. **Paper 25.1** describes the application of neural networks to software reliability growth modeling. **Paper 25.2** presents a neural network approach to detecting high-risk software modules during the software design effort. **Paper 25.3** proposes a neural network approach to software size estimation.

A Neural Network Approach for Software Reliability Growth Modeling In the Presence of Code Churn

N. Karunanithi

Room: 2E-378, Bellcore

445 South Street, Morristown, NJ 07960

(201) 829-4466

Email: *karun@faline.bellcore.com*

Abstract

One of the key assumptions made in most of the time-domain based software reliability growth models is that the complete code for the system is available before testing starts and that the code remains frozen during testing. However, this assumption is often violated in large software projects. Thus, the existing models may not be able to provide an accurate description of the failure process in the presence of code churn. Recently, Dalal and McIntosh [3] developed an extended stochastic model by incorporating continuous code churn into a standard Poisson process model and observed an improvement in the model's estimation accuracy. This paper demonstrates the applicability of the neural network approach to the problem of developing an extended software reliability growth model in the face of continuous code churn. In this preliminary study, a comparison is made between two neural network models, one with the code churn information and the other without the code churn information, for the accuracy of fit and the predictive quality using a data set from a large telecommunication system. The preliminary results suggest that the neural network model that incorporates. the code churn information is capable of providing a more accurate prediction than the network without the code churn information.

Keywords: Software reliability growth modeling, Extended stochastic models, Neural network models, Continuous code churn, Complex models.

1 Introduction

There exists a large number of analytic software reliability growth models for estimating reliability growth of software systems. Existing analytic models describe the failure process as a function of execution time (or calendar time) and a set of unknown parameters. Some of the attractive features of the analytic models are that they are easy to analyze, interpret and make inferences. However, analytic models are based on many simplifying assumptions [9, 12]. For example, one of the key assumptions made in many of the existing analytic models (although this is often not stated explicitly) is that the code size remains unchanged during testing. This assumption may not be valid for most large software systems because the program undergoes change (or evolves) during development. Programs can evolve due to either requirements changes or integration of parts during development. Requirement changes may occur due to enhancement of features, adaptation of the system to changing hardware and software, optimization of the system to realize performance improvement etc. Evolution of code may also occur during development for several reasons such as: parallel development of component systems by different groups, conducting tests in a step-by-step (or feature-by-feature) fashion, performing tests as and when subsystems are ready, and starting tests before the interfaces between subsystems are incomplete.

Evolving programs can introduce a variety of complications for both software engineers and the software reliability estimate. For software engineers, an evolving program becomes a moving target during testing. Furthermore, the testing team cannot have uniform confidance on all parts of an evolving program because the code which is included early on would be exercised more often than the parts that are included later. From software reliability estimation point of view, the program evolution introduces complications in efforts such as data collection, modeling, analysis and interpretation. Thus, in the face of program evolution, existing execution time based software reliability growth models may not be able to provide a

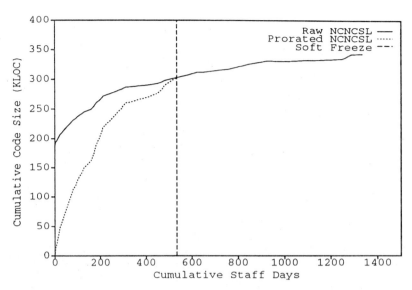

Figure 1: Code Churn Vs. Cumulative Staff Days.

trustworthy estimate without proper extensions.

To make a model more reliable one must incorporate relevant information about the evolutionary process of the code. Incorporating such additional information into a model can help the model to provide a more realistic picture of the failure process than a model that relies solely on the assumptions made by the model developer. Musa et al. [12] discuss three general approachs for tackling the issue of program evolution. However, all those approachs do not directly deal with continuous program evolution. Recently, Munson et al. [11] proposed an approach to incorporate the functional program complexity of the software into dynamic reliability growth models. The functional complexity of a system (under testing) represents the expected value of the relative complexity metrics of modules under a particular operational profile. However, this approach requires both a static analysis of the code as well as a precise definition of the operational profile of the software. In order to deal with a continuously evolving code (or "code churn") Dalal and McIntosh [3] proposed a simple extension to a Poisson process model proposed by Dalal and Mallows [1, 2]. (Their definition of "code churn" includes both new additions of code as well as changes in the existing code due to fault fixes.) In their approach, the size of the code churn was considered as one of the free variables of the model. They validated their extended model by applying it to a large telecommunication software project. Their empirical results clearly demonstrate that adding the code churn information can improve the fit of the model.

This paper demonstrates the applicability of the neural network approach to the problem of modeling software reliability growth in the face of continuous code churn. The idea is inspired by the work of Dalal and McIntosh [3]. In this preliminary study, a comparison is made between two neural network models, one with the code churn information and the other without the code churn information, for the accuracy of fit and the predictive quality using a data set from a large telecommunication system. The preliminary results suggest that the neural network model that incorporates the code churn information is capable of providing a more accurate prediction than the network without the code churn information. The rest of the paper is as follows. Section 2 describes the data set used in this study. Section 3 reviews the extended model developed by Dalal and McIntosh [3] and discusses the applicability of the neural network approach for developing extended software reliability growth models. Section 4 presents preliminary results from the neural network approach in terms of the fit of the models and their predictive quality. Section 5 concludes the paper with a summary of results and future extensions.

2 The Data Set

The data set used for this study is from a large telecommunication system consisting of approximately 7 million non-commentary source lines [3]. The particular release for which the reliability model

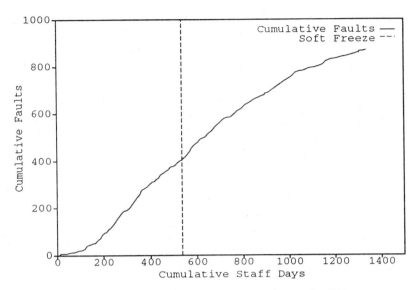

Figure 2: Cumulative Faults Vs. Cumulative Staff Days.

is applied had around 400,000 new or changed non-commentary source lines (NCNCSL). Since the testing was performed in a highly distributed environment the time was measured in "staff days". The "staff day" metric represents the amount of time a tester actually spends every day on testing the current release. It should be noted that a staff day is not exactly the same as the calendar time. To collect the staff day data, the testing organization used a custom built login procedure to prompt the tester to enter the time information for the previous day when they logged on each morning. The code churn took place in two ways: first, the developers delivered code on daily basis; and second, testing in the early stages occurred by groups of subsystems. At the initial stages of testing the system contained only some of the modifications and additions of the code; not all of the subsystems were tested at once. As testing progressed, more additions and modifications were included. Figure 1 illustrates the continuous code churn as a function of staff days. The vertical (dashed) line indicates the date on which the system was frozen. After the "soft freeze", no functionality was added to the system and subsequent changes reflect only fault fixes. To make the graph continuous, they used a simple linear interpolation for those days in which there was no code churn. Since they considered modifications in the code due to fault fixes also as part of the code churn, the system had a non-trivial code churn even after the soft freeze. Though several subsystems were delivered at the start of the testing, only a subset of them were actually tested. This necessitated a proper adjustment

to the initial NCNCSL. So the initial NCNCSL was prorated across the NCNCSL received after the start of testing but before the soft freeze. The dotted line in Figure 1 shows the adjusted code size. Figure 2 illustrates the actual failure history of the system as a function of time.

In the model developed by Dalal and McIntosh [3] as well as the neural network approach examined in this paper, the code size is used as one of the free variables. Figure 3 illustrates the relationship between the cumulative faults and the cumulative code size. Note that nearly half of the faults were observed before the soft freeze and the amount of additional code added due to fault fixes constitutes about one sixth of the entire code.

3   Model Development

3.1   Dalal and McIntosh Model

If one assumes a continuous code churn and fits a basic model at each interval, the resulting cumulative fault vs. time curve will look like a waterfall (a cascade of exponentially decaying curves). This will also lead to an unmanageable number of parameters. In order to make the model computationally tractable, Dalal and McIntosh [3] make the following assumptions. Let the testing be divided into n intervals $(t_0, t_1), (t_1, t_2), \ldots, (t_{n-1}, t_n)$ and each code delivery corresponds to the start of a new interval. Let the number of faults N_i in each interval i be a Poisson random variable with mean α_i and that it satisfies

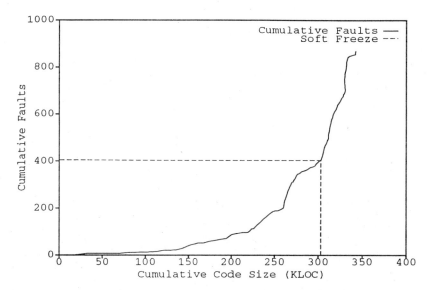

Figure 3: Cumulative Faults Vs. Cumulative Code Size.

the usual exponential assumptions. Let c_i be the size of the code added at the end of the i-th interval. If there was no code added in an interval then the corresponding $c_i = 0$. Since all code should undergo at least some testing, it is assumed that there were no further additions of code beyond interval $k \leq n - 1$. The basic model of Dalal and Mallows [1, 2] on which the extended model was built is given by

$$\mu(t_i) = \alpha_i(1 - e^{-\beta(t_i - t_{i-1})})$$

where $\mu(t_i)$ is the mean number of faults found at time t_i, α_i is the number of faults at the beginning of the i-th interval and β is the rate parameter. The number of remaining faults at time t_i is equal to $\alpha_i e^{-\beta(t_i - t_{i-1})}$. The extended model, which incorporates code churn c_i, is given by,

$$\alpha_{i+1} = g(\alpha_i e^{-\beta(t_i - t_{i-1})}, c_i, \theta) \qquad i = 1, \ldots, n$$

where $g(x, c, \theta)$ is a general (yet unspecified) function. Typically, the extended model can also be expressed as

$$g(x, c, \theta) = x + g_1(c, \theta) + g_2(x, c, \theta)$$

with $g_1 = g_2 = 0$ whenever $c = 0$. This formulation can be interpreted as follows:
The number of faults in the code
after the code churn =
{ the number of faults immediately before the code churn } +
{ the number of faults in newly delivered code } +
{ the number of faults in the code because of the interactions between the two sets of faults}.

As a first step approximation, it is assumed that the function $g_2(x, c, \theta) = 0$. This is equivalent to saying that there is no additional faults due to interaction of the existing code and the newly added code. Next, the structure of g_1 is assumed to be an identity function and c is equal to NCNCSL at the i-th delivery (i.e., $g_1(c, \theta) = \theta g_1(c)$). Finally, the model is simplified by assuming that the number of faults in the added code is proportional to the size of this code. Thus, the resulting model is given by,

$$g(\alpha_i e^{-\beta(t_i - t_{i-1})}, c_i, \theta) = \alpha_{i+1} = \alpha_i e^{-\beta(t_i - t_{i-1})} + \theta c_i$$

where α_{i+1} is the number of faults in the system at the beginning of $(i + 1)$st interval. Their formulation also includes a maximum likelihood equation for estimating the parameters of the extended model and an economic heuristic to decide when one should stop testing. Observe that the estimate of the parameters α and β can very over time. The corresponding expression for the cumulative fault, $M(t_i)$, is given by,

$$M(t_i) = M(t_{i-1}) + \alpha_i(1 - e^{-\beta(t_i - t_{i-1})})$$

where $M(t_{i-1})$ is the cumulative faults found at the end of the $(i - 1)$st interval. Note that the above expression has the structure of an autoregressive process. One of the important claims of their study is that the fit of the extended model is considerably superior than that of the basic model.

3.2 The Neural Network Approach

Applicability of neural network models to software reliability growth prediction has been demonstrated

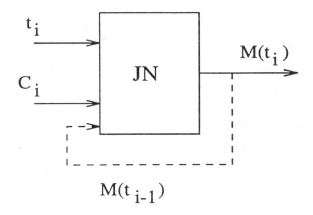

Figure 4: A Modified Jordan Style Neural Network.

by Karunanithi et al. [6, 7, 8]. (For more details on neural network models and their implementation refer to [6, 7, 8] and other references recommended therein.) Two important conclusions of the earlier studies are: i) the neural network approach is a "black box" approach (i.e., the neural networks are capable of developing an appropriate model for the failure process from the training data) and ii) the modified Jordan style [5] networks with "Teacher Forced" training are capable of providing more accurate predictions than the feed-forward networks. Also, it was hypothesized that one can easily realize a complex software reliability growth model by incorporating additional information into the neural network framework. This paper verifies the later hypothesis by adding the code churn information to the existing neural networks framework.

The network models used in the previous research[6, 7, 8] had the accumulated time (t_i) as the free variable and the cumulative faults ($M(t_i)$) as the dependent variable. From the modeling point of view, they are analogous to the traditional execution time based software reliability growth models. However, the networks used in the present study have an additional input (C_i) for the cumulative code churn. Figure 4 represents an abstract model of the modified Jordan style network used in this study. The dotted line in Figure 4 represents the feed-back from the output ($M(t_{i-1})$) required for realizing the Jordan style network. For simplicity, it is assumed that the network operates only in discrete time-steps. The "box" (JN) represents the neural network.

The function mapping of the network can be expressed as,

$$M(t_i) = f(M(t_{i-1}), t_i, C_i)$$

where f is an unknown mapping developed by the neural network. According to this model, the cumu-

lative faults at time t_i is a function of the cumulative time, the cumulative code churn and the cumulative faults at the previous time step. This realization of the model is analogous to the extended model developed by Dalal and McIntosh [3].

4 Results

4.1 Fit of the Model

To evaluate the quality of the fit of the neural network approach, we constructed two different Jordan style networks. The first network had the staff day as the only external input. The second network, on the other hand, had both the staff day and the cumulative code churn as external inputs. Figure 4 shows the schematic representation of the second network model. The network had a clipped linear unit [8] in the output layer and sigmoidal units in the hidden layer. The network was constructed and trained using the Cascade-Correlation algorithm. The Cascade-Correlation algorithm is a constructive algorithm that can be used not only to train a network but also to construct a suitable network. During training, the Cascade-Correlation starts with a minimal network (i.e., a network with no hidden units) and progressively adds the required number of hidden units until the learning is successfully completed. However, the number of hidden units added to the network and the final weights of a trained network can vary depending on the random weight values used at the beginning of the training. This can introduce statistical variation in the fit as well as the predictions of the model. To reduce such variations and to get a better statistics we constructed and trained networks using 50 different initial weight vectors. The results reported in this

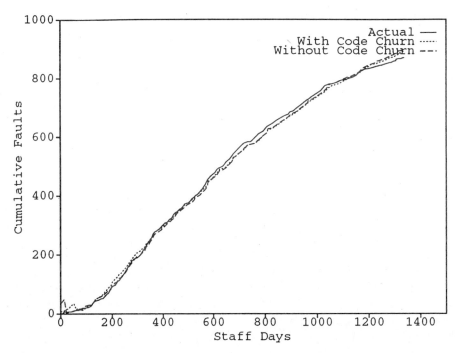

Figure 5: Fit of the Neural Network Models.

section are based on the averages obtained from 50 trials. The final fit of the networks with and without the code churn information are shown in Figure 5. The solid line in Figure 5 represents the actual cumulative faults observed. The dotted line is the fit of the network with the code churn input. The fit of the network without the code churn information is represented in a dash line. Note that both fits look almost similar. However, a closer look at these fits revealed that the network that used the code churn information is closer to the actual data than the network without the code churn information. This observation agrees with the result of Dalal and McIntosh [3].

4.2   A Diagnostic Plot

In order to check whether there are bias in the fit of the models, a simple diagnostic plot was constructed using the residuals from the final fit of the models. For the purpose of illustration, the diagnostic plot for the network with the code churn information is shown in Figure 6.

The residuals in Figure 6 represent the difference between the change in the observed number of cumulative faults and the change in the number of cumulative faults of the fit of the model. The residuals for the plot are obtained as follows:

$$Residuals = \{(M(t_i) - M(t_{i-1})) - (\hat{M}(t_i) - \hat{M}(t_{i-1}))\}$$

where $M(t)$ and $\hat{M}(t)$ represent the observed faults and the fit of the model respectively. The residuals are analogous to the derivative of $M(t)$ and reflect the sensitivity (or bias) of the local behavior of the fit. The diagnostic plot suggests that there is no overall major trend in the fit of the neural network model.

4.3   Prediction Results

Even if the fit of a model is good, that does not guarantee that its predictions will always be accurate. A good model also should provide accurate predictions of future faults. In order to assess the predictive capability of the model we used two extreme prediction horizons: the *next-step prediction* (NSP), for the cumulative faults at the end of the next time step; and the *end-point prediction* (EPP), for the cumulative faults at the end of the test phase. When an extended model like the one developed in this paper is used for predicting future events, one has to know not only the execution time corresponding to a future day but also a precise information about the code churn. We solved this issue by using the size of the code corresponding to the final value of the code churn in the training data to all future predictions (i.e., the value of the code size of the last point in the training data was considered as the size of the final code). Note that this issue does not arise if we do not use the code

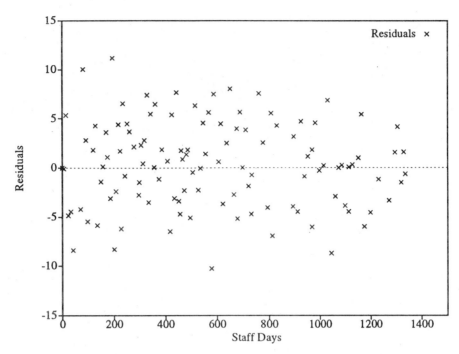

Figure 6: Diagnostics: Residuals vs. Staff Days.

churn information.

The neural networks cannot predict well without sufficient training data. This is analogous to using insufficient data to estimate the parameters of a stochastic model. In our prediction experiment, the size of the training set was gradually increased from a minimal set consisting of all data points before the "soft freeze" up to a set with all but the last point in the failure history. In order to gauge the predictive quality of the neural network model we used the average relative error (ARE) used by Malaiya et al. [10]. The average relative error measure is defined as

$$ARE = \frac{1}{n-k-1} \sum_{i=k+1}^{n-1} \left| \frac{M(t_i) - \hat{M}(t_i)}{M(t_i)} \right|$$

where n is the number of points in data set, k is the number of points in the training set corresponding to the soft freeze and $n-k-1$ is the prediction window. ARE provides a summary of how well the model predicts across a window of the future failure history. The predictive performance of the neural network models for the two extreme prediction horizons are summarized in Table 1. The "Mean" and "SD" represent the mean and the standard deviation of the ARE measure over 50 trials. These results suggest that the network with the code churn information is capable of providing a more accurate prediction than the network

without the code churn information.

5 Conclusion

We demonstrated that one can easily extend the execution time based neural network framework to incorporate the code churn information. Our preliminary results suggest that incorporating the code churn information can help both the fit as well as the predictive accuracy of the neural network models. However, we do note that the results presented here are preliminary and they have yet to be compared with the results of the existing models. This will be explored in future.

Dalal and Mallows [1, 2] proposed and integrated an economic model to decide when one should stop testing. The economic model is based on the tradeoff between the cost of testing software (i.e., not releasing in time) and the cost of releasing it. In the future, we plan to integrate their economic model with the neural network framework.

Often, one is interested in predicting not only the cumulative faults but also other quantities such as the rate of occurrence of failure, mean time to failure etc. The extended neural network model developed in this study represent only the cumulative faults. However, if one is interested in the failure rate expression, it is straightforward to derive it from the expression for the

Neural Network	NSP		EPP	
Model	Mean	SD	Mean	SD
Without Code Churn	3.834	1.883	26.342	8.417
With Code Churn	2.955	1.803	17.27	5.837

Table 1: A Summary of Prediction Results in Terms of *ARE*.

cumulative faults using the method outlined in [8].

There are several advantages with an extended software reliability growth model:

- From a modeling point of view, it demonstrates how one can extend a time-domain based model, whether it is based on the neural network framework or the standard stochastic approach, by incorporating continuous code churn information.

- From an information theoretic point view, the extended model is appealing because it is based on more information about the failure process than the traditional execution time-based model. As a first approximation, we directly included the code size in the extended model. However, this need not be the case; one can preprocess the code (i.e., perform a static analysis on the code to extract relevant static complexity measures) and then use the preprocessed outputs to build a more sophisticated software reliability growth model.

- One can also use the extended model in the early stages of the software development cycle because the model does not require the existence of code for the complete system.

References

[1] S. R. Dalal and C. L. Mallows, "When Should One Stop Testing Software?", *J. Am. Statist. Assoc.*, 83, pp. 872-879, 1988.

[2] S. R. Dalal and C. L. Mallows, "Some Graphical Aids for Deciding When to Stop Testing Software", *IEEE J. Selected Areas in Communications.*, Vol. 8, No. 2, pp. 169-175, 1990.

[3] S. R. Dalal and A. A. McIntosh, "Reliability Modeling and When to Stop Testing for Large Software Systems in the Presence of Code Churn: Analysis and Results for TIRKS Release 16.0", *Bellcore, TM-ARH-021705*, Aug. 1992.

[4] S. E. Fahlman and C. Lebiere, "The Cascaded-Correlation Learning Architecture", School of Computer Science, Carnegie Mellone University, Tech. Rep. CMU-CS-90-100, Feb. 1990.

[5] M. I. Jordan, "Attractor Dynamics and Parallelism in a Connectionist Sequential Machine", *Proc. of the 8th Annual Conf. of the Cog. Science*, pp. 531-546, 1986.

[6] N. Karunanithi, D. Whitley, and Y. K. Malaiya, "Prediction of Software Reliability Using Connectionist Models", *IEEE Trans. on Software Eng.*, Vol. 18, No. 7, pp. 563-574, July 1992.

[7] N. Karunanithi, D. Whitley, and Y. K. Malaiya, "Using Neural Networks in Reliability Prediction", *IEEE Software*, Vol. 9, No. 4, pp. 53-59, July 1992.

[8] N. Karunanithi and Y. K. Malaiya, "The Scaling Problem in Neural Networks for Software Reliability Prediction", *Proc. 1992 Int. Symp. on Soft. Rel. Eng.*, pp. 76-82, Oct. 1992.

[9] B. Littlewood, "Theories of Software Reliability: How Good Are They and How Can They Be Improved?", *IEEE Trans. on Software Eng.*, Vol. SE-6, No. 5, pp. 489-500, Sep. 1980.

[10] Y. K. Malaiya, N. Karunanithi, and P. Verma, "Predictability of Software Reliability Models", *IEEE Trans. Reliability*, Vol. 41, No. 4, pp. 539-546, Dec. 1992.

[11] J. C. Munson and T. M. Khoshgoftaar, "The Functional Problem Complexity Metrics for Software Reliability Models", *Proc. 1991 Int. Symp. on Soft. Rel. Eng.*, pp. 2-11, May 1991.

[12] J. D. Musa, A. Iannino, and K. Okumoto, **Software Reliability - Measurement, Prediction, Applications**, McGraw-Hill, 1987.

A Neural Network Modeling Methodology for the Detection of High-Risk Programs

Taghi M. Khoshgoftaar
Dept. of Computer Science & Engineering
Florida Atlantic University
Boca Raton, FL 33431
Email: taghi@cse.fau.edu

David L. Lanning
IBM
1000 NW 51st Street
Boca Raton, Florida 33432
Email: lanningd@cse.fau.edu

Abhijit S. Pandya
Dept. of Computer Science & Engineering
Florida Atlantic University
Boca Raton, FL 33431
Email: abhi@cse.fau.edu

Abstract

The profitability of a software development effort is highly dependent on both timely market entry and the reliability of the released product. To get a highly reliable product to the market on schedule, software engineers must allocate resources appropriately across the development effort. Software quality models based upon data drawn from past projects can identify key risk or problem areas in current similar development efforts. Knowing the high-risk modules in a software design is a key to good design and staffing decisions. A number of researchers have recognized this, and have applied modeling techniques to isolate fault-prone or high-risk program modules early in the development cycle. Discriminant analytic classification models have shown promise in performing this task. In this paper, we introduce a neural network classification model for identifying high-risk program modules, and we compare the quality of this model with that of a discriminant classification model fitted with the same data. We find that the neural network techniques provide a better management tool in software engineering environments.

1 Introduction

To be profitable, a software development effort must get a highly reliable product to the market in a reasonable time. Products having low reliability are typically shunned by the market, and they incur high maintenance costs. Late arriving products must lure market share from established products by providing more functionality and better value. Since quality and schedule act in opposition, it is difficult to hit the market on time with a highly reliable product. To achieve this goal, software engineers must allocate resources appropriately across the development effort.

Typically, few of the modules comprising a software system tend to be complex. For example, LeGall *et al.* observed several software systems and found that only 4 to 6% of the modules were complex, 32 to 36% were simple, and the remaining modules fell between these extremes [8]. Design decisions based upon risk potential can reduce the time-to-market for software products, and improve the customer's perception of product quality. A design having characteristics similar to passed designs that have lead to implementation and maintenance problems is likely to cause similar problems in similar development efforts. Further, considering risk potential can improve staffing decisions. The skill level of those assigned to implement, test, and maintain high-risk modules should meet the complexity of these modules.

A number of researchers have noted the value in identifying the high-risk program modules early in the development process. Two distinct approaches have appeared in the literature: models based upon discriminant analysis, and models based upon decision trees. Munson and Khoshgoftaar introduced the application of discriminant analytic models that detect high-risk modules based on the values of orthogonal domain metrics [13]. Porter and Selby investigated the use of metric based decision trees to model high-risk characteristics of program modules, and to identify high-risk modules [15]. Briand *et al.* applied a similar modeling process based on both statistics and machine learning principles [1].

In this paper, we present a neural network model for the detection of high-risk programs, and compare its performance with that of a discriminant analytic model. For both of these approaches, we build models that predict high-risk modules based upon software complexity metric and fault data. The discriminant model uses domain metrics derived from the complex-

879

ity metric data. The data is collected from a large military telecommunications system.

2 Classification Methodology

Classification models optimally assign objects to two or more labeled classes based upon object attributes that vary somewhat from class to class. A classification modeling technique attempts to derive models that produce the fewest misclassifications in a sample of objects with known attributes and known class memberships. This sample of objects is the *training* or *calibration* data set. The process of deriving the model with this set is often referred to as *training* in neural network circles, and as *fitting* in statistical circles. A fitted, or trained, model can classify objects with known object attributes, but unknown class memberships.

Classifying program modules as either high-risk or low-risk applies a restricted classification model in which there are only two classes. The objects are program modules, the class labels are high-risk and low-risk, and the object attributes are a selection of software complexity metrics. A suitable period of testing and field experience reveals the class memberships of the modules comprising a software system. The criterion for classifying a module, the criterion variable, is the number of faults found in the module. Those found to contain many faults are high-risk; those found to contain few faults are low-risk. A classification model is derived to optimally classify a collection of modules with known complexity metric values and known class memberships. It is expected that this model will achieve a low misclassification rate in a similar software development environment for untested program modules with known complexity metric values.

In this study we compare a model derived using statistical discriminant analysis techniques with a model derived using neural network techniques. Section 2.1 discusses statistical discriminant analysis techniques. Section 2.2 discusses neural network techniques. Since we apply two-class models, we restrict our discussions in these sections to classification models having two classes.

2.1 Discriminant Modeling Methodology

In this study we derive a discriminant model that classifies program modules as either high-risk or low-risk based upon software complexity metric values. There are several discriminant analytic techniques. The technique that is appropriate for a given analysis depends on the types of the independent variables. The independent variables may be all quantitative, all qualitative, or a mixture of these two types. Applicable models in each of these cases use, respectively, linear, discrete, and logistic discrimination techniques [2]. Since all of the software complexity metrics in this study are quantitative, we use a linear discriminant model and restrict our discussion to techniques of this type.

In our linear discriminant model, an observation, $\mathbf{x}$, is a vector of software complexity metrics. Let $\bar{\mathbf{x}}_j$ represent the mean of a class $j = 1, 2$. Then the squared distance from an observation to the mean of class j is

$$D_j^2(\mathbf{x}) = (\mathbf{x} - \bar{\mathbf{x}}_j)^T \Sigma^{-1} (\mathbf{x} - \bar{\mathbf{x}}_j)$$

where Σ is the pooled covariance matrix. Thus the posterior probability of membership of $\mathbf{x}$ in class j is

$$p_j(\mathbf{x}) = \frac{e^{-\frac{1}{2}D_j^2(\mathbf{x})}}{\sum_{i=1}^{2} e^{-\frac{1}{2}D_i^2(\mathbf{x})}}$$

The model assigns an observation, $\mathbf{x}$, to the class, j, having greater posterior probability of membership; that is, the model selects j such that $p_j(\mathbf{x}) = \max(p_1(\mathbf{x}), p_2(\mathbf{x}))$.

In a large selection of complexity metrics, it is likely that some metrics will have strong correlations [11]. Yet, regression and discriminant analyses assume that the independent variables have no linear relationships. Deviations from this assumption can result in models with highly unstable regression coefficients. At the same time, an understanding of the most important attributes of software complexity requires consideration of a large selection of complexity measures [17]. We avoid this dilemma by using *domain metrics* as the independent variables in our discriminant model.

Munson and Khoshgoftaar found that software complexity metrics are actually linear combinations of a small number of underlying orthogonal metric domains [11]. A principal components analysis of complexity data isolates these domains. Let Σ be the covariance matrix for a set of m complexity metrics. Then Σ is a real symmetric matrix, and, assuming that it has distinct roots, may be decomposed as

$$\Sigma = \mathbf{P}\Lambda\mathbf{P}^T$$

where Λ is a diagonal matrix with the eigenvalues $\lambda_1, \lambda_2, \ldots, \lambda_m$ on its diagonal, $\mathbf{P}$ is an orthogonal matrix where column j is the eigenvector associated with λ_j, and $\mathbf{P}^T$ is the transpose of $\mathbf{P}$. The m eigenvectors in $\mathbf{P}$ give the coefficients that define m uncorrelated linear combinations of the original complexity metrics. These orthogonal linear combinations are the principal components of Σ. An element p_{ij} of $\mathbf{P}$ gives the coefficient of the ith complexity metric in the jth principle component. λ_j gives the amount of complexity metric variance that is explained by the jth principle component. In principal components analysis, the eigenvalues along the diagonal of Λ form a decreasing sequence that explains all of the complexity data variance, that is, $\lambda_1 > \lambda_2 > \cdots > \lambda_m$, and $\sum_{j=1}^{m} \lambda_j$ gives the total variance in the complexity metric data.

The first few principal components typically explain a large proportion of the total explained variance. Thus restricting attention to the first few principal components can achieve a reduction in dimensionality with an insignificant loss of explained variance. A stopping rule selects $p < m$ principal components such that each one contributes significantly to the total explained variance, and the p selected components collectively account for a large proportion of this variance. A typical stopping rule extracts principle components with associated eigenvalues greater than one. The relationship of each of the m metrics to each of the p significant principal components is given by the standardized transformation matrix, $\mathbf{T}$. Given that $\mathbf{x}_i$ is the vector of m complexity measures for module i, and that $\bar{\mathbf{x}}$ and $\mathbf{x}_s$ are, respectively, the vector mean and vector variance of these complexity measures, $\mathbf{z}_i = (\mathbf{x}_i - \bar{\mathbf{x}})/\mathbf{x}_s$ is the vector of standardized complexity measures for module i, and

$$\mathbf{D}_i = \mathbf{z}_i \mathbf{T}$$

is a new vector of p domain metrics for module i. The domain metrics represent each significant source of variance in the complexity data, and satisfy the independence assumptions of regression modeling [5].

2.2 Neural Network Modeling Methodology

Recent advances in artificial neural network programming techniques have attracted the attention of software engineers. Researchers have applied neural networks to several applications related to software quality control. Karunanithi *et al.* developed neural network models of software reliability growth, and demonstrated that these models have better predictive quality than some analytic models [4]. Khoshgoftaar *et al.* proposed a neural network approach for predicting the number of faults in program modules [6]. This article focuses on feed-forward neural network classifiers for static patterns with continuous-valued inputs. The input patterns are the software complexity metrics associated with program modules. The neural network classifies the modules as either high-risk or low-risk.

In a neural network, knowledge is represented by weighted connections, or interconnection strengths, between the neurons. Finding the best weights for a classification model is an unconstrained optimization problem [14] [16]. Let W_{ij} be the interconnection strength between neurons i and j. The summed input at neuron i is

$$net_i = \sum_j W_{ij} * Out_j + \theta_i$$

where θ_i is the threshold of neuron i. The output at neuron i is based on the logistic function:

$$Out_i = 1/(1 + e^{-net_i/T})$$

where net_i is the summed input at neuron i, and T adjusts the gain of the function.

A vector of interconnection weights, $\mathbf{W}$, is sought that minimizes the network's error,

$$E(\mathbf{W}) = \sum_{m=1}^{2} \sum_{l=1}^{L_m} \sum_{k=1}^{N} (Ideal_{mlk} - Out_{mlk})^2,$$

where N is the number of output neurons, L_m is the number of samples in the mth class, and Out_{mlk} and $Ideal_{mlk}$ are, respectively, the actual and the desired output for the kth output neuron for the lth observation belonging to class m.

Figure 1 shows the two phases of the neural network application. During the training phase, the network iterates through the training data set adjusting its connection weights to reduce its error on each observation. Let $W_{ij}(n)$ be the interconnection strength between neuron j in layer l and neuron i in layer $(l-1)$ after the nth iteration through the training data set. The backward propagation algorithm adjusts the connection weights as follows:

$$W_{ij}(n+1) = W_{ij}(n) + \eta * Out_i * \delta_i + \\ \alpha * (W_{ij}(n) - W_{ij}(n-1))$$

where

$$\delta_j = (Ideal_j - Out_j) * Out_j * (1 - Out_j)$$

for the output layer, and

$$\delta_j = (\sum_k \delta_k * W_{kj}) * Out_j * (1 - Out_j)$$

for the hidden layers and backward propagation of the error. Here k is the running index for neurons in layer $(l-1)$. η and α are constants which set the learning and momentum rates, respectively. The algorithm iterates through all of the inputs until a desired error tolerance is achieved or until a user defined maximum number of iterations are completed. If the desired error tolerance is achieved, the network is said to have converged and it is ready to evaluate the data sets for which it has been trained. If the network does not converge, one could repeat the training phase after varying a learning parameter, η or α, or after selecting a new training data set.

3 Experimental Methods

In this study we develop and compare two classification models that identify high-risk program modules: a neural network model, and a discriminant analytic model. We develop both models using data collected on the Command and Control Communications System (CCCS), a large military telecommunications system implemented in Ada. Software complexity metric data were collected from the program text. Fault data were collected from the problem tracking reports generated during the CCCS system integration and test

Training Phase

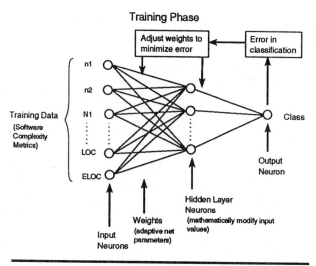

Prediction Phase

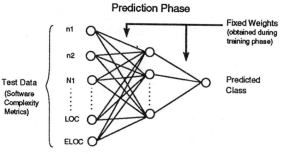

Figure 1: Two Phases of Neural Network Operation

phase, and during its first year of deployment. After removing the outliers in this data set, 282 observations remained. Modules with more than four faults are considered high-risk. Those with no faults are considered low-risk.

The collection of complexity metrics includes:
- Unique operator count (η_1) [3]
- Unique operand count (η_2) [3]
- Total operator count (N_1) [3]
- Total operand count (N_2) [3]
- Halstead's estimated program length $(\hat{N})$ where $\hat{N} = \eta_1 log_2\eta_1 + \eta_2 log_2\eta_2$ [3]
- Halstead's effort metric (E) [3]
- Program volume $(V = N log_2(\eta_1 + \eta_2))$ [3]
- McCabe's Cyclomatic complexity $(VG1)$ [10]
- Extended Cyclomatic complexity $(VG2 = VG1 +$ number of logical operators)
- Number of procedures in a package $(PROCS)$
- Number of comment lines (COM)
- Number of blank lines $(BLNK)$
- Number of lines of code (LOC)
- Number of executable source lines of code $(ELOC)$.

Note that some of the metrics in this collection are derived from others. For example, $\hat{N}$ is derived from η_1 and η_2. Metrics that are not derived from other metrics are primitive metrics; those that are derived from others are non-primitive. Since, in a collection of complexity metrics, non-primitive metrics that are derived from primitive metrics in the collection do not measure any program attributes that are not measured by the primitive metrics [12], we develop the models using the primitive metrics: η_1, η_2, N_1, N_2, $VG1$, $VG2$, LOC, and $ELOC$.

There are two aspects of quality in classification models. First, a model must be successful in classifying program modules having known complexity data, but unknown fault data. Second, a model must be able to perform this classification with little uncertainty. The misclassification rates of a model measure its success in classifying program modules. A model can commit two types of classification errors. A Type 1 error occurs when a low-risk module is classified as high-risk. This could result in some wasted attention paid to low-risk modules. A Type 2 error occurs when a high-risk module is classified as low-risk. This could result in an extension of the scheduled release date as more effort is required than planned for, or the release of a lower quality product. The nature of the impacts of these error types suggests that the Type 2 error rate is more important than the Type 1 error rate in considering the quality of a classification model.

On each classification, the model assigns a module to one of the two classes based upon some function of the module's complexity metric data. Modules with values of this function above some cutoff value fall in one class; the remaining modules fall in the other class. For some modules the function value will fall far from the cutoff value that determines class membership. These modules have a high probability of falling in the assigned class. For other modules the function value will fall close to the cutoff value. These modules have a relatively low probability of falling in the assigned class. For correct classifications, the model probability of membership in the opposite class is the uncertainty in the classification.

To measure misclassification rates and uncertainty we applied the data splitting technique. We randomly split the data into two sets, two thirds of the observations forming the training data set, and the remaining third forming the testing data set. This split left 188 observations in the training data set, and 94 observations in testing data set. The testing data set simulates application of the model to present program development with unknown outcomes. Note that the models are trained without access to the observations in this data set. After training the models, we used the 94 observations in the testing data set to measure both the misclassification rates and the uncertainty of the models.

To magnify the difference between the class of modules with characteristics that resulted in few faults, and the class with characteristics that resulted in many faults, we biased the training data set before fitting the models [13]. We achieved this by removing all of the modules with between one and four faults from the set. After removing these modules, 121 observations were left: 93 low-risk modules and 28 high-risk modules. These observations were used to train both models.

4 The Discriminant Model Results

We used a linear discriminant model that assigns modules to one of two classes based upon the module's posterior probability of membership in each of the classes. Such a model could compute posterior probabilities using either raw complexity metric values, or domain metric values. By considering models based upon both of these choices, we found that the domain metric based model was superior. Thus the model in this study assigns each module to the class to which it has the greater posterior probability of membership based upon the values of domain metrics. The domain metrics were derived from the primitive metrics collected from the program source code. Thus the first step in deriving the discriminant model was principal components analysis of the primitive complexity metric data, and derivation of the domain metrics.

The principal components analysis revealed two complexity domains with eigenvalues greater than one. Table 1 gives the rotated domain patterns of these two domains. This table shows the degree of relationship between each of the primitive metrics and the two domains. The larger the number at the intersection between a domain and a metric, the stronger the relationship between this metric and domain. One of the two domains will dominate each metric. Table 1 shows the dominating values in bold print. Domain 1 loads on η_1, η_2, N_1, N_2, LOC, and $ELOC$, metrics related to the program **size**. Domain 2 loads on the $VG1$ and $VG2$, metrics related to **control**. Domain 1, the **size**

Metric	Domain 1 Size	Domain 2 Control
η_1	**0.841**	0.261
N_2	**0.831**	0.507
N_1	**0.827**	0.528
LOC	**0.812**	0.511
η_2	**0.785**	0.557
$ELOC$	**0.752**	0.641
$VG1$	0.395	**0.911**
$VG2$	0.451	**0.885**
Eigenvalues	4.284	3.199
% Variance	53.550	39.987
Cumulative % Variance	53.550	93.537

Table 1: **Rotated Domain Pattern**

Metric	Domain 1 Size	Domain 2 Control
η_1	0.511	-0.425
N_2	0.288	-0.127
N_1	0.266	-0.099
LOC	0.268	-0.106
η_2	0.205	-0.029
$ELOC$	0.102	0.099
$VG1$	-0.446	0.727
$VG2$	-0.374	0.648

Table 2: **Standardized Transformation Matrix**

domain, accounts for about 54% of the variability in the primitive metrics. Domain 2, the **control** domain, accounts for an additional 40% of this variability. Together these two domains account for about 94% of the variability seen in the primitive metrics.

Table 2 gives the standardized transformation matrix, **T**, for the domains. Using this matrix, and the vectors of standardized complexity measures, we derived two domain metric values for each of the 121 modules in the training data set. The discriminant model was fitted using these domain metric values. Domain metrics represent simplified and uncorrelated measures on the complexity space.

Before using the fitted model to classify the modules in the testing data set, we used the standardized transformation matrix and the vectors of standardized complexity measures to derive domain metrics for the 94 modules in this data set. The model assigned class membership based upon the domain metric values. The model misclassified 3 of the 48 low-risk modules giving a Type 1 error rate of 6.25%. The model misclassified 4 of the 15 high-risk modules giving a Type 2 error rate of about 26.7%. The average uncertainty for both low-risk and high-risk classifications is about 5%. Overall this model misclassified about 11% of the modules in the testing data set, and demonstrated an average uncertainty of about 5%.

5 The Neural Network Model Results

The neural network used for this project contains a single hidden layer, and one output neuron. Both the input and the hidden layer have eight neurons, one for each primitive metric used as input to the model. The network is constructed with logistic-function units that yield an output between 0.0 and 1.0 so the input data are scaled to this range by dividing each complexity metric value by the metric's highest observed value. The network trains using backward error propagation. Training began with connection weights initialized to random values between -1.0 and 1.0. Training using several different random weight initializations produced nearly identical results. The learning and momentum rates were set to $\eta = 1.5$ and $\alpha = 0.7$, respectively. The output neuron value will fall between zero and one. An output closer to one than to zero classifies a module as high-risk. An output closer to zero than to one classifies a module as low-risk. The amount of deviation from zero or one represents the uncertainty in the classification.

The neural network did not achieve good results with a standard training algorithm. Observations with software metrics resembling those of the opposite class prevented the network from converging, and the last training iteration often did not yield connection weights that would result in the minimum number of misclassifications on the training data set. Therefore, the learning algorithm for the network was modified in two ways. First, training is allowed to proceed for a set period, rather than for a set number of iterations. Second, the training algorithm is not allowed to modify the connection weights on every iteration through the data set. On odd iterations, the algorithm finds the number of misclassifications on the training data set using the current connection weights. If this number improves over the number found in previous iterations, then the algorithm records the connection weights. On even iterations, the algorithm modifies the connection weights. In this way, the algorithm finds the connection weights that produce the fewest misclassifications during the training period.

The network was trained with the modified training algorithm with α and η values of 0.7 and 1.5, respectively. After training, the network was executed on the testing data set with the weights set to the values recorded during the training iteration with the fewest misclassifications. The model misclassified 6 of the 48 low-risk modules giving a Type 1 error rate of 12.5%. There is no uncertainty in correct low-risk classifications. The model misclassified 1 of the 15 high-risk modules giving a Type 2 error rate of about 6.7%. The average uncertainty in correct high-risk classifications is 2%. Overall this model misclassified about 11% of the modules in the testing data set, and demonstrated an average uncertainty of 0.5%. We have seen similar results for other data sets, one collected from the development of a 400,000 line commercial software system [9], and another collected from the development of a subsystem of a general-purpose operating system [7].

6 Comparing the Models

Table 3 summarizes the findings of the previous two sections. This table compares the discriminant and neural network classification models along three dimensions: Type 1 errors, Type 2 errors, and overall errors. We see that the discriminant model has a better Type 1 error rate, the neural network model has a better Type 2 error rate, and the overall error rates of the two models are equivalent. These observations are misleading since they do not consider the uncertainty of the two models. While the Type 1 error rate of the discriminant model is better than that of the neural network model, the neural network model achieves its Type 1 error rate with no uncertainty. The discriminant model has an average of 5% uncertainty in correct low-risk classifications, with extreme values of 25, 33, and 34%. While the overall misclassification rates of two models are identical, the overall uncertainty in correct classifications is about 5% for the discriminant model, and negligible for the neural network model. Thus, the neural network model achieved better separation of the two classes.

Decisions based on Type 1 errors result in suboptimal test resource allocations, and thus increase the cost of the test phase. Decisions based on Type 2 errors can extend the scheduled release date, or lower the reliability of the released product. Thus Type 2 errors have greater cost than Type 1 errors. Since the Type 2 error rate for the neural network model was superior to that of the discriminant model, the neural network model would serve as the better management tool.

7 Conclusions

In this paper we introduced the neural network approach to the detection of high-risk modules, and compared this approach to the discriminant analytic approach. The distributions of misclassifications in the two models indicated that the neural network model would serve as the better management tool. The neural network model also achieved a lower level of uncertainty, indicating that the neural network model achieved better separation of the two classes.

The neural network model's Type 2 error rate was lower than that of the discriminant model. Models of this quality allow great confidence that the high-risk modules of a software product can be identified early in the development process. Models can be built using complexity metric data collected during either the design or the implementation phase. Design phase models allow designers to isolate areas of their designs

Error Type	Model	
Error Type	Discriminant	Neural Network
Type 1		
Count	3	6
Rate	6.25%	12.50%
Uncertainty	5%	0%
Type 2		
Count	4	1
Rate	26.67%	6.67%
Uncertainty	5%	2%
Overall		
Count	7	7
Rate	11.11%	11.11%
Uncertainty	5.1	0.5%

Table 3: **Comparative Performance Data for the Models**

that are likely to cause reliability problems. With this information they can consider alternate designs, and software product managers can assign experienced development staff members to areas of high complexity. Implementation phase models allow the management team to allocate more testing resources to high-risk modules. It is often difficult to estimate the impacts of design changes that are proposed during the implementation phase. By considering the distribution of high-risk modules both with and without the proposed design change, project managers can develop a better understanding of the risks associated with these design changes.

Finally, neural network models have none of the data assumptions that are common to statistical models. Thus they are particularly suited for modeling of software complexity data, and offer an effective alternative to regression techniques that are often weakened in this environment by assumptions that are not met. This project has shown that neural networks show great promise in predicting high-risk modules based on software complexity metrics.

ACKNOWLEDGEMENT

We appreciate the numerous suggestions, leading to substantial improvements in the original manuscript, by the anonymous referees. We also would like to thank Mr. Ron Weir and Hemant More for helping us prepare this manuscript and to our colleagues (anonymous) in the aerospace industry for providing the Command and Control Communication System data. The work of Dr. Khoshgoftaar was supported in part by a research grant from the Florida High Technology and Industry Council Applied Grants Program.

References

[1] L. C. Briand, V. R. Basili, and C. J. Hetmanski, "Providing an Empirical Basis for Optimizing the Verification and Testing Phases of Software Development," in *Proceedings of the Third International Symposium on Software Reliability Engineering*, pp. 329–338, Research Triangle Park, North Carolina, October 1992.

[2] W. R. Dillon and M. Goldstein. *Multivariate Analysis: Methods and Applications*. Wiley, New York, 1984.

[3] M. H. Halstead. *Elements of Software Science*. Elsevier North-Holland, New York, 1977.

[4] N. Karunanithi, D. Whitley, and Y. K. Malaiya, "Using Neural Networks in Reliability Prediction," *IEEE Software*, vol. 9, no. 4, pp. 53–59, July 1992.

[5] T. M. Khoshgoftaar and J. C. Munson, "Predicting Software Development Errors Using Complexity Metrics," *IEEE Journal of Selected Areas in Communications*, vol. 8, no. 2, pp. 253–261, February 1990.

[6] T. M. Khoshgoftaar, A. S. Pandya, and H. B. More, "A Neural Network Approach for Predicting Software Development Faults," in *Proceedings of the Third International Symposium on Software Reliability Engineering*, pp. 83–89, Research Triangle Park, North Carolina, October 1992.

[7] B. Kitchenham and L. Pickard, "Towards a Constructive Quality Model," *Software Engineering Journal*, vol. , pp. 114–119, July 1987.

[8] G. LeGall, M. F. Adam, H. Derriennic, B. Moreau, and N. Valette, "Studies on Measuring Software," *IEEE Journal of Selected Areas in Communications*, vol. 8, no. 2, pp. 234–245, 1990.

[9] R. K. Lind and K. Vairavan, "An Experimental Investigation of Software Metrics and their Relationship to Software Development Effort," *IEEE Transactions on Software Engineering*, vol. 15, no. 5, pp. 649–651, May 1989.

[10] T. J. McCabe, "A Complexity Metric," *IEEE Transactions on Software Engineering*, vol. 2, no. 4, pp. 308–320, December 1976.

[11] J. C. Munson and T. M. Khoshgoftaar, "The Dimensionality of Program Complexity," in *Proceedings of the Eleventh International Conference on Software Engineering*, pp. 245–253, Pittsburgh, PA, May 1989.

[12] J. C. Munson and T. M. Khoshgoftaar, "Some Primitive Control Flow Metrics," in *Proceedings of the Annual Oregon Workshop on Software Metrics*, Silver Falls, Oregon, March 1991.

[13] J. C. Munson and T. M. Khoshgoftaar, "The Detection of Fault-Prone Programs," *IEEE Transactions on Software Engineering*, vol. 18, no. 5, pp. 423–433, May 1992.

[14] A. S. Pandya and R. Sazabo, "A Fast Learning Algorithm for Neural Network Applications," in *The IEEE Conference on Systems, Man, and Cybernetics*, pp. 1569–1573, 1991.

[15] A. A. Porter and R. W. Selby, "Empirically Guided Software Development Using Metric-Based Classification Trees," *IEEE Software*, vol. 7, no. 2, pp. 46–54, March 1990.

[16] D. E. Rumelhart, G. E. Hinton, and R. J. Williams. *Parallel Distributed Processing: Explorations in the Microstructure of Cognition*, volume 1, pp. 318–362. MIT Press, Cambridge MA, 1986.

[17] H. Zuse. *Software Complexity: Measures and Methods*. Walter De Gruyter, New York, 1991.

Neural Networks in Specification Level Software Size Estimation

Juha Hakkarainen, Petteri Laamanen, and Raimo Rask

University of Joensuu, Department of Computer Science, Finland

Abstract

This paper presents a neural network approach to software size estimation. A multilayer feedforward network is trained using backpropagation algorithm. The training and testing data consist of randomly generated Structured Analysis (SA) descriptions as input data and corre-sponding algorithm based size metric values as output data. The size metrics used in the experiments are Albrecht's Function Points, Symons's Mark II Function Points, and DeMarco's Function Bang metric. The experiments indicate that neural networks can learn to calculate software size estimates. In each of our experiments we found that the results depend on the features of the input data, the metric, and the convergence criteria used. The results also encourage to develop a general input set to represent size related features of graph based system descriptions.

1: Introduction

We can define *metrics* as scales or units in which a quantitative attribute can be measured [13]. A *software metric* is a measure of the extent or degree to which a software product or process possesses and exhibits a given attribute. Thus, software metrics are *measurable indications* of some quantitative aspects of a software system [8] and they can be divided into two functional categories [6], [13]: product and process metrics.

Process metrics quantify attributes of the development process and of the development environment. They are often concerned with resources. *Product metrics* are measures of the software product. They can be based on requirements, design, documentation, or source code. A general relationship between process and product metrics can be written [6]:

$$(1) \qquad y = f(x_1, x_2, \dots, x_n),$$

where the dependent variable y is a process metric of interest, such as the total effort or development cost. It is a function of the independent variables $x_1, x_2, \dots, x_n$, which can be either product- or process-related.

In this study we will concentrate on *product size metrics* which can be used for cost estimation purposes. We are interested in automating the production of size estimates from specification level descriptions. In chapter 2 we give a short introduction to the metrics used in this paper: Albrecht's [1] Function Point Analysis, Symons's [19] Mark II Function Point Analysis, and DeMarco's [8] Function Bang metric. In chapter 3 we then describe the neural network training and testing environment for these metrics and show the results from our experiments. Finally, in chapter 4 we draw our conclusions and explain the needs for future research.

2: Specification level size metrics

2.1: DeMarco´s Function Bang metric

DeMarco [8] discusses the measurement principles that can be applied during the requirements specification phase. The principles can be applied to the techniques of DeMarco's [7] Structured Analysis. A function metric, *Function Bang*, for a so-called function-strong system can be counted:

$$(2) \qquad \text{CFP} = \sum w_i * \text{CFPI}_i.$$

In (2) each term CFPI_i is calculated by formula (3) derived from Halstead's [11] model for counting a program length:

$$(3) \qquad (\text{TC}_i * \log_2 (\text{TC}_i))/2.$$

In (3) each term TC_i represents the number of data tokens around the boundary of the *i*th functional primitive in a dataflow diagram (DFD). A token is a data item that need not be subdivided within the functional primitive. To adjust the variations in the complexity of each functional primitive the term $CFPI_i$ must be multiplied by a constant weight w_i in formula (2). In defining the weights DeMarco [8] suggests 16 categories in which each functional primitive must be assigned. Each category has its own constant weight w_j (j=1,2,...,16).

As a size measure, Function Bang is based on the complexity of the dataflows and the types of operations (functions) operating on these dataflows. The volume of each dataflow affects the complexity of the corresponding functional primitive and thus the processing complexity of a software system.

Recently, Bourque and Côté [5] have published values 0.892 and 0.563 for coefficients of multiple determination between Function Bang and lines of code (LOC) using data obtained from two target systems. Hence, Function Bang can in some situations suggest reasonable estimates of the product size.

2.2: Function Point Analysis

Albrecht [1] has developed a widely used measurement method called *Function Point Analysis* (FPA). FPA sizes an application from an end-user perspective. A *function point* is defined as one end-user business function.

To calculate an *unadjusted value* of function points we first identify, classify and weight the user functions. The functions are organized into the following five groups [2], [9]: external inputs, external outputs, external inquiries, logical internal files, and external interface files.

An *external input* is a unique user data or control input that enters the application boundary and also updates (adds to, changes, or deletes from) a logical internal file [9]. An external input may also trigger an output which is not a part of an external inquiry though the input does not update any logical internal file. An input is considered unique if (1) it has a different format, or (2) it has the same format as another input, but requires different processing logic. For example, transactions such as add, delete, or change may have exactly the same screen format but they should be counted as unique inputs if they require different processing logic [1]. The complexity classification of input functions depends on two things - the number of files referenced and the number of data items referenced.

An *external output* is a unique user data or control output which is procedurally generated and leaves the application boundary. An output is considered unique if it has a different format, or it has the same format as another output, but requires a different processing logic. According to Dreger [9] each report format (total and detail level) and different processing period need to be

counted separately. The complexity classification of output functions depends on the same things as the classification of input types - the number of files referenced and the number of data items referenced.

External inquiries include each unique input/output combination where the on-line input causes and generates an immediate on-line output from a data base or a master file [9]. The inquiry performs no updates; data is not entered except for control purposes and therefore only transaction logs are altered [1]. An inquiry is considered unique if (1) it has a format different from other inquiries either in its input or in its output; or (2) it has the same format, both in input and in output, as another inquiry, but requires a different processing logic in either. The classification is applied separately to both input and output part and the complexity of an inquiry function is the greatest of the complexities of its two parts.

A *logical internal file* refers to a major logical group of user data or control information maintained within the application boundary [1], [9]. After Dreger [9], each key or data base view is counted as one logical internal file. For example, a customer file requiring a separate index file because of the access method would be regarded as one logical file, not two. An alphabetical index file to aid in establishing customer identity, however, would be considered as a separate file [1]. The complexity classification of each file depends on two things: the number of data items referenced by the measured application and either the number of different record formats within the file or the number of logical relationships this file is associated with.

External interface files consist of major logical files or similar logical groups of user-approved data or control information within the application boundary that are sent to, shared with, or received from another application [2], [9]. A file shared between two (or more) applications is counted both as an internal file and as an interface within each application that actually uses the file. Thus, each interface file must also be a logical internal file of either (1) the measured application itself, or (2) some of its external applications, or (3) both; or (4) it must be a transaction file. Complexity classification principles for the external interfaces are the same as with logical internal files although a transaction file is not a file per se. Figure 1 summarizes the possible connections between the measured application A and an external application B.

Interfaces in Figure 1 can represent any of the following three situations:

1. File-A is passed from application A to application B. File-A would receive both file and interface credit.
2. File-A is passed from application B to application A. File-A would receive interface credit only.

3. File-A is shared with applications A and B. File-A would receive both file and interface credit. Actually both applications, A and B, are maintaining the same file-A.

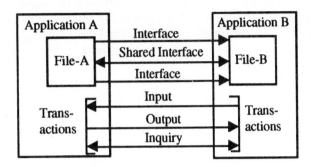

Figure 1. Connections between applications [9].

If applications are exchanging information by means of *transactions* they will obtain input, output, and/or inquiry points - and possibly also interface points. A transaction file sent from one application to another may indicate an additional interface function depending on whether or not a *conversion* is required to match the record or file layout of the receiving application. If a transaction file is received from application B, we would count one input for application A if no data conversion is required. Correspondingly we would count one output if a transaction file is sent to application B and no conversion is required. If a conversion is required within application A we would count both input and interface, or output and interface for application A.

The *total unadjusted function point value* (TUFPV) is produced by summing up the user functions weighted by the complexity factors or weights:

(4) $TUFPV = \sum F_i * CF_i.$

The functions are graouped based on the function type (input, output, inquiry, internal file, or interface) and the complexity classification principles within each function type. F_i in formula (4) is the number of functions in the *i*th group and CF_i is the weight of the group.

The implementation effort of a logical system may vary depending on the objectives and the available hardware/software environment. Because of this there are 14 environmental *adjusting factors* to calibrate TUFPV into the *final function point value* (FFPV). This is derived using the following formula:

(5) $FFPV = TUFPV * (0.65 + TDI/100),$

where TDI depicts *total degree of influence* determined

by the sum of the adjusting factors describing the target hardware/software platform.

There are several studies reporting a good correlation between Function Points and lines of code (LOC) (e.g., [2]). Moreover, by analyzing data from a large survey of Dutch organizations, Heemstra and Kusters [12] have found that FPA was the most popular model used in cost estimation.

The function groups in FPA, external and internal ones, make FPA an all-inclusive approach to size an application. Although the counting procedure is largely based on an external complexity, it takes into account an internal complexity of an application, too.

2.3: Mark II Function Points

Symons [19] criticizes Albrecht's FPA because of the classification of all system component types, the choice of the classification weights, the way internal or processing complexity is taken into account, and the differences between function point values resulting from an integrated system description and those resulting from separate system descriptions. At the same time he gives a new alternative, *Mark II*, for estimating the system size (in his recent book Symons [20] uses the name "Mk II FPA Method"). This metric contains the following assumptions:

- a system consists of logical input/process/output combinations,
- interfaces at the logical level will be treated as any other input or output,
- inquiries will be considered just as any other input/ process/output combination, and
- a logical file concept is interpreted at the logical transaction level as an entity, that is anything in the real world about which the system provides information.

The task then is to find properties of input, process, and output components of each logical transaction. The complexity of the *process* component can be counted as a number of entities referenced (created, updated, read, or deleted) by the transaction. For the *input* and *output* components of each transaction the number of data element types forms the size of the component.

The Mark II formula for information processing size expressed in unadjusted function points (UFP) can be written as follows [19], [20]:

(6) $UFP = N_I W_I + N_E W_E + N_O W_O,$

where

N_I = number of input data element types,
W_I = weight of an input data element type,
N_E = number of entity type references,
W_E = weight of an entity type reference,
N_O = number of output data element types, and
W_O = weight of an output data element type.

Based on Albrecht's Function Point Analysis and industrial calibration material, Symons [19], [20] has defined values of the weights for formula (6):

(7) $UFP = 0.44N_I + 1.67N_E + 0.38N_O$, or

(8) $UFP = 0.58N_I + 1.66N_E + 0.26N_O$

To get the final size of the target software system, Symons [20] proposes to use the *technical complexity adjustment* (TCA) by adding five general application characteristics to those of Albrecht's environmental adjusting factors. Moreover, the user of the Mark II method is free to extend the list of adjusting factors. The TCA is evaluated by the formula:

(9) $TCA = 0.65 + C * TDI$,

where TDI depicts *total degree of influence* determined by the sum of the (extended) adjusting factors. The current industry-average value of 'C' is 0.005. The final system size, *function point index* (FPI), can be obtained:

(10) $FPI = UFP * TCA$.

Clearly, Symons's Mark II metric (UFP) is easier to understand and calculate when compared with Albrecht's metric (TUFPV). Mark II contains fewer function types and the functions need not to be classified and weighted. The principles to calculate Albrecht's final function point value (FFPV) and Symons's function point index (FPI) do not differ significantly.

Symons [20] investigates also the conversion from Albrecht's FPA to Mark II by remarking that the conversion problem deals only the problem of the product size component of function points as measured by unadjusted function points. The input and output parts of logical transactions according to the Mark II view are roughly equivalent to the input and output, and the input/output parts of inquiries of the Albrecht view. The Mark II views the processing dimension of the transactions by counting each data entity once every time it is referenced in a logical transaction. Instead, in Albrecht's FPA we count each internal logical file and external interface file once, irrespective of how often they are used in transactions.

According to the Symons's own comparisons [19], [20] Albrecht's metric and Mark II unadjusted function points do not correlate very well. He found that it would not be possible to forecast the Mark II size value from the Albrecht's FPA size accurately, because the scatter diagram is nearly random. Moreover, the Mark II method seems to give systematically higher UFP scores as a function of system size compared with Albrecht's method.

3: Neural network approach to software size estimation

As shown in the previous chapter, the symbolic calculation of a metric value can be a complicated task. In addition, we have found in our earlier experiments (e.g., [16]) that because different metrics take into account different features of SA descriptions, the metric values do not always correlate. Therefore, we try to develop more general and more accurate method to software size estimation by using neural networks.

3.1: Data generation for training and testing purposes

Because we had no possibility to get real material from software industry to carry out the experiments, we decided to generate a test material using randomized SA descriptions to simulate a real industrial material. By randomizing we mean here generating a random local data dictionary for each DFD. Figure 2 shows the phases of the data generation.

The global data dictionary, common to all SA specifications, is generated taking into account the distribution of file sizes as presented in FPA. The upper limit of the size of each data specification is 69 primitive data items. The global dictionary contains these 69 different primitive data item names and the different combinations of these.

The *basic* dataflow diagrams in our study contain inputs, outputs, internal files, and processes [15]. The number of processes is from one to seven and the number of files does not exceed the number of processes. The upper limit for the number of processes is based on the distribution of file relationships in FPA. Each data store (file) is updated by one or more input dataflows and each data store is used by one or more input/output combinations. The number of dataflows around data stores and around the processes is minimized.

For one process we can draw only one basic DFD. Figure 3 shows the possible diagrams when we have two processes. When we have three processes and one data store, it is possible that either two processes update the

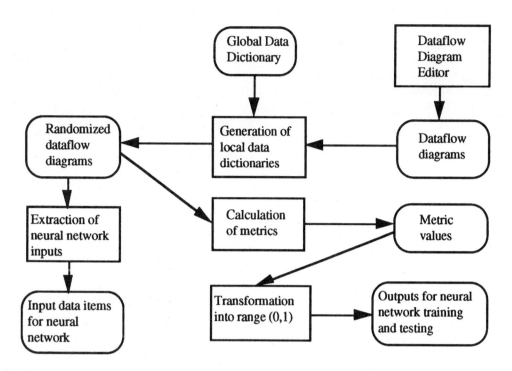

Figure 2. Data generation process.

data store and one process uses it, or one process updates the data store and two processes use it. When we form all possible combinations based on these principles the total number of basic dataflow diagrams grows up to 113.

Each data store of a randomized dataflow diagram contains 1-69 primitive data items one of which is a primary key. One data store may contain several logical internal files depending on the number of separate access keys used; if the dataflow that references a file is not named, the access key is supposed to be the same as the primary key of the data store. Each output dataflow contains 1-24 primitive data items and each input

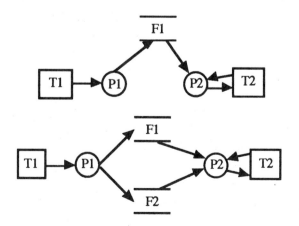

Figure 3. Two examples of test dataflow diagrams.

dataflow contains 1-19 primitive data items. These upper limits are based on the distributions of data items referenced in FPA. The number of file relationships is produced randomly. The upper limit here is the number of data stores minus one.

Besides these basic DFDs we wanted to include different system features: inquiries, interfaces, and process chains. To add the effect of *inquiries* we replaced each input/output combination of the basic diagrams by an external inquiry symbol. Based on the principles of FPA, an external inquiry can not update a data store. To add the effect of *process chains* we doubled the primitive processes in each basic diagram. In this paper we call the group of basic, inquiry, and process chain diagrams a *preliminary test material*. All file references within this preliminary test material were unnamed.

To add the effect of *interfaces* and *naming of file references*, we added one instance of each interface type (transaction file, shared file, and external file) into each basic diagram. Together with preliminary test material we call this source data group an *extended test material*. Naming of file references affects also the number of internal logical files in FPA. To get more diversified test material, part of the file references in this extended experiment were named.

To randomize the local data dictionaries we used a normal distribution. By normalization we tried to reduce the effect of extreme values. For example, we wanted to avoid situations when a data store contains only one data item. Normalization thus gives a more realistic data to simulate a real industrial data.

The range of the diagram sizes in unadjusted function point values (TUFPV) is from 14 to 242. In this respect the material fits in with the materials published with the empirical studies in the literature (e.g., [2], [4], [14]).

3.2: The neural network model

Figure 4 illustrates the basic network architecture used in our experiments.

The *feedforward network* used has three layers: one input, one hidden, and one output layer. The nodes in each layer are fully connected to nodes in the next layer. Each node takes a weighted sum of its inputs, plus a bias weight and passes the result through an output function. More precisely, the output of node j is:

(11) $o_j = f(w_{j0} + \Sigma w_{ji} o_i)$.

In our simulations we use the sigmoid output function:

(12) $f(x) = 1/(1 + e^{-x})$,

which has an output range (0,1). The network gets a set of numeric features of a SA description as an input and produces an estimate for the software size as an output.

The network was trained by using the *backpropagation* algorithm [17], which is the most commonly used learning algorithm today. It has been used to solve several interesting problems like speech generation [18], classification of sonar signals [10], performing logical inferences [3], etc.

The algorithm tries to minimize the error function

(13) $E = 1/2 \: \Sigma\Sigma \: (t_{pj} - o_{pj})^2$,

where o_{pj} is a network output value and t_{pj} is a target value. The network weights are changed according to the formula:

(14) $\Delta w_{ji}(t) = -\alpha \: \partial E / \partial w_{ji}(t-1) + \gamma \: \Delta w_{ji}(t-1)$,

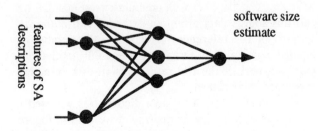

Figure 4. The structure of the network.

where t is an iteration number, α is a learning rate (steplength) constant and γ is an inertia (momentum) term which smooths the weight changes. The standard value for γ is about 0.9. In our experiments we used the value 0.95. The choice of α is problem-dependent. If the size of α is too small the algorithm converges very slowly; if it is too large, algorithm may not converge at all.

To test the neural networks capability to learn to calculate software size estimates, we did experiments with different sets of input data items. The input data items presented the most important features of the SA descriptions to be measured.

In each experiment the neural network was *trained* by using algorithm based metric values as targets. Values were converted into range (0,1), as shown in Figure 2. The network was trained until the absolute difference between the output value given by the network and its associated target was less than the convergence criteria.

To *test* how well the trained network could actually solve the metric values, we generated additional SA descriptions, from which we formed the set of input data items with same features as we had in the training phase. Then we let the network solve the metrics, and compared the results with the algorithm based "correct" results.

3.3: Experiment I: a preliminary test

In our first experiment we used the preliminary training and testing material described in section 3.1. The initial set of data items of our experiment consisted of the following 13 data items counted from each SA description to be measured:

1.   The number of primitive processes.
2.   The number of input dataflows.
3.   The number of output dataflows.
4.   The number of inquiries.
5.   The number of data stores.
6.   The total number of dataflows around the primitive processes.
7.   The total sum of the sizes of the dataflows around the primitive processes.
8.   The total sum of the sizes of the input dataflows.
9.   The total sum of the sizes of the output dataflows.
10. The total sum of the sizes of the inquiry dataflows (both input and output part).
11. The total sum of the sizes of data stores.
12. The total sum of data store references within all transactions.
13. The total sum of all references between data stores in a dataflow diagram.

The items are based partially on the specific characters

of each metric, and partially on the features of SA descriptions. To emphasize the diversity of different components in SA descriptions, we added the corresponding averages and standard deviations to the initial set of input data items. The preliminary test then was carried out by using the following 21 data items as input to the neural network:

1-5. Data items 1-5 above,
6-13. Averages of each data item 6-13 above,
14-21. Standard deviations of each data item 6-13 above.

The total number of randomized SA descriptions was 337. These descriptions were further grouped randomly into training material and testing material sets as shown in section 3.1. The training data set contained 150 randomly selected SA descriptions.

Selecting the number of units in hidden layer is a difficult problem. Normally, increasing the number of hidden units increases performance in the training set but may decrease it in the test set. After some trials we selected the number of hidden units to be five and the learning rate α to be 0.0005.

Table 1 shows the results of the preliminary experiment. The error percentage indicates the portion of test cases in which the absolute value of difference between network output and the corresponding algorithm based target metric value is greater than the testing accuracy shown in Table 1. For example, from Table 1 we can see that in 52.7 % of the test cases the network

failed to solve the Albrecht's FPA metric (TUFPV) with the convergence criteria 0.1 and the testing accuracy 0.02. On the other hand, the best TUFPV result was reached with convergence criteria 0.02 and testing accuracy 0.1: the network was able to calculate TUFPV correctly from all test descriptions.

In all, the network learned to calculate Albrecht's FPA (TUFPV) and Symons's Mark II (UFP) values accurately enough for measuring purposes in practice. Instead, the training of DeMarco's Function Bang metric (CFP) turned out to be more complicated and the desirable zero value for error percentage could not be achieved with any testing accuracy used. However, the error percentage 0.7 means that the testing material contained only one metric value that the trained network could not solve.

3.4: Experiment II: an extended test

In our second experiment we added new features to the preliminary test material to produce an extended test material, as described in section 3.1. The total number of training data was 300 SA descriptions and the total number of testing descriptions was 264. In this experiment we got best results when the network had six nodes in the hidden layer and the learning rate α was 0.04.

Table 1. Error % when compared with algorithm based metric values: Experiment I.

Metric	Convergence criteria	Testing accuracy				
		0.02	0.04	0.06	0.08	0.10
TUFPV	0.1	52.7	21.3	4.0	1.3	0.7
	0.08	44.0	11.3	1.3	0.7	0.7
	0.06	44.3	11.3	1.3	0.7	0.7
	0.04	29.3	4.0	1.3	0.7	0.7
	0.02	17.3	4.7	1.3	1.3	0.0
UFP	0.1	72.0	42.0	22.0	10.7	5.3
	0.08	70.0	34.7	20.0	8.7	4.0
	0.06	44.7	17.3	4.0	2.7	0.0
	0.04	34.7	10.0	4.0	0.0	0.0
	0.02	26.7	6.7	1.3	0.0	0.0
CFP	0.1	48.0	24.0	11.3	5.3	3.3
	0.08	40.7	14.7	7.3	4.0	1.3
	0.06	26.0	9.3	1.3	1.3	1.3
	0.04	25.3	6.0	2.7	1.3	1.3
	0.02	17.3	2.7	0.7	0.7	0.7

Table 2. Error % when compared with algorithm based metric values: Experiment II.

Metric	Convergence criteria	Testing accuracy				
		0.02	0.04	0.06	0.08	0.10
TUFPV	0.1	52.3	18.9	6.1	1.1	0.0
	0.08	51.9	17.8	6.8	1.5	0.4
	0.06	56.1	26.1	13.3	6.8	2.7
	0.04	61.4	31.4	14.8	9.5	4.6
	0.02*	59.5	32.2	20.5	15.2	11.4
UFP	0.1	25.4	5.7	3.0	1.1	0.4
	0.08	21.2	9.1	3.4	1.1	0.4
	0.06	22.7	8.7	3.8	1.1	0.8
	0.04	23.1	8.0	4.2	1.5	0.4
	0.02	23.1	12.9	7.2	5.7	3.0
CFP	0.1	15.5	7.6	2.7	1.1	0.8
	0.08	20.1	4.9	1.1	0.8	0.4
	0.06	10.6	1.9	1.1	0.4	0.0
	0.04	5.7	1.5	0.4	0.0	0.0
	0.02	3.0	0.4	0.4	0.0	0.0

* The training was stopped after 620 000 000 iterations although the network had not converged.

The input for the neural network contained the following 27 numeric data items, including the new features of the extended test material:

1. The number of logical files.
2. The number of input dataflows.
3. The number of output dataflows.
4. The number of inquiry dataflows.
5. The number of data stores.
6. The total number of shared data stores with external applications.
7. The total number of external input files from external applications.
8. The total number of external output files to external applications.
9. The total number of conversions from/to external applications.
10. The total number of primitive processes.
11-27. Mean and standard deviation for the following components:
    - the sizes of inputs, outputs, and inquiries
    - the number of logical record formats
    - the number of references to internal logical files
    - the sizes of internal logical files
    - the number of references for each entity
    - the sizes of functional primitives.

Table 2 contains the results from the extended experiment. The results from testing Albrecht's FPA (TUFPV) show an *over-fitting* phenomenon: too much training destroys networks capability to generalize. The Mark II (UFP) metric in this experiment was too difficult for the network to learn completely, in terms of any convergence criteria or testing accuracy used. Now, however, the Function Bang (CFP) test results were the most accurate ones.

3.5: Experiment III: a generalized input data set

In our last experiment our goal was to find a more general input data set for the neural network. By generality we mean a graph theoretical approach where the input data set is formed by means of graph components: nodes and edges.

In a dataflow diagram we have three types of nodes: data stores, primitive processes, and external entities. In addition, we have three types of edges: dataflows between two primitive processes, dataflows between primitive processes and data stores, and dataflows between the system and the environment. Based on these generalizations, we formed the following 12 input data items:

1. The number of primitive processes.
2. The number of data stores.
3. The number of input dataflows.
4. The number of output dataflows.
5. The number of inquiry dataflows.
6. The number of dataflows between processes.
7. The number of dataflows between processes and data stores.
8-12. Mean and standard deviation for the following components:
    - the sizes of inputs, outputs, an inquiries
    - the sizes of dataflows between processes
    - the sizes of dataflows between processes and data stores.

By using this kind of representation it could be possible to get rid of the metric and development method specific characters concerning the neural network input data items. By finding a general graph based representation for neural network input data we could generalize the size measurement also from system descriptions other than those of SA.

Table 3. Error % when compared with algorithm based metric values: Experiment III.

Metric	Conver-gence criteria	Testing accuracy				
		0.02	0.04	0.06	0.08	0.10
TUFPV	0.1	40.7	10.7	1.3	0.7	0.7
	0.08	31.3	6.7	0.7	0.7	0.0
	0.06	26.7	4.7	1.3	0.0	0.0
	0.04	21.3	2.7	0.7	0.0	0.0
	0.02	14.7	3.3	1.3	0.0	0.0
UFP	0.1	64.0	30.0	17.3	8.0	2.7
	0.08	68.0	41.3	18.7	8.7	6.0
	0.06	68.7	42.7	16.7	8.7	5.3
	0.04	56.0	27.3	10.7	4.0	2.0
	0.02	24.7	4.7	2.0	1.3	0.7

In this third experiment we used the training and testing material, and the network similar to the preliminary experiment in section 3.3. The results are shown in Table 3. When training the Function Bang metric the network did not converge. This means that the generalization trial was partly failed. However, the selected input data items made possible to train the neural network to solve TUFPVs. The results from training Mark II are also promising: there was only one case when the trained network gave wrong answer with testing accuracy 0.1.

4: Summary and conclusions

The experiments in this paper indicate, that neural networks are capable to learn to calculate software size estimates. In our earlier experiments we have found that the system features affect the correlation between different metrics [16]. By using neural networks it is possible to calculate the metric values by using the same input set for all three metrics introduced in this study.

The input set in Experiment I was based on the specific characters of each metric and on the features of SA components. In Experiment II we enlarged the preliminary input set by more metric specific features. In Experiment III the input set was formed by means of graph components, only.

From Experiments I and II we can conclude that a neural network can learn the metrics quite well, depending on the convergence criteria in the training phase and the desired accuracy. However, neural networks can be overtrained as seen in Experiment II with training of Albrecht's FPA metric.

The problem with neural networks in software size estimation is to find an input data set general and small, but covering enough to calculate software size estimates. In Experiment III the network was not able to learn the Function Bang metric. This was caused by excluding too many metric specific features from SA descriptions to be measured. Although our generalization trial was partly failed, it seems possible to find a general set of primitive features, common to different metrics and graph based system description techniques. This set of primitive features could then be used as a basis for software size estimation using neural network environment.

Acknowledgement

The simulations were done by using the Aspirin/ MIGRAINES Software Tools, release V5.0, MITRE Corporation.

References

[1] Albrecht A. J., "Measuring application development productivity," *Proceedings, Joint SHARE/GUIDE/IBM Application development symposium*, pp. 83-92, Oct. 1979.

[2] Albrecht A. J. & Gaffney J. E., "Source Lines of Code, and Development Effort Prediction: A Software Science Validation," *IEEE Transactions on Software Engineering*, SE-9(6), pp. 639-648, Nov. 1983.

[3] Bechtel W. & Abrahamsen A., *Connectionism and the Mind*. Basic Blackwell Inc., 1991.

[4] Behrens C. A., "Measuring the Productivity of Computer Systems Development Activities with Function Points," *IEEE Transactions on Software Engineering*, SE-9(6), pp. 648-652, Nov. 1983.

[5] Bourque P. & Côté V. , "An Experiment in Software Sizing with Structured Analysis Metrics," *Journal of Systems Software*, 15, pp. 159-172, 1991.

[6] Conte S. D., Dunsmore H. E., and Shen V. Y. , *Software Engineering Metrics and Models*. The Benjamin/ Cummings Publishing Company, 1986.

[7] DeMarco T., *Structured analysis and system specification*. Yourdon Press, 1978.

[8] DeMarco T., *Controlling Software Projects*. Yourdon Press, 1982.

[9] Dreger J. B., *Function Point Analysis*. Prentice-Hall, 1989.

[10] Gorman R. P. & Sejnowski T. J., " Analysis of Hidden Units in Layered Network Trained to Classify Sonar Targets," *Neural Networks*, 1, pp. 75-89, 1988.

[11] Halstead M. H., *Elements of Software Science*, Elsevier, 1977.

[12] Heemstra F. J. & Kusters R. J., "Function point analysis: evaluation of a software cost estimation model," *Eur. J. Inf. Systs.*, 1(4), pp. 229-237, 1991.

[13] Hunter R., "Lecture 1: Software Measurement," *Software Tools 1990: The Practical Use of Software Metrics*. Wembley Conference Centre, London, 12-14, June, Blenheim Online, 1990.

[14] Low C. G. & Jeffery D. R., "Function Points in the Estimation and Evaluation of the Software Process," *IEEE Transactions on Software Engineering*, 16(1), pp. 64-71, Jan. 1990.

[15] Rask R. & Laamanen P., "Test Material for the Automatic Comparison of Albrecht's Function Point and DeMarco's Function Bang Metrics," *Report B-1991-1*. University of Joensuu, Department of Computer Science, 1991.

[16] Rask R., Laamanen P., and Lyytinen K., "A Comparison of Albrecht's Function Point and Symons's Mark II Metrics, 1992 (to be published).

[17] Rumelhart D. E., Hinton G. E., and Williams R. J., "Learning Internal Representations by Error Propagation," *Parallel Distributed Processing* (Eds. Rumelhart D. E., McClelland J., and the PDP Research Group). MIT Press, 1986.

[18] Sejnowski T. J. & Rosenberg C. R., "NETtalk: a parallel network that learns to read aloud," *Technical Report JHU/EECS-86/01*. The Johns Hopkins University Electrical Engineering and Computer Science, 1986.

[19] Symons C. R., "Function point analysis: difficulties and improvements," *IEEE Transactions on Software Engineering*, 14(1), pp. 2-11, 1988.

[20] Symons C. R., *Software Sizing and Estimating, Mk II FPA (Function Point Analysis)*. John Wiley & Sons, 1991.

Part VII: Vehicles

The final part of this book is dedicated to vehicle applications of neural networks. The two chapters in this part describe applications to robot navigation (Chapter 26) and automobiles (Chapter 27). Other vehicles such as aircraft, ships, and submarines have used neural networks, but are not represented in this part because they either fell more naturally into other areas or they were not resident in the available set of papers.

Chapter 26:   Robot Navigation

Chapter 26
Robot Navigation

Path planning, obstacle avoidance, environment modeling and many other aspects of navigation must be conquered for untethered robots to become functional. This chapter describes several neural network applications to robot navigation. **Paper 26.1** describes a vision-guided navigation system called NEURO-NAV that employs neural network and expert system hybrids for determining the proper course of operation. **Paper 26.2** reports on an approach to environment modeling that uses sonar sensors and reinforcement learning neural networks for processing the data. **Paper 26.3** presents a neural network approach to environment modeling that mimics the behavior of a bee.

NEURO-NAV: A Neural Network Based Architecture For Vision-Guided Mobile Robot Navigation Using Non-Metrical Models of the Environment

Min Meng and A. C. Kak

Robot Vision Laboratory
1285 EE Building
Purdue University
W. Lafayette, IN 47907-1285

Abstract

In this paper we describe a vision-guided mobile robot navigation system, called NEURO-NAV, that is "human-like" in the following two senses: First, the robot can make do with non-metrical models of the environment in much the same manner as humans. In other words, the robot does not need a geometric model of the environment; it is sufficient if the environment is modeled by the order of appearance of various landmarks and by adjacency relationships. Second, the robot can respond to human-supplied commands like "Follow the corridor and turn right at the second T junction." This capability is achieved by an ensemble of neural networks whose activation and deactivation are controlled by a supervisory controller that is rule-based. The individual neural networks in the ensemble are trained to interpret visual information and perform primitive navigational tasks such as hallway following and landmark detection.

1: Introduction

Over the past several years, basically two approaches have emerged for vision-guided mobile robot navigation. The first approach may be called a deliberative approach and involves model-based reasoning and Kalman filtering using highly geometric models of the environment. The models of the environment may either be hand-compiled or built using map-making algorithms on the data collected by on-board sensors. A recent example of the deliberative approach, presented in [1], presents a highly robust reasoning and control architecture that allows a robot to navigate indoors at speeds around 8 m/min in the presence of moving and stationary clutter. Other examples of the deliberative approach are described in [2,3,4].

When geometric models of the environment are available, the deliberative approaches work fine. However, when such models are not available or when map-making algorithms are inadequate for the job, the deliberative approaches are certainly at a disadvantage.

In contrast with the deliberative approach, the second approach consists of imparting to the robot a reactive behavior that is driven by visual stimuli. Obviously, if vision is to be used in a reactive mode, the processing of vision data must be fast, which on most computing platforms today precludes the use of conventional symbolic reasoning architectures. For this reason, the work done to date in the second approach has relied on neural networks, the main idea being that appropriately preprocessed vision data fed into task-specific neural networks can instantaneously tell the robot which way to steer in pursuit of its goals. Using this approach, in the work reported by Pomerleau [5], a reduced-resolution raw image and range data for road scenes were fed into a 2-layer feed-forward neural network to produce direction output for a mobile robot. While clearly a pioneering effort, the proposed architecture suffers from the shortcoming that a monolithic neural network is used to generate the final decisions for the vehicle. Monolithic neural networks are not amenable to interaction with higher level supervisory control in an autonomous system. In contrast, as we will demonstrate in this paper, when a control architecture uses an ensemble of neural networks, each dedicated to some primitive task, control becomes much more flexible and more receptive to the incorporation of possible heuristic knowledge supplied by a human expert.

In this paper, our approach to vision-guided mobile robot navigation is inspired by our intuitive understanding of how human navigators operate. While navigating, a human navigator does not need to know the exact location of the edges of the road or the edges of the floor in a hallway; in other words, precise geometrical detail appears

*This work was partly supported by the Office of Naval Research under Grant ONR N00014-93-1-0142.

unnecessary for navigation. Instead humans respond to visual stimuli such as the approximate location and orientation of road edges or that of landmarks, which may be doors, bulletin boards, etc. It appears that humans possess a hierarchical system for the extraction of information from visual images. While priority is given to the information that appears most relevant to the task at hand, the contextual information that is of a related nature is stored away and can be retrieved if problems arise with the fulfillment of the task.

Based on these observations, we have designed a vision-guided mobile robot navigation system, called NEURO-NAV, that is more "human-like". In this system, a collection of neural networks is trained to interpret visual information and perform primitive navigational tasks such as hallway following, landmark detection, etc. Each neural network is trained to perform one primitive task. The output of these networks can activate higher level reasoning in a hybrid rule-based expert system architecture. NEURO-NAV operates in two modes: autonomous and human-supervised. In the autonomous mode, the robot is given an initial and destination position. The path planner then produces a sequence of symbolic directions such as *"Follow the corridor, then turn right at the next T junction"* using information about the hallway from a non-metrical model of the hallway. Given these directions, the neural networks that perform primitive tasks and the expert system that provides high level supervisory control work together to accomplish the navigational task. In the human-supervised mode, a human supervisor gives the non-metrical commands directly.

In this paper we present the architecture of NEURO-NAV for vision-guided indoor (hallway) navigation. In the rest of this paper, Section 2 deals with the overall reasoning and control architecture of NEURO-NAV where each module of the architecture is described. In Section 3, experimental results are shown. Finally, the conclusions are presented in Section 4.

2: Architecture of NEURO-NAV

As depicted in Fig. 1, the reasoning and control architecture of our vision-guided mobile robot navigation system includes a non-metrical model of the hallway, a path planner, a human supervisor, a hallway follower, a landmark detector, an obstacle-avoidance module, and a rule-based supervisory controller. In the rest of this section, we will briefly describe the functions of the modules shown in Fig. 1.

2.1: Hallway modeler

Historically, hallway modeling is an integral part of scene interpretation in model-based indoor mobile robotic

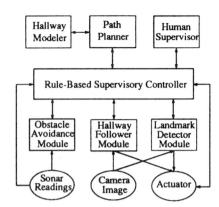

Fig. 1   Architecture of NEURO-NAV

systems. To locate its position in the hallway, a mobile robot compares feature entities from its camera image with those of a model database or those of a rendered image produced from the model of the hallway. Consequently, how the hallways are modeled seriously affects the computational efficiency of the entire navigation system.

Traditional modeling techniques are geometry based; an important aspect of these systems is the precision with which all the relevant measurements are captured. For example, a hallway can be represented by a faceted boundary representation, or modeled in a CSG (constructive solid geometry) representation where the hallway is viewed as a Boolean combination of volumetric primitives. Although these basic techniques have been used widely for many years for 3-D object recognition in computer vision systems, they are time consuming and therefore ill-suited for mobile robot navigation systems. More recently, Kosaka and Kak have presented a simpler data structure for the geometric modeling of hallways which, although hand-compiled, can render a scene in just a few seconds on a 16 MIPS machine [1].

Clearly, given the missions of NEURO-NAV, geometric modeling is not what we need. As mentioned before, NEURO-NAV views a task, such as hallway following, as a reactive behavior, which means the motions of the robot will be triggered by visual cues such as the orientation of the hallway floor edges with respect to the direction of the robot. A task such as hallway following, therefore, has no need for the usual metrical details of a geometry-based modeler. For these reasons, in the modeling needed for NEURO-NAV we have eschewed geometry in favor of a more non-metrical approach. The components of a hallway model in NEURO-NAV are determined more by their semantic and functional significance rather than by geometry. What we mean by this statement is made clear by what we have to say next.

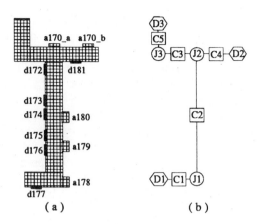

(a)   (b)

Fig. 2 (a)A hallway section. (b) Representation of the hallway section in (a). C_i's are corridors, J_i's junctions, and D_i's dead-ends in a non-metrical attributed-graph representation.

name:	C2
primary direction:	north
left node:	door, d176
	door, d175
	door, d174
	door, d173
	door, d172
right node:	power_panel, p3
	alcove, a179
	power_panel, p2
	alcove, a180
	bulletin_board, b2
behind node:	junction, J1
beyond node:	junction, J2

Fig. 3 The data structure used for the node that represents the corridor C2 in Fig. 2 (b).

For the purpose of illustrating our modeler, consider the hallway segment shown in Fig. 2(a) and its corresponding model, represented as an attributed graph, in Fig. 2(b). As shown there, the nodes of this graph consist of corridors, junctions, dead-ends, doors, and other "servoable" landmarks, meaning landmarks for which it is possible to design a neural network for visual servoing. The links of the graph, also attributed, contain the information regarding the physical distance between the landmarks represented by the nodes at the two ends of the link.* A node is represented by a list of attribute names and pointers. For example, a corridor node contains the attributes *name, primary direction,* and pointers to the four nodes which correspond to the faces, junctions, etc., that define the corridor. These four pointers are stored in the order: *left node, right node, behind node,* and *beyond node.* These pointers point, in turn, to a list of landmarks (e.g. doors, junctions, alcoves) that are on the entity represented by that node. An example of a corridor node, corridor C2 in Fig. 2 (b) in the hallway model, is shown in Fig. 3. The attributed graph for a hallway structure is stored in the computer memory as an adjacency matrix whose columns and rows point to the nodes and whose elements point to the attribute-value frames for the links. For example, if *adj_matrix* designates the adjacency matrix representation of the hallways in Fig. 2a, the item stored at *adj_matrix[5][1]* contains a pointer to a record

---
* Given NEURO-NAV's commitment to non-metrical models, the reader is probably looking askance at this incorporation of what is clearly a piece of metrical information. Compared to the metrical detail that goes into a geometrical modeler (and the geometrical details that are needed by a deliberative approaches as in [1-4]), the distance between the nodes is a minimal metrical cue. As is explained later in this paper, the distance between nodes is needed by the Path Planner module.

whose main entry is the distance of 8.5 meters; in this example, node 5 is the junction J1, node 1 is corridor C2 whose length is 17 meters. Therefore, in a sense, each extended node, such as the corridor C2, is assumed to be centered at its middle point, making the distance between C2 and J1 equal to half the length of the corridor. This is done merely to facilitate path planning. NEURO-NAV itself is fully aware of the fact that C2 is an extended physical entity.

As the reader has surely surmised from our description, a hallway model is defined with respect to a particular direction of travel for each of its corridors; this points to an interesting difference between the traditional geometrical models and the non-metrical models such as ours. In a geometrical model, various features such as doors, windows, etc., are mathematically defined surface or volume elements, with mathematical formulas governing their precise placement in the model. In a non-metrical model, on the other hand, doors, windows, etc., are merely symbolic entities and care has to be taken to ensure that, regardless of the orientation of the robot or the direction of its travel, proper relationships are maintained between the physical objects corresponding to the symbolic entities. For this reason, we have found it necessary that each node in the hallway model be defined with respect to a particular direction of travel. Of course, the robot is free to traverse the hallways in directions opposite to those that are incorporated in the model, if the path planner says so. If the path planner finds it necessary to send the robot in a direction inconsistent with what is in the model, what the robot expects to see on its left or right is reversed. In other words, each segment of a planned path points to what the robot should see on its left and right and in what order. And, for reasons mentioned, this information can be opposite of what is in the model data structures.

We mentioned above that each node in the hallway model is defined with respect to a particular direction of travel. While that is certainly true of the corridor and dead-end junctions, in order to make the task of the path planner less challenging we have found it desirable to store at each junction node the relevant information for all possible directions of travel. For example, for the case of the hallways shown in Fig. 2a, for junction J2 the stored information consists of three different lists, one for the case the robot is approaching the junction via corridor C3, the other when the robot is approaching via C4, and yet another for the case of approach via C2. Each list is a list of pointers, as in Fig. 3.

2.2: Path planner

A path planner plans a path from an initial position to a destination position. There are basically two approaches to path planning. In the mobile robotics context, the first approach, called the configuration space based approach, may be implemented by first constructing a binary array whose non-zero elements correspond to the floor of the hallways and then modifying the binary array in such a manner that, from the standpoint of collision avoidance, the motion of the mobile robot on the floor is equivalent to the motion of a point object in the hallways. This approach was pioneered by the work of Lozano-Perez and Wesley [6] in the context of path planning for arm robots. For a recent report on how the configuration space based approach can be used for mobile robot path planning, the reader is referred to [1]. While notable characteristics of a configuration space based approach are that a calculated path is a set of non-overlapping segments and that each segment is defined precisely by the coordinates of its end points, its major disadvantage is the need for path replanning whenever the robot deviates from its originally computed path, as is wont to happen during collision avoidance exercises.

The need for replanning is eliminated in a second approach to path planning; in this approach each object is considered to give rise to a potential field and a path to the goal is calculated by searching through the valleys of the overall potential field. Although in recent years this approach, pioneered originally by Khatib [7], has proved popular in a number of different domains, nonetheless it is not suitable for our purposes since, like the configuration space based approaches, it is highly demanding of the detailed geometrical knowledge of the navigational environment.

Our path planner differs fundamentally from both the configuration space approach used earlier in the FINALE system [1] and the potential field based approaches. The new path planner, reported here only very briefly, simulates human cognition in the sense that the paths produced

are less geometrical and more descriptive and yet useful enough for a mobile robot to use to get to its destination. For example, for the hallway shown in Fig. 2, if the robot is placed initially facing north in corridor C2 and its destination is in front of the dead-end D2, the path planner will output the following string of symbols: *"follow corridor, turn right at next T-junction, stop at next dead-end"*. It is important to realize that this path to the destination is semantically rich and is essentially devoid of explicit geometry, at least in the sense geometry is used in, say, CAD-based systems. It would not be far fetched to say that the output of the path planner shares many similarities with how a human navigator might communicate with the driver of a vehicle.

We will next briefly describe our approach to path planning. The initial and the destination positions of the robot, given by a human supervisor, are specified relative to landmarks in the hallway model. Suppose the robot is going to navigate in the hallway shown in Fig. 2. The position of the robot can be described using symbol streams like:

(landmark: X ; node: Y ; direction: Z)

or, just,

(node: Y ; direction: Z)

The first choice is evidently more specific than the second for describing the initial position or the desired destination position of the robot. As an example, when the robot is in the vicinity of door d176 in Fig. 2a facing north, the position would be described by the list *(landmark: d176; node: C2; direction: north)*. On the other hand, if the human did not wish to be specific about the precise location of the robot, the path planner would not complain if the position of the robot is described by the list *(node: C2; direction: north)*. The reader should note that, as with some other aspects of NEURO-NAV, this manner of inputing the robot position into the path planner makes for a human-like interface with the robot. (Our explanation here should not be construed to imply that we use compass directions, north, south, etc., for interacting with the robot. We believe that humans do not use compass directions for navigation inside buildings, yet humans do seem to maintain a landmark-based frame of reference for reasoning about interior directions. We have tried to approximate that capability by first making a list of all different directions in a hallway structure; assigning different symbolic tags to the directions; and then using these tags to reason about the orientation of the robot and its direction of travel.)

Given the initial and destination locations specified as above, the path planner then examines the adjacency matrix data structure for the hallways. The Dijkstras's algorithm [8] is used to traverse the adjacency matrix using the distances between nodes as cost functions and to

Table 1 Command Menu Available to a Human Supervisor

	name	argument		name	argument
	Commands				
1	turn left	(degrees)	12	stop	T junction
2	turn right	(degrees)	13	turn left	left_T junction
3	go straight	(meters)	14	go straight	left_T junction
4	stop		15	stop	left_T junction
5	follow	corridor	16	turn right	right_T junction
6	stop	dead-end	17	go straight	right_T junction
7	turn left	junction	18	stop	right_T junction
8	turn right	junction	19	turn left	intersection
9	stop	junction	20	turn right	intersection
10	turn left	T junction	21	go straight	intersection
11	turn right	T junction	22	stop	intersection

produce a sequence of nodes as solutions. This sequence of nodes where the first node is the initial node and the last node the destination node represents the shortest path between the initial and destination positions. The path planner subsequently translates this sequence of path nodes into a sequence of descriptive commands. For example, when the initial and the destination positions are given by *(landmark: d176; node: C2; direction: north)* and *(node: D2; direction: east)*, respectively, the command sequence output by the path planner is *(follow corridor, turn right at next T junction,* and *stop in front of the dead-end)*. Associated with each command in this sequence are lists of landmarks on the left and the right faces, and on the behind and the beyond junctions. These landmarks are listed in the order of appearance to be seen by the robot.

Before closing the subject of path planning, we want to mention that when the calculated paths are described using semantically rich descriptors, path replanning becomes unnecessary. Since the description of the path along which the robot is moving is not burdened by geometrical precision, the robot now has latitude in locating itself with respect to its environment. To elaborate, as long as the robot can see a particular set of landmarks, each possibly recognized by a special neural network, the robot knows where it is with respect to the final goal. In the manner of a human, the robot would not compute its exact location, but would still know how to get to its destination.

2.3: Human supervisor

The human supervisor in NEURO-NAV has two different roles. When the robot is in autonomous mode, the human supervisor specifies the initial and the destination positions of the robot and this information is passed on to the path planner, which then outputs a command sequence. When the robot is in human-supervised mode, the human supervisor directly gives out the commands in the form of a sequence that is similar to what is produced

by the path planner when the robot is in the autonomous mode. The menu of commands that is available to a human supervisor is shown in Table 1. The first four commands are explicit directions for the robot to follow. The remaining eighteen commands are implicit and the robot executes them with the help of the hallway follower, the landmark detector, and the rule-based supervisory controller.

2.4: Hallway follower and landmark detector

Given commands from the path planner or the human supervisor, the robot must be able to execute them using its ability to perform primitive navigational tasks such as hallway following, i.e. navigating down a hallway without running into walls, and landmark detection. These primitive navigational capabilities are implemented using neural networks.

The Hallway Follower Module and the Landmark Detector Module in Fig. 1 are composed of collections of neural networks, each collection trained to perform a specific task. The Hallway Follower Module consists of three submodules, the Corridor Follower, the Junction_Left Follower, and the Junction_Right Follower, each consisting of two neural networks. (The reason why two neural networks are necessary in each submodule will be explained shortly.) The function of the Corridor Follower is to keep the robot going straight down a hallway and do so even when the robot is forced by obstacles to deviate from a straight path. The function of the Junction_Left Follower is to ensure that the robot is able to navigate through a junction that turns to the left. The function of the Junction_Right Follower is the same, except that now the robot has to turn right through the junction.

The Landmark Detector Module consists of a single neural network that is capable of detecting both junctions and dead-ends, and, at the same time, of making a qualitative estimate of the distance between the robot and the junction/dead-end. The distance estimate is qualitative in the sense that the output nodes of this neural network correspond to "far," "at," and "near," and the estimation is in terms of these semantic labels.

When an approaching junction is detected, the appropriate networks are activated depending on what the next direction for the robot is. Suppose the next direction is to follow the junction that turns to the left. In that case, the robot will follow the right hallway floor edge to turn using the "right" network for junction following, and at the same time monitor the left hallway floor edge using the "left" network for corridor following. If, say, the robot makes too large a left turn during this maneuver, the "left" network of the corridor follower module will issue

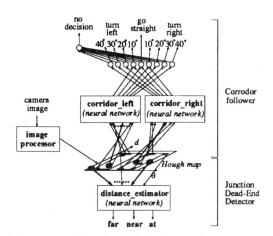

Fig. 4 The structure of the Corridor Follower is shown here. As shown, the disjoint regions of a Hough map are fed into two different neural networks for corridor following. Other regions of the Hough map feed into the Junction/Dead-End Detector.

forth a correction.

We will now explain in greater detail the structure of the Corridor Follower. Its design is based on the rationale that i) in order for a robot to go straight down a hallway, the perspective projection in the camera image of either the left or the right hallway edge must be within a certain angular range; and ii) if the robot is not headed straight down the hallway – a condition that could be caused by an attempt at collision avoidance – there exists a correlation between the turn the robot must make back towards the straight-down-the-hallway direction and the extent to which the perspective projection of the hallway edge is outside the previously stated angular range. This rationale evidently dictates that it be possible to extract line features from images and, since the robot has to servo with respect to the line features, it be possible to carry out a fast extraction of these line features. These considerations have led to the Corridor Follower shown in Fig. 4. The input to the two neural networks shown there consists of the left and the right regions of the Hough map derived from a single camera image. For readers conversant with vision algorithms, a robust method for detecting edges that may be continuous or broken consists of first applying an edge detector to an image and then mapping all the edge points into what is called a Hough space, whose each cell is indexed by the slope of an edge and by the perpendicular distance of a line through that edge from the image center. In order to speed up this process, in NEURO-NAV the camera image is downsampled from a 512x480 matrix to a 64x60 matrix without any noticeable effects on the abilities of the Corridor Follower.

To understand why different regions of the Hough map are fed into different neural networks in Fig. 4, we must first explain the purpose of the *corridor_left* and the *corridor_right* neural networks shown there. Note the goal of corridor following is to navigate down the corridor without running into the walls on the left or the right of the robot. In Fig. 4, one neural network, *corridor_left*, is trained to be sensitive to the left hallway floor edge; while the other neural network, *corridor_right*, is sensitive to the right hallway floor edge. Each of these two networks produces six output commands representing steering angles of 10° apart. The output of the two neural networks compete to contribute to the final decision using the principle of "maximum takes all". If neither network can produce a decisive output (i.e. values of all output nodes are below some threshold), a "no decision" output is rendered. Now back to the explanation regarding the segmentation of the Hough map, it can be shown that the Hough map can be structured in such a manner that even for significant deviations in the orientation of the robot from its ideal direction, all the edge features corresponding to the left wall will be in the left half of the Hough space and all the edge features corresponding to the right wall in the right half of the Hough space. Therefore, it is sufficient to feed into the *corridor_left* only those Hough cells that are in the left half plane, and into the *corridor_right* only those that are in the right half plane. Fig. 5 shows a typical downsampled hallway image, all the detected edges are shown in (b), the extracted floor edges in (c), and finally the Hough space representation of the floor edges used as input to the neural networks is shown in (d).

To give the reader an example of how landmark detection works in NEURO-NAV, we will now briefly present the main point on which the design of Junction/Dead-End Detector, a part of the Landmark Detector module in Fig. 1, is based. Clearly, as the robot is approaching a hallway junction, say junction J2 in Fig. 2a, the numerous horizontal edges that define what the robot sees straight ahead as it approaches the junction will exhibit a downward motion in the camera image. This fact is exploited for the qualitative estimation of the distance between the robot and a junction/dead-end by first applying a difference operator to Hough space representation of successive images; the difference operator is applied to only those regions of the Hough space that are populated by the horizontal lines in the image. (For the configuration of the camera on our robot, the first few columns and the last few columns in the Hough map correspond to the horizontal edges.) The output nodes of this network, as was mentioned before, stand for the labels "far," "at," and "near," these labels being qualitative estimates of the distance of the robot from far wall of the junction. The Junction/Dead-End Detector has also been shown in Fig. 4.

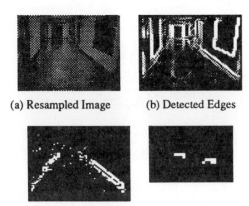

(a) Resampled Image (b) Detected Edges

(c) Extracted Floor Edges (d) Corresponding Hough Space

Fig. 5 Floor edges are extracted and mapped into the Hough space for corridor following. Vertical edges, not necessary for corridor following, are not included in the Hough representation.

The neural networks for junction following share similarities with the Corridor Follower. To elaborate, a Junction_Left Follower, used for turning left through a junction, consists of two neural networks, one tracks the right edge of the floor and the other of the left edge. In actual execution, the latter network is initially ineffective as it either sees nothing or whatever it sees is in the wrong cells of the Hough map. However, as the robot comes close to finishing up a left turn, this network keeps the robot from overturning. In a similar fashion, Junction_Right Follower consists of two neural networks also.

All the neural networks we have mentioned are 3-layer feed-forward networks and are trained by the backpropagation learning algorithm. Readers who wish to know more about the structure of these networks and the parameters used for the learning algorithm are referred to [9].

2.5: Rule-based supervisory controller

The job of the Supervisory Controller in Fig. 1 is to coordinate the activation and deactivation of the various neural networks in the system. In addition, the Supervisory Controller invokes the sensors that are most appropriate to the task at hand. Furthermore, the Supervisory Controller orchestrates the motions of the robot in order to enable the robot to look for the scene features that are relevant to the goal at hand. To further explain these functions of the Supervisory Controller, let's assume that the initial position of the robot is in the vicinity of door d176, facing north, in the hallway C2 in Fig. 2a. Let's also assume that the human supervisor has declared the dead-end d2 to be the destination. For this case, the Path Planner will produce the sequence of motion commands described in Section 2.2.

The robot will now respond to each command in the sequence produced by the Path Planner, while being cognizant of the next goal in the sequence. Therefore, at the very outset, the robot will initiate motion in response to *(follow corridor)* while it "knows" that the next goal is *(turn right at next T-junction)*. Speaking more generally, the next goal always acts as a termination condition for the current goal.

To show how the Rule-Based Supervisory Controller comes into play, let's now assume that the robot detects an obstacle while approaching the junction J2, the detection being reported by the ultrasonic sensors that have a high interrupt priority. The Supervisory Controller will now suspend all vision processing. As soon as the Collision Avoidance Module reports all free, the Supervisory Controller reverts back to the usual vision-based servoing.

The Supervisory Controller also carries out perception planning when forward vision fails to produce the steering commands for the robot. To explain, as the robot is approaching the junction J2, assume that the image preprocessor fails to produce strong enough edges for the rest of the Hallway Follower to work. In that case, the Supervisory Controller turns the robot around, facing south, and reactivates the Hallway Follower. This action sends the robot back to a position where it is facing straight down the hallway, although facing in the opposite direction. Once there, the Supervisory Controller turns the robot back around and the original mission is continued.

An important and novel aspect of the Supervisory Controller is the use of neural networks for antecedents of some of the rules. The need to represent rule antecedents directly by neural networks, as opposed to by the more traditional statements of symbolic logic, is dictated by the difficulty in specifying the criteria for initiating decision-making processes. For example, let's say that we want to encode the following rule in our vision-guided mobile robot navigation system:

IF approaching junction, THEN slow down.

One of the problems with a traditional rule-based system would be the design of articulatable criteria for detecting an approaching junction in the camera image. Our solution to this problem is to represent the entire antecedent by a neural network which is trained by showing features extracted from many images containing junctions and feeding these into a neural system that then sets up its own criteria (which never have to be made explicit) for deciding when a junction is approaching.

3: Experimental results

NEURO-NAV is implemented on our Cybermotion mobile robot controlled by a MC68030 processor. Using laboratory computing hardware consisting of a 16 MIPS machine, NEURO-NAV can process a camera image and produce a navigational output, meaning a steering command, within 2 seconds.

Although the ultimate proof of the NEURO-NAV system lies in our experimental demonstrations on the Cybermotion platform, we now would like to state the importance of computer simulations to the design of NEURO-NAV. First a couple of words about the functionality of the simulator we have designed. This simulator uses a 3D model of the hallways to render images from any desired viewpoint in the hallways. These images are then used as input in the learning phase of the neural networks.* Given an initial and the destination position for the robot, the simulator first calls upon the Path Planner in Fig. 1 and then actually simulates the motion of the robot and the associated vision servoing in response to the commands spit out by the path planner. In other words, the simulator invokes the 3D model of the hallways to generate the images that the camera mounted on the robot would see, processes these images in a manner similar to what is done to real images, and then finally feeds these into the appropriate neural networks.

Shown in Fig. 6 are the trajectories of the robot in a simulated run in the hallway using vision feedback derived from the rendering package and the CAD model. Although at times incorrect steering commands were generated as shown in Fig. 6, (these are perhaps not too discernible in the figure) the robot was able to detect the error in its subsequent moves and correct its course. And when a "no decision" output was produced (approximately 4% of the total output), the NEURO-NAV system instructed the robot to turn slightly with the chance that the new viewing angle might produce a more useful output in terms of a steering angle. Also displayed in Fig. 6 are the directions for the robot to follow, some scenes seen by the robot, features extracted from those scenes, and their corresponding Hough maps that were used as input to the neural networks.

4: Conclusions

In this paper we presented an architecture for vision-guided mobile robot navigation that uses an ensemble of neural networks whose activation and deactivation are orchestrated by a rule-based supervisory controller. The fact that this system uses non-metrical models of the environment is one of its more unique features.

---
* We must hasten to add that 3D hallway modeling is not necessary to NEURO-NAV in the same sense it is necessary to the FINALE system in [1]; however, such modeling if available does make it easier to train the neural networks.

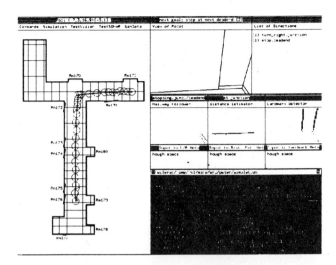

Fig. 6 Simulation of vision-guided mobile robot navigation using the NEURO-NAV control architecture.

References

[1] A. Kosaka and A. C. Kak, "Fast vision-guided mobile robot navigation using model-based reasoning and prediction of uncertainties," *Computer Vision, Graphics, and Image Processing – Image Understanding,*" November 1992, pp. 271-329.

[2] J. R. Beveridge and E. M. Riseman, "Hallway navigation in perspective," *Working Notes of 1991 AAAI Symposium on Sensory Aspects of Robotic Intelligence,* 1991, pp.125-132.

[3] T. Tsubouchi and S. Yuta, "Map assisted vision system of mobile robots for reckoning in a building environment," *Proc. 1987 IEEE Int. Conf. Robotics & Automation,* 1987, pp.1978-1984.

[4] D. J. Kriegman, E. Triendl, and T. O. Binford, "Stereo vision and navigation in buildings for mobile robots," *IEEE Transactions on Robotics and Automation,* Vol. 5, No. 6, 1989, pp. 792-803.

[5] D. A. Pomerleau, "ALVINN: An autonomous land vehicle in a neural network," tech. report, CMU-CS-89-107, 1989.

[6] T. Lozano-Perez and M. A. Wesley, "An algorithm for planning collision-free paths among polyhedral obstacles," *CACM,,* Vol.22, No.10, October 1979, pp.560-570.

[7] O. Khatib, "Real-time obstacle avoidance for manipulators and mobile robots," *The Int. Journal Robotics Research,* Vol.5, No.1, 1986, pp.90-98.

[8] A. V. Aho, J. E. Hopcroft, and J. D. Ullman, *The Design and Analysis of Computer Algorithms,* Addison-Wesley, 1974.

[9] M. Meng and A. C. Kak, "Fast vision-guided mobile robot navigation using neural networks," *Proc. IEEE Int. Conf. Systems, Man, and Cybernetics,* 1992, pp. 111-116.

Exploration and Model Building in Mobile Robot Domains

Sebastian B. Thrun [1]

University of Bonn, Institut für Informatik III

Römerstr. 164, D-5300 Bonn 1, Germany

E-mail: thrun@uran.informatik.uni-bonn.de

Abstract— I present first results on COLUMBUS, an autonomous mobile robot. COLUMBUS operates in initially unknown, structured environments. Its task is to explore and model the environment efficiently while avoiding collisions with obstacles. COLUMBUS uses an instance-based learning technique for modeling its environment. Real-world experiences are generalized via two artificial neural networks that encode the characteristics of the robot's sensors, as well as the characteristics of typical environments the robot is assumed to face. Once trained, these networks allow for the transfer of knowledge across different environments the robot will face over its lifetime. COLUMBUS' models represent both the expected reward and the confidence in these expectations. Exploration is achieved by navigating to low confidence regions. An efficient dynamic programming method is employed in background to find minimal-cost paths that, executed by the robot, maximize exploration. COLUMBUS operates in real-time. It has been operating successfully in an office building environment for periods up to hours.

I. INTRODUCTION

I report first results on robot exploration in mobile robot domains. In contrast to many other approaches to robot learning, I consider a robot that has no other task than maximizing its knowledge about the initially unknown environment, while avoiding negative reward. The robot at hand, COLUMBUS (Figure 1), is a wheeled mobile robot equipped with a proximity sensor, a sonar sensor that allows to sense distances to objects next to the robot by emitting sonar signals, and a motion sensor for monitoring the motion of the wheels and detecting collisions. COLUMBUS operates in environments such as office buildings or private homes and has to avoid negative reward that will be received when colliding with obstacles. It operates in real-time.

COLUMBUS employs a local, instance-based learning technique to model its environment. Rather than fitting a global monolithic model, experiences are remembered explicitly, and functions are approximated locally with the help of artificial neu-
ral networks. Many global approaches to function fitting (e.g., with a single monolithic neural network) in mobile robot domains either fail in complex environments due to effects like un-/relearning, or demand many well-distributed training examples and have often been tested in simplified simulations only [2, 9, 15, 18]. Modularized, local and instance-based approaches to function approximation have often been reported to generalize better from fewer or ill-distributed examples [1, 5, 6, 7, 10, 12]. Instance-based curve fitting techniques have also been applied successfully to fairly complex robot control learning problems, including the work by Atkeson and Moore. In COLUMBUS' approach to model building, experiences are remembered explicitly. They are generalized via two artificial neural networks, one for *sensor interpretation* and one for *confidence assessment*. These networks encode the specific characteristics of the sensors as well as those of typical environments of a mobile robot, thus capturing knowledge independent of any particular environment the robot might face. Once trained, they provide an efficient way of knowledge transfer from previously explored environments to new environments. For example, based on knowledge acquired in previously explored environments COLUMBUS was found to avoid collisions almost completely in new environments. In contrast, tabula rasa learning methods will cause collisions in any new, unknown environment, before the robot eventually learns to avoid them.

COLUMBUS top-level goal is efficient exploration. The approach taken in this paper is motivated by earlier research on exploration in the context of reinforcement learning [18]. Theoretical results on the efficiency of exploration indicate the importance of the exploration strategy for the amount of knowledge gained, and for the efficiency of learning control in general. It has been shown that for certain hard deterministic environments, that an autonomous robot can face, exploration strategies such as random walk result in an expected learning time that scales at least exponentially with the number of states the environment can take [19]. In contrast, more thoughtful exploration techniques, such as *"go to the least explored location,"* have been shown to reduce the complexity to a small polynomial function in the size of the state space [8, 17]. While these results may be theoretically significant, their relevance and implications for practical research in robot exploration are unclear. This is because the best known worst-case bounds for the complexity of exploration are still too large to be of any practical meaning,

[1] This research was done while the author was with Carnegie Mellon University, School of Computer Science, Pittsburgh PA 15213.

This research was sponsored in part by Siemens Corporation. The views and conclusions contained in this document are those of the author and should not be interpreted as representing the official policies, either expressed or implied, of Siemens Corp.

Figure 1: (a) COLUMBUS is a wheeled HERO-2000 robot with a manipulator and a gripper. It is equipped with a sonar sensor on the top of the robot that can be directed by a rotating mirror to give a full 360° sweep (24 values). Sonar sensors return approximate echo distances. Such sensors are inexpensive but very noisy. (b) COLUMBUS explores an unknown environment. Note the obstacle in the middle of the laboratory. Our lab causes many malicious sonar values, and is a hard testbed for sonar-based navigation. For example, some of the chairs absorb sound almost completely, and are thus hard to detect by sonar.

given the complexity of environments and state spaces faced by a robot acting in the real world. Furthermore, the theoretical results ignore the ability of mobile robots to gain knowledge by sensing its environment, which allows the robot to make predictions for neighboring locations. Such predictions, of course, may reduce the number of exploration steps drastically. However, the intuition behind the theoretical results carries over to mobile robot domains. An efficiently exploring robot should not explore by selecting actions randomly. Instead, it should actively maneuver to poorly explored parts of the environment, in order to maximize knowledge gain. COLUMBUS' exploration strategy follows this principle. Its model keeps track of how well its environment is explored, and based on this knowledge the robot is maneuvered to poorly explored regions.

II. Modeling the Environment

In this section, the instance-based model building technique developed for COLUMBUS is described. Let x_i denote the *location* (position, state)[2] of the mobile robot at time step i, s_i denote the vector of *sensations* (sonar measurements in the case of COLUMBUS) at this time, and r_i (the collision) reward received at this time. Generally speaking, an *adaptive model* $\mathcal{M}$ is a function that generalizes from a finite set of examples (data points) $\{\langle x_i, s_i, r_i \rangle | i = 1 \ldots n\}$ to arbitrary new positions x in the domain:

$$r = \mathcal{M}(\{\langle x_i, s_i, r_i \rangle | i = 1 \ldots n\}, x)$$

In our case, r denotes the expected reward received when entering location x.

Different model identification procedures differ in the way in which they combine and interpolate between points (inductive bias). The approach taken in COLUMBUS is to split the function $\mathcal{M}$ into n pieces, one for each data point. More specifically, $\mathcal{M}$

is realized using a pair of artificial neural networks: the *sensor interpretation network* $\mathcal{R}$ and the *confidence estimation network* $\mathcal{C}$. These networks are trained using the backpropagation training procedure [13] to encode the specific characteristics of the sensors as well as those of typical environments of a mobile robot.

More specifically, the **sensor interpretation network**

$$r_i = \mathcal{R}(s_i, x - x_i) = \mathcal{R}(s_i, \Delta x)$$

(c.f. Fig. 2a) maps a *single* experience (x_i, s_i) to an estimation of reward at x. Here Δx is the difference between x_i and x, making $\mathcal{R}$ independent of absolute coordinate values. Fig. 3a illustrates the output of $\mathcal{R}$ in the mobile robot domain. Here the distance measurements from the sonar sensor are mapped to expected reward (generalized occupancy). $\mathcal{R}$ is trained in a supervised manner: The robot operates and takes sensor measurements in a *known* environment where regions which the robot can physically not enter are labeled with negative reward.[3]

Instead of *one* estimate of expected reward $r = \mathcal{M}(x)$ at location x, $\mathcal{R}$ returns n estimates r_i, one for each data point (s_i, x_i). There are several reasons why combining multiple interpretations r_i is necessary. First, many sensors such as sonars are noisy, and often fail to sense the environment accurately. Second, $\mathcal{R}$ models an inherently unpredictable function. For example, a sonar sensor cannot "look through a wall." Thus if the query point x and x_i are separated by an obstacle, r_i will usually be wrong. In what follows, a scheme for combining multiple interpretations based on estimating confidence is described.

The **confidence network** (Fig. 2b)

$$c_i = \mathcal{C}(s_i, \Delta x)$$

---

[2]Throughout this section it will be assumed that there is an accurate way to estimate the location x_i of the robot in some global coordinate frame. This assumption is relaxed in section IV. , where a technique for re-estimating the location of the robot based on sensations is described.

---

[3]Note that in the current implementation, this is done with a simulator that models sonar sensors as well as sensor noise. Simulation is significantly cheaper and faster than real-world experimentation, and I empirically found $\mathcal{R}$ to be accurate enough even if trained on simulated data. All results displayed in figures, however, are generated from real-world data.

In general, training these networks can be interleaved with exploration, allowing for cross-environment transfer of learned knowledge for model identification.

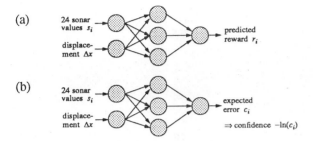

(a)

24 sonar values s_i

displacement Δx

predicted reward r_i

(b)

24 sonar values s_i

displacement Δx

expected error c_i

$\Rightarrow$ confidence $-\ln(c_i)$

Figure 2: (a) sensor interpretation network $\mathcal{R}$ and (b) confidence network $\mathcal{C}$.

maps a single experience (x_i, s_i) to a scalar in $(0, 1)$, again with $\Delta x = x - x_i$. Note that the interpretation network $\mathcal{R}$ will never generalize perfectly, i.e., its error will never approach zero. This effect is utilized for training the confidence network. Using an independent test set for $\mathcal{R}$ (after training), $\mathcal{C}$ is trained to estimate the *expected error* $|\mathcal{R}(s_i, \Delta x) - reward(x)|$ of $\mathcal{R}$ (normalized to $[0, 1]$). Since $\mathcal{C}$ estimates the expected error of r_i, the confidence in r_i is low if c_i is large and vice versa. It is straightforward to use this error estimate in the integration of the r_i by weighting interpretations r_i with their *confidences*, defined as $-\ln(c_i)$.

Figure 3b illustrates confidence estimations, corresponding to the reward estimations shown in Figure 3a. Note that predictions of freespace and walls usually have high confidence, whereas for example the confidence in predictions behind walls is low. As can be seen from some of the examples in this figure, the confidence network deals with noise by assigning low confidence to potentially noisy sensations.

Finally, reward estimates r_i are combined according to their confidence estimates $-\ln c_i$, using the formula.

$$\mathcal{M}(x) = \frac{\sum_i -\ln c_i(x) \cdot r_i(x)}{c_{\mathcal{M}}(x)} \quad \text{with} \quad c_{\mathcal{M}}(x) = \sum_i -\ln c_i(x)$$

The term $c_{\mathcal{M}}(x)$ is called the *cumulative confidence* at x. Knowing that COLUMBUS' sonar sensors have a maximum range of perception (10.5 feet), $i \in \{1 \ldots n\}$ sums only over those data points that are close enough to x, i.e., for which $|x-x_i|$ is smaller than the maximal sonar perception range. In Figure 4b, a compiled model after 27 exploration steps is shown.

III. Anytime Planning for Exploration in Real-Time

Exploring and modeling initially unknown environments is the top-level goal of COLUMBUS. In order to find low-cost paths to the unexplored, the model is discretized yielding a grid representation of the environment, and dynamic programming is employed to propagate exploration utility through this discretized model [3, 16]. More specifically, this is done in the following way: To each grid point x in the discretized model there is a real-valued *exploration utility* $U(x)$ associated. Initially, the exploration utility of x is set to the negative cumulative confidence $-c_{\mathcal{M}}(x)$. Cumulative confidence (c.f. Equation (1)) is a straightforward measure to estimate the utility of exploring a location: The lower $c_{\mathcal{M}}(x)$, the less explored is x and the higher is the (initial) exploration utility of x, and vice versa. All grid points are then iteratively updated according to the maximum

(a) sensor interpretation

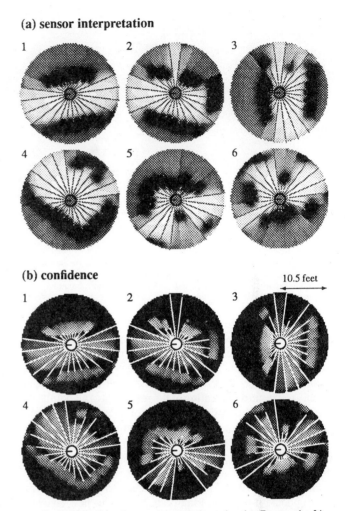

(b) confidence

10.5 feet

Figure 3: (a) Examples of sensor interpretation using the $\mathcal{R}$ network. Lines indicate sonar measurements (distances), and the region darkness represents the expected collision reward for surrounding areas (dark values indicate negative reward). Examples are: 1. hallway, 2. hallway with open door. 3. hallway with human walking by, 4. corner of a room, 5. corner with obstacle, 6. several obstacles. (b) The corresponding confidences C in the interpretations shown in a. The darker the color, the larger the expected error and the lower the confidence. Low confidence regions include the boundary region between freespace and obstacles, as well as regions beyond obstacles.

exploration utility of their neighbors y of the grid:

$$U(x) \longleftarrow -L(x) + \max_y U(y)$$

Here the expected (negative) reward by the model functions as *costs*[4] $L(x) > 0$ of moving from x to y, and is used for weighting the flow of exploration utilities. This implies that exploration utilities are predominantly propagated through freespace, while places with negative predicted reward such as walls and obstacles block the flow of utility. The resulting exploration utilities represent anytime plans for arbitrary robot locations, given that the robot applies steepest ascent therein. Figure 4 displays a model and the corresponding exploration utility landscape after 27 steps of exploration.

---

[4]The actually implemented cost function is a complex monotonically decreasing function of the expected reward.

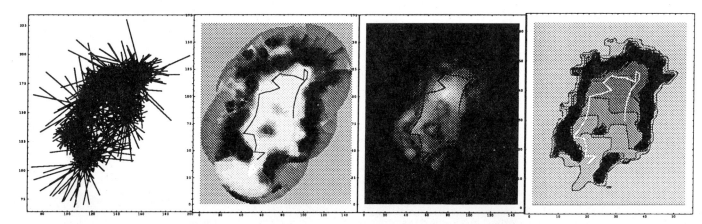

Figure 4: Integration of several measurements along an exploration path: (a) Raw, noisy sensor input on an exploration path with 27 measurements. (b) Resulting model, corresponding to the lab shown in Figure 1b (lab doorway is toward bottom left). The path of the robot is also plotted (from right to left), demonstrating the exploration of the initially unknown lab. (c) Cumulative confidence. (d) Exploration utilities. By local gradient descent in exploration utility space (i.e., moving to the brightest reachable location), the robot moves to the closest unexplored region on a minimal-cost path. In the next steps, the robot will pass the door of the lab and explore the hallway.

Because COLUMBUS shall explore in real-time, actions are immediately generated once the previous action execution is finished, regardless whether the propagation of exploration utility has converged or not. In principle this may lead to non-optimal actions. However, since the exploration values are propagated not only to the current location of the robot, but to all points in the discretized model, they can be reused for later planning once the robot location has been changed. Reusing plans was observed to result in optimal plans after surprisingly short planning times, although plain dynamic programming is known to be slow in complex domains.[5]

Since COLUMBUS' model of the environment is continuously updated during exploration according to new sensor information, dynamic programming has to be modified to deal efficiently with the resulting changes in the cost function and the cumulative confidence. In general, dynamic programming may cause long planning time if the model changes during planning. More specifically, the problem that may occur when changing the cost function or the cumulative confidence is the *overestimation problem* for exploration utilities: Assume the planner assigns high utility to two adjacent grid points that, after updating the model based on new sensor information, will now have low utility. Dynamic programming may take many iterations before converging to the lower utilities. This is because each of the large exploration utilities will be updated with a large value, justified by the observation that there is an adjacent grid point with a large utility. Only the costs of moving from one grid point to another can cause the utilities to decay over time. This effect was frequently observed to cause very long planning durations. In order to overcome the overestimation problem, COLUMBUS' planner works in three phases:

1. If a new sensation is received, the grid representation of both the model and the confidence map is updated according to this sensor information, using the networks $\mathcal{R}$ and $\mathcal{C}$.

2. Each overestimated utility, i.e., each utility that would have been set to a smaller value by the next dynamic programming step, is set to $-\infty$. This step is repeated until no overestimated utility can be identified, resulting in a strictly underestimating set of exploration utilities.

3. Finally, dynamic programming is applied to propagate exploration utilities as discussed above.

Whenever the robot finishes the execution of an action, a simple search procedure that maximizes exploration utility is employed to determine the next action, using the current estimate of exploration utilities. This ensures that COLUMBUS operates in real-time: Even if planning is not completed, actions are generated and executed. It should be noted that this planner can also be, and in fact is in the current implementation, used for planning paths to goal locations specified by the user.

IV. EXPERIMENTAL DESIGN AND RESULTS

In Section II. it was assumed that the location of the robot can always be determined accurately. However, real-world robots usually suffer from cumulative control errors caused by inaccurate effectors. After some time of operation, location estimates based on dead-reckoning are usually significantly wrong. COLUMBUS uses the networks $\mathcal{R}$ and $\mathcal{C}$ also for relocating itself on-the-fly with respect to its model. This is done by building a *local model* (interpretation) from the most recent sensation, s_{n+1}, and then maximizing the match between this local model and the current global model obtained from the previous n sensations $\{s_1, s_2, \ldots, s_n\}$. In COLUMBUS, gradient descent search is used to estimate the location of the robot x_{n+1}. More specifically, the squared deviation of the global and the local model (weighted by prediction confidences) is measured over a set of randomly drawn nearby sample points. Online position control is achieved by minimizing this match error. Since neural networks represent differentiable functions, these error gradients can be propagated through the sensor interpretation network, resulting

---

[5]The planning speed benefits also from the fact that the internal representation of the environment is only two-dimensional, neglecting COLUMBUS' rotational degree of freedom.

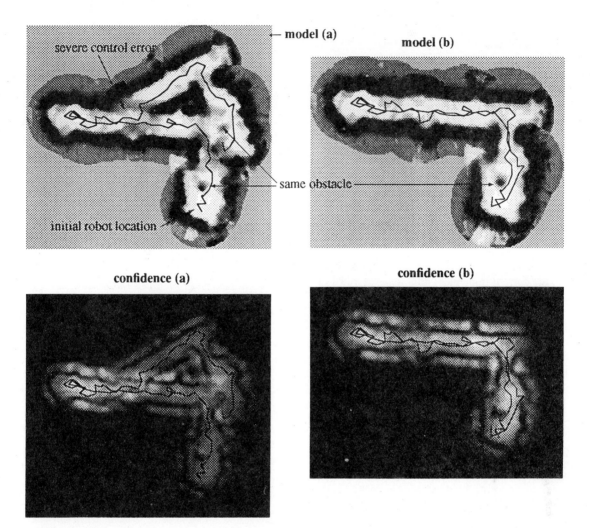

model (a) ← | model (b)

severe control error

same obstacle

initial robot location

confidence (a) | confidence (b)

Figure 5: Online position control: (a) In this experiment, I invoked one severe control error by rotating the robot manually, in addition to the normal cumulative control errors. Without correction, the resulting model is wrong and therefore useless. (b) By maximizing the match between the global model and the interpretation of the most recent sonar values (local model), control errors can be successfully identified and corrected. Note that in this experiment, the robot was told to return to the lab after some exploration.

in the derivatives of the match error with respect to the input values of these networks. These gradients are used for gradient descent search in the location space of the robot. By iteratively adjusting the internal belief of the location of the robot, the match error is minimized. This online position control procedure was found to work successfully even in the presence of severe errors in dead-reckoning. An example is shown in Figure 5.

Both the sensor interpretation function $\mathcal{R}$ and the confidence estimation function $\mathcal{C}$ were represented by backpropagation networks with one hidden layer and eight hidden units. Instead of processing all 24 sonar values by these networks, only the four to a query point x nearest sonar values were provided as an input. By ignoring most of the sensor information, the processing time was significantly reduced when updating the discretized versions of the model, as was the number of training examples required for training $\mathcal{R}$ and $\mathcal{C}$. However, omitting sensor values is only valid, if these are independent of the expected reward at point x. This is approximately the case for COLUMBUS.

Additional speedup was obtained by ignoring COLUMBUS' rotational degree of freedom, as mentioned above. Henceforth the dimensionality of the model was two, and the cost of rotations was considered to be 0. Introducing a third dimension would have had a negative impact on memory requirements and planning times in COLUMBUS. The grid size in the planner was 4 inches. COLUMBUS planner can deal with large areas (500 000 square feet and more), limited only by the memory capacity of the workstation used for planning.

COLUMBUS actual implementation is modularized and distributed. Modules (map builder, planner, position controller, central controller and graphical user interface) are connected using the Task Control Architecture [14], which allows to execute the programs on several SUN SPARC workstations in parallel. Robot actions take usually between 3 and 12 seconds, plus approximately 3 seconds for transmitting sensor and control information by a radio link. During extensive experimentation I observed roughly the following timing behavior: 1.5 sec for updating the discretized version of the model, 2 to 20 sec for complete planning from scratch, and between 0 and 4 for planning when reusing earlier plans (planning took up to 120 sec without the utility reset mechanism described in the previous section). The position control mechanism described above did run endlessly in the background, interrupted only by new sensor information.

V. DISCUSSION

COLUMBUS is an autonomous mobile robot, whose goal it is to explore and model unknown environments efficiently. It employs an instance-based approximation technique based on neural networks for modeling the environment, and an anytime planner based on dynamic programming for planning low-cost paths to poorly explored areas. COLUMBUS has been successfully operated in the hallways and labs at CMU for periods up to hours.[6] In order to do so in dynamic environments such as a office buildings, the current implementation features a fast obstacle detection and avoidance mechanism that is not described here. However, COLUMBUS' models assumes static environments. It seems to be feasible to extend this approach to slowly changing environments (e.g., by decaying confidence over time).

In principle, the artificial neural networks $\mathcal{R}$ and $\mathcal{C}$ employed for model building and exploration allow for knowledge transfer and thus a synergy effect across multiple environments. This is because these network represent robot-specific knowledge that is independent of particular environments at hand. However, in the current real-world implementation this synergy effect has been only partially demonstrated, since the networks are pretrained in simulation. One of the main limitations of this approach is that these networks have to be trained in a supervised manner, requiring a *known* environment. Although in principle COLUMBUS is able to label its environment autonomously by sensing collisions directly (using the motion sensors of its wheels), I preferred simulation, since it facilitates supervised learning, and since real-world collisions will ultimately damage the robot.

In order to operate in real-time, COLUMBUS features an anytime planner based on dynamic programming. I have empirically found that this planner generates appropriate actions in real-time, even though the dynamic programming process might not have fully converged. This planner, however, operates on a two-dimensional representation of the environment. In order to scale up to higher dimensional environments the approach taken has to be modified.

Future research will also include comparisons to other approaches to model building and path planning, for example [4, 11].

ACKNOWLEDGMENT

I thank Tom Mitchell and Alex Waibel for invaluable advice, and Long-Ji Lin, Hans Moravec, and the ODYSSEUS team at CMU, namely Reid Simmons, Charalambos Athanassiou, John Cheng, Lonnie Chrisman, Richard Goodwin, Goang-Tay Hsu, and Hank Wan, for being an excellent team as well as for many discussions. Furthermore, I thank Reid Simmons and Chris Fedor for providing the Task Control Architecture software

REFERENCES

[1] Christopher A. Atkeson. Using locally weighted regression for robot learning. In *Proceedings of the 1991 IEEE International Conference on Robotics and Automation*, pages 958–962, Sacramento, CA, April 1991.

[2] Jonathan R. Bachrach. A connectionist learning control architecture for navigation. In R. P. Lippmann, J. E. Moody, and D. S. Touretzky, editors, *Advances in Neural Information Processing Systems 3*, pages 457–463, San Mateo, 1991. Morgan Kaufmann.

[3] Andy G. Barto, Steven J. Bradtke, and Satinder P. Singh. Real-time learning and control using asynchronous dynamic programming. Technical Report COINS 91-57, Department of Computer Science, University of Massachusetts, MA, August 1991.

[4] Alberto Elves. Sonar-based real-world mapping and navigation. *IEEE Journal of Robotics and Automation*, RA-3(3):249–265, June 1987.

[5] Dieter Fox, Volker Heinze, Knut Möller, Sebastian B. Thrun, and Gerd Veenker. Learning by error-driven decomposition. In Simula, Kohonen, editors, *Proceedings of International Conference on Artificial Neural Networks*, Amsterdam, 1991. Elsevier Publisher.

[6] Jerome H. Friedmann. Multivariate adaptive regression splines. *Annals of Statistics*, 19(1):1–141, March 1991.

[7] Robert A. Jacobs and Michael I. Jordan. A modular connectionist architecture for learning piecewise control strategies. In *Proceedings of the American Control Conference*. Dept. of Brain and Cognitive Sciences, MIT, 1991.

[8] Sven Koenig. The complexity of real-time search. Technical Report CMU-CS-92-145, Carnegie Mellon University, April 1992.

[9] Long-Ji Lin. Programming robots using reinforcement learning and teaching. In *Proceedings of AAAI-91*, Menlo Park, CA, July 1991. AAAI Press / The MIT Press.

[10] Andrew W. Moore. *Efficient Memory-based Learning for Robot Control.* PhD thesis, Trinity Hall, University of Cambridge, England, 1990.

[11] Hans P. Moravec. Sensor fusion in certainty grids for mobile robots. *AI Magazine*, pages 61–74, Summer 1988.

[12] Steven J. Nowlan. Competing experts: An experimental investigation of associative mixture models. Technical Report CRG-TR-90-5, Dept. of Computer Science, University of Toronto, Canada, September 1990.

[13] David E. Rumelhart, Geoffrey E. Hinton, and Ronald J. Williams. Learning internal representations by error propagation. In D. E. Rumelhart and J. L. McClelland, editors, *Parallel Distributed Processing. Vol. I + II.* MIT Press, 1986.

[14] Reid Simmons. Concurrent planning and execution for autonomous robots. *IEEE Control Systems*, 12(1):46–50, February 1992.

[15] Satinder P. Singh. The efficient learning of multiple task sequences. In J. E. Moody, S. J. Hanson, and R. P. Lippmann, editors, *Advances in Neural Information Processing Systems 4*, pages 251–258, San Mateo, CA, 1992. Morgan Kaufmann.

[16] Richard S. Sutton. Integrated architectures for learning, planning, and reacting based on approximating dynamic programming. In *Proceedings of the Seventh International Conference on Machine Learning, June 1990*, pages 216–224, 1990.

[17] Sebastian B. Thrun. Efficient exploration in reinforcement learning. Technical Report CMU-CS-92-102, Carnegie Mellon University, Pittsburgh, PA 15213, January 1992.

[18] Sebastian B. Thrun. The role of exploration in learning control. In David A. White and Donald A. Sofge, editors, *Handbook of intelligent control: neural, fuzzy and adaptive approaches*, Florence, Kentucky 41022, 1992. Van Nostrand Reinhold.

[19] Steven D. Whitehead. A study of cooperative mechanisms for faster reinforcement learning. Technical Report 365, University of Rochester, Computer Science Department, Rochester, NY, March 1991.

---

[6] In fact, COLUMBUS' approach to model building and position control has been successfully used as part of the CMU entry "ODYSSEUS" in the first AAAI robot competition in California, 1992.

Bee-havior in a Mobile Robot:
The Construction of a Self-Organized Cognitive Map and its Use in Robot Navigation within a Complex, Natural Environment

Ashley Walker†, John Hallam†, David Willshaw‡

†Department of Artificial Intelligence, ‡Centre for Cognitive Science

†5 Forrest Hill , ‡2 Buccleuch Place

University of Edinburgh, Edinburgh †EH1 2QL ‡EH8 9LW, Scotland

Abstract--In this work, we model a mobile robotic control system on the spatial memory and navigatory behaviors attributed to foraging honey bees in an effort to exploit some of the robustness and efficiency these insects are known to enjoy. Our robot uses a self-organizing feature-mapping neural network to construct a topographically ordered map from ultra-sound range images collected while exploring the environment. This map is then annotated with metric positional information from a dead reckoning system. The resulting cognitive map can be used by the robot to localize in the world and to plan safe and efficient routes through the environment. This system has been thoroughly tested in simulation and is currently being implemented on the robot.

I. INTRODUCTION

A fundamental skill possessed by most animals is the ability to move around within their environments. Small insects, e.g., central place foraging honey bees (Apis mellifera), provide an excellent example of a robust navigational system which enables its user to travel along circuitous outbound journeys (e.g., covering distances up to 10 000 meters round trip [1]) in search of food and to return home along highly efficient routes--which are determined primarily by internal mechanisms, rather than by external sensory cues (e.g., chemical gradients). Furthermore, these insects have short range navigational abilities that allow them to pinpoint the small opening to their hive and to orient precisely toward the food bearing portion of a flower. Purposeful motion of this sort requires that the traveling agent have a system for representing spatial information which is integrated with its navigation, locomotive and motivational mechanisms [2].

The way in which insects (and "higher" animals) create, store, and use spatial memory is a subject of great interest and debate. In the particular case of the honey bee, nearly half a century of research has resulted in the development of coherent and structured models of this behavior. In the last two decades, it has been possible to use computer simulation to test the plausibility of these models and to compare different algorithms for achieving similar effects [3], [4], [5], [6]. In addition to increasing our understanding the operational principles involved in natural information processing, implementing models of animal behavior (in computer simulations and, moreover, in mobile robots) allows us to extract useful engineering knowledge which can be applied to the creation of more robust and efficient artificial systems designed to achieve similar functions.

This work has the latter goal in mind and addresses the task of (i) what sort of basic environmental spatial representation(s) may underlie robust, obstacle-free navigation and (ii) what sort of computational structure can provide an intelligent agent with a reliable and easily accessible memory for recording spatial information. In choosing spatial primitives, we do not employ a representation which requires formal recognition or reasoning about landmarks, obstacles and/or areas. Instead, we consider a simple, unprocessed representation of the patterns of environmental free space detected by the robot's sensors. As a spatial memory, we examine a distributed, decentralized neural network based structure which can easily be learnt by the robot using a self-organization process [7].

Our robotic map-building and navigation system was inspired by some elegant strategies utilized by foraging honey bees. These are modeled at a behavioral, rather than a neurophysiological, level of analysis. In the following subsections we provide an overview of these mechanisms.

A. Spatial Information utilized by Foraging Honey Bees
Honey bees navigate over long distances via dead reckoning (or path integration). The bee performs dead reckoning by monitoring the angles it steers (using an internal compass calibrated to the sun) and the distances it travels (using proprioceptive information) and then integrating this data into a vector pointing toward the hive. Due to the inaccuracies associated with dead reckoning, global localization--a visual image comparison process--is used to identify target locations once the bee has arrived in their vicinity [8]. Global localization requires that the bee record visual images, or "snapshots[1]" of important regions in its environment. As the bee approaches one of these sites, e.g., the hive, it recalls the relevant snapshots and compares them to its current retinal image in order to produce a set of motion vectors which will accurately align it with the entrance to the hive.

B. Spatial Memory mechanisms of Foraging Honey Bees
The way that these sensory inputs are organized in the honey bee's memory is not fully understood. Some researchers believe that snapshots are simply associated with the compass bearing along which the bee was traveling when the snapshots was taken. This implies snapshots may only be used serially to guide path specific navigation [8]. At the other

---

1 Snapshots are not completely unprocessed retinal images. Studies by [6] have shown that at least some amount of filtering is used to eliminate, for example, distant objects from snapshots used to give fine motion guidance near to a target.

extreme, it has been suggested that snapshots and the metric outputs of a dead reckoning process are combined within an internal cognitive map [9], [10]. In general, a cognitive map is an internal representation of the spatial relationships among observable points in an animal's environment which can be used to plan movements through that environment. In this scenario, goal locations have a map position which can be "looked up" and a route between the animal's current location and the goal location can be planned when some other internal motivational source encourages goal pursuit behavior.

In this work, we employ relevant features of the latter hypothesis--not in an effort to assess the validity of this invertebrate behavior theory--but because it yields insight into a more robust and efficient way to organize spatial information in a navigating robot. We suppose that bees may possess a cognitive map because it would endow the bee (and our robot) with the ability to (i) recover its positional information after displacement or a failure in the dead reckoning system, (ii) plan efficient, novel routes throughout the environment and (iii) make discriminating choices about routes based on known topography.

II SYSTEM DESIGN AND ARCHITECTURE

This research was conducted aboard a transputer based mobile robot called "Ben Hope." Earlier work [11] resulted in the creation of a parallel, distributed software control architecture (based upon that proposed by Brooks [12]) for the coordination of behaviors aboard the robot. Three basic behaviors exist to enable purposeful movement of the robot within its environment. The lowest layer of behavioral competence, WANDER, allows the robot to investigate the environment by pursuing motion in any (initially arbitrary) direction. Ben Hope is biased to seek out regions of free space in that if an AVOID module detects an obstacle(s) in the robot's direction of forward motion, an EXPLORE-FREE-SPACE behavior is triggered. The latter facilitates selection of the new direction of travel to be the one containing the most free space (as detected by acoustic range sensors).

A. Spatial Information utilized by Ben Hope

In implementing honey bee navigation mechanisms on this system, a DEAD-RECKONING module is created to monitor high resolution position encoders on the robot's wheels and to continually update a vector pointing towards its start-up position, or home. In order to facilitate global localization, Ben Hope is equipped with 12 ultra-sonic range sensors with a (combined) 360° field of view. Thus, the robot has an orientation independent view of the world, which allows it to recognize features therein regardless of its direction of travel.

Acoustic range data is chosen (instead of visual data) to underlie global localization in this real-time system due to the relative ease of interpretation of their returned signal. As with all sensors, sonar range data is subject to uncertainties which must be properly understood in order for the data to be used in a meaningful fashion. Due to specular reflection, a true range cannot be reliably obtained from these devices when measuring an acoustically smooth surface at an angle of incidence more than 1/2 of the beamwidth [13]. Two of the

most common ways to combat this sonar uncertainty include (i) engineering the environment so as to eliminate the problem (e.g., using acoustic retroreflectors as in [13]) or (ii) building a model of the uncertainty expected. The latter approach requires the robot to identify landmarks by matching their range signatures to stored templates [14]. Static model matching approaches require both a precise robot positioning system and a sophisticated matching algorithm to reason about uncertainty and error.

It is argued here (and elsewhere [15], [16]) that uncertainty may be dealt with more simply by relying on the dynamic, rather than the static, properties of these signals. Much uncertainty may be filtered out of a system which exploits the time averaged derivative of sensory signals--accumulated by an agent as it moves around in its world--in a way which forces larger changes in the sensor readings than those contributed by noise [15]. Mataric's [2] boundary tracing robot takes such a dynamic approach to sonar landmark detection by identifying semantic spatial primitives (e.g., "left-wall," "corridor," etc,) defined as combinations of its motion and sensory input averaged over time.

Our handling of sonar data intrinsically capitalizes on the dynamic character of the sensory information. We use an unsupervised neural network to extract the qualitative features of this data by statistically classifying sonar readings into general feature categories. Classifications are built up over training time and the final character of each feature category will represent an average of similar sonar images. This process enables the creation of a memory structure which, like the honey bee's spatial memory, supports a robust kind of pattern matching and does not require formal recognition of the contents of an image.

B. Spatial Memory mechanisms utilized by Ben Hope

In order to mimic the presupposed cognitive mapping capabilities of the honey bee, our robot must order the elements (or patterns) perceived in its environment into a topographically coherent and useful form. To this end, Ben Hope's MAP-BUILDING behavioral module utilizes a self-organizing feature-mapping (SOFM) neural network to map from external sensory space to an internal spatial representation. A modified version of Kohonen's Algorithm [17], [18] is used to perform the mapping because it seeks to produce an order reminiscent of the neurophysiology organization of the honey bee's memory, i.e., bees are thought to store their snapshots somewhere in the optic lobe or mushroom bodies--both of which contain topographical maps of the retina [19].

1. Organization of the Memory Map

The details of the mapping process are specified below.

• The cognitive map is represented in the robot's memory as a 2-dimensional output array of network nodes. Each individual node in this array contains a 12-dimensional weight vector (equivalent to the dimensionality of each sonar image) whose weight elements are randomly initialized. This corresponds to initially haphazard connections between the imaging surface and the map surface before learning.

• As prescribed by Kohonen [18], input vectors (i.e., 12-dimensional sonar readings) are presented to the network in a random order. In order to perform the mapping in real-time (i.e., while the robot is exploring), initiation of the mapping procedure is delayed with respect to the commencement of exploration so as to allow a pool of sensory information to accumulate in memory from which to draw individual vector elements at random. Once this condition is met, mapping proceeds continuously for the duration of the exploration session.

• Kohonen's SOFM learning algorithm organizes this grid of map nodes into local neighborhoods which classify features in the input sensory data. The algorithm achieves this organization by determining which map node contains the weight vector most similar (in Euclidean distance) to a current input (i.e., the "winning node") and then selectively optimizing an area of the map surrounding that winning node such that it comes to represent an average of the training data for that class of feature

• We found it necessary to modify Kohonen's proposed weight update scheme by introducing inhibitory, as well as the standard excitatory, weight updating. In full, we enhance the weights of nodes within a rectangular optimization neighborhood surrounding the winning node and, at the same time, spread an equivalent amount of inhibition to nodes outside this region. Employing inhibition in this way serves to push the values of dissimilar weight vectors yet further away from the current input vector .

• This form of Hebbian learning is used to update weights by an amount proportional to the magnitude of the input. Kohonen decreases the proportionality term (i.e., the "learning rate") with training time to curtail learning. However, in this application, the learning rate remains constant so that the robot continues to learn about its environment for the duration of the exploration.

• Convergence of the map to a stable order is facilitated by decreasing the size of the optimization area (i.e., "neighborhood update zone") to the single node which is most excited upon stimulation by a particular input.

As training proceeds over several iterations, each map node learns to encode a particular pattern of free space visible from certain vantage points within the room. (See Figure 1.) Beginning from a grid of map nodes containing 12-dimensional randomly initialized weight vectors, an ordered map is created such that input vectors which are similar in 12-dimensional external sensory space are clustered to similar positions on the 2-dimensional internal array of map nodes.

2. Association of Position Metrics

In order for this map to underlie the sorts of useful navigatory behavior attributed to bees, metric information need be incorporated. The bee is thought to associate compass bearings [8], [10] with snapshots stored in memory. For our purposes, a more useful metric is positional information. The robot's dead reckoning system keeps a record of the (x,y) coordinate position from which each sonar sensor reading is taken. In the current implementation of the system, each of the unique acoustic image features classified by individual network nodes is associated with the coordinate position from which that feature can be seen within the natural environment. A Willshaw Net [20] is used to make these associations. Although the positions encoded by the system are specific coordinate values, the concept of a feature's associated

position is used loosely in this system. In actuality, each unique sonar feature is visible within a small area in the room which is, on average, 5% of the total room area.

This is an acceptable resolution for a sonar based navigation system operating in a cluttered laboratory environment. The topographically ordered map, with this metric annotation, need only facilitate navigation to a position within the sensing range of a goal location. An exact goal position can be reached by augmenting the robot with special purpose sensors (e.g., a simplified compound eye) and fine motion planning (e.g., based on visual information processing algorithms proposed for bees [3], [4]).

III. RESULTS

In this section, we examine the topographical order encoded within cognitive maps constructed as described in the previous section. Furthermore, the utility of this map to underlie obstacle-free navigation and efficient route planning is described. The results illustrated here were obtained from computer simulation using real data collected by the robot. Since the time of this writing, the MAP-BUILDING algorithm has been implemented on the robot's transputer control system and deployment of the NAVIGATION behavioral module will shortly follow.

A. The Cognitive Map Illustrated

In order to describe the character of the spatial memory map, we developed an original method for viewing the high dimensional weight vectors contained in each node of our completed cognitive map. In this representation, the 12x12 output array of cognitive map nodes is reduced to 36 node areas by averaging the contents of four adjacent nodes. The remaining 36 representative weight vectors are then thresholded such that individual weights above a thresholding parameter are turned ON--signifying a relatively long and unobstructed sonar view, or turned OFF--indicating that an obstacle was relatively close at hand. This new binary weight matrix representation is then examined, and, for each set of three bits (corresponding to a 90° field of view on the robot), the viewing area is deemed OPEN if two (or more) of the three bits were ON, otherwise it is labeled OBSTRUCTED. In Figure 1, a small circular robot symbol--with four viewing quadrants--is placed in each node area. A quadrant is shaded where visibility is OPEN and a blackened where the robot's encoded view is OBSTRUCTED. (For simplicity, no associated positional information is displayed.)

The cognitive map of Figure 1 is a guide to the types and locations of free space in Ben Hope's laboratory environment. The sonar readings vary smoothly across the map--which is evidence of the neighborhood preserving character of the mapping. The fidelity of the mapping can be further confirmed by examining the positions associated with each node. For example, it is the case that the cluster of totally obstructed views in the lower, left corner of the map are associated with coordinate positions which map to a highly cluttered area between two tables and a wall.[2]

---

2 As a final confirmation, we employed Rank, or Nonparametric, Correlation to statistically determine whether nodes which are

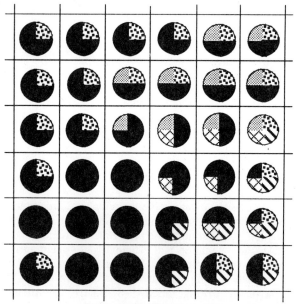

Figure 1: The Cognitive Map

The algorithm to produce these maps runs in real time. Exploration and mapping (in the laboratory environment tested) can be satisfactorily accomplished in approximately one hour. However, the quality of the map will, of course, increase with training time. Maps built up over a longer training period will be both more robust to the effects of sensor noise and will learn to ignore the positional changes of insignificant items (e.g., rubbish bins, empty boxes, etc.) and transient aspects of the environment (e.g., occasional students rushing through the laboratory). The latter will fade from memory because they receive no re-enforcement.

B. Map Based Route Planning:

Some model of the world (e.g., a map) is required by all agents who wish to navigate toward locations which cannot be sensed from their current position. Gould [9] and Gallistel [10] believe bees use a cognitive map to localize their position in the world and then may employ vector addition to perform route planning. This method of path finding seems to be very efficient navigation strategy for any animal whose physiology and environmental topography make obstacle avoidance along "bee-line" paths between targets possible. In the cluttered environment of our relatively large and less maneuverable robot, there are certain configurations of obstacles and objects which prevent straight line travel between two points. Noting this discrepancy between the artificial and

close together on the map do indeed correspond to world places that are close--i.e., acoustically and geographically similar. Kendall's rank correlation coefficient yields a value, τ, between -1 (data is anti- correlated-- e.g., close map places are associated with widely separated world distances) and 1 (data is positively associated). In our cognitive map, the degree of correlation between map distances and high dimensional world distances is positive, $\tau=0.352$, and differs quite significantly (d=30.4) from the null hypothesis of $\tau=0$, or no correlation.

natural systems, we decided to pursue navigation along two parallel lines of research. The first aligns itself with the biological approach of performing relatively simple path planning (e.g., simple vector addition constrained by known topography) and using rather more enroute sensing to avoid obstacles. This method could not be simulated and therefore will not be considered further in this paper. The second approach is motivated by engineering concerns, and seeks to exploit the rich source of information about unobstructed world paths that the robot discovered in the exploration and mapping phase of learning. This information is incorporated into the cognitive map.

To this end, we employ a graphical representation of location connectivity relations discovered during exploration. Between all pairs of nodes in the map, an edge is defined if, during exploration, the robot discovered that these nodes encode the sonar features of adjacent world places. Since each node has an associated world position, the cost associated with each of these edges is simply the difference between the two coordinate points in the world. In the current implementation, we use an A* search algorithm to find the shortest path between the current node and the goal node. Such a path will necessarily be globally obstacle-free because it consists of path segments that were traveled during training.

It is safe to assume that local obstacle avoidance will be required to correct for the uncertainty in the positioning system and for the small scale drift of moveable objects (e.g., chairs). By tracking its corresponding map position as it moves through the world, the robot can use patterns of free space encoded in the map to make intelligent decisions about low cost local detours.

Figures 2 and 3 show two routes (embolded) planned by our navigation simulator. The faint projections emanating from the start node illustrate paths considered but eventually rejected as their cost built up. The coordinates of the room and all of the large-scale objects in the room were overlaid on the paths generated. (Objects depicted include: ▭ tables, ▨ shelves, ▦ desks, ▥ other.)

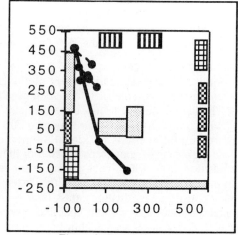

Figure 2: Sample Route 1

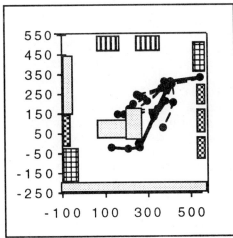

Figure 3: Sample Route 2

In the robot, the NAVIGATION module begins route planning by correlating the robot's current position with its encoded map position using an excitation based matching process. This involves comparing new sonar information with that stored in the map and computing an index of stimulation for each node. Nodes that respond most strongly encode sonar features that are most similar to those at the currently sensed world position. The robot localizes by selecting the single node which is most excited over several readings. (As each node encodes positional information, global localization may be used to re-calibrate the dead reckoning system using this procedure.) Once a correlation is made, the active node can spread expectation to nodes which encode neighboring world features and thereby decrease the pool of possible matches in subsequent localizations [2].

IV. DISCUSSION

These results suggest that a cognitive map created through self-organization can underlie robust and efficient navigation in a mobile robotic system employing dead reckoning and global localization. This map utilizes local sensory information to create a qualitative representation of the permanent features in the environment. The ability of this map to robustly and reliably encode spatial information lies in the qualitative nature of the representation. The map making algorithm does not depend on the accuracy of the sonar sensors or on precise positioning of the robot. Instead, sensor uncertainty is filtered through dynamic averaging. Similarly, small scale and transient environmental features are filtered from the final representation.

Formal recognition of objects and areas is not required by this system. Our review of honey bee information processing revealed that a lower level "primitive" such as patterns of free-space (or, alternatively, patterns of obstacle constellations) projected on a retina (or detected through a sonar ranging device) is a more simple and robust representation of spatial information.

Finally, by employing an unsupervised neural network to organize sensory information, we enable our robot to process only those aspects of the world that are relevant to it. In this way, we have constructed a theoretical tool which, as recommended by Brooks [15], uses aspects that the creature is sensing as the primary formal notion.

V. FUTURE DIRECTIONS

The first step in the future development of this system is the implementation of a NAVIGATION module in the robot's transputer control architecture. We can then better assess the limitations of the navigation system described and compare it to the more biologically plausible method of weak planning and strong sensing. It has also been suggested [Harry Barrow, personal communication] that connectionist path finding strategies be investigated at this stage.

Furthermore, once the robot begins navigating, we may need to redefine our notion of localization. At present, the robot correlates its current world location with its map equivalent by comparing a series of images taken from that vantage point with the image features encoded in the map in order to calculate a single representative node. It may be the case that a more distributed approach will prove to be more robust. Such a scheme would employ some measure of the excitation across the entire map to localize. This may resemble the way that the hippocampus of a rat encodes places via a pattern of firing across many distinct CA neurons.

One of the most important differences between a biologically inspired system such as this and a real biological system is that the latter learns constantly. Our robotic system would be more robust if it continued to learn during navigation, or could be triggered to learn when its sensory readings perceived that the world had changed significantly since the last mapping session. Another element which could add to the biological plausibility and autonomousity of the system would be to add, to the control architecture, a motivational system which could encourage goal pursuit behavior.

When motivations are included, the robot should seek out meaningful places (e.g., a battery recharging outlet). Our objective thus far has been to design a coarse scale learning algorithm which allows the robot to create a robust spatial representation of its environment and then to perform map based navigation to within the sensing range of the goal location. In order to reach these more exact goal locations, we plan to employ a compound eye sensor which can perform pattern matching tasks more faithful to those that have been proposed for the honey bee.

ACKNOWLEDGMENT

We would like to thank Hugh Cameron, Sandy Colquhoun, Peter Forster, Douglas Howie and Martin Hughes for technical assistance and Beau Lotto for reviewing this manuscript.

REFERENCES

[1] Visscher, P.K., and T.D. Seeley. 1982. "Foraging strategy of honeybee colonies in a temperate deciduous forest". Ecology. 63 : 1790-1801.

[2] Mataric, M. J. 1991. "Navigating with a rat brain: a neurobiologically-inspired model for spatial representation".

International Conference on the Simulation of Adaptive Behaviour: from Animals to Animats. 169-175.

[3] Anderson, A. M. 1977. "A model for landmark learning in the honey-bee". Journal of Comparative Physiology. 114 : 335-355.

[4] Cartwright, B.A., and T.S. Collett. 1983. "Landmark learning in bees". Journal of Comparative Physiology. 151 : 521-543.

[5] Cartwright, B. A., and T. S. Collett. 1987. "Landmark maps for honey bees". Biological Cybernetics. 57 : 85-93.

[6] Cheng, K., T.S. Collett, A. Pickhard, and R. Wehner. 1987. "The use of visual landmarks by honeybees: bees weight landmarks according to their distance from the goal". Journal of Comparative Physiology. 161 : 469-475.

[7] Walker, V. A.. 1991. "Bee-haviour in a mobile robot". Unpublished M.Sc. Thesis, University of Edinburgh, Department of Artificial Intelligence.

[8] Wehner, R., and R. Menzel. 1990. "Do insects have cognitive maps?". Annual Review of Neuroscience. 13 : 403-414.

[9] Gould, J. L. 1986. "The locale map of honey bees: do insects have cognitive maps?". Science. 232 (16 May 1986) : 861-863.

[10] Gallistel, R.C. 1990. "The cognitive map". In The Organization of Learning. 102-172. Cambridge, MA: MIT Press.

[11] Forster, P. 1991. "A transputer-based autonomous mobile robot". Technical Paper #6, University of Edinburgh, Department of Artificial Intelligence.

[12] Brooks, R.A. 1986. "A robust layered control system for a mobile robot". IEEE Journal of Robotics and Automation. RA-2 (April) : 14-23.

[13] Steer, B. and T. Atherton. 1990. "Design for navigation". IEEE International Conference on Robotics and Automation. : 942-947.

[14] Kuipers, B. 1987. "A qualitative approach to robot exploration and map learning". AAAI Workshop on Spatial Reasoning and Multisensor Fusion.

[15] Brooks, R. A. 1991. "Challenges for complete creature architecture". International Conference on the Simulation of Adaptive Behaviour: from Animals to Animats. : 434-443.

[16] Malcolm, C., T. Smithers, and J. Hallam. 1989. "An emerging paradigm in robotic architecture". Invited paper at the Intelligent Autonomous Systems Conference.

[17] Willshaw, D.J., and C. von der Malsburg. 1976. "How patterned neural connections can be set up by self-organization". Proceedings of the Royal Society of London B. 194 : 431-445.

[18] Kohonen, T. 1988. "Self-Organization and Associative Memory". Springer, Berlin.

[19] Mobbs, P.G. 1982. "The brain of the honeybee Apis mellifera. I. The connections and spatial organization of the mushroom bodies". Philosophical Transactions of the Royal Society of London B. 198 : 309-354.

[20] Willshaw, D. J., O. P. Buneman, and H. C. Longuet-Higgins. 1969. "Non-holographic associative memory". Nature. 222 : 960-962.

Chapter 27:   Automobiles

Chapter 27
Automobiles

Neural networks have been cautiously approached by the automobile industry. The thought that a computer is performing tasks that it learned, but is unable to explain its actions, was too risky for serious consideration. As the analysis techniques for neural networks have improved, the reluctance to use neural networks in an automobile has dissipated. This chapter contains five papers that describe different aspects of neural network applications to automobiles. **Paper 27.1** is a survey paper that describes a wide variety of opportunities for neural networks in intelligent vehicles. **Paper 27.2** describes a collision avoidance system that employs two types of neural networks. **Paper 27.3** presents a survey of fuzzy logic and fuzzy neural network applications that can be embedded within the automobile. **Paper 27.4** describes a method for parameter estimation for shock absorbers. **Paper 27.5** reports on a neural network that utilizes electrochemical impedance data to assess the damage to paint finishes caused by stones.

Neural Networks for Intelligent Vehicles

Dean A. Pomerleau

Carnegie Mellon University, School of Computer Science

5000 Forbes Ave., Pittsburgh, PA 15213-3890

Phone: (1)412-268-3210, Fax: (1)412-621-1970, Internet: pomerleau@cmu.edu

Abstract

This paper is a survey of current research in applying artificial neural networks to the domain of intelligent vehicles. It describes work in three areas: video-based traffic monitoring, monitoring and control of onboard systems, and vision-based lateral control. In each of these domains, successful preliminary systems demonstrate that artificial neural networks have the potential to make significant improvements in the state-of-the-art. Because of the simplicity and uniformity of the neural network architectures and algorithms employed in these systems, they each have the potential to be implemented efficiently in hardware, which could eventually make them commercially viable.

1. Introduction

Artificial neural networks are a powerful technique for solving non-linear mapping and classification tasks. They have proven capable of solving problems ranging from speech and handwritten character recognition [29] [26] to medical diagnosis [2]. Recently neural networks have even begun to appear in consumer products such as washing machines and vacuum cleaners [17].

Two attributes of artificial neural networks make them useful for a wide variety of problems, including intelligent vehicles. The first beneficial attribute is their ability to adapt to new tasks and circumstances with relatively little effort on the part of the user or developer. In their most common form, namely multilayer perceptrons, neural networks learn to map input patterns to particular output patterns or classes based on many examples of the desired mapping. For instance, the input pattern in character recognition is typically a bitmap image of a character, and the output is the identity of the character. The system developer need not entirely specify the relevant features or processing required for the task, but instead needs only provide the network with numerous examples of the mapping to be performed (e.g. bitmaps paired with their identities). Neural network training algorithms, such as back-propagation [25] or radial basis function learning [19] can automatically determines from these examples the relevant input attributes and how to process them to perform the task. This ability to learn complex tasks through observation makes neural networks well suited to domains like intelligent vehicles, where the problems are often ill understood and constantly changing.

The second important attributed of artificial neural networks is their computational simplicity. In general, artificial neural networks are composed of many very simple computing elements, called units, which interact with each other through weighted connections. The simplicity and uniformity of this computing paradigm makes efficient implementations possible on both serial and parallel computers [13] [33] [31]. In addition, the regular nature of the neural network processing makes hardware implementations particularly attractive. The ability to implement a trained neural network on a single chip both reduces cost and increases reliability, two crucial factors in determining commercial viability. Nowhere is the need for inexpensive, reliable systems more acute than in the domain of intelligent vehicles, where the potential market includes the millions of cars sold each year, and where the cost of failure can be catastrophic.

This paper discusses three applications of artificial neural networks to the domain of intelligent vehicles: video-based traffic monitoring, monitoring and control of onboard systems, and vision-based lateral control. None of these systems is yet commercially available, but each has the potential to greatly improve the safety and efficiency of road travel.

2. Traffic Monitoring

The task in traffic monitoring is to detect traffic level and flow rates at key points, such as traffic lights and tunnels. The most common approach to traffic monitoring is install mechanical or electrical devices placed on top or embedded in the roadway. There are three disadvantages to such systems. First, they are expensive to install, particularly if they must be embedded in the pavement like the electrical inductance "loop" detectors typically used at traffic lights. Second, they are prone to mechanical failure due to pavement cracking. Third, they often can only "see" a single lane of traffic, or if they can detect traffic in multiple lanes, can not discriminate traffic on one lane versus another.

More recently, people have begun to investigate the use of machine vision techniques for traffic monitoring [5] [28]. These systems have the advantages of being easy to install, and being able to provide much more specific information about traffic conditions, including queue length and lane distribution. These systems generally employ simple image processing like image thresholding, image differencing, and template matching. As a result, they suffer from several problems, including sensitivity to lighting conditions and camera perspective. While more sophisticated image processing system which use optical flow and appearance models for different vehicle types are under development, they generally suffer from brittleness under changing

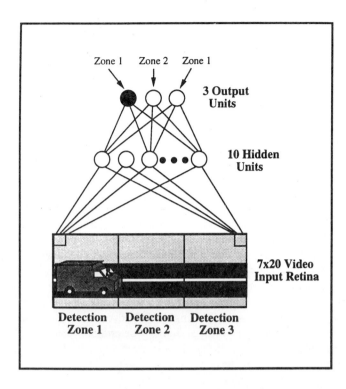

Figure 1: Network for Vehicle Detection.

conditions.

An alternative which may prove more robust is to use neural network-based image processing. Just such a system is being developed by Bullock, Garrett and Hendrickson [6]. The idea is to train a network to monitor a scene and indicate when the image contains a vehicle and where the vehicle is located. The network receives a reduced resolution video image of the scene as input, and has a number of output units each trained to respond to the presence of a vehicle in a particular region of the image (See Figure 1). The particular architecture used in this experiment had a 7x20 pixel input retina, 10 hidden units, and 3 output units corresponding to three "detection zones".

The network was trained on 233 images digitized from a two hour videotape of a public street. The images contained large amounts of visual noise including heavy shadows, bicycles, pedestrians and joggers, as well as many types of vehicles including cars and trucks of different makes, models and colors. The network was trained using a variation of the back-propagation learning algorithm called quickprop [10].

The trained network was tested on a disjoint test set of 83 images digitized from the same videotape. The network's performance was measured using the following criteria. The network was considered to have made a mistake if:

- a vehicle is present in a zone, but the corresponding output unit has an activation less than 0.6

- a vehicle is not present in a zone, but the corresponding output is greater than 0.4

- one of the outputs is between 0.4 and 0.6, a range considered indeterminant.

Using this criterion, the network had an error rate of 12How-ever all 9 of the mistakes occurred when a vehicle was transitioning from one zone to another. All 9 error were eliminated when the temporal activation pattern of the output units was examined.

These results are very preliminary, in that the system does not take into account multiple vehicles in the scene at once, and do not address the problem of vehicle identification (cars vs. trucks). However they do demonstrate that neural networks are capable of effective traffic monitoring, even in the presence of changing lighting conditions.

3. Vehicle Control Systems

A second successful application of artificial neural networks to the domain of intelligent vehicles has been in the area of monitoring, diagnosis and control of vehicle control systems. Increasing demands for performance, safety and fuel economy and lead to increasingly complex and sophisticated vehicle control systems in today's automobiles. A few of these advances include electronic ignition, anti-lock braking and active suspension systems. To achieve the full benefit of these advances requires sophisticated monitoring and control. What makes these applications particularly challenging is that they require very rapid responses, often based on quite limited amounts of data. Artificial neural networks have demonstrated an ability to perform well within these severe constraints.

3.1. Ignition Timing Estimation

A prime example of the effect use of neural networks for vehicle control system monitoring is the work of Willson, Whitham and Anderson [30]. They have focused on the task of neural network based engine control using information such as cylinder pressure, manifold pressure, engine temperature, engine speed and engine emissions. Their preliminary work has focused on on-line estimation of ignition timing, a crucial factor contributing to fuel economy and vehicle performance. With the proper equipment, ignition timing is straightforward to measure. Unfortunately such equipment is difficult to integrate into a moving vehicle. Recent development of high speed piezoelectric and fiber optic pressure sensors have made it possible to indirectly measure ignition timing by recording cylinder pressure at various crank angles. However the relationship between the time course of cylinder pressure and ignition timing is highly nonlinear due to its dependence on engine speed, air/fuel ratio and throttle setting.

Willson, Whitham and Anderson employed a single hidden layer network similar in many respects to the network used for traffic monitoring. However in their network, they employed 36 input units represented representing cylinder pressure at 36 different crank angles between −40° and +40° of top dead center. The best network architecture they found for the task had 16 hidden units and a single output unit representing the spark timing, which ranged from 5° to 35° before top dead center.

The network was trained on cylinder pressure data collected from a 350 in.^{3} Chevrolet engine running at 4000 RPMs with various spark timings. After training, the network was able to estimate the ignition timing on a disjoint test set collected from the same engine to within an average of 0.66°. While quite encouraging, the network's preformance under different conditions (e.g. different engine RPM or air/fuel ratio) remains to be tested.

3.2. Anti-lock Brake System Control

Another area of vehicle controls where early experiments suggest neural networks can be effectively applied is in the control of anti-lock braking systems [9]. In this task, the goal is to stop the vehicle as quickly as possible. As anyone who has driven on ice or snow realizes, the optimum braking strategy is not to slam on the brakes. This response will cause the wheels to "lock-up" and slide with much less friction than will occur when moderate braking is applied. The task is complicated by the fact that braking performance is heavily dependent on road conditions and true vehicle velocity, factors which are difficult to measure accurately.

The Davis et al. anti-lock braking system employs a two stage training system typical of neural network control systems. In the first stage, a "plant identification" network is trained to predict the behavior of the physical system under a variety of conditions. They trained a recurrent network to predict the wheel and vehicle velocity in the next time step based on the current wheel and vehicle velocity, and the current braking command. The training algorithm used was the dynamic decoupled extended Kalman filter (DDEKF) algorithm described in [11].

Once the identification network was trained to predict the vehicle's behavior, it was used to train a second recurrent network to produce the braking command for optimal stopping. The controller network learned from the vehicle model just how much braking force can be applied before the wheels lock under a variety of road conditions and vehicle speeds. After training in simulation using the identification network as the vehicle model, the controller network was trained on-line using a real vehicle driven on a test track. The controller network was also trained using the DDEKF algorithm.

Results showed that the network was able to learn to keep the vehicle's brakes from locking and the wheel slippage quite close to the theoretical optimal under a variety of road conditions (coefficients of friction between 0.2 to 1.0). While this performance is encouraging, Davis et al. did not report any comparison between the stopping distance achieved by the neural network controller and existing anti-lock braking systems.

Similar promising results have been achieved in active suspension control and detection of engine misfires [15]. In the later domain, a feedforward multi-layer perceptron was able to detect all but four of 150 misfires in a test set of 7600 engine measurements recorded from a vehicle in a wide variety of conditions (potholed roads, rapid acceleration and braking). It exhibited only 13 false alarms on the 7450 normal engine readings. This was in fact the first successful automated misfire detection system operating on a vehicle.

Figure 2: The CMU Navlab autonomous navigation testbed vehicle.

4. Vision-based Lateral Control

Perhaps the most widely studied application of neural networks to intelligent vehicles has been in vision-based lateral control. The goal in this task is to steer the vehicle based on input from an onboard video camera.

There are a number of neural network-based vision systems for autonomous vehicle control. Some rely primarily on color information [32] [16] to determine where the road is in the scene, while others use texture variations [7] in the image of the scene ahead of the vehicle to make steering decisions. The neural network architectures and algorithms employed by these systems also varies considerably. Many rely on standard feedforward networks and the back-propagation algorithm for training [32] [16], while others use recurrent networks [7] or radial basis functions [1].

The first and most successful neural network-based autonomous driving system is the ALVINN system developed by Pomerleau [24]. The ALVINN system is designed to drive the CMU Navlab autonomous navigation testbed shown in Figure 2. The vehicle is equipped with a video camera, and motors on the steering wheel, brake and accelerator pedal, enabling computer control of the vehicle's trajectory.

4.1. Neural Network Model

The connectionist model for autonomous road following used in the ALVINN system [23] is the feedforward multi-layer perceptron shown in Figure 3. The input layer consists of a single 30x32 unit "retina" onto which a video image is projected. Each of the 960 input units is fully connected to the four unit hidden layer, which is in turn fully connected to the output layer. The 30 unit output layer is a linear representation of the currently appropriate steering direction. The centermost output unit represents the "travel straight ahead" condition, while units to the left and right of center represent successively sharper left and right turns.

To drive the Navlab, an image from the video camera is reduced to 30x32 pixels and projected onto the input layer. After propagating activation through the network, the output layer's activation profile is translated into a vehicle steering command.

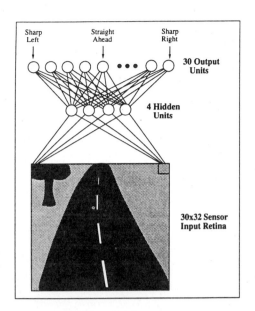

Figure 3: Architecture of the network designed for autonomous driving.

4.2. Training "On-the-Fly"

The most interesting and novel aspect of the ALVINN system is the method used to train it. In this technique, called training "on-the-fly" the network is taught to imitate the driving reactions of a person. As a person drives, the network is trained with back-propagation using the latest video image as input and the person's steering direction as the desired output.

To facilitate generalization to new situations, variety is added to the training set by shifting and rotation the original camera image in software to make it appear that the vehicle is situated differently relative to the road ahead. The correct steering direction for each of these transformed images is created by altering the person's steering direction for the original image to account for the altered vehicle placement. So for instance, if the person was steering straight ahead, and the image was transformed to make it appear the vehicle is off to the right side of the road, the correct steering direction for this new image would be to steer towards the left in order to bring the vehicle back to the road center. Adding these transformed patterns to the training set teachs the network to recover from driving mistakes, without requiring the human trainer to explicitly stray from the road center and then return.

4.3. ALVINN Driving Performance

Running on two Sun Sparcstations onboard the Navlab, training on-the-fly requires about two minutes during which a person drives over about a 1/4 to 1/2 mile stretch of training road. During this training phase, the network typically is presented with approximately 50 real images, each of which is transformed 15 times to create a training set of 750 images.

Once it has learned, the network can accurately traverse the length of the road used for training, and also generalize to drive along parts of the road not encountered during training under

Figure 4: Video images taken on three of the roads ALVINN has been trained to handle.

a variety of weather and lighting conditions. In addition, since determining the steering direction from the input image merely involves a forward sweep through the network, the system is able to process 20 images per second, and drive at up to 55 mph. This is over five times as fast as any non-connectionist system as driven using comparable hardware [14] [8].

The flexibility provided by the neural network has allowed ALVINN to learn to driving in a wide variety of situations. Individual networks have been trained to drive on single-lane dirt and paved roads, two-lane suburban and city streets, and multi-lane divided highways. Images taken from three of these domains are shown in Figure 4. On the highway, ALVINN has driving for for up to 21 miles without human intervention. Measurements of the ALVINN systems driving accuracy show it is able to keep the vehicle within 6.9cm of the center of its lane on average [22]. This compares favorably with human driving performance, which has been measured to average 5.7cm from the center of the lane on average [3].

The eventual goal of the ALVINN project is to create an advanced cruise control system which controls both longitudinal and lateral motion of the vehicle. The system will be trained by watching the person drive for several minutes. After training, the person will push a button and ALVINN would take over all vehicle controls. However this fully autonomous system is still a long way off. In the nearer term, the ALVINN system will be used as a lane excursion warning device, sounding an alarm when the driver starts to swerve out of his lane. In fact, a single chip hardware implementation of the ALVINN system, integrating both the CCD array for image capture and the neural network for image processing, is currently under development at Carnegie Mellon University. This hardware implementation should provide an inexpensive and reliable platform on which to develop a practical lane excursion warning device.

5. Conclusion

Artificial neural networks have the potential to make large contributes to the field of intelligent vehicles. Their ability to learn complex non-linear mappings allow neural networks to perform many difficult intelligent vehicle tasks, including traffic monitoring, mechanical system monitoring and control, and vision-based lateral motion monitoring and control.

While such applications of neural networks are still in the experimental stages, their preliminary success, when coupled with the fact that their simplicity allows them to be implemented cheaply and reliably, should result in commercially viable intelligent vehicle products. Such commercial neural networks are already available in certain consumer products including models of washing machines, vacuum cleaners and air conditioners sold by Panasonic [17]. A single chip implementation of the ALVINN neural network vision system is currently under development for use as a lane excursion warning system.

However there are several factors currently limiting the widespread application of neural networks to real world problems, including those of intelligent vehicles. The first is a general lack of rigorous performance comparisons with alternative methods. While there has been some limited experiments comparing the driving accuracy of the ALVINN system with that of people, in general intelligent vehicle applications of neural networks have only reported qualitative results. Part of this lack of rigor stems from the fact that it is often difficult to find good metrics for performance in domains like traffic monitoring, and once they are found, it is difficult to measure a system's performance. For example, measuring the accuracy of the ALVINN driving system involved painstaking experiments in which water was dripped from the center of the vehicle and then the position of the water drops were measured relative to the road center. While such quantitative measurements are difficult to perform, they are absolutely necessary if neural network solutions to problems are to be accepted.

The need for rigorous performance characterization is increased by the inherent difficulty in analyzing artificial neural networks. Neural networks are computationally a very powerful technique, in fact they are able to represent arbitrarily complex real-valued mappings from inputs to outputs [4]. But as a result of this power, the internal representations they develop are often quite hard to interpret, and the processing they perform can be quite difficult to understand. A number of techniques are under develop which can provide greater insight into the processing and representations of neural networks, including cluster analysis [12], sensitivity analysis [21], explanation based neural networks [18], and reliability estimation techniques [20]. When perfected and widely employed, these techniques should mitigate many of the concerns over the "black-box" nature of neural networks and allow them to be applied to critical real world tasks like intelligent vehicles.

6. Acknowledgements

The principle support for the Navlab has come from DARPA, under contracts DACA76-85-C-0019, DACA76-85-C-0003 and DACA76-85-C-0002. This research was also funded in part by a grant from Fujitsu Corporation.

References

[1] Aste, M., and Caprile, B. (1992) Learning autonomous navigation abilities using radial basis function networks. In *Proceedings of the 1992 Intelligent Vehicles Symposium*, I. Masaki (ed.), pp 241-246.

[2] Baxt W. (1993) The Application of the artificial neural network to clinical decision making. *Advances in Neural Information Processing Systems 5*, Giles, C.L., Hanson, S.J., and Cowan, J.D. (ed.), Morgan Kaufmann.

[3] Blaauw, G.J. (1982) Driving experience and task demands in simulator and instrumented car: A validation study, *Human Factors, Vol. 24*, pp. 473-486.

[4] Baldi, P. (1991) Computing with arrays of bell-shaped and sigmoid functions. *Advances in Neural Information Processing Systems 3*, R.P. Lippmann, J.E. Moody, and D.S. Touretzky (ed.), Morgan Kaufmann, pp. 735-742.

[5] Blosseville, J., Krafft, C., Lenoir, F., Motyka, V., and Beucher, S. (1989) TITAN: A traffic measuring system using image processing techniques. *Second Int. Conf. on Road Traffic Monitoring*, pp. 84-88.

[6] Bullock, D., Garrett, J. and Hendrickson C. (1991) A prototype neural network for vehicle detection. *Artificial Neural Networks in Engineering*.

[7] Catala, A., Grau, A., Morcego, B., Fuertes, J. (1992) A neural network texture segmentation system for open road vehicle guidance. In *Proceedings of the 1992 Intelligent Vehicles Symposium*, I. Masaki (ed.), pp 247-252.

[8] Crisman, J.D. and Thorpe, C. (1990) Color Vision for Road Following. *Vision and Navigation: The CMU Navlab* C. Thorpe (Ed.), Kluwer Academic Publishers, Boston.

[9] Davis, L., Puskorius, G., Yuan, F., and Feldkamp L. (1992) Neural network modeling and control of an anti-lock brake system. In *Proceedings of the 1992 Intelligent Vehicles Symposium*, I. Masaki (ed.), pp 179-184.

[10] Fahlman, S.E. (1988) Faster-learning variations on back-propagation: an empirical study. *Proceedings of the Connectionist Summer School*, Morgan Kaufmann.

[11] Feldkamp, L., Puskorius G., Davis, L., and Yuan, F. (1991) Decoupled Kalman training of neural and fuzzy controllers for automotive systems. *Proc. of the Fuzzy and Neural Systems and Vehicle Applications Conference*, Tokyo, Japan.

[12] Gorman, R.P. and Sejnowski, T.J. (1988) Analysis of hidden units in a layered network trained to classify sonar targets. *Neural Networks Vol. 1*, pp. 75-89.

[13] Gusciora, G.L., Pomerleau, D.A., Touretzky, D.S., Kung, H.T. (1990) Back-propagation on Warp. *Artificial Neural Networks: Applications and Implementations*, Ben Wah, Manoel F. Tenorio, Pankaj Mehra and Jose A.B. Fortes (Eds.) IEEE Computer Society Press.

[14] Kluge, K. and Thorpe, C. (1990) Explicit models for robot road following. *Vision and Navigation: The CMU Navlab* C. Thorpe (Ed.), Kluwer Academic Publishers, Boston.

[15] Marko, K.A. (1991) Neural network application to diagnostics and control of vehicle control systems. In *Advances in Neural Information Processing Systems 3*, R.P. Lippmann,

J.E. Moody, and D.S. Touretzky (ed.), Morgan Kaufmann, pp. 537-543.

[16] Marra, M., Dunlay, T.R., Mathis, D. (1988) Terrain classification using texture for the ALV. Martin Marietta Information and Communications Systems technical report 1007-10.

[17] Maruno S. (1993) Smart consumer products using neural networks in Japan. Invited talk *Neural Networks for Computing*, Snowbird, Utah.

[18] T.M. Mitchell and S.B. Thrun (1993) Explanation-based neural network learning for robot control. To appear in *Advances in Neural Information Processing Systems 5*, Giles, C.L., Hanson, S.J., and Cowan, J.D. (eds.) Morgan Kaufmann.

[19] Poggio, T., and Girosi, F. (1990) Regularization algorithms for learning that are equivalent to multilayer networks. *Science, Vol. 247* pp. 987-982.

[20] Pomerleau, D.A. (1993) Input Reconstruction Reliability Estimation. *Advances in Neural Information Processing Systems 5*, Giles, C.L., Hanson, S.J., and Cowan, J.D. (eds.) Morgan Kaufmann.

[21] Pomerleau, D.A. and Touretzky, D.S. (1993) Understanding Neural Network Internal Representations through Hidden Unit Sensitivity Analysis. *Proceedings of the International Conference on Intelligent Autonomous Systems*, C.E. Thorpe (ed.), IOS Publishers, Amsterdam.

[22] Pomerleau, D.A. (1992) Neural network perception for mobile robot guidance. PhD. Dissertation. Carnegie Mellon technical report CMU-CS-92-115.

[23] Pomerleau, D.A. (1991) Efficient Training of Artificial Neural Networks for Autonomous Navigation. In *Neural Computation 3:1*.

[24] Pomerleau, D.A. (1989) ALVINN: An Autonomous Land Vehicle In a Neural Network. *Advances in Neural Information Processing Systems 1*, D.S. Touretzky (ed.), Morgan Kaufmann.

[25] Rumelhart, D. E., Hinton, G. E., and Williams, R. J. (1986) Learning internal representations by error propagation. In D. E. Rumelhart & J. L. McClelland (Eds.), *Parallel Distributed Processing: Explorations in the Microstructure of Cognition. Vol. I: Foundations* pp. 318-362, Bradford Books/MIT Press, Cambridge, MA.

[26] Schenkel, M., Weissman, H., Guyon, I., Nohl, C., Henderson, D., Boser, B., and Jackel, L (1993) *Advances in Neural Information Processing Systems 5*, Giles, C.L., Hanson, S.J., and Cowan, J.D. (ed.), Morgan Kaufmann.

[27] Seitzma, J., and Dow, R. (1991) Creating Artificial Neural Networks that Generalize. *Neural Networks, Vol. 4* pp. 67-79, Pergamon Press.

[28] Shimizu, K., and Shigehara, N. (1989) Image processing system using cameras for vehicle surveillance. *Second Int. Conf. on Road Traffic Monitoring*, pp. 61-65.

[29] Waibel, A., Hanazawa, T., Hinton, G., Shikano, K., and Lang K. (1987) Phoneme recognition using time-delay neural networks. ATR Technical Report TR-I-0006.

[30] Willson B., Whitham, J., and Anderson C. (1992) Estimating ignition timing from engine cylinder pressure with neural networks. In *Proceedings of the 1992 Intelligent Vehicles Symposium*, I. Masaki (ed.), pp 108-113.

[31] Witbrock, M. and Zagha, M. (1989) An implementation of back-propagation learning on the GF-11, a large SIMD parallel computer. Carnegie Mellon University tech report CMU-CS-89-208.

[32] Wright, W.A. (1989) Contextual road finding with a neural network. British Aerospace Advanced Information Processing Department technical report.

[33] Zhang, X., Mckenna, M., Misirov, J., and Waltz, D. (1990) An efficient implementation of the back-propagation algorithm on the connection machine CM-2. *Advances in Neural Information Processing Systems 2*, D. Touretzky (ed.), Morgan Kaufmann.

Action planning for the collision avoidance system using neural networks

Manzoor A Arain * Raglan Tribe * Edgar An ** and Chris Harris **

* Control Systems, Lucas Advanced Engineering Centre, Dog Kennel Lane, Shirley Solihull
West Midlands B90 4JJ, UK. Fax (+44) 021 733 3001 email: MAA@LISHIRL1.LI.CO.UK.

** Dept. of Aeronautics and Astronautics, Southampton University SO9 5NH, UK.

Abstract

An understanding of the scenario in complex traffic situations is essential in order to give an early warning, or in an autonomous system, to intervene in the urban or motorway environment. A collision avoidance system needs both to predict possible collisions or hazards and to plan a less hazardous move in a critical situation. A crucial factor in the success of the system is the use of *a priori* knowledge. The classical problem with a knowledge-based decision making system is the acquisition and representation of the knowledge. It is difficult to design and develop a system for real time auto-piloting in varied traffic environments.

Neural networks are ideally suited for applications where a large training set is available because they can apply human decision-making criteria in different situations. The learning processes encapsulate a wide variety of drivers' reactions to various scenarios. Neural networks' ability to generalise their training to new scenarios in the light of driving experience and to make emotion-free decisions leads to a system that is adaptive and closely which resembles human action strategy.

Recognition of a scenario is achieved by acquiring data about a scene from a variety of sensors. Visual data is pre-processed and features are extracted using a real-time image processing system, while microwave radar provides obstacle information and distances. This paper described an early warning system and suggests possible responses to various traffic situations.

The paper focuses on various learning algorithms for decision-making which is based on the current model and immediate history only. It would help if we could always recognise the dominant threat at every instant and avoid it by either slowing down or changing direction. In our analysis of situations using neural networks, the test cases show that reasonably such behaviour can be generated.

In order to validate the auto pilot it is tested in parallel with expert drivers to assess the drivers' action in a number of scenarios. The network's intervention control is verified by independent observers. The intervention strategies are based on a number of rules by which an intervention controller is trained to generate various actions. These rule are fine tuned on-line to achieve reliable and repeatable actions.

Introduction

An ideal auto pilot would be capable of operating over a range of car speeds and road conditions to maintain a required heading and with the ability to perform overtaking manoeuvres. These manoeuvres should be completed rapidly with a minimum of overshoot and a fast convergence to the new lane. While overtaking, the trajectory error should be minimum under all circumstances. In the case of heading without a change of path the vehicle should maintain a desired speed and safety region between itself and the vehicle in front. In order to achieve this understanding of the scenario, an assessment of the situation is essential. In order to identify various scenarios, an automatic collision avoidance system must monitor the environment, its own vehicle and the human driver. Monitoring of the driver is essential to prevent the system from performing any actions which are contradictory to the driver's wishes. This paper discusses methods for learning the driver's response to different scenarios using neural networks. Having adapted to the driver's behaviour, the system can predict to a high level of accuracy the driver's likely response to a particular scenario. For the problem of continuous decision making in a dynamic and constantly changing environment, a good solution will depend both on the local models (i.e. current snapshot of the environment) and the global models. Decision making in a dynamic environment is a complex issue. A good decision depends on three representational models:

A current situation model describing the current values of the parameters involved in decision making

A history model which records the fluctuation of the parameter in the past

A prediction model predicting the expected values based on the pattern exhibited in the past history.

This paper focuses on learning algorithms for decision making based on the current situation model only. It would help if we can always recognise the dominant threat at every instant and stay away from it by either slowing down or changing lane. In our analysis of the situation using neural networks, the test cases show that reasonably good behaviour can be generated.

Neural Networks as a decision making technique

Neural network models represent a new approach that is robust and fault tolerant. It is well known that operators such as association, optimisation, feature extraction, recognition etc. can be performed using artificial neural networks. Consideration of neural networks for identification of scenario and planning a control strategy seems an ideal choice. In such applications they can learn from many situations and thus have the ability to make the decisions needed to survive in dangerous ones. The potential benefits of neural networks include the high computation rates provided by massive parallelism. Neural networks also typically provide a greater degree of robustness or fault tolerance than the conventional Von Neumann type sequential computers because there are many more processing nodes each with primary local connections. Therefore damage to a few nodes or links need not impair overall performance significantly.

A neural network is an array of processors linked by connections that can be strengthened or weakened. The concept takes its inspiration from the interconnected neurons of the brain. A neural network is trained by being given a series of examples of correct responses and then the connections between its processor are strengthened or weakened according to its success in reproducing what is wanted. The neural network is never given an explicit body of rules to follow; its program is contained in the strengths and weakness of the different links in the network.

Since a single hidden layer (a layer of nodes between input layer and output layer) is adequate to approximate any continuous function it follows that the same property is also enjoyed by networks with more than one hidden layer. However, as in the case of optimisation techniques which are polynomials, Fourier series and general orthogonal functions, the network theorems do not provide a recipe for the choice of the number of terms needed to achieve the approximation i.e. the number of layers and number of nodes in each layer in the network. These have to be determined by trial and error in a specific context[6].

Since polynomials, orthogonal functions and splines can also be used, in principle it is not readily apparent why neural network should be preferred. Extensive computer studies carried out during the past few years have revealed that Multilayer Neural Networks, Cerebeller Model Articulated Controllers (CMAC)[9] and Radial Basis Function networks [4] all have some advantages over conventional methods for approximation. For example, polynomial approximations do not have good scaling properties and, in addition, are difficult to implement in hardware because of signal saturation effects of analog circuits[6]. Further more, when the polynomial is too high order and the magnitude of the input variable exceeds unity, the output can be very large resulting in numerical instabilities during the determination of coefficients.

Multi-Layer Networks

Multi layer networks using error backpropagation [1] have several advantages: (i) given enough neurons, they can approximate any well-behaved bounded function to an arbitrarily high degree of accuracy and can even approximate the less well-behaved functions needed in direct inverse control; (ii) VLSI chips exist to implement Multi-Layer Perceptrons (MLPs) and several other neural network designs with a very high computational throughput, equivalent to a super computer on a chip[12].

This second property is crucial to many applications. MLPs are also feed forward networks which means that we can calculate their output by proceeding from neuron to neuron (or from layer to layer) without having to solve systems of non-linear equations.

A multi layer neural network using error backpropagation learning rules is shown in figure 1.

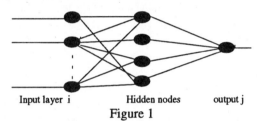

Input layer i   Hidden nodes   output j

Figure 1

In such a network the outputs of the units in layer i are multiplied by appropriate weights w_{ji} which in turn become the inputs to the next layer. The output of a unit in layer j is

$$Y_j = f(x_{j-1})$$

The sigmoid function (a monotonic S-shaped function mapping numbers in the interval $(-\infty, +\infty)$ to a finite interval such as (-1,+1) or (0,1)) is expressed in the form

$$y_i = f(x_j) = \frac{1}{(1 + e^{-(\delta \frac{E_j}{T})})}$$

Where $\delta \frac{E_j}{T} = x_j + h_j$ is an energy gap between the current and the new states, h_j being the internal threshold for unit j sub i and T is the temperature of the system.

The error backpropogation learning algorithm adjusts the weights to obtain a minimised system energy function. This is done by repeatedly propagating backwards the difference between the actual and desired outputs to the hidden layer. There the weight of each unit is adjusted in relation to the derivative of the error function, i.e. the ones used to adjust the weights for the output layer units. The error at any output unit in layer k is

$$e_k = t_k - y_k$$

where t_k is the desired output for that unit and y_k is the actual output. The total error function can be written as

$$E = \frac{1}{2} \sum_k (t_k - y_k)^2$$

The error is minimised by starting with any set of weights and repeatedly changing each weight by an amount proportional to $\frac{\partial E}{\partial W}$

$$\delta w_{kj} = -e \frac{(\partial E)}{(\partial W_{kj})} = \delta_k y_j$$

where the error signal ∂k is given by

$$\delta k = (t_k - y_k) y_k (1 - y_k)$$

at an output unit k and

$$\delta = y_j (1 - y_j) \frac{\Sigma}{K} \partial K W_{kj}$$

at any hidden unit j. The thresholds learn by taking h_j to be equivalent to another weight W_{ji} thereby connecting the unit j to a bias unit which is always active. As the learning parameter ε tends to zero and the number of updates tend to infinity, the learning algorithm is aggravated to find the optimum set of weights that gives the least mean square error of the total error function. In practice, a momentum term is added so that the learning rate ε can be increased without causing oscillations

$$\Delta W_{jk}^{(n+1)} = \varepsilon \delta K y_j + \alpha \Delta W_{kj}^n$$

where the momentum parameter α determines the effect of past weights changes on the current direction of movement in weight space. This provides a kind of momentum in weight space that effectively filters out high frequency variations of the error surface in the weight space. During the learning phase when the new pattern is presented to the network, it does not wipe out the stored pattern but it modifies slightly the connection strengths. This is achieved by adjusting the weight very slightly. Back-propagation training begins by presenting an input patterns vector X to the network sweeping forward through the system to generate an output response vector Y and computing the errors at each output. The next step involves sweeping the effects of the errors backwards through the network to associate a the error derivative in order to compute a gradient from each Delta and finally update the weights of each node based upon the corresponding gradient. Initially there weight values are normally set to small random numbers.

Cerebeller Model Articulated Controller (CMAC)

The standard CMAC network can be constucted using ρ layers of non-overlapping receptive fields, with each layer offset diagonally relative to each other in the bounded input space (R^N). The offsetting scheme can be defined using a relative displacement vector, $\underline{d}$, in which d_i is the relative offset value along the ith axis in terms of the number of discretization intervals in each input axis. Thus, similar

inputs produce similar outputs while dissimilar inputs produce indenpendent outputs. It is important to notice that the linkage between the number of layers and the field width is a unique feature in the CMAC structure. ρ is a critical network parameter which affects the generalization ability and the regularity of the field placement. For a larger ρ, the network generalization is stronger at at the expense of sparse and less uniform placement, and vice versa. New offsetting schemes with different $\underline{d}$ has been proposed which improve the regularity of the lattice placement[7],[10]. Figure 2 shows an example of a two-input CMAC network with ρ chosen to be 3.

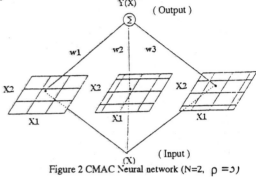

Figure 2 CMAC Neural network (N=2, ρ =3)

The univariate field shape is traditionally rectangular although higher order piecewise polynomials can also be used to generate a smoother network output[8]. A multi-dimensional receptive field ($\underline{f}$) is formed using the minimum operator. For example, $\underline{f}$ is a pyramid for a 2D input.

Learning Rule

Based on the fact that receptive fields in each layer do not overlap, any input can excite only one receptive field in each layer at any time. Thus, exactly ρ active receptive fields will be used in any training instances. The only adaptable parameters in the network are the receptive field weights or heights ($\underline{w}$). The network output is an inner product of $\underline{f}$ and $\underline{w}(\sum_{i=1}^{\rho} w_i f_i(x))$. As the output is linear with w, the error surface is well-defined in that there is only one global minimum. Well known optimization techniques, such as conjugate-gradient, gradient-descent, and Newton method can be be used to adjust $\underline{w}$.

In order to achieve real-time learning, the instantaneous cost function (c), can be used, and is defined as $\frac{1}{2}(y_d - y)^2$, where y_d is the desired output and y is the network output. Least mean square (LMS) or normaliized LMS method

$$\delta w_i = -\frac{\beta \frac{\partial c}{\partial w_i}}{\sum_{i=1}^{\rho} f_i(x)^2} = \frac{\beta((y_d - y) f_i(x)}{\sum_{i=1}^{\rho} f_i(x)^2}$$

can be used to adjust the active w. For completeness, the convergence properties of the CMAC network for different training schemes has been established [11]. Detail treatment on the CMAC network is referred to [9],[11].

Scenario and environment understanding

Any autonomous vehicle requires a control module to provide it with a collision free path through an environment consisting of fixed or stationary obstacles. Safety envelopes are established to handle uncertainties in the motion of the obstacles. The ideas adapted here is to establish a safety envelope around each moving obstacle and then treat these envelopes as stationary obstacles. Certain envelopes represent forbidden regions which are defined on the basis of a high likelihood of collision. The vehicle is equipped with a radar and a camera which scans the space ahead to provide samples of moving obstacle positions in the safety envelope. The different columns in the safety envelope represent the intended direction of movement, and rows indicate distance with respect to the vehicle. The calculation and action criteria will be based on the likelihood of the obstacle behaving in a predicted manner. The actions of collision avoidance systems depend on three factors: 1) The obstacle is losing velocity, 2) The obstacle has started a possible collision motion, 3) The obstacle will behave in an unpredicted manner.

Let $(x_j(t_i), y_j(t_i))$ be the sensed position of an object O_j at time T_i. The driving space is represented by a grid of square elements of size alpha. Suppose O_j renews its position every delta seconds. Based on O_j's behaviour in the time interval $\{t_i + 1 - t_i\}$, a collision zone is defined. The distance moved by is O_j in the time interval $\{t_i + 1 - t_i\}$ is modelled as a random vector $R_n = (X_n, Y_n)$ which can be written as a sum of n random vectors k=1,2....n; . The random vector is represented in a two dimensional matrix. The distance being represented by rows in terms of three classes: a) over braking distance, b) below braking distance and c) possible colliding distance. The behaviour of the obstacle in the safety envelope is monitored. The response to the obstacle changing its behaviour takes place on successive parameter changes. The duration of delay is approximately 100 millisecs. In order to avoid unnecessary control actions the system first establishes the development of a scenario leading to required safety manoeuvres. It also allows sufficient time for frontal vehicle sensors to establish reliability that behaviour's due to a change by the target vehicle. In the case of a false reading no action is taken.

The system developed has short-range path planning (navigation) which is responsible for selecting the actual path to be traversed through the surrounding safety envelope in front of the vehicle. It should be a track of safe passage, avoiding obstacles as they are detected by both the visual resources of the system and the microwave radar. Short navigation involves updating the position with respect to the safety envelope and modifying the contents of this safety envelope either by the vision sensor or microwave radar. Thus it resembles a kind of short term planning the trajectory.

To achieve a short range travel capability, the safety envelope must be provided with (or have extracted) the column of free space through which a detailed path is planned. This safety envelope and the obstacles detected within it, are represented within a safety envelope band surrounding the envelope. This band surrounding the safety envelope implies an encoding of positional information and should also allow for other attributes to be associated with objects such as their names, velocities and time to contact . The visual resources were used for obstacle detection and localisation and the microwave radar for accurate range information and relative velocity of the obstacles.

The vision system as a whole is responsible for perceiving objects of interest (e.g. roads, vehicles in front, lane markings and number of lanes) and the microwave radar provides range and number-of-objects in front. The image processing module is responsible for extracting symbolic representation of the environment from individual images. A data fusion system combines the symbolic representation of the image with the microwave radar range and number-of-obstacles information and is responsible for establishing the overall obstacle information and updating the safety envelope table.

Experiments on simulation

A number of experiments were performed using simulated data where the network was trained on various scenarios. The scenarios deal with a situation where a two lane road is simulated and traffic is approaching from opposite directions. The network was trained for assessment of the situation where the vehicle in front slows down significantly or becomes stationary. The network was then trained to make a decision to reduce speed, brake or overtake in order to keep a safe heading. A number of scenarios created a network which was trained to make decisions. If the decision is to overtake the obstacle causing the threat, the system works out a safe trajectory for overtaking and provides the time and acceleration required the length of trajectory and a cost factor representing the level of risk associated with such a move. If the cost factor is too high for such a move than the decision is not executed and a second move is chosen e.g. to slowdown or brake.

During the experiments multi layer networks were used. It was found that the generalisation ability of network was good in that it recognised more than 95% of the scenario which presented. It is important to consider more complex situations for path searching and environment. In order to speed up the decision making process it is important that the scenario identification , simulation evaluation and path searching be carried out in parallel. This will improve the confidence level of decisions and update the path information available .

Control of throttle

In order to travel safely in a traffic column while maintaining a safety gap between the vehicle and any obstacle in front, a network must be trained for throttle control on a driver modeling.   The words "driver modeling" for throttle control are being used here initially to mean for decision making activities including whether to accelerate or decelerate in order to maintain the safety gap. The decision of making changes to the current state of throttle is based on an assessment of the current model (current situation of environment). The neural network is trained on the data which consists of the current value and two previous values of range, relative velocity and vehicle speed. Data was logged on a test track, with maximum vehicle speed of 75 kph and a vehicle in front up to 50 meters away. The selection of a 50 meters maximum range limit is based on the provision that a vehicle beyond such range does not cause any threat.   The network was then trained on a number of examples extracted from the different situations. The network learned to behave as a throttle controller. The results are shown using different neural networks in figures 3,4,5 for error backpropagation with fast learning techniques [2,3] and in figures 6,7,8 for the CMAC. It was found that the networks followed the driver very closely where changes on throttle control were based on variations in the range and relative velocity of the obstacle.   In a number of examples when the network identifies a threat, it showed response to the control of throttle.

The network behaviour was found to be very interesting when the range starts to falls. The network responded positively to the changes by reducing the throttle. As the range started to increase, the network increased it output (throttle control) to reach the desired speed. The behaviour of the network tested on recorded data with different driving profile and similar behaviour was observed The result is shown in figure 3.

The model described above is an illustration of a technique for decision making in a dynamic environment. The important aspect is that decisions are very similar to human ones because the network was trained on human reactions.

The techniques does show great potential for the application of decision making to an auto pilot. It is also a powerful pattern recognition tool for identification of scenarios as particular patterns start to build which cause a threat in the heading.

Conclusion

Experiments on the simulation data produced interesting results; in particular the network generalisation ability was good. The network recognised more then 95% of scenarios presented. An improvement on the 5% error could be achieved by using different network structures and especially by considering associative memory networks or increasing in number of input parameters. So far, the result

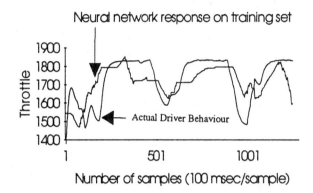

Figure 3

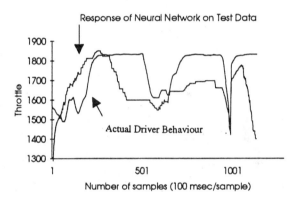

Figure 4

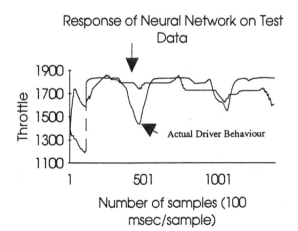

Figure 5

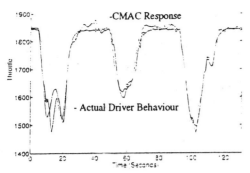

Figure 6 CMAC response on training set

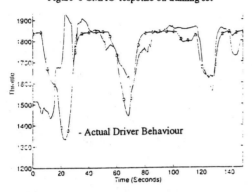

Figure 7 CMAC response on test data

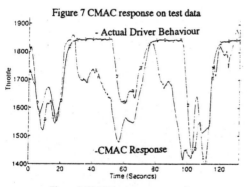

Figure 8 CMAC response on test data

on path planning look encouraging but more complex scenarios also need to be investigated.

For the driver modelling we used two different types of network to compare the generalisation ability and performance. CMAC is very quick to train compared with MLP which even with using fast learning rule [2,3] training, was slow. The significant advantage MLP has shown during the experiments over CMAC is that it is less sensitive to range peaks and noise in the data.

The experiments on the driver model aimed to identify the scenarios which lead to the situation where action is required. The network was used as a recognition device to identify the situation and then to produce an output indicating what the throttle position should become. In the case of range reducing quickly, the network responded quickly to the threat. Also during the modelling we found the network responded well to the change in driving style.

Further work is required on modelling of brakes, steering and on the scenario assessments and identification of more complex situations. The final system will be implemented by number of networks running in parallel and a supervisor network monitoring the action strategy. In order to make the system robust enough for a fully autonomous systems there will be a rule-based system running in parallel validating the networks' decisions.

References

[1] Rumelhart D.E., McClelland J.L., 1986. Parallel Distributed Processing Vol. 1, MIT Press.

[2] Samd T., 1988 Backpropogation is Significantly faster if the Expected Value of the Source Unit is used for update. International Neural Network Society Conference Abstract.

[3] Samad T., Back Propogation Extension, Honeywell SSDC Techanical report, 1000 Boone Ave.N. Golden Valley MN 55427

[4] Billings S., Chen S., 1992 Neural Networks and System Identification in Neural Networks for Control and Systems Edited by Warrick K., Irwin W. and Hunt K.J. IEE UK.

[5] Arain M.A. Tribe R., 1990. Application of Neural Networks For Traffic Scenario Identification. 4th Prometheus Workshop, University of Compiegne, Paris, France.

[6] Narendra K.S., 1992. Adaptive Control of Dynamical Systems Using Neural Networks, Handbook of Intelligent Control Edited by White D.A., Sofge D.A., Van Nostrand Reihold NY

[7] An P.E., Miller W.T., Parks P.C. 1991. Design Improvements in Association Memories for Cerebeller Model Articulation Controllers (CMAC), Proc. Intl.Conf. on Artificial Neural Networks, Helsinki, North Holland Vol.2 pp. 1207-1210.

[8] Lane S.H., Handelman D.A., Gelfand J.J., 1992. Theory and Development of Higher-order CMAC Neural Networks, IEEE Control Systems, April, pp.1561-1567.

[9] Miller W.T., Glanz F.H., Kraft L.G. 1990. CMAC: An Associative Neural Network Alternative to Backpropagation, Proc. IEEE, Vol.78, pp.1561-1567.

[10] Parks P.C., Militzer J. 1991. Improved Allocation of Weights for Associative Memory Storage in Learning Control Systems, Proc.1 IFAC Symp. on Design Methods of Control Systems, Zurich, Peragamon Press, Vol.2 pp 777-782.

[11] Parks P.C., Militzer J., 1992. A Comparison of five Algorithms for the Training of CMAC Memories for Learning Control Systems, Automatica, Vol. 28, No.5, pp.1027-1035.

[12] Mead C., 1989. Analog VLSI and Neural Systems, Addison Wesley, Reading, MA.

FUZZY LOGIC AND NEUROFUZZY TECHNOLOGIES IN EMBEDDED AUTOMOTIVE APPLICATIONS

Constantin von Altrock and Bernhard Krause

Inform Software Corporation, 1840 Oak Avenue, Evanston, IL 60201, Fax (708) 886-1839

INFORM GmbH, Pascalstrasse 23, D-52076 Aachen, Fax +49-2408-6090

ABSTRACT: Most advanced control algorithms in automotive engineering can benefit from fuzzy logic and neurofuzzy techniques. Either by speeding up the development cycle or by rendering functionalities not achieved by other advanced control techniques, fuzzy logic complements conventional control by incorporating engineering "know-how" in the design process. Typical embedded applications are in the area of ABS, ASR, 4WD/4WS, suspension and powertran control. This paper focusses on the implementational and design issues special to automotive applications. The integration of high-speed fuzzy logic software implementations into existing hardware platforms and the optimization and verification strategies for fuzzy logic systems are discussed with a case study of an anti-skid steering system implemented in a model car at the University of Aachen.

1. INTRODUCTION

Fuzzy Logic Control -- invented 20 years ago [3] -- proved to be an efficient way to implement engineering heuristics into a control solution [1]. Especially japanese automotive companies already make extensive use of fuzzy logic control to implement complex control strategies for various components, such as anti-locking-braking (ABS), traction control (ASR), engine control and others [4, 5, 6, 7, 8, 12]. Rather than showing these applications in detail, we will present the technologies needed to design, optimize and verify fuzzy logic systems in complex control applications. As an illustration for such a complex control system, we will use anti-skid-steering control, implemented in a model car at the University of Aachen, in cooperation with Inform GmbH and a German automotive manufacturer. In this paper, we assume that the reader is familiar with the basic concepts of fuzzy logic. If not, please refer to standard literature [1, 13].

2. ADVANCED FUZZY LOGIC CONTROL FOR ANTI-SKID STEERING CONTROL

To implement active stability control systems in cars has a long history. As a first step, anti-locking brakes were used to improve the braking performance by reducing the amount of brake force set by the driver to the maximum amount which can be taken by the road. This avoids sliding and results in shorter braking distances. The second step in active stability control systems was to introduce traction control systems which do essentially the same, just not for braking but for the acceleration. By reducing the engine power applied to the wheels to the amount which can be taken by the road, acceleration of the car is maximized and tyre wear is minimized. The next logical step, after skid-controlled braking and skid-controlled accelerating, is skid-controlled steering. Such an anti-skid steering system (ASS) has to reduce the steering angle to the amount the road can take, thereby it optimizes the steering action and avoids sliding. A sliding car is very hard to restabilize, especially for drivers which are not used to it.

Figure 1: Model car for high-speed driving experiments

Though an anti-skid steering systemmakes a lot of sense from a technical point of view, such a system will be hard to market. In contrast to ABS systems, where it can be proven, that it never performs worse than a traditional brake system, that would be very hard to prove for an ASS system. Also, it may be hard to sell customers a car, which in emergency situations "takes over the steering". Even ABS faced a long period of rejection by customers, because they felt uneasy about a system inhibiting their brake action.

For this reasons, it may take a long time before an ASS system will be implemented in a production car. Our reason to choose this example in this paper is that we can show how such a very complex control problem benefits from implementation of engineering expertise using fuzzy logic technologies.

3. THE TEST VEHICLE

Real experiments were made on a standard-size sedan and on a 20" model car (fig. 1). In this paper, we will only present the results with the model car. To perform skidding and sliding experiments in extreme situations at high speeds, the car is powered by a one-horsepower electric motor, rendering the power-to-weight-ratio of a race car. On dry surface, it reaches a velocity of 20 mph in just 3.5 seconds, with top speed up to 50 mph. Most experiments are carried out between 20 and 30 mph. Each wheel is suspended individually, having separate shock absorbers, and the car is equipped with disk brakes and a lockable differential [2].

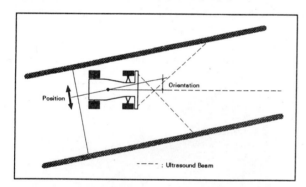

Figure 2: To guide the car in the test track, three ultrasonic sensors are used

For the control of the car, the motherboard of a notebook PC is conneted to an inferface board which drives the actors (power steering, brake servo and pulswidth power control), and the sensors (ultrasonic distance sensors for track guidance and infrared reflex sensors in every wheel for speed). To investigate NeuroFuzzy adaption technologies for tuning the fuzzy logic controller in real time, we implemented a four node transputer net on the car (seen as spoiler in fig. 1). This high-performance parallel computer was neccessary, since all learning technologies -- such as NeuroFuzzy -- are computationally intensive when used in real-time [10]. The 200 rules fuzzy logic controller requires 6 ms computing time on the notebook's 286 CPU (12 MHz), and the control loop time is set to 10 ms [2].

To measure the dynamic state of the car, such as skidding and sliding, the invividual speed of all four wheels is measured by infrared sensors. By evaluating the wheel speed differences, the fuzzy logic system interprets the current situation. Since the car has been designed for autonomous operation, three fixed mounted ultrasonic sensors measure the distance to the next obstacle to the front, the left and the right. Intentionally, low-cost sensors have been used in this study rather than CCD cameras and picture recognition techniques, because we wanted to show, that in some cases, expensive sensors can be replaced by putting more intelligence into the control strategy.

Fig. 2 shows the example of a practical experiment involving the model car. We place an obstacle (block) right after the curve, so that the ultrasonic sensors of the car will "see" the obstacle very late. To not hit the obstacle, the car has to decide for a very rapid turn. To optimize the steering effect, the anti-skid controller has to reduce the desired steering angle to the maximum the road can take, avoiding sliding and hitting the obstacle.

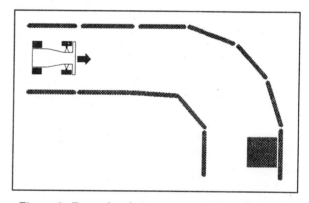

Figure 3: Example of an experiment. The ultrasonic sensors of the car will detect the obstacle placed right after the curve very late, making a quick turn necessary.

4. MODEL BASED SOLUTION VS. FUZZY LOGIC CONTROL

In theory, it is possible to build a mechanical model for the car and to derive a mathematical model based on differential equations to implement a model based controller. In reality, the complexity of this approach would be overwhelming and the resulting controller would be very hard to tune. Here is the point for fuzzy logic: race car drivers can perform this control taks very well without solving differential equations. This proves that there must be an alternative way for anti-skid steering control.

Though there are multiple ways of expressing engineering heuristics, fuzzy logic has proven to be very effective, due to the following reasons:

- Engineering heuristics and expertise very often can be formulated in "if-then" causalities. The "if" part usually represents a certain state of a process while the "then" part represents the action to be taken in this case.
- In contrast to other methods of expressing "if-then" causalities, such as expert systems, the computation in a fuzzy logic system is quantitative rather than symbolic. Hence, a few rules can express complex situations, while a conventional expert systems requires to have a rule for every possible situation.
- Fuzzy logic allows to design a systems in which every element is self-explanatory. Linguistic variables come very close to the human representation of continous concepts, and fuzzy inference and fuzzy operators combine these concepts very much the way humans do.
- Fuzzy logic is non-linear and multi-parametral by nature. So it can better cope with complex control problems which are also non-linear and involve multiple parameters.
- Fuzzy logic can be efficiently implemented in embedded control applications. Even on a standard microcontroller, a fuzzy logic system can outperform a comparable conventional solution both by code size and computing speed.

5. DESIGN AND IMPLEMENTATION OF A FUZZY LOGIC CONTROLLER

Fig. 3 shows the first prototype of a fuzzy logic controller for the car. The first objective, we tried to implement, was the autonomous guidance of the car in the track at slow speed, where no skidding and sliding occures. In fig. 3, the lower rule block uses the distances measured by the three ultrasonic sensors to determine the steering angle. The upper rule block implements a simple speed control by using the distance to the next obstacle measured by the front ultrasonic sensor and the speed of one front wheel only. Due to the slow speed we assume that no skidding or sliding occurs, hence, we consider all wheel speeds the same. The fuzzy logic system contained about 200 rules and has been implemented in a very short period.

After the succesful implementation of the heuristics that guide the autonomous ride, we implemented a more complex fuzzy logic system for dynamic stability control, including anti-locking brakes, traction and anti-skid steering control (fig. 5). It was neccessary to implement two stages of the fuzzy inference. The first stage, represented by the three left rule blocks, estimates the state variables of the dynamic situation of the car out of the sensor data. The two lower rule blocks estimate skidding and sliding states out of speed sensor signals, while the upper rule block estimates position and orientation of the car in the test track. Note, that the output of the left three rule blocks is linguistic rather than numerical. An estimated state of the car therefore could be: "the position is rather left, while the orientation is strongly to the right, and the car skids over the left front wheel".

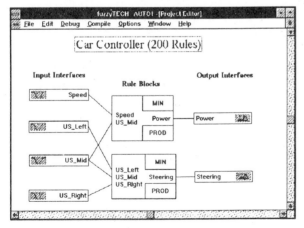

Figure 4: First prototype with 200 rules in two rule blocks. The four left boxes indicate input interfaces for sensors, the two right boxes indicate output interfaces for the actors and the two large boxes in the middle represent fuzzy logic rule blocks

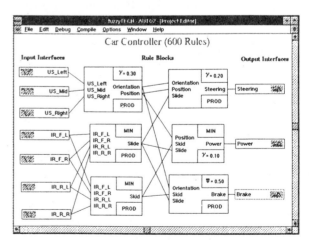

Figure 5: Optimized fuzzy fogic controller using Advanced Fuzzy Technologies

The second stage, represented by the three right rule blocks, uses these estimations as inputs to determine the best control action for this situation. The upper rule block determines the steering angle, the middle one the engine power to be applied, and the lower one controls the brake. Such a two-stage control strategy represents well the human behaviour to first analyze the situation and then determine the action. Also, this allows for efficient optimization, since the total of 600 rules is structured in 6 rule blocks, which can be designed and optimzed indepently.

In contrast to the first controller implemented, which was just able to guide the car (fig. 3), the second controller, able to dynamically stabilize the car's cruise, required a long optimization and test period before it performed well in all situations. Also, the standard fuzzy inference methods proved to be inefficient, and we employed advanced fuzzy inference methods such as the Gamma aggregational operator and the FAM inference [2].

6. EXPEDITET DESIGN WITH "ONLINE" DEVELOPMENT

For the definition of the fuzzy logic system, a standard software tool was used. After the graphical definition of the system structure (fig. 3, 5), the linguistic variables and the rule bases, the compiler of the software tool generates the system as C code. This code was compiled and implemented on the microprocessor of the car. To optimize the system "on-the-fly", the Online module of the software tool was used [11]. Fig. 6 shows the structure of the optimization test bed. Conventional C code was used to programm the sensor data preprocessing and the postprocessing of the outputs of the fuzzy logic controller for driving the actors. The fuzzy logic code is separated into two segments. One contains all "static" code, i.e. code that does not need to be modified for system optimizations. The other one contains all "dynamic" code, i.e. the code containing the membership functions of the linguistic variables, the inference structure, and the rules. The "dynamic" segment is doubled, with only one of the segments active at the same time. With this, the parser, linked to the development PC via a communications manager, can modify the inactive code segment, so modifications can be made on the running system without halting or compiling. At the same time, the entire inference flow inside the fuzzy logic controller is graphically visualized on the PC, since the communications manager also transfers all real-time data.

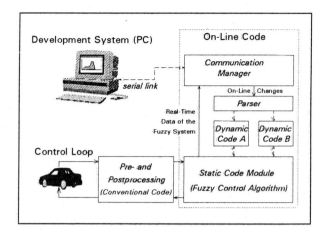

Figure 6: To visualize and optimize a running system "on-the-fly", the fuzzyTECH Online module has been employed. By doubling the code segments containing membership functions and rules on the target system, real-time optimization is made possible

7. IMPLEMENTATION ON STANDARD MICROCONTROLLER

In the past, the implementation of fuzzy logic control techniques either required a powerful microcontroller -- due to the computational inefficiency of the early software implementation -- or the use of a dedicated hardware, such as a fuzzy logic coprocessor. Since the resulting cost increase imposes restrictions on the use of fuzzy logic in cost sensitive applications, a cooperation between the U.S. semiconductor manufacturer Intel and the German fuzzy design software house Inform was set up to optimize the fuzzy logic algorithms.

Microcontroller	Test Systems		
	7 rules 2 in / 1 out	20 FAM rules 2 in / 1 out	80 FAM rules 3 in / 1 out
80C196KD / 20Mhz: code by fuzzyTECH MCU-96 Edition	0.19 ms 0.73 KB ROM 54 Byte RAM	0.29 ms 0,87 KB ROM 63 Byte RAM	0.43 ms 1.2 KB ROM 69 Byte RAM
8051 / 12 MHz: code by fuzzyTECH MCU-51 Edition,	1ms 0.45 KB ROM 21 Byte RAM	1.5 ms 0,58 KB ROM 25 Byte RAM	4.4 ms 1 KB ROM 29 Byte RAM

Figure 7: Device performance comparison for two standard microcontrollers. The 8051 is an example for a medium-performance 8 bit microcontroller, the 80C196 an example for a high-performance 16 bit microcontroller. Both devices are common in automotive applications

Fig. 7 shows a comparison between two different microcontroller families running different fuzzy logic controller. The computing time of less than half a millisecond for a medium-sized (80 rules) fuzzy system as found in ABS systems is fast enough for most practical applications. With a code size of 1.2 KB ROM for such a system, this fuzzy controller can be integrated with other controller code in on-chip ROM [11].

8. CONCLUSION

On the example of a anti-skid steering system, we have shown the applicability of fuzzy logic technologies for a complex control problem found in automotive industry. The design of the fuzzy logic system has been done straighforward without a mathematical model of the process. Existing engineering heuristics were implemented in fuzzy logic rules and linguistic variables. During optimization, we found the control strategy easy to optimize due to the linguistic representation in the fuzzy logic system. Tests and verification were expedited due to the transparency of the controller. The poor computational performance of early fuzzy logic software solutions has been overcome with the new generation of software implementation tools.

9. LITERATURE

[1]   von Altrock, C., "Fuzzy Logic: Band 1 - Die Technologie", Oldenbourg, München (1993).

[2]   von Altrock, C., Krause, B. und Zimmermann, H.-J. "Advanced fuzzy logic control of a model car in extreme situations", Fuzzy Sets and Systems, Vol 48, Nr 1 (1992), p. 41 - 52.

[3]   Assilian, P. und Mamdani, E. H., "An experiment in linguistic synthesis with a fuzzy logic controller", International Journal of Man-Machine Studies 7 (1975), p. 1 - 13.

[4]   Feldkamp, L. und Puskorius, G., "Trainable fuzzy and neural-fuzzy systems for idle-speed control", Second IEEE International Conference on Fuzzy Systems, ISBN 0-7803-0615-5, p. 45 - 51.

[5]   Ikeda, H. et. al., "An intelligent automatic transmission control using a one-chip fuzzy inference engine", Proceedings of the International Fuzzy Systems and Intelligent Control Conference in Louisville (1992), p. 44 - 50.

[6]   Kawai, H. et al., "Engine control system", Proc. of the Int'l Conf. on Fuzzy Logic &

Neural Networks, IIZUKA, Japan (1990), p. 929 - 937.

[7]   Matsumoto, N. et. at., "Expert antiskid system", IEEE IECON'87 (1987), p. 810 - 816.

[8]   Murayama, Y. et. al., "Optimizing control of a diesel engine", in Sugeno (Hsg.) "Industrial Applications of Fuzzy Control" (1985), p. 63 - 72, Amsterdam, Ney York.

[9]   N.N., "fuzzyTECH 3.0 MCU Edition Manual", INFORM GmbH Aachen (1992).

[10]   N.N., "fuzzyTECH 3.0 NeuroFuzzy-Module Manual", INFORM GmbH Aachen (1993).

[11]   N.N., "fuzzyTECH 3.0 Online Edition Manual", INFORM GmbH Aachen (1993).

[12]   Sakaguchi, P. et. al., "Application of fuzzy logic to shift scheduling method for automatic transmission", Second IEEE International Conference on Fuzzy Systems, ISBN 0-7803-0615-5, p. 52 - 58.

[13]   Zimmermann, H.-J., "Fuzzy Set Theory -- and its applications", Zweite Revidierte Auflage (1991), Boston, Dordrecht, London, ISBN 0-7923-9075-X.

Parameter Estimation of Shock Absorbers with Artificial Neural Networks

S. Leonhardt[*], J. Bußhardt[*],
R. Rajamani[**], K. Hedrick[**],
and R. Isermann[*]

[*] Technical University of Darmstadt
Institute of Control Engineering
Landgraf-Georg-Str. 4
6100 Darmstadt, FRG
e-mail : LEO@IRT1.RT.E-TECHNIK.TH-DARMSTADT.DE

[**] University of California at Berkeley
Department of Mechanical Engineering
6185 Etcheverry Hall
Berkeley, CA 94720, USA

Abstract

A method for identification of adjustable shock absorbers is presented which combines a modern QR-RLS parameter estimation algorithm (DSFI) with an artificial neural network (ANN) for classification purposes. The parameter estimation algorithm is based on a discrete-time linear model. Thus, no state variable filter (SVF) as for continuous time identification problems is required. For the ANN, a multilayer feedforward perceptron trained by backpropagation is used.

The method was tested by simulation and with data drawn from shock absorber test stands at UC Berkeley and TU Darmstadt.

1. Introduction

Shock absorbers are one of the most important parts of a vehicle suspension system. Besides the spring, the tire and other components, the shock absorber influences the performance of a vehicle in a large range and is mainly responsible for driving safety and comfort.

Today, some of the modern shock absorbers are capable of somehow adjusting their damping coefficients. There are three basic concepts : passive, semi-active and active dampers. The first two concepts deal with those dampers which do not put energy into the system and adjust their dynamics passively, often by changing the valve diameter of a hydraulic bypass. Semi-active dampers are faster, though, their adjusting frequency is in the range of the vertical eigendynamics resulting in modified overall dynamics. For reference see [1] or [2]. Active dampers are different in the way that they use external energy supply, see e.g. [3]. Within the scope of this paper, only passive and semi-active dampers are concerned.

To design proper control rules for adjustable dampers, a good knowledge of the actual physical parameters is desirable. On-line identification schemes to estimate unknown or non-measurable vehicle coefficients (damping coefficient, masses, stiffnesses) by measuring vertical movements (e.g. suspension deflection, wheel or body acceleration) have recently been developed, see e.g. [1]. The method presented in this work combines such an estimation scheme with an artificial neural network (ANN) which allows to further interpret the estimation results, see Fig. 1.

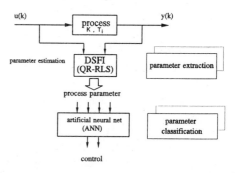

Fig. 1 : general estimation scheme

The presented scheme requires a linear mathematical model of the vertical vehicles dynamics in z- and s-domain. For the extraction of characteristics (z-domain model parameters), a recursive QR-RLS algorithm (DSFI) is used. Afterwards, the estimated parameters are classifed by a perceptron featuring backpropagation training.

The concept has been tested by simulation and by measurements taken on the half car test rig of UC Berkeley and the quarter car test stand of TU Darmstadt and may be applied on-board for real-time control of suspension and vehicle components.

2. Physical Models

For rigorous testing of new control and estimation schemes, a test stand allowing to simulate realistic vehicle conditions is required. In the following, the test rigs of UC at Berkeley and of TU Darmstadt will shortly be presented.

At the Institute of Control Engineering of the Technical University of Darmstadt, a quarter car test rig has been designed. Fig. 2 gives a block diagram.

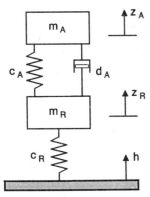

Fig. 2 : scheme of quarter car

From first principles, the following equations are obtained

$$m_A \ddot{z}_A = c_A (z_R - z_A) + d_A (\dot{z}_R - \dot{z}_A) \qquad (1)$$

$$m_R \ddot{z}_R = - c_A (z_R - z_A) - d_A (\dot{z}_R - \dot{z}_A) \\ + c_R (h - z_R) \qquad (2)$$

Note that c_R stands for tire stiffness and that c_A counts for the shock absorber spring. d_A denotes the damping coefficient, m_R and m_A stand for wheel and body mass, respectively. Eq. (3) and (4) give the transfer functions for the vehicle body

$$G_A(s) = \frac{(z_R - z_A)}{\ddot{z}_A} = \frac{\dfrac{m_A}{c_A}}{1 + \dfrac{d_A}{c_A} s} \qquad (3)$$

and for wheel and body

$$G_R(s) = \frac{z_R - z_A}{h - z_R} = \frac{\dfrac{m_A c_R}{c_A (m_R + m_A)}}{1 + \dfrac{d_A}{c_A} s + \dfrac{m_A m_R}{c_A (m_A + m_R)} s^2} \qquad (4)$$

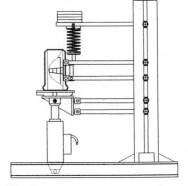

Fig. 3 : quarter car test stand

In Fig. 3, the physical construction of the test stand is shown. The input (road displacement h) is generated by a hydraulic actuator.

The half-car test rig at UC Berkeley is a full-scale model incorporating both pitch and heave dynamics for the sprung mass. Fig. 4 gives the block diagram.

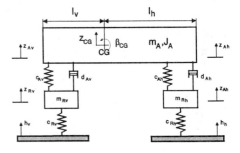

Fig. 4 : scheme of half car

For the dynamic behaviour, model equations can again be derived from first principles, see [4]. Let m_A, m_{Rv} and m_{Rh} be physical parameters (body mass and wheel masses, respectively). Let further be J_A the moment of inertia relative to the body center of gravity. Three masses and an additional rotational degree of freedom would lead to four equations. However, only two shall be given here

$$m_A \ddot{z}_{CG} = c_{Av} (z_{Rv} - z_{Av}) + d_{Av} (\dot{z}_{Rv} - \dot{z}_{Av}) \\ + c_{Ah} (z_{Rh} - z_{Ah}) + d_{Ah} (\dot{z}_{Rh} - \dot{z}_{Ah}) \qquad (5)$$

$$J_A \ddot{\beta}_{Rh} = l_h c_{Ah} (z_{Rh} - z_{Ah}) + l_h d_{Ah} (\dot{z}_{Rh} - \dot{z}_{Ah}) \\ - l_v c_{Av} (z_{Rv} - z_{Av}) - l_v d_{Av} (\dot{z}_{Rv} - \dot{z}_{Av}) \qquad (6)$$

For small angles β_{CG}, the following geometric relationships are valid

$$z_{Av} = z_{CG} - l_v \beta_{CG} , \quad z_{Ah} = z_{CG} + l_h \beta_{CG} \qquad (7)$$

Taking derivates of eq. (7) and plugging in eq. (5) and

(6), the following two equations are obtained

$$\ddot{z}_{Av} = a_{0vv}(z_{Rv} - z_{Av}) + a_{1vv}(\dot{z}_{Rv} - \dot{z}_{Av}) + a_{0hv}(z_{Rh} - z_{Ah}) + a_{1hv}(\dot{z}_{Rh} - \dot{z}_{Ah}) \quad (8)$$

$$\ddot{z}_{Ah} = a_{0vh}(z_{Rv} - z_{Av}) + a_{1vh}(\dot{z}_{Rv} - \dot{z}_{Av}) + a_{0hh}(z_{Rh} - z_{Ah}) + a_{1hh}(\dot{z}_{Rh} - \dot{z}_{Ah}) \quad (9)$$

where the a_{ijk} are functions of the physical parameters.

3. QR-RLS Parameter Estimation

For extracting characteristics from a dynamical system, recursive parameter estimation algorithms have often been applied during the last decades. For example, within adaptive controllers RLS estimators are often used, see e.g. [5].

Let b_i, a_i represent a discrete time model where input and output signals are given by $u(k)$ and $y(k)$, respectively. A dc offset shall be named y_∞. Let the process order be n with m the order of the numerator ($m \leq n$). Let d denote a possible discrete time delay. This leads to the following model

$$y(k) = \psi^T(k)\ \theta \quad (10)$$

with the data vector

$$\psi^T(k) = [-y(k-1),...,-y(k-m), \\ u(k-d-1),...,u(k-d-m),1] \quad (11)$$

and the parameter vector

$$\theta = [a_1,...,a_m,b_1,...,b_m,y_\infty]^T \quad (12)$$

After N+1 samples one can construct a $(N+1)$-dimensional output vector $Y(k)$ and a rectangular data matrix Ψ with dimension $(N+1, m+n+1)$. The error vector $\varepsilon(k)$ and the loss function $V(k)$ are given by

$$\varepsilon(k) = Y(k) - \Psi(k)\ \theta_{est}(k-1) \quad (13)$$

$$V(k) = \varepsilon^T(k)\ \varepsilon(k) = \|I\ \varepsilon\|^2 \quad (14)$$

Minimizing eq. (14) solves the Least Squares (LS) estimation problem and leads to the "normal equation"

$$\theta_{est} = [\ \Psi^T\ \Psi\ ]^{-1}\ \Psi^T\ Y \quad (15)$$

When using the LS algorithm recursively, the inversion of the squared data matrix may be avoided by applying the matrix inversion lemma. The resulting algorithm is the well established Recursive Least Square algorithm (RLS), see e.g. [5]. However, squaring the data matrix may cause numerical instability. In such cases, so called QR-RLS algorithms are a good alternative. In this study, a specific algorithm referred to as DSFI (Discrete Square Root Filter in the Information Form) was used which directly factorizes Y into Ω R (with R an upper triangular and Ω an orthogonal matrix).

$$Y = \Psi\ \theta \quad \begin{matrix} \Omega \\ \Rightarrow \end{matrix} \quad \begin{bmatrix} R \\ \underline{0} \end{bmatrix} \theta = \Omega\ Y = \begin{bmatrix} c \\ d \end{bmatrix} \quad (16)$$

$$\Leftrightarrow \quad \theta = R^{-1}\ c \quad (17)$$

This algorithm actually avoids squaring the data matrix by applying the orthogonal transformation as shown in eq. (16) and (17) and then directly solves the resulting system of linear equations. QR transformations are usually either a Householder transformation or, as in this study, a set of Givens rotations, see [6]. Details on the recursive implementation can be found in [7].

4. Artifical Neural Networks (ANNs)

ANNs are motivated by biological central nervous systems (CNS). Here, the central processing element is a cell called neuron which actually integrates input signals in space and time and sends out a frequency coded output signal if a certain threshold is reached. When building artificial neural networks, however, some major simplifications are made. Most artifical neurons do not integrate over space and are synchronized with system time. Also, frequency coding is substituted by a nonlinear activation function **f**.

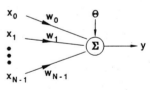

Fig. 5 : artificial neuron

The resulting neuron is known as the McCulloch-Pitts neuron (1943), see Fig. 5 and eq. (18).

$$y(k) = f\left(\sum_{i=0}^{N-1} w_i\ x_i(k) - \theta\right) = f(a) \quad (18)$$

When "backpropagation", see [8], is used for training, the network "learns" data by adjusting its weights w_{ji} to minimize the quadratic loss function

$$E = \frac{1}{2}\sum_j (g_j - y_j)^2 \qquad (19)$$

g_j stand for the desired output while y_j is the current output of the network. Usually, a gradient descent method is used for weight adjusting

$$w_{ji}(n+1) = w_{ji}(n) - \eta\, \frac{\partial E}{\partial w_{ji}(n)} \qquad (20)$$

with the learning rate η. Each iteration, the weight adjustment propagates backwards from output to the input layers. Fig. 6 shows a feedforward multilayer network.

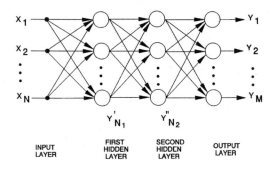

Fig. 6 : multilayer perceptron

Thus, the network actually performs a nonlinear mapping. For reference on classification with ANNs see e.g. [9].

5. Experimental Results

Static Damping Curves
Fig. 7 shows the characteristic curves of the damper used for the experiments in Darmstadt.

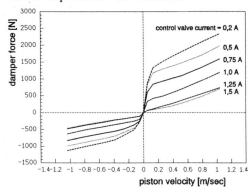

Fig. 7 : damping curve of Darmstadt shock absorber

Note that the linear model asumption in section 2 actually linearizes these curves by an average slope.

The following setup was used
- body mass m_A : 200 - 300 kg
- wheel m_R : 32 kg
- tire : radial-ply tire 195/65 VR 15
- tire stiffness c_R : 203 kN/m at 2.0 bar, adjustable by changing air pressure
- damper : continuously adjustable double-tube gas pressure shock absorber
- input : hydraulic, 200 mm at 10 kN

Fig. 8 shows different damping curves for the damper used for the experiments in Berkeley. Numbers 1 .. 20 indicate different settings of the stepper motor.

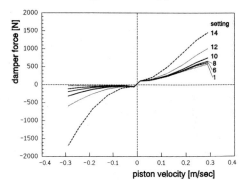

Fig. 8 : damping curves of shock absorber

The following setup was used for the first shock absorber (the second was an active one):

- body mass m_A : 580 kg
- moment of inertia J : 770 kg m^2
- unsprung mass m_R : 59.5 kg
- tire stiffness c_R : 190000 N/m
- spring stiffness c_A : 16812 N/m
- damper : 22-state double tube shock absorber using a stepper motor to switch between states
- input : hydraulic actuators using a supply pressure of 1500 psi

Classification of Parameter Changes
For the quarter car test rig of TU Darmstadt, the following changes were implemented

- ◆ class 1/2 : damping coefficient d_A too high/low
- ◆ class 3/4 : tire stiffness c_R too high/low

Classes 3 and 4 indicate a wrong tire air pressure resulting in a different tire stiffness. Together with class 0 (no changes), one finds a total of 5 classes which were mapped on a binary coded 4-dimensional output vector. The parameters of the discrete-time model, a_1, a_2, b_1 and b_2 form the 4-dimensional input vector. Fig. 9 shows the decision regions of the (reduced) parameter space a_1 and b_1 when damping coefficient or tire stiffness were changed (the complete 4-dimensional parameter space can not be plotted for obvious reasons).

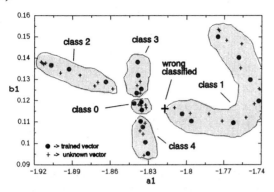

Fig. 9 : decision regions in parameter space

The artificial neural network was trained with 21 input vectors. Best convergence (288 iterations) was obtained for a 4-16-4 network. After training, the ability to generalize was tested by 32 unknown input vectors and found to be correct except for one input, see fig. 9.

At Berkeley, only the damping coefficient of the passive shock absorber was modified (the second absorber was an active one). Fig. 10 gives the variation of discrete-time parameters a'_{0v} and a'_{0h} as a function of the damping coefficient. Three classes were formed

◆ class 1 : weak damping (1, 6, 8)
◆ class 2 : medium damping (10, 12)
◆ class 3 : stiff damping (14, 16, 18, 20)

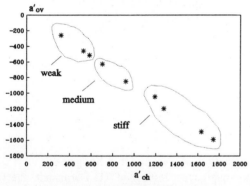

Fig. 10 : half car shock absorber variations

6. Conclusions

The combined algorithm presented in this work has been shown to work successfully on two specific shock absorbers. Despite the fact that the two processes are actually nonlinear, a parameter estimation based on a discrete linear model works satisfactory. Furthermore, feedforward multilayer ANNs proved to be useable for

classification of process properties. Both techniques may well be used for adaptive control and supervision of shock absorbers.

Acknowledgements

The cooperation between our two research groups was partly funded by grants from German Research Foundation (DFG) and by the UC Berkeley - TU Darmstadt academic exchange program.

References

[1] **Bußhardt, J., Isermann, R.**, "Adaptive and Semi-active Shock Absorbers Based on Real-time Parameter Estimation", 24. Fisita Congress 92 "Automotive Technology Serving Society", London, June 07-11, 1992.

[2] **Butsuen, T.**, "The Design of Semiactive Suspensions for Automation Vehicles", Ph.D. thesis, Mass. Inst. of Technology, 1989.

[3] **Alleyne, A., Hedrick, J.K.**, "Nonlinear Control of a Quarter Car Active Suspension", American Control Conference, Chicago, July 24-26, 1992, pp. 21-25.

[4] **Rajamani, R., Hedrick, K.**, "Semi-active Suspension - a comparison between theory and experiment", 12th IAVSD Symposium on the dynamics of vehicels on roads and on tracks, Lyon, Aug. 26-30, 1991

[5] **Isermann, R.**, "Identifikation dynamischer Systeme", Springer Verlag, Berlin, 1988.

[6] **Strang, G.**, "Introduction to Applied Mathematics", Wellesley-Cambridge Press, Wellesley, USA, 1986.

[7] **Leonhardt, S.**, "A Parallel Algorithm for Process Identification", 9th IFAC Symposium on Ident. and System Parameter Estimation, Budapest, Hungary, July 8-12, 1991.

[8] **Rummelhart, D. E., McCleland, J.L.**, "Parallel Distributed Processing", MIT Press, Cambridge, 1989.

[9] **Barschdorff, D., Becker, D.**, "Neuronale Netze als Signal- und Musterklassifikatoren", Technisches Messen (tm) 57, No. 11, 1990, pp. 437-444.

STONE IMPACT DAMAGE TO AUTOMOTIVE PAINT FINISHES - A NEURAL NET ANALYSIS OF ELECTROCHEMICAL IMPEDANCE DATA

A. C. Ramamurthy* and Mirana Uriquidi-Macdonald**
BASF Corporation, 26701, Telegraph Road, Southfield, MI 48086
** Department of Engineering Science and Mechanics
The Pennsylvania State University, University Park, PA, 16802

ABSTRACT- Automotive car bodies are subject to impact by stones either lofted from tires or launched by other passing vehicles. Impact can result either in physical loss of paint and the possibility of failure at the metal/phosphate - Polymer interface. Corrosion brought about as a result of impact is referred to as Impact Induced Corrosion or IIC. Electrochemical Impedance is very sensitive to delamination at the metal - polymer interface and is able to discern the influence of velocity, angle of impact, the type of coating and ambient temperature. Neural Network analysis of electrochemical impedance data are presented.

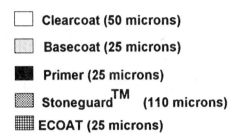

Fig 1. Paint layers for Modern Automobiles

I . INTRODUCTION

A common source of damage to automotive paint finishes is due to impact of small stones either lofted by tires or from other passing vehicles. Stone impact damage can result in either physical loss of paint or delamination at the metal-polymer interface [1,2]. Physical loss of paint is a "cosmetic" issue while delamination leads to corrosion beneath the coating which can ultimately lead to perforation. We refer to corrosion due to impact as Impact Induced corrosion or IIC. Figure 1 shows a typical multilayer automotive paint system. The ECOAT layer serves as barrier for corrosion protection, Stoneguard^{TM} as an "anti" stone chip layer, the Basecoat contains all the color pigments and the Clearcoat serves as glossy scratch and UV resistance layer.

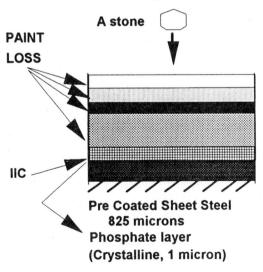

II. ADVANCED EXPERIMENTAL AND ANALYSIS TECHNIQUES

Recently, several single impact test methods have been implemented by the automobile manufacturers to systematically evaluate paint systems. These techniques have the ability to precisely control velocity, angle of incidence of the projectile and operate over a wide temperature range.

Single impact methods have also led to the use of advanced post impact damage techniques such as digital image analysis, thermal imaging, ultrasonic microscopy and EIS [3] to estimate percent paint loss and impact induced corrosion. The ultimate goal of this analysis is to discern the effects of impact variables and be able to construct an "impact response surface" for any given substrate/coating system.

Impact phenomenon of which IIC is a part of, is a complex non-linear threshold phenomenon and Table I shows a partial list of variables that are known to affect impact response. Given a complex phenomenon such as impact damage, a coatings formulator typically resorts to a well planned statistical design to, A) design new impact resistant coating systems and B) efficiently carry out impact experiments. These procedures takes into account all the chemical and experimental variables necessary to design new coating systems based on the impact response. Analysis of the data [4,5] can provide insight into main effects, two and three factor interactions between the variables that may influence the phenomenon. This insight offers suggestions to the coatings designer to make the required polymer/pigment modifications (in one or more layers) which would "weaken" the effect on the variables, e.g., temperature or type of pigments, which adversely affect impact response.

Table I : Complexity of impact damage phenomenon

VARIABLES	ATTRIBUTES
Projectile	Size Density Shape Modulus Poisson's ratio
Impact	Velocity Angle of incidence
Environment	Temperature Humidity Corrosion cycle
Coating	Viscoelsatic properties Adhesion Fracture toughness
Fixture	Stiffness
Substrate	Type Thickness High strain rate- properties

Besides this capability, it is also desirable to be able to predict damage response outside the range of conditions chosen for the laboratory simulation. Predictions outside the range, if found reliable via independent experiments, can help set confidence & tolerance limits for a given substrate/coating system. Since there exists no deterministic approach to account for our observations on impact induced corrosion, we suggest the application of Neural Networks (NN) as a predictive tool. It is our intention to show in the present work , the feasibility of using NN to account for the intrinsic complex relation between the input variables and the observed impact response.

Neural networks are relatively new mathematical techniques for solving complex non linear problems frequently encountered in science and engineering [6]. A typical NN may contain from few to several hundred simulated neurons. Each connection is associated with a number or weight, and each neuron associated with a transfer function. NN's can be trained to operate either in the supervised or unsupervised mode. In the supervised mode as used in the present work, NN "learns" adjusting its weights when given the input and target values.

In this work we introduce Electrochemical Impedance Spectroscopy as a sensitive tool to detect and quantify impact induced corrosion. Also, in this work, we present our first attempt to rationalize impact response (for IIC) using Neural Network methods. To the best of our knowledge, this work is the first investigation reported on the application of EIS for detecting IIC and to present a preliminary approach for data analysis.

III. EIS BODE PLOTS AS AN IIC DIAGNOSTIC [11]

It is well known that electrochemical impedance is a very sensitive technique for detecting delamination at the metal-polymer interface [7]. Since the objective of this work is not to discern the mechanistic aspects of IIC, EIS merely serves as a quantitative diagnostic tool. Figure 2 shows a typical Bode magnitude plot for a coated metal in contact with an electrolyte solution. Under impact loading, if the Metal-Polymer interface remains intact, one typically observes a straight line with a slope -1 and the low frequency impedance magnitude (typically at 0.1 Hz) would exceed 10^9 ohms . cm^2. If impact causes delamination at the metal/phosphate - ECOAT (refer to Figure 1) interface, one expects impedance magnitude at low frequencies, to be in the range 10^3 to 10^5 ohms. cm^2 .

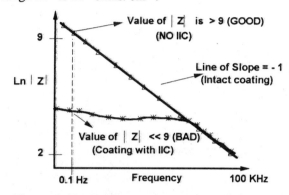

Figure 2: Typical Bode plots for an intact coating and for a system exhibiting impact induced corrosion

This work exploits the measurement of impedance, $|Z|$ at low frequencies as measure of IIC. The lower the $|Z|$ value at 0.1 Hz, the greater the degree of IIC. Visualization of interaction effects of impact variables (velocity and angle of incidence) and ambient temperature is not straightforward by examining raw impedance data. Our preliminary approach which involved viewing superimposed Bode plots obtained under various experimental conditions failed to provide any insight on the influence of variables which effect IIC. In the present work we propose to use $|Z|$ measured at 0. 1 Hz for Neural Net analysis.

III. EXPERIMENTAL

The test matrix consisted of only variations in the ECOAT layer and phosphate pre treatment. TABLE II shows the test matrix and impact conditions chosen in the present study. TYPE A and TYPE B ECOAT's were model systems in which significant changes in polymer structure were implemented while TYPE C was a commercial system currently used in the industry.

The impact device used in this work was developed and is marketed by VIANOVA resins in GRAZ, Austria and is described in the literature [8].

Table II : Impact matrix and parameters

ECOAT	PHOSPHATE	PIGMENT	IMPACT VARIABLES
TYPE A	+	P	Velocity: 60, 80 and 120 km/hr.
	-	C	Angle of Incidence: 45, 60 and 80 degree.
TYPE B	+	P	
	-	C	Temperature: -20, 0 and + 20 Celsius.
TYPE C (Commercial)	+	P	

+ : Phosphated Cold Rolled Steel.
- : Bare Cold Rolled Steel
P : Pigmented ECOAT.
C : Clear ECOAT.
Cold Rolled Steel supplied by ACT, Hillsdale, MI.
Phosphate : Gardobond 24 by CHEMETALL, Frankfurt, Germany.

IV. DATA ANALYSIS

A Forward-Backward propagation Neural Network with two hidden layer of neurons was used in the analysis. Neural Works Professional II/PLUS (Neural Ware, Pittsburgh, PA) running on a Macintosh II ci computer was used in this work. During training, the artificial neural net learns from input vectors (temperature, projectile velocity, projectile angle of incidence), and output vectors (measured impedance).

During the test mode only the input vectors are used, and the net predicted the results (impedance). The total data set had nine metal-polymer interfaces for which the magnitude of the impedance at 0.1 Hz was measured at three temperatures, three projectile velocities and three angles of incidence. The data set was divided into two sections. The first section consisted of approximately 66 % of the total data while second one with 34 %. The selection process was random. The former section went into the "training" mode the latter section serving as the "test" mode.

The analysis was carried out on the entire data set (for all the nine systems), averaging the measured impedance for all the tests at given temperature, angle and velocity. Figure 3 shows the NN predictions trend for TYPE a (+) coating. |Z| decreases with increase in velocity (Figure 3 A) and temperature (Figure 3 B) while exhibiting a minimum at 60 degree angle of impact (Figure 3 C) These trends observed however are not the same for each one of the nine individual systems investigated in this study.

V. RESULTS AND DISCUSSION

Figures 4 to 6 show typical Bode plots illustrating the influence of velocity, angle of incidence, ambient temperature. It is clear from these representative plots, EIS is able to clearly discern the influence of the variables at the levels chosen in this study.

NN analysis indicate the best correlation between predicted and measured data are obtained for Type A (+)

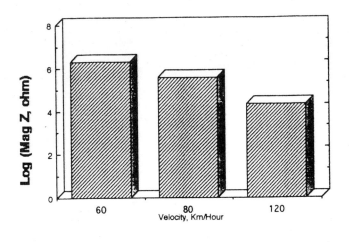

Fig. 3 A

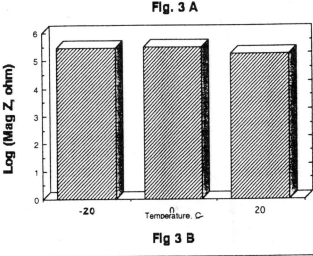

Fig 3 B

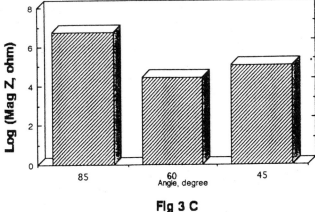

Fig 3 C

system (Figure 7). For the other eight systems NN predictions are very good for higher |Z| values but at the lower end predicted values are higher than measured values. This discrepancy is due to the quality of data. Since the various coating systems behave differently with velocity, angle and temperature, it is not clear at this stage of research

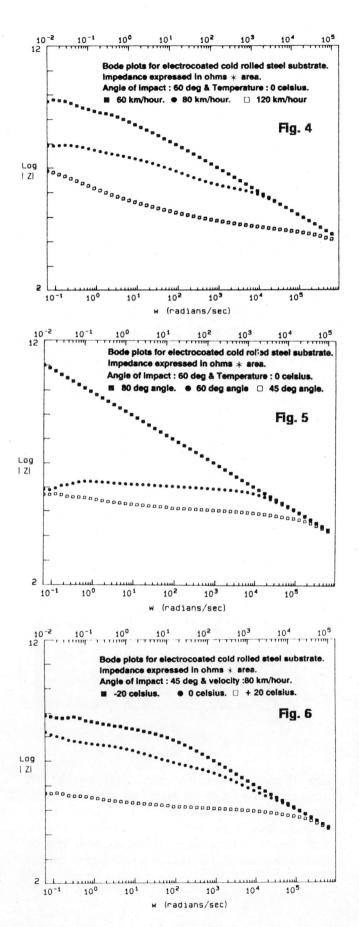

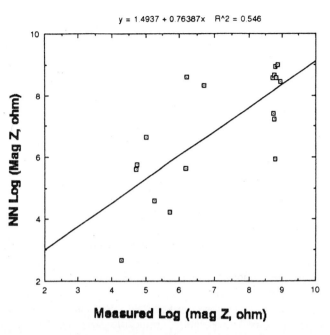

Fig 7. Correlation between NN predicted impedance and measured impedance for TYPE A (+) system.

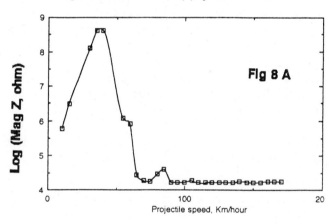

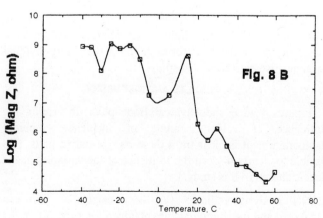

Fig 8 A & B : NN predicted impedance's for TYPE A (+) system as a function of velocity and temperature.

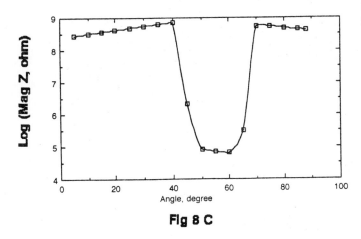

Fig 8 C

Figure 8 C : NN predicted impedance's for TYPE A(+) system as a function of angle of incidence.

if the trends in the observed impedance are real and within experimental error. Furthermore, the value of experimental error is unknown and the data set is small. Due to the above considerations, data for Type A + was used to train the NN and to explore its predictions.

Figure 8 shows NN predictions of impedance as function of temperature, velocity and angle for TYPE A (+) system. The oscillations observed in the temperature plot are due to poor quality of data as pointed out above. NN predictions follow a trend indicated by the dashed line, which is in agreement with experimental observations.

For velocities above 35 km/hr, NN predictions with experimental observations are good. NN also predicts a constant impedance reached at higher velocities which is supported by experimental observations. The discrepancy at low velocities may be due to the fact that impact damage is a threshold phenomenon and the data set is not trained in this regime. NN predictions with the variable, angle of incidence, are good and are supported by our experimental observations.

VI. CONCLUSIONS

This study has been able to show that EIS is a very sensitive post impact diagnostic probe to detect delamination at the metal-polymer boundary. Considering the noisy quality of data, the learning of the NN was good. We have been able to show that NN is able to make predictions that are in agreement with independent experimental observations. Based on this preliminary work, future use of NN as predictive tools will rely on a comprehensive data set

obtained under rigorous experimental conditions using stone projectiles, alternate treatments of impedance data and also taking into account parameters such as stone shape, mass, and density.

VII. REFERENCES

1. A. C. Ramamurthy, W. I. Lorenzen, S. Bless and N. S. Brar, Proceedings of the American Chemical Society, Division of PMSE. 67, 114 (1992).

2. U. Zroll, Farbe und Lack. 91, 1123 (1985).

3. A. C. Ramamurthy, T. Ahmed, L. D. Favro, R. L. Thomas, D. K. Hohnke and R. P. Cooper, SAE paper # 930051, Presented at the 1993 Annual Congress, Detroit, MI.

4. G. E. P. Box, W. G. Hunter and J. S. Hunter , Statistics for experimenters, Part III, John Wiley (1978).

5. R. V. Lenth, Technometrics, 31, 469 (1989).

6. J. M. Zurada , Introduction to Artificial Neural Systems, West (1992).

7. F. Mansfeld and M. W. Kendig, Werkstoffe und Korrosion. 36, 473, (1985)

8. E. Ladstadter, Farbe und Lack. 90, 577 (1984).

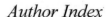

Subject Index

Tissue classification, 421–22
Torque ripple minimization, 36–42
Total luminescent spectroscopy, 819–24
Traffic monitoring, 927–32
Traffic prediction, 608–15
Trajectory generation, 130–35
Transformer oil diagnosis, 810–13
Transient state operation, 49
Transmission control, 191–95

U

Ultrasound, in vivo liver differentiation, 425–30

V

Vehicle control, 185–201, 927–32
Vehicles, 927–53
Velocity dispersion, 425–30
Vision, 903–10
Viterbi decoder, 724–27
Voiced-stop-consonant recognition, 673–77
Voltage control, 207–25, 307–10
Voltage instability, 307–10

W

Wafer-to-wafer process control, 89–92
Waste water process control, 97–101

X

Webster rating scale, 356–61
Welding, 65–70
Weld pool sensing, 65–70
Well-logs, 665–68
Word recognition, 695–704
Word splitting, 724–27

X-ray, lung nodule detection, 415–20

Patrick K. Simpson

Patrick K. Simpson was born in Cordova, AK, a small fishing community on the Prince William Sound. From 1974 to 1986, Mr. Simpson worked with his family on fishing boats, starting as a crew member and working his way up to captain.

Mr. Simpson received his Bachelor of Arts degree in Computer Science from the University of California at San Diego in 1986. Since college, Mr. Simpson has distinguished himself in the application of neural networks, fuzzy systems, and artificial intelligence to difficult defense-related problems in areas such as electronic intelligence, radar surveillance, sonar signal identification, and various aspects of automated diagnostics.

In addition to his career as an engineer, Mr. Simpson has written several archival papers, taught several courses, written a text book that has been used in college courses around the United States, and lectured on the theory and application of neural networks and fuzzy systems world wide.

Recently, Mr. Simpson has combined his past with the present and formed Scientific Fishery Systems, Inc., a small business dedicated to the conversion of defense technologies to the fisheries.